Adolescence

Eighth Edition

Adolescence

Laurence Steinberg
Temple University

Boston   Burr Ridge, IL   Dubuque, IA   Madison, WI   New York   San Francisco   St. Louis
Bangkok   Bogotá   Caracas   Kuala Lumpur   Lisbon   London   Madrid   Mexico City
Milan   Montreal   New Delhi   Santiago   Seoul   Singapore   Sydney   Taipei   Toronto

McGraw-Hill
Higher Education

Published by McGraw-Hill, an imprint of The McGraw-Hill Companies, Inc., 1221 Avenue of the Americas, New York, NY 10020.

This book is printed on acid-free paper.

1 2 3 4 5 6 7 8 9 0 CCI/CCI 0 9 8 7

ISBN: 978-0-07-340548-3
MHID: 0-07-340548-5

Editor in Chief: *Emily Barrosse*
Publisher: *Beth Mejia*
Executive Editor: *Mike Sugarman*
Executive Marketing Manager: *Sarah Martin*
Director of Development: *Dawn Groundwater*
Senior Developmental Editor: *Judith Kromm*
Development Editor for Supplements: *Meghan Campbell*
Production Editor: *Holly Paulsen*
Manuscript Editor: *Thomas L. Briggs*
Creative Director: *Jeanne Schreiber*
Senior Design Manager: *Cassandra Chu*
Text Designer: *Maureen McCutcheon*
Cover Designer: *Maureen McCutcheon*
Art Editor: *Emma Ghiselli*
Illustrator: *Emma Ghiselli*
Photo Research Coordinator: *Natalia Peschiera*
Photo Research: *Toni Michaels, PhotoFind, LLC*
Senior Production Supervisor: *Rich DeVitto*
Digital Project Manager: *Magdalena Corona*
Composition: *10/12 Minion by Aptara*
Printing: *45# Publishers Matte Plus, Courier Inc.*

Cover: © Bloomimage/Corbis

Credits: The credits section for this book begins on page C-1 and is considered an extension of the copyright page.

Library of Congress Cataloging-in-Publication Data

Steinberg, Laurence D.
    Adolescence / Laurence Steinberg.—8th ed.
       p. cm.
    Includes bibliographical references and indexes.
    ISBN-13: 978-0-07-340548-3 (hardcover : alk. paper)
    ISBN-10: 0-07-340548-5 (hardcover)
    1. Adolescent psychology—Textbooks. I. Title.

BF724.S75 2008
305.235—dc22   2007017014

The Internet addresses listed in the text were accurate at the time of publication. The inclusion of a Web site does not indicate an endorsement by the authors or McGraw-Hill, and McGraw-Hill does not guarantee the accuracy of the information presented at these sites.

For Wendy and Ben

About the Author

LAURENCE STEINBERG, Ph.D., is the Distinguished University Professor and Laura H. Carnell Professor of Psychology at Temple University. He graduated from Vassar College in 1974 and from Cornell University in 1977, where he received his Ph.D. in human development and family studies. He is a Fellow of the American Psychological Association, former President of the Society for Research on Adolescence, and the current President of the Division of Developmental Psychology of the American Psychological Association. Dr. Steinberg has been on the editorial boards of many major journals, including *Developmental Psychology* and *Child Development,* where he served as Associate Editor. He is a member of the National Academy of Science's Board on Children, Youth, and Families and its Committee on the Science of Adolescent Health and Behavior, and has been a frequent consultant to state and federal agencies and lawmakers on child labor, secondary education, and juvenile justice policy. His work was cited numerous times by the U.S. Supreme Court in its 2005 landmark decision that abolished the juvenile death penalty.

Dr. Steinberg is one of the most highly cited scholars in the field of developmental psychology. His own research has focused on a range of topics in the study of contemporary adolescence, including parent–adolescent relationships, adolescent employment, high school reform, and juvenile crime and justice. He has been the recipient of numerous honors, including the John P. Hill Award for Outstanding Contributions to the Study of Adolescence, given by the Society for Research on Adolescence, the Society for Adolescent Medicine's Gallagher Lectureship, and the American Psychological Association's Urie Bronfenbrenner Award for Lifetime Contribution to Developmental Psychology in the Service of Science and Society. Dr. Steinberg also has been recognized for excellence in research and teaching by the University of California, the University of Wisconsin, and Temple University, where he was honored in 1994 as one of that university's Great Teachers. He has taught undergraduate and graduate courses in adolescence for more than 30 years and has served as the doctoral advisor to more than 30 students, many of whom have gone on to become influential scholars in the field in their own right in the field of adolescence.

In addition to *Adolescence*, Dr. Steinberg is the author or co-author of more than 200 scholarly articles on growth and development during the teenage years, as well as the books *You and Your Adolescent: A Parent's Guide for Ages 10 to 20* (with Ann Levine); *When Teenagers Work: The Psychological and Social Costs of Adolescent Employment* (with Ellen Greenberger); *Crossing Paths: How Your Child's Adolescence Triggers Your Own Crisis* (with Wendy Steinberg); *Studying Minority Adolescents: Conceptual, Methodological, and Theoretical Issues* (co-edited with Vonnie McLoyd), *Beyond the Classroom: Why School Reform Has Failed and What Parents Need to Do* (with Bradford Brown and Sanford Dornbusch), the *Handbook of Adolescent Psychology* (co-edited with Richard Lerner), and *The Ten Basic Principles of Good Parenting*.

Brief Contents

About the Author vi
Preface xv

Introduction The Study of Adolescent Development   3

PART 1
The Fundamental Changes of Adolescence 21

1 Biological Transitions 23
2 Cognitive Transitions 61
3 Social Transitions 93

PART 2
The Contexts of Adolescence 127

4 Families 129
5 Peer Groups 161
6 Schools 197
7 Work, Leisure, and Mass Media 231

PART 3
Psychosocial Development During Adolescence 265

8 Identity 267
9 Autonomy 301
10 Intimacy 333
11 Sexuality 367
12 Achievement 403
13 Psychosocial Problems in Adolescence 433

Glossary G-1
References R-1
Credits C-1
Name Index I-1
Subject Index I-28

Contents

About the Author   vi

Preface   xv

Introduction
The Study of Adolescent
Development   3

A MULTIDISCIPLINARY APPROACH TO
ADOLESCENCE   5

THE BOUNDARIES OF ADOLESCENCE   6

Early, Middle, and Late Adolescence   7

A FRAMEWORK FOR STUDYING ADOLESCENT
DEVELOPMENT   8

The Fundamental Changes of Adolescence   8

The Contexts of Adolescence   9

Psychosocial Development of Adolescence   12

THEORETICAL PERSPECTIVES ON
ADOLESCENCE   14

Biosocial Theories   14

Organismic Theories   15

Learning Theories   16

Sociological Theories   17

Historical and Anthropological Theories   17

STEREOTYPES VERSUS SCIENTIFIC STUDY   19

PART 1
The Fundamental Changes of
Adolescence   21

Chapter 1
Biological Transitions   23

PUBERTY: AN OVERVIEW   24

The Endocrine System   25

What Triggers Puberty?   26

How Hormones Influence Adolescent
Development   27

SOMATIC DEVELOPMENT   28

Changes in Stature and the Dimensions
of the Body   28

Sexual Maturation   30

THE TIMING AND TEMPO OF PUBERTY   34

Variations in the Timing and Tempo of Puberty   34

Genetic and Environmental Influences
on Pubertal Timing   35

THE PSYCHOLOGICAL AND SOCIAL
IMPACT OF PUBERTY   38

The Immediate Impact of Puberty   39

The Impact of Specific Pubertal Events   44

The Impact of Early or Late Maturation   45

EATING DISORDERS   49

Obesity   49

Anorexia Nervosa and Bulimia   51

PHYSICAL HEALTH AND HEALTH CARE
IN ADOLESCENCE   55

   The Paradox of Adolescent Health   55

   Causes of Mortality in Adolescence   56

   Promoting Adolescent Health   57

Chapter 2
Cognitive Transitions   61

CHANGES IN COGNITION   62

   Thinking About Possibilities   62

   Thinking About Abstract Concepts   64

   Thinking About Thinking   65

   Thinking in Multiple Dimensions   66

   Adolescent Relativism   67

THEORETICAL PERSPECTIVES ON ADOLESCENT
THINKING   68

   The Piagetian View of Adolescent
   Thinking   68

   The Information-Processing View of
   Adolescent Thinking   71

THE ADOLESCENT BRAIN   73

   What Changes in Adolescence?   74

   Implications for Adolescent Behavior   77

INDIVIDUAL DIFFERENCES IN INTELLIGENCE
IN ADOLESCENCE   78

   The Measurement of IQ   78

   Types of Intelligence   78

   Intelligence Test Performance in
   Adolescence   80

   Culture and Intelligence   81

ADOLESCENT THINKING IN CONTEXT   83

   Changes in Social Cognition   83

   Adolescent Risk Taking   86

   Adolescent Thinking in the Classroom   90

Chapter 3
Social Transitions   93

SOCIAL REDEFINITION AND PSYCHOSOCIAL
DEVELOPMENT   94

THE ELONGATION OF ADOLESCENCE   95

ADOLESCENCE AS A SOCIAL INVENTION   96

   The "Invention" of Adolescence   97

   Emerging Adulthood: A New Stage of Life or
   a Luxury of the Middle Class?   99

CHANGES IN STATUS   103

   Changes in Interpersonal Status   103

   Changes in Political Status   103

   Changes in Economic Status   104

   Changes in Legal Status   104

THE PROCESS OF SOCIAL REDEFINITION   106

   Common Practices in the Process of Social
   Redefinition   107

VARIATIONS IN SOCIAL TRANSITIONS   109

   Variations in Clarity   109

   Variations in Continuity   112

THE TRANSITION INTO ADULTHOOD
IN CONTEMPORARY SOCIETY   118

   Special Transitional Problems of Poor and
   Minority Youth   119

   The Effects of Poverty on the Transition
   into Adulthood   120

   What Can Be Done to Ease the Transition?   120

THE INFLUENCE OF NEIGHBORHOOD CONDITIONS
ON ADOLESCENT DEVELOPMENT   121

   Processes of Neighborhood Influences   122

PART 2
The Contexts of Adolescence   127

Chapter 4
Families   129

IS CONFLICT BETWEEN TEENAGERS AND PARENTS
INEVITABLE?   130

The Generation Gap: Fact and Fiction   130

What Do Adolescents and Parents
Usually Fight About?   131

FAMILY RELATIONSHIPS AT ADOLESCENCE   133

A Time of Reorganization and Change   133

The Adolescent's Parents at Midlife   133

Changes in Family Needs and Functions   135

Transformations in Family Relations   135

Sex Differences in Family Relationships   137

FAMILY RELATIONSHIPS AND ADOLESCENT
DEVELOPMENT   138

Parenting Styles and Their Effects   138

Ethnic Differences in Parenting Practices   142

Autonomy and Attachment in
the Adolescent's Family   143

Adolescents' Relationships with Siblings   143

BEHAVIORAL GENETICS AND ADOLESCENT
DEVELOPMENT   145

Genetic and Environmental Influences
on Adolescent Development   145

Why Are Siblings Often So Different?   146

THE ADOLESCENT'S FAMILY IN A CHANGING
SOCIETY   148

The Changed and Changing Nature
of Family Life   148

Adolescents and Divorce   150

The Specific Impact of Marital Conflict   152

The Longer-Term Effects of Divorce   153

Custody, Contact, and Conflict Following
Divorce   154

Remarriage   155

Economic Stress and Poverty   156

THE IMPORTANCE OF THE FAMILY IN
ADOLESCENT DEVELOPMENT   159

Chapter 5
Peer Groups   161

THE ORIGINS OF ADOLESCENT PEER GROUPS
IN CONTEMPORARY SOCIETY   163

The Educational Origins of Adolescent Peer
Groups   163

Work, Family Life, and Adolescent
Peer Groups   164

Changes in the Population   164

THE ADOLESCENT PEER GROUP: A PROBLEM
OR A NECESSITY?   167

Is There a Separate Youth Culture?   167

The Need for Peer Groups in
Modern Society   168

THE NATURE OF ADOLESCENT
PEER GROUPS   169

Changes in Peer Groups During
Adolescence   169

Cliques and Crowds   171

Changes in Clique and Crowd
Structure over Time   173

ADOLESCENTS AND THEIR CROWDS   177

The Social Map of Adolescence   177

Crowds as Reference Groups   177

ADOLESCENTS AND THEIR CLIQUES   179

Similarity Among Clique Members   179

Common Interests Among Friends   182

Similarity Between Friends: Selection
or Socialization?   185

POPULARITY AND REJECTION IN ADOLESCENT
PEER GROUPS   187

Determinants of Popularity and Rejection   187

Relational Aggression   189

Victimization and Harassment   191

THE PEER GROUP AND PSYCHOSOCIAL
DEVELOPMENT   194

Chapter 6
Schools   197

THE BROADER CONTEXT OF U.S. SECONDARY
EDUCATION   199

The Origins of Compulsory Education   199

The Rise of the Comprehensive
High School   200

School Reform: Past and Present   201

What Should Schools Teach?   202

Education in the Inner Cities   204

THE SOCIAL ORGANIZATION OF SCHOOLS   204

School Size and Class Size   205

Age Grouping and School Transitions   206

Tracking   210

Ethnic Composition   213

Public Schools and Private Schools   215

CLASSROOM CLIMATE   217

   The Best Classroom Climate for
Adolescents   217

   Teacher Expectations and Student
Performance   218

   The Importance of Student Engagement   219

   Intervening to Change a School's Climate   221

   School Violence   222

BEYOND HIGH SCHOOL   223

   The College Bound   223

   The Non-College Bound   226

SCHOOLS AND ADOLESCENT DEVELOPMENT   227

   Characteristics of Good Schools   227

   The Effects of Schools on Adolescent
Development   228

Chapter 7
Work, Leisure, and
The Mass Media   231

ADOLESCENTS' FREE TIME IN CONTEMPORARY
SOCIETY   232

   Patterns of Time Use in Contemporary
America   232

   Patterns of Time Use in Other Countries   234

ADOLESCENTS AND WORK   235

   School and Work in the Early
Twentieth Century   235

   The Emergence of the Student-Worker   235

   Teenage Employment in America and in Other
Nations   236

   The Adolescent Workplace Today   238

   Employment and Adolescent
Development   239

   Youth Unemployment   243

ADOLESCENTS AND LEISURE   245

   Adolescents' Free Time and Their Moods   245

   Structured Leisure Activities   246

   Unstructured Leisure Time   250

   Promoting Positive Youth Development   252

ADOLESCENTS AND THE MASS MEDIA   253

   Patterns of Media Use   253

   Theories of Media Influence and Use   256

   The Impact of Adolescents' Exposure to
Controversial Media Content   258

   Mass Media and Sex-Role Socialization   260

   The Adolescent Consumer   261

FREE TIME AND ADOLESCENT DEVELOPMENT   262

PART 3
Psychosocial Development
During Adolescence   265

Chapter 8
Identity   267

IDENTITY AS AN ADOLESCENT ISSUE   268

CHANGES IN SELF-CONCEPTIONS   270

   Changes in the Content and Structure of
Self-Conceptions   270

   Dimensions of Personality in Adolescence   273

CHANGES IN SELF-ESTEEM   274

   Stability and Changes in Self-Esteem   274

   Sex, Class, and Ethnic Differences
in Self-Esteem   278

   Antecedents and Consequences of High
Self-Esteem   281

THE ADOLESCENT IDENTITY CRISIS   283

   Erikson's Theoretical Framework   283

   Identity Versus Identity Diffusion   283

   The Social Context of Identity
Development   284

   Resolving the Identity Crisis   285

   Problems in Identity Development   286

RESEARCH ON IDENTITY DEVELOPMENT   287

Determining an Adolescent's Identity
Status   287

Studying Identity Development over
Time   289

Shifts in Identity Status   290

THE DEVELOPMENT OF ETHNIC IDENTITY   291

The Process of Ethnic Identity
Development   291

Multiethnic Adolescents   292

Alternative Orientations to Ethnic Identity   294

Discrimination and Its Effects   296

GENDER-ROLE DEVELOPMENT   297

Gender-Role Socialization During
Adolescence   297

Masculinity, Femininity, and Androgyny   298

Chapter 9
Autonomy   301

AUTONOMY AS AN ADOLESCENT ISSUE   303

THE DEVELOPMENT OF EMOTIONAL
AUTONOMY   305

Emotional Autonomy and Detachment   305

Emotional Autonomy and Individuation   306

Research on Emotional Autonomy   306

Emotional Autonomy and Parenting
Practices   309

THE DEVELOPMENT OF BEHAVIORAL
AUTONOMY   311

Changes in Decision-Making Abilities   311

Changes in Susceptibility to Influence   314

Ethnic and Cultural Differences in Expectations
for Autonomy   319

Changes in Feelings of Self-Reliance   320

THE DEVELOPMENT OF VALUE AUTONOMY   320

Moral Development During Adolescence   321

Prosocial Reasoning, Prosocial Behavior, and
Volunteerism   326

Political Thinking During Adolescence   327

Religious Beliefs During Adolescence   328

Chapter 10
Intimacy   333

INTIMACY AS AN ADOLESCENT ISSUE   334

THEORETICAL PERSPECTIVES ON ADOLESCENT
INTIMACY   336

Sullivan's Theory of Interpersonal
Development   336

Erikson's View of Intimacy in Adolescence   338

Attachment in Adolescence   340

THE DEVELOPMENT OF INTIMACY
IN ADOLESCENCE   343

Changes in the Nature of Friendship   343

Changes in the Display of Intimacy   345

Sex Differences in Intimacy   346

Changes in the Targets of Intimacy   348

Friendships with the Other Sex   353

DATING AND ROMANTIC RELATIONSHIPS   356

Dating and the Development of Intimacy   358

The Development of Dating Relationships   360

The Impact of Dating on Adolescent
Development   362

INTIMACY AND PSYCHOSOCIAL
DEVELOPMENT   364

Chapter 11
Sexuality   367

SEXUALITY AS AN ADOLESCENT ISSUE   368

HOW SEXUALLY PERMISSIVE IS CONTEMPORARY
SOCIETY?   369

Sexual Socialization in Restrictive
Societies   370

Sexual Socialization in Semirestrictive
Societies   370

Sexual Socialization in Permissive
Societies   371

SEXUAL ACTIVITY DURING ADOLESCENCE   371

Stages of Sexual Activity   372

Sexual Intercourse During Adolescence   373

Changes in Sexual Activity over Time   374

THE SEXUALLY ACTIVE ADOLESCENT   376

Psychological and Social Characteristics of
Sexually Active Adolescents   376

Hormonal and Contextual Influences
on Sexual Activity   377

Parental and Peer Influences
on Sexual Activity   378

Sex Differences in the Meaning of Sex   382

Homosexuality During Adolescence   383

Sexual Harassment, Rape, and Sexual Abuse During Adolescence   386

Contraceptive Use   387

AIDS and Other Sexually Transmitted Diseases   391

TEENAGE PREGNANCY AND CHILDBEARING   393

The Nature and Extent of the Problem   393

Causes and Correlates of Teen Pregnancy   395

The Role of the Father   396

Consequences for Mother and Child   396

Teenage Pregnancy Prevention and Intervention Programs   398

Chapter 12
Achievement   403

ACHIEVEMENT AS AN ADOLESCENT ISSUE   404

ACHIEVEMENT MOTIVES AND BELIEFS   406

The Motive to Achieve   406

The Importance of Beliefs   407

ENVIRONMENTAL INFLUENCES ON ACHIEVEMENT   412

The Influence of the Home Environment   412

The Influence of Friends   414

EDUCATIONAL ACHIEVEMENT   416

The Importance of Socioeconomic Status   416

Ethnic Differences in Educational Achievement   418

Changes in Educational Achievement over Time   421

Dropping Out of High School   423

OCCUPATIONAL ACHIEVEMENT   426

The Development of Occupational Plans   426

Influences on Occupational Plans   427

Chapter 13
Psychosocial Problems in Adolescence   433

SOME GENERAL PRINCIPLES ABOUT PROBLEMS IN ADOLESCENCE   434

PSYCHOSOCIAL PROBLEMS: THEIR NATURE AND COVARIATION   436

Comorbidity of Externalizing Problems   437

Comorbidity of Internalizing Problems   440

SUBSTANCE USE AND ABUSE   440

Prevalence of Substance Use and Abuse   441

Causes and Consequences of Substance Use and Abuse   446

Prevention and Treatment of Substance Use and Abuse   448

EXTERNALIZING PROBLEMS   450

Categories of Externalizing Problems   450

Developmental Progression of Antisocial Behavior   452

Changes in Juvenile Offending over Time   453

Causes of Antisocial Behavior   455

Prevention and Treatment of Externalizing Problems   459

INTERNALIZING PROBLEMS   460

The Nature and Prevalence of Depression   461

Sex Differences in Depression   462

Suicide   464

Causes of Depression and Internalizing Disorders   466

Treatment and Prevention of Internalizing Problems   467

STRESS AND COPING   468

Glossary   G-1
References   R-1
Credits   C-1
Name Index   I-1
Subject Index   I-28

Preface

I BEGAN MY GRADUATE WORK at Cornell University in 1974, just as the field of adolescence was beginning to emerge as a distinct area of study within the discipline of human development. My mentors were two scholars who have probably influenced the contemporary study of adolescence more than anyone else: John Hill, who modernized the scientific study of adolescence and was the founding president of the Society for Research on Adolescence, and Urie Bronfenbrenner, who was the father of the ecological perspective on human development. There is a lot of each of these great thinkers in this book. Its organization comes directly from Hill's framework for the study of adolescence, and the perspective is indisputably ecological.

I've taught adolescent development at both the undergraduate and graduate levels for more than 30 years, and I know firsthand how exhilarating and exasperating teaching adolescence can be. Every student comes into class an expert; for many of them, adolescence wasn't very long ago. No good instructor wants to squelch the interest and curiosity most students bring with them when they first come into a class. But no conscientious teacher wants to see students leave with little more than the preconceptions they came in with and an even firmer conviction that social scientists who study human development are out of touch with the "real" world.

Bronfenbrenner once wrote that the science of child development had found itself caught between "a rock and a soft place"—between rigor and relevance. Teachers of adolescent development find themselves in the same boat. How do you present scientific research on adolescent development in ways students find interesting, believable, relevant, and worth remembering when the term is over? I hope this book will help.

My goals for this book are fourfold: to provide students with the most current, most thorough coverage of the scientific literature on adolescent development; to help students understand how the context in which adolescents come of age shapes the way in which they develop; to help students see how what they are learning about adolescence can be applied to improve the lives of young people and their families; and, most importantly, to get students to really think about what adolescence is and why it is a unique period in the human life span. For some, this understanding will make them better teachers, health care providers, or counselors, because they will really grasp how adolescents are different from children and from adults, and how they should take these differences into account when they interact with youth. For some, this will mean being smarter researchers, because they will know the research literature and the importance of separating science from stereotype. For some, this will mean designing better programs or policies that affect young people, because they will understand what adolescents need to grow up healthy. And for most, this understanding will mean being better mothers and fathers, because they will know what to expect and how to respond as their sons and daughters mature from childhood into adulthood.

Adolescent Development in Context

If there is a guiding theme to *Adolescence*, it is this: Adolescent development cannot be understood apart from the context in which young people grow up. Identity crises, generation gaps, and peer pressure may be features of adolescent life in contemporary society, but their prevalence has more to do with the nature of our society than with the nature of adolescence as a stage in the life cycle. In order to understand how adolescents develop in contemporary society, students need first to understand the world in which adolescents live and how that world affects their behavior and social relationships. I have therefore devoted a good deal of attention in this book to the contexts in which adolescents live—families, peer groups, schools, neighborhoods, and work and leisure settings—to how these contexts have changed and are changing, and to how these changes are transforming the nature of adolescence.

A Few Words About Diversity

Perhaps the greatest expansion of knowledge during the past decade has been about adolescents from ethnic minority groups, from disadvantaged communities, and from parts of the world other than North America. This has permitted increased coverage in this edition of the ways in which development during adolescence is affected by culture, class, and region.

Authors take different approaches to handling issues of diversity. Whereas some choose to present this material in a separate chapter on ethnicity or culture, I am not convinced that this is the best way to help students understand when, how, and why patterns of adolescent development vary across ethnicity and region of the world. Moreover, the literature on psychological development of ethnic minority and non-American adolescents has expanded so rapidly during the past 10 years that it would be impossible to provide adequate coverage of this material in just one chapter.

Others take what I think of as the "travelogue" approach, sprinkling boxes on the nature of adolescence in various ethnic groups or different parts of the world (the more remote and exotic, the better) throughout the text, in which they discuss adolescence as if everyone from that culture or country were the same. I think it is both patronizing and misleading to take this approach. (As a character in the Woody Allen movie *Annie Hall* said sarcastically, "I just love being reduced to a cultural stereotype.") There isn't any such thing as "the" Mexican adolescent or "the" Indian adolescent, any more than there is such a thing as "the" American adolescent.

My approach is to integrate discussions of ethnicity and culture throughout *every single chapter,* focusing not only on ethnic differences in development but also on similarities that cut across adolescents from different social, economic, and cultural backgrounds. There are important differences in the experiences of adolescents from different backgrounds, to be sure, but, as I point out often in the book, many studies indicate that influences on adolescent development are far more similar than different across ethnic and cultural groups. Factors that influence school achievement, risky sexual behavior, and drug use, for instance, are virtually iden-

tical across ethnic groups. In other words, "diversity" doesn't necessarily equal "difference." In fact, one of the consequences of the globalization of adolescence that has taken place in the last decade is that technological innovation has made adolescence more similar around the world, not more different.

My emphasis is on getting students to think critically about whether and why ethnicity matters, rather than simply assuming that it does. You will not find a separate chapter labeled "culture" or "ethnicity" in this book. What you will find are extensive and thoughtful discussions of such issues as ethnic identity, ethnicity and family relationships, cross-ethnic peer relations, ethnic differences in achievement, and ethnic differences in problem behaviors throughout the book, as well as comprehensive coverage of research on adolescent development in the context of economic disadvantage. I treat gender in a similar fashion. Gender influences virtually *every* aspect of adolescent development. That's why I discuss it in *every* chapter.

About the Eighth Edition

Although the book's original organization has been retained, the material in each chapter has been thoroughly updated and revised. Nearly 1,000 new studies have been cited since the seventh edition alone—studies that my research assistants and I culled from the several thousand we reviewed to prepare for this edition. We work from a list of about 50 scientific journals from the fields of psychology, education, sociology, psychiatry, economics, law, neuroscience, medicine, history, and anthropology, and we review the abstract of every single article involving adolescents published since the last edition of the textbook. If the abstract looks interesting, I read the entire article and decide whether it contains information that students need to know.

Like the field of adolescence itself, some things about this book have changed very little over the years, and others have been completely transformed. In addition to the increase in our knowledge about adolescents from different cultural groups and different parts of the world, which, as noted earlier, pervades every chapter, our understanding of adolescent brain development, sleep, risk-taking, romance, religious development, conduct disorder, and media use (including use of the Internet) has expanded substantially since the last edition, as has our knowledge about neighborhood influences on development and the prolonged extension of late adolescence (what some writers have called "emerging adulthood"). Sections on these topics have been either added or completely rewritten.

This edition of *Adolescence* drops a feature that ran throughout the past several editions. In those editions, in each chapter, a box titled "The Scientific Study of Adolescence" examined one particular study in detail. In consulting with many users of the previous edition, I came to the conclusion that it was unwise to include any important material in a boxed insert, because instructors told me that students often skipped over these. In this edition, I've moved the most important content that had been contained in these boxes into the text. I've retained the use of interim summaries—called "Recaps"—and thought-provoking questions—called "Food for Thought"—based on the positive feedback I've received from users. I've learned that some instructors use the "Food for Thought" questions as a launching pad for class discussions or as essay questions on examinations.

I also worked especially hard to make the writing more accessible. Some reviewers noted that, with the addition of more and more research with each edition—an addition that was necessary because of the expansion of scientific knowledge—the text had become a little encyclopedic. I've fixed that in this edition and have added more subheadings to help guide students through each chapter. We've also opened up the design of the book and given the pages a new, fresh look.

Organization and Learning Aids

The overall organization of this book has not changed since the previous edition. Specifically, the chapters about psychosocial development during adolescence are separate from those about the contexts of adolescence. In this way, the psychosocial concerns of adolescence—identity, autonomy, intimacy, sexuality, and achievement—are presented as central developmental concerns that surface across, and are affected by, different settings.

This book contains an Introduction and 13 chapters, which are grouped into three parts: the fundamental biological, cognitive, and social changes of the period (Part 1); the contexts of adolescence (Part 2); and psychosocial development during the adolescent years (Part 3). The Introduction presents a model for studying adolescence that serves as both the organizational framework for the text and an overview of some of the basic disciplinary perspectives on the period. I have found the framework to be extremely helpful in teaching adolescent development, and I highly recommend using it. However, if the model does not fit with your course outline or your own perspective on adolescence, it is possible to use the text without using the framework. Each chapter is self-contained, and so it is not necessary to assign chapters in the sequence in which

they are ordered in the text. Most users of this book assign the chapters in the order in which they appear, but some assign the chapters in a sequence that pairs an aspect of psychosocial development with the context that most influences it (for example, "Schools" with "Achievement," or "Peer Groups" with "Intimacy"), and that has worked well for them.

Theory and Methods

Although the Introduction reviews how different disciplines (such as psychology, sociology, anthropology, and history) approach the study of adolescence, it does not provide detailed examinations of particular theories or research methods. My preference is to integrate material on theory and methods when it is most relevant, in a way that shows students how research and theory are related. At the beginning of the chapter on intimacy, for instance, several perspectives on close relationships (for example, attachment theory and Sullivan's perspective on psychosocial development) are presented, and then the relevant research is examined. Similarly, the research methods and tools employed in the study of adolescence are discussed in the context of specific studies that illustrate the powers—or pitfalls—of certain strategies.

Supplements
FOR THE INSTRUCTOR

The supplements for the eighth edition have been carefully revised and updated by Elizabeth Cauffman and Elizabeth Davis, both from the University of California, Irvine. All the instructor supplements can be found on the text's password-protected Online Learning Center at www.mhhe.com/steinberg8. Please ask your McGraw-Hill representative for access information.

- **Instructor's Manual** includes learning objectives, lists of key terms, notable changes from last edition, chapter overviews, lecture topics and supplementary readings, background readings, classroom activities, Web links, and lists of films and videos.
- **Test Bank** includes approximately 100 test questions per chapter, comprised of multiple-choice and Essay questions. This computerized test bank is available in EZ-Test, McGraw-Hill's computerized testing software.
- **PowerPoint presentations** have been enhanced to include more figures and tables from the text. For additional images, go to the **Image Gallery,** where you can download and embed images into your PowerPoint presentations and course Web site.

FOR THE STUDENT

The student Online Learning Center features chapter-by-chapter multiple-choice, true/false, and short-answer questions that allow students to test their understanding of the text. For access go to www.mhhe.com/steinberg8.

Acknowledgments

Revising a textbook at a time when so much new information is available is a challenge that requires much assistance. Over the years, my students (as well as many who have written to me from other institutions) have suggested numerous ways in which the text might be improved, and I have learned a great deal from listening to them. I am especially grateful to Kate Monahan and Joanna Lee, who ably tracked down and organized much of the new research published in the three years between editions. I also acknowledge with appreciation the following colleagues, whose feedback on the seventh edition helped shape the eighth edition:

John H. Bickford, Jr., *University of Massachusetts, Amherst*

Jane Dwyer, *Rivier College*

Roger Gaddis, *Gardner-Webb University*

Lisa Jack, *Augsburg College*

Erin Kraan, *Miami University of Ohio*

Steven Kohn, *Valdosta State University*

Nan McJamerson, *Grambling State University*

Mike Pecanic, *California State University, Fullerton*

Amanda Rabidue, *University of Arizona*

J. Blake Snider, *East Tennessee State University*

Claudia Whitley, *Stephen F. Austin State University*

A special thanks goes to Elizabeth Cauffman, at the University of California, Irvine, who read and critiqued each revised chapter in detail.

I also wish to thank my colleagues at McGraw-Hill, including Mike Sugarman, executive editor; Judith Kromm, senior developmental editor; Holly Paulsen, production editor; Natalia Peschiera, photo research coordinator; Cassandra Chu, senior designer; Rich DeVitto, production supervisor; Emma Ghiselli, art editor; and Sarah Martin, executive marketing manager.

In addition, I am grateful to the many colleagues and students across the country who took the time during the past 25 years to send me comments and suggestions based on their firsthand experiences using *Adolescence* in the classroom. They have improved the text with each edition.

I wrote the first edition of this book exactly 25 years ago, when I was teaching at the University of California, Irvine, sitting at a desk in a small alcove of a tiny 1930s beach cottage a few blocks from the ocean, with our Springer spaniel, Oscar, at my feet each day. This revision was written under similar circumstances, although in a different Southern California house and with a different Springer under my desk. Like his predecessor, Smuckers showed little interest in the book, but his loyal presence was always reassuring.

Laurence Steinberg

Adolescence

The Study of Adolescent Development

A MULTIDISCIPLINARY APPROACH TO ADOLESCENCE

THE BOUNDARIES OF ADOLESCENCE

Early, Middle, and Late Adolescence

A FRAMEWORK FOR STUDYING ADOLESCENT DEVELOPMENT

The Fundamental Changes of Adolescence

The Contexts of Adolescence

Psychosocial Development of Adolescence

THEORETICAL PERSPECTIVES ON ADOLESCENCE

Biosocial Theories

Organismic Theories

Learning Theories

Sociological Theories

Historical and Anthropological Theories

STEREOTYPES VERSUS SCIENTIFIC STUDY

ON OCTOBER 13, 2004, the line to get into the gallery of the U.S. Supreme Court started forming long before dawn. People had come from all over the country to hear oral arguments for what was probably the most important case concerning teenagers in the Court's history. The justices were going to decide whether it was constitutional to execute individuals for crimes they had committed when they were under 18. At the time, the United States was one of only two countries in the world—the other being Somalia—that still had the so-called juvenile death penalty. Previous Supreme Court rulings had banned capital punishment for individuals under 16. But in 2004, in the United States, it was still legal to execute anyone who was 16 or older. At issue in this case, *Roper v. Simmons*, was whether the ban against capital punishment should be extended to 16- and 17-year-olds.

I was one of the lucky ones who did not have to wait in line that morning. As the lead scientific consultant to the American Psychological Association on this issue, I had helped author the organization's *amicus brief*—a document that is submitted to the Court before a case is argued that tries to influence the justices' thinking—and I had a reserved seat in the gallery, along with many others who had been actively involved in the case. In our brief, we had argued that scientific research on adolescent development was consistent with the idea that 16- and 17-year-olds were psychologically less mature than adults—so much so that they should not be held to the same standards in court or subject to the same degree of punishment (Steinberg & Scott, 2003). The Court had ruled a few years earlier that mentally retarded individuals could not be executed, because they were not as responsible for their behavior as individuals of ordinary intelligence. By this logic, we wrote, the same should be true for minors. After all, society prohibits 16- and 17-year-olds from voting, serving on juries, or purchasing alcohol, on the grounds that they are not as mature as adults. In our view, it simply wasn't fair to say that teenagers were too immature to vote but mature enough to be treated like adults when they had committed a crime.

I had a special interest in the case. For the past 10 years, my collaborators and I have been trying to figure out where, on the basis of scientific study, we should draw the line between adolescence and adulthood. This is not just an abstract, academic exercise. How we answer this question has far-reaching ramifications for society and, of course, for teenagers. How old does someone have to be in order to be tried and sentenced as an adult for a crime he has committed? At what age should a pregnant adolescent be able to obtain an abortion without parental permission? How old should individuals have to be to obtain contraception, see a psychologist, or have cosmetic surgery without their parents knowing? Have we picked the right ages in deciding where to draw the line as to who can drive, see R-rated movies, or buy cigarettes? Is there an age by which you think individuals are mature enough to make these sorts of decisions on their own? Or should we have different ages for different decisions?

And how should we respond to young offenders? "Do the adult crime, do the adult time," may sound fair from the perspective of crime victims, but does it make sense in light of what we know about adolescent development? Can a 12-year-old fully appreciate the consequences of his actions? Does someone this age understand court procedures enough to be competent to stand trial? Should adolescents who are found guilty of crimes receive the same punishment as adults who have committed similar offenses? If capital punishment is legal for adults who have committed murder, why shouldn't it be legal for teenage killers as well? After all, it hurts just as much to be shot by a 16-year-old as it does to be shot by a 26-year-old.

As I waited for the justices to file into the court, I worried about how the arguments would go. The outcome was difficult to predict. Everyone knew where seven of the nine justices stood. It was common knowledge that Chief Justice Rehnquist and Justices Scalia and Thomas were all in favor of permitting the execution of individuals for crimes they had committed when they were 16 or 17. In contrast, Justices Breyer, Ginsburg, Stevens, and Souter had publicly stated that they thought that capital punishment for teenagers was unconstitutional. That made the count 4–3 in favor of abolishing the juvenile death penalty. We needed either Justice Kennedy or Justice O'Connor to vote to ban the juvenile death penalty to obtain a majority.

The questions posed by the justices during oral arguments did not reveal what either Justice Kennedy or Justice O'Connor was thinking. Both justices asked questions, but neither commented in a way that revealed his or her leanings. As I left the court with my colleagues, we agreed that the ultimate vote was still impossible to predict.

On March 1, 2005, the Court announced its decision. By a vote of 5–4, it ruled that the juvenile death penalty was unconstitutional—that it violated the Eighth Amendment's prohibition against "cruel and unusual punishment." Justice Kennedy had joined with the other four justices who had previously announced their opposition to capital punishment for minors. Not only did Justice Kennedy write for the majority, he cited our studies of adolescent development five times in his opinion. Thanks in part to the scientific study of adolescent development, no American under the age of 18 would ever face the death penalty again.

FOOD FOR THOUGHT
What do you think about the Supreme Court decision? Should 16- and 17-year-olds who commit serious crimes be punished the same way as adults who commit comparable offenses?

A Multidisciplinary Approach to Adolescence

What is the nature of adolescents' identity development in a changing world? How should society deal with problems of youth unemployment, underage drinking, teenage pregnancy, and juvenile crime? What is the best way to prepare young people for the work, family, and citizenship roles of adulthood? How should the criminal justice system treat violent juvenile offenders like Christopher Simmons, the defendant who potentially faced the death penalty as a result of his murder conviction?

Answering these questions requires a thorough understanding of adolescents' psychological development, and in this book, we will examine how—and why—people's hopes and plans, their fears and anxieties, and their questions and concerns change as they grow into adulthood. Answering these difficult questions requires more than an understanding of the ways in which individuals change psychologically as they move through adolescence, though. It also requires knowledge of how they develop physically, how their brain matures, how their relationships with others change, how as a group they are viewed and treated by society, how adolescence in our society differs from adolescence in other cultures, and how the nature of

One significant aspect of the transition from childhood into adolescence is the young person's entry into the labor force.

adolescence itself has changed over the years. In other words, a complete understanding of adolescence in contemporary society depends on being familiar with biological, social, sociological, cultural, and historical perspectives on adolescence (Dahl & Hariri, 2005).

In this book, we will look at adolescence from a *multidisciplinary* perspective—a perspective that draws on a variety of disciplines. Each provides a view of adolescence that, in its own way, helps further our understanding of this period of the life cycle. We will look at contributions to the study of adolescence made by biologists, psychologists, educators, sociologists, historians, and anthropologists. The challenge here is not to try to determine which perspective on adolescence is best, but to find ways in which to integrate contributions from different disciplines into a coherent and comprehensive viewpoint on the nature of adolescent development in contemporary society.

The Boundaries of Adolescence

Let's begin with a fairly basic question: When does adolescence begin and end? Perhaps we can gain some insight into this question by examining the word itself.

The word *adolescence* is derived from the Latin *adolescere,* which means "to grow into adulthood" (Lerner & Steinberg, 2004). In all societies, adolescence is a time of growing up, of moving from the immaturity of childhood into the maturity of adulthood, of prepa-

ration for the future (Larson & Wilson, 2004). **Adolescence** is a period of transitions: biological, psychological, social, economic. During adolescence, individuals become interested in sex and become biologically capable of having children. They become wiser, more sophisticated, and better able to make their own decisions. They become more self-aware, more independent, and more concerned about what the future holds. They are permitted to work, to get married, to drive, and to vote. Think for a moment about how much you changed between elementary school and college. I'm sure you'll agree that the changes you went through were remarkable.

For the purposes of this book, adolescence is defined, roughly speaking, as the second decade of the life span. Although at one time "adolescence" may have been synonymous with the teenage years (from 13 to 19), the adolescent period has been lengthened considerably in the previous century, both because young people mature earlier physically (you'll read about this in the next chapter) and because so many individuals delay entering into work and marriage until their mid-20s (Settersten, Furstenberg, & Rumbaut, 2005). It therefore makes more sense to think of adolescence as beginning around age 10 and ending in the early 20s.

As you can see in Table I.1, there are a variety of boundaries we might draw between childhood and adolescence, and between adolescence and adulthood. Whereas a biologist would place a great deal of emphasis on the attainment and completion of puberty, an

TABLE I.1   The boundaries of adolescence. One problem that students of adolescence encounter early is a fundamental one: deciding when adolescence begins and ends, or what the boundaries of the period are. Different theorists have proposed various markers, but there is little agreement on the issue. Here are some examples of the ways in which adolescence has been distinguished from childhood and adulthood that we shall examine in this book. Which boundaries make the most sense to you?

Perspective	When Adolescence Begins	When Adolescence Ends
Biological	Onset of puberty	Becoming capable of sexual reproduction
Emotional	Beginning of detachment from parents	Attainment of separate sense of identity
Cognitive	Emergence of more advanced reasoning abilities	Consolidation of advanced reasoning abilities
Interpersonal	Beginning of shift in interest from parental to peer relations	Development of capacity for intimacy with peers
Social	Beginning of training for adult work, family, and citizen roles	Full attainment of adult status and privileges
Educational	Entrance into junior high school	Completion of formal schooling
Legal	Attainment of juvenile status	Attainment of majority status
Chronological	Attainment of designated age of adolescence (e.g., 10 years)	Attainment of designated age of adulthood (e.g., 21 years)
Cultural	Entrance into period of training for ceremonial rite of passage	Completion of ceremonial rite of passage

adolescence   The second decade of life.

attorney would look instead at important age breaks designated by law, and an educator might draw attention to differences between students enrolled in different grades in school. Is a biologically mature fifth-grader an adolescent or a child? Is a 20-year-old college student who lives at home an adolescent or an adult? There are no right or wrong answers to these questions. It all depends on the boundaries we use to define the period. Determining the beginning and ending of adolescence is more a matter of opinion than absolute fact.

Rather than argue about which boundaries are the correct ones, it makes more sense to think of development during adolescence as involving a *series* of transitions from immaturity into maturity (Settersten et al., 2005). Some of these passages are long and some are short; some are smooth and others are rough. And not all of them occur at the same time. Consequently, it is quite possible—and perhaps even likely—that an individual will mature in some respects before he or she matures in others. The various aspects of adolescence have different beginnings and different endings for every individual. An individual can be a child in some ways, an adolescent in other ways, and an adult in still others.

FOOD FOR THOUGHT

What boundaries make the most sense to you? How would you draw the line between childhood and adolescence? Between adolescence and adulthood?

EARLY, MIDDLE, AND LATE ADOLESCENCE

Although adolescence may span a 10-year period, because so much psychological and social growth takes place during this decade, most social scientists and practitioners argue that it makes more sense to view the adolescent years as composed of a series of phases than as one single stage. The 12-year-old whose time and energy is wrapped up in hip-hop, IM-ing, and soccer, for example, has little in common with the 20-year-old who is involved in a serious romance, worried about pressures at work, and looking for an affordable apartment.

Social scientists who study adolescence usually differentiate among **early adolescence** (about ages 10–13), **middle adolescence** (about ages 14–17), and **late adolescence** (about ages 18–21). These divisions, as you may have guessed, correspond to the way in which our society groups young people in educational institutions; they are the approximate ages that customarily mark attendance at middle or junior high school, high school, and college. In discussing devel-

opment during adolescence, we will need to be sensitive not only to differences between adolescence and childhood, or between adolescence and adulthood, but to differences among the various phases of adolescence itself. Some writers also have suggested that a new phase of life, called **emerging adulthood** (Arnett, 2004) or "youthhood" (Côté, 2000), now characterizes the early and mid-20s. However, despite the popularity of this idea in the mass media, there is little evidence that this is a universal stage of life or that the majority of young people in their mid-20s are in some sort of psychological or social limbo (Shanahan, Porfeli, Mortimer, & Erikson, 2005). Indeed, what is most striking about the transition from adolescence to adulthood today is just how many different pathways there are. Some individuals—those we might label "emerging adults"—spend their 20s single, dependent on their parents, and bouncing from job to job, while others leave adolescence and go straight into marriage, full-time employment, and economic independence (Osgood, Ruth, Eccles, Jacobs, & Barber, 2005). As you'll see in Chapter 3, the pathways through adolescence and into adulthood are equally varied.

RECAP

- The study of adolescence draws on different disciplines, including psychology, biology, sociology, anthropology, and education.
- *Adolescence* comes from the Greek word meaning "to grow into adulthood."
- There is no single accepted way to define the beginning or end of adolescence—it has different boundaries depending on how one chooses to define the period.
- Most social scientists distinguish among three stages of adolescence: early (10–13), middle (14–17), and late (18–22).
- Some writers have suggested that a new phase of life, called "emerging adulthood," now characterizes the early and mid-20s.

early adolescence   The period spanning roughly ages 10–13, corresponding roughly to the junior or middle high school years.

middle adolescence   The period spanning roughly ages 14–17, corresponding to the high school years.

late adolescence   The period spanning roughly ages 18–21, corresponding approximately to the college years.

emerging adulthood   The period spanning roughly ages 18–25, during which individuals make the transition from adolescence to adulthood.

A Framework for Studying Adolescent Development

In order to organize information from a variety of different perspectives, this book uses a framework that is based largely on a model suggested by the late psychologist John Hill (1983). The framework is organized around three basic components: (1) the fundamental changes of adolescence, (2) the contexts of adolescence, and (3) the psychosocial developments of adolescence.

THE FUNDAMENTAL CHANGES OF ADOLESCENCE

What, if anything, is distinctive about adolescence as a period in the life cycle? According to Hill, three features of adolescent development give the period its special flavor and significance: (1) the onset of puberty, (2) the emergence of more advanced thinking abilities, and (3) the transition into new roles in society. We refer to these three sets of changes—biological, cognitive, and social—as the *fundamental changes* of adolescence. And they are changes that occur universally; virtually without exception, all adolescents in every society go through them.

▌ **Biological Transitions**   The chief elements of the biological changes of adolescence—which collectively are referred to as **puberty**—involve changes in the young person's physical appearance (including breast development in girls, the growth of facial hair in boys, and a dramatic increase in height for both sexes) and the development of the ability to conceive children (Susman & Rogol, 2004).

Chapter 1 not only describes the biological changes that occur in early adolescence but also examines how puberty affects the adolescent's psychological development and social relationships. The adolescent's self-image, for example, may be temporarily threatened by marked changes in physical appearance. When your body and face are changing, not surprisingly, the way you look at yourself changes as well. In addition, relationships inside the family are transformed by adolescents' greater need for privacy and their interest in forming intimate relationships with peers. Girls may suddenly feel uncomfortable about being physically affectionate with their fathers, and boys with their mothers. And, of course, adolescents' friendships are altered by newly emerging sexual impulses and concerns. In short, puberty is not just a biological event.

The implications of the cognitive changes of adolescence are far-reaching.

▌ **Cognitive Transitions**   The word *cognitive* is used to refer to the processes that underlie how people think about things. Memory and problem solving are both examples of cognitive processes. Changes in thinking abilities, which are dealt with in Chapter 2, make up the second of the three fundamental changes of the adolescent period. The emergence of more sophisticated thinking abilities is one of the most striking changes to take place during adolescence. Compared with children, for example, adolescents are much better able to think about hypothetical situations (that is, things that have not yet happened but might, or things that may not happen but could) and about abstract concepts, such as friendship, democracy, or morality (Keating, 2004). As you'll read, groundbreaking research on brain development is beginning to shed light on the ways in which these and other changes in thinking during adolescence result from the maturation of particular brain regions and systems.

The implications of these cognitive changes are also far-reaching. The ability to think more capably in hypothetical and abstract terms affects the way adolescents think about themselves, their relationships, and the world around them. We will see, for example, that teenagers' abilities to plan ahead, argue with their parents, solve algebra equations, and resolve moral dilemmas are all linked to changes in the way they think. Even the way day-to-day decisions are made is affected. For the first time, individuals become able to think in logical ways about what their lives will be like in the future, about their relationships with friends and family, and about politics, religion, and philosophy.

puberty   The biological changes of adolescence.

Social scientists who study adolescence usually differentiate among three periods: early adolescence (approximately ages 10–13), middle adolescence (14–17), and late adolescence (18–21).

▎**Social Transitions** All societies distinguish between individuals who are thought of as children and those who are seen as ready to become adults. Our society, for example, distinguishes between people who are "underage," or minors, and people who have reached the age of majority. It is not until adolescence that individuals are permitted to drive, marry, and vote. Such changes in rights, privileges, and responsibilities—which we'll examine in Chapter 3—constitute the third set of fundamental changes that occur at adolescence: social changes. In some cultures, the social changes of adolescence are marked by a formal ceremony—a **rite of passage.** In most contemporary industrialized societies, though, the transition is less clearly marked. But everywhere, a change in social status is a universal feature of adolescence (Ford & Beach, 1951).

FOOD FOR THOUGHT

In contemporary society, we do not have formal ceremonies that designate when a person has become an "adult." Do we have more informal ways to let individuals know when they have made the transition?

As the young person's treatment by society changes, so do relationships around the home, at school, and in the peer group. Changes in social status also permit young people to enter new roles and engage in new activities, such as marriage and work, that dramatically alter their self-image and relationships with others. The adolescent, on the verge of becoming an adult, has important decisions to make and new options to choose among. Even something as simple as being able to drive has implications for the adolescent's relationships with parents and friends.

RECAP

- The three features of adolescence that make the period unique are called the "fundamental changes of adolescence."
- One fundamental change is biological and involves the physical changes of puberty.
- A second fundamental change is cognitive and involves changes in thinking abilities.
- The third fundamental change is social and involves changes in the way that society defines the individual.

THE CONTEXTS OF ADOLESCENCE

Although all adolescents experience the biological, cognitive, and social transitions of the period, the *effects* of these changes are not uniform for all young people. Puberty makes some adolescents feel attractive

rite of passage A ceremony or ritual marking an individual's transition from one social status to another, especially marking the young person's transition to adulthood.

and self-assured, but it makes others feel ugly and self-conscious. Being able to think in hypothetical terms makes some teenagers thankful that they grew up with the parents they have, but it prompts others to run away in search of a better life. Reaching 18 prompts some teenagers to enlist in the military or apply for a marriage license, but for others, becoming an adult is frightening and unsettling.

If the fundamental changes of adolescence are universal, why are their effects so varied? Why aren't all individuals affected in the same ways by puberty, by cognitive development, and by changes in social and legal status? The answer lies in the fact that the psychological impact of the biological, cognitive, and social changes of adolescence is shaped by the environment in which the changes take place. In other words, psychological development during adolescence is a product of the interplay between a set of three very basic, universal changes and the context in which these changes are experienced. According to the **ecological perspective on human development,** whose main proponent has been Urie Bronfenbrenner (1979), we cannot understand development without examining the settings, or context, in which it occurs. I always laugh to myself when parents ask me how their children are going to be affected by puberty, because the only honest answer I can give them is, "It depends."

Consider, for example, two 14-year-old girls growing up in neighboring communities. When Diane went through puberty, around age 13, her parents responded by restricting her social life because they were afraid she would become too involved with boys and neglect her schoolwork. Diane felt that her parents were being unfair and foolish. She rarely had a chance to meet any boys she wanted to date, because all the older boys went to the high school across town. Even though she was in the eighth grade, she was still going to school with fifth-graders. And she couldn't meet anyone through work, either, because her school would not issue work permits to any student under the age of 16.

Maria's adolescence was very different. For one thing, when she had her first period, her parents took her aside and discussed sex and pregnancy with her. They explained how different contraceptives worked and made an appointment for Maria to see a gynecologist in case she ever needed to discuss something with a doctor. Although she was still only 14 years old, Maria knew that she would begin dating soon, because in her

community, the junior and senior high schools had been combined into one large school, and the older boys frequently asked the younger girls out. In addition, since there was no prohibition at her school against young teenagers working, Maria decided to get a job; she knew she would need money to buy clothes if she was going to start dating.

Two teenage girls. Each goes through puberty, each grows intellectually, and each moves closer in age to adulthood. Yet each grows up under very different circumstances: in different families, in different schools, with different groups of peers, and in different communities. Both are adolescents, but their adolescent experiences are markedly different. And as a result, each girl's psychological development will follow a different course.

Diane's and Maria's worlds may seem quite different from each other. Yet the two girls share many things in common, at least in comparison to two girls growing up in different parts of the world or in different historical eras. Imagine how different your adolescence would have been if you had grown up a century ago and, instead of going to high school, had to work full-time from the age of 12. Imagine how different it might be to grow up 100 years from today. And imagine how different adolescence is for the teenager whose family is very poor versus one whose family is wealthy. Even siblings growing up within the same family have different growing-up experiences, depending on their birth order in the family and various other factors, such as differences in the way their parents treat them (Hetherington, Reiss, & Plomin, 1994). It is impossible to generalize about the nature of adolescence without taking into account the surroundings and circumstances in which young people grow up.

For this reason, the second component of our framework is the *context* of adolescence. In modern societies, there are four main contexts in which young people spend time: families, peer groups, schools, and work and leisure settings. But it is not enough to consider these settings in isolation, because they themselves are located within a neighborhood or community, which influences how they are structured and what takes place in them. It would be naïve, for example, to discuss the impact that "school" has on adolescent development without recognizing that a school in an affluent suburb is likely very different from one in the inner city or in a remote rural area. Moreover, the community in which these settings are located is itself embedded in a broader context that is shaped by culture, geography, and historical forces (Bronfenbrenner, 1979). The nature and structure of these contexts—both proximal and distant—dramatically affect the ways in which the fundamental changes of adolescence

ecological perspective on human development   A perspective on development that emphasizes the broad context in which development occurs.

are experienced. To the extent that one adolescent's world differs from another's, the two young people will have very different experiences during the adolescent years.

Most social scientists interested in adolescent development study young people in one setting at a time. Researchers traditionally have looked at family relations or at peer relations, at school or at work, at home or in the community. Increasingly, however, researchers have begun to acknowledge the linkages among the different contexts of adolescence, and they are beginning to ask questions about the nature of these connections. Instead of asking how adolescents are affected in the home environment, for example, studies might ask how events in the home environment affect events in the peer group.

This change in orientation reflects, in part, the increased importance of the ecological perspective on development (Bronfenbrenner, 1979, 1989). From this perspective, we focus not only on the developing individual but also on the interrelations between the individual and his or her contexts, and on the interconnections among the contexts themselves. According to Bronfenbrenner, the ecology of adolescent development can be thought of as having four distinct levels: (1) each of the immediate settings in which adolescents live (such as the family and the school), which he calls **micro-systems;** (2) the system of relations between these immediate settings (such as the family–peer group link and the home–school link), which he calls the **meso-system;** (3) the settings that do not contain the adolescent but that affect him or her indirectly (such as the parent's workplace), which he calls the **exo-system;** (4) and the broader context of culture and historical time (such as the country and era in which an adolescent lives), which he calls the **macro-system.** Most research on adolescent development has focused on either the micro-system or the macro-system; far less attention has been paid to the meso-system and the exo-system.

Although young people growing up in modern America share some experiences with young people all over the world, their development is distinctly different from that of young people in other societies, especially those in less affluent and less industrialized nations, because their families, peer groups, schools, work settings, and social institutions are different (Brown, Larson, & Saraswathi, 2002). In other words, the contexts of adolescence are themselves shaped and defined by the larger society in which young people live. In this book, we'll be especially interested in how the contexts of adolescence have changed in contemporary industrialized society and what the implications of these changes are for adolescent development. Key contexts include the following:

▌ **Families**   Adolescence is a time of dramatic change in family relationships (Collins & Laursen, 2004). In addition, frequent moves, high rates of divorce, and increasing numbers of single-parent households and working mothers have altered aspects of family life in contemporary America (Hernandez, 1997). In Chapter 4, we examine how changes in the family system, and in the context of family life, affect young people's psychological development.

▌ **Peer groups**   Over the past 100 years, the peer group has come to play an increasingly important role in the socialization and development of teenagers (B. Brown, 2004). But has the rise of peer groups in contemporary society been a positive or negative influence on young people's development? In Chapter 5, we discuss how peer groups have changed adolescence, for better and for worse.

▌ **Schools**   Chapter 6 examines schools as a context for adolescent development. Contemporary society depends on schools to occupy, socialize, and educate adolescents. But how good a job are schools doing?

FOOD FOR THOUGHT

Think about the context in which you went through adolescence, and compare it to that in which your parents went through the same period of development. How do these contexts differ from each other? What difference might it have made for psychological development?

micro-systems   In the ecological perspective on human development, the immediate settings in which adolescents develop, such as the family or the peer group.

meso-system   In the ecological perspective on human development, the layer of the environment formed by two or more immediate settings, as in the home–school linkage.

exo-system   In the ecological perspective on human development, the layer of the environment that does not directly contain the developing person but that affects the setting in which the person lives.

macro-system   In the ecological perspective on human development, the outermost layer of the environment, containing forces such as history and culture.

As family life has changed, so has the context in which adolescents develop.

What should schools do to help prepare adolescents for adulthood? And how should schools for adolescents be structured (Eccles, 2004)? These are three of the many difficult questions we will be examining.

▮ **Work, leisure, and the mass media**   If you've been to a large shopping mall or fast-food restaurant lately, you know that many of today's teenagers are working (Staff, Mortimer, & Uggen, 2004). In Chapter 7, we look at the world of adolescent work and at how part-time jobs are affecting young people's psychological development and well-being. We also discuss the influence of various leisure activities, including extracurriculars, mass media, and the Internet (Roberts, Henriksen, & Foehr, 2004).

RECAP
- According to Urie Bronfenbrenner's ecological perspective on human development, we cannot understand development without examining the settings, or context, in which it occurs.

psychosocial   Referring to aspects of development that are both psychological and social in nature, such as developing a sense of identity or sexuality.

- Although the fundamental biological, cognitive, and social changes of adolescence are universal, their effects depend on the context in which they take place.
- The immediate, or proximal, contexts of adolescent development are the family, the peer group, school, and work and leisure settings.
- What takes place in these immediate settings is influenced by the broader context in which they are contained, including the community, the culture, and the historical era in which people grow up.

PSYCHOSOCIAL DEVELOPMENT OF ADOLESCENCE

The third, and final, component of our framework concerns the major *psychosocial developments* of adolescence—identity, autonomy, intimacy, sexuality, and achievement—as well as certain psychosocial problems that may arise in adolescence. Social scientists use the word **psychosocial** to describe aspects of development that are both psychological and social in nature. Sexuality, for instance, is a psychosocial issue because it involves both psychological change (that is, changes in the individual's emotions, motivations, and behavior) and changes in the individual's social relations with others.

Identity, autonomy, intimacy, sexuality, and achievement are not concerns that arise only during the adolescent years, of course, and psychological or social problems can and do occur during all periods of the life cycle. These five sets of issues are present throughout the life span, from infancy through late adulthood. They represent basic developmental challenges that all people face as they grow and change: (1) discovering and understanding who they are as individuals —**identity,** (2) establishing a healthy sense of independence—**autonomy;** (3) forming close and caring relationships with other people—**intimacy;** (4) expressing sexual feelings and enjoying physical contact with others—**sexuality;** and (5) being successful and competent members of society—**achievement.**

Although these issues are not unique to adolescence, development in each of these areas takes a special turn during this stage. Understanding how and why such psychosocial developments take place during adolescence is a special concern of social scientists interested in this age period. We know that individuals form close relationships before adolescence, for example, but why is it that intimate relationships with opposite-sex friends first develop during adolescence? We know that infants struggle with learning how to be independent, but why during adolescence do individuals need to be more on their own and make some decisions apart from their parents? We know that children fantasize about what they will be when they grow up, but why is it that these fantasies are not transformed into serious concerns until adolescence?

Part Three of this book discusses changes in each of the five psychosocial areas and examines several common psychosocial problems.

▌ **Identity** Chapter 8 deals with changes in identity, self-esteem, and self-conceptions. In adolescence, a variety of important changes in the realm of identity occur (Nurmi, 2004). The adolescent may wonder who he or she really is and where he or she is headed. Coming to terms with these questions may involve a period of experimentation—a time of trying on different personalities in an attempt to discover one's true self. As you will read, the adolescent's quest for identity is a quest not only for a personal sense of self but for recognition from others and from society that he or she is a special, unique individual.

▌ **Autonomy** Adolescents' struggle to establish themselves as independent, self-governing individuals— in their own eyes and in the eyes of others—is a long and occasionally difficult process, not only for young people but for those around them, especially their parents. Chapter 9 focuses on three sorts of concerns about autonomy that are of special importance during

adolescence: becoming less emotionally dependent on parents, learning to make independent decisions, and establishing a personal code of values and morals (Eisenberg & Morris, 2004; Steinberg, 1990).

▌ **Intimacy** During adolescence, important changes take place in the individual's capacity to be intimate with others, especially with peers. As we'll see in Chapter 10, friendships emerge for the first time during adolescence that involve openness, honesty, loyalty, and exchange of confidences, rather than simply sharing activities and interests (B. Brown, 2004; Collins & Steinberg, 2006). Dating takes on increased importance, and as a consequence, so does the capacity to form romantic relationships that are trusting and loving (Collins, 2003; Furman, Brown, & Feiring, 1999).

▌ **Sexuality** Sexual activity generally begins during the adolescent years (Savin-Williams & Diamond, 2004). Becoming sexual is an important aspect of development during adolescence—not only because it transforms the nature of relationships between adolescents and their peers but also because it raises for the young person a range of difficult questions. Chapter 11 discusses these concerns, including efforts to incorporate sexuality into a still-developing sense of self, the need to resolve questions about sexual values and morals, and the need to come to terms with the sorts of relationships into which the adolescent is prepared—or not prepared—to enter. We also look at sex education, contraceptive use, the dangers of sexually transmitted diseases, and adolescent childbearing.

▌ **Achievement** In Chapter 12, we examine changes in individuals' educational and vocational behavior and plans. Important decisions—many with long-term consequences—about schooling and careers are made during adolescence. Many of these decisions depend on adolescents' achievement in school, on their evaluations of their own competencies and capabilities, on their aspirations and expectations for the future, and on the direction and advice they receive from parents, teachers, and friends (Eccles, 2004).

identity The domain of psychosocial development involving self-conceptions, self-esteem, and the sense of who one is.

autonomy The psychosocial domain concerning the development and expression of identity.

intimacy The psychosocial domain concerning the formation, maintenance, and termination of close relationships.

sexuality The psychosocial domain concerning the development and expression of sexual feelings.

achievement The psychosocial domain concerning behaviors and feelings in evaluative situations.

█ **Psychosocial Problems**   Historically, the scientific study of adolescence has focused much attention on the problems that some young people have during this time, despite the fact that most adolescents move through the period without getting into serious trouble (Steinberg & Morris, 2001). In Chapter 13, we'll look at three sets of problems typically associated with adolescence: drug and alcohol use and abuse (Chassin et al., 2004), delinquency and other "externalizing problems" (Farrington, 2004), and depression and other "internalizing problems" (Graber, 2004). In each case, we examine the prevalence of the problem, the factors believed to contribute to its development, and approaches to prevention and intervention.

RECAP

- Five main psychosocial issues are especially important in adolescence.
- Identity involves changes in the ways individuals see, evaluate, and think about themseves.
- Autonomy involves the development of emotional, behavioral, and moral independence.
- Intimacy involves the development of the ability to form close and satisfying relationships with others.
- Sexuality involves the development of the ability to express sexual feelings and enjoy physical contact with others.
- Achievement involves the development of beliefs and abilities that permit one to be a competent and successful member of society.
- Some individuals experience psychological problems during adolescence—most commonly depression, delinquency, and substance abuse—although the majority of individuals move through the period without serious difficulties.

Theoretical Perspectives on Adolescence

The study of adolescence is based not just on empirical research but on theories of development. You will read more about different theories of adolescence throughout this book, but an overview of the major ones may be helpful.

I find it useful to organize theoretical perspectives on adolescence around a question that has long dominated discussions of human development: How much is due to "nature," or biology, and how much is due to "nurture," or the environment. Some theories of adolescence emphasize biology, others emphasize the environment, and still others fall somewhere between the two extremes (see Figure I.1). The purpose of this brief overview is not to argue for one approach over another, but rather to demonstrate how each of these views has helped us gain a better understanding of the nature of adolescence. We'll begin with a look at the most extremely biological perspectives and work our way across a continuum toward the other extreme—perspectives that give primacy to the role of the environment.

BIOSOCIAL THEORIES

The fact that biological change during adolescence is noteworthy is not a matter of dispute—how could it be, when puberty is such an obvious part of adolescence? But how important this biological change is in defining the psychosocial issues of the period is something that students of adolescence disagree about. Theorists who have taken a biological or, more accurately, "biosocial" view of adolescence stress the hormonal and physical changes of puberty as driving forces. The most important biosocial theorist was G. Stanley Hall (1904), considered the "father" of the scientific study of adolescence.

█ **Hall's Theory of Recapitulation**   G. Stanley Hall, who was very much influenced by the work of Charles Darwin, the author of the theory of evolution, believed that the development of the individual paralleled the development of the human species, a notion referred to as his theory of recapitulation. Infancy, in his view, was equivalent to the time during our evolution when we were primitive, like animals. Adolescence, in contrast, was seen as a time that paralleled the evolution of our species into civilization. For Hall, the development of the individual through these stages was determined primarily by instinct—by biological and genetic forces within the person—and hardly influenced by the environment.

FIGURE I.1   Theories of adolescence range from the extremely biological, like that of G. Stanley Hall, to the extremely environmental, like that of Ruth Benedict.

The most important legacy of Hall's view of adolescence is the notion that it is inevitably a period of "storm and stress". He believed that the hormonal changes of puberty cause upheaval, both for the individual and for those around him or her. Because this turbulence was biologically determined, it was unavoidable. The best that society could do was to find ways of managing the young person whose "raging hormones" would invariably lead to difficulties.

Although scientists no longer believe that adolescence is an inherently stressful period, or that the hormonal changes of puberty cause emotional problems, much contemporary work continues to emphasize the role that biological factors play in shaping the adolescent experience. More than 100 years ago, in fact, Hall speculated about brain maturation, hormonal influences on behavior, and changes in patterns of sleep during adolescence—all very hot topics in the study of adolescence today (Dahl & Hariri, 2005). Current work in the biosocial tradition, also influenced by Hall and his followers, explores the genetic bases of individual differences in adolescence and the evolutionary bases of adolescent behavior.

ORGANISMIC THEORIES

Our next stop on the continuum is in the domain of what are called "organismic" theorists. Like biosocial theorists, organismic theorists stress the importance of the biological changes of adolescence. But unlike their biosocial counterparts, organismic theories also take into account the ways in which contextual forces interact with and modify these biological forces.

If you have had previous course work in developmental psychology, you have undoubtedly encountered the major organismic theorists, since they have long dominated the study of human development more generally. Three of these theorists, in particular, have had a great influence over the study of adolescence: Sigmund Freud (1938), Erik Erikson (1968), and Jean Piaget (Inhelder and Piaget, 1958). Although these theorists share in common an organismic orientation, the theories they developed emphasized different aspects of individual growth and development.

Freudian Theory   For Freud, development was best understood in terms of the psychosexual conflicts that arise at different points in development. Like Hall, Freud saw adolescence as a time of upheaval. According to Freud, the hormonal changes of puberty upset the psychic balance that had been achieved during the prior psychosexual stage, called "latency." Because the hormonal changes of puberty were responsible for marked increases in sex drive, the adolescent was temporarily thrown into a period of intrapsychic crisis, and old psychosexual conflicts, long buried in the unconscious, were revived. Freud and his followers believed that the main challenge of adolescence was to resolve these conflicts and restore a psychic balance. Although the process was driven by the hormonal changes of puberty, the specific conflicts faced by the young person were seen as dependent on his or her early experiences in the family.

Sigmund Freud himself actually had very little to say specifically about adolescence. But his daughter, Anna Freud (1958), extended much of her father's thinking to the study of development during the second decade of life. This work has been carried on by neo-Freudians such as Peter Blos (1979), whose theories of adolescent autonomy we explore in detail in Chapter 9.

Eriksonian Theory   In Erikson's theory, the emphasis was on the psychosocial crises characteristic of each period of growth. Like Freud, Erikson believed that internal, biological developments moved the individual from one developmental stage to the next. But unlike Freud, Erikson stressed the psychosocial, rather than the psychosexual, conflicts faced by the individual at each point in time. Whereas Freud emphasized the development of the id—that part of the psyche believed to be dominated by instinctual urges—Erikson emphasized the development of the ego—that part of the psyche believed to regulate thought, emotion, and behavior.

Erikson proposed eight stages in psychosocial development, each characterized by a specific "crisis" that arose at that point in development because of the interplay between the internal forces of biology and the unique demands of society. In Erikson's theory, which we look at in detail in Chapter 8, adolescence is seen as a period that revolves around the identity crisis, a crisis that is shaped both by the changes of puberty and by the specific demands that society places on young people to make decisions about the future. According to Erikson, the challenge of adolescence is to resolve the identity crisis and to emerge with a coherent sense of who one is and where one is headed.

▌ **Piagetian Theory** Freud and Erikson both emphasized emotional and social development. For Jean Piaget, in contrast, development could best be understood by examining changes in the nature of thinking, or cognition. Piaget believed that, as children mature, they pass through stages of cognitive development, and in each stage, from birth to adolescence, their ways of thinking are qualitatively distinct. In his view, understanding the distinctive features of thought and reasoning at each stage can give us insight into the overall development of the individual at that point in time.

In Piaget's theory, which is discussed in detail in Chapter 2, adolescence marks the transition from concrete to abstract thought. According to this model, adolescence is the period in which individuals become capable of thinking in hypothetical terms, a development that permits a broad expansion of logical capabilities. As you will see, many of the familiar changes in behavior that we associate with adolescence have been attributed to these changes in cognitive abilities. Piaget's views have been applied to the study of moral development, social development, and education.

As is the case with the other organismic theories, Piaget's theory of cognitive development emphasizes the interplay between biological and contextual forces. The development of abstract thinking in adolescence, for example, is influenced both by the internal biological changes of the developmental period and by changes in the intellectual environment encountered by the individual.

LEARNING THEORIES

As we move across the theoretical continuum from extreme biological views to extreme environmental ones, we encounter a group of theories that shift the emphasis from biological forces to environmental ones. Whereas organismic theorists tend to emphasize the interaction between biological change and environmental demands, learning theorists stress the context in which behavior takes place. The capacity of the individual to learn from experience is assumed to be a biological given that is in place long before adolescence. What is of interest to learning theorists is the content of what is learned.

Learning theorists are not especially developmental in their approach and, as a consequence, have little to say specifically about adolescence as a developmental period. Indeed, for learning theorists, the basic processes of human behavior are the same during adolescence as during other periods of the life span. But learning theorists have been extremely influential in the study of adolescent development because they have helped us understand how the specific environment in which an adolescent lives can shape his or her behavior.

▌ **Behaviorism** There are two general categories of learning theorists. One group, known as behaviorists, emphasizes the processes of reinforcement and punishment as the main influences on adolescent behavior. The main proponent of this view was B. F. Skinner (1953), whose theory of operant conditioning has had a tremendous impact on the entire field of psychology. Within an operant conditioning framework, reinforcement is defined as the process through which a behavior is made more likely to occur again, whereas punishment is defined as the process through which a behavior is made less likely to occur again. From this vantage point, adolescent behavior is nothing more or less than the product of the various reinforcements and punishments to which the individual has been exposed. An adolescent who strives to do well in school, for example, does so because in the past she or he has been reinforced for this behavior or has been punished for not behaving this way. Similarly, a teenager who continues to experiment with risky behavior must be being reinforced for this sort of activity or punished for being especially cautious.

▌ **Social Learning Theory** A related approach is taken by social learning theorists such as Albert Bandura (Bandura & Walters, 1959) Social learning theorists also emphasize the ways in which adolescents learn how to behave, but in contrast to behaviorists, they place more weight on the processes of modeling and observational learning. According to these theorists, adolescents learn how to behave not simply by being reinforced and punished by forces in the environment but also by watching and imitating those around them. As is clear throughout the text, social learning approaches to adolescence have been very influential in explaining how adolescents are affected by the child-rearing methods employed by their parents and by the influence, or pressure, of their peers. From this vantage point, an adolescent who strives to do well in school or who takes a lot of risks is probably imitating peers, family members, or actors portrayed in the mass media.

SOCIOLOGICAL THEORIES

The emphasis of the biosocial, organismic, and learning theories is mainly on forces within the individual, or within the individual's specific environment, that shape development and behavior. In contrast, sociological theories of adolescence attempt to understand how adolescents, *as a group*, come of age in society. Instead of emphasizing differences among individuals in their biological makeups or their experiences in the world, sociological theorists focus on the factors that all adolescents or groups of adolescents have in common by virtue of their age, gender, ethnicity, social class, or some other demographic factor.

▌ **Adolescent Marginality** Sociological theories of adolescence often have focused on relations between the generations and have tended to emphasize the difficulties young people have in making the transition from adolescence to adulthood, especially in industrialized society. Two themes have dominated these discussions. One theme, concerning the marginality of young people, emphasizes the difference in power that exists between the adult and the adolescent generations. Two important thinkers in this vein are Kurt Lewin (1951) and Edgar Friedenberg (1959). Although the view that adolescents are "second-class citizens" was more influential 50 years ago than today, contemporary applications of this viewpoint stress the fact that many adolescents are prohibited from occupying meaningful roles in society and therefore experience frustration and restlessness. Some writers have noted that many of the problems we associate with adolescence have been created, in part, by the way in which we have structured the adolescent experience and isolated young people from adults (Furstenberg, 2000).

A modification of this view focuses on differences within the adolescent population. According to this viewpoint, the adolescent's social class, or socioeconomic status, as it is formally known, structures his or her experience of growing up. Theorists such as August Hollingshead ([1949] 1975) and Robert Havighurst (1952) have emphasized the fact that the experience of adolescence differs markedly as a function of the young person's family background. They argue that it is impossible to generalize about the "nature" of adolescence because it varies so much depending on the resources of the adolescent's family.

▌ **Intergenerational Conflict** The other theme in sociological theories of adolescence concerns intergenerational conflict, or as it is more commonly known, the generation gap. Theorists such as Karl Mannheim (1952) and James Coleman (1961) stressed the fact that adolescents and adults grow up under different social circumstances and therefore develop different sets of attitudes, values, and beliefs. As a consequence, there is inevitable tension between the adolescent and the adult generations. Some writers, like Coleman, have gone so far as to argue that adolescents develop a different cultural viewpoint—a counterculture—that may be hostile to the values or beliefs of adult society. We'll look more closely at this idea in Chapter 5.

Although sociological theories of adolescence clearly place the emphasis on the broader context in which adolescents come of age, there is still a theme of inevitability that runs through their approach. Mannheim, for example, believed that because modern society changes so rapidly, there will always be problems between generations, because each generation grows up with different experiences and beliefs. American adults who were teenagers in the late 1960s, for instance, when "sex, drugs, and rock 'n' roll" was the mantra, may find themselves arguing with their children, who may have come of age during a time of extreme political conservatism, such as the 1980s. Similarly, Lewin believed that marginality is an inherent feature of adolescence because adults always control more resources and have more power than young people.

HISTORICAL AND ANTHROPOLOGICAL THEORIES

Our final stop on the continuum takes us to the extreme environmental position. Historians and anthropologists who study adolescence share with sociologists an interest in the broader context in which young people come of age, but they take a much more relativistic stance. Historical perspectives, such as those offered by Glen Elder (1980), Joseph Kett (1977), and Thomas Hine (1999), stress the fact that adolescence as a developmental period has varied considerably from one historical era to another. As a consequence, it is impossible to generalize about such issues as the degree to which adolescence is stressful, the developmental tasks of the period, or the nature of intergenerational relations. Historians would say that these issues all depend on the social, political, and economic forces present at a given time. Even something as basic to our view of adolescence as the "identity crisis," they say, is a social invention that arose because of industrialization and the prolongation of schooling. Prior to the Industrial Revolution, when most adolescents followed in their parents' occupation, people didn't have "crises" over who they were or what they were going to do in life.

▌ **Adolescence as an Invention** One group of theorists has taken this viewpoint to its logical extreme, arguing that adolescence is *entirely* a social invention (Bakan, 1972). They believe that the way in which we

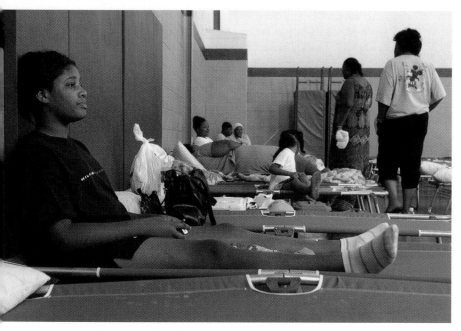

Dramatic historical events, such as a major hurricane, can transform the nature of adolescence.

Anthropological Perspectives A similar theme is echoed by anthropologists who study adolescence, the most important of whom were Ruth Benedict (1934) and Margaret Mead (1928). Benedict and Mead, whose work is examined in Chapter 3, pointed out that societies vary considerably in the ways in which they view and structure adolescence. As a consequence, these thinkers viewed adolescence as a culturally defined experience—stressful and difficult in societies that saw it this way, but calm and peaceful in societies that had an alternative vision. Benedict, in particular, drew a distinction between continuous and discontinuous societies. In continuous societies (typically, nonindustrialized societies with little social change), the transition from adolescence to adulthood is gradual and peaceful. In discontinuous societies (typically, industrialized societies characterized by rapid social change), the transition to adulthood is abrupt and difficult. In Chapter 3, we'll look at whether the nature of development differs for individuals in continuous versus discontinuous societies.

divide the life cycle into stages—drawing a boundary between childhood and adolescence, for example—is nothing more than a reflection of the political, economic, and social circumstances in which we live. They point out that, although puberty has always been a feature of human development, it was not until the rise of compulsory education that we began treating adolescents as a special and distinct group. This suggests that social conditions, not biological givens, define the nature of adolescent development. We noted earlier that contemporary writers debate whether a new phase of life, "emerging adulthood," actually exists. Writers who believe that different stages of life are social inventions would say that, if emerging adulthood does exist, it does so because society has made it so, not because people have really changed in any fundamental way.

RECAP

- Theoretical perspectives on adolescence range from those that emphasize the role of biology to those that emphasize the role of the environment.
- Biosocial theorists view development in adolescence as the inevitable outcome of the physical changes of puberty. One of the most important, Hall, believed that adolescence was necessarily a period of storm and stress.
- Organismic theorists like Freud, Erikson, and Piaget view development as the product of an interaction between biology and the environment. Freud and his followers emphasized the internal psychological conflicts brought on by puberty. Erikson viewed adolescence as a time of "identity crisis." Piaget emphasized the development of abstract thinking.
- Learning theorists like Skinner and Bandura view development in adolescence as the result of exposure to forces that reinforce, punish, or model particular behaviors.
- Sociological theorists focus more on the ways in which adolescents as a group, rather than individuals, are treated by society. They emphasize differences between the adolescent and adult generations in power, attitudes, and values.
- Historical theorists focus on the ways in which adolescence differs during different periods.

FOOD FOR THOUGHT

Some writers have argued that the stage of life we call adolescence is a social invention. What do they mean by this? Could you say this about other periods of development? Is infancy a social invention? Is middle age?

They emphasize the fact that adolescence is at least in part a social "invention," whose characteristics depend on the way in which young people are viewed at that point in time.

- Anthropological theorists emphasize the diversity of adolescent experiences across different cultures. Like historical theorists, they believe that the nature of adolescence is determined by the conditions under which people grow up.

Stereotypes Versus Scientific Study

One of the oldest debates in the study of adolescence is whether adolescence is an inherently stressful time for individuals. As we noted earlier, G. Stanley Hall, who is generally acknowledged as the father of the modern study of adolescence, likened adolescence to the turbulent, transitional period in the evolution of the human species from savagery into civilization. "Adolescence is a new birth," Hall wrote. "Development is less gradual, suggestive of some ancient period of storm and stress" (1904, p. 6). Long before Hall, in the eighteenth century, the French philosopher Jean-Jacques Rousseau had described adolescence by drawing an analogy to a violent storm. "As the roaring of the waves precedes the tempest, so the murmur of rising passions announces the tumultuous change. . . . Keep your hand upon the helm," he warned parents, "or all is lost" (Rousseau, [1762] 1911, pp. 172–173).

Although neither Hall nor Rousseau had any scientific evidence that adolescence was any more stormy than childhood or adulthood, their portrayal of teenagers as passionate, fickle, and unpredictable individuals persists today. For example, people still tend to think of adolescence as a difficult and stressful time. Once, when working with a family that was having problems, the 12-year-old girl I was counseling told me that her mother had been telling her that she was going to go through a difficult time when she turned 14—as if some magical, internal alarm clock was set to trigger storm and stress on schedule.

The girl's mother wasn't alone in her view of adolescence, of course. Sometime this week, turn on the television or go to a movie and note how teenagers are depicted. If they are not portrayed as juvenile delinquents—the usual role in which they are cast—adolescents are depicted as sex-crazed idiots (if they are male), giggling fools (if they are female), or

tormented lost souls, searching for their place in a strange, cruel world (if they aren't delinquent, sex-crazed, or giggling). It's not only fictionalized portrayals of teenagers that are stereotyped—studies of local newscasts find that the majority of stories on youth are about violence (Dorfman, Woodruff, Chavez, & Wallack, 1997; Gilliam & Bales, 2001). Scholars, too, have been influenced by this viewpoint—a disproportionate number of scientific studies of adolescents have focused on young people's problems rather than their normative development (Steinberg & Morris, 2001).

Adolescents are one of the most stereotyped groups in contemporary society and, as a consequence, are one of the most misunderstood (Males, 1998). These stereotypes have important implications for how teenagers are treated—by teachers, by shopkeepers, and by parents. One study, for example, measured mothers' general beliefs about adolescence to see how well these preconceptions predicted how they raised their own teenager (Buchanan, 2003). The more likely a mother was to believe that teenagers are conforming, risk taking, and rebellious, the more likely she was to expect adolescence to be difficult for her own child—regardless of her own child's actual behavior. In contrast, the more likely a mother was to believe that adolescents as a group are kind and moral, the more likely she was to expect that she would have a positive relationship with her own child. This finding is important because, as you'll read in Chapter 4, parent–teenager relations are influenced by the expectations they have about each other.

The tremendous growth of the scientific literature on adolescence over the past two decades has, fortunately, led to more accurate views of normal adolescence among practitioners who work with young people (Stoller, Offer, Howard, & Koenig, 1996), although a trip to the "Parenting" section of your local bookstore will quickly reveal that the storm-and-stress stereotype is still alive and well (Steinberg, 2001). (I once saw a book titled *Surviving Your Dog's Adolescence*!) Today, most experts do not dismiss the storm-and-stress viewpoint as entirely incorrect but do see the difficulties that some adolescents have as due largely to the cultural context within which they grow up. Studies show that adolescents are more stressed in contemporary industrialized societies, for example, than they are in nonindustrialized, traditional ones, although this may change as globalization brings some of the more stressful aspects of adolescence to less industrialized parts of the world (Larson & Wilson, 2004). Indeed, one of the most striking trends of the past several decades is that globalization has made adolescence in different parts of the world increasingly similar (National Research Council, 2005).

FOOD FOR THOUGHT

If adolescence is not inevitably a period of storm and stress, why is it so often portrayed this way?

You have no doubt come into this course with many convictions of your own about adolescence. These beliefs are based in part on your own experiences as a teenager (Buchanan & Holmbeck, 1998) and in part on the images of adolescents to which you have been exposed over the years—in books, on film, and in television. As several writers have pointed out, even social scientists' portrayal of teenagers is influenced by the broader social and historical context in which they work. To the extent that we *want* to see adolescents as being different from adults, we exaggerate the differences between teenagers and their elders and portray young people as "out of control due to hormonal storms" (Lesko, 1996, p. 157). During periods of economic downturn, for instance, when jobs are scarce, scholars depict adolescents as immature, unstable, and undereducated, whereas during periods of war, the same age group is portrayed as mature, responsible, and competent (Enright, Levy, Harris, & Lapsley, 1987). Presumably, these characterizations serve a broader, if hidden, agenda—during depressions, there are fewer jobs to go around, and adults may "need" to see adolescents as incapable of working, whereas the reverse is true during wartime, when adolescents are needed to take on jobs and serve in the military.

The truth of the matter is that most characteristics of adolescence as a developmental stage have both positive and negative elements (Siegel & Scovill, 2000). Young people's willingness to challenge authority, for instance, is both refreshing (when we agree with them) and bothersome (when we do not). Their propensity to take risks is both admirable and frightening. Their energy and exuberance is both exciting and dangerous.

In many respects, then, whatever "story" adult society tells about adolescence at any given moment is one that portrays young people in a way that best serves the needs of adults. Adolescent "irresponsibility" is cast in a favorable light by advertisers trying to sell soft drinks (e.g., our product will make you as carefree and fun loving as a teenager), but in a negative light in order to justify policies like mandating community service for high school students or spending money to build more juvenile detention facilities. Today's calls for treating youthful offenders as adults—"adult time for adult crime"—have more to do with politicians' desires to take advantage of public concerns about crime than with any real changes that have taken place in young people themselves (Scott & Woolard, 2004).

Sadly, recent public opinion polls indicate that American adults today view adolescents very negatively, describing them as rude, irresponsible, wild, and disrespectful (Public Agenda, 1999). Part of this is due, no doubt, to the overly negative picture of adolescents presented in the contemporary mass media, which exaggerates the prevalence of adolescents' involvement in crime, drug use, promiscuous sex, and various forms of risk taking (Males, 1998). Unfortunately, there are signs that as globalization has spread these images beyond America, stereotypes of adolescents have become more negative around the world (Larson & Wilson, 2004). There is even an obscure word for the irrational fear of adolescents: **ephebephobia**!

One of the goals of this book is to provide you with a more realistic understanding of adolescent development in contemporary society—an understanding that reflects the best and most up-to-date scientific knowledge. As you read the material, you should think about your personal experiences as an adolescent, but you should also try to look beyond them and be willing to question the "truths" about teenagers that you have grown accustomed to over the years. This does not mean that your experiences were not valid, or your recollections inaccurate. Rather, your experiences as a teenager were the product of a unique set of forces that have made you the individual you are today. The person who sits next to you in class—or the person who right now, in some distant region of the world, is thinking back to his or her adolescence—was probably exposed to different forces than you were and probably had a different set of adolescent experiences as a consequence.

RECAP

- Adolescents are one of the most stereotyped groups in society.
- Many stereotypes about adolescence are excessively negative, portraying teenagers as sex-crazed, foolish, irresponsible, difficult, or troubled.
- The scientific study of adolescence has not provided evidence in support of these stereotypes.
- One goal of this book is to foster an objective understanding of adolescence that is grounded in solid research and theory.

ephebephobia   The irrational fear of adolescents.

PART 1

1 | Biological Transitions   2 | Cognitive Transitions   3 | Social Transitions

The Fundamental Changes of Adolescence

CHAPTER 1

Biological Transitions

PUBERTY: AN OVERVIEW
>   The Endocrine System
>   What Triggers Puberty?
>   How Hormones Influence Adolescent Development

SOMATIC DEVELOPMENT
>   Changes in Stature and the Dimensions of the Body
>   Sexual Maturation

THE TIMING AND TEMPO OF PUBERTY
>   Variations in the Timing and Tempo of Puberty
>   Genetic and Environmental Influences on Pubertal Timing

THE PSYCHOLOGICAL AND SOCIAL IMPACT OF PUBERTY
>   The Immediate Impact of Puberty
>   The Impact of Specific Pubertal Events
>   The Impact of Early or Late Maturation

EATING DISORDERS
>   Obesity
>   Anorexia Nervosa and Bulimia

PHYSICAL HEALTH AND HEALTH CARE IN ADOLESCENCE
>   The Paradox of Adolescent Health
>   Causes of Mortality in Adolescence
>   Promoting Adolescent Health

ACCORDING TO AN OLD JOKE, there are only two things in life that one can be sure of—death and taxes. To this brief list, we might add puberty—the physical changes of adolescence—for, of all the developments that take place during the second decade of life, the only truly inevitable one is physical maturation. Not all adolescents experience identity crises, rebel against their parents, or fall madly in love, but virtually all undergo the biological transitions associated with maturation into adult reproductive capability.

Puberty, however, is considerably affected by the context in which it occurs. Physical development is influenced by a host of environmental factors, and the timing and rate of pubertal growth vary across regions of the world, socioeconomic classes, ethnic groups, and historical eras. Today, in contemporary America, the average girl reaches **menarche**—the time of first menstruation—at about age 12$\frac{1}{2}$. But among the Lumi people of New Guinea, the typical girl does not reach menarche until after 18 years of age (Eveleth & Tanner, 1990). Imagine how that five-year difference transforms the nature of adolescence. Picture how different high school would be if sexual maturation did not occur until after graduation!

Physical and sexual maturation profoundly affects the ways in which adolescents view themselves and are viewed and treated by others. Yet the social environment exerts a tremendous impact on puberty and its psychological and social consequences; indeed, as you will read in this chapter, the social environment even affects the timing of puberty (that is, whether a person matures early or late). In some societies, pubertal maturation brings with it a series of complex and public initiation rites that mark the passage of the young person into adulthood, socially as well as physically. In other societies, recognition of the physical transformation from child into adult takes more subtle forms. Parents may merely remark, "Our little boy has become a man," when they discover that he needs to shave, or "Our little girl has grown up," when they learn that she has gotten her first period. Early or late maturation may be cause for celebration or cause for concern, depending on what is admired or derogated in a given peer group at a given point in time. In the fifth grade, developing breasts may be a source of embarrassment, but in the ninth grade, it may be just as embarrassing not to have developed breasts.

In sum, even the most universal aspect of adolescence—puberty—is hardly universal in its impact on the young person. In this chapter, we examine just how and why the environment in which adolescents develop exerts its influence even on something as fundamental as puberty.

Puberty: An Overview

Puberty derives from the Latin word *pubertas*, which means "adult." Technically, the term refers to the period during which an individual becomes capable of sexual reproduction. More broadly, however, puberty encompasses all the physical changes that occur in the growing girl or boy as the individual passes from childhood into adulthood.

Puberty has five chief physical manifestations (Marshall, 1978):

1. A rapid acceleration in growth, resulting in dramatic increases in both height and weight

2. The development of primary sex characteristics, including the further development of the gonads, or sex glands, which are the testes in males and the ovaries in females

3. The development of secondary sex characteristics, which involves changes in the genitals and breasts, and the growth of pubic, facial, and body hair

4. Changes in body composition—specifically, in the quantity and distribution of fat and muscle

5. Changes in the circulatory and respiratory systems, which lead to increased strength and tolerance for exercise

Each of these sets of changes is the result of developments in the endocrine and central nervous systems, many of which begin years before the external signs of puberty are evident—some occur even before birth. Puberty may appear to be rather sudden, judging from its external signs, but in fact it is part of a gradual process that begins at conception (Susman & Rogol, 2004). You may be surprised to learn that no new hormones are produced and no new bodily systems develop at puberty. Rather, some hormones that have been present since before birth increase, and others decrease.

menarche   The time of first menstruation, one of the most important changes to occur among females during puberty.

THE ENDOCRINE SYSTEM

The **endocrine system** produces, circulates, and regulates levels of hormones in the body. **Hormones** are highly specialized substances secreted by one or more endocrine glands, after which they enter the bloodstream and travel throughout the body. **Glands** are organs that stimulate particular parts of the body to respond in specific ways. Just as specialized hormones carry "messages" to particular cells in the body, so are the body's cells designed to receive hormonal messages selectively. Many of the hormones that play important roles at puberty carry their instructions by activating very specific types of neurons in the brain, called **gonadotropin-releasing hormone (GnRH) neurons** (Sisk & Foster, 2004).

■ **The Hormonal Feedback Loop** The endocrine system receives its instructions to increase or decrease circulating levels of particular hormones from the central nervous system, mainly through the firing of GnRH neurons in the brain. The system works like a thermostat. Hormonal levels are "set" at a certain point, which may differ depending on the stage of development, just as you might set a thermostat at a certain temperature (and use different settings during different seasons or different times of the day). By setting your room's thermostat at

60°F, you are instructing your heating system to go into action when the temperature falls below this level. Similarly, when a particular hormonal level in your body dips below the endocrine system's **set point** for that hormone, secretion of the hormone increases; when the level reaches the set point, secretion temporarily stops. And, as is the case with a thermostat, the setting level, or set point, for a particular hormone can be adjusted up or down, depending on environmental or internal bodily conditions.

Such a **feedback loop** becomes increasingly important at the onset of puberty. Long before early adolescence—in fact, before birth—a feedback loop develops involving the **pituitary gland** (which controls hormone levels in general), the **hypothalamus** (the part of the brain that controls the pituitary gland, and where there is a concentration of GnRH neurons), and the **gonads** (in males, the **testes;** in females, the **ovaries**). This feedback loop is known as the **HPG axis** (for Hypothalamus, Pituitary, Gonads). The gonads release the "sex" hormones—**androgens** and **estrogens** (see Figure 1.1). Although

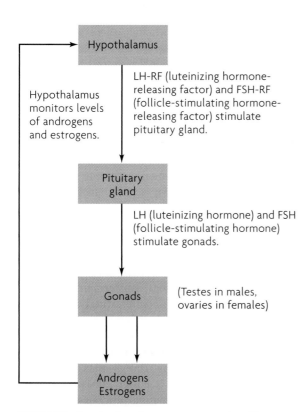

FIGURE 1.1 Levels of sex hormones are regulated by a feedback system composed of the hypothalamus, pituitary gland, and gonads. (Grumbach et al., 1974)

endocrine system The system of the body that produces, circulates, and regulates hormones.

hormones Highly specialized substances secreted by one or more endocrine glands.

glands Organs that stimulate particular parts of the body to respond in specific ways to particular hormones.

gonadotropin-releasing hormone (GnRH) neurons Specialized neurons that are activated by certain pubertal hormones.

set point A physiological level or setting (e.g., of a specific hormone) that the body attempts to maintain through a self-regulating system.

feedback loop A cycle through which two or more bodily functions respond to and regulate each other, such as that formed by the hypothalamus, the pituitary gland and the gonads.

pituitary gland One of the chief glands responsible for regulating levels of hormones in the body.

hypothalamus A lower part of the brain stem that controls the functioning of the pituitary gland.

gonads The glands that secrete sex hormones; in males, the testes; in females, the ovaries.

testes The male gonads.

ovaries The female gonads.

HPG (hypothalamic-pituitary-gonadal) axis the neurophysiological pathway that involves the hypothalamus, the pituitary gland, and the gonads.

androgens A class of sex hormones secreted by the gonads, found in both sexes, but in higher levels among males than females following puberty.

estrogens A class of sex hormones secreted by the gonads, found in both sexes, but in higher levels among females than males following puberty.

you may think of androgens as "male" hormones and estrogens as "female" hormones, both types of hormones are produced by each sex, and both are present in males and females at birth. During adolescence, however, the average male produces more androgens than estrogens, and the average female produces more estrogens than androgens (Petersen & Taylor, 1980).

The hypothalamus responds to the levels of sex hormones circulating in the body. Your HPG axis is set to maintain certain levels of androgens and estrogens. When these levels fall below the set points, the hypothalamus no longer inhibits the pituitary, thus permitting it to stimulate the release of sex hormones by the gonads and other, puberty-related hormones by the adrenal gland. When sex hormone levels reach the set point, the hypothalamus responds by inhibiting its stimulation of the pituitary gland. As you will see, puberty occurs when it does because several different signals—genetic as well as environmental—instruct the brain to change the set point (Sisk & Foster, 2004). Just as you might change the setting on your heating thermostat automatically every November 1, or when your utility bill has gotten too expensive, your brain is constantly monitoring a variety of signals and adjusting your hormonal set points in response.

▮ **Adrenarche**   During and just before puberty, the pituitary also secretes hormones that act on the thyroid and on the adrenal cortex and hormones that stimulate overall bodily growth. The release of these substances is also under the control of the hypothalamus. The thyroid and adrenal cortex, in turn, secrete hormones that cause various bodily changes to take place at puberty. Research also indicates that early feelings of sexual attraction to others—most individuals, not only in America but around the world, report that their first sexual attraction took place at the "magical age of 10," before they went through puberty—may be stimulated by maturation of the adrenal glands, called **adrenarche** (Herdt & McClintock, 2000). Changes at puberty in the brain system that regulates the adrenal gland are also important because this is the brain system that controls how we respond to stress. One reason that adolescence may be a period of great vulnerability for the onset of many serious mental disorders is that an adverse side effect of the hormonal changes of puberty is to make us more responsive to stress (Steinberg et al., 2005; Walker, Sabuwalla, & Huot, 2004).

adrenarche   The maturation of the adrenal glands that takes place during adolescence.

cortisol   A hormone produced when we are exposed to stress.

leptin   A protein produced by the fat cells that may play a role in the onset of puberty.

This leads to excessive secretion of the stress hormone **cortisol,** a substance that at high and chronic levels can cause brain cells to die. Keep in mind that there is a difference between saying that adolescence is an inherently stressful time (which it is not) and saying that adolescence is a time of heightened vulnerability to stress (which it is).

FOOD FOR THOUGHT

Do you remember your first feelings of sexual attraction for someone? How old were you?

WHAT TRIGGERS PUBERTY?

Although the HPG axis is active before birth, it is relatively quiet during much of childhood. Something happens during middle childhood, though, that reawakens the HPG axis and signals it that the body is ready for puberty. Some of this is due to a clock whose "puberty alarm" is set very early in life by information coded in the genes (as you will see, the age at which someone goes through puberty is largely inherited). But some of the reawakening of the HPG axis at puberty is due to multiple signals that tell the brain it is time to "get the childbearing show on the road." These signals indicate whether there are sexually mature mating partners in the environment, whether there are sufficient nutritional resources to support a pregnancy, and whether the individual is physically mature and healthy enough to begin reproducing.

For example, some evidence suggests that rising levels of a protein produced by fat cells, **leptin,** may be the most important signal, at least in females (Susman & Rogol, 2004). This idea is consistent with observations that individuals may not go through puberty until they have accumulated a certain amount of body fat. Research also shows that stress, illness, nutritional deficiencies, excessive exercise, and excessive thinness can all delay the onset of puberty (Frisch, 1983; McClintock, 1980), and that puberty tends to occur earlier among girls who are obese (Kaplowitz, Slora, Wasserman, Pedlow, & Herman-Giddens, 2001). (Interestingly, obesity is associated with *earlier* puberty among girls but with *later* puberty among boys [Wang, 2002].) The signal carried by rising levels of leptin instructs the hypothalamus to stop doing things that have been inhibiting puberty (Sisk & Foster, 2004). As a result of these genetic and signaling processes, the GnRF neurons are excited, and the hypothalamus initiates a cascade of hormonal events that ultimately result in sexual maturation.

Excessive exercise can delay the onset of puberty among girls.

HOW HORMONES INFLUENCE ADOLESCENT DEVELOPMENT

Hormones play two very different roles in adolescent development: an **organizational role** and an **activational role** (Coe, Hayashi, & Levine, 1988). Most people understandably think that changes in behavior at puberty result from changes in hormones that occur at that time. But this is only partially correct. Long before adolescence—in fact, before birth—hormones shape, or *organize*, the brain in ways that may not be manifested in behavior until childhood or even adolescence. Generally, until about eight weeks after conception, the human brain is "feminine" unless and until it is exposed to certain "masculinizing" hormones, like testosterone. Because levels of testosterone are higher among males than females while the brain is developing, males usually end up with a more "masculinized" brain than females. This sex difference in brain organization predetermines certain patterns of behavior, many of which may not actually appear until much later (Collaer & Hines, 1995). Studies of sex differences in aggression, for example, show that even though

some of these differences may not appear until adolescence, they likely result from the impact of prenatal hormones, rather than from hormonal changes at puberty.

In other words, the presence or absence of certain hormones early in life may "program" the brain and the central nervous system to develop in certain ways and according to a certain timetable later on (Sisk & Foster, 2004). Because we may not see the resulting changes in behavior until adolescence, it is easy to conclude, mistakenly, that the behaviors result from hormonal changes that take place at the time of puberty. In reality, however, exposure to certain hormones before birth may set a sort of alarm clock that does not go off until adolescence. Just because the alarm clock rings at the same time that puberty begins does not mean that puberty *caused* the alarm to go off.

Many changes in behavior at adolescence occur, however, because of changes in hormone levels at puberty; these hormonal changes are said to *activate* the changes in behavior. For instance, the increase in certain hormones at puberty is thought to stimulate the development of secondary sex characteristics, such as the growth of pubic hair. Other hormonal changes at adolescence, controlled by the adrenal gland, may stimulate an increase in individuals' sex drive (McClintock & Herdt, 1996).

Still other changes during puberty are likely to be results of an *interaction* between organizational and activational effects of hormones (Collaer & Hines, 1995). Hormones that are present during the development of the fetus may organize a certain set of behaviors (for example, our brains may be set up to have us later engage in sexual behavior), but certain changes in those hormones at puberty may be needed to activate the pattern; that is, individuals may not become motivated to engage in sex until puberty.

RECAP

- Puberty has five main physical manifestations: a rapid acceleration in growth, the development of primary sex characteristics, the development of secondary sex characteristics, changes in body composition, and changes in the circulatory and respiratory systems.

organizational role (of hormones) The process through which early exposure to hormones, especially prenatally, organizes the brain or other organs in anticipation of later changes in behavior or patterns of growth.

activational role (of hormones) The process through which changes in hormone levels, especially at puberty, stimulate changes in the adolescent's behavior, appearance, or growth.

- Puberty is regulated by a hormonal feedback loop that includes the hypothalamus, the pituitary gland, and the gonads.
- Many important changes at puberty involve a process called "adrenarche," which involves the regulation of the adrenal gland rather than the gonads.
- The onset of puberty is triggered by several factors, including a biological "alarm" that is coded in the individual's genes and various environmental signals, which let the body know that it is ready to begin reproduction.
- Physical and behavioral changes at puberty result from two different hormonal processes: organizational, which take place long before adolescence, and activational, which result from changes in hormones when puberty takes place.

Somatic Development

The effects of the hormonal changes of puberty on the adolescent's body are remarkable. Consider the dramatic changes in physical appearance that occur during early adolescence. The individual enters puberty looking like a child but within four years or so has the physical appearance of a young adult. During this relatively brief period, the average individual grows about 10 inches taller, matures sexually, and develops an adult-proportioned body. Along with many other organs, the brain changes in size, structure, and function at puberty, a series of developments we'll discuss in Chapter 2.

CHANGES IN STATURE AND THE DIMENSIONS OF THE BODY

▌ **The Adolescent Growth Spurt**   The simultaneous release of growth hormones, thyroid hormones, and androgens stimulates rapid acceleration in height and weight. This dramatic increase in stature is referred to as the **adolescent growth spurt.** What is most incredible about the adolescent growth spurt is

adolescent growth spurt   The dramatic increase in height and weight that occurs during puberty.

peak height velocity   The point at which the adolescent is growing most rapidly.

epiphysis   The closing of the ends of the bones, which terminates growth after the adolescent growth spurt has been completed.

not so much the absolute gain of height and weight that typically occurs but the speed with which the increases take place. Think for a moment of how quickly very young children grow. At the time of **peak height velocity**—the time at which the adolescent is growing most rapidly—he or she is growing at the same rate as a toddler. For boys, peak height velocity averages about 4 inches (10.3 centimeters) per year; for girls, it's about 3.5 inches (9.0 centimeters). Puberty is also a time of significant increase in weight—nearly half of one's adult body weight is gained during adolescence (Susman & Rogol, 2004).

Figure 1.2 shows just how remarkable the growth spurt is in terms of height. The graph on the left presents information on absolute height and indicates that, as you would expect, the average individual increases in height throughout infancy, childhood, and adolescence. As you can see, there is little gain in height after age 18. But look now at the right-hand graph, which shows the average increase in height per year (i.e., the *rate* of change) over the same age span. Here you can see the acceleration in height at the time of peak height velocity.

Figure 1.2 also indicates quite clearly that the growth spurt occurs, on average, about two years earlier among girls than among boys. In general, as you can see by comparing the two graphs, boys tend to be somewhat taller than girls before age 11; then girls tend to be taller than boys between ages 11 and 13; and finally, boys tend to be taller than girls from about age 14 on. You may remember what this was like during the fifth and sixth grades. Sex differences in height can be a concern for many young adolescents when they begin socializing with members of the opposite sex, especially if they are tall, early-maturing girls or short, late-maturing boys.

FOOD FOR THOUGHT

Think back to a time when the girls in your elementary school class tended to be taller than the boys. What impact, if any, did this have on social relationships?

During puberty, the skeletal structure also changes, with bones becoming harder and more brittle. One marker of the conclusion of puberty is the closing of the ends of the long bones in the body, a process called **epiphysis,** which terminates growth in height. Interestingly, there are ethnic differences in some of these skeletal changes, with bone density increasing

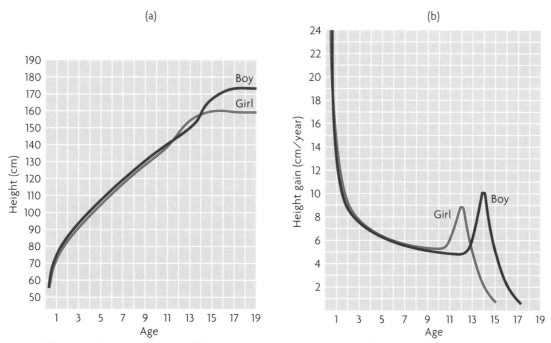

FIGURE 1.2 (a) Height (in centimeters) at different ages for the average male and female youngster. (b) Gain in height per year (in centimeters) for the average male and female youngster. Note the adolescent growth spurt. (Adapted from Marshall, 1978)

significantly more during puberty among African American than among white youngsters. Some experts believe that this ethnic difference in adolescence may account for the fact that, during adulthood, African American women are less likely than white women to develop osteoporosis and have fewer bone fractures (Gilsanz, Roe, Mora, Costin, & Goodman, 1991).

Much of the height gain during puberty results from an increase in torso length rather than in leg length. The sequence in which various parts of the body grow is fairly regular. Extremities—the head, hands, and feet—are the first to accelerate in growth. Then accelerated growth occurs in the arms and legs, followed by torso and shoulder growth. As one classic article put it, "A boy stops growing out of his trousers (at least in length) a year before he stops growing out of his jackets" (J. Tanner, 1972, p. 5).

Young adolescents often appear to be out of proportion physically—as though their nose or legs were growing faster than the rest of them. No, it's not an optical illusion. The parts of the body do not all grow at the same rate or at the same time during puberty. This can lead to an appearance of awkwardness or gawkiness in the young adolescent, who may be embarrassed by the disproportionate growth of different body parts. It is probably little consolation for the young adolescent going through this to be told that an attractive balance probably will be

restored within a few years, but fortunately, this is what usually happens.

■ **Sex Differences in Muscle and Fat**   The spurt in height during adolescence is accompanied by an increase in weight that results from an increase in both muscle and fat, but there are important sex differences in body composition. Before puberty, there are relatively few sex differences in muscle development and only slight sex differences in body fat. In both sexes, muscular development is rapid during puberty, but muscle tissue grows faster in boys than girls. In contrast, body fat increases for both sexes during puberty, but more so for females than for males, especially during the years just before puberty. For boys, there is actually a slight decline in body fat just before puberty. The end result of these sex differences is that boys finish adolescence with a muscle-to-fat ratio of about 3 to 1, but the comparable ratio for girls is approximately 5 to 4. This has important implications for understanding why sex differences in strength and athletic ability often appear for the first time during adolescence. According to one estimate, about half of the sex difference in athletic performance during early adolescence results simply from the difference in body fat (Smoll & Schutz, 1990).

Accompanying the gains in strength that occur during early adolescence are increases in the size and capacity of the heart and lungs and, consequently, in exercise tolerance. In all these areas, the rate and magnitude of the gains favor males over females. By the end of puberty, boys are stronger and have "larger hearts and lungs relative to their size, a higher systolic blood pressure, a lower resting heart rate, a greater capacity for carrying oxygen to the blood, . . . a greater power for neutralizing the chemical products of muscular exercise, such as lactic acid," higher blood hemoglobin, and more red blood cells (Petersen & Taylor, 1980, p. 129).

It is tempting to attribute these sex differences purely to hormonal factors, because androgens, which are present at higher levels in the prenatal environments of males versus females, and which increase during puberty in males at a much faster rate than in females, are closely linked to growth in aspects of the body that influence athletic ability. But with age, environmental factors like diet and exercise become increasingly important influences on sex differences in physical performance (Smoll & Schutz, 1990). As Petersen and Taylor (1980) point out, there are strong social pressures on girls to curtail "masculine" activities—including some forms of exercise—at adolescence, and studies show that girls are more likely than boys to markedly reduce their physical activity in preadolescence, with a very large proportion of adolescent girls failing to meet national guidelines for exercise (Goran et al., 1998; Savage & Scott, 1998). Moreover, adolescent girls' diets, especially those of African Americans, are generally less adequate nutritionally than the diets of boys, particularly in important minerals like iron (Johnson, Johnson, Wang, Smiciklas-Wright, & Guthrie, 1994). Both factors could result in sex differences in muscular development and exercise tolerance. Thus, sex differences in physical ability are influenced by a variety of factors, of which hormonal differences are but one part of a complex picture.

▌ Body Dissatisfaction Among Adolescent Girls

The rapid increase in body fat that occurs among females in early adolescence frequently prompts young girls to become overly concerned about their weight— even when their weight is within the normal range for their height and age (Smolak, Levine, & Gralen, 1993). Although the majority of girls diet unnecessarily during this time in response to the increase in body fat, the girls who are most susceptible to feelings of dissatisfaction with their bodies during this phase of development are those who mature early, begin dating early, and

come from relatively more affluent families (Dornbusch et al., 1981; Smolak, Levine, & Gralen, 1993). Girls who spend a lot of time talking about their looks with their friends are especially vulnerable to feelings of body dissatisfaction. In fact, for girls, it is comparing themselves with their friends, and not just being exposed to media portrayals of thinness, that leads to dissatisfaction (Carlson Jones, 2004). In contrast, boys' feelings about how they look revolve around how muscular they are and do not seem to be affected by comparisons with peers.

There are also important ethnic differences in the ways in which adolescent girls feel about their changing bodies (Yates, Edman, & Aruguete, 2004). African Americans seem less vulnerable to these feelings of body dissatisfaction than other girls, and consequently they are less likely to diet, presumably because of ethnic differences in conceptions of the ideal body type. Even among African Americans, however, dieting is common in early adolescence (Halpern & Udry, 1994). As you will read later in this chapter, many studies point to adolescence as the period of greatest risk for the development of eating disorders such as anorexia and bulimia.

FOOD FOR THOUGHT

Given the nature of sex differences in the physical changes of puberty, is body dissatisfaction inevitable among adolescent girls? Can anything be done to make young women feel better about their appearance?

SEXUAL MATURATION

Puberty brings with it a series of developments associated with sexual maturation. In both boys and girls, the development of the **secondary sex characteristics** is typically divided into five stages, often called **Tanner stages,** after the British pediatrician who devised the categorization system. Figure 1.3 shows the relative timing of the somatic and hormonal changes of puberty.

▌ Sexual Maturation in Boys

The sequence of developments in secondary sex characteristics among boys is fairly orderly (see Table 1.1). Generally, the first stages of puberty involve growth of the testes and scrotum, accompanied by the first appearance of pubic hair. Approximately one year later, the growth spurt in height begins, accompanied by growth of the penis and

secondary sex characteristics   The manifestations of sexual maturity at puberty, including the development of breasts, the growth of facial and body hair, and changes in the voice.

Tanner stages   A widely used system used to describe the five stages of pubertal development.

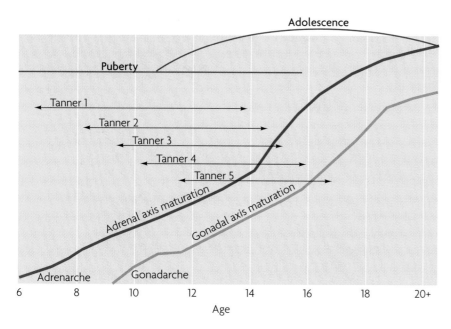

FIGURE 1.3 The biological changes we associate with adolescence actually unfold over a long period of time, beginning with the maturation of the adrenal axis during childhood and ending with the maturation of the gonadal axis in the early 20s. (Adapted from Dorn et al., 2006)

TABLE 1.1 The sequence of physical changes at puberty

Boys		Girls	
Characteristic	Age of First Appearance (Years)	Characteristic	Age of First Appearance (Years)
1. Growth of testes, scrotal sac	10–13½	1. Growth of breasts	7–13
2. Growth of pubic hair	10–15	2. Growth of pubic hair	7–14
3. Body growth	10½–16	3. Body growth	9½–14½
4. Growth of penis	11–14½	4. Menarche	10–16½
5. Change in voice (growth of larynx)	About same time as penis growth	5. Underarm hair	About two years after pubic hair
6. Facial and underarm hair	About two years after pubic hair appears	6. Oil- and sweat-producing glands	About same time as underarm hair
7. Oil- and sweat-producing glands, acne	About same time as underarm hair		

Source: Goldstein, 1976.

further development of pubic hair—now of a coarser texture and darker color. The five Tanner stages of penis and pubic hair growth in boys are shown in Figure 1.4.

The emergence of facial hair—first at the corners of the upper lip, next across the upper lip, then at the upper parts of the cheeks and in the midline below the lower lip, and finally along the sides of the face and the lower border of the chin—and body hair are relatively late developments in the pubertal process. The same is true for the deepening of the voice, which is gradual and generally does not occur until very late

adolescence. During puberty, there are changes in the skin as well. The skin becomes rougher, especially around the upper arms and thighs, and there is increased development of the sweat glands, which often gives rise to acne, pimples, and increased oiliness of the skin.

During puberty, there are slight changes in the male breast—to the embarrassment of many boys. Breast development is largely influenced by the estrogen hormones. As noted earlier, both estrogens and androgens are present in both sexes and increase in both sexes

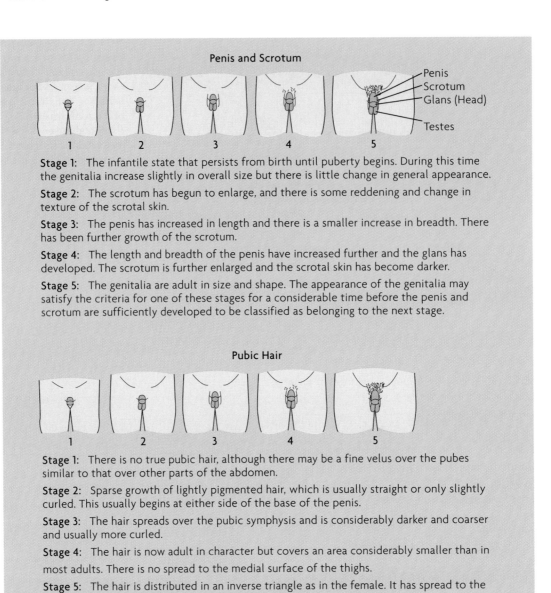

FIGURE 1.4   The five pubertal stages for penile and pubic hair growth. (From Morris & Udry, 1980)

at puberty, although in differing amounts. In the male adolescent, the areola (the area around the nipple) increases in size, and the nipple becomes more prominent. Some boys show a slight enlargement of the breast, although in the majority of cases this is temporary.

Other, internal changes occur that are important elements of sexual maturation. At the time that the penis develops, the seminal vesicles, the prostate, and the bilbo-urethral glands also enlarge and develop. The first ejaculation of seminal fluid generally occurs about one year after the beginning of accelerated penis growth, although this is often determined culturally rather than biologically, since for many boys first ejaculation occurs as a result of masturbation (J. Tanner,

1972). One interesting observation about the timing and sequence of pubertal changes in boys is that boys are generally fertile (i.e., capable of fathering a child) before they have developed an adultlike appearance. As you will read in the next section, the opposite is true for girls.

■ Sexual Maturation in Girls   The sequence of development of secondary sex characteristics among girls (shown in Table 1.1) is less regular than it is among boys. Generally, the first sign of sexual maturation in girls is the elevation of the breast—the emergence of the so-called breast bud. In about one-third of all adolescent girls, however, the appearance of pubic hair

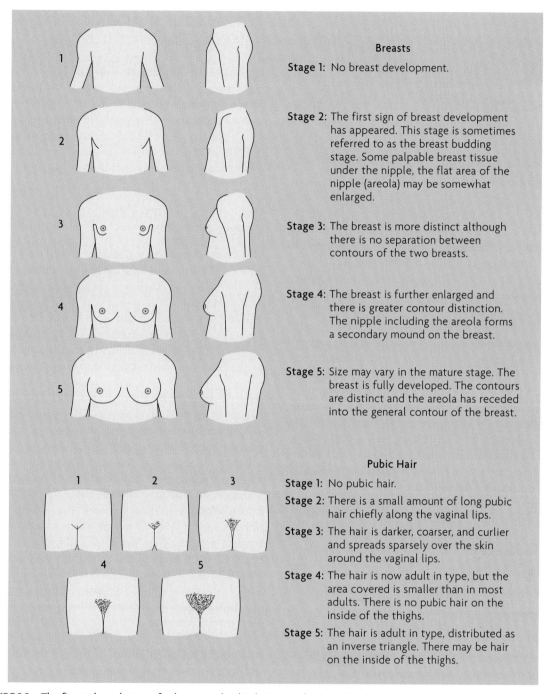

Breasts

Stage 1: No breast development.

Stage 2: The first sign of breast development has appeared. This stage is sometimes referred to as the breast budding stage. Some palpable breast tissue under the nipple, the flat area of the nipple (areola) may be somewhat enlarged.

Stage 3: The breast is more distinct although there is no separation between contours of the two breasts.

Stage 4: The breast is further enlarged and there is greater contour distinction. The nipple including the areola forms a secondary mound on the breast.

Stage 5: Size may vary in the mature stage. The breast is fully developed. The contours are distinct and the areola has receded into the general contour of the breast.

Pubic Hair

Stage 1: No pubic hair.

Stage 2: There is a small amount of long pubic hair chiefly along the vaginal lips.

Stage 3: The hair is darker, coarser, and curlier and spreads sparsely over the skin around the vaginal lips.

Stage 4: The hair is now adult in type, but the area covered is smaller than in most adults. There is no pubic hair on the inside of the thighs.

Stage 5: The hair is adult in type, distributed as an inverse triangle. There may be hair on the inside of the thighs.

FIGURE 1.5 The five pubertal stages for breast and pubic hair growth. (From Marshall & Tanner, 1969)

precedes breast development. The development of pubic hair in females follows a sequence similar to that in males—generally, from sparse, downy, light-colored hair to denser, curlier, coarser, darker hair. Breast development often occurs concurrently and generally proceeds through several stages. In the bud stage, the areola widens, and the breast and nipple are elevated as a small mound. In the middle stages, the areola and nipple become distinct from the breast and project beyond the breast contour. In the final stages, the areola is recessed to the contour of the breast, and only the nipple is elevated. The female breast undergoes these changes at puberty regardless of changes in breast size. For this reason, changes in the shape and definition of the areola and nipple are far better indicators of sexual maturation among adolescent girls than is breast growth alone. The five Tanner stages of breast and pubic hair growth in girls are shown in Figure 1.5.

As is the case for boys, puberty brings important internal changes for adolescent girls that are associated with the development of reproductive capacity. In girls, these changes involve development and growth of the uterus, vagina, and other aspects of the reproductive system. In addition, there is enlargement of the labia and clitoris.

As is apparent in Table 1.1, the growth spurt is likely to occur during the early and middle stages of breast and pubic hair development. Menarche, the beginning of menstruation, is a relatively late development that reflects the culmination of a long series of hormonal changes (Dorn et al., 1999). Therefore, it is incorrect to use menarche as a marker for the onset of puberty among girls, because a great deal of pubertal development has taken place long before the adolescent girl begins to menstruate. Generally, full reproductive function does not occur until several years after menarche, and regular ovulation follows menarche by about two years (Hafetz, 1976). Unlike boys, therefore, girls generally appear physically mature before they are capable of becoming pregnant.

RECAP

- The adolescent growth spurt, which takes place about two years earlier among girls than boys, involves a rapid increase in height and weight.
- Puberty brings with it changes in ratio of muscle to fat, with marked gender differences in the way in which body composition changes. The increase in fat, which is greater among females than males, is a source of concern to many girls.
- Sexual maturation in both sexes is measured according to Tanner stages, which are used to chart the development of secondary sex characteristics.

The Timing and Tempo of Puberty

You may have noted that, thus far, no mention has been made of the "normal" ages at which various pubertal changes are likely to take place. This is because variations in the timing of puberty (the age at which puberty begins) and in the tempo of puberty (the rate at which maturation occurs) are so great that it is misleading to talk even about average ages.

VARIATIONS IN THE TIMING AND TEMPO OF PUBERTY

The onset of puberty can occur as early as age 7 in girls and 9½ in boys, or as late as age 13 in girls and 13½ in boys. In girls, the interval between the first sign of puberty and complete physical maturation can be as short as a year and a half or as long as six years. In boys, the comparable interval ranges from about two to five years (J. Tanner, 1972). Think about it: Within a totally normal population of young adolescents, some individuals will have completed the entire sequence of pubertal changes before others have even begun. In more concrete terms, it is possible for an early-maturing, fast-maturing youngster to complete pubertal maturation by age 10 or 11—two years before a late-maturing youngster has even begun puberty, and seven years before a late-maturing, slow-maturing youngster has matured completely!

There is no relation between the age at which puberty begins and the rate at which pubertal development proceeds. The timing of puberty may have a small effect on one's ultimate height or weight, however, with late maturers, on average, being taller than early maturers as adults, and early maturers, on average, being somewhat heavier—at least among females (St. George, Williams, & Silva, 1994). Adult height and weight are far more strongly correlated with height and weight before childhood than with the timing of puberty, however (Pietiläinen et al., 2001).

Within the United States, there are ethnic differences in the timing and rate of pubertal maturation. Several large-scale studies of U.S. youngsters indicate that African American females mature significantly earlier than Mexican American girls, who, in turn, mature earlier than white girls (Chumlea et al., 2003; Herman-Giddens et al., 1997) (see Figure 1.6). Although the reasons for this ethnic difference are not known, it does not appear to be due to ethnic differences in income, weight, or area of residence (Anderson, Dallal, & Must, 2003). One possible explanation for the earlier maturation of nonwhite girls is that they may be more frequently exposed to chemicals in the

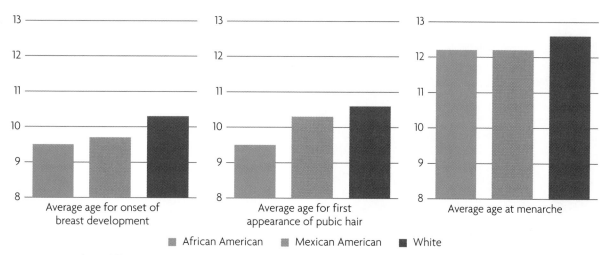

FIGURE 1.6   Ethnic differences in the timing of different aspects of puberty. (From Wu, Mendola, & Buck, 2002)

environment that stimulate earlier puberty, such as animal hormones contained in certain hair care products, although this has not been studied systematically (Wu, Mendola, & Buck, 2002).

GENETIC AND ENVIRONMENTAL INFLUENCES ON PUBERTAL TIMING

Why do some individuals mature relatively early and others relatively late? Researchers who study variability in the onset and timing of puberty approach the issue in two ways. One strategy involves the study of differences among individuals (i.e., studying why one individual matures earlier or faster than another). The other involves the study of differences among groups of adolescents (i.e., studying why puberty occurs earlier or more rapidly in certain populations than in others). Both sets of studies point to both genetic and environmental influences on the timing and tempo of puberty.

■ **Individual Differences in Pubertal Maturation** Differences in the timing and rate of puberty among individuals growing up in the same general environment result chiefly, but not exclusively, from genetic factors. Comparisons between individuals who are genetically identical (identical twins) and individuals who are not indicate that the timing and tempo of an individual's pubertal maturation are largely inherited (Dick, Rose, Pulkkinen, & Kaprio, 2001; Mustanski, Viken, Kaprio, Pulkkinen, & Rose, 2004).

Despite this powerful influence of genetic factors, the environment plays an important role. In all likelihood, every individual inherits a predisposition to develop at a certain rate and to begin pubertal maturation at a certain time. But this predisposition is

best thought of as an upper and lower age limit, not a fixed absolute. Whether the genetic predisposition that each person has to mature around a given age is actually realized, and when within the predisposed age boundaries she or he actually goes through puberty, is subject to the influence of many external factors. In this respect, the timing and rate of pubertal maturation are the product of an interaction between nature and nurture, between one's genetic makeup and the environmental conditions under which one has developed.

By far the two most important environmental influences on pubertal maturation are nutrition and health. Puberty occurs earlier among individuals who are better nourished throughout their prenatal, infant, and childhood years. Not surprisingly, then, whereas girls who are taller or heavier than their peers mature earlier (St. George et al., 1994), delayed puberty is more likely to occur among individuals with a history of protein and/or caloric deficiency. Chronic illness during childhood and adolescence is also associated with delayed puberty, as is excessive exercise. For example, girls in ballet companies or in other rigorous training programs often mature later than their peers (Frisch, 1983). Generally, then, after genetic factors, the most important determinant of the timing of puberty is the overall physical well-being of the individual from conception through preadolescence (Marshall, 1978).

■ **Familial Influences on Pubertal Timing** Interestingly, a number of studies suggest that social and physical factors in the environment may influence the onset of maturation, especially in girls. According to a comprehensive review of the literature, puberty occurs somewhat earlier among girls who grew up in

The age at which individuals go through puberty varies around the world. Teenagers in highly industrialized countries, such as Japan, mature earlier than their counterparts in developing countries, where health and nutritional problems slow physical growth.

father-absent families, in less cohesive or more conflict-ridden households, or with a stepfather (Ellis, 2004). One explanation for the finding that distant family relations may accelerate pubertal maturation is that distance in the family may induce a very small amount of stress, which, in turn, may affect hormonal secretions in the adolescent. Puberty may be sped up by *small* amounts of stress; a great deal of stress, however, is likely to slow maturation. In addition, the presence of a stepfather may expose the adolescent girl to **pheromones** (a class of chemicals secreted by animals that stimulate certain behaviors in other members of the species) that stimulate pubertal maturation. In general, among humans and other mammals, living in proximity to one's close biological relatives appears to slow the process of pubertal maturation, whereas exposure to unrelated members of the opposite sex may accelerate it.

Although it may seem surprising that something as biological as puberty can be influenced by factors in the social environment, scientists have long known that our social relationships can indeed affect our biological functioning. One of the best-known examples of this is that women who live together—such as dormitory roommates—find that their menstrual periods begin to synchronize over time (Graham, 1991; McClintock, 1980).

FOOD FOR THOUGHT

Why might the timing of puberty in girls be more influenced by social factors than is the case among boys?

Group Differences in Pubertal Maturation

Researchers typically study group differences in puberty by comparing average ages of menarche in different regions. Most of these studies have indicated that genetic factors play an extremely small role in determining group differences in pubertal maturation (Eveleth & Tanner, 1990). Differences among countries in the average rate and timing of puberty are more likely to reflect differences in their environments than differences in their populations' gene pools (Morabia, Costanza, & World Health Organization, 1998).

The influence of the broader environment on the timing and tempo of puberty can be seen in more concrete terms by looking at three sorts of group comparisons: (1) comparisons of the average age of menarche across countries, (2) comparisons among socioeconomic groups within the same country, and (3) comparisons within the same population during different eras. (Although menarche does not signal the onset of puberty, researchers often use the average age of menarche when comparing the timing of puberty across different groups or regions, because it can be measured more reliably than other indicators.)

First, consider variations in the age of menarche across different regions of the world. The average age at menarche generally is lower in those countries where individuals are less likely to be malnourished or to suffer from chronic disease. For example, in western Europe and in the United States, the median menarcheal age ranges from about 12½ to 13½ years. In Africa, however, the median menarcheal age ranges from about 14 to 17 years. The range is much wider across Africa because of the greater variation in environmental conditions there.

pheromones   A class of chemicals secreted by animals that stimulate certain behaviors in other members of the species.

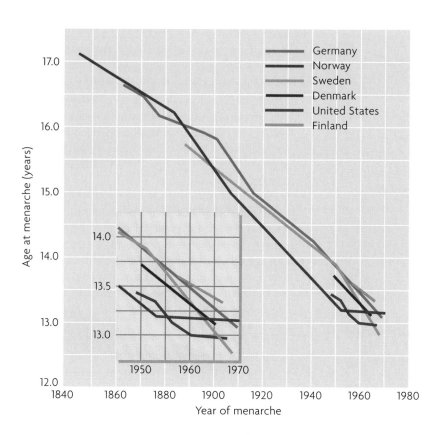

FIGURE 1.7 The age at menarche has declined considerably over the past 150 years. This decline is known as the secular trend. (Adapted from Eveleth & Tanner, 1990)

When we look *within* a specific region, we find that, almost without exception, girls from affluent homes reach menarche before economically disadvantaged girls. In comparisons of affluent and poor youngsters from the United States, Hong Kong, Tunis, Baghdad, and South Africa, for example, differences in the average menarcheal ages of economically advantaged and disadvantaged youngsters within each of these regions range from about 6 to 18 months (Eveleth & Tanner, 1990).

▌ **The Secular Trend** Finally, we can examine environmental influences on the timing of puberty by looking at changes in the average age of menarche over the past two centuries. Because nutritional conditions have improved during the past 150 years, we would expect to find a decline in the average age at menarche over time. This is indeed the case, as can be seen in Figure 1.7. This pattern, known as the **secular trend,** is attributable not only to improved nutrition but also to better sanitation and better control of infectious diseases. In most European countries, maturation has become earlier by about three to four months per decade. For example, in Norway 150 years ago, the average age of menarche may have been about 17 years. Today, it is between 12 and 13 years. Similar

declines have been observed over the same period in other industrialized nations and, more recently, in developing countries as well. The secular trend is less well documented among boys, in part because there is no easily measured marker of puberty, like menarche. But there is some evidence that the age of onset of puberty among American boys may have dropped very slightly during the second half of the twentieth century (Karpati, Rubin, Kieszak, Marcus, & Troiano, 2002; Slyper, 2006).

FOOD FOR THOUGHT

Some studies indicate that the secular trend has been more dramatic among females than males. Why might this be the case?

secular trend The tendency, over the past two centuries, for individuals to be larger in stature and to reach puberty earlier, primarily because of improvements in health and nutrition.

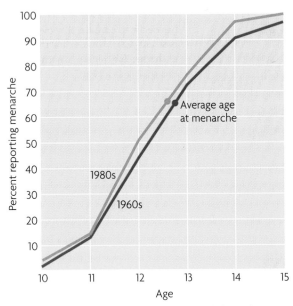

FIGURE 1.8   The age at which American girls have their first period (menarche) continued to drop in the late twentieth century. (From Anderson, Dallal, & Must, 2003)

RECAP

- The timing of puberty, as well as the rate with which it occurs, is highly variable.
- The timing of puberty is influenced by both genetic and environmental factors. Among the most important environmental influences are health and nutrition. Generally, individuals who are healthier and better nourished begin puberty at a relatively younger age than their less healthy or more poorly nourished peers.
- Some evidence suggests that girls growing up in single-parent families, stepfamilies, or families in which there is a high level of conflict go through puberty somewhat earlier than their peers.
- The age at which puberty occurs has declined over time, a phenomenon known as the "secular trend." Scientists disagree about whether the secular trend is still taking place in contemporary industrialized societies.

Scientists disagree about whether the secular trend has continued in the United States in recent years and, if so, whether the trend toward earlier puberty is greater in some ethnic groups than in others. Studies using indicators such as breast or genital maturation or the appearance of pubic hair find no change on average but a decline in the age of puberty among white boys and among Mexican American boys and girls (Sun et al., 2005). In contrast, other studies have found that the average age of menarche among American girls dropped by about two and a half months between the 1960s and 1990s (see Figure 1.8), most probably because of increased rates of obesity (Anderson, Dallal, & Must, 2003) or changes in diet (Slyper, 2006), and that the decline has been especially marked among African American girls (Chumlea et al., 2003). One reason for these discrepancies is that puberty can be measured in many ways (Dorn, Dahl, Woodward, & Biro, 2006), and what we conclude about the average age of puberty depends on what indicator is used. Because the development of pubic hair (which is influenced by androgens) is affected by different factors than is menarche (which is influenced by estrogen and progesterone), patterns of change over time in each would not necessarily be identical (Biro et al., 2006). In general, though, most scientists agree that any changes in the average age of puberty have been much less dramatic in recent decades than they were in the early twentieth century, when the average age of menarche dropped by about four months every decade.

The Psychological and Social Impact of Puberty

Puberty can affect the adolescent's behavior and psychological functioning in a number of ways (Brooks-Gunn, Graber, & Paikoff, 1994) (see Figure 1.9). First, the biological changes of puberty can have a direct effect on behavior. Increases in testosterone at puberty are directly linked, for example, to an increase in sex drive and sexual activity among adolescent boys (Halpern, Udry, & Suchindran, 1996). (The impact of hormonal change on girls' sex drive and sexual activity is more complicated, as you'll see in Chapter 11.)

Second, the biological changes of puberty cause changes in the adolescent's self-image, which, in turn, may affect how he or she behaves. For example, a boy who has recently gone through puberty may feel more grown up as a result of his more adultlike appearance. This, in turn, may make him seek more independence from his parents. He may ask for a later curfew, a larger allowance, or the right to make decisions about things that previously were decided by his parents. As we will see later in this chapter, the physical changes of puberty often spark conflict between teenagers and their parents, in part because of the ways in which puberty affects the adolescent's desire for autonomy.

Finally, biological change at puberty transforms the adolescent's appearance, which, in turn, may elicit changes in how *others* react to the teenager. These changes in reactions may provoke changes in the

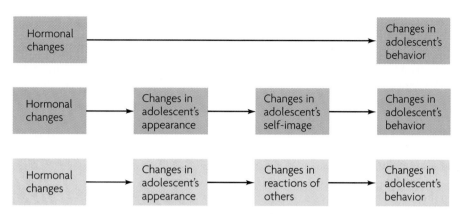

FIGURE 1.9 The biological changes of puberty can affect the adolescent's behavior in at least three ways.

adolescent's behavior. An adolescent girl who has recently matured physically may find herself suddenly receiving the attention of older boys who had not previously paid her much heed. She may feel nervous about all the extra attention and confused about how she should respond to it. Moreover, she must now make decisions about how much time she wishes to devote to dating and how she should behave when out on a date.

Young people's reactions to the changes brought on by puberty, and others' reactions to them, are influenced by the broader social environment, in which messages about physical attractiveness, sexuality, and sexual maturation change, often markedly, from era to era. Although it is difficult to imagine an era in which adolescents, especially girls, did not obsess about their shape, size, and sexual allure, adolescent females' preoccupation with their body is a relatively recent phenomenon, created largely by marketers of clothing, undergarments, cosmetics, weight loss programs, and "feminine" products (Brumberg, 1997). Contemporary society's views of puberty and physical maturation are expressed through television commercials, newspaper and magazine advertisements, and depictions of young adolescents in films and other media. People cannot help but be influenced by these images, and the expectations they associate with puberty, as well as the meaning they give it, determine the reactions puberty brings out in them. Consider, for example, the treatment of menstruation in magazine advertisements, and the sorts of reactions these ads might foster.

Researchers have generally taken two approaches to studying the psychological and social consequences of puberty. One approach is to look at individuals who are at various stages of puberty, either in a **cross-sectional study** (in which groups of individuals are compared at different stages of puberty) or in a **longitudinal study** (in which the same individuals are tracked over time as they move through the different stages of puberty). Studies of this sort examine the impact of puberty on young people's psychological development and social

relations. Researchers might ask, for example, whether youngsters' self-esteem is higher or lower during puberty than before or after.

A second approach compares the psychological development of early and late maturers. As noted previously, there is large variation in pubertal timing, and individuals of the same chronological age, who are in the same grade in school, may be at very different stages of puberty. Researchers have been tremendously interested in whether the timing of puberty affects the adolescent's psychological development. The focus of these studies is not so much on the absolute impact of puberty as on the effects of differential timing of the changes. Here, a typical question might be whether early maturers are more popular in the peer group than late maturers are.

THE IMMEDIATE IMPACT OF PUBERTY

Studies of the psychological and social impacts of puberty indicate that physical maturation, regardless of whether it occurs early or late, affects the adolescent's self-image, mood, and relationships with parents. As you will see, however, the short-term consequences of puberty may be more taxing on the adolescent's family than on the adolescent.

▌ **Puberty and Self-Esteem** Although research suggests that puberty can be a potential stressor with temporary adverse psychological consequences, this is only true when it is coupled with other changes that necessitate adjustment (Simmons & Blyth, 1987). In this respect, the impact of puberty on adolescents' psychological functioning is to a great extent shaped by the social context in which puberty takes place (Susman,

---

cross-sectional study A study that compares two or more groups of individuals at one point in time.

longitudinal study A study that follows the same group of individuals over time.

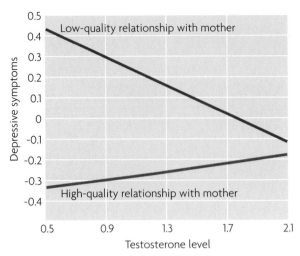

1997). The impact of puberty on mental health varies by gender and across ethnic groups, with girls more adversely affected than boys, and with white girls, in particular, at greatest risk for developing a poor body image (Siegel, Yancey, Aneshensel, & Schuler, 1999). Given the premium in contemporary society placed on thinness, the increase in body dissatisfaction among white girls that takes place at puberty is, not surprisingly, linked to specific concerns that girls have about their hips, thighs, waist, and weight (Rosenblum & Lewis, 1999). Interestingly, the way adolescents feel about their physical appearance when they begin adolescence remains remarkably stable over time, regardless of whether their actual attractiveness changes (Rosenblum & Lewis, 1999).

▌ **Puberty and Adolescent Moodiness** Although an adolescent's self-image can be expected to change during a time of dramatic physical development, self-esteem or self-image can also be reasonably stable, with long and sturdy roots reaching back to childhood. For this reason, some researchers have turned their attention to the impact of puberty on more transient states, such as mood. One reason for this focus is that adolescents are thought to be moodier, on average, than either children or adults. One study, in which adolescents' moods were monitored repeatedly by electronic pagers, for example, showed that their moods fluctuate during the course of the day more than the moods of adults do (Csikszentmihalyi & Larson, 1984). Many adults assume that adolescent moodiness is directly related to the hormonal changes of puberty (Petersen, 1985). Is there any scientific evidence that the hormonal changes of puberty cause adolescents to be moody or, for that matter, that these hormonal changes affect the adolescent's psychological functioning or behavior at all?

According to several comprehensive reviews of research on hormones and adolescent mood and behavior, the direct connection between hormones and mood is not very strong (Buchanan, Eccles, & Becker, 1992; Flannery, Torquati, & Lindemeier, 1994). When studies do find a connection between hormonal changes at puberty and adolescent mood or behavior, the effects are strongest early in puberty, when the process is being "turned on" and when hormonal levels are highly variable. For example, studies indicate that *rapid* increases in many of the hormones associated with puberty—such as testosterone, estrogen, and various adrenal androgens—especially when the increases take place very early in adolescence, may be associated with increased irritability, impulsivity, aggression (in boys), and depression (in girls). One interpretation of these findings is that it is not so much the absolute increases in these hormones during

FIGURE 1.10 Low testosterone in boys is associated with more symptoms of depression, but only among boys who have a low-quality relationship with their mother.
(From Booth et al., 2003)

puberty but their rapid fluctuation early in puberty that may affect adolescents' moods. Once the hormone levels stabilize at higher levels, later in puberty, their negative effects appear to wane (Buchanan et al., 1992). There is also evidence, discussed in Chapter 2, that important changes take place around the time of puberty in regions of the brain that play major roles in the processing of emotion, although the specific ways in which hormones contribute to this is not yet fully understood (Nelson, Leibenluft, McClure, & Pine, 2005).

Even still, most researchers agree that the impact of hormonal change on mood and behavior in adolescence is greatly influenced by environmental factors (Booth, Johnson, Granger, Crouter, & McHale, 2003; Susman, 1997). For example, although rapid increases in hormones early in puberty are associated with depressed mood in girls, it turns out that stressful life events, such as problems in the family, in school, or with friends, play a far greater role in the development of depression than do hormonal changes (Brooks-Gunn, Graber, & Paikoff, 1994). Similarly, while high levels in testosterone have been associated with impulsivity and aggression and low levels with depression, these associations are weaker among adolescents who have positive family relationships (Booth et al., 2003) (see Figure 1.10).

Interestingly, not only is there little evidence that adolescents' moodiness results from the "storm and stress" of raging hormones, but there is also research that questions the very idea that adolescents are inherently moodier than children. Psychologists Mihaly Csikszentmihalyi and Reed Larson (1984; Larson & Lampman-Petraitis, 1989) had teenagers carry

TABLE 1.2 Five patterns of adolescent moodiness

Pattern	Size of Mood Change	Rate of Mood Change	Typical Mood	Intensity of Mood
I	Very large	Very fast	Positive	Very high
II	Small	Average	Positive	Low
III	Small	Slow	Negative	Very low
IV	Very large	Average	Negative	High
V	Average	Slow	Very negative	High

Source: Bence, 1992.

electronic pagers, and the researchers paged them periodically throughout the day. When the adolescents were paged, they filled out forms noting how they were feeling, what they were doing, where they were, and whom they were with. By looking at changes in mood across activities and settings, the researchers were able to determine the correlates of adolescent moodiness.

Their findings suggest that adolescent mood swings parallel their changes in activities. Over the course of a day, a teenager may shift from elation to boredom, back to happiness, and then to anger. But these shifts in mood appear to have more to do with shifts in activities—elated when seeing a girlfriend, bored in social studies class, happy when having lunch with friends, and angry when assigned extra work at the fast-food restaurant—than with internal, biological changes. More important, comparisons of youngsters ages 9–15 did not show increases in moodiness during the transition into adolescence.

How can we reconcile these scientific studies, which provide little support for the notion that adolescents are especially prone to mood swings, with the popular portrayals of teenagers as exceedingly moody? One possibility is that there is a great deal of variability within the adolescent population in terms of moodiness. In one study of adolescents, for example, five distinct patterns of mood change were identified (Bence, 1992) (see Table 1.2). One group showed considerable fluctuation in mood over the course of a week, but these teenagers typically were in a positive mood (they bounced back up to positive moods quickly after being in a bad mood). A second group was, on average, as positive as the first, but showed much less mood fluctuation. The third group was similar to the second, in that members showed little fluctuation in mood; but in contrast to the second group, this group was generally in a slightly bad mood. The fourth group, like the first, showed considerable fluctuation in mood but was generally in a bad mood (that is, members dropped back down to a negative mood quickly after being in a positive mood). Finally, the fifth group was composed of youngsters whose mood did not fluctuate greatly but who were in an extremely negative mood most of the time. Thus, the answer to the question of whether puberty makes adolescents moody depends on the person and on factors in his or her environment.

▌ Puberty and Changes in Patterns of Sleep

One fascinating finding on hormones and behavior in adolescence concerns adolescents' sleep preferences (Fredriksen, Rhodes, Reddy, & Way, 2004). Many parents complain that their teenage children go to bed too late in the evening and sleep in too late in the morning. It now appears that the emergence of this pattern—called a **delayed phase preference**—is driven by the biological changes of puberty (Carskadon, Acebo, Richardson, Tate, & Seifer, 1997).

Falling asleep is caused by a combination of biological and environmental factors. One of the most important is the secretion of a hormone in the brain called **melatonin.** Melatonin levels change naturally over the course of the 24-hour day, mainly in response to the amount of light in the environment. Feelings of sleepiness increase and decrease with melatonin levels—as melatonin rises, we feel sleepier, and as it falls, we feel more awake. Over the course of the day, we follow a sleep-wake cycle that is calibrated to changes in light and regulated by melatonin secretion.

During puberty, the time of night at which melatonin levels begin to rise changes, becoming later and later as individuals mature physically. In fact, the nighttime increase in melatonin starts about two hours later among adolescents who have completed puberty than among those who have not yet entered puberty (Carskadon & Acebo, 2002). As a result of this shift, individuals become able to stay up later before feeling sleepy. In fact, when allowed to regulate their own sleep schedules (as on weekends), most teenagers will stay up until around 1:00 A.M. and sleep until

delayed phase preference A pattern of sleep characterized by later sleep and wake times, which usually emerges during puberty.

melatonin A hormone secreted by the brain that contributes to sleepiness.

about 10:00 A.M. Because the whole cycle of melatonin secretion is shifted later at puberty, this also means that adolescents who have gone through puberty are more sleepy early in the morning than those who are still prepubertal.

Falling asleep is affected by the environment as well—as you know, it is much easier to fall asleep when a room is dark than when it is bright. But when preadolescents get into bed at night, they tend to fall asleep very quickly—even if there is something that they want to stay up for—because their melatonin levels are already high. After going through puberty, though, because of the delayed timing of the increase in melatonin, it is easier for individuals to stay up later, so that if there is something more exciting to do—surf the Internet, watch a DVD, talk on the phone—it is not difficult to remain awake (Taylor, Jenni, Acebo, & Carskadon, 2005). Thus, the tendency for adolescents to stay up late is due to the interaction of biology (which delays the onset of sleepiness) and the environment (which provides an impetus to stay up). This shift in sleep preferences, to a later bedtime and a later wake time, begins to reverse around age 20, but at a slightly earlier age among females than males (Roenneberg et al., 2004).

If getting up early the next day were not an issue, staying up late would not be a problem. Unfortunately, most teenagers need to get up early on school days, and the combination of staying up late and getting up early leads to sleep deprivation and daytime sleepiness. The shift in the timing of the melatonin cycle contributes to this, because the decrease in melatonin that takes place in the middle of the night happens later after puberty than before. This means that when teenagers get out of bed early in the morning, their melatonin levels are relatively higher than they are at the same time of day for preadolescents. Indeed, one study found that adolescents were least alert between the hours of 8:00 and 9:00 A.M. (when most schools start) and were most alert after 3.00 P.M., when the school day is over (Allen & Mirabell, 1990). Sleep researchers estimate that, because of early school start times, adolescents get two fewer hours of sleep per night when the school year begins than they did during the preceding summer months (Hansen, Janssen, Schiff, Zee, & Dubocovich, 2005). This has prompted some communities to delay their school starting time for teenagers (Mitru, Millrood, & Mateika, 2002).

Interestingly, the tendency for individuals to go to bed later as they become teenagers has become

Important changes in the sleep cycle take place after puberty. This "delayed phase preference" causes adolescents to want to stay up later at night and feel more tired in the early morning hours.

stronger over the past 30 years (Iglowstein, Jenni, Molinari, & Largo, 2003), perhaps because the availability of television, the Internet, and other mass media during the late night and early morning hours has increased (Van den Bulck, 2004). This suggests that the late-night hours kept by many adolescents are at least somewhat voluntary, made easier by the changes in the sleep centers of the brain. (There is also evidence that exposure to light depresses melatonin secretion, so that staying up late with the lights on will delay the rise in melatonin even more.) Whatever the explanation, because teenagers' wake time has not changed, but their bedtime has gotten later, today's teenagers get significantly less sleep than their counterparts did several decades ago. Excessive daytime sleepiness is rampant among American teenagers, a finding that has been replicated in several countries, including Japan and Taiwan (Gau, Soong, & Merikangas, 2004; Ohida et al., 2004)

Although individuals' preferred bedtime gets later as they move from childhood into adolescence, the amount of sleep they need each night remains constant, at around nine hours. Yet, one study of more than 3000 Rhode Island high school students found that only one-fifth of the students got at least eight hours of sleep on an average school night and that nearly half got seven hours or less (Wolfson & Carskadon, 1998). A more recent study of Chicago middle school students found, similarly, that the average eighth-grader got about seven hours of sleep on school nights (Fredriksen et al., 2004). There is now a clear consensus among scientists that most teenagers are not getting enough sleep, and that inadequate sleep is associated in adolescence with poorer mental health (more depression and anxiety) and lowered school performance (Fredriksen et al., 2004). In the Rhode Island study, for example, students who were earning grades of C or lower were going to bed 40 minutes later and sleeping about 25 minutes less each night than their classmates whose grade point averages were B or better. The students with poorer grades also reported staying up considerably later on weekends than they did on school nights. Despite many adolescents' belief that catching up on their sleep on weekends will make up for sleep deprivation during the week, research indicates that having markedly different bedtimes on weekends versus weekdays contributes to further sleep-related problems (Wolfson & Carskadon, 1998). (Actually, the best thing teenagers can do to avoid problems waking up on school days is to force themselves to get up at the same time on the weekend as on school days, regardless of how late they have stayed up.) Not surprisingly, sleep-related difficulties among teenagers are also linked to the consumption of caffeine (Pollack & Bright, 2003) and tobacco (Patten, Choi, Gillin, & Pierce, 2002), both of which are stimulants. About 10 percent of teenagers report chronic insomnia (Johnson, Roth, Schultz, & Breslau, 2006).

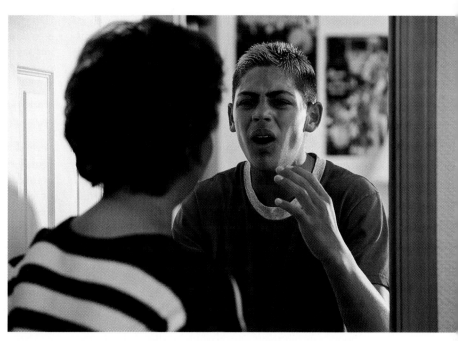

Studies indicate that parent–adolescent conflict may increase at puberty.

FOOD FOR THOUGHT

Some policymakers have called for delaying the time at which the high school day begins, in view of new studies on changing patterns of sleep during adolescence. Do you think this is a good idea?

■ **Puberty and Family Relationships**   Research into the impact of puberty on family relationships has pointed to a fairly consistent pattern, namely, that puberty appears to increase conflict and distance

between parents and children. You should be aware, however, that the "distancing" effect of puberty on adolescent–parent relationships is not as strong in single-parent homes (Anderson, Hetherington, & Clingempeel, 1989) and not as consistently observed in ethnic minority families (Molina & Chassin, 1996; Sagrestano, McCormick, Paikoff, & Holmbeck, 1999). Among white families, however, several studies show that as youngsters mature from childhood toward the middle of puberty, emotional distance between them and their parents increases, and conflict intensifies, especially between the adolescent and his or her mother (Laursen, Coy, & Collins, 1998; Ogletree, Jones, & Coyl, 2002). The change that takes place is reflected in an increase in "negatives" (e.g., conflict, complaining, anger) and, to a lesser extent, a decrease in "positives" (e.g., support, smiling, laughter) (e.g., Flannery et al., 1994; Holmbeck & Hill, 1991). Although negative interchanges may diminish after the adolescent growth spurt, adolescents and their parents do not immediately become as close as they were before the adolescents entered puberty. Interestingly, puberty increases distance between children and their parents in most species of monkeys and apes, and some writers have suggested that the pattern seen in human adolescents may have some evolutionary basis (Steinberg, 1987b).

Because this connection between pubertal maturation and parent–child distance is not affected by the age at which the adolescent goes through puberty—in other words, the pattern is seen among early as well as late maturers—it suggests that something about puberty in particular may transform the parent–child bond. To date, we do not know whether this effect results from the hormonal changes of puberty, from changes in the adolescent's physical appearance, or from changes in adolescent psychological functioning that, in turn, affect family relationships. Moreover, because few studies of family relationships at puberty have examined multiple aspects of adolescent development simultaneously, it is difficult to say whether the patterns of change in family relationships that many studies have found do, in fact, result from puberty and not from some other change taking place at the same time in the adolescent or in the parent (Paikoff & Brooks-Gunn, 1991).

Whatever underlying mechanism is involved, one interpretation of these studies is that developments occurring around the time of puberty can upset interpersonal balances that are established during childhood, causing temporary periods of disruption in the family system. During a son's or daughter's childhood, families develop patterns of relationships that are comfortable and workable, but they may find that puberty disrupts the patterns to which they have grown accustomed. They have developed a certain way of discussing things and a certain way of including the children in discussions. But as the children go through puberty, they may want to be treated more like adults and have a greater say in family decisions. Consequently, families may experience a temporary period of conflict or tension when sons and daughters enter early adolescence. It may take some time for the individual and the family to achieve a new equilibrium that takes into account the changes brought on by puberty.

▌ Pubertal Maturation and Peer Relationships

Puberty may have an effect on relationships in the peer group, too. One study of adolescents' social networks—the people they are most likely to see and spend time with—found that adolescents who were physically mature were less likely than their less developed peers to name adults as people who were important to them, and they were more likely to name other adolescents (Garbarino, Burston, Raber, Russell, & Crouter, 1978). This finding suggests that pubertal maturation may play an important role in shifting adolescents' interests and energies toward the peer group. Boys and girls who are physically mature are more likely than less mature age-mates to be involved in cross-sex romantic activities such as having a boyfriend or girlfriend or going out on dates (Compian, Gowen, & Hayward, 2004), although this depends on the social norms of the adolescent's peer group and the prevailing expectations about the age at which teenagers should begin dating

(Dornbusch et al., 1981; Gargiulo, Attie, Brooks-Gunn, & Warren, 1987). Interestingly, pubertal maturation is *not* associated with having platonic relationships with opposite-sex peers (Compian et al., 2004).

THE IMPACT OF SPECIFIC PUBERTAL EVENTS

Several studies have focused specifically on adolescents' attitudes toward and reactions to particular events at puberty, such as girls' reactions to menarche or breast development, and boys' reactions to their first ejaculation.

In general, most adolescents react positively to the biological changes associated with puberty, especially those associated with the development of secondary sex characteristics. One study of adolescent girls' attitudes toward breast development, for example, found that the majority of girls greeted this change positively (Brooks-Gunn, Newman, Holderness, & Warren, 1994).

Girls' reactions to menarche are more varied, however, in part because the onset of menstruation is "not just one of a series of physiological events during puberty, but is also a sociocultural event ... imbued with special meaning" (Brooks-Gunn & Ruble, 1979, p. 1). Cultural beliefs concerning menarche and the specific information that an adolescent receives from parents, teachers, friends, and health practitioners all influence how she greets and experiences menarche (Brooks-Gunn & Ruble, 1982).

Adolescent girls' attitudes toward menarche are less negative today than they appear to have been in the past (Greif & Ulman, 1982; Ruble & Brooks-Gunn, 1982), a change that may be attributable to the increase in information about menstruation in schools and in the media in recent years (Merskin, 1999). In general, among today's adolescent girls, menarche is typically accompanied by gains in social maturity, peer prestige, and self-esteem—as well as by heightened self-consciousness (Brooks-Gunn & Reiter, 1990). Nevertheless, many young women have developed a negative image of menstruation before reaching adolescence, and they enter puberty with ambivalent attitudes about menarche—a mixture of excitement and fear (Moore, 1995; Ruble & Brooks-Gunn, 1982).

Interestingly, one set of studies indicates that a strong negative bias toward menstruation before menarche may actually be associated with greater menstrual discomfort. Menstrual symptoms are reported to be more severe among women who expect menstruation to be uncomfortable, among girls whose mothers lead them to believe that menstruation will be an unpleasant or uncomfortable experience, and in cultures that label menstruation as an important event. In Mexico and in China, for example, where attitudes toward menarche may be especially ambivalent, menarche may have an adverse effect on girls' mental health, an effect not generally observed in the United States (Benjet & Hernandez-Guzman, 2002; Tang, Yeung, & Lee, 2003). In addition, girls who experience menarche early, relative to their peers, or who are otherwise unprepared for puberty report more negative reactions to the event (Koff & Rierdan, 1996; Tang, Yeung, & Lee, 2004).

Far less is known about boys' reactions to their first ejaculation, an experience that we might consider analogous to menarche in girls. Although most boys are not very well prepared for this event by their parents or other adults, first ejaculation does not appear to cause undue anxiety, embarrassment, or fear. Interestingly, however, in contrast to girls, who generally tell their mothers shortly after they have begun menstruating and tell their girlfriends soon thereafter, boys, at least in the United States, do not discuss their first ejaculation with either parents or friends (Gaddis & Brooks-Gunn, 1985; Stein & Reiser, 1994). In other cultures, the event may be experienced somewhat differently. For example, one study of first ejaculation among adolescent boys in Nigeria found not only that boys were not upset by the event but also that they told their friends about the experience very soon after it occurred (Adegoke, 1993). Cultural differences in boys' responses to their first ejaculation are likely related to differences in how cultures view masturbation. As is the case with girls and menarche, boys' reactions to their first ejaculation are more positive when they have been prepared for the event (Stein & Reiser, 1994).

These adolescents are the same chronological age, despite their markedly different physical appearances. Among boys, early maturation is associated with greater popularity and higher self-esteem. Among girls, early maturation is also associated with greater popularity, but it is linked as well with a higher incidence of emotional problems.

THE IMPACT OF EARLY OR LATE MATURATION

Adolescents who mature relatively early or relatively late stand apart from their peers physically and may, as a consequence, elicit different sorts of reactions and expectations from those around them. Moreover, individual adolescents may be all too aware of whether they are early or late relative to their age-mates, and their feelings about themselves are likely to be influenced by their comparisons. One recent study found that early-maturing adolescents were more likely to be "pseudomature"—wishing they were older, hanging around with older peers, less involved in school, and more oriented toward their peers (Galambos, Barker, & Tilton-Weaver, 2003). Indeed, adolescents' *perceptions* of whether they are an early or a late maturer are more strongly related to their feelings about their physical maturation than whether they actually are early or late (Dubas, Graber, & Petersen, 1991). Further, adolescents' behavior is related to how old they

feel, and not simply to how physically mature they actually are (Galambos, Kolaric, Sears, & Maggs, 1999). Nevertheless, early and late maturers are often treated differently by others and view themselves differently, and they may, as a result, behave differently. As we shall see, however, early and late maturation have different consequences in the immediate present and in the long run, different consequences in different contexts, and, most important, different consequences for boys and girls.

▮ Early Versus Late Maturation Among Boys

Over the past 50 years, research on boys' pubertal timing has consistently shown that early-maturing boys feel better about themselves and are more popular than their late-maturing peers (Graber, Lewinsohn, Seeley, & Brooks-Gunn, 1997; Jones & Bayley, 1950). Consistent with this, boys who are more physically mature than their peers report more frequent feelings of positive affect, attention, strength, and being in love (Richards &

Larson, 1993). Interestingly, studies of boys with delayed puberty indicate that their feelings of competence, especially in the realms of work and sports, increased following the administration of hormone treatments (Schwab et al., 2001).

At the same time, however, early-maturing boys are more likely than their peers to get involved in antisocial or deviant activities, including truancy, minor delinquency, and problems at school (Duncan, Ritter, Dornbusch, Gross, & Carlsmith, 1985). They are also more likely to use drugs and alcohol and engage in other risky activities (Dick, Rose, Pulkkinen, & Kaprio, 2001; Weisner & Ittel, 2002; Wichstrom, 2001). Interestingly, although all adolescents are adversely affected by being bullied by their peers, the impact of victimization is greater for early maturers, perhaps because being picked on when one is larger than average is all the more embarrassing (Nadeem & Graham, 2005). The impact of early maturation on adolescents' antisocial behavior is comparable among African American, Mexican American, and white boys (Cota-Robles, Neiss, & Rowe, 2002). One reasonable explanation is that boys who are more physically mature develop friendships with older peers and that these friendships lead them into activities that are problematic for the younger boys (Andersson & Magnusson, 1990). Once involved with these older peer groups, the early maturers' higher rate of delinquency and substance use increases over time through their social contacts (Silbereisen et al., 1989). Thus, early puberty seems to play a role in the initiation, but not intensification, of substance use.

Clearly, early-maturing boys enjoy some psychological advantages over late maturers during early adolescence, when some boys have matured physically but others have not. But what about later during adolescence, when the late maturers have caught up? At least one study points to some interesting advantages for late-maturing boys, despite their initially lower popularity. Although early and late maturers exhibit similar psychological profiles before they enter adolescence, during the time of pubertal onset, and one year later as well, late maturers show significantly higher ratings on measures of intellectual curiosity, exploratory behavior, and social initiative. While they are in the midst of puberty, early maturers experience more frequent and more intense temper tantrums and depression (Ge, Brody, Conger, Simons, & Murry, 2002; Ge et al., 2003).

Why might this be? One explanation is that late maturers have the advantage of a longer preadolescent period, giving them more time to "prepare" psychologically for the onset of puberty (Peskin, 1967). This preparation may be important if, as noted earlier, rapid increases in hormones at puberty provoke changes in mood. Many theorists believe that the middle-childhood and preadolescent years are extremely important periods for the development of coping skills—skills that prove valuable during adolescence and adulthood. Although puberty by no means marks the end of the growth of coping abilities, it does come as an abrupt interruption to the more relaxed preadolescent era. A later puberty, and hence a longer preadolescence, might allow for coping skills to develop more fully before adolescence. This may account in part for the apparently better coping skills demonstrated by late maturers—not only during puberty but, as you will read, during adulthood as well.

Do the psychological and interpersonal differences that are observed between early and late maturers during adolescence persist into adulthood? In order to answer such questions, a series of follow-up studies some 25 years later looked at the adult personalities of males who had been studied during adolescence (Livson & Peskin, 1980). At age 38, the early maturers were more responsible, cooperative, self-controlled, and sociable. At the same time, though, they had grown up to be more conforming, conventional, and humorless. The late maturers, in contrast, remained somewhat more impulsive and more assertive but turned out to be more insightful, inventive, and creatively playful. What had happened?

One interpretation is that, because of their more adultlike appearance, the early-maturing boys were pushed into adult roles earlier than their peers. They were more likely to be asked to assume responsibility, to take on leadership positions, and to behave in a more grown-up manner. But this early press toward adulthood may have come too soon and may have stifled a certain amount of creativity and risk taking.

Have you gone to any gatherings of former high school classmates? Did you discover that some of the people whom you remembered as being extremely mature and socially successful during high school had turned out to be not all that interesting? Perhaps too much leadership, responsibility, social success, and maturity during the high school years interferes with the sort of psychological development that makes for interesting and creative adults. As we shall see in a later chapter, many psychologists believe that adolescents may benefit in the long run from having an extended period of time during which they are *not* being pushed into adulthood.

■ **Early Versus Late Maturation in Girls** In contrast to the generally positive impact that early maturation has on the psychological well-being of boys, early-maturing girls have more emotional difficulties than their peers, including lowered self-image and higher rates of depression, anxiety, eating disorders, and panic attacks (Aro & Taipale, 1987; Ge et al., 2003; Stice, Presnell, & Bearman, 2001). These difficulties seem to have a great deal to do with girls' feelings about their weight, because early maturers are, almost by definition, heavier than their later-maturing peers (Petersen, 1988). In societies that define as physically attractive the thin, "leggy" woman, a late-maturing girl will look more like this image than an early-maturing girl will. In addition, early maturation in girls may lead to heightened emotional arousal, which, in turn, may leave them more vulnerable to emotional problems (Graber, Brooks-Gunn, & Warren, 2006).

The ultimate impact of early maturation on the young girl's feelings about herself appears to depend on the broader context in which maturation takes place, however. For example, studies of American girls generally find that early-maturing girls have lower self-esteem and a poorer self-image, because of our cultural preference for thinness and our ambivalence about adolescent sexuality (Brooks-Gunn & Reiter, 1990). In Germany, however, where sex education is more open and attitudes toward adolescent sexuality are less conflicted, early-maturing girls are found to have *higher* self-esteem (Silbereisen, Petersen, Albrecht, & Kracke, 1989).

Interestingly, even *within* the United States, the impact of physical maturation appears to depend on the social context in which teenagers live (Dyer & Tiggemann, 1996). One study of suburban Chicago youngsters, for example, found that girls' body image was significantly higher in one community than in another—despite comparable levels of physical maturation between the two groups. One factor that differentiated the two communities was "cliquishness": In the more cliquish high school, girls were less satisfied with the way they looked, perhaps because cliquish girls place more emphasis on physical appearance in determining popularity (Richards, Boxer, Petersen, & Albrecht, 1990).

Although some early-maturing girls may have self-image difficulties, their popularity with peers is not jeopardized. Indeed, some studies indicate that early maturers are more popular than other girls, especially, as you would expect, when the index of popularity includes popularity with boys (Simmons, Blyth, & McKinney, 1983). Interestingly, one study of girls with delayed puberty found that hormone treatments improved girls' perceptions of their romantic appeal (Schwab et al., 2001). Ironically, it may be in part because the early maturer is more popular with boys that she reports more emotional upset: Early pressure to date and, perhaps, to be involved in a sexual relationship may take its toll on the adolescent girl's mental health. Consistent with this, research indicates that early-maturing girls are more vulnerable to emotional

distress when they have relatively more opposite-sex friendships (Ge et al., 1996) and when they are in schools with older peers (for example, sixth-graders who are in a school that has seventh- and eighth-graders, too) (Blyth, Simmons, & Zakin, 1985). Again, we see the importance of context.

Psychologists have offered several explanations for the fact that early maturation appears to be harder on girls than boys. One explanation might be termed the "maturational deviance" hypothesis (Simmons & Blyth, 1987). Simply put, youngsters who stand far apart from their peers—in physical appearance, for instance—may experience more psychological distress than adolescents who blend in more easily. Because girls mature earlier than boys, on average, early-maturing girls mature earlier than both their male and female peers. This makes them stand out at a time when they would rather fit in and, as a result, may make them more vulnerable to emotional distress. This explanation would also account for the lower self-esteem of late-maturing boys, who deviate toward the other extreme.

A second explanation for the sex difference in the impact of early maturation focuses on "developmental readiness." If puberty is a challenge that requires psychological adaptation by the adolescent, perhaps younger adolescents are less ready to cope with the challenge than older ones. Because puberty occurs quite early among early-maturing girls, it may tax their psychological resources. Early maturation among boys, because it occurs at a later age, would pose less of a problem. This also helps to explain why late-maturing boys seem better able than early maturers to control their temper and their impulses when they are going through puberty: They are relatively older and psychologically more mature (Peskin, 1967). If the developmental readiness hypothesis is true, both girls and boys should experience more difficulty if they are early maturers than if they are on time or late, but the difficulty should be temporary. This appears to be the case among boys (for whom the negative effects of early puberty occur during puberty itself, but then fade), but not for girls (for whom the negative effects of early puberty persist) (Ge et al., 2003).

A final explanation for the relatively greater disadvantage of early maturation for girls concerns the cultural desirability of different body types (Petersen, 1988). Early maturation for girls means leaving behind the culturally admired state of thinness. As noted previously, among girls, the ratio of fat to muscle increases dramatically at puberty, and many girls are distressed when they mature because they gain weight. Early maturers experience this weight gain at a time when most of their peers are still girlishly thin. One interesting study showed that in

FIGURE 1.11 Early-maturing girls are more likely to use tobacco, alcohol, and other drugs than girls who mature on time or late. (From Dick et al., 2000)

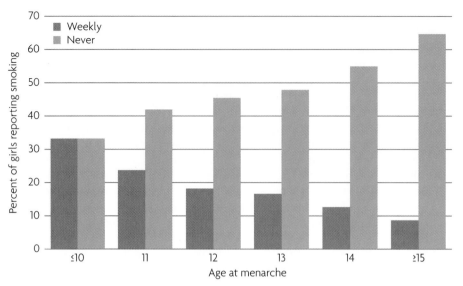

ballet companies—where thinness is even more important than in the culture at large—late maturers, who can retain the "ideal" shape much longer than earlier maturers, have fewer psychological problems than even on-time girls (Brooks-Gunn & Warren, 1985). In contrast, at puberty, boys move from a culturally undesirable state for males (short and scrawny) to a culturally admired one (tall and muscular). Early maturers enjoy the special advantage of being tall and muscular before their peers—a special benefit in a society that values males' athletic prowess—and therefore are more likely to react well to puberty. The fact that the effects of early maturation on girls' self-esteem vary across cultures suggests that contextual factors need to be taken into account in explaining this pattern of sex differences.

Whatever the explanation, it's important for parents and school counselors to bear in mind that early-maturing girls are at heightened risk for psychological problems, at least in the United States. Unfortunately, as long as our culture overvalues thinness and encourages the view that females should be judged on the basis of their physical appearance rather than their abilities, values, or personality, the risks of early puberty will probably endure. Adults can help by being supportive, by helping the early-maturing girl recognize her strengths and positive features—physical and nonphysical alike—and by preparing her for puberty before it takes place.

Like their male counterparts, early-maturing girls are also more likely to become involved in problem behavior, including delinquency and drugs and alcohol use; are more likely to have school problems; and are more likely to experience early sexual intercourse (Dick et al., 2000; Stice, Presnell, & Bearman, 2001;

Wichstrom, 2001) (see Figure 1.11). This is true in Europe and the United States (Silbereisen et al., 1989), and across ethnic groups within the United States (Deardorff, Gonzales, Christopher, Roosa, & Millsap, 2005). These problems appear to arise because early-maturing girls are more likely to spend time with older adolescents, especially older adolescent boys, who initiate them into activities that might otherwise be delayed (Haynie, 2003; Magnusson, Statin, & Allen, 1986). Girls with a history of problem behavior prior to puberty appear most susceptible to the adverse effects of early maturation (Caspi & Moffitt, 1991).

Again, however, it is important to consider the role of context in interaction with pubertal change. Although early-maturing girls generally are more likely to engage in delinquent behavior than their late-maturing peers, a study of New Zealand youngsters indicates that this may only hold true for girls who attend coeducational high schools (Caspi, Lynam, Moffitt, & Silva, 1993). Early-maturing girls in all-female schools are no more likely than late maturers to be involved in delinquent activities, presumably because there are far fewer opportunities for delinquency in same-sex schools. Thus, while early puberty may predispose girls toward more frequent and earlier deviance, this predisposition may be realized only in an environment that permits the behavior—such as a school that places early-maturing girls in close contact with older boys. Similarly, among both boys and girls, the impact of early maturation on problem behavior or depression is accentuated when adolescents have many stressful life events, live in disadvantaged urban neighborhoods, or have harsh and inconsistent parents (Ge, Brody, Conger, Simons, & Murry, 2002; Ge, Conger, &

FOOD FOR THOUGHT

Consider the research on the psychological consequences of early versus late maturation in males and females. Most of this research has been done in the United States. Are the effects of being early, on time, or late likely to be similar in different parts of the world?

Elder, 2001; Obeidallah, Brennan, Brooks-Gunn, & Earls, 2004).

One study of the adult personalities of women who were either early or late maturers suggests some interesting parallels between the personality development of early-maturing girls and late-maturing boys (Peskin, 1973). Both sets of youngsters may have self-esteem problems during adolescence, but both appear to be somewhat more psychologically advanced than their peers during adulthood. Like the late-maturing boys, the early-maturing girls may be forced to develop coping skills during adolescence that have some long-term positive effects.

At the same time, however, more recent research indicates that the earlier involvement of early-maturing girls in problem behavior may adversely affect their long-term educational achievement and mental health. In one study of Swedish girls, for example, the researchers found that the school problems of early-maturing girls persisted over time, leading to the development of negative attitudes toward school and lower educational aspirations. In young adulthood, there were marked differences between the early- and late-maturing girls' levels of education; for example, the late-maturing girls were twice as likely as early-maturing girls to continue beyond the compulsory minimum number of years of high school (Magnusson, Stattin, & Allen, 1986). In a different study of American girls, researchers found that women who had been early maturers reported higher levels of psychological distress and were more likely than others to have experienced a serious mental disorder at some point in adolescence or young adulthood (Graber, Seeley, Brooks-Gunn, & Lewinsohn, 2004).

RECAP

- Although going through puberty in and of itself is not ordinarily stressful, some evidence suggests that adolescents may be moodier during periods of rapid changes in pubertal hormones. In general,

though, stress in the environment is a much stronger influence on adolescent mental health than is puberty.
- Important changes in patterns of sleep take place at puberty. As the result of the emergence of a "delayed phase preference," after puberty, adolescents tend to stay up later at night and sleep later in the morning.
- Family relationships frequently become temporarily more strained and distant during the early stages of puberty.
- Among boys, early maturation is associated with popularity, higher self-esteem, and more self-confidence, but also with higher rates of problem behavior.
- Among girls, early maturation is associated with higher rates of problem behavior, with psychological distress, and emotional difficulties.
- In both sexes, the impact of early or late maturation depends on the social context in which it takes place.

Eating Disorders

Although a variety of nutritional and behavioral factors can lead to weight gain during adolescence, weight gain can sometimes result directly from the physical changes of puberty. Not only does the ratio of body fat to muscle increase markedly during puberty, but the body's **basal metabolism rate**—the minimal amount of energy one uses when resting—also drops about 15 percent. A person's weight is partly dependent on this rate.

Because adolescence is a time of dramatic change in physical appearance, teenagers' overall self-image is very much tied to their body image. In light of the tremendous emphasis that contemporary society places on being thin, particularly for females, the normal weight gain and change in body composition that accompanies puberty leads many adolescents, especially girls, to become extremely concerned about their weight.

OBESITY

Many adolescents, of course, have legitimate concerns about being overweight. The easiest way to determine whether someone is overweight is to calculate his or

basal metabolism rate   The minimal amount of energy used by the body during a resting state.

Obesity is by far the most common eating disorder among adolescents.

her **body mass index (BMI),** which is done by dividing the person's weight, measured in kilograms, by the square of the person's height, measured in meters. Individuals are considered obese if their BMI is at or above the 95th percentile for people of the same age and gender, at great risk for obesity if their BMI is at or above the 90th percentile, and overweight if their BMI is at or above the 85th percentile (Zametkin, Zoon, Klein, & Munson, 2004). (Charts showing the BMI cutoffs for males and females of different ages can be found at www.cdc.gov/growthcharts.) Using this definition, 16 percent of adolescents in the United States are obese, and another 15 percent are at great risk for obesity (Institute of Medicine, 2006), a rate that has *tripled* since 1980 (see Figure 1.12). Compared to their peers in the mid-1960s, the average 15-year-old boy today is 15 pounds heavier, and the average 15-year-old girl is 10 pounds heavier—increases that are far greater than could possibly be due to changes in height. Obesity is now considered the single most serious public health problem afflicting American teenagers.

▌ **Influences on Obesity** Current research indicates that obesity is a result of the interplay of genetic and environmental factors (Zametkin et al., 2004). Obesity is especially prevalent among African American girls, for both genetic and environmental reasons. Compared to their peers, African American girls have a lower basal metabolism rate and, in addition, spend less time exercising and more time watching television (where they are exposed to commercials promoting unhealthy foods) (Alleyne & LaPoint, 2004).

Research on the psychological consequences of obesity has not led to consistent conclusions. Some studies show higher levels of psychological distress (such as depression and low self-esteem) among obese individuals, especially during adolescence, but many studies show no such effect, and some research indicates that depression leads to obesity, rather than vice versa (Zametkin et al., 2004). In all likelihood, the psychological impact of obesity is highly dependent on the cultural context in which an adolescent grows up, because obesity is stigmatized far more in some ethnic groups than others. Nevertheless, because nearly 80 percent of obese adolescents will be obese adults, obesity during adolescence places the individual at much higher risk for other health problems, including hypertension (high blood pressure), high cholesterol levels, and diabetes (Institute of Medicine, 2006). The high rates of obesity among African American females, in particular, represent a serious threat to the cardiovascular health of this group (Kimm et al., 2002).

Although genetic factors are important contributors, the dramatically increased prevalence of adolescent obesity over such a short time period indicates that the problem has strong environmental causes. Indeed, it is not at all difficult to understand why so many American adolescents today are overweight. Studies show that too few children and adolescents are physically active (spending far too much time with television, video games, or the computer), and that too many eat far too much high-calorie, high-fat food (drinking far too many sugary soft drinks and consuming far too much junk food). The combination of inadequate exercise and poor nutrition is a recipe for obesity (Institute of Medicine, 2006).

▌ **Preventing and Treating Obesity** Much recent attention has focused on the availability of unhealthy foods and beverages in American schools, and in May 2006, the beverage industry announced that it would voluntarily stop selling high-calorie soft drinks in schools (Mayer, 2006). Manufacturers of high-calorie and high-fat foods also have been criticized for marketing these products to younger children, because food preferences are known to develop largely during early childhood (Institute of Medicine, 2006). Of course, although schools and advertisers undoubtedly influence what children and adolescents eat and drink, the bulk of what children and adolescents put into their mouths comes from their own homes. Even among adolescents, who spend far more time away from their family than do younger children, about two-thirds of their daily caloric intake comes from things they consume in their own home (Institute of Medicine, 2006). Taken together, these studies indicate that preventing

body mass index (BMI) A measure of an individual's body fat, the ratio of weight to height; used to gauge overweight and obesity.

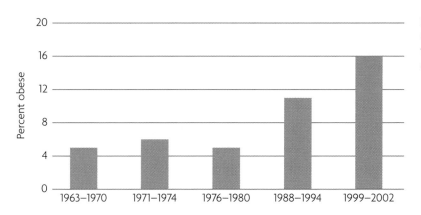

FIGURE 1.12 The rate of obesity among American adolescents has more than tripled since 1970. (From Institute of Medicine, 2006)

obesity will require multifaceted efforts involving parents, the mass media, food and beverage manufacturers, restaurants, and schools.

Research has also evaluated a variety of approaches to individual weight loss, including behavioral therapy designed to gradually alter patterns of diet and exercise, and medications designed to promote weight loss. Several evaluations indicate that the combination of behavior modification and weight loss medication is more effective than either component by itself (Berkowitz, Wadden, Tershakovec, & Cronquist, 2003; Chanoine, Hampl, Jensen, Boldrin, & Hauptman, 2005). Radical approaches to weight control—fad diets and the like—actually increase, rather than decrease, obesity (Stice, Presnell, Shaw, & Rohde, 2005).

ANOREXIA NERVOSA AND BULIMIA

Health care professionals are concerned not only about adolescents who are obese but also about adolescents who have unhealthy attitudes toward eating and toward their body image (French, Story, Downes, Resnick, & Blum, 1995). Only about one-fourth of American adolescents are highly satisfied with their body (Kelly, Wall, Eisenberg, Story, & Neumark-Sztainer, 2005). Egged on by advertisers, who promote the idea that "thin is beautiful"—middle-class white girls define bodily perfection as being 5 feet 7 inches tall and weighing 110 pounds—many adolescents respond to normal bodily changes at puberty by dieting, often unnecessarily (Brumberg, 1997). More than half of all adolescent girls consider themselves overweight and have attempted to diet (Fisher et al., 1995). One recent study found that 14 percent of female college undergraduates were so concerned about eating that they were embarrassed at buying a chocolate bar in a store (Rozin, Bauer, & Catanese, 2003). Gender differences in concerns about weight emerge long before adolescence (Phares, Steinberg, & Thompson, 2004).

■ **Disordered Eating** Psychologists use the term **disordered eating** to refer to unhealthy eating attitudes and behaviors. Disordered eating can range from unnecessary preoccupation with weight and body image to full-blown clinical eating disorders, such as anorexia and bulimia. Studies show that disordered eating is associated with a range of stress-related psychological problems, including poor body image, depression, alcohol and tobacco use, and poor interpersonal relationships (French et al., 1995; Graber, Brooks-Gunn, Paikoff, & Warren, 1994; Neumark-Sztainer, Story, Dixon, & Murray, 1998). It is not clear, however, whether these problems precede or follow from disordered eating (Leon, Fulkerson, Perry, Keel, & Klump, 1999).

In contemporary America, as the expression goes, one can never be too rich or too thin. Studies of magazines aimed at women and adolescent girls reveal clear and consistent messages implying that women cannot be beautiful without being slim and promoting a range of weight loss products. Between 1970 and 1990, moreover, images presented in these magazines' advertisements changed, with the "ideal" body shape becoming slimmer and less curvaceous (Guillen & Barr, 1994). Exposure to commercials containing images of females with idealized thin bodies increases girls' dissatisfaction with their own bodies (Hargreaves & Tiggemann, 2003). Interestingly, among Hispanic American girls, those who are more acculturated ("Americanized") are significantly more likely to develop disordered eating than those who are less acculturated (Gowen, Hayward, Killen, Robinson, & Taylor, 1999). Girls whose mothers have body image problems are especially likely to engage in extreme weight loss behaviors (Ogle & Damhorst, 2003), as are those who report more negative relationships with their parents (Archibald, Graber, & Brooks-Gunn,

disordered eating Mild, moderate, or severe disturbance in eating habits and attitudes.

1999). Ironically, research indicates that adolescents' attempts to control their weight through intensive dieting, the use of laxatives and appetite suppressants, and deliberate vomiting lead to weight *gain,* not loss (Stice, Cameron, Killen, Hayward, & Taylor, 1999).

Not everyone is genetically or metabolically meant to be as thin as fashion magazines tell people they should be, however. Some young women become so concerned about gaining weight that they take drastic—and dangerous—measures to remain thin. Some go on eating binges and then force themselves to vomit to avoid gaining weight, a pattern associated with an eating disorder called **bulimia.** In the more severe cases, young women who suffer from an eating disorder called **anorexia nervosa** actually starve themselves in an effort to keep their weight down. Adolescents with these sorts of eating disorders have an extremely disturbed body image: They see themselves as overweight when they are actually underweight. Some anorexic youngsters may lose between 25 and 50 percent of their body weight. As you might expect, bulimia and anorexia, if untreated, lead to a variety of serious physical problems; in fact, nearly 20 percent of anorexic teenagers inadvertently starve themselves to death.

Anorexia and bulimia each began to receive a great deal of popular attention during the 1980s, because of their dramatic nature and their frequent association in the mass media with celebrities. Perhaps because of this attention, initial reports characterized these eating disorders as being of epidemic proportion. Although unhealthy eating and unnecessary dieting are prevalent among teenagers, careful studies indicate that the incidence of genuine anorexia and genuine bulimia is rather small (Fisher et al., 1995). Fewer than one-half of 1 percent of adolescents are anorexic, and only about 3 percent are bulimic (American Psychiatric Association, 1994). Rates among females are substantially higher than among males—clinically defined anorexia and bulimia are 10 times more prevalent among adolescent girls than boys (Jacobi, Hayward, de Zwaan, Kraemer, & Agras, 2004), although the female-to-male ratio is substantially smaller when less severe forms of these disorders are considered (Muise, Stein, & Arbess, 2003; Ricciardelli & McCabe, 2004).

■ **Body Dissatisfaction**   Although the incidence of anorexia and bulimia is small, the proportion of adoles-

cents who are unhappy with their body shape or weight is not. In one study, for example, more than one-third of girls whose weight was considered normal by medical and health standards believed that they were overweight—including 5 percent who actually were *underweight* by medical criteria. (In contrast, fewer than 7 percent of normal-weight boys and no underweight boys described themselves as being overweight.) In this study, more than 70 percent of the girls reported that they would like to be thinner than they are (as opposed to one-third of the boys), and more than 80 percent said that being thinner would make them happier, more successful, and more popular (Paxton et al., 1991). Dissatisfaction with body shape and weight is likely to lead to the development of eating problems (Attie & Brooks-Gunn, 1989), depression (Stice & Bearman, 2001; Stice, Hayward, Cameron, Killen, & Taylor, 2000), and the initiation of smoking (Austin & Gortmaker, 2001; Fulkerson & French, 2003; Stice & Shaw, 2003). According to a recent study, more than half of high school girls engaged in some form of unhealthy behavior (e.g., fasting, smoking, vomiting after eating, using diet pills) in order to lose weight (Croll, Neumark-Sztainer, Story, & Ireland, 2002). Taken together, these findings have led some writers to suggest that we think about disordered eating on a continuum, ranging from dieting that may be perfectly sensible and healthy, to disordered eating that is unhealthy but not psychopathological (i.e., at a level requiring treatment) to full-blown anorexia or bulimia (Tyrka, Graber, & Brooks-Gunn, 2000).

Unfortunately, many girls gain weight during puberty, and for early adolescent girls, being overweight is highly correlated with being seen as unattractive by others (Rosenblum & Lewis, 1999). Despite adults' wishes that girls not place so much emphasis on being thin, research indicates that the widespread belief among adolescent girls that being slim will increase their popularity, especially with boys, is in fact based in reality (see Figure 1.13) (Halpern, Udry, Campbell, & Suchindran, 1999). That is, the pressure girls feel to be thin in order to attract boys does not just come from television, movies, and magazines—it comes from their actual experience. Indeed, one recent analysis found that, regardless of a girl's ethnicity, each 1-point increase in a young woman's BMI (an index of the degree to which she is overweight) was associated with a 6 percent decrease in the probability of her being in a romantic relationship (Halpern, King, Oslak, & Udry, 2005). This places many girls in a difficult situation, as one team of researchers noted:

> Most girls in our sample reported that having a boyfriend was either somewhat or very important to them, and virtually all girls saw physical attractiveness as important. As adolescent girls experience the weight

bulimia   An eating disorder found primarily among young women, characterized by a pattern of binge eating and self-induced vomiting.

anorexia nervosa   An eating disorder found chiefly among young women, characterized by dramatic and severe self-induced weight loss.

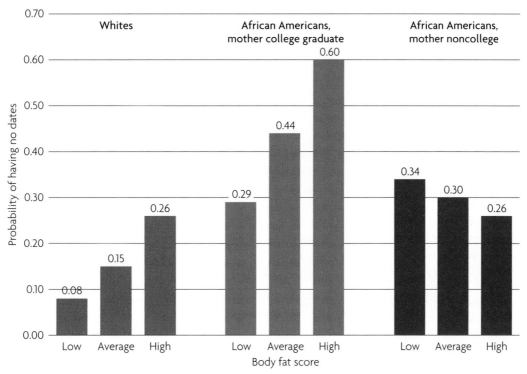

FIGURE 1.13 White girls and middle-class black girls are significantly less likely to date when they are not as slim as their peers. The same is not true for less affluent black girls, however. (Adapted from Halpern et al., 1999)

and fat gains that accompany and follow puberty, they must reconcile these gains with their belief that slimness is an important factor in dating and popularity with boys. . . . For White girls and Black girls with college-educated mothers, more body fat, even among non-obese girls, strongly lowered the probability of dating. . . . The 5 ft 3 in. girl who weighed 110 pounds was twice as likely to date as a girl of the same height and level of pubertal maturity who weighed 126 pounds. . . . Obviously, these adolescent girls had not carried out the sort of probability calculations that we have presented here, but adolescents, White adolescents in particular, believe that slimness is important to the likelihood of dating. Our data indicate that they are right. (Halpern et al., 1999, p. 732)

█ Prevalence and Causes of Anorexia and Bulimia Initial reports on the prevalence of disordered eating among adolescent girls led to the conclusion that eating disorders were especially common among affluent, suburban, white, and Asian American girls (e.g., Condit, 1990). More recent studies do not support this contention, however. Contemporary research indicates that disordered eating and body dissatisfaction have been reported among poor as well as affluent teenagers and among African American and Hispanic American as well as Asian American and white youngsters (Jacobi et al., 2004). Although less is known about the causes and consequences of body

dissatisfaction among adolescent males, evidence suggests that many contemporary adolescent boys feel pressure to be especially muscular and engage in unhealthy behaviors, such as anabolic steroid use, in order to develop an appearance that is more similar to the idealized male body type (Ricciardelli & McCabe, 2004).

A recent analysis of historical and cross-cultural trends in the prevalence of anorexia and bulimia points to important differences between the two disorders (Keel & Klump, 2003). Whereas anorexia has been observed all over the world, bulimia has been reported almost exclusively in Western cultures or in cultures exposed to strong Western influences. And whereas anorexia has increased in prevalence steadily over time, the prevalence of bulimia increased significantly between 1970 and 1990 but has declined somewhat since then—interestingly, paralleling trends in females' reported body dissatisfaction, which also peaked in the early 1990s, despite the fact that individuals' BMI continued to increase (Cash, Morrow, Hrabosky, & Perry, 2004). This suggests that bulimia is a much more culturally determined disorder than is anorexia. Consistent with this, the degree to which anorexia is an inherited disorder is far more comparable from one culture to another than is the case for bulimia.

Several theories have been proposed to account for the onset of anorexia and bulimia during adolescence (see Jacobi et al., 2004, for a review). Traditional views emphasized psychological factors and, in particular, aspects of the parent–child relationship. Early writers who observed patterns of dysfunctional relationships in families with anorexic girls proposed that anorexia is related to the adolescent's attempts to assert her autonomy within an overly controlling family system in which parents are overprotective and highly critical (e.g., Bruch, 1973; Minuchin, Rosman, & Baker, 1978). According to a recent comprehensive review of studies of risk factors for eating disorders, however, evidence in support of these theories is sparse, and the same familial factors that have been proposed to cause eating disorders have been shown to influence a wide variety of psychological disorders (Jacobi et al., 2004). In addition, longitudinal studies have shown that negative family relationships often follow from, rather than precede, the onset of disordered eating, raising questions about which causes which (Archibald, Linver, Graber, & Brooks-Gunn, 2002).

A second school of thought views eating disorders as part of a more general syndrome of psychological distress. Many studies have pointed to links between eating disorders and other serious mental health problems, such as depression, obsessive-compulsive disorders, or substance abuse; many anorexic and bulimic women display such psychological problems along with their eating disorder (French et al., 2001; Jacobi et al., 2004; Stice, Burton, & Shaw, 2004). These studies suggest that anorexia and bulimia may be best understood not as independent or unique disorders, but as particular manifestations of a more general underlying psychological problem—called "internalized distress"—that can be displayed in a variety of ways. (As you'll see in Chapter 13, many different psychological disorders in adolescence occur together, or "covary.") In support of this view, some evidence suggests that the same medications that are successful in treating depression and obsessive-compulsive disorder are useful in treating bulimia (but, interestingly, not anorexia) (Walsh et al., 2006).

FOOD FOR THOUGHT

Although obesity is a far more prevalent disorder than either anorexia or bulimia, until fairly recently, obesity attracted far less media attention. Now, however, childhood obesity is constantly in the news. Why do you think this change in media coverage has taken place?

Finally, because anorexia and bulimia are 10 times more common in females than males, broader social forces are probably a main factor in the development of these eating disorders (Keel & Klump, 2003). Research indicates, for example, that girls who are early maturers and early daters are likely to report greater dissatisfaction with their body and to be at greater risk for disordered eating (Cauffman & Steinberg, 1996; Smolak, Levine, & Gralen, 1993; Swarr & Richards, 1996); that girls who perceive that they are under pressure to be thin or who have accepted thinness as an ideal toward which to strive are more susceptible to eating disorders (Stice & Whitenton, 2002); and that girls who turn to popular magazines, such as *Seventeen, Sassy,* and *Glamour,* for information about dieting and appearance are more likely to have a high drive for thinness, low body satisfaction, and disturbed patterns of eating (Jones, Vigfusdottir, & Lee, 2004; Levine, Smolack, & Hayden, 1994). As noted earlier, cultural influences on the development of bulimia are especially strong.

Adolescents' beliefs about ideal body types are also shaped by the people they spend time with. One interesting study showed, for example, how bulimia became socially "contagious" in a college sorority (Crandall, 1988). This researcher found that over the course of the academic year, women's eating behavior became more and more like that of their sorority friends—even in a sorority in which binge eating was the norm. Other research indicates that girls' attitudes toward eating and dieting are influenced by the attitudes of their parents (especially their mothers) and friends (Mukai, 1996; Ogle & Damhorst, 2003). African American girls whose peer group is ethnically mixed, for example, are more likely to endorse mainstream American cultural stereotypes about the desirability of thinness than are those whose peers are predominantly African American (Abrams & Stormer, 2002).

Just because cultural conditions contribute to the development of disordered eating doesn't mean that individual characteristics do not play a role as well. Cultural conditions may predispose females more than males toward anorexia and bulimia, and girls and young women who have certain genetic vulnerabilities, psychological traits (such as proneness to depression or low self-esteem), physical characteristics (such as early pubertal maturation), familial characteristics (such as strained relations with parents), or social concerns (such as a strong interest in dating) may be more likely to develop problems (e.g., Cauffman & Steinberg, 1996; Frank & Jackson, 1996; Ricciardelli & McCabe, 2001). The onset of eating disorders, like so many aspects of adolescent development, is likely the product of a complex interaction between individual and contextual factors.

A variety of therapeutic approaches have been employed successfully in the treatment of anorexia and bulimia, including individual psychotherapy and cognitive-behavioral modification, group therapy, family therapy, and, more recently, antidepressant medications (Agras, Schneider, Arnow, Raeburn, & Telch, 1989; Condit, 1990; Killian, 1994; Vigersky, 1977). The treatment of anorexia often requires hospitalization initially in order to ensure that starvation does not progress to fatal or near-fatal levels (Mitchell, 1985).

RECAP

- The most common eating disorder in adolescence is obesity. About one in six American adolescents are obese, and another one in six are at great risk for obesity. Obesity is associated with a wide array of serious health problems.
- Anorexia and bulimia are eating disorders that do not appear until adolescence and that are far more prevalent among females than males.
- Many girls with anorexia or bulimia develop the disorder as a result of dissatisfaction with the way in which their body has changed following puberty, especially within a culture that idealizes thinness among women.
- Anorexia and bulimia are often accompanied by other emotional problems, such as depression, anxiety, or obsessive-compulsive disorder.

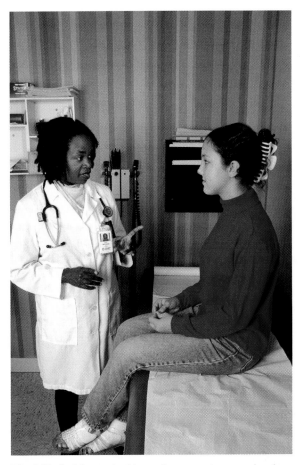

The field of adolescent health care has grown in recent decades, as medical practitioners have come to recognize the special health care needs of adolescents.

Physical Health and Health Care in Adolescence

Although puberty is undoubtedly the most important biological development of adolescence, concerns about the physical health and well-being of young people are far broader than those involving reproductive maturation. In the past two decades, the field of **adolescent health care** has grown rapidly, as health educators and health care practitioners have come to better understand that the health care needs of adolescents differ from those of children and adults in important respects (Williams, Holmbeck, & Greenley, 2002).

THE PARADOX OF ADOLESCENT HEALTH

Adolescence is a paradox as far as physical health is concerned. On the one hand, adolescence is one of the healthiest periods in the life span, characterized by a relatively low incidence of disabling or chronic illnesses (such as asthma or cancer), fewer short-term hospital stays, and fewer days in which individuals stay home sick. Nonetheless, in the United States, nearly 1 in 15 adolescents has at least one disabling chronic illness, with the main causes of disability being mental disorders such as depression, respiratory illnesses such as asthma, and muscular and skeletal disorders such as arthritis (Ozer, Macdonald, & Irwin, 2002). Fortunately, in the past 50 years, rates of death and disability resulting from illness and disease during adolescence have decreased substantially, and new medical technologies and better health care delivery have improved the physical well-being of children, especially those with chronic illnesses and disabling medical conditions (Williams et al., 2002). Adolescents are far less likely than individuals of any other age to seek

adolescent health care A field of study and health care devoted to understanding the health care needs of individuals during the second decade of life.

and receive medical care through traditional office visits to practitioners however, and there are large socioeconomic and ethnic disparities in adolescents' access to health care, with poor and ethnic minority youths far less likely to have adequate health insurance and health care access than affluent or white youths (Ozer et al., 2002).

The most virulent threat to adolescent health comes from unhealthy behaviors (such as drug use), violence (both self-inflicted and inflicted by others), and risky activity (such as unprotected sexual intercourse or reckless driving) (Williams et al., 2002). In some senses, then, many of the improvements in preventing and treating the traditional medical problems of the period—those having to do with chronic illnesses—have been offset by what some scientists call the "new morbidity and mortality" of adolescence (Hein, 1988a). Contributors to this new morbidity and mortality include accidents (especially automobile accidents), suicide, homicide, substance abuse (including tobacco and alcohol use), and sexually transmitted diseases (including AIDS).

CAUSES OF MORTALITY IN ADOLESCENCE

The contrast between the old and new mortalities of adolescence is readily apparent. Fifty years ago, illness and disease accounted for more than twice as many deaths among teenagers as violence or injury, but the reverse is true today. A recent analysis of the causes of mortality among adolescents and young adults indicates that unintentional injuries are the leading cause of death worldwide, followed by AIDS, infectious disease, homicide, and suicide, in that order (Blum & Nelson-Mmari, 2004). According to recent estimates, approximately 45 percent of all teenage deaths in the United States result from car accidents and other unintentional injuries, and another 30 percent are a result of homicide or suicide (Ozer et al., 2002). Adolescents are involved in more driving accidents than adults, primarily because they are less experienced behind the wheel (at any age, new drivers are more likely to have accidents than seasoned drivers), but also because they are more likely to take chances while driving (Cvijanovich, Cook, Mann, & Dean, 2001; Dee & Evans, 2001; Harré, 2000). Two of the most important con-

tributors to serious car accidents involving teenage drivers are driving at night and driving with other teenagers in the car (Simons-Morton, Hartos, Leaf, & Preusser, 2005). This finding has led many states to implement graduated driver-licensing programs, which place restrictions on when and with whom teenagers can drive until they have gained sufficient experience; these programs have reduced automobile fatalities (Foss, Feaganes, & Rodgman, 2001; Shope, Molnar, Elliott, & Waller, 2001). One piece of good news: Although alcohol contributes greatly to automobile accidents among young drivers, the rate of alcohol-related traffic fatalities among young people has dropped dramatically in recent years (Dee & Evans, 2001).

The consensus among health care experts, then, is that the most significant threats to the health of today's youths arise from psychosocial rather than from natural causes (Ozer et al., 2002). Unlike many other periods of the life span (such as infancy or old age), when we are more vulnerable to disease and illness, most of the health problems of teenagers are preventable. Moreover, patterns of diet, drug use, and exercise established during adolescence persist into adulthood (Williams et al., 2002). As a result of this recognition, the focus in the field of adolescent health has shifted away from traditional medical models (in which the emphasis is on the assessment, diagnosis, and treatment of disease) and toward more community-oriented, educational approaches (in which the emphasis is on the prevention of illness and injury and the promotion of good health) (Millstein, Petersen, & Nightingale, 1993; Susman, Koch, Maney, & Finkelstein, 1993).

FOOD FOR THOUGHT

Although most adolescent health problems are caused by teenagers' own behavior, getting adolescents to change how they live has proven remarkably difficult. Why do you think this is the case?

In other words, instead of asking how we can best treat sick adolescents, experts in adolescent health care are now asking how we can encourage adolescents to take the steps necessary to prevent illness and disability. How can we help adolescents reduce **health-compromising behaviors,** such as violence, drug use, unsafe driving, and unprotected sexual intercourse, and increase **health-enhancing behaviors,** such as

health-compromising behaviors   Behaviors that place individuals at risk for health problems.

health-enhancing behaviors   Behaviors that lessen individuals' risk for health problems or that increase well-being.

eating properly, exercising adequately, and wearing seat belts? Current efforts include providing teenagers with education about alcohol and drug use, accident prevention, safe sex, and proper nutrition, as well as encouraging health care professionals to do more direct screening for risky health practices among their adolescent patients—as one group of experts put it, "Don't ask, they won't tell" (Blum, Beuhring, Wunderlich, & Resnick, 1996, p. 1767).

PROMOTING ADOLESCENT HEALTH

A variety of new, wide-reaching strategies for promoting adolescent health have been attempted in recent decades. Among the most popular are **school-based health centers.** Located in or adjacent to schools, they provide such services as physical examinations, the treatment of minor injuries, health education programs, dental care, and counseling related to substance abuse, sexuality, and mental health. They often are set up to serve poor youth, who generally are less likely to receive medical and dental care than their more affluent counterparts.

School-based health centers have become increasingly popular because they are positioned to address the most pressing problems in adolescent health care: that most adolescent health problems are preventable, that adolescents underutilize conventional medical services, and that adolescents often want their health care needs to remain confidential. Although the development of these centers has generated controversy in a number of communities because some school-based health centers distribute contraceptives (a practice, that, as we shall see in a later chapter, upsets many adults), studies show that the vast majority of visits to these centers are for injuries, acute illnesses (such as influenza or strep throat), and mental health services (such as counseling). Visits for family planning services account for only 10 percent of visits to school-based clinics (Scales, 1991).

How well are school-based clinics working? Recent evaluations of several school-based health programs—including those designed to improve adolescents' physical and mental health, those designed to reduce drug and alcohol use, and those designed to reduce teenage pregnancy—have been inconsistent. Although most programs have shown some success in increasing adolescents' understanding of health-related issues (for example, how AIDS is spread) or knowledge about health risks (for example, the dangers of cocaine use), few programs have been markedly successful in changing adolescents' *behavior,* particularly after the program was completed (Kisker & Brown, 1996; Millstein et al., 1993). Why is this so? As is the case in studies of adults, studies of adolescents indicate that it is far easier to alter what individuals know than it is to change how they behave.

As many experts point out, health behavior is influenced by a number of factors, of which knowledge is only one component (e.g., Leventhal & Keeshan, 1993). Changes in the context in which adolescents live (such as the accessibility of handguns, the availability of illicit drugs, or the role models to which young people are exposed) must accompany changes in adolescents' knowledge and understanding if lasting health promotion is to be accomplished (Nation et al., 2003). For example, recent investigations of the impact of changing one element of the broader context of adolescent health—the legal drinking age—have found that raising the age leads to a significant decline in accidental death rates among young automobile drivers and pedestrians, as well as in the rates of unintentional injuries not involving cars and homicides (Jones, Pieper, & Robertson, 1992). Similarly, the single most effective policy for reducing teen smoking has been raising the price of cigarettes (Gruber & Zinman, 2001).

Improving the health of young people is an especially important concern among those working with adolescents who are poor or from ethnic minority groups, because these youngsters are at greater risk for many of the old and new morbidities and mortalities of adolescence (Ozer et al., 2002; Singh & Yu, 1996). Nonwhite youngsters, for example, are relatively more likely than white youngsters to suffer from a chronic illness (Ozer et al., 2002), to be obese or to have high blood pressure or high cholesterol levels (National Heart, Lung, and Blood Institute Growth and Health Study Research Group, 1992), to be physically inactive (Wolf et al., 1993), to be victims of violent crimes (Earls, Cairns, & Mercy, 1993), to contract AIDS (Sells & Blum, 1996), to die from drowning (Warneke & Cooper, 1994), and to be murdered (Sorenson, Richardson, & Peterson, 1993). Homicide is the leading cause of death for African-American adolescents, accounting for almost half of all deaths in this ethnic group, and homicide is also largely responsible for higher mortality rates among Hispanic youth (Ozer et al., 2002). American Indian/Alaska Native males have suicide rates four times higher than that of any other racial/ethnic group (Ozer et al., 2002). Yet, despite their generally poorer health, minority youngsters are less likely to have access to sources of medical care, less likely to visit the doctor when ill, and less likely to have health insurance (Newacheck, Park, Brindis, Biehl, & Irwin, 2004).

school-based health centers A relatively new approach to the delivery of health care services to adolescents that places health care providers in offices located in or adjacent to schools.

The combination of poor health and limited access to health care is even more concentrated among the sizable proportion of adolescents who live in poverty, a disproportionate number of whom are from ethnic minority backgrounds (Klerman, 1993). There is now convincing evidence that the links between health and socioeconomic status are strong and pervasive across different sorts of health problems, with physical and mental health problems increasing linearly as one moves down the socioeconomic ladder (Adler et al., 1994; Keating & Hertzman, 2000). Because increases in the size of the adolescent population over the next several decades worldwide will be concentrated among poor and minority youth (Fussell & Greene, 2002), the most daunting challenge facing health care providers and policymakers will be finding ways of minimizing or even eliminating the socioeconomic and ethnic disparities in health and health care that currently exist around the world (Call et al., 2002; Ozer et al., 2002).

RECAP

- The most important physical health problems afflicting adolescents have behavioral rather than natural causes.
- The leading cause of mortality among adolescents around the world is unintentional accidents.
- Experts in adolescent health care argue that it is important to focus on changing adolescents' behavior in order to prevent health-compromising activities and encourage health-promoting ones.
- Among the most important innovations in adolescent health care are school-based clinics.

CHAPTER 2

Cognitive Transitions

CHANGES IN COGNITION

Thinking About Possibilities

Thinking About Abstract Concepts

Thinking About Thinking

Thinking in Multiple Dimensions

Adolescent Relativism

THEORETICAL PERSPECTIVES ON ADOLESCENT THINKING

The Piagetian View of Adolescent Thinking

The Information-Processing View of Adolescent Thinking

THE ADOLESCENT BRAIN

What Changes in Adolescence?

Implications for Adolescent Behavior

INDIVIDUAL DIFFERENCES IN INTELLIGENCE IN ADOLESCENCE

The Measurement of IQ

Types of Intelligence

Intelligence Test Performance in Adolescence

Culture and Intelligence

ADOLESCENT THINKING IN CONTEXT

Changes in Social Cognition

Adolescent Risk Taking

Adolescent Thinking in the Classroom

CHANGES IN COGNITION, or thinking, represent the second of three fundamental changes that occur during adolescence—the others being the biological changes of puberty and the transition into new social roles. Like developments in the other two domains, the cognitive transitions of adolescence have far-reaching implications for the young person's psychological development and social relations. Indeed, the expansion of thought during adolescence represents as significant an event and as important an influence on the adolescent's development and behavior as puberty. In the view of some writers, adolescence is a critical period for the development of more complex and sophisticated ways of reasoning about the world (Keating, 2004).

In recent years, scientists have made tremendous gains in understanding brain maturation during adolescence through the use of imaging techniques that permit us to look inside the adolescent brain, just as an X-ray permits physicians to look directly at bones. Although this understanding is still developing—and almost as fast as an adolescent in the midst of a growth spurt!—we now have a good idea of how the brain changes during the adolescent years and the implications of these changes for behavioral, emotional, and, of course, cognitive development. Later in this chapter, we'll look at brain maturation in adolescence in detail. But let's begin by simply describing how adolescents think and, more importantly, how their thinking differs from that of children.

Changes in Cognition

Most people would agree that adolescents are "smarter" than children. Not only do teenagers know more than children—after all, the longer we live, the more opportunities we have to acquire new information—but they actually think in ways that are more advanced, more efficient, and generally more effective. In general, during adolescence, individuals develop an "executive suite" of capabilities that permit thinking that is more deliberate and more controlled (Keating, 2004). This can be seen in five chief ways:

1. Adolescents are better able than children to think about what is possible, instead of limiting their thought to what is real.
2. Adolescents are better able than children to think about abstract things.
3. Adolescents think more often than children about the process of thinking itself.
4. Adolescents' thinking, compared to children's, is more often multidimensional, rather than limited to a single issue.
5. Adolescents are more likely than children to see things as relative, rather than as absolute.

Let's look at each of these advantages—and some of their implications for adolescent's behavior—in greater detail.

THINKING ABOUT POSSIBILITIES

Adolescents' thinking is less bound to concrete events than is that of children. Children's thinking is oriented to the here and now—that is, to things and events that they can observe directly. But adolescents are able to consider what they observe against a backdrop of what is possible. Put another way, for the child, what is possible is what is real; for the adolescent, what is real is just a subset of what is possible. Consider how individuals think about themselves. Children generally do not wonder, the way adolescents often do, about how their personalities might change in the future, or how their lives might be affected by different career choices, or how they might have been different had they grown up under different circumstances. As a young child, you simply are who you are. But as an adolescent, who you are is just one possibility of who you could be.

This does not mean that children are incapable of imagination or fantasy. Even young children have vivid imaginations. Nor does it mean that children are unable to conceive of things being different from the way they observe them to be. Rather, the advantage that adolescents enjoy over children when it comes to thinking about possibilities is that adolescents are able to move easily between the specific and the abstract, to generate alternative possibilities and explanations systematically, and to compare what they actually observe with what they believe is possible.

The adolescent's ability to reason systematically in terms of what is possible comes in handy in a variety of mathematical, scientific, and other problem-solving contexts. For instance, the study of mathematics in junior and senior high school (algebra, geometry, and trigonometry) often requires that you begin with an abstract or theoretical formulation—for example, "the square of a right triangle's hypotenuse is equal to the sum of the squares of the other two sides" (the Pythagorean theorem). This theorem, after all, is a proposition about the possible rather than the real. It is a statement about all *possible* right triangles, not just triangles that you might actually observe. In mathematics, you learn how to apply these theorems to concrete examples (that is, real triangles). Scientific experimentation—in biology, chemistry, and physics—also involves the ability to generate possibilities systematically. In a chemistry experiment in which you are trying to identify an unknown substance by performing various tests, you must first be able to imagine alternative possibilities for the substance's identity in order to know what tests to conduct.

FOOD FOR THOUGHT

In what ways did your high school classes take advantage of the advanced thinking abilities that develop in adolescence? In what ways were opportunities to do this missed?

The adolescent's use of this sort of thinking is not limited to scientific problem solving. We see it in the types of arguments adolescents employ, in which they are better able than younger children to envision and therefore anticipate the possible responses of an opponent and to have handy a counterargument or series of counterarguments (Clark & Delia, 1976). Many parents believe that their children become more argumentative during adolescence. What probably happens, though, is that their children become *better arguers.* An adolescent does not accept other people's points of view unquestioningly—including his or her parents' viewpoints—but instead evaluates them against other theoretically possible beliefs. As you'll see in Chapter 4, this improvement in the adolescent's intellectual ability likely contributes to the bickering and squabbling that often occur between teenagers and their parents (Smetana, 1989).

▌ **Deductive and Inductive Reasoning** One manifestation of the adolescent's increased facility with thinking about possibilities is the development of **deductive reasoning.** Deductive reasoning is a type of logical reasoning in which you draw logically necessary conclusions from a general set of premises, or givens. Consider the following problem:

All hockey players wear mouth guards.

Kim is a hockey player.

Does Kim wear a mouth guard?

Individuals who reason deductively understand that the correct conclusion (that Kim wears a mouth guard) necessarily follows from the first two statements. No additional knowledge about hockey or about Kim is necessary to reach the correct answer. Adolescents are also better able than children to recognize when a log-

ical problem does not provide sufficient information and to respond by saying that the question can't be answered with any certainty. Suppose we were to change the problem to read like this:

All hockey players wear mouth guards.

Kim is wearing a mouth guard.

Is Kim a hockey player?

If you answer this type of question quickly, without thinking it through, you might say that Kim is indeed a hockey player. But, in fact, this is not necessarily the case. Whereas children are easily fooled by such problems, adolescents are more likely to say that there is no way of knowing whether Kim plays hockey, because we are not told that the *only* people who wear mouth guards are hockey players. One reason for their superior performance on these sorts of problems is that adolescents are better able to catch themselves before they incorrectly answer the question—something that scientists refer to as "inhibiting a prepotent response"—and pause a moment before responding (Daniel & Klaczynski, 2006). Interestingly, the ability to stop yourself before acting automatically (and perhaps incorrectly) is controlled by a region of the brain that has been shown to mature during adolescence (Luna, Garver, Urban, Lazar, & Sweeney, 2004).

Often in life, we make educated guesses even though our hunches cannot be supported by deductive reasoning. Consider the following problem:

Kim, John, Julie, Tom, Liz, and Kendra are hockey players.

Kim, John, Julie, Tom, Liz, and Kendra all wear mouth guards.

Do all hockey players wear mouth guards?

This problem cannot be solved using deductive reasoning because no certain answer to the question necessarily follows from the first two statements. Instead, this problem is likely to be solved using **inductive reasoning,** in which an inference is made based on the accumulated evidence. For this problem, your answer to the question would likely vary depending on how many people were listed in the first two statements, your knowledge of hockey, your own experience playing contact sports, and so on. And rather than being certain of your answer, you would have different degrees of confidence in your conclusion depending on the amount of information you had. In other

deductive reasoning A type of logical reasoning in which one draws logically necessary conclusions from a general set of promises, or givens.

inductive reasoning Reasoning that involves drawing an inference from the evidence that one has.

words, whereas the conclusions derived from deductive inferences are guaranteed to be true by virtue of their inherent logic, conclusions derived from inductive inferences vary in their likelihood of being true (Galotti, Komatsu, & Voelz, 1997). Inductive reasoning is used by people of all ages, even very young children (Jacobs & Portenza, 1991). Indeed, we all use inductive reasoning in everyday situations (for example, you find out that many of your classmates have gotten poor grades on a test, so you start to worry that you will, too). Deductive reasoning is seldom used before adolescence, however. Indeed, the development of deductive reasoning is seen by many researchers as the major intellectual accomplishment of adolescence (Klaczynski & Narasimham, 1998; Morris & Sloutsky, 2001).

▮ **Hypothetical Thinking**   Related to the development of deductive reasoning is the emergence of hypothetical, or "if-then," thinking. In order to think hypothetically, you need to see beyond what is directly observable and apply logical reasoning to anticipate what might be possible. The ability to think through hypotheses is an enormously powerful tool. Being able to plan ahead, to see the future consequences of an action, and to provide alternative explanations of events are all dependent on being able to hypothesize effectively.

Thinking in hypothetical terms also permits us to suspend our beliefs about something in order to argue in the abstract. Being capable of assuming a hypothetical stance is important when it comes to debating an issue, since doing so permits us to understand the logic behind the other person's argument without necessarily agreeing with its conclusion. Playing devil's advocate, for example—as when you formulate a position contrary to what you really believe in order to challenge someone else's reasoning—requires the ability to think in hypothetical terms. Studies show that prior to adolescence, individuals have difficulty in dealing with propositions that are contrary to fact, unless they are part of a larger fiction (Markovits & Valchon, 1989). For example, a 7-year-old would have trouble answering the question "Where would flying cows build nests?" He might say, "Cows don't fly," unless he had heard about flying cows in a story that was clearly fantasy-based.

Of course, hypothetical thinking also has implications for the adolescent's social behavior. It helps the young person to take the perspective of others by enabling him or her to think through what someone else might be thinking or feeling, given that person's point of view ("If I were in that person's situation, I would feel pretty angry"). Hypothetical thinking helps in formulating and arguing a viewpoint, because it allows adolescents to think a step ahead of the opposition—a cognitive tool that comes in quite handy when dealing with parents ("If they come back

with 'You have to stay home and clean up the garbage,' then I'll remind them about the time they let my sister go out when *she* had chores to do"). And hypothetical thinking plays an important role in decision making, because it permits the young person to plan ahead and to foresee the consequences of choosing one alternative over another ("If I go out for the soccer team, then I am going to have to give up my part-time job"). As we will see, scientists now believe that the development of the ability to think ahead is closely tied to the maturation of a region of the brain that changes dramatically during adolescence (Steinberg, 2005).

THINKING ABOUT ABSTRACT CONCEPTS

The appearance of more systematic, abstract thinking is the second notable aspect of cognitive development during adolescence. We noted earlier that children's thinking is more concrete and more bound to observable events and objects than is that of adolescents. This difference is clearly evident when we consider the ability to deal with abstract concepts—things that cannot be experienced directly through the senses.

For example, adolescents find it easier than children to comprehend the sorts of higher-order abstract logic inherent in puns, proverbs, metaphors, and analogies. When presented with verbal analogies, children are more likely than adolescents to focus on concrete and familiar associations among the words than on the abstract, or conceptual, relations among them.

Consider the following analogy:

Sun : Moon : : Asleep : ?

a. Star

b. Bed

c. Awake

d. Night

Instead of answering "awake"—which is the best answer of the four—children would be more likely to respond with "bed" or "night," since both of these words have stronger associations with the word "asleep." It is generally not until early adolescence that individuals are able to discern the abstract principles underlying analogies—in the one above, the principle involves antonyms (opposites)—and therefore solve them correctly (Sternberg & Nigro, 1980).

The adolescent's greater facility with abstract thinking also permits the application of advanced reasoning and logical processes to social and ideological matters. This is clearly seen in the adolescent's increased facility and interest in thinking about interpersonal relationships, politics, philosophy, religion, and morality—topics that involve such abstract concepts as friendship, faith, democracy, fairness, and honesty. As some writers have pointed out, the ability to think abstractly may prompt many adolescents to spend time thinking about the meaning of life itself (Hacker, 1994). The growth of social thinking—generally referred to as "social cognition"—during adolescence is directly related to the young person's improving ability to think abstractly. Later in this chapter, we will examine the ways in which social thinking improves in adolescence.

THINKING ABOUT THINKING

A third noteworthy gain in cognitive ability during adolescence involves thinking about thinking itself, a process sometimes referred to as **metacognition.** Metacognition often involves monitoring your own cognitive activity during the process of thinking—for example, when you consciously use a strategy for remembering something (such as *Every Good Boy Deserves Fun,* for the notes of the treble clef in music notation) or when you appraise your own comprehension of something you are reading before going on to the next paragraph. Studies show that using such strategies significantly aids adolescents in problem-solving situations (Chalmers & Lawrence, 1993). In addition, interventions designed to improve adolescents' metacognitive skills have been shown to enhance reading, writing, test taking, and performance on homework (Williams et al., 2002).

FOOD FOR THOUGHT

What metacognitive tools do you use to aid in your own studying?

Not only do adolescents "manage" their thinking more than children do, but they are also better able to explain to others the processes they are using. When asked, adolescents can explain not only *what* they know but *why* knowing what they know enables them to think differently and solve problems more effectively (Reich, Oser, & Valentin, 1994). Adolescence is an important time for changes in our understanding of what knowledge is and how it is acquired (Schommer, Calvert, Gariglietti, & Bajaj, 1997). In addition, adolescents are much better able than children to understand that people do not have complete control over their mental activity. One study found, for example, that adolescents and adults were much more likely than children to understand that

it is impossible to go for a long period of time without thinking about anything, that we often have thoughts that we do not want to have, and that unwanted thoughts we try to get rid of often return (Flavell, Green, & Flavell, 1998).

Another interesting way in which thinking about thinking becomes more apparent during adolescence is in increased introspection, self-consciousness, and intellectualization. When we are introspective, after all, we are thinking about our own emotions. When we are self-conscious, we are thinking about how others think about us. And when we intellectualize, we are thinking about our own thoughts. All three processes play an important role in the adolescent's psychological growth. As we'll see in Chapter 8, for example, these processes permit the sorts of self-examination and exploration that are important components of the young person's attempt to establish a coherent sense of identity.

Adolescent Egocentrism These intellectual advances may occasionally result in problems for the young adolescent, particularly before she or he adjusts to having such powerful cognitive tools. Being able to introspect, for instance, may lead to periods of extreme self-absorption—a form of "adolescent egocentrism" (Elkind, 1967). Adolescent egocentrism results in two distinct problems in thinking that help to explain some of the seemingly odd beliefs and behaviors of teenagers (Goossens, Seiffge-Krenke, & Marcoen, 1992).

The first, the **imaginary audience,** involves having such a heightened sense of self-consciousness that the teenager imagines that his or her behavior is the focus of everyone else's attention. For example, a teenager who is going to a concert with 4,000 other people may worry about dressing the right way because "everybody will notice." Given the cognitive limitations of adolescent egocentrism, it is difficult indeed to persuade the young person that the "audience" is not all that concerned with his or her behavior or appearance. According to a recent study (Rankin, Lane, Gibbons, & Gerrard, 2004), feelings of self-consciousness, which on average are more intense among girls than boys, increase during early adolescence, peak around age 15, and then decline, presumably as the adolescent gains more social confidence. And evidence from recent studies of brain maturation suggests that the part of the brain that processes social information—such as perceptions of what others are thinking—undergoes significant change during early adolescence, just when

---

metacognition   The process of thinking about thinking itself.

imaginary audience   The belief, often brought on by the heightened self-consciousness of early adolescence, that everyone is watching and evaluating one's behavior.

Adolescent egocentrism brought on by the cognitive changes of the period can contribute to a heightened sense of self-consciousness.

self-consciousness is increasing (Nelson, Leibenluft, McClure, & Pine, 2005).

A second problem resulting from adolescent egocentrism is called the **personal fable.** The personal fable revolves around the adolescent's egocentric (and erroneous) belief that her or his experiences are unique. For instance, an adolescent whose relationship with a girlfriend has just ended might tell his sympathetic mother that she could not possibly understand what it feels like to break up with someone—even though breaking up is something that most people have experienced plenty of times during their adolescent and young adult years. In some respects, adherence to a personal fable of uniqueness provides some protective benefits, in that it enhances adolescents' self-esteem and feelings of self-importance. Sometimes, however, holding on to a personal fable can be dangerous, as in the case of a sexually active adolescent who believes that pregnancy simply won't happen to her or a reckless driver who believes that he will defy the laws of nature by taking hairpin turns at breakneck speed.

FOOD FOR THOUGHT

Think about the changes in secondary sex characteristics that take place at puberty in humans. Why might we have evolved so that puberty occurs outside as well as inside the body?

Although some writers have suggested that much of the risk-taking behavior engaged in by adolescents can be explained partly in terms of the personal fable (Lapsley, Flannery, Gottschlich, & Raney, 1996), several researchers have found it difficult to confirm that the various manifestations of adolescent egocentrism actually peak in early adolescence as predicted (Gray & Hudson, 1984; Riley, Adams, & Neilsen, 1984). Instead, certain aspects of adolescent egocentrism, such as the personal fable, may persist through the adult years (Frankenberger, 2000; Goossens et al., 1992; Quadrel, Fischhoff, & Davis, 1993). Ask any *adult* cigarette smoker if she or he is aware of the scientific evidence linking cigarette smoking with heart and lung disease, and you'll see that the personal fable is quite common among many individuals who have long since left adolescence.

One problem with many of these studies of adolescent egocentrism is that they rely on fairly simple questionnaires to assess rather complicated belief systems invoked in real-life situations (Elkind, 1985). For example, it is easy to imagine that the same adolescent who worried about being seen by "everyone" at a rock concert might not appear so egocentric in his or her responses to a hypothetical dilemma posed in a questionnaire. This difference, of course, would raise doubts about whether adolescent egocentrism is an entirely cognitive phenomenon, since we would expect that cognitive deficiencies would show up in questionnaire assessments. One guess is that adolescents are egocentric for emotional and social, not cognitive, reasons. Another is that adolescents are overly concerned about what others think of them not because they are cognitively compromised, but because, in the highly social world in which they live, other peoples' opinions have genuine and important consequences (Bell & Bromnick, 2000). It's like the old joke: "Just because you're paranoid doesn't mean that people aren't following you."

THINKING IN MULTIPLE DIMENSIONS

A fourth way in which thinking changes during adolescence involves the ability to think about things in a multidimensional fashion. Whereas children tend to think about things one aspect at a time, adolescents can see things through more complicated lenses. For instance, when a certain hitter comes up to the plate in a baseball game, a preadolescent who knows that the hitter has a good home-run record might exclaim that the batter will hit the ball out of the park. An adolescent, however, would consider the hitter's record in relation to the specific pitcher on the mound and would weigh both factors, or dimensions, before making a prediction

personal fable   An adolescent's belief that he or she is unique and therefore not subject to the rules that govern other people's behavior.

(perhaps this player hits homers against left-handed pitchers but strikes out against righties).

The ability to think in multidimensional terms is evident in a variety of situations. Obviously, adolescents can give much more complicated answers than children to questions such as "Why did the Civil War begin?" or "How did Jane Austen's novels reflect the changing position of women in European society?" Thorough answers to these sorts of questions require thinking about several dimensions simultaneously.

The development of a more sophisticated understanding of probability is also made possible by an improved ability to think in multidimensional terms. Suppose I give you a set of beads that contain both blue and yellow ones. Now I ask you to divide them into two containers so that the containers have different numbers of beads overall but the probability of reaching into a container and picking a blue bead is the same for each. In order to do so, you would have to vary the number of blue beads *and* the number of yellow beads between the two containers, since the probability of drawing a blue bead is a function of both the number of blue beads and the number of yellow beads. It is not until early adolescence that individuals can solve this sort of problem successfully (Falk & Wilkening, 1998).

As is the case with other gains in cognitive ability, the increasing capability of individuals to think in multiple dimensions also has consequences for their behavior and thinking outside of academic settings. As you will see, adolescents describe themselves and others in more differentiated and complicated terms ("I'm both shy and extroverted") and find it easier to look at problems from multiple perspectives ("I know that's the way you see it, but try to look at it from her point of view"). Understanding that people's personalities are not one-sided or that social situations can have different interpretations, depending on one's point of view, permits the adolescent to have far more sophisticated—and far more complicated—self-conceptions, as well as relationships with other people.

▌ Sarcasm and South Park One interesting manifestation of adolescents' ability to look at things in multiple dimensions concerns the development of children's understanding of sarcasm. As an adult, you understand that the meaning of a speaker's statement is communicated by a combination of what is said, how it is said, and the context in which it is said. If I turned to you during a boring lecture, rolled my eyes, and said, in an exaggeratedly earnest tone, "This is the most interesting lecture I've ever heard," you would know that I actually meant just the opposite. But you would know this only if you paid attention to my

inflection and to the context, as well as the content, of my statement. Only by attending simultaneously to multiple dimensions of speech can we distinguish between the sincere and the sarcastic. Because our ability to think in multidimensional terms improves during adolescence, we would predict improvements as well in the ability to understand when someone is being sarcastic.

In one study designed to look at this question, children, adolescents, and adults were presented with different stories, in which an interaction between two people was followed by a remark that was sincere, deliberately deceptive, or sarcastic (Demorest, Meyer, Phelps, Gardner, & Winner, 1984). The participants in the study were then asked what the true meaning and intent of the remark were. Before the age of 9, children had difficulty picking out sarcastic remarks. Individuals' understanding of sarcasm increased somewhat between ages 9 and 13, and continued to increase during the adolescent years.

Why do young adolescents laugh hysterically when characters in movies aimed at their age group say things like, "He said 'erector set'"? Adolescents' increased facility in thinking along multiple dimensions permits them to appreciate satire, metaphor, and the ways in which language can be used to convey multiple messages, as in double entendres—expressions that have two meanings, one of them typically rude or crude. Teenagers' newfound ability to use and appreciate sarcasm and satire helps to explain why shows like *Beavis and Butthead, The Simpsons, South Park,* and *The Family Guy,* as well as publications like *Mad* magazine, have always had such strong appeal in this age group. (Not to mention that they are often pretty funny to adults, too. Our son's school once summoned his class's parents to watch an "offensive" episode of *South Park,* to show us how our children were being harmed by television; the demonstration ended prematurely, though, because we were laughing too hard.)

ADOLESCENT RELATIVISM

A final aspect of cognition that changes during adolescence concerns the way in which adolescents look at things. Children tend to see things in absolute terms—in black and white. Adolescents, in contrast, tend to see things as relative. They are more likely to question others' assertions and less likely to accept "facts" as absolute truths.

This increase in relativism can be particularly exasperating to parents, who may feel as though their adolescent children question everything just for the sake of argument. Difficulties often arise, for example, when adolescents begin seeing parents' values that they had previously considered absolutely correct ("Moral people do not have sex before they are married") as completely relative ("Welcome to the twenty-first century, Dad").

Adolescents' belief that everything is relative can become so overwhelming that they may become extremely skeptical about many things (Chandler, 1987). In fact, once adolescents begin to doubt the certainty of things that they had previously believed, they may come to believe that everything is uncertain, that no knowledge is completely reliable. Some theorists have suggested that adolescents pass through such a period of extreme skepticism on the way toward reaching a more sophisticated understanding of the complexity of knowledge.

RECAP

- One of the most important changes in thinking during adolescence is the increased ease with which individuals think about what is possible or hypothetical.
- Being able to think about what is possible, and not just what is real, is reflected in improvements in deductive reasoning—reasoning that is based on principles of logic.
- Adolescence is a time of improvements in thinking about abstract concepts.
- During adolescence, individuals become better able to engage in "thinking about thinking," or metacognition.
- Compared with children, adolescents are better able to think in multiple dimensions.
- Adolescents often go through a stage of relativistic thinking, during which they question the validity of absolutes.

cognitive-developmental view   A perspective on development, based on the work of Piaget, that takes a qualitative, stage-theory approach.

sensorimotor period   The first stage of cognitive development, according to Piaget, spanning the period roughly between birth and age 2.

preoperational period   The second stage of cognitive development, according to Piaget, spanning roughly ages 2–5.

concrete operations   The third stage of cognitive development, according to Piaget, spanning the period roughly between age 6 and early adolescence.

formal operations   The fourth stage of cognitive development, according to Piaget, spanning the period from early adolescence through adulthood.

Theoretical Perspectives on Adolescent Thinking

Although there is general agreement that adolescents' thinking is different and more advanced than children's in the ways we have just described, there is far less consensus about the processes underlying the cognitive differences between children and adolescents. Part of the lack of agreement stems from the fact that it is unlikely no one single factor distinguishes thinking during adolescence from thinking during childhood (Keating, 2004). And part of the lack of agreement stems from the different points of view that theorists have taken toward the issue of cognitive development in general. Because researchers working from different theoretical perspectives have posed different research questions, used different tasks to measure cognitive growth, and emphasized different aspects of cognitive activity, their studies provide different, but still theoretically compatible, pictures of mental development during adolescence.

The two theoretical viewpoints that have been especially important are the Piagetian perspective and the information-processing perspective. Although these two views of adolescent thinking begin from different assumptions about the nature of cognitive development in general, they each provide valuable insight into why thinking changes during adolescence.

THE PIAGETIAN VIEW OF ADOLESCENT THINKING

▍Piaget's Theory of Cognitive Development
Generally, theorists who adopt a Piagetian perspective and take a **cognitive-developmental view** of intellectual development argue that cognitive development proceeds through a fixed sequence of qualitatively distinct stages, that adolescent thinking is fundamentally different from the type of thinking employed by children, and that during adolescence, individuals develop a special type of thinking that they use in a variety of situations.

According to Piaget, cognitive development proceeds through four stages: (1) the **sensorimotor period** (from birth until about age 2), (2) the **preoperational period** (from about age 2 until about age 5), (3) the period of **concrete operations** (from about age 6 until early adolescence), and (4) the period of **formal operations** (from adolescence through adulthood). These stages are presented in Table 2.1. Each stage is characterized by a particular type of thinking, with earlier stages of thinking being incorporated into new, more advanced, and more adaptive forms of reasoning. According to Piaget, transitions into higher stages

TABLE 2.1 The four stages of cognitive development according to Piaget

Stage	Approximate Ages	Chief Characteristics
Sensorimotor	Birth–2 years	Discovery of relationships between sensation and motor behavior
Preoperational	2–6 years	Use of symbols to represent objects internally, especially through language
Concrete operations	6–11 years	Mastery of logic and development of rational thinking
Formal operations	11+ years	Development of abstract and hypothetical reasoning

of reasoning are most likely to occur when the child's biological readiness and the increasing complexity of environmental demands interact to stimulate more advanced thinking.

Given the emphasis that Piaget placed on the interaction between biological change and environmental stimulation in provoking intellectual growth, it comes as no surprise that early adolescence—a time of dramatic biological maturation and equally noteworthy changes in environmental demands—is viewed in Piagetian theory as an extremely important period in cognitive development.

Piaget believed that at the heart of formal-operational thinking is the use of an abstract system of **propositional logic**—a system based on theoretical, or formal, principles of logic (hence the term *formal operations*). Formal reasoning can be applied just as easily to hypothetical events as to real ones, is just as effective in dealing with abstract concepts as with concrete things, and is just as useful for thinking about alternatives to what really exists as it is for thinking about reality itself.

Consider the significance of being able to understand the following example of propositional logic:

If *A* is true or *B* is true, then *C* is true.

This is a logical relationship that is encountered in all sorts of situations, ranging from scientific problem solving ("If the solution turns blue or yellow, then it must contain the mineral copper") to understanding social relationships ("If Bob asks Susan out or if Judy calls me to do something this Friday night, then Bob and Judy must have broken up"). Once the form of the logic is understood—that either *A* or *B* is sufficient to demonstrate that *C* is true—it can be applied to all sorts of events (real as well as hypothetical, concrete as well as abstract) merely by changing what *A, B,* and *C* stand for. While concrete-operational thinkers are able to imagine alternative and hypothetical situations, they are unable to think about them in as systematic a way as formal-operational thinkers can.

Just because adolescents can employ propositional logic, however, does not mean that they are always consciously aware of doing so. In the example given above, for instance, we would hardly expect that an adolescent who is trying to figure out whether two friends are still dating consciously runs through the *A*'s, *B*'s, and *C*'s of propositional logic. But you do not have to be aware of doing so to use propositional logic effectively.

Piagetian theorists believe that the use of propositional logic—the foundation of formal-operational thinking—is the chief feature of adolescent thinking that differentiates it from the type of thinking employed by children. This is not unlike the claim, discussed earlier, that the ability to use deductive reasoning is the defining feature of adolescent cognition. We noted that adolescents' thinking can be distinguished from the thinking of children in several respects—among them, in thinking about possibilities, in thinking multidimensionally, and in thinking about abstract concepts. The connection between these types of thinking and the development of formal operations is clear: In order to think about alternatives to what really exists, in order to think in multidimensional terms, and in order to systematically think about concepts that are not directly observable, you must have a system of reasoning that works just as well in abstract, imagined, and complicated situations as it does in concrete ones. The system of propositional logic provides the basis for precisely this sort of reasoning.

The Growth of Formal-Operational Thinking
The development of formal thinking appears to take place in two steps. During the first step, characteristic of early adolescence, formal thinking is apparent, but it has a sort of "Now you see it, now you don't" quality to it. Young adolescents may demonstrate formal thinking at some times but at others may think only in concrete terms; they may use formal operations on some tasks but not on others; they may reason formally under some but not all testing situations (Markovits et al.,

propositional logic An abstract system of logic that forms the basis of formal operational thinking.

1996). Virtually all adolescents go through this period of "emergent formal operations" (Kuhn, Langer, Kohlberg, & Haan, 1977). It is not until middle or even late adolescence that formal-operational thinking becomes consolidated and integrated into the individual's general approach to reasoning (Markovits & Valchon, 1990).

While virtually all adolescents have the potential to develop formal-operational thinking, and most can and do demonstrate it from time to time, not all adolescents (or, for that matter, all adults) develop formal-operational thinking or employ it regularly and in a variety of situations. At least some research suggests that adolescents who as children had more secure relationships with their parents are more likely to display formal thinking than their insecure peers (Jacobsen, Edelstein, & Hofmann, 1994), as are young people who have received explicit instruction in deductive reasoning (Morris & Sloutsky, 1998). Consistent with the notion that certain types of instruction may facilitate the development of formal reasoning, one analysis of French students' reasoning abilities found that adolescents in the 1990s performed significantly better than their counterparts who were tested 20 or 30 years earlier, a change that must be related to changes in schooling (Flieller, 1999).

The Competence–Performance Distinction

More important, the extent to which formal-operational thinking is displayed consistently by an individual depends a great deal on the conditions under which his or her reasoning is assessed (Overton, 1990). It is important, therefore, to differentiate between *competence* (that is, what the adolescent is capable of doing) and *performance* (that is, what the adolescent actually does in the assessment situation). Much research, on adults as well as adolescents, indicates that gaps between individuals' logical reasoning abilities and their actual use of logical reasoning in everyday situations are very large, with everyday decision making fraught with logical errors that cannot be explained by cognitive incompetence (Klaczynski, 2000, 2001). For example, if asked whether they would rather try to pull a lucky lottery ticket from an envelope of 10 tickets, of which only 1 is lucky, versus an envelope of 100 tickets, of which 10 are lucky, most people select the second option—even though, if quizzed, they know that the mathematical odds of pulling a lucky ticket are identical in the two scenarios.

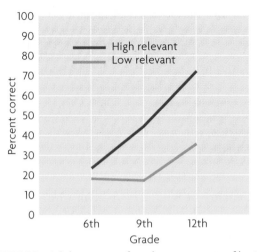

FIGURE 2.1   Adolescents perform better on tests of basic cognitive competence when they are familiar with the material than when they are not. (From Ward & Overton, 1990)

The **competence–performance distinction** is nicely illustrated in a series of studies by Willis Overton and colleagues. In one study (Ward & Overton, 1990), the researchers presented sixth-, ninth-, and twelfth-grade students with a mixture of logical problems that varied in their relevance to adolescents' lives. The problems were all of the same type—they tested deductive reasoning abilities, just like the mouth guard and hockey player problems you read about earlier—but they were about different topics. The most relevant problem concerned students' misbehavior in school; the least relevant concerned the situation of older individuals who had retired from work. The researchers hypothesized that having relevant problems to solve would improve adolescents' performance, but only among older adolescents, who were likely to have the underlying competence to reason formally.

This is precisely what the researchers found, as you can see in Figure 2.1. Among the sixth-graders, only about 20 percent of the problems were solved correctly, regardless of whether the task was relevant. The ninth- and twelfth-graders, however, were more than twice as successful when given relevant problems than when given less relevant ones. The researchers concluded that the competence to reason deductively does not become available until early adolescence and that the relevance of the content of tasks used to assess logical reasoning is an important factor that influences adolescents' performance, once they have achieved the necessary level of competence.

Although its influence has waned considerably over the past two decades (see Bjorklund, 1997; Keating, 2004), the Piagetian perspective on cognitive development during adolescence has stimulated a great deal of

competence–performance distinction   The distinction between what individuals are capable of and what they actually do, important in the study of cognitive development.

research on how young people think (Lourenço & Machado, 1996). Generally, the concept of formal operations as defined by Piaget and his followers describes many of the changes in thinking observed during the adolescent years. Specifically, the theory helps to explain why adolescents are better able than children to think about possibilities, to think multidimensionally, and to think about thoughts.

Where the Piagetian perspective on adolescent cognitive development falls short is in its claim that cognitive development proceeds in a stagelike fashion and that the stage of formal operations is the stage of cognitive development characteristic of adolescence (Keating, 2004). Rather, research suggests that advanced reasoning capabilities develop gradually and continuously from childhood through adolescence and beyond, probably in more of a gradual fashion than was proposed by Piaget (that is, more like a ramp than like a staircase). Rather than talking about a stage of cognitive activity characteristic of adolescence, then, it is more accurate to depict these advanced reasoning capabilities as skills that are employed by older children more often than by younger ones, by some adolescents more often than by others, and by individuals when they are in certain situations (especially familiar ones) more often than when they are in other situations (Kuhn, Garcia-Mila, Zohar, & Andersen, 1995).

THE INFORMATION-PROCESSING VIEW OF ADOLESCENT THINKING

Some scientists point out that the Piagetian approach has not been especially helpful in pinpointing exactly *what* it is that changes as individuals mature into and through adolescence. If we are left only with the conclusion that cognitive growth between childhood and adolescence reflects changes in "logical reasoning abilities," we have not moved a great deal closer to understanding which *specific* aspects of intellectual development during adolescence are the most important ones. Just what is it about the ways adolescents think about things that makes them better problem solvers than children? This question has been the focus of researchers working from a second theoretical vantage point: the **information-processing perspective.**

Information-processing researchers apply the same techniques to understanding human reasoning that computer scientists employ in writing software that strings together a series of subprograms. They argue that it is possible to look at human intelligence in much the same way. When broken down into its component processes, human thinking involves such "subprograms" as paying attention to a stimulus, encoding

information, retrieving information, comparing different pieces of information, and making decisions based on such comparisons. Deficiencies in any of these component functions, or in the way in which they are strung together, will interfere with accurate problem solving.

Studies of changes in specific components of information processing have focused on five areas in which improvement occurs during adolescence: attention, working memory, processing speed, organization, and metacognition. Studies show that improvements in all of these areas take place as individuals move from childhood through adolescence, mainly during the first half of the adolescent decade (Demetriou, Christou, Spanoudis, & Platsidou, 2002; Keating, 2004). Taken together, these gains help to explain why adolescents are better than children at abstract, multidimensional, and hypothetical thinking.

Attention First, there are advances in individuals' ability to pay attention. Improvements are seen both in **selective attention,** in which adolescents must focus on one stimulus (such as a reading assignment) and tune out another (such as the electronic beeping of a younger brother's video game), and in **divided attention,** in which adolescents must pay attention to two sets of stimuli at the same time (such as studying while listening to music) (Higgins & Turnure, 1984; Schiff & Knopf, 1985). Improvements in attention mean that adolescents are better able than children to concentrate and stay focused on complicated tasks, such as reading and comprehending difficult material (Casteel, 1993).

Memory Second, during adolescence, memory abilities improve. This is reflected both in **working memory,** which involves the ability to remember something for a brief period of time, such as 30 seconds, and in **long-term memory,** which involves being able to recall something from a long time ago (Keating, 2004).

information-processing perspective A perspective on cognition that derives from the study of artificial intelligence and attempts to explain cognitive development in terms of the growth of specific components of the thinking process (such as memory).

selective attention The process by which we focus on one stimulus while tuning out another.

divided attention The process of paying attention to two or more stimuli at the same time.

working memory That aspect of memory in which information is held for a short time while a problem is being solved.

long-term memory The ability to recall something from a long time ago.

Improvements in selective attention and divided attention enable adolescents to tune out interference and focus on the task at hand.

When we think of the importance of memory in problem solving, we typically think of having to retrieve facts that we deliberately have memorized—one aspect of long-term memory. For example, can you recall the name of the stage of thinking that precedes the stage of formal operations in Piaget's theory? (If not, refer to page 68.)

But working memory is extremely important in problem solving as well. For example, in order to answer multiple-choice questions, you need to be able to remember each option long enough to compare it with the other choices as you read them. Think for a moment of how frustrating it would be to try to solve a multiple-choice problem if, by the time you had read the final potential answer, you had forgotten the first one! Studies show that working memory skills for both verbal and visual information increase between childhood and adolescence and over the course of adolescence (Hale, Bronik, & Fry, 1997). This increase in our ability to hold information in "temporary storage" contributes to the development of reading skills during adolescence (Siegel, 1994).

FOOD FOR THOUGHT

Suppose you were designing a curriculum for early adolescents. Would you emphasize different things if you were more Piagetian in your orientation than if you leaned more toward information-processing perspectives?

▌ **Speed**   A third component of information processing that may be closely related to the observed improvements in thinking is an increase in the sheer speed of information processing (Hale, 1990; Kail, 1991a, 1991b; Kail & Hall, 1994). Regardless of the type of cognitive task employed, researchers find that older adolescents process the information necessary to solve the problem faster than early adolescents, who, in turn, process information faster than preadolescents. This fact would certainly help explain age differences in performance on timed tests, such as standardized achievement tests. Generally, the increase in the speed of information processing that occurs with age becomes smaller over the course of adolescence. Therefore, the difference in speed between a 9-year-old and a 12-year-old is greater than that between a 12-year-old and a 15-year-old, which, in turn, is greater than that between a 15-year-old and an 18-year-old (Kail, 1991a). In fact, speed of processing does not appear to change very much between middle adolescence and young adulthood (Hale, 1990).

▌ **Organization**   A fourth type of information-processing gain seen in adolescence involves improvements in individuals' organizational strategies (Siegler, 1988). Adolescents are more "planful" than children—they are more likely to approach a problem with an appropriate information-processing strategy in mind and are more flexible in their ability to use different strategies in different situations (Plumert, 1994). The use of mnemonic devices (such as using HOMES to remember the names of the Great Lakes—Huron, Ontario, Michigan, Erie, and Superior) and other organizational strategies helps to account for differences in the performance of older and younger children on tasks requiring memory (Brown, 1975). For instance, think for a moment about how you approach learning the information in a new textbook chapter. After years of studying, you are probably well aware of particular strategies that work well for you (underlining, highlighting, taking notes, writing in the margins), and you begin a reading assignment with these strategies in mind. Because children are not as "planful" as adolescents, their learning is not as efficient. Developmental differences in levels of planning during childhood and adolescence can be seen quite readily by comparing individuals' approaches to the guessing game 20 Questions. With age, individuals' strategies become increasingly more efficient—when guessing the name of a person, an adolescent might begin by asking whether the person is dead or alive, whereas a young child might just start throwing out the names of specific people (Drumm & Jackson, 1996).

▌ **Metacognition** Finally, individuals' knowledge about their own thinking processes improves during adolescence. We noted earlier that one of the most important gains in adolescence is in the realm of metacognition—thinking about thinking. Adolescents are more likely than children to think about their own thoughts—a tendency, as we saw, that helps to explain their greater self-consciousness. One explanation for this emphasizes adolescents' greater sensitivity to social information. But from an information-processing perspective, adolescents' heightened self-consciousness results from advances in basic metacognitive abilities. For the first time, the adolescent is capable of "thinking about thinking about thinking." Once you begin thinking about what other people might think you are thinking, it is hard to avoid becoming self-conscious.

Of course, advances in metacognition are more a blessing than a curse. Because adolescents are better able to think about their own thoughts, they are much better at monitoring their own learning processes. For example, during the course of studying, adolescents are more able than children to step back and assess how well they are learning the material. Doing this enables them to pace their studying accordingly—to speed up and skim the material if they feel that they are learning it easily, or to slow down and repeat a section if they feel that they are having a hard time (e.g., Baker & Brown, 1984).

Most basic information-processing skills, like working memory or attention, as well as logical reasoning abilities, increase throughout childhood and early adolescence and then level off around age 15 (Gathercole, Pickering, Ambridge, & Wearing, 2004; Keating, 2004; Luciana, Conklin, Hooper, & Yarger,

2005). In other words, by the time they have turned 15, adolescents are just as proficient as adults in these basic skills. Where adolescents of this age are lacking, relative to adults, and where cognitive development continues beyond age 15 and into young adulthood, is in more sophisticated cognitive skills, such as planning ahead or judging the relative costs and benefits of a risky decision, and in the coordination of cognition and emotion, when feelings might interfere with logical reasoning (for example, when you have to make a decision when you are angry or when faced with peer pressure). In fact, much of what we have learned about brain maturation in adolescence—the subject of the next section—leads to the conclusion that the development of these advanced abilities may not be complete until individuals reach their mid-20s.

RECAP

- The two dominant theoretical perspectives in the study of adolescent cognition are the Piagetian perspective and the information-processing perspective.
- According to Piaget, adolescence is a period characterized by the stage of formal operations.
- Although Piaget theorized that thinking during adolescence was qualitatively different from thinking during childhood, research shows that changes in cognition during this time are more gradual.
- The information-processing perspective focuses on the specific components of thinking, such as memory and attention, and asks whether and to what extent these improve in adolescence.
- In general, there are major improvements in basic cognitive processes in early adolescence, but by the time individuals have reached age 15 or so, their basic thinking and reasoning abilities are comparable to those of adults.

The Adolescent Brain

No area of adolescence research in recent years has generated as much attention or excitement as the study of brain development during adolescence. Fascination with the adolescent brain quickly spread from scientific journals to the popular press, as a cover story in *Time* magazine titled "Inside the Teen Brain" attests (e.g., Wallis, 2004). Educators, parents, highway safety experts, and even the U.S. Supreme Court wanted to know whether the emerging science of adolescent brain development could be used to inform how we teach, raise, and regulate teenagers.

Interest in brain development during adolescence is not new. Scientists have long wondered whether the sorts of changes in thinking and behavior that occur during adolescence can be linked to actual changes in the brain. After all, we've long known that early adolescence is a time of tremendous improvement in abstract thinking. For many years, researchers searched for evidence that the sheer growth in the size of the brain that takes place around puberty was somehow related to the expansion of intellectual abilities. These attempts proved futile, however (Keating, 1990).

Recent improvements in the study of brain maturation—including studies of brain growth and development in other animals, studies of changes in brain chemistry in humans and other species, and perhaps most important, studies of human brains using various imaging techniques, such as **functional magnetic resonance imaging (fMRI)**, **positron emission tomography (PET)**, or **diffusion tensor imaging (DTI)**—have shed new light on this issue. These techniques allow researchers to take pictures of individuals' brains and compare their structure and functioning. Studies using fMRI and, to a lesser extent, DTI have been especially important, because, unlike PET, which requires that dye be injected into the participant in order to see brain activity, these techniques are noninvasive and can be used with children as well as adults. Using fMRI, researchers have looked at activity in various regions of the brain while individuals are performing a variety of tasks (for example, tests of memory, vision, or problem solving). It is possible, therefore, to study whether adolescents and adults show different patterns

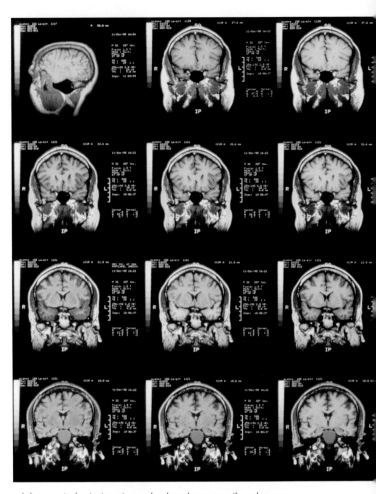

Advances in brain imaging technology have contributed to our understanding of how the brain changes at adolescence. These images are created through a process known as functional magnetic resonance imaging, or fMRI.

of brain activity while performing the very same task (e.g., Pine et al., 2000a). Using DTI, scientists are able to see the ways in which various regions of the brain are connected and compare patterns of interconnections among people at different ages. This allows us to better understand how "communication" patterns linking different regions of the brain change with development.

WHAT CHANGES IN ADOLESCENCE?

New research on the brain points to several aspects of brain maturation in adolescence that may be linked to behavioral, emotional, and cognitive development during this period (Steinberg, 2005). First, there appears to be considerable "remodeling" of the brain through the processes of **synaptic pruning,** which is the elimination of unused connections between nerve cells, or **neurons,** and **myelination,** in which the neuronal projections that connect to

functional magnetic resonance imaging (fMRI) A technique used to produce images of the brain, often while the subject is performing some sort of mental task.

positron emission tomography (PET) A technique used to produce image's of the brain, often while the subject is performing some sort of mental task; it is more invasive than fMRI.

diffusion tensor imaging (DTI) A technique used to produce images of the brain that shows connections among different regions.

synaptic pruning The process through which unnecessary connections between neurons are eliminated, improving the efficiency of information processing.

neurons Nerve cells.

myelination The process through which brain circuits are insulated with myelin, which improves the efficiency of information processing.

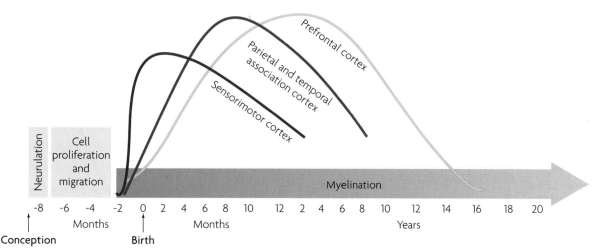

FIGURE 2.2   Grey matter density in different brain regions. Synaptic pruning takes place in different brain regions at different ages. (From Casey et al., 2005)

form brain circuits become encased within a sheath of myelin, a white fatty substance that provides a sort of insulation that makes the transmission of impulses flow much more effectively. Both synaptic pruning and myelination lead to much more efficient and more focused information processing (Giedd et al., 1999).

▌ **Remodeling the Brain**   Although synaptic pruning takes place throughout infancy, childhood, and adolescence, different regions of the brain are pruned at different points in development. As Figure 2.2 illustrates, the part of the brain that is pruned in adolescence is the **prefrontal cortex,** the region of the brain most important for sophisticated thinking abilities, such as planning, thinking ahead, weighing risks and rewards, and controlling impulses (Casey, Tottenham, Liston, & Durston, 2005). Although you might think that a loss of synapses would necessarily be associated with worse, rather than better, information processing, this is not always the case. Indeed, we now know that, early in life, many more synapses are produced in the brain than are necessary for competent information processing, and that information processing is improved by the selective pruning of excessive and unnecessary neuronal connections. Over time, the synaptic connections that are used most frequently become stronger, and those that are not used often are eliminated. (Think of it as replacing a system of many single-lane dirt roads with a smaller number of six-lane interstate highways, or of pruning a garden that has become overgrown and less attractive.) Scientists believe that this pruning accounts for many of the cognitive advances that take place in adolescence.

There is also continued myelination of the prefrontal cortex throughout adolescence (Paus et al.,

1999; Sowell, Trauner, Gamst, & Jernigan, al., 2002). Like synaptic pruning, myelination is affected by experience (Bengtsson et al., 2005). By the end of adolescence, the brain circuits that are active during high-level cognitive tasks are functioning far more efficiently than they were during childhood. Interestingly, adolescents whose prefrontal cortical development is less mature than normal are more likely to have conduct problems (Bauer & Hesselbrock, 2002). Imaging studies have also shown that there is a significant increase in connectivity between the prefrontal cortex and other areas of the brain, suggesting better "communication" between brain regions as individuals mature (Cunningham, Bhattacharyya, & Benes, 2002; Luna et al., 2001).

Studies of brain development also help explain why certain intellectual abilities decline in adolescence. For example, whereas brain regions that are known to play a major role in language acquisition continue to grow rapidly during preadolescence, they stop growing around the time of puberty. This is consistent with evidence indicating that individuals find it far more difficult to learn a new language as teenagers than as children (Thompson et al., 2000).

▌ **The Prefrontal Cortex**   We now know that full maturation of the prefrontal cortex is not complete until the mid-20s (Casey et al., 2005; Hooper, Luciana, Conklin, & Yarger, 2004; Segalowitz & Davies, 2004). The prefrontal cortex is the part of the brain that is active when we are engaged in complicated cognitive

prefrontal cortex   The part of the brain responsible for many higher-order cognitive skills, such as decision making and planning.

activities such as planning, decision making, goal setting, and metacognition. Of special importance are developments in the **dorsolateral prefrontal cortex,** the outer and upper areas of the front of the brain, which is important for skills such as planning ahead and controlling impulses (Casey et al., 2005); the **ventromedial prefrontal cortex,** the lower and central area of the front of the brain, which is important for more gut-level, intuitive decision making, and which has strong connections with the limbic system, where emotions and social information are processed (Bechara, 2005); and the **orbitofrontal cortex,** the area of the brain directly behind the eyes, which is important for evaluating risks and rewards (May et al., 2004) (see Figure 2.3). In contrast to changes in the limbic system, which take place early in adolescence, around the time of puberty, the maturation of the prefrontal cortex is still ongoing in early adulthood (Steinberg, 2005). One recent study found a relation between intelligence and patterns of synaptic growth and pruning in the cortex, with relatively more intelligent adolescents showing a more dramatic and longer period of production of synapses before adolescence, and a more dramatic pruning of them after (Shaw et al., 2006).

▌ **The Limbic System**   There are also changes in levels of several **neurotransmitters** (the chemicals that permit the transfer of electrical charges between neurons), including dopamine and serotonin, in the parts of the brain that process emotional stimuli—most notably, areas of the **limbic system.** These changes may make individuals more emotional, more responsive to stress (see page 26), and, at the same time, more interested in, but less responsive to, rewards (i.e., seeking rewards but getting less of a "rush" from them) (Ernst et al., 2005; Spear, 2000). In other words, there may be a neurochemical basis for adolescents' frequent complaints of boredom! More seriously, though, some scientists believe that changes in the limbic system may stimulate adolescents to seek higher levels of novelty, take more risks, and experiment with drugs, in an effort

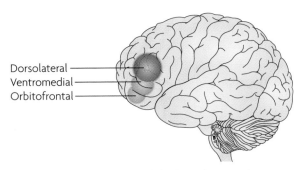

FIGURE 2.3   Three regions of the frontal cortex that undergo major change in adolescence are the dorsolateral prefrontal cortex, the ventromedial prefrontal cortex, and the orbitofrontal cortex.

to get the same levels of positive feelings from the environment that they were able to get more easily before adolescence (Martin et al., 2002). Changes in the limbic system are also thought to increase individuals' vulnerability to substance abuse (because they seek higher levels of reward), depression (because of their increased vulnerability to stress), and other mental health problems (because of their easily aroused emotions, including anger and sadness) (Steinberg et al., 2006).

Changes in levels of neurotransmitters in the limbic system in early adolescence may also help explain why adolescents' concerns about what their peers think increase during this time, because the limbic system is important for the processing of social information (Nelson et al., 2005). Conceivably, this may make adolescents more susceptible to peer pressure, a topic we'll look at in Chapter 9. In one recent and very clever study, researchers imaged the brains of adolescents who thought they were participating in a Facebook-style task, networking with other teenagers who were being imaged at the same time in different locations (Nelson et al., 2007). (Inside the fMRI equipment was a computer screen, on which the researchers could show any images of their choosing.) While being imaged, the adolescents were shown pictures of the other teenagers and asked to rate how interested they were in chatting with them online. The adolescents, who were told that their own photograph was "posted" online, received what they thought was feedback from the other teenagers. In reality, though, there were no other teenagers connected to the network, and the feedback the adolescents received was rigged to be positive (interested in chatting) half the time and negative (not interested in chatting) half the time. When the adolescents were told that other teenagers were interested in them, areas of their brain known to be sensitive to rewards like food and money were activated, suggesting that social rewards may be processed during adolescence in ways similar to the ways in which we process other types of rewards.

dorsolateral prefrontal cortex   The outer and upper areas of the front of the brain, important for skills such as planning ahead and controlling impulses.

ventromedial prefrontal cortex   The lower and central area at the front of the brain, important for gut-level decision making.

orbitofrontal cortex   The region of the brain located directly behind the eyes, important for the evaluation of risk and reward.

neurotransmitters   Chemical substances in the brain that carry electrical impulses across synapses.

limbic system   An area of the brain that plays a role in emotional experience.

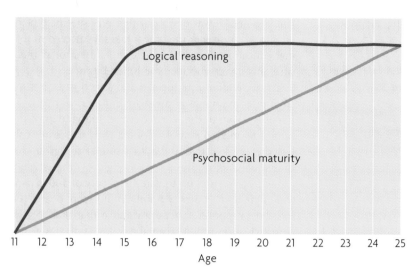

FIGURE 2.4 Although logical reasoning abilities reach adult levels by age 16, psychosocial capacities, such as impulse control, future orientation, and resistance to peer influence, continue to develop into young adulthood. This graph shows the hypothetical growth pattern of each. (Steinberg, 2007)

FOOD FOR THOUGHT

How important is it that we document changes in brain structure and function in order to understand adolescent thinking? Is it not enough simply to show that cognitive abilities change during this period? What do we gain by studying brain maturation?

IMPLICATIONS FOR ADOLESCENT BEHAVIOR

The relatively late maturation of the prefrontal cortex, particularly in relation to the changes that take place in the limbic system at puberty, has been the subject of much discussion among those interested in risk taking and behavioral problems in adolescence (Steinberg, 2004). In essence, the brain changes in ways that may provoke individuals to seek novelty, reward, and stimulation several years before the complete maturation of the brain systems that control judgment and decision making (Steinberg, 2007)(see Figure 2.4). This gap may help explain why adolescence is a period of heightened experimentation with risk. In the words of one team of writers, it's like "starting the engines with an unskilled driver" (Nelson et al., 2002, p. 515).

Although scientists agree about the ways in which the structure of the brain changes during adolescence, the implications of these changes for adolescent development are still the subject of a great deal of ongoing research and considerable speculation, because few studies have directly linked changes in brain images with changes in thought, emotion, or behavior. One question that is often asked is when adolescents begin to think like adults. As you now know, this is a hard question to answer based on brain science alone,

because it depends on which aspects of thinking one is concerned about. When it comes to relatively more sophisticated cognitive abilities, such as thinking ahead, envisioning the future consequences of a decision, balancing risks and rewards, or controlling impulses—all of which are governed mainly by the prefrontal cortex—research on brain maturation certainly suggests that these capabilities are still developing well after individuals enter their 20s. But when it comes to more basic abilities, such as those involving memory, attention, and logical reasoning, especially under optimal conditions, brain and behavioral studies indicate that the average 15-year-old performs no worse than the average adult. Where we draw the boundary between adolescence and adulthood—at least as far as cognitive development is concerned—should probably depend on why the boundary is being drawn and on what specific abilities are relevant to the behavior in question.

RECAP

- New imaging techniques, especially functional magnetic resonance imaging (fMRI), have enabled scientists to chart changes in the structure and function of the brain in adolescence.
- Among the most important changes in the brain to take place in adolescence is the elimination of unnecessary synapses, a process called synaptic pruning, particularly in the prefrontal cortex. This is thought to lead to improvements in many advanced thinking abilities, known as executive functions.
- Adolescence is also a time of increased myelination of the brain, which permits more efficient connections within and between brain regions.
- A second important change in brain at adolescence involves neurotransmitters in the part of the brain known as the limbic system. This is

thought to increase sensation seeking and emotional arousal, and to make adolescents more sensitive to social information.

- The combination of heightened sensation seeking and a still-maturing prefrontal cortex may make adolescence a period of experimentation with risky activity.

Individual Differences in Intelligence in Adolescence

For the most part, theorists who have studied adolescent cognitive development from either a Piagetian or an information-processing framework have focused on the universals in adolescent intellectual growth. These theorists ask, How does thinking change as individuals move into adolescence? What processes drive cognitive development as children become teenagers? What cognitive competencies do all adolescents share?

In contrast, other theorists have been more interested in studying individual differences in intellectual abilities. They ask, How can we account for different patterns of intellectual growth within the adolescent population? How large are individual differences in intelligence in adolescence? Are some adolescents brighter than others? If so, why, and in what ways?

THE MEASUREMENT OF IQ

To answer questions about the relative intelligence of individuals, psychologists have had to devise ways of assessing intelligence—no easy feat given the considerable disagreement over what "intelligence" really is. Today, the most widely used measures are intelligence tests, or IQ (for "intelligence quotient") tests. A variety of such tests exists, including the Stanford-Binet, the Wechsler Intelligence Scale for Children (WISC-IV), and the Wechsler Adult Intelligence Scale (WAIS-III). An individual's IQ is computed by dividing his or her mental age by his or her chronological age and then multiplying the result by 100.

The IQ test is one of the most widely used—and most widely misused—psychological instruments. Initially developed in France in 1905, the first intelligence test was devised in response to the French government's interest in better predicting which children would and would not profit from formal schooling. Although the test—and the many others that would be developed over the years—was designed to yield a measure of

"intelligence," it was devised with a very specific type of intelligence in mind: the type it takes to succeed in formal education. Even the best IQ tests used today measure only a very specific type of intelligence.

An individual's performance on an IQ test is usually presented not as a raw score but as a relative score in comparison to the scores of other individuals of the same age and generation. Comparison scores are collected every so often, so that the comparison group for individuals taking the test at any given time is valid, representative, and up to date. The score of 100 is used to designate the midway point. An IQ score below 100 indicates a poorer test performance than half of the comparison group; a score above 100 indicates a better performance than half the comparison group. In other words, the higher an individual's IQ, the smaller the number of age-mates who perform equally or better on the same test.

Although an individual's score on an intelligence test is often reported in terms of her or his overall IQ, intelligence tests actually comprise a series of tests, and it is usually possible to look at performance in different areas independently. The WISC-IV and the WAIS-III, for example, each contain two groups of tests: verbal tests, which include measures of vocabulary, general information, comprehension, and arithmetic abilities; and performance tests, which include measures of memory, perceptual reasoning, and picture completion.

The IQ test represents only one of many ways of assessing intelligence in adolescence. Indeed, many theorists have argued that its exclusive focus on "school smarts"—the sorts of abilities that are related to scholastic success—yields a one-sided picture of what it means to be an intelligent person. Two of the better-known attempts to expand on this narrow definition come from the work of Robert Sternberg (1988) and Howard Gardner (1983). Many of Sternberg and Gardner's ideas formed the basis for the best-selling book *Emotional Intelligence,* by journalist Daniel Goleman (1996).

TYPES OF INTELLIGENCE

Sternberg's "Triarchic" Theory   Sternberg proposed a triarchic, or three-part, theory of intelligence. He argued that a thorough assessment of an individual's intellectual capabilities requires that we look at three distinct but interrelated types of intelligence: (1) componential intelligence, which involves our abilities to acquire, store, and process information (as described in the previous section about information processing); (2) experiential intelligence, which involves our abilities to use insight and creativity; and (3) contextual intelligence, which involves our ability to think practically. Componential intelligence is closest

Critics of standardized testing argue that these tests measure just one type of intelligence—"school smarts"—and neglect other, equally important skills, such as emotional intelligence, creativity, and "street smarts."

to the type of intelligence measured on traditional intelligence tests. Experiential intelligence is closest to what we call "creativity." And contextual intelligence is closest to what we might call "street smarts." All individuals have all three types of intelligence, but some individuals are stronger in one respect than in others. You probably can think of individuals who are good test takers but who are not particularly creative or sensible. According to Sternberg's model, these individuals would be high in componential intelligence but low in experiential and contextual intelligence.

More importantly, Sternberg's view forces us to look at individuals who are not good test takers but who are creative or street smart as being just as intelligent as individuals who score high on IQ tests—but intelligent in a different way. Sternberg argued that society needs individuals with all types of intelligence and that it is time we started assessing—and encouraging—experiential and contextual intelligence as much as we do componential intelligence (Matthews & Keating, 1995).

▌ Gardner's Theory of Multiple Intelligences

Howard Gardner's theory of multiple intelligences also stresses that there is more to being smart than being "book smart." Gardner proposed that there are seven types of intelligence: verbal, mathematical, spatial, kinesthetic (movement), self-reflective, interpersonal, and musical. According to his view, for example, outstanding athletes such as basketball legend Michael Jordan or soccer superstar Mia Hamm have a well-developed kinesthetic intelligence, which allows them to control their bodies and process the movements of others in extraordinary ways. Although conventional tests of intelligence emphasize verbal and mathematical abilities, these are not the only types of intelligence that we possess—nor are they the only types that we should value.

FOOD FOR THOUGHT

What particular intellectual strengths do you have that might not be picked up by conventional measures of intelligence?

INTELLIGENCE TEST PERFORMANCE IN ADOLESCENCE

Although the existence of different forms of intelligence is an increasingly popular idea, most research in the psychometric tradition has employed traditional IQ tests to investigate the nature of intelligence during adolescence. Assessments based on IQ tests have been used to examine two seemingly similar but actually very different questions: (1) How *stable* are IQ scores during adolescence? and (2) Do the sorts of mental abilities that are assessed via intelligence tests *improve* during adolescence?

It is easy to confuse these questions, because at first glance, they seem to be asking the same thing. But consider this: Individuals' IQ scores remain remarkably stable during the adolescent years; yet, during the same period, their mental abilities improve dramatically. Although this might seem contradictory, it is not. Studies of stability examine changes in individuals' *relative* standing over time, whereas studies of change examine changes in individuals' *absolute* scores.

Take height, for example. Children who are taller than their peers during middle childhood are likely to be taller than their peers during adulthood as well; children who are average in height remain so throughout childhood and adulthood; and children who are shorter than their peers at one time are likely to be shorter than their peers later on. Height, therefore, is a very stable trait. But this does not mean that individuals don't grow between childhood and adolescence.

Like height, scores on intelligence tests are characterized by high stability and a good deal of change during childhood and adolescence. To the first question posed above—about how stable IQ scores are during adolescence—the answer, then, is very stable. Youngsters who score higher than their peers on intelligence tests during early adolescence are likely to score higher throughout the adolescent years. In fact, recent research indicates that certain measures of intellectual performance taken during the first year of life—not IQ tests, but measures of speed of information processing—are significantly predictive of IQ test performance in early adolescence (Rose & Feldman, 1995). This does not mean, however, that individuals' intellectual performance remains fixed or is not susceptible to change—as you will see in a moment.

A 10-year-old boy whose score is average for his age would have an IQ of about 100. If his score were stable—that is, if he remained average in comparison with his peers—his IQ would remain at about 100. Even if he became more intelligent over time, as any normal child would, his IQ score probably would not change very much, because the score would always reflect his performance relative to his peers. If his

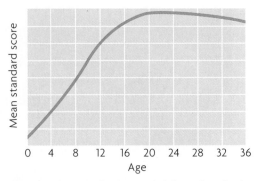

FIGURE 2.5 The growth of mental abilities from birth to age 36, as measured by standardized IQ tests. (Adapted from Bayley, 1949)

abilities increased at the same rate as his age-mates', his relative standing would not change. In other words, when an individual's IQ scores are fairly stable, a graph of those scores over time produces a relatively straight horizontal line. For most individuals, this is indeed what happens. Although some individuals show fluctuation in IQ scores between childhood and adolescence, ultimately, most adolescents end up with IQ scores that are not very different from their scores as children. In one study, for example, the average amount of change over a seven-year period (from age 7 to age 13) among all of the individuals whose scores fluctuated to *any* degree was only 5 IQ points, which is not a change of much practical significance (Moffitt, Caspi, Harkness, & Silva, 1993).

In absolute terms, however, do mental abilities increase during adolescence? Figure 2.5 shows the growth of mental abilities as assessed by standardized tests. As you can see, abilities assessed by conventional IQ tests increase dramatically through childhood and adolescence, reaching a plateau sometime in mid-to-late adolescence. Thus, despite the fact that IQ scores remain stable over time, individuals do become smarter as they get older—a fact that argues strongly in favor of educational interventions, especially in early childhood, because they have been shown to improve intellectual performance during adolescence (Campbell, Pungello, Miller-Johnson, Burchinal, & Ramey, 2001). In addition, research shows that extended schooling during adolescence itself enhances individuals' performance on standardized tests of intelligence (Ceci & Williams, 1999). Whereas individuals who had dropped out of school early showed unchanging—and relatively lower—scores on intelligence tests during adolescence, students who remained in school, especially those in the more advanced tracks, showed impressive gains in verbal ability over time. As you read in the previous section, on brain maturation in adolescence, scientists believe that much of the synaptic pruning that takes place in the frontal lobe during the mid-adolescent years is affected by experience (Casey, Tottenham, Liston, & Durston, 2005).

■ **The SAT** Another widely used—and equally controversial—measure of aptitude in adolescence is the SAT. The SAT is intended not to measure adolescents' present level of academic achievement but to predict their likelihood of success in college. Like the IQ test, therefore, the SAT is a measure of "school smarts," and scores on this test should be so viewed. The SAT does not measure such important characteristics as insight, creativity, or practical intelligence.

Given that the SAT was created in order to predict high school students' college success, it is only fair that it be evaluated in this light. How well does the SAT predict academic success in college? The answer is, well, but not perfectly. Knowing an individual's SAT scores helps to foretell how well he or she will do in college, but SAT scores are only one of many useful predictive factors. Because of this, most college admissions committees rely on many additional pieces of information about an applicant's academic record, including the difficulty of the high school curriculum and the student's class rank (Moll, 1986).

Interestingly, one study found that scores on the mathematics section of the SAT may be a more valid predictor of college math grades for males than for females (Wainer & Steinberg, 1992). In this study, the researchers began with a sample of 47,000 college men and women who were then matched on their performance in college math classes (and on the difficulty of the math classes they took). If the SAT is an equally valid predictor of achievement for males and females, the researchers reasoned, then males and females who earn comparable grades in math classes should have had comparable SAT scores. This was not the case, however. Among college students earning A's in math classes, for example, the men had scored 36 points higher on the math portion of the SAT than had the women. A college admissions committee that rejects a woman in favor of a man on the basis of SAT math scores makes an ill-informed decision.

Actually, studies comparing the performance of males and females on various tests of intelligence have found few reliable sex differences. Although it was once the case that males performed better on tests of mathematical ability, and females on tests of verbal ability, these sex differences disappeared about 20 years ago (Jacklin, 1989). The only reliable sex difference in mental abilities during adolescence is in the area of spatial ability, where males outperform females

by a slight margin. You may recall taking standardized tests in which you were asked to imagine how an irregular three-dimensional object would appear if it were rotated in certain ways; this is a test of spatial ability. The male advantage on many tests of spatial performance emerges before age 10 and is more or less constant during the adolescent years (Johnson and Meade, 1987; Voyer, Voyer, & Bryden, 1995).

CULTURE AND INTELLIGENCE

■ **Vygotsky's Perspective** Much of our current thinking about the nature of intelligence has been influenced by the work of the late Russian psychologist Lev Vygotsky ([1930]1978), who emphasized the broader context in which intellectual development occurs. According to this view, it is essential that we understand the nature of the environment in which an adolescent develops in terms of its demands for intelligent behavior and its opportunities for learning. Individuals develop and use intellectual skills not simply as a function of their cognitive maturation but in response to the everyday problems they are expected to solve. Young street merchants in Brazil, for example, who might not perform well on standardized tests of math knowledge, nevertheless use sophisticated mathematical skills during transactions with customers (Guberman, 1996). The very same children who perform poorly on school-based tests of knowledge may excel when faced with an equally challenging test of competence in the real world—such as figuring out the most efficient route between school and home through a dangerous neighborhood.

Vygotsky argued that children and adolescents learn best in everyday situations when they encounter tasks that are neither too simple nor too advanced, but just slightly more challenging than their abilities permit them to solve on their own. Within this so-called **zone of proximal development,** young people, through close collaboration with a more experienced instructor (whether an adult or another child), are stimulated to "reach" for the more advanced level of performance. The role of the instructor is to help structure the learning situation so that it is within the reach of the student—a structuring process called **scaffolding.** If you watch good parents, teachers, or coaches at work, you will probably observe a great deal of scaffolding.

zone of proximal development In Vygotsky's theory, the level of challenge that is still within the individual's reach but that forces an individual to develop more advanced skills.

scaffolding Structuring a learning situation so that it is just within the reach of the student.

▌**Culture-Fair Testing**   Studying cognitive development in context clearly points out the problems in measuring intelligence through standardized testing. Indeed, the problem of defining intelligence adequately is perhaps no more readily apparent than when issues of ethnic or racial differences in intelligence are raised. In general, studies find that African American and Hispanic American youngsters typically score lower on standardized IQ tests than do their white peers (Anastasi, 1988). But how are we to interpret this finding? Does this mean that minority youngsters are less "intelligent" than white youths? Or does it mean that the tests used to assess intelligence are unfairly biased against minority children?

In recent years, experts have leaned toward the latter explanation. They point out that IQ tests, which were initially developed and standardized for populations of individuals of European descent, are loaded with questions that reflect the experiences and values of middle-class whites. These critics suggest that white individuals would do similarly poorly on intelligence tests designed by and for ethnic minority individuals (Miller-Jones, 1989). In addition, language differences between minority and nonminority youths (especially if English is not the minority youngster's first language) may lead to apparent differences in intelligence when the testing is performed in English. These criticisms have lead to calls for **culture-fair tests**—intelligence tests that attempt to reduce sources of ethnic or cultural bias. Such tests tend to be based less on verbal skills (thus avoiding the language problems of many tests) and more oriented toward the sorts of items included on the performance scales of traditional IQ tests.

One fascinating study of the SAT demonstrates how a relatively simple change in the way the test is scored can significantly reduce the gap between white and ethnic minority test takers (Freedle, 2003). The researcher hypothesized that the items with the greatest cultural bias would be the easier items on the test, because these items refer to concepts that are likely learned outside school, where culture plays a strong role in influencing what children learn. In contrast, more difficult items are more likely to refer to concepts that are learned in school, where cultural differences between students with respect to what they learn are much smaller, because students in the same class use the same textbooks and are exposed to the same curriculum (although tracking can certainly introduce ethnic differences into what students are exposed to in school). For example, an item using the word "golf" would be considered an easy item, because it is a common word, yet adolescents from different cultural groups likely have different degrees of familiarity with the sport. Although an item with the infrequently used word "anathema" would be considered hard, it is not one that most people are exposed to in everyday life, and most adolescents familiar with the word would have learned it in a more culture-neutral context. Sure enough, when the researcher compared SAT scores of ethnic minority and white students using two different scoring procedures—one that used the whole test, and one that used only the difficult items—ethnic differences in performance changed.

Even with the advent of culture-fair testing, the notion that there is such a "thing" as intelligence and that it is the same in all cultural and ethnic groups is a difficult one to swallow. The skills that contribute to intelligent behavior in a nonindustrialized farming and hunting community, or on the streets of an inner-city community, are likely very different from those that contribute to intelligence in a high school science class. Yet the standardized tests used in assessing intelligence place nearly exclusive emphasis on the intellectual skills that are chiefly helpful in educational settings. It is essential for practitioners to keep in mind that any assessment of a youngster's intelligence must take into account the nature and purpose of the test used, the circumstances of the assessment, the background of the child, and the context in which the child has developed (Keating, 1995).

RECAP

- The IQ test measures the specific type of intelligence that is predictive of success in school. IQ scores are remarkably stable during adolescence
- According to theorists like Sternberg and Gardner, there are other types of intelligence important to success in life that are not captured on conventional IQ tests
- Sex differences in intellectual abilities have largely disappeared and are limited to differences in spatial ability
- Experts agree that it is essential to view and assess intelligence in a way that takes into account the cultural context in which the adolescent has grown up. An important influence on this perspective has been Vygotsky.

---

culture-fair tests   Standardized tests that do not, by virtue of their construction, favor one cultural or ethnic group over another.

Adolescent Thinking in Context

Just as it is important to ask how the broader context influences adolescents' cognitive development, it is also important to ask how their cognitive development influences their interactions with their environment. After all, most of the thinking adolescents do occurs in everyday situations, not just when they are taking tests designed to see how able they are.

As our understanding of adolescent thinking has expanded, researchers have begun to look beyond laboratory experiments and standardized tests to examine how the cognitive changes of adolescence actually affect teenagers' day-to-day thoughts and actions. Do advances in deductive reasoning or information-processing abilities make a difference in the real world? To answer this question, psychologists and educators have studied the practical side of adolescent thinking in three domains: in social situations, in risk taking, and in the classroom.

CHANGES IN SOCIAL COGNITION

Many of the examples of adolescent thinking that we have looked at in this chapter have involved reasoning about scientific problems or physical objects. But the same sorts of gains in intellectual abilities that are observed in young people's thinking in these realms are apparent in their reasoning about social phenomena. **Social cognition** involves such cognitive activities as thinking about people, thinking about social relationships, and thinking about social institutions (Lapsley, 1989).

It is not difficult to imagine that adolescents' advanced abilities in thinking about possibilities, thinking in multiple dimensions, and thinking about abstract concepts make them more sophisticated when it comes to reasoning about social matters. Compared with those of children, adolescents' conceptions of interpersonal relationships are more mature, their understanding of human behavior is more advanced, their ideas about social institutions and organizations are more complex, and their ability to figure out what other people are thinking is far more developed. As we shall see in subsequent chapters, gains in the area of social cognition help account for many of the psychosocial advances typically associated with adolescence—advances in the realms of identity, autonomy, intimacy, sexuality, and achievement. Individual differences in social cognitive abilities also help explain why some adolescents have more social problems than others (Lenhart & Rabiner, 1995).

Studies of social cognition during adolescence typically fall into three categories: (1) studies of impression formation, which examine how individuals form and organize judgments about other people; (2) studies of social perspective taking, which examine how, and how accurately, individuals make assessments about the thoughts and feelings of others; and (3) studies of morality and social conventions, which examine individuals' conceptions of justice, social norms, and guidelines for social interaction.

▌ **Impression Formation** During preadolescence and adolescence, individuals' impressions of other people develop in five main directions (Hill & Palmquist, 1978). First, impressions become progressively more differentiated. Adolescents are more likely than children to describe people—themselves as well as others—in more narrowly defined categories and with more differentiated attributes. Whereas children tend to use fairly global descriptors, such as in terms of gender and age, adolescents are more likely to describe people in terms of such things as interests and personality characteristics, although the particular sets of attributes adolescents use to describe other people may vary across cultures (Crystal, Watanabe, Weinfurt, & Wu, 1998). Second, impression formation tends to be less egocentric. Adolescents are more likely to be aware that their impressions of others are personal viewpoints and therefore are subject to disagreement. Third, impressions of other people become more abstract; that is, they become less rooted in such concrete attributes as physical characteristics or personal possessions and more tied to such abstract things as attitudes and motives. Fourth, individuals come to make greater use of inference in their impressions of others. Compared with children, adolescents are more likely to interpret the feelings of others and to infer their motives, beliefs, and feelings, even when specific information of this sort is not directly observable. Finally, adolescents' impressions of others are more highly organized. Adolescents are more likely than children, for example, to make judgments of others that link personality traits to the situations in which they are likely to be expressed ("She's impatient when she works with other people") and to reconcile apparently discrepant information about people into a more complex impression ("He's friendly toward girls but not toward boys").

Together, these gains in impression formation mark the beginning of the development of an **implicit personality theory**—a theory of why people are the

social cognition   The aspect of cognition that concerns thinking about other people, about interpersonal relations, and about social institutions.

implicit personality theory   An intuitive understanding of human behavior and motivation that emerges during early adolescence.

Advances in social cognition enhance adolescents' ability to reason with others.

way they are (Barenboim, 1981). This can be seen in how adolescents talk about others and in the plots and character development in stories they write (McKeough & Genereaux, 2003). As we shall see in Chapter 10, the development of this implicit personality theory has important implications for the development of intimate relationships.

▌ **Social Perspective Taking**   Related to these gains in impression-formation abilities are considerable improvements in adolescents' **social perspective taking**—the ability to view events from the perspective of others. According to Robert Selman (1980), who has studied this aspect of development extensively, children become better able as they grow older to recognize that others may view an event from a different, but equally valid, perspective. Not only are adolescents more capable of discerning another person's perspective on some issue or event, but they are also better able to understand that person's perspective on their own point of view. Interestingly, the fact that individuals' ability to look at things from another person's perspective increases in adolescence does not mean that individuals become more tolerant of the beliefs of those with whom they disagree. People's tolerance for diversity in viewpoint depends more on the particular issue involved than on age (Wainryb, Shaw, Laupa, & Smith, 2001).

social perspective taking   The ability to view events from the perspective of others.

mutual role taking   In Selman's theory, the stage of social perspective taking during which the young adolescent can be an objective third party and can see how the thoughts or actions of one person can affect those of another.

According to Selman, the development of social perspective taking progresses through a series of stages. In the preadolescent stage, youngsters can put themselves in others' shoes but do not yet see how the thoughts and feelings of one person may be related to the thoughts and feelings of another. During early adolescence, with the progression into what Selman calls **mutual role taking,** the young adolescent can be an objective third party and can see how the thoughts or actions of one person might influence those of another. In thinking about two friends, for instance, an adolescent at this level would be able to look at the friends' relationship and see how each person's behavior affects the other's.

Later in adolescence, perspective taking achieves an in-depth, societal orientation. The adolescent at this level understands that the perspectives which people have on each other are complicated, are often unconscious, and are influenced by larger forces than individuals can control—including each person's position in society or within a social institution. For example, you are able to understand that your perspective on the instructor teaching your class is influenced not only by your own personality and by the instructor's but also by forces inherent in the professor–student relationship.

Ultimately, adolescents' gains in social perspective–taking abilities lead to improvements in communication, as they become more capable of formulating arguments in terms that are more likely to be understood by someone whose opinion is different. One study (Clark & Delia, 1976), for example, looked at how well youngsters of different ages were able to persuade other people to do something for them—such as convincing their parents to buy them a new stereo. The researchers found that adolescents were more likely to use reasoning that pointed out advantages to their parents ("If I have my own stereo in my room, you won't be bothered by my music") than reasoning that simply stated the case from their own point of view ("I really need to have my own stereo. All the other kids do"). Note that a major shift in reasoning takes place during early adolescence, coinciding with the transition into the stage of mutual role taking. Although you might think that parents find it more difficult to deal with a teenager who is more persuasive, studies suggest that when adolescents are able to take their parents' perspective in an argument, family communication becomes more effective and more satisfying (Silverberg, 1986).

▌ **Conceptions of Morality and Social Convention**   The realization that individuals' perspectives vary, and that their opinions may differ as a result, leads to changes in the ways that adolescents approach issues regarding morality and social convention. Changes in moral reasoning during adolescence have been investigated extensively, and we'll examine this body of research in detail in Chapter 9. Briefly, during childhood, moral guidelines are seen as absolutes emanating from such authorities as parents or teachers; judgments of right and wrong are made according to concrete rules. During adolescence, however, such absolutes and rules are questioned, as the young person begins to see that moral standards are subjective and are based on viewpoints that are subject to disagreement. Later in adolescence comes the emergence of reasoning that is based on such moral principles as equality, justice, and fairness—abstract guidelines that transcend concrete situations and can be applied across a variety of moral dilemmas (Eisenberg & Morris, 2004).

The development of individuals' understanding of **social conventions**—the social norms that guide day-to-day behavior—follows a similar course (Smetana, in press). During middle childhood, social conventions—such as waiting in line to buy movie tickets—are seen as arbitrary and changeable, but adherence to them is not; compliance with such conventions is based on rules and on the dictates of authority. When you were 7 years old, you might not have understood why people had to wait in line to buy movie tickets, but when your parents told you to wait in line, you waited. By early adolescence, however, conventions are seen as arbitrary and changeable in terms of both origins and enforcement; conventions are merely social expectations. As an adolescent, you begin to realize that people wait in line because they are expected to, not because they are forced to. Indeed, young adolescents often see social conventions as *nothing but* social expectations and, consequently, as insufficient reasons for compliance. You can probably imagine youngsters in their midteens saying something like this: "Why wait in a ticket line simply because other people are lined up? There isn't a *law* that forces you to wait in line, is there?"

Gradually, however, adolescents begin to see social conventions as the means by which society regulates people's behavior. Conventions may be arbitrary, but we follow them because we share an understanding of how people are expected to behave in various situations. In fact, high schoolers see conventions as so ingrained in the social system that individuals follow them partly out of habit. We wait in line for theater tickets not because we want to comply with any rule, but because it is something we are accustomed to doing.

Ultimately, individuals come to see that social conventions serve a function in coordinating interactions among people. Social norms and expectations are derived from and maintained by individuals' having a common perspective and agreeing that, in given situations, certain behaviors are more desirable than others, because such behaviors help society and its institutions function more smoothly. Without the convention of waiting in line to buy movie tickets, the pushiest people would always get tickets first. Older adolescents can see that waiting in line not only benefits the theater by keeping order but also preserves everyone's right to a fair chance to buy tickets. In other words, we wait in line patiently because we all agree that it is better if tickets are distributed fairly.

Changes in adolescents' understanding of social conventions, and in the ways in which they distinguish between moral issues and conventional ones, have important implications for their relationships with parents and peers (Smetana, in press). With age, individuals increasingly distinguish between moral issues (such as whether it is acceptable to steal from someone else) and conventional ones (such as whether one eats dessert before or after the main course). As adolescents begin to see that social conventions are far less absolute than morals, they may come to question their parents' authority in various contexts. Issues that had been viewed as matters of right and wrong start to seem like matters of personal opinion without any genuine moral basis. For example, parents' rules about things like the cleanliness of the adolescent's bedroom or how late she or he can stay up on school nights, which had been accepted as matters of right and wrong, start to seem like arbitrary conventions that are open to debate. Similarly, "rules" that had governed relationships with peers (for example, that if one has a party, no one from class can be excluded) may come to be seen as conventions that don't necessarily have to be followed. Excluding another classmate from a social activity no longer seems like an ethically wrong thing to do, but simply a matter of personal choice. As we'll see in Chapter 4, one main source of conflict between adolescents and their parents involves disagreements over whether certain issues involve moral questions or conventional ones.

Table 2.2 summarizes some of the important differences in social cognitive abilities between preadolescents and adolescents. As you can see, across all four domains, thinking becomes more abstract, more hypothetical, and more relativistic between childhood and adolescence.

Together, these gains in social cognitive abilities help to account for gains in individuals' social competence during adolescence. As you will see in Chapter 10, adolescents who have more sophisticated social cognitive abilities (that is, more advanced perspective-taking

social conventions The norms that govern everyday behavior in social situations.

TABLE 2.2   Differences between preadolescent and adolescent thinking in four social cognitive domains

Domain	Preadolescent Thought	Adolescent Thought
Impressions of others (e.g., Barenboim)	Impressions are global, egocentric, concrete, disorganized, and haphazard.	Impressions are differentiated, objective, and abstract, and are organized into a coherent whole.
Role taking (e.g., Selman)	Child is able to put self in other's shoes but has difficulty seeing how one person's perspective affects another's.	Adolescent is able to take third-party perspective and to see bigger societal picture.
Moral reasoning (e.g., Kohlberg)	Morals are based on concrete rules handed down by authorities.	Morals come out of agreements between people or out of abstract principles.
Social conventions (e.g., Turiel)	Conventions are based on rules and dictates of authorities.	Conventions are based on expectations or grow out of social norms.

abilities and more sophisticated impression formation skills) actually behave in more socially competent ways (Eisenberg & Morris, 2004; Lenhart & Rabiner, 1995). Although there is more to social competence than social cognition, being able to understand social relationships is an important component of social maturity.

▌ **Adolescent Wisdom**   One of the most important ways in which improvements in social cognition are manifested during adolescence is in the development of wisdom. *Wisdom* has been defined as rich knowledge about life that permits "exceptional insight, judgment, and advice about complex and uncertain matters" (Pasupathi, Staudinger, & Baltes, 2001, p. 351). Wisdom requires social perspective–taking skills that do not develop until midadolescence. In a recent study of the development of wisdom, individuals between the ages of 14 and 37 were interviewed about a series of dilemmas that required sophisticated insight, reasoning, and judgment but that did not have clear-cut solutions, such as those concerning complex interpersonal problems or the meaning of life. One such dilemma was this: "A teenager learns that his or her parents want to divorce. What could one or the teenager do and think in such a situation?" The interviews were transcribed and coded for the presence of various aspects of wisdom. Although we tend to associate the development of wisdom with adulthood rather than adolescence, the researchers found that wisdom increased steadily between the ages of 14 and 25, and then leveled off. In other words, it is during the transition between adolescence and adulthood that individuals acquire the sort of wisdom we associate with age (Pasupathi et al., 2001).

ADOLESCENT RISK TAKING

A second practical application of research into adolescent thinking involves the study of adolescent risk taking. In Chapter 1, you read that many of the health problems of adolescence are the result of behaviors that can be prevented—behaviors such as substance abuse, reckless driving, and unprotected sex. The Centers for Disease Control and Prevention, a federal agency that monitors the health of Americans, now surveys American teenagers annually and asks whether they had engaged in various behaviors during the previous 30 days (Centers for Disease Control and Prevention, 2006). Risk taking is common among adolescents. Recent surveys have revealed, for example, that although most high school students regularly use a seat belt, of those teenagers who ride motorcycles, 37 percent report rarely or never wearing a helmet, and of those who ride bicycles, 83 percent report rarely or never wearing a helmet. Nearly 80 percent of boys and 60 percent of girls take unnecessary risks while skateboarding or riding bikes, close to one-third of both sexes have been passengers in cars driven by intoxicated drivers, and one-tenth have driven while drinking (Centers for Disease Control and Prevention, 2006; Ozer, Macdonald, & Irwin, 2002). In general, risk taking is much more common among males than females, although some evidence suggests that this gender gap has been narrowing over time (Byrnes, Miller, & Schafer, 1999).

Some writers have suggested that we look at these behaviors as resulting from decisions that adolescents make—for instance, decisions to drink alcohol, to drive fast, or to have intercourse without using contraception—and that we need to better understand the cognitive processes behind such decision making. One line of research has attempted to examine whether adolescents make risky decisions because of deficiencies in their developing cognitive abilities (Furbey & Beyth-Marom, 1992).

▌ **Behavioral Decision Theory**   A number of writers have looked at adolescent risk taking from a

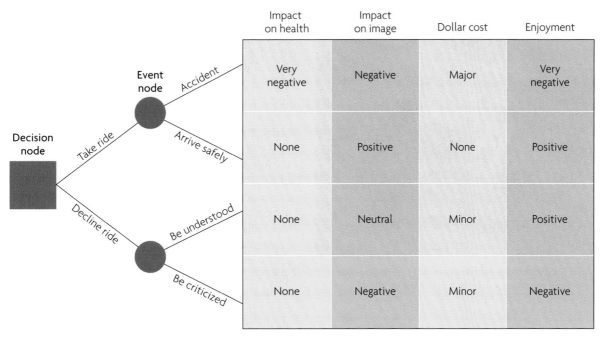

FIGURE 2.6   The process of deciding whether to accept a ride home from a friend who has been drinking, according to behavioral decision theory. (Fischoff & Quadrel, 1995)

perspective called **behavioral decision theory** (Fischhoff & Quadrel, 1995; Kahneman, Slovic, & Tversky, 1982; Reyna & Farley, 2006). In this perspective, which draws heavily on economics, decision making is a rational process in which individuals calculate the costs and benefits of alternative courses of action and behave in ways that maximize the benefits and minimize the costs (Gruber, 2001). According to this theory, all behaviors, including risky ones, can be analyzed as the outcome of a process involving five steps: (1) identifying alternative choices, (2) identifying the consequences that might follow from each choice, (3) evaluating the costs and benefits of each possible consequence, (4) assessing the likelihood of each possible consequence, and (5) combining all this information according to some decision rule (Beyth-Marom, Austin, Fischhoff, Palmgren, & Jacobs-Quadrel, 1993).

So, for example, an adolescent girl who is trying to decide whether to accept a ride home from a party with friends who have been drinking will (1) identify the choices (to accept the ride or not), (2) identify the consequences ("If I accept the ride, and we get into an accident, I could be seriously hurt, but if I don't accept the ride, my friends will make fun of me for being a 'loser'"), (3) evaluate the desirability of each consequence ("Appearing like a 'loser' to my friends is bad, but being in an accident would be terrible"), (4) assess the likelihood of each consequence ("My friends probably won't really change their opinion of me just

because I turn down the ride, and my friend who is driving is so drunk that he really might get into an accident"), and (5) combine all the information according to some decision rule ("All things considered, I think I won't take the ride"). Figure 2.6 shows what this decision-making process might look like.

From the perspective of behavioral decision theory, then, it is important to ask whether adolescents use different processes than adults in identifying, estimating, and evaluating behavioral options and consequences. If risky decisions are the result of faulty information processing—in attention, memory, metacognition, or organization, for example—perhaps it would make sense to train adolescents in these basic cognitive abilities as a means of lessening their risk taking.

FOOD FOR THOUGHT

What risky behavior did you engage in during adolescence that you would be reluctant to engage in today? If you did, why do you think you took those risks? What has changed that has made you more risk averse?

---

behavioral decision theory   An approach to understanding adolescent risk taking, in which behaviors are seen as the outcome of systematic decision-making processes.

Recent research on cognitive development in adolescence has been aimed at understanding the thinking behind risk-taking behavior.

As we have seen, however, adolescents, at least by the time they are 15 or so, make decisions using the same basic cognitive processes that adults use (Beyth-Marom et al., 1993; Furbey & Beyth-Marom, 1992). This is true even for issues as complicated as deciding whether to abort a pregnancy (Lewis, 1987). The major gains in the cognitive skills that affect decision making appear to occur between childhood and adolescence, rather than between adolescence and adulthood (Steinberg & Cauffman, 1996). Thus, educating adolescents in how to make "better" decisions is not likely to reduce risk taking (Steinberg, 2004).

■ **Do Adolescents Really Feel Invulnerable?**   A second possibility that is often suggested is that adolescents are more likely to feel invulnerable—more likely, that is, to subscribe to the personal fable that they will not be harmed by potentially harmful activities. However, as you read earlier, there is no evidence for the widely held belief that adolescents are more likely to subscribe to personal fables than are adults (Quadrel, Fischhoff, & Davis, 1993). More importantly, studies indicate that young adolescents are *less* likely than young adults to see themselves as invulnerable—if anything, young adolescents *overestimate* the risks involved in potentially harmful behavior (Millstein & Halpern-Felsher, 2002). By middle adolescence, individuals have begun to underestimate their likelihood of being hurt by potentially harmful activities, but they are no more likely to do this than adults (Quadrel et al., 1993). Interestingly, however, research indicates that adolescents vary far more than adults in how they interpret words and phrases used to describe risk—

words like "probably," "likely," or "a very low chance"—suggesting that health educators and practitioners should not take for granted that an adolescent's understanding of a message about risk is what they think it is (Biehl & Halpern-Felsher, 2001). Similarly, just because an adolescent says that she knows that having "safe sex" can protect her against sexually transmitted diseases doesn't necessarily mean that she knows the specific behaviors that constitute safe sex (Reyna & Farley, 2006).

■ **Age Differences in Values and Priorities**   If adolescents use the same decision-making processes as adults, and if adolescents are no more likely than adults to think of themselves as invulnerable, why, then, do they behave in excessively risky ways? One answer may involve the different ways in which adolescents and adults evaluate the desirability of different consequences (Moore & Gullone, 1996). For example, an individual's decision to try cocaine at a party may involve evaluating a number of different consequences, including the legal and health risks, the pleasure the drug may induce, and the way in which he or she will be judged (both positively and negatively) by the other people present. An adult and an adolescent may both consider all these consequences, but the adult may place relatively more weight on the health risks of trying the drug, while the adolescent may place relatively more weight on the social consequences of not trying it. Although an adult may see an adolescent's decision to value peer acceptance more than health as irrational, an adolescent may see the adult's decision as equally incomprehensible. Behavioral decision theory reminds us that all decisions—even risky ones—can be seen as rational once we understand how an individual estimates and evaluates the consequences of various courses of action.

One very important difference between adolescents and adults, for instance, is that, when weighing the costs and benefits of engaging in a risky behavior, adolescents are more attuned to the potential rewards than adults are (Ben-Zur & Reshef-Kfir, 2003; Millstein & Halpern-Felsher, 2002). This difference is consistent with what we now know is taking place in the limbic system around the time of puberty. One recent study of delinquents found, for instance, that adolescents' criminal activity was more strongly related to their beliefs about the potential rewards of the activity (for example, being seen as "cool") than to their perceptions of the activity's riskiness (for example, the chances of being arrested) (Matsueda, Kreager, & Huizinga, 2006). As several writers have pointed out, this has important implications for the prevention of risky behavior among adolescents. It may be more important to convince adolescents that the rewards of

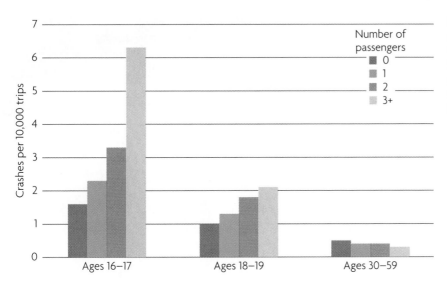

FIGURE 2.7   Crash rates are significantly higher when teenage drivers have passengers in the car. This is less true for college-age drivers and not at all true for middle-aged adults, however. (Williams, 2003)

a risky activity are small (for example, that few people will actually look up to you for being violent) than to persuade them that the costs are large (for example, that being incarcerated will be terrible).

In all likelihood, of course, neither adolescents' nor adults' decisions are always made in as straightforward or rational a way as suggested by behavioral decision theory. Nevertheless, this approach has opened up a new way of thinking about adolescent risk taking. Instead of viewing risky activities as the result of irrational or faulty judgment, experts are now trying to understand where and how adolescents obtain the information they use in reaching their conclusions, and how accurate the information is. If, for example, adolescents underestimate the likelihood of getting pregnant following unprotected sex, sex education efforts might focus on teaching teenagers the actual probability. (Of course, this presumes that adolescents' decisions about whether to have sex are made rationally, which may not be the case [Levine, 2001].) From the perspective of public policy, adolescent risk taking could be reduced by increasing the actual costs of risky behavior (for instance, by raising the price of cigarettes or alcohol; by limiting the supply of illegal drugs, which would make them more expensive; or by making the penalties for reckless driving more severe) (Gruber, 2001).

■ **Emotional and Contextual Influences on Risk Taking**   We should also keep in mind that emotional and contextual factors, as well as cognitive ones, contribute to adolescent risk taking. Several researchers have noted that adolescents may differ from adults in important ways that are not captured by measures of logical reasoning, such as susceptibility to peer pressure, impulsivity, orientation to the present rather than the

future, or fun seeking (Maggs, Almeida, & Galambos, 1995; Robbins & Bryan, 2004; Scott, Reppucci, & Woolard, 1995; Steinberg & Cauffman, 1996). In fact, differences between adolescents and adults in these respects were used to argue against the juvenile death penalty (Steinberg & Scott, 2003). With respect to emotional factors, for example, studies show that individuals who are confident, competitive, and high in **sensation seeking**— that is, they enjoy novel and intense experiences—are more likely to engage in various types of risky behaviors than their peers (Miller & Byrnes, 1997).

The context in which individuals spend time matters, too. Keep in mind that a good deal of adolescents' risk taking takes place in contexts in which they are unsupervised by adults and exposed to tremendous peer pressure to engage in risky behavior (Byrnes, 1997). As noted earlier, individuals' susceptibility to peer pressure increases during early and middle adolescence, and then declines, suggesting that one reason for teenagers' greater risk taking is the fact that they spend so much time in the peer group. Most adolescent risk taking, including delinquency, drinking, and reckless behavior, occurs when other teenagers are present (Steinberg, 2004)

The effect of peers on adolescent risk taking is clearly evident in studies of driving accidents. As Figure 2.7 shows, having multiple passengers in the car increases the risk of crashes dramatically among 16- and 17-year-old drivers, significantly among 18- and 19-year-old drivers, and not at all among adults. Consistent with this, in one recent experiment, in which adolescents, college undergraduates, and adults who

sensation seeking   The enjoyment of novel and intense experiences.

were either alone or in a room with their friends played a video driving game that permitted risky driving—for instance, driving through an intersection after a traffic light had turned yellow—found that the mere fact of having friends watching their performance increased risk taking among adolescents and undergraduates, but not adults (Gardner & Steinberg, 2005). In that study, the presence of peers also increased adolescents' stated willingness to take all sorts of risks, including shoplifting, stealing, and allowing friends to bring drugs into their house. Contrary to popular belief, alcohol is not the main contributor to the increased rate of automobile accidents among teenagers—in fact, adolescents are *less* likely to drink and drive than adults. Driving with other teenagers in the car and speeding are far more important factors (Williams, 2003).

ADOLESCENT THINKING IN THE CLASSROOM

Given the sorts of changes in thinking that occur during the adolescent years, we might hope that schools and teachers would adapt their methods and curricula to better mesh with the developing cognitive abilities of their students. In theory, adolescents' ability to think in more advanced ways—whether in terms of abstraction, multidimensionality, relativism, or some other dimension—should permit them to think more critically about a wide range of issues. Yet the prevalence of **critical thinking** among American high school students—thinking that is in-depth, analytical, and discriminating—is less than staggering, as we shall see in later chapters about school and achievement. Most assessments of adolescent achievement in recent years indicate that American youths have difficulty thinking in the sophisticated ways that our theories and research suggest they ought to be capable of. Part of the reason, some critics contend, is simply that adolescents are rarely asked to think in this fashion (Ravitch, 1995).

According to some writers, our educational system does not encourage or stimulate the type of thinking that adolescents have the potential for. Although research indicates that it is possible, for example, to stimulate the development of formal-operational thinking (e.g., Danner & Day, 1977; Siegler, Liebert, & Liebert, 1973), few junior or senior high school classes are set up to do so. Rather than encouraging adolescents to think in abstract or relativistic ways, for instance, most secondary school classes reward the rote memorization of facts and the parroting back of the teacher's "correct" answer (Sternberg, 1994). According to one

One reason so many teenagers complain of boredom in school is that few school hours are spent in activities that engage them intellectually or encourage critical thinking.

expert, opportunities for real give-and-take in adolescents' schools account for less than 10 percent of the total time spent on instruction (Sternberg, 1994). At a time when individuals are becoming capable of seeing that most issues are too complicated to have one right answer, an educational program that stifles this developing ability works against adolescents' developmental inclinations. Although attempts have been made to make the instruction of adolescents more compatible with our understanding of their cognitive development, these efforts have not been widespread. Yet, studies show that teaching that takes advantage of adolescents' developing reasoning abilities can result in students' more sophisticated understanding of the subject matter, especially in science classes (Linn & Songer, 1991, 1993). For example, opportunities to engage in hands-on experiments contribute to adolescents' understanding of scientific principles (Penner & Klahr, 1996).

FOOD FOR THOUGHT

Many have criticized schools for failing to promote critical thinking. But do you think that most adolescents really want educational practices to change?

The gap between what adolescents can do (i.e., their *competence*) and their actual school achievement (i.e., their *performance*) may be especially large among

---

critical thinking   Thinking that is in-depth, analytical, and discriminating.

youths who attend English-speaking schools but who speak another language or dialect when not in school, as one study of native Hawaiian youths indicates (Feldman, Stone, & Renderer, 1990). Although these students attended schools where the instruction was in Standard English, they spoke Hawaiian Creole–English at home and with their friends. The researchers found that, even though the students were functioning at a high cognitive level, they were uncomfortable speaking in class because of their language background, and this lack of verbal engagement interfered with their learning. One hypothesis is that speaking in class aids in the process of encoding the information, which facilitates learning. Presumably, all groups of youngsters whose in-school and out-of-school languages are different may be at risk for this disadvantage.

Criticisms also have been leveled against schools' lack of attempts to deliberately enhance adolescents' information-processing skills. As our society becomes more information-dependent—some social commentators have talked about information overload—it is important that adolescents learn how to better manage and utilize this wealth of data. A number of writers have argued that schools can and should teach adolescents ways of focusing attention, improving short- and long-term memory, organizing information, and monitoring thought processes (Williams et al., 2002). In other words, these experts believe that metacognitive skills can be taught and that educators

should make a more conscious effort to do so. Moreover, they point to recent advances in research on adolescent information processing as providing the foundation for an overhaul of our secondary school curricula.

RECAP

- Contemporary researchers have been interested in the ways in which the cognitive changes of adolescence play out in everyday activities.
- One domain in which improvements in thinking are evident is the realm of social cognition.
- Scientists who have examined the underlying reasons for the higher rate of risk taking among adolescents have noted that this is not due to deficiencies in basic cognitive abilities. More likely causes are age differences in priorities, in psychosocial factors, and in the contexts in which adolescents and adults spend time.
- Despite evidence that the development of advanced thinking abilities can be stimulated, schools do a very poor job of encouraging their development or stimulating critical thinking.

BALLOTS

CHAPTER 3

Social Transitions

SOCIAL REDEFINITION AND PSYCHOSOCIAL DEVELOPMENT

THE ELONGATION OF ADOLESCENCE

ADOLESCENCE AS A SOCIAL INVENTION

The "Invention" of Adolescence

Emerging Adulthood: A New Stage of Life or a Luxury of the Middle Class?

CHANGES IN STATUS

Changes in Interpersonal Status

Changes in Political Status

Changes in Economic Status

Changes in Legal Status

THE PROCESS OF SOCIAL REDEFINITION

Common Practices in the Process of Social Redefinition

VARIATIONS IN SOCIAL TRANSITIONS

Variations in Clarity

Variations in Continuity

THE TRANSITION INTO ADULTHOOD IN CONTEMPORARY SOCIETY

Special Transitional Problems of Poor and Minority Youth

The Effects of Poverty on the Transition into Adulthood

What Can Be Done to Ease the Transition?

THE INFLUENCE OF NEIGHBORHOOD CONDITIONS ON ADOLESCENT DEVELOPMENT

Processes of Neighborhood Influences

WHAT EVENTS IN YOUR LIFE told you—and others around you—that you were no longer a child, and had finally become an adolescent? Was it when you turned 13? Finished elementary school? Went to your first boy– girl party? Were allowed to be out at the mall without an adult?

And what signaled, or will signal, that you are an adult? Turning 18? Turning 21? Getting your first full-time job? Getting your driver's license? Graduating from college? Getting your first apartment? Getting married?

Each of these social transitions is not just an event. Each is also a source of information—to the individual and those in his or her life—about the individual's stage of development. Parents may treat their children differently once they start high school, even if their appearance and behavior haven't changed. Neighbors might look at a child who has grown up next door differently once they see him or her driving. Adolescents may feel differently about themselves once they have started working at a "real" job.

In all societies, adolescence is a period of social transition for the individual. Over the course of the adolescent years, the individual ceases to be viewed by society as a child and comes to be recognized as an adult. This chapter is about the ways in which individuals are redefined during adolescence and the implications of this process for psychological development. Although the specific elements of this social passage from childhood into adulthood vary across time and space, the recognition that the individual's status has changed—a **social redefinition** of the individual—is universal.

In this chapter, we will look at a third fundamental feature of adolescence—changes in the way in which society defines who that person is and determines what rights and responsibilities she or he has as a result. Along with the biological changes of puberty and changes in thinking abilities, changes in social roles and social status constitute yet another universal feature of development during adolescence. As you will read, some theorists have argued that the nature of adolescent development is far more influenced by the way in which society defines the economic and social roles of young people than by the biological or cognitive changes of the period.

The study of social transitions in adolescence provides an interesting vehicle through which to compare adolescence across different cultures and historical epochs. Puberty, after all, is pretty much the same everywhere (although its timing and meaning may vary across contexts). Abstract thinking and logical reasoning don't differ from one society to the next (although *what* people think and reason about certainly does). The social transitions of adolescence are not the same, however. Although the social passage from childhood into adulthood is universal, considerable differences exist between the processes of social redefinition in industrialized society and in more traditional cultures. In examining some of these differences, you will come to understand better how the way in which society structures the transition of adolescents into adult roles influences the nature of psychosocial development during the period.

Social Redefinition and Psychosocial Development

Like the biological and cognitive transitions of adolescence, the social transitions have important consequences for the young person's psychosocial development. Indeed, from a sociological or anthropological perspective, the social redefinition of the individual has the most profound impact on development and behavior. In the realm of identity, for example, attainment of adult status may transform a young woman's

self-concept, causing her to feel more mature and to think more seriously about future work and family roles. Similarly, the first time an individual reports to work, goes into a bar, drives without an adult in the car, or votes, may make him or her feel older and more mature. In turn, these new activities and opportunities may prompt self-evaluation and introspection.

Becoming an adult member of society, accompanied as it is by increases in responsibilities and freedom, also has an impact on the development of autonomy, or independence. In contrast to the child, the adolescent-turned-adult faces a wider range of decisions that may have serious long-term consequences (Scott & Woolard, 2004). An individual who has reached the drinking age,

social redefinition   The process through which an individual's position or status is redefined by society.

for example, must decide how to handle this new privilege. Should he go along with the crowd and drink every weekend night, follow his parents' example and abstain from drinking, or chart a middle ground? And in return for the privileges that come with adult status, the adolescent-turned-adult is expected to behave in a more responsible fashion. For example, receiving a driver's license carries with it the obligation of driving safely. Thus, the attainment of adult status provides chances for the young person to exercise autonomy and to develop a greater sense of independence.

FOOD FOR THOUGHT

Which fundamental change of adolescence—biological, cognitive, or social—do you think has the most powerful effect on psychological development? Why?

Changes in social definition often bring with them changes in relationships with others. Social redefinition at adolescence is therefore likely to raise new questions and concerns for the young person about intimacy—including such matters as dating and marriage. Many parents prohibit their children from dating until they have reached an "appropriate" age, and not until the **age of majority** (the legal age for adult status) are individuals allowed to marry without first gaining their parents' permission. In certain societies, young people may even be *required* to marry when they reach adulthood, entering into a marriage that may have been arranged while they were children.

Changes in status at adolescence may also affect development in the domain of sexuality. In contemporary society, for example, laws governing sexual behavior (such as the definition of statutory rape) typically differentiate between individuals who have and have not attained adult status. By becoming an adult in a legal sense, the young person may be confronted with the need for new decisions about sexual activity. One problem continuing to face contemporary society is whether sexually active individuals who have not yet attained adult legal status should be able to make independent decisions about such adult matters as abortion and contraception (Scott & Woolard, 2004).

Finally, reaching adulthood often has important implications in the realm of achievement. For instance, in contemporary society, it is not until adult work status is attained (typically at age 16 in the United States) that young people can enter the labor force as a full-time employee. And not until young people have

reached a designated age are they permitted to leave school of their own volition. In less industrialized societies, becoming an adult typically entails entrance into the productive activities of the community. Together, these shifts are likely to prompt changes in the young person's skills, aspirations, and expectations.

RECAP

- Changes in social definition—in how society views the individual—constitute a third set of fundamental changes that define adolescence.
- Although societies vary in how the transition from childhood to adulthood is signified, all cultures have some way of recognizing that the individual's rights and responsibilities have changed once he or she becomes an adult.
- Changes in social definition may have profound effects on development in the realms of identity, autonomy, intimacy, sexuality, and achievement.

The Elongation of Adolescence

One of the most striking aspects of the social transition experienced by adolescents today is the sheer length of the time it takes to travel from childhood to adulthood. By virtually any indicator, adolescence lasts longer today than ever before, because young people go through puberty (one marker of the beginning of adolescence) earlier and enter into adult roles of work and family (one way to define the end of adolescence) later. Although this is more true in industrialized societies than in developing ones, there is evidence that adolescence lasts longer in developing countries as well (National Research Council, 2005).

In previous eras, when puberty occurred around age 15 and individuals left school and went to work just a few years later, adolescence, at least by these markers, lasted only a few years. Today, in contrast, young people are caught between the world of childhood and the world of adulthood for an extremely long time, often longer than a decade, and frequently with only a vague sense of when—and how—they become adults. Indeed, in the minds of many social scientists who study adolescence in modern society, the social passage of young people into adult roles is too long, too vague,

age of majority   The designated age at which an individual is recognized as an adult.

and too rocky (Chisholm & Hurrelmann, 1995; Nightingale & Wolverton, 1993). And, as we shall see, the passage from adolescence into adulthood is especially difficult for young people growing up in poverty.

FOOD FOR THOUGHT

The time between the age when individuals become sexually mature and when they marry was much shorter in previous generations than it is today—because sexual maturity takes place so much earlier now and marriage takes place so much later. As a result the admonition to "wait until you're married" to have sex was probably a lot easier to do 150 years ago than it is today. Do you agree?

The lengthening of adolescence as a developmental period has had important implications for how young people see themselves, relate to others, and develop psychologically. Consider just a few examples:

- Parents used to "launch" their children from home very close to the age of puberty. As a consequence, individuals spent very little time living under the same roof with their parents once they had become sexual beings. In contemporary society, however, individuals live with their parents long after they have become sexually mature. What impact might this have on parent–child relationships?

- Adolescents today probably aren't any less emotionally mature than they were 100 years ago—if anything, growing up under many of the pressures to which individuals are exposed in today's world has made them more mature at a younger age. But because they are expected to stay in school for such a long period, adolescents' economic "maturity" (that is, their ability to support themselves without help from their parents) lags far behind their psychological maturity (that is, their ability to behave responsibly). What implications does this have? How does it feel to be an adult psychologically but a child financially?

- One of the main reasons that adolescence has been lengthened is that much more formal education is now necessary in order to make a successful transition into adult work roles. School, however, is not something that all individuals

enjoy equally. How might forcing all adolescents to follow the same pathway into adulthood may benefit some but not others?

RECAP

- The length of adolescence as a developmental period has increased dramatically due to the earlier onset of puberty and the prolongation of formal education, which delays many of the role transitions that mark the beginning of adulthood.
- Many observers of adolescence in contemporary society believe that the transition into adulthood is too long, too vague, and too disorderly, and that this has had harmful effects on adolescents' development and well-being, especially those for whom formal schooling is not a fulfilling experience.

Adolescence as a Social Invention

Many writers have argued that adolescence, as a period in the life cycle, is mainly a social invention (e.g., Fasick, 1994; Lapsley, Enright, & Serlin, 1985). These writers, often referred to as **inventionists,** point out that, although the biological and cognitive changes characteristic of the period are important in their own right, adolescence is defined primarily by the ways in which society recognizes (or does not recognize) the period as distinct from childhood or adulthood.

Many of our images of adolescence are influenced by the fact that society draws lines between adolescence and childhood (for instance, the boundary between elementary and secondary school) and between adolescence and adulthood (for instance, the age at which one can hold a job). Inventionists stress that it is because we see adolescence as distinct that it exists as such. They point to other cultures and other historical periods in which adolescence either is not recognized at all or is viewed very differently. Many of these theorists view the behaviors and problems characteristic of adolescence in contemporary society as having to do with the particular way that adolescence is defined by society, rather than the result of the biological or cognitive givens of the period. As you know, this is an entirely different view than that espoused by writers such as G. Stanley Hall, who saw the psychological changes of adolescence as driven by puberty and, as a result, by biological destiny.

inventionists   Theorists who argue that the period of adolescence is mainly a social invention.

THE "INVENTION" OF ADOLESCENCE

Have there always been adolescents? Although this may seem like a simple question with an obvious answer, it is actually a very complicated issue. Naturally, there have always been individuals between the ages of 10 and 20, or who just passed through puberty, or whose frontal lobes were still maturing. But according to the inventionist view, adolescence as we know it in contemporary society did not really exist until the Industrial Revolution of the mid-nineteenth century (Fasick, 1994). Prior to that time, in the agricultural world of the sixteenth or seventeenth century, children were treated primarily as miniature adults, and people did not make precise distinctions among children of different ages ("child" referred to anyone under the age of 18 or even 21). Children provided important labor to their families, and they learned early in their development the roles they were expected to fill later in life. The main distinction between children and adults was not based on their age or their abilities but on whether they owned property (Modell & Goodman, 1990). As a consequence, there was little reason to label some youngsters as "children" and others as "adolescents"—in fact, "adolescent" was not widely used prior to the nineteenth century.

■ **The Impact of Industrialization** With industrialization came new patterns of work, education, and family life. Adolescents were among those most dramatically affected by these changes. First, because the economy was changing so rapidly, away from the simple and predictable life known in agrarian society, the connection between what individuals learned in childhood and what they would need to know in adulthood became increasingly uncertain. Although a man may have been a farmer, his son would not necessarily follow in his footsteps. One response to this uncertainty was that parents, especially in middle-class families, encouraged adolescents to spend time within societal institutions, such as schools, preparing for adulthood. Instead of working side by side with their parents and other adults at home, as was the case before industrialization, nineteenth-century adolescents were increasingly more likely to spend their days with their peers, preparing for the future. As you will read in later chapters, this change was one factor that led to the increased importance of peer groups and youth culture.

Inventionists are quick to point out that the redefinition of adolescence as a time of preparation rather than participation suited society's changing economic needs as well (Fasick, 1994). One initial outcome of industrialization was a shortage of job opportunities, because machines were replacing workers. Although adolescents provided inexpensive labor, they were competing with adults for a limited number of jobs. One way of protecting adults' jobs was to remove adolescents from the labor force, by turning them into full-time students. To accomplish this, society needed to begin discriminating between individuals who were "ready" for work and those who were not. And although there was little factual basis for the distinction, society began to view adolescents as less capable and more in need of guidance and training—as a way of legitimizing what was little more than age discrimination. Individuals who earlier in the century would have been working next to adults were now seen as too immature or too unskilled to carry out similar tasks—even though the individuals themselves hadn't changed in any meaningful way. As noted in the introductory chapter, society's view of adolescents' capability and maturity has changed dramatically when their labor was sorely needed, such as during wartime (Enright, Levy, Harris, & Lapsley, 1987).

A less cynical view of the events of the late nineteenth century emphasizes the genuine desire of some adults to protect adolescents from the dangers of the new workplace, rather than the selfish desire to protect adults' jobs from teenagers. Industrialization brought with it worrisome changes in community life, especially in the cities. Many factories were dangerous working environments, filled with new and unfamiliar machinery. The disruption of small farming communities and the growth of large urban areas because of the shift from agriculture to industry was accompanied by increases in crime and in "moral degeneracy." **Child protectionists** argued that young people needed to be kept away from the labor force for their own good. In addition to the rise of schools during this time, the early twentieth century saw the growth of many organizations aimed at protecting young people, such as the Boy Scouts and other adult-supervised youth clubs (Modell & Goodman, 1990).

■ **The Origins of Adolescence as We Know It Today** For whatever the reason, it was not until the late nineteenth century—little more than 100 years ago—that adolescence came to be viewed as it is today: a lengthy period of preparation for adulthood, in which young people, in need of guidance and supervision, remain economically dependent on their elders. This view started within the middle class—where parents had more to gain by keeping their children out of the labor force and educating them for a better adulthood—but it spread quickly throughout society. Because the workplace has continued to change in ways that make the future uncertain, the idea of adolescence

child protectionists Individuals who argued, early in the twentieth century, that adolescents needed to be kept out of the labor force in order to protect them from the hazards of the workplace.

as a distinctive period of preparation for adulthood has remained intact. Adolescence, as a transitional stage between childhood and adulthood, now exists in virtually all societies (Larson & Wilson, 2004).

FOOD FOR THOUGHT

In your view, is adolescence a social invention?

Although adolescence was invented during the late nineteenth century, it was not until the middle of the twentieth century that our present-day image of the teenager was created. An important contributor to this image were the mass media—magazines such as Seventeen *cultivated the picture of the happy-go-lucky teenager as a way of targeting advertisements toward an increasingly lucrative adolescent market.*

Two other modifications of the definition of adolescence also gave rise to new terminology and ideas. The first of these concerns the use of the term **teenager,** which was not employed until about 50 years ago. In contrast to adolescent, teenager suggests a more frivolous and lighthearted age, during which individuals concern themselves with such things as cars and cosmetics. An important social change that led to the development of the concept of teenager was the increased affluence and economic freedom enjoyed by American adolescents during the late 1940s and early 1950s (Fasick, 1994; Hine, 1999). Advertisers recognized that these young people represented an important consumer group and, with the help of the new publications such as *Seventeen* magazine, began cultivating the image of the happy-go-lucky teenager as a means of targeting ad campaigns toward the lucrative adolescent market (Greenberger & Steinberg, 1986). Interestingly, although the image of the American teenager—fun-loving, irresponsible, and independent—now appears all over the world, in some societies it is viewed favorably, while in others it is held up as an example of what adults do *not* want their children to become (Larson & Wilson, 2004).

A second term whose acceptance grew as a result of social change is **youth,** which was used long before "adolescent." But, prior to industrialization, youth had a vague, imprecise meaning and could refer to someone as young as 12 or as old as 24 (Modell & Goodman, 1990). Gradually, and during the 1960s in particular, the growth of the college population and the rise in student activism focused attention on individuals who were somewhere between adolescence and young adulthood—those in the 18- to 22-year-old range.

Many adults referred to the changes they saw in attitudes and values among college students as the "youth movement." One theorist went so far as to argue that youth is a separate stage in the life cycle, psychologically as well as chronologically distinct from adolescence and adulthood (Keniston, 1970). Indeed, many college students are unsure about whether they are adolescents or adults, since they may feel mature in some respects (for example, keeping up an apartment or being involved in a serious relationship) but immature in others (for example, having to depend on parents for economic support or having to have an advisor approve class schedules). Although it may strike you as odd to think of 22-year-olds as adolescents, the lengthening of formal schooling in contemporary society has altered the way we define adolescence, because the majority of young people continue their education past high school and are forced to delay their transition into many adult work and family roles (Furstenberg, 2000). By this definition, many 22-year-olds (and many individuals who are even older) are still not yet adults.

teenager   A term popularized about 50 years ago to refer to young people; it connoted a more frivolous and lighthearted image than did "adolescent."

youth   Today, a term used to refer to individuals ages 18–22; it once referred to individuals ages 12–24.

FOOD FOR THOUGHT

Historians agree that social conditions during the second half of the nineteenth century led to the creation of adolescence as we know it today. What changes in the nature of adolescence have taken place since that time? How might adolescence change in the twenty-first century?

EMERGING ADULTHOOD: A NEW STAGE OF LIFE OR A LUXURY OF THE MIDDLE CLASS?

The transition to adulthood has become so delayed in many industrialized societies that some have suggested that there is a new stage in life—emerging adulthood—that may last for some individuals until their mid-20s (Arnett, 2004). The main proponent of this idea has been psychologist Jeffrey Arnett, who contends that the period from ages 18 to 25 is neither adolescence nor adulthood, but a unique developmental period in its own right, characterized by five main features:

1. The exploration of possible identities before making enduring choices
2. Instability in work, romantic relationships, and living arrangements
3. A focus on oneself and, in particular, on functioning as an independent person
4. The subjective feeling of being between adolescence and adulthood
5. The subjective sense that life holds many possibilities

Is Emerging Adulthood Universal?   This profile certainly describes many young people in contemporary society, particularly those whose parents can foot the bill while their "emerging adults" are figuring out what they want to do with their lives. Exploring the limitless possibilities of one's life while figuring out who one is and where one is headed is an expensive proposition. As Arnett himself points out (2000), however, emerging adulthood does not exist in all cultures—in fact, it exists in very few (the United States, Canada, Australia, New Zealand, Japan, and the more affluent nations of western Europe). A recent study of Chinese college students, for instance, found that the majority feel they have reached adult status in their early 20s (Nelson, Badger, & Bo, 2004). And even within countries in which there are significant numbers of emerging adults, the majority of individuals cannot afford to delay the transition from adolescence into full-fledged adulthood for a half decade. Several recent analyses indicate that there is a great deal of variability among people in their mid-20s with respect to the dimensions of emerging adulthood. As one team of researchers put it, "It is a mistake to think that a sample of youth in their midtwenties are all emerging adults" (e.g., Shanahan, Porfeli, Mortimer, & Erickson, 2005, p. 251). According to one study of Michigan working- and middle-class youths in their mid-20s (Osgood, Ruth, Eccles, Jacobs, & Butler, 2005), for example, six distinct lifestyle patterns, each characterized by different degrees of commitment to adultlike work, romantic, and residential arrangements, were evident: fast starters (12 percent), parents without careers (10 percent), educated partners (19 percent), educated singles (37 percent), working singles (7 percent), and slow starters (14 percent) (see Figure 3.1). The group that most resembled emerging adults, the "educated singles," made up about 40 percent of the sample.

It is also important to note that the existence of emerging adulthood is not entirely an economic phenomenon. Many emerging adults live the way they do because the economy forces them to, but many simply do it by choice—that is, they want to take some time before assuming full adult responsibilities. As one recent analysis of patterns of marriage and residential arrangements indicates, the lifestyle associated with emerging adulthood—delaying marriage and parenthood, living alone or cohabiting, changing jobs frequently, and "finding" oneself—is more prevalent in some communities than in others. The researchers, using U.S. census data, looked at differences between states in patterns of marriage, household formation, and so forth (Lesthaeghe & Neidert, 2006). They found that in some states a substantial number of individuals appeared to be living the life of the quintessential emerging adult, but in other states this was not very common. The specific pattern was fascinating and suggests that the existence of emerging adulthood may have a lot to do with values and priorities. Young adults in states that voted for George W. Bush in 2004—states that are generally more conservative, politically and socially—were far less likely to follow the emerging-adulthood pattern, in contrast to young adults in states that voted for John Kerry. If you want to speak to an emerging adult in the United States, you are better off looking on either of the coasts than in the middle of the country!

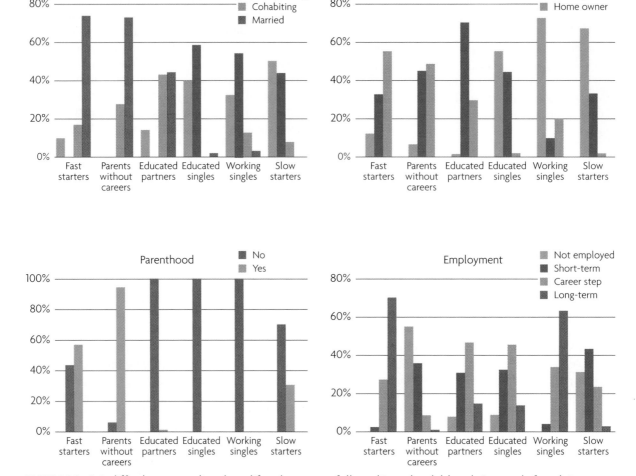

FIGURE 3.1   It is difficult to generalize about lifestyle patterns followed in early adulthood. One study found six distinct clusters who varied in their relationships, living arrangements, employment, and transition to parenthood. (Osgood et al., 2005)

FOOD FOR THOUGHT

What do you think of the concept of "emerging adulthood"? If it is a choice, rather than an inevitable consequence of economic change, why do you think some, but not all, people choose it?

▌ **Psychological Well-Being in Emerging Adulthood**   Very little research has examined psychological development and functioning during emerging adulthood. The profile described by Arnett suggests both a difficult time, characterized by floundering and financial instability, and a time of carefree optimism and independence. By all accounts, the second picture

seems to be more accurate than the first, at least among American and Canadian youth. Several studies show that the period is generally one of positive and improving mental health (see Figure 3.2), although, naturally, not all individuals show this pattern (Galambos, Barker, & Krahn, 2006; Kim, Capaldi, & Stoolmiller, 2003).

One recent study followed a national sample of American youths from age 18 to their mid-20s. The researchers compared four groups of individuals: (1) those who reported positive well-being across the entire interval, (2) those who reported negative well-being across the entire interval, (3) those whose well-being started low but increased, and (4) those whose well-being started high but decreased (Schulenberg, Bryant, & O'Malley, 2004). (There also was a large group whose well-being was average to begin with and

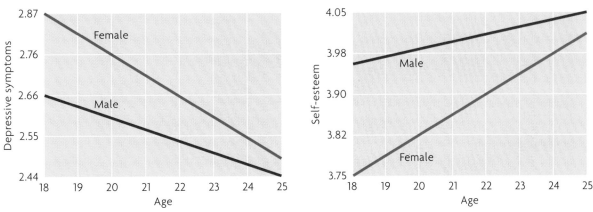

FIGURE 3.2 Early adulthood is a time of improved mental health, as indicated by decreases in depression and increases in self-esteem. (Galambos et at., 2006)

stayed that way.) They then looked to see whether these patterns of well-being over time were related to indicators of individual functioning, by rating whether individuals had been succeeding, maintaining, or stalling as they moved into adulthood (see Table 3.1). Three main findings emerged. First, over 80 percent of the sample showed great stability in their well-being over the period. This is consistent with findings from many other studies indicating that psychological functioning in childhood and adolescence is highly predictive of success later in life (e.g., Shanahan & Bauer, 2004). That is, success in one stage (doing well in high school) usually leads to success in the next stage (getting into a good college), and some fundamental "resources" predict success throughout the lifespan—it helps to have a high IQ, money, and good parents (e.g., Masten, Burt, & Roisman, 2004). Second, for more than a sixth of the sample, this period was one of substantial change in mental health—about 7 percent of the sample were well-functioning adolescents whose mental health declined, and another 10 percent were troubled adolescents who became "exemplary" young adults. Finally, experiences in the domains of work, romance, and citizenship—but not in the domains of school or finances—were especially linked to changes in well-being. Other studies have also found that success in the worlds of work and romance are related to well-being during this time (Galambos et al., 2006).

Has a new stage of life actually arisen? How widespread does a pattern of behavior have to be for us to conclude that a new stage of development has emerged? Does emerging adulthood exist if it is common in Boston or Berkeley, but not in Biloxi, Baghdad, or Beijing? It is hard to say. "Midlife" is a stage that we take for granted in contemporary America but that doesn't exist everywhere, or at least, not as we

think of it (Schweder, 1998). Nevertheless, the notion that individuals go through a distinct and unique set of psychological transitions during middle age has become widely accepted (if perhaps less supported by hard evidence than journalists and other writers in the popular media suggest).

Clearly, on average, in some parts of the world, and in some segments of society, the transition between adolescence and adulthood has been lengthened—that much is indisputable. More individuals attend college than in previous eras, which delays their entrance into the world of work, and more postpone getting married, which delays their settling into a more stable lifestyle. But whether this means that the psychological functioning of 23-year-olds who follow this pattern of a delayed and prolonged transition is significantly different from that of 23-year-olds who transition from college directly into full-time employment and marriage is anyone's guess, because it hasn't been studied. Whether a *psychological* stage of emerging adulthood really exists has yet to be established.

Note that when we say that adolescence (or the teenager, or youth, or emerging adulthood) is in part a social invention, we do not mean that its significance is in any way diminished or that it is somehow less real than if it were an entirely biological phenomenon. Democracy, after all, is a social invention, too, but its creation and development have had profound effects on the way that we live. As with other social inventions, the notion that there should be a distinct period of adolescence has endured over time and has had important and concrete repercussions. But as with other social constructs, the nature of adolescence changes over time, and it will continue to change as we revise our notions of what it means to grow from childhood into adulthood.

TABLE 3.1 Descriptions of developmental task domains

Domain	Succeeding	Maintaining	Stalling
Education	• Graduated from 4-year college by age 26, or • Expected to graduate from 2-year college and received 2-year degree	• Expected to graduate from 4-year college and received 2-year degree, or • Did not expect 2- or 4-year degree and did not receive either degree, or • Expected 2-year degree and did not receive 2-year degree by age 26	• Expected 4-year college degree and did not receive either 2- or 4-year degree by age 26
Work	• No unemployment at age 22 or 26, and • Working 10+ months/year at full-time job by age 26, and • High job confidence at age 26	• Neither succeeding nor stalling (e.g., homemaker or otherwise not working and not looking for work outside home)	• Some unemployment at age 22 and/or 26, and • Low job confidence at age 26
Financial autonomy	• Self and/or spouse providing all resources at age 26	• Some resources come from other than self or spouse (and not stalling)	• At age 26, less than half of support is from self and/or spouse, and/or • Live with parents and receive some financial help (>20%) from them
Romantic involvement	• At age 26, married or engaged (with or without cohabitation), and • No divorce history	• At age 26, cohabiting, or • Dating more than once a month, and/or • Divorced, but remarried	• At age 26, not married, not engaged not cohabiting, and • Dating once a month or less
Peer involvement	• Goes out two or more times a week for fun and recreation at age 22 and age 26	• Neither succeeding nor stalling	• Goes out one or fewer times a week for fun and recreation at age 22 and age 26
Substance abuse avoidance (healthy coping/life style)	Four indicators of substance use: cigarettes (current use), binge drinking (past 2 weeks), marijuana (current use) and other illicit drugs (12-month use): • No substance use at any age (18, 22, 26)	• Some substance use, but less than stalling	• Use of two or more substances at all three ages (18, 22, 26), and/or • Use of three or more substances at age 26
Citizenship	Three indicators reported at age 22 and age 26: social conscience, charity, and awareness of social/political events • Measures indicate at least one strong connection at age 22 and at least two strong connections at age 26	• Measures indicate some strong connections but not as frequent as at succeeding level	• Measures indicate no strong connections at age 26

Source: Schulenberg et al., 2004.

RECAP

- Inventionists argue that adolescence is more a social invention than a biological or cognitive phenomenon.
- Our conception of adolescence—whether it exists as a separate period and what its nature is—is determined largely by forces in the broader social environment. Changes in the broader environment, therefore, can change the very nature of adolescence.
- Adolescence as we know it today is largely a product of the Industrial Revolution of the late nineteenth century.
- Some writers have suggested that a new stage of life, called emerging adulthood, has arisen in recent years. Evidence for the existence of emerging adulthood as a widespread phenomenon is mixed.
- Although there is not a great deal of research on psychological development during the years immediately following adolescence, several studies indicate that for most people, especially those who successfully move into adult work and romantic roles, this is a time of increasing well-being and positive mental health.

Changes in Status

"The most casual survey of the ways in which different societies have handled adolescence makes one fact inescapable," wrote anthropologist Ruth Benedict in her classic work *Patterns of Culture.*

> Even in those cultures which have made the most of the trait, the age upon which they focus their attention varies over a great range of years. . . . The puberty they recognize is social, and the ceremonies are a recognition in some fashion or other of the

child's new status of adulthood. . . . In order to understand [adolescence]. . . we need . . . to know what is identified in different cultures with the beginning of adulthood and their methods of admitting to the new status. (Benedict, 1934, p. 25)

Changes in social definition at adolescence typically involve a two-sided modification in the individual's status. On the one hand, the adolescent is given certain privileges and rights that are typically reserved for the society's adult members. On the other hand, this increased power and freedom generally are accompanied by increased expectations for self-management, personal responsibility, and social participation.

We can find examples of this double shift in social status in all societies, across a variety of interpersonal, political, economic, and legal arenas (see Table 3.2)

CHANGES IN INTERPERSONAL STATUS

In many societies, individuals who have been recognized as adults are usually addressed with adult titles. They also are expected to maintain different sorts of social relationships with their parents, with the community's elders, and with young people whose status has not yet changed. On holidays such as Thanksgiving, for example, some large families set two tables: a big table for the adults and a smaller, children's table. When a young person is permitted to sit at the big table, it is a sign that he or she has reached a new position in the family. These interpersonal changes are typically accompanied by new interpersonal obligations—for example, being expected to take care of and set a proper example for the younger members of the family.

CHANGES IN POLITICAL STATUS

With the attainment of adult status, the young person is often permitted more extensive participation in the community's decision making. Among the Navaho, for example, it is only following a formal

TABLE 3.2 Some consequences of attaining adult status

	In Traditional Societies	In Contemporary Societies
Interpersonal	Addressed with adult title by other members of community	Permitted to sit with grown-ups for special occasions
Political	Permitted to participate in community decision making	Eligible to vote
Economic	Permitted to own property	Permitted to work
Legal	Permitted to consume certain foods	No longer dealt with in separate juvenile justice system

initiation ceremony that adolescents are considered members of the Navaho People and are permitted full participation in ceremonial life (Cohen, 1964). In contemporary America, attaining the age of majority brings the right to vote. But along with this increased power usually come new obligations. In most societies, young adults are expected to serve their communities in cases of emergency or need, and in many cultures, training for warfare is often demanded of young people once they attain adult status (Benedict, 1934).

CHANGES IN ECONOMIC STATUS

Attaining adult status also has important economic implications that again entail obligation as well as privilege. In some societies, only adults may own property and maintain control over their income (N. Miller, 1928). In many American states, for example, any income that a youngster earns before the age of 16 is technically the property of the young person's parents. (This may come as a surprise to many working teenagers.) Before adulthood, individuals are not permitted to enter into contracts, and a contract signed by someone younger than 18—such as a lease or a car loan—is not legally enforceable (Scott & Woolard, 2004).

Entrance into certain work roles is also restricted to adults. Among the Tikopia (Melanesia), one of the first privileges accorded boys when they reach adolescence is accompanying older males on fishing expeditions (Fried & Fried, 1980). In most industrialized societies, employment is regulated by child labor laws, and the attainment of a prescribed age is a prerequisite to employment in certain occupations. In most societies, once they have attained the economic status and rights of adults, young people are expected to contribute to the economic well-being of their community—to participate in the community's productive activities and to carry out the labor expected of adults. In contemporary society, the young adult's economic responsibilities to

the broader community may entail having to pay taxes for the first time. In some families, adolescents who are permitted to work must contribute to their family's support.

CHANGES IN LEGAL STATUS

In most societies, not until adult status is attained is the young person permitted to participate in a variety of activities that are typically reserved for adults. Gambling, purchasing alcoholic beverages, and seeing X-rated films are but three of the many privileges we reserve in America for individuals who have reached the legal age of adulthood. In many cultures, the eating of certain foods is restricted to individuals who have been admitted to adult society (Mead, 1928).

Once an adolescent is designated as an adult, however, she or he is also subject to a new set of laws and will be treated differently by the legal institutions of the society than would be a child. In some instances, attaining adult status brings with it more lenient treatment under the law, whereas in others, it may be associated with harsher treatment. In the United States, for example, certain activities that are permissible among adults, such as not showing up for school (truancy) or leaving one's home without informing others (running away), are considered offenses when they are committed by young people. (Indeed, we use the term **status offense** to refer to a behavior that is problematic because of the young person's *status* as a juvenile.) As a college student, you cannot be legally punished for not showing up for class, as would have been the case when you were in high school, and if you decide you don't want to return home when you are on a break, you don't have to, at least not as far as the law is concerned. Certain crimes, when committed by a minor, are adjudicated in a separate **juvenile justice system,** which operates under different rules and principles than the **criminal justice system** that applies to adults. Although being tried in the juvenile justice system usually results in a less severe sanction than being found guilty of the same crime in adult court, this, interestingly, is not always the case (Kurlychek & Johnson, 2004).

The legal regulation of adolescent behavior in the United States has been quite controversial in recent years. Part of the problem is that development during adolescence is so rapid and so variable between individuals that it is difficult to know at what chronological age a line should be drawn between legally viewing someone as an adult versus viewing him or her as a child (Scott & Woolard, 2004; Steinberg & Cauffman, 1996; Steinberg & Scott, 2003). This problem is compounded by the fact that we draw the boundary at different places for different purposes (for example,

initiation ceremony   The formal induction of a young person into adulthood.

status offense   A violation of the law that pertains to minors but not adults.

juvenile justice system   A separate system of courts and related institutions developed to handle juvenile crime and delinquency.

criminal justice system   The system of courts and related institutions developed to handle adult crime.

driving at 16, voting at 18, buying alcohol at 21, and so on). This inconsistency makes it hard to point to any specific age and say with certainty that there is consensus about where the legal boundary should be drawn.

FOOD FOR THOUGHT

At what age do you think we should draw the line between legal adolescence and legal adulthood? Should this age be the same for all activities, or should different activities have different age boundaries?

█ **Adolescents as Criminal Defendants** There is especially great disagreement about how we should view and treat young people who commit serious violent offenses (Fagan & Zimring, 2000; Grisso & Schwartz, 2000). Should juveniles who commit crimes be viewed as less blameworthy than adults because they are less able to foresee the consequences of their actions or resist the pressure of others to engage in antisocial activity? Or should we hold adolescents and adults to the same standards of criminal responsibility? If a youngster has committed a violent crime, should he or she be treated as a child (and processed as a delinquent) or tried as an adult (and processed as a criminal)? Should young teenagers and adults who are convicted of the same crime receive the same penalties? As noted in the Introduction to this book, in 2005, the U.S. Supreme Court raised the age at which individuals can be exposed to the death penalty from 16 to 18 (*Roper v. Simmons*, 2005).

One issue that arises in cases in which a juvenile might be tried as an adult is whether the adolescent is competent to stand trial. In the United States, it is not permissible to try someone in a criminal proceeding if the individual does not understand the charges against him or her, does not understand the nature of the trial, or is unable to make reasoned decisions about the case (for example, whether to take the stand in his or her own defense). Historically, questions about a defendant's competence to stand trial have only been raised in cases in which the individual is mentally ill or mentally retarded. Now that more and more juveniles are being tried as adults at younger and younger ages, however, experts have asked whether some young defendants may be incompetent to stand trial simply because of cognitive or emotional immaturity. One recent study of this issue examined the competence to stand trial of a large

During the mid-1990s, many states changed their laws to permit adolescents accused of violent crimes to be tried as adults.

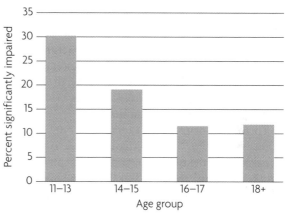

FIGURE 3.3 Significant numbers of juveniles under the age of 16 may not be competent to stand trial as adults. Shown are the proportions of individuals at different ages whose trial competence is as impaired as mentally ill adults who have been found incompetent. (Grisso et al., 2003)

sample of individuals between the ages of 11 and 24 (Grisso et al., 2003). The researchers found that about one-third of those ages 13 and younger, and one-fifth of 14- and 15-year-olds, were as impaired in their abilities to serve as a competent defendant as were mentally ill adults who had been found not competent to stand trial (see Figure 3.3). This study suggests that courts should not assume that younger adolescents, even those who are not mentally ill or retarded, are necessarily competent to be tried as adults, and that juveniles' competence to stand trial should be evaluated before their cases can be heard in adult court. Research also indicates that juveniles are less likely than adults to understand their rights when being questioned by the police, more likely to confess to a crime than remain silent, and less likely to discuss disagreements with their attorneys (Redlich, Silverman, & Steiner, 2003; Viljoen, Klaver, & Roesch, 2005).

Inconsistencies in Adolescents' Legal Status

Many other issues surrounding the legal status of adolescents in the United States remain vague and confusing. Two U.S. Supreme Court cases indicate just how inconsistent our views of adolescents' status are (Moshman, 1993). In one case, *Hazelwood v. Kuhlmeier*, the Court ruled that a public high school can censor articles written by students for their school newspaper, on the grounds that adolescents are so "immature" that they need the protection of "wiser" adults. Yet the same Court also ruled, in *Board of Education v. Mergens*, that students who wanted to form a Bible study group had the right to meet on campus because high school students are "mature" enough to understand that a school can permit the expression of ideas that it does not necessarily endorse. Similarly, in *Hodgson v. Minnesota*, the Court ruled that, because of their maturity, adolescents do not need to obtain parental consent to get an abortion. Yet the Court also ruled, in *Roper v. Simmons*, that adolescents should not be subject to the death penalty, because their immaturity makes them less responsible for their criminal behavior (and therefore less "punishable").

There are many other examples of this sort of inconsistency. For example, courts have ruled that teenagers have the right to obtain contraceptives without their parents' approval. But they also have upheld laws forbidding adolescents access to cigarettes or to magazines that, although vulgar, are not considered so obscene that they were outlawed among adults (Zimring, 1982). As you know, the age at which adolescents are permitted to engage in various adult behaviors—driving, voting, drinking, viewing R-rated movies, smoking—varies considerably from one domain to the next. Is there a pattern to this inconsistency? In general, legal decisions tend to set the age boundary high, in order to restrict the behavior of adolescents when the behavior in question is viewed as potentially damaging to the young person (for example, buying cigarettes), but have supported the concept of adolescent autonomy

and set the age boundary low when the behavior is viewed as having potential benefit (for example, having access to contraceptives).

RECAP

- Changes in the individual's social definition at adolescence typically revolve around changes in status in four domains: interpersonal, political, economic, and legal. In each of these domains, individuals are given greater privileges but are expected to take increased responsibility for self-management and participation in adult society.
- In contemporary society, there is great inconsistency in where we draw age boundaries between childhood and adulthood. Different ages are used for different purposes.
- An especially controversial issue concerns whether juveniles who commit serious crimes should be treated as children or tried as adults.

The Process of Social Redefinition

Social redefinition during adolescence is not a single event but, like puberty or cognitive maturation, is a series of events that often occur over a relatively long time. In contemporary America, the process of redefinition typically begins at age 15 or 16, when the young person is first permitted to drive, to work, and to leave school. But in most states, the social redefinition of the adolescent continues well into the young-adult years. Some privileges of adulthood, such as voting, are not conferred until the age of 18, and others, such as purchasing alcoholic beverages, are not conferred until the age of 21, five or six years after the redefinition process begins. Even in societies that mark the social redefinition of the young person with a dramatic and elaborate initiation ceremony, or rite of passage, the social transformation of the individual from child into adult may span many years, and the initiation ceremony may represent just one element of the transition (Markstrom & Iborra, 2003). In fact, the initiation ceremony usually marks the beginning of a long period of training and preparation for adulthood, and not the adolescent's final passage into adult status (Cohen, 1964).

In many cultures, the social redefinition of young people occurs in groups. That is, the young people of a community are grouped with peers of approximately the same age—a **cohort**—and move through the series

cohort   A group of individuals born during the same general historical era.

of status transitions together. One of the results of such age-grouped social transitions is that very strong bonds are formed among youngsters who have shared certain rituals. In many American high schools, for example, attempts are made to create class spirit or class unity by fostering bonds among students who will be graduated together. In many Latino communities, adolescent girls participate together in an elaborate sort of "coming-out" celebration, called the **quinceañera.** On college campuses, fraternities and sororities may conduct group initiations that involve difficult or unpleasant tasks, and special ties may be forged between "brothers" or "sisters" who have pledged together.

The Navaho initiation ceremony for females, called Kinaaldá, provides a nice illustration of a coming-of-age ritual and the importance of this type of ceremony for social redefinition (Markstrom & Iborra, 2003). From an early age, Navaho girls are taught about Kinaaldá and its significance. The ceremony, which lasts four days, takes place during the adolescent girl's first or second menstrual period, during which time her powers are thought to be greatest. Although menarche is the main external sign of the girl's readiness to be initiated, the Navaho also believe that there is an advance in logical thinking just before puberty that enables her to take on the adult responsibilities for which she is being prepared. The girl is separated from her family and community, and assigned a mentor—called Ideal Woman—who massages every part of the girl's body and oversees the girl's purification (by washing her hair and jewelry) and physical transformation (by painting her with white clay). She is dressed and painted to resemble a figure called Changing Woman. During the four days, the girl is expected to perform certain physical feats, including grinding corn; running several times each day, often for long distances; and taking part in an all-night sing. In the final stages of the ceremony, the girl serves a corn cake, made from the corn she has ground (which symbolizes her new fertility and signifies her understanding of the role of women in providing sustenance for others) and is given a new name (to signify her new status as an adult).

COMMON PRACTICES IN THE PROCESS OF SOCIAL REDEFINITION

Although the specific ceremonies, signs, and timetables of social redefinition during adolescence vary from one culture to another, several general themes,

In many nonindustrialized societies, a formal initiation ceremony is used to mark the beginning and end of adolescence.

evident in the Navaho initiation ceremony just described, characterize the process in all societies.

■ Real or Symbolic Separation from Parents
First, social redefinition usually entails the real or symbolic separation of young persons from their parents. In traditional societies, this may take the form of a practice known as **extrusion:** During late childhood, children are expected to begin sleeping in households other than their own. Youngsters may spend the day with their parents but spend the night with friends of the family, with relatives, or in a separate residence reserved for preadolescents (Cohen, 1964). In America, during earlier times, it was customary for adolescents to leave home temporarily and live with other families in the community, either to learn specific occupational skills (as apprentices) or to work as domestic servants (Kett, 1977). Interestingly, the "placing out" of adolescents from their parents' home often coincided with puberty (which, as you now know, occurred at a much later age at this time in history) (Katz, 1975). In contemporary societies, the separation of adolescents from their parents takes somewhat different forms. They are sent to summer camps, to boarding schools, or, as is more common, to college.

quinceañera   An elaborate sort of "coming-out" celebration for adolescent girls that is practiced in many Latino communities.

extrusion   The practice of separating children from their parents and requiring them to sleep in other households, part of the process of social redefinition at adolescence in many societies.

Formal rites of passage from childhood into adolescence, or from adolescence into adulthood, are rare in contemporary industrialized societies. Certain religious ceremonies, such as the Bar Mitzvah (pictured here) or confirmation, are as close as we come to initiation rites in today's society.

■ **An Emphasis on Differences Between the Sexes** A second aspect of social redefinition during adolescence entails the accentuation of physical and social differences between males and females (Ford & Beach, 1951; Schlegel & Barry, 1991). This accentuation of differences occurs partly because of the physical changes of puberty and partly because adult work and family roles are generally highly sex-differentiated. Many societies separate males and females during religious ceremonies, have individuals begin wearing sex-specific articles of clothing (rather than clothing permissible for either gender), and keep males and females apart during initiation ceremonies. Some traditional societies employ a practice known as **brother–sister avoidance:** After puberty, a brother and sister may not have any direct contact or interaction until one or both are married (Cohen, 1964).

Still, in many non-Western societies today, the privileges extended to males and females once they have reached puberty are so different that adolescence often is an entirely different phenomenon for boys and girls (Larson & Wilson, 2004). Examples of the differential

treatment of adolescent boys and girls in non-Western cultures abound, but in general, girls' behavior is more subject to the control of adults, whereas boys are given more freedom and autonomy. Girls are expected to remain virgins until marriage, for example, whereas boys' premarital sexual activity is tolerated. Girls are expected to spend time preparing for domestic roles, whereas boys are expected to acquire vocational skills for employment outside the home. And formal schooling is far less available to girls than to boys, especially in rural societies.

The separation of males and females in adolescence is not limited to non-Western societies. In earlier times in America (and to a certain extent in many other industrialized societies today), during adolescence, males and females were separated in educational institutions, either by excluding adolescent girls from secondary and higher education, grouping males and females in different schools or different classrooms, or having males and females follow different curricula. In present-day America, many of these practices have been discontinued because of legal rulings prohibiting sex discrimination, but some elements of accentuated sex differentiation and sex segregation during adolescence still exist—for example, in residential arrangements, styles of dress, athletic activities, and household chores (Hill & Lynch, 1983; Medrich, Roizen, Rubin, & Buckley, 1982; White & Brinkerhoff, 1981). And many contemporary ceremonies designed to recognize the young person's passage into adulthood are either limited to one sex or the other (for example, debutante balls or the quinceañera, each of which is for young women) or somehow differentiate between males and females (for example, the **Bar Mitzvah** and the **Bas Mitzvah** ceremonies for Jewish males and females, respectively).

FOOD FOR THOUGHT

Social redefinition in contemporary society is often so familiar that we overlook it. Can you think of examples of social definition practices within your personal experience that parallel practices in more traditional cultures?

brother–sister avoidance The avoidance of any contact or interaction between brothers and sisters from the onset of puberty until one or both persons are married, part of the process of social redefinition at adolescence in many societies.

Bar (Bas) Mitzvah In Judaism, the religious ceremony marking the young person's transition to adulthood.

■ **The Passing on of Information from the Older Generation** A third aspect of social redefinition during adolescence typically entails the passing on of cultural, historical, and practical information from the adult generation to the newly inducted cohort of young people. This information may concern (1) matters thought to be important to adults but of limited utility to children (for example, information about the performance of certain adult work tasks), (2) matters thought to be necessary for adults but unfit for children (for example, information regarding sex), or (3) matters concerning the history or rituals of the family or community (for example, how to perform certain ceremonies). In traditional societies, initiates are often sent to some sort of "school" in which they are instructed in the productive activities of the community (hunting, fishing, or farming). Following puberty, boys and girls receive instruction about sexual relations, moral behavior, and societal lore (Fried & Fried, 1980; N. Miller, 1928).

In contemporary society, too, adolescence is a time of instruction in preparation for adulthood. Elementary school students, for example, are generally not taught a great deal about sexuality, work, or financial matters; such course work is typically reserved for high school students. We also restrict entrance into certain "adult" activities (such as sexually explicit movies) until adolescents are believed old enough to be exposed to them.

Because formal initiation ceremonies are neither very common nor very meaningful in modern society, students sometimes overlook important similarities between the processes of social redefinition in traditional and contemporary societies. Practices like extrusion, brother–sister avoidance, and **scarification**—the intentional creation of scars on some part or parts of the body, often done as part of an initiation ceremony—may seem alien to us. But if we look beneath the surface, at the meaning and significance of each culture's practices, we find many common threads. In contemporary society, for example, our own form of brother–sister avoidance begins at puberty: Once adolescents have reached puberty, brothers and sisters are much more likely to seek privacy from each other when dressing or bathing. And while we do not practice anything as "alien" as scarification, we do have our share of body rituals which often are not seen until adolescence and which might seem equally alien to someone unfamiliar with our society: the punching of holes in earlobes or other parts of the body (ear or body piercing), the scraping of hair from faces or legs (shaving), the permanent decoration of skin (tattoos), and the application of brightly colored paints to lips, eyes, and cheeks (putting on makeup).

RECAP

- Certain themes are common to the process of social redefinition across many societies. These include the real or symbolic separation of young people from their parents, the accentuation of differences between males and females, and the

passing on of cultural, historical, or practical information deemed important for adulthood.
- Although these themes are more explicit in the formal initiation ceremonies practiced in traditional societies, they are evident in the process through which individuals are redefined in contemporary industrialized society as well.

Variations in Social Transitions

Different societies recognize and orchestrate the passage into adult status at different times and in different ways. In this respect, although the presence of social redefinition in a general sense is a universal feature of adolescent development, there is considerable diversity in the nature of the transition. Examining social redefinition from cross-cultural and historical perspectives provides a valuable means of contrasting the nature of adolescence in different social contexts. Two very important dimensions along which societies differ in the process of social redefinition are in the explicitness, or clarity, of the transition and in the smoothness, or continuity, of the passage.

VARIATIONS IN CLARITY

Initiation ceremonies are in many ways religious ceremonies. As such, they are most often employed in societies in which a shared religious belief unites the community and structures individuals' daily experiences. Universal, formal initiation ceremonies therefore have never been prevalent in American society, largely because of the cultural diversity of the population and the general separation of religious experience from everyday affairs.

There are, however, factors other than the presence of formal rites of passage that determine how clear the transition into adult status is to young persons and to society. One such factor concerns the extent to which various aspects of the status change occur at about the same time for individuals and during the same general period for adolescents growing up together (Elder, 1980). When transitions into adult work, family, and citizenship roles occur close in time, and when most members of a cohort experience these transitions at

scarification The intentional creation of scars on some part or parts of the body, often done as part of an initiation ceremony.

about the same age, the passage into adulthood takes on greater clarity. If all young people were to graduate from high school, enter the labor force, and marry at the age of 18, this age would be an implicit boundary between adolescence and adulthood, even without a formal ceremony. But when different aspects of the passage occur at different times, and when adolescents growing up in a similar environment experience these transitions in different order and along different schedules, the boundary between adolescence and adulthood becomes cloudier.

■ **The Clarity of Social Redefinition in Contemporary Society** When did you become an adolescent? When did you (or when will you) become an adult? If you are like most individuals in contemporary society, your answers to these questions will not be clear-cut. One study, for example, found that, when asked, "Do you feel that you have reached adulthood?" nearly half of all 12- to 17-year-olds and nearly three-fifths of 18- to 25-year-olds answered, "Yes and no" (Arnett, 2000). We have no formal ceremonies marking the transition from childhood into adolescence, nor do we have any way to mark the passage from adolescence into adulthood. Although in many religious, cultural, and social groups, the young American adolescent may undergo an initiation ceremony of sorts—the confirmation, the Bar or Bas Mitzvah, the quinceañera, and the coming-out parties of debutantes are some examples—rarely does such a rite have much significance outside the youngster's family, circle of friends, or religious community. School graduation ceremonies perhaps come the closest to universal rites of passage in contemporary society, but school graduation does not bring with it many meaningful or universal changes in social status, responsibilities, or privileges. As a result, social redefinition in contemporary society does not give adolescents any clear indication of when their responsibilities and privileges as an adult begin. As we noted earlier, laws governing the age at which individuals can and cannot do "adult" activities are inconsistent. In many states, for example, the age for starting employment is 15; for driving, 16; for attending restricted (R-rated) movies without parents, 17; for voting, 18; and for drinking, 21. In some states, the age at which someone can be tried as an adult for a serious violent crime is as low as 10 (Hartney, 2006).

In short, we have few universal markers of adulthood—adolescents are treated as adults at different times by different people in different contexts. A young person may be legally old enough to drive, but his parents may feel that 16 is too early and may refuse to let him use the family car. Another may be treated like an adult at work, where she works side by side with people three times her age, but be treated like a child at home. A third may be viewed as an adult by her mother but as a child by her father. It is little wonder, in light of the mixed and sometimes contradictory expectations facing young people, that for many adolescents the transition into adult roles is a difficult passage to navigate. In the middle of the twentieth century, social psychologist Kurt Lewin (1948) introduced the term **marginal man** to describe the adolescent's position in society—caught in a transitional space between childhood and adulthood. Many commentators believe that adolescents continue to be marginalized today.

■ **Adolescents' Views of Themselves** Because contemporary society does not send clear or consistent messages to young people about when adolescence ends and adulthood begins, young people living within the same society can have widely varying views of their own social status and beliefs about age-appropriate behavior (Arnett, 1994; Nurmi, 1993). For this reason, it is instructive to ask people what they think defines the transition to adulthood, as a way of gauging the way in which adult status is conceptualized by the broader society. Psychologist Jeffrey Arnett has examined conceptions of adulthood in contemporary North America and has contrasted them with the ways in which adult status has been viewed in other cultures and at other points in time (Arnett, 1998). His analysis points to three interesting trends.

First, in modern industrialized society, adolescents place relatively less of an emphasis than is the case in traditional societies on the attainment of specific roles (for example, worker, spouse, parent) as defining characteristics of adulthood and relatively more emphasis on the development of various character traits indicative of self-reliance (for example, responsible, independent, self-controlled). Consistent with this, in one recent study of individuals ages 17–29, the best predictor of subjective age—that is, what age they *felt* they were, regardless of how old they actually were—was their level of psychosocial maturity (Galambos, Turner, & Tilton-Weaver, 2005). Among contemporary American youths, for instance, "accepting responsibility for one's self" is the most frequently mentioned criterion for being an adult; among Inuit adolescents in the Canadian Arctic, the most important is the establishment of a marriagelike relationship by moving into a separate household with a prospective mate. Of the role-related transitions viewed as important among contemporary youth, being able to support oneself financially was the most important defining criterion

marginal man Lewin's term that refers to the transitional nature of adolescence—poised on the margin of adulthood.

of adulthood (Arnett, 1998). Perhaps for this reason, less than one-third of college undergraduates see themselves unambiguously as adults. Interestingly, indicators of entering into adultlike roles of romantic partner and worker at age 20—basically, successfully holding down a job and being involved in an emotionally close romantic relationship—are not especially good predictors of later adult competence, according to a longitudinal study that tracked individuals from age 20 to age 30 (Roisman, Masten, Coatsworth, & Tellegen, 2004). Far better predictors of later adult success were more "adolescent" indicators of competence—doing well in school, having an active social life, and staying out of trouble.

Second, over time, there has been a striking decline in the importance of family roles—marriage and parenthood—as defining features of the transition from adolescence to adulthood. In early American society, for example, the role of head of household was an especially important indicator of adult status for males, and entering the roles of wife and mother defined adulthood for females. In contrast, in Arnett's surveys of contemporary youth, in which he asked whether certain accomplishments were necessary for an individual to be considered an adult, only 17 percent of the respondents indicated that being married was necessary, and only 14 percent indicated that it was necessary to become a parent (Arnett, 1998).

Finally, the defining criteria of adulthood have become more or less the same for males and females in contemporary industrialized society, unlike the case in traditional societies or during previous eras. In nonindustrialized cultures, the requirements for male adulthood were to be able to "provide, protect, and procreate," whereas for females, the requirements for adulthood were to care for children and run a household. Contemporary youth, in contrast, view the various indicators of adult status as equally important (or equally unimportant) for males and females (Arnett, 1998).

Given the absence of clear criteria that define adult status in contemporary North America, it is not surprising that, among people of the same age, some may feel older than their chronological age-mates, while others might feel younger. How old an adolescent feels affects his or her behavior, with adolescents who feel older spending more time with opposite-sex peers, feeling more autonomous, spending more time with antisocial peers, and engaging in more problem behavior (Galambos, Kolaric, Sears, & Maggs, 1999). Psychologist Nancy Galambos has been interested in changes in individuals' subjective age and, more specifically, in when individuals make the transition from feeling older than they really are (as most teenagers do), to feeling younger than they really are

(as most adults do) (Galambos et al., 2005). In her research on Canadian youth, Galambos found that this shift takes place around age 25, for both males and females.

■ **The Clarity of Social Redefinition in Traditional Cultures** Unlike the case in contemporary society, social redefinition during adolescence is clearly recognized in most traditional cultures. Typically, the passage from childhood into adolescence is marked by a formal initiation ceremony, which publicly proclaims the young person's assumption of a new position in the community (Ford & Beach, 1951). For boys, such ceremonies may take place at puberty, at a designated chronological age, or at a time when the community decides that the individual is ready for the status change. For girls, initiation is more often linked to puberty and, in particular, to the onset of menstruation. In both cases, the initiation ceremony serves to ritualize the passing of the young person out of childhood and, if not directly into adulthood, into a period of training for it.

In many initiation ceremonies, the adolescent's physical appearance is changed, so that other members of the community can distinguish between initiated and uninitiated young people. For example, new types of clothing may be worn following initiation, or some sort of surgical operation or scarification may be performed to create a permanent means of marking the individual's adult status. Unlike the case in contemporary society, where we one often can't tell who is a juvenile and who is an adult by physical appearance alone, in most traditional societies, there is no mistaking which individuals are adults and which are still children. We have grown accustomed to seeing teenagers who try to dress like adults, and adults who try to dress like teenagers, but such a state of affairs would be highly uncommon in traditional cultures.

■ **The Circumcision Controversy** One practice involving the physical transformation of the adolescent that has generated a great deal of controversy is circumcision. **Circumcision** is a procedure in which some part of the genitals is cut and permanently altered. There are important differences between male and female circumcision. In the United States, male circumcision, in which the foreskin around the penis is removed during infancy, is very common and is performed both for religious reasons (mainly among Jews) and for health reasons, because male circumcision is associated with decreased risk of urinary tract infections and sexually transmitted diseases, including HIV infection. There is

circumcision A procedure in which some part of the genitals is cut and permanently altered.

no evidence that men are harmed emotionally by being circumcised, and complications from the procedure are minimal and far fewer than the health risks associated with not being circumcised (Schoen, Wiswell, & Moses, 2000).

Female circumcision, which involves the cutting or removal of the clitoris, and often, the labia, is rarely practiced outside of North Africa (where, in some countries, such as Mali, Somalia, and Egypt, virtually all women have been circumcised, usually during childhood or preadolescence). Unlike male circumcision, female circumcision—some have called it "genital mutilation"—has no associated health benefits and carries many risks, including infection and chronic pain during urination, menstruation, and sexual intercourse. After circumcision, it is virtually impossible for a woman to achieve an orgasm during sex (Althaus, 1997). Many international groups, citing female circumcision as a human rights violation, have called for a worldwide prohibition against the practice.

▍ The Clarity of Social Redefinition in Previous Eras
Two old friends meet on the street. The first one asks, "How's your wife?" The second one replies, "Compared to what?"

What is the transition to adulthood like today? Well, compared to what? We often use the **baby boom** generation—individuals who were adolescents in the late 1950s and 1960s—as an implicit point of comparison when characterizing today's young people, perhaps because the baby boom generation has provided the basis for so many of the images of modern family life that are deeply embedded in our cultural psyche. (How often have you heard someone use the television show *Leave It to Beaver*, which ran from 1957 to 1963, as a comparison point in discussions of family life?) But the baby boomers' transition to adulthood was highly unusual in many respects. Let's look at life in 1960, during the middle of *Leave It to Beaver*'s run on television, as an example:

- In 1960, the average age of marriage was 20 for women and 22 for men; today, it is 26 and 27, respectively (U.S. Bureau of the Census, 2006).
- In 1960, about 20 percent of 22-year-old women and about 30 percent of 22-year-old men lived with their parents; in 2000, the figures were 35 percent and 40 percent.
- In 1960, a very high proportion of adolescents went directly from high school into the military or full-time employment, and only one-third of

American high school graduates went directly to college; today, close to two-thirds do so.

In other words, in 1960, three key elements of the transition to adulthood—finishing school, moving out of the parents' home, and getting married—all occurred relatively early, and all took place within a fairly constricted time frame. By that standard, today's transition to adulthood looks excessively long and vaguely defined. Indeed, one recent study of patterns of schooling, work, romance, and residence during emerging adulthood found that individuals frequently move back and forth between periods of independence and dependence. This suggests that the progression from adolescence to adulthood today not only is long but occurs in fits and starts (Cohen, Chen, Hartmark, & Gordon, 2003). It's little wonder that 60 percent of people in their mid-20s today don't know if they are adolescents or adults.

Compared to the situation 50 years ago, then, today's transition to adulthood is long and rocky. But the transition into adulthood was just as disorderly and prolonged during the nineteenth century. According to historian Joseph Kett (1977), many young people at that time moved back and forth between school, where they were viewed as children, and work, where they were viewed as adults. Moreover, timetables for the assumption of adult roles varied considerably from one individual to the next, because they were highly dependent on family and household needs rather than on generally accepted age patterns of school, family, and work transitions. An adolescent might have been working and living away from home, but if his family needed him—because, let's say, someone became ill—he would leave his job and move back in with his parents. During the middle of the nineteenth century, in fact, many young people were neither enrolled in school nor working, occupying a halfway stage that was not quite childhood but not quite adulthood (Katz, 1975). And age at first marriage was just about the same among males at the turn of the twentieth century as it is today (age at first marriage among females actually is much older today than it was a century ago) (U.S. Bureau of the Census, 2006). Although the notion of "emerging adulthood" may ring true today, it is by no means a new phenomenon. At least in industrialized societies, the brief and clear transition into adulthood experienced by many baby boomers in the mid-twentieth century was the exception, not the rule. It's important not to lose sight of that.

VARIATIONS IN CONTINUITY

The well-known anthropologist Ruth Benedict (1934), after surveying many different societies, pointed out that a second way in which the process of social

---

baby boom   The period following World War II, during which the number of infants born was extremely large.

redefinition varies across cultural and historical contexts is along the dimension of *continuity*—the extent to which the adolescent's transition into adulthood is gradual or abrupt. Gradual transitions, in which the adolescent assumes the roles and status of adulthood bit by bit, are referred to as **continuous transitions.** Transitions that are not so smooth, in which the young person's entrance into adulthood is more sudden, are referred to as **discontinuous transitions.** For example, children who grow up working on the family farm and continue this work as adults have a continuous transition into adult work roles. In contrast, children who do not have any work experience while they are growing up and who enter the labor force for the first time when they graduate from college have a discontinuous transition into adult work roles.

The Continuity of the Adolescent Passage in Contemporary Society

In contemporary society, we tend to exclude young people from the world of adults; we give them little direct training for adult life and then thrust them rather abruptly into total adult independence. Transitions into adulthood in contemporary society are therefore more discontinuous than in other cultural or historical contexts. Consider, for example, three of the most important roles of adulthood that individuals are expected to carry out successfully—the roles of worker, parent, and citizen. In all three cases, we find that adolescents in contemporary society receive little preparation for these positions.

For instance, young people are segregated from the workplace throughout most of their childhood and early adolescent years, and they receive little direct training in school relevant to the work roles they will likely find themselves in as adults. As you will read in Chapter 7, the sorts of jobs available to teenagers today, such as working the counter of a fast-food restaurant, bear little resemblance to the jobs they will hold as adults. The transition into adult work roles, therefore, is fairly discontinuous for most young people in industrialized society, and, according to many employers, a high proportion of young people leave school without adequate preparation for the workplace.

All modern societies face the challenge of helping young people move from the world of school into the world of work, but societies vary in how they approach this issue (Shanahan, Mortimer, & Krueger, 2002). Numerous writers (e.g., Kazis, 1993; Rosenbaum et al., 1992; Stern, Finkelstein, Stone, Latting, & Dornsife, 1994) have argued that many individuals have difficulty making this transition successfully because only one acceptable way of making this passage actually exists—through higher education—and

not all individuals can, or want to, make the transition via this route. Studies have found, for example, that most high school counselors steer all students toward college, regardless of their interests or plans (Krei & Rosenbaum, 2001). As you will read in Chapter 6, this is one reason that many American students enroll in college but drop out before obtaining their degree.

Is it possible to create a route from high school to adult work that doesn't involve college? Many critics of the American educational system say that there is. They point out that in other industrialized countries high school students have many options other than going to college, including, most importantly, taking a formal **youth apprenticeship;** this provides structured, work-based learning that will likely lead to a high-quality job. Typically, a high school student combines time in an apprenticeship with time in school as he or she gradually makes the transition from school to work. Among the most successful models of youth apprenticeships are those developed in Germany, in which young people during their last few years of high school can spend one or two days per week in school and the remainder of the week at a job supervised by master workers (Hamilton & Hamilton, 2004). Unlike American high school students, who have difficulty finding good jobs after graduation, German graduates who complete a youth apprenticeship program usually enter a high-quality job within a few days of finishing school (Rosenbaum et al., 1992). Although some writers have questioned whether the German model can be directly copied in the United States, there is hope that some version of an apprenticeship system can be developed. At the very least, some critics have argued that, for many young people in the United States, high school as it now exists lasts far too long (Botstein, 1997).

The transition of young people into adult family roles is even more abrupt than is their transition into work roles. Before actually becoming parents, most young people have little training in child rearing or other related matters. Families are relatively small today, and youngsters are likely to be close in age to their siblings; as a result, few opportunities exist for participating in child care activities at home. Schools generally offer little, if any, instruction in family relationships and domestic activities. And with childbirth

continuous transitions Passages into adulthood in which adult roles and statuses are entered into gradually.

discontinuous transitions Passages into adulthood in which adult roles and statuses are entered into abruptly.

youth apprenticeship A structured, work-based learning experience that places an adolescent under the supervision of a skilled adult.

In societies in which hunting, farming, and fishing are the primary work activities, young people are often taught the skills they will need as adult workers by accompanying and observing their elders in daily activities, rather than by attending classes in school.

generally taking place in hospitals rather than at home, few young people today have the opportunity of observing a younger sibling's birth.

Passage into adult citizenship and decision-making roles is also highly discontinuous in contemporary Western society. Adolescents are permitted few opportunities for independence and autonomy in school, and are segregated from most of society's political institutions until they complete their formal education. Young people are permitted to vote once they turn 18, but they receive little preparation for participation in government and community roles prior to this time.

It is little surprise, then, that some young people today have difficulty in assuming adult roles and responsibilities. Instead of being gradually socialized into work, family, and citizenship positions, adolescents in modern society typically are segregated from activities in these arenas during most of their childhood and youth. Yet young people are expected to perform these roles capably on reaching the age of majority. With little experience in meaningful work, adolescents are expected to find, get, and keep a job immediately after completing their schooling. With essentially no training for marriage or parenting, they are expected to form their own families, manage their own households, and raise their own children soon after they reach adulthood. And without any previous involvement in community activities, they are

expected on reaching the age of majority to vote, pay taxes, and behave as responsible citizens.

▌ The Continuity of the Adolescent Passage in Traditional Cultures   The high level of discontinuity found in contemporary America is not characteristic of adolescence in traditional societies. Consider the socialization of young people in Samoa, described in detail by the late anthropologist Margaret Mead in her classic book *Coming of Age in Samoa* (1928). From early childhood on, Samoan youngsters are involved in work tasks that have a meaningful connection to the work they will perform as adults. They participate in the care of younger children, in the planting and harvesting of crops, and in the gathering and preparation of food. Their entrance into adult work roles is gradual and continuous, with work tasks being graded to their skills and intelligence. They are charged with the socialization of their infant brothers and sisters, particularly during middle childhood, when they are not yet strong enough to make a substantial contribution to the community's fishing and farming activities. Gradually, they are taught the fundamentals of weaving, boating, fishing, building, and farming. By the time they reach late adolescence, Samoan youngsters are well trained in the tasks they will need to perform as adults.

Such continuity is generally the case in societies in which hunting, fishing, and farming are the chief work activities. As Mead observed, the emphasis in these societies is on informal education in context rather than on formal education in schools. Children are typically not isolated in separate educational institutions, and they accompany the adult members of their community in daily activities. Adolescents' preparation for adulthood, therefore, comes largely from observation and hands-on experience in the same tasks that they will carry out as adults. Typically, boys learn the tasks performed by adult men, and girls learn those performed by adult women. When work activities take adults out of the community, it is not uncommon for children to accompany their parents on these expeditions (N. Miller, 1928).

As Reed Larson and Suzanne Wilson (2004) point out, however, modernization and globalization have made the transition from adolescence to adulthood longer and increasingly more discontinuous all over the world. As successful participation in the workforce increasingly has come to require formal education, parents have become less able to provide their children with advice on how best to prepare for adulthood. Increasingly, school, rather than hands-on experience in the workplace, is how individuals all over the world are expected to prepare for adult work (National Research Council, 2005). How these changes are affecting the psychological development of young people in developing countries is a question that researchers are only now beginning to examine.

FOOD FOR THOUGHT

Many commentators have remarked on the tremendous discontinuity characteristic of the adolescent transition in modern society. But in light of the nature of adult roles in contemporary society, is it really possible to make the transition more continuous than it currently is? If so, what changes would you recommend?

The Continuity of the Adolescent Passage in Previous Eras

During earlier periods in American history, the transition into adult roles and responsibilities began at a younger age and proceeded along a more continuous path than generally is the case today. This is especially true with regard to work. During the eighteenth century and the early nineteenth century, when many families were engaged in farming, a good number of adolescents were expected to work on the family farm and to learn the skills necessary to carry on the enterprise. Boys often accompanied their fathers on business trips, learning the nuances of salesmanship and commerce (Kett, 1977)—a pattern reminiscent of that found in many traditional societies.

Many other young people left home relatively early—some as early as age 12—to work for nonfamilial adults in the community or in nearby villages (Katz, 1975; Kett, 1977). Even as recently as the mid-nineteenth century, young adolescents commonly worked as apprentices, learning skills and trades in preparation for the work roles of adulthood; others left home temporarily to work as servants or to learn domestic skills. The average nineteenth-century youngster in Europe or America left school well before the age of 15 (Chisholm & Hurrelmann, 1995; Modell, Furstenberg, & Hershberg, 1976).

However, census data and historical documents—such as letters, diaries, and community histories—indicate that although adolescents of 100 years ago took on full-time employment earlier in life than they typically do today, they were likely to live under adult supervision for a longer period than is usual in contemporary society. That is, although the transition into work roles may have occurred at a younger age in the nineteenth century than in the twentieth, this transition was made in the context of semi-independence rather than complete emancipation (Katz, 1975; Kett, 1977; Modell & Goodman, 1990). This semi-independent period—which for many young people spanned the decade from about ages 12 to 22, and often beyond—may have increased the degree of continuity of the passage into adulthood by providing a time during which young people could assume certain adult responsibilities gradually (Katz, 1975). The semi-independence characteristic of adolescence in the nineteenth century had largely disappeared by 1900, however (Modell & Goodman, 1990). It is worth noting, though, that although many contemporary commentators (and many college graduates) complain about the increasing prevalence of unpaid internships as a bridge between college and full-time paid employment (e.g., Kamenetz, 2006), this transitional pathway into the world of adult work is not unlike what existed in the nineteenth century.

Socialization for family and citizenship roles may also have been more continuous in previous eras. Living at home during the late-adolescent and early-adult years, particularly in the larger families characteristic of households 100 years ago, contributed to the preparation of young people for future family life. It was common for the children in a family to span a wide age range, and remaining at home undoubtedly placed the older adolescent from time to time in child-rearing roles (President's Science Advisory Committee, 1974). As opposed to today's adolescents, who typically have little experience with infants, adolescents 100 years ago were more likely to have fed, dressed, and cared for their younger siblings. They were also expected to assist their parents in maintaining the household (Modell et al., 1976), which no doubt benefited young people when they eventually established a home separate from their parents. This pattern also likely strengthened sex-role stereotypes, because leaving their parents' home earlier and living independently before marriage encourages young women to develop less traditional attitudes, values, and plans than their counterparts who live with their parents as young adults (Waite, Goldscheider, & Witsberger, 1986). Interestingly, individuals from single-parent homes, stepfamilies, adoptive families, and foster homes tend to leave home at an earlier age than do their peers whose biological parents remain married (Aquilino, 1991; Mitchell, Wister, & Burch, 1989).

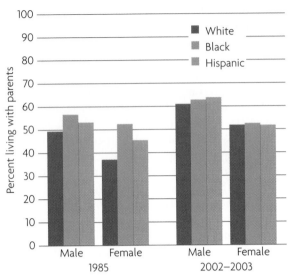

FIGURE 3.4   In general, a higher proportion of young adults (ages 20–22) live with their parents today than was the case two decades ago. (Hil & Holzer, 2006)

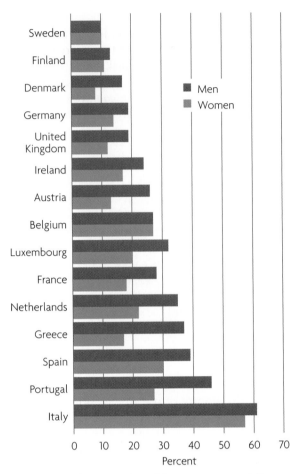

FIGURE 3.5   The proportion of European young adults (ages 18–34) living with their parents varies considerably from country to country. (European Quality of Life Survey, 2003)

■ **Current Trends in Home Leaving**   Recent reports of changes in home leaving are noteworthy, however, and suggest that this aspect of the transition into adulthood may be changing in many industrialized countries. On average, individuals are living with their parents longer today than in recent years (see Figure 3.4). More than 55 percent of all American 20- to 22-year-olds (more than 60 percent of males, and about 50 percent of females) either live with or are supported by their parents (Hill & Holzer, 2007). Most experts attribute this trend to the increased costs of housing and transportation, which make it difficult for individuals to move out of their parents' home (or give up their parents' financial support) and establish a separate residence.

A similar trend is evident in western Europe, where there was a substantial increase during the 1980s in the proportion of youth who were living with their parents well into their mid-20s (Chisholm & Hurrelmann, 1995). However, as Figure 3.5 illustrates, there is considerable variability across European countries in young people's living arrangements. For example. relatively few Scandinavian young adults live at home, whereas doing so is quite common in the southern European countries.

How living with their parents in late adolescence affects their psychological development and mental health likely depends on the extent to which this experience is seen as normative within the cultural group. In the United States, where a premium is placed on becoming independent from one's parents, living at home may have a negative impact on a young adult's well-being and contribute to conflict in the parent–adolescent relationship. One study of middle-class African American young women found that those who

had left home had relatively better relationships with their parents (Smetana, Metzger, & Campione-Barr, 2004). Among Asian and Latin American young adults, who are more likely to have been raised in a culture that places special importance on family obligations, however, living with one's parents in late adolescence and early adulthood may be characterized by positive feelings and close family relationships (Fuligni & Pedersen, 2002). In one recent study of adolescents in the People's Republic of China, a sense of family obligation was associated with more positive family relationships and better school performance (Fuligni & Zhang, 2004), although other studies, of American adolescents, have found that family obligations can detract from school performance (Tseng, 2004).

The current impact of the economy on adolescents' home leaving reaffirms the importance of looking at the broader context in defining what normal adolescence is. In 1960, because it was the exception for adolescents to live at home past high school, we tended to view individuals who did so as being less independent

In postindustrial societies, economic changes often force adolescents in rural or working-class areas to choose between staying home near friends and family or leaving in search of better opportunities. Adolescents in Herrin, Illinois, may face such a choice after this Maytag plant closed in December 2006 after 60 years, taking with it over 1,000 jobs.

or less mature than their peers. But now that living at home has become the norm, we no longer view it as an index of maturity. Above all, we need to keep in mind that, because adolescence is in part defined by society, its nature changes along with society.

Recent economic changes in many postindustrial societies have had a particularly strong effect on the expectations and plans of working-class adolescents (Bettis, 1996) and those living in rural areas (Crockett & Bingham, 2000). Many such teenagers are anxious and uncertain about their future, given the shrinking number of well-paying, blue-collar jobs and the limited economic opportunities for individuals without a college degree. Rural adolescents, especially those with high aspirations, often face a difficult choice between leaving their community in search of better opportunities and staying near home, where social supports are stronger (Johnson, Elder, & Stern, 2005).

Historic events, such as the economic recession of the early 1980s, the 2003 war in Iraq, and Hurricane Katrina, may temporarily alter the nature of the adolescent passage and may produce exceptions to general historical trends. One such event was the Great Depression of the early 1930s. Sociologist Glen Elder, Jr., has examined the impact of growing up during this era on adolescents' behavior and development (Elder, 1974), and many of his findings are relevant to the issue of continuity in the adolescent passage. Elder looked at the data collected during the Depression as part of a

longitudinal study of individuals living in Oakland, California. Members of the group Elder focused on were born between 1920 and 1921 and thus were preadolescents during the worst years of the Depression.

Elder found that youngsters whose families experienced economic hardship during these years were more likely to be involved in adultlike tasks at an earlier age than were their more privileged peers. Boys, for example, were more likely to work and to help support their families; girls were more likely to play a major role with household chores; and both boys and girls were more likely to marry and enter into full-time employment relatively early. Thus, some aspects of the semi-independent stage of adolescence that had become uncommon by 1930 may have reappeared during the Depression. For many youngsters growing up during this period, the adolescent passage may have resembled that of an earlier era.

Research on contemporary German and Polish youngsters by Rainer Silbereisen and colleagues (Silbereisen, Schwarz, Nowak, Kracke, & von Eye, 1993) indicates that, even today, growing up under adversity is associated with an earlier transition into adult roles and behaviors. Whether "earlier" means "better" is a matter of some debate, however. As you'll read in Chapter 8, some writers believe that adolescents profit psychologically from having a relatively long period of time to develop without being burdened by adult responsibilities.

RECAP

- The process of social definition varies from society to society in terms of its clarity.
- In most traditional societies, adolescence is marked by a formal initiation ceremony and specific rites of passage. In contemporary industrialized society, however, the transition from childhood into adulthood is vague and poorly defined.
- Contemporary adolescents are more likely to define adulthood with respect to psychological achievements than to role transitions.
- Societies vary in the extent to which the passage into adulthood is continuous or discontinuous. In a continuous passage, the adolescent assumes the roles and status of adulthood bit by bit, with a good deal of preparation and training along the way. In a discontinuous passage, the adolescent is thrust into adulthood abruptly, with little prior preparation.

The Transition into Adulthood in Contemporary Society

We do not know for certain whether today's prolonged and discontinuous passage into adulthood impedes or enhances adolescents' psychosocial development. Much probably depends on whether the adolescent has access to the resources necessary for such a protracted transition. Indeed, many commentators have noted that there is not one transition into adulthood in contemporary America, but three very different transitions: one for the "haves," one of the "have-nots," and one for those who are somewhere in between (Furstenberg, 2006). As one writer recently put it:

> The lack of societal support for [the] most vulnerable youth stands in stark contrast to the extensive support provided to the best situated, most-likely-to-succeed young adults—the 25 to 30 percent of all youth who attend four-year colleges and obtain bachelor's degrees.
>
> The great majority of these youth are embedded in networks—families, friends, and communities—that provide guidance, support, and help, both financial and otherwise, when they face the crises that are an inevitable part of the transition. The majority live in households with higher incomes. Beyond what their parents provide, society invests billions of dollars in these youth and provides them with an extensive support system. . . . While students attending two-year colleges have fewer support services, they too benefit

from a system designed to aid their development and transition. Colleges also convey to their students a sense of being special, a message that is rarely, if ever, conveyed to vulnerable youth, who are ignored at best and demonized at worst. (Wald, 2005, pp. ix–x)

Observers of adolescence in America have suggested that the discontinuity in the passage into adulthood has become so great that many youngsters, especially those not bound for college, are having tremendous problems negotiating the passage into adult roles (Hamburg, 1986; National Research Council, 1993; Osgood, Anderson, & Shafer, 2005). One national commission found that society had so neglected the needs of non-college-bound adolescents that its report called them "The Forgotten Half" (William T. Grant Foundation, 1988). Another prestigious panel, in a disheartening report, estimated that about one-quarter of American 10- to 17-year-olds are at risk of failing to lead productive adult lives (National Research Council, 1993).

These observers point to problems that the most vulnerable young people in society face in developing a coherent sense of identity, establishing a healthy sense of autonomy, and making informed decisions about commitments to family and work. They note that the lack of clarity and continuity in the transition into adulthood may contribute to some of the problems faced by adolescents in contemporary society and may also contribute to some of the problems faced by contemporary society in dealing with young people. Many social scientists believe that our relatively high rates of divorce, family violence, youth unemployment, juvenile delinquency, and teenage alcoholism stem in part from the confusing and contradictory nature of the passage into adulthood in modern society (National Research Council, 1993).

As we look to the future, we can point to two specific societal trends that are reshaping the nature of the transition from adolescence to adulthood (Mortimer & Larson, 2002). First, as we have noted throughout this chapter, the length of the transitional period is increasing. As the labor force continues to shift toward jobs that demand more and more formal education, the amount of time individuals need to spend as economically dependent students will increase, which will delay their assumption of all sorts of adult roles, including family roles. (One of the reasons that individuals are marrying at a later age today than in the past is that it takes longer to accumulate enough wealth to establish a separate residence or start a family.) Today, the transition between childhood and adulthood takes longer than it did in the past century. Tomorrow, however, it will take even longer.

Second, as success in the labor force comes to be more and more dependent on formal education, the

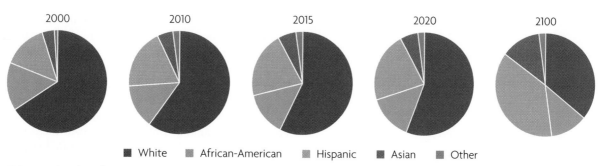

FIGURE 3.6   The ethnic composition of the United States will continue to change dramatically over the twenty-first century. (Federal Interagency Forum on Child and Family Statistics, 2005)

division between the haves—those who have access to money, schools, and information technology—and have-nots—those who are poor, less well educated, and cut off from important resources, will grow. This division will be seen both between countries (that is, the nature of adolescence will differ markedly in wealthy and poor nations) and within countries (that is, within any given country, adolescence will differ markedly between the affluent and the poor). Already in the United States, for example, we can see dramatic differences in what it means to be an adolescent when we compare young people growing up in suburban affluence with those growing up in urban or rural poverty, or between relatively more privileged adolescents and those whose transition to adulthood is impeded by mental illness, disability, severe learning problems, or involvement with the foster care or justice systems (Osgood et al., 2005). One extremely important international trend concerns different birthrates in different parts of the world: Because the birthrate in poor and developing countries is so much higher than it is in wealthy nations, the distribution of the world's adolescents is changing dramatically. As we move further into the twenty-first century, relatively fewer and fewer of the world's teenagers will come from affluent parts of the world, and relatively more and more will live in impoverished countries (Larson & Wilson, 2004).

SPECIAL TRANSITIONAL PROBLEMS OF POOR AND MINORITY YOUTH

No discussion of the transitional problems of young people in America today would be complete without noting that youngsters from some minority groups—African American, Hispanic American, and American Indian youth, in particular—have more trouble negotiating the transition into adulthood than do their white and Asian American counterparts. This is due to many factors, including poverty, discrimination, segregation, and disproportionate involvement with the justice system (Garcia Coll et al., 1996; Osgood et al., 2005).

Youngsters from minority backgrounds make up a substantial and growing portion of the adolescent population in America. At the beginning of this century, about two-thirds of American adolescents were white. Today, about 19 percent of American adolescents are Hispanic American, 14 percent African American, 5 percent Asian American or Pacific Islanders, and 2 percent American Indian, Native Alaskan, or bi-ethnic youth. In other words, about 40 percent of American adolescents are from ethnic minority groups. Because the population of Hispanic American and Asian American youth is increasing especially rapidly, by the year 2020, ethnic minority children will account for nearly 45 percent of all U.S. adolescents (Federal Interagency Forum on Child and Family Statistics, 2005). By the end of this century, the U.S. Census Bureau estimates that nearly two-thirds of American adolescents will be nonwhite and that Hispanic adolescents will be the largest ethnic group in the country (see Figure 3.6).

Many American adolescents were not born in the United States, of course. One curiosity within studies of ethnic minority youth and the transition to adulthood concerns the better-than-expected mental health and school performance of immigrant adolescents in the United States. For reasons not entirely understood, foreign-born adolescent immigrants have better mental health, exhibit less problem behavior, and perform better in school than do adolescents from the same ethnic group who are native-born Americans (Harris, 1999; Kao, 1999; Rumbaut, 1997; Schmid, 2001). Indeed, one of the most interesting findings to emerge from research on immigrant adolescents is that their "Americanization" appears to be associated with worse, not better, outcomes. For example, the longer a foreign-born adolescent has lived in the United States, the more likely he or she is to smoke cigarettes or binge drink (Gfroerer & Tan, 2003). Similarly, a study of Latino adolescents in Los Angeles found that those who spoke English exclusively (an index of Americanization) were more likely to drink alcohol, smoke cigarettes, and engage in sexual intercourse than were

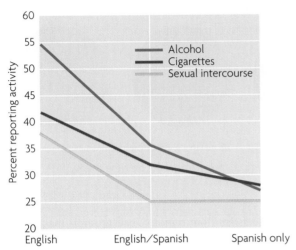

FIGURE 3.7 Latino adolescents who are relatively more acculturated, as indexed by their primary language, are more likely to engage in problem behavior than those who are less acculturated. (Ebin et al., 2001)

those who spoke a mixture of English and Spanish, who, in turn, were more likely to engage in these behaviors than those who spoke Spanish exclusively (Ebin et al., 2001) (see Figure 3.7). Although there are many possible explanations for this, one reason is that when adolescents from immigrant families become more Americanized, this leads to family conflict and increased distance between adolescent and parents, which, in turn, leads to problem behavior (McQueen, Getz, & Bray, 2003). For example, highly Americanized Asian American adolescents who have strong attachments to their parents are not at heightened risk for problems (Hahm, Lahiff, & Guterman, 2003).

THE EFFECTS OF POVERTY ON THE TRANSITION INTO ADULTHOOD

Growing up in poverty may profoundly impair youngsters' ability to move easily between adolescence and adulthood. Poverty is associated with failure in school, unemployment, and out-of-wedlock pregnancy, all of which contribute to transitional difficulties (Guldi, Page, & Stevens, 2007; National Research Council, 1993; Schoon et al., 2002). Because minority youngsters are more likely than other teenagers to grow up in poverty, they are also more likely to encounter transitional problems during middle and late adolescence.

Experiencing poverty during adolescence has an especially negative effect on adolescents' school achievement (Guo, 1998). As you will see in later chapters, school dropout rates are much higher among Hispanic American and American Indian teenagers than among other groups, and college enrollment is lower among African American, Hispanic American, and

American Indian youth. In addition, unemployment is much higher among African American, Hispanic American, and American Indian teenagers; African American and Hispanic American youth are more likely to be victimized by crime and exposed to violence; and rates of out-of-wedlock births are higher among African American and Hispanic American teenagers than among white teenagers. All these factors disrupt the transition into adulthood by limiting individuals' economic and occupational success. Poverty impedes the transition to adulthood among all teenagers, regardless of race, of course; but because minority youth are more likely to grow up poor, they are also more likely to have transition problems.

As William Julius Wilson documented in his widely cited book *The Truly Disadvantaged*, the situation is particularly grave for poor minority youngsters growing up in the inner city (Wilson, 1987). Many of these young people grow up without knowing a single adult "whose stable employment supports an even modest standard of family life" (Wilson, cited in Nightingale & Wolverton, 1993, p. 480).

WHAT CAN BE DONE TO EASE THE TRANSITION?

A variety of suggestions have been offered for making the transition into adulthood smoother for all young people, especially those who are not college-bound, including restructuring secondary education, expanding work and volunteer opportunities, and improving the quality of community life for adolescents and their parents. Some groups have called for expanded opportunities in the workplace as a way of making the high school years more of a "bridge" between adolescence and adulthood (Kazis, 1993). Others have suggested that adolescents be encouraged to spend time in voluntary, nonmilitary service activities—such as staffing day care centers, working with the elderly, or cleaning up the environment—for a few years after high school graduation so that they can learn responsibility and adult roles (Children's Defense Fund, 1989; McLellan & Youniss, 2003). Still others have pointed out that adolescents cannot come of age successfully without the help of adults and that programs are needed to strengthen families and communities and to bring adolescents into contact with adult mentors (National Research Council, 1993). Overall, most experts agree that a comprehensive approach to the problem is needed and that such an approach must simultaneously address the educational, employment, interpersonal, and health needs of adolescents from all walks of life (Dryfoos, 1990).

In recent years, there has been growing interest in mentoring programs for at-risk adolescents, many of

A variety of psychological and social problems are more common among adolescents who grow up amidst poverty.

whom have few relationships with positive adult role models (DuBois, Holloway, Valentine, & Cooper, 2002; Rhodes, 2004). Adolescents who lack positive adult role models are more likely to have psychological and behavioral problems (Bryant & Zimmerman, 2003; Zimmerman, Bingenheimer, & Notaro, 2002). Among the best-known mentoring programs is Big Brothers/Big Sisters, which has more than 500 branches across the United States. Mentoring programs seek to pair adults with young people through community- or school-based efforts designed to facilitate positive youth development, improve academic achievement, and deter antisocial behavior.

Evaluations of mentoring programs indicate that they have a small, but significant positive effect on youth development. On average, adolescents who have been mentored are less likely to have problems in school and at home, less likely to use drugs and alcohol, and less likely to get into trouble with the law (Rhodes, Grossman, & Resche, 2000). Not surprisingly, the impact of mentoring varies as a function of characteristics of the mentor, the young person, and their relationship (DuBois et al., 2002; Grossman & Rhodes, 2002). In general, mentoring tends to be more successful when the mentor maintains a steady presence in the youth's life over an extended period (at least two years), has frequent contact with the youngster, and involves the adolescent in a wide range of recreational, social, and practical activities (Langhout, Rhodes, & Osborne, 2004; Roth, Brooks-Gunn, Murray, & Foster, 1998). It is important to note, however, that although mentoring may benefit adolescents, other influences in their lives are also important, and mentoring alone is not sufficient to meet the needs of at-risk youth

(DuBois & Silverthorn, 2005). One potentially important influence, to which we now turn, is the neighborhood in which the adolescent lives.

RECAP

- There are three very different "transitions" to adulthood in contemporary America, one for the haves, one for the have-nots, and one for those who are somewhere in between the extremes.
- The discontinuous and prolonged nature of the adolescent passage in contemporary society has caused difficulties for many of today's youth, especially poor, minority youth living in pockets of concentrated poverty.
- Mentoring programs have a small, but significant positive effect on the development of at-risk adolescents, but mentoring alone is not sufficient to help poor adolescents make a successful transition to adulthood.
- Most experts agree that a comprehensive approach to the problem is needed and that such an approach must simultaneously address adolescents' educational, employment, interpersonal, and health needs.

The Influence of Neighborhood Conditions on Adolescent Development

One factor contributing to the especially worrisome situation of poor and minority youth in the United States is that poverty has become much more concentrated over the past 40 years, with greater and greater clustering of poor families into economically and racially segregated communities. In response to this, and taking the lead from Wilson's discussion about the devastating impact of concentrated poverty in his book *The Truly Disadvantaged*, a number of researchers have turned their attention to the study of the ways in which neighborhoods influence adolescent development (Leventhal & Brooks-Gunn, 2004). Although other characteristics of neighborhoods in addition to poverty certainly could potentially affect adolescents' development (for example, the ethnic composition, crime rate, or availability of social service programs), far more is known about the effects of

FIGURE 3.8 Neighborhood conditions influence adolescents' development by shaping the norms to which adolescents are exposed; by influencing the quality of the relationships they have with others, including their parents; and by facilitating or limiting adolescents' and families' access to economic and institutional resources.

neighborhood poverty than about any other neighborhood factor (e.g., Brooks-Gunn, Duncan, Klebanov, & Sealand, 1993; Coulten & Pandy, 1992; Duncan, 1994; Ensminger, Lamkin, & Jacobson, 1996; Sampson, 1997). Exposure to neighborhood poverty is an especially prevalent problem among nonwhite adolescents. Close to 90 percent of all residents of the poorest neighborhoods in the United States are from ethnic minority groups (National Research Council, 1993).

Studying neighborhood influences on adolescent development is tricky business. Because poor families tend to live in poor neighborhoods, it is not always easy to separate the effects of neighborhood disadvantage from the effects of family disadvantage. To do this, researchers have had to compare adolescents whose family situations are similar, but who live in very different types of neighborhoods. This is not always easy to do—as you can imagine, there are few affluent families that live in poor neighborhoods, and few poor families that live in affluent ones.

There is also the problem of cause and effect. If families in a good neighborhood seem to be functioning better than families in a poor one, it might simply reflect the fact that better-functioning families choose to live in better neighborhoods (rather than indicate that the neighborhood actually influenced family functioning). There have been a few experiments in which the researchers took this into account, by randomly assigning families from poor neighborhoods to either remain where they were living or be relocated into more advantaged neighborhoods, and then tracking the psychological development and behavior of adolescents in the two groups. These studies have found mixed effects of relocation, with some studies showing positive effects, others showing no effect, and some actually showing negative effects (Kling, Ludwig, &

Katz, 2005; Leventhal, Fauth, & Brooks-Gunn, 2005; Ludwig, Duncan, & Hirschfield, 2001).

Despite these cautions, evidence suggests that growing up in a poor neighborhood has negative effects on adolescent behavior and mental health, and that these effects are above and beyond those attributable to growing up in a poor family or attending a poor school (Harding, 2003). Adolescents growing up in impoverished urban communities are more likely than their peers from equally poor households but better neighborhoods to bear children as teenagers, to become involved in criminal activity, and to achieve less in, or even drop out of, high school—factors that, as you will read in later chapters, seriously interfere with the successful transition into adulthood (Leventhal & Brooks-Gunn, 2004; Wickrama, Merten, & Elder, 2005). Interestingly, the absence of affluent neighbors, rather than the presence of poor neighbors, seems to place adolescents in impoverished communities at greatest risk (Duncan, 1994; Ensminger et al., 1996; Leventhal & Brooks-Gunn, 2004). Although virtually all neighborhood research has focused on urban adolescents, studies find that growing up in poor rural communities also places adolescents at risk (Farmer et al., 2004).

PROCESSES OF NEIGHBORHOOD INFLUENCE

How might neighborhood conditions affect the behavior and development of adolescents? Three different mechanisms have been suggested (Leventhal & Brooks-Gunn, 2004) (see Figure 3.8).

■ **Collective Efficacy** First, neighborhood conditions shape the norms that guide individuals' values and behaviors. Poverty in neighborhoods breeds social isolation and social disorganization, undermining a neighborhood's sense of **collective efficacy**—the extent to which neighbors trust each other, share common

collective efficacy A community's social capital, derived from its members' common values and goals.

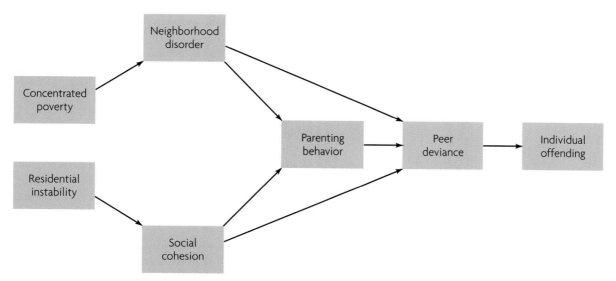

FIGURE 3.9   Neighborhood disadvantage diminishes parental effectiveness, which leads adolescents to affiliate with deviant peers and get involved in crime and delinquency. (Chung & Steinberg, 2006)

values, and count on each other to monitor the activities of youth in the community (Sampson, Raudenbusch, & Earls, 1997). As a consequence, it is easier for deviant peer groups to form and to influence the behavior of adolescents in these communities. Rates of teen pregnancy, school failure, and antisocial behavior are all higher in neighborhoods that have low levels of collective efficacy (Ainsworth, 2002; Bowen & Bowen, 2002; Brooks-Gunn, Duncan, Klebanov, & Sealand, 1993; Herrenkohl et al., 2000; Paschall & Hubbard, 1998; Sampson, 1997; Sampson & Laub, 1994; Simons, et al., 1996; Tolan, Gorman-Smith, & Henry, 2003). Living in a neighborhood high in collective efficacy—where adults monitor the behavior of all adolescents, not just their own—is especially important for adolescents whose parents are themselves not very vigilant (Browning, Leventhal, & Brooks-Gunn, 2005).

Some writers (e.g., Crane, 1991; Simons, et al., 1996) suggest that, under conditions of low collective efficacy, social problems are contagious—they spread from one adolescent to another in a pattern not unlike a disease epidemic. To the extent that poverty increases behavior problems, for example, adolescents living in poor neighborhoods will come into contact with deviant peers more often. Adolescents who associate with delinquent peers are more likely to be drawn into criminal and delinquent activity (Simons et al., 1996). Similarly, adolescents who live in neighborhoods characterized by high rates of teenage childbearing grow up exposed to large numbers of peers who are relatively more tolerant of this behavior, which affects their own attitudes toward premarital childbearing (Baumer & South, 2001; South & Baumer, 2000). Adolescents who see nothing but poverty and unemployment in their communities have little reason to be hopeful about their own future, and they may feel that they have little to lose by having a baby, dropping out of school, or becoming involved in criminal activity (Kirby, Coyle, & Gould, 2001; LeBlanc, 2003). Interestingly, neighborhood poverty has an impact on adolescents' sexual behavior and decisions about whether to abort a pregnancy—with those living in poor neighborhoods more likely to be sexually active at an early age and to have the baby—but not on their likelihood of getting pregnant or using contraception (Cubbin, Santelli, Brindis, & Braveman, 2005; South & Baumer, 2001).

▌ **The Impact of Stress**   Second, the stresses associated with poverty undermine the quality of people's relationships with each other. Poverty, we know, interferes with parents' ability to be effective parents. Psychologist Vonnie McLoyd, who has done extensive research on the impact of poverty on African American youth, has shown in numerous studies that both the financial strain and the neighborhood stress associated with poverty undermines the quality of parenting in a family, which, in turn, leads to adolescent maladjustment. Indeed, across all ethnic groups, poverty is associated with harsh, inconsistent, and punitive parenting, and these factors, in turn, are linked to adolescent misbehavior (Bradley, Corwyn, Pipes McAdoo, & Garcia-Coll, 2001; Gutman, McLoyd, & Tokoyawa, 2005; Ramirez-Valles, Zimmerman, & Juarez, 2002). When parents are not effective in supervising and monitoring their teenagers, for example, and when teenagers have little social support from parents or other adults, the teenagers are more likely to associate with antisocial peers and get into trouble (see Figure 3.9)

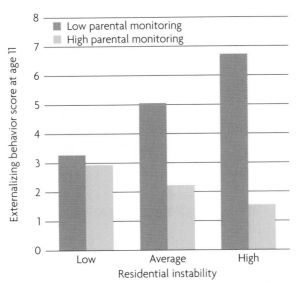

FIGURE 3.10 Under conditions of neighborhood stability, parental monitoring is unrelated to adolescent misbehavior. But when neighborhoods are unstable, parental monitoring is extremely important. (Beyers et al., 2003)

(Chung & Steinberg, 2006; Hoffman, 2003; Lynam et al., 2000; Tolan, Gorman-Smith, & Henry, 2003).

Consistent with this, the harmful effects of exposure to negligent or harsh parenting are even more pronounced in disadvantaged neighborhoods (see Figure 3.10) (Beyers, Bates, Pettit, & Dodge, 2003; Brody et al., 2003; Browning, Leventhal, & Brooks-Gunn, 2005; Cleveland, 2003; Knoester & Haynie, 2005). Studies of whether good parenting is affected by neighborhood conditions have not yielded consistent results. Some studies show that good parenting is more effective in good neighborhoods (e.g., Simons, Simons, Burt, Brody, & Cutrona, 2005), while others show the reverse (Cleveland, Gibbons, Gerrard, Pomery, & Brody, 2005).

The impact of poverty on levels of neighborhood violence is especially devastating. Adolescents who grow up in poor neighborhoods are far more likely than other youth to be exposed to chronic community violence, and repeated exposure to violence and other types of stress increases the risk of behavioral, emotional, and even physical health problems (Farrell & Sullivan, 2004; Shahinfar, Kupersmidt, & Matza, 2001; Stevenson, 1998; Vermeiren, Ruchkin, Leckman, Deboutte, & Schwab-Stone, 2002). Perhaps not surprisingly, adolescents who grow up in poor neighborhoods are more likely to interpret ambiguous situations as threatening and to show increases in blood pressure and heart rate as a consequence, placing them at risk for heart disease (Chen, Langer, Raphaelson, & Matthews, 2004).

Exposure to violence is pervasive in poor neighborhoods. One study of young adolescents in Philadelphia,

for example, indicated that 96 percent of the students in an urban middle school knew someone who had been robbed, beaten, stabbed, shot, or murdered. Two-thirds of these students had been personally robbed, beaten up, stabbed, shot, or caught in gun cross fire. Nearly three-quarters of the youngsters reported hearing gunfire in their neighborhood (Campbell & Schwartz, 1996). In another study, of poor New York City teenagers, half of the students reported knowing someone who had been murdered, 61 percent had witnessed a robbery, 59 percent had witnessed a beating, 37 percent had witnessed a shooting, and 31 percent had witnessed a stabbing (Pastore, Fisher, & Friedman, 1996).

Adolescents who themselves have been exposed to violence are more likely to engage in violent behavior, to think about killing themselves, and to report symptoms of depression, posttraumatic stress disorder, hopelessness, and substance abuse (Bolland, Lian, & Formichella, 2005; Campbell & Schwartz, 1996; DuRant, Pendergrast, & Cadenhead, 1994; DuRant, Getts, Cadenhead, & Woods, 1995; Gorman-Smith & Tolan, 1998; Ozer, 2005; Pastore et al., 1996; Youngstrom, Weist, & Albus, 2003). One recent study found that witnessing gun violence *doubles* an adolescent's risk for committing violence in the future (Bingenheimer, 2005). Not all adolescents who are exposed to violence go on to commit antisocial acts, of course; among the factors that help protect against the harmful effects of exposure to violence are having parental support and strong religious beliefs (Brookmeyer, Henrich, & Schwab-Stone, 2005; Pearce, Jones, Schwab-Stone, & Ruchkin, 2003).

FOOD FOR THOUGHT

Inner-city neighborhoods typically come to mind when we think of adolescents growing up in poverty, but many poor adolescents live in rural, not urban, areas. In what ways is poverty different for urban versus rural youth? How might this affect the nature of adolescence in each type of community?

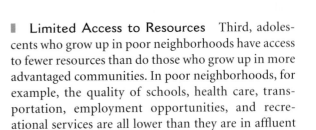

■ **Limited Access to Resources**   Third, adolescents who grow up in poor neighborhoods have access to fewer resources than do those who grow up in more advantaged communities. In poor neighborhoods, for example, the quality of schools, health care, transportation, employment opportunities, and recreational services are all lower than they are in affluent

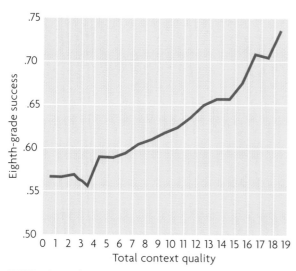

FIGURE 3.11   The more positive features an adolescent's context contains, the more likely he or she is to succeed. (Cook et al., 2002)

neighborhoods. As a result, adolescents in poor communities have fewer chances to engage in activities that facilitate positive development and fewer chances to receive services when they are having difficulties (Leventhal & Brooks-Gunn, 2004). Adolescents who live in communities with relatively greater resources, such as higher-quality schools, are less likely to become involved in antisocial behavior (Kowaleski-Jones, 2000). Interestingly, in neighborhoods with higher levels of resources and greater feelings of cohesion, adults' beliefs about teenagers tend to be more favorable, probably because the casual interactions that take place between adults and adolescents in these settings are more positive (Zeldin & Topitzes, 2002). The presence of institutional resources, then, often goes hand in hand with the presence of positive social relationships.

Most of the effects of neighborhoods on adolescent development are indirect, transmitted through the impact of the neighborhood on the more immediate settings in which adolescents spend time (Chung & Steinberg, 2006; Jones, Forehand, Brody, & Armistead, 2002; Teitler & Weiss, 2000). For example, neighborhood disorder affects the way that parents behave, and this, in turn, affects adolescents' development and mental health. Consistent with the ecological perspective on human development discussed in the Introduction, then, neighborhoods influence individuals by transforming what takes place within the more immediate contexts that are embedded in them.

Is one setting—the family, the peer group, the school—a more influential transmitter of neighborhood effects than others? A recent study by Thomas Cook and his colleagues shows that no single context alone provides a complete explanation of why some adolescents have an easier time making a successful transition into adulthood than do others (Cook, Herman, Phillips, & Settersten, 2002). Each setting contributes modestly and independently to the course of adolescent development, and it is the cumulative impact of multiple contexts that matters most. As Figure 3.11 illustrates, the greater the number of positive features an adolescent's environment contains, the better off he or she will be. By the same token, the more sources of contextual risk an adolescent is exposed to, the greater his or her chances are of developing problems (Morrison, Gutman, Sameroff, & Eccles, 2002; Jones et al., 2002; Prelow, Danoff-Burg, Swenson, & Pulgiano, 2004; Prelow & Loukas, 2003).

In the next set of chapters, we'll look in detail at the immediate contexts in which adolescents spend time—the family, the peer group, the school, and work and leisure settings—and at the features of each that help or hinder healthy adolescent development.

RECAP

- Neighborhoods affect adolescents through three interrelated processes: by influencing the sorts of norms to which adolescents are exposed, by altering the nature of interpersonal relationships inside and outside the family, and by facilitating or limiting adolescents' access to economic and institutional resources.

- To date, most research on neighborhood influences has focused on the impact of growing up in a poor neighborhood, which has been shown to have adverse effects on adolescents' development, above and beyond the adverse effects of growing up in a poor family.

- Exposure to violence is an especially severe problem for adolescents in poor neighborhoods.

- The impact of the neighborhood on adolescent development occurs through the neighborhood's influence on the more immediate settings in which adolescents spend time.

- The more positive features an adolescent's context contains, the more likely he or she is to succeed.

PART 2

4 | Families   5 | Peer Groups   6 | Schools   7 | Work, Leisure, and Mass Media

The Contexts of Adolescence

CHAPTER 4

Families

IS CONFLICT BETWEEN TEENAGERS AND PARENTS INEVITABLE?

The Generation Gap: Fact and Fiction

What Do Adolescents and Parents Usually Fight About?

FAMILY RELATIONSHIPS AT ADOLESCENCE

A Time of Reorganization and Change

The Adolescent's Parents at Midlife

Changes in Family Needs and Functions

Transformations in Family Relations

Sex Differences in Family Relationships

FAMILY RELATIONSHIPS AND ADOLESCENT DEVELOPMENT

Parenting Styles and Their Effects

Ethnic Differences in Parenting Practices

Autonomy and Attachment in the Adolescent's Family

Adolescents' Relationships with Siblings

BEHAVIORAL GENETICS AND ADOLESCENT DEVELOPMENT

Genetic and Environmental Influences on Adolescent Development

Why Are Siblings Often So Different?

THE ADOLESCENT'S FAMILY IN A CHANGING SOCIETY

The Changed and Changing Nature of Family Life

Adolescents and Divorce

The Specific Impact of Marital Conflict

The Longer-Term Effects of Divorce

Custody, Contact, and Conflict Following Divorce

Remarriage

Economic Stress and Poverty

THE IMPORTANCE OF THE FAMILY IN ADOLESCENT DEVELOPMENT

THE NEXT TIME you are in a bookstore, take a look at the books in the section on parent–adolescent relationships. Judging from the titles—ones like *When We're in Public, Pretend You Don't Know Me; Get Out of My Life—But First, Could You Drive Me and Cheryl to the Mall; I'm Not Mad, I Just Hate You; Surviving Your Adolescents;* and *Yes, Your Teen Is Crazy*—you would think that stress and strain between teenagers and their parents is commonplace, even normal. In contrast to advice books on infancy, which emphasize normative development, books for parents of teenagers tend to focus on problems (Steinberg, 2001). This is unfortunate, for two reasons. First, as you'll read, the stereotype presented in these writings isn't true. And second, the more parents believe in the stereotype of adolescents as difficult, the more they expect their own child to conform to it, and the worse their relationship with their teenager is (Jacobs, Chin, & Shaver, 2005). In other words, parents believing that they are going to have a difficult time with their child once he or she enters adolescence can become what psychologists call a **self-fulfilling prophecy**—an expectation that is realized because parents act in ways that make it happen.

In truth, scientific studies indicate that, on average, there is very little emotional distance between young people and their parents (Collins & Laursen, 2004). Although some adolescents and their parents have serious interpersonal problems, the overwhelming majority of adolescents feel close to their parents, respect their parents' judgment, feel that their parents love and care about them, and have a lot of respect for their parents as individuals (Steinberg, 2001). In fact, one-fifth of American teenagers say that their top concern is that they don't spend *enough* time with their parents; ironically, less than one-tenth of parents say that *their* top concern is that they don't spend enough time with their kids (YMCA, 2000).

To be sure, there are times when adolescents and parents have their problems. But there are times when younger children and their parents have problems, and when adults and their parents do, too. No systematic studies demonstrate that family problems are any more likely to occur during adolescence than at other times in the life span. Most research indicates that among the 25 percent of teenagers and parents who report having problems, about 80 percent had problematic relations during childhood (Rutter, Graham, Chadwick, & Yule, 1976). The bottom line: Only about 5 percent of families who enjoy positive relations during childhood can expect to develop serious problems during adolescence.

In this chapter, we'll look at the family as a context for adolescent development, with three broad questions in mind. First, how do relationships in the family change during adolescence—that is, what is the effect of adolescence on the family? Second, how are adolescents affected by their experiences in the family—in other words, what is the effect of the family on adolescents? And third, how have changes in family life during the past half century affected the adolescent experience?

FOOD FOR THOUGHT

Portrayals of adolescent–parent relationships in the popular press suggest that the period is much more difficult and unpleasant than research indicates. Why might there be a "disconnect" between what research finds and what the public is led to believe?

Is Conflict Between Teenagers and Parents Inevitable?

It is impossible to discuss adolescents' relationships with their parents without talking about parent–adolescent conflict, a topic that not only dominates popular writings on the period but also has been the focus of decades of research by scholars of adolescence (Steinberg, 2001).

THE GENERATION GAP: FACT AND FICTION

Most people believe that adolescents and adults hold different values and attitudes, a phenomenon known

---

self-fulfilling prophecy   The idea that individuals' behavior is influenced by others' expectations for them.

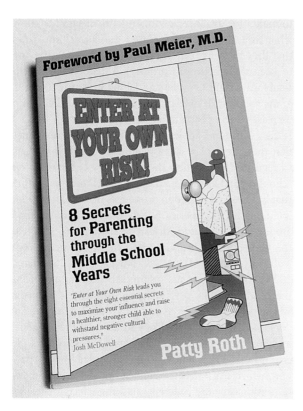

Many popular advice books for parents of teenagers, such as this one, incorrectly portray adolescence as an inherently difficult time.

as the **generation gap,** and that this is a constant source of difficulty for young people and their parents. However, this is not the case. Systematic studies of teenagers and their parents find that they usually have surprisingly similar beliefs about such things as the importance of hard work, educational and occupational ambitions, and the personal characteristics and attributes that they feel are important and desirable (Gecas & Seff, 1990; Knafo & Schwartz, 2003). Indeed, when it comes to basic, core values—concerning religion, work, education, and so on—diversity *within* the adolescent population is much more striking than are differences between the generations.

Why is this so? Because adolescents and their parents share a common social, regional, and cultural background, and these are the factors that shape our central beliefs. Socioeconomic background, for instance, has a much stronger influence on individuals' values and attitudes than does age, and adolescents are more likely to share their parents' values than those of other teenagers who are from a different background. Wealthy adolescents growing up in affluent suburbs, for example, have educational and career plans that resemble their parents' plans for them, and their plans are very different from those of poor adolescents growing up in less prosperous areas.

Although there is not much of a generation gap when it comes to core values, there is often a gap between the generations in matters of personal taste, most clearly evident in styles of dress, preferences in music, and patterns of leisure activity (Collins & Laursen, 2004; Montemayor, 1983). The explanation for a gap of this sort is not surprising: Unlike basic values, which develop gradually over time and are shaped from an early age, preferences and tastes for things like clothing, music, and hairstyles are far more transitory and subject to the immediate influences of the social environment. Adolescents are more likely to be influenced by their friends than by their parents in these matters, and as a consequence, disagreements and differences in opinion between old and young often result. Because adolescents spend a great deal of time with their friends (and because a good deal of that time is spent in social activities in which taste in clothes, music, and so on is especially important), teenagers' preferences are likely to be shaped to a large measure by forces outside the family.

WHAT DO ADOLESCENTS AND PARENTS USUALLY FIGHT ABOUT?

If parents and teenagers typically don't argue over "big" issues, what do they fight about? Studies find that they squabble about things like teenagers' curfews, leisure time activities, clothing, and the cleanliness of their rooms. These have been the major sources of disagreement in families with teenagers for at least as long as scientists have been studying the issue (Montemayor, 1983). And, although conflict between adolescents and parents over these mundane matters is generally less frequent in ethnic minority than in white families, the topics of disagreement are similar across ethnic groups and cultures (Barber, 1994; Kupersmidt, Burchinal, Leff, & Patterson, 1992; Smetana, Daddis, & Chuang, 2003). A recent study of adolescents in the People's Republic of China and Hong Kong, for example, found that the most common sources of conflict between adolescents and parents were everyday issues, such as time spent on schoolwork, household chores, and choice of friends (Yau & Smetana, 2003).

Why do parents and teenagers argue over such mundane matters? According to research by Judith Smetana (1995, 2000; Smetana & Asquith, 1994; Yau & Smetana, 2003), a major contributor to adolescent–parent bickering is the fact that teenagers and their parents define the issues of contention very differently—a finding that has been replicated across several cultural and ethnic

generation gap The popular phrase for the alleged conflict between young people and adults over values and attitudes.

One source of conflict between parents and teenagers involves differences in the way they define issues. Making sure that the adolescent's bedroom is tidy is seen by parents as an area over which parents should have jurisdiction. Teenagers, however, tend to see their bedroom as their own private space and decisions about neatness as matters of personal choice.

groups. Smetana studies parent–adolescent relations by videotaping parents and teenagers discussing various issues and then analyzing the conversations. Parents view many issues as matters of right and wrong—not in a moral sense, but as matters of custom or convention. Adolescents, in contrast, are likely to define these same issues as matters of personal choice. A mother who disapproves of her daughter's outfit says, "People just don't dress that way to go to school." The daughter responds, "*You* wouldn't dress this way for school, but *I* do."

▌ **Rebels with a Cause**   Contrary to stereotype, though, adolescents rarely rebel against their parents just for the sake of rebelling. In fact, they are willing to accept their parents' rules as legitimate when they agree that the issue is a moral one (whether it is permissible to cheat on a school test) or one involving safety (whether it is permissible to smoke cigarettes or drink alcohol), but they are less inclined to accept their parents' authority when they view the issue as personal (how one dresses to go to a party) (Jackson, 2002; Smetana & Daddis, 2002). In other words, rather than resisting all of their parents' attempts to make and enforce rules (the stereotype that many people have of teenagers), adolescents draw distinctions between parental rules that they think their parents have a right

to make (for instance, having to let their parents know what time they'll be home after going out) and rules that they think are out of bounds (for example, having to keep their bedroom orderly), a distinction that in many ways is quite understandable (Smetana, 2005).

As you'll read, conflict between parents and children increases during early adolescence. One reason for this is that, with time, adolescents see more and more issues that they previously saw as legitimate for their parents to regulate (for example, how late they can stay up on school nights) as matters of personal choice—a finding that has been replicated in numerous parts of the world, including North America, South America, and Asia, and among both white and African American adolescents in the United States (e.g., Hasebe, Nucci, & Nucci, 2004; Milnitsky-Sapiro, Turiel, & Nucci, 2006; Smetana, 2005). And how parents respond to this change affects their adolescent's psychological health: Adolescents whose parents attempt to regulate what they believe are personal issues are more likely to describe their parents as being overly controlling. Perhaps because of this, the effects of feeling psychologically controlled by their parents, which has a negative impact on adolescents' mental health, are very different than the effects of feeling that their activities are monitored, which has a positive impact (Hasebe, Nucci, & Nucci, 2004; Silk, Morris, Kanaya, & Steinberg, 2003; Smetana, Campione-Barr, & Daddis, 2004; Smetana & Daddis, 2002).

In other words, teenagers and their parents often clash more over the definition of the issue (that is, whether something is a moral or safety issue versus a matter of personal choice) than over the specific details. The struggle, then, is over who has the authority—and whose jurisdiction the issue falls into. Because early adolescence is a time when adolescents' reasoning abilities are changing, the ways that individuals understand family rules and regulations change as well. As a consequence of normal cognitive development, a 9-year-old child who is willing to accept his parents' views of right and wrong—who doesn't question his mother when she says, "We do not leave clothes on the floor"—grows into an adolescent who understands that some issues are matters of personal choice, rather than social convention ("It's my room, so why should it bother you?").

RECAP

- Although popular books for parents of teenagers present adolescence as a problematic time for the family, the notion that a wide gap exists between the generations in fundamental values is largely a myth.
- When parents and adolescents disagree, it tends to be over mundane, day-to-day issues, not over major values or priorities.

- Many disagreements between parents and teenagers stem from the different perspectives that they bring to the discussion: The same issues that parents see as matters of right or wrong may be seen by adolescents as matters of personal choice.
- Conflict between parents and children may increase in early adolescence because adolescents change their perspective on many issues that they had previously viewed as ones their parents had legitimate authority to regulate.

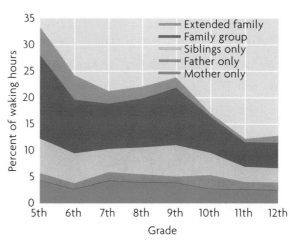

FIGURE 4.1 Age differences in the amount of time adolescents spend with family members. (Larson et al., 1996)

Family Relationships at Adolescence

Although it is incorrect to characterize adolescence as a time of high conflict in most families, it is important to keep in mind that adolescence is nevertheless a period of change and reorganization in family relationships and daily interactions (Collins & Laursen, 2004). As they develop, adolescents spend increasingly less time in family activities, especially in activities with the family as a group (see Figure 4.1) (Larson, Richards, Moneta, Holmbeck, & Duckett, 1996).

A TIME OF REORGANIZATION AND CHANGE

According to **family systems theory,** relationships in families change most dramatically during those times when individual family members or the family's circumstances are changing, since it is during these times that the family's previously established equilibrium, or balance, will be upset. Not surprisingly, one period in which family relationships usually change a great deal is adolescence. One study of interactions between adolescent boys and their parents found that the peak time for this equilibrium to be upset was around age 13 or 14; the researchers speculate that, because some of this transformation may be driven by puberty, in families with girls, this "disequilibrium" is more likely to occur earlier, around age 11 or 12 (Granic, Hollenstein, Dishion, & Patterson, 2003).

The specific concerns and issues characteristic of families at adolescence arise not just because of the changing needs and concerns of the young person but also because of changes in the adolescent's parents and because of changes in the needs and functions of the family as a unit. You already have some understanding of what changes adolescents go through and how these may affect the family system. But to fully understand the changing nature of family relationships during the adolescent years, we must take into account not only characteristics of the developing young person but characteristics of the adolescent's parents and of families at this stage as well. The quality of the parent–child relationship affects not just the adolescent's well-being—it affects the parent's well-being, too (Knoester, 2003).

THE ADOLESCENT'S PARENTS AT MIDLIFE

Because people typically have their first child around age 30, most parents are in their early 40s when the first child enters early adolescence. Some research suggests that this time of life can be a potentially difficult time for many adults, whether they have children or not. Indeed, some theorists have gone so far as to describe it as a time of **midlife crisis** (Farrell & Rosenberg, 1981; Levinson, 1978).

▌ **Midlife Meets Adolescence**   If we look at the nature of these midlife crises in some detail, we find that the developmental concerns of parents and adolescents are complementary (Steinberg & Steinberg, 1994). First, consider the issue of biological change. At the same time that adolescents are entering into a period of rapid physical growth, sexual maturation, and, ultimately, the period of the life span that society has labeled one of the most physically attractive, their parents are beginning to feel increased concern about

family systems theory A perspective on family functioning that emphasizes interconnections among different family relationships (such as marital, parent–child, sibling).

midlife crisis A psychological crisis over identity believed to occur between the ages of 35 and 45, the age range of most adolescents' parents.

For many adults, their child's adolescence coincides with their own passage through midlife. Not all adults experience a "midlife crisis," but for many, this is a time of heightened introspection and self-doubt. The collision of adolescence and midlife may make the period an especially challenging one in some families.

their own bodies, about their physical attractiveness, and about their sexual appeal (Gould, 1972). One mother of an early-adolescent girl once remarked, in an interview with my research staff, that it was jarring to realize that when she and her daughter walked down the street, men now looked at her daughter, and not at her.

A second overlap of crises concerns perceptions of time and the future. At the same time that adolescents are beginning to develop the capability to think systematically about the future and do, in fact, begin to look ahead, their parents are beginning to feel that the possibilities for changes in their own lives are limited. An important shift in time perspective takes place during midlife. Before this phase in the life cycle, individuals tend to measure time in terms of how long they have been alive; after midlife, they are more likely to see things in terms of how much longer they have to live (Neugarten & Datan, 1974). One reason for this shift may be that at midlife adults are reminded of their mortality because they see their own parents aging. Whatever the reason, it is not hard to imagine that the naïve optimism of adolescence may clash with the hardened pragmatism of middle age.

Finally, consider the issue of power, status, and entrance into the roles of adulthood. Adolescence is the time when individuals are on the threshold of gaining a great deal of status. Their careers and marriages lie ahead of them, and choices may seem limitless. For their parents, in contrast, many choices have already been made—some successfully, others perhaps less so. Most

adults reach their "occupational plateau"—the point at which they can tell how successful they are likely to be—during midlife, and many must deal with whatever gap exists between their early aspirations and their actual achievements (Gould, 1972). In sum, for adolescents, this phase in the family life cycle is a time of boundless horizons; for their parents, it is a time of coming to terms with choices made when they were younger.

This overlap of crises is likely to have an impact on family relationships (Hamill, 1994; Steinberg & Steinberg, 1994). A father who is worried about his own physical health may suddenly feel uncomfortable about playing tennis each weekend with his growing son, as they did for years when the boy was younger. They may have to find new activities that they can share. An adolescent girl with big plans for the future may find it difficult to understand why her father seems so cautious and narrow-minded when she asks him for advice. She may react by turning to her friends more often. Or an adolescent boy may find his mother's constant attention annoying; he doesn't see that, to her, his interest in independence signifies the end of an important stage in her career as a parent. The adolescent's desire for autonomy may be especially stressful for parents (Small, Eastman, & Cornelius, 1988).

This generalization about the collision of adolescence and midlife must be tempered by the fact that recent decades have seen important changes in both the age at which individuals marry and the age at which they have their first child. The average age at marriage has increased, and proportionately more couples today are delaying childbearing until they have become established in their careers. As a consequence, adults tend to be older today when their children reach adolescence than was the case two decades ago. Although psychologists have studied the impact of this change on parents' relationships with their infants (e.g., Parke, 1988), we do not know how being an older parent affects relationships during adolescence.

■ **The Mental Health of Parents** What we do know is that in families with middle-aged adults, adjusting to adolescence may take more of a toll on the mental health of parents than on the mental health of adolescents (Steinberg & Steinberg, 1994). One study found that nearly two-thirds of mothers and fathers described adolescence as the most difficult stage of parenting (Pasley & Gecas, 1984), and several studies have found this period in the family life cycle to be a low point in parents' marital and life satisfaction (Gecas & Seff, 1990). Parents who are deeply involved in work outside the home or who have an especially happy marriage may be buffered against some of these negative consequences, however, whereas single mothers may be especially vulnerable to these effects (Silverberg, Marczak, & Gondoli, 1996; Silverberg

& Steinberg, 1987, 1990; Steinberg & Silverberg, 1987; Steinberg & Steinberg, 1994). In fact, a strained relationship between a midlife parent and his or her adolescent child may drive the parent to devote relatively more time to work (Fortner, Crouter, & McHale, 2004).

By the way, the notion that parents' mental health declines when they enter the "empty nest" stage is a myth, especially among mothers. Parents' mental health is worse when their teenage children are living at home than it is once they have moved out, and when children leave home, it is fathers, not mothers, who typically feel the greatest sense of loss (Steinberg & Steinberg, 1994).

FOOD FOR THOUGHT

Many studies have found that marital satisfaction is lower when parents' first-born child is a teenager than at any other point in the marriage. Why do you think this might be?

CHANGES IN FAMILY NEEDS AND FUNCTIONS

It is not only individual family members who undergo change during the family's adolescent years. The family as a unit changes as well in its economic circumstances, its relationship to other social institutions, and its functions. One of the most important changes is financial, with family finances likely to be strained during adolescence. Children grow rapidly during puberty, and clothing for adolescents is expensive. Keeping up with the accoutrements of the peer culture—the DVDs, cosmetics, clothes, cell phones, and high-priced home video, computer, and stereo equipment—may push a family budget to the limit. Many families also begin saving money for large anticipated expenditures, such as the adolescent's college education. And in some families, parents may find themselves having to help support their own parents at a time when their children are still economically dependent. The financial demands placed on parents in the "sandwich generation" (that is, sandwiched between their adolescent children and their aging parents) require considerable adjustment.

In addition to these financial pressures, the adolescent's family must cope with the increasing importance of the peer group (Larson & Richards, 1994). During the early stages of the life cycle, the child's social world is fairly narrow, and the family is the central setting. During late childhood and early adolescence, however, the peer group becomes a setting in which extremely close

ties are forged, and parents and adolescents may argue about the teenager's reluctance to give up time with her or his friends for family activities. How adolescents and parents adjust to this shift in orientation is likely to vary across ethnic groups, since certain cultures are more likely to stress family obligations—like helping with household chores—than others (Fuligni, Yip, & Tseng, 2002; Lee, 2001). Differing expectations about family obligations between parents and teenagers are an important source of stress for adolescents, especially those whose parents grew up outside the United States, with different expectations about children's duties (Crane, So, Larson, & Hafen, 2005; Phinney & Ong, 2002).

Finally, important changes in family functions also take place during adolescence. During infancy and childhood, the functions and responsibilities of the family are fairly clear: nurturance, protection, and socialization. While all these roles are still important during adolescence, adolescents are more in need of support than nurturance, of guidance more than protection, of direction more than socialization. Making the transition from the family functions of childhood to the family functions of adolescence is not necessarily easy. The transition is further complicated in contemporary society, in which preparation for adulthood—one of the chief tasks of adolescence that was once carried out primarily by the family—is increasingly performed in other institutions, such as the school. Many families may feel at a loss to figure out just what their role during adolescence is.

TRANSFORMATIONS IN FAMILY RELATIONS

Together, the biological, cognitive, and social transitions of adolescence, the changes experienced by adults at midlife, and the changes undergone by the family during this stage in the family life cycle, set in motion a series of transformations in family relationships. In most families, there is a movement during adolescence away from patterns of influence and interaction that are asymmetrical and unequal, and toward ones in which parents and adolescents are on a more equal footing. And some evidence suggests that early adolescence—when this shift toward more egalitarian relationships first begins—may be a time of temporary disruption in the family system.

■ **Changes in the Balance of Power** Studies of family interaction suggest that early adolescence may be a time during which young people begin to try to play a more forceful role in the family but parents may not yet acknowledge adolescents' input. As a result, young adolescents may interrupt their parents more often but have little impact. By middle adolescence, however, teenagers act and are treated much more like adults. They have more influence over family decisions, but they do not

Early adolescence is often a time of heightened conflict between parents and teenagers. Bickering between adolescents and their parents increases during preadolescence, peaks in early adolescence, and then begins to subside.

need to assert their opinions through interruptions and similarly immature behavior (Grotevant, 1997).

Increases in the assertiveness and influence of adolescents as they get older are consistent with their changing needs and capabilities. To adapt to the changes triggered by the child's entrance into adolescence, family members must have some shared sense of what they are experiencing and how they are changing. Yet studies show that in many families parents and children live in "separate realities," perceiving their day-to-day experiences in very different ways (Larson and Richards, 1994). A mother and son, for example, may have a conversation about the boy's schoolwork, and while she may experience the conversation as a serious discussion, he may perceive it as an argument. One recent study of African American families, in which mothers, teenagers, and researchers all rated a videotape of the mother and teenager having a discussion, found that the teenagers rated their mother's behavior far more negatively than did either the mother or the researcher (Campione-Barr & Smetana, 2004). One interesting finding to emerge from recent research on brain maturation in adolescence is that young adolescents may be especially sensitive—perhaps even overreactive—to the emotional signals transmitted by others. A parent may speak to an adolescent in a serious voice, but the adolescent may experience it as anger (Nelson, Leibenluft, McClure, & Pine, 2005).

▌ **The Role of Puberty**   The adolescent's biological and cognitive maturation likely play a role in unbalancing the family system during early adolescence. Several researchers have demonstrated that family relationships change during puberty, with bickering between adolescents and their parents increasing, and closeness between adolescents and their parents diminishing (Baer, 2002; Holmbeck, 1996; Larson, Richards, Moneta, Holmbeck, & Duckett, 1996; McGue, Elkins, Walden, & Iacono, 2005).

Although puberty seems to distance adolescents from their parents, it is not associated with familial "storm and stress," and rates of outright conflict between parents and children are not dramatically higher during adolescence than before or after (Laursen, Coy, & Collins, 1998). Rather, disputes between parents and teenagers are typical of the sorts of arguments people have when a more powerful person (in this case, the parent) is trying to get a less powerful one (in this case, the adolescent) to do something (Adams & Laursen, 2001). Similarly, the diminished closeness is more likely to be manifested in increased privacy on the part of the adolescent and diminished physical affection between teenagers and parents, rather than any serious loss of love or respect between parents and children (Collins & Laursen, 2004; Montemayor, 1983, 1986). Research suggests that the distancing that takes place between parents and teenagers in early and middle adolescence is temporary, and that parent–child relationships may become less conflicted and more intimate during late adolescence (Thornton, Orbuch, & Axinn, 1995). Nevertheless, studies indicate that the more frequent bickering characteristic of early adolescence may take a modest toll on parents' mental health (Steinberg, 2001).

Patterns of conflict and closeness in the family at adolescence may vary across ethnic groups. One study found that in Asian American households, there is an increase in conflict, as in non-Asian families, but not until later in adolescence (Greenberger & Chen, 1996). Patterns of conflict and closeness in immigrant families may also differ as a function of the language used by adolescents and parents to communicate: Conflict is less frequent, and cohesion higher, in households where teenagers and their parents communicate in their native language (Tseng & Fuligni, 2000). Because the disagreements parents and adolescents have typically revolve around issues of parental control, patterns of squabbling and bickering will likely vary across cultural groups whose timetables for adolescent independence differ.

In any event, it is probably fair to say that the first half of adolescence may be a somewhat more strained time for the family than earlier or later. Part of the problem may be that conflicts between teenagers and parents tend to be resolved not through compromise but through one party giving in or walking away, neither of which enhances the quality of the relationship or contributes to the adolescent's or the parent's well-being (Laursen & Collins, 1994; Tucker, McHale, & Crouter, 2003).

▌ **Violations of Expectations**   Several researchers have studied changes in adolescents' cognitive abilities and how these changes may reverberate throughout the family. We noted earlier in this chapter that changes in the ways adolescents view family rules and regulations may contribute to increased conflict between them and their parents (Smetana, 1989). Research also indicates that early adolescence is a time of changes in youngsters' views of family relationships and in family members' expectations of each other (Lanz, Scabini, Vermulst, & Gerris, 2001). For example, one study asked adolescents of different ages to characterize their actual and ideal families in terms of how close and dominant different family members were (Feldman & Gehring, 1988). With age, the gap between adolescents' actual and ideal portraits widened, indicating that as they became older, adolescents became more aware of their families' shortcomings—at least in comparison to what they believed a perfect family was like. This realization does not necessarily lead adolescents to reject their parents, but it does lead to a more balanced, and probably more accurate, appraisal of them (Youniss & Smollar, 1985).

Psychologist W. Andrew Collins (1988, 1990) has examined changes in children's and parents' expectations for each other during adolescence and how "violations" of these expectations can cause family conflict. A child may enter adolescence expecting that it will be a time of great freedom, for example, whereas the parents may view the same period as one in which tighter reins are necessary. Alternatively, another child, perhaps influenced by television sitcoms portraying happy families, may imagine that adolescence will be a time of increased closeness and shared activities in the family, only to find that his or her parents have been looking forward to having time to themselves. It is easy to see how differences in expectations about what adolescence is going to be like can escalate into arguments and misunderstandings. When questioned about whether adolescents were expected to disclose secrets to their parents, for example, adolescents' expectations for secrecy were much greater than parents' (Smetana, Metzger, Gettman, & Campione-Barr, 2006). For this reason, psychologists have been studying what sorts of beliefs children and parents have about adolescence, what influences these beliefs, and where they turn for sources of information (Steinberg, 2001; Whiteman & Buchanan, 2002).

SEX DIFFERENCES IN FAMILY RELATIONSHIPS

In general, differences between the family relations of sons and daughters are minimal. Although there are occasional exceptions to the rule, sons and daughters report similar degrees of closeness to their parents, similar amounts of conflict, similar types of rules (and disagreements about those rules), and similar patterns of activity. And observational studies of interactions between parents and adolescents indicate that sons and daughters interact with their parents in remarkably similar ways (Steinberg & Silk, 2002).

Family relationships may be similar for sons and daughters, but they could not be more different for mothers and fathers. Indeed, the consistency with which studies of parents and adolescents uncover different patterns of relations for mothers and fathers is striking—especially in light of changes that have taken place in sex roles in contemporary society. Teenagers—males and females alike—relate very differently to mothers and to fathers (Collins and Russell, 1991; Holmbeck, Paikoff, & Brooks-Gunn, 1995). Adolescents tend to be closer to their mother, to spend more time alone with their mother, and to feel more comfortable talking to their mother about problems and other emotional matters; as a consequence, mothers tend to be more involved than fathers in their adolescents' lives (Updegraff, McHale, Crouter, & Kupanoff, 2001; Williams & Kelly, 2005). Fathers often rely on mothers for information about their adolescent's activities, but the reverse is uncommon (Crouter, Bumpus, Davis, & McHale, 2005; Waizenhofer, Buchanan, & Jackson-Newsom, 2004). Fathers are more likely to be perceived as relatively distant authority figures who may be consulted for objective information (such as help with homework) but who are rarely sought for support or guidance (such as help with problems with a boyfriend or girlfriend). Interestingly, adolescents also fight more often with their mothers than with their fathers, but this higher level of conflict does not appear to jeopardize the closeness of the mother–adolescent relationship. Relationships between adolescents and their mothers are more emotionally intense in general, and this intensity has both positive and negative manifestations (Apter, 1990; Larson & Richards, 1994).

RECAP

- Transformations in family relations are sparked by the biological, cognitive, and social maturation of the adolescent, by the changes of parents at midlife, and by changes in the needs and functions of the family.
- Adolescence is a time of reorganization in family relationships, with adolescents gaining increasingly more power and becoming increasingly more assertive.
- Many of the changes in family relations that occur at adolescence affect the psychological well-being of the adolescent's middle-aged parents as well as the teenager; indeed, in some regards, adolescence may be a more difficult time for the parents than the teenager.
- Although the family relations of adolescent males and females are very similar, studies show that mothers and fathers have very different relationships with their teenagers, regardless of the teenagers' gender.

Family Relationships and Adolescent Development

Thus far, we have looked at the sorts of issues and concerns faced by most families during the adolescent years. In our focus on those experiences that all families share, however, we have not addressed the very important questions of how relationships differ from family to family and whether these differences have important consequences for the developing adolescent. Some parents are stricter than others. Some adolescents are given a great deal of affection, while others are treated more distantly. In some households, decisions are made through open discussion and verbal give-and-take; in other households, parents lay down the rules, and children are expected to follow them. To what extent are different patterns of family relationships associated with different patterns of adolescent development? Are some styles of parenting more likely to be associated with healthy development than others?

Before we try to answer these questions, several cautions are in order. Although our tendency is to see children's behavior as the result of their parents' behavior, socialization is actually a two-way, not a one-way, street (Collins, Maccoby, Steinberg, Hetherington, & Bornstein, 2000). Just as parents affect their adolescents' behavior, so do adolescents affect their parents' behavior, thereby playing a role in shaping their own development (Ge, Conger, Lorenz, Shanahan, & Elder, 1995; Lerner, Castellino, & Perkins, 1994). One nine-year longitudinal study found, for example, that adolescents' and parents' negative feelings toward each other had a reciprocal relationship over time—the more negative adolescents felt, the more this led to negative feelings on the part of their parents, and vice versa (Kim, Conger, Lorenz, & Elder, 2001).

In addition, various types of parenting affect different adolescents differently. For example, although it is well established that adolescents whose parents are hostile or aloof are more likely to exhibit antisocial behavior (e.g., Dobkin, Tremblay, & Sacchitelle, 1997), the link between negative parenting and adolescent problem behavior is far stronger among teenagers who are temperamentally more impulsive; among adolescents who are temperamentally more introverted, the same sort of negative parenting leads to anxiety and depression (Stice & Gonzales, 1998; Van Leeuwen,

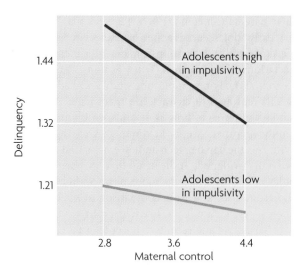

FIGURE 4.2   Adolescents who are temperamentally different are affected in different ways by the same parenting. Too little control by mothers predicts delinquency among adolescents who are impulsive but not among their peers who have more self-control. (Adapted from Stice & Gonzales, 1998)

Mervielde, Braet, & Bosmans, 2004) (see Figure 4.2). Furthermore, adolescents who have a greater genetic risk for developing problems (by virtue of their family history) are more likely to evoke from their parents the sort of behavior that has been shown to lead to the development of behavior problems (O'Connor, Deater-Deckard, Fulker, Rutter, & Plomin, 1998). Researchers who study parent–adolescent relationships have become increasingly aware of the need to look not only at the impact of parenting on the adolescent but also at the ways in which experiences in the family and in other contexts interact with genetic factors in influencing behavior and development (Collins, Maccoby, Steinberg, Hetherington, & Bornstein, 2000; Rutter, 1997). One recent study, for example, found that the impact of child abuse on later antisocial behavior depended on the presence or absence of a particular gene (Caspi et al., 2000).

PARENTING STYLES AND THEIR EFFECTS

There are a variety of ways to characterize parents' behavior toward their children. One of the most useful approaches derives from the work of psychologist Diana Baumrind (1978). According to her work and that of others in this vein, two aspects of the parent's behavior toward the adolescent are critical: parental responsiveness and parental demandingness (Maccoby & Martin, 1983). **Parental responsiveness** refers to the degree to which the parent responds to the child's needs in an accepting, supportive manner.

parental responsiveness   According to Baumrind, one of the two important dimensions of parenting; responsiveness refers to the degree to which the parent responds to the child's needs in an accepting, supportive manner.

Demandingness

	High	Low
Responsiveness High	Authoritative	Indulgent
Low	Authoritarian	Indifferent

FIGURE 4.3 A scheme for classifying parenting types.
(From Maccoby and Martin, 1983)

Parental demandingness refers to the extent to which the parent expects and demands mature, responsible behavior from the child. Parents vary on each of these dimensions. Some are warm and accepting, while others are unresponsive and rejecting; some are demanding and expect a great deal of their child, while others are permissive and demand very little.

■ **Four Styles of Parenting** Because parental responsiveness and demandingness are more or less independent of each other—that is, it is possible for a parent to be demanding without being responsive, and vice versa—it is possible to look at various combinations of these two dimensions (see Figure 4.3). Many studies of parents and children indicate that the fourfold classification scheme presented in Figure 4.3 is very important in understanding the impact of parents' behavior on the child, and psychologists have given labels to the four different prototypes presented in the figure.

Parents who are both responsive and demanding are authoritative. **Authoritative parents** are warm but firm. They set standards for the child's conduct but form expectations that are consistent with the child's developing needs and capabilities. They place a high value on the development of autonomy and self-direction but assume the ultimate responsibility for their child's behavior. Authoritative parents deal with their child in a rational, issue-oriented manner, frequently engaging in discussion and explanation over matters of discipline. Authoritative parents strive to raise a child who is self-reliant and who has a strong sense of initiative.

Parents who are very demanding but not responsive are authoritarian. **Authoritarian parents** place a high value on obedience and conformity. They tend to favor more punitive, absolute, and forceful disciplinary measures. Verbal give-and-take is not common in authoritarian households, because the underlying belief of authoritarian parents is that the child should accept without question the rules and standards established by the parents. They tend not to encourage independent behavior and, instead, place a good deal of importance on restricting the child's autonomy. Authoritarian parents place a premium on obedience.

A parent who is very responsive but not at all demanding is indulgent. **Indulgent parents** behave in an accepting, benign, and somewhat more passive way in matters of discipline. They place relatively few demands on the child's behavior, giving the child a high degree of freedom to act as he or she wishes. Indulgent parents are more likely to believe that control is an infringement on the child's freedom that may interfere with her or his healthy development. Instead of actively shaping their child's behavior, indulgent parents are more likely to view themselves as resources that the child may or may not use. Indulgent parents tend to be especially concerned with raising a happy child.

Parents who are neither demanding nor responsive are indifferent. **Indifferent parents** try to do whatever is necessary to minimize the time and energy they must devote to interacting with their child. In extreme cases, indifferent parents may be neglectful. They know little about their child's activities and whereabouts, show little interest in their child's experiences at school or with friends, rarely converse with their child, and rarely consider their child's opinion when making decisions. Rather than raising their child according to a set of beliefs about what is good for the child's development (as do the other three parent types), indifferent parents are "parent centered"—they structure their home life primarily around their own needs and interests.

■ **The Power of Authoritative Parenting** Few areas of research in the field of adolescent development have received as much attention as the link between what parents do and how adolescents turn out, and the findings of this body of work are amazingly consistent (Steinberg, 2001). Generally, young people who have been raised in authoritative households are more psychosocially mature than peers who have been raised in authoritarian, indulgent, or indifferent homes.

parental demandingness According to Baumrind, one of two important dimensions of parenting; demandingness refers to the degree to which the parent expects and insists on mature, responsible behavior from the child.

authoritative parents Parents who use warmth, firm control, and rational, issue-oriented discipline, in which emphasis is placed on the development of self-direction.

authoritarian parents Parents who use punitive, absolute, and forceful discipline, and who place a premium on obedience and conformity.

indulgent parents Parents who are characterized by responsiveness but low demandingness, and who are mainly concerned with the child's happiness.

indifferent parents Parents who are characterized by low levels of both responsiveness and demandingness.

Adolescents raised in authoritative homes are more responsible, more self-assured, more adaptive, more creative, more curious, more socially skilled, and more successful in school. Adolescents raised in authoritarian homes, in contrast, are more dependent, more passive, less socially adept, less self-assured, and less intellectually curious. Adolescents raised in indulgent households are often less mature, more irresponsible, more conforming to their peers, and less able to assume positions of leadership. Adolescents raised in indifferent homes are often impulsive and more likely to be involved in delinquent behavior and in precocious experiments with sex, drugs, and alcohol (for a review, see Collins & Steinberg, 2006).

Although occasional exceptions to these general patterns have been noted, the evidence linking authoritative parenting and healthy adolescent development is remarkably strong, and it has been found in studies of a wide range of ethnicities, social classes, and family structures, not only within the United States (e.g., Clark, Novak, & Dupree, 2002; Cleveland, Gibbons, Gerrard, Pomery, & Brody, 2005; Kim & Ge, 2000; Luthar & Latendresse, 2005; Matza, Kupersmidt, & Glenn, 2001) but in parts of the world as diverse as Iceland (Adalbjarnardottir & Hafsteinsson, 2001), the Czech Republic (Dmitrieva, Chen, Greenberger, & Gil-Rivas, 2004), India (Carson, Chowdhury, Perry, & Pati, 1999), China (Pilgrim, Luo, Urberg, & Fang, 1999), Israel (Mayseless, Scharf, & Sholt, 2003), Switzerland (Vazsonyi, Hibbert, & Snider, 2003), and Palestine (Punamaki, Qouta, et al., 1997). Indeed, the evidence in support of the advantages of authoritative parenting is so strong that some experts have suggested that the question of which type of parenting benefits teenagers the most need not be studied anymore (Steinberg, 2001). Indeed, research shows that educational programs designed to teach parents how to be more responsive and more demanding are effective in fostering healthy adolescent development and behavior (e.g., Brody et al., 2005). Table 4.1 summarizes the 10 basic principles of good parenting.

At the other extreme, parenting that is indifferent, neglectful, or abusive has been shown consistently to have harmful effects on the adolescent's mental health and development, leading to depression and a variety of behavior problems, including, in cases of physical abuse, aggression toward others (Crittenden, Claussen, & Sugarman, 1994; Pittman & Chase-Lansdale, 2001; Sheeber, Hops, Alpert, Davis, & Andrews; 1997; Strauss & Yodanis, 1996). Severe psychological abuse (excessive criticism, rejection, or emotional harshness) appears to have the most deleterious effects (Dube et al., 2003; Haj-Yahia, Musleh, & Haj-Yahia, 2002; McGee, Wolfe, & Wilson, 1997; Rohner,

TABLE 4.1 The 10 basic principles of good parenting

Several years ago, after reviewing decades of research on parenting and child development, I came to the conclusion that we really did know what sort of parenting is most likely to help children and adolescents grow up in healthy ways. I summarized this evidence in a book called *The 10 Basic Principles of Good Parenting* (Steinberg, 2005). Here's what all parents, regardless of their child's age, should keep in mind:

1. What You Do Matters
2. You Can Not Be Too Loving
3. Be Involved in Your Child's Life
4. Adapt Your Parenting to Fit Your Child
5. Establish Rules and Set Limits
6. Help Foster Your Child's Independence
7. Be Consistent
8. Avoid Harsh Discipline
9. Explain Your Rules and Decisions
10. Treat Your Child With Respect

Source: Steinberg, 2005b.

Bourque, & Elordi, 1996; Simons, Johnson, & Conger, 1994).

■ **How Authoritative Parenting Works** Why is authoritative parenting associated with healthy adolescent development? First, authoritative parents provide an appropriate balance between restrictiveness and autonomy, giving the adolescent opportunities to develop self-reliance while providing the sorts of standards, limits, and guidelines that developing individuals need (Rueter & Conger, 1995a, 1995b). Authoritative parents, for instance, are more likely to give children more independence gradually as they get older, which helps children develop self-reliance and self-assurance. Because of this, authoritative parenting promotes the development of adolescents' competence (Glasgow, Dornbusch, Troyer, Steinberg, & Ritter, 1997; Steinberg, Elmen, & Mounts, 1989) and enhances their ability to withstand a variety of potentially negative influences, including life stress (Barrera, Li, & Chassin, 1995; Hagan, MacMillan, & Wheaton, 1996; McCabe, 1997; Pearce, Jones, Schwab-Stone, & Ruchkin, 2003; Wagner, Cohen, & Brook, 1996) and exposure to antisocial peers (Galambos, Barker, & Almeida, 2003; Kim, Hetherington, & Reiss, 1999; Mason, Cauce, Gonzales, & Hiraga, 1994; Mounts & Steinberg, 1995; Walker-Barnes & Mason, 2004).

Second, because authoritative parents are more likely to engage their children in verbal give-and-take, they are likely to promote the sort of intellectual development that provides an important foundation for the development of psychosocial maturity (Rueter & Conger, 1998; Smetana, Crean, & Daddis, 2002). Authoritative parents, for example, are less likely than other parents to assert their authority by turning adolescents' personal decisions (such as over what type of music they listen to) into "moral" issues (Smetana, 1995; Smetana & Asquith, 1994). Family discussions in which decisions, rules, and expectations are explained help the child understand social systems and social relationships. This understanding plays an important role in the development of reasoning abilities, role taking, moral judgment, and empathy (Baumrind, 1978; Eisenberg & Morris, 2004; Krevans & Gibbs, 1996).

Authoritative parents are warm, firm, and fair. They strike a balance between exercising their authority over the adolescent and granting an appropriate degree of independence.

FOOD FOR THOUGHT

Our discussion has focused mainly on the consequences of growing up with parents who use different styles of parenting. But what makes parents choose the sort of parenting they use? Why are some parents authoritative but others not?

Third, because authoritative parenting is based on a warm parent–child relationship, adolescents are more likely to identify with, admire, and form strong attachments to their parents, which leaves them more open to their parents' influence (Bogenschneider, Small, & Tsay, 1997; Darling & Steinberg, 1993; Mackey, Arnold, & Pratt, 2001; Mounts, 2002; Sim, 2000). Adolescents who have had warm and close relationships with their parents are more likely, for example, to have similar attitudes and values (Brody, Moore, & Glei, 1994). Adolescents who are raised by nonauthoritative parents, in contrast, often end up having friends their parents disapprove of, including those involved in problem behavior (Adamczyk-Robinette, Fletcher, & Wright, 2002; Kim et al., 1999).

Finally, the child's own behavior may play a role in shaping authoritative parenting practices (Cook, 2001; Lewis, 1981a; Stice & Barrera, 1995). Children who are responsible, self-directed, curious, and self-assured elicit from their parents warmth, flexible guidance, and verbal give-and-take. In contrast, children who are aggressive, dependent, or less psychosocially mature in other ways may provoke parents' behavior that is excessively harsh, passive, or distant (Rueter & Conger, 1998). Parents may enjoy being around children who are responsible, independent, and willing to tell them about their activities and whereabouts, and they may treat them more warmly as a result. Thus, although evidence suggests that active parental monitoring does deter adolescent problem behavior (Fletcher, Steinberg, & Williams-Wheeler, 2004; Waizenhofer et al., 2004), some of what often appears to be "effective parental monitoring" may actually be the end result of a parent–adolescent relationship in which the adolescent willingly discloses information to the parent (Kerr & Stattin, 2000; Soenens, Vansteenkiste, Luyckx, & Goossens, 2006; Stattin & Kerr, 2000). In contrast, children who are continually acting up make their parents short-tempered, impatient, or distant. In one recent study, for instance, the researchers found that when parents had little knowledge of their adolescent's behavior, this led to an increase in delinquency, but that increases in delinquency, in turn, led to decreases in parental knowledge (Laird, Pettit, Bates, & Dodge, 2003) (see Figure 4.4). In other words, the relationship between adolescent competence and authoritative parenting may be the result of a reciprocal cycle in which the child's psychosocial maturity leads to authoritative parenting, which, in turn, leads to the further development of

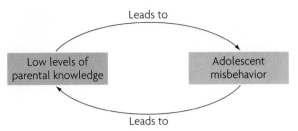

FIGURE 4.4 The relation between parenting and adolescent behavior is often reciprocal. (Adapted from Laird et al., 2003)

maturity (Lerner, Castellino, & Perkins, 1994; Repetti, 1996; Steinberg et al., 1989). In contrast, nonauthoritative parenting may lead to the development of emotional and behavioral problems, which may lead parents to disengage even more (Dishion, Nelson, & Bullock, 2004).

ETHNIC DIFFERENCES IN PARENTING PRACTICES

A number of researchers have asked whether parents from different ethnic groups vary in their child rearing and whether the relation between parenting and adolescent outcomes is the same across different ethnic groups. These, of course, are two different questions: The first concerns average differences between groups in their approaches to parenting (for example, whether ethnic minority parents are stricter than white parents), whereas the second concerns the correlation between parenting practices and adolescent adjustment in different groups (for example, whether the effect of strictness is the same in ethnic minority families as it is in white families).

In general, researchers find that authoritative parenting, as defined earlier in this chapter, is less prevalent among African American, Asian American, or Hispanic American families than among white families, no doubt reflecting the fact that parenting practices are often linked to cultural values and beliefs (Dornbusch et al., 1987; Smetana & Chuang, 2001; Steinberg, Dornbusch, & Brown, 1992; Yau & Smetana, 1996). Nevertheless, even though authoritative parenting is less common in ethnic minority families, as noted earlier, its effects on adolescent adjustment are beneficial in all ethnic groups (Amato & Fowler, 2002; Knight, Virdin, & Roosa, 1994; Mason, Cauce, Gonzales, & Hiraga, 1996; Steinberg et al., 1992; Walker-Barnes & Mason, 2001). In other words, ethnic minority youngsters benefit from parenting that is responsive and demanding, just as their nonminority peers do (Steinberg, 2001).

Research also indicates that authoritarian parenting (high in demandingness but low in responsiveness) is more prevalent among ethnic minority than

Research indicates important ethnic differences in parenting practices during adolescence. In general, Asian American parents are stricter than their counterparts from other cultural groups.

among white families, even after taking ethnic differences in socioeconomic status into account (Chao, 1994; Dornbusch et al., 1987; Steinberg, Lamborn, Dornbusch, & Darling, 1992). As opposed to research on authoritative parenting, however, which suggests similar effects across ethnic groups, research on authoritarian parenting indicates that the adverse effects of this style of parenting may be greater among white youngsters than among their ethnic minority counterparts (Chao, 1994; Morrison Gutman et al., 2002; Lamborn, Dornbusch, & Steinberg, 1996; Ruiz, Roosa, & Gonzales, 2002; Schweingruber & Kalil, 2000; Steinberg, Lamborn, Darling, Mounts, & Dornbusch, 1994). Several explanations have been offered for this finding.

First, because ethnic minority families are more likely to live in dangerous communities, authoritarian parenting, with its emphasis on control, may not be as harmful and may even offer some benefits (Steinberg, Blatt-Eisengart, & Cauffman, 2006). Second, as several researchers (Chao, 1994, 2001; Gonzales, Cauce, & Mason, 1996) have pointed out, the distinction between authoritative versus authoritarian parenting may not always make sense when applied to parents from other cultures. For example, nonwhite parents frequently combine a very high degree of strictness (like white authoritarian parents) with warmth (like white authoritative parents) (Formoso, Ruiz, & Gonzales, 1997; Smetana & Gaines, 2000; Supple, Peterson, & Bush, 2004). Because most of the research on parenting and adolescent development has been conducted by white researchers, other ethnic groups' approaches to child rearing (which appear very controlling, but which are neither aloof nor hostile) may be mislabeled as authoritarian (Gonzales et al., 1996). Similar arguments have been made about the misinterpretation of strictness among American parents from all ethnic groups who are conservative Protestants (Gunnoe, Hetherington, & Reiss, 1999, 2006; Wilcox, 1998). Nevertheless, it is important to keep in mind that the conclusion to be drawn from these studies is not that authoritarian parenting is better than authoritative parenting for ethnic minority adolescents, but rather that it is not as harmful in these groups as it has been shown to be among white adolescents (Collins & Steinberg, 2006).

AUTONOMY AND ATTACHMENT IN THE ADOLESCENT'S FAMILY

Several studies of conversations between adolescents and their parents have examined factors in the nature of parent–adolescent communication that contribute to healthy adolescent development. In these studies, families were asked to discuss a problem together, and their interaction was videotaped and later analyzed. Generally, families with psychologically competent teenagers interact in ways that permit family members to express their autonomy and individuality while remaining attached, or connected, to other family members (Grotevant, 1997; Rathunde, 1996; Silverberg, Tennenbaum, & Jacob, 1992). In these families, verbal give-and-take is the norm, and adolescents (as well as parents) are encouraged to express their own opinions, even if this sometimes leads to disagreements. At the same time, however, the importance of maintaining close relationships in the family is emphasized, and individuals are encouraged to consider how their actions may affect other family members (Rueter & Conger, 1995a, 1995b). Indeed, adolescents who are permitted to assert their own opinions within a family context that is secure and loving develop higher self-esteem and more mature coping abilities. Adolescents whose autonomy is squelched are at risk for developing feelings of depression and low self-esteem, whereas those who do not feel connected are more likely than their peers to develop behavior problems (Allen, Hauser, Bell, & O'Conner, 1994; Aquilino & Supple, 2001; Barber, 1996; Boykin, McElhaney & Allen, 2001).

Rather than posing attachment and autonomy as opposites, studies of family interaction indicate that the path to healthy psychological development during adolescence is likely to combine the two. In other words, adolescents appear to do best when they grow up in a family atmosphere that permits the development of individuality against a backdrop of close family ties (Grolnick, Kurowski, Dunlap, & Hevey,

2000; Grotevant & Cooper, 1986; Walsh, Shulman, Bar-On, & Tsur, 2006). In these families, conflict between parents and adolescents can play a very important and positive role in the adolescent's social and cognitive development, because individuals are encouraged to express their opinions in an atmosphere that does not risk severing the emotional attachment (Cooper, 1988). Perhaps for this reason, adolescents whose perceptions of their family differ from those of their parents a little bit are better adjusted than those whose views are either identical to their parents' or extremely divergent (Feinberg, Howe, Reiss, & Hetherington, 2000).

ADOLESCENTS' RELATIONSHIPS WITH SIBLINGS

Far more is known about adolescents' relations with their parents than about their relations with brothers and sisters. In recent years, however, research on adolescence and the family has moved beyond studies of parent–adolescent relationships to also focus on the family system (e.g., Rueter & Conger 1995a, b), the extended family (e.g., Spieker & Bensley 1994), and siblings. There has been a particular surge of interest in sibling relationships and the ways in which siblings influence adolescent development.

▌ **The Nature of Sibling Relationships in Adolescence** In general, sibling relationships during adolescence have characteristics that set them apart from both other family relationships (such as those between adolescents and their parents) and relationships with peers (such as those between adolescents and their close friends) (Furman & Buhrmester, 1985; Raffaelli & Larson, 1987). In one study, young adolescents were asked to rate several types of relationships (for example, with parents, siblings, friends, and grandparents) along similar dimensions. Adolescents rated their sibling relationships similarly to those with their parents with regard to measures of companionship and importance, but sibling relationships were rated more like friendships with respect to power, assistance, and their satisfaction with the relationship.

FOOD FOR THOUGHT

Did you grow up with siblings? How did your relationship with them change as you moved through adolescence?

Young adolescents often have emotionally charged relationships with siblings that are marked by conflict and rivalry, but also by nurturance and support (Lempers & Clark-Lempers, 1992). As children mature from childhood to early adolescence, sibling conflict increases (Brody, Stoneman, & McCoy, 1994), with adolescents reporting more negativity in their sibling relationships compared to their relationships with peers (Buhrmester & Furman 1990) and less effective conflict resolution than with their parents (Tucker, McHale, & Crouter, 2003a). Over the course of adolescence, adolescents' relationships with siblings, and especially with younger siblings, become more egalitarian but also more distant and less emotionally intense (Buhrmester & Furman, 1990; Cole & Kerns, 2001). As with the parent–adolescent relationship, siblings become less influential as adolescents expand their relations outside the family (Hetherington, Henderson, & Reiss, 1999). Sibling relationships improve as individuals leave adolescence and move into young adulthood, however (Scharf, Shulman, & Avigad-Spitz, 2005). Despite these changes over time, there is considerable stability in the quality of sibling relationships between childhood and adolescence, and

Because siblings live in close proximity to each other, they have added opportunities for both positive and negative interactions.

siblings who are relatively closer during middle childhood are relatively closer as adolescents (Dunn, Slomkowski, & Beardsall, 1994).

■ **A Network of Relationships** Several researchers have uncovered important links among parent–child, sibling, and peer relations in adolescence, and these findings indicate that it is helpful to think of the adolescent's interpersonal world as consisting of a web of interconnected relationships (see Figure 4.5). A body of research indicates that the quality of the parent–adolescent relationship influences the quality of relations among adolescent brothers and sisters (e.g., Brody et al., 1994; East & Khoo, 2005; Hoffman, Kiecolt, & Edwards, 2005; Matthews & Conger, 2004; Paley, Conger, & Harold, 2000; Reese-Weber, 2000). Harmony and cohesiveness in the parent–adolescent relationship are associated with less sibling conflict and a more positive sibling relationship (e.g., Hetherington et al., 1999). In contrast, adolescents who experience maternal rejection and negativity are more likely to display aggression with siblings.

By the same token, children and adolescents learn much about social relationships from sibling interactions, and they bring this knowledge and experience to friendships outside the family (Brody, Stoneman, & McCoy, 1994; McCoy, Brody, & Stoneman, 1994; Updegraff, McHale, & Crouter, 2000). In poorly functioning families, aggressive interchanges between unsupervised siblings may provide a training ground within which adolescents learn, practice, and perfect antisocial and aggressive behavior (Bank, Reid, & Greenley, 1994; Criss & Shaw, 2005; Snyder, Bank, & Burraston, 2005). The reverse is true as well—the quality of adolescents' relationships with their friends influences how they interact with their siblings (Kramer & Kowal, 2005).

The quality of the sibling relationship affects not only adolescents' peer relations but their adjustment in general (Seginer, 1998; Stocker, Burwell, & Briggs, 2002). Positive sibling relationships contribute to adolescent school competence, sociability, autonomy, and self-worth (e.g., Hetherington et al., 1999; Yeh & Lempers, 2004). Having a close sibling relationship can partially ameliorate the negative effects of not having friends in school (East & Rook, 1992), and siblings can serve as sources of advice and guidance (Kolburn

FIGURE 4.5 Adolescents' relationships inside the family affect their relationships with peers.

Quality of parent–adolescent relationship → Quality of adolescent's relationships with siblings → Quality of adolescent's relationships with friends

Kowal & Blinn-Pike, 2004; Tucker, Barber, & Eccles, 1997; Tucker, McHale, & Crouter, 2001). Of course, siblings can influence the development of problems as well (Bank, Burraston, & Snyder, 2004; Conger et al., 1997). For example, younger sisters of childbearing adolescents are more likely to engage in early sexual activity and to become pregnant during adolescence (e.g., East & Jacobson, 2001; East & Kierman, 2001). Siblings also influence each other's drug use and antisocial behavior (e.g., Ardelt & Day, 2002; Bullock & Dishion, 2002; Haynie & McHugh, 2003; Rowe, Rodgers, & Meseck-Bushey, 1989).

RECAP

- Psychologists have identified four basic styles of parenting during adolescence: authoritative (responsive and demanding), authoritarian (demanding but not responsive), indulgent (responsive but not demanding), and indifferent (neither demanding nor responsive).
- In general, adolescents from authoritative homes fare best on measures of psychological adjustment, whereas adolescents from indifferent homes fare worst.
- Studies of parent–adolescent interaction show, as well, that the healthiest families are those that permit the adolescent to develop a sense of autonomy while staying emotionally attached to the family.
- Over the course of adolescence, adolescents' relationships with siblings become more equal but more distant and less emotionally intense.
- The quality of the adolescent's sibling relationships are affected by the quality of the parent–child relationship and, as well, the quality of adolescent–sibling relationships affects adolescents' mental health and peer relationships.

Behavioral Genetics and Adolescent Development

One topic of interest to researchers who study adolescents and their siblings concerns how closely siblings resemble each other in various characteristics, such as intelligence, personality, and interests. Recent advances in the study of **behavioral genetics** have provided new insights into this issue, as well as a host of others concerning the joint impact of genes and environment on development.

Researchers examine this issue by studying adolescents who are twins, to see whether identical twins are more similar than fraternal twins (e.g., McGue, Elkins, Walden, & Iacono, 2005); by studying adolescents who have been adopted, to see whether adopted adolescents are more like their biological parents than like their adoptive parents (e.g., Abrahamson, Baker, & Caspi, 2002; Deater-Deckard & Plomin, 1999); and by studying adolescents and their siblings in stepfamilies, to see whether similarity between siblings varies with their biological relatedness (e.g., Hetherington et al., 1994; Neiderhiser et al., 2004). In addition to examining whether and how much given traits are genetically versus environmentally determined, researchers also ask how these two sets of factors interact (for example, whether the same environment affects people with different genetic makeups in different ways, or whether people with different genetic makeups evoke different reactions from their environment) (Collins et al., 2000).

GENETIC AND ENVIRONMENTAL INFLUENCES ON ADOLESCENT DEVELOPMENT

In studies of genetic and environmental influences on adolescent development, researchers distinguish between two types of environmental influences. **Shared environmental influences** are factors in the environment that individuals, such as siblings, have in common and that make the individuals similar in personality and behavior. **Nonshared environmental influences** are factors in the environments of individuals that are not similar and that, as a consequence, make the individuals different from one another (Plomin & Daniels, 1987). In studies of siblings, nonshared environmental influences can include factors within the family as well as outside of it. For example, if two siblings are treated very differently by their parents, this would be considered a nonshared environmental influence. Indeed, some evidence suggests that this sort of nonshared environment—that is, the nonshared environment that results from people having different experiences within what would appear to be the same context—may be the most important (Turkheimer & Waldron, 2000). Studies indicate that both genetic and nonshared environmental influences,

behavioral genetics   The scientific study of genetic influences on behavior.

shared environmental influences   Nongenetic influences that make individuals living in the same family similar to each other.

nonshared environmental influences   The nongenetic influences in individuals' lives that make them different from people they live with.

such as differential parental treatment, peer relations, and school experiences, are particularly strong in adolescence. In contrast, shared environmental factors, such as parental personality, family socioeconomic status, or the neighborhood in which two siblings live, are less influential (McGue, Sharma, & Benson, 1996; Pike et al., 1996).

Studies of siblings have revealed that genetic factors strongly influence many qualities that have been assumed to be shaped mainly by the environment. Evidence suggests that aggressive behavior is especially driven by genetic influences, although shared and nonshared environmental influences on adolescents' antisocial behavior, including aggression, also have been found (Deater-Deckard & Plomin 1999; Eley, Lichenstein, & Stevenson 1999; Spotts, Neiderhiser, Hetherington, & Reiss, 2001). Genetic factors also have been linked to emotional distress in adolescence, such as risk for suicide and depression (Jacobson & Rowe, 1999). Research also has found strong genetic influences on adolescent competence, self-image, and intelligence. Adolescents' self-perceptions of their scholastic competence, athletic competence, physical appearance, social competence, and general self-worth are moderately heritable, with little evidence for shared environmental influences (McGuire et al., 1994, 1999).

Intelligence in adolescence (as indexed by IQ) is also under strong genetic control, with genetic influences compounding over time and ultimately becoming more influential than the family environment, although genetic influences on school performance, in contrast to intelligence, are more modest (Loehlin, Neiderhiser, & Reiss, 1989; Teachman, 1997). In general, genetic influences on intelligence are stronger in families with highly educated parents, consistent with the general notion that the influence of genes is typically higher in more favorable environments (Rowe, Jacobson, & Van den Oord, 1999).

When researchers study the impact of the family context on adolescent development, they assume that they are studying an environmental, rather than a genetic, influence. But one of the most interesting findings to emerge in recent years is that assessments of the adolescent's family may also reflect features of the adolescent's and parents' genetic makeup. Actual and reported levels of conflict, support, and involvement in the family, for example, are significantly influenced by adolescents' genetic makeup (Neiderhiser, Pike, Hetherington, & Reiss, 1999). This results in part because adolescents who display hostile and antisocial behaviors are more likely than adolescents not prone to these problems to elicit negative behaviors from

their parents (Ge et al., 1996), and in part because the same genetic factors that may make adolescents prone to fighting (for instance, irritability) may make them prone to be critical of their parents when questioned about their family (McGue et al., 2005; Neiderhiser, Pike, et al., 1999). Because of this, it is important to be cautious when interpreting research on adolescent development in the family context. Indeed, growing evidence suggests that at least some of the impact of parenting on adolescent adjustment, depression, and antisocial behavior can be explained by the genetic transmission of these characteristics from parents to their children (Neiderhiser, Pike, et al., 1999; Neiderhiser, Reiss, et al., 2004).

WHY ARE SIBLINGS OFTEN SO DIFFERENT?

Given the fact that the environment plays an important role in shaping development, and in view of research suggesting that the family context is an important influence, how can we explain the fact that siblings who grow up in the same family often turn out to be very different from one another? One answer is that siblings may have very different family experiences, both because they are treated differently by their parents and because they often perceive similar experiences in different ways (Feinberg & Hetherington, 2000; Mekos, Hetherington, & Reiss, 1996; O'Connor, Hetherington, Reiss, & Plomin, 1995; Plomin and Daniels, 1987; Tucker, McHale, & Crouter, 2003b). For example, one brother may describe his family as very close-knit, while another may have experienced it as very distant. One girl may describe her family life as plagued with argument and conflict, while her sister describes it as peaceful and agreeable. In other words, even though we may assume that children growing up in the same family have shared the same environment, this is not necessarily the case.

As you might expect, unequal treatment from mothers or fathers often creates conflict among siblings (Brody, Stoneman, & Burke, 1987) and is linked to problem behaviors, such as depression, antisocial behavior, and early pregnancy (East & Jacobson, 2003; Reiss et al., 1995). Studies also show that differences in siblings' real and perceived family experiences are related to different patterns of development (Anderson, Hetherington, Reiss, & Howe, 1994; Barrett-Singer & Weinstein, 2000; Conger & Conger, 1994; Mekos et al., 1996). In general, better-adjusted adolescents are more likely than their siblings to report that their relationship with their mother was close, that their relations with brothers or sisters were friendly, that they were involved in family decision making, and that they were given a high level of responsibility around the house (Daniels, Dunn, Furstenberg, & Plomin, 1985).

Despite this evidence for differential treatment and its potentially adverse influence on adolescent development, adolescents report that 75 percent of parental treatment is not differential. Interestingly, studies show that youngsters, especially as they get older, generally appreciate the reasons for parents treating siblings differently, and that sibling relationships are strained only when this differential treatment is perceived as unfair (Feinberg, Neiderhiser, Simmens, Reiss, & Hetherington, 2000; Kowal & Kramer, 1997).

Oddly, treating siblings differently may actually be a good thing for parents to do, so long as each sibling is treated well. There is some evidence that when siblings are treated differently by their parents, they get along better—presumably because this differential treatment makes them feel unique and lessens **sibling rivalry** (Feinberg, McHale, Crouter, & Cumsille, 2003). Perhaps you have a brother or sister whom you resemble more than you'd like—so much, in fact, that you have had a hard time establishing your own personality. When siblings feel this way, they often deliberately try to be different from each other—a phenomenon known as **sibling deidentification**. An adolescent whose brother or sister is a star athlete, for instance, may shun sports and focus on cultivating other types of talents, perhaps in academics or in the arts, a strategy that will diminish feelings of competition. Differential treatment by parents may have similar effects.

FOOD FOR THOUGHT

The proportion of adolescents growing up as only children has increased substantially in recent decades. How might growing up without siblings influence development in adolescence?

In addition to having different experiences inside the family, siblings also may have very different experiences outside the family—at school, with friends, in the neighborhood. These contexts provide yet another source of nonshared environmental influence. Because factors other than the family environment shape adolescent development and behavior—as you will see in the next few chapters—siblings may turn out very different if they have divergent experiences outside the home.

■ **Adolescents and Adoption** Studies of the psychological development of adolescents who have been adopted have yielded mixed and often contradictory results. On average, adopted individuals show higher rates of delinquency, substance use, psychological difficulties, and poorer school performance, but the actual magnitude of the difference between adopted and nonadopted adolescents is small, especially when other factors, like family resources, are taken into account (Miller, Fan, Christensen, Grotevant, & van Dulmen, 2000; Slap, Goodman, & Huang, 2001; Sun, 2003). One reason for the mixed results and relatively modest effects is that there is a good deal of variability among adopted adolescents in their adjustment and in their feelings about being adopted. For instance, adopted adolescents who are preoccupied with having been adopted are relatively more alienated from and mistrustful of their adoptive parents (Kohler, Grotevant, & McRoy, 2002).

RECAP

- Researchers have examined genetic and environmental influences by studying adolescents who are twins, adolescents who have been adopted, and adolescents and their siblings in stepfamilies.
- Researchers distinguish between two types of environmental influences: shared environmental influences, which make individuals in the same environment similar, and nonshared environmental influences, which make them different.
- Although genetic influences on a wide range of characteristics have been documented, adolescent development is the product of the interaction between genetics and environment.
- Siblings often differ from each other because they have different experiences both inside and outside the family, and because they sometimes deliberately strive to be different.

sibling rivalry Competition between siblings, often for parental attention.

sibling deidentification The process through which siblings deliberately try to be different from each other.

The Adolescent's Family in a Changing Society

If there is one word that best characterizes the nature of family life in America as we have moved into the twenty-first century, that word is *diversity*. As you read in Chapter 3, a large and growing proportion of American adolescents are from ethnic minority families, and a large number of these youngsters are foreign-born or recent immigrants. In addition to this ethnic diversity, today's adolescents grow up in a vast array of family forms, from the traditional two-parent, stay-at-home-mother structure that dominated the demographic landscape of the 1950s, to the blended, dual-career stepfamilies that gained prominence in the 1990s. Some adolescents have parents who are in their mid-40s (the most common age among parents of teenagers), but some have parents who are younger than 30, and a substantial number have parents who are in their 50s or 60s. About one-fifth of youngsters are only-children, but one-sixth have three or more siblings. One-sixth of American adolescents today grow up in poverty, and another one-fifth are from low-income homes, but at least one-fifth of American teenagers live in families whose circumstances can be described as relatively luxurious.

THE CHANGED AND CHANGING NATURE OF FAMILY LIFE

In America and in many other industrialized countries, the family has undergone a series of profound changes during the past half century that have diversified its form and, as a result, adolescents' daily experiences. Increased rates of divorce and childbearing outside of marriage, and maternal employment, as well as a changing international economy and accelerating geographic mobility, have dramatically altered the world in which children and adolescents grow up. Although some of the most striking trends in family life slowed during the early 1990s, they did not reverse by any means. The divorce rate, the proportion of single-parent families, and the rate of maternal employment, all of which skyrocketed during the 1970s and 1980s, stabilized at their historically high levels at the beginning of the 1990s and have changed relatively little since then (Hernandez, 1997; Kilborn, 1996).

Questions about whether these changes have weakened the family's influence over young people or, in one way or another, have harmed young people continue to generate heated debate. According to some

observers, the all-too-familiar problems of young people—low achievement test scores, high rates of alcohol and drug use, sexual precocity, violence in the schools—have been due to changes in the family (e.g., Cornwell, Eggebeen, & Meschke, 1996). Others, less pessimistic, note that today's families are strong in their own ways, and that it is the quality of relationships in the adolescent's life, not the number of adults in his or her household, that matters most (Parke & Buriel, 1998; Weisner & Garnier, 1995). According to many, supporting and strengthening today's families—in all their diversity—is more important than wringing our hands over the passing of the family forms of the 1950s.

Just how dramatic have the changes in American family life been over the past half century? Consider five of the most important indicators of family circumstances: divorce, single parenthood, remarriage, maternal employment, and poverty.

▌ **Divorce**   As Figure 4.6 shows, the divorce rate increased markedly beginning in the 1960s, rising steadily, and at times rapidly, until 1980. (The divorce rate increased most dramatically after 1965 and peaked around 1980.) Although the accompanying figure shows that, for the population as a whole, the divorce rate declined slightly after 1980, looking only at the average trend masks an important difference between college graduates and nongraduates. Between 1980 and 2005, the divorce rate remained steady among individuals who did not graduate from college but dropped considerably among college graduates (Hurley, 2005). **Demographers**—social scientists who study changes in the composition of the population—note that during the 1990s, close to half of all first marriages were likely to disrupt through divorce or separation. As a consequence, nearly half of all American children born during the 1990s—today's teenagers—will experience their parents' divorce and will spend approximately five years in a single-parent household before turning 18 (Hetherington, Henderson, & Reiss, 1999).

▌ **Single Parenthood**   In addition to adolescents who live in a single-parent household as a consequence of their parents' divorce, a sizable percentage of youngsters will spend time in a single-parent household from birth; indeed, today, the number of American children in single-parent households who live with a parent who has never married is about the same as the number who live with a parent who has been married and divorced (Fields, 2003). Keep in mind, though, that a substantial number of adolescents who are classified as living in single-parent households actually live with more than one adult, often with the unmarried partner of the child's parent (Fields, 2003). When youngsters live with

demographers   Social scientists who study large-scale changes in the makeup of the population.

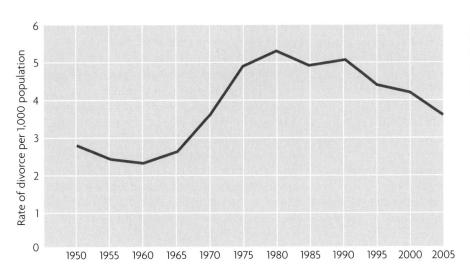

FIGURE 4.6 The divorce rate in America increased steadily during the 1970s, remained stable for several years, and began declining in the mid-1980s.

only one of their biological parents, either in single-parent or in two-parent households, it is nearly always with the mother; only about 15 percent of children who live with one parent live with their father (U.S. Bureau of the Census, 2006).

There are important racial and ethnic differences in these patterns of family life, however. African American youngsters are far more likely than other youngsters to experience parental divorce and to be born outside of marriage, but they are far less likely to experience their parents' remarriage (Hetherington, Bridges, & Insabella, 1998). As a consequence, African American adolescents spend longer periods of time in single-parent households than do other adolescents. Whereas close to 80 percent of all Asian American children, 75 percent of all white children, and 67 percent of all Hispanic American children live with two parents, only 35 percent of African American children do (U.S. Bureau of the Census, 2006).

■ **Remarriage** Because more than three-fourths of divorced men and two-thirds of divorced women remarry, the majority of youngsters whose parents separate also experience living in a stepfamily at some time. Of the young people living in two-parent families, a substantial number—close to 15 percent—live with only one of their biological parents (Hernandez, 1997). And, because the divorce rate is higher for second marriages than first marriages, the majority of youth whose parents remarry will experience a *second* divorce. Moreover, because divorces generally occur faster in remarriages—one-fourth happen within five years—many children confront a second divorce before they have finished adapting to having a stepparent (Hetherington et al., 1999).

■ **Maternal Employment** Another trend worth noting concerns maternal employment. Among women with school-aged children, full-time employment has increased steadily since 1950. Today, about 80 percent of all women with adolescent children are employed, and nearly half of these mothers work full-time. More than 80 percent of single mothers with adolescent children are employed outside the home, and more than half of these mothers are employed full-time. Among elementary school children, three-quarters have mothers in the labor force, nearly 40 percent in full-time jobs (U.S. Census Bureau, 2002).

■ **Poverty** Finally, approximately 16 percent of all children in the United States grow up in abject poverty, and an additional 22 percent grow up in low-income families (National Center for Children in Poverty, 2002). Although the proportion of children living in poverty declined during the 1990s, it began to rise again in 2000. Perhaps more importantly, the gap between the very poor and the very wealthy has widened substantially in the past 30 years (Hernandez, 1997). Poverty, as we noted in Chapter 3, is much more likely to touch the lives of nonwhite children; approximately 30 percent of African American and Hispanic American children grow up in poverty. One reason for the large disparity in poverty rates between white and nonwhite children, in fact, is the racial disparity in rates of single parenthood: Because nonwhite children are more likely to be raised in single-parent homes, they are more likely to be poor (Hernandez, 1997).

To what extent has the changed nature of the American family changed the nature of adolescent development? How do divorce, single parenthood, remarriage, maternal employment, and poverty affect adolescents' development?

Many individuals are certain that the answer to these questions is, "For the worse." But before we jump to this conclusion, it is important to raise two considerations. First, although increases in adolescents' problems between 1950 and 1980—as indexed by such indicators as drug use, suicide, and poor school achievement, for example—occurred alongside many of these shifts in family life, it is difficult to say that the family changes caused the changes in adolescent behavior. Social scientists who argue that the decline in family life has led to these problems (e.g., Uhlenberg & Eggebeen, 1986) have had a hard time explaining why adolescents' psychological and behavioral well-being took a turn for the better in the early 1980s, despite the continued "demise" of the family (see Furstenberg, 1990a). Moreover, the one group of young people whose psychological and behavioral profile improved most markedly in the past 10 years— poor, minority youngsters—experienced the most dramatic "decline" in family life during this time.

Second, because the conditions under which divorce, single parenthood, remarriage, and maternal employment take place vary tremendously from family to family, it is hard to generalize about their effects on adolescents. (In contrast, it is relatively easy to generalize about the effects of poverty on adolescents, which are almost always negative.) For some young people, divorce may bring a welcome end to family conflict and tension; for others, it may be extremely disruptive psychologically. Some young people living with only their mother actually see their father more often than do their peers who live in homes where the father ostensibly is present. And although, for some adolescents, having an employed mother may mean curtailed family time and less contact with her, for others, a mother who is employed may provide an important role model, needed income, and added opportunities to take on responsibility around the household. In other words, the variations within different family structures are likely to be more important than the differences among them. This is readily apparent when we look at how adolescents are affected by parental divorce.

ADOLESCENTS AND DIVORCE

At one time, any discussion of adolescents and divorce would likely have started with the assumption that living with one parent was not as good as living with two, and consequently, that children whose parents divorced would be at a distinct disadvantage, relative to those whose parents remained married. Over time, however, researchers' ideas about divorce and its impact adolescents have changed dramatically, as new and better studies have challenged, clarified, and tempered the conclusions of past research. While most social scientists still agree that adolescents from divorced homes have more difficulties than those from nondivorced homes, the explanation for this effect is far more complicated than the conventional wisdom

that "Two parents are better than one" or "All children need a mother and a father."

▌ The Effect of Divorce Is Small in Magnitude
Five sets of findings have questioned these simple assertions. First, although divorce clearly diminishes youngsters' well-being, the average effect size is quite small (Amato & Keith, 1991a). It is possible in a study with a large sample for a small effect to be statistically significant. There are statistically significant differences between children from divorced versus nondivorced homes in school achievement, behavior problems, psychosocial adjustment, and family relations—all favoring individuals from nondivorced homes—but the absolute difference in the groups' scores is seldom substantial. In general, the effects of divorce tend to be stronger for school-aged individuals than for preschoolers or college students; interestingly, the effects are comparable for boys and girls. One especially intriguing finding is that the effects of divorce seem to be smaller among youngsters from the United States than among those from other countries. The explanation: Divorce is more common in the United States than abroad, and as a consequence, American children from divorced homes are less likely to be stigmatized and more likely to have access to psychological services, such as counseling, that may attenuate the negative impact of family disruption.

▌ Quality Matters
Second, the quality of the relationships the young person has with the important adults in her or his life matters more than the number of parents present in the home (Buchanan, Maccoby, & Dornbusch, 1996; Hines, 1997; Mandara & Murray, 2000; McKeown et al., 1997). Adolescents from stepfamilies, for example, have as many, if not more, problems than those from single-parent homes, even though adolescents in stepfamilies have the ostensible benefit of two parents in the home (Allison & Furstenberg, 1989; Hetherington et al., 1999; Hoffmann, 2002; Jeynes, 1999). In addition, youngsters from single-parent families that have not experienced divorce (for example, youngsters who have lost a parent through death, or youngsters with a single mother who never married) have fewer difficulties than their counterparts from divorced or remarried homes (Demo & Acock, 1996). Finally, adolescents in two-parent homes do not always have warm and close relationships with their parents. Indeed, adolescents living in father-absent homes have higher self-esteem than adolescents who live in two-parent homes but who feel that their father has little interest in them (Clark & Barber, 1994). In fact, adolescents in divorced, single-parent families describe their parents as friendlier than do adolescents whose parents are married (Asmussen & Larson, 1991)

and are in a relatively more positive mood when with their family than when with friends (Larson & Gillman, 1996). Adolescents and their parents argue less often in single-parent households, perhaps because single parents tend to be more permissive in their child rearing, which may make for less parent–adolescent conflict (Smetana, Yau, Restrepo, & Braeges, 1991).

■ **Adaptation to Divorce**   Third, it is the process of going through a divorce, not the resulting family structure, that matters most for adolescents' mental health (Buchanan, Maccoby, & Dornbusch, 1996; Hetherington, Bridges, & Insabella, 1998). In general, most studies show that the period of greatest difficulty for most adolescents is, as you would think, right around the time of the disruption itself (Jeynes, 2001). Although many young people show signs of difficulty immediately after their parents divorce or remarry—among them, problems in school, behavior problems, and increased anxiety—by the time two years have passed, the majority of these children have adjusted to the change and behave comparably to their peers whose biological parents have remained married (Hetherington et al., 1998). Although adolescents whose parents have divorced have, on average, more problems than those whose parents remain married, the vast majority of individuals with divorced parents do not have significant problems (Hetherington et al., 1998).

■ **Conflict and Stress**   Fourth, research has linked the adverse consequences of divorce to a number of factors not specifically due to having a single parent (see Hetherington et al., 1998, for a review). These include the exposure of the children to marital conflict (Amato & Keith, 1991a; Forehand et al., 1991; Vandewater & Lansford, 1998), disorganized or disrupted parenting (Forehand, Thomas, Wierson, Brody, & Fauber, 1990; Hetherington et al., 1992; Shucksmith, Glendinning, & Hendry, 1997), and marked increases in the degree of stress experienced by the household, often due to loss of income (Hetherington et al., 1998; Pong & Ju, 2000; Sun & Li, 2002; Thomson, Hanson, & McLanahan, 1994). As you will read, adolescents living in two-parent families in which no divorce has occurred are also harmed by marital conflict, disrupted parenting (especially parenting that is too lenient, too harsh, or inconsistent), and loss of income. In other words, the adverse temporary effects of divorce or remarriage on youngsters' well-being appear to reflect the heightened conflict, disorganization, and stress surrounding the event, not the divorce or remarriage per se. Experts now believe that the most important pathway through which divorce may adversely affect adolescent adjustment is via its direct and indirect impact on the quality of parenting to which the child is exposed (Amato & Sobolewski, 2001; Hetherington et al., 1998).

■ **Genetic Influences**   Finally, although some of the apparent effects of parental divorce are the result of exposure to such stressors as marital conflict or disorganized parenting, at least some of the differences between adolescents whose parents have divorced and those whose parents have not are due to genetic differences between the teenagers. At least part of the reason that adolescents from divorced homes have, on average, more problems than their peers is that they have inherited from their divorced parents some of the same traits that influenced their parents' divorce (O'Connor, Caspi, DeFries, & Plomin, 2000). Adults who divorce are different from those who do not with respect to many traits that have strong genetic origins—such as aggression, antisociality, and predispositions to different sorts of emotional and behavioral problems, like depression—and these traits are passed on from parents to children.

■ **Individual Differences in the Effects of Divorce**   There also are interesting differences among children in how vulnerable they are to the short-term effects of divorce. In general, immediate problems are relatively more common among boys, younger children, children with a difficult temperament, children who do not have supportive relationships with adults outside the immediate family, and youngsters whose parents divorce during childhood or preadolescence (Davies & Windle, 2001; Rodgers & Rose, 2002). Especially interesting, if somewhat disheartening, is the finding that contact after the divorce between the child and his or her noncustodial father does not invariably reduce the adverse effects of marital dissolution, and sometimes may make things worse, especially in African American families (Coley, 2003; Thomas, Farrell, & Barnes, 1996). Financial support from fathers, however, is associated with less problem behavior and higher academic achievement (Furstenberg, Morgan, & Allison, 1987; Menning, 2002).

Studies of African American youth indicate that social support from friends and relatives outside the family may be an especially important resource for inner-city children growing up in single-parent homes (Lamborn & Nguyen, 2004; Mason, Cauce, Gonzales, Hiraga, & Grove, 1994; Salem, Zimmerman, & Notaro, 1998; Taylor, 1996; Taylor & Roberts, 1995). Support from kin, in particular, appears to increase single parents' effectiveness in child rearing, and this, in turn, tends to limit adolescents' misbehavior. This support can come from relatives living apart from, or within, the adolescent's household. For example, several studies of African American youngsters found that children growing up in home environments that include a grandparent as well as a parent fare significantly better than did those growing up in single-parent homes or in stepfamilies;

152   PART 2   The Contexts of Adolescence

Contact with members of the extended family may play an especially important role in the socialization of African American youth.

FIGURE 4.7 The effects of exposure to marital conflict are both direct and indirect through its negative impact on parenting.

however, adolescents raised without either biological parent tend to fare worse than their peers, even if a grandparent is present (Barbarin & Soler, 1993; Hamilton, 2005; Sun, 2003). These studies, as well as others, remind us that relatives other than parents may play an extremely important role in adolescents' lives, especially within ethnic groups that historically have placed a great deal of importance on maintaining close ties to extended family members. Single parenthood and extensive contact with the extended family have been salient features of African American family life for more than 100 years (Ruggles, 1994).

THE SPECIFIC IMPACT OF MARITAL CONFLICT

Although divorce is generally associated with short-term difficulties for the adolescent, several studies show that at least some of the differences between adolescents from divorced versus nondivorced homes were present before the parents divorced (Cherlin et al., 1991; Sun, 2001). In one sample of British youngsters who were followed from birth into adulthood, 7-year-olds whose parents eventually divorced had more educational and behavioral problems than did 7-year-olds whose parents did not divorce (Cherlin, Chase-Lansdale, & McRae, 1998; Elliott & Richards, 1991). One explanation for this is that the children in the households that later divorced were exposed to higher levels of marital unhappiness and conflict and strained parent–child relationships, both of which are known to increase children's difficulties (Amato & Booth, 1996; Forehand, Neighbors, Devine, & Armistead, 1994) (see Figure 4.7).

The recognition that exposure to marital conflict, apart from and in addition to divorce itself, has harmful effects on children's development has prompted many researchers to study why and how the quality of the adolescent's parents' marriage affects the teenager's mental health and behavior (Cui, Conger, & Lorenz, 2005; Erel & Burman, 1995; Feldman & Fisher, 1997; Fincham, 1994; Harold & Conger, 1997; Rogers & Holmbeck, 1997). Several conclusions have emerged from this research. First, children are more adversely affected by marital conflict when they are aware of it than when it is more covert (Feldman & Wentzel, 1995; Harold & Conger, 1997). For this reason, marital conflict is particularly harmful when it is especially hostile, physically violent, or frightening (Buehler et al., 1998; Gordis, Margolin, & St. John, 1997; Harold & Conger, 1997; Osofsky, 1995). Exposure to overt marital conflict and domestic violence has been linked to a wide range of adolescent problems, including depression (especially in girls), aggression, delinquency, and other types of externalizing (especially in boys) (Davies & Lindsay, 2004; Harold & Conger, 1997; Krishnakumar & Cuehler, 1996; Sim & Vuchinich, 1996).

Second, children are more negatively affected when the marital conflict leads to feelings of insecurity or self-blame. Adolescents who blame themselves for their parents' conflict, whose feelings of security are challenged, or who are drawn into their parents' arguments are more likely to feel anxious, depressed, and distressed (Buehler, Krishnakumar, Anthony, Tittsworth, & Stone, 1994; Davies & Cummings, 1994; Grych, Raynor, & Fosco, 2004; Tschann et al., 2002).

Finally, marital conflict more adversely affects the adolescent when the conflict disrupts the quality of the parent–child relationship (Amato & Sobolewski, 2001). Adolescents are directly affected by exposure to their parents' conflict, to be sure, but several studies have found as well that tension between spouses spills over into the parent–child relationship, making mothers and fathers more hostile, more irritable, and less effective as parents (Buehler, Benson, & Gerard, 2006; Davies & Cummings, 1994; Doyle & Markiewicz, 2005; Fine & Kurdek, 1995; Mahoney, Donelly, Boxer, & Lewis, 2003). As you will read later in this chapter, adolescents who perceive their parents as hostile or uncaring are more likely to report a wide range of emotional and behavioral problems than are their peers.

FOOD FOR THOUGHT

Based on the available research, what advice would you give to parents of teenagers who are considering divorce?

THE LONGER-TERM EFFECTS OF DIVORCE

Social scientists have also looked at the longer-term (more than two or three years) consequences of divorce. These studies, for example, might look at elementary school children whose parents divorced when their child was in preschool, or at adolescents whose parents split up during the youngster's elementary school years. Presumably, if the adverse effects of divorce are solely attributable to the immediate problems of adjusting to a new household structure, or due to exposure to intense marital conflict before and during the divorce, these effects will dissipate within a few years.

Research on the longer-term consequences of parental divorce has yielded very interesting findings. Some studies show that individuals whose parents divorce during preadolescence and adolescence often demonstrate adjustment difficulties later, even after two or three years (e.g., Hetherington, 1993). The problems typically seen in greater frequency among individuals from divorced homes include higher rates of drug and alcohol use, more behavior problems, precocious sexual activity, and poorer school performance (Allison & Furstenberg, 1989; Astone & McLanahan, 1991; Hetherington & Stanley-Hagan, 1995; Sandefur,

McLanahan, & Wojtkiewicz, 1992; Zimiles & Lee, 1991); poorer interpersonal relationships with members of the opposite sex in late adolescence and young adulthood, including more negative attitudes toward marriage and higher rates of divorce (McLanahan & Bumpass, 1988; Summers, Forehand, Armistead, & Tannenbaum, 1998; Tasker & Richards, 1994; Wallerstein & Blakeslee, 1989); and, with the exception of African American and Hispanic American males, lower levels of occupational attainment as adults (Amato & Keith, 1991b). Some research indicates that individuals whose parents divorced during childhood or adolescence continue to have adjustment problems well into their 30s (see Figure 4.8) (Cherlin et al., 1998). These effects do not appear to be ameliorated by parental remarriage; adolescents from stepfamilies score similarly, or worse, on measures of longer-term adjustment, as do adolescents from single-parent, divorced homes (Allison & Furstenberg, 1989; Hetherington et al., 1998).

▌ **Sleeper Effects** To what can we attribute these "sleeper" effects—effects of divorce that may not be apparent until much later in the child's development? Two possible explanations come to mind. The first is that the ways in which adjustment difficulties might be expressed may not surface until adolescence. For example, social scientists believe that increased drug use and higher rates of early pregnancy are consequences of the lower level of parental monitoring found in divorced homes (e.g., Dornbusch et al., 1985; McLanahan & Bumpass, 1988; Moore & Chase-Lansdale, 2001). But because younger children—even poorly monitored ones—are unlikely to use drugs or be sexually active, no matter what their family background, the effect of the poor monitoring is not seen until adolescence, when individuals might begin using drugs and having sex.

A second explanation concerns the particular developmental challenges of adolescence (Sessa & Steinberg, 1991). Adolescence is a time when individuals first begin experimenting with intimate, sexual relationships. If having one's parents divorce or being exposed to marital conflict early in life affects one's conceptions of relationships or views of romantic commitment (Belsky, Steinberg, & Draper, 1991; Tasker & Richards, 1994; Woodward, Fergusson, & Belsky, 2000), it makes sense that some of the effects of early parental divorce will not be manifested until the adolescent begins dating and getting seriously involved with others of the opposite sex. These initial forays into intimate relationships may recall old and difficult psychological conflicts that had remained latent for some time (Wallerstein & Blakeslee, 1989).

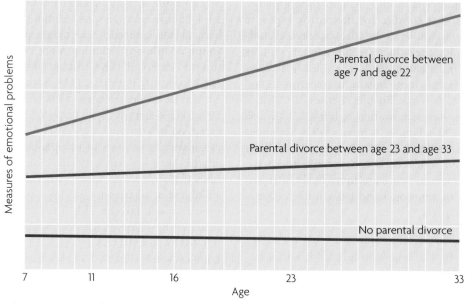

FIGURE 4.8   A long-term study of British individuals illustrates two interesting points about the effects of divorce on the development of emotional problems. First, at age 7, individuals whose parents eventually divorced *already* had more emotional problems than other children. Second, the emotional problems associated with parental divorce during childhood or adolescence increased over time and persisted well into adulthood. (Cherlin, Chase-Lansdale, & McRae, 1998)

CUSTODY, CONTACT, AND CONFLICT FOLLOWING DIVORCE

After a divorce, do adolescents fare better or worse in different kinds of living arrangements? Does contact with the nonresidential parent contribute to the adolescent's well-being?

Studies to date indicate that it is the nature of the relationship between the adolescent's divorced parents, and not which one he or she lives with, that makes a difference (Buchanan et al., 1996; Downey, Ainsworth-Darnell, & Dufur, 1998; Hetherington et al., 1998). In the years immediately following a divorce, children may fare a bit better in the custody of the parent of the same sex, but these effects are not long-lasting; over time, both male and female adolescents fare equally well either in dual custody or in the sole custody of their mother (Buchanan et al., 1996; Donnelly & Finkelhor, 1992; Downey, 1995). More important, especially for adolescents who have dual residences, are two factors: whether the ex-spouses continue to fight and place the child between them, and whether the adolescent's discipline is consistent across the two households. Adolescents whose parents have a congenial, cooperative relationship and who receive consistent and appropriate discipline from both homes report less emotional difficulty and fewer behavioral problems than those whose parents fight or are inconsistent with each other (Buchanan, Maccoby, & Dornbusch, 1996; Coiro & Emery, 1996; Donnelly &

Finkelhor, 1992; Simons, Whitbeck, Beaman, & Conger, 1994).

Adolescents whose parents have divorced also vary in the extent to which they have contact with the parent they no longer live with, typically their father. Generally, contact between adolescents and their father following a divorce diminishes very quickly after the father moves out and continues to decline over time, especially among men who remarry or enter into a new romantic relationship (Stephens, 1996). Although conventional wisdom suggests that adolescents ought to benefit from maintaining a close relationship with their nonresidential parent, research on this has been inconsistent. Some studies find that adolescents benefit from regular postdivorce contact with their nonresidential parent, but others find that such contact matters very little, and still others find that extensive postdivorce contact with the nonresidential parent can actually have harmful effects on children's well-being. The critical factors appear to be the level of conflict between the divorced parents and the nature of the adolescent's relationship with the nonresidential parent before the divorce (Amato & Rezac, 1994; Hetherington & Stanley-Hagan, 1995; Stewart, 2003; Videon, 2002). Adolescents benefit from contact with their nonresidential parent when conflict between their parents is minimal, but suffer from such contact when parental conflict is intense. Similarly, adolescents benefit when they have frequent contact with a nonresidential parent with whom they had a close relationship when their parents were married, but suffer from contact with one whom they didn't get along with prior to the divorce.

■ What Divorced Parents Tell Their Teenagers

Psychologist Susan Koerner and colleagues have examined the sorts of disclosure that takes place between recently divorced mothers and their children (Koerner, Jacobs, & Raymond, 2000; Koerner, Wallace, Lehman, Lee, & Escalante, 2004). To the researchers' surprise, mothers were equally like to talk to sons and daughters, and their conversations were similar, consistent with a point made earlier, namely, that for the most part adolescent males and females are treated similarly. Koerner has been especially interested in two topics of conversation: the mother's complaints about and anger toward her ex-husband, and the mother's concerns about finances (both common concerns among recently divorced women).

Among mothers who disclosed these sorts of feelings, an important motive for doing so turned out not to be the mother's need for a confidante, but rather her desire to shape her daughter's impression of her and the circumstances surrounding the divorce. Here's one example:

> I talk to her about anything. Complaints I have about her father. [Alison] thinks the divorce is all my fault. Her Dad has been absent for two years. He called on occasion and sent presents on Christmas and B-Days. While he was gone Alison turned him into some sort of God in her mind. Now that he has returned to the area he wants little or nothing to do with his kids. When Alison complains, I make statements like, "Alison, you're starting to see the side of your Dad that I was married to" or "He never gave me any time either." (Koerner et al., 2000, p. 305)

Not all mothers shared their feelings about these topics with their child. As one put it:

> I try really hard not to say anything negative about my ex-husband to my children. We agreed when we got divorced to always do what was best for our children. So far, so good. (Koerner et al., 2000, p. 305)

Consistent with other research indicating that adolescents fare worse when they are drawn into their divorced parents' conflict, adolescents whose mothers complain to them about their ex-husbands or discussed their financial concerns report more psychological distress, in the form of anxiety, depression, tension, and psychosomatic complaints. It's not hard to see why. As several adolescents explained:

> I was thinking, my gosh, my dad doesn't care about me—he's not paying it [child support]! I felt like going and calling my dad and yelling at him because I think he doesn't care about it. (11-year-old daughter, quoted in Koerner et al., 2004, p. 52)

> My mom constantly rags on and on about how my dad is such a jerk and won't pay her as much as she thinks he should. It disturbs me incredibly because my dad is very kind when I visit him and I don't think my mom is fair. (15-year-old son, quoted in Koerner et al., 2004, p. 52)

> My mom talks to me about how we don't have extra money. I don't really like to hear how little money we have. . . . I feel sad and kinda angry when we talk about money cause before the divorce this topic never, really came up to talk about. . . . (13-year-old daughter, quoted in Koerner et al., 2004, p. 52)

REMARRIAGE

Adolescents growing up in stepfamilies—especially if the remarriage occurred during early adolescence rather than childhood—often have more problems than their peers, a finding that holds regardless of whether the stepparents are legally married or cohabiting (Hetherington et al., 1999; Manning & Lamb, 2003). For example, youngsters growing up in single-parent homes are more likely than those in intact homes to be involved in delinquent activity, but adolescents in stepfamilies are even more at risk for this sort of problem behavior than are adolescents in single-parent families (Dornbusch et al., 1985; Steinberg, 1987c). This results, in part but not entirely, because they are exposed to a "double dose" of marital conflict—normal, everyday conflict between the parent and stepparent, and additional conflict between ex-spouses (Hanson, McLanahan, & Thomson, 1996; MacDonald & DeMaris, 1995)—and because they are exposed to a new set of potentially difficult issues that arise in the blending of children from two different marriages (Hetherington et al., 1999).

Like the short-term effects of divorce, the short-term effects of remarriage vary among children, although not necessarily in the same ways. In general, girls have more difficulty in adjusting to remarriage than do boys, and older children have more difficulty than younger ones (Hetherington, 1993; Lee, Burkham, Zimiles, & Ladewski, 1994; Needle, Su, & Doherty, 1990; Vuchinich, Hetherington, Vuchinich, & Clingempeel, 1991; Zimiles & Lee, 1991). One explanation for this is that both boys and younger children have more to gain from their mother's remarriage than do girls or older children, who may have become accustomed to having a single mother (Hetherington, 1991). Over time, however, gender differences in adjustment to remarriage disappear, and in remarriages that last more than five years, the adjustment of male and female children is similar (Hetherington et al., 1999). One interesting finding, especially in light of the growing number of young adults who depend on their parents' financial support, is that remarried parents and stepparents are

Studies show that each time a family goes through a marital transition, such as divorce or remarriage, the adolescent is placed at some risk for minor adjustment difficulties.

less inclined than other parents to provide money to their children over the transition to adulthood (Aquilino, 2005).

▌ Difficulties Adjusting to Parental Remarriage

Remarriage during the adolescent years may be extremely stressful when families are unable to accommodate the new stepparent relationship. Given what we know about family reorganization and change during adolescence, having to integrate a new type of relationship into a family system that is already undergoing a great deal of change may be more than some families can cope with (Kurdek & Fine, 1993). Many adolescents find it difficult to adjust to a new authority figure moving into the household, especially if that person has different ideas about rules and discipline, and particularly if the new authority figure is not legally married to the child's biological parent (Buchanan et al., 1996; Hetherington et al., 1999). This appears to be especially true when the adolescent in question is already somewhat vulnerable, either because of previous psychological problems or because of a recent divorce or other stressful event.

By the same token, many stepparents find it difficult to join a family and not be accepted immediately by the children as the new parent. Stepparents may wonder why love is not forthcoming from their stepchildren, who often act critical, resistant, and sulky (Vuchinich et al., 1991). Although many stepfathers and their adolescent stepchildren do establish positive relationships, the lack of a biological connection between stepparent and stepchild—coupled with the stresses associated with divorce and remarriage—may make this relationship especially vulnerable to problems

(Hetherington et al., 1999). Adolescents in remarried households fare better when their stepparent can establish a consistent, supportive, authoritative style of discipline (Crosbie-Burnett & Sims, 1994; Henry & Lovelace, 1995; Hetherington et al., 1999).

This research underscores the need—particularly as remarriage becomes a more common part of American family life—to understand the special problems that may arise in the course of family reorganization. Several studies indicate that children's adjustment declines somewhat each time they must cope with a change in their family's household composition (e.g., Adam & Chase-Lansdale, 2002; Albrecht & Teachman, 2003; Kim, Conger, et al., 2003; Kurdek, Fine, & Sinclair, 1995), in part because parenting may become less effective during each family transition (Forgatch, DeGarmo, & Knutson, 1994; Kurdek & Fine, 1993). As our understanding of stepfamily relationships grows, it should become easier to anticipate stepfamily problems before they occur, to prepare families in the process of reorganization for the transition they are about to make, and to provide special services for families who need help. Given the fact that the benefits of authoritative parenting are just as strong in divorced and remarried families as they are in other homes, experts believe that clinicians who work with families that have undergone marital transitions should help parents learn and adopt this parenting style (Hetherington et al., 1999).

One factor that seems to make a very big difference in the adjustment of children in stepfamilies is the nature of the relationship they have with their noncustodial parent—that is, the biological parent with whom they do not live. Children in stepfamilies fare better when there is consistency in discipline between their custodial and noncustodial parents, and when they have a good relationship with the noncustodial parent, especially in the years immediately following the remarriage (Anderson, 1992; Bray, Berger, Tiuch, & Boethel, 1993; Buchanan & Maccoby, 1993; Gunnoe, 1994). Having a close relationship with the noncustodial parent does not appear to undermine the relationship with the custodial parent (Buchanan & Maccoby, 1993). Indeed, one study found that boys who felt close to both their father and stepfather were more optimistic about the prospect of their own future marriage (Risch, Jodl, & Eccles, 2004).

ECONOMIC STRESS AND POVERTY

In recent years, there has been an upsurge in interest in the relationship between parents' unemployment and adolescents' well-being—in particular, in the ways in which adolescents' mental health is affected by changes in their family's financial situation. To date,

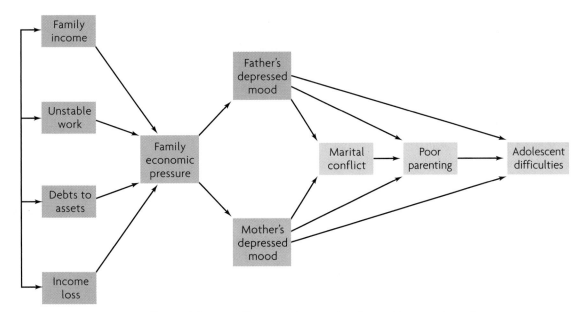

FIGURE 4.9   Economic strain affects adolescent adjustment via several pathways. (Conger et al., 1993)

the studies of family income loss and adolescent adjustment suggest a number of parallels with the research on divorce and remarriage.

■ **The Effects of Financial Strain**   Like divorce, income loss tends to be associated with disruptions in parenting, which, in turn, lead to increases in adolescent difficulties, including a diminished sense of mastery, increased emotional distress, academic and interpersonal problems, and delinquency (Barrera et al., 2002; Conger, Conger, Matthews, & Elder, 1999; Cui, Conger, Bryant, & Elder, 2002; Elder, Caspi, & van Nguyen, 1986; Kloep, 1995; Lempers, Clark-Lempers, & Simmons, 1989). Although males and females alike are adversely affected by their family's economic problems, the pathways through which this occurs may differ between the sexes. For girls, financial difficulty is likely to lead to more demands for maturity and increased responsibility around the house (perhaps to assume some of mother's duties while she works or looks for employment) (Elder, 1974; Flanagan, 1990). This may contribute to their developing more pessimistic expectations about their own occupational futures, since they may develop more traditional views and find it difficult to envision a satisfying career outside the home (Galambos & Silbereisen, 1987). For boys, in contrast, disruptions in family finances seem to lead to more frequent conflict, especially with fathers (Elder, van Nguyen, & Caspi, 1985; Flanagan, 1990). Boys whose fathers have been laid off may lose respect for them and challenge their authority. The resulting disruption in family functioning may lead to

more involvement in problem behavior and heightened irresponsibility.

A series of studies of rural families during the American farm crisis of the 1980s by sociologists Rand Conger and Glen Elder sheds light on some of the processes through which economic strain on the family can adversely affect adolescents' psychological development (Conger et al., 1999; Conger, Conger, Elder, et al., 1992, 1993; Conger, Ge, Elder, Lorenz, & Simons, 1994; Elder, Conger, Foster, & Ardelt, 1992; Ge & Conger, 1995) (see Figure 4.9). Financial strain increases mothers' and fathers' feelings of depression, worsens parents' marriages, and causes conflicts between parents and adolescents over money. These consequences, in turn, make parents more irritable, which adversely affects the quality of their parenting. Studies show that parents under economic strain are less involved, less nurturing, harsher, and less consistent in their discipline (McLoyd, 1990).

The family climate created by economic strain puts adolescents at risk for a variety of problems. As you now know, adolescents who are exposed to harsh, uninvolved, and inconsistent parenting are at greater risk for a wide range of psychological and behavioral problems. When adolescents are repeatedly exposed to marital conflict—especially when it is not resolved—they are more likely to become aggressive and depressed (Cummings, Ballard, El-Sheikh, & Lake, 1991). And when adolescents themselves are the recipients of aggressive parenting, they are likely to imitate this behavior in their relationships with siblings (Conger, Conger, & Elder, 1994) and, later, in their own marriage (Straus & Yodanis, 1996) and with their children (Simons, Whitbeck, Conger, & Chyi-In, 1991).

■ **The Impact of Chronic Poverty**   Researchers have also studied the impact on adolescents of growing up amidst chronic economic disadvantage (Brody et al., 1994; Felner et al., 1995; Gutman, McLoyd, & Tokoyama, 2005; McLoyd, Jayaratne, Ceballo, & Borquez, 1994). In general, persistent poverty, like temporary economic strain, undermines parental effectiveness, making mothers and fathers harsher, more depressed, less vigilant, less consistent, and more embroiled in conflict. These consequences all have negative effects on adolescent adjustment, which are manifested in increases in anxiety and depression, more frequent conduct problems, and diminished school performance (Conger, Patterson, & Ge, 1995; Kim & Brody, 2005; Taylor, Rodriguez, Seaton, & Dominguez, 2004; Wadsworth & Compas, 2002).

Interestingly, there appear to be few differences in the behavior, values, or family relationships between adolescents in families that are on welfare and those that are not, calling into question the notion that welfare undermines parental effectiveness, contributes to adolescents' development of undesirable beliefs and values about work, or encourages problem behavior among teenagers (Kalil & Eccles, 1998). At the same time, studies of the impact of requiring women who have been on welfare to enter the labor force find very few effects—positive or negative—on adolescent development or behavior (Chase-Lansdale, et al., 2003). Some evidence suggests that adolescents whose mothers have been required to go off public assistance and go to work show somewhat worse school performance as a result, but this effect is most pronounced when the adolescent has a younger sibling, presumably because of the added household responsibilities the mother's employment created for the teenager (Gennetian et al., 2004).

Growing up poor affects adolescents' mental health in a variety of ways. As we discussed in Chapter 3, poor adolescents are more likely to be exposed to violence (Sheidow, Gorman-Smith, Tolan, & Henry, 2001), to feel more alienated from school (Felner et al., 1995), and to be exposed to high levels of stress (Felner et al., 1995; Masten, Miliotis, Graham-Bermann, Ramirez, & Neeman, 1993). Although few scientific studies have been conducted on homeless adolescents, research suggests that these youngsters share many of the same problems with other youth who experience chronic poverty, including higher rates of depression and suicidal thoughts, academic difficulties, and behavior problems (Masten et al., 1993; Unger, Kipke, Simon, Montgomery, & Johnson, 1997; Whitbeck, Hoyt, & Bao, 2000; Zima, Wells, & Freeman, 1994).

An estimated 5 percent of American adolescents experience at least one night of homelessness each year (Ringwalt, Greene, Robertson, & McPheeters, 1998).

FOOD FOR THOUGHT

Most research on economic conditions, family functioning, and adolescent development has focused on poverty. Do you think there are negative effects of growing up under extreme *affluence*?

Studies of families living in poverty also tell us what parents living in poor neighborhoods can do to help protect their children from the adverse consequences of growing up in poor inner-city or rural neighborhoods (Brody, Stoneman, & Flor, 1996; Early & Eccles, 1994; Elder & Ardelt, 1992; Furstenberg, 1996; Jarrett, 1995). In general, families fare better when they have adequate sources of social support (Mason et al., 1994; Taylor, 1996; Taylor & Roberts, 1995) and when they have strong ties to religious institutions (Brody, Stoneman, Flor, & McCrary, 1994; Brody et al., 1996). In addition, two specific sets of family management strategies employed by parents in poor neighborhoods seem to work: promotive strategies, which attempt to strengthen the adolescent's competence through effective child rearing within the home environment or through involving the child in positive activities outside the home, and restrictive strategies, which attempt to minimize the child's exposure to dangers in the neighborhood (Crosnoe, Mistry, & Elder, 2002; Furstenberg, Cook, Eccles, Elder, & Sameroff, 1999; Jarrett, 1995). Studies indicate that a combination of promotive strategies and moderately (but not overly) restrictive strategies may be especially beneficial to adolescents living in impoverished communities. Although adolescents in poor neighborhoods benefit from consistent parental monitoring—perhaps even from monitoring that is more vigilant than that used by families in more advantaged communities—they do not thrive when their parents exercise excessive control (McCarthy et al., 1992).

RECAP

- Five demographic trends that have changed the nature of family life in adolescence over the past half century have been increases in rates of divorce, single parenthood, remarriage, maternal employment, and poverty.
- Research on divorce indicates that the period of greatest difficulty for adolescents whose parents

divorce is the time immediately after the event and that this is largely attributable to the exposure of the child to marital conflict, disrupted parenting, and family stress.

- It is the nature of the relationship between the adolescent's divorced parents, and not which one he or she lives with, that makes a difference.
- Because adolescents' mental health suffers somewhat each time their family situation changes, young people growing up in stepfamilies are at even greater risk for problems than their peers in single-parent, divorced homes.
- Research on economic strain and its impact on adolescents indicates that the main effects of financial stress are transmitted to the adolescent through the negative impact they have on parents' mental health and marital relations.

The Importance of the Family in Adolescent Development

As you have seen, there is considerable diversity among families with adolescents—diversity in background, in income, in parenting style, and in household composition. Yet no factor seems to influence adolescent adjustment more than the quality of relationships at home (Garnefski, 2000). As one team of experts concluded on the basis of a comprehensive study of the lives, behavior, and health of 90,000 American teenagers:

> Across all of the health outcomes examined, the results point to the importance of family and the home environment for protecting adolescents from harm. What emerges most consistently as protective is the teenager's feeling of connectedness with parents and family. Feeling loved and cared for by parents matters in a big way. (Blum & Rinehart, 2000, p. 31)

Study after study finds that adolescents who believe their parents or guardians are there for them—caring, involved, and accepting—are healthier, happier, and more competent than their peers, however health,

happiness, or competence is assessed. This conclusion holds true regardless of the adolescent's sex, ethnicity, social class, or age, and across all types of families, whether married or divorced, single-parent or two-parent, rich or poor (Dornbusch, Erickson, Laird, & Wong, 2001). This has led many psychologists, including myself, to call for widespread efforts to increase the quality of parenting that children and adolescents receive as a way of preventing emotional and behavioral problems and promoting healthy development (Kumpfer & Alvarado, 2003). As I have written elsewhere, we know what the basic principles of good parenting are (Steinberg, 2005). The challenge facing us is to figure out how best to disseminate this information to the people who need it most—parents.

Despite the tremendous growth and psychological development that take place as individuals leave childhood on the road toward adulthood, despite society's pressures on young people to grow up fast, despite all the technological and social innovations that have transformed family life, and contrary to unsupported claims that parents don't really make a difference—that by adolescence, parents' influence is overshadowed by the peer group or the mass media (e.g., Harris, 1998)—the fact remains that adolescents continue to need the love, support, and guidance of adults who genuinely care about their development and well-being. Being raised in the presence of caring and committed adults is one of the most important advantages a young person can have in life.

RECAP

- No factor seems to influence adolescent adjustment more than the quality of his or her relationships at home.
- Even after reaching adolescence, young people continue to need the love, support, and guidance of adults who genuinely care about their development and well-being.
- We know what the basic principles of good parenting are. The challenge facing us is to figure out how best to disseminate this information to parents.

CHAPTER 5

Peer Groups

THE ORIGINS OF ADOLESCENT PEER GROUPS IN CONTEMPORARY SOCIETY
  The Educational Origins of Adolescent Peer Groups
  Work, Family Life, and Adolescent Peer Groups
  Changes in the Population

THE ADOLESCENT PEER GROUP: A PROBLEM OR A NECESSITY?
  Is There a Separate Youth Culture?
  The Need for Peer Groups in Modern Society

THE NATURE OF ADOLESCENT PEER GROUPS
  Changes in Peer Groups During Adolescence
  Cliques and Crowds
  Changes in Clique and Crowd Structure over Time

ADOLESCENTS AND THEIR CROWDS
  The Social Map of Adolescence
  Crowds as Reference Groups

ADOLESCENTS AND THEIR CLIQUES
  Similarity Among Clique Members
  Common Interests Among Friends
  Similarity Between Friends: Selection or Socialization?

POPULARITY AND REJECTION IN ADOLESCENT PEER GROUPS
  Determinants of Popularity and Rejection
  Relational Aggression
  Victimization and Harassment

THE PEER GROUP AND PSYCHOSOCIAL DEVELOPMENT

IT IS ABOUT 8:00 A.M. A group of teenagers congregates in the hallway in front of their first-period classroom, discussing their plans for the weekend. As the first-period bell sounds, they enter the classroom and take their seats. For the next four hours (until there is a break in their schedule for lunch), they will attend class in groups of about 25 adolescents to 1 adult.

At lunch, the clique meets again to talk about the weekend. They have about 45 minutes until the first afternoon period begins. After lunch, they spend another two hours in class—again, in groups of about 25 adolescents and 1 adult. The school day ends, the clique convenes yet again, and they go to someone's house to hang out for the rest of the day. Everyone's parents are working; they are on their own. At about 6:00 P.M., they disperse and head home for dinner. A few will talk on the phone that night. Some will get together to study. And they will see one another first thing the next morning.

When you think about it, adolescents in modern society spend a remarkable amount of time with their peers. High school students in the United States and Europe spend twice as much of their time each week with peers as with parents or other adults—even discounting time in class (Brown, 2004; Larson & Verma, 1999). Virtually all adolescents spend most of each weekday with their peers while at school, and the vast majority also see or talk to their friends in the late afternoon, in the evening, and over the weekend (Larson & Verma, 1999). Even when adolescents work at part-time jobs, they are more likely to work with people their own age than with adults (Greenberger & Steinberg, 1986). And studies show that adolescents' moods are most positive when they are with their friends, that time spent with friends becomes more rewarding over the course of adolescence, and, as Figure 5.1 illustrates, that

teenagers' moods become more positive over the course of the week, as the weekend approaches (Larson, 1983; Larson & Richards, 1991, 1998).

American society is highly age segregated. From the time youngsters stop spending their full day at home—certainly by age 5, but for many, as early as the first year of life if they go to a day care center—until they graduate high school at age 18 or so, they are grouped with children their own age. Other than relatives, they have little extended contact with people who are older or younger. Because schools play such an important role in determining children's friendships, age grouping carries over into after-school, weekend, and vacation activities. Little League, scouting, after-school programs, church groups—all are structured in a way that groups people by age.

In contemporary society, **peer groups**—groups of people who are roughly the same age—have become an increasingly important context in which adolescents spend time (Harris, 1995). Modernization has led to more and more age segregation—in schools, in the workplace, and in the community. Today's teenagers spend far more time in the exclusive company of their peers than their counterparts did in the past. Indeed, the rise of peer groups in modern society gives adolescence in contemporary society some of its most distinctive features. And the role of peers in shaping adolescent psychosocial development has become increasingly important.

For these reasons, understanding how adolescent peer groups form and what takes place within their boundaries is critical to understanding adolescent development in contemporary society. No discussion of adolescent identity development is complete without an examination of how and why teenagers derive part of their identity from the group they spend time with.

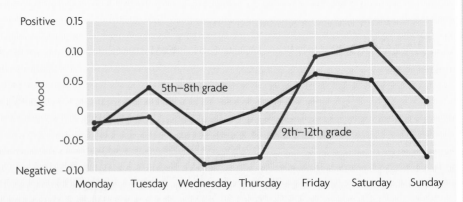

FIGURE 5.1   As the weekend approaches and adolescents anticipate spending more time with their friends, their mood takes a marked turn for the better. (Larson & Richards, 1998)

peer groups   Groups of individuals of approximately the same age.

No discussion of the development of autonomy is complete without consideration of how adolescents learn to be independent decision makers when they are with their friends. No discussion of intimacy is complete without an understanding of teenagers' cliques and how they are formed. No discussion of adolescent sexuality is complete without an examination of how, and when, peer groups change from same-sex groups to mixed-sex groups. And no discussion of the development of achievement in adolescence can ignore the role that friends play in influencing each other's attitudes toward school.

The Origins of Adolescent Peer Groups in Contemporary Society

Contact between adolescents and their peers is found in all cultures, of course. But not all societies have peer groups that are as narrowly defined and age segregated as those in contemporary America. Although adolescent peer relationships are universal, age-segregated peer groups are not. In earlier times, for example, interactions among youngsters occurred largely in the context of mixed-age groups composed of infants, children, and adolescents (Hartup, 1977). And much interaction among children occurred in the presence of their parents, because adults and children were not isolated from one another during the day.

Even today, in societies that are less industrialized and in many Asian countries, young people spend a good part of the day in contact with their parents. For example, in India, adolescents spend about 40 percent of their waking hours with family members. In the United States, in contrast, by the time an adolescent is a senior in high school, less than 15 percent of his or her waking hours are spent with family (Larson & Verma, 1999). In contemporary America and Europe, age segregation is the norm (Brown, 2004; Larson & Verma, 1999).

THE EDUCATIONAL ORIGINS OF ADOLESCENT PEER GROUPS

Educators first developed the idea of free public education, with students grouped by age—a practice known as **age grading**—in the middle of the nineteenth century. In so doing, they established an arrangement that would eventually touch all American youngsters and encourage the development and maintenance of age-segregated peer groups. It was not until the second quarter of the twentieth century, however, that most adolescents were directly affected by educational age grouping. Attending elementary school may have been common before 1900, but until 1930 or so, high school was a luxury available only to the affluent. In other words, adolescent peer groups based on friendships formed in school were not prevalent until well into the twentieth century.

What about adolescents prior to 1930? Did they have peer groups similar to those that adolescents have today? We do not know for sure. But we can be fairly certain that the forces encouraging adolescents to associate almost exclusively with people of exactly the same age were not as strong at the beginning of the twentieth century as they are today. Youngsters who were not in school were generally working and living at home, where they were likely to have a good deal of contact with adults and children of all ages (Modell, Furstenberg, & Hershberg, 1976). Even those youngsters from families wealthy enough to send their children to high school typically attended academies where children of different ages were mixed together; during the nineteenth century, it was not uncommon for peer groups to be composed of individuals ranging in age from 14 to 20 (President's Science Advisory Committee, 1974). Today, in contrast, virtually all American youngsters spend the years between ages 6 and 18 in age-graded schools.

The physical separation of teenagers and adults has increased over the past six decades, due to changing patterns of housing and employment. In contemporary society, many adolescents spend most of their free time without contact with adults.

age grading The process of grouping individuals within social institutions on the basis of age.

The impact of this educational age grading on adolescents' social life has been staggering. In one survey, in which seventh- through tenth-grade students were asked to list the people who were important to them, over two-thirds of the same-sex peers they mentioned were from the same grade in their school (Blyth, Hill, & Thiel, 1982). Participation in organized activities outside of school also contributes to age segregation. One study found that close to 80 percent of sixth-graders are involved in at least one nonschool club, extracurricular activity group, or youth organization in which they are likely to have contact only with peers of the same age (Medrich, Roizen, Rubin, & Buckley, 1982). When students are free to mix with people of different ages while at school, they are more likely to do so during early adolescence (Gray & Feldman, 1997), perhaps because there is such wide variability in physical development at this point in development.

WORK, FAMILY LIFE, AND ADOLESCENT PEER GROUPS

A second set of factors related to the rise of adolescent peer groups concerns changes in the workplace, or more precisely, changes in the relationship between work and other aspects of daily life. With industrialization came more stringent and more carefully monitored child labor laws, which restricted adolescents' participation in the world of work (Bakan, 1972; Modell & Goodman, 1990). Because the implementation of tougher child labor laws coincided with the rise of secondary education, adolescents and adults (who had once shared the same daily activity—work) went their separate ways. Adolescents spent the day in school, while adults went to work.

FOOD FOR THOUGHT

Has the increase in the number of adolescents in single-parent households had any impact on the rise of peer groups in modern society?

The segregation of adolescents from adults also was fueled by the rise in maternal employment during the last few decades of the twentieth century. The movement of mothers out of the home and into the workplace furthered the trend—already set in motion by suburbanization—toward the development of residential neighborhoods dominated by young people during weekday mornings and afternoons. Today,

Changes in work and family life have resulted in a large number of young people who are not supervised by their parents after school. Affluent, suburban, and white children are most likely to be home alone.

approximately 14 million school-aged youngsters come home from school to houses with no adults present, and an additional half million care for themselves in the morning, before school begins (National Institute on Out-of-School Time, 2006). We'll look at the implications of after-school activities for adolescent development in Chapter 7, when we look at how adolescents spend their free time.

CHANGES IN THE POPULATION

Perhaps the most important factor influencing the rise of adolescent peer groups in recent years was the rapid growth of the teenage population between 1955 and 1975, a trend that is now repeating itself. Following the end of World War II, many parents wanted to have children as soon as possible, creating what has been called the postwar **baby boom.** The products of this baby boom became adolescents during the 1960s and early 1970s, creating an "adolescent boom" for about 15 years. As you can see from Figure 5.2, the size of the population ages 15–19 nearly doubled between 1955 and 1975 and, more important, rose from less than 7 percent of the total population to over 10 percent. During the mid-1970s, in fact, more than 1 out of every 6 Americans was a teenager! One reason for the growth of peer groups, therefore, was the sheer increase in the number of peers that young people had.

baby boom   The period following World War II, during which the number of infants born was extremely large.

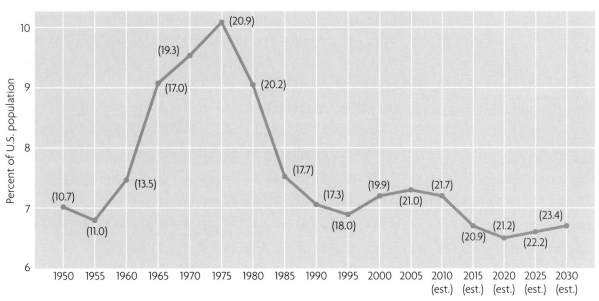

FIGURE 5.2 The percentage of the U.S. population made up of 15- to 19-year-olds reached its highest level in 1975. It began to increase again in 1995. Figures in parentheses indicate the number of 15- to 19-year-olds, in millions. (U.S. Bureau of the Census, 2000)

This trend, as you can see, turned downward in 1975, and the relative size of the adolescent population decreased until 1995. But during the last decade of the twentieth century—when the products of the baby boom began raising adolescents of their own—the size of the teenage population began increasing once again, although in relative terms it has remained, and will continue to remain, at around 7 percent of the U.S. population. In the year 2000, the population of 15- to 19-year-olds in the United States numbered about 20 million. An additional 20 million individuals were between ages 10 and 14 at that time, meaning that as we entered the twenty-first century, approximately 1 in 7 individuals in the United States were adolescents. The proportion of the U.S. population that is adolescent is estimated to remain at about this level through the next half century (U.S. Bureau of the Census, 2000). Patterns of change in the size of the adolescent population vary considerably around the world, mainly because of different birthrates.

Social scientists are interested in tracking the size of the adolescent population for several reasons. First, changes in the size of the adolescent population may warrant changes in the allocation of funds for social services, educational programs, and health care, since adolescents' needs are not the same as those of children or adults. Second, changes in the size of the adolescent population have implications for understanding the behavior of cohorts. A cohort is a group of individuals born during a particular period, such as the baby boomers (born in the late 1940s and early to mid-1950s), "Gen X" (born in the early 1970s), or the "Millennial generation" (the adolescent children of the baby boomers, born in the 1980s and early 1990s) (see Table 5.1). Baby boomers, many of whom were adolescents in the early and mid-1970s, for example, were members of a very crowded cohort, which meant that they encountered a relatively high degree of competition for places in college, jobs, and so on. The size of this cohort also meant that it could attract a great deal of public attention, from politicians to advertisers. In contrast, members of Gen X, who were adolescents in the late 1980s and early 1990s, were members of a much smaller cohort, with less competition among individuals but also with far less clout in the larger society. Because it is considerably larger than Gen X, the Millennial generation, who are teenagers today, will likely be more influential.

RECAP

- In contemporary society, adolescents spend a great deal of time with age-mates, or peers.
- Peer groups are a far more important influence on adolescent development today than in previous eras, when age segregation was not as pervasive.
- Many factors contributed to the rise of peer groups during the twentieth century, including the spread of compulsory secondary education, changes in the workplace that segregated young from old, and changes in the relative size of various cohorts of adolescents.

TABLE 5.1 Cohorts, periods, and ages

Cohort Name	Became Young Adults (16–30)	Key Events at That Time	Ages in Census Year										
			1900	1910	1920	1930	1940	1950	1960	1970	1980	1990	2000
Millennial generation	1992–2015	Information era: economic growth and global politics											16–24
Gen X	1982–2005	Reagan era: economic polarization, political conservatism										16–24	25–30
Late baby boomers	1972–95	Watergate era: economic recession, employment restructuring									16–24	25–30	
Early baby boomers	1962–85	Hippies: social movements, campus revolts								16–24	25–30		
Happy days generation	1952–75	Family and conformity: baby boom and Cold War/ McCarthy era							16–24	25–30			
Happy days/ greatest generation	1942–65	Family and conformity: baby boom and Cold War/ McCarthy era						16–24	25–30				
Greatest generation/ children of Great Depression	1932–55	Hard times: economic depression and World War II					16–24	25–30					
Children of Great Depression	1922–45	Hard times: economic depression and World War II				16–24	25–30						
Lost generation	1912–35	World War I and Roaring Twenties, Prohibition			16–24	25–30							
…	1902–25	Age of invention and World War I		16–24	25–30								
…	1892–1915	Age of invention, urbanization	16–24	25–30									

Source: Adapted from Farly, 1996.

The Adolescent Peer Group: A Problem or a Necessity?

Is the rise of peer groups in modern society a problem that needs to be remedied, or is it an inevitable—perhaps even necessary—part of life in contemporary America? This question has sparked some of the hottest debates in the study of adolescence over the past 25 years (Brown, 2004). On one side are those who claim that age segregation has led to the development of a separate youth culture, in which young people maintain attitudes and values that are different from—even contrary to—those of adults. On the other side are those who argue that industrialization and modernization have made peer groups more important, that adults alone can no longer prepare young people for the future, and that peer groups play a vital role in the socialization of adolescents for adulthood (Harris, 1995). Let's look at both sides of the debate.

IS THERE A SEPARATE YOUTH CULTURE?

The belief that age segregation has fueled the development of a separate—and troublesome—youth culture was first expressed by sociologist James Coleman, whose book *The Adolescent Society* (1961) presented the findings of an extensive study of the social worlds of 10 American high schools. Even though this book was published nearly 50 years ago, many of the concerns expressed by Coleman have echoed repeatedly over the past four decades. Indeed, when adults today complain about the questionable morals and poor character of today's young people, they are saying nothing different from what Coleman and other commentators were asserting in the middle of the twentieth century. Indeed, there probably has not been a generation of adults that hasn't complained about the character and behavior of the young.

Coleman worried about the relatively low value the adolescents in his study placed on academic success. Although the parents he surveyed felt that academic achievement should be a priority for their youngsters, the adolescents lived in a social world in which academic success was frowned on, in which doing well in school did not earn the admiration of peers. Whereas their parents may have been pleased by straight-A report cards, the high school students in the study said that being a good student carried little weight with their friends. Although Coleman's study is close to 50 years old, its findings still ring true. It probably is fair to say that academic achievement is not valued any

Studies show that in most high schools athletic and social success are more reliable routes to popularity than is academic success.

more by American teenagers today than it was a half century ago (Bishop, 1999; Meyer, 1994; Steinberg, Brown, & Dornbusch, 1996).

Do Adolescents Inhabit a Separate World?

What should we make of the fact that, relative to adults, adolescents do not place a great deal of emphasis on doing well in school? According to some observers, age segregation has so strengthened the power of the peer group that American adolescents have become alienated from and unfamiliar with the values of adults. No longer are young people interested in the things their parents want for them, these commentators say. In fact, teenagers have become separated from adult society to such an extent that they have established their own society—a separate youth culture that undermines parents' efforts to encourage academic excellence and instead emphasizes sports, dating, and partying.

According to this view, problems such as youth unemployment, teenage suicide, juvenile crime and delinquency, drug and alcohol use, and premarital pregnancy can be attributed to the rise of peer groups and the isolation of adolescents from adults. Many observers of the adolescent scene have noted that all these problems increased dramatically since the 1940s, as peer groups became more prominent and age segregation became more prevalent (e.g., Bronfenbrenner, 1974). The argument, then, is that the rise in adolescents' problems can be directly linked to the rise in the power of adolescent peer groups. Although this view is widely held among adults, at least one study indicates that it may not be entirely true.

In this study, the researcher contrasted the peer orientation of young people at three different points in time. Identical questionnaires assessing how much adolescents looked to their parents and friends for advice on a range of issues were given to groups of teenagers from the same community in 1963, 1976, and 1982 (Sebald, 1986). As might have been predicted, between 1963 and 1976, adolescents became more oriented toward their peers and less toward their parents. Between 1976 and 1982, however—a time during which rates of adolescent problems increased—this trend reversed itself somewhat, as adolescents' orientation toward their peers diminished. During this period, boys' orientation toward their parents increased, but girls' continued to decline, although at a less dramatic rate. Adolescents' values were more similar to those of their parents during the early 1980s than they were during the late 1960s and early 1970s (Gecas & Seff, 1990).

As B. Bradford Brown (2004), an expert on adolescent peer groups, has noted, the nature and strength of adolescent peer influence varies a great deal from one historical period to the next. We must be cautious about generalizing images of adolescent peer pressure derived from one point in time to all generations of young people. The strength of peer influence also may vary from one context to another. One study of Canadian adolescents, for example, found that the majority of students preferred to be remembered as outstanding students (rather than as great athletes or popular adolescents), and other studies have found that students' preferences for how they will be remembered vary a great deal by sex, age, and their place in the social structure of the school (Brown, 1990).

■ **Has the Youth Culture Harmed Adolescents?**
These cautions notwithstanding, it seems obvious to even the most casual observer that peers play a more important role in the lives of adolescents in modern society than they did in previous eras. But has the rise of adolescent peer groups in modern society really caused so many problems?

Unfortunately, this question is very difficult to answer. While age segregation certainly has increased over the past 60 years, society has changed in other ways during this same time—ways that may also have contributed to increases in such problems as crime and drug use. In many regards, the world is a far more stressful place to grow up in now than it was in the past. Families move every few years. Divorce is commonplace. Adolescents experience enormous pressures from parents, peers, and the mass media (Meyer, 1994). More importantly, as you will read in later chapters, rates of many adolescent problem behaviors—crime and drug use are good examples—have fluctuated

considerably over the past quarter century, but there has not been a reversal of the trend toward age segregation. If age segregation were the "true" cause of adolescents' problems, this would not be the case.

To be sure, contemporary adolescents spend more time in peer groups than adolescents did in past eras. But we do not know if today's young people are any more susceptible to the influence of their friends than their counterparts were previously, nor do we know if teenagers are any worse off because peer groups have come to play a more prominent role in modern society. In fact, studies of peer pressure indicate that most teenagers feel that their friends are likely to pressure them *not* to use drugs or to engage in sexual activity. Adolescents do, however, report a good deal of pressure to drink alcohol—pressure that increases during the adolescent years (Brown, Clasen, & Eicher, 1986)—while few adolescents report that their friends pressure them to do well in school (Steinberg, Brown, & Dornbusch, 1996). Thus, adolescents exert both positive and negative influences on each other; it is simply incorrect to describe the peer group as a monolithic, negative influence (Brown, 2004). More to the point, some theorists have suggested that peer groups—regardless of how they influence adolescent behavior—are inevitable and necessary by-products of modernization, and essential to the transmission of cultural information (Harris, 1995). Let's look at their point of view.

THE NEED FOR PEER GROUPS IN MODERN SOCIETY

The family is a less influential institution today than it was in the past. In less industrialized societies, political, economic, and social institutions revolve around the family. Occupation, choice of spouse, place of residence, treatment under the law, and participation in community governance—all are tied to who one's relatives are. Individuals' family ties determine with whom they can trade and how much they pay for various commodities. In short, how adults are expected to behave depends on which family they come from.

■ **Particularistic Versus Universalistic Norms**
Because not all adults are expected to behave in the same way in these kinship-based societies, it is not possible to educate or socialize all young people in one large group, since they all have to learn somewhat different sets of norms. When norms for behavior vary from person to person, they are called **particularistic norms.** Suppose the laws governing driving were particularistic—that the rules of the road were different for every person. Perhaps people from families who had

---

particularistic norms Guidelines for behavior that vary from one individual to another; more commonly found in less industrialized societies.

lived in the community for a long time would be allowed to drive at 75 miles an hour, but people from families who were new to the area would have to drive at 55. Under a particularistic system such as this, having driver education courses for high school students wouldn't make much sense, because each student would have to learn a different set of rules.

In societies in which norms are particularistic, grouping adolescents by age and sending them off to school is not an effective strategy for socializing them for adulthood, since their family ties, not their age, determine what their rights and responsibilities are. The socialization of adolescents in kinship-based societies is best accomplished in family groups, where elders can pass on the family's particular values and norms to their younger relatives.

In contemporary societies, things are quite different. Modernization has eroded much of the family's importance as a political, social, and economic unit. Generally, in modern society, all individuals are expected to learn the same set of norms, because the rules governing behavior apply equally to all members of the community. These norms are called **universalistic norms.** When you walk into a grocery store to buy something or when you go to a polling place to vote, it generally makes no difference who your relatives are. Whom you may marry, what kind of work you do, where you live, and how you are treated under the law are not based on family lineage. The norms that apply to you apply to everyone.

Under these circumstances, it is not wise to limit the socialization of adolescents to the family, because doing so does not ensure that all youngsters will learn the same set of norms (Harris, 1995). In societies that require individuals to learn universalistic norms, it is more efficient to group by age all the individuals who are to be socialized (Eisenstadt, 1956). Teaching is better done in schools than left up to individual families. One of the reasons we have driver education classes, for example, is that our rules for driving are universalistic—the same for everyone—and we need to make sure that individuals learn a common set of regulations, not simply the ones their parents teach them.

As the family has become a less important political and economic institution, universalistic norms have come to replace particularistic ones. And this has required a change in the way in which adolescents are prepared for adulthood. Not only has modernization created age groups, it has made them absolutely necessary. Without systematic age grouping in schools, it would be impossible to prepare young people for adulthood. And because age grouping in schools carries over into activities outside of school, the need for universal, school-based education has created age-segregated peer groups.

FOOD FOR THOUGHT

Can you think of examples from your own experience that support the argument that age-graded peer groups are a necessary, even beneficial, influence on adolescent development? Has this had any effect on relationships between adolescents and adults?

Do these analyses mean that the adolescents of the future will cease to profit from having close relationships with adults? Of course not. As we saw in the previous chapter, young people will always need the support, affection, and advice of their elders. But understanding how modernization has necessitated peer groups casts the issue of age segregation in a new light. Despite whatever problems may have been caused by the rise of peer groups in contemporary society, there may be little we can—or should—do to make adolescent peer groups less important.

RECAP

- Social scientists have long debated whether the prominent role played by peer groups in the socialization of young people is a cause for concern or celebration.
- Some commentators have suggested that the rise of peer groups has contributed to the development of a separate youth culture that is hostile toward adult values. Others point to the necessary and valuable educational role played by peer groups in rapidly changing societies like ours.
- Peer groups are especially important in societies that are governed by universalistic norms, where individuals are educated mainly outside the family.

The Nature of Adolescent Peer Groups

CHANGES IN PEER GROUPS DURING ADOLESCENCE

Visit any elementary school playground, and you will readily see that peer groups are an important feature of the social world of childhood. But even though peer

universalistic norms Guidelines for behavior that apply to all members of a community; more common in industrialized societies.

groups exist well before adolescence, during the teenage years, they change in significance and structure. Four specific developments stand out (Brown, 1990, 2004).

In What Ways Do Peer Groups Change?

First, as noted earlier, there is a sharp increase during adolescence in the sheer amount of time individuals spend with their peers and in the relative time they spend in the company of peers versus adults. If we count school as being a setting in which adolescents are mainly with age-mates, well over half of the typical American adolescent's waking hours are spent with peers, as opposed to only 15 percent with adults—including their parents (a good deal of the remaining time is spent alone or with a combination of adults and age-mates). Indeed, during the transition into adolescence, there is a dramatic drop in the amount of time adolescents spend with parents; for boys, this is mainly replaced by time spent alone, whereas for girls, it is replaced by time alone and by time with friends (see Figure 5.3) (Larson & Richards, 1991). There are important ethnic and gender differences in patterns of time use, however. For example, the decline in time spent with family members and the dramatic increase in time spent with peers in early adolescence are more striking among white girls than among boys or African American youth (Larson, Richards, Sims, & Dworkin, 2001).

When asked to list the people in their lives who are most important to them—what psychologists call their significant others—nearly half the people adolescents mention are the same age. By sixth grade, adults other than parents account for less than 25 percent of the typical adolescent's social network—the people whom she or he interacts with most regularly. And among early-maturing teenagers, this figure is only about 10 percent (Brown, 1990). Naturally, not all adolescents are equally interested in spending time with peers. One recent study identified four distinct groups, based on their social self-perceptions: confident, anxious, unconcerned, and desperate. Confident and desperate adolescents spent far more time with peers than did anxious or unconcerned ones (Jacobs, Vernon, & Eccles, 2004).

Second, during adolescence, peer groups function much more often without adult supervision than they do during childhood, partly because adolescents are more mobile and partly because they seek, and are granted, more independence (Brown, 1990). Groups of younger children typically play in the presence of adults or in activities organized or supervised by adults

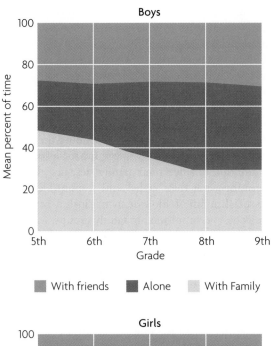

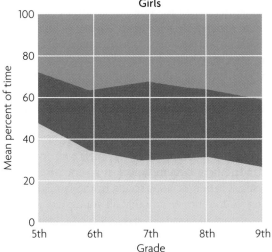

FIGURE 5.3 There are significant changes in how individuals spend leisure time during early adolescence. (Larson and Richards, 1991)

(for example, Little League, youth soccer, Brownies), whereas adolescents are granted far more independence. A group of teenagers may go off to the mall or to the movies on their own, or will deliberately congregate at the home of someone whose parents are absent.

Third, during adolescence, increasingly more contact with peers is with opposite-sex friends. During childhood, peer groups are highly sex segregated, a phenomenon known as **sex cleavage.** This is especially true of children's peer activities in school and other settings organized by adults, although somewhat less so of their more informal activities, such as neighborhood play (Maccoby, 1990). During adolescence, however, an increasingly larger proportion of an individual's

sex cleavage The separation of boys and girls into different cliques, common during late childhood and early adolescence.

significant others are opposite-sex peers, even in public settings (Brown, 2004). As we will see in a later section, this movement toward opposite-sex peers seems to stimulate changes in the structure of the peer group.

Finally, whereas children's peer relationships are limited mainly to relatively small groups—at most, three or four children at a time, for example—adolescence marks the emergence of larger collectives of peers, or crowds. (Adolescents still have close friendships, of course, which we'll look at in Chapter 10.) In junior high school cafeterias, for example, the "popular" crowd sits in one section of the room, the "brains" in another, and the "druggies" in a third (see Eder, 1985). These crowds typically develop their own minicultures, characterized by particular styles of dressing, talking, and behaving. Studies show that it is not until early adolescence that individuals can confidently list the various crowds in their schools and reliably describe the stereotypes that distinguish the different crowds from one another (Brown, Mory, & Kinney, 1994).

Most adolescents belong to at least one clique, a group of about a half-dozen close friends.

▌ What Causes Peer Groups to Change?

These changes in peer relations have their origins in the biological, cognitive, and social transitions of adolescence. Puberty, as we have seen, stimulates adolescents' interest in opposite-sex relationships and serves to distance them from their parents, which helps to explain why adolescents' social networks increasingly include more opposite-sex peers and fewer adults. The cognitive changes of adolescence permit a more sophisticated understanding of social relationships, an understanding that may allow the sort of abstract categorization that leads to grouping individuals into crowds. And changes in social definition may stimulate changes in peer relations as a sort of adaptive response: The larger, more anonymous social setting of the secondary school, for instance, may force adolescents to seek out individuals whom they perceive as having common interests and values, perhaps as a way of re-creating the smaller, more intimate groups of childhood (Brown, 2004). Instead of floundering in a large, impersonal high school cafeteria, the adolescent who belongs to the "cheerleader" crowd, or even the "nerds," may head directly for her or his place at a familiar table.

CLIQUES AND CROWDS

To better understand the significance of peer relations during adolescence, it is helpful to think of adolescents' peer groups as organized around two related, but different, structures (Brown, 2004). **Cliques** are small groups of between 2 and 12 individuals—the average is about 5 or 6—generally of the same sex and, of course, the same age (Dunphy, 1969; Hollingshead, [1949] 1975). Cliques can be defined by common

activities (for example, the "drama" group or a group of students who study together regularly) or simply by friendship (e.g., a group of girls who have lunch together every day or a group of boys who have known each other for a long time). The importance of the clique, whatever its basis, is that it provides the main social context in which adolescents interact with one another. The clique is the social setting in which adolescents hang out, talk to each other, and form close friendships. Some cliques are more open to outsiders than others (that is, the members are less "cliquish"), but virtually all cliques are small enough that the members feel they know each other well and appreciate each other more than people outside the clique do (Brown, 2004).

▌ How Cliques Structure Social Networks

One study of the structure, prevalence, and stability of cliques among ninth-graders in five different high schools within a large American school district illustrated the ways in which cliques structure adolescents' friendship networks (Ennett & Bauman, 1996). Based on interviews with students over a one-year period, the researchers categorized adolescents as clique members (individuals who have most of their interactions with the same small group of people), liaisons (individuals who interact with two or more adolescents who are members of cliques, but who themselves are not part of a clique), and isolates (individuals who have few or no links to others in the network) (see Figure 5.4). Three interesting patterns

cliques Small, tightly knit groups of between 2 and 12 friends, generally of the same sex and age.

FIGURE 5.4   A map of an adolescent social network: cliques, liaisons, and isolates. (From Ennett and Bauman, 1996)

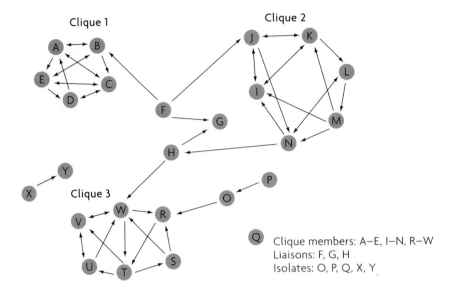

Clique members: A–E, I–N, R–W
Liaisons: F, G, H
Isolates: O, P, Q, X, Y

emerged. First, despite the popular image of adolescents as "cliquish," fewer than half the adolescents in any school were members of cliques. Second, girls were more likely than boys to be members of cliques, whereas boys were more likely than girls to be isolates (see also Urberg, Değirmencioğlu, Tolson, & Halliday-Scher, 1995). Finally, adolescents' positions in their school's social network was relatively stable over time: Adolescents who were members of cliques in the ninth grade were clique members in tenth grade; ninth-grade isolates remained, for the most part, isolates one year later. This does not mean that the composition of specific cliques is stable—typically, it is not—but only that individuals who were members of some clique at one point of time were members of some clique one year later. In other words, there is stability in adolescents' tendency to join cliques, but not in the makeup of particular groups (Brown, 2004). In one recent study, about 75 percent of seventh-graders were members of cliques and about 15 percent were isolates; very few were liaisons or connected to just one other adolescent in a dyad (Ryan, 2001). Not surprisingly, the more recently a student has arrived at a school, the less "well connected" he or she is likely to be; developing a social network is especially hard on students whose families move frequently (South & Haynie, 2004)

▋ **How Adolescents Sort into Crowds**   Cliques are quite different in structure and purpose from crowds. **Crowds** are based on "the identification of adolescents who share a similar image or reputation

among peers, or who have a common feature such as ethnicity or neighborhood, even if they do not consider each other friends or spend much time interacting with each other" (Brown, 2004). In contemporary American high schools, typical crowds include "jocks," "brains," "nerds," "populars," and "druggies." The labels for these crowds may vary from school to school ("nerds" versus "geeks," "populars" versus "preps"), but their generic presence is commonplace, at least in the United States and Canada. If you grew up in one of these two countries, you can probably recognize these different types of crowds from your own school experience. In contrast to cliques, crowds are not settings for adolescents' intimate interactions or friendships but instead serve three broad purposes: to locate adolescents (to themselves and to others) within the social structure of the school, to channel adolescents into associations with some peers and away from others, and to provide contexts that reward certain lifestyles and disparage others (Brown, 1996, 2004; Brown, Dolcini, & Leventhal, 1995; Brown, Mory, & Kinney, 1994).

Interestingly, most European schools have the crowds that Americans call "populars" and "druggies," as well as crowds organized around certain types of music (for example, "metalheads") and antisocial crowds, but athletically oriented crowds ("jocks") and academically oriented crowds ("brains" and "nerds") are rarely found (Arnett, 2002). The absence of a "jock" crowd is attributable to the absence of school-sponsored sports teams in Europe (adolescents join sports clubs in the community instead). The absence of "brains" and "nerds" is likely due to the different sorts of attitudes that European and American teenagers have toward achievement—students who try hard in school are made fun of in the United States but not,

crowds   Large, loosely organized groups of young people, composed of several cliques and typically organized around a common shared activity.

for the most part, in other countries. In other countries, therefore, there is no need to single people out on the basis of how much they care about doing well in school.

Membership in a crowd is based mainly on reputation and stereotype, rather than on actual friendship or social interaction. This is very different from membership in a clique, which, by definition, hinges on shared activity and friendship. In concrete terms—and perhaps ironically—an adolescent does not have to actually have "brains" as friends, or hang around with "brainy" students, to be one of the "brains." If he dresses like a "brain," acts like a "brain," and takes honors courses, then he is a "brain" as far as his crowd membership goes. The fact that crowd membership is based on reputation and stereotype can be very difficult for individual adolescents, who—if they do not change their reputation early on in high school—may find themselves stuck, at least in the eyes of their peers, in a crowd that they do not wish to belong to (or that they do not see themselves as a part of) (Brown, Freeman, Huang, & Mounts, 1992). This also means that some individuals can be members of more than one crowd simultaneously, if their reputation is such that they fit into them (Brown, 2004; Mory, 1994). According to recent estimates, close to half of high school students are associated with one crowd, about one-third are associated with two or more crowds, and about one-sixth do not clearly fit into any crowd (Brown, 2004).

The images adolescents have of various crowds in their schools are often highly stereotyped and caricatured, and adolescents tend to inflate the positive qualities of their own crowd while exaggerating the negative qualities of others (Mory, 1992). In one study (cited in Brown et al., 1994), in which teenagers were asked about the crowds in their school, responses such as these were given:

> "Oh, yeah; they all wear these tight-fitting jeans and sit around the commons in between classes like they own the place"

> "You'd be crazy to walk down the B-wing by yourself because the headbangers, they, like, attack you."

> "They all wear glasses and kiss up to teachers, and after school they all tromp uptown to the library, or they go over to somebody's house and play some stupid computer game until 9:00 at night—and then they go right to bed, 'cause their mommies make 'em!"

Whether each and every "popular" wears tight-fitting jeans, each and every "headbanger" stalks other adolescents, or each and every "nerd" goes to sleep at 9:00 P.M.

doesn't really matter. What is more important, perhaps, is that their peers believe that they do.

Although an adolescent's closest friends are almost always members of the same clique, some of them may belong to a different crowd, especially when one crowd is close in lifestyle to the other (Urberg et al., 1995). Thus, for example, a "brain" will have some friends who are also "brains" and some who are "nerds" but few, if any, who are "druggies" (Brown et al., 1994).

More importantly, crowds are not simply clusters of cliques; the two different structures serve entirely different purposes. Because the clique is based on activity and friendship, it is the important setting in which the adolescent learns social skills—how to be a good friend, how to communicate effectively, how to be a leader, how to enjoy someone else's company, or even how to break off a friendship that is no longer satisfying. These and other social skills are important in adulthood as well as in adolescence. In contrast, because crowds are based more on reputation and stereotype than on interaction, they probably contribute more to the adolescent's sense of identity and self-conception—for better and for worse—than to his or her actual social development.

CHANGES IN CLIQUE AND CROWD STRUCTURE OVER TIME

Studies of the structure of adolescents' peer groups often make use of a research technique called **participant observation.** In this approach, the researcher establishes rapport with a group of individuals in order to infiltrate and eventually join the group. In *Inside High School* (Cusick, 1973), which, incidentally, provided much of the material for the movie *Fast Times at Ridgemont High*, the author pretended to be a newcomer to the community and attended high school for a year to learn more about the adolescents' social world. As an observer who is also a participant, the researcher can observe the group's behavior under conditions that are more natural and more private than would otherwise be the case. Overhearing a 10-minute conversation in a high school locker room can be more informative than interviewing a student for three hours, if the student feels uncomfortable or uneasy.

▌ How Romance Changes the Peer Group

Observational studies of young people indicate that there are important changes in the structure of cliques

participant observation   A research technique in which the researcher "infiltrates" a group of individuals in order to study their behavior and relationships.

By late adolescence, same-sex peer groups have mainly disintegrated. Adolescents are more likely to spend their leisure time as members of couples.

and crowds during the adolescent years, driven in large measure by the increased importance of romantic relationships (e.g., Connolly, Furman, & Konarski, 2000; Kuttler & La Greca, 2004). During early adolescence, adolescents' activities revolve around same-sex cliques. Adolescents at this stage are not yet involved in "partying" and typically spend their leisure time with a small group of friends, playing sports, talking, or simply hanging out.

Somewhat later, as boys and girls become more interested in one another romantically—but before romantic relationships actually begin—boys' and girls' cliques come together. This is clearly a transitional stage. Boys and girls may go to parties or hang out together, but the time they spend there actually involves interaction with peers of the same sex. When youngsters are still uncomfortable about dealing with members of the opposite sex, this setting provides an opportunity in which they can learn more about opposite-sex peers without having to be intimate and without having to risk losing face. It is not unusual, for example, at young adolescents' first mixed-sex parties, for groups of boys and girls to position themselves at opposite sides of a room, watching each other but seldom interacting.

The peer group then enters a stage of structural transformation, generally led by the clique leaders. As youngsters become interested in romance, part of the group begins to split off into mixed-sex cliques, while other individuals remain in the group but in same-sex cliques. This shift is usually led by the clique leaders,

with other clique members following along. For instance, a clique of boys whose main activity is playing basketball may discover that one of the guys they look up to has become more interested in going to mixed-sex parties Saturday nights than in hanging out with the guys. Over time, they will begin to follow his lead, and their all-male activities will become more infrequent.

During middle adolescence, mixed-sex and mixed-age cliques become more prevalent (Cooksey, Mott, & Neubauer, 2002). In time, the peer group becomes composed entirely of mixed-sex cliques. One clique might consist of the drama students—male and female students who know each other from acting together in school plays. Another might be composed of four girls and four boys who like to drink on weekends. The prominent athletes—male and female— might make up a third.

Finally, during late adolescence, peer crowds begin to disintegrate. Pairs of adolescents who see themselves as couples begin to split off from the activities of the larger group. The larger peer group is replaced by loosely associated sets of couples. Adolescents begin to shift some of their attention away from friends and toward romantic partners (Kuttler & La Greca, 2004). Groups of couples may go out together from time to time, but the feeling of being in a crowd has disappeared. This pattern—in which the couple becomes the focus of social activity—persists into adulthood.

When viewed from a structural point of view, the peer group's role in the development of intimacy is quite clear. Over time, the structure of the peer group changes, in keeping with adolescents' changing needs and interests. As we'll see in Chapter 10, the adolescent's capacity for close relationships develops first through friendships with peers of the same sex. Only later does intimacy enter into opposite-sex relationships. Thus, the structure of the peer group changes during adolescence in a way that parallels the adolescent's development of intimacy: As the adolescent develops increasing facility in intimate relationships, the peer group moves from the familiarity of same-sex activities to contact with opposite-sex peers, but mainly in the safety of the larger group. It is only after adolescent males and females have been slowly socialized into dating roles—primarily by modeling their higher-status peers—that the safety of numbers is no longer needed and adolescents begin pairing off.

■ **Changes in Crowds**   There also are changes in peer crowds during this time. Many of these changes reflect the growing cognitive sophistication of the adolescent, as described in Chapter 2. For example, as adolescents mature intellectually, they come to define crowds more in terms of abstract, global characteristics ("preppies," "nerds," "jocks") than in terms of concrete, behavioral features ("the ballet crowd," "the Play Station crowd," "the kids who play basketball on 114th Street") (O'Brien & Bierman, 1988). As you know, this shift from concrete to abstract is a general feature of cognitive development in adolescence. In addition, as adolescents become more cognitively capable, they become more consciously aware of the crowd structure of their school and their place in it (Brown, 2004).

Over the course of adolescence, the crowd structure also becomes more differentiated, more permeable, and less hierarchical, which allows adolescents more freedom to change crowds and enhance their status (Brown, 2004; Horn, 2003). For example, in a study of peer crowds in one small midwestern city, the researcher found that over the course of adolescence, the crowd structure shifted between middle school, early high school, and late high school (Kinney, 1993). During middle school, there clearly was a small in-group ("trendies") and a larger out-group ("dweebs"). During early high school, there was one high-status crowd ("trendies"), two other socially acceptable crowds ("headbangers" and "normals"), and two less desirable groups ("grits" and "punkers"). And during late high school, the status differences among "trendies," "normals," and "headbangers" were negligible, and "hybrid" crowds (for example, "grit-headbangers") were common. This change over time permitted some individuals who were low in status during middle school to "recover" during high school.

■ **The Transformation of the Nerds**   In one fascinating study of the day-to-day experiences of "nerds" and their interactions with other students, sociologist David Kinney conducted an **ethnography** of the social interaction and peer culture in a high school in a small midwestern city. In contrast to survey or experimental research, which is typically quantitative in nature (that is, the data collected can be quantified), ethnographic research is qualitative. The researcher spends a considerable amount of time observing interactions within the setting, interviewing many adolescents, and writing up field notes, much as an anthropologist would do in studying a foreign culture. Ethnographic approaches can be extremely useful in studying social relationships, because they provide rich, descriptive data.

Here, for example, is an excerpt of an interview Kinney conducted with two students who had been "nerds" in middle school:

Ross: And middle school—

Ted: We were just nerds. I mean—

Ross: Yeah—

Ted: People hated us.

Ross: Well, they didn't hate us, but we weren't—

Ted: Popular. Which was either you were popular or you weren't.

Ross: In middle school it's very defined. There's popular people and unpopular people. It's just very—rigid. You were popular or unpopular. That's it.

Ted: And there wasn't people that were in between.

Ross: Oh no!

Ted: You just had one route [to becoming popular], and then there was the other. And we were the other, and—basically you were afraid of getting laughed at about anything you did because if you did one thing that was out of the ordinary, and you weren't expected to do anything out of the ordinary, then you were laughed at and made fun of, and you wouldn't fit the group at all, and then, of course, you were excluded and then you didn't even exist.

Ross: You got "nuked," so to speak. (Kinney, 1993, p. 27)

Kinney discovered, however, that many individuals who had been "nuked" in middle school had managed to transform themselves from "nerds" into "normals" sometime during high school. For some, this transition was accomplished because the high school peer structure was more differentiated and more permeable. As opposed to middle school, where there were only two groups—the popular and the unpopular—in high school, there were more socially acceptable groups with which to affiliate. For others, the transition to "normal" came about through gains in self-assurance that came with physical and social development. And for still others, the transformation was facilitated by the development of a more cognitively sophisticated, confident view of the social hierarchy—one that permitted them to reject the premise that whatever the "trendies" valued was necessarily desirable. As one woman put it:

---

ethnography   A type of research in which individuals are observed in their natural settings.

If you have confidence, you can overlook people who put you down 'cause there are always people who are going to put you down. And [when you have confidence], you don't have to worry about what I think are the more trivial things in life, like appearance or being trendy. (Kinney, 1993, p. 33)

In essence, the transformation of "nerds" to "normals" was enabled by a combination of factors both within the context (for example, the increasing differentiation and permeability of the peer crowd system) and within the adolescent (for example, the physical, cognitive, and social maturation of the individual) (Brown, 1996). Kinney's study, as well as other ethnographies of peer groups (for example, Merten's [1996] study of a group of nerdy outcasts known as the "Mels"), reminds us of the potential for growth and change during the adolescent years, even for individuals who begin the period at a social disadvantage.

The Waxing and Waning of Crowds As crowds become increasingly more salient influences on adolescents' view of their social world, they come to play an increasingly important role in structuring adolescent social behavior (O'Brien & Bierman, 1988). By ninth grade, there is nearly universal agreement among students in a school about their school's crowd structure, and students' assessment of the strength of peer group influence is very high. Between ninth and twelfth grades, however, the significance of the crowd structure begins to decline, and the salience of peer pressure wanes.

In a recent study, students were presented with several scenarios asking if it was all right to exclude someone from a school activity (cheerleading, basketball, student council) because the person was a member of a certain crowd ("jock," "gothic," "preppie") (Horn, 2003). They were also asked whether it was acceptable to deny individuals resources (for example, a scholarship) on the basis of their crowd membership. Consistent with the decline in the salience of peer crowds between mid- and late adolescence, ninth-graders were more likely to say that excluding someone from an activity on the basis of his or her crowd was all right. Students of all ages agreed that it was less acceptable to deny students resources because of crowd membership (which virtually all students viewed as immoral) than to exclude them from an activity (which was less often seen as a moral issue).

As we'll see in Chapter 9, this pattern of an increase and then a decline in the salience of peer crowds parallels developmental changes in adolescents' susceptibility to peer pressure. In other words, as crowds become more important between early and middle adolescence in defining the teenager's social world, the individual becomes more likely to accede to their influence. As crowds become less

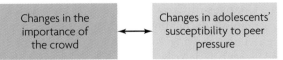

important, however, between middle and late adolescence, their influence over the individual's behavior weakens as well (Brown, 2004; Gavin and Furman, 1989). Most probably, the interplay between changes in the importance of the crowd and changes in adolescent's susceptibility to peer influence is reciprocal (see Figure 5.5).

FIGURE 5.5 As crowds become more important, they exert more pressure on adolescents to conform; in turn, as adolescents become more susceptible to peer pressure, crowds become more important.

FOOD FOR THOUGHT

Think back to your own high school experience. What were the major crowds in your school? What common characteristics did you share with the people who were in your clique?

Just as the changes in the structure of cliques play a role in the development of intimacy during adolescence, changes in the salience of crowds over the adolescent years play an important role in adolescent identity development. In Chapter 8, we'll see that adolescence is frequently a time for experimentation with different roles and identities. During the early adolescent years, before adolescents have "found" themselves, the crowd provides an important basis for self-definition (Newman & Newman, 2001). By locating themselves within the crowd structure of their school—through style of dress, language, or choice of hangouts—adolescents wear "badges" that say, "This is who I am." At a time when adolescents may not actually know just who they are, associating with a crowd provides them with a rudimentary sense of identity.

As adolescents become more secure in their identity as individuals, however, the need for affiliation with a crowd diminishes. Indeed, by the time they have reached high school, older adolescents are likely to feel that remaining a part of a crowd stifles their sense of identity and self-expression (Larkin, 1979; Varenne, 1982). The breakup of the larger peer group in late adolescence may both foreshadow and reflect the emergence of each adolescent's unique and coherent sense of self (Brown, 2004).

RECAP

- As individuals move into adolescence, there is an increase in the amount of time they spend in the exclusive company of their peers, their peer groups function increasingly outside adult supervision, and they spend more time with opposite-sex peers.
- Social scientists distinguish between crowds and cliques. Cliques are small groups of friends; crowds, in contrast, are larger and more vaguely defined groups that are based on reputation.
- Cliques, which begin as same-sex groups of individuals, gradually merge to form larger, mixed-sex groups, as adolescents develop romantic relationships and start socializing with peers of the opposite sex. In late adolescence, these groups begin to break down, as adolescents' social lives start to revolve more around couple-based activities.
- Crowds, which peak in importance during midadolescence, become more differentiated and more permeable during high school, and their influence becomes less salient.

Adolescents and Their Crowds

THE SOCIAL MAP OF ADOLESCENCE

We noted earlier that the idea of a single youth culture has not held up very well in recent research. Most ethnographic studies of high schools indicate that the social world of adolescents is far more multifaceted than this (e.g., Cusick, 1973). One helpful scheme for mapping the social world of adolescent crowds was suggested by Rigsby and McDill (1975) and later modified by Brown (1990).

According to this model, adolescents' crowds can be placed along two dimensions: how involved they are in the institutions controlled by adults, such as school and extracurricular activities, and how involved they are in the informal, peer culture (see Figure 5.6). "Jocks" and "populars," for example, are quite involved in the peer culture, but they are also very involved in the institutions valued by adults (sports and school organizations, for example). "Brains" and "nerds," in contrast, are also involved in adult-controlled organizations (in their case, academics), but they tend to be less involved in the peer culture. "Partyers" are on the opposite side of the map from "nerds": These adolescents are very involved in the peer culture but are not involved in

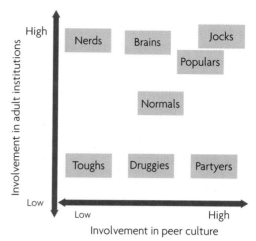

FIGURE 5.6   A model for mapping the social world of adolescent peer groups. (From Brown, 1990)

adult institutions. "Toughs" and adolescents who are members of delinquent gangs are not involved in either the peer culture or adult institutions. Other crowds, such as "normals" or "druggies," fall somewhere between these extremes. This conceptualization points to an important limitation of Coleman's view of a monolithic adolescent society: His description of adolescents as fun loving and anti-intellectual accurately described one segment of the adolescent society—a segment known in some schools as "partyers"—but not all young people in general.

CROWDS AS REFERENCE GROUPS

Knowing where an adolescent fits into the social system of the school can often tell us a fair amount about the individual's behavior and values. This is because crowds contribute to the definition of norms and standards for such things as clothing, leisure, and tastes in music. Being a "jock" means more than simply being involved in athletics; it means wearing certain types of clothes, listening to certain types of music, spending Saturday nights in certain hangouts, and using a particular slang. These adolescents accept many of the values of the adults around them but also value many elements of the contemporary peer culture.

FOOD FOR THOUGHT

Think back on your own adolescent experience. What crowd were you in? Did you change crowds, or do you know someone who did? How was this accomplished? Do you know anyone who tried to change crowds but failed? Why did this happen?

Another way of putting this is that adolescents' crowds serve as **reference groups.** They provide their members with an identity in the eyes of other adolescents. Adolescents judge one another on the basis of the company they keep, and they become branded on the basis of whom they hang out with. Such labels as "jocks," "brains," "populars," "druggies," and "skaters" serve as shorthand notations—accurate or inaccurate— to describe what someone is like as a person and what he or she holds as important.

▋ Crowd Membership and Adolescent Identity

Crowd membership is important not only because crowds are used by adolescents when talking about one another but also because membership in a crowd is often the basis for an adolescent's own identity (Newman & Newman, 2001). A girl who runs with the "preppies" identifies herself as such by wearing their "uniform," shopping in their stores, and speaking their language. After a while, preppiness becomes part of her own self-concept; she wouldn't think of dressing or talking any other way. Or consider the boys whose clique is held together by a dislike of school. Since this attitude toward school is continuously reinforced by the clique, each boy's feelings about school become strengthened, and not liking school becomes part of each boy's identity. Even if something very positive happens at school, it becomes difficult for someone in the clique to admit that it makes him feel good about himself. Doing well on a test or receiving a compliment from a teacher is likely to be dismissed as unimportant.

Because the adolescent's peer group plays such an important role as a reference group and a source of identity, the nature of the crowd with which an adolescent affiliates is likely to have an important influence on his or her behavior, activities, and self-conceptions (Prinstein & La Greca, 2002; Sussman et al., 1994). Brown and his colleagues have studied how peer group membership—that is, which peer group the adolescent affiliates with—may affect the adolescent's development and behavior (Brown, 1996). Although most adolescents feel pressure from their friends to behave in ways that are consistent with their crowd's values and goals, the specific nature of the pressure varies from one crowd to another. Adolescents who are part of the "druggie" crowd report much more peer pressure to engage in misconduct, for example, than do adolescents from the "jock" crowd (Clasen & Brown, 1985).

Crowd membership can also affect the way adolescents feel about themselves. Adolescents' self-esteem is higher among students who are identified with peer groups that have relatively more status in their school. In the high schools that Brown studied, the "jocks" and "socies" were highest in status, and the "druggies" and "toughs" were lowest. Students who were identified with the higher-status groups had higher self-esteem than did those who were identified with the lower-status groups (Brown & Lohr, 1987). As the authors wrote, "Crowds are not merely fertile grounds for bolstering self-esteem through identity testing or building supportive social relationships. Crowd labels also provide one feedback on one's comparative standing among peers, which in turn may enhance or depreciate self-esteem" (1987, p. 53). One recent study, for example, found that over the course of adolescence, symptoms of psychological distress declined among the "populars" and "jocks" but increased among the "brains" (Prinstein & La Greca, 2002). Of course, the longer-term consequences of crowd membership during adolescence are not necessarily the same as their immediate impact. One study that examined the young-adult (age 24) outcomes of high school crowd membership found that both "brains" and "jocks" showed the most favorable patterns of psychological adjustment over time (Barber, Eccles, & Stone, 2001). Not surprisingly, individuals who had been members of antisocial peer groups fared the worst.

▋ Ethnicity and Crowd Membership

Researchers do not know how the social structure of adolescent crowds differs for minority and nonminority adolescents, because most of the research to date has been conducted in predominantly white high schools (Brown, 2004). Some research indicates that at least some of the basic distinctions among crowds that have been found in studies of predominantly white high schools (for example, academically oriented crowds, partying crowds, deviant crowds, trendy crowds) also exist among adolescents from ethnic minority groups (see Brown & Mounts, 1989; Fordham & Ogbu, 1986). Some evidence, however, suggests that in multiethnic high schools, the adolescents may first divide across ethnic lines and then form into the more familiar adolescent crowds within ethnic groups. Thus, in a large urban high school, there may be separate groups of African American "jocks" and white "jocks," of Hispanic American "populars" and African American "populars," and so on (Steinberg et al., 1996). Interestingly, in multiethnic schools, adolescents from one ethnic group are less likely to see crowd distinctions within other ethnic groups than they are within their own group. Thus, to white students, all Asian American adolescents are part of the "Asian" crowd, whereas the Asian American students see themselves as divided into "brains," "populars," and so on (Brown & Mounts, 1989).

reference groups   A group against which an individual compares him- or herself.

There is also reason to believe that the meaning associated with belonging to different crowds may vary among ethnic and socioeconomic groups, although this varies considerably from school to school (Tyson, Darity, & Castellino, 2005). Although one widely cited study reported that high-achieving African American students are ostracized for "acting white" (Fordham & Ogbu, 1986), many studies do not find this to be typical (e.g., Horvat & Lewis, 2003; Tyson et al., 2005). In many schools, *all* students who are highly committed to school, regardless of their ethnicity, are teased or excluded for being "nerds" or "brains." Consider the following interchange between Carrie, a white eighth-grader, and an interviewer:

In multiethnic high schools, peer groups often divide along ethnic lines.

> *Carrie*: I think—they don't— some people don't like to be known as smart. I don't know why, but that's just how they feel.
>
> *Interviewer*: Are these people that you're thinking of, are they in fact "smart," or are they people who are not— who don't think of themselves as smart?
>
> *Carrie*: They are smart. They are really smart and they can be—like a bunch of people chose not to be in [the AP] class, because they didn't—they just didn't want to be known as one of the smart kids, I guess. I don't know. Which, I mean, I just don't see—there's nothing wrong with it. It's something to be proud of. (Tyson et al., 2005, pp. 598–599)

Similarly, in some schools it may be admirable to be a "jock," while in others it may be frowned upon. Thus, the values we associate with being in one crowd as opposed to another may not be constant across all school contexts.

RECAP

- Although the specific crowd names may differ from one school to another, and from one ethnic group to the next, most high schools have relatively similar crowd structures, with some version of "jocks," "populars," "brains," "nerds," and "toughs."

- Adolescents' crowds can be mapped on two distinct dimensions: how involved they are in adult institutions, such as school, and how involved they are in the peer culture.
- Because they often serve as reference groups, crowds play an important role in the adolescent's identity development.

Adolescents and Their Cliques

What draws adolescents into one clique and not another? Because cliques serve as a basis for adolescents' friendships and play an important role in their social development, many researchers have studied the determinants of clique composition.

SIMILARITY AMONG CLIQUE MEMBERS

The most important influence on the composition of cliques is similarity. Adolescents' cliques typically are composed of people who are of the same age and the same race, from the same socioeconomic background, and—at least during early and middle adolescence— of the same sex (Ennett & Bauman, 1996).

▌**Age Segregation**   Age grouping in junior and senior high schools makes it unlikely that an individual will have friends who are substantially older or younger. A tenth-grader who is enrolled in tenth-grade English, tenth-grade math, tenth-grade history, and tenth-grade science simply does not have many opportunities to meet adolescents who are in different grades. Age segregation in adolescents' cliques does, indeed, appear to result mostly from the structure of schools (Shrum, Cheek, & Hunter, 1988). When an adolescent's friends come from a different school, those friends are just as likely to be younger or older as to come from the same grade (Blyth, Hill, & Thiel, 1982).

▌**Sex Segregation**   During the early and middle adolescent years, cliques also tend to be composed of adolescents of the same sex (Ennett & Bauman, 1996). This sex cleavage begins in childhood and continues through most of adolescence, though it is stronger among white students than among African American students (Filardo, 1996; Hallinan, 1981; Sagar, Schofield, & Snyder, 1983), and it weakens later in adolescence (Shrum et al., 1988). The causes of sex segregation in adolescents' cliques are more interesting than the causes of age segregation, because schools seldom separate boys and girls into different classes. Why, then, do adolescent males and females separate themselves into different cliques? Psychologist Eleanor Maccoby, an expert on gender and development, has suggested several reasons (Maccoby, 1990).

First, cliques are formed largely on the basis of shared activities and interests. Generally, preadolescent and early adolescent boys and girls are interested in different things. Not until adolescents begin dating do boys' cliques and girls' cliques mix, presumably because dating provides a basis for common activity.

A second reason for the sex cleavage in adolescent peer groups concerns young adolescents' sensitivity about sex roles. Over the course of childhood, boys and girls become increasingly concerned about behaving in ways judged to be sex-appropriate. When boys show an interest in dolls, they are often told either explicitly (by parents, friends, and teachers) or implicitly (by television, books, and other mass media), "Little boys don't play with dolls—those are for girls." And when girls start wrestling or roughhousing, they are often reprimanded and told to "act like ladies."

As a consequence of these continual reminders that there are boys' activities and girls' activities, early adolescents—who are trying to establish a sense of identity—are very concerned about acting in sex-appropriate ways (Galambos, 2004). This makes it very difficult for an adolescent girl to be part of a boys'

clique, in which activities are likely to be dominated by athletics and other physical pursuits, or for a boy to be a part of a girls' clique, in which activities are likely to revolve around clothing, grooming, and talking about boys (Schofield, 1981). Adolescents who go against prevailing sex-role norms by forming friendships with members of the opposite sex may be teased about being "fags" or may be ostracized by their peers because they are "perverts." (Interestingly, gay male adolescents typically have more cross-sex friendships than same-sex friendships [Diamond & Dube, 2002].) Ironically, once dating becomes the norm, adolescents who don't have relationships with peers of the opposite sex become the objects of equally strong suspicion and social rejection.

▌**Social Class Segregation**   One of the most important studies ever undertaken of adolescents' peer groups is *Elmtown's Youth* (Hollingshead, [1949] 1975). In this study of adolescents in the midwestern community of "Elmtown," sociologist August Hollingshead examined the relation between the social position of adolescents' families and the composition of teenagers' cliques. He was interested in determining whether adolescents' cliques were segregated along class lines.

Hollingshead used such indicators as income, residence, and reputation in the community to sort families into five different groups defined by social class. In the highest class were families who were very affluent, lived in the best neighborhoods, and were seen in the community as powerful and respected. These upper-class families had lived in the community for a long time and belonged to all the exclusive clubs and organizations. In the "lower class" were families who were poor, lived on the "wrong" side of town, and were not highly regarded in the community. Between these extremes were three groups of families: the hard-working but not very well off "working-class" families, the comfortable but not especially affluent "middle-class" families, and the "upper-middle-class" families, who had money but did not quite have the reputation and prestige of the families in the highest class.

Hollingshead found that adolescents do, in fact, associate chiefly with peers from the same social class. More than 60 percent of "close" friendships in Elmtown High School were between teenagers from the same background. Of the remaining clique relationships, the vast majority were between adolescents of adjacent social classes (for example, between middle-class and upper-middle-class adolescents). Almost never did adolescents from one social class associate with students from a class that was *two* ranks higher or lower. Hollingshead found similar patterns

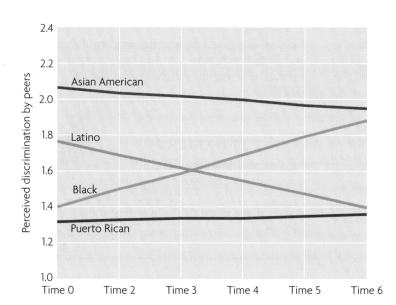

FIGURE 5.7 Black students report increasingly more discrimination by other students over time, whereas it declines among Latino students. Asian American students report the highest level of peer discrimination. (Greene et al., 2006)

when he looked at adolescents' best friends and dating relationships: Rarely were social class lines crossed, and, when they were, it was virtually always between adolescents of adjacent classes. Moreover, adolescents became even more class conscious as they got older.

Several studies conducted since the time of *Elmtown's Youth* have confirmed the enduring importance of social class in influencing adolescents' positions in the peer network of the high school. In the five-school study of cliques discussed earlier, for example, cliques were just as class segregated as they were found to be by Hollingshead many decades earlier. Within each clique, about 60 percent of adolescents came from the same social class, even though each school was considerably more diverse in its social class composition as a whole (Ennett & Bauman, 1996). Clique-based friendships between adolescents who were from very different social backgrounds were seldom observed.

▌**Ethnic Segregation** Ethnicity is not a strong determinant of clique composition during childhood, but like social class, it becomes increasingly powerful as youngsters get older, at least within the United States (Shrum et al., 1988). By middle and late adolescence, adolescents' peer groups typically are ethnically segregated, with very few ethnically mixed cliques present in most high schools (Ennett & Bauman, 1996). This appears to be the case, although somewhat less so, even within schools that have been desegregated. One recent study of a multiethnic New York City public high school found, for example, that nearly three-quarters of the Latino students, two-thirds of the African American students, and 85 percent of the

Asian American students had friends who were predominantly from the same ethnic group (Way & Chen, 2000). In fact, cross-ethnic friendships are less common in ethnically diverse schools than in schools where one ethnic group predominates (Moody, 2001; Quillian & Campbell, 2003).

A recent analysis of data from a large, nationally representative sample of adolescents found that race continues to be an enormously powerful determinant of friendship patterns—far more powerful than socioeconomic status (Quillian & Campbell, 2003). The rift between African American students and students from all other ethnic groups, especially whites and Asian Americans, is especially strong, and African American students' reports of being discriminated against by other students increases over time (although Asian American students report the highest degree of discrimination by peers) (see Figure 5.7) (Greene, Way, & Pahl, 2006). In fact, students are more likely to have friends of the same ethnicity who come from the opposite end of the socioeconomic spectrum than to have friends from the same social class but a different ethnic group. Studies of whether cross-ethnic friendships are more common among Asian American and Hispanic American adolescents who are American born than among their peers who are immigrants have found that immigrants are less likely to have cross-ethnic friendships, perhaps because of language barriers (Hamm, Brown, & Heck, 2005). But even among ethnic minority youth whose families have been in the United States for generations, there still exists a strong preference for same-ethnicity friends (Quillian & Campbell, 2003).

It is difficult to know why such strong ethnic segregation persists in adolescents' friendship selection.

Although adolescents' cliques are often segregated along socioeconomic lines, this does not account for their ethnic segregation, which persists even after socioeconomic factors are taken into account. One strong possibility is that some ethnic segregation in friendship patterns is due to differential levels of academic achievement of adolescents from different ethnic groups (Hamm et al., 2005). As you'll read in Chapter 12, on average, white and Asian American adolescents earn significantly higher grades in school than do African Americans or Hispanic Americans (Steinberg, Dornbusch, & Brown, 1992). Adolescents who are friends usually have similar attitudes toward school, similar educational aspirations, and similar school achievement levels (Brown, 2004). Racial differences in school achievement may lead to racial separation in adolescent peer groups (Hallinan & Williams, 1989). Cross-ethnic friendships are more rare, for instance, in schools that frequently separate students into different academic tracks (Stearns, 2004).

A second reason for racially segregated peer groups—according to one study of adolescents in a recently desegregated school—is attitudinal. In this school, the white adolescents perceived their African American peers as aggressive, threatening, and hostile. The African American students, in turn, saw the white students as conceited, prejudiced, and unwilling to be friends with them. These perceptions, which fed on each other, made the formation of interracial peer groups unlikely. The more the white students believed that the African American students were hostile, the more the white students acted distant and kept to themselves. But the more the white students acted this way, the more likely the African American students were to feel rejected, and the more hostile they became. In general, white students are less apt to initiate contact with African American students and to select them as friends than vice versa (Quillian & Campbell, 2003; Sagar et al., 1983). In many schools, adolescents' lack of familiarity with youngsters from other racial groups results in misperceptions of the others' attitudes and motives, and this misunderstanding limits interracial interaction (Schofield, 1981). This finding also has been reported in recent studies of Arab and Jewish students in Israel (Pitner, Astor, Benbenishty, Haj-Yahia, & Zeira, 2003).

One way out of this cycle of misunderstanding is to bring white and African American youngsters together from an early age, before they have had time to build up prejudices and lock onto stereotypes. Interracial school busing, for example, has been far more successful in communities that began such programs during elementary school than in districts that implemented them for the first time at the high school level.

If white and African American children grow up together from an early age, they are less likely to misunderstand each other and less likely to split off into separate peer groups purely on the basis of race.

FOOD FOR THOUGHT

As you now know, the ethnic composition of the American adolescent population is changing dramatically. What impact, if any, might this have on friendship patterns?

Indeed, one study of Canadian adolescents indicated that racial segregation in adolescent peer relationships is far less common in Canada than in the United States (Maharaj & Connolly, 1994). According to the researchers, one reason for this is that the broader cultural context in Canada is more supportive of multicultural tolerance and more aggressive in its approach to multicultural education and ethnic integration.

Of course, not all adolescents have especially strong preferences for friends from the same ethnic background. One comparison of two Chinese immigrant girls in a U.S. high school illustrates this point nicely (Shih, 1998). One of the girls, Christine, had a strong preference for friends who not only were Chinese but were Chinese immigrants. Although she initially was open-minded about having friends who were not Chinese, she came to feel psychologically distant from them—that she had little in common with them and that they made fun of her speech and behavior. Denise, in contrast, was eager to become Americanized and so went out of her way to acquire the slang, customs, and attitudes of mainstream adolescent culture. She saw having non-Chinese friends as a way of facilitating her Americanization and actively sought them for this reason.

COMMON INTERESTS AMONG FRIENDS

Thus far, we have seen that adolescents' cliques are usually composed of individuals who are the same age, in the same grade, from the same social class, and of the same race. But what about factors beyond these? Do adolescents who associate with one another also share certain interests and activities? Generally, they do. Three factors appear to be especially important in determining adolescent clique membership and friendship patterns: orientation toward school, orientation toward the teen culture, and involvement in antisocial activity (Crosnoe & Needham, 2004). In general, this is true for both white youth (e.g., Berndt, 1982) and nonwhite youth (e.g., Tolson, Halliday-Scher, & Mack, 1994).

■ **Orientation Toward School** Adolescents and their friends tend to be similar in their attitudes toward school, in their school achievement, and in their educational plans (Berndt, 1982; Epstein, 1983a; Wentzel & Caldwell, 1997), although this tends to be more true among whites and Asian Americans than among African Americans (Hamm, 2000). Adolescents who earn high grades, study a great deal, and plan to go on to college usually have friends who share these characteristics and aspirations. One reason for this is that how much time students devote to schoolwork affects their involvement in other activities. Another is that students' friendships are often drawn from the peers with whom they have classes, and if schools track students on the basis of their academic achievement, their friends will be more likely to have similar records of school performance (Crosnoe, 2002). Someone who is always studying will not have many friends who stay out late partying, because the two activities conflict. By the same token, someone who wants to spend afternoons and evenings out having fun will find it difficult to remain friends with someone who prefers to stay home and study.

Students also may influence each other's academic performance. Given two students with similar records of past achievement, the student whose friends do better in school is likely to achieve more than the one whose friends do worse (Epstein, 1983a). Similarly, adolescents whose friends are disruptive in school tend to become more disruptive over time (Berndt & Keefe, 1995).

■ **Orientation Toward the Teen Culture** Adolescents and their friends generally listen to the same type of music, dress alike, spend their leisure time in similar types of activities, and share patterns of drug use (Berndt, 1982; Hamm, 2000). It would be very unlikely, for example, for a "jock" and a "druggie" to be part of the same clique, because their interests and attitudes are so different. In most high schools, it is fairly easy to see the split between cliques—in how people dress, where they eat lunch, how much they participate in the school's activities, and how they spend their time outside of school. Indeed, similarity in patterns of substance use is such a strong influence that it often serves as the basis for forming cross-ethnic group friendships, which, as we noted earlier, are not common (Hamm, 2000).

■ **Involvement in Antisocial Activity** A number of studies, involving both boys and girls from different

ethnic groups, indicate that antisocial, aggressive adolescents may gravitate toward each other, forming deviant peer groups (Cairns, Cairns, Neckerman, Gest, & Gariepy, 1988; Dishion, Patterson, Stoolmiller, & Skinner, 1991; Espelage, Holt, & Henkel, 2003; Kiesner, Cadinu, Poulin, & Bucci, 2002; Kreager, 2004; Laird, Pettit, Dodge, & Bates, 1999). That is, contrary to the popular belief that antisocial adolescents do not have friends or that they are interpersonally inept, these youngsters do have friends, but their friends tend to be antisocial as well, a finding that was recently replicated in a study of Italian early adolescents (Kiesner & Pastore, 2005). Although adolescents with deviant friends show some of the same emotional problems as adolescents without friends, those with deviant friends, not surprisingly, are less lonely than their friendless peers (Brendgen, Vitaro, & Bukowski, 2000).

■ **Gangs** Although we would not necessarily want to call all of these peer groups "delinquent," since they are not always involved in criminal activity, understanding the processes through which antisocial peer groups form provides some insight into the development of delinquent peer groups, or gangs. **Gangs** are deviant peer groups that can be identified by name (often denoting a neighborhood or part of the city) and common symbols ("colors," tattoos, hand signs, jewelry, etc.) (Branch, 1995; Harris, 1994; Winfree, Bäckström, & Mays, 1994). Adolescents who belong to gangs are at greater risk for many types of problems in addition to antisocial behavior, including elevated levels of psychological distress and exposure to violence (Li et al., 2002). This is also true for female adolescents who hang around with male gangs, which increases their involvement in high-risk sexual behavior, drug use, and crime. Here is one girl's description of another girl's rape, taken from a recent study of Mexican American females who associated with gang members in San Antonio:

> She was already drunk when she came to the party. I think she was 17, but I'm not too sure. She was a new girl. She didn't know nothing about the Brothers [male gang]. She didn't know nothing at all, nothing about gangs, drugs. All she knew about was drinking, and drinking, and drinking, and that's it.
>
> The Brother, he just took her to a bedroom. He was telling her that he wanted to show her something. She went up to the room after he told her that he had a diamond ring for her. So she went upstairs. He put alcohol on some rag and covered her face. That's all I heard. My homeboy said just go home, and I went. He told me that he didn't want nothing to happen to me, and I just went home. (Cepeda & Valdez, 2003, p. 99).

gangs Organized peer groups of antisocial individuals.

FIGURE 5.8 Poor parenting leads adolescents to affiliate with deviant peers, which increases teenagers' risk for antisocial behavior.

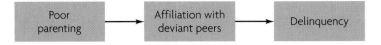

Are adolescent gangs merely a peer group whose focus is on antisocial activity, or do they have unique characteristics? Research indicates that gangs both resemble and differ from other sorts of peer groups. On the one hand, as one study of Mexican American female gang members, or *cholas,* points out, adolescent gangs look much like other types of adolescent cliques, in that they are groups of adolescents who are similar in background and orientation, share common interests and activities, and use the group to derive a sense of identity (Harris, 1994). On the other hand, the processes that lead adolescents to join gangs are not the same as those that lead to membership in other sorts of peer groups. More specifically, gang members tend to be more isolated from family, to have more emotional and behavioral problems, and to have poorer self-conceptions than other adolescents, including those who are not gang members but who are involved in antisocial activity (Dukes, Martinez, & Stein, 1997; Esbensen, Deschenes, & Winfree, 1999; Harper & Robinson, 1999). But a study of Puerto Rican male adolescents from New York City suggests that the actual relationships that antisocial adolescents have with their clique-mates may be less satisfying than are those between other adolescents and their friends (Pabon, Rodriguez, & Gurin, 1992). Although these antisocial peers spent a great deal of time together, they did not describe their relationships as emotionally close or intimate. Rather, most of the boys felt estranged from each other. As the researchers point out, this finding has implications for the design of interventions aimed at controlling delinquency by involving antisocial peer groups in positive activities; in the absence of their shared interest in antisocial activities, delinquent peers may have little reason to maintain their friendship.

▎ **The Role of Parents** According to several studies (Dishion et al., 1991; Garnier & Stein, 2002; Kim, Hetherington, & Reiss, 1999; Scaramella, Conger, Spoth, & Simons, 2002; Tolan, Gorman-Smith, & Henry, 2003), the process of antisocial peer group formation in adolescence begins in the home during childhood (see Figure 5.8). Problematic parent–child relationships—ones that are coercive and hostile—lead to the development of an antisocial disposition in the child, and this disposition contributes, in elementary school, to both school failure and rejection by classmates (Dishion et al., 1991; Pardini, Loeber, & Stouthamer-Loeber, 2005). (As you will read in a later

section, aggression in elementary and middle school often leads to peer rejection.) Rejected by the bulk of his classmates, the aggressive boy "shops" for friends and finds that he is accepted only by other aggressive boys. Once these friendships are formed, the boys, like any other clique, reward each other for participating in a shared activity—in this case, antisocial behavior. Interestingly, improvements in parenting during adolescence reduce teenagers' association with antisocial peers, which, in turn, reduces problematic behavior (Simons, Chao, Conger, & Elder, 2001).

The family and peer contexts are connected through other processes as well. As psychologist Nina Mounts has pointed out (2002, 2004), parents often "manage" their adolescent's friendships by monitoring the individuals their child spends time with, guiding their child toward peers they like, prohibiting contact with peers they dislike, and supporting friendships they approve of (Tilton-Weaver & Galambos, 2003). Parents also act as "consultants," helping their teenagers work out problems with their friends. Adolescents whose parents act as consultants in this way are less likely to be involved in drug use and delinquent activity, and report more positive relationships with their friends (Mounts, 2004). Rather than viewing the family and peer contexts as separate worlds, it is important to keep in mind that what takes place in one setting often has an impact on what occurs in others.

The role of the family in friendship choice has also been described in studies of crowds (Brown, Mounts, Lamborn, & Steinberg, 1993; Curtner-Smith & MacKinnon-Lewis, 1994; Mason, Cauce, Gonzales, & Hiraga, 1996; Melby, 1995). One of the factors that influences the crowd an adolescent belongs to is her or his upbringing. Parents play a role in socializing certain traits in their children, and these orientations, whether toward aggression or academic achievement, predispose adolescents toward choosing certain friends or crowds with which to affiliate. Once in these cliques or crowds, adolescents are rewarded for the traits that led them there in the first place, and these traits are strengthened. Thus, a child who is raised to value academics will perform well in school and will likely select friends who share this orientation. Over time, these friends will reinforce the youngster's academic orientation and strengthen his or her school performance. By the same token, antisocial adolescents, who are drawn toward other antisocial peers, become more antisocial over time as a result (Vitaro,

Tremblay, Kerr, Pagani, & Bukowski, 1997). Even when adolescents have relatively more antisocial friends, having better relationships at home and a stronger attachment to school will make them less susceptible to their friends' negative influence—even in the context of a gang (Crosnoe, Erickson, & Dornbusch, 2002; Vitaro, Brendgen, & Tremblay, 2000; Walker-Barnes & Mason, 2004).

The finding that adolescents become more antisocial when they spend time with antisocial peers has prompted some experts to question the wisdom of group-based interventions for adolescents with conduct problems (Dishion, McCord, & Poulin, 1999). Several studies of programs designed to diminish adolescents' delinquency or aggression, for example, have found that, instead of having the desired effect, the programs actually increased participants' problem behavior; that is, they had what scientists call iatrogenic effects (Mahoney, Stattin, & Lord, 2004). **Iatrogenic effects** are the undesirable consequences of well-intentioned treatments—for example, when the side effects of a medication are far worse than the problem it is intended to treat. Evidently, when antisocial adolescents spend time with like-minded peers, even in therapeutic settings, they may teach each other how to be "more effective" delinquents and may reward each other for misbehavior. Several writers have described this process as "deviancy training" (e.g., Capaldi, Dishion, Stoolmiller, & Yoerger, 2001; Dishion, Nelson, Winter, & Bullock, 2004). Knowing that group treatments for antisocial behavior have iatrogenic effects is obviously important for the design of programs for delinquent and aggressive youth.

SIMILARITY BETWEEN FRIENDS: SELECTION OR SOCIALIZATION?

Because antisocial activities seem to be such a strong determinant of clique composition, many adults have expressed concern over the influence of peers in the promotion of delinquent activity and drug and alcohol use. Parents often feel that if their youngster runs with the wrong crowd, he or she will acquire undesirable interests and attitudes. They express concern, for instance, when their child starts spending time with peers who seem to be less interested in school or more involved with drugs. But which comes first—joining a clique or being interested in a clique's activities? Do adolescents develop interests and attitudes because their friends influence them in this direction, or is it more the case that people with similar interests and tastes are likely to become friends?

This question has been examined in several large-scale studies that have tracked adolescents and their friendships over time (e.g., Curran, Stice, & Chassin,

Members of cliques are generally similar when it comes to their orientation toward school, toward teen culture (including styles of dress and preferences in music), and toward antisocial activity.

1997; Dobkin, Tremblay, Mâsse, & Vitaro, 1995; Ennett & Bauman, 1994; Kandel, 1978; Mounts & Steinberg, 1995; Poulin, Dishion, & Haas, 1999; Stein, Newcomb, & Bentler, 1987). By tracing patterns of attitudinal and behavioral change over time, and comparing these shifts with patterns of friendship formation and change, the researchers could determine whether adolescents are attracted to one another because of their initial similarity (what social scientists refer to as *selection*), whether they become similar because friends influence each other (what is referred to as *socialization*), or a combination of the two. It is also important to consider how peer similarity is measured; when similarity is measured by asking adolescents about their friends' behavior ("How often do your friends drink alcohol?"), estimates of similarity are higher than when friends when researchers ask directly, because adolescents tend to overestimate their similarity to their friends. Some researchers have concluded that once

iatrogenic effects Unintended adverse consequences of a treatment or intervention.

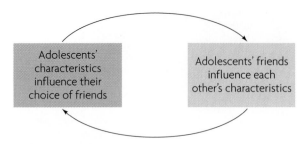

FIGURE 5.9   Adolescents' choice of friends both influences and is influenced by their traits and interests.

this tendency is taken into account, the actual size of genuine peer influence on problem behavior is quite small (Jaccard, Blanton, & Dodge, 2005).

In general, studies indicate that both selection and socialization are at work, across a variety of attitudinal and behavioral domains, including school achievement, drug use, mental health, and delinquency (Brown, 2004) (see Figure 5.9). Adolescents who use alcohol or tobacco, for example, are more likely to choose other alcohol or tobacco users as friends, especially when they attend schools with a large number of substance-using students (an example of selection). By the same token, spending time with friends who use these substances increases the adolescents' own use as well (an example of socialization) (Bryant & Zimmerman, 2002; Cleveland & Wiebe, 2003; Ennett et al., 2006; Urberg, Değirmencioğlu, & Pilgrim, 1997). The more substance-using friends an adolescent has, and the closer he or she feels to them, the more the adolescent is likely to use alcohol and drugs (Hussong & Hicks, 2003). Similarly, adolescents who report more depressive symptoms are likely to choose other depressed adolescents as friends, which, in turn, negatively affects their own mood and that of their friends (Baker, Milich, & Manolis, 1996; Hogue & Steinberg, 1995; Stevens & Prinstein, 2005). Adolescents who are bullies are more likely to have friends who themselves are bullies (Espelage, Holt, & Henkel, 2003). Conversely, antisocial adolescents who have few friends, and few aggressive friends in particular, are likely to become less antisocial over time (Adams, Bukowski, & Bagwell, 2005; Botvin & Vitaro, 1995), whereas those with antisocial friends who become even more antisocial themselves become more delinquent (Werner & Silbereisen, 2003).

Parents, of course, are inclined to blame the peer group for any of their adolescent's misbehavior, but studies that look simultaneously at selection and socialization suggest that this may not be justified. When it comes to antisocial activities, such as delinquency or drug use, it appears as if "birds of a feather flock together," at least to some extent.

How much of adolescents' similarity to their friends is due to selection and how much is due to

socialization? The answer depends on what and who is being studied. Peer influence (socialization) is far stronger over day-to-day preferences in things like clothing or music than over many of the behaviors that adults worry about, such as binge drinking or risky sex (Jaccard et al., 2005). In terms of problem behavior, selection may be a somewhat stronger factor at least as far as delinquency and gang membership are concerned (Dobkin et al., 1995; Gordon, et al., 2004; Haynie & Osgood, 2005), whereas selection and socialization are about equally influential when it comes to drug use (Curran et al., 1997; Dishion & Owen, 2002; Ennett & Bauman, 1994; Kandel, 1978). And peer influence on antisocial behavior is generally stronger among white adolescents than in other cultural groups, a finding that has emerged in several studies conducted at different historical times and in different parts of the world (Chen, Greenberger, Lester, Dong, & Guo, 1998).

One recent analysis of a data from a large, nationally representative sample of adolescents found that adolescents' friendship groups fall into one of four profiles: high functioning (a network of high-achieving friends who were involved in school-based extracurricular activities and who reported low use of alcohol and few symptoms of depression), maladjusted (friends showed the opposite pattern), disengaged (friends were not engaged in much of anything, including drinking), and engaged (friends were engaged in school, achieved decent grades, and neither abstained from nor abused alcohol) (see Figure 5.10). More importantly, an individual adolescent's behavior could be predicted on the basis of her or his friendship group's profile (Crosnoe & Needham, 2004). Adolescents' socioeconomic background and family situation were strongly related to characteristics of their friendship network, with teenagers from more educated, two-parent families more likely to fall into the high-functioning and engaged groups.

■ **Stability of Adolescent Friendships**   How stable are adolescents' friendships over time? In general, adolescents' cliques show only moderate stability over the course of the school year—with some members staying in the clique, others leaving, and new ones joining—although cliques become more stable later in high school (Cairns, Leung, Buchanan, & Cairns, 1995; Değirmencioğlu, Tolson, & Urberg, 1993). Although the actual composition of adolescents' cliques may shift over time, the defining characteristics of their cliques or their best friends do not (Hogue & Steinberg, 1995; Luo, Urberg, Rao, & Fang, 1995; Neckerman, Cairns, & Cairns, 1993). That is, even though some members of an adolescent's clique may leave and be replaced by others, the new members are likely to have attitudes and values that are

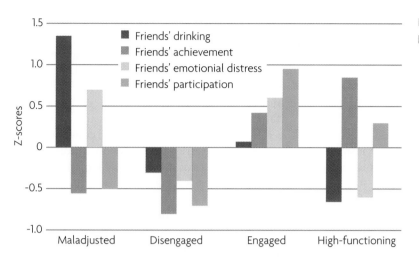

FIGURE 5.10 Four friendship group profiles. (Crossnoe & Needham, 2004)

quite similar to the former members' (Brown, 2004). Even "best friendships" are likely to change during the school year. One study found that only about one-third of students who were best friends in the fall of a school year renamed the same person as their best friend in the spring, although that person was typically listed as a friend (Değirmencioğlu et al., 1993; Değirmencioğlu, Urberg, Tolson, & Richard, 1998). Only half of all reciprocated best friendships (in which each person names the other as a best friend) that exist at the beginning of a school year exist at the end; surprisingly, staying friends over the course of a school year has nothing to do with the quality of the friendship (Bowker, 2004).

RECAP

- Cliques are small groups of adolescents who are friends and who see each other regularly.
- Unlike crowds, cliques play an important role in the development of social skills and intimacy.
- Generally, adolescents form cliques with peers who are similar in background, in orientation toward school and the peer culture, and in their level of involvement in antisocial activities.
- Although clique members influence each other's behavior and values, research also shows that adolescents initially select their friends on the basis of similarity.

Popularity and Rejection in Adolescent Peer Groups

Thus far, our discussion has focused on how and why crowds and cliques serve as the basis for adolescents' social activities. But what about the internal structure

In general, popularity in the adolescent peer group is most strongly associated with social competence—popular teenagers are friendly, cheerful, and funny. Status in the peer group, in contrast, has more to do with leadership and capability in the activities valued by the group.

of peer groups? Within a clique or a crowd, what determines which adolescents are popular and which are not?

DETERMINANTS OF POPULARITY AND REJECTION

The chief determinant of an adolescent's popularity is his or her social skills. Popular adolescents act appropriately in the eyes of their peers, are skilled at perceiving and meeting the needs of others, and are confident without being conceited. Additionally, popular adolescents are friendly, cheerful, good-natured, humorous, and—you may be surprised to learn—

intelligent (Hartup, 1983). Popular adolescents and adolescents with satisfying friendships are more knowledgeable specifically about what it takes to make and keep friends than are adolescents who are less well accepted by their peers (Jarvinen & Nicholls, 1996; Wentzel & Erdley, 1993). Because of their social skill, popular adolescents also are good at adjusting their behavior to maintain their favored social standing when peer group norms change. If, for instance, smoking marijuana becomes something that is valued by the peer group, popular adolescents will start getting high more regularly (Allen, Porter, McFarland, Marsh, & McElhaney, 2005). While many determinants of popularity are common across cultures, some differ. Shyness, for example, which is clearly a social liability in American peer groups, may be an asset among children in China (Chen, Rubin, & Li, 1995).

■ **Popularity and Aggression** Despite these broad generalizations about the determinants of popularity, it is important to note that there are many routes to popularity within adolescent peer groups. One study of preadolescent and young adolescent boys indicates that there are at least two distinct types of popular boys (Rodkin, Farmer, Pearl, & Van Acker, 2000). One group, whom the researchers described as "model" boys, had the characteristics typically identified in studies of popular youth: They were physically and academically competent, friendly, and neither shy nor aggressive. A second group of popular boys, however, whom the researchers described as "tough," were extremely aggressive, physically competent, and average or below average in friendliness, academic competence, and shyness. Contrary to the notion that aggressive children are invariably rejected by their classmates—which psychologists had long assumed—some youngsters, both boys and girls, are both aggressive and popular (Bowker, Bukowski, Hymel, & Sippola, 2000; Bukowski, Sippola, & Newcomb, 2000). Other research suggests that it is not aggression alone, but the combination of aggression and poor emotion regulation or a lack of social skills, that leads to problems with peers (Farmer, Estell, Bishop, O'Neal, & Cairns, 2003; Pope & Bierman, 1999). Consistent with this, aggressive adolescents who use their aggression deliberately—what is referred to as **instrumental aggression**—are much more popular than aggressive adolescents whose aggression is unplanned—what is referred to as **reactive aggression** (Little, Brauner, Jones, Nock, & Hawley, 2003; Prinstein & Cillessen, 2003).

instrumental aggression Aggressive behavior that is deliberate and planned.

reactive aggression Aggressive behavior that is unplanned and impulsive.

■ **The Dynamics of Popularity** Two ethnographic studies of early adolescent girls provide insight into the dynamics of popularity. Ethnographer Donna Eder (1985) spent two years in a middle school observing interactions among early adolescent girls in various extracurricular and informal settings (in the cafeteria, in the hallway, at school dances). In this school, the cheerleaders were considered the elite crowd, and girls who made the cheerleading squad were immediately accorded social status. Other girls then attempted to befriend the cheerleaders as a means of increasing their own status. This, in turn, increased the cheerleaders' popularity within the school, as they became the most sought-after friends. The girls who were successful in cultivating friendships with the cheerleaders then became a part of this high-status group and became more popular themselves. This popularity had a price, however, as one eighth-grader explained to the researcher:

> "A lot of times, people don't talk to the popular kids because they're kind of scared of them and they don't know their real personality. So that's kind of a bummer when you're considered to be popular because you don't usually meet a lot of other people because they just go, 'Oh.'" (Eder, 1985, p. 162)

Paradoxically, popularity in many cases led to these girls' being disliked. As Eder explains:

> There are limits to the number of friendships that any one person can maintain. Because popular girls get a high number of affiliative offers, they have to reject more offers of friendship than other girls. Also, to maintain their higher status, girls who form the elite group must avoid associations with lower-status girls. . . . These girls are likely to ignore the affiliative attempts of many girls, leading to the impression that they are stuck-up. . . . Shortly after these girls reach their peak of popularity, they become increasingly disliked. (Eder, 1985, p. 163)

In another study, the researcher spent time observing and interviewing a group described by teachers as the "dirty dozen" (Merten, 1997). This group of girls was "considered 'cool,' 'popular,' and 'mean.' They are a combination of cute, talented, affluent, conceited, and powerful" (1997, p. 178). The researcher was interested in understanding "why a clique of girls that was popular and socially sophisticated was also renowned for its meanness" (1997, p. 188). The answer, he discovered, was that meanness was one of the ways that the clique ensured that no one member became stuck-up as a result of her popularity in the eyes of her classmates. Thus, while it was important for clique members to maintain their popular image, if any clique member appeared to become too popular, the other members would turn on her, undermining her standing with other girls by gossiping, starting rumors, and deliberately attempting to disrupt her friendships. The following quote, from a girl whose friends turned on her, will sound all too familiar:

> Gretchen was starting to get really mad at me. I talked to her about it and I asked her what was wrong. She just said, "Oh, I heard something you said about me." But I didn't say anything about her. Sara was mad at me. I don't know why. She started being mad at me and then she started making things up that [she said] I said. Sara told Brenda and Gretchen so that they would get mad at me, too. So now I guess Gretchen has made up something and told Wellesley. They are all mad at me and laughing and everything. (Merten, 1997, p. 182)

Ironically, then, one of the potential costs of being popular in adolescence is that, if one's popularity becomes too great, one faces the very real possibility of being the object of other classmates' meanness.

Although popularity clearly has some costs, in general, the advantages of being popular far outweigh the disadvantages. Being popular (accepted or well liked by a large number of people) is not the same as having close and intimate friendships (Asher, Parker, & Walker, 1996), but the two often go hand in hand (Franzoi, Davis, & Vasquez-Suson, 1994). Compared with their less popular age-mates, popular adolescents are more likely to have close and intimate friendships, participate in social activities with peers, take part in extracurricular activities, and receive more social recognition (such as being selected as the leader of a school organization) (Franzoi et al., 1994). Part of the overlap between social acceptance and friendship no doubt stems from the fact that many of the characteristics that make adolescents popular are the same ones that make them sought after as friends—chief among them, having good social skills.

It is also important to note that some adolescents who are unpopular in school may have a well-developed network of friends outside of school. Because most research on adolescents' peer networks has been limited to school-based friendships, however, we know relatively little about the nature of nonschool friendships. We do know that many adolescents have a social life outside of school that is quite different from their life in school. Because the characteristics of an adolescent's after-school friends are more predictive of the adolescent's out-of-school behavior, studies that examine the impact of friends on adolescent development may miss important information if they do not include information about the number and characteristics of the adolescent's nonschool friends. One study of Italian middle school students found that having friends outside school buffered the harmful consequences of having few friends in school (Kiesner, Poulin, & Nicotra, 2003).

■ **Rejected Adolescents**   Social scientists have shown that it is important to distinguish among three types of unpopular, or disliked, adolescents (Bierman & Wargo, 1995; Coie, Terry, Lenox, Lochman, & Hyman, 1995; French, Conrad, & Turner, 1995; Hatzichristou and Hopf, 1996; Hymel, Bowker, & Woody, 1993; Olweus, 1993; Parkhurst & Asher, 1992). One set of unpopular adolescents is overly aggressive; they are likely to get into fights with other students, are more likely to be involved in antisocial activities, and often are involved in bullying. A second set is withdrawn; these adolescents are exceedingly shy, timid, and inhibited and, interestingly, are themselves more likely to be the victims of bullying. A third group is aggressive-withdrawn. Like other aggressive youngsters, aggressive-withdrawn children have problems controlling their hostility, but like other withdrawn children, they tend to be nervous about initiating friendships with other adolescents.

RELATIONAL AGGRESSION

Most studies of the peer relations of aggressive children have focused on children who are overtly aggressive (either physically or verbally). This has led researchers to focus relatively more attention on the social relationships of rejected boys than girls, because boys exhibit more overt aggression than girls. A series of studies by psychologist Nikki Crick, however, indicates that girls also act aggressively toward peers, but their aggression is often social, not physical, in its expression (Crick, 1996; Crick, Bigbee, & Howes, 1996; Crick & Grotpeter, 1995). In particular, Crick has studied the use of **relational aggression**—aggression intended to harm other adolescents through deliberate manipulation of their social standing and relationships. Individuals who use relational aggression try to hurt others by excluding them from social activities, damaging their reputations with others, or withdrawing attention and friendship.

■ **"Mean Girls"**   Although relational aggression was first noticed in observations of girls, recent research in the United States and abroad suggests that both genders employ it but that girls are more aware of and distressed by it (French, Jansen, & Pidada, 2002; Galen & Underwood, 1997; Paquette & Underwood, 1999). One recent study of adolescents' reasoning about excluding people from group activities found, for example, that girls are more likely than boys to say that it is morally wrong to exclude someone simply on the basis of the

relational aggression   Acts intended to harm another through the manipulation of his or her relationships with others, as in malicious gossip.

Although boys are more physically aggressive than girls, girls often engage in what has been called relational aggression—an attempt to harm someone by ruining their reputation or disrupting their friendships.

crowd to which he or she belongs (Horn, 2003). Although relational aggression is more covert than fighting or yelling, the use of relational aggression is nevertheless associated with rejection by peers (Crick, 1996; Rys & Bear, 1997). Interestingly, adolescents whose aggression is atypical for their gender (that is, girls who are highly physically aggressive and boys who are highly relationally aggressive) show more maladjustment than their peers whose aggression is more gender-typical (Crick, 1997).

Girls' use of relational aggression has attracted a great deal of popular attention, as reflected in the best-selling books *Odd Girl Out* (Simmons, 2003) and *Queen Bees and Wannabees* (Wiseman, 2003), which served as the basis for the movie *Mean Girls*. Perhaps in response, educators are expressing concerns about "meanness" in school environments, noting that teachers have devoted far more attention to preventing overt aggression, like physical fighting, than relational aggression—despite the fact that victims of relational aggression also suffer harm as a result. Some have called for educational programs designed to help teachers understand, assess, prevent, and respond to the problem when it arises in their classroom, as well as schoolwide programs designed to teach tolerance and acceptance, and to encourage students to disapprove of relational aggression when they see it. Changing students' attitudes about relational aggression—which many see as fine, even if they object to physical aggression—is important, because adolescents' attitudes about the acceptability of relational aggression

(for example, agreeing with the statement "In general, it is OK to not let someone sit with your group of friends at the lunch table") predict their use of it (Werner & Nixon, 2005). In the opinion of most experts, middle schools ought to be the focus of such interventions (Yoon, Barton, & Taiarol, 2004).

FOOD FOR THOUGHT

Is relational aggression something that is especially common in adolescence? If so, why might this be? If not, is it expressed differently among adults?

As psychologist Amanda Rose has pointed out, however, preventing relational aggression is easier said than done (Rose, Swenson, & Waller, 2004). She has shown that adolescents who use relational aggression are more popular than their peers. In some ways, this is hardly surprising, because the whole *point* of using relational aggression is to enhance one's status and popularity, and because the same social skills that make one popular (learning how to "read" other people, being able to adjust one's behavior to maintain one's status, etc.) are useful when one is spreading rumors, gossiping, or trying to undermine someone else's reputation. In fact, Rose's findings suggest that the reason some physically aggressive boys are often more popular than their peers is that physical aggression and relational aggression may go hand in hand, and it is their relational aggression, not their physical aggression, that contributes to their popularity. One thing that adolescents are reluctant to do is to stop doing something that makes them popular, even if it is at the expense of someone else.

▌ Consequences of Rejection Being unpopular has negative consequences for adolescents' mental health and psychological development—peer rejection is associated with subsequent depression, behavior problems, and academic difficulties (DeRosier, Kupersmidt, & Patterson, 1994; French & Conrad, 2001; Kupersmidt, Burchinal, & Patterson, 1995; Kupersmidt & Coie, 1990; Morison & Masten, 1991; Olweus, 1993; Parker & Asher, 1987; Patterson & Stoolmiller, 1991; Wentzel, 2003). But studies show that the specific consequences of peer rejection may differ for rejected youth who are aggressive versus those who are withdrawn. Among African American and white children alike, aggressive individuals who are rejected are at risk for conduct problems and involvement in antisocial activity as adolescents (Feldman, Rosenthal, Brown, & Canning, 1995; French et al., 1995; Laird, Petit, & Dodge, 2005; Rubin, Chen, McDougall, Bowker, & McKinnon, 1995; Underwood, Kupersmidt, & Coie, 1996). In contrast, withdrawn children who are rejected are likely to feel exceedingly lonely and are at risk for low self-esteem, depression, and diminished social competence (Hoza, Molina, Bukowski, & Sippola, 1995; Rubin et al., 1995). Rejection is especially likely to lead to depression in adolescents who place a lot of importance on their standing in the peer group and who believe that they, rather than the peers who reject them, are at fault (Prinstein & Wargo, 2004). Adolescents who are both aggressive and withdrawn are at the greatest risk of all (Morison & Masten, 1991; Parkhurst & Asher, 1992; Rubin, LeMare, & Lollis, 1990).

Many psychologists believe that unpopular youngsters lack some of the social skills and social understanding necessary to be popular with peers. According to findings from an extensive program of research by Kenneth Dodge and his colleagues, unpopular aggressive children are more likely than their peers to think that other children's behavior is deliberately hostile, even when it is not (Crick & Dodge, 1994, 1996; Dodge, 1986; Dodge & Coie, 1987). Numerous studies have now confirmed that this so-called **hostile attributional bias** plays a central role in the aggressive behavior of rejected adolescents (Astor, 1994; Courtney & Cohen, 1996; Crick and Dodge, 1994; Waldman, 1996). When accidentally pushed while waiting in line, for instance, unpopular aggressive children are more likely than others to believe that the person who did the pushing did it on purpose and, consequently, to retaliate. Studies of African American adolescents find that deficits in social information processing may characterize overly aggressive African American youngsters as well (Graham, 1993; Graham & Hudley, 1994).

Not surprisingly, the inferences that adolescents draw from the behavior of others vary in part as a function of their ethnic and cultural backgrounds. Compared to Latino students, for instance, African American students are more likely to be described by other students as aggressive (Graham & Juvonen, 2002). In one fascinating study, the reactions of African American and Mexican American adolescents to videotapes of different social situations were compared (Rotheram-Borus & Phinney, 1990). In one situation, for example, a boy was rejected for a team. Whereas the African American adolescents said that in a similar situation they would get angry or leave, the Mexican American youngsters said that they would feel hurt but would not leave. In another

vignette, two teenagers were working at a table on which the necessary supplies were closer to one adolescent than the other. The Mexican American adolescents were more likely to say simply that the adolescent who was closer to the supplies should hand them to the other teenager, whereas the African American adolescents were more likely to say that if they were the adolescent farther from the supplies, they would be upset and would reach over and get what they needed. These differences in social information processing likely reflect cultural differences in the emphases placed on group solidarity and cooperation—two qualities that tend to be highly valued in Mexican American families.

VICTIMIZATION AND HARASSMENT

What about unpopular withdrawn children? What are their social skills deficits? In general, research shows that unpopular withdrawn children are excessively anxious and uncertain around other children, often hovering around the group without knowing how to break into a conversation or activity (Rubin et al., 1990). Their hesitancy, low self-esteem, and lack of confidence makes other children feel uncomfortable, and their submissiveness makes them easy targets for bullying (Olweus, 1993; Salmivalli, 1998). Many of these youngsters are especially sensitive to being rejected, a trait that may have its origins in early experiences with parents (Downey, Lebolt, Rincón, & Freitas, 1998). Unfortunately, the more these children are teased, rejected, and victimized, the more hesitant they feel, and the more they blame themselves for their victimization, which only compounds their problem—creating a sort of cycle of victimization (Graham & Juvonen, 1998; Hymel, Rubin, Rowden, & LeMare, 1990).

FOOD FOR THOUGHT

What can be done to reduce victimization in schools? If you were asked to design an intervention, what would it entail?

■ **Victims and Bullies** Young adolescents who are victimized by their peers typically develop problems that lead to further peer rejection and victimization

hostile attributional bias The tendency to interpret ambiguous interactions with others as deliberately hostile.

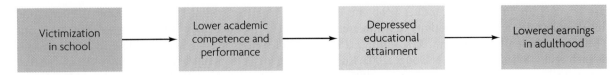

FIGURE 5.11   **Being victimized in school can affect income in adulthood.** (Macmillan & Hagan, 2004)

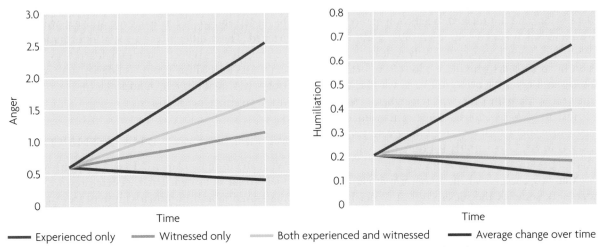

FIGURE 5.12   **Being victimized has negative consequences, but so does witnessing other students' victimization.** (Nishina & Juvonen, 2005)

(Hodges & Perry, 1999). One of the most pernicious effects of victimization is that it undermines feelings of academic competence, academic performance and school engagement, which has cascading effects well beyond adolescence—even after taking into account background factors, victimization during adolescence is associated with lower educational attainment and, as a consequence, diminished earnings in adulthood (see Figure 5.11) (Macmillan & Hagan, 2004). Interestingly, children who are victimized but who have a best friend are less likely to be caught in this vicious cycle than those who are friendless (Hodges, Boivin, Vitaro, & Bukowski, 1999).

Peer harassment is something that students can be exposed to both directly (when they are the victims) or indirectly (when they witness harassment but aren't themselves victimized). According to one recent study, these two different types of experience can have both similar and dissimilar effects (Nishina & Juvonen, 2005). Being victimized or witnessing the harassment of others makes students anxious, but witnessing the harassment of others appears to buffer some of the harmful effects of being victimized. As Figure 5.12 indicates, adolescents who were victims of harassment but who did not see anyone else being victimized were more likely to feel humiliated and angry than those who were both victims and witnesses on the same day. Presumably, being singled out for harassment feels worse than being one of many who are picked on.

For this reason, studies find that in ethnically diverse schools victimized students whose ethnic group is in the minority are not as harmed psychologically as are victimized students whose ethnic group is in the majority, who are less able to attribute their victimization to their ethnicity and more likely to attribute it to their own shortcomings as individuals (Graham, Bellmore, Nishina, & Juvonen, in press).

Although relationships between adolescents who dislike each other have not been studied extensively, such mutual antipathies are not uncommon among teenagers (Abecassis, Hartup, Haselager, Scholte, & Van Lieshout, 2002). Such relationships frequently involve bullies and victims, with one adolescent repeatedly harassing another. Studies of American and European youth indicate that about one-third of students report having been bullied at some time during the past year, although in some studies, the percentage of students who report having been victimized has been considerably higher (Haynie et al., 2001; Nansel et al., 2001). Not surprisingly, students who are harassed by their classmates report a range of adjustment problems, including low self-esteem, depression, and academic difficulties, whereas those who report frequent bullying are more likely to show problems in social skills and in the control of aggression (Ando, Asakura, & Simons-Morton; Haynie et al., 2001; Juvonen, Nishina, & Graham, 2000) One recent study found that the effects of being harassed in middle school were still observed in high school

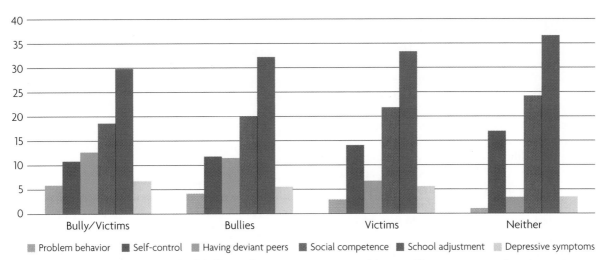

FIGURE 5.13 Adolescents who are both bullies and victims report more problems and less competence than those who are exclusively bullies or exclusively victims. (Adapted from Haynie et al., 2001)

(Rusby, Forrester, Biglan, & Metzer, 2005). One finding that has now been replicated in several different countries is that many of the same adolescents who report having been victimized also report bullying others and that these adolescents have the greatest adjustment problems, consistent with the finding discussed earlier, that children who are both aggressive and withdrawn are the most disturbed (see Figure 5.13) (Juvonen, Graham, & Schuster, 2003; Kim, Koh, & Leventhal, 2005).

■ **Helping Unpopular Teens** Can unpopular adolescents be helped? In recent years, several teams of psychologists have experimented with different sorts of interventions designed to improve the social skills of unpopular adolescents. These social competence training programs have focused on three different strategies. One type of program has been designed to teach social skills—self-expression, leadership, and the questioning of others about themselves (Kelly & de Armaa, 1989; Repinski & Leffert, 1994). These social skills intervention programs have been shown to improve adolescents' abilities to get along with peers. A second approach has been to have unpopular adolescents participate in group activities with popular ones under the supervision of psychologists. Programs like this have been shown to improve adolescents' self-conceptions and their acceptance by others (Bierman & Furman, 1984). Finally, some social competence programs focus on a combination of behavioral and cognitive abilities, including social problem solving (e.g., Greenberg & Kusche, 1998; Weissberg, Caplan, & Harwood, 1991). Social problem-solving programs, such as PATHS (Promoting Alternative THinking Strategies), are designed to improve individuals' abilities to judge social situations and figure out acceptable ways of behaving. Adolescents are taught to calm down and think before they react, to decide what the problem is, to figure out what their goal is, and to

think of positive approaches toward reaching that goal. Instead of lashing out at a classmate who grabbed the last basketball from a gym closet, for example, a hot-tempered boy who had been through this sort of social skills program might calm himself down, tell himself that his goal is to play basketball rather than get into a fight, and approach another student to ask if he can get into a game. PATHS has been shown to effectively reduce behavioral problems among elementary school children (Conduct Problems Prevention Research Group, 1999).

RECAP

- Popular adolescents tend to be socially skilled, intelligent, humorous, and friendly.
- Unpopular adolescents tend to fall into three categories: aggressive adolescents (especially those who have difficulty controlling their emotions), withdrawn adolescents, and adolescents who are both aggressive and withdrawn.
- In general, adolescents who are rejected by their peers are at risk for a wide variety of psychological and behavioral problems, including academic failure, conduct problems, and depression.
- Victimization and harassment by peers, whether through physical bullying or relational aggression, have harmful and enduring consequences for individuals' mental health.
- Numerous interventions have been designed to improve adolescents' social competence, including those that focus on improving unpopular adolescents' social skills and their social understanding.

The Peer Group and Psychosocial Development

Regardless of the structure or norms of a particular peer group, peers play an extremely important role in the psychological development of adolescents. Problematic peer relationships are associated with a range of serious psychological and behavior problems during adolescence and adulthood. Individuals who are unpopular or who have poor peer relationships during adolescence are more likely than their socially accepted peers to be low achievers in school, to drop out of high school, to have a range of learning disabilities, to show higher rates of delinquent behavior, and to suffer from an array of emotional and mental health problems as adults (Savin-Williams & Berndt, 1990). Although it is likely that poorly adjusted individuals have difficulty making friends, good evidence also suggests that psychological problems result from—as well as cause—problems with peers (Bagwell, Newcomb, & Bukowski, 1998; Brendgen, Vitaro, & Bukowski, 2000; Buhrmester & Yin, 1997; Coie et al., 1995; Hymel et al., 1990; Kupersmidt & Coie, 1990; McCoy, 1996; Parker & Asher, 1987; Parker & Seal, 1996; Windle, 1994; Woodward & Ferguson, 1999).

Peers also play a crucial role in promoting normal psychosocial development. In the realm of identity, for example, peers provide the sorts of models and feedback that adolescents cannot get from adults (Brown, 2004). In the context of the peer group, young people can try on different roles and personalities and can experiment with different identities with greater ease than at home. And, as we saw earlier, the peer group may serve as a way station in the development of identity as adolescents begin to establish a separate sense of self, one that is differentiated from the family (Brown et al., 1986). Experience in the peer group also can be an important influence on adolescents' self-image.

Experience in the peer group also is vital for the development and expression of autonomy. The process of developing more mature and more independent relationships with parents is accompanied by the establishment of more mature relationships with peers. In addition, the peer group provides a context for adolescents to test out decision-making skills in an arena where there are no adults present to monitor and control their choices (Hill & Holmbeck, 1986).

Intimacy and sexuality, of course, are much more common between peers than between adolescents and adults, for a variety of reasons. Perhaps most critical is that both intimacy and sexuality require interaction between two individuals who are relative equals. Moreover, sexual relationships and close intimacy within the family context would be likely to disrupt important functions of family relationships (Hartup, 1977). It is therefore the adolescent's peer group that generally plays the central role in socializing youngsters in appropriate sexual behavior and in developing the capacity for intimate friendship (Sullivan, 1953a).

Finally, peers are an important influence on adolescent achievement, especially in countries where high schools tend not to be specialized or separated according to student ability, like the United States, Spain, or Korea. In countries like France, Germany, and Switzerland, in contrast, where students are assigned to different schools depending on their ability and aspirations (for example, vocational schools versus college prep schools), peers are a less important influence on achievement (Buchmann & Dalton, 2002). Although peers play a less prominent role than parents or teachers in influencing adolescents' long-term educational and occupational plans, adolescents' classmates are a significant influence on their day-to-day school behaviors and feelings, including how much they value school, how much effort they devote to their studies, and how well they perform in class (Epstein, 1983b; Ryan, 2001; Steinberg et al., 1996). Peers seem to be an especially important influence on the achievement of ethnic minority youth (Steinberg, Dornbusch, & Brown, 1992).

Adolescents consider the time they spend with peers to be among the most enjoyable parts of the day (Csikszentmihalyi & Larson, 1984). One reason is that activities with friends are typically organized around having a good time, in contrast to activities with parents, which are more likely to be organized around household chores and the enforcement of parental rules (Larson, 1983; Montemayor, 1982). Rather than being competing institutions, the family and peer group mainly provide contrasting opportunities for adolescent activities and behaviors. The family is organized around work and other tasks, and it may be important in the socialization of responsibility and achievement. The peer group provides more frequent opportunities for interaction and leisure, which contributes to the development of intimacy and enhances the adolescent's mood and psychological well-being.

RECAP

- Problematic peer relationships are associated with a range of serious psychological and behavior problems during adolescence and adulthood.
- Peers play a crucial role in the development of identity, autonomy, intimacy, sexuality, and achievement in adolescence.
- Rather than being competing institutions, the family and peer group mainly provide contrasting opportunities for adolescent activities and behaviors.

CHAPTER 6

Schools

THE BROADER CONTEXT OF U.S. SECONDARY EDUCATION
The Origins of Compulsory Education
The Rise of the Comprehensive High School
School Reform: Past and Present
What Should Schools Teach?
Education in the Inner Cities

THE SOCIAL ORGANIZATION OF SCHOOLS
School Size and Class Size
Age Grouping and School Transitions
Tracking
Ethnic Composition
Public Schools and Private Schools

CLASSROOM CLIMATE
The Best Classroom Climate for Adolescents
Teacher Expectations and Student Performance
The Importance of Student Engagement
Intervening to Change a School's Climate
School Violence

BEYOND HIGH SCHOOL
The College Bound
The Non-College Bound

SCHOOLS AND ADOLESCENT DEVELOPMENT
Characteristics of Good Schools
The Effects of School on Adolescent Development

BECAUSE OF THE IMPORTANT and multifaceted role it has come to play in modern society, the secondary educational system—**secondary education** refers to middle schools, junior high schools, and high schools—has been the target of a remarkable amount of criticism, scrutiny, and social science research. It's not easy to design a perfect school for adolescents—or even agree on what one would look like. If you think otherwise, consider the following questions:

- How universal should our curriculum be? Should all high schools across the country teach the same courses with the same content (as is the case in most countries), or should we leave this up to local communities to decide (as is the case in the United States)?

- How stringently should we enforce standards? Should we require that all students pass a standardized examination before being promoted or receiving a diploma (a policy that has become increasingly widespread), or should we promote students based on their age (the system that has been in place for nearly a century in the United States)?

- What topics should be included in a middle or high school curriculum? Should schools restrict their activities to the teaching of basic academic subjects, such as writing and mathematics, or should they also spend time on other topics, such as music, art, and health? And what about value-laden subjects, like sex education? When budgets are tight, what subjects, if any, should be cut?

- How should students be separated by age? Should young adolescents attend schools with preadolescents (as they did early in the twentieth century), with older adolescents, or only with their peers?

- Should students be grouped by ability level, or should students at all levels of achievement be educated together?

Parents, teachers, administrators, and researchers have debated all of these issues, and many more, for decades—and they continue to do so today. Although these questions are remarkably difficult to answer—if they weren't, we wouldn't be still debating them—they remain extremely important. Secondary school touches the lives of all adolescents in industrialized societies, as well as an increasingly larger proportion of the population in the developing world. Virtually all American adolescents under the age of 17 and nearly all 17- and 18-year-olds are enrolled in school. And schooling is as time-consuming as it is pervasive. During most of the year, the typical American student spends more than one-third of his or her waking hours each week in school or in school-related activities (Larson & Verma, 1999). Even in the poorest parts of the world—sub-Saharan Africa, for example—close to two-thirds of 10- to 14-year-olds and 40–50 percent of 15- to 19-year-olds are enrolled in school. In most developing countries, attending high school is much more common among children of the wealthy, often because poor families need their adolescents to work (National Research Council, 2005). As you'll read in Chapter 12, how far youngsters go in school—in poor countries, whether they go to high school, and in more advantaged ones, whether they go to college—is tremendously influenced by their social class.

Not only are schools the chief educational arena for adolescents, but, at least in the United States, they also play an extremely important role in defining the young person's social world and in shaping her or his psychosocial development. Naturally, the development of achievement—motivation, aspirations, and expectations—is profoundly affected the adolescents' experiences in school. (Just think about the differences between attending a good school and a bad one.) But schools influence psychosocial development far beyond the domain of achievement. How adolescents do in school influences their academic self-conceptions and occupational choices—shaping their identity. The way in which a school is organized affects the adolescent's sense of independence, and the way a classroom is run affects the extent to which the adolescent learns to *think* independently. Schools often define adolescents' social networks, thereby influencing the development of interpersonal relationships. And the majority of adolescents, at least in the United States, learn about sexuality in school. You can not understand adolescence as a developmental period without understanding the ways in which schools shape the adolescent experience.

secondary education   The system of middle schools, junior high schools, and high schools.

In this chapter, we will examine the organization and workings of secondary schools at multiple levels of analysis. Perhaps your first inclination is to think about what takes place in the classroom. And while this is important, as Jacquelynne Eccles, one of the world's experts on adolescents and education, has noted, a thorough understanding of schooling and its impact on adolescent development requires an examination that goes beyond the classroom (Eccles, 2004). What takes place in the classroom is influenced by the way in which the school is organized, and the way in which the school is organized, in turn, is influenced by the needs and demands of the community and of society. Unlike the family or peer group, whose structure is not under the direct or deliberate control of society, schools are environments created to serve specific purposes. In many respects, the schools we have today—for all their strengths and weaknesses—are the schools we designed, by making some decisions and by avoiding others. This is abundantly clear when we look at the history of secondary education in America.

The Broader Context of U.S. Secondary Education

Consider the data presented in Figure 6.1. Today, virtually all young people ages 14–17 are enrolled in school. But in 1930, only about half of this age group were students, and at the turn of the century, only 1 in 10 attended school (D. Tanner, 1972; William T. Grant Foundation, 1988).

Not only are there considerably more youngsters enrolled in school today than there were 50 years ago, but today's students also spend more days per year in school. In 1920, for example, the average school term was 162 days, and the average student attended for only 121 days, or 75 percent of the term. By 1968, however, the school term had been lengthened to nearly 180 days, which remains the national average, and the typical student today attends close to 90 percent of the term (National Center for Education Statistics, 2003). And in many other countries, the school year is even longer than it is in the United States. In England, for example, high school students spend 220 days in school each year, and in Japan, adolescents are in school 240 days each year (Consortium on Productivity in the Schools, 1995).

Although some critics of American schools have called for lengthening the school year (National Commission on Excellence in Education, 1983), others have pointed out that simply expanding the school year, without changing what takes place in school, may be misguided (National Education Commission on Time and Learning, 1994). For example, although today the typical school offers a six-period day with about 5.6 hours of classroom time, studies have shown that students spend only 40 percent of their time on such core academic subjects as math, English, history, and science—about half the time devoted to basic academic instruction in European schools (Consortium on Productivity in the Schools, 1995; National Education Commission on Time and Learning, 1994). Clearly, then, it would be possible to increase the amount of time students spend on academic matters considerably without lengthening the school day at all.

Not only is the school year longer today than it was in the past, but adolescents also remain in school for more years now than they did in previous eras. In 1924, fewer than 33 percent of all youngsters entering the fifth grade eventually graduated from high school; today, more than 75 percent of all fifth-graders will eventually graduate on time, and a substantial number of those who do not graduate on schedule eventually get their diploma, either by completing high school at a later date or through equivalency programs or continuation schools.

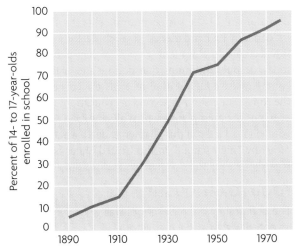

FIGURE 6.1   The proportion of the 14- to 17-year-old population enrolled in school increased dramatically between 1910 and 1940. Today, nearly 95 percent of individuals this age are in school. (D. Tanner, 1972; William T. Grant Foundation, 1988)

THE ORIGINS OF COMPULSORY EDUCATION

The rise of secondary education in America was the result of several historical and social trends that converged at the turn of the twentieth century. Most important were industrialization, urbanization, and immigration.

Following widespread industrialization during the late nineteenth century, the role of children and young adolescents in the workplace changed dramatically. With the economy expanding, many families that at one time had needed their children in the labor force for financial reasons were able to make ends meet without the labor of their young. Furthermore, as the nature of the workplace changed, employers recognized that they needed workers who were more skilled and more reliable than youngsters. The few unskilled jobs that remained required strength beyond the capacity of many youth (Church, 1976). Social reformers also expressed concerns about the dangers children faced working in factories, and organized labor—an increasingly powerful force in the early 1900s—sought to protect not only the welfare of children but also the security of their own employment. In response, child labor laws narrowed and limited the employment of minors (Bakan, 1972). Together, these changes in the workplace kept many youngsters out of the labor force.

During this same period, the nature of life in American cities was also changing markedly. Industrialization brought with it urbanization and, along with the rising rate of immigration during the early twentieth century, new problems for urban centers. The effects of a rapidly expanding economy were seen in the tenements and slums of America's cities: poor housing, overcrowded neighborhoods, crime. Eager to improve living conditions for the urban masses, social reformers envisioned education as a means of improving the life circumstances of the poor and working classes. And eager to ensure that the problems of cities did not get out of hand, many saw compulsory secondary education as a means of social control. High schools would take many thousands of idle young people off the streets, it was argued, and place them in a social institution in which they could be supervised and kept out of trouble. In addition, anxious to see that foreign-born immigrants were well socialized to the American way of life, reformers presented universal secondary education as a necessary part of the process of Americanization: It was a way of homogenizing a population characterized by increasing—and to many, increasingly uncomfortable—ethnic and cultural diversity (Church, 1976; D. Tanner, 1972). By 1915, the idea of universal compulsory education for adolescents had gained widespread acceptance.

THE RISE OF THE COMPREHENSIVE HIGH SCHOOL

Prior to the early twentieth century, before secondary education became compulsory, high schools were designed for the elite. In curriculum, staff, and student composition, they were similar to the colleges of the day, with the emphasis mainly on classical liberal arts instruction (Church, 1976; D. Tanner, 1972).

By 1920, however, educators saw a need for curricular reform. Compulsory secondary education had changed the social composition of the schools, and many educators argued for a corresponding diversification in the secondary school curriculum. Now that secondary education was aimed at the masses, schooling was seen not merely as a means of intellectual training but also as a way of preparing youth for life in modern society. It was argued that education, especially for the majority, should include preparation for the roles of work and citizenship.

The 1920s marked the birth in the United States of what came to be known as the **comprehensive high school,** an educational institution that promised to meet the needs of a diverse and growing population of young people. Classes in general education, college preparation, and vocational education were all housed under one roof. As you saw in Figure 6.1, the proportion of high school–aged individuals enrolled in school jumped dramatically in the years between World War I and World War II—from 32 percent in 1920 to over 73 percent in 1940. This was also a time of tremendous change in the high school curriculum. During these years, new courses were added in music, art, family life, health, physical education, and other subjects designed to prepare adolescents for family and leisure as well as work roles.

The high school had come a long way from its exclusive focus at the turn of the century on the intellectual development of the socioeconomic elite. By the 1950s, its concern had broadened to include the social and intellectual development of all young people. And today, despite continuing questioning and criticism, the comprehensive high school remains the cornerstone of the American system of secondary education. It is, however, not the exemplar to which all countries aspire—as you will read later in this chapter. Indeed, what we think of as the "high school" in the United States is in many regards a distinctively American institution.

FOOD FOR THOUGHT

The comprehensive high school was invented within a specific historical context. Does it make sense within today's society? If not, what alternative or alternatives would you suggest?

comprehensive high school   An educational institution that evolved during the first half of the twentieth century, offering a varied curriculum and designed to meet the needs of a diverse population of adolescents.

SCHOOL REFORM: PAST AND PRESENT

Although we naturally think of schools as institutions whose primary goal is education, they are much more than this. Schools are also potentially important tools of social intervention, because it is through schools that the greatest number of young people can most easily be reached. For this reason, the study of schools is extremely important to social scientists and policymakers who are interested in influencing adolescent development. In fact, one way to understand the ways in which adults want adolescents to change is to look at the ways that schools have been reformed over the years.

During the 1950s, for example, when politicians felt that the United States had lost its scientific edge to the former Soviet Union, schools were called upon to offer more courses in math and science (Conant, 1959). When social scientists felt that adolescents were growing up unfamiliar with the world of work—as they did in the 1970s—schools were asked to provide opportunities for work–study programs and classes in career education (President's Science Advisory Committee, 1974). In the 1990s, as society grappled with a broad array of social problems affecting and involving youth—problems such as violence, AIDS, and drug abuse—we once again looked to schools for assistance, asking schools to implement an array of preventive interventions (Dryfoos, 1993).

■ **No Child Left Behind** Toward the end of the 1990s, amidst growing concerns that our inner-city schools were not producing graduates who could compete for high-skills jobs, and in response to a public increasingly interested in alternatives to conventional public education, such as charter schools or home schooling, schools were called upon to raise standards for all students (e.g., Ravitch, 2001). In January 2002, President Bush signed into law the No Child Left Behind Act, a sweeping and controversial piece of legislation mandating that states ensure that all students, regardless of their economic circumstances, achieve academic proficiency (U.S. Department of Education, 2006). No Child Left Behind required that schools create and enforce academic standards by annually testing all students and by reporting the results of students' performance to the public. Underperforming schools—schools where students' test scores did not improve—initially would be given an opportunity to do a better job the following year, by providing additional instruction, tutoring, or special services for students who needed them. But schools that continued to fail eventually would have funding taken away and could even be forced to close.

On the face of it, No Child Left Behind sounds like a reasonable strategy. As you'll read in Chapter 12, a huge proportion of American students do not meet even minimal standards for academic performance, and poor performance is disproportionately seen among disadvantaged, African American, Hispanic, and American Indian students. Many commentators had criticized the practice of **social promotion**—moving students from one grade to the next regardless of their academic performance—arguing that poor and ethnic minority youth especially were being cheated out of a good education and graduated without the skills necessary to succeed in college or in the labor force (Steinberg et al., 1986). Forcing schools to regularly assess student progress and publicize how their students were faring would give parents and the community the information they needed to put pressure on schools to do better. No one could disagree with the basic idea that all students—regardless of their background—deserve a high-quality public education.

Although No Child Left Behind sounded good in principle, in practice it has proven problematic and has met with tremendous resistance. States have complained that they simply do not have the resources to conduct the mandated assessments or to respond to failing students' poor performance. Teachers and parents have complained that the focus on standardized testing adversely affects what takes place in the classroom—if a school's financial future depends on its students' reading and math test scores, why should teachers do anything other than teach to the test? (Be honest—how much effort do *you* devote to learning material in your classes that you know you won't be tested on?) What happens to the teaching of subjects that will not appear on the test, like current events, or to the teaching of skills that are impossible to assess through standardized exams, such as critical thinking? Who determines how tough the tests are or what level of achievement on them is acceptable? If schools are to be punished for poor student performance, isn't it in their best interest to set the bar low, so that a high proportion of their students pass? And, with millions of dollars at stake, what's to stop schools from manipulating their average scores, by encouraging poor-performing students to be absent on testing days or by actually helping students cheat on the tests (Levitt & Dubner, 2005)?

It is difficult to forecast what the next wave of school reform proposals will bring, but we can be sure that, as we move further into the twenty-first century, schools will continue to play a central role in the development and implementation of a wide range of social policies concerning young people. Whether this use of our educational system is proper or misguided has been a matter of considerable debate for more than a century (Ravitch, 2000).

social promotion The practice of promoting students from one grade to the next automatically, regardless of their school performance.

Higher-order thinking is stimulated when students are encouraged to interpret, analyze, and evaluate information, rather than simply memorize it or use it in a routine way.

FOOD FOR THOUGHT

What do you think about mandating that all students pass a standardized examination before being promoted to the next grade or before being granted a diploma? What are the possible positive and negative effects of this policy?

WHAT SHOULD SCHOOLS TEACH?

Suppose you are asked to list the things you think young people need to know in order to function as competent, responsible, satisfied adults. Which items on your list should be the responsibility of high schools? Should high school curricula be limited to the traditional academic subjects, or should schools play a broader role in preparing young people for adulthood by providing instruction more directly relevant to work, family, leisure, and citizenship? Should students receive instruction only in English, mathematics, science, and social studies, or should they take courses as well in "general education"—in subjects such as art, home economics, health, sex education, driver education, and personal finance? Which courses should be required, and which should be left as electives? If you were to discuss these questions with your classmates, you would probably find little agreement.

critical thinking Thinking that involves analyzing, evaluating, and interpreting information, rather than simply memorizing it.

Over the last decade or so, politicians and parents have sounded the cry for schools to scale down their general education offerings and place greater emphasis on the traditional academic subjects: English, mathematics, science, social studies, and a new "basic"—computer science (Consortium on Productivity in the Schools, 1995; Consortium on Renewing Education, 1998; National Education Commission on Time and Learning, 1994; Ravitch, 1995). Several social commentators have argued that educators—in high schools and colleges alike—have lost sight of the common core of knowledge and values that serves as the intellectual foundation of our society (Bloom, 1987; Botstein, 1997; Hirsch, 1996).

■ **Back to Basics** During the 1980s, many commentators called for a return to a curriculum that stressed the basics. Why? The achievement test scores of American high school students had been falling steadily. International comparisons of student achievement consistently found that American youngsters were faring poorly. Partly in response to these worrisome findings, several proposals called for more demanding curricula (e.g., Finn, 1991). One set of writers bemoaned what they called the "shopping-mall high school," where students were given too much freedom in choosing courses and schools were more concerned with keeping students happy than with ensuring that genuine and important learning took place (Powell, Farrar, & Cohen, 1985). Noting that America was losing its competitive edge in the world market, reformers called for more academic rigor in the schools as a means of preparing young people for the workplace of the future. For example, one group called for schools to implement more demanding academic requirements, tougher standards for graduation, and longer school days (National Commission on Excellence in Education, 1983). Another recommended that schools spend at least 5.5 hours daily on instruction in core academic subjects (National Education Commission on Time and Learning, 1994). Whereas school reformers of the 1970s had demanded more relevant curricula, reformers of the 1980s demanded more rigorous ones.

■ **Critical Thinking** During the late 1980s, yet another type of school reform received widespread attention. This time, however, the focus shifted from the content of the curriculum to the process of learning. Education reformers called for more emphasis in the classroom on critical thinking—whether in the teaching of basics or in the teaching of electives (Newmann, 1992;

Newmann, Marks, & Gamoran, 1996). **Critical thinking** is stimulated when students are encouraged to interpret, analyze, and evaluate information, rather than simply memorizing or applying it in a routine way. In social studies, for example, asking students to discuss *why* political revolts occur may stimulate critical thinking, whereas asking them simply to memorize (and regurgitate) the dates of important political events probably will not. At least one study has found that students' learning is greater when they are encouraged to collaborate with classmates on projects, probably because such collaboration facilitates more understanding of the material than does mere memorization (Fall, Webb, & Chudowsky, 2000).

Whether these reforms have produced a more intelligent public is unclear. By the mid-1990s, it had become apparent that vast numbers of American students were graduating from high school deficient not only in critical-thinking abilities but in basic academic skills and knowledge. According to the National Assessment of Educational Progress, in the mid-1990s, the percentage of students who scored at or above proficiency on reading and mathematics ranged from about 10 percent in Louisiana, California, and the District of Columbia to around 35 percent in North Dakota, Maine, and Minnesota (Education Trust, 1996). The need for remedial education—on college campuses and in the workplace—had risen substantially (Steinberg, 1998).

■ **Standards-Based Reform**   As we entered the twenty-first century, school reformers continued to call for schools to place a greater emphasis on critical thinking, but stressed that this focus needed to be accompanied by a return to rigorous and universal performance standards. Many commentators argued that schools had become so focused on the process of learning by the late 1980s that they had lost sight of the importance of having a strong and challenging curriculum (Consortium on Renewing Education, 1998; Hirsch, 1996; Ravitch, 1995). **Standards-based reform** became the focus of heated debates among educators and politicians.

Although state after state began to implement standardized examinations to ensure that high school graduates actually knew what they were supposed to know, problems still arose. First, educators could not agree on the body of knowledge and skills that comprised what high school graduates should know and be able to do. Second, as states soon discovered, large numbers of students did not fully acquire the knowledge and capabilities assessed on standardized graduation examinations. And it is not at all clear what to do when one-third or one-half of a state's high school seniors fail their state's graduation exam.

Today, many observers continue to question whether the comprehensive public high school should—or can—continue to play a central role in the education of adolescents. Some claim that insufficient financial support has crippled public schools. Others, like educational historian Diane Ravitch (2000), argue that the problem has been a lack of focus, not a lack of funding. She notes that three beliefs, in particular, have interfered with successful educational reform: that the schools can solve any social or political problem (which has led to our diverting schools from their most important mission—academic instruction), that only a portion of youngsters are capable of benefiting from a high-quality education (which has led to our having vastly different standards for students from different backgrounds), and that imparting knowledge is relatively unimportant and that schools should focus on engaging students in activities and experiences (which has watered down the curriculum and led to an approach to instruction that is all process and no content).

Amid widespread disappointment over the state of public education in America, increasing numbers of parents have begun to look at other options—among them, **charter schools** (public schools that are given more freedom to set their own curricula), schools that are run by private corporations rather than local school boards, and government-subsidized **school vouchers** (which can be used for private school tuition). Although all of these alternatives gained popularity during the past decade, research on the costs and benefits of charter schools, privatization, and vouchers has been inconclusive (Loveless, 2002). As is the case with public schools, which vary tremendously in their quality and level of student achievement, there is considerable variability among charter, for-profit, and private schools. The bottom line is that what takes place within a school is probably more important than the nature of its funding and oversight.

FOOD FOR THOUGHT

How do you feel about vouchers? About charter schools? What are the costs and benefits of each, to students and to society?

standards-based reform   Policies designed to improve achievement by holding schools and students to a predetermined set of standards measured by achievement tests.

charter schools   Public schools that have been given the autonomy to establish their own curricula and teaching practices.

school vouchers   Government-subsidized vouchers that can be used for private school tuition.

EDUCATION IN THE INNER CITIES

Although concerns about the demise of American education raged during the late 1990s, some commentators argued that the problem of low student achievement was not an across-the-board problem, but one that was concentrated mainly among poor and minority youngsters living in inner cities (Berliner & Biddle, 1995).

Although other critics (e.g., Stedman, 1998; Steinberg et al., 1996) disagreed with this assessment, arguing that poor achievement was indeed a problem everywhere, virtually all social scientists concurred that the education crisis and its implications for the future of the labor force had become distressingly urgent within inner-city public schools. Indeed, the achievement gap between white and nonwhite youngsters, which had been closing for some time, grew wider during the 1990s, especially in large urban school districts. In the District of Columbia, for example, which serves a predominantly African American population, only 5 percent of all eighth-graders are judged proficient in math. In California, white students who are proficient in math outnumber Latino youngsters by a ratio of 5 to 1. In New York, proficient white students outnumber proficient African-American students by a ratio of 8 to 1. As one set of writers pointed out, "Many people now dismiss urban schools 'as little more than human storehouses to keep young people off the streets'" (Kantor & Brenzel, 1992, pp. 278–279). Although there have been occasional success stories, inner-city schools in America continue to have tremendous problems.

Why has school reform failed in so many urban schools in particular? Experts point to several reasons. First, the increasing concentration of poverty in certain inner-city communities (see Chapter 3) has produced a population of students with very grave academic and behavioral problems—problems for which few schools are equipped or able to address. Recent surveys of American high school students indicate that so many are afraid of being victimized that 15 percent of boys and 8 percent of girls across the country carry a gun to school, with even higher percentages doing so in inner-city schools (Centers for Disease Control, 2006). Second, many urban school districts are burdened by huge administrative bureaucracies that often impede reform and hinder educational innovation. Third, students in urban schools report less of a sense of "belonging" to their school (Anderman, 2002). Finally, the erosion of job opportunities in inner-city communities has left many students with little incentive to remain in school or to devote a great deal of effort to academic pursuits (Kantor & Brenzel, 1992).

RECAP

- Schools play an extremely important role in structuring the nature of adolescence in modern society. In most of the industrialized world, virtually all 14- to 17-years-olds are enrolled in school, a pattern that is becoming increasingly prevalent in the developing world as well.
- A number of social forces combined to lead to the development of compulsory education for adolescents in America, including industrialization, immigration, and urbanization.
- During the 1920s, the high school as we know it in the United States today—the comprehensive high school—was born.
- Educators have long debated whether and how high schools should be reformed. The pendulum has swung back and forth between eras in which teaching basic academic skills was emphasized and those during which the emphasis was on making the school's curriculum relevant.
- At the turn of the twenty-first century, calls for the implementation and enforcement of rigorous academic standards became widespread, as the public grew increasingly worried about the competitiveness of American students in an international economy that is increasingly reliant on high-tech, high-skill jobs.
- There is broad consensus that inner-city public schools, which mainly serve disadvantaged ethnic minority adolescents, are in especially dire straits.

The Social Organization of Schools

In addition to debating curricular issues, social scientists interested in school reform have discussed the ways in which secondary schools should be organized. Because the organization of a school affects students' day-to-day experiences, variations in school organization can have profound effects on adolescents' development and behavior. In this section, we examine the research on five key aspects of school organization: (1) school and classroom size, (2) different approaches to age grouping and, in particular, how young adolescents should be grouped, (3) tracking, or the grouping of students in classes according to their academic abilities, (4) the ethnic composition of schools, and (5) public versus private schools.

SCHOOL SIZE AND CLASS SIZE

As the idea of the comprehensive high school gained widespread acceptance, educators attempted to deliver a wider range of courses and services under a single roof. As a consequence, schools became larger and larger over the course of the twentieth century. By the end of the 1990s, in many metropolitan areas, students attended enormous schools, with enrollments of several thousand students. One advantage enjoyed by larger schools is that they can offer a more varied curriculum—a large high school, for instance, may be able to offer many specialized courses that a small school would be unable to staff.

▌ Is Bigger Better?

When it comes to school size, however, is bigger necessarily better? Do students who attend larger schools reap any educational or psychological advantages as a result? A fair amount of research conducted over the past 40 years says, "No." Indeed, one of the most consistent conclusions to emerge from recent evaluations of school reform efforts is that student performance and interest in school improves when their schools are made less bureaucratic and more intimate. Numerous studies indicate that students achieve more when they attend smaller schools that create a cohesive sense of community (Lee, Smith, & Croninger, 1997; Ready, Lee, & Welner, 2004; Roeser, Midgley, & Urdan, 1996).

At the same time, however, there is no evidence that school size alone influences students' sense of belonging. School size may affect academic outcomes, but it does not necessarily affect students' emotional attachment to the institution (Anderman, 2002) or their mental health (Watt, 2003), perhaps because some large schools are able to maintain a more intimate climate by dividing students into smaller groups. Indeed, in recent years, many educators have recommended that large schools be broken down into **schools within schools,** and many districts have followed this recommendation. Although few such transformations have been studied systematically, the existing research indicates both advantages and disadvantages to this approach. On the positive side, creating schools within schools does lead to the development of a more positive social environment; on the negative side, though, if not done carefully, schools may inadvertently create "schools" within one school that vary considerably in their educational quality.

Although the move to reorganize large secondary schools into more personal institutions gained wider acceptance during the 1990s, researchers have been studying the pros and cons of large versus small high schools for nearly a half century (Barker & Gump,

1964; Elder & Conger, 2000). Actually, the most interesting findings of this research concern participation in extracurricular activities, not achievement in the classroom.

You might expect that, in addition to providing a more varied curriculum, large schools would be able to offer more diverse extracurricular activities to their students—and indeed they do. Large schools can support more athletic teams, after-school clubs, and student organizations. But because large schools also contain so many more students, actual rates of participation in different activities are only half as high in large schools as in smaller ones. As a result, in larger schools, students tend more often to be observers than participants in school activities. For instance, during the fall, a small school and a large school might each field teams in football, soccer, and cross-country running, together requiring a total of 100 students. An individual's chances of being 1 of those 100 students are greater in a school that has only 500 students than in a school with an enrollment of 4,000.

▌ The Strengths of Small Schools

Because students in small schools are more likely than students in large schools to be active in a wider range of activities, they are more likely to report doing things that help them develop their skills and abilities, allow them to work closely with others, and make them feel needed and important. In a small school, chances are, sooner or later, most students will find themselves on a team, in the student government, or in an extracurricular organization. Students in small schools also are more likely to be placed in positions of leadership and responsibility, and they more often report having done things that made them feel confident and diligent. School size especially affects the participation of students whose grades are not very good. In large schools, academically marginal students often feel like outsiders, and rarely get involved in school activities. In small schools, however, these students feel a sense of involvement and obligation equal to that of more academically successful students.

In short, although large schools may be able to offer more diverse curricula and provide greater material resources to their students, the toll that school size may take on student learning and engagement appears to exceed the benefits of size (Lee & Smith, 1995). Some evidence also suggests that there is more inequality in students' educational experiences in larger schools, where students may be sorted into tracks of differing quality. In small schools, in contrast,

---

schools within schools   Subdivisions of the student body within large schools created to foster feelings of belongingness.

Research has shown that adolescents in large classes learn just as much as adolescents in small classes. An important exception, however, is remedial education. Here, adolescents benefit from smaller classes and one-on-one instruction.

it is more likely that all students are exposed to the same curriculum, if only because the school cannot afford to offer more than one. Experts now agree that the ideal size of a school for adolescents is between 500 and 1,000 students (Entwisle, 1990; Ready et al., 2004).

■ **Variations in Class Size** Unfortunately, policymakers do not always implement social science findings in ways that accurately reflect the research evidence. Encouraged by the results of research on smaller *schools*, many politicians began calling for smaller *classes*. However, in contrast to studies of schools, studies of classrooms indicate that variations within the typical range of classroom sizes—from 20 to 40 students—do not generally affect students' scholastic achievement once they have reached adolescence. Small classes may benefit young elementary school children (that is, up until third grade), who may need more individualized instruction (Finn, Gerber, & Boyd-Zaharias, 2005), but adolescents in classes with 40 students learn just as much as students in classes with 20 students (Mosteller, Light, & Sachs, 1996).

An important exception to this finding involves situations that call for highly individualized instruction or tutoring, in which case smaller classes do appear to be more effective. For example, in remedial education classes, where teachers must give a great deal of attention to each student, small classes are valuable. One implication of these findings is that it may be profitable for schools that maintain regular class sizes of 25–30 students to increase the sizes of these classes by a student or two in order to free instructors, and to

trim the sizes of classes for students who need specialized, small-group instruction (Rutter, 1983).

■ **The Problem of Overcrowding** One certain impediment to delivering high-quality education, especially in large metropolitan school districts, is overcrowding (Ready et al., 2004). According to national surveys, nearly 15 percent of secondary schools in the United States are overcrowded—that is, the size of the student body is at least 6 percent larger than the school was designed to house—and an additional 8 percent are "severely overcrowded," with the student body 25 percent above capacity. Schools with more than 50 percent ethnic minority students are especially likely to be overcrowded. California, which has a very high proportion of ethnic minority students, has some of the most overcrowded schools in the country. Achievement is lower in overcrowded schools because of stress on both students and teachers, the use of facilities for instruction that were not designed to serve as classrooms (such as gyms), and inadequate resources.

Educators have attempted to reduce the adverse effects of overcrowding through a variety of measures—some successful, others not. Many school districts use temporary structures, such as trailers, to provide additional classroom space. Unfortunately, many such portable units, especially older ones, are constructed with materials that are harmful to students' physical health, and the tight quarters and poor ventilation common in these structures can create toxic environments (Ready et al., 2004). Other districts—most famously, Los Angeles—have created multitrack programs, whereby schools are used year-round, and students are organized into groups, with one group on vacation at any given point in time. Evaluations of this approach have been mixed.

AGE GROUPING AND SCHOOL TRANSITIONS

A second issue that social scientists have examined in the study of school structure and organization concerns the ways in which schools group students of different ages and the frequency with which students are expected to change schools.

Early in the twentieth century, most school districts separated youngsters into an elementary school (which had either six or eight grades) and a secondary school (which had either four or six grades). Students changed schools once (after either sixth or eighth grade). However, many educators felt that the two-school system was unable to meet the special needs of young adolescents, whose intellectual and emotional maturity was greater than that expected in elementary school, but not yet at the level necessary for high school. During the early years of compulsory secondary education, the establishment of separate schools for young adolescents began, and the **junior high school** (which contained the seventh, eighth, and sometimes ninth grades) was born (Hechinger, 1993). In more recent years, the **middle school**—a three- or four-year school housing the seventh and eighth grades with one or more younger grades—has gained in popularity, replacing the junior high school in many districts.

▌ **The Transition into Secondary School** One of the most commonly reported findings is that students' academic motivation and school grades drop as they move from elementary into middle or junior high school (Eccles, 2004; Gentry, Gable, & Rizza, 2002; Gutman & Midgley, 2000; Murdock, Anderman, & Hodge, 2000). (Interestingly, scores on standardized achievement tests do not decline during this same time, suggesting that the decline in grades may be more a reflection of changes in grading practices and student motivation than in students' knowledge [Eccles, 2004]). One well-publicized report on this subject was issued by the Carnegie Corporation's Council on Adolescent Development (1989). Among its most important recommendations were to divide middle schools into units of 200–500 students in order to reduce students' feelings of anonymity, hire teachers who have special training in adolescent development, and strengthen ties between schools and the communities in which they are located.

FOOD FOR THOUGHT

When you were a young adolescent, did you go to school with older adolescents, with preadolescent children, or only with people your age? How do you think your experience was affected by this arrangement?

Researchers also have examined how changing schools affects student achievement and behavior. In many of these studies, researchers compared school arrangements in which students remain in elementary school until eighth grade—that is, where they have one school change—with arrangements in which they move from elementary school, to middle or junior high school, and then to high school—where they change schools twice. In general, this research suggests that school transitions, whenever they occur, can disrupt the academic performance, behavior, and self-image of adolescents, although this effect may be stronger among white students than their ethnic

minority peers (Kuperminc, Blatt, Shahar, Henrich, & Leadbeater, 2004). This disruption is generally temporary, however. Over time, most youngsters adapt successfully to changing schools, especially when other aspects of their life—family and peer relations, for example—remain stable and supportive, and when the new school environment is well suited for adolescents (Anderman & Midgley, 1996; Gillock & Reyes, 1996; Lord, Eccles, & McCarthy, 1994; Seidman, Lambert, Allen, & Aber, 2003; Teachman, Paasch, & Carver, 1996).

Researchers do not agree about whether the drop in academic motivation and achievement that occurs after elementary school is due to the school transition itself (that is, students suffer *whenever* they have to change schools) or to the difference between elementary school, on the one hand, and middle or junior high school, on the other. Specifically, some experts believe that the poor showing of middle and junior high schools is due primarily to their failure to meet the particular developmental needs of young adolescents (Barber & Olsen, 2004; Eccles, 2004).

▌ **How Secondary Schools Differ from Elementary Schools** Psychologist Jacquelynne Eccles and her colleagues have conducted the most comprehensive research to date on school transitions during the early adolescent years (Eccles et al., 1993; Eccles, Lord, & Midgley, 1991; Eccles, Roeser, Eccles, & Freedman-Doan, 1999). Eccles has argued that the classroom environment in the typical middle school or junior high school is quite different from that in the typical elementary school. Not only are junior high schools larger and less personal, but middle and junior high school teachers also hold different beliefs about students than do elementary school teachers—even when they teach students of the same chronological age (Midgley, Berman, & Hicks, 1995). For example, teachers in junior high schools are less likely to trust their students and more likely to emphasize discipline, which creates a mismatch between what students at this age desire (more independence) and what their teachers provide (more control). Teachers in junior high schools also tend to be more likely to believe that students' abilities are fixed and not easily modified through instruction—a belief that interferes with their students' achievement. In addition, teachers who teach in junior high or middle schools are less likely than other teachers to feel confident about their teaching ability (Eccles, 2004).

junior high school An educational institution designed during the early era of public secondary education, in which young adolescents are schooled separately from older adolescents.

middle school An educational institution housing seventh- and eighth-grade students along with adolescents who are one or two years older.

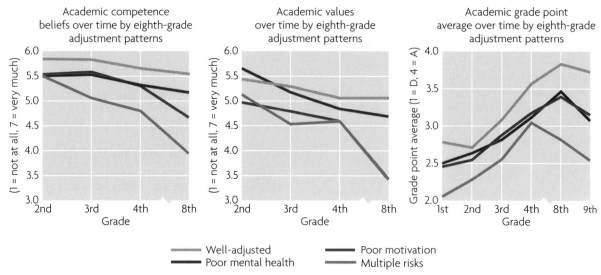

FIGURE 6.2   Although many studies find a general drop in school performance and academic engagement during the transition into middle school, not all adolescents show this pattern. (Roeser et al., 1999)

Eccles points out that it is hardly surprising that students experience a drop in achievement motivation when they enter middle or junior high school, given the change in environments they experience and the mismatch between what adolescents need developmentally and what the typical school context provides. The issue, according to Eccles, is not that the adolescents must make a transition; it is the *nature* of the transition they must make. Indeed, although students' self-esteem drops during the transition into middle or junior high school, it increases somewhat during the early high school years, suggesting that the initial decline reflects students' temporary difficulties in adapting to the new environment (Wigfield, Eccles, MacIver, Reuman, & Midgley, 1991). Consistent with this, middle school students attending more personal, less departmentalized schools do better than their peers in more rigid and more anonymous schools (Lee & Smith, 1993). Not surprisingly, changing schools is easier on students who move into small rather than large institutions (Russell, Elder, & Conger, 1997).

Why do junior high school teachers differ from those who teach elementary school? At this point, the answer is not clear-cut. The individuals who choose to become junior high teachers do not seem to differ all that much from those who choose to teach younger grades. Rather, Eccles has suggested that the organization and anonymity of junior high schools have a negative effect on the teachers who work in them, which, in turn, affects the way they interact with students. This is consistent with a large body of evidence that students are more engaged in school when their teachers themselves are more engaged in their work (Louis & Smith, 1992).

Eccles also points out that cultural stereotypes about adolescence may have a negative influence on junior high school teachers' beliefs. As we saw in the Introduction, many adults believe that adolescence is an inevitably difficult time—not only for teenagers themselves but also for those who work with them. To the extent that teachers come into the classroom with negative images of adolescence as a stage in the life cycle—that teenagers are inherently unruly, or unteachable, or perplexing—their preconceptions may interfere with their work as educators (Midgley, Feldlaufer, & Eccles, 1988). (Recall that this same sort of process affects parents who hold negative stereotypes about adolescence.) As we shall see in a later section, one of the most important influences on the adolescent's experience in school is the classroom climate.

■ **Individual Differences in the Extent of Transitional Problems**   It is important to remember that although some aspects of the transition into secondary school may be difficult for students to negotiate, not all students experience the same degree of stress (Fenzel, 2001). One study identified four distinct groups of students (see Figure 6.2) (Roeser et al., 1999). About 30 percent of the children were highly motivated, well adjusted, and high achieving while in elementary school, and they did not have difficulties making the transition into secondary school. A second group (about 10 percent of the sample), who had multiple academic and psychological problems before the transition, had particular difficulty with the transition from elementary to middle school, but no special problems with the transition into high school, presumably because they were already disengaged from academics entirely. Indeed, by the time these young adolescents were ready for high school, they had become so alienated from school and discouraged about their own ability that they viewed school as uninteresting and unimportant. A third group of students (another 30 percent) showed declines in their motivation and feelings of competence during the transition out of elementary school, and declines in their school performance and mental health during the transition into high school. Finally, a fourth group (another 30 percent) showed increases in psychological distress over the course of the transition, but no appreciable changes in academic motivation or performance. One possibility is that aspects of the transition unrelated to academics (e.g., changes in peer relations) distressed these adolescents.

A study of students in Quebec, Canada, found similar variability in trajectories of achievement during the transition from elementary into secondary school (Duchesne, Larose, Guay, Vitaro, & Tremblay, 2005). In this study, however, the proportion of students whose achievement declined significantly was relatively small (14 percent), whereas the proportions of students whose achievement remained stable before, during, and after the transition were far greater: 23 percent were low achievers in fourth grade and stayed that way, and 63 percent were high achievers in fourth grade and stayed that way.

Not surprisingly, students who have more academic and psychosocial problems before making a school transition cope less successfully with it (Berndt & Mekos, 1995; Carlson et al., 1999; Little & Garber, 2004; Murdock et al., 2000; Roeser et al., 1999). Factors other than students' prior record may also influence the nature of their transition to middle or high school. Students who experience the transition earlier in adolescence have more difficulty with it than those who experience it later (Simmons & Blyth, 1987). And adolescents who have close friends before and during the transition adapt more successfully to the new school environment (Wentzel, Barry, & Caldwell, 2004), although the benefits of staying with their friends may accrue only to students who had been doing well previously; students who had been doing poorly adjust better if they enroll in a different school than their friends (Schiller, 1999).

Evidently, then, the transition into secondary school is not the sort of stressor that has uniform effects on all students. More vulnerable adolescents, adolescents with fewer sources of social support, and adolescents moving into more impersonal schools may be more susceptible to the adverse consequences of this transition than their peers are. Not surprisingly, studies of poor, inner-city youngsters found significant negative

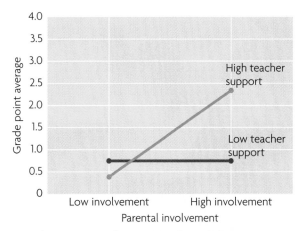

FIGURE 6.3 During the transition from elementary to middle school, students fare best when they report high levels of both parental involvement and teacher support. (Gutman & Midgley, 2000)

effects of the school transition on their self-esteem, achievement, classroom preparation, perceptions of the school environment, reports of social support, and participation in extracurricular activities (Eccles, 2004; Seidman, Aber, Allen, & French, 1996; Seidman, Allen, Aber, Mitchell, & Feinman, 1994). One study of Texas adolescents found that African American and, especially, Mexican American youngsters were more likely than their white peers to experience a variety of difficulties during the transition out of elementary school—including receiving poor grades, getting into trouble with teachers, and being hassled by other students (Munsch & Wampler, 1993).

Low-income students' adjustment to middle school may be enhanced as a result of an intervention targeted at their parents, according to one study (Bronstein et al., 1998). The researchers had parents participate in an 11-week program designed to increase their understanding of adolescent development and their effectiveness as parents. The children whose parents participated in the program were functioning better psychologically and behaviorally, both immediately after the program and one year later, than were their counterparts whose parents did not participate. Moreover, the children whose parents participated did not show the decline in functioning that often is associated with the transition into middle school. In general, parental support and involvement are associated with better adolescent adjustment during school transitions (Isakson & Jarvis, 1999). One study of low-income African American students found that students who fare best during the transition, however, have both supportive teachers and parents who are involved in their education (Gutman & Midgley, 2000) (see Figure 6.3).

Research on tracking suggests that it has positive effects on the achievement of students in the more advanced tracks, but negative effects on students in the lower tracks.

TRACKING

In some schools, students with different academic abilities and interests do not attend classes together. Some classes are designated as more challenging and more rigorous, and are reserved for students identified as especially capable. Other classes in the same subject area are designated as average classes and are taken by most students. Still others are designated as remedial classes and are reserved for students having academic difficulties.

The process of separating students into different levels of classes within the same school is called ability grouping, or **tracking.** Not all high schools use tracking systems. In some schools, students with different abilities take all their classes together. Even among schools that use tracking, there are important differences in the implementation of the tracking system (Jones, Vanfossen, & Ensminger, 1995). Some schools are more inclusive in their tracking, permitting a relatively high proportion of students into the highest track (even, perhaps, some students whose abilities do not warrant such placement). Other schools are more exclusive, limiting the places in the highest track to a privileged few (even if this means placing some high-ability students in the lower tracks). And still other schools are "meritocratic," placing students in tracks that accurately match their abilities.

tracking The grouping of students, according to ability, into different levels of classes within the same school grade.

■ **Pros and Cons of Tracking** Educators have debated the pros and cons of tracking for years, but research provides no definitive answers about its overall effects (Eccles, 2004). Proponents of tracking note that ability grouping allows teachers to design class lessons that are more finely tuned to students' abilities; tracking may be especially useful in high school, where students must master certain basic skills before they can learn such specialized subjects as science, math, or foreign languages (Rutter, 1983). Critics of tracking point out, however, that students who are placed in the remedial track generally receive not just a different education but a poorer-quality education than those in the more advanced tracks (Eccles, 2004). Moreover, the effects of tracking are not limited to academic outcomes. Because schools play such an important role in influencing adolescents' friendships, when students are tracked, they tend to socialize only with peers from the same academic group (Rosenbaum, 1976). Tracking can thereby contribute to the polarization of the student body into different subcultures that are hostile toward each other.

FOOD FOR THOUGHT

Tracking seems to have different effects on students in the more advanced and less advanced tracks. In view of this, should schools engage in ability grouping?

Some critics of tracking also point out that decisions about track placements often discriminate against poor and ethnic minority students, and may hinder rather than enhance their academic progress (Ayalon, 1994; Oakes, 1995; Rosenbaum, 1976; Wells & Serna, 1996). Some school counselors assume, for example, that ethnic minority or poor youngsters are not capable of handling the work in advanced classes and may automatically assign them to average or remedial classes, where less material is covered and the work is less challenging (Vanfossen, Jones, & Spade, 1987). Not all research indicates that track placements are biased, however. Other studies have found that students' ability has a stronger influence than their background on initial track placement (Alexander & Cook, 1982; Dauber, Alexander, & Entwisle, 1996), but that middle-class and white students initially placed in lower tracks are more likely to be moved into higher ones, in part because their parents frequently succeed in "lobbying" their child's school for a changed track placement (Hallinan, 1996; Oakes, 1995; Wells & Serna, 1996).

One arena in which track assignments seem to be influenced by factors other than ability is in math, where boys are more likely than girls to be placed in more advanced classes. Although elementary school girls generally outscore boys on tests of math achievement, junior and senior high school boys are more likely to be enrolled in advanced math classes (Davenport et al., 1998). Some evidence suggests that tracking biases in the math curriculum operate against the assignment of girls to high-ability math classes. In one study, researchers examined mathematics ability-group assignments in a large sample of fourth-through seventh-graders (Hallinan & Sorensen, 1987). They were interested in whether assignment to the high-ability group was influenced by the student's math ability, by his or her gender, or by a combination of the two. They found, not surprisingly, that students' ability weighed heavily in the assignment process, with more able students being more likely to be assigned to the high-ability group. But they also found that high-ability girls were less likely to be assigned to the high-ability group than were boys of comparable talent. Studies also show that girls are less likely than boys to be moved from a lower math track into a higher one (Hallinan, 1996).

■ **Tracking, Sexism, and Single-Sex Schools** Is this sort of sexism diminished in single-sex schools? According to one investigation involving 60 private schools—20 coeducational, 20 boys' schools, and 20 girls' schools—not necessarily (Lee, Marks, & Byrd, 1994). The researchers observed classes in these schools and carefully noted both subtle and blatant forms of sexism, such as a teacher's ignoring a young woman's interest in science or providing female students with less challenging math instruction than was warranted. Somewhat surprisingly, these sorts of practices existed even in girls' schools, despite the hope that girls might encounter less sexist instruction in a single-sex environment.

Although a number of academically demanding girls' schools were less sexist than the norm, there was considerable variation among the girls' schools studied. For example, the researchers observed teachers in girls' schools "talking down to girls, making academic activities more palatable by 'wrapping calculus in a nontechnical package,' setting up expectations that students would have difficulty with assignments by offering help before it was required or requested, or

promulgating an attitude that 'trying hard is as important as succeeding' with difficult undertakings" (Lee et al., 1994, p. 114). In contrast, boys' schools were more likely to use an aggressive style of teaching that encouraged students to state their views assertively and to expect the intense scrutiny of their teachers and peers. Sexism was just as pronounced in coeducational schools, however, especially in science classes. For example, in one chemistry class, the female teacher responded positively to boys who spoke out without raising their hands but reprimanded girls for the exact same behavior. Another chemistry teacher at a different coeducational school told the researchers that he believed "girls are not suited to 'do' science" (Lee et al., 1994, p. 108).

The biased assortment of youngsters into math tracks has long-term implications for future course selection. An adolescent girl who is not assigned to a high-ability math class—despite her talent—may come to develop more negative attitudes toward math than she might have otherwise and may miss opportunities to pursue certain careers that require advanced mathematics training. Indeed, girls are less likely than boys to receive advice, encouragement, and counseling to take advanced courses in math or to prepare for careers that would require these courses (Lee et al.,1994).

■ **On the Wrong Track** In many respects, then, early track placements set in motion an educational trajectory that is often difficult to change without the deliberate intervention of the student's parents (Alexander & Cook, 1982; Dauber, Alexander, & Entwisle, 1996; Dornbusch, 1994; Hallinan, 1992, 1996; Stevenson, Schiller, & Schneider, 1994). And the ways in which students' schedules are arranged may lead students to be tracked in several different subject areas simply because they are tracked in one class, which makes the effects of tracking even more substantial (Heck, Price, & Thomas, 2004). If, for example the only class period during which advanced math is offered is the same as the class period during which remedial English is taught, a student who is assigned to remedial English will not be able to take advanced math (Lucas & Berends, 2002).

Research on tracking in high schools indicates quite clearly that students in different tracks have markedly different opportunities to learn (Gamoran, 1987, 1996; Stevenson et al., 1994). Students in the more advanced tracks receive more challenging instruction and better teaching, and they are more likely to engage in classroom activities that emphasize critical thinking rather than rote memorization. Being placed in a more advanced track has a positive influence on school achievement (how much the student actually learns over time), on subsequent course selection (what curriculum the student is exposed to), and on ultimate educational attainment (how many years of schooling the student completes) (Gamoran & Mare, 1989; Lee & Bryk, 1989; Natriello, Pallas, & Alexander, 1989). Interestingly, although students in the more advanced tracks begin high school with a stronger interest in school than do students in remedial tracks, the advanced students lose interest over time, whereas the remedial students do not. Trajectories of parental involvement in school show similar patterns, with parents of advanced students, but not parents of remedial students, becoming less involved over time (Crosnoe, 2001).

Because students are assigned to different tracks initially on the basis of test scores and other indicators of aptitude, and because students in the lower tracks receive an inferior education, the net effect of tracking over time is to increase preexisting differences among students. The students who need the most help are assigned to the tracks in which the quality of instruction is the poorest; not surprisingly, studies find that students in lower tracks exert less effort, which, in turn, limits their learning (Callahan, 2005; Carbanaro, 2005). In other words, in a school that uses tracking, the academically rich get richer, and the poor get poorer. Although students in the lower tracks usually get the short end of the educational stick, there are some exceptions—for example, schools in which classes in the lower tracks are taught by strong teachers who insist on maintaining high standards (Gamoran, 1993; Hallinan, 1994).

■ **The Effects of Tracking on Student Achievement**   Literally hundreds of studies have been done on the impact of tracking on student achievement (Hallinan, 1996). Unfortunately, this research suggests both positive and negative effects and, more importantly, different effects among students in different tracks. More specifically, tracking has positive effects on the achievement of high-track students, negative effects on low-track students, and negligible effects on students in the middle (Fuligni, Eccles, & Barber, 1995; Hallinan, 1996). Because of this, decisions about whether to implement tracking in nontracked schools, or whether to "detrack" schools that use ability grouping, are typically quite controversial; not surprisingly, parents of students in the higher tracks favor the

practice, while parents of students in the lower tracks oppose it (Wells & Serna, 1996).

Even in schools that do not have formal tracking, of course, teachers may group students within the same class into ability groups. In such an arrangement, students may have a wider range of peers with whom to compare themselves than they would in separate tracks, since their classes are much more diverse in composition. The impact of this comparison process on both students and teachers is quite interesting. For high-ability students, within-classroom ability grouping raises their expectations for achievement and raises their teachers' evaluations of them; for low-ability students, the opposite is true: They have lowered expectations and get worse grades from their teachers (Reuman, 1989). Presumably, both adolescents and teachers make their evaluations based on unstated comparisons. In mixed classes with ability groups, the high-ability students look better, and the low-ability students look worse, than they would in a conventionally tracked school or in a school in which ability grouping is not used (Marsh, Chessor, Craven, & Roche, 1995). As is the case with tracking, within-classroom ability grouping also exposes students in different groups to different levels of educational quality, with students in the high-ability groups receiving more challenging instruction and more engaging learning experiences (Catsambis, 1992).

■ **Students at the Extremes**   Related to the issue of tracking are questions concerning the placement of individuals who are considered **gifted students** and of those who have a **learning disability.** Adolescents who score 130 or higher on an intelligence test are gifted. Adolescents with a learning disability are those whose actual performance is significantly poorer than their expected performance (based on intelligence tests and the like) and whose difficulty with academic tasks cannot be traced to an emotional problem, such as coping with a parental divorce, or sensory dysfunction, such as a visual or hearing impairment. Most learning disabilities are presumed to be neurological in origin (Lovitt, 1989).

Educators have debated whether gifted students and those with learning disabilities are best served by instruction in separate classes (for example, in enriched classes for gifted students or in special education classes for students with a learning disability) or by **mainstreaming,** the integration of all students with special needs into regular classrooms. Pros and cons of each approach have been identified. On the one hand, separate special education programs can be tailored to meet the specific needs of students and can target educational and professional resources in a cost-effective way. On the other hand, segregating students on the basis of academic ability may foster social

gifted students   Students who are unusually talented in some aspect of intellectual performance.

learning disability   A difficulty with academic tasks that cannot be traced to an emotional problem or sensory dysfunction.

mainstreaming   The integration of adolescents who have educational handicaps into regular classrooms.

isolation and stigmatization—either for being "stupid" or for being a "brainiac."

Generally, educators have tended to favor mainstreaming over separate classrooms for adolescents with special needs. (In the case of adolescents with disabilities, mainstreaming, whenever possible, is required by federal law.) Proponents of mainstreaming argue that the psychological costs of separating adolescents with special academic needs from their peers outweigh the potential academic benefits. Studies of gifted youngsters have found, for example, that those who were integrated into regular classrooms have more positive academic self-conceptions than did those assigned to special classes (Marsh et al., 1995; Schneider, Clegg, Byrne, Ledingham, & Crombie, 1989). One downside to being placed with students of high academic ability is that when other students compare themselves to their high-achieving classmates, they don't feel as competent as they would if their point of comparison were students who were not so smart. This phenomenon, called the **big fish–little pond effect,** has been documented around the world, most recently in an analysis of data from over 100,000 students attending schools in 26 different countries (Marsh & Hau, 2003). Being a big fish in a little pond is also helpful for admission to college. One recent study of some 45,000 applications to three elite universities found that applicants' chances of being accepted are greater when they come from high schools with a relatively lower proportion of other high-achieving students than when applicants with the same credentials come from high schools with many other high achievers (Espenshade, Hale, & Chung, 2005).

Whereas the big fish–little pond effect suggests that gifted students might not be better off psychologically in classes restricted to high-achieving students—and argues in favor of mainstreaming them—it poses a dilemma for those who favor mainstreaming students with learning disabilities. Low-achieving students, when mainstreamed, will end up comparing themselves to students whose performance is better than their own, and they may end up feeling worse about themselves than had they been separated into special classes with comparably achieving peers (Marsh & Hau, 2003). Perhaps because of this, studies find that, even with mainstreaming, adolescents who have learning disabilities may suffer psychological consequences related to their problems in school. Compared with average-achieving students, adolescents with learning disabilities report more social and behavioral difficulties and, not surprisingly, more problems in coping with school. They are also more likely than other adolescents to have poor peer relations, are less likely to participate in school-based extracurricular activities,

and are more likely to drop out of school (Lovitt, 1989). Given the tremendous importance society places on school success, it is not difficult to see why students who have difficulties learning would suffer psychological as well as scholastic problems.

ETHNIC COMPOSITION

Since the landmark U.S. Supreme Court rulings in *Brown v. Board of Education of Topeka* (1954, 1955), many school districts have adopted measures designed to make schools more ethnically diverse, through strategies designed to encourage voluntary desegregation (for example, permitting families to choose among different schools within a large catchment area rather than assigning students to specific schools on the basis of residence). Other districts have enacted policies aimed at mandatory desegregation (for example, assigning students from different racial backgrounds to specific schools in order to create predetermined racial balances) (Bradley & Bradley, 1977). Despite these measures, many schools in the United States remain segregated because of strong and continuing residential segregation (Rivkin, 1994).

In past decades, school districts in many parts of the country used information on students' racial background when making school assignments, generally in attempts to better balance the racial composition of schools in areas where residential segregation would otherwise produce very imbalanced schools. (For example, in a city with highly segregated neighborhoods, some students from each neighborhood might be bused out of their community in order to make the schools less segregated.) Debates about whether schools can or should use race as a factor in decisions about student assignment to schools have surfaced in recent years, however, as questions have been raised about the constitutionality of policies designed to alter the ethnic composition of schools. In 2006, the U.S. Supreme Court agreed to hear two new cases involving school districts in the states of Kentucky and Washington, where race was a factor in determining how students would be assigned to various schools in the district. Educators watched these cases closely.

▌ **Effects of Desegregation**   Does transforming the ethnic composition of a school make a big difference in student achievement? Studies of the short-term effects of desegregation on high school students have been mixed. On the one hand, research indicates that

---

big fish–little pond effect   Phenomenon whereby individuals who attend high school with high-achieving peers feel worse about themselves than comparably successful individuals with lower-achieving peers.

desegregation has surprisingly little impact on the achievement levels of either minority or white youngsters (Entwisle, 1990). In addition, some evidence suggests that minority youngsters' self-esteem is higher when they attend schools in which they are in the majority—a phenomenon true not only for African American youth but for all youth; in general, students fare better psychologically when the cultural environment of their neighborhood is consonant with the cultural environment of their school (Gray-Little & Carels, 1997; Goldsmith, 2004; Hudley, 1995; Nieto et al., 1996; Rosenberg, 1975). Consistent with this, students who attend schools that use busing report weaker feelings of attachment to their school than do students whose schools draw directly from the local neighborhood (Anderman, 2002). Similarly, students' attachment to school is higher when they attend schools where relatively more of their classmates are from the same ethnic group; interestingly, the ethnic composition of a school affects students' emotional attachment to it, but not their level of engagement in classroom activities (Johnston, Crosnoe, & Elder, 2001). And, as we saw in Chapter 5, interracial contact even in desegregated schools is rare (Quillian & Campbell, 2003; Way & Chen, 2000). Within multiethnic schools, however, students feel safer, less lonely, and less harassed in relatively more diverse schools (i.e., where the proportions of students from different ethnic groups are similar) than in schools that are less balanced (Juvonen, Nishina, & Graham, 2006).

■ **Being in the Minority**   The difficulties associated with attending school where one is in a distinct minority were tellingly illustrated in a study by Patricia Phelan and colleagues (Phelan, Yu, & Davidson, 1994). Consider these excerpts from the researchers' interviews with students:

> Ivonne, Mexican American female: Well, I kind of feel uncomfortable. Not many Mexicans and Hispanics are in [my] classes. They [other students] probably think of me as weird, because they probably have this view that most Hispanics are dumb or something. They have that opinion, you know, [Hispanics] get bad grades. So, I don't know why I feel uncomfortable. I just ... it means you're not really with any other ... many people. Maybe by the end of the year they will realize that I belong. (Phelan et al., 1994, p. 425)

> Trinh, Vietnamese American female: [Because I'm Vietnamese] I notice the little things more often than other people. Just like, I don't really get noticed by all the popular people. OK, everyone in the class, I know their names and everything. ... Like being Vietnamese ... like they have a lot of Americans in here. That there are more of them, and when you're alone, you're nervous over little things. (Phelan et al., 1994, p. 425)

> Sonia, Mexican American female: Yeah, it's weird, 'cause most teachers, you know—white teachers— some of them are kind of prejudiced. ... It's probably the way they look at you, the way they talk, you know when they're talking about something—about something like when they talk about the people who are going to drop out, and they ... look around, look around [at you].
>
> And then Mr. Kula, when he's talking about teenage pregnancy or something like that. He turns around and he looks at us. It's like—he tries to look around the whole room, so we won't notice but like he mostly like tries to tell us, tries to get it through our heads, you know. Sometimes I think he's prejudiced. And sometimes I think he's trying to help us. (Phelan et al., 1994, p. 431)

As several commentators have pointed out, focusing on the short-term impact of desegregation on achievement or self-esteem may provide only a very narrow means of assessing its costs and benefits, however (Braddock, 1985; Wells, 1995). For example, African Americans who have attended desegregated high schools are more likely to graduate and to continue their education in desegregated institutions, and African American students who have attended racially mixed high schools adjust more successfully to integrated colleges than their peers who attended segregated high schools (Adan & Felner, 1995). Because African Americans graduating from predominantly white colleges earn more when they enter the labor force than do those who attend predominantly minority colleges, it would seem that youngsters who attend desegregated high schools reap advantages in the labor force later on as young adults. Moreover, African American graduates of predominantly white schools are more likely to work in integrated environments, have integrated networks of friends, and live in integrated neighborhoods during adulthood (Wells, 1995). Together, these studies suggest that desegregated high school programs do benefit minority youth but that the benefits may not be apparent until adulthood. Furthermore, these studies suggest that desegregation during high school does help break down racial barriers in society at large.

It also may not be advisable to make generalizations about the impact of school desegregation without looking further at the processes inside the school and how they are affected (or not affected) by its racial composition. Not all desegregated schools are the same (Campbell, 1977). De facto segregation may be maintained even in desegregated schools through tracking, seating assignments, ability grouping within classrooms, and class scheduling (Entwisle, 1990; Mickelson, 2001). To assess the situation, we would need information about how the school's policies and procedures were changed, and about how students, teachers, and administrators responded to the changes. Consider, for example, the differences between two desegregated schools. Each has achieved racial balance. But in one school, minority and white students are taught in different classes; in the other, the classes are all integrated. Obviously, it makes little sense to view these schools as having similar environments merely because they are both classified as desegregated.

Finally, not all children and families respond in the same way to changes in the racial composition of their school. Some parents and students are enthusiastic about such changes, whereas others are apprehensive. Thus, in any comprehensive study of the effects of school desegregation, it would be important to know how children of different ages are affected, how children from different racial and socioeconomic backgrounds are affected, how parents' attitudes toward desegregation affect their child's reaction, and so forth. These and other factors are likely to mediate the impact of desegregation on the adolescent (St. John, 1975).

PUBLIC SCHOOLS AND PRIVATE SCHOOLS

While the vast majority of students attending secondary school in America are enrolled in public schools, a substantial minority attend private schools, either parochial (that is, with a religious affiliation) or independent. In the past, researchers cared little about studying differences between private and public schools. But, as we noted earlier, during the late 1980s and 1990s, many education policymakers suggested that one way to improve schools would be to give parents more of a choice in determining where their child was enrolled, in order to force schools to compete for the best students. One concrete suggestion in this spirit was that states provide parents with school vouchers that could be used to "purchase" education at a school of their choosing—private or public. Another suggestion was that states permit the development of charter schools—independent public schools that are freer to operate as they wish, without some of the constraints imposed by the state's education bureaucracy. In light of these suggestions, researchers became interested in whether some types of schools produced more high-achieving students than others.

Initial investigations of this by sociologist James Coleman and his colleagues, conducted some 20 years ago (e.g., Coleman & Hoffer, 1987; Coleman, Hoffer, & Kilgore, 1982), pointed to advantages for students attending private high schools, especially those attending Catholic schools. The studies found

Although social scientists disagree over their interpretation, studies have shown that adolescents who attend parochial schools generally achieve at a higher rate than those attending public schools.

that students from private schools achieved more, even after taking into account many preexisting differences between public and private students that could explain their achievement differences. (For example, we know that IQ scores are positively correlated with social class and that wealthier families can better afford private schools; and even within social classes, parents may be more likely to invest money in the education of more capable students.) The higher achievement of students in private schools was especially evident in comparisons of juniors and seniors (Entwisle, 1990).

More recent research using more powerful statistical techniques than were available two decades ago suggests, however, that private schools may not be much more effective than public schools once a full array of students' background characteristics are taken into account (Braun, Jenkins, & Grigg, 2006; Rumberger & Palardy, 2005). (These studies, as well as a large body of older research on the topic, indicate that students' family background is a far more powerful influence on their

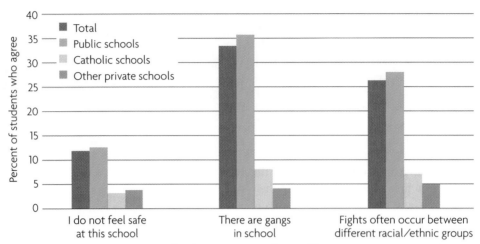

FIGURE 6.4 Students in private schools report more safety and less exposure to gangs and fighting than do students in public schools. (National Center for Education Statistics, 2002)

achievement than is the quality of the school they attend.) Consistent with this, evaluations of the impact of charter schools and voucher programs on student achievement, once students' background characteristics are taken into account, have not produced consistent results; at the very least, research indicates that these are not likely to be "silver bullets" in the effort to raise American student achievement (Howell & Peterson, 2002; Loveless, 2002). This is also true in disadvantaged urban areas, where it had been hoped that charter schools might be the solution to the many problems that plague education in the inner city.

One thing we do know is that the climate of public and private schools, especially Catholic schools, is often very different. As many writers have pointed out, a Catholic school is a part of a community in which parents, teachers, and students all share similar values and attitudes. Strong communities, whether based in neighborhoods or schools, generate what has been called **social capital**—interpersonal resources that, like financial capital, give "richer" students advantages over "poorer" ones. Students profit from the social capital associated with attending a Catholic school, for example, because the lessons taught in school are reinforced at home, at church, and in the neighborhood, and because the links between home and school are stronger (Teachman et al., 1996). In addition, private schools typically assign more homework and are more orderly and disciplined (as you will read, an important element of the climate in good schools) (Coleman et al., 1982). As Figure 6.4 illustrates, for example, students who attend private schools (Catholic or otherwise) are substantially less likely to report feeling unsafe, being

exposed to gangs, or witnessing fighting between ethnic groups (National Center for Education Statistics, 2002).

RECAP

- Generally, smaller schools, although not necessarily smaller classes, are more effective than larger ones.
- The transition from elementary school into secondary school, or from one secondary school to another, can be difficult for some students, especially those who have academic or behavioral problems at the time of the transition.
- Researchers point to features of the middle or junior high school environment that may be problematic and, more generally, to a mismatch between the school environment and the developmental needs of young adolescents.
- Research on tracking reveals that the academically rich get richer and poor get poorer. Students who are placed in the more advanced tracks or in high-ability groups in classrooms achieve more than those in lower tracks, in part because the quality of instruction in the higher tracks is superior.
- In general, the effects of changing the ethnic composition of a school on student achievement are very modest.
- There appear to be advantages for students who attend Catholic schools, but not necessarily all types of private schools. Students in Catholic schools profit from the more orderly environment and from the greater degree of social capital characterizing the families who use them.

social capital   The interpersonal resources available to an adolescent or family.

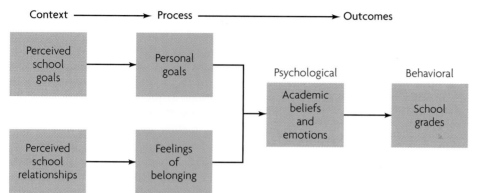

FIGURE 6.5   A positive school climate fosters students' feeling of belonging and strengthens their feelings of academic efficacy. These feelings, in turn, lead to better school performance. (Roeser et al., 1996)

Classroom Climate

Thus far, we have seen that certain elements of the school's social organization—size, age grouping, tracking, and so forth—can affect students' motivation, behavior, and achievement. But these factors are important mainly because they influence what takes place in classrooms and in other school settings. Indeed, most social scientists and educators now agree that the school-related factors that are most important in influencing learning and psychosocial development during adolescence concern the more immediate environment of the school and classroom.

Various aspects of the school climate have important effects on youngsters' learning and achievement (Rutter, 1983). Specifically, how teachers interact with students, how classroom time is used, and what sorts of standards and expectations teachers hold for their students are all more important than the size of the school, the way age groups are combined, or the racial composition of the school. One reason that tracking makes a difference, for example, is that classes in different tracks have very different climates.

THE BEST CLASSROOM CLIMATE FOR ADOLESCENTS

What sort of climate brings out the best in students? Considered together, the results of several studies indicate that the same factors that influence positive adolescent adjustment at home are important at school. Specifically, students achieve and are engaged more in school when they attend schools that are responsive and demanding. Moreover, academic functioning and psychological adjustment affect each other, so that a positive school climate—such that relationships between students and teachers are positive, and teachers are both supportive and demanding—enhances adolescents' psychological well-being as well as their achievement (Blum & Rinehart, 2000; Eccles, 2004; Gutierrez, 2000; Reddy, Rhodes, & Mulhall,

2003; Roeser, Eccles, & Sameroff, 1999; Rowan, Chiang, & Miller, 1997).

Generally, both students and teachers are more satisfied in classes that combine a moderate degree of structure with high student involvement and high teacher support, a finding that has emerged in studies of both white and nonwhite students from various socioeconomic backgrounds (Langer, 2001; Vieno, Perkins, Smith, & Santinello, 2005; Way & Robinson, 2003; Wentzel, 2002). In these classes, teachers encourage their students' participation but do not let the class get out of control. Classes that are too task oriented—particularly those that also emphasize teacher control—tend to make students anxious, uninterested, and unhappy (Moos, 1978). The pattern of classroom variables associated with positive student behavior and attitudes, then, is reminiscent of the authoritative family environment (see Chapter 4) (Pellerin, 2005). Similarly, an overemphasis on control in the classroom in the absence of support is reminiscent of the authoritarian family, while a lack of clarity and organization is reminiscent of both the indulgent family and the indifferent family—and these styles in the classroom appear to affect adolescents detrimentally, just as they do at home. Students do best when their teachers spend a high proportion of time on lessons (rather than on setting up equipment or dealing with discipline problems), begin and end lessons on time, provide clear feedback to students about what is expected of them and about their performance, and give ample praise to students when they perform well (Rutter, 1983). A good high school teacher, in other words, bears a striking resemblance to a good parent (Wentzel, 2002).

Students in schools in which teachers are supportive but firm and maintain high, well-defined standards for behavior and academic work have stronger bonds to their school and more positive achievement motives; these beliefs and emotions, in turn, lead to fewer problems, better attendance, lower rates of delinquency, more supportive friendships, and higher scores on tests of achievement (see Figure 6.5) (Eccles,

2004; Roeser, Midgley, & Urdan, 1996; Ryan & Patrick, 2001; Way & Pahl, 2001). This pattern is remarkably similar to that uncovered in studies comparing public and private high schools (Coleman, Hoffer, & Kilgore, 1982). In these studies, too, students' achievement was higher in schools that were somewhat more structured and demanding—no matter whether the school was public or private.

TEACHER EXPECTATIONS AND STUDENT PERFORMANCE

In addition to research on school climate, several studies also point to the importance of teachers' expectations. When teachers expect more of their students, the students actually learn more; when teachers expect less, they learn less—another example of what psychologists call a "self-fulfilling prophecy" (Rosenthal & Jacobson, 1968).

Although researchers have documented a link between teachers' expectations for their students and the students' performance, it is not clear whether this connection exists because teacher expectations create self-fulfilling prophecies that ultimately influence student achievement or, instead, because teachers' expectations are genuinely accurate reflections of students' ability. One study of nearly 2,000 early adolescents in Michigan attempted to disentangle these two explanations.

Psychologists Lee Jussim and Jacquelynne Eccles gathered information from teachers and students at several points in time in order to look at the over-time relation between teacher expectations and student performance. A longitudinal study, in which the same students were followed over time, was necessary for this research because a cross-sectional study, which might examine the correlation at one point between teacher expectations and student performance, would not reveal which came first (that is, whether expectations preceded performance or vice versa). Because the researchers had information about student achievement both before and after the assessment of teacher expectations, they were able to look at both possible pathways.

Data about student achievement were gathered at the end of fifth grade, at the beginning of sixth grade, and again at the end of sixth grade and the beginning of seventh grade. Data about teacher expectations were gathered during October of the students' sixth-grade year. If teachers' expectations are accurate, the researchers argued, there should be a correlation between student achievement before sixth grade and teacher expectations in October. If teachers' expectations really influence students' achievement, the researchers reasoned, the October expectations should predict student performance later in the year, even

after taking into account student performance before teacher expectations were measured.

The researchers found support for both possibilities. The teachers' expectations were accurate, in that student achievement in the fifth grade predicted both teacher expectations in the sixth grade and student achievement in the sixth grade. Yet, these very expectations, in turn, further influenced student performance, because teacher expectations in October predicted whether and how much student achievement changed over the course of the year. Which pathway was more powerful? The researchers concluded that about 80 percent of the connection between teacher expectations and student achievement results from teachers' having accurate perceptions, and about 20 percent is an effect of the self-fulfilling prophecy. The self-fulfilling prophecy appears to be somewhat stronger for academically weaker students, whose performance is more tied to teacher expectations (Madon, Jussim, & Eccles, 1997).

Even though the self-fulfilling prophecy effect is relatively small, it may be quite powerful, as the researchers point out, when accumulated over years of schooling. If teachers' expectations are unfairly based on characteristics such as students' gender, ethnicity, or socioeconomic background, the over-time effect of having teachers with low expectations may be quite substantial.

Because teachers' expectations influence students' performance, it is important to understand where these expectations come from. Unfortunately, research suggests that teachers are likely to base their expectations in part on students' ethnic and socioeconomic background. In much the same way that these factors sometimes influence tracking decisions, as we saw earlier, they may consciously and unconsciously shape teachers' expectations, which, in turn, affect students' learning. Thus, for example, teachers may call on poor or minority students less often than they call on affluent or white students—conveying a not-so-subtle message about whose responses the teacher believes are more worthy of class attention (Good & Brophy, 1984). Several studies report that African American and Latino students perceive their teachers as having low expectations and holding stereotypes about their likelihood of misbehaving (Spencer, 2005). Some evidence also suggests that white teachers rate the misbehavior of black students more harshly than do black teachers (Downey & Pribesh, 2004). It is not difficult to see how years of exposure to this sort of treatment can adversely affect students' self-concepts and interest in school. Indeed, teachers' biases against lower-class or minority adolescents may make it difficult for students from these groups to attain a level of academic accomplishment that permits upward mobility. In

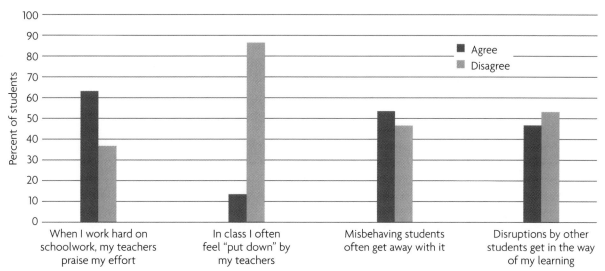

FIGURE 6.6   Students describe their teachers in positive terms but have less kind things to say about their peers' classroom behavior. (National Center for Education Statistics, 2002)

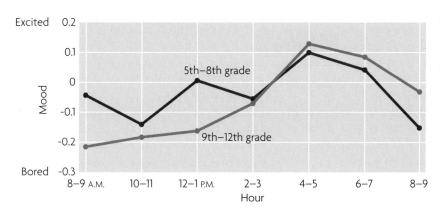

FIGURE 6.7   Studies of fluctuations in adolescents' mood over the course of the day show that students—especially high school students—feel bored most of the time they are in school. (Larson & Richards, 1998)

addition, biased treatment by teachers—having low expectations for some ethnic groups and high expectations for others—can contribute to feelings of hostility between students from different ethnicities (Rosenbloom & Way, 2004).

THE IMPORTANCE OF STUDENT ENGAGEMENT

It is important to keep in mind, of course, that students, as well as teachers, influence the classroom climate. In much the same way that the relationship between parents and adolescents is reciprocal—parents influence how their teenagers develop, but teenagers influence what their parents do—so is the relationship between teachers and their students. Effective teachers can engage and excite their students, and engaged and excited students can motivate their teachers to be more effective. According to national surveys, however, levels of student engagement and excitement in American schools are not high. About half of all high school sophomores say that disruptive students get in the way

of their learning and that students who misbehave are permitted to get away with it (see Figure 6.6) (National Center on Education Statistics, 2002). Studies also show that levels of student engagement in American high schools are very low, that many students are mainly going through the motions when they are in school, and that high school teachers often confront a roomful of students who are physically present but psychologically absent (Steinberg et al., 1986).

■ **Boring Classes, Bored Students**   In view of this, several writers have suggested that if we want to understand the impact of classroom climate on student achievement, we need to better understand how to enhance student engagement—the extent to which students are psychologically committed to learning and mastering the material rather than simply completing the assigned work (Newmann, 1992; Newmann et al., 1996; Steinberg et al., 1996). Students frequently say they are bored while in school—especially high school students, who find school far more boring than do middle school students. As you can see in Figure 6.7,

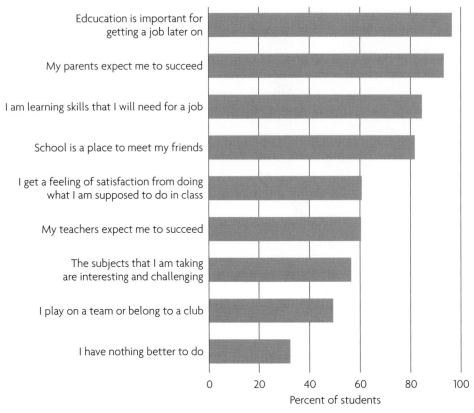

FIGURE 6.8   **Students give a variety of reasons for attending school.** (National Center for Education Statistics, 2002)

students are bored for most of the time on weekdays between 8:00 A.M. and 3:00 P.M., and the improvement in their mood seems to have more to do with the school day ending than with any special activity that takes place in the evening. Many experts believe that the make-work, routinized, rigid structure of most class-rooms, in which teachers lecture at students rather than engage them in discussion, alienates most students from school and undermines their desire to achieve. Only about half of American sophomores agree with the statement "The subjects that I am taking are inter-esting and challenging," and one-third say that they come to school because "I have nothing better to do" (see Figure 6.8) (National Center for Education Statis-tics, 2002). As one student explains:

What do I like least about school? Basically, it's boring. Like English. What we do in there—we're supposed to read something, and then maybe do something in your notebook, when you could do everything at home. So I don't really have to show up. So, I'd say that class could be about 10 minutes long. (Brown, Lamborn, & New-mann, 1992)

The notion that many students feel disengaged from school—unchallenged and bored—has been borne out in numerous studies of contemporary

American students (e.g., Owen, 1995; Steinberg et al., 1996). According to one study, titled *Getting By: What American Teenagers Really Think About Their Schools*:

Students routinely admitted—some with bravado and some with chagrin—that they calibrate their efforts, often meticulously, to do only as much as it takes to get the grade they can live with. For youngsters aiming for private colleges or elite public universities, this concept of "getting by" implies a certain grade-point average. . . . Other youngsters . . . seem satisfied with any passing grade. . . . [S]tudents from across the country repeat-edly said that they could "earn" acceptable grades, pass their courses, and receive a diploma, all while investing minimal effort in their school work. . . [A]lmost two-thirds of teens across the country (65 percent) say they could do better in school if they tried harder. (Public Agenda, 1997, p. 20)

Think back to your own high school experience. What distinguished the good classes from the tedious ones? Newmann (1992) suggests a number of specific factors that contribute to student engagement. First, teachers need to provide opportunities for students to genuinely display their competencies. Second, schools should try to facilitate students' feelings of belonging to their school. Finally, and most importantly, teachers should assign work that is "authentic"—work that is interesting, fun, and relevant to the real world (Marks, 2000). There is nothing more alienating to students than being asked to perform tasks that are boring, uninteresting, and irrelevant. Students who are disengaged from school are also more likely to misbehave (Schmidt, 2003).

FOOD FOR THOUGHT

Research has revealed the elements of school climate that are favorable to learning. Given the consistency with which these factors appear in research on good schools, why might classrooms in which students feel genuinely engaged be so rare? What impediments make it difficult for teachers to create classroom environments in which adolescents are engaged?

■ **Out-of-School Influences on Student Engagement**   Teachers and school personnel, of course, are not the only influences on adolescents' behavior in school. Several writers have noted that the peer group's values and norms also exert an important influence, especially in high school (Bishop, 1999; Steinberg, 1996). In *The Adolescent Society* (1961), for example, James Coleman reported that high schools vary a great deal in the extent to which the prevailing peer culture emphasizes academic success as a route toward status and popularity. In schools in which academic success is not valued by the student body, students are less likely to achieve grades that are consonant with their tested ability. In other words, a bright student who attends a school in which getting good grades is frowned upon by other students will actually get lower grades than he or she would in a school in which scholastic success is generally admired.

As we noted in Chapter 5, however, cliques and crowds differ enormously in the extent to which they encourage or discourage academic success (Clasen & Brown, 1985). It therefore is misleading to generalize about the impact of peer groups on adolescents' engagement in school without knowing more about the specific peer group in question. Some peer groups (for instance, the "brains") may place a great deal of pressure on their members to succeed in school and may engage in behaviors (such as studying together) that promote academic success. Other groups, in contrast, may actively discourage scholastic efforts and success.

Other researchers have focused on adolescents' experiences outside of school—at home, at work, and in extracurricular activities—and on the impact of

those experiences on their school achievement and engagement. This research demonstrates that the impact of school on adolescent achievement cannot be understood in isolation. Studies show, for example, that students whose parents are involved in school activities (such as parent–teacher conferences and "back-to-school" nights), who encourage and emphasize academic success, and who use authoritative parenting practices (see Chapter 4) do better in secondary school than do their peers (Dornbusch, Ritter, Liederman, Roberts, & Fraleigh, 1987; Gregory & Weinstein, 2004; Steinberg, Lamborn, Dornbusch, & Darling, 1992; Stevenson & Baker, 1987). In Chapter 7, we'll look more closely at the effects of employment and extracurricular participation on school achievement. Suffice it to say here that students who overextend themselves on the job or the playing field may inadvertently jeopardize their school performance (Eccles, 2004; Staff, Mortimer, & Uggen, 2004).

INTERVENING TO CHANGE A SCHOOL'S CLIMATE

The most ambitious attempt to date to improve student achievement by changing the school climate has been the Comer School Development Program (Comer, Haynes, Joyner, & Ben Avie, 1996). This intervention, designed by psychologist James Comer, has many components, but perhaps the most unique is the implementation within each school of a School Planning and Management Team, which consists of school administrators, teachers, other school staff, parents, and sometimes students; a Social Support Team, which includes counselors, nurses, social workers, special education teachers, and psychologists; and a Parent Team, which attempts to mobilize parent involvement and support for the school. Comer's approach to school reform is markedly different from most other models, because it places greater emphasis on the broader social context of the school than on what takes place in individual classrooms. His perspective is consistent with research indicating that what takes place in families, peer groups, and neighborhoods may be a stronger influence on student achievement than what takes place in classrooms (Steinberg et al., 1996).

Although the Comer program has been implemented in schools across the United States, until recently, there had been no independent evaluation of its impact on student learning and well-being. Several years ago, sociologist Thomas Cook and colleagues conducted rigorous and objective evaluations of the impact of the Comer program on school climate and student achievement in Chicago elementary schools (Cook, Murphy, & Hunt, 2000) and in middle schools in a Maryland suburb of Washington, DC (Cook et al.,

1999). In Chicago, schools that adopted the Comer program were superior to those that did not with respect to student and teacher perceptions of the school climate, reading and math achievement, and student misbehavior. In Maryland, in contrast, few differences between the Comer and comparison schools were found. No one knows for sure why the intervention worked in one setting but not another. One hypothesis is that in Maryland, over the course of the evaluation, many of the comparison schools implemented changes that made them more "Comer-like," something the researchers could not prevent, but that reduced the differences between the experimental schools and the control group. Another possibility is that the Comer program is more effective in elementary than in middle schools. In any case, these two evaluations show how difficult it is to replicate programs and their effects across different sites and how hard it is to assess the effects of a complex and wide-ranging intervention. Nevertheless, the evaluation of the Comer model in Chicago indicates that changes in the school climate aimed at enhancing adolescents' psychological well-being can lead to improvements in student behavior and school achievement.

SCHOOL VIOLENCE

Unfortunately, many students attend schools in which serious disruption—even violence—is an all-too-prevalent feature of the school climate (Noguera, 1995; Vaughan et al., 1996). According to a national survey of secondary school students in American public schools, one out of every four students has been a victim of violence in or around school, and one out of six is worried about being physically attacked or hurt while in school. One recent study found that nearly half of all middle schoolers had been threatened at school (Flannery, Weseter, & Singer, 2004). In another study, of sixth-graders attending a multiethnic school in Los Angeles, half the students surveyed reported having been verbally harassed during the previous two weeks, and about one-fifth said they had been physically victimized (Nishina & Juvonen, 2005). Violence is more common in overcrowded schools located in poor urban neighborhoods (Khoury-Kassabri, Benbenishty, Astor, & Zeira, 2004).

One study of violence in a multiethnic, urban high school found that Asian American students were often the victims of violence and verbal harassment at the hands of their African American and Latino classmates, in part because of perceptions that teachers favored Asian Americans and discriminated against their non-Asian classmates (Rosenbloom & Way, 2004). According to the researchers:

> Students reported random "slappings" by male and female peers as they walked through the hallways. Slappings are quick, pop shots, often to the head or body as students passed one another in the hall or anywhere else. Asian Americans described them as unnerving, randomly occurring, and humiliating violations that are particularly harrowing for the boys when girls slap them. . . . Along with the slappings, Asian American students were observed and reported being pushed, punched, teased, and mocked by their non-Asian American peers. The racial slur "chino" or "geek" was often heard as Asian American students passed by. (Rosenbloom & Way, p. 433)

Fifty years ago, teachers expressed concerns about such disciplinary problems as students chewing gum, talking out of turn, or making noise; today, when teachers are surveyed about disciplinary problems in their schools, they list things like rape, robbery, and assault (Toch, 1993). Experts disagree about how best to respond to violence in schools. Some educators have suggested that schools should refer aggressive students to law enforcement, and many schools have police officers on duty to deter assaults and arrest students who cause trouble. But some writers contend that the new, get-tough approach to violence prevention in schools—referred to as **zero tolerance**—has only made the situation worse, and that school violence is more effectively reduced through programs that attempt to create a more humane climate (Fox & Harding, 2005; Noguera, 1995). One unintended consequence of zero-tolerance policies is that many students end up with arrest records and contact with the justice system for acts that in the past would have been treated as disciplinary infractions by school officials (Casella, 2003).

Lethal School Violence A series of widely publicized school shootings in the United States during the late 1990s—such as the school shootings at Columbine High School in Littleton, Colorado—drew national attention to the problem of lethal school violence (Moore, Petrie, Braga, & McLaughlin, 2003). As with many topics that generate a great deal of attention in the media, much of what was asserted about school shootings has turned out not to be the case. Although violence in schools is indeed a significant problem, lethal school shootings are extremely rare events, especially when you consider the number of schools and students in the United States (there are about 50 million schoolchildren in the United States, and fewer than 20 students are killed in American schools each year) (Anderson et al., 2001). In fact, you may be surprised to learn that the number of school

zero tolerance   A get-tough approach to adolescent misbehavior that responds seriously or excessively to the first infraction.

shootings has actually declined since the early 1990s; there has been an increase in the number of student deaths in schools, but this is due to the use of automatic weapons (which tends to leave more victims), and not to any increase in the number of shootings (Anderson et al., 2001).

Actually, far more children and adolescents are killed at home or in the community than in or around school; indeed, schools are among the *safest* places for adolescents to be (Mulvey & Cauffman, 2001). In fact, an American adolescent is four times more likely to be struck by lightning than to be shot in school (Steinberg, 2001)! In addition, although the school shootings that garnered public attention generally involved white youth, a disproportionate number of homicides in schools involve nonwhite youth, both as perpetrators and victims (Anderson et al., 2001). Perhaps most importantly, it is virtually impossible to predict which students will commit acts of lethal violence (Mulvey & Cauffman, 2001). Boys, students with mental health problems, and adolescents who have easy access to guns are more likely than others to be involved in school shootings (Moore et al., 2003), but identifying the specific students with these characteristics who will commit lethal crimes in school is a different matter altogether. Obviously, the vast majority of boys with mental health problems and access to guns never hurt anyone (Steinberg, 2000). Most experts believe that, in the absence of a proven means of identifying in advance adolescents who will commit acts of lethal violence in school, the most effective policy involves limiting adolescents' access to guns and identifying and treating young people with mental health problems (Moore et al., 2003).

Interviews with students who live in communities where violence is common illuminate the ways in which these youngsters manage their day-to-day activities to avoid exposing themselves to harm (Irwin, 2004). Some make sure that they steer clear of students who have reputations for violent behavior and go out of their way to act friendly if they can't avoid them. Others learn which parts of town to avoid. Still others befriend peers who can serve as protectors, as this 16-year-old Latina did after someone at her school threatened to kill her:

> I got so scared. I didn't know what to do. I ran in the house and called my friend Daryl and I was really crying and [said] "I don't know what to do." And Daryl's all, "What's his number? What's his number?" And I gave it to him. Since that day, that same guy will leave me alone because Daryl went up to him and told him he better leave me alone or else something is going to happen to him and his family. (Irwin, 2004, pp. 467–468)

RECAP

- Researchers agree that the climate of the school is more important than its organization or structure.
- Effective teachers are like authoritative parents—they are warm, firm, and fair, and they have high expectations for student performance.
- Several writers have suggested that if we want to understand the impact of the classroom environment on student achievement, we need to better understand how to enhance student engagement—the extent to which students are psychologically committed to learning and mastering the material.
- Students perform better in school when their parents are involved in their education, when their peers value academic achievement and when their involvement in activities that compete with school is kept to a minimum. Unfortunately, many studies of American high school students indicate that they find school boring and undemanding.
- The most ambitious attempt to date to improve student achievement by changing the school climate has been the Comer School Development Program.
- Many students attend schools in which serious disruption—even violence—is an all-too-prevalent feature of the school climate. Zero-tolerance policies, which harshly punish students for any act of violence, have been shown to have unintended and often harmful effects.

Beyond High School

THE COLLEGE BOUND

The early twentieth century was an important time in the development not only of secondary schools but also of postsecondary educational institutions in the United States. Although colleges and, to a lesser extent, universities had existed for some time previously, not until the latter part of the nineteenth century did diversity in institutions of higher education begin to develop. Early postsecondary institutions were typically small, private, liberal arts academies, often with a strong theological emphasis. But during a relatively brief period bridging the nineteenth and twentieth centuries, these colleges were joined by a host of other types of institutions, including large private

FIGURE 6.9 College enrollments in the United States continue to increase, especially among females. (National Center for Education Statistics, 2006)

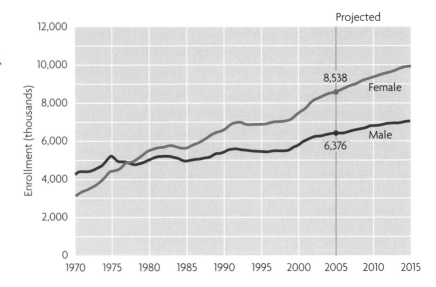

universities, technical colleges, professional schools, publicly financed state universities, land grant colleges, urban universities, and two-year community colleges (Brubacher & Rudy, 1976).

◼ **The Growth of College Enrollment**   Although postsecondary educational institutions multiplied and became more varied during the early twentieth century, enrollment in college was still a privilege enjoyed by very few young people. In 1900, only 4 percent of the 18- to 21-year-old population was enrolled in college; and by 1930, the proportion had grown only to 12 percent. Even as recently as 1950, fewer than one in five young people were enrolled in college (Church, 1976). During the first half of the twentieth century, then, colleges and universities were not prominent in the lives of most American youth.

How different the state of affairs is today! Paralleling the rise of secondary education between 1920 and 1940, postsecondary education grew dramatically between 1950 and 1970. By 1960, one-third of all young people were entering college directly from high school. College enrollments, which numbered about 1 million in 1930, had risen to more than 3 million by 1960, 8.5 million by 1970, and 16 million by 2008 (see Figure 6.9) (National Center for Education Statistics, 2006). Today, three-fourths of high school graduates enroll in college, two-thirds of them immediately after graduation (National Center for Education Statistics, 1999; Pennington, 2003). Although there were large increases in the enrollment of minority youth in higher education during the 1970s, the proportion fell during the early 1980s, primarily because of reductions in the availability of financial aid (Baker & Velez, 1996). The proportion of African American and Hispanic American high school graduates enrolled in college has increased

The vast majority of high school graduates in the United States enter college, but nearly one-third leave after just one year. About half of them will return at some later time.

somewhat in recent years, however (National Center for Education Statistics, 2006). Today, close to 70 percent of white high school graduates and more than 60 percent of African American and Hispanic American high school graduates go directly into college (see Figure 6.10). Youth from immigrant families, despite the fact that their parents typically did not attend American colleges themselves, and despite often having to support their family financially, are just as likely to enroll in and succeed in

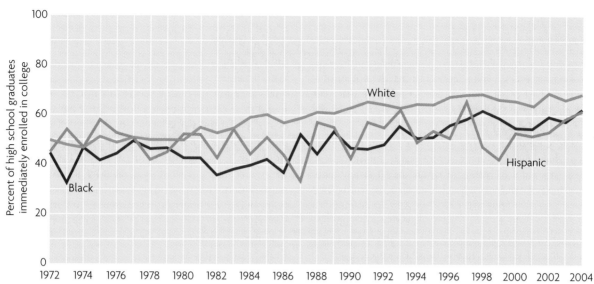

FIGURE 6.10   Today, nearly two-thirds of all American high school graduates go immediately to college. (National Center for Education Statistics, 2006)

college as are American-born youth (Fuligni & Witkow, 2004).

American Postsecondary Education   If there are two dominant characteristics that distinguish the development of postsecondary education in contemporary America from that in other parts of the world, they are diversity and accessibility (Brubacher & Rudy, 1976). In countries other than the United States, postsecondary education is likely to be monopolized by monolithic public universities (President's Science Advisory Committee, 1974). Individuals are often separated into college- and non-college-bound tracks early in adolescence, typically on the basis of standardized national examinations. In fact, rather than housing all high school students in comprehensive high schools such as those found in the United States, many European nations separate students during early adolescence into schools for college-bound youngsters and schools designed to provide vocational and technical education. In the United States, the postsecondary education system is composed of a wide variety of public and private two- and four-year institutions, some emphasizing a liberal arts education and others focusing more on technical, vocational, and preprofessional training.

The goals of students attending college also vary greatly. The population of individuals enrolled in community college, for instance, which tends to be older than that attending four-year institutions, includes highly committed students who intend to transfer to a four-year college or are working toward a specific associate's degree or certificate (together, about half of all community college students). But it

also includes students who are less committed and not sure why they are going to school (and whose attendance is sporadic), as well as some who are just taking a course here or there out of interest in the subject matter (National Center for Education Statistics, 2006). Similar variability in commitment and goals likely characterizes the population of students enrolled in four-year colleges and universities.

Although the accessibility and diversity of its postsecondary educational institutions have been commended by many, the American system of higher education has its critics (Brubacher & Rudy, 1976). Some observers have suggested that educational diversity is gained at the expense of quality. With so many options and electives for young people to choose among, it is difficult for colleges to ensure that all students receive a high-quality education. Others have pointed out that it is difficult for many young people to obtain adequate information about the range of alternatives open to them and that students are often poorly matched with the colleges they enter (Boyer, 1986). The large enrollments of many high schools make it difficult for school counselors to give each student individualized advice.

The Transition from High School to College
In some respects, the transition from high school to college parallels the transition from elementary to secondary school. For many students, going to college means entering an even larger, more formidable, and more impersonal environment. For some, the transition may coincide with other life changes, such as leaving home, breaking off or beginning an important

relationship, or having to manage their own residence or finances for the first time.

As a consequence of all these factors, although many more American adolescents enroll in college today than in previous years, a very large number do not graduate. Only half of all students who enroll in a four-year college complete their degree within six years (National Center for Education Statistics, 2006). Perhaps as a consequence of increasing accessibility, poor matching, and a lack of "consumer" knowledge among college applicants, rates of college attrition are extremely high: One-third of students who enter college in the United States drop out after just one year. And while many of the students who leave after one year do eventually finish their degree program, one-third of all students who enroll in college never finish. In other words, although a great deal has been done to make college entrance more likely, rates of college graduation lag far behind rates of enrollment (Pennington, 2003).

FOOD FOR THOUGHT

A large proportion of students who enter college leave after one year. Based on your own experience in college, what might be done to help more students stay enrolled?

THE NON-COLLEGE BOUND

The problems associated with moving from high school to college pale in comparison with the problems associated with not going to college at all. In general, college graduates earn substantially more income over their lifetime than do individuals who attend college but do not graduate, and these individuals, in turn, earn much more than students who do not attend college at all (Halperin, 2001; William T. Grant Foundation, 1988). Individuals who drop out of high school before graduation suffer a wide range of problems, which we'll examine in detail in Chapter 12.

One of the unfortunate by-products of our having made postsecondary education so accessible—and so expected—is that we have turned our backs on individuals who do not go directly to college, even though they compose *one-third* of the adolescent population. As many writers have noted, our secondary schools are geared almost exclusively toward college-bound youngsters (Krei & Rosenbaum, 2001).

We noted earlier that opportunities for learning and for critical thinking are much greater in college-prep classes than in the general or vocational tracks. In addition, students who are not headed for college—some by choice, others by unavoidable circumstance—find that their high schools have not prepared them at

all for the world of work. Even those who complete school and earn a diploma—who have done what they were supposed to do as adolescents—may have a hard time finding employment and a nearly impossible time finding a satisfying, well-paying job. As a consequence, many individuals who do not go to college spend their early adult years floundering between periods of part-time work, underemployment (for example, working at a job that is less challenging than they would like), and unemployment. By the time they are 25 or so, most have found steady, if low-paying, employment. But they may have spent six or seven years living very close to the edge, if not in genuine poverty. Rates of depression are significantly higher among young adults who are not in school than among those who are, and they are especially high among individuals who are neither in school nor steadily employed (Aseltine & Gore, 2005).

One important contributing factor to the continuing difficulties faced by adolescents who do not go to college has been the change in the world of work mentioned earlier in this chapter: As manufacturing jobs began to be replaced by minimum-wage service jobs, the chances of making a decent living without at least two years of college experience worsened appreciably. Today, young adults without college experience often must try to make ends meet on minimum-wage jobs—jobs that offer little in the way of promotion or advancement. The economic problems faced by non-college-bound youth have been compounded by the escalating costs of such essentials as housing and health care.

Given the high dropout rate already characteristic of most colleges, the answer to the problem does not seem to be simply to encourage more individuals to continue their education past high school. Obviously, for those who want a postsecondary education, we should make every attempt to see that they can obtain and afford it. But what about those adolescents who just are not interested in a college degree? How can these individuals be helped?

Experts believe that one potential answer involves strengthening the links between the worlds of school and work during high school, as discussed in Chapter 3 (Hamilton & Hamilton, 2004). In most other industrialized countries, non-college-bound youth begin apprenticeships during their last two years of compulsory school, so that by the time they have completed their formal schooling, they are well trained to take on skilled jobs (Hamilton & Hamilton, 2004). Instead of simply dumping such adolescents into the labor force at graduation, as we do in America, schools and communities provide training, career counseling, and job placement services throughout high school. In most contemporary American high schools, counseling is geared toward helping college-bound students continue their education. Billions of dollars, in the form of financial aid and subsidized public college tuition, are given to these students. Some critics have suggested that we should spend just as much time and money helping the other third of the adolescent population make their transition into adulthood as smooth as possible (Wald, 2006).

RECAP

- About three-quarters of all American adolescents go on to some form of postsecondary education, but many students drop out after their first year, probably because of a mismatch between their needs and the school environment.
- High schools as they are presently structured do not serve non-college-bound adolescents very well. As a result, one-third of the country's adolescents complete their formal education without adequate preparation for the world of work they hope to enter.
- Experts believe that one potential answer to the transition problems of students who do not go from high school to college involves strengthening the links between the worlds of school and work during high school.

Schools and Adolescent Development

CHARACTERISTICS OF GOOD SCHOOLS

Despite all the debate about how secondary schools ought to be organized and reformed, there is a fair degree of consensus among experts about the characteristics of good schools for adolescents, at least as far as student achievement is concerned (as you will read in Chapter 12, the characteristics of schools with high rates of student achievement are not the same as those with low rates of dropping out) (Linney & Seidman, 1989; Rumberger & Palardy, 2005).

First and foremost, good schools emphasize intellectual activities (Ravitch, 1995, 2000). They create this atmosphere in different ways, depending on the nature and size of the student body, but in these good schools, a common purpose—quality education—is valued and shared by students, teachers, administrators, and parents (Lee, Smith, & Croninger, 1997). Learning is more important to students than athletics or extracurricular activities, and seeing that students learn is more important to teachers and administrators than seeing that they graduate.

Second, good schools have teachers who are committed to their students and who are given a good deal of freedom and autonomy by administrators in the way that this commitment is expressed in the classroom (Lee & Smith, 1996; Lee et al., 1997). In all schools, of course, teachers have curricular requirements that they must fulfill. But in good schools, teachers are given relatively more authority to decide how their lessons are planned and how their classes are conducted. When teachers are given this sort of say in school governance, they may find it easier to commit to the shared values of the institution.

Third, good schools constantly monitor themselves and their students in order to become even better. Rather than viewing questions and concerns about school policies and practices as threatening, principals and other administrators welcome opportunities for dialogue and discussion. When school personnel encourage flexibility, openness to change, and the exchange of ideas, they set a tone for the entire school that may even affect the classroom and may result in more stimulating student–teacher interactions (Goodlad, 1984).

Fourth, good schools are well integrated into the communities they serve (Coleman & Hoffer, 1987). Active attempts are made to involve parents in their youngsters' education, which is an important influence on student achievement and a deterrent against students dropping out (Rumberger & Palardy, 2005). Links are forged between the high school and local colleges and universities, so that advanced students may take more challenging and more stimulating courses for high school credit. Bridges are built between the high school and local employers, so that students begin to see the relevance of their high school education to their occupational futures.

Finally, and perhaps obviously, good schools are composed of good classrooms. In good classrooms, students are active participants in the process of education, not passive recipients of lecture material. The atmosphere is orderly but not oppressive. Innovative projects replace rote memorization as a way of encouraging learning. Students are challenged to think critically and to debate important issues, rather than being asked simply to regurgitate yesterday's lessons (Newmann, Marks, & Gamoran, 1996).

FOOD FOR THOUGHT

Based on the criteria of good schools discussed in this chapter how would you rate the high school that you attended?

THE EFFECTS OF SCHOOL ON ADOLESCENT DEVELOPMENT

Whatever the shortcomings of schools, staying in school is preferable to dropping out, not only in terms of future earnings but in terms of cognitive development as well. One study contrasted the performance of dropouts and graduates on a battery of standardized tests of achievement administered during late adolescence (Alexander, Natriello, & Pallas, 1985). The study took into account differences in achievement levels that existed before the dropouts had left school (two years before the assessment was conducted), because dropouts are more likely than graduates to show achievement problems early in their education. Compared with the dropouts, adolescents who stayed in school gained far more intellectually over the two-year interval in a variety of content areas. More importantly, the results showed that the adverse effects of dropping out were most intense among socioeconomically disadvantaged youth. Paradoxically, then, those students who are most likely to leave school prior to graduation may be most harmed by doing so.

One other way of assessing the contribution of schools to adolescents' intellectual development is by comparing early adolescents' intellectual gains during the school year with their gains during the summer. Several studies have done just this (e.g., Cooper, Charlton, Valentine, & Muhlenbruck, 2000). Using information about the academic progress of students measured at three points in time—the beginning of the school year, the end of the school year, and the beginning of the next year—researchers were able to see how the academic progress of students during the summer compared with their academic progress during the school session. Among students with higher socioeconomic status (SES), rates of academic progress during the school year and during the summer were comparable. Among disadvantaged students, however, the pattern was different. Although rates of progress during the school year were more or less equal to those of higher-SES students, during the summer months, disadvantaged students' scores declined. In other words, if it were not for the effects of school on cognitive development, the discrepancy between affluent and poor youngsters' achievement scores would be much greater than it currently is. One benefit of summer school for disadvantaged students is that it diminishes the decline in achievement that would otherwise occur between the spring and fall semesters (Cooper et al., 2000).

Far less is known about the impact of schools on the psychosocial development of adolescents. Commenta-tors have long noted that most schools are not structured to promote psychosocial development, given their excessive focus on conformity and obedience, and their lack of encouragement for creativity, independence, and self-reliance (Friedenberg, 1967). This certainly comes through loud and clear when adolescents are asked about their classroom experiences. But there are many good schools in which students not only learn the academic material taught in classes but also learn about themselves, their relationships with others, and their society. Schools differ from each other, and it may be difficult to generalize about the impact of schools on adolescent development without knowing more about the particular school in question.

It is also important to recognize that despite adults' intentions and objectives, students do not view school solely in terms of its academic agenda. In one study, the researchers asked a sample of seventh- through twelfth-graders to list the best and worst things about school. The best things? "Being with my friends" and "Meeting new people." The worst? Homework, tests, and the restrictive atmosphere of the school (Brown, Lamborn, & Newmann, 1992). Adults may evaluate schools in terms of their contribution to adolescents' cognitive and career development, but for the typical adolescent, school is a primary setting for socializing. When we ask about the consequences of leaving school early, then, we must take into account the impact this may have on the individual's social, as well as cognitive, development.

Studies also show that students' experiences within a school can vary widely according to the track they are on, the peer group they belong to, and the extracurricular activities they participate in. It seems safe to say that academically talented and economically advantaged students have a more positive experience in school than their less capable or less affluent counterparts do—positive not only with respect to what they learn in class but also with respect to the impact of school on their feelings about themselves as individuals. They receive more attention from their teachers, are more likely to hold positions of leadership in extracurricular organizations, and are more likely to experience classes that are engaging and challenging. In other words, the structure of a school—its size, its tracking policy, its curricula—provides different intellectual and psychosocial opportunities for students who occupy different places within that structure. The best answer to the question "How do schools affect adolescent development?" then, is another question: "Which schools, which adolescents, and in what ways?"

RECAP

- Good schools have five characteristics: (1) They emphasize intellectual activities, (2) they have committed teachers who are given autonomy, (3) they monitor their own progress, (4) they are well integrated into their community, and (5) they have a high proportion of classrooms in which students are active participants in their education
- Evidence suggests that attending high school does, in fact, contribute to adolescents' intellectual development. However, critics of contemporary secondary schools have noted that most schools, with their focus on conformity and obedience and their lack of encouragement for creativity, independence, and self-reliance, are not structured to promote adolescents' psychosocial development.
- The ways in which adolescents are affected by school depend a great deal on the characteristics of the schools they attend. College-bound students in the more advanced tracks have markedly different experiences than non-college-bound students in the lower tracks.

CHAPTER 7

Work, Leisure, and the Mass Media

ADOLESCENTS' FREE TIME IN CONTEMPORARY SOCIETY

Patterns of Time Use in Contemporary America

Patterns of Time Use in Other Countries

ADOLESCENTS AND WORK

School and Work in the Early Twentieth Century

The Emergence of the Student-Worker

Teenage Employment in America and Other Nations

The Adolescent Workplace Today

Employment and Adolescent Development

Youth Unemployment

ADOLESCENTS AND LEISURE

Adolescents' Free Time and Their Moods

Structured Leisure Activities

Unstructured Leisure Time

Promoting Positive Youth Development

ADOLESCENTS AND THE MASS MEDIA

Patterns of Media Use

Theories of Media Influence and Use

The Impact of Adolescents' Exposure to Controversial Media Content

Mass Media and Sex-Role Socialization

The Adolescent Consumer

FREE TIME AND ADOLESCENT DEVELOPMENT

THERE IS NO QUESTION that the settings we have looked at in the past three chapters—the family, the peer group, and the school—exert a profound influence on the development and behavior of adolescents. Yet it may surprise you to learn that today's teenagers spend more time in leisure activities than they do in the "productive" activities of school, more time alone than with members of their family, about four times the number of hours each week on a part-time job as on homework, and considerably more time "wired" to music, the Internet, or television than "tuned into" the classroom (Csikszentmihalyi & Larson, 1984; Roberts, Henriksen, & Fochr, 2004; Shanahan & Flaherty, 2001; Staff, Mortimer, & Uggen, 2004). In this chapter, we look at these other important contexts of adolescence—the contexts of work, leisure, and the mass media.

Social scientists have only recently begun to study systematically the ways in which work, leisure, and the mass media influence adolescent development (Brown & Cantor, 2000a; Mahoney, Larson, Eccles, & Lord, 2005; Roberts et al., 2004; Staff et al., 2004; Verma & Larson, 2003). Perhaps because historically we have considered school to be the most important activity of adolescence in contemporary society, we have paid far less attention to what adolescents do in their spare time than to what they do in school—even though their spare time occupies much more of their waking hours than does their time in school. As you know, however, one of the hallmarks of teenage life in industrialized society is that adolescents have considerable amounts of time and money to devote to activities of their choosing. Among the most popular are working at a part-time job, participating in an after-school extracurricular activity, shopping, hanging out with friends, and enjoying one or more of the mass media, including television, radio, movies, recorded music and video, video games, and, increasingly, the Internet.

Adolescents' Free Time in Contemporary Society

The abundance of free time in the lives of contemporary adolescents has several origins. Ironically, one of the most important contributors was the development of compulsory schooling. Prior to this, adolescents were expected to work full-time, and most maintained schedules comparable to adults, working long hours each week. With the spread of secondary schools during the early decades of the twentieth century, however, adolescents were in effect barred from the labor force; the part-time jobs held by teenagers that are familiar to us today—working behind fast-food counters, for instance—simply did not exist in large numbers, making after-school employment opportunities rare.

One indirect effect of compulsory high school, then, was to increase the amount of free time available to young people—time that previously would have been occupied by work. Indeed, at the turn of the twentieth century, adults were so worried about the free time available to adolescents that they began to organize various youth clubs and activities—such as the Boy Scouts and organized sports—in order to occupy their "idle hands" (Hine, 1999; Modell & Goodman, 1990). In some respects, organized leisure became an institutionalized part of adolescence as a supplement to school and a replacement for full-time employment.

A second influence on the rise of free time for adolescents in contemporary society was the increased affluence of Americans following World War II. As noted in Chapter 3, the invention of the "teenager"—and, more importantly, the discovery of the teenager by those in advertising and marketing—changed the nature of adolescence in modern society. As adolescents gained more autonomy, they came to be recognized as consumers with plenty of discretionary income to spend on recreation, an accurate image that persists today (Zollo, 2004). How adolescents spend their free time has become a central focus and defining feature of the sociocultural landscape. This week, notice the commercials and advertisements aimed at teenagers on television shows, in magazines, on radio stations, or on the Internet. You'll see that much of the advertising targeted toward young people concerns leisure expenditures: music, movies, restaurants, electronic gadgets, cosmetics, athletic equipment, and so on.

FOOD FOR THOUGHT

Free time has not always played such an important role in the lives of teenagers. How do you think it has changed the nature of adolescence?

PATTERNS OF TIME USE IN CONTEMPORARY AMERICA

How much time do adolescents spend in various sorts of activities? In one study, early adolescents were asked to monitor their time use with electronic

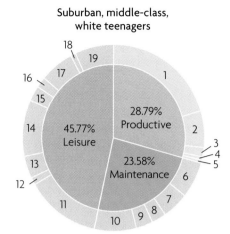

Suburban, middle-class, white teenagers

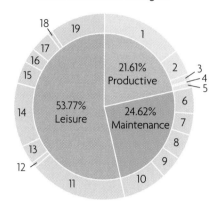

Urban, poor, African American teenagers

	Suburban, middle-class, white teenagers	Urban, poor, African American teenagers
1 Classwork	19.92%	14.74%
2 Homework	6.23%	4.48%
3 Extracurricular activities (includes school assemblies)	1.58%	1.13%
4 Working for pay (includes babysitting)	0.56%	0.27%
5 Religious activities	0.49%	0.99%
6 Eating	6.19%	4.53%
7 Transportation (includes walking)	4.63%	3.76%
8 Resting	2.52%	4.46%
9 Chores and errands	2.92%	3.99%
10 Personal maintenance	7.33%	7.89%
11 Television viewing	13.00%	17.53%
12 Music listening	1.27%	0.83%
13 Creative activities	3.82%	3.34%
14 Talking	9.58%	11.12%
15 Playing	2.62%	3.97%
16 Playing games	1.83%	2.55%
17 Playing sports (includes exercise, swimming, and other physical activities)	5.96%	3.73%
18 Public leisure (includes leisure shopping, attending a movie, outings)	0.89%	0.77%
19 Idling (includes doing nothing, thinking, waiting)	6.79%	9.94%

FIGURE 7.1   How suburban and urban adolescents spend their time. (Larson et al., 2001)

pagers (the adolescents were "beeped" periodically throughout the day and prompted to fill out questionnaires about what they were doing at the time). The results are presented in Figure 7.1 for two very different groups: suburban, middle-class, white teenagers, and urban, poor, African American teenagers. What is perhaps most striking about these data is how similar the groups' time allocation is, despite their very different backgrounds and living circumstances. In both groups, leisure activities, such as socializing, watching TV, and playing sports, account for about half their waking time; the balance is divided roughly evenly between productive activities, such as attending class and studying, and maintenance activities, such as grooming, eating, and running errands (Larson, Richards, Sims, & Dworkin, 2001) (see Figure 7.1).

Group averages can be deceptive, however, because there are wide variations even among teenagers from similar socioeconomic and ethnic backgrounds in how they spend their free time. In one study, which tracked adolescents' time use over their high school years, the researchers identified several distinct groups of students (Shanahan & Flaherty, 2001). One especially busy group—about one-third of the sample in all grades—spent considerable time in a wide range of activities, including extracurricular activities, paid work, schoolwork, time with friends, and household chores. A second group, about one-fourth of the sample, was similarly busy but did not hold a paying job. A third group, whose numbers increased from about 12 percent in the ninth grade to 20 percent in the twelfth grade, devoted substantial time to a paying job but spent little time on other activities. A fourth group spent no time

FIGURE 7.2   In one study of urban adolescents, most participants focused on one particular domain of activity, such as sports or academics. About one-fourth had multiple commitments, and about one-tenth had none (Adapted from Pederson et al., 2005)

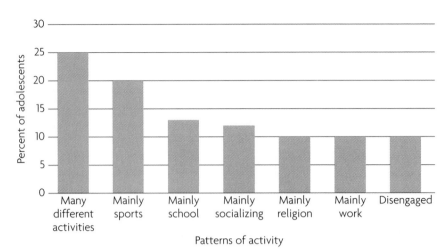

in work or extracurricular activities, but a substantial amount of time hanging around with friends.

Although the study found that adolescents' time use patterns changed somewhat with age (not surprisingly, as adolescents got older, they were more likely to spend at least some of their free time working at a paid job), individuals who were busy ninth-graders were likely to be busy throughout high school. Overall, the results suggest that adolescents' free time is not best thought of as a "zero sum" phenomenon, whereby involvement in one activity necessarily displaces involvement in another. Rather, there appear to be very busy, well-rounded adolescents who have substantial time commitments across many different activities, and not-so-busy adolescents who do not. Generally, most studies, regardless of adolescents' socioeconomic or ethnic background, find that relatively busier adolescents are better adjusted and more achievement oriented than their classmates, but whether their better adjustment is caused by or results from their busy schedules is not clear (Bartko & Eccles, 2003). (Most likely, it is a combination of the two.)

A recent study of poor, predominantly Hispanic American and African American urban youth found similar diversity in students' patterns of activity (Pedersen et al., 2005). As Figure 7.2 indicates, about 25 percent of the sample was highly engaged across a wide range of different activities (for example, school, athletics, socializing, work, religion). Other students tended to "specialize," reporting high involvement in either sports (20 percent), school (13 percent), socializing (12 percent), religion (10 percent), or work (10 percent) but not in much else. About 10 percent of the sample was disengaged from pretty much everything. Overall, adolescents who were engaged in multiple contexts reported better mental health than those whose commitment was more narrowly focused, who in turn reported better mental health than students who were disconnected. Interestingly, some forms of engagement—athletics, for example—were associated with positive outcomes when

combined with a second type of engagement (for example, academics), but with negative outcomes if it was the only activity an adolescent was involved in.

PATTERNS OF TIME USE IN OTHER COUNTRIES

Patterns of time use differ considerably in different parts of the world. Generally, American adolescents spend far more time on leisure, and far less time in productive activities, than their counterparts in other countries. American students' use of their free time for school-related activities is especially low. For instance, the average American high school student spends fewer than five hours per week on homework; in Asian countries such as India, Taiwan, and Japan, the average is between four and five hours *per day* (Larson & Verma, 1999). And European and Asian adolescents spend almost three times as many hours each week reading for pleasure as do American adolescents (Larson & Verma, 1999). In contrast, American teenagers spend relatively more time playing sports, socializing with friends, caring for their physical appearance, and working in after-school jobs (Alasker & Flammer, 1999; Flammer, Alasker, & Noack, 1999; Larson & Seepersad, 2003; Larson & Verma, 1999).

What is the effect of all this free time on adolescents' behavior and development? Are they learning about the real world from their part-time jobs? Are their extracurricular activities as character building as adults believe they are? Are they being driven toward sex and violence by the mass media? Are they really affected by the lyrics of rock music, the images on MTV and BET, or the brutality of many video games? Has the increase in time that they spend on-line adversely affected their ability to relate to others in person? These are some of the questions we will address in this chapter. We begin by examining how teenagers are affected by after-school employment.

RECAP

- The rise of compulsory schooling and the increasing affluence of American society in the second half of the twentieth century contributed to the increased importance of free time in the lives of contemporary adolescents.
- Adolescents' time out of school is spent working in part-time jobs, engaging in a variety of leisure activities, and using the mass media.
- Today's American adolescents spend about half their time in leisure activities—far more than is the case in most other industrialized countries (where more time is devoted to school) and in developing nations (where more time is devoted to work).
- There is considerable variability in how individual adolescents spend their free time; some are very busy with structured extracurricular activities, while others' time is far more unstructured.

Adolescents and Work

Today, in the United States, it is commonplace to see teenagers working in restaurants and retail stores. Indeed, almost 80 percent of today's high school students will have worked before graduating (Staff, Mortimer, & Uggen, 2004). Although working while attending high school may currently be the norm, only in the past four decades has part-time employment become widespread among American adolescents. As you will read, the employment of students in present-day America represents an important break from past eras, in which going to school and working were mutually exclusive activities.

SCHOOL AND WORK IN THE EARLY TWENTIETH CENTURY

Prior to 1925—when continuing on in high school was the exception, not the rule—teenagers from all but the most affluent families left school between the ages of 12 and 15 and became full-time workers (Horan and Hargis, 1991; Modell, Furstenberg, & Hershberg, 1976). In other words, a century ago, adolescents were either students or workers, but not both. During the second quarter of the twentieth century, however, school began to replace the workplace as the setting in which most adolescents spent their weekdays.

As secondary education became more widespread among different socioeconomic segments of American society, more youngsters remained in school well into middle and late adolescence, and fewer elected to work. Compulsory education laws were passed in most states that required individuals to remain in school until at least the age of 16, part-time jobs were not plentiful, and a variety of child labor laws were enacted to restrict youngsters' employment (Kett, 1977). As a result of these social and legislative changes, the employment of American teenagers in the formal labor force declined steadily during the first four decades of the twentieth century. In 1940, for example, only 5 percent of 16- and 17-year-old male high school students and less than 2 percent of female students worked during the school year (U.S. Department of Commerce, 1940).

THE EMERGENCE OF THE STUDENT-WORKER

The situation began to change between 1940 and 1950. Following the end of World War II, and as a result of the economic growth that took place in the postwar years, sectors of the American economy that needed large numbers of part-time employees expanded rapidly (Ginzberg, 1977). More than three out of every five new jobs created between 1950 and 1977 were in retail trade or services, where many jobs are part-time. Employers, particularly in businesses such as fast-food restaurants, needed workers who were willing to work part time for relatively low wages and for short work shifts. Many employers looked to teenagers to fill these jobs—and, in the mid-1970s, as you read in Chapter 5, teenagers were plentiful, making up a larger proportion of the population than they had in previous decades.

As shown in Figure 7.3, the proportion of American high school students holding part-time jobs rose dramatically between 1940 and 1980. By 1980, about two-thirds of all high school seniors and about half of all high school sophomores held part-time jobs during the school year (Lewin-Epstein, 1981). More recent estimates indicate that the proportion of working high school students has not changed appreciably since this time (Mortimer & Johnson, 1998; Staff et al., 2004). By current estimates, at any one time during the school year, well over 6 million American high school students are working.

When you think of the typical working teenager, what image comes to mind? An adolescent from a poor family that relies on the teenager's income to make ends meet? Wrong.

In the past, it was young people from less affluent families who were more likely to work; today this is no longer the case. Working during high school is just as common among middle-class teenagers as it is among poor youth (National Center for Education Statistics, 2006). Working is also more common among white

FIGURE 7.3   The proportion of U.S. high school students with jobs rose dramatically between 1940 and 1980. For the past 20 years, the majority of U.S. high school students have held part-time jobs during the school year.

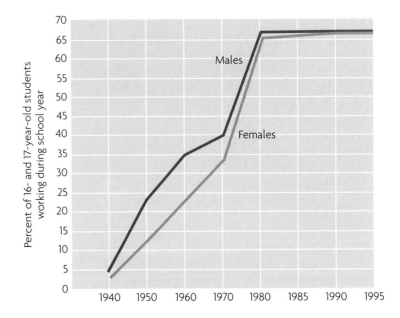

than among nonwhite students, with employment rates being lowest among African American youth. Male and female adolescents are equally likely to be employed, although they often work in very different types of jobs (McNeal, 1997; Steinberg & Cauffman, 1995).

Not only are more high school students working today than ever before, but they work for considerably more hours than adolescents did in the past (Mortimer, 2003; National Research Council, 1998). The average high school sophomore puts in about 15 hours per week at a job, and the average senior about 20 (Mortimer, 2003). Considering that the average school day runs for about 6 hours, today's typical working adolescent is busy with school or work commitments for close to 50 hours a week.

Although youngsters in contemporary America do not enter the formal labor force until age 15 or 16, many individuals will have worked on an informal basis during childhood, doing chores around the house; this pattern is especially common in less industrialized societies and, among industrialized nations, more common in Western than Asian countries (Larson & Seepersad, 2003; Larson & Verma, 1999). In virtually all countries around the world, but especially in developing countries, household chores are more likely to be assigned to adolescent girls than boys, especially as they get older. In one study of urban adolescents in Mexico, for example, the amount of time devoted to household chores by boys remained steady between ages 12 and 17 (at about 7 hours per week) but rose considerably among girls, from about 11 hours per week to 17 (National Research Council, 2005). By early adolescence, many youngsters begin to take on informal employment outside the home for other family members or neighbors. Babysitting is a common

source of income for many young adolescent girls, and gardening and lawn work for young adolescent boys (Greenberger & Steinberg, 1983; McNeal, 1997).

TEENAGE EMPLOYMENT IN AMERICA AND IN OTHER NATIONS

The extent and nature of teenage employment vary considerably from country to country (Verma & Larson, 2003). In most nonindustrialized societies, work life and family life are not as distinct as they are in contemporary America, and youngsters are typically integrated into the world of work before they reach adolescence (Whiting & Whiting, 1975). If the society subsists on farming, children are taught how to farm at an early age; if the society subsists on hunting, children are taught how to hunt. Although young people who are still acquiring work skills may be given tasks that are more elementary than those performed by their elders, adolescents and adults work side by side, and a distinctively adolescent workplace—such as that in the United States today—is uncommon.

In developing nations where industrialization is still in a relatively early stage and a large percentage of the population is poor, adolescents generally leave school early—at least by American standards. In many parts of the developing world, work obligations may take precedence over schooling, as a recent study of rural Bolivian children described (Punch, 2004). In these countries, most adolescents enter into full-time employment by age 15 or 16, in jobs similar to the ones they will hold as adults. Very often, adolescents work for their families. The pattern in these countries closely resembles that found in America during an earlier stage in its history: school for adolescents of the extremely affluent, and work for the rest (Larson & Verma, 1999). The trade-off between school and work is common in the developing world, and as more and more adolescents from developing nations are enrolled in school, the number of adolescents in these countries' labor force declines at about the same rate. In China, for example, where educational opportunities have expanded rapidly in recent decades, especially outside urban centers, about half of all 16-year-olds were employed in 1989, but fewer than one-quarter were employed in 1997 (National Research Council, 2005).

Other comparably industrialized countries provide the most interesting contrast to the United States, because in these countries, social and economic conditions are more similar to those affecting American adolescents. In these nations, however, adolescents are far more likely to defer paid employment until their education is completed. Thus, whereas about three-quarters of American high school juniors hold jobs during the school year, only one-quarter of Japanese and Taiwanese juniors do (Larson & Verma, 1999). Paid employment during the school year is even rarer in most European countries and virtually nonexistent in many, such as France, Hungary, Russia, and Switzerland; in European countries where adolescents are employed during the school year, they tend to work very few hours each week and to be employed in more informal jobs, like babysitting (Flammer & Schaffner, 2003). In other industrialized countries, then, young people generally move from school directly into full-time employment without an intervening period of formal part-time work. In the United States, in contrast, it is more common for youngsters to move from full-time school with no formal employment (during early adolescence), to a combination of school and part-time work (during middle and late adolescence), to full-time work (sometime during late adolescence or early adulthood) (Mortimer, 2003).

Although European adolescents are less likely than their American counterparts to hold paying part-time jobs during the school year, they are more likely to work in school- or government-sponsored apprenticeships (Hamilton & Hamilton, 2004; Mortimer, 2003). In many countries, such as Germany, these apprenticeships play an extremely important role in preparing adolescents for the transition into adult employment, especially for students who are not bound for college. It is important to remember as you read this chapter that the studies of teen employment in the United States are typically studies of students who are working in part-time jobs that have little to do with the careers they hope to pursue after they complete their education, and most of what we know about the impact of employment on youth development comes from studies of American teenagers. In contrast, in Europe, students' work experience is much more continuous with the roles they will assume as adults (Hamilton & Hurrelmann, 1994).

How can we account for these differences between the United States and other industrialized countries in rates of student employment? First, part-time employment opportunities are not as readily available elsewhere as they are in America. Fast-food restaurants, although increasingly popular in other countries, are not seen on every major street. Second, the scheduling of part-time jobs in other countries is not well suited to the daily routines of students. In Europe, for example, the school day lasts well into the late afternoon, and relatively few shops are open in the evenings. In the United States, many adolescents leave school early in the afternoon and go straight to their part-time jobs, where they work until 9:00 or 10:00 P.M. Third, in most other industrialized countries, the employment of children is associated with being poor, and there is a strong stigma attached to having one's children work. Many middle-class parents do not feel that it is appropriate for their children to have jobs while attending school. Fourth, schools in countries other than the United States require much more out-of-school time for homework (Larson & Seepersad, 2003; Steinberg, 1996). Finally, as noted in Chapter 6, American schools have not done a very good job of anticipating the needs of adolescents who do not intend to go to college. Because formal apprenticeship programs, such as those found in most other industrialized countries, are quite rare in the United States, one of the only ways for American adolescents to gain work experience is through part-time jobs. The school-to-work transition is far more systematic, and far more effective, in most European countries than in the United States (Hamilton & Hamilton, 2004).

Although having a part-time job while in high school has a positive impact on employment in young adulthood, the effect is very small (Mortimer, 2003). And as you will read, whatever modest long-term benefits employment during high school may have are accompanied by what some commentators believe are short-term costs (Carr, Wright, & Brody, 1996; Greenberger & Steinberg, 1986).

FOOD FOR THOUGHT

Student employment during the school year is far more common in the United States than elsewhere. How might this make the nature of adolescence different in the United States than in other parts of the world?

The vast majority of contemporary teenagers are employed in a small number of different occupations, generally in retail stores or restaurants.

THE ADOLESCENT WORKPLACE TODAY

▍**Common Adolescent Jobs**   The range of jobs open to American adolescents who wish to work in the formal labor force is rather limited. The vast majority of teenagers are employed in the retail and service industries, although, as you might expect, there are important differences as a function of region, age, and sex. In general, older students are more likely to hold formal jobs (for example, retail or restaurant work) than are younger students, who are more likely to hold informal jobs (such as babysitting or yard work) (Mortimer, 2003). As expected, working teenagers in rural areas are more likely to be employed in agricultural occupations than are their urban or suburban counterparts. Also, boys are more likely to work in manual labor than are girls, who are more likely than boys to work in service positions (Greenberger & Steinberg, 1986; McNeal, 1997).

These differences notwithstanding, it is important to recognize that a limited number of types of jobs accounts for a very large proportion of today's student workers. According to data from government surveys, nearly 60 percent of employed eighth-graders work in one of two jobs: babysitting or yard work (Schneider & Shouse, 1991). And job opportunities are just as restricted for older workers: Restaurant work (such as a counter worker in a fast-food restaurant) and retail sales work (such as a cashier in a clothing store) account for nearly 60 percent of all working students' jobs (Mortimer, 2003; Steinberg, Fegley, & Dornbusch, 1993). Very few teenagers are employed on farms or in factories anymore (Charner & Fraser, 1987).

▍**The Adolescent Work Environment**   What do adolescents actually do—and learn—on the job? In one series of studies of adolescents who work, a team of researchers examined teenagers' work environments (Greenberger & Steinberg, 1981; Greenberger, Steinberg, & Ruggiero, 1982). Most of the workers studied were employed in one of five types of work: food service (fast-food counter worker), clerical (file clerk in an office), retail (cashier in a store), manual labor (gardener), and skilled labor (assistant automobile mechanic). Using an elaborate coding system to record on-the-job activities, the researchers observed what went on in the work settings. They recorded the tasks that the adolescents performed (for example, "cleans table"), the things they said ("May I help you?"), and the people with whom they interacted ("adult customer"). They also interviewed the adolescent workers and had them complete a series of questionnaires about their experiences at work.

Although this research was conducted more than 25 years ago, the researchers' observations still ring true today. Unlike adolescents in traditional societies, whose work typically brings them into extensive contact with adults, the young people who were observed in these studies spent as much time on the job interacting with other adolescents as they did with their elders. In the typical fast-food restaurant, for example, nearly all the workers were teenagers, the supervisor was usually not much older, and the customers were often young people, too. Few of the teenage workers surveyed reported having formed close relationships with adults at work. They were unlikely to see their adult supervisors or co-workers outside of work, felt reluctant to go to the adults at work with personal problems, and reported feeling less close to adults at work than to other people in their lives (Greenberger & Steinberg, 1981).

The studies also indicated that most teenagers' jobs are fairly dreary. Few jobs permit adolescents to behave independently or make decisions; they receive little instruction from their supervisors, and they are rarely required to use the skills they have been taught in school (Greenberger & Steinberg, 1986). With occasional exceptions, most teenagers' jobs are repetitive, monotonous, and intellectually unstimulating. Some are even highly stressful, requiring that youngsters work under intense time pressure without much letup and exposing them to potential injury and accidents (National Research Council, 1998). Not all jobs are this tedious or dangerous, of course, and some researchers have argued that adolescents in better jobs—jobs in which they can learn genuinely useful skills, for example—benefit from employment as a result (Mortimer, Pimentel, Ryu, Nash, & Lee, 1996;

Schulenberg & Bachman, 1993). While this may be true, the fact is that the proportion of adolescents who hold good jobs—jobs in which there is ample opportunity to learn new or higher-level skills—is quite small.

FOOD FOR THOUGHT

Think back to your own work experiences as an adolescent, either during the summer or the school year. What were the best jobs you had? Which ones were the worst? Why?

It is important to note, however, that this characterization of adolescents' jobs as dreary is not something that teenagers themselves report. Indeed, the majority of adolescent workers describe their jobs in favorable terms, saying that they learned things, liked the people with whom they worked, had opportunities to exercise responsibility, and were satisfied with their pay. As Jeylan Mortimer, one of the leading researchers in this area, noted, "[T]here is cause for concern for the minority of youth who find their jobs completely lacking in learning opportunities or chances to be helpful to others. . . . Still, it is remarkable, given the widespread characterization of the jobs available to young people as menial or 'bad' jobs, how positive young workers are when asked to comment on the qualities of their work" (Mortimer, 2003, p. 67).

The contrast between adults' conceptions of adolescents' work environments and teenagers' own descriptions of their experiences is noteworthy. Perhaps compared to school, which as you saw in the previous chapter is a context in which adolescents are frequently bored and seldom challenged, even the jobs that adults consider menial are comparatively satisfying. And perhaps there is something about earning money and having some responsibility, regardless of how modest, that makes adolescents feel better about themselves and translates into a positive description of their work experience.

EMPLOYMENT AND ADOLESCENT DEVELOPMENT

The impact of employment in the psychological development of adolescents has been the focus of numerous studies (Staff et al., 2004). Three broad questions have been asked in this research: whether working helps adolescents develop a sense of responsibility and prepares them for the transition to adulthood, whether working interferes with other activities, such as school, and whether working promotes the development of negative behaviors, such as drug and alcohol use. As you will read, the answer to the question of how adolescents are affected by working depends on many factors, including the nature of the job, the number of hours worked each week, and the aspect of development studied.

▍ **The Development of Responsibility** Most people believe that working builds character, teaches adolescents about the real world, and helps them prepare for adulthood, but these assumptions are not generally supported by research. Indeed, studies indicate that the benefits of working during adolescence have probably been overstated and that intensive employment during the school year may even negatively affect young people's development and preparation for adult work.

Studies of contemporary youth, for example, generally do not support the view that holding a job makes adolescents become more personally responsible (Mortimer & Johnson, 1998; Steinberg et al., 1993; Wright, Cullen, & Williams, 1997). Although working may help adolescents become more responsible when their work makes a genuine contribution to their family's welfare (Elder, 1974), this condition does not characterize the situation of most contemporary middle-class adolescents, who work mainly to earn spending money.

Moreover, adolescents who have jobs often express cynical attitudes toward work and endorse unethical business practices, two aspects of "character building" that few adults would be pleased with. For example, workers are more likely than nonworkers to agree with such statements as "People who work harder at their jobs than they have to are a little crazy" and "In my opinion, it's all right for workers who are paid a low salary to take little things" (Steinberg, Greenberger, Garduque, Ruggiero, & Vaux, 1982). One study found high rates of misconduct among adolescent workers (for example, stealing from employers, lying about the number of hours worked), even in the early months of their first jobs (Ruggiero, Greenberger, & Steinberg, 1982). And adolescents who work long hours (20-plus hours weekly) are less satisfied with their lives than are adolescents who work fewer hours (Fine, Mortimer, & Roberts, 1990). In smaller doses (less than 20 hours per week), however, working does not seem to have any effect, either positive or negative, on adolescents' psychological development (Staff et al., 2004).

What can we make of these findings? Why would working long hours make youngsters more cynical about work and less satisfied with their lives? Perhaps

Few adolescents who work save a large percentage of their earnings for their future education, and fewer still use their income to help their family with household expenses. Most working teenagers spend most of their earnings on clothing, cars, entertainment, and food.

the answer has something to do with the nature of the work most adolescents perform. Think for a moment about the job environment of most teenagers—or perhaps even the environment you worked in as a teenager if you had a job. As you read earlier, the work generally is dull and monotonous, and sometimes stressful. Even if you have never worked in such a job, you can certainly imagine how working under these conditions might make people feel cynical and protective of their own interests.

As is the case with research on adolescents' work environments, however, studies that ask adolescents directly whether working has helped them become more responsible suggest that adolescents' own perceptions of how work has affected them differ from what objective assessments indicate (Mortimer, 2003). Many individuals say that their jobs as teenagers helped them learn things like punctuality or ways to deal effectively with strangers. Here's how one young adult put it, looking back: "It taught me a lot about

responsibility, I mean I had to be there on time. If there was a shift or a time that I couldn't work, I was responsible for making sure that it got covered" (Mortimer, 2003, p. 152).

We should not be surprised at discrepancies between what people say about an experience (as when people are interviewed about what they got out of their adolescent jobs) and what researchers conclude from objective assessments (as when adolescents fill out standardized questionnaires measuring their sense of responsibility), nor should we assume that the objective assessments are wrong simply because they differ from people's subjective appraisals. For one thing, people aren't always accurate in how they account for their own development; an adolescent may have become more responsible while working during high school and may attribute this to her job experience, but it could easily be that she would have become more responsible anyway, just as a result of growing older. In addition, when people are asked to recall earlier experiences, they are often selective in what they remember. Most studies of human behavior find that subjective reports and objective assessments are only modestly correlated (for instance, it is possible for you to believe that you have learned a great deal from a course but perform poorly on a test of what the course covered), and most social scientists believe that objective and subjective measures provide different, but nevertheless valid, information.

One specific aspect of responsibility that working is believed to affect is money management. Because the average working teenager earns around $400 per month, holding a job may provide many opportunities for learning how to budget, save, and spend money responsibly. Although about half of all adolescents are given an allowance by their parents (most often, these are younger adolescents who are not employed), parents exert more control over purchases made from allowances than they do over purchases made from job earnings (Greenberger & Steinberg, 1986; Miller & Yung, 1990).

Research indicates, however, that few teenagers exercise a great deal of responsibility when it comes to managing their earnings. The majority of working teenagers spend most of their wages on their own needs and activities (Steinberg et al., 1993). Few adolescents who work save a large percentage of their income for their education, and fewer still use their earnings to help their families with household expenses. Instead, the picture of the contemporary working teenager that emerges from these studies is one of self-indulgent materialism. Wages are spent on designer clothing, expensive stereo equipment, movies, and eating out (Steinberg et al., 1993). And a fair proportion of the earnings are spent on drugs and alcohol (Greenberger & Steinberg, 1986). According to one social scientist, many working teenagers may suffer from **premature affluence**—"affluence because [$400] or more per month represents a lot of 'spending money' for a high school student, and premature because many of these individuals will not be able to sustain that level of discretionary spending once they take on the burden of paying for their own necessities" (Bachman, 1983, p. 65).

What might be some of the effects of premature affluence? These might include increased cynicism about the value of hard work and a lack of interest in working harder than is absolutely necessary, increased interest in buying drugs and alcohol, and a tendency to develop more materialistic attitudes (Greenberger & Steinberg, 1986; Mihalic & Elliott, 1997). Importantly, adolescents who have earned (and spent) a lot from their jobs are less satisfied with their financial situations as young adults, probably because they had become accustomed to living in an unrealistic world, one in which they had a large amount of discretionary income and few financial obligations (Bachman, 1983). Ironically, the very experience that many adults believe builds character may, in reality, teach adolescents undesirable lessons about work and the meaning of money.

Perhaps the most reasonable conclusion we can draw about the impact of working on the development of responsibility is that it depends largely on the nature of the job (Mortimer, 2003). In jobs in which adolescents are given genuine responsibility, make important decisions, and perform challenging tasks, they are more likely to come away feeling more mature, competent, and dependable. In jobs in which the work is repetitive, stressful, or unchallenging, however, adolescents may well be harmed by the experience (Greenberger, Steinberg, & Vaux, 1981; Mortimer, 2003). Along similar lines, adolescents who work in a family business may be affected differently than those who work in a different context (Hansen & Jarvis, 2000). Thus, while it is *possible* for an adolescent to benefit psychologically from working, it is not *probable*, given the nature of most adolescents' jobs.

The Impact on Schooling A second question that has received a fair amount of research attention concerns the impact of working on adolescents' involvement in other activities, most notably, schooling. Here, studies indicate that the issue is not whether a teenager works, but how much (Staff et al., 2004).

Many experts now believe that working more than 20 hours a week may jeopardize adolescents' school performance and engagement (National Research Council, 1998). Youngsters who work long hours are absent from school more often, are less likely to

Participation in extracurricular activities, such as performing in a school musical, is less common among students who work long hours at a part-time job.

participate in extracurricular activities, report enjoying school less, spend less time on their homework, and earn lower grades. These results occur both because youngsters who are less interested in school choose to work longer hours and because working long hours leads to disengagement from school (Mihalic & Elliott, 1997; Safron, Sy, & Schulenberg, 2003; Schoenhals, Tienda, & Schneider, 1998; Warren, 2002). There is no evidence that summer employment, even for long hours, affects school performance, however, suggesting that the negative impact of working on school performance may be due to the time demands of having a job while going to school (Oettinger, 1999).

Working long hours also seems to lead to increased absenteeism and decreased time spent on homework and other school activities. In addition, intensive involvement in a part-time job early in a student's education—during the sophomore year in high school, for example—may actually increase the likelihood of dropping out of school, although this does not seem to be true among students in informal jobs, like babysitting or yard work (Carr et al., 1996; Damico, 1984; McNeal, 1997). Students who work a good deal have less ambitious plans for further education while in high school, and they complete fewer years of college (Marsh et al., 2005; Mortimer & Finch, 1986), due in part to the fact that students with low aspirations for the future choose to work longer hours than their peers (Safron et al., 2003).

premature affluence Having more income than one can manage maturely, especially during adolescence.

Although the impact of working on students' actual grades and achievement test scores is small (Barton, 1989), several studies indicate that extensive employment during the school year may take its toll on students in ways that are not revealed by looking only at grade point averages. Students who work a great deal, for example, report paying less attention in class, exerting less effort on their studies, and skipping class more frequently (Steinberg & Dornbusch, 1991). Additionally, when students work a great deal, they often develop strategies for protecting their grades. These strategies include taking easier courses, cutting corners on homework assignments, copying homework from friends, and cheating (Greenberger & Steinberg, 1986; McNeil, 1984; Steinberg & Dornbusch, 1991). Teachers express concern about the excessive involvement of students in after-school jobs (Bills, Helms, & Ozcan, 1995), and some teachers may respond to an influx of students into the workplace by lowering classroom expectations, assigning less homework, and using class time for students to complete assignments that otherwise would be done outside of school (Bills et al., 1995; McNeil, 1984). As a consequence, when large numbers of students in a school are employed, even nonworkers' schooling may be affected.

■ **The Promotion of Problem Behavior**   Some studies have examined the time-honored belief that having a job deters youngsters from delinquent and criminal activity—that keeping teenagers busy with work will keep them out of trouble. Contrary to popular belief, however, employment during adolescence does not deter delinquent activity (Steinberg & Cauffman, 1995). Indeed, several studies suggest that working long hours may actually be associated with *increases* in aggression, school misconduct, precocious sexual activity, and minor delinquency, including engaging in petty theft, joyriding, carrying a weapon, and buying stolen goods (Gottfredson, 1985; Rich & Kim, 2002; Wright et al., 1997). However, at least one study reports that the higher rate of problem behavior among working adolescents is due to the fact that delinquent youth are simply more likely to choose to work long hours than their peers (Paternoster, Bushway, Brame, & Apel, 2003).

Many studies also have found that rates of smoking, drinking, and drug use are higher among teenage workers than nonworkers, especially among students who work long hours (Bachman & Schulenberg, 1993; Mihalic & Elliott, 1997; Mortimer & Johnson, 1998; Steinberg et al., 1993; Wu, Schlenger, & Galvin, 2003). Although some writers have proposed that adolescents who are already inclined toward smoking or using drugs and alcohol are more likely to choose to work long hours (e.g., Bachman & Schulenberg, 1993), recent analyses suggest that alcohol and drug use both

leads to and follows from intensive employment. That is, students who use alcohol and other drugs are more likely to want to work long hours, but increases in work hours tend to lead to increases in cigarette, drug, and alcohol use (Mortimer et al., 1993; Paschall, Flewelling, & Russell, 2004; Safron et al., 2003; Steinberg et al., 1993).

A variety of explanations have been proposed for the connection between working and smoking, drinking, and using drugs. The impact of extensive employment on adolescent drug and alcohol use probably reflects the fact that adolescents who work long hours have more discretionary income and, hence, greater opportunity to purchase drugs and alcohol. In addition, drug and alcohol use are more common among adolescents who work under conditions of high job stress than among their peers who work for comparable amounts of time and money but under less stressful conditions—and many adolescents work in stressful work settings, like fast-food restaurants (Greenberger et al., 1981). It may also be the case that when adolescents work long hours, this disrupts their relationship with their parents, which, in turn, is associated with problem behavior (Roisman, 2002; Steinberg et al., 1993). Whatever the reason, the impact of school-year employment on drug and alcohol use persists over time; individuals who worked long hours as teenagers drink and use drugs more in their late 20s than their peers who worked less or not at all (Mihalic & Elliott, 1997). About the only positive thing we can say about job stress in adolescence is that it may help individuals cope better with job stress in young adulthood (Mortimer & Staff, 2004).

One point of debate among researchers who study adolescent employment concerns the differential impact of working on middle-class versus poor youth. Some researchers have found that working, even in the sorts of minimum-wage jobs available to teenagers, may not lead to increased problem behavior and, in fact, may have benefits for inner-city adolescents from poor families (Leventhal, Graber, & Brooks-Gunn, 2001; Newman, 1999; Sullivan, 1989). However, working during junior high school or the early high school years (as opposed to later in high school) may increase the chances of poor minority youth dropping out of school and engaging in problem behavior (Entwisle, Alexander, & Olson, 2005; Olatunji, 2005; Roche, Ensminger, Chilcoat, & Storr, 2003). Why might this be? One possibility is that working in early adolescence may make school seem less important, whereas working in later adolescence, when making the transition to adult work roles is more salient, may make school seem more so.

In sum, although teenagers generally enjoy working, there is little evidence that doing so contributes in significant ways to their psychosocial development, and some evidence that the psychological costs of working may outweigh the benefits. Studies of work and adolescent development point to a complicated pattern of cause and effect that unfolds over time. In general, adolescents who are less attached and committed to school, and who are more involved in problem behavior, are more likely to choose to work long hours. Working long hours, in turn, leads to more disengagement from school and increased problem behavior. In other words, intensive employment during the school year most threatens the school performance and psychological well-being of those students who can least afford to suffer the consequences of overcommitment to a job.

FOOD FOR THOUGHT

How do you reconcile findings from research on the impact of adolescent employment, which do not indicate many positive effects on psychological development, and the reports of teenagers, who say they have benefited from their jobs?

YOUTH UNEMPLOYMENT

Although the employment of teenagers has become commonplace in contemporary America, some young people who wish to work are unable to find jobs. In general, however, youth unemployment is not very widespread, once the proportion of young people who are in school is taken into account. According to the U.S. Census Bureau (2005), in 2004, for example, 55 percent of all 16- to 24-year-olds were enrolled in school (either in high school or college); of the remaining 45 percent who were not in school, more than 70 percent were employed. Overall, then, only a small percentage of 16- to 24-year-olds—about 14 percent—are neither in school nor employed, and many of these are young parents who are at home full-time and not actively seeking work. Only 4 percent of young people are not enrolled in school, unemployed, and actively looking for work. Moreover, young people who are out of school and out of work are typically unemployed for only short periods of time. The majority of unemployed youth are high school dropouts. Although high school dropouts constitute only about 14 percent of the population of 18- to 21-year-olds, they account for about half of the unemployed people in this age bracket.

Minority youth are far more likely to experience unemployment than are white youth. Among the reasons for this are the relatively higher proportion of minority youth who drop out of high school or college (as you will read in Chapter 12, dropout rates are especially high among Hispanic American youth) and the relatively lower proportion of minority high school graduates who attend college. In 2003, for example, a little more than half of all whites and about half of all African Americans ages 18–21 were in school, compared with about 40 percent of Hispanic American youth (U.S. Bureau of the Census, 2004). And, whereas only 6 percent of white 16- to 19-year-olds were both out of school and out of work in 2004, nearly twice the percentage of African American and Hispanic American youth were (Federal Interagency Forum on Child and Family Statistics, 2006).

Most studies show that unemployment during adolescence and young adulthood results primarily from a combination of economic and social factors, rather than from a lack of motivation on the part of unemployed individuals (Freeman & Wise, 1982). Perhaps more importantly, the consequences of unemployment during adolescence and young adulthood appear to be worse in the short term than in the long run. Most people who have been unemployed as teenagers are eventually able to secure stable full-time employment. Youth unemployment is a problem among individuals not in school mostly because it is associated with higher rates of crime, drug abuse, and violence (Freeman & Wise, 1982).

Many different approaches have been taken over the years in trying to solve the youth unemployment problem. One set of proposals concerns the nearly one-third of all adolescents who do not go on to college. As noted in this chapter and in Chapter 6, American secondary schools do little to prepare non-college-bound youngsters for the world of work. These youngsters, of course, are far more likely to experience unemployment during their late adolescent years. Many experts therefore believe that the youth unemployment problem is attributable mainly to the lack of clear linkages between school and work. They point out that there are so many "cracks" in the transition from school to work that it is easy for students who are not in school to fall into periods of unemployment.

Several suggestions have been made to combat this problem (Rosenbaum, 1996). Many commentators have argued that expanding opportunities for **community service** will help integrate adolescents into the community, enhance their feelings of confidence and responsibility, and put them in contact with adult role models. Studies of **service learning**—nonpaid

community service   The involvement of young people in activities that serve some social or economic need of society.

service learning   Structured educational experiences that involve volunteering in the community.

programs, sometimes connected with school, that place adolescents in volunteer positions in the community—indicate that some volunteer experiences may enhance adolescents' self-esteem and feelings of efficacy, impart academic and career skills, enhance community involvement, improve mental health, and deter problem behavior. These positive results are most likely to occur in programs in which adolescents have good relationships with their supervisors, are given sufficient autonomy, are psychologically engaged in the activity, and have adequate time to reflect on and learn from their experience (Hansen, Larson, & Dworkin, 2003; McGuire & Gamble, 2006; Scales, Blyth, Berkas, & Kielsmeier, 2000; Stukas, Clary, & Snyder, 1999).

A second suggestion is that communities improve their employment and counseling services for young people and strengthen youth organizations. In Europe, for example, local communities provide much better employment services for youth—including job placement—than is the case in the United States. Such community programs might also help with career and college counseling, summer employment, and placement in volunteer activities. In most American high schools, guidance counselors are so busy counseling students for college that they rarely pay attention to the non-college-bound population.

Finally, it has been proposed that American schools experiment with apprenticeship programs modeled after those found in Europe (Hamilton & Hamilton, 2004). These programs would introduce young people to the world of work early in high school and would gradually move them from full-time school, into a mixture of school and work, and finally into full-time employment. Instead of working in the dead-end jobs of the adolescent workplace, teenagers would combine schooling and on-the-job training with employers likely to offer them full-time, career-oriented jobs after graduation. However, although these programs have been successful abroad, many scholars have questioned whether they can be successfully imported to the United States (Kantor, 1994).

What about the substantial proportion of adolescents who do not graduate from high school, who are at the greatest risk of experiencing unemployment? To date, many different types of interventions have been tried, but few have succeeded (Smith, 1993). Despite some 30 years of government programs designed to train unemployed youth and place them in the labor force, most evaluations of these efforts find that high school dropouts who participate in such programs are no more likely to find full-time employment than are dropouts who do not participate in the programs (Foster, 1995). This is quite disconcerting, since the programs that have been evaluated have tried a wide array of approaches,

including work experience, job training, job placement, and instruction in labor market skills (such as interviewing and job seeking). In light of this evidence, most experts believe that efforts should be redirected away from providing work experience programs and toward helping youngsters who are at risk for dropping out of school stay in school and graduate (Foster, 1995; Kantor, 1994).

RECAP

- The student-worker emerged in the United States during the second half of the twentieth century, as the need for cheap, part-time labor in the service and retail industries grew. Today, the majority of American teenagers hold part-time jobs during the school year, and many work more than 15–20 hours weekly.
- Part-time work during the school year is much less common in other parts of the world. In most other countries, students do not combine school and work, except in apprenticeship programs designed to help them find career-related jobs after they finish high school.
- Most employed U.S. adolescents work in retail jobs or in restaurants. Although observational studies suggest that the work they do is highly routine and uninteresting, adolescents' own descriptions of their jobs are generally favorable.
- The impact of work on adolescent development depends on the nature of the job and the number of hours worked each week. Working generally has few effects on adolescents' psychological development, but working long hours may increase rates of delinquency and drug and alcohol use, and take a toll on schooling.
- Many social commentators have worried about the high rate of youth unemployment, especially among poor, minority youth. Among the suggestions offered for combating youth unemployment are increasing adolescents' opportunities to perform community service, strengthening counseling and career services for high school students, encouraging the development of apprenticeship programs like those found in Europe, and, above all, encouraging all adolescents to complete high school.

Adolescents and Leisure

The average American middle-class teenager feels bored more then 25 percent of the time, and some complain of boredom more than 50 percent of the time (Larson & Richards, 1991). As one expert noted, "The litany of explanations for this boredom—'algebra sucks,' 'I'm always bored on Sunday,' 'there's nothing to do,' 'the *Odyssey* is boring'—reads like a script from Bart Simpson" (Larson, 2000, p. 170). Boredom is much more commonly reported by relatively more affluent students—in one study, more than one-third of the middle-class respondents were chronically bored, compared with only one-tenth of the students from poor families (Hunter & Csikszentmihalyi, 2003).

One context in which boredom is seldom reported by teenagers is leisure. In some regards, this is good news, because young people in the United States and other Western countries spend nearly half their waking hours in leisure activities (Mahoney, Larson, Eccles, & Lord, 2005). As noted earlier, leisure occupies more of the typical adolescent's waking hours than do school and work combined (Larson, 2000). Leisure activities include socializing with friends, playing sports and games, watching television and listening to music, surfing the Internet, playing video games, practicing a musical instrument, shopping, working on hobbies, hanging out with friends, and just plain "chilling."

One important difference between leisure and other activities is that adolescents choose their leisure activities, whereas their time at school and work is dictated by others (teachers, supervisors, etc.). Perhaps as a consequence, and not surprisingly, studies show that adolescents report being in a better mood during leisure activities than during school or work (Csikszentmihalyi & Larson, 1984). Leisure activities that are both structured and voluntary—such as sports, hobbies, artistic activities, and clubs—seem to provide special psychological benefits (Larson, 2000).

ADOLESCENTS' FREE TIME AND THEIR MOODS

Studying adolescents' moods through the conventional methodologies of observational or questionnaire research is difficult. Questions concerning adolescents' emotional states, for instance, are especially tricky, because individuals' emotions change during the day and may not be, at the time of a researcher's assessment, reflective of their moods at other points in the day. Suppose a researcher wanted to know how adolescents' moods were affected by various activities—such as attending school, watching television, or having dinner with the family. Although it would be possible to interview respondents and ask them to recall their moods at different points in the day, we cannot be sure whether their recollections would be entirely accurate.

■ **The Experience Sampling Method** One of the most interesting innovations in the contemporary study of adolescence was designed to overcome this and other sorts of methodological problems. Using a technique called the **experience sampling method (ESM)**, researchers can collect much more detailed information about adolescents' experiences over the course of the day, and thereby illuminate many different aspects of the adolescent experience. The ESM has been used to chart adolescents' moods, to monitor their social relationships, and to catalogue their activities in far greater detail than has been previously available.

The use of the ESM in the study of adolescent development was pioneered by psychologist Reed Larson and colleagues (Larson & Lampman-Petraitis, 1989; Larson & Richards, 1991). In studies using this method, adolescents carry electronic pagers and, when they are signaled, report on whom they are with, what they are doing, and how they are feeling (Larson & Richards, 1991); in the early days of ESM, adolescents filled out written questionnaires every time they were "beeped." Today, many researchers give adolescents personal digital assistants (PDAs), which can be programmed to allow the youngster to input data directly into the device every time he or she is signaled.

In one early ESM study, Larson had nearly 500 adolescents ages 9–15 carry pagers and booklets of self-report forms for one week, and asked them to fill out a form each time they were signaled. The form contained a series of questions about companionship ("Who were you with [or talking to on the phone]?"), location ("Where were you?"), activity ("What were you doing?"), and mood (the adolescents used a checklist to report their feelings). The adolescents were beeped seven times each day, once within every two-hour block between 7:30 A.M. and 9:30 P.M. By examining the adolescents' many reports, the researchers were able to chart changes in activities, companionship, and mood over the course of the week and to relate variations in activity, companionship, and mood to one another. Thus, the method permitted the researchers to ask how activities, companionship, and mood varied as a function of age; how mood varied as a function of what the adolescent was doing; and how both activity and mood varied as a function of whom the adolescent was with. One of the questions asked was how adolescents' moods varied as a function of whom they were with (parents, peers, or no one) and

experience sampling method (ESM) A method of collecting data about adolescents' emotional states, in which individuals are paged and asked to report on their mood and activity.

FIGURE 7.4 Average affect reported by girls and boys at different ages when alone, with friends, and with family.
(Larson & Richards, 1991)

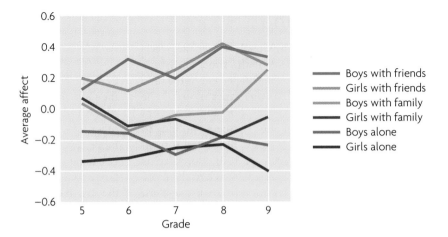

whether the connection between mood and companionship changed with age. The results are presented in Figure 7.4

As you can see, adolescents' moods are generally most positive when they are with their friends and least positive when they are alone; their moods when with their family fall somewhere in between. More interesting, perhaps, is that between grades 5 and 9, adolescents' moods while with friends become more positive, whereas their moods while with their family follow a **curvilinear pattern** (a curvilinear pattern can either can be U-shaped or can look like an inverted U). That is, their moods while with their family become more negative between elementary and middle school (between grades 5 and 7) and then rise between middle school and high school (between grades 8 and 9). As Larson and Richards point out, this dip parallels findings from other research on family relations (see Chapter 4) that point to early adolescence as a time of heightened strain in the parent–child relationship.

▌ **Solitude** The data on adolescents' moods when they were alone are somewhat surprising. Given the fact that adolescents spend increasingly more time alone as they get older, you might expect that solitude would be associated with more positive—not more negative—affect. Although the researchers could not explain this finding easily, one hypothesis is that, when alone, adolescents spend a good deal of time thinking about themselves and working through the events of the day (Larson, 1990). Some of the time spent alone is spent listening to music, and some of the music adolescents listen to may have sad or depressing themes (unrequited love, broken relationships, etc.). Interestingly, other studies using the ESM (e.g., Csikszentmihalyi & Larson,

1984) have found that adolescents feel better after being alone and that, with age, solitude tends to become associated with more positive feelings (Larson, 1990, 1997). Together, these findings suggest that periods of solitude may be associated with negative mood in the short term but with positive mood in the long term.

Adolescents' moods are strongly influenced by where they are and whom they are with. As Figure 7.5 indicates, when adolescents are in school, they report moderate levels of concentration but very low levels of motivation or interest in what they are doing, consistent with other studies indicating that most American teenagers do not find high school engaging (e.g., Steinberg et al., 1996). When they are with friends, teenagers report moderate levels of motivation and interest but low levels of concentration. It is only when adolescents are playing sports or involved in the arts, a hobby, or an extracurricular organization that they report high levels of both concentration and interest. While they are in unstructured leisure activities, like watching TV, adolescents tend to show the same pattern of moderate interest but low concentration as when they are socializing with friends. Moreover, participation in structured extracurricular activities, such as hobbies or sports, has been shown to be the most positive way for adolescents to spend free time, in terms of their current and future psychological development (McHale, Crouter, & Tucker, 2001; Zaff, Moore, Papillo, & Williams, 2003).

STRUCTURED LEISURE ACTIVITIES

For many adolescents around the world, school-sponsored extracurricular activities provide the context for much of their leisure activity (Stevenson, 1994). According to recent surveys, about two-thirds of American high school students participate in one or more extracurricular activities, although the participation rate varies greatly from school to school.

curvilinear pattern In statistical analyses, a pattern of relations between two variables that resembles a U-shaped or an inverted U-shaped curve.

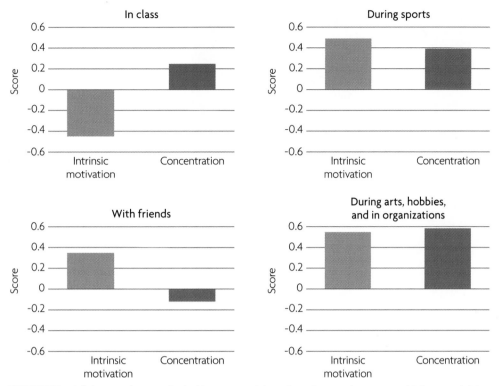

FIGURE 7.5　Adolescents' state of mind is more positive when they are in structured leisure activities than when they are in class or with friends. (Larson, 2000)

The most popular extracurricular activity in the United States is athletics, in which about half of all adolescents participate. The other two main activities in which many adolescents participate are those related to music (such as band, chorus, orchestra, or glee club; about one-fifth of all adolescent students participate in these) and those related to academic or occupational interests (such as science clubs, language clubs, or clubs oriented toward certain careers; about one-fifth participate in these). The average American high school sophomore spends about five hours each week in extracurricular activities—about twice as much time as reading for pleasure and the same amount of time as doing homework, but only one-third as much time as working for pay (National Center for Education Statistics, 2002).

Participation in extracurricular activities is influenced by a number of factors. In general, participation is somewhat more prevalent among adolescents from middle-class families, among students who earn better grades, and among students from smaller schools and smaller, more rural communities, where school activities often play a relatively more central role in the lives of adults and adolescents alike (for example, where an entire community may turn out for a school's Friday night football or basketball game). Whereas boys are more likely than girls to participate in athletic

activities, the reverse is true for nonathletic activities (Berk, 1992). Adolescents whose parents are themselves involved in the community or who reinforce their children's interests are also more likely to participate (Fletcher, Elder, & Mekos, 2000; Huebner & Mancini, 2003).

■ **The Impact of Extracurricular Participation on Development**　Researchers have spent considerable time studying the impact of extracurricular participation on adolescent development, but it has been difficult to draw any firm conclusions, because few studies separate cause and effect. For example, although researchers generally find that participants have higher self-esteem than nonparticipants, it isn't clear whether students with high self-esteem are more likely to go out for extracurricular activities to begin with, whether participation makes students feel better about themselves, or whether some other factor, like having positive family relationships, is associated both with extracurricular participation and with better mental health (Gore, Farrell, & Gordon, 2001; Markstrom, Li, Blackshire, & Wilfong, 2005; Spreitzer, 1994). However, the few studies that have tried to get at cause and effect by tracking students over time suggest that participation in an extracurricular activity—especially athletics or the arts—seems to improve students'

Participation in extracurricular activities may lead to increased academic achievement, better adjustment, and less problem behavior. One exception is participation in sports, which may increase alcohol consumption.

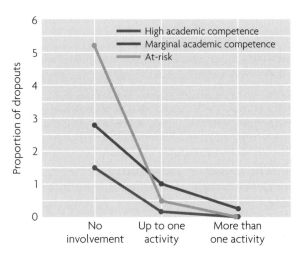

FIGURE 7.6   Participation in athletic extracurricular activities benefits less competent students more than their academically talented counterparts. (McNeal, 1995)

performance in school and reduce the likelihood of dropping out; to deter delinquency, drug use, and other types of risk taking; and to enhance students' psychological well-being and social status (Broh, 2002; Eder & Kinney, 1995; Guest & Schneider, 2003; Mahoney & Cairns, 1997; Savage & Holcomb, 1999). The one exception to this uniformly positive picture is involvement in team sports, which is associated

with an increase in alcohol use, especially among boys who participate in school-sponsored, male-dominated sports, like football or wrestling (Eccles & Barber, 1999; Moore & Werch, 2005; Savage & Holcomb, 1999). Participation in extracurricular activities is especially beneficial among adolescents whose network of friends also participates in the same activity, an indicator, perhaps, of membership in a peer group involved in prosocial activities that revolve around the school (Mahoney, 2000).

As Figure 7.6 illustrates, a positive link between athletic participation and academic performance—a so-called spillover effect—is found mainly among adolescents who are poorer students and in schools in poor communities (Guest & Schneider, 2003; Mahoney & Cairns, 1997). This is not the case for other types of extracurricular participation, which have similar effects across different types of students and schools. Extracurricular activities also may provide greater opportunities for cross-racial friendship than does the regular school day, and African American adolescents in integrated schools who participate in extracurricular activities show better mental health as a result. Extracurricular participation in high school also seems to be linked to extracurricular participation in college and to community involvement in adulthood—just as youngsters who are involved in extracurricular activities as ninth-graders are likely to be similarly busy throughout high school, "do-ers" as adolescents tend to remain so in young and middle adulthood. Along similar lines, individuals who participate in sports during adolescence are likely to continue athletic activities in adulthood (Perkins, Jacobs, Barber, & Eccles, 2003).

Researchers speculate that the generally positive impact of extracurricular participation is because these activities increase students' contact with teachers and other school personnel who may reinforce the value of school (as when a coach or advisor counsels a student about plans for college), and because participation itself may improve students' self-confidence and self-esteem. Some educators believe that extracurricular participation also helps bond students and parents to their school, especially in the case of adolescents who are not achieving academically; for many of them, their extracurricular activity is what keeps them coming to school each day (Berk, 1992; Broh, 2002; Mahoney & Cairns, 1997; Marsh & Kleitman, 2002).

Several serious cautions have been raised about adolescents' participation in athletics, however. As extracurricular sports have become more competitive, the number of young people injured during these activities has risen substantially. According to some estimates, around 25 percent of all adolescent athletes are injured while playing organized sports (Over-baugh & Allen, 1994). There is a clear need for more rigorous injury prevention education among athletes, coaches, and parents (Dalton, 1992). In addition, many adolescents feel anxious and tense within the competitive atmosphere that has come to dominate after-school sports in many communities. Thus, while competitive athletics are a source of consider-able pleasure for some adolescents, they are a source of equally considerable stress for others (Scanlan, Babkes, & Scanlan, 2005).

FOOD FOR THOUGHT

Why are the apparent effects of participation in extracurricular activities different from those associated with part-time employment? How might these two sets of experiences differ?

■ Sex Roles and Extracurricular Activities

Many leisure activities—especially those organized and controlled by adults—are designed to socialize adolescents into adult roles, including, quite often, traditional sex roles. Sociologist Donna Eder (Eder & Kinney, 1995; Eder & Parker, 1987) has studied sex-role socialization in high school extracurricular activities. In an extensive ethnographic study of a secondary school, Eder and colleagues examined how different extracurricular activities were viewed within the school and what values were communicated to adolescents through them.

In the school they studied, as in many others, athletics were the chief route to popularity and status for boys. But which values were communicated through team sports? An analysis of interactions during practice and during other free periods (for example, lunchtime) revealed that the culture of boys' athletics emphasizes achievement, toughness, dominance, and competition—all traits that society has traditionally valued in the socialization of adult males. Consider the following observation taken from the researchers' field notes during football practice:

> A player came up to a coach as practice was just begin-ning and complained that another player was starting a fight with him. The coach seemed aggravated at having to deal with this and told him to "knock his socks off in practice." This player was not particularly satisfied with the suggestion but realized that was all he could get from Coach James. (Eder & Parker, 1987, p. 205)

In contrast, although aggression and competitive-ness were valued within girls' sports, athletics were not a route toward popularity or status for girls in the school, and as a consequence, these traits were less likely to be socialized among girls. For instance, on days when "big" games were to be played by the boys' teams, team members wore their athletic jerseys to school so that they would be recognized by their peers. On days when the girls' teams had "big" games, how-ever, team members did not wear their jerseys. One reason was that being a member of an athletic team actually *detracted* from a girl's popularity (Eder & Kin-ney, 1995).

The main route toward popularity for girls in this school was through cheerleading. Are the traits that were valued in this activity the ones traditionally stressed in the socialization of adult women? Consider the following observation recorded during cheerlead-ing tryouts:

> At one point, Mrs. Tolson started to tell them what they were going to be judged on, saying they would get 10 points (out of 50) for a "sparkle," which was their smile, personality, bubbliness, appearance, attractive-ness—not that all cheerleaders had to be attractive, but it was important to have a clean appearance, not to be sloppy, have messy or greasy hair, because that doesn't look like a cheerleader. (Eder & Parker, 1987, p. 207)

These traits—appearance, neatness, and "bubbli-ness"—are all characteristics traditionally socialized in women. In essence, the popularity accorded male ath-letes rewarded boys for behaving in ways stereotypical for men, while the popularity accorded female cheer-leaders rewarded girls for behaving in ways stereotyp-ical for women.

You may be thinking that this difference in empha-sis makes perfect sense, because football requires aggres-sion and toughness, and cheerleading requires "sparkle." But as the researchers point out, it is "interesting that neatly combed hair was emphasized [in cheerleading tryouts], given the physical nature of this activity, which includes cartwheels and backflips. It is also interesting to compare the focus on neatness during cheerleading with the absence of this concern during male and female athletics" (p. 207). According to these researchers, an important reason for the difference between the emphases of football and cheerleading concerns the function of extracurricular activities in the socialization of male and female sex roles. Along similar lines, male and female athletes are more likely to be admired when they participate in "sex-appropriate" sports (Holland & Andre, 1994).

Interestingly, participation in athletics (until recently, a male-dominated activity) enhances the science achievement of high school girls, whereas participation in cheerleading (still today a female-dominated activity) hampers it. In contrast, boys' science achievement is unaffected by their athletic participation (Hanson & Kraus, 1998). One reason for this pattern of findings may be that female athletes acquire certain traits through athletic participation—independence, competitiveness, and aggression—that help them compete in academic disciplines historically dominated by males. High school boys presumably have many opportunities in addition to sports to develop these characteristics, since these are often socialized in males from an early age.

UNSTRUCTURED LEISURE TIME

One important distinction that is consistent with adults' preconceptions about leisure time and its impact on adolescent development is that between structured leisure activities, like school- or community-sponsored extracurricular activities, which are run and supervised by adults, and unstructured leisure activities, such as hanging out with friends without any organized activity in mind. Whereas participation in structured leisure activities tends to have positive effects on adolescent development, time spent in unstructured leisure activities does the reverse (Osgood, Anderson, & Shaffer, 2005).

■ **Routine Activity Theory** Sociologist Wayne Osgood and colleagues (e.g., Osgood & Anderson, 2004) have argued that the combination of a lack of structure, socializing with peers, and the absence of adult supervision is a recipe for the encouragement of delinquency and other problem behaviors. Their view, called **routine activity theory,** is that "the less structured an activity, the more likely a person is to encounter opportunities for problem behavior in the simple sense that he or she is not occupied doing something else" (Osgood et al., 2005, p. 51). Because most adolescence is a time of heightened peer pressure and heightened susceptibility to peer influence (as you will read in Chapter 9), and because one of the strongest deterrents against problem behavior is the presence of an adult, it is hardly surprising that unstructured peer activity without adult supervision is associated with all sorts of problems—delinquency, drug and alcohol use, and precocious sexual activity.

Even something as positive sounding as attendance at a community recreation center can increase adolescents' problem behavior if their time there is unstructured and minimally supervised (Mahoney & Stattin,

2000; Mahoney, Stattin, & Lord, 2004). Hanging out with friends in the absence of adult supervision at night increases the likelihood of adolescents' engaging in problem behavior substantially; one study found that adolescents who spent five or more evenings out in an average week, for instance, were at least four times more likely than those who went out fewer than twice a week to be involved in antisocial activity (Gage, Overpeck, Nansel, & Kogan, 2005). As one team of writers succinctly put it, "Whether you like or dislike your father, it will be more convenient to smoke marijuana when he isn't around" (Osgood, Wilson, O'Malley, Bachman, & Johnston, 1996, p. 640).

■ **Time After School** One prime time for unstructured and unsupervised leisure is during the afternoon on school days—after school has let out but before parents have returned home from work. The changes in patterns of school, work, and family life discussed in previous chapters have resulted in a large number of young people—somewhere around 8 million school-aged youngsters—who are not supervised by their parents after school. While some of these youngsters are involved in school- or community-based programs that provide adult supervision, others spend their after-school hours away from adults, in their homes, with friends, or simply hanging out in neighborhoods and shopping malls (Carnegie Council on Adolescent Development, 1992). Affluent, suburban, and white children are most likely to be home unsupervised, and poor, minority, and urban and rural children are least likely (U.S. Bureau of the Census, 1994).

Psychologists have debated whether so-called latchkey youth profit from these opportunities for self-management (e.g., Rodman, Pratto, & Nelson, 1988) or potentially are heading for trouble (Richardson et al., 1989, 1993). In general, most studies show that children who care for themselves after school do not differ from their peers when it comes to psychological development, school achievement, and self-conceptions (e.g., Galambos & Garbarino, 1985; Vandell & Corasaniti, 1988). These studies argue against the view that having to care for oneself contributes in positive ways to the development of self-reliance or personal responsibility—findings reminiscent of those reported in studies of part-time employment.

More importantly, perhaps, several studies, including a study of nearly 4,000 youngsters from a variety of ethnic backgrounds (Richardson et al., 1993), suggest that children in self-care are more socially isolated, more depressed, more likely to be involved in problem behavior, more likely to be sexually active at earlier ages, and likely to use more drugs and alcohol than young people who are supervised after school by

routine activity theory A perspective on adolescence that views unstructured, unsupervised time with peers as a main cause of misbehavior.

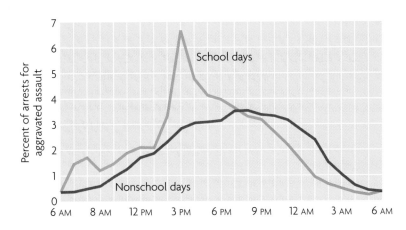

FIGURE 7.7   More arrests occur during school day afternoons than at any other time, presumably because this is the time when adolescents are least likely to be supervised. (Osgood et al., 2005)

adults (Carnegie Council on Adolescent Development, 1992; Cohen, Farley, Taylor, Martin, & Schuster, 2002; Galambos & Maggs, 1991; Richardson et al., 1989, 1993). Together, these studies seem to suggest that latchkey arrangements may have more costs than benefits. As Figure 7.7 indicates, for instance, delinquency is more common on weekday afternoons than at any other time (Osgood et al., 2005).

One limitation of studies of latchkey youth is that they typically lump together all children who take care of themselves after school, even though there are important differences within the latchkey population and among after-school programs (Mahoney et al., 2005). Several studies have shown, for example, that the setting in which adolescents care for themselves makes a difference: Latchkey youngsters who go straight home after school are far less likely to engage in problem behavior than are their peers who go to a friend's house or who just hang out (Galambos & Maggs, 1991; Richardson et al., 1993; Steinberg, 1986). In addition, latchkey youngsters who are raised by authoritative parents and who are monitored by their parents from a distance—via telephone check-ins, for example—are no more susceptible to problem behavior than are children whose parents are home with them after school (Galambos & Maggs, 1991; Steinberg, 1986; Vandell & Ramanan, 1991). As noted earlier, one of the most consistent findings in studies of how adolescents spend their free time is that spending free time with peers in unstructured activities in the absence of adult supervision is associated with increased problem behavior (Mahoney & Stattin, 2002; McHale et al., 2001; Osgood et al., 1996).

Several recent studies indicate that spending time after school with friends in unsupervised settings is more problematic under some circumstances than others. One study found, for example, that it was not simply spending unsupervised time with peers that increased an adolescent's likelihood of alcohol and drug use; it was the combination of lacking supervision,

having friends who liked to party and use drugs, and being especially susceptible to peer pressure that was most damaging (Caldwell & Darling, 1999). A second study found that the harmful effects of low parental monitoring were especially bad in neighborhoods low in collective efficacy, where other adults were unlikely to provide supervision if parents were not around (discussed in Chapter 3) (Coley, Morris, & Hernandez, 2004). In another study, the researchers examined rates of problem behavior among seventh-graders as a function of three factors: whether they spent their after-school time in unsupervised settings, whether they had parents who monitored their activities and whereabouts, and whether they lived in a neighborhood that was considered safe (Pettit, Bates, Dodge, & Meece, 1999). In all groups, being closely monitored by parents was a deterrent against problem behavior. And, not surprisingly, adolescents who reported spending a lot of after-school time with peers in unsupervised settings were more likely to show problem behavior one year later than were other teenagers. But the negative effects of low parental monitoring and unsupervised peer group activity were especially pronounced among teenagers living in unsafe neighborhoods. Indeed, in safe neighborhoods, adolescents who spent time in unsupervised peer activities were not at greater risk for developing problems, even if they were not monitored closely by their parents. This study serves as a reminder of the importance of looking at the broader context in which adolescents live in order to fully understand how they are affected by parents, peers, and other influences.

Taken together, these studies suggest that self-care after school probably does not hold great benefits for youngsters and, under some conditions, may cause problems if adolescents' parents do not promote the development of responsible behavior when they are with their child. What should parents who have no choice but to leave their youngsters in self-care do? Experts advise parents to provide clear instructions

TABLE 7.1   The Five C's of Positive Youth Development

Five C's	Definition
Competence	A positive view of one's actions in domain-specific areas including social, academic, cognitive, and vocational. Social competence pertains to interpersonal skills (e.g., conflict resolution). Cognitive competence pertains to cognitive abilities (e.g., decision making). School grades, attendance, and test scores are part of academic competence. Vocational competence involves work habits and career choice explorations.
Confidence	An internal sense of overall positive self-worth and self-efficacy; one's global self-regard, as opposed to domain-specific beliefs.
Connection	Positive bonds with people and institutions that are reflected in bidirectional exchanges between the individual and peers, family, school, and community in which both parties contribute to the relationship.
Character	Respect for societal and cultural rules, possession of standards for correct behaviors, a sense of right and wrong (morality), and integrity.
Caring/compassion	A sense of sympathy and empathy for others.

Source: Lerner et al., 2005.

about the child's after-school activities and where-abouts, asking the child to check in with an adult as soon as he or she gets home, and teaching the child how to handle emergencies, should they arise (Steinberg & Levine, 1991).

FOOD FOR THOUGHT

Most studies link unstructured leisure time with adolescent problem behavior. But is there no value for adolescents in simply hanging out with friends, without having adults organizing their activities for them? Is all unstructured leisure time bad?

PROMOTING POSITIVE YOUTH DEVELOPMENT

In light of evidence that certain types of extracurricular activities appear to benefit adolescents, and in view of the potential dangers of leaving adolescents unsupervised after school, many experts have called for better and more readily available after-school programming for adolescents. They argue that well-designed programs not only will deter problem behavior by providing adolescents with adult supervision but will promote **positive youth development** (Lerner et al., 2005; Small & Memmo, 2004). Experts' interest in helping young people develop strengths, rather than

simply preventing them from getting into trouble, has burgeoned in recent years. Many models of positive youth development have been proposed, but they generally focus on the same concepts. According to psychologist Richard Lerner, there are five fundamental aspects to positive youth development: competence, confident, connection, character, and caring compassion (see Table 7.1).

These characteristics, in one form or another, are often the focus of contemporary community-based programming for youth, including programs emphasizing community service, volunteer activity, mentoring, and skill building. Although the label "positive youth development" is new, the concept is not. Indeed, the goals espoused by proponents of positive youth development programs today bear a striking resemblance to the stated goals of youth programs that have been around for ages, like the YMCA (founded in London in 1844 and transported to the United States in 1851), the Boys and Girls Clubs of America (with the first club founded in 1860), 4-H clubs (founded at the turn of the twentieth century), and scouting (founded in 1910). Indeed, in 1866, the YMCA of New York City announced that its purpose was "the improvement of the spiritual, mental, social and physical condition of young men" (YMCA, 2006).

RECAP

- In most industrialized countries, leisure occupies more time in adolescence than do school and work combined.
- It is important to distinguish between participation in structured leisure activities, such as organized extracurricular activities, and unstructured leisure, such as hanging out with friends.

positive youth development   The goal of programs designed to facilitate healthy psychosocial development and not simply to deter problematic development.

- Adolescents' moods are better when they are engaged in structured leisure activities than at any other time. In addition, participation in school-sponsored extracurricular activities may enhance adolescents' well-being and strengthen their attachment to school.
- Having large amounts of unstructured leisure time increases adolescents' risk for engagement in problem behavior. Because many adolescents' parents work, self-care during the after-school hours can be problematic. The greatest risk for problem behavior after school is found among teenagers who live in unsafe neighborhoods, spend a lot of time in unsupervised activity with peers, and are poorly monitored by their parents.
- Many experts have called for better and more readily available after-school programming that will not simply deter problem behavior but promote positive youth development.

Adolescents and the Mass Media

PATTERNS OF MEDIA USE

In 2004, a major study on media usage among American children and adolescents was conducted in which a nationally representative sample of more than 2,000 American students were surveyed; a similar survey had been conducted by these researchers in 1999, so it was possible to examine how media usage had changed over the five-year period (Roberts, Foehr, & Rideout, 2005). The findings were staggering in several respects.

▌ **Media Saturation** First, the availability of media in young people's homes was remarkable—as the authors commented, today's adolescents live in a context that is not simply "media-rich" but absolutely "media-saturated." For example, while it is not surprising to learn that 99 percent of all American adolescents live in homes with a television, the survey indicated that the proportion of homes with a VCR or CD player is nearly as high (97 percent and 98 percent, respectively), and the vast majority of teenagers' homes have a video game player (83 percent), cable or satellite TV (82 percent), and a computer (86 percent). As of 2004, three-quarters of all adolescents' homes had Internet access, and the majority of adolescents without home Internet have access to the Internet at school or at friends' houses. With the exceptions of computers and Internet access, very few differences in media availability were found

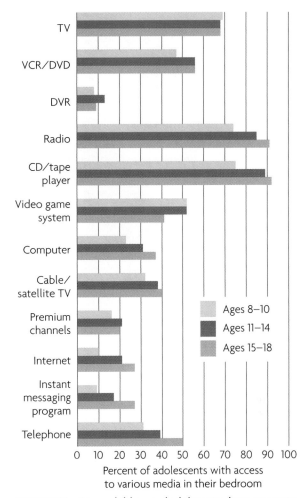

FIGURE 7.8 Many children and adolescents have access to a variety of mass media in their own bedroom. (Roberts et al., 2005)

among adolescents from different social or ethnic backgrounds. As you would expect, computers and Internet access are more common in more affluent homes; even still, 80 percent of all lower-class homes have a computer, and two-thirds have Internet access. There may have been a "digital divide" (different access to computer technology among the social classes) in the 1990s, but it had largely disappeared by 2004.

The majority of adolescents have access to many of these media in their own bedrooms, as Figure 7.8 indicates. Thus, the context in which many adolescents view TV, listen to music, play video games, or surf the Internet is one that makes parental monitoring very difficult. Interestingly, many more parents (61 percent) than teenagers (38 percent) say that their adolescent's Internet usage is monitored (Wang, Bianchi, & Raley, 2005). Whether this is because parents think they know more about their teenagers' Internet usage than they actually do or because teenagers are not aware of the extent to which their parents monitor their Internet usage is not

The average adolescent uses one or more mass media, like television, approximately seven hours each day.

clear, but studies find that adolescents' media usage is lower in households where parents have and enforce rules limiting the amount of time youngsters can spend watching television, playing video games, or using the computer (Roberts et al., 2005).

Second, television in particular is ever-present in adolescents' homes. More than 70 percent of adolescents live in homes with three or more TVs. Two-thirds of adolescents report that the TV is on during meals, and half of all adolescents live in what might be called a "constant television environment," in which the TV remains on throughout the day, regardless of whether anyone is watching it.

Third, adolescents' total media exposure—the amount of time they spend each day using one of the mass media—is extremely high. The average adolescent spends more than six hours each day using one or more media, and this includes time spent using different media simultaneously (that is, where one hour watching TV while surfing the Internet and talking on a cell phone would be recorded as only one hour of media use). Among teenagers, most of this time is spent watching TV or videos (three hours per day), followed by listening to music (about two hours each day). In contrast, reading occupies far less time—less than an hour per day, on average—and fewer than half of all adolescents read more than 30 minutes each day (this includes books, magazines, and newspapers, but not homework).

One of the most significant changes to take place between 1999 and 2004 was in the amount of time adolescents spend each day on the computer—this increased

from 30 minutes per day in 1999 to one hour in 2004 (Roberts et al., 2005). Among high school students, one-third of this time is spent instant messaging, one-fourth playing games, and one-fourth visiting websites. Although adults have become increasingly concerned about teenagers' exposure to chat rooms, the amount of time youngsters actually spend doing this—about three minutes each day—is far less than the amount of time they spend watching TV (three hours daily), listening to music (nearly two hours daily), or talking on the phone (about an hour each day), and only half as much time as they spend each day reading the newspaper—a statistic that would probably surprise most adults. Generally, exposure to video media (TV, VCR, movies, video games) declines as individuals age. Exposure to music media follows the opposite pattern, increasing linearly throughout childhood and adolescence (see Figure 7.9).

The amount of time adolescents spend watching TV and other electronic media is important not only because of the content to which they are exposed but also because the amount of time they spend watching TV and playing video games is inversely linked to the amount of time they spend in physical activity (Motl, McAuley, Birnbaum, & Lytle, 2006). Most experts believe that the high and worrisome rate of obesity among American teenagers is due, in part, to the large amount of time young people spend in sedentary activities, like watching TV, playing video games, and using the computer for recreation. On average, the typical American adolescent spends at least six hours each day sitting in front of one sort of screen or another, but only 90 minutes exercising or playing sports (Roberts et al., 2005). Interestingly, however, adolescents who report wanting to look like celebrities are more physically active than are other media users (Taveras et al., 2004).

▎ **Television Viewing During Adolescence** According to psychologist Reed Larson (1994), one of the reasons that television viewing declines and listening to music increases during adolescence is that TV viewing is far less satisfying to adolescents. TV, he argues, is created by adults for a general audience, while many types of popular music (for example, rap, alternative rock) are created specifically for adolescents. Not surprisingly, studies of teenagers' emotional states indicate that they often feel vacant while watching TV but are more aroused (either positively or negatively) while listening to music (Larson, 1994; Thompson & Larson, 1995). Indeed, nearly two-thirds of high school students say that when

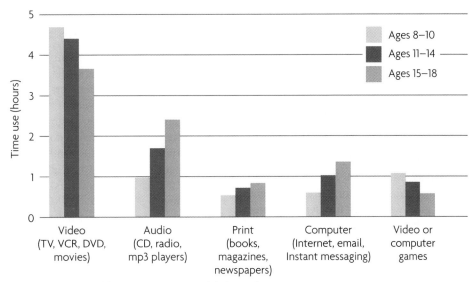

FIGURE 7.9　Age differences in patterns of daily media use. (Adapted from Roberts et al., 2005)

they are watching TV, they are very often just killing time (Roberts & Foehr, 2003).

In addition, Larson finds that TV tends to link adolescents with their families (in part because adolescents, especially young adolescents, often watch TV with other family members), whereas listening to music is often a solitary activity. (Watching TV with parents becomes less frequent during the course of adolescence, however [Roberts & Foehr, 2003].) Indeed, typical teenagers spend 13 percent of their waking hours in their bedroom—second only to their time spent at school—and much of that time is spent listening to music (J. Brown, 1994). Over the course of adolescence, there is a substantial increase in the amount of time adolescents spend alone, although this increase is greater for boys than for girls (Larson & Richards, 1991; Wong & Csikzentmihalyi, 1991; refer back to Figure 5.3). Solitude, with or without music or television in the background, can actually be a positive contributor to adolescents' mental health (Larson, 1995, 1997; Steele & Brown, 1995; Thompson & Larson, 1995).

▌ **Media Content Preferred by Adolescents**
Given the fact that adolescents spend so much time watching television, listening to music, and playing video games, it is reasonable to ask what they are watching, listening to, and playing. The most popular TV shows among teenagers in 2004 were comedies (of the 80 percent of respondents who watched TV on the day prior to the survey, one-third had watched a TV comedy the previous day), followed by movies (23 percent), reality shows (19 percent), entertainment/variety shows (19 percent), dramas (17 percent), and sports (13 percent) (Roberts et al., 2005). Generally, there are few substantial social class or ethnic differences in the types of

shows adolescents watch, although there is one huge sex difference: Boys are four times more likely than girls to watch sports. And, as anyone who has been to a movie theater lately knows, action movies and comedies top the list of teenagers' film preferences.

With respect to music, the 2004 survey found that rap and hip-hop continue to lead the list (listened to by 65 percent of teenagers), followed by alternative rock (32 percent), hard rock/metal (27 percent), ska/punk (23 percent), and country-and-western (18 percent). Ethnic differences in music preferences are not as large as many adults think—rap and hip-hop are the overwhelming choices of youth from all ethnic backgrounds, although some music genres are clearly preferred by some ethnic groups more than by others. For instance, rock music (whether alternative, hard, or soft) is listened to much more often by white teenagers, reggae and R&B by African American teenagers, and salsa and Latin music by Hispanic American teenagers.

Among the most popular websites visited by adolescents in 2006 were so-called social networking sites, such as myspace.com (open to people of all ages, and the most popular website among adolescents) or facebook.com (originally designed for college students, but increasingly used by high school students as well), which permit individuals to create their own web pages with personal information and photographs that can be viewed by others, or sites like xanga.com, which post individuals' "blogs," or on-line journals. These sites have generated a good deal of controversy, however. Despite their popularity with teenagers, some adults have expressed concerns about the fact that strangers who might wish to harm young people, such as sexual predators, could use this publicly posted information to establish relationships and initiate sexual contact with them. According to the Youth Internet Safety Survey, conducted by the U.S. Department of Justice in 2005, about 13 percent of young people received an unwanted sexual solicitation on-line each year (a decline since the previous survey, a few years earlier), and 4 percent reported that the on-line solicitation was followed by an attempt to contact them through some means other than the computer; these attempts were almost never successful, and no one in the survey was actually assaulted (Finkelhor, Mitchell, & Wolak, 2005; Wolak, Mitchell, & Finkelhor, 2006). Most at risk for unwanted solicitation were adolescent high school–aged girls who were frequent Internet users, were often in chat rooms, and reported higher-than-average rates of depression or life stress.

Although adults often express concerns about adolescents' using the Internet to view pornography, much of the pornographic material on the Internet to which adolescents are exposed is unwanted rather than actively sought; in 2005, one-third of all adolescents reported receiving unwanted sexual material, although less than 10 percent of adolescents said that they had received material that upset them (Wolak et al., 2006). Adolescents are far more likely to visit entertainment websites (for example, disneychannel.com) or sports (espn.com) than pornographic ones. Indeed, many of the most popular websites among teenagers are the ones also visited frequently by adults: yahoo (no. 2 among adolescents), google (no. 3), hotmail (no. 4), and ebay (no. 5) (Teen Research Unlimited, 2006).

The frequent use of social networking websites and chat rooms focused on relationships indicates that many teenagers may be using the Internet to get and give advice on a range of personal matters. The extent to which this is helpful (because it allows adolescents to connect with others who have similar concerns) or harmful (because the advice and information provided may be erroneous, misguided, or even dangerous) is not known. Some evidence suggests that adolescents with relatively more psychological problems and poorer family relationships are more likely than their peers to form close on-line relationships, but we do not know whether having on-line relationships leads to or follows from maladjustment (Wolak, Mitchell, & Finkelhor, 2003; Ybarra, Alexander, & Mitchell, 2005). That is, it is quite plausible that adolescents who have problems simply are more likely to seek out relationships with people over the Internet (Gould, Munfakh, Lubell, Kleinman, & Parker, 2002).

cultivation theory   A perspective on media use that emphasizes the impact media exposure have on individuals.

uses and gratification approach   A perspective on media use that emphasizes the active role users play in selecting the media to which they are exposed.

THEORIES OF MEDIA INFLUENCE AND USE

Given the considerable amount of time adolescents spend exposed to the mass media, not surprisingly, the impact of the media on teenagers' behavior and development has been the subject of much debate. Unfortunately, little of the debate is grounded in conclusive scientific research. One tremendous problem in interpreting studies of media use and adolescent development is that it is extremely difficult to disentangle cause and effect, because adolescents choose which mass media they are exposed to (Roberts et al., 2004). Although it has been speculated that violent film images and heavy metal music provoke aggression, for example, it is just as likely, if not more so, that aggressive adolescents are more prone to choose to watch violent images (Arnett, 1996; Roe, 1995). Similarly, sexual behavior may be correlated with listening to "sexy" music, but it is impossible to say which causes which. And, although the major study of media use discussed earlier (Roberts et al., 2005) found that adolescents who listen to a lot of music or play a lot of video games were significantly more troubled (bored, unhappy, in trouble at home or school) than adolescents who used these media less often, it is not known whether large doses of mass media cause problems or, more plausibly, whether adolescents with more problems listen to more music and play more video games, perhaps as a way of distracting themselves from their troubles.

There are three basic schools of thought concerning the media's impact (or lack thereof) on adolescent development. One school of thought argues that adolescents are influenced by the content to which they are exposed, with respect to their knowledge about the world, their attitudes and values, and their behavior. You've no doubt heard contentions like these thousands of times: Playing violent video games makes adolescents aggressive, watching sexy movies makes adolescents sex-crazed, being exposed to Internet pornography affects the ways that adolescents think about gender roles, listening to rap lyrics encourages adolescents to engage in violence and crime, viewing beer commercials during the Super Bowl makes adolescents drink beer, and so on. According to this view, the media shape adolescents' interests, motives, and beliefs about the world—a view known as **cultivation theory** (Gerbner, Gross, Morgan, & Signorelli, 1993).

A second school of thought, called the **uses and gratifications approach** (Katz, Blumler, & Gurevitch, 1974), emphasizes the fact that adolescents choose the media to which they are exposed. Any correlation between what adolescents are exposed to and what they do or think is due not to the influence of the media, but to the fact that individuals with particular inclinations choose media that are consistent with their interests. According to this view, adolescents deliberately choose the media they use, either for entertainment, information, bonding with others, or developing a sense of identity. Thus, aggressive adolescents are more likely to purchase violent video games because they enjoy being aggressive; teenagers who are interested in sex are more likely to surf the Internet looking for pornography because they want to masturbate or feel sexually aroused; beer-drinking adolescents are more likely to watch football and to be exposed to beer commercials (which, after all, is why beer companies advertise during football games and not on the Animal Planet network); and adolescents who are involved with drugs like to listen to music that glorifies drug use. According to this view, adolescents' preexisting interests and motives shape their media choices.

According to the third school of thought, the links between adolescents' preferences, on the one hand, and their media exposure, on the other, are reciprocal (that is, they affect each other); moreover, adolescents not only choose what they are exposed to but interpret the media in ways that shape their impact. This view is referred to as the **media practice model** (Steele & Brown, 1995). Imagine two adolescents who accidentally stumble onto a sexually explicit website while surfing the Internet. One, a sexually experienced teenager who is curious about pornography, views the website with interest—perhaps it even makes him feel aroused. The other, who isn't interested in sex, sees the very same content and feels repulsed. Not only is the experience not arousing, it makes this adolescent even less interested in having sex than he was before landing on the site. One teenager sees a beer commercial and thinks, "That's how I want to party when I can drink." Another sees the exact same images and thinks, "What morons those people are—look how stupid beer makes you act." Two adolescents are channel surfing—one, who collects rap music, sees a flash of a music video that piques her interest and stops flipping channels to watch; the other, who is into country music, doesn't even notice the clip. According to this third view, the ways in which media do (or do not) affect adolescents depends on the ways in which the media are experienced and interpreted.

These problems in distinguishing among **correlation** (when two things go hand in hand), **causation** (when one thing actually causes another), **reverse causation** (when the correlation between two things is due not to the first thing causing the second, but to the reverse), and **spurious causation** (when the correlation between two things is due to the fact each of them is correlated with some third factor) make it almost impossible to say for sure whether media exposure genuinely affects adolescent development (see Figure 7.10).

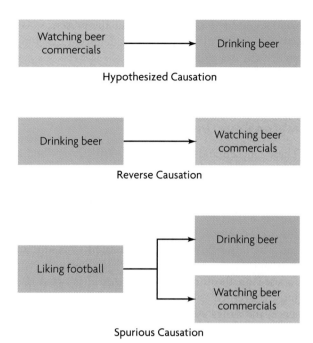

FIGURE 7.10 Two things can be correlated because the first causes the second (the hypothesized correlation), the second causes the first (reverse causation), or some third factor causes both of them (spurious causation). Research on media "effects" on adolescent development has a hard time separating the three.

The only sure way to demonstrate cause and effect where media influence is concerned is to conduct an experiment in which people are randomly assigned to be (or not be) exposed to the medium of interest and see how it affects them. But experiments of this sort are rare, because they are difficult to do well. Even the most ardent believers in the power of media influence generally acknowledge that one exposure to a commercial, a movie, or an Internet site is unlikely to change someone's behavior. But if the impact of media exposure is incremental and cumulative—perhaps taking years of exposure to have an effect—it may be quite powerful, but impossible to demonstrate in a brief experiment. All of this is to say that

media practice model A perspective on media use that emphasizes the fact that adolescents not only choose what media they are exposed to but also interpret the media in ways that shape their impact.

correlation When two things go hand in hand.

causation When one thing actually causes another.

reverse causation When the correlation between two things is due not to the first thing causing the second, but to the second causing the first.

spurious causation When the correlation between two things is due to the fact that each of them is correlated with some third factor.

you should view any claims about the presence—or absence—of media influence on adolescent development with tremendous caution.

THE IMPACT OF ADOLESCENTS' EXPOSURE TO CONTROVERSIAL MEDIA CONTENT

These chicken-and-egg problems notwithstanding, a few generalizations about media usage and adolescent development have enough supporting evidence, however indirect, to generate some consensus among experts in the area. Most of the relevant research has focused on television (as a consequence, we know virtually nothing about the impact of other media on development), and the bulk of the research has focused on the three topics about which adults are most concerned (some might say obsessed): sex, violence, and drugs. Although scientists debate the long-term effects of adolescents' exposure to sex, violence, and drug use in the media, there is no question that the exposure is considerable.

■ **Sex**   Sexual themes are ubiquitous on television, with more than *70 percent* of all shows popular among teenagers containing sexual content, and with an average of nearly seven sexual scenes per hour (Kunkel et al., 2005). Although it may be hard to believe, the prevalence of sexual content in shows popular among adolescents actually declined between 2000 and 2005, most likely because of the increase in popularity of reality shows like *American Idol* and *America's Next Top Model,* which have displaced shows with more sexual content (usually dramas) on the list of programs most watched by teenagers. Generally, sex on TV is portrayed as pleasurable and carefree (Ward & Friedman, 2006). Most sexual content on prime-time TV is not composed of graphic images of individuals having sex, but instead is made up of humorous and suggestive comments. On daytime television, however, a lot of sexual imagery is of individuals engaging in passionate kissing and erotic touching. Sexual content is also very common in music videos (Ward, 2003).

The most common sexual messages concern men seeing women as sex objects ("Look at the body on that chick"; "In case she's a dog, I can fake a heart attack"), sex as a defining aspect of masculinity ("I slept with 10 girls last week." "Oh, that's one afternoon for me"), sex as a competition ("You're supposed to be keeping score, not trying to score"), and sex as fun and exciting ("It's so romantic, all that passion, when you have to make love every minute of the day") (Ward, 1995). This message—that woman are sexual objects—is one that teenagers seem especially susceptible to (Ward & Friedman, 2006). Similar messages

are carried in most MTV videos, in which men are shown as aggressive and dominant, and women are seen as the subservient objects of men's sexual advances (Roberts et al., 2004). One issue that has concerned many sex educators is the relative absence of messages concerning the possible physical consequences of sex (for example, pregnancy, STDs), although these are more common now than in the past (Kunkel et al., 2005).

■ **Violence**   Adolescents are also exposed to a great deal of violent imagery on television, in movies, in certain music genres, and in video games (Roberts et al., 2004). More than 60 percent of TV programming contains violence; as a consequence, young people see an estimated 10,000 acts of media violence each year, and more than one-fourth of all violent incidents on TV involve guns. One analysis of MTV videos indicated that more than one-fifth portrayed overt violence and one-quarter showed weapons (Strasburger & Donnerstein, 1999).

Precise estimates of the amount of violent imagery in the most popular video games or other visual media are not available, but concerns have been raised over the impact of violent video games on young people's behavior and attitudes (Cantor, 2000). Studies have found that adolescents who spend a lot of time playing violent video games get into more fights and arguments than do their peers (e.g., Gentile, Lynch, Linder, & Walsh, 2004), but it is difficult to know whether playing such games makes adolescents more hostile or whether adolescents who are more hostile to begin with are simply more likely to want to play these sorts of games. Although controlled experiments have shown that exposure to the lyrics of violent songs increases individuals' aggressive thoughts (Anderson, Carnagey, & Eubanks, 2003), many experts doubt that playing violent video games or listening to music with violent lyrics causes adolescents to engage in the sorts of serious violent acts that alarmists have raised concerns about. As some have noted, given the millions of copies of violent games that have been sold, if playing video games had a significant impact on real-world violence, we'd likely be in the midst of a violence epidemic—yet juvenile violence has declined steadily since peaking in the early 1990s (Reichhardt, 2003).

■ **Drugs**   Finally, many analyses have shown that alcohol and tobacco use are ubiquitous in the mass media to which adolescents are exposed. As one team of experts noted, "Alcohol, tobacco, or illicit drugs are present in 70 percent of prime time network dramatic programs, 38 out of 40 top-grossing movies, and half of all music videos." Nearly 10 percent of the commercials that young people see on TV are for beer or wine—and for every public service announcement discouraging alcohol use, teenagers will view 25–50 ads for alcoholic beverages. And alcohol and tobacco companies have an increasing presence on the Internet, sponsoring numerous websites and specially designed chat rooms (Strasburger & Donnerstein, 1999). The tobacco industry spends approximately $1 million each year on Internet advertising, and the alcohol industry spends more than $1 billion in traditional advertising and an additional $1 million on Internet ads (Roberts et al., 2004). Adolescents are also exposed to alcohol and tobacco through films, which frequently depict actors smoking and drinking. Teenagers are more likely to smoke if their favorite film star is a smoker (Roberts et al., 2004).

Studies that unequivocally demonstrate that exposure to messages about sex, violence, and drugs causes changes in adolescents' behavior are harder to find than simple documentation of exposure. The strongest evidence is in the area of violence, where numerous studies have shown that repeated exposure to violent imagery on television leads to aggressive behavior in children and youth, especially among those who have prior histories of aggression (Johnson, Cohen, Smailes, Kasen, & Brook, 2002) (see Figure 7.11). It is important to note, however, that other factors, such as experiences in the family or community, likely play a far greater role in serious violence than does media exposure (Strasburger & Donnerstein, 1999). Nevertheless, exposure to TV violence in childhood has been linked

in adolescence and adulthood to aggressive behavior toward others, a heightened tolerance of violence, and greater desensitization to the effects of violence on others, although most of this effect is likely due to the tendency for people with aggressive tendencies to choose to watch violent programming (Cantor, 2000; Huesmann, Moise-Titus, Podolski, & Eron, 2003; Roberts et al., 2004). One recent longitudinal study of African American girls found that those who had greater exposure to rap music videos, especially "gangsta rap," were more likely to hit a teacher and be arrested, as well as have multiple sex partners, contract a sexually transmitted disease, and use drugs and alcohol over the course of the following year (Wingood et al., 2003). Again, though, this shows only that exposure to violence and antisocial behavior are correlated, not that one causes the other.

■ **Misleading Media Messages**   Data linking exposure to messages about sex and drugs to actual sexual activity or drug use are considerably weaker than those concerning violence (Strasburger & Donnerstein, 1999). Yet, although it has not been conclusively shown that exposure to messages about sex and drugs alters adolescents' behavior, repeated exposure affects their attitudes, beliefs, and intentions (L'Engle, Brown, & Kenneavy, 2006; Roberts et al., 2004; Ward, 2003). For example, adolescents who watch a lot of music videos have more tolerant attitudes toward sexual harassment and more sex-stereotyped attitudes about sexual relationships (Strouse, Goodwin, & Roscoe, 1994; Ward, Hansbrough, & Walker, 2005). Along similar lines, one study found that college students who frequently watched soap operas (which have a high sexual content) gave higher estimates than nonviewers did of the number of real-life extramarital affairs, children born out of wedlock, and divorces. Another study found that high school students who believed that TV characters have highly satisfying sex were less likely themselves to feel that sex is satisfying, presumably because the images they saw on TV created false expectations (Roberts, 1993). Similarly, prolonged exposure to pornography leads to exaggerated beliefs about the extent of sexual activity in the real world (Zillman, 2000). Studies of exposure to ads for alcohol and tobacco, as well as antismoking commercial messages (such as those conveyed in the "Truth" campaign), have shown that they are effective in changing teenagers' attitudes about drinking and smoking, and in developing brand recognition (Farrelly, Davis, Haviland, Healton, & Messeri, 2004; Roberts et al., 2004; Straub, Hills, Thompson, & Moscicki, 2003). Evidence showing that exposure to advertising actually causes adolescents to begin using cigarettes or alcohol is far less compelling, however.

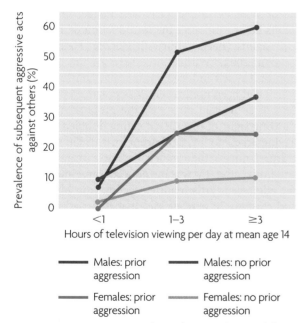

FIGURE 7.11   **Exposure to violent television during adolescence is associated with increased aggression in young adulthood, especially among individuals who had a prior history of aggression.** (Johnson et al., 2002)

FOOD FOR THOUGHT

Politicians often argue that adolescents' development is being adversely affected by the mass media and regularly propose legislation that would restrict adolescents' access to media they believe is dangerous. What do you think about this? What policies, if any, do you support that would affect adolescents' access to mass media?

Others have noted that many of the messages communicated to adolescents about the world via mass media are just plain inaccurate. One analysis of the content of popular TV shows about families, for example, found that the portrayal of the families was markedly different from reality. On TV, nonconventional families (single-parent families, families with adopted children, families composed of children and nonparental guardians) were greatly overrepresented, and men were depicted as being much more involved in family roles than is generally the case. Difficult issues like poverty, family conflict, divorce, and stress were generally sidestepped (Moore, 1992). Daytime soap operas, which are especially popular among adolescents, often present single mothers as having far more comfortable lives than is actually the case (Larson, 1996). Another analysis, of the presentation of work, found that TV shows overrepresent and glamorize more prestigious, exciting, and adventurous jobs (for example, lawyers, doctors, entertainers). Interestingly, adolescents who watch a great deal of TV are more likely to aspire to such jobs, and to believe that such jobs are easy and lucrative and permit one to take long vacations (Signorelli, 1993).

It is important to note that discussions of media effects often fail to distinguish between what adolescents actually perceive and remember and what adults believe adolescents see and remember. After all, media are not simply viewed or heard—they are interpreted. Studies of "violent" video games, for example, find that adolescents, college students, and parents rate the same games very differently (Funk, Flores, Buchman, & Germann, 1999). Adolescents are not exposed to the mass media as blank slates; rather, they bring preexisting values, beliefs, and expectations to the experience of watching or listening, and these preexisting states influence what they perceive and remember (Roberts et al., 2004). One extensive study of girls' responses to sexual media content found, for instance, that some girls were disinterested in sexual media, others were intrigued, and still others resisted the sexual imagery to the point of criticizing it.

MASS MEDIA AND SEX-ROLE SOCIALIZATION

Several commentators have raised concerns about the messages to which young women are exposed in mass media aimed at adolescent girls, especially in light of evidence (discussed in Chapter 1) of widespread body dissatisfaction among adolescent females (Brumberg, 1997; Evans, Rutberg, Sather, & Turner, 1991). The majority of articles in these magazines focus on dating and heterosexual relationships, and most emphasize the importance of physical attractiveness and thinness, in particular, for young women. This sort of content has increased considerably over time—the proportion of items mentioning sexuality in *Seventeen* magazine rose from about 30 percent in 1974 to more than 50 percent in 1994 (Ward, 2003). According to researchers, the articles and advertisements contained in such magazines convey a clear message that attracting males by being physically beautiful is the road to true happiness for women. Interestingly, adolescent girls who frequently read fashion magazines are more dissatisfied with their body than are girls who do not, and controlled experiments have indicated that showing girls images of thin models increases their body dissatisfaction (Roberts et al., 2004).

Similar results are reported in studies of girls' responses to appearance-related commercials on television, which, like ads in fashion magazines, typically feature thin models. In a fascinating study of the impact of TV on adolescent girls' body image, the researchers examined girls' self-image and eating habits before and after the introduction of TV to the Fiji islands (Becker, Burwell, Herzog, Hamburg, & Gilman, 2002). Within three years of the introduction of TV, self-induced vomiting to control weight, which had been nonexistent, was practiced by 11 percent of adolescent girls, and the proportion of girls showing signs of disordered eating doubled. Prior to having access to TV, adolescent girls in Fiji endorsed cultural norms that valued having a large appetite and body; after TV was introduced, three-quarters of the adolescent girls reported feeling "too big or fat," and close to 70 percent said that they had dieted to lose weight.

In contrast to the emphasis on physical appearance, little space in magazines aimed at teenage girls is devoted to issues of ethics, education, or self-improvement in other than physical ways. Another analysis, of the fiction appearing in *Seventeen,* found that in the majority of the stories the main character did not solve her own problems but depended on someone else to solve them for her. In these stories as well, occupations were portrayed in traditionally sex-stereotyped terms (Pierce, 1993).

THE ADOLESCENT CONSUMER

A final, and very important, aspect of adolescent media use is economic. The size of the adolescent population, the prevalence of student employment, and the fact that adolescents save less than any other age group make young people an attractive target for a variety of businesses (Fine et al., 1990). In 2008, teenagers were projected to spend more than $200 billion of their own money and to influence $340 billion more in additional household spending (Zollo, 2004). More than three-quarters of teenagers visit a shopping mall each week. The average adolescent has more than $400 per month in spending money—and spends nearly all of it (girls, who spend more than $100 per week, spend slightly more than boys). Not surprisingly, virtually all of adolescents' money is spent on purchases related to leisure activities. Girls spend their money on clothes, food, and cosmetics, in that order; boys use their money for food and clothes, and they also save for big-ticket items, like cars and stereo equipment (Meyer, 1994). And, unfortunately, many adolescents spend money on alcohol and cigarettes—according to one estimate, more than $22 billion is spent each year on alcohol consumed by underage drinkers in the United States (Foster, Vaughan, Foster, & Califano, 2003).

We can certainly debate the merits of cultivating such strong consumer urges among the young and impressionable. Some critics contend that advertising aimed at teenagers takes advantage of the fact that they are more impulsive and self-conscious than adults (see Pechmann, Levine, Loughlin, & Leslie, 2005). On the other hand, America's economy is driven by consumer spending, and the segments of our economy that are devoted to leisure and recreation depend on the adolescent market. Among the most important industries are those connected with movies, music, sports, and television. Teenagers make up a large, and therefore influential, segment of the consumers of these products—as a glance at the local movie or TV listings or a trip through a music store will readily attest. And, of course, the jobs held by millions of adults who work in these sectors of the economy depend on adolescents' purchases.

Supporters of adolescent consumerism also have been quick to point out the strong influence that teenagers have on each other when it comes to purchases—and new ways of tapping into this influence that take advantage of the Internet and other new technologies, referred to as **viral marketing,** have been explored by businesses wishing to expand their share of the teen consumer market. Viral marketing refers to a strategy that encourages people to pass on a marketing message to others, "creating the potential for exponential growth in the message's exposure and influence. Like viruses, such strategies take advantage of rapid multiplication to explode the message to thousands, to millions" (Wilson, 2005). Because adolescents are likely to use technologies that can easily and instantly connect them to thousands of other teenagers, using young people to spread the word about new products is a highly effective marketing strategy. (Think of how quickly Gmail, an Internet mail service, went from a new, unknown service to one of the largest email services in the world—this is a classic example of viral marketing.)

FOOD FOR THOUGHT

Have you been the recipient of viral marketing? What product was marketed, and how did you find out about it?

The influence of the adolescent market extends well beyond the youth cohort, however—as evidenced by the uncanny predictability with which adult tastes in clothing and music often follow those of teenagers, albeit in a toned-down fashion. Teenagers often have considerable influence over their parents' purchases, which gives added incentive for advertisers to market products with young people's tastes in mind (Zollo, 2004). Interestingly, the power of adolescents as consumers has increased in recent decades, owing to the growth in the proportion of single-parent and dual-worker households. In many such homes, adolescents influence both day-to-day and major purchases—in part because adolescents themselves may do a fair amount of the family's shopping (Graham, 1988).

RECAP

- Today's adolescents live in a media-saturated environment, with the average adolescent exposed to the mass media more than six hours each day, and with television the most used medium.
- One of the most significant changes in recent years has been in the amount of time adolescents spend each day on the computer. Among high school students, one-third of this time is spent instant messaging, one-fourth playing games, and one-fourth visiting websites.
- Many observers of the adolescent scene are concerned about the high level of adolescents'

viral marketing A way of promoting products or services by encouraging individuals to pass information on to others.

exposure to messages about sex, violence, and drug use through the mass media.

- Although adults have worried about the corrupting influence of the mass media, it has been difficult to document such alleged effects. Media exposure may influence adolescents, but adolescents choose which media they use and actively interpret what they see and hear.

- Several studies have shown that exposure to media violence does lead to more aggressive behavior and that exposure to images of drug and alcohol use and sex does affect adolescents' attitudes and beliefs about these matters.

- Adolescents wield enormous power as consumers, both because they have a great deal of discretionary income of their own and because they influence how their families spend money.

Free Time and Adolescent Development

Adults have mixed feelings about adolescents' activities outside of school. On the positive side, adults take pride in watching their children's sports teams and creative activities, and they believe that these productive uses of leisure time help build character and teach important skills, such as teamwork and perseverance. (Think about all the movies you have seen about the character-building benefits of team sports). Similarly, most adults view holding a part-time job as a worthwhile activity that provides opportunities for learning and for the development of a sense of responsibility.

On the other hand, adults view many adolescent leisure activities as wasted time, or worse, as preludes to trouble: They worry about groups of teenagers cruising the mall; they poke fun at groups of girls sequestered in front of a mirror trying on an array of cosmetics; they cringe at images of adolescents plugged into their MP3 players, mindlessly staring off into space; and they worry about adolescents' exposure to sex and violence on television, in film, in music, and on the Internet. Although we might wish for the "good old days" before the advent of cell phones, email, iPods®, satellite television, DVD players, and personal computers, those good old days are long gone. And keep in mind that even during those supposed good old days, adults worried about how adolescents spent their idle time and about the corrupting influence of

such evils as rock 'n' roll, dime-store romances, and comic books.

This mixed view of adolescents' free time reflects an interesting paradox about the nature of adolescence in modern society. Because industrialized society has "given" adolescents a good deal of free time, adults expect them to use it productively. But by definition, free time is supposed to be time that can be used for purposes other than being productive. As you will read in the next chapter, some theorists of adolescence believe that the existence of large blocks of uncommitted time is one feature of adolescence in modern society that has the potential to contribute in positive ways to young people's development; one potential benefit of participation in leisure activities is that this may help adolescents explore different sides of themselves (Barber, Stone, Hunt, & Eccles, 2005).

Nevertheless, many misconceptions about the pros and cons of various uses of free time abound. Most adults view participation in structured extracurricular activities as a good thing, and this seems to be the case. But most people are equally sure that working is good for teenagers, even though studies show that the costs of intensive involvement in part-time work during the school year may outweigh the benefits. And, although adults believe that the mass media have a negative effect on adolescents' behavior, studies show that it is more likely that adolescents' interests affect their media use than the reverse.

The impact of the mass media on adolescent development has become especially controversial as the role of technology in adolescents' lives has expanded. Most adults, especially parents, are absolutely certain that nothing good comes from adolescents' exposure to television, movies, popular music, or the Internet, and often blame the mass media for a wide array of adolescents' problems—despite the fact that parents themselves exert a far greater influence on adolescent development than do any of the media about which they are often so alarmed. Moreover, as you now know, because adolescents choose the media to which they are exposed, it has been very difficult to demonstrate that adolescents are actually affected by what they see and hear. This is not to say that the media have no impact on adolescents' behavior and well-being, but it is to suggest that we should be careful not to confuse cause and effect. It is also important to keep in mind that the mass media can be used to promote positive behavior and healthy development, to provide information about a rapidly changing world, and to facilitate communication with others.

By valuing adolescents' free time only when it is used productively, adults may misunderstand the important functions that leisure time serves in the psychosocial development of young people. For example, studies show that a moderate amount of solitude (during which daydreaming is a central activity) is positively related to high school students' psychological well-being (Csikszentmihalyi & Larson, 1984; Larson, 1997). Free time plays an important role in helping young people develop a sense of themselves, explore their relationships with each other, and learn about the society around them (Coatsworth et al., 2005). And, for better or for worse, the mass media are globalizing adolescence, contributing to the development of a common culture that gives adolescents all over the world much to share.

RECAP

- Adults' ambivalence about adolescents' free time reflects an interesting paradox about the nature of adolescence in modern society. Because industrialized society has "given" adolescents a good deal of free time, adults expect them to use it productively. But by definition, free time is supposed to be time that can be used for purposes other than being productive.
- Many misconceptions about the pros and cons of various uses of free time abound. Some of the activities that adults believe are uniformly good for adolescents, like employment, have more costs than benefits. Other activities that adults believe are harmful, like watching television, listening to popular music, and surfing the Internet, are probably not as bad for teenagers as they are often assumed to be.
- Leisure plays an important role in helping young people develop a sense of themselves, explore their relationships with each other, and learn about the society around them.

8 | Identity   9 | Autonomy   10 | Intimacy
11 | Sexuality   12 | Achievement   13 | Psychosocial Problems

Psychosocial Development During Adolescence

CHAPTER 8

Identity

IDENTITY AS AN ADOLESCENT ISSUE

CHANGES IN SELF-CONCEPTIONS

Changes in the Content and Structure of Self-Conceptions

Dimensions of Personality in Adolescence

CHANGES IN SELF-ESTEEM

Stability and Changes in Self-Esteem

Sex, Class, and Ethnic Differences in Self-Esteem

Antecedents and Consequences of High Self-Esteem

THE ADOLESCENT IDENTITY CRISIS

Erikson's Theoretical Framework

Identity Versus Identity Diffusion

The Social Context of Identity Development

Resolving the Identity Crisis

Problems in Identity Development

RESEARCH ON IDENTITY DEVELOPMENT

Determining an Adolescent's Identity Status

Studying Identity Development over Time

Shifts in Identity Status

THE DEVELOPMENT OF ETHNIC IDENTITY

The Process of Ethnic Identity Development

Multiethnic Adolescents

Alternative Orientations to Ethnic Identity

Discrimination and Its Effects

GENDER-ROLE DEVELOPMENT

Gender-Role Socialization During Adolescence

Masculinity, Femininity, and Androgyny

AS YOU MAY RECALL from your own adolescence, there are few experiences as trying—or as exhilarating—as questioning who you really are and, more important, who you would like to be. Some, but not all, adolescents share the feelings of self-consciousness and confusion expressed in the statement below. For these young people, adolescence is a time of identity crisis. For other adolescents, though, this period is one of more gradual and more subtle changes. Here's how a 15-year-old girl responded when asked to describe herself:

> What am I like as a person? You're probably not going to understand. I'm complicated! With my really close friends, I am very tolerant. I mean, I'm understanding and caring. With a group of friends, I'm rowdier. I'm also usually friendly and cheerful but I can get pretty obnoxious and intolerant if I don't like how they're acting. I'd like to be friendly and tolerant all of the time, that's the kind of person I want to be, and I'm disappointed when I'm not. At school, I'm serious, even studious every now and then, but on the other hand I'm a goof-off too, because if you're too studious, you won't be popular. So I go back and forth, which means I don't do all that well in terms of my grades. But that causes problems at home, where I'm pretty anxious when I'm around my parents. They expect me to get all A's, and get pretty annoyed with me when report cards come out. I care what they think about me, and so then I get down on myself, but it's not fair! I mean, I worry about how I probably should get better grades, but I'd be mortified in the eyes of my friends if I did too well. So I'm usually pretty stressed out at home, or sarcastic, since my parents are always on my case. But I really don't understand how I can switch so fast. I mean, how can I be cheerful with my friends, then coming home and feeling anxious, and then getting frustrated and sarcastic with my parents. Which one is the real me? I have the same question when I'm around boys. Sometimes I feel phony. Say I think some guy might

> be interested in asking me out. I try to act different, like Madonna. I'll be a real extrovert, fun loving and even flirtatious, and think I am really good-looking. And then everybody, I mean everybody else is looking at me like they think I'm totally weird! They don't act like they think I'm attractive, so I end up thinking I look terrible. I just hate myself when that happens. Because it gets worse! Then I get self-conscious and embarrassed and become radically introverted, and I don't know who I really am! Am I just acting like an extrovert, am I just trying to impress them, when really I'm an introvert? But I don't really care what they think anyway. I mean, I don't want to care, that is. I just want to know what my close friends think. I can be my true self with my close friends. I can't be my real self with my parents. They don't understand me. What do they know about what it's like to be a teenager? They treat me like I'm still a kid. At least at school people treat you more like you're an adult. That gets confusing, though. I mean, which am I, a kid or an adult? . . . I have a part-time job and the people there treat me like an adult. I want to make them approve of me, so I'm very responsible at work. . . . But then I go out with my friends and I get pretty crazy and irresponsible. So which am I, responsible or irresponsible? How can the same person be both? . . . So I think a lot about who is the real me, and sometimes I try to figure it out when I write in my diary, but I can't resolve it. There are days when I wish I could just become immune to myself! (Harter, 1999, pp. 67–68)

Because changes—whether gradual or abrupt—take place during adolescence in the ways young people view and feel about themselves, the study of identity development has been a major focus of research and theory on adolescents. In this chapter, we examine whether adolescence is indeed a time of major changes in identity and how the course of adolescent identity development is shaped by the nature of life in contemporary society.

Identity as an Adolescent Issue

Changes in the way in which we view and feel about ourselves occur throughout the life cycle. You have probably heard and read about the so-called midlife crisis, for example—an identity crisis thought to occur during middle age. And certainly, important changes in self-conceptions and in self-image take place

throughout childhood. When a group of 4-year-olds and a group of 10-year-olds are asked to describe themselves, the older children provide a far more complex self-portrait. Whereas young children restrict their descriptions to lists of what they own or what they like to do, older children are more likely to tell you about their personality as well.

If changes in identity occur throughout the life cycle, why have researchers who are interested in identity development paid so much attention to adolescence? One reason is that the changes in identity that take place during adolescence involve the first substantial reorganization and restructuring of the individual's sense of self at a time when he or she has the intellectual capability to appreciate fully just how significant the changes are. Although important changes in identity certainly occur during childhood, the adolescent is far more self-conscious about these changes and feels them much more acutely.

■ **Puberty and Identity Development** Another reason for the attention that researchers and theorists have given the study of identity development during adolescence concerns the fundamental biological, cognitive, and social changes characteristic of the period. Puberty, as we saw in Chapter 1, brings with it dramatic changes in physical appearance and alters the adolescent's self-conceptions and relationships with others. It is not hard to see why puberty plays an important role in provoking identity development during adolescence. When you change the way you look— for example, when you have your hair colored or cut in a different way, lose a great deal of weight, or dramatically change your style of dress—you sometimes feel as though your personality has changed, too. During puberty, when adolescents are changing so dramatically on the outside, they understandably have questions about changes that are taking place on the inside. For the adolescent, undergoing the physical changes of puberty may prompt fluctuations in self-image and a reevaluation of who he or she really is.

■ **Cognitive Change and Identity Development** Just as the broadening of intellectual capabilities during early adolescence provides new ways of thinking about problems, values, and interpersonal relationships, it also permits adolescents to think about themselves in new ways. We saw in Chapter 2 that it is not until adolescence that the young person is able to think in systematic ways about hypothetical and future events. This is manifested in two specific ways that have implications for identity development. First, adolescents become much more able to imagine their **possible selves**—the various alternative identities that they may adopt (Markus & Nurius, 1986). Second, there is an impressive increase in their **future orientation**—the ability and tendency to consider the long-term consequences of their decisions and imagine what their life might be like in the years to come (Nurmi, 2004). For this reason, it is not until adolescence that individuals typically begin to wonder, "Who will I become?" or "What am I really like?" Because the preadolescent child's thinking is concrete, it is difficult for him or her to think seriously about being a different person.

Adolescence is often a time when individuals ask questions about who they are and where they are headed. Concerns with physical appearance often intensify.

But the changes in thinking that take place during adolescence open up a whole new world of alternatives.

■ **Social Roles and Identity Development** Finally, as we saw in Chapter 3, the changes in social roles that occur at adolescence open up a new array of choices and decisions for the young person that were not concerns previously. In contemporary society, adolescence is a time of important decisions about work, marriage, and the future. Facing these decisions about their place in society does more than provoke questions about who they are and where they are headed—it *necessitates* the questions. At this point in the life cycle, young people must make important choices about their careers and their commitments to other people, and thinking about these questions prompts them to ask more questions about themselves: "What do I really want out of life?" "What things are important to me?" "What kind of person would I really like to be?" Questions about the future, which inevitably arise as the adolescent prepares for adulthood, raise questions about identity.

Identity development is complex and multifaceted. Actually, it is better understood as a series of interrelated developments—rather than one single development— that all involve changes in the way we view ourselves in relation to others and in relation to the broader society in which we live. Generally, researchers and theorists have taken three different approaches to the

possible selves The various identities an adolescent might imagine for him- or herself.

future orientation The extent to which an individual is able and inclined to think about the potential consequences of decisions and choices.

question of how the individual's sense of identity changes over the course of adolescence. Each approach, examined in detail later in this chapter, focuses on a different aspect of identity.

The first approach emphasizes changes in **self-conceptions**—the ideas that individuals have of themselves with regard to various traits and attributes. An entirely different approach focuses on adolescents' **self-esteem,** or self-image—how positively or negatively they feel about themselves. Finally, a third approach emphasizes changes in the **sense of identity**—the sense of who one is, where one has come from, and where one is going.

RECAP

- Although changes in the way we see and feel about ourselves occur throughout the life cycle, the study of identity development has been a prominent issue in the field of adolescent development in particular.
- One reason for this attention concerns the impact that the biological, cognitive, and social definitional changes of adolescence have on the young person's ability to engage in self-examination, and on his or her interest in doing so.
- Researchers have traditionally distinguished among three aspects of identity development in adolescence: changes in self-conceptions, changes in self-esteem, and changes in the sense of identity.

Changes in Self-Conceptions

During adolescence, important shifts occur in the way individuals think about and characterize themselves—that is, in their self-conceptions. As individuals mature intellectually and undergo the sorts of cognitive changes described in Chapter 2, they come to conceive of themselves in more sophisticated and more differentiated ways. As we saw in that chapter, adolescents are much more capable than children of thinking

self-conceptions   The collection of traits and attributes that individuals use to describe or characterize themselves.

self-esteem   The degree to which individuals feel positively or negatively about themselves.

sense of identity   The extent to which individuals feel secure about who they are and who they are becoming.

about abstract concepts and considerably more proficient in processing large amounts of information. These intellectual capabilities affect the way in which individuals characterize themselves. Compared with children, who tend to describe themselves in relatively simple, concrete terms, adolescents are more likely to employ complex, abstract, and psychological self-characterizations (Harter, 1999).

CHANGES IN THE CONTENT AND STRUCTURE OF SELF-CONCEPTIONS

Self-conceptions change in structure and content during the transition from childhood into and through adolescence. Structurally, self-conceptions become more differentiated and better organized (Byrne & Shavelson, 1996; Marsh, 1989a; Montemayor & Eisen, 1977). Let's first consider the idea that self-conceptions become more differentiated.

■ **Differentiation of the Self-Concept**   In answer to the question "Who am I?" adolescents are more likely than children to link traits and attributes that describe themselves to specific situations, rather than using them as global characterizations. While a preadolescent child might say, "I am nice" or "I am friendly," but not specify when or under what conditions, an adolescent is more likely to say, "I am nice if I am in a good mood" or "I am friendly when I am with people I have met before." The realization that their personality is expressed in different ways in different situations is one example of the increased differentiation that characterizes the self-conceptions of youngsters as they mature toward adulthood.

There is another way in which self-conceptions become more highly differentiated at adolescence. As opposed to characterizations provided by children, adolescents' self-descriptions take into account who is doing the describing (Harter, 1999). Teenagers differentiate between their own opinions of themselves and the views of others. Suppose you ask a group of youngsters to describe how they behave when they are with other people. Instead of saying, "I am shy" or "I am outgoing," an adolescent is more likely to say, "People think I'm not at all shy, but most of the time, I'm really nervous about meeting other kids for the first time." Adolescents also recognize that they may come across differently to different people, another type of differentiation in self-conceptions that does not appear until this point in time—for example, "My parents think I'm quiet, but my friends know I really like to party a lot."

■ **Organization and Integration of the Self-Concept**   With this shift toward increased differentiation in self-conceptions comes better organization and integration (Harter, 1999; Marsh, 1989a). When

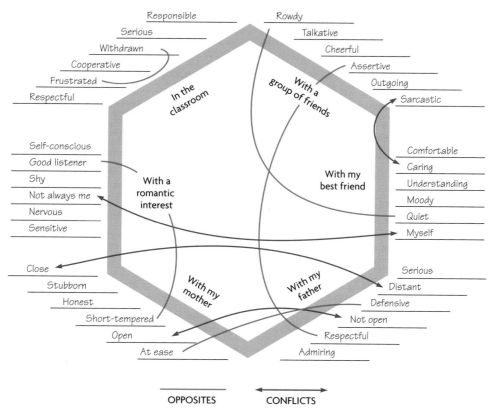

FIGURE 8.1   The multiple selves of a 15-year-old girl. Some opposing traits are experienced as clashing with each other (indicated by lines with arrowheads), while others are not. (Harter, 1999)

children are asked to describe themselves, the traits and attributes they list remain somewhat disorganized, like items haphazardly placed on a grocery list. Adolescents, in contrast, are likely to organize and integrate different aspects of their self-concept into a more logical, coherent whole. Whereas a younger child may list a sequence of several traits that appear to be contradictory ("I am friendly, and I am shy"), an adolescent will attempt to organize apparently discrepant bits of information into more highly organized statements ("I am shy when I first meet people, but after I get to know them, I'm usually pretty friendly").

Although it does not appear that self-conceptions become even more differentiated after early adolescence (Marsh, 1989a), the movement toward more abstract and more psychological self-conceptions continues well into the high school years, as the 15-year-old's self-description at the beginning of this chapter clearly indicates. The increased abstraction and psychological complexity of self-conceptions may present some difficulties for middle adolescents, though, who may be able to recognize—but not yet quite understand or reconcile—inconsistencies and contradictions in their personality. The proportion of adolescents who give opposite traits in self-descriptions, who feel conflicts over such discrepancies, and who feel confused over

such discrepancies increases markedly between seventh and ninth grades, and then declines somewhat (Harter & Monsour, 1992). In one study, when asked to reflect on contradictions in their personalities, early, middle, and late adolescents responded in very different ways, as in the following examples (Harter, 1990, p. 358):

> I guess I just think about one thing about myself at a time and don't think about the other until the next day. (11–12 years old)

> I really think I am a happy person and I want to be that way with everyone, but I get depressed with my family and it really bugs me because that's not what I want to be like. (14–15 years old)

> You can be shy on a date, and then outgoing with friends because you are just different with different people; you can't always be the same person and probably shouldn't be. (17–18 years old)

In another series of studies, psychologist Susan Harter (1999) and colleagues asked adolescents to describe their personalities by listing the traits they thought characterized themselves in different settings. The adolescents were also asked to identify opposite traits, either within or across settings, by connecting them with a line and to indicate opposite traits that clashed with each other by drawing arrowheads on the line. Figure 8.1 shows the diagram constructed by a 15-year-old girl.

Although the recognition that one's personality is multifaceted—even contradictory—may initially cause some distress, in the long run, it probably has a number of advantages. Indeed, some psychologists have suggested that the development of a more complicated view of the self is one way that individuals cope with the recognition of their faults and weaknesses, a recognition that comes with the increased self-awareness of adolescence ("I'm not really a nasty person, I just act mean when people tease me"). Consistent with this, adolescents who have more complex self-conceptions are less likely to be depressed (Evans, 1993; Jordan & Cole, 1996).

One additional advantage of having a more differentiated self-concept is that the adolescent is now able to distinguish among his or her actual self (who the adolescent really is), ideal self (who the adolescent would like to be), and feared self (who the adolescent most dreads becoming). According to one view, being able to make these distinctions provides a motive for adolescents to improve—either to bring their actual self more into line with the ideal self or to strive to become their ideal self and avoid becoming their feared self (Markus & Nurius, 1986; Oyserman & Markus, 1990). An important aspect of having a healthy self-concept is having an ideal self to balance a feared self. One study found, for example, that delinquent adolescents were less likely than nondelinquent youth to have this sort of balanced view; although delinquent adolescents might dread becoming criminals, for instance, they may not have a positive hoped-for self (for example, to be successfully employed) to balance this fear (Oyserman & Markus, 1990). Interestingly, adolescents tend to imagine more similarity between their present and future selves than they say exists between their past and present selves (Hart, Fegley, & Brengelman, 1993).

▌ **False-Self Behavior**   Another interesting consequence of adolescents' recognition that they are not always consistent in their personality concerns their ability to distinguish between their true and false selves (that is, their authentic and inauthentic selves). Adolescents are most likely to behave inauthentically in romantic and dating situations and with classmates, and they are least likely to put on a false front with close friends. Interestingly, **false-self behavior**—acting in a way that one knows is inauthentic—occurs less often with parents than with dates, but more often with parents than with close friends (Harter, 1990). Although adolescents sometimes say that they dislike false-self behavior, they also say that sometimes it is acceptable, such as when trying to impress another person or hide an aspect of their personality that

others do not like. You can easily imagine how the ability to put on a false front would come in handy on a date, at school, or with your parents.

Adolescents differ, of course, in the degree to which they present false fronts and in their reasons for doing so. In general, adolescents who report less emotional support from parents and peers, those who have low self-esteem, and those who are relatively more depressed and hopeless than their peers are more likely to engage in false-self behavior. Whereas some adolescents engage in false-self behavior because they are low in self-esteem, others experience a drop in self-esteem because they knowingly put on a false front. Depression and hopelessness are highest among adolescents who engage in false-self behavior because they genuinely devalue their true self, in contrast to those who put on a false front because they want to please others or because they are experimenting with different personalities (Harter, Marold, Whitesell, & Cobbs, 1996).

Studies of young adults have also found that individuals vary in the extent to which they present themselves authentically or inauthentically. One study of Israelis in their early and mid-20s found three distinct groups: a group that had not yet developed a stable and well-integrated self-concept, a group that had a good understanding of who they are and were genuine in their presentation of themselves to others (even their weak points), and a third group that was characterized by a reluctance to share their true self with others (Shulman, Feldman, Blatt, Cohen, & Mahler, 2005). One member of this latter group, a 25-year-old woman, told the researchers:

> For example, my parents, though they are very close to me, they don't really know who I am. I behave, let's say, when I am at my parents' place, I behave according to their expectations. They expect me to behave in a certain way and I try to show them that I am OK. . . . At other places, I don't know if I behave totally differently. But I act according to . . . I do not know [if] according to the context or according to how they would like to see me. (Shulman et al., 2005, p. 591)

FOOD FOR THOUGHT

There have been relatively few studies of false-self behavior among adults. When was the last time you put on a false self? What was your motivation?

Understanding how self-conceptions change during adolescence helps to explain why issues of identity begin to take on so much importance at this stage in the life span. As self-conceptions become more abstract, and as young people become more able to see themselves in

---

false-self behavior   Behavior that intentionally presents a false impression to others.

psychological terms, they become more interested in understanding their own personalities and why they behave the way they do. The distress caused by recognizing one's inconsistencies may spur identity development. You may recall having wondered as a teenager about your personality development, about the influences that shaped your character, about how your personality had changed over time: "Am I more like my father or like my mother? Why do my sister and I seem so different? Will I always be so shy?" Although these sorts of questions may seem commonplace to you now, in all likelihood, you did not think about these things until adolescence, when your own self-conceptions became more abstract and more sophisticated.

DIMENSIONS OF PERSONALITY IN ADOLESCENCE

While many researchers have studied adolescent personality development by examining young people's views of themselves, others have administered standardized inventories designed to assess the most important aspects of personality. Most researchers now approach the study of personality using the **five-factor model** (McCrae & John, 1992). This model is based on the observation that there are five critical personality dimensions, often referred to as the "big five": extraversion (how outgoing and energetic someone is), agreeableness (how kind or sympathetic someone is), conscientiousness (how responsible and organized someone is), neuroticism (how anxious or tense someone is), and openness to experience (how curious and imaginative someone is). Although the five-factor model was developed through research on adults, it has been successfully applied to adolescents as well (Caspi, 1997; McCrae et al., 2002). For example, delinquent adolescents are more likely than their peers to score high in extraversion and low in agreeableness and conscientiousness, whereas adolescents who are high achievers in school score high in conscientiousness and openness (John, Caspi, Robins, Moffitt, & Stouthamer-Loeber, 1994). In general, the structure of personality appears comparable across groups of adolescents from different ethnic backgrounds (Markstrom-Adams & Adams, 1995; Rowe, Vazsonyi, & Flannery, 1994).

Researchers point to both genetic and environmental influences on individual differences in personality (e.g., Rose, 1988). Individuals may inherit temperamental predispositions (such as a high activity level or an inclination to be sociable), which are observable early in life, and these predispositions may "harden" and become organized into personality traits partially in response to the environment (Caspi, 2000; Gest, 1997; John et al., 1994). Thus, an active and sociable child who enjoys interacting with others may be rewarded for doing so and, over time, become extraverted. Longitudinal studies show that both temperament and personality become increasingly stable as we grow older, in part because we tend to spend time in environments that reward and reinforce the traits that draw us to these settings (Roberts & DelVecchio, 2000). As a result, we become more like ourselves every day! There is also evidence that, between adolescence and young adulthood, individuals on average become more extraverted, more conscientious, and more emotionally stable (Roberts, Walton, & Viechtbauer, 2006).

In sum, a good deal of evidence indicates that many core personality traits, such as impulsivity or timidity, are quite stable between childhood and adolescence and between adolescence and young adulthood (McCrae et al., 2002; Roberts, Caspi, & Moffitt, 2001). Although the external manifestations of these traits may change with age (for example, anxiety may appear as bed-wetting in early childhood but as nervous talkativeness in adolescence), our basic, underlying traits are quite stable over time. For example, individuals who displayed relatively higher levels of aggression in preadolescence, temper tantrums during childhood, or negative emotions during infancy are more likely to behave aggressively as adolescents (Cairns, Cairns, & Neckerman, 1989; Caspi et al., 1995; Hart, Hofman, Edelstein, & Keller, 1997). Similarly, individuals who had difficulty controlling their impulses as preschoolers are more likely to be impulsive, aggressive, and danger seeking as adolescents and young adults, while individuals who were inhibited as young children tend to be relatively more timid, anxious, and shy as teenagers. Not surprisingly, then, individuals who are judged to be well adjusted in early and middle childhood tend to be resilient and competent in adolescence (Caspi & Silva, 1995; Gest, 1997; Gjerde, 1995; Hart et al., 1997; Shiner, Masten, & Tellegen, 2002).

FOOD FOR THOUGHT

Why is there continuity in personality over childhood and adolescence? Do you see elements of yourself that have always been present in your personality? Thinking about yourself, would you agree with the statement "The person who enters adolescence is basically the same as that who exits it."

five-factor model   The theory that there are five basic dimensions to personality: extraversion, agreeableness, conscientiousness, neuroticism, and openness to experience.

Despite popular stereotypes about adolescence as a time of "rebirth," research has not supported the view that adolescence is a time of tumultuous upheaval in personality. Far from it. Indeed, as one team of researchers put it, "The person who enters adolescence is basically the same as that who exits it" (Dusek & Flaherty, 1981, p. 39).

RECAP

- During the transition into adolescence, self-conceptions become increasingly complex, abstract, and psychological.
- Adolescents' self-conceptions are more differentiated and better organized than those of children.
- Although having more complex self-conceptions may be unsettling to adolescents initially, it ultimately provides for a more sophisticated and more accurate view of themselves.
- Adolescents are able to distinguish between their actual and their imagined selves, and between their authentic and false selves.
- There are five basic personality dimensions in adolescence and adulthood, often referred to as the big five: extraversion, agreeableness, conscientiousness, neuroticism, and openness to experience.
- Longitudinal studies show strong links between early temperament and adolescent personality, and stability in basic personality traits over time.

Researchers differentiate between baseline self-esteem, which does not fluctuate across situations, and barometric self-esteem, which does.

Changes in Self-Esteem

One of the manifestations assumed to result from the "storm and stress" of adolescence involves problems in adolescents' self-esteem—how they evaluate themselves. As you will read, although there is no dramatic drop in self-esteem in adolescence, research indicates that adolescents' feelings about themselves fluctuate from day to day, particularly during the early adolescent years. From about eighth grade on, however, self-esteem remains highly stable.

STABILITY AND CHANGES IN SELF-ESTEEM

As you read in Chapter 2, the stability of a trait (like intelligence or self-esteem) has nothing to do with the degree to which people change with age, because stability merely refers to the extent to which individuals'

relative standing stays more or less the same over time. Height, for instance, is a stable trait (tall children tend to become tall adults) that nevertheless changes a great deal with age (individuals grow taller between childhood and adulthood). Asking whether self-esteem changes during adolescence (that is, whether on average people's view of themselves become more positive or negative) is not the same as asking whether self-esteem is stable during this period (that is, whether individuals with high self-esteem as children are likely to have high self-esteem as adolescents). In general, self-esteem tends to become increasingly more stable between childhood and early adulthood, suggesting that adolescents' feelings about themselves gradually consolidate over time, becoming less likely to fluctuate in response to different experiences (Alasker & Olweus, 1992; Trzesniewski, Donnellan, & Robins, 2003). Along similar lines, day-to-day fluctuations in mood tend to become smaller between early adolescence and late adolescence (Larson, Moneta, Richards, & Wilson, 2002).

Studies of changes in self-esteem as individuals move through adolescence have not yielded consistent findings, partly because researchers have focused on

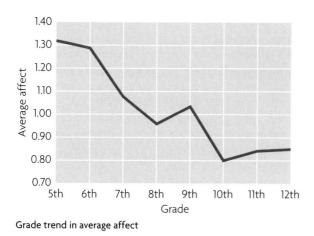

Grade trend in average affect

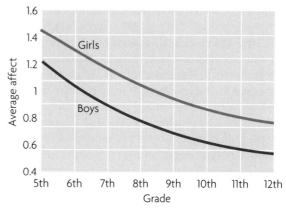

Estimated time trends of mean affect across grades for girls and boys

FIGURE 8.2   On average, individuals become less positive in their mood between fifth and ninth grades. Around tenth grade, however, this decline in mood starts to level off. (Larson et al., 2002)

different aspects of individuals' self-image. As a consequence, some studies find that individuals' feelings about themselves decline over the course of adolescence (e.g., Jacobs, Lanza, Osgood, Eccles, & Wigfield, 2002), but others find that they increase (Cole et al., 2001). In general, however, *changes* in self-perceptions (whether positive or negative) are greater during early adolescence than during middle or late adolescence; from middle adolescence through young adulthood, self-esteem either remains at about the same level or increases (Block & Robins, 1993; Harter, 1997; Nottelmann, 1987; O'Malley & Bachman, 1983; Rosenberg, 1986; Savin-Williams & Demo, 1984). Interestingly, although there is a general trend for individuals' average mood to become less positive over the course of adolescence (that is, on average, children are usually in a more positive mood than young adolescents, who are generally in a better mood than older adolescents), this trend begins to level off around tenth grade, around the time that self-esteem seems to stop changing as well (Larson et al., 2002) (see Figure 8.2).

Although adolescence is not a time of storm and stress, some evidence suggests that for a brief period during early adolescence, minor problems in self-image may arise. Some 35 years ago, Roberta Simmons and colleagues conducted a series of now-classic studies that shed light on when and why these problems in self-image are likely to occur (Simmons, Rosenberg, & Rosenberg, 1973). The researchers assessed three aspects of adolescents' self-image: their self-esteem (how positively or negatively they feel about themselves), their **self-consciousness** (how much they worry about their self-image), and their **self-image stability** (how much they feel that their self-image changes from day to day). They hypothesized that young adolescents would show the lowest levels of

self-esteem, the highest levels of self-consciousness, and the shakiest self-image.

Consistent with their expectations, the researchers found that fluctuations in adolescents' self-image are most likely to occur between the ages of 12 and 14. Compared with older adolescents (15 years and older) and with preadolescents (8–11 years old), early adolescents have lower self-esteem, are more self-conscious, and have a more unstable self-image than do other youngsters. Younger adolescents are also more prone to feel ashamed than older individuals, which may result from and contribute to their heightened self-consciousness (Reimer, 1996; Reimer, Overton, Steidl, Roscastein, Horowitz, 1996). Generally, the small but reliable differences between the preadolescents and the early adolescents are greater than those between the younger and the older adolescents, which indicates that the most marked fluctuations in self-image occur during the transition into adolescence, rather than over the course of adolescence itself (Simmons et. al., 1973). Consistent with this, a recent study of poor, urban students in New York City, Baltimore, and Washington, DC, found that the transition from elementary into junior high school was more likely to disrupt adolescents' self-esteem than was the transition into high school (Seidman & French, 2004),

▌ **Barometric and Baseline Self-Esteem**   How can we reconcile these findings about fluctuations in self-esteem with studies indicating that self-esteem is

self-consciousness   The degree to which an individual is preoccupied with his or her self-image.

self-image stability   The degree to which an individual feels that his or her self-image changes from day to day.

quite stable during adolescence? According to sociologist Morris Rosenberg (1986), it is important to differentiate between two aspects of self-perception in looking at studies of self-esteem. **Barometric self-esteem** refers to that aspect of our feelings about ourselves that fluctuates rapidly from moment to moment. Perhaps you can remember times as a teenager—or even as an adult—when you entered a room full of people feeling confident but suddenly felt nervous and insecure, only to engage in a pleasant interaction with someone an hour later and feel confident once again. You were experiencing fluctuations in your barometric self-esteem.

Baseline self-esteem, in contrast, is less transitory and less likely to fluctuate from moment to moment. This aspect of self-image is relatively stable over time and is unlikely to be easily influenced by immediate experiences. Even if you feel momentarily insecure when entering a room full of new people, your deep-down, or baseline, self-esteem has not shifted. Indeed, individuals with high baseline self-esteem would readily dismiss transient feelings of insecurity as having more to do with the situation than with themselves.

Studies that report very high stability in self-esteem over adolescence are likely tapping the individual's baseline self-esteem, which is unlikely to change dramatically over time. This may be because the determinants of baseline self-esteem are themselves relatively stable factors such as social class (middle-class adolescents have higher self-esteem than do less affluent peers), sex (boys have higher self-esteem than girls), birth order (oldest or only children have higher self-esteem), and academic ability (more able adolescents have higher self-esteem) (Bachman & O'Malley, 1986; Jackson, Hodge, & Ingram, 1994; Savin-Williams & Demo, 1983). In contrast, studies that show fluctuation and volatility in self-image during early adolescence are probably focusing on barometric self-image, which by definition is more likely to fluctuate.

FOOD FOR THOUGHT

What makes barometric self-esteem more volatile in some individuals than others? Is it possible to have high baseline self-esteem but very volatile barometric self-esteem?

In other words, although individuals' baseline self-image does not change markedly over adolescence, early adolescence is a time of increased volatility in barometric self-image (Rosenberg, 1986). Oddly, the extent to which an individual's barometric self-esteem is volatile is itself a fairly stable trait; that is, young adolescents whose self-image fluctuates a lot from moment to moment are likely to develop into older adolescents who experience the same thing (Savin-Williams & Demo, 1983).

Although an individual's baseline self-image is probably a better overall indicator of how the person feels about him- or herself, fluctuations in barometric self-image can be distressing and uncomfortable—as most of us know well (Rosenberg, 1986). Consistent with this, studies indicate that young adolescents report higher levels of depressed mood than preadolescents or older teenagers do (Simmons et al., 1973). Moreover, young adolescents with the most volatile self-image report the highest levels of anxiety, tension, psychosomatic symptoms, and irritability (Rosenberg, 1986). This is especially likely among adolescents who have a great deal of stress in their day-to-day lives (Tevendale, DuBois, Lopez, & Prindiville, 1997). In other words, having a volatile self-image may make individuals especially vulnerable to the effects of stress.

Volatility in barometric self-image during early adolescence probably is due to several interrelated factors. First, the sort of egocentrism common in early adolescence, discussed in Chapter 2, may make young adolescents painfully aware of others' reactions to their behavior. Second, as individuals become more socially active, they begin to learn that people play games when they interact, and consequently they learn that it is not always possible to tell what people are thinking on the basis of how they act or what they say. This ambiguity may leave young adolescents—who are relatively unskilled at this sort of "impression management"—puzzled and uncomfortable about how they are really viewed by others. Finally, because of the increased importance of peers in early adolescence, young adolescents are especially interested in their peers' opinions of them. For the first time, they may have to come to terms with contradictions between the messages they get from their parents ("I think that hairstyle makes you even more beautiful") and the messages they get from their peers ("You'd better wear a hat until your hair grows back!"). Hearing contradictory messages probably generates a certain degree of uncertainty about themselves (Rosenberg, 1986).

■ **The Wrong Question?**   Some researchers have argued that the question of whether self-esteem is stable during adolescence is a poor one. According to several studies (Diehl, Vicary, & Deike, 1997; Hirsch &

barometric self-esteem   The aspect of self-esteem that fluctuates across situations.

baseline self-esteem   The aspect of self-esteem that is relatively stable across situations and over time.

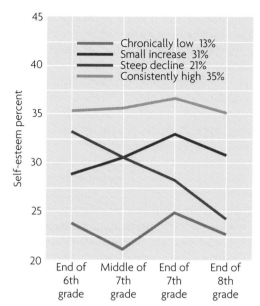

FIGURE 8.3 Research indicates that individuals follow different self-esteem trajectories during early adolescence. (Adapted from Hirsch & DuBois, 1991)

DuBois, 1991; Zimmerman, Copeland, Shope, & Dielman, 1997), some adolescents show very high stability in self-esteem over time, whereas others do not. In one study, the researchers identified four dramatically different patterns of self-esteem over time that were followed by youngsters during the transition into junior high school (see Figure 8.3). Approximately one-third of the adolescents were classified as consistently high in self-esteem, and approximately one-sixth were classified as chronically low. Half the sample, however, showed impressive patterns of change over just a two-year period: About one-fifth were categorized as steeply declining, and nearly one-third showed a small but significant increase in self-esteem. Boys may be disproportionately overrepresented in the group of adolescents whose self-esteem increases, whereas girls may be overrepresented in the group whose self-esteem declines—even though the majority of boys and girls show stability rather than dramatic change in self-esteem during adolescence (Block & Robins, 1993; Koenig, 1995; Zimmerman et al., 1997). Not surprisingly, adolescents with better family and peer relationships are more likely than their peers to maintain positive self-esteem or develop enhanced self-esteem over time (Diehl et al., 1997).

Some critics of studies of the stability of self-esteem in adolescence also question the validity of examining self-esteem in such a global, or general, sense. Although most research on adolescent self-esteem has focused on teenagers' overall feelings about themselves, most researchers today believe that young people evaluate themselves both globally (which may be a good indicator of general psychological well-being) and along several distinct dimensions, such as academics, athletics, appearance, social relationships, and moral conduct (which may indicate specific areas of strength and weakness) (Andrews, Hops, Davis, & Duncan, 1995; DuBois, Felner, Brand, Phillips, & Lease, 1996; Harter, 1999; Graziano, Jensen-Campbell, & Finch, 1997; Masten et al., 1995; Owens, 1994). As a consequence, it is possible for an adolescent to have, say, high self-esteem when it comes to academic abilities, low self-esteem when it comes to athletics, and moderate self-esteem when it comes to physical appearance, social relationships, or moral conduct. The following comments, spoken by the adolescent girl whose remarks opened the chapter, are fairly typical:

How much do I like the kind of person I am? Well, I like some things about me, but I don't like others. I'm glad that I'm popular since it's really important to me to have friends. But in school I don't do as well as the really smart kids. That's OK, because if you're too smart you'll lose your friends. So being smart is just not that important. Except to my parents. I feel like I'm letting them down when I don't do as well as they want. But what's really important to me is how I look. If I like the way I look, then I really like the kind of person I am. Don't get me wrong. I mean, I don't exactly look like Madonna even though I try to act like her. But compared to the other girls in my school, I'm sort of good-looking. There's another thing about how much I like the kind of person I am. It matters what other people think, especially the other kids at school. It matters whether they like you. I care about what my parents think about me too. I've also changed. It started when I went to junior high school. I got really depressed. I thought it was going to be so great, like I'd feel so grown-up, and then I saw all of these new, older kids who really had it together and I didn't. So I felt terrible. There was this one day when I hated the way I looked, and I didn't get invited to this really important party, and then I got an awful report card, so for a couple of days I thought it would be best to just end it all. I mean, why bother getting up the next morning? What's the point? Who cares? I was letting my parents down, I wasn't good-looking anymore, and I wasn't that popular after all, and things were never going to get better. I talked to Sheryl, my best friend, and that helped some, but what does she really know? I mean, she's my best friend, so of course she likes me! I mean, her opinion doesn't really count. It's what all the other kids think and want that counts. It was a lot easier for my brother. He got involved in this gang and just decided that what they thought was what was really important, and he stopped caring about the kids in school, or my parents, or even society. That's what he did, and he likes himself fine. But I really don't, not right now. (Harter, 1990, pp. 364–365)

Most researchers believe that self-esteem is multidimensional and that adolescents evaluate themselves along several dimensions simultaneously. As a consequence, it is possible to have high self-esteem when it comes to one's athletic abilities but low self-esteem when it comes to other things, like academics or physical attractiveness.

❚ **Components of Self-Esteem** Even within the broad domains of self-esteem mentioned previously (for example, academics, athletics, social relationships), adolescents may have quite differentiated views of themselves. Studies show, for example, that adolescents' evaluations of their social competence within the context of their relationships with their parents may be very different from the way they see themselves in the context of their relationships with teachers, which in turn may differ from their evaluations of themselves in the context of their friendships with peers (Harter, Waters, & Whitesell, 1998). Even within the realm of peer relationships, adolescents' social self-esteem may vary depending on whether they are thinking about their friendships or their romantic relationships (Connolly & Konarski, 1994). Therefore, it may be misleading to characterize an adolescent's social self-esteem as low or high without specifying the context of the relationship. The same goes for academic self-esteem: Because students evaluate their abilities in specific subject areas both in comparison to other students ("I am terrible at math compared to everyone else in this class")

and relative to their abilities in other subject areas ("I am so much better at math than I am at history"), making sweeping statements about an adolescent's overall academic self-image is often unwise (Marsh & Hau, 2004). Much depends on the basis of comparison.

Do some aspects of self-esteem contribute more to an adolescent's overall self-image than others? The answer appears to be yes. In general, adolescents' physical self-esteem—how they feel about their appearance—is the most important predictor of overall self-esteem, followed by self-esteem about relationships with peers (Harter, 1999). Less important are self-esteem about academic ability, athletic ability, or moral conduct. Interestingly, although researchers find that adolescents' physical self-esteem is the best predictor of their overall self-esteem, adolescents, when asked, say that their physical appearance is one of the least important contributors to how they feel about themselves. In other words, adolescents may be unaware of the degree to which their self-worth is based on their feelings about their appearance (DuBois, Tevendale, Burk-Braxton, Swenson, & Hardesty, 2000). It is important to note both that physical self-esteem is a more important influence on overall self-esteem among girls than among boys (Harter, 1990; Usmiani & Daniluk, 1997) and that girls' physical self-esteem is on average lower than boys' (Cole et al., 2001; Harter, 1999) (see Figure 8.4). Taken together, these findings help to explain why there are sex differences in the extent to which adolescents' experience self-image difficulties and, as we'll see in Chapter 13, depression.

SEX, CLASS, AND ETHNIC DIFFERENCES IN SELF-ESTEEM

❚ **Sex Differences in Self-Esteem** Not all adolescents undergo the same degree of fluctuation in self-esteem, nor are all adolescents' levels of self-esteem comparable. Several studies have shown that early adolescent girls are more vulnerable to disturbances in the self-image than any other group of youngsters. Specifically, early adolescent girls' self-esteem is lower, their degree of self-consciousness is higher, and their self-image is shakier than is the case for boys. As a consequence, girls also are more likely than boys to say negative things about themselves, to feel insecure about their abilities, and to worry about whether other people like being with them. Sex differences in adolescents' self-perceptions become smaller over the course of adolescence (Fredricks & Eccles, 2002).

Although sex differences in self-esteem are most pronounced among white adolescents, similar patterns have been found among Puerto Rican adolescents but not, for the most part, among African Americans

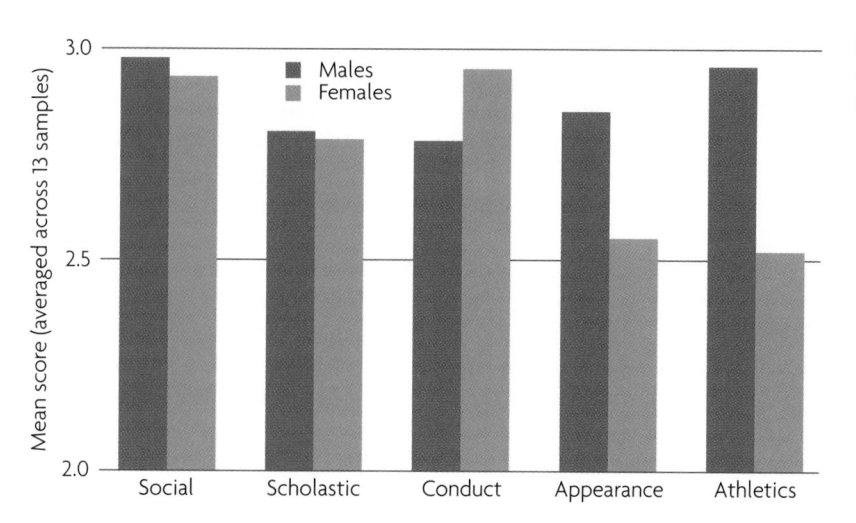

FIGURE 8.4 Sex differences in various domains of self-esteem. (Harter, 1999)

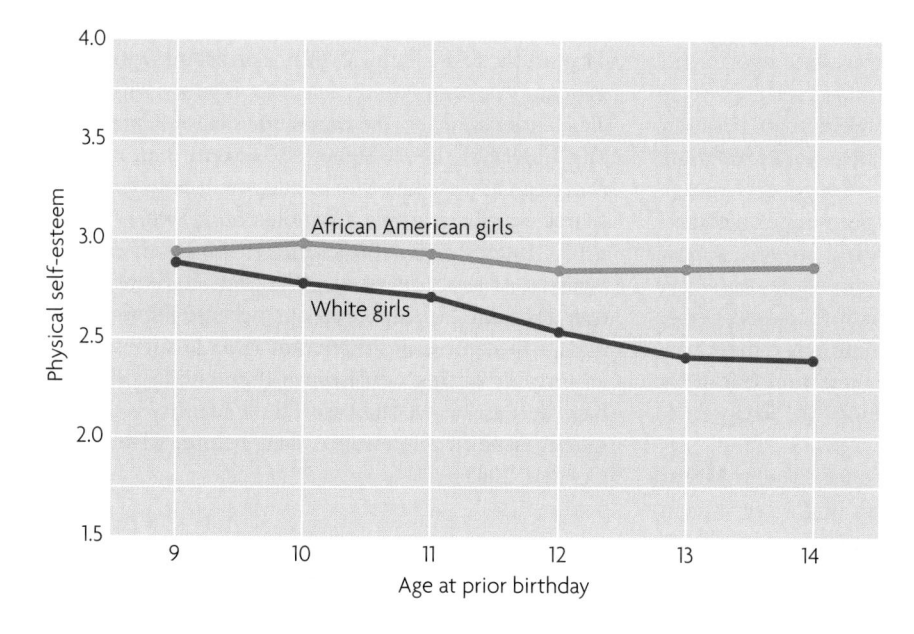

FIGURE 8.5 Race differences in patterns of change in physical self-esteem. (Brown et al., 1998)

(Erkut, Szalacha, Garcia Coll, & Alarcon, 2000; Harter, 1999; Kling, Hyde, Showers, & Buswell, 1999). Studies of African American girls do not find the same sort of self-esteem vulnerability as is found in studies of white girls, in part because African American girls do not experience the same drop in body image during puberty (Brown et al., 1998) (see Figure 8.5).

Why would girls have greater self-esteem problems during early adolescence than boys? The answer may be related to the special significance of physical self-esteem and self-esteem about acceptance by peers, as discussed earlier. Compared with other youngsters, young girls seem to worry a great deal about their looks and about dating and being popular in school. Yet they are also worried about doing well academically. Other adolescents care about these things, of course, but they have a more casual attitude.

Young adolescent girls may feel caught in a bind between pressures to do well academically and pressures to do well socially, especially as they move into secondary school. As we saw in Chapter 5, getting good grades in school is at the bottom of the list of attributes that adolescent girls feel are important for being accepted into the leading crowd (Coleman, 1961). Several studies have shown that adolescents who worry a lot about being popular are most likely to feel self-conscious and to have unstable views of themselves (Simmons & Rosenberg, 1975). Because young girls appear to be more concerned than boys about physical attractiveness, dating, and peer acceptance, they may experience a greater number of self-image problems. Because African American girls do not feel as negatively about their appearance as white or Hispanic American girls, they have higher overall self-esteem and show less of a decline in self-esteem over adolescence (Gray-Little & Hafdahl, 2000; Malanchuk & Eccles, 1999; Prosser & Carlson, 1999).

Social Class Differences in Self-Esteem

Studies also indicate that an adolescent's social class—as indexed by his or her parents' occupations, education, and income—is an important determinant of self-esteem, especially as the individual moves into middle and later adolescence. In general, middle-class youngsters have higher self-esteem than their less-affluent peers, and this discrepancy grows greater over the course of adolescence. One explanation for this is that middle-class youngsters do better in school than their less affluent peers, and this success leads to enhanced self-esteem (Demo & Savin-Williams, 1983).

Ethnic Differences in Self Esteem

Most research indicates that African American adolescents have higher self-esteem than white adolescents, who, in turn, tend to have higher self-esteem than Hispanic American, Asian American, or Native American youth (Gray-Little & Hafdahl, 2000; Twenge & Crocker, 2002). Although less research has been done on adolescents from other ethnic minority groups, several studies indicate that Asian American adolescents have significantly lower self-esteem than their peers (e.g., Herman, 2004), a finding that some researchers have attributed to higher rates of peer rejection (recall the discussion of peer discrimination in Chapter 5) (Greene & Way, 2005).

A number of researchers have asked why African American adolescents have such high self-esteem, given the prevalence of prejudice in American society and the generally disadvantaged position of African Americans in the workplace and school, two institutions where individuals' performance influences their self-image. Three main explanations for the relatively high self-esteem of African American adolescents have been offered.

First, some writers have argued that, despite their encounters with racism and prejudice, African American teenagers benefit from the support and positive feedback of adults in the African American community, especially in the family (Barnes, 1980). This is not surprising, given the wealth of research showing that the approval of significant others is an especially powerful influence on adolescents' self-esteem—much more so than the opinion of the broader society (e.g., Felson & Zielinski, 1989; Gray-Little & Hafdahl, 2000; Luster & McAdoo, 1995; Robinson, 1995).

Second, other researchers suggest that all teenagers—minority and otherwise—tend to shift their priorities over time so that they come to value those activities at which they excel. In doing so,

adolescents are able to protect their self-esteem by focusing on areas of strength instead of weakness. For example, a boy who is an outstanding student but who feels physically unattractive and does not do well in sports will likely derive positive self-esteem from his school achievement and not restrict his self-evaluation to his looks or performance on the playing field (Luster & McAdoo, 1995). One way that African American adolescents may respond to their relatively poorer school performance is to change their feelings about the importance of doing well in school, which weakens the connection between academic success and self-esteem.

Finally, several writers have suggested that the very strong sense of ethnic identity (which we look at later in this chapter) among African American adolescents serves to enhance their overall self-esteem (DuBois, Burk-Braxton, Swenson, Tevendale, & Hardesty, 2002; Gray-Little & Hafdahl, 2000). Consistent with this, African American adolescents who identify with popular black characters on television (such as Darrell, on *The Hughleys*) report higher self-esteem than African American adolescents who identify with popular white characters (for example, Chandler, on *Friends*) (Ward, 2003). Interestingly, ethnic differences in self-esteem, favoring African American adolescents, have increased over the past 25 years (perhaps because ethnic identity has become a more relevant issue in society) and are greater during adolescence than childhood (perhaps because, as we shall see, ethnic identity is a more salient issue in adolescence than before) (Twenge & Crocker, 2002).

FOOD FOR THOUGHT

Studies of ethnic differences in self-esteem, indicating relatively higher self-esteem among African American adolescents and lower self-esteem among Asian American adolescents, have almost all been conducted in the United States. Do you think similar patterns would emerge in research conducted in other countries?

Ethnic differences also exist in patterns of change in self-esteem during adolescence. In one recent study of African American, Latino, and Asian American urban adolescents, the researchers found that African American students and biracial students (mainly black/Latino) had higher self-esteem in early adolescence, and this remained high throughout the adolescent years. In contrast, Latino students had relatively

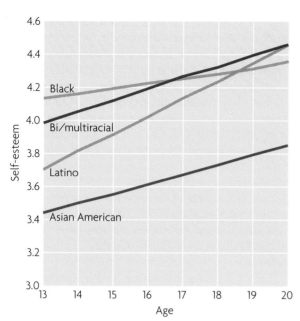

FIGURE 8.6 Ethnic differences in patterns of self-esteem over time. (Greene & Way, 2005)

lower self-esteem early in adolescence, but caught up with their African American peers by the end of high school. Asian American students began with the lowest self-esteem, and it remained lower than that of other groups over time (see Figure 8.6). Interestingly, and in contrast to studies of white adolescents, there were no sex differences in levels or patterns of change in self-esteem in this sample of ethnic minority adolescents.

The context in which adolescents develop has a substantial impact on their self-image, however. Some research indicates, for example, that high school students who live in a social environment or go to a school in which their ethnic or socioeconomic group is in the minority are more likely to have self-image problems than those who are in the majority (Rosenberg, 1975). This seems to be true with regard to religion, socioeconomic status, ethnicity, and household composition. African American teenagers, for example, have a higher opinion of themselves when they go to schools in which African American students are a majority than when they attend predominantly white schools, where they may feel out of place and under pressure to play down their cultural heritage. By the same token, Jewish adolescents have higher self-esteem in schools in which there are many other Jewish students than in schools in which Jews compose a small minority of the student body. Similarly, levels of maladjustment are higher among both Hispanic American and non–Hispanic American youngsters when they are in the minority in their school (Kaufman, Gregory, & Stephan, 1990). Consistent with this, adolescents' psychological well-being

is adversely affected by discrimination and prejudice. Adolescents who report frequent experiences of being insulted, excluded, and teased about their race or ethnicity have relatively more psychological problems than do their nondiscriminated-against peers (Caldwell, Kohn-Wood, Schmeelk-Cone, Chavous, & Zimmerman, 2004; DuBois et al., 2002; Sellers, Copeland-Linder, Martin, & Lexis, 2006).

ANTECEDENTS AND CONSEQUENCES OF HIGH SELF-ESTEEM

Several researchers have examined the link between self-esteem and adolescent behavior, in an attempt to see whether certain sorts of experiences contribute— either positively or negatively—to adolescents' feelings about themselves. Others have posed the question in reverse: Does having high (or low) self-esteem lead adolescents to behave in particular ways?

Influences on Self-Esteem Regarding the first question, studies find that self-esteem is enhanced by having the approval of others, especially of parents and peers, and by succeeding in school (Bachman & O'Malley, 1986; DuBois et al., 2002; Luster & McAdoo, 1995; Roberts et al., 2000; Wilkinson, 2004). These correlates of high self-esteem have been found in virtually all ethnic and cultural groups, although the self-esteem of Asian American youngsters seems especially influenced by their academic success (e.g., Szesulski, Martinez, & Reyes, 1994). Thus, even though there are ethnic differences in average levels of self-esteem, the correlates of self-esteem are different in different ethnic groups (Rowe et al., 1994).

Adolescents whose self-esteem is too wrapped up in the approval of others—especially the approval of peers—may be at risk for developing self-image problems, since peer acceptance may fluctuate over time, leading to temporary drops in self-esteem (Harter, Stocker, & Robinson, 1996). Consistent with this, adolescents who tend to derive their self-esteem relatively more from peers, as opposed to teachers or parents, show more behavioral problems and poorer school achievement (DuBois, Felner, Brand, & George, 1999; DuBois, Bull, Sherman, & Roberts, 1998; DuBois et al., 2002). In fact, one explanation for the increase in problem behavior that takes place over the course of adolescence is that adolescents tend to look relatively more to their peers for social support as they get older (DuBois et al., 2002).

Consequences of High Self-Esteem How does having high self-esteem influence adolescents' adjustment and behavior? Although it once was believed that enhanced self-esteem leads to school

Adolescents who attend schools in which they are in the ethnic minority may suffer greater self-esteem problems than their peers who attend schools in which they are in the majority. Although desegregation may have a positive impact on minority adolescents' academic achievement, this benefit may be counterbalanced by the apparently negative impact of desegregation on minority students' self-image.

success, there actually is little evidence for this, and a good deal of evidence for the opposite (e.g., Liu, Kaplan, & Rosser, 1992; Rosenberg, Schooler, & Schoenback, 1989; Schmidt & Padilla, 2003). That is, academic success leads to improvements in how adolescents feel about themselves, not the other way around. These findings cast doubt on the logic behind programs designed to raise teenagers' school performance by increasing their self-esteem. High self-esteem during adolescence does enhance adolescents' well-being, however, whereas low self-esteem may lead to involvement in deviant activity, psychological distress, and victimization, both in the short run (Andrews, Alpert, Hops, & Davis, 1996; DuBois & Tevendale, 1999; Egan & Perry, 1998; Liu et al., 1992; Rosenberg et al., 1989) and well into adulthood (Trzesniewski et al., 2006).

Actually, the relation between low self-esteem and emotional and behavioral problems is complicated (Cole, Peeke, Dolezal, Murray, & Canzoniero, 1999; Gerard & Buehler, 2004; Tram & Cole, 2000). Low self-esteem is one of several symptoms of depression, but it is not clear whether depression leads to low self-esteem, or vice versa. The answer, it seems, depends on the individual. For about half of all adolescents, having low self-esteem leads to depression and other forms of emotional distress. For the other half, however, the reverse is true—depression leads to low self-esteem (Harter, 1999). One reason that low self-esteem may lead to depression is that adolescents with negative feelings about themselves are less likely to seek positive feedback from others (Cassidy, Ziv, Mehta, & Feeney, 2003).

The link between self-esteem and behavior problems (as opposed to emotional problems) is even less clear. Although low self-esteem initially may impel some adolescents toward delinquency, involvement with delinquent peers actually may lead to an increase in self-esteem, perhaps because involvement in delinquency earns teenagers approval from certain peers (Dishion, Andrews, & Crosby, 1995; Jang & Thornberry, 1998; Mason, 2001; Rosenberg et al., 1989). Furthermore, adolescents with high self-esteem are more likely to experiment with alcohol than are those with low self-esteem (Scheier, Botvin, Griffin, & Diaz, 2000), most probably because high self-esteem is associated with being in the more popular, social crowds, in which drinking is more common.

RECAP

- Researchers have differed in their approach to the study of self-esteem. While some have studied adolescents' general, or global, feelings about themselves, others have stressed the multidimensional nature of self-esteem.
- Adolescence is a time of gradual rather than tumultuous change in individuals' self-image. For most individuals, global self-esteem is quite stable during adolescence and, contrary to popular belief, increases slightly.
- During early adolescence, individuals may experience periods of heightened self-consciousness, and their self-image may fluctuate more than during other periods.
- Generally, males, middle-class adolescents, and African American adolescents have higher self-esteem than females, less affluent youth, or adolescents from other ethnic groups, although sex differences in self-esteem are much more pronounced among white teenagers. Asian American

adolescents have especially low self-esteem relative to their peers.

- Across all demographic groups, high self-esteem is related to parental approval, peer support, and success in school. Although it is difficult to disentangle cause and effect, high self-esteem is associated with better mental health, whereas low self-esteem is correlated with a number of emotional problems.

The Adolescent Identity Crisis

Many of the twentieth century's most important novels, from James Joyce's *Portrait of the Artist as a Young Man* to J. D. Salinger's *The Catcher in the Rye*, revolve around an adolescent's identity crisis. Indeed, the coming-of-age novel is a classic literary genre. One of the most memorable fictional accounts of an adolescent's struggle to find her identity is told in Carson McCullers's *The Member of the Wedding*. Set in the South during the mid-1940s, the story revolves around the identity development of Frankie Addams, a 12-year-old girl who has her first encounter that summer with the sort of self-examination and introspection that we have come to associate with the adolescent years. Here is Frankie speaking to her confidante, Berenice:

> Listen. . . . What I've been trying to say is this. Doesn't it strike you as strange that I am I, and you are you? I am F. Jasmine Addams. And you are Berenice Sadie Brown. And we can look at each other, and touch each other, and stay together year in and year out in the same room. Yet always I am I, and you are you. And I can't ever be anything else but me, and you can't ever be anything else but you. Have you ever thought of that? And does it seem to you strange? (McCullers, 1946, p. 109)

If you were asked to write a novel about your own identity development, what sorts of things would you mention? Perhaps you would talk about the development of a sense of purpose, or the clarification of your long-term plans and values, or the growing feeling of knowing who you really are and where you are headed. If these are the sorts of things that come to mind when you think about identity development in adolescence, you are thinking about an aspect of development that psychologists refer to as the sense of identity. The dominant view in the study of adolescent identity development emphasizes precisely these aspects of psychosocial development, and the theorist whose work has been most influential in this area is Erik Erikson.

ERIKSON'S THEORETICAL FRAMEWORK

Erikson's (1959, 1963, 1968) theory developed out of his clinical and cross-cultural observations of young people at various stages of development. He viewed the developing person as moving through a series of eight psychosocial crises over the course of the life span. Each crisis, although present in one form or another at all ages, takes on special significance at a given period of the life cycle because biological and social forces interact to bring the crisis into prominence. Erikson believed that the establishment of a coherent sense of identity—what he called the crisis of **identity versus identity diffusion**—is the chief psychosocial crisis of adolescence.

IDENTITY VERSUS IDENTITY DIFFUSION

Prior to adolescence, the child's identity is like patches of fabric that have not yet been sewn together. But by the end of adolescence, these patches will be woven into a patchwork quilt that is unique to the individual. As Erikson described it, "From among all possible and imaginable relations, [the young person] must make a series of ever-narrowing selections of personal, occupational, sexual, and ideological commitments" (1968, p. 245). The maturational and social forces that converge at adolescence force young people to reflect on their place in society, on the ways that others view them, and on their options for the future. Achieving a balanced and coherent sense of identity is an intellectually and emotionally taxing process. In fact, according to Erikson, it is not until adolescence that one even has the mental or emotional capacity to tackle this task.

The key to resolving the crisis of identity versus identity diffusion, argued Erikson, lies in the adolescent's interactions with others. By responding to the reactions of people who matter, the adolescent selects and chooses from among the many elements that could conceivably become a part of his or her adult identity. The other people with whom the young person interacts serve as a mirror that reflects back to the adolescent information about who he or she is and ought to be. As such, the responses of these significant others shape and influence the adolescent's developing sense of identity. Through others' reactions, adolescents learn whether they are competent or clumsy,

identity versus identity diffusion   According to Erikson, the normative crisis characteristic of the fifth stage of psychosocial development, predominant during adolescence.

attractive or ugly, socially adept or tactless. Perhaps more importantly—especially during periods when their sense of identity is still forming—they learn from others what they do that they ought to keep doing, and what they do that they ought to stop doing.

One process through which this occurs is via the sharing of important memories with others. When we tell stories to friends or family members about our previous experiences, we do so for a variety of reasons, one of which is to help ourselves understand who we are and how we were changed by the experience. In one recent study of college undergraduates (McLean, 2005), students were asked to describe occasions in the past year in which they shared an important memory with another person. One participant described the following event, which took place when he was in high school:

> I was at my friend's house one night with my main group of friends. They were all smoking marijuana and drinking. I did not feel comfortable with trying marijuana. They tried hard to get me to try it, but I chose not to. One of my friends (my best) supported my choice. *I learned who my real friends were. But more important, I learned that I can be strong with my decisions if I choose to, regardless of the outside influence.*

He then described telling his college friends about the event:

> The subject of drugs came up and so I explained the above story to them. They seemed to enjoy the story and applauded me on my resiliency. Now, my friends here [at college] will ask me if I want to do anything and they will not harass me about it, regardless of my answer. *It pays to be strong when you want to.* (McLean, 2005, p. 687; italics in original)

In other words, developing an identity is a social as well as mental process. Erikson placed a great deal of weight on the role of society (and, especially, on those individuals who have influence over the adolescent) in shaping the adolescent's sense of self. The adolescent's identity is the result of a mutual recognition between the young person and society: The adolescent forges an identity, but, at the same time, society identifies the adolescent.

THE SOCIAL CONTEXT OF IDENTITY DEVELOPMENT

The social context in which the adolescent attempts to establish a sense of identity exerts a tremendous impact on the nature and outcome of the process. Clearly, if adolescents' identities are forged out of a recognition on the part of society, society will play an

important role in determining which sorts of identities are possible alternatives; and of those identities that are genuine options, society will influence which are desirable and which are not.

As a consequence, the course of identity development will vary in different cultures, among different subcultures within the same society, and over different historical eras (Kroger, 1993). For example, the career options open to women in contemporary American society have changed dramatically in the past 40 years and, consequently, so has the nature of adolescent girls' identity development. In the past, most young women assumed that their adult identity would be exclusively tied to marriage and family life. But today, many more alternative identities are open to women. As a result, the process of choosing among different alternatives has become more complicated than it once was.

The social context in which an adolescent develops also determines to a large extent whether the youngster's search for self-definition will take the form of a full-blown crisis or whether it will be a more manageable challenge, Generally, the more alternatives available to the young person, and the more arenas in which decisions must be made, the more difficult establishing a sense of identity will be. Growing up in contemporary America, where adolescents have a range of careers to decide among, for example, is far more likely to provoke an occupational identity crisis than is growing up in a small agrarian community in which each young person continues farming the family's land.

The rapid rate of social change in most of the industrialized world has raised new and more complex sets of questions for young people to consider—questions not only about occupational plans but also about values, lifestyles, and commitments to other people. Today, adolescents must ask themselves if they want to remain single, live with someone, or marry; if and when they want to have children; and how they plan to incorporate these choices into their career plans. Consequently, the likelihood of going through a prolonged and difficult identity crisis is probably greater today than it has ever been.

The Psychosocial Moratorium According to Erikson, the complications inherent in identity development in modern society have created the need for a **psychosocial moratorium**—a "time out" during adolescence from the sorts of excessive responsibilities and obligations that might restrict the young person's pursuit of self-discovery. Adolescents in contemporary America are given a moratorium of sorts by being encouraged to remain in school for a long time, where they can think seriously about their plans for the future without making irrevocable decisions.

psychosocial moratorium A period during which individuals are free from excessive obligations and responsibilities, and can therefore experiment with different roles and personalities.

Role experimentation during adolescence often involves trying on different looks, images, and patterns of behavior. According to theorists such as Erik Erikson, having the time and freedom to experiment with different roles is an important prelude to establishing a coherent sense of identity.

During the psychosocial moratorium, the adolescent can experiment with different roles and identities in a context that permits and encourages this sort of exploration. The experimentation involves trying on different postures, personalities, and ways of behaving—sometimes to the consternation of the adolescent's parents, who may wonder why their child's personality seems so changeable. One week, an adolescent girl will spend hours putting on makeup; the next week, she will insist to her parents that she is tired of caring so much about the way she looks. An adolescent boy will come home one day with a shaved head and pierced ear, and a few weeks later he will discard this image for that of a preppie. Many parents worry about their teenage children going through these sorts of phases. Much of this behavior, however, is actually normal experimentation with roles and personalities.

Having the time to experiment with roles is an important prelude to establishing a coherent sense of identity. But role experimentation can take place only in an environment that allows and encourages it (Gallatin, 1975). Without a moratorium, a full and thorough exploration of the options and alternatives available to the young person cannot occur, and identity development will be somewhat impeded. In other words, according to Erikson, adolescents must grow into an adult identity—they should not be forced into one prematurely.

It is clear, however, that the sort of moratorium Erikson described is an ideal; indeed, some might even consider it to be a luxury of the affluent. Many young people—perhaps even most—do not have the economic freedom to enjoy a long delay before taking on the responsibilities of adult life. For many youngsters, alternatives do not exist in any realistic sense, and introspection only interferes with the more pressing task of survival. Does the 17-year-old who must drop out of school to work a full-time factory job go through life without a sense of identity? Do youngsters who cannot afford a psychosocial moratorium fail to resolve the crisis of identity versus identity diffusion?

Certainly not. But from an Eriksonian point of view, the absence of a psychosocial moratorium in some adolescents' lives—either because of restrictions they place on themselves, restrictions placed on them by others, or their life circumstances—is truly lamentable. The price these youngsters pay has to do not with failure to develop a sense of identity but with lost potential. You may know people whose parents forced them into prematurely choosing a certain career or who had to drop out of college and take a job they really did not want because of financial pressures. According to Erikson, without a chance to explore, to experiment, and to choose among options for the future, these young people may not realize all that they are capable of becoming.

RESOLVING THE IDENTITY CRISIS

Is establishing a sense of identity something that is conscious? According to Erikson, it is. It is experienced as a sense of well-being, a feeling of "being at home in one's body," a sense of knowing where one is going, and an inner assuredness of recognition from those who count. It is a sense of sameness through time—a feeling of continuity between the past and the future.

FOOD FOR THOUGHT

Have you experienced the sort of identity crisis described by Erikson? If so, when did it happen, and what did it feel like? Was it triggered by anything in particular?

Establishing a coherent sense of identity is a lengthy process. Most writers on adolescence and youth believe that identity exploration continues well into young adulthood. But rather than thinking of the adolescent as going through a single identity crisis, it probably makes more sense to view the phenomenon as a series of crises that may concern different aspects of the young person's identity and that may surface—and resurface—at different points in time throughout the adolescent and young-adult years. As Erikson wrote, "A sense of identity is never gained nor maintained once and for all" (1959, p. 118). Indeed, during adolescence, the feeling of well-being associated with establishing a sense of identity is often fleeting. Ultimately, however, the identity crisis of adolescence, when successfully resolved, culminates in a series of basic life commitments: occupational, ideological, social, religious, ethical, and sexual (Bourne, 1978a).

PROBLEMS IN IDENTITY DEVELOPMENT

Given the wide variations in developmental histories that individuals bring to adolescence and the wide variations in the environments in which they develop, it is not surprising to find differences in the ways in which individuals approach and resolve the crisis of identity versus identity diffusion. Problems in identity development can result when an individual has not successfully resolved earlier crises or when the adolescent is in an environment that does not provide the necessary period of moratorium. Three sorts of problems received special attention from Erikson: identity diffusion, identity foreclosure, and negative identity.

■ **Identity Diffusion**   **Identity diffusion,** is characterized by an incoherent, disjointed, incomplete sense of self. Identity diffusion can vary in degree from a mild state of not quite knowing who one is while in the midst of an identity crisis to a more severe, psychopathological condition that persists beyond a normal period of exploration. It is marked by disruptions in the individual's sense of time (some things seem to happen much faster than they really do, while others seem to take forever); excessive self-consciousness, to the point that it is difficult to make decisions; problems in work and school; difficulties in forming intimate relationships with others; and concerns over sexuality. In other words, identity diffusion is reflected not only in problems of identity but also in the areas of autonomy, intimacy, sexuality, and achievement.

A classic example of an adolescent in the throes of identity diffusion is Holden Caulfield in the 1951 novel *The Catcher in the Rye*. He has flunked out of several prep schools, has severed most of his friendships, and has no sense of where he is headed. At one point in the book, for example, walking up Fifth Avenue in New York City, Holden says, "Every time I came to the end of a block and stepped off the goddam curb, I had this feeling that I'd never get to the other side of the street. I thought I'd just go down, down, down, and nobody'd ever see me again. Boy, did it scare me" (Salinger, [1951] 1964, pp. 197–198).

■ **Identity Foreclosure**   Some young people bypass—either willingly or unwillingly—the period of exploration and experimentation that precedes the establishment of a healthy sense of identity. Instead of considering a range of alternatives, these adolescents prematurely commit themselves to a role, or series of roles, and settle upon a certain identification as a final identity. In essence, these individuals are not given—or do not take advantage of—a psychosocial moratorium. For example, a college freshman who made up her mind about becoming a doctor at the age of 13 may enroll in a rigid premed curriculum without considering other career possibilities. The circumvention of the identity crisis is called **identity foreclosure.**

Typically, the roles adopted in the process of identity foreclosure revolve around the goals set for the young person by parents or other authority figures. The adolescent may be led into these roles directly or may be forced into them indirectly by being denied a true psychosocial moratorium. Perhaps the parents of the would-be doctor have arranged their child's school schedule and summer vacations so that all of her spare time is spent taking extra science courses. No time is left for role experimentation or introspection. Individuals who have bypassed the identity crisis have made commitments, but they have not gone through a period of experimentation before making them. Identity foreclosure is an interruption of the identity development process, an interruption that interferes with the individual's discovery of his or her full range of potentials.

FOOD FOR THOUGHT

The broader context in which adolescents develop affects the nature of their identity development. Are there any aspects of today's environment that might make the resolution of the identity crisis especially difficult?

identity diffusion   The incoherent, disjointed, incomplete sense of self characteristic of not having resolved the crisis of identity.

identity foreclosure   The premature establishment of a sense of identity, before sufficient role experimentation has occurred.

Negative Identity Occasionally, adolescents appear to select identities that are obviously undesirable to their parents and their community. The examples are familiar: the daughter of the local police chief who repeatedly gets into trouble with the law, the son of prestigious and successful parents who refuses to go to college, or the child of a devoutly religious family who insists that he or she is a confirmed atheist. Because the establishment of a healthy sense of identity is so intimately tied to the recognition of the adolescent by those who count in her or his life, the adoption of a so-called **negative identity** is a sign that problems in identity development have arisen. The adolescent who adopts a negative identity is recognized by those around him or her, but not in a way that fosters healthy development.

Usually, selecting a negative identity represents an attempt to forge some sense of self-definition in an environment that has made it difficult to establish an acceptable identity. This appears to be especially likely when, after repeatedly trying and failing to receive positive recognition from those who are important in their lives, adolescents turn to a different, perhaps more successful, route to being noticed—adopting a negative identity. Consider this example: The son of successful parents is a good student but not quite good enough to please his excessively demanding parents. He feels he is a nobody in his parents' eyes, so he drops out of school to play guitar in a band—something his parents vehemently oppose. To paraphrase Erikson, this adolescent, like most youngsters, would rather be somebody "bad" than nobody at all.

RECAP

- According to Erikson, the major psychosocial issue of adolescence revolves around the identity crisis—coming to terms with who one is and where one is headed.
- To resolve the identity crisis, the young person needs some time out from excessive responsibilities—a psychosocial moratorium—in order to engage in identity exploration and experimentation.
- Some adolescents have trouble resolving the identity crisis. The three most common problems described by Erikson are identity diffusion, identity foreclosure, and negative identity.
- Problems in identity development can result when the individual has not resolved earlier crises or when the adolescent is in an environment that does not provide the necessary period of psychosocial moratorium.

		Commitment: Present	Commitment: Absent
Exploration	Present	Identity achievement	Moratorium
	Absent	Identity foreclosure	Identity diffusion

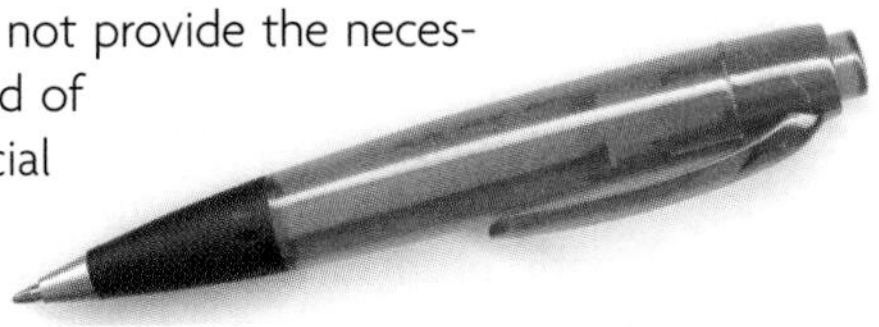

FIGURE 8.7 Identity status categories derived from Marcia's (1966) measure.

Research on Identity Development

DETERMINING AN ADOLESCENT'S IDENTITY STATUS

The term "identity status" refers to the point in the identity development process that characterizes an adolescent at a given time. In order to determine an individual's identity status, most researchers have used an approach developed by James Marcia (1966, 1976), which focuses on identity exploration in three areas—occupation, ideology (values and beliefs), and interpersonal relations. Based on responses to an interview or questionnaire, individuals are rated on two dimensions: (1) the degree to which they have made commitments and (2) the degree to which they engaged in a sustained search in the process (see Figure 8.7). On the basis of these ratings, the researchers assign young people to one of four categories: (1) identity achievement (the individual has established a coherent sense of identity, that is, has made commitments after a period of crisis and experimentation), (2) moratorium (the individual is in the midst of a period of crisis and experimentation), (3) identity foreclosure (the individual has made commitments but without a period of crisis or experimentation), or (4) identity diffusion (the individual does not have firm commitments and is not currently trying to make them). Within each of these categories, it is also possible to draw somewhat finer distinctions—for example, between foreclosed individuals whose foreclosure seems temporary and those whose foreclosure appears "firm" (Kroger, 1995).

Generally, research employing this approach has supported many aspects of Erikson's theory (see Berzonsky & Adams, 1999; Meeus, Iedema, Helsen, & Vollebergh, 1999; Meeus, Iedema, & Vollebergh, 1999; van Hoof, 1999; Waterman, 1999a, 1999b; Zimmerman & Becker-Stoll, 2002). The strongest support for the

negative identity The selection of an identity that is obviously undesirable in the eyes of significant others and the broader community.

theory comes from studies that show a pattern of correlations between various traits and the different identity statuses that are consistent with predictions based on Erikson's model. As you might expect, for example, identity achievers are psychologically healthier than other individuals on a variety of measures: They score highest on measures of achievement motivation, moral reasoning, intimacy with peers, reflectiveness, and career maturity. Individuals in the moratorium category score highest on measures of anxiety, show the highest levels of conflict over issues of authority, and are themselves the least rigid and least authoritarian. Individuals classified as being in the foreclosure group have been shown to be the most authoritarian and most prejudiced, and to have the highest need for social approval, the lowest level of autonomy, and the greatest closeness to their parents. Individuals in a state of identity diffusion display the highest level of psychological and interpersonal problems: They are the most socially withdrawn and show the lowest level of intimacy with peers (Adams, Gullotta, & Montemayor, 1992; Fulton, 1997; Meeus, 1997; Wallace-Broscious, Serafica, & Osipow, 1994).

■ **Ways of Resolving the Identity Crisis** Several researchers have also described the ways in which different individuals approach the resolution of the identity crisis (e.g., Berzonsky, 2004). According to this framework, it is possible to differentiate among individuals who tend to actively seek information and approach identity-related decisions with an open mind (described as having an "informational" orientation), those who attempt to conform to family and other social expectations and try to get identity-related decisions over as quickly as possible (described as having a "normative" orientation), and those who tend to procrastinate and avoid making identity-related decisions (described as having a "diffuse/avoidant" orientation). Not surprisingly, the informational orientation is more characteristic of identity achievers, the normative orientation is more characteristic of individuals who are identity foreclosed, and the diffuse/avoidant orientation is more characteristic of individuals who exhibit identity diffusion.

More evidence of this sort comes from a study that attempted to link classifications based on a measure of identity development with scores on the personality dimensions tapped within the five-factor model of personality discussed earlier (Clancy & Dollinger, 1993). As expected, adolescents who were classified as identity achievers were higher in extraversion and less neurotic than other adolescents; foreclosed adolescents were less open; and diffused adolescents were more neurotic, less open, and less agreeable. It was not clear from this study

whether different personality constellations led to different patterns of identity development or, alternatively, whether different patterns of identity development influenced subsequent personality. Given what we know about the childhood antecedents of personality traits, however, the former explanation (that personality affects identity development) seems more likely than the latter.

One of the defining characteristics of individuals who have achieved a coherent sense of identity, at least in contemporary American society, is that they approach life's decisions with a strong sense of **agency**—they take responsibility for themselves, they feel in control of their decisions, and they have confidence that they will be able to overcome obstacles along the way (Côté, 2000). In recent studies of college students from different ethnic groups, psychologist James Côté and colleagues have shown that a strong sense of personal agency is predictive of identity achievement across ethnic and socioeconomic groups (e.g., Schwartz, Côté, & Arnett, 2005). Being "in charge" of one's life may be especially important in contemporary industrialized society, where the transition to adulthood is prolonged and where individuals are faced with a tremendous number of identity-related decisions. Consistent with this, individuals in their late teens or early 20s who, when asked whether they are adolescents or adults, say they are not sure, are less likely to have achieved a sense of identity than are those who are certain that they have reached adulthood (Nelson & Barry, 2005). It is not clear whether having a coherent sense of identity leads one to think of oneself as an adult or, instead, whether seeing oneself as an adult leads one to have a more coherent sense of identity. But it does seem that becoming an adult, at least in industrialized society, is a psychological transition as well as one characterized by entering the formal roles of adulthood.

What sorts of parenting practices are associated with different identity statuses? Generally, individuals whose identity development is healthy are more likely to come from authoritative homes characterized by warm, but not excessively constraining, relations, a finding that has been replicated in both white and Latino samples (Berzonsky, 2004; Grotevant & Cooper, 1986; Perosa, Perosa, & Tam, 1996; Schwartz, Pantin, Prado, Sullivan, & Szapocznik, 2005). As we saw in Chapter 4, individuals who grow up in these environments are encouraged to assert their individuality but remain connected to their families at the same time. Typically, the absence of parental warmth is associated with problems in making commitments—the most extreme case being identity diffusion—whereas the absence of parental encouragement of individuality is associated with problems in engaging in extensive exploration (Campbell, Adams, & Dobson, 1984).

agency   The sense that one has an impact on one's world.

STUDYING IDENTITY DEVELOPMENT OVER TIME

In order to examine the development of a sense of identity, researchers have done both cross-sectional studies (comparing individuals of different ages) and longitudinal studies (following the same individuals over a period of time). Many of these studies have raised questions about the accuracy of the identity status model. Perhaps the most significant finding to emerge from this research is that a coherent sense of identity generally is not established before age 18, let alone earlier in adolescence, as originally hypothesized (Marcia, 1980). In general, when comparisons are made among groups of youngsters of different ages over the span from ages 12 to 24, differences in identity status are most frequently observed between groups in the 18- to 21-year-old range. Few consistent differences emerge in comparisons of teenagers in the middle adolescent years, suggesting that, although self-examination may take place throughout adolescence, the consolidation of a coherent sense of identity does not begin until very late in the period (Adams & Jones, 1983; Archer, 1982; Luyckx, Goossens, & Soenens, 2006; Reis & Youniss, 2004). The late teens and early 20s appear to be the critical times for the crystallization of a sense of identity (Nurmi, 2004; Schwartz et al., 2005).

The movement toward identity achievement that occurs between ages 18 and 21 among college students appears to be primarily in the area of occupational commitments. During the college years, vocational plans solidify, but religious and political commitments are not as clearly established. More specifically, individuals emerge from college with more clearly defined occupational plans but no firm religious or political commitments (Waterman, 1982). In fact, college seems to *undermine* students' traditional religious beliefs—the beliefs they acquired from their parents—without replacing them. Students who enter college as devout Catholics, for example, may graduate from college having lost some of their commitment to Catholicism but without having developed any new religious commitments. This pattern may not hold for adolescents from all religious groups, however. One study of Mormon adolescents, for example, found that these youngsters were much more likely than their peers to maintain a strong—even foreclosed—commitment to their religious upbringing (Markstrom-Adams, Hofstra, & Dougher, 1994).

Most research indicates that the chief period for identity development is in late adolescence, when many individuals are enrolled in college.

The freshman year of college can be an important time in the process of identity development (Montemayor, Brown, & Adams, 1985). In one study, a group of students was assessed before entering college and again toward the end of their freshman year. Before entering college, 50 percent of the adolescents were judged to be in a state of identity diffusion, and 40 percent were judged to be in a state of moratorium—consistent with the notion that the identity crisis is unlikely to be resolved during high school (Nurmi, 2004). Another 8 percent were in the identity achievement status, and the rest were judged to be foreclosed.

What happened to these individuals as college freshmen? Over the first year of college, the most common pathway was either remaining diffused or in a state of moratorium or moving from one of the committed statuses (identity achievement or identity foreclosure) to one of the noncommitted statuses (diffusion or moratorium). In other words, while the freshman year may "shake up some students and cause them to reexamine previously held commitments, students who are uncertain to begin with. . . remain so. . . . The freshman year appears to produce uncertainty in many students but does not help to resolve it" (Montemayor, Brown, & Adams, 1985, p. 7). For many young people, college may prolong the psychosocial moratorium, especially in matters of political and religious beliefs.

SHIFTS IN IDENTITY STATUS

As you will recall, Erikson theorized that the sense of identity that is developed during adolescence is constantly lost and regained, that the identity challenge is not resolved once and for all at one point in time. If, according to Erikson's model, identity crises surface and resurface throughout the life cycle, we ought to find that individuals move from one identity status to another, particularly during the adolescent and young-adult years.

This appears to be precisely the case. In a longitudinal study of Dutch youth ages 12–14, for example, nearly 60 percent of the individuals classified as diffused with respect to their educational and occupational identity were no longer classified that way four years later, and nearly 75 percent of individuals who were in the midst of a moratorium at the beginning of the study were no longer in this category at the later assessment (Meeus et al., 1999). Nearly 67 percent of individuals who had apparently foreclosed the identity development process were in the midst of an identity crisis four years later, suggesting that foreclosure may be a temporary stage, at least for some adolescents. Other longitudinal studies of adolescents have revealed similar findings (Adams & Fitch, 1982; Waterman, Geary, & Waterman, 1974; Waterman & Goldman, 1976).

FOOD FOR THOUGHT

Why does research indicate that most identity development occurs in late adolescence or early adulthood, rather than in early or middle adolescence, as Erikson proposed?

Much of this shifting is understandable and perfectly consistent with Erikson's view of adolescent identity development. But how can we account for the fact that in these same longitudinal studies, a large proportion of the identity achievement group also shifted status over the course of the study? In the Dutch study, for example, half of the adolescents who were classified as identity-achieved at the first assessment were not classified this way four years later. How could some individuals who at one point had apparently resolved their identity crisis actually not have resolved it—at least, not in any final sense? According to some writers, these sorts of regressions to a less mature identity status are part of the normal process through which individuals ultimately establish a coherent sense of self (Kroger, 1996). That is, we

should not view the achievement of a sense of identity in adolescence as a final state, but rather as a step on a long route toward the establishment of a mature sense of self.

Because little research has focused on the processes through which identity development occurs, the factors associated with changing from one identity status to another are not well understood (Kroger & Green, 1996; LaVoie, 1994). Indeed, it is fair to say that psychologists have been much better at describing the various stages that adolescents move through over the course of their identity development than explaining why or how individuals' sense of identity changes when it does. The little research that has been done on this subject indicates that turning points in the development of a sense of identity are provoked both by internal factors—discontent with one's life, for example—and by specific life events or changes in life circumstances, such as making the transition into or out of high school (Kalakoski & Nurmi, 1998; Kroger & Green, 1996).

One recent attempt to extend the model of identity formation in a way that focuses somewhat more on the underlying process has led researchers to propose that there are actually two different processes going on simultaneously, one in which individuals explore various identities before making commitments, and one in which individuals explore their commitments in depth after having made them, perhaps resulting in a reevaluation and questioning of their initial commitments (Luyckx et al., 2006). According to this view, which actually is closer to Erikson's belief that identity development is an ongoing process, rather than one that leads an individual to an identity that never changes, identity development doesn't follow a straight line, with a steady increase in commitments, but rather is a process characterized by alternating periods of increasing commitment and exploration. On average, people's identity strengthens over time, but at any given moment, an individual may be in a period of uncertainty and reevaluation.

RECAP

- The predominant influence on the study of identity development in adolescence was Erik Erikson, who suggested that the major psychosocial issue of adolescence revolves around the identity crisis—coming to terms with who one is and where one is headed.
- To resolve this crisis successfully, young people need some time out from excessive responsibilities—a psychosocial moratorium—in order to engage in identity exploration and experimentation.

- Some adolescents have difficulty in successfully resolving the identity crisis. Among the three most common problems described by Erikson are identity diffusion, identity foreclosure, and negative identity.
- Research on identity development from Erikson's theoretical perspective, which has been heavily influenced by the work of James Marcia, has generally supported his model.
- Most studies indicate that the major developments in identity occur in late adolescence and young adulthood, rather than earlier during the adolescent decade.

The Development of Ethnic Identity

For all individuals who are not part of the majority culture, integrating a sense of **ethnic identity** into their overall sense of personal identity is likely to be an important task of late adolescence, perhaps as important as establishing a coherent occupational, ideological, or interpersonal identity (Newman, 2005; Phinney & Alipuria, 1987). Over the past two decades, an extensive literature has been amassed on the process through which ethnic identity develops and on the implications of having a strong versus weak sense of ethnic identity for adolescent adjustment and behavior. Ethnic identity has been studied in samples of African American, Hispanic American, American Indian, Asian American, and white youth (Marshall, 1995; Newman, 2005; Phinney & Devich-Navarro, 1997; Spencer & Markstrom-Adams, 1990; Stevenson, 1995; Vega, Khoury, Zimmerman, Gil, & Warheit, 1995). In America, white youth generally have a weaker sense of ethnic identity than their non-white peers, but many white adolescents identify strongly with a particular ethnic group (such as, German, Irish, Italian, Jewish) and derive part of their overall sense of self from this identification (Martinez & Dukes, 1997; Roberts et al., 1999). Nevertheless, if given a list of labels to identify their own ethnic background, white adolescents in the United States are less likely than ethnic minority adolescents to choose labels based on their specific heritage (for example, "German," "Italian-American") and more likely to use generic "panethnic" labels (for example, "white") or simply to identify themselves as "American" (Fuligni, Witkow, & Garcia, 2005).

THE PROCESS OF ETHNIC IDENTITY DEVELOPMENT

According to several writers (Cross, 1978; Kim, 1981, cited in Phinney & Alipuria, 1987; Newman, 2005), the process of ethnic identity development follows the process of identity development in general, with an unquestioning view of oneself being displaced or upset by a crisis. Following the crisis, the individual may become immersed in his or her own ethnic group and may turn against the majority culture. Eventually, as the value of having a strong ethnic identity becomes clear, the individual establishes a more coherent sense of personal identity that includes this ethnic identity, and with growing confidence, he or she attempts to help others deal with their own struggles with ethnic identity. Consistent with this, a recent study of ethnic identity development among students attending urban public schools found that adolescents' feelings about their own ethnic group rose during both early and middle adolescence (when ethnic identity first becomes salient and individuals become immersed in their own culture), but that actual identity exploration did not really begin until middle adolescence, perhaps because it was at that point that students began to prepare to make the transition from relatively homogeneous schools into much more diverse ones (French, Seidman, Allen, & Aber, 2006).

Some research indicates that moving through the early stages of ethnic identity development may be speeded up somewhat when parents take a more deliberate approach to racial, or ethnic, socialization (Marshall, 1994; Quintana, Castaneda-English, & Ybarra, 1999). **Racial socialization** refers to the process through which parents attempt to teach their children about their ethnic identity and about the special experiences they may encounter within the broader society as a result of their ethnic background (Stevenson, Reed, Bodison, & Bishop, 1997; Thornton, Chatters, Taylor, & Allen, 1990). According to one model, ethnic socialization in minority families focuses on three themes: understanding one's culture, getting along in mainstream society, and dealing with racism (Boykin & Toms, 1985). However, although racial socialization by parents may speed up the process of ethnic identity development, it does not appear to lead adolescents to an ultimately stronger sense of ethnic identity (DeBerry, Scarr, & Weinberg, 1996; Marshall, 1995; Phinney & Chavira, 1995). Nor is more racial socialization necessarily better; in one

ethnic identity The aspect of individuals' sense of identity concerning ancestry or racial group membership.

racial socialization The process through which individuals develop an understanding of their racial or ethnic background.

Having a strong sense of ethnic identity is an important part of adolescents' psychosocial development, especially among young people who are members of an ethnic minority group.

study, the best-adjusted African American adolescents came from homes in which their mothers provided a moderate number of racial socialization messages, rather than many or few (Frabutt, Walker, & MacKinnon-Lewis, 2002). Interestingly, having positive attitudes about one's own ethnic group is correlated with having positive attitudes about adolescents from other ethnic groups, suggesting that racial socialization may enhance, rather than upset, interracial relations (Phinney, Ferguson, & Tate, 1997).

Do members of ethnic minorities have more difficulty than white adolescents in resolving the identity crisis? Researchers are just now beginning to examine this question, and the answer is not known. The little research that has been done suggests more similarities than differences in the process through which ethnic identity development occurs. One difference, though, appears to be quite important, if perhaps not very surprising: Having a strong ethnic identity is consistently associated with higher self-esteem, stronger self-efficacy,

and better mental health among minority youngsters, whereas the link between ethnic identity and mental health is weaker among white youth (Blash & Unger, 1992; DeBerry et al., 1996; Deyhle, 1995; DuBois et al., 2002; Martinez & Dukes, 1997; McCreary, Slavin, and Berry, 1996; McMahon & Watts, 2002; Phinney and Alipuria, 1987; Reviere & Bakeman, 1992; Smith, 1996; Verkuyten, 1995). One study of drug use found, for instance, that ethnic pride was associated with less use among African American, Mexican American, and biracial adolescents, but with more use among white adolescents (Marsiglia, Kulis, & Hecht, 2001). It would seem, therefore, that establishing a sense of ethnic identity is more important for individuals who are part of an ethnic minority than for those who are part of a majority (Gray-Little & Hafdahl, 2000). Indeed, among white American adolescents, having a strong sense of ethnic identity is highly correlated with identifying oneself as American (Phinney, Cantu, & Kurtz, 1997).

As many writers have noted, the task of developing a coherent sense of identity is much more complicated for minority adolescents than for their majority counterparts (Gray-Little & Hafdahl, 2000; Spencer & Dornbusch, 1990; Stevenson et al., 1997). Because identity development is profoundly influenced by the social context in which the adolescent lives, the development of minority adolescents must be understood in relation to the specific context that nonmajority youngsters face in contemporary society (Garcia Coll et al., 1996). All too often, this context includes racial stereotypes, discrimination, and mixed messages about the costs and benefits of identifying too closely with the majority culture. Not surprisingly, a number of studies suggest that the incidence of identity foreclosure is more prevalent among minority youth (e.g., Hauser & Kasendorf, 1983).

MULTIETHNIC ADOLESCENTS

One understudied group of adolescents for whom developing a sense of ethnic identity may be especially challenging are **biracial** youth—adolescents whose parents are not from the same ethnic or racial group. Understanding psychological development among biracial adolescents has taken on increased importance as their numbers have grown. In the 1970s, for example, 1 out of every 100 children was born to parents of different races; by 2000, this had increased to 1 out of 20 (Herman, 2004).

You've probably filled out many forms and applications asking you to indicate your racial or ethnic background, and for the majority of individuals, this is not an especially challenging task. But what about individuals who are of mixed heritage? Today, when

biracial Having two parents of different ethnic or racial backgrounds.

TABLE 8.1 Percent of Multiracial Respondents Who Self-Identify in Each Monoracial Category and Counts of Multiracial Respondents Using Alternative Categorization Methods

	% Black	% White	% Asian	% Hispanic	% Other	% No choice	Precise *N*	Parsimonious *N*
Black-Asian	57	15	7	7	7	7	60	30
Black-Hispanic	56	7	1	25	7	4	70	52
Other-Asian	11	14	23	15	37	1	89	27
Asian-Hispanic	13	15	15	40	12	5	101	55
Other-Hispanic	9	9	2	46	33	0	117	46
Other-Black	61	11	3	4	20	1	159	91
Black-White	68	16	1	2	4	9	160	160
White-Asian	4	33	43	6	10	4	298	250
Other-White	5	62	1	8	25	0	450	324
White-Hispanic	3	38	1	52	1	5	485	461
Total							1,989	1,496

Note: Precise counts each respondent in as many race categories as befit his or her parentage; parsimonious counts each respondent in only one category according to norms of hypodescent.

Source: Herman, 2004.

questionnaires ask individuals to provide information on their ethnic background, they typically provide respondents with the opportunity to indicate that they are multiracial, by permitting them to select more than one answer. Prior to 2000, however, even the U.S. Census forced people to choose an identification from one of several broad categories (for example, Asian, Black, Latino, White, Other). The problem, of course, is that a forced choice of this sort demands that multiracial individuals either select one of the ethnic groups or use the category "Other," neither of which allows them to be identified as multiracial. Moreover, each ethnic category will include individuals with two parents from that group as well as multiracial individuals who have an especially strong identification with one of their parents' ethnic heritage. It is little wonder that we know so little about multiracial adolescents, given the fact that in many studies they are impossible to identify.

A recent study by sociologist Melissa Herman took advantage of a unique opportunity to examine what biracial adolescents do when forced to choose an ethnic identity and whether biracial adolescents who choose one ethnicity to describe themselves differ from adolescents with parents of the same two ethnic backgrounds who choose the other ethnicity for self-description (Herman, 2004). In a survey that I conducted many years ago with Sanford Dornbusch and Bradford Brown, we accidentally asked adolescents about their ethnic background twice: once when we asked them to tell us the ethnic background of each of their parents, and once when we asked them to identify their own ethnic background but did not permit them to choose more than one category. (To be

honest, this was a mistake that we overlooked when developing the questionnaire, but the truth is that researchers' mistakes often lead to more interesting discoveries than their deliberate choices.)

Capitalizing on our error, Herman was able to identify biracial adolescents (based on their descriptions of each of their parents) and examine how they described themselves. For instance, some adolescents with a white father and a Hispanic mother, when forced to choose, described themselves as white, others said they were Hispanic, and a third group chose neither. Table 8.1 shows the results; the left-most column gives the parental combination (such as Black-Asian), and the remaining columns indicate the proportion of adolescents with that combination who chose a specific ethnic group for self-identification. For instance, the top row of the table indicates that 57 percent of adolescents with one black and one Asian parent identified themselves as black, whereas only 7 percent identified themselves as Asian. (Adolescents who did not choose either of their parents' ethnicity usually did so because one of their parents was multiethnic.) Two patterns in the table are noteworthy. First, individuals with one black parent were significantly more likely to identify themselves as black than as a member of the second group. Second, individuals with one white and one ethnic minority parent were more likely to identify themselves as a member of the ethnic minority group, regardless of the ethnicity.

Herman then asked whether certain factors, beyond the ethnicities of his or her parents, predicted which ethnic group an adolescent chose. Although few variables operated the same across all ethnic groups, two that did were the adolescent's physical appearance

FIGURE 8.8 A two-dimensional model of identification with two cultures. (Phinney et al., 1994)

Identification with majority group	Identification with ethnic group	
	Strong	Weak
Strong	Bicultural	Assimilated
Weak	Separated	Marginal

(based on ratings of a yearbook photo) and the ethnic background of the adolescent's friends. Biracial adolescents who appeared white to the yearbook raters were more likely to identify themselves as white, and biracial adolescents who reported that the majority of their friends were from an ethnic minority group were less likely to identify themselves as white. Individuals with one or two black parents reported the highest levels of discrimination (these groups did not differ from each other), and those with two white parents reported the lowest.

ALTERNATIVE ORIENTATIONS TO ETHNIC IDENTITY

According to psychologist Jean Phinney and colleagues (e.g., Phinney, Devich-Navarro, DuPont, Estrada, & Onwughala, 1994), minority youth have four possibilities in dealing with their ethnicity: assimilation (trying to adopt the majority culture's norms and standards while rejecting those of their own group), marginality (living within the majority culture but feeling estranged and outcast), separation (associating only with members of their own culture and rejecting the majority culture), or biculturalism (maintaining ties to both the majority and the minority cultures) (see Figure 8.8).

In the past, minority youth were encouraged by majority society to assimilate as much as possible. Assimilation, however, has not proven to be as simple as many nonminority individuals imagine (Gil, Vega, & Dimas, 1994). First, although minority youth are told to assimilate, they may be tacitly excluded from majority society on the basis of their physical appearance or language (Vega et al., 1995). This leads to a situation of marginality, in which the minority youth is on the edge of majority society but is never really accepted as a full-status member.

Second, minority youth who do attempt to assimilate are often scorned by their own communities for trying to "act white." Partly in reaction to this, many minority youth in predominantly white schools adopt strategies of separation and **biculturalism,** especially as they get older (Hamm & Coleman, 2001). This is especially common among African American adolescents, who are often the victims of especially intense discrimination and prejudice (see Figure 8.9) (Phinney, Devich-Navarro et al., 1994; Sellers et al., 2006; Spencer, 2005).

A few studies have compared the ethnic identity orientations of Asian American, African American, Hispanic American, and white adolescents. In one such study (Rotherham-Borus, 1990), as expected, white youngsters were more likely to characterize themselves as assimilated (or "mainstream") than were minority students, who were more likely to characterize themselves as bicultural (between 40 and 50 percent) than as either mainstream or embedded solely within their ethnic group. African American and Puerto Rican adolescents are relatively more likely to be ethnically embedded, whereas Mexican American and Asian American adolescents are more likely to be bicultural (e.g., Phinney, DuPont, Espinosa, Revill, & Sanders, 1994).

More interesting, however, is the finding that although adolescents' ethnic attitudes differed among the mainstream, bicultural, and strong ethnic groups, their psychological functioning did not. Adolescents with all three orientations had equal self-esteem, grades in school, and feelings of social competence. Similar findings were reported in a study that further separated bicultural adolescents into groups that differed in the ways they expressed their bicultural orientation (for example, having a strong American identity with recognition of one's ethnic heritage versus having a strong ethnic minority orientation with recognition of one's American citizenship) (Phinney, DuPont et al., 1994). The benefits of biculturalism are seen, as well, among recent immigrants to the United

biculturalism The successful maintenance of an identification with more than one cultural background.

Percent of sample reported experiencing hassle

FIGURE 8.9 Common race-related "hassles" reported by African American high school students. (Sellers et al., 2006)

States from European cultures and among Asian immigrants to European countries (Birman, Trickett, & Vinokurov, 2002; Liebkind, Jasinskaja-Lahti, & Solheim, 2004). In general, then, positive mental health among ethnic minority adolescents is associated with having a strong, positive ethnic identity and a healthy awareness of the potential for discrimination, but not with outright rejection of the mainstream culture (Birman, 1998; Gil et al., 1994; Pillay, 2005; Smith & Lalonde, 2003; Umaña-Taylor, 2004; Yasui, Dorham, & Dishion, 2004).

FOOD FOR THOUGHT

How strong is your own sense of ethnic identity? Have there been points in your life when it was especially important?

Several researchers have focused on the special situation of ethnic minority youth who are recent immigrants to a new culture (e.g., Gil et al., 1994; Phinney, Romero, Nava, & Huang, 2001; Rumbaut & Cornelius,

1995). One study of Armenian, Vietnamese, and Mexican immigrant families in Los Angeles found both similarities and differences in the factors that influence the strength of adolescents' ethnic identity. In all three groups, proficiency in one's ethnic language and interacting with peers from the same ethnic group were associated with having a stronger ethnic identity. Parents' deliberate attempts to shape their adolescents' sense of ethnic identity played a much more important role among Armenian adolescents than among Vietnamese or Mexican adolescents, however (Phinney et al., 2001).

Interestingly, foreign-born ethnic minority adolescents tend to express more positive feelings about mainstream American ideals than do their counterparts whose families have been in the United States longer, and foreign-born ethnic minority youth perform better in school and are less likely to be involved in delinquent behavior or have physical, emotional, and behavioral problems than are their more acculturated peers (Kulis, Marsiglia, & Hurdle, 2003; Rumbaut, 1997; Vega et al., 1995). One interpretation of this is that ethnic minority immigrants arrive in America idealistic about the "melting pot" society, only to discover that they are objects of prejudice and discrimination.

This realization may prompt a strengthening of ethnic identity, a desire for separatism, cynicism about endorsing mainstream American values, and increased conflict within the family (Phinney, DuPont et al., 1994; Samaniego & Gonzales, 1999). Another explanation for the higher achievement and better mental health of immigrant adolescents is that newly arrived immigrant parents provide relatively closer supervision of their children (Harker, 2001).

DISCRIMINATION AND ITS EFFECTS

The relationship among ethnic identity, perceived discrimination, and mental health among African Americans is extremely complicated. Psychologist Robert Sellers and colleagues developed the **multidimensional model of racial identity** to help make sense out of a complex web of findings (Sellers et al., 2006). According to this model, we need to take into account three different aspects of racial identity: racial centrality (how important race is in defining individuals' identity), private regard (how individuals feel about being a member of their race), and public regard (how individuals think others view their race).

It is well established that individuals—from any group—who report experiencing high levels of discrimination suffer psychologically as a result, but it is also true that individuals vary both in the extent to which they feel discriminated against and in the extent to which they are adversely affected by it (Greene, Way, & Pahl, 2006; Oppedal, Røysamb, & Sam, 2004; Sellers et al., 2006). Not surprisingly, African Americans who have experienced discrimination firsthand are more likely to believe that the public has low regard for African Americans. However, African Americans who believe that the public has low regard for African Americans are more sensitive to racial cues, which, in turn, may heighten their experience of discrimination. This is not to say that individuals with heightened sensitivity to discrimination are simply imagining it; rather, individuals with heightened sensitivity may be better at perceiving more subtle signs of genuine racial bias.

How all of this works together to affect adolescents' mental health is tricky. Not surprisingly, having positive feelings about their race, believing that others feel positively about their race, and having race as a central part of their identity are all positively linked to psychological well-being (Caldwell, Sellers, Bernat, &

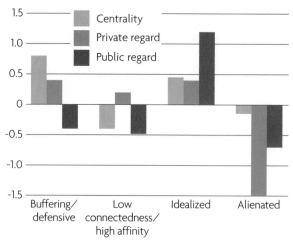

FIGURE 8.10   Racial identity groups among African American adolescents, as indicated by feelings of centrality, private regard, and public regard. (Chavous et al., 2003)

Zimmerman, 2004; Sellers et al., 2006). But having race as a central part of their identity has two other, opposite effects: It makes adolescents more sensitive to discrimination (which hurts their mental health), but it also makes them more able to cope with it (which helps) (Greene et al., 2006; Sellers & Shelton, 2003). And, to complicate things further, believing that the public has a positive view of their race intensifies the effects of discrimination—perhaps because they feel especially wounded when they don't expect to encounter it.

A recent study of ethnic identity and academic achievement illustrates how racial centrality, private regard, and public regard work together to influence African American adolescents' school performance and motivation (Chavous et al., 2003). The researchers identified four distinct clusters within their sample of 600 students: buffering/defensive (high centrality, high private regard, low public regard; 29 percent of the sample), low connectedness/high affinity (low centrality, high private regard, low public regard; 21 percent), idealized (high on all three dimensions; 31 percent), and alienated (low on all three dimensions; 19 percent) (see Figure 8.10). Alienated students were the most disengaged from school and most likely to drop out, while idealized students were more likely to hold positive beliefs about school. But it was the buffering/defensive group that were the least likely to drop out and the most likely to be enrolled in college two years after graduation. The researchers speculated that the success of this group was due to the combination of strong feelings of group pride and a realistic expectation of facing discrimination. Sadly, as long as discrimination persists in American society, students who are its victims will need to protect themselves against its pernicious effects.

multidimensional model of racial identity (MMRI)   Sellers's perspective on ethnic identity, which emphasizes three different phenomena: racial centrality (how important race is in defining individuals' identity), private regard (how individuals feel about being a member of their race), public regard (how individuals think others feel about their race).

RECAP

- Many researchers have studied the process through which ethnic identity develops and the implications of having a strong versus weak sense of ethnic identity for adolescent adjustment and behavior.
- The process of ethnic identity development follows the process of identity development in general, with an unquestioning view of the self being displaced or upset by a crisis that is later resolved, as a more coherent sense of ethnic identity emerges.
- Racial socialization is the process through which parents attempt to teach their children about their ethnic identity and about the special experiences they may encounter within the broader society as a result of their ethnic background.
- One understudied group of adolescents for whom developing a sense of ethnic identity may be especially challenging are biracial youth—adolescents whose parents are not from the same ethnic or racial group. Today, 1 out of every 20 children born in America is biracial.
- Positive mental health among ethnic minority adolescents is associated with having a strong, positive ethnic identity and an awareness of the potential for discrimination, but not with outright rejection of the mainstream culture.
- Adolescents who report experiencing high levels of discrimination suffer psychologically as a result, but individuals vary both in the extent to which they feel discriminated against and in the extent to which they are adversely affected by it.

Gender-Role Development

Like ethnicity, gender is a critical component of individuals' identity. From birth, boys and girls are socialized to behave in "sex-appropriate" ways—that is, to conform to society's standards for acceptable masculine and acceptable feminine behavior. In American society, strong gender-role stereotypes prevail among children, adolescents, and adults. Traits such as logic, independence, ambition, and aggressiveness are considered masculine; and traits such as gentleness, sociability, empathy, and tenderness are considered feminine (Broverman, Vogel, Broverman, Clarkson, & Rosenkrantz, 1972).

Individuals vary in their degrees of masculinity and femininity. Some are decidedly more masculine than feminine, and others are decidedly more feminine than masculine. But some people have a high degree of both masculinity and femininity. For instance, some people are both highly ambitious (a trait usually considered masculine) and highly sensitive (a trait usually considered feminine). Individuals who are both highly masculine and highly feminine are said to be high in **androgyny** (Bem, 1975).

Many researchers have been interested in the relation between gender-role stereotypes and adolescent identity development. Are teenagers, for example, pressured more than children to behave in stereotypically masculine or feminine ways? If so, to what extent does a person's compliance with prevailing gender-role stereotypes affect his or her self-image?

GENDER-ROLE SOCIALIZATION DURING ADOLESCENCE

Pressures to behave in sex-appropriate ways may temporarily intensify during adolescence, especially for girls (Crouter, Manke, & McHale, 1995; Huston & Alvarez, 1990; Loebel, Nov-Krispin, Schiller, Lobel, & Feldman, 2004). This idea, called the **gender intensification hypothesis** (Hill & Lynch, 1983), is that many of the sex differences observed between adolescent boys and girls result from an acceleration in their socialization to act in stereotypically masculine and feminine ways. Even though individuals' beliefs about gender roles may become more flexible as they move through adolescence, social pressures may drive teenagers toward more gender-stereotypic behavior (Alfieri, Ruble, & Higgins, 1996; Katz & Ksansnak, 1994). For example, at adolescence, achievement behavior becomes more gender-stereotyped, with girls beginning to disengage from math and science (Hill & Lynch, 1983). And over the course of adolescence, boys become less emotionally expressive, while girls become more so (Polce-Lynch, Myers, Kilmartin, Forssmann-Falck, & Kliewer, 1998; Polce-Lynch, Myers, Kliewer, & Kilmartin, 2001). However, not all studies find an increase in gender stereotyping in early adolescence (e.g., Jacobs et al., 2002; McHale, Kim, Whiteman, & Crouter, 2004). One reason for these discrepancies is that the extent to which gender-stereotypic behavior becomes more pronounced in early adolescence likely depends on the realm of behavior studied, the developmental history of the adolescent, and the broader context in which the adolescent lives (Galambos, 2004; McHale, Shanahan, Updegraff, Crouter, & Booth, 2004: Watt, 2004). One very good possibility is that the

androgyny The combination of both highly masculine and highly feminine traits.

gender intensification hypothesis The idea that pressures to behave in sex-appropriate ways intensify during adolescence.

gender intensification hypothesis, which was advanced about 25 years ago, was more true then than it is now.

If sex differences in gender-role attitudes do, in fact, increase in early adolescence, these increases seem more tied to chronological age than to the onset of puberty (Galambos, Almeida, & Petersen, 1990). The entry into early adolescence may mark the emergence of new behaviors, which, in turn, may elicit more sex-differentiated behavior from others. As teenagers begin to date, for example, it may become more important for them to act in ways that are consistent with gender-role expectations and that meet with approval in the peer group. Boys who do not act masculine enough and girls who do not act feminine enough may be less popular with and less accepted by their same- and opposite-sex peers (Smith & Leaper, 2005). Studies also suggest that gender-role intensification may be more likely to occur in families in which the adolescent has a younger, opposite-sex sibling (Crouter et al., 1995).

According to psychologists Carol Gilligan (Gilligan, Lyons, & Hanmer, 1990) and Annie Rogers (1993), who have argued that adolescence is a critical turning point in female psychological development, the mixed messages that adolescent girls receive about desirable behavior are confusing and not easily reconciled. Girls, they argue, arrive at adolescence more likely than boys to prize intimacy and interpersonal communication. Throughout childhood, they have been rewarded for this more "relational" orientation. At adolescence, however, social cognitive abilities grow, and girls begin to realize that the very traits they have been socialized for are not valued in the male-dominated broader society. As a consequence, girls feel caught between what they have been told is correct for their gender (being caring and nurturant) and what they can see is valued by society at large (being assertive and independent). Overwhelmed by ambivalence, many girls become less confident and less sure of themselves—they lose their "voice" (Gilligan, 1993). This does not appear to happen to all girls but is more likely to happen to those with an especially feminine gender-role identity (Harter, Waters, Whitesell, & Kastelic, 1998). As you will read in Chapter 13, some theorists believe that this conflict may contribute to the greater prevalence of depression among females than males both in adolescence and in adulthood.

FOOD FOR THOUGHT

In recent years, many popular books have argued that boys, not girls, are the more psychologically vulnerable group of adolescents. Do you agree with this?

MASCULINITY, FEMININITY, AND ANDROGYNY

If gender-role socialization becomes more intense during adolescence, we would expect to find that conformity to gender-role expectations is an important influence on adolescents' self-image. Do more feminine girls and more masculine boys feel better about themselves than do their peers, or are boys and girls both better off being somewhat androgynous—as some psychologists suggest (Bem, 1975; Spence & Helmreich, 1978)?

Recent research on gender-role identity during adolescence suggests that the answer to this question may differ for males and females (Galambos, 2004). Although boys and girls who behave in gender-typical ways are more accepted than their peers whose behavior does not conform with gender-role stereotypes—and feel better about themselves as a result of this peer acceptance—the costs of being gender-atypical are greater for boys than girls (Smith & Leaper, 2005). Put another way, the relative benefits of androgyny to youngsters' self-image are greater for girls than for boys. This is because it is specifically the masculine component of androgyny that is associated with better mental health in adolescence (Markstrom-Adams, 1989). Interestingly, this is not the case during childhood, when aspects of both masculinity and femininity are linked to well-being for both sexes (Allgood-Merten & Stockard, 1991), or during young adulthood, when both femininity and masculinity are predictive of well-being among young women (Stein, Newcomb, & Bentler, 1992).

Although masculinity is predictive of mental health among both adolescent males and females, androgynous girls feel better about themselves than either very masculine or very feminine girls, whereas masculine boys—not androgynous boys—show the highest levels of self-acceptance, a finding that has emerged in studies of both Western and non-Western youth (Frome & Eccles, 1996; Lau, 1989; Orr & Ben-Eliahu, 1993). This may be because peer acceptance during adolescence is highest for androgynous girls and masculine boys (Massad, 1981). These findings suggest that it is easier for girls to behave sometimes in masculine ways during adolescence than it is for boys to act occasionally in feminine ways. Consistent with research on younger children (Lynn, 1966), during adolescence—at least in contemporary American society—males who do not conform to traditionally masculine gender-role norms are judged more deviant than are females whose behavior departs from exclusively feminine roles. Interestingly, however, boys who have a more traditionally masculine orientation, while higher in self-acceptance than other boys, are more likely to be involved in various types of problem behavior—perhaps because part of being masculine in contemporary society involves being "macho" enough to experiment with delinquency, drugs and alcohol, and unprotected sex (Kulis, Marsiglia, & Hurdle, 2003; Pleck, Sonenstein, & Ku, 1994), or because boys who live in difficult environments, where problem behavior is prevalent, adopt a more "macho" posture to survive in the community (Cunningham, 1999). Conversely, girls who have a more traditionally feminine gender-role orientation are more likely to develop more traditionally feminine sorts of psychological problems, such as disordered eating (McHale, Corneal, Crouter, & Birch, 2001).

Given that pressures to conform with gender-role norms affect both girls and boys during adolescence, why is it that boys suffer greater self-image problems when they deviate from what is viewed as appropriate behavior for their sex? The answer is that although girls may be pressured to adopt (or maintain) certain feminine traits during adolescence, they are not necessarily pressured to relinquish all elements of masculinity. In contrast, boys are socialized from a very early age not to adopt feminine traits and are judged deviant if they show signs of femininity. Consistent with this, boys are more likely to see themselves as "typical males" than girls are to see themselves as "typical females," more likely to be content to be male than girls are to be female, and more pressured to act in stereotypically male ways than girls are to act in stereotypically female ways (Egan & Perry, 2001).

In other words, girls can be highly pressured during adolescence to behave in feminine ways without necessarily being punished or labeled deviant for exhibiting some masculine traits at the same time; thus, for girls, androgyny is a viable alternative to exclusive femininity. Girls may feel increasingly pressured to dress nicely and to wear makeup when they reach adolescence, but they are not pressured to give up athletics or other typically masculine interests. Boys, however, from childhood on, are pressured not to behave in feminine ways—even if the femininity is in the context of androgyny. Their gender-role socialization does not intensify during adolescence as much as it does for girls because it is so intense to begin with.

RECAP

- An important aspect of adolescent identity involves gender-role development.
- Although individuals grow more flexible during adolescence in the way that they think about gender roles, adolescents may feel especially strong pressure to adhere to stereotypic gender roles.
- In general, among both males and females, many traits traditionally labeled as masculine are associated in adolescence—but not in childhood or young adulthood—with better adjustment and greater peer acceptance. As a result, androgynous females and masculine males report higher self-esteem than their peers do.

CHAPTER 9

Autonomy

AUTONOMY AS AN ADOLESCENT ISSUE

THE DEVELOPMENT OF EMOTIONAL AUTONOMY

Emotional Autonomy and Detachment

Emotional Autonomy and Individuation

Research on Emotional Autonomy

Emotional Autonomy and Parenting Practices

THE DEVELOPMENT OF BEHAVIORAL AUTONOMY

Changes in Decision-Making Abilities

Changes in Susceptibility to Influence

Ethnic and Cultural Differences in Expectations for Autonomy

Changes in Feelings of Self-Reliance

THE DEVELOPMENT OF VALUE AUTONOMY

Moral Development During Adolescence

Prosocial Reasoning, Prosocial Behavior, and Volunteerism

Political Thinking During Adolescence

Religious Beliefs During Adolescence

You are about to leave the house:

"Where are you going?"

"Out."

"Out where?"

"Just out."

"Who are you going with?"

"A friend."

"Which friend?"

"Mom, just a friend, okay? Do you have to know everything?"

"I don't have to know everything. I just want to know who you're going out with."

"Debby, okay?"

"Do I know Debby?"

"She's just a friend, okay?"

"Well, where are you going?"

"Out." (Ephron, 1981)

FOR MOST ADOLESCENTS, establishing a sense of autonomy is as important a part of becoming an adult as is establishing a sense of identity. Becoming an autonomous person—a self-governing person—is one of the fundamental developmental tasks of adolescence.

Although we often use the words *autonomy* and *independence* interchangeably, in the study of adolescence, they mean slightly different things. Independence generally refers to individuals' capacity to behave on their own. The growth of independence is surely a part of becoming autonomous during adolescence, but, as you will see in this chapter, autonomy has emotional and cognitive as well as behavioral components. In other words, autonomy is not just about acting independently—it is also about feeling independent and thinking independently.

During adolescence, there is a movement away from the dependency typical of childhood and toward the autonomy typical of adulthood. But the growth of autonomy during adolescence is frequently misunderstood. Autonomy is often confused with rebellion, and becoming an independent person is often equated with breaking away from the family. This perspective on autonomy goes hand in hand with the idea that adolescence is inevitably a time of stress and turmoil. But as we have seen in previous chapters, the view that adolescence is a period of storm and stress has been questioned repeatedly by scientific research.

The demands on young people to behave independently are greater today than ever before. This adolescent is expected to begin preparing dinner each day after school.

The same sort of rethinking has taken place with regard to the development of autonomy. Rather than viewing adolescence as a time of spectacular rebellion, researchers now see the growth of autonomy during adolescence as gradual, progressive, and—although important—relatively undramatic.

Because today's adolescents spend so much time away from the direct supervision of adults, either by themselves or with their peers, learning how to govern their own behavior in a responsible fashion is a crucial task. As we saw in previous chapters, with increasing numbers of single-parent and two-career households, more young people are expected to supervise themselves for a good part of the day. Many young people feel pressured—by parents, by friends, and by the media—to grow up quickly and to act like adults at an earlier age. One 13-year-old must make plane reservations to fly back and forth between his separated parents' homes. Another is pregnant and, afraid to tell her parents, must seek counseling on her own. A third is expected to take care of his younger siblings each afternoon because both of his parents work. In many regards, the demands on young people to behave independently are greater today than ever before.

There is a curious paradox in all of this, however. At the same time that adolescents have been asked to become more autonomous psychologically and socially, they have become less autonomous economically. Because of the extension of schooling well into the young-adult years for most individuals, financial independence may not come until long after psychological independence has been established.

Many young people who are emotionally independent find it frustrating to discover that they have to abide by their parents' rules as long as they are being supported economically. They may believe that the ability to make their own decisions has nothing to do with financial dependence. A 16-year-old who drives, has a part-time job, and has a serious relationship with his girlfriend, for example, may be independent in these respects, but he is nonetheless still dependent on his parents for food and shelter. His parents may feel that as long as their son lives in their home, they should decide how late he can stay out at night. But the adolescent may feel that his parents have no right to tell him when he can come and go. This sort of difference of opinion can be a real source of problems and confusion for teenagers and their parents, particularly when they have difficulty agreeing on a level of independence for the adolescent. Disagreements over autonomy-related concerns are at the top of the list of things that provoke quarrels between adolescents and parents (Collins & Laursen, 2004; Holmbeck & O'Donnell, 1991; Montemayor, 1986; Steinberg, 2001).

Autonomy as an Adolescent Issue

Like identity, autonomy is a psychosocial concern that surfaces and resurfaces during the entire life cycle. The development of independent behavior begins long before puberty. Erik Erikson (1963), whose ideas about identity we examined in the previous chapter, believed that autonomy is the central issue of toddlerhood, just as identity is the central issue of adolescence. Young children, he observed, try to establish an initial sense of autonomy when they begin to explore their surroundings on their own and assert their desire to do as they please. If you spend any time with 3-year-olds, you know that one of their favorite expressions is "No!" In some regards, the early adolescent's behavior that is captured in the excerpt at the beginning of this chapter is quite similar. The toddler who insists on saying "No!" and the young adolescent who insists on keeping her whereabouts secret are both demonstrating their growing sense of independence and autonomy. And just as psychologists see toddlers' oppositional behavior as normal—however frustrating it might be to parents—they also see adolescents' interest in privacy as normal, too—however frustrating *that* might be to *their* parents.

Although childhood and adolescence are important periods for the development of autonomy, it is a mistake to suggest that issues of autonomy are resolved once and for all upon reaching young adulthood. Questions about their ability to function independently arise whenever individuals find themselves in positions that demand a new degree of self-reliance. Following a divorce, for example, someone who has depended on a spouse over the years for economic support, guidance, or nurturance must find a way to function more autonomously and more independently. During late adulthood, autonomy may become a significant concern of the person who suddenly finds it necessary to depend on others for assistance and support.

If establishing and maintaining a healthy sense of autonomy is a lifelong concern, why has it attracted so much attention among scholars interested in adolescence? When we look at the development of autonomy in relation to the biological, cognitive, and social changes of adolescence, it is easy to see why.

Puberty and the Development of Autonomy
Consider first the impact of puberty. Some theorists, like Anna Freud (1958), have suggested that the physical changes of early adolescence trigger changes in the young person's emotional relationships at home (Collins & Laursen, 2004; Holmbeck, 1996). Adolescents' interest in turning away from their parents and toward their peers for emotional support—a development that is part of establishing adult independence—may be sparked by their emerging interest in sexual relationships and by their concerns over such things as

dating and intimate friendships. In some senses, then, puberty drives the adolescent away from exclusive emotional dependence on the family. Furthermore, the changes in stature and physical appearance occurring at puberty may provoke changes in how much autonomy the young person is granted by parents and teachers. Youngsters who simply look more mature may be given more responsibility by the adults around them.

▌ Cognitive Change and the Development of Autonomy

The cognitive changes of adolescence also play an important role in the development of autonomy. Part of being autonomous involves being able to make independent decisions. When individuals turn to others for advice, they often receive conflicting opinions. For example, if you are trying to decide between staying home to study for an exam and going out to a party, your professor and the person throwing the party will probably give you different advice. As an adult, you are able to see that each individual's perspective influences his or her advice. The ability to see this, however, calls for a level of intellectual abstraction that is not available until adolescence. Being able to take other people's perspectives into account, to reason in more sophisticated ways, and to foresee the future consequences of alternative courses of action all help the young person to weigh the opinions and suggestions of others more effectively, and to reach his or her independent decisions. The cognitive changes of adolescence also provide the logical foundation for changes in the young person's thinking about social, moral, and ethical problems. These changes in thinking are important prerequisites to the development of a system of values based on the individual's own sense of right and wrong, and not merely on rules and regulations handed down by parents or other authority figures (Mazor & Enright, 1988; Mazor, Shamir, & Ben-Mosche, 1990).

▌ Social Roles and the Development of Autonomy

Finally, changes in social roles and activities during adolescence are bound to raise concerns related to independence, as the adolescent moves into new positions that demand increasing degrees of responsibility and self-reliance. Being able to work, marry, drive, drink, and vote—to name just a few activities that are first permitted during adolescence—all require the ability to manage oneself responsibly in the absence of monitoring by parents or teachers. Becoming involved in new roles and taking on new responsibilities place the adolescent in situations that require and stimulate the development of independent decision-making abilities and the clarification of personal values. A teenager might not really think much about the responsibilities associated with taking a job, for example, until she actually ends up in one. Choosing whether to drink does not become an important question until the adolescent begins to approach the legal drinking age. And deciding what his political beliefs are becomes a more pressing concern when the young person realizes that he will soon have the right to vote.

FOOD FOR THOUGHT

Many psychologists contend that the two periods of life during which autonomy is an especially salient issue are early adolescence and toddlerhood. What do these periods share in common that might account for the importance of autonomy during each?

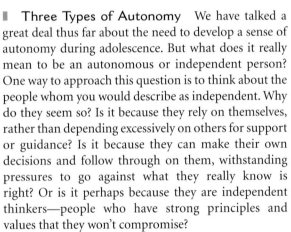

▌ Three Types of Autonomy

We have talked a great deal thus far about the need to develop a sense of autonomy during adolescence. But what does it really mean to be an autonomous or independent person? One way to approach this question is to think about the people whom you would describe as independent. Why do they seem so? Is it because they rely on themselves, rather than depending excessively on others for support or guidance? Is it because they can make their own decisions and follow through on them, withstanding pressures to go against what they really know is right? Or is it perhaps because they are independent thinkers—people who have strong principles and values that they won't compromise?

Each of these characterizations is a reasonable enough description of what it means to be independent, and yet each describes a different sort of independence (Douvan & Adelson, 1966; Noom, Dekovic, & Meeus, 2001). The first characterization involves what psychologists call **emotional autonomy**—that aspect of independence related to changes in the individual's close relationships, especially with parents. The second characterization corresponds to what is sometimes called **behavioral autonomy**—the capacity to make independent decisions and follow through on them. The third characterization involves an aspect of independence that is referred to as **value autonomy,** which is more than simply being able to resist pressures to go along with the demands of others; it means

---

emotional autonomy   The establishment of more adultlike and less childish close relationships with family members and peers.

behavioral autonomy   The capacity to make independent decisions and to follow through with them.

value autonomy   The establishment of an independent set of values and beliefs.

having a set of principles about right and wrong, about what is important and what is not. In this chapter, we will examine these three aspects of autonomy.

RECAP

- Although the development of autonomy is an important psychosocial issue throughout the life span, it is especially salient during adolescence because of the physical, cognitive, and social changes of the period.
- Emotional autonomy (feeling independent) refers to emotional independence in relationships with others, especially parents.
- Behavioral autonomy (acting independently) refers to the development of independent decision-making abilities.
- Value autonomy (thinking independently) concerns the development of independent beliefs and principles.

The Development of Emotional Autonomy

The relationship between children and their parents changes repeatedly over the course of the life cycle. Changes in the expression of affection, the distribution of power, and patterns of verbal interaction, to give a few examples, are likely to occur whenever important transformations take place in the child's or parents' competencies, concerns, and social roles.

By the end of adolescence, individuals are far less emotionally dependent on their parents than they were as children. We can see this in several ways. First, older adolescents do not generally rush to their parents when they are upset, worried, or in need of assistance. Second, they do not see their parents as all-knowing or all-powerful. Third, they often have a great deal of emotional energy wrapped up in relationships outside the family; in fact, they may feel more attached to a boyfriend or a girlfriend than to their parents. And finally, older adolescents are able to see and interact with their parents as people—not just as their parents. Many parents find, for example, that they can confide in their adolescent children, something that was not possible when their children were younger, or that their adolescent children can easily sympathize with them when they have had a hard day at work. These sorts of changes in the adolescent–parent

relationship all reflect the development of emotional autonomy (Steinberg, 1990).

EMOTIONAL AUTONOMY AND DETACHMENT

Psychoanalytic Theory and Detachment Early writings about emotional autonomy were influenced by psychoanalytic thinkers such as Anna Freud (1958), who argued that the physical changes of puberty cause substantial disruption and conflict inside the family system. The reason, Freud believed, is that intrapsychic conflicts that have been repressed since early childhood are reawakened at early adolescence by resurgent sexual impulses. (These conflicts, according to psychoanalytic theory, revolve around the young child's unconscious attraction toward the parent of the opposite sex and ambivalent feelings toward the parent of the same sex.) The reawakened conflicts are expressed as increased tension among family members, an increase in arguments, and a certain degree of discomfort around the house. As a consequence of this tension, early adolescents are driven to separate themselves, at least emotionally, from their parents, and they turn their emotional energies to relationships with peers—in particular, peers of the opposite sex. Psychoanalytic theorists call this process of separation **detachment,** because to them it appears as though the early adolescent is attempting to sever the attachments that have been formed during infancy and strengthened throughout childhood.

Detachment, and the accompanying storm and stress inside the family, were viewed by Freud and her followers as normal, healthy, and inevitable aspects of emotional development during adolescence. In fact, Freud believed that the absence of conflict between an adolescent and his or her parents signified that the young person was having problems growing up. This view was compatible with the idea that adolescence was an inherently tumultuous time—a perspective that, as you know, dominated ideas about adolescence for many, many years.

Research on Detachment Studies of adolescents' family relationships have not supported Freud's idea, however. In contrast to predictions that high levels of adolescent–parent tension are the norm, that adolescents detach themselves from relationships with their parents, and that adolescents are driven out of the household by unbearable levels of family conflict, every major study done to date of teenagers' relations with

detachment In psychoanalytic theory, the process through which adolescents sever emotional attachments to their parents or other authority figures.

In contrast to the view that tension between adolescents and their parents is the norm, every major study done to date of family relations in adolescence has shown that most teenagers and their parents get along quite well.

their parents has shown that most families get along quite well during the adolescent years (Steinberg, 2001). Although parents and adolescents may bicker more often than they did during earlier periods of development, there is no evidence that this bickering significantly diminishes closeness between them in any lasting way (Grotevant, 1997; Hill & Holmbeck, 1986). One team of researchers, for example, who asked adolescents and children of different ages to rate how close they were to their parents, found that 19-year-old college students reported being just as close to their parents as did fourth-graders (Hunter & Youniss, 1982). Most individuals report becoming closer to their parents in late adolescence, especially after they have made the transition into college (Lefkowitz, 2005).

The psychic and interpersonal tension believed to arise at puberty does not show up in markedly strained family relationships, then. Although adolescents and their parents undoubtedly modify their relationships during adolescence, their emotional bonds are by no means severed. This is an important

distinction, for it means that emotional autonomy during adolescence involves a *transformation*, not a breaking off, of family relationships (Guisinger & Blatt, 1994). In other words, adolescents can become emotionally autonomous from their parents without becoming detached from them (Collins & Laursen, 2004; Grotevant, 1997; Steinberg, 1990). Interestingly, adolescents who are better able to balance autonomy and connectedness in their relationships with their parents are also better able to balance autonomy and intimacy in their romantic relationships (Taradash, Connolly, Pepler, Craig, & Costa, 2002).

EMOTIONAL AUTONOMY AND INDIVIDUATION

As an alternative to the classic psychoanalytic perspective on adolescent detachment, some theorists have suggested that the development of emotional autonomy be looked at in terms of the adolescent's developing sense of **individuation** (Blos, 1967). The process of individuation, which begins during infancy and continues into late adolescence, involves a gradual, progressive sharpening of the young person's sense of self as autonomous, competent, and separate from her or his parents. Individuation, therefore, has a great deal to do with the development of a sense of identity, in that it involves changes in how adolescents come to see and feel about themselves.

Individuation does not involve stress and turmoil, however. Rather, individuation entails relinquishing childish dependencies on parents in favor of a more mature, more responsible, and less dependent relationship. Adolescents who establish a sense of individuation can accept responsibility for their choices and actions instead of looking to their parents to do it for them (Josselson, 1980). For example, rather than rebelling against her parents' midnight curfew by deliberately staying out later, a girl who has a healthy sense of individuation might take her parents aside before going out and say, "This party tonight may last longer than midnight. If it does, I'd like to stay a bit longer. Suppose I call you at eleven o'clock and let you know when I'll be home? That way, you won't worry as much if I come home a little later."

RESEARCH ON EMOTIONAL AUTONOMY

Studies indicate that the development of emotional autonomy is a long process, beginning early in adolescence and continuing into young adulthood. In one study (Steinberg & Silverberg, 1986), a questionnaire measuring four aspects of emotional autonomy was administered to a sample of 10- to 15-year-olds. The four components were (1) the extent to which

individuation The progressive sharpening of an individual's sense of being an autonomous, independent person.

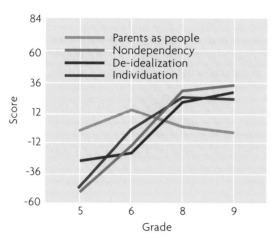

FIGURE 9.1 Age differences in four aspects of emotional autonomy. (Steinberg & Silverberg, 1986)

adolescents' de-idealized their parents ("My parents sometimes make mistakes"), (2) the extent to which adolescents were able to see their parents as people ("My parents act differently with their own friends than they do with me"), (3) nondependency, or the degree to which adolescents depended on themselves, rather than on their parents, for assistance ("When I've done something wrong, I don't always depend on my parents to straighten things out"), and (4) the degree to which the adolescent felt individuated within the relationship with his or her parents ("There are some things about me that my parents do not know"). As you can see in Figure 9.1, scores on three of the four scales—all except "parents as people"—increased over the age period studied.

Similar findings have emerged in other studies. In one, for example, the researchers found that as adolescents aged the number of their friends whom their parents knew declined significantly, reflecting greater individuation and privacy on the part of the adolescents (Feiring & Lewis, 1993). In another study, in which adolescents were interviewed about their family relationships, the researchers found that older adolescents were also more likely to de-idealize their parents. For example, one adolescent said this about his father: "I used to listen to everything. I thought he was always right. Now I have my own opinions. They may be wrong, but they're mine and I like to say them" (Smollar & Youniss, 1985, p. 8). A third study, which examined adolescent boys' reports of homesickness during summer camp, found that homesickness—which was experienced by youngsters as anxiety and depression—became less prevalent during middle adolescence than it had been in early adolescence or preadolescence (Thurber, 1995). Finally, one study found that adolescents' willingness to express negative emotions in front of their parents—for example, anger

and sadness—was lower during early adolescence than before or after, perhaps because keeping some emotional distance from one's parents is a part of the individuation process (Zeman & Shipman, 1997).

De-Idealization Psychologists believe that the de-idealization of parents may be one of the first aspects of emotional autonomy to develop, because adolescents may shed their childish images of their parents before replacing them with more mature ones. Yet, although middle adolescents are less likely than young adolescents to hold onto idealized pictures of their parents, when it comes to seeing their parents as individuals, 15-year-olds are no more emotionally autonomous than are 10-year-olds. In other words, de-idealization is the beginning, not the end, of a long process that gradually leads adolescents to adopt more realistic views of their parents. Even during the high school years, adolescents appear to have some difficulty in seeing their parents as individuals beyond their roles as parents. This aspect of emotional autonomy may not develop until much later—perhaps not until young adulthood (Smollar & Youniss, 1985; White, Speisman, & Costos, 1983). Seeing one's parents as people also appears to develop later in adolescents' relations with their fathers than with their mothers, because fathers seem to interact less often with their adolescents in ways that permit them to be seen as individuals (Smollar & Youniss, 1985).

FOOD FOR THOUGHT

Why does it take relatively longer for individuals to develop more sophisticated views of their parents as people than it does to develop other types of emotional autonomy?

The Importance of Maintaining the Connection Interestingly, and in contrast to the old view that adolescents needed to sever their ties with their parents in order to grow up healthily, a number of studies find that the development of emotional autonomy, and individuation in particular, may have different psychological effects on adolescents depending on whether the parent–child relationship is a close one. Adolescents who become emotionally autonomous, but who also feel distant or detached from their parents, score poorly on measures of psychological adjustment, whereas adolescents who demonstrate the same degree of emotional autonomy, but who still feel close and attached to their parents, are psychologically healthier than their peers (Allen, Hauser, O'Connor, Bell, & Eickholt, 1996;

Lamborn & Steinberg, 1993; Mahoney, Schweder, & Stattin, 2002; Ryan & Lynch, 1989).

In one recent study of African American, Mexican American, and white adolescents, for example, young people from all ethnic groups who reported greater feelings of separation from their parents and higher levels of family conflict (a combination indicative of detachment) also showed increases in alcohol use over time, whereas alcohol use declined among those who reported higher levels of individuation and family cohesion (Bray, Adams, Getz, & Baer, 2001). In essence, whereas detachment has negative effects on adolescents' mental health, individuation has positive ones. Taken together, these studies remind us that it is important to distinguish between separating from one's parents in a way that nevertheless maintains emotional closeness in the relationship (which is healthy) versus breaking away from one's parents in a fashion that involves alienation, conflict, and hostility (which is unhealthy) (Beyers, Goossens, Vansant, & Moors, 2003). Consistent with this, lying to one's parents and concealing undesirable things from them, which may be more an indicator of detachment than of healthy individuation, is associated with psychological problems (Finkenauer, Engels, & Meeus, 2002; Frijns, Finkenauer, Vermulst, & Engels, 2005). Not surprisingly, as individuals make the transition from adolescence into adulthood and work through much of the individuation process, they increasingly see lying to their parents as unacceptable (Jensen, Arnett, Feldman, & Cauffman, 2004).

■ **What Triggers Individuation?** What triggers the process of individuation? Two different models have been suggested (Collins & Laursen, 2004). According to several researchers, puberty is the main catalyst (e.g., Holmbeck, 1996; Steinberg, 1989). Changes in the adolescent's physical appearance provoke changes in the way that adolescents are viewed—by themselves and by their parents—which, in turn, provoke changes in parent–child interaction. As we saw in Chapter 4, shortly after puberty, most families experience an increase in bickering and squabbling. Some writers have suggested that this increase in conflict helps adolescents see their parents in a different light and develop a sense of individuation (Cooper, 1988; Holmbeck & Hill, 1991; Steinberg, 1990). Consistent with this, adolescents' feelings of connectedness to their parents may decline in early adolescence, when bickering is more frequent, but increase in late adolescence after this temporary period of heightened squabbling is over (Pinquart & Silbereisen, 2002).

Other authors believe that adolescents' movement toward higher levels of individuation is stimulated by their social-cognitive development (Collins, 1990;

Smetana, 1988a). As you read in Chapter 2, social cognition refers to the thinking we do about ourselves and our relationships with others. The development of emotional autonomy in adolescence may be provoked by young people's development of more sophisticated understandings of themselves and their parents. Prior to adolescence, individuals accept their parents' views of themselves as accurate ("My parents think I am a good girl, so I must be"). But as individuals develop more differentiated self-conceptions in early and middle adolescence (recall the discussion of this in Chapter 8), they come to see that their parents' view is but one of many—and one that may not be entirely accurate ("My parents think I am a good girl, but they don't know what I am really like"). By late adolescence, individuals are able to see that these apparent discrepancies between their self-conceptions and their parents' views are perfectly understandable ("There are sides of me that my parents know and sides of me that they don't") (see Mazor & Enright, 1988).

This is not to suggest that the process of individuation is always a smooth one. Some writers have suggested that as adolescents de-idealize their parents, they may begin to feel both more autonomous and more insecure—what one research team labeled a "double-edged sword" (Frank, Pirsch, & Wright, 1990). That is, even though their childish images of their parents as being all-knowing and all-powerful may be inaccurate, the images still provide a degree of emotional comfort. Leaving such images behind can be both liberating and frightening, for parents as well as teenagers. Indeed, some researchers have found that the development of emotional autonomy is associated not only with insecurity for adolescents but also with increased feelings of anxiety and rejection on the part of parents (Hock, Eberly, Bartle-Haring, Ellwanger, & Widaman, 2001; Ryan & Lynch, 1989; Steinberg & Steinberg, 1994). Difficulties in the process of individuation may also arise when adolescents push for independence at an earlier age than parents are willing to grant it. One recent study found, for example, that adolescents believe that individuals should be granted autonomy earlier than parents do (Ruck, Peterson-Badali, & Day, 2002).

Several writers have explored the ways in which the process of developing autonomy may differ for adolescents whose parents have divorced (Feldman & Quatman, 1988; Sessa & Steinberg, 1991; Wallerstein & Kelly, 1974; Weiss, 1979). These writers argue that having divorced parents prompts adolescents to grow up faster—to de-idealize parents at an earlier age, because observing their parents during the process of divorce may reveal their flaws and failings. To the extent that de-idealization of their parents is the first step in the individuation process, adolescents from divorced homes may do this somewhat earlier than their peers. Whether this has positive or negative consequences, however, is not known.

EMOTIONAL AUTONOMY AND PARENTING PRACTICES

Whether provoked by puberty or by the development of more advanced cognitive skills, and whether approached with confidence or with trepidation, one fact is certain: Healthy individuation and positive mental health are fostered by close, not distant, family relationships (Allen, Hauser, Eickholt, Bell, & O'Connor, 1994; Bomar & Sabatelli, 1996; Foster & Ritter, 1995; Grotevant & Cooper, 1986; Keener & Boykin, 1996). Tense family relationships during adolescence indicate problems, not positive development (Fuhrman & Holmbeck, 1995). Researchers have found, for example, that adolescents who feel the most autonomous— that is, those who are most likely to feel that they have been granted enough freedom by their parents—are not the ones who have severed relationships at home. In fact, just the opposite is true: Autonomous adolescents report that they are close to their parents, enjoy doing things with their families, have few conflicts with their mothers and fathers, feel free to turn to them for advice, and say they would like to be like their parents (Kandel & Lesser, 1972). Rebellion, negativism, and excessive involvement in the peer group are more common among psychologically immature adolescents than among mature ones (Josselson, Greenberger, & McConochie, 1977a, 1977b). Even during college years, students who live away from home (which is in its own way a type of autonomy)—as opposed to remaining in their parents' home and commuting to school—report more affection for their parents, better communication, and higher levels of satisfaction in the relationship (Holmbeck, Durbin, & Kung, 1995; Sullivan & Sullivan, 1980). Strained family relationships appear to be associated with a lack of autonomy during adolescence, rather than with its presence (Bomar & Sabatelli, 1996).

At the same time, adolescents whose parents are emotionally close to the point of being intrusive or overprotective—that is, parents who use a lot of **psychological control**—may have difficulty individuating from them, which may lead to depression, anxiety, and diminished social competence (Allen & McElhaney, 2000; Bean, Bush, McHenry, & Wilson, 2003; Holmbeck et al., 2000). Adolescents whose parents impede the individuation process are more likely to show signs of anxiety, depression, and other forms of psychological distress (Barber, 1996; Steinberg, 1990). Overprotectiveness may be especially harmful for adolescents who are less competent to begin with

(Thompson & Zuroff, 1999). As a consequence, the impact of parental psychological control is even more harmful when it is accompanied by negative self-evaluations by the adolescent; adolescents who do not feel good about themselves and who have very intrusive parents are especially vulnerable to depression (Pomerantz, 2001).

FOOD FOR THOUGHT

Studies show that parents' behavior can help or impede the development of emotional autonomy. Based on what you've read, what advice would you give the parents of a preadolescent in this regard?

Individuation in the Context of Closeness Psychologists now know that emotional autonomy develops best under conditions that encourage both individuation and emotional closeness. The need for parents to strike the right balance can be seen quite clearly in the work of Stuart Hauser and Joseph Allen, who have studied videotapes of parents and adolescents in discussions and have examined whether certain types of interaction are more or less facilitative of healthy adolescent development (Allen & McElhaney, 2000; Allen et al., 1994, 1996; Hauser, Powers, & Noam, 1991). In this research, the tapes were coded for two specific types of behavior: enabling behavior and constraining behavior. Parents who use a lot of enabling behavior accept their adolescent and at the same time help the teenager to develop and state his or her own ideas through questions, explanations, and the tolerance of differences of opinion. In contrast, parents who use constraining behavior have difficulty accepting their child's individuality and react to expressions of independent thinking with remarks that are distracting, judgmental, or devaluing. After hearing an adolescent's opinion that differs from his own, for example, an enabling father might ask for more clarification or might genuinely probe the adolescent's logic, whereas a constraining father might cut off further discussion by saying that the adolescent is wrong or ignorant.

Not surprisingly, adolescents whose parents use a great deal of enabling and relatively little constraining are more likely to develop in healthy ways: They are more individuated and score higher on measures of identity development and psychosocial competence. This is in line with other research showing that healthy

psychological control　Parenting that attempts to control the adolescent's emotions and opinions.

development—in adolescence and beyond—is more likely to occur within families in which adolescents are encouraged both to be connected to their parents and to express their own individuality (Cooper, Grotevant, & Condon, 1983; Grotevant & Cooper, 1986), and that adolescents fare best when their relationships at home strike the right balance between autonomy and connectedness (Bell & Bell, 2005; Hodges, Finnegan, & Perry, 1999). Adolescents who grow up in families that inhibit individuation are more likely to report feeling anxious and depressed, while adolescents from families with low levels of closeness are more likely to display behavioral problems, such as poor impulse control (Allen et al., 1994; Pavlidis & McCauley, 1995). One recent study that followed individuals ages 16–25 found that the negative effects of having parents who constrain the development of autonomy during adolescence even persist into young adulthood—adolescents whose parents were overly intrusive were relatively more hostile and angry as young adults (Allen, Hauser, O'Connor, & Bell, 2002).

■ **Emotional Autonomy and Parenting Style**   As we saw in Chapter 4, adolescents' development is affected differently by different styles of parenting. In particular, independence, responsibility, and self-esteem are all fostered by parents who are authoritative (friendly, fair, and firm) rather than authoritarian (excessively harsh), indulgent (excessively lenient), or indifferent (aloof to the point of being neglectful). Let us now look more closely at these findings in light of what we know about the development of emotional autonomy.

In authoritative families, guidelines are established for the adolescent's behavior, and standards are upheld, but they are flexible and open to discussion. Moreover, these standards and guidelines are explained and implemented in an atmosphere of closeness, concern, and fairness. Although parents may have the final say when it comes to their child's behavior, the decision that is reached usually comes after consultation and discussion—with the child included. In discussing an adolescent's curfew, for example, authoritative parents will sit down with their child and explain how they arrived at their decision and why they picked the hour they did. They will also ask the adolescent for his or her suggestions and consider them carefully in making a final decision.

It is not difficult to see why the sort of give-and-take that is found in authoritative families is well suited to the healthy development of emotional autonomy. Because standards and guidelines are flexible and adequately explained, it is not hard for the family to adjust and modify them as the child matures, physically, emotionally, and intellectually (Smetana & Asquith, 1994). Gradual changes in family relations that permit the young person more independence and encourage more responsibility, but that do not threaten the emotional bond between parent and child—in other words, changes that promote increasing emotional autonomy—are relatively easy to make for the family that has been flexible and has been making these sorts of modifications in family relationships all along (Baumrind, 1978; Vuchinich, Angeletti, & Gatherum, 1996).

In authoritarian households, in contrast, where rules are rigidly enforced and seldom explained to the child, adjusting to adolescence is more difficult for the family. Authoritarian parents may see the child's increasing emotional independence as rebellious or disrespectful, and they may resist their adolescent's growing need for independence rather than accepting it. For example, authoritarian parents, on seeing that their daughter is becoming interested in boys, may implement a rigid curfew in order to restrict her social life. Instead of encouraging autonomy, authoritarian parents may inadvertently maintain the dependencies of childhood by failing to give their child sufficient practice in making decisions and being responsible for his or her actions. In essence, authoritarian parenting may interfere with adolescent individuation.

When closeness, as well as support for autonomy, is absent, the problems are compounded. In families in which excessive parental control is accompanied by extreme coldness and punitiveness, the adolescent may rebel against parents' standards explicitly, in an attempt to assert her or his independence in a visible and demonstrable fashion (Hill & Holmbeck, 1986). Accordingly, adolescents whose parents refuse to set reasonable curfews are the ones who typically stay out the latest. Such rebellion is not indicative of genuine emotional autonomy, though; it is more likely a demonstration of the adolescent's frustration with his or her parents' rigidity and lack of understanding. And, as noted earlier, when adolescents attempt to establish emotional autonomy within the context of a cold or hostile family, the effect on their mental health is likely to be negative (Lamborn & Steinberg, 1993). In fact, adolescents from hostile or stressful family environments may do best when they actively detach themselves from their parents (Fuhrman & Holmbeck, 1995).

In both indulgent families and indifferent families, a different sort of problem arises. These parents do not provide sufficient guidance for their children, and as a result, the youngsters do not acquire adequate standards for behavior. Someone who has never had to abide by her or his parents' rules as a child faces tremendous difficulty learning how to comply with rules as an adult. In the absence of parental guidance and rules, permissively reared teenagers often turn to their peers for advice and emotional support—a practice that can be problematic when the peers are themselves still relatively young and inexperienced. Not surprisingly, adolescents whose parents have failed to provide sufficient guidance are likely to become psychologically dependent on their friends—emotionally detached from their parents, perhaps, but not genuinely autonomous (Devereux, 1970). The problems of parental permissiveness are exacerbated by a lack of closeness, as is the case in indifferent families.

Some parents who have raised their children permissively until adolescence are caught off guard by the consequences of not having been stricter earlier on. The greater orientation toward the peer group of permissively raised adolescents may involve the young person in behavior that his or her parents disapprove of. As a consequence, some parents who have been permissive throughout a youngster's childhood shift gears when he or she enters adolescence, becoming autocratic in an attempt to control a youngster over whom they feel they have lost control. For instance, parents who have never placed any restrictions on their daughter's afternoon activities during elementary school may suddenly begin monitoring her social life once she enters junior high school. Shifts like these can be extremely hard on adolescents—just at the time when they are seeking greater autonomy, their parents become more restrictive. Having become accustomed to relative leniency, adolescents whose parents change the rules in the middle of the game may find it difficult to accept standards that are being strictly enforced for the first time.

RECAP

- Although adolescence historically has been viewed as a time during which individuals need to break away from and rebel against their parents, research indicates that the growth of emotional autonomy is typically smoother and less tumultuous than stereotypes suggest.
- Instead of emphasizing the young person's need for detachment, contemporary psychologists stress the more gradual process of individuation, which may be triggered by the physical and cognitive changes of early adolescence.
- One of the first signs of individuation may be the adolescent's de-idealization of his or her parents.
- Healthy individuation is fostered by close, not distant, family relationships, with adolescents encouraged to develop and assert their individuality.
- Adolescents who are raised in authoritative homes in which their parents are both accepting and

tolerant of the young person's individuality enjoy many psychological advantages over their peers, including a more fully developed sense of emotional autonomy.

The Development of Behavioral Autonomy

One of the most popular misconceptions about adolescent development is that adolescents demonstrate autonomy by rebelling against the wishes of their parents. But in many instances, teenagers rebelling against their parents or other authorities is done not out of independence but out of a desire to conform to their peers. During early adolescence, in fact, individuals become more emotionally autonomous from their parents but more dependent on their friends (Steinberg & Silverberg, 1986). Merely substituting one source of influence (the peer group) for another (the family), though, is hardly evidence of growth toward independence. After all, excessive adherence to the pressures of one's friends is no more autonomous than is excessive adherence to the pressures of one's parents. Moreover, as we saw earlier in this chapter, rebellion is associated with immaturity, not with healthy development. Just what is meant, then, by behavioral autonomy?

All individuals—at any age—are susceptible to the pressures of those around them. The opinions and advice of others, especially people whose knowledge and judgment we respect, are and should be, important influences on our choices and decisions. Surely, then, we would not want to say that the behaviorally autonomous adolescent is entirely free from the influence of others. Rather, the individual who is behaviorally autonomous is able to turn to others for advice when it is appropriate, can weigh alternative courses of action based on his or her own judgment and the suggestions of others, and can reach an independent conclusion about how to behave (Hill & Holmbeck, 1986). Let's look more closely at why and how changes in behavioral autonomy occur during adolescence. Researchers have looked at changes in three domains: in decision-making abilities, in susceptibility to the influence of others, and in feelings of self-reliance.

CHANGES IN DECISION-MAKING ABILITIES

As you read in Chapter 2, the more sophisticated reasoning processes employed by adolescents permit them to hold multiple viewpoints in mind simultaneously,

Adolescence is an important time for the development of mature judgment and decision-making skills.

allowing comparisons among the viewpoints to be drawn—an ability that is crucial for weighing the opinions and advice of others. In addition, because adolescents are better able than children to think in hypothetical terms, they are more likely to consider the possible long-term consequences of choosing one course of action over another. And the enhanced role-taking capabilities of adolescence permit teenagers to consider another person's opinion while taking into account that person's perspective. This is important in determining whether someone who gives advice has special areas of expertise, particular biases, or vested interests that the young person should keep in mind. Taken together, these cognitive changes result in improved decision-making skills and, consequently, in the individual's greater ability to behave independently.

▌ **Improvements in Decision-Making Abilities**
A now-classic study by Catherine Lewis (1981b) sheds a good deal of light on these issues. She presented over 100 adolescents ages 12–18 with a series of problems they were to help another teenager solve. The problems concerned such things as becoming involved in different sorts of risky situations, revising an opinion of someone who had previously been respected, or reconciling different pieces of advice from two "experts." One of the problems, for example, focused on a teenager's indecision about whether to have cosmetic surgery.

Lewis looked at adolescents' responses along five dimensions: whether adolescents were aware of risks; whether they were aware of likely future consequences; whether parents, peers, or outside specialists were recommended as consultants; whether attitudes were revised in light of new information; and whether the

adolescents recognized and cautioned against the vested interests of people giving advice. The adolescents were grouped by grade level, with seventh- and eighth-graders forming one group, tenth-graders a second group, and twelfth-graders a third group. The results of the study are shown in Figure 9.2.

The age groups differed along four of the five dimensions studied, with older adolescents demonstrating more sophisticated decision-making abilities. The older adolescents were more likely to be aware of risks, more likely to consider future consequences, more likely to turn to an independent specialist as a consultant, and more likely to realize when someone's vested interests existed and to raise cautions about accepting advice from people who might be biased. A recent study of adolescents' and adults' decision making using a similar methodology found comparable results: Compared to adolescents, adults are more likely to consider risks and benefits associated with the decisions they make, and are more likely to suggest seeking the advice of an independent specialist (Halpern-Felsher & Cauffman, 2001).

In other words, decision-making abilities improve over the course of adolescence, with gains continuing through the later years of high school and into young adulthood. These developments provide the cognitive tools for behavioral autonomy: being able to look ahead and assess risks and likely outcomes of alternative choices, being able to recognize the value of turning to an independent expert, and being able to see that someone's advice may be tainted by his or her own interests.

▌ **Legal Decision Making** Several studies of adolescents' legal decision making provide additional evidence of these changes (Grisso et al., 2003; Schmidt, Reppucci, & Woolard, 2003). In these studies, adolescents and adults were presented with vignettes involving an individual who had gotten into trouble with the law and asked how the individual should handle different situations—being interrogated by the police, consulting with an attorney, deciding whether to plead guilty in return for a lesser sentence versus going to trial, or taking her or his chances on the outcome. Researchers' analyses of individuals' responses to these sorts of scenarios indicate that adolescents are less likely than adults to think about the long-term implications of their decisions, more likely to focus on the immediate consequences, and less able to understand the ways in which other people's positions might bias their interests. For example, when asked what a guilty individual should do when being interrogated by the police, younger adolescents are more likely than adults to say that they should confess (which is not what most attorneys would recommend) rather than remain silent (which most attorneys would

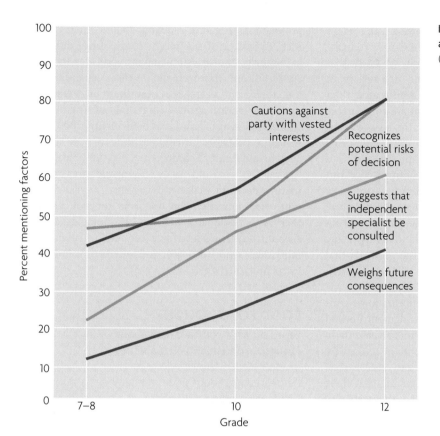

FIGURE 9.2   Decision-making abilities improve during adolescence. (Derived from Lewis, 1981b)

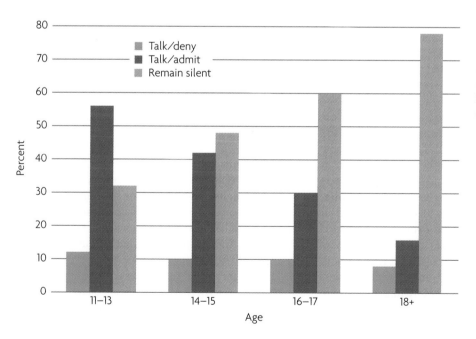

FIGURE 9.3   Age differences in how individuals believe one should respond to a police interrogation when one has committed a crime. (Grisso et al., 2003)

say is the most advisable thing to do). The younger adolescents are thinking about the immediate consequences of their actions ("If I tell the police the truth, they'll let me go home"), and not the longer-term implications ("If I confess, this information can be used against me in court") (see Figure 9.3).

The recognition that individuals' decision-making skills improve over the course of adolescence has prompted numerous debates about young people's abilities to make decisions in the real world—for example, with regard to having access to medical care without their parents' approval or functioning as competent defendants in court. However, this is an area in which the evidence is sufficiently fuzzy to make drawing firm conclusions very difficult. We know that older adolescents (those ages 16 and up) reason in ways that are significantly more sophisticated than those of younger adolescents and that are comparable to those demonstrated by adults. On the basis of this, youth advocates have argued that older adolescents should have the right to seek health care services (including abortions and contraception) without parental knowledge or consent (Blum, Resnick, & Stark, 1990; Gardner, Scherer, & Tester, 1989; Melton, 1990; Scherer & Gardner, 1990). Ironically, however, the exact same evidence has been used to justify trying adolescent offenders as adults, on the grounds that adolescents' decision making is not all that different from adults' (Grisso & Schwartz, 2000).

At the same time, because there appears to be continued improvement in maturity of judgment beyond age 15 or 16—due not so much to improvements in cognitive abilities but to improvements in things like impulse control, planning ahead, and risk assessment—and in light of evidence suggesting that there is continued maturation through late adolescence of regions of the brain that have been implicated in the development of these capacities (see Chapter 2), individuals who are opposed to trying juvenile offenders as adults use this evidence to argue in favor of keeping adolescents in the juvenile justice system and sentencing juveniles less harshly than adults because of their immature judgment (Fried & Reppucci, 2001; Steinberg & Scott, 2003).

▌ Cognitive and Psychosocial Influences on Decision Making

Mature decision making is the product of both cognitive abilities (such as being able to reason logically) and psychosocial factors (such as being able to control one's impulses), and these aspects of development appear to proceed along somewhat different timetables (Steinberg, 2004). As you read in Chapter 2, the maturation of basic cognitive abilities is complete at around age 16, but the process of psychosocial maturation continues well into adulthood. Consequently, there is a period during which adolescents may *think* like adults but *behave* in a much more immature way.

The fact of the matter is that, although experts agree that adolescents' decision-making tools improve with age, there is little consensus about whether the improvement is sufficient to permit adolescents to be treated as adults or at what age the boundary should be drawn (Steinberg & Cauffman, 2000). As a consequence, laws governing adolescents' autonomous access to health care are often inconsistent and highly variable from state to state, as are those governing their criminal

prosecution (Fagan & Zimring, 2000; Gittler, Quigley-Rick, & Saks, 1990). A recent study of age differences in maturity and decision making indicates that there are significant improvements in these capabilities over the adolescent years but that there is tremendous variability within groups of individuals of the same chronological age (Cauffman & Steinberg, 2000). Thus, while it is probably correct to assume that the "average" 15-year-old is not as competent a decision maker as the "average" 20-year-old, many 15-year-olds are capable of mature decision making, and many 20-year-olds are quite irresponsible. The dilemma for policymakers, then, is to create laws that take chronological age into account but that allow for exceptions to be made for individuals whose behavior and judgment is not typical for people their age.

FOOD FOR THOUGHT

Based on what you have read about changes in decision-making abilities in adolescence, should adolescents be treated like adults under the law? If you were a lawmaker, where would you draw the line for issues concerning access to health care? For issues concerning criminal activity? Would you favor laws holding parents legally responsible for the behavior of their teenage children?

CHANGES IN SUSCEPTIBILITY TO INFLUENCE

As adolescents come to spend more time outside the family, the opinions and advice of others—not only peers but adults as well—become more important. For example, at a certain point, adolescents seek the advice of friends rather than their parents concerning how to dress. They may turn to a teacher or guidance counselor for advice about what courses to take in school, instead of bringing such questions home. Understandably, a variety of situations arise in which adolescents may feel that their parents' advice may be less valid than the opinions of others.

There also are issues that might be talked over with more than one person. For example, a teenage girl who is trying to decide whether to take a part-time job after school might discuss the pros and cons with her parents but also ask friends for their advice. When friends and parents disagree, adolescents must reconcile the differences of opinion and reach their own independent conclusions.

Adolescents are more likely to conform to their peers' opinions when it comes to short-term, day-to-day, and social matters, such as styles of dress. When it comes to long-term issues or decisions that concern basic values, however, parents remain more influential than peers.

In situations in which parents and peers give conflicting advice, do teenagers tend to follow one group more often than the other? Adolescents are often portrayed as being extremely susceptible to the influence of peer pressure—more so than children or young adults—and as being stubbornly resistant to the influence of their parents. But is peer pressure really more potent during adolescence than during other times in the life cycle?

■ **The Influence of Parents and Peers** Researchers have studied conformity and peer pressure during adolescence by putting adolescents in situations in which they must choose either between the wishes of their parents and those of their peers or between their own wishes and those of others—typically, parents or friends. For example, an adolescent might be told to imagine that he and his friends discover something that looks suspicious on the way home from school. His friends tell him that they should keep it a secret. But the youth tells his mother about it, and she advises him to report it to the police. He then would be asked by the researcher to say what he would do.

In general, studies that contrast parents' and peers' influences indicate that in some situations, peers' opinions are more influential, but that in other situations, parents' opinions are more powerful. Specifically, adolescents are more likely to conform to their peers' opinions when it comes to short-term, day-to-day, and social matters—styles of dress, tastes in music, choices among leisure activities, and so on. This is particularly true during the junior high school and early high school years. When it comes to long-term questions concerning educational or occupational plans, however, or to issues concerning values, religious beliefs, or ethics, teenagers are primarily influenced by their parents (Brittain, 1963; Young & Ferguson, 1979). Some studies also have looked at adolescents' willingness to seek advice from adults outside their family. These studies indicate that in situations calling for objective information (such as facts about getting admitted to a particular college) rather than opinion (such as whether the college is supposed to be a friendly place), teenagers are likely to turn to outside experts, such as their teachers (Young & Ferguson, 1979).

Similar findings emerge from studies of the consultants adolescents turn to when they have problems (Morrison, Laughlin, Miguel, Smith, & Widaman, 1997; Wintre, Hicks, McVey, & Fox, 1988). In general, when adolescents' problems center on a relationship with a friend, they to turn to a peer, a preference that becomes stronger with age. But adolescents' willingness to turn to an adult for advice with problems—especially problems that involve adolescents and their parents—remains very strong and increases as individuals move toward late adolescence. This suggests that older adolescents are quite willing to turn to adult experts whose advice they value.

These findings are consistent with some of the findings we looked at earlier regarding changes in adolescents' decision-making abilities. With age, adolescents become increasingly likely to turn to experts for advice. On social matters, the experts are friends; on issues requiring specific objective information, teachers and other adults likely to have the necessary knowledge are the authorities; and on questions of values, ethics, and plans, parents remain the advisors of choice. More importantly, the results of these studies indicate that peer pressure—or, for that matter, parental pressure—is likely to be ineffective in some situations and powerful in others. In short, adolescents turn for advice to different people in different situations (Finken & Jacobs, 1996).

Nevertheless, youngsters' views of adult authority clearly change over the course of adolescence (Helwig, Arnold, Tan, & Boyd, 2003). Preadolescents, for example, are more likely to believe that parents and teachers have authority over a wide range of decisions, that the rules made by adults are important and legitimate, and that breaking these rules—even in the interest of preserving a relationship with a friend—is wrong.

As most parents and teachers can attest, however, over time, adolescents become more questioning of adult authority, more likely to see some issues as personal (and out of the jurisdiction of adults), and more likely to allow their friendships with peers to be important determinants of their decision making (Smetana & Bitz, 1996; Tisak, Tisak, & Rogers, 1994).

■ **Responding to Peer Pressure**   Studies that contrast the influence of peers and adults do not really reveal all there is to know about peer pressure, however, because most peer pressure operates when adults are absent from the scene—when adolescents are at a party, on the way home from school, or on a date. To get closer to this issue, researchers have studied how adolescents respond when they must choose between the pressure of their friends and their own opinions of what to do. For example, an adolescent boy might be asked whether he would go along with his friends' pressure to vandalize some property even though he did not want to do so (Berndt, 1979).

In general, most studies using this approach show that conformity to peers is higher during early and middle adolescence (it peaks around age 14) than during preadolescence or later adolescence (Berndt, 1979; Brown, 1990; Krosnick & Judd, 1982; Steinberg & Silverberg, 1986), although the specific age pattern varies somewhat depending on the domain of behavior studied (Sim & Koh, 2003). The heightened susceptibility to peer pressure of individuals around age 14 is most often seen when the behavior in question is antisocial—such as cheating, stealing, or trespassing—and it is especially true for boys (Erickson, Crosnoe, & Dornbusch, 2000). These findings are in line with studies of delinquent acts, which are often committed by boys in groups, during middle adolescence (Berndt, 1979). Several studies indicate that, compared with their more autonomous friends, adolescents who are more susceptible to peer pressure to engage in delinquent activity actually are more likely to misbehave (Brown, Clasen, & Eicher, 1986). Susceptibility to antisocial peer pressure is also higher among relatively more acculturated Latino adolescents than their less acculturated peers, and higher among Latino adolescents who were born in the United States than those who were born abroad, consistent with research showing higher rates of delinquency among more acculturated adolescents (Umaña-Taylor & Bámaca-Gómez, 2003; Wall, Power, & Arbiona, 1993).

One interesting application of research on adolescents' susceptibility to social pressure concerns adolescents' false confessions to police officers. In several well-publicized cases involving adolescents who had confessed to crimes—such as the case of the Central Park jogger, in which a group of adolescents confessed to assaulting a woman who was running through the

New York City park—it was subsequently discovered that the juveniles had given false confessions to the police. Although most of us find it hard to understand why someone would confess to a crime that he or she did not commit, studies that simulate police interrogations have found that it is not at all unusual for adolescents to do so when questioned under pressure. In one such study (Redlich & Goodman, 2003), subjects of different ages participated in an experiment that involved typing letters on a computer as they were read by the experimenter. Before beginning the experiment, subjects were instructed not to touch the ALT key, because doing so would crash the computer and ruin the experiment. The experiment was rigged, however, so that the computer would crash after a set amount of time, even without the subject touching the ALT key. After the computer crashed, the experimenter questioned the subjects about whether they had hit the ALT key. When subjects denied doing so, the experimenter presented false evidence "proving" that the ALT key had been pressed. The subjects were then questioned once again about what they had done. In the face of false evidence, significantly more young adolescents (ages 12–16) than young adults confessed to having hit the ALT key, even when they actually had not (see Figure 9.4).

Although we know that conformity to peer pressure is greater during early adolescence than before or after, it is not clear why this is so. One interpretation is that adolescents are more susceptible to peer influence during this time because of their heightened orientation toward the peer group. Because they care more about what their friends think of them, they are more likely to go along with the crowd to avoid being rejected (Brown et al., 1986). This heightened conformity to

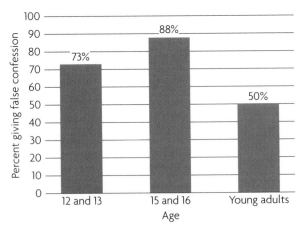

FIGURE 9.4   In a controlled experiment, adolescents were more likely than adults to provide false confessions when confronted with fake "evidence" that they had made a computer crash when they actually had not. (Redlich & Goodman, 2003)

Conformity to peers—especially in situations involving antisocial or delinquent behavior—is higher during early and middle adolescence than before or after. Some forms of delinquency may result from this heightened susceptibility to the influence of friends.

peer pressure during early adolescence may be a sign of a sort of emotional "way station" between becoming emotionally autonomous from parents and becoming a genuinely autonomous person (Steinberg & Silverberg, 1986). In other words, these adolescents may become emotionally autonomous from their parents before they are emotionally ready for this degree of independence and may turn to peers to fill this void. Each of these accounts suggests that susceptibility to peer pressure increases as youngsters move into early adolescence, peaks at around age 14, and declines thereafter (Brown et al., 1986; Steinberg & Silverberg, 1986).

A different version of the same story focuses on changes in the sheer strength of peer pressure. For instance, individuals' susceptibility to peer pressure may remain constant over adolescence even as the peer pressure itself strengthens and then weakens over the period. Early adolescent peer groups may exert more pressure on their members to conform than do groups of younger or older individuals, and the pressure may be strong enough to make even the most autonomous teenagers comply. Although this is an attractive alternative explanation—particularly to adolescents who

appeal to their parents by saying, "No one will talk to me if I don't do it!"—studies have not borne it out. In fact, peer pressure to misbehave seems to increase steadily throughout adolescence, beyond the age at which it would be expected to diminish (Brown et al., 1986).

When we put together the research about peer pressure, peer conformity, and parental conformity, the following picture emerges: During childhood, boys and girls are highly oriented toward their parents and far less oriented toward their peers, and peer pressure is not especially strong. As they approach adolescence, children become somewhat less oriented toward their parents and more oriented toward their peers, and peer pressure begins to escalate. As a result, during preadolescence, there is little net gain in behavioral autonomy—overall levels of conformity do not change, but the source of influence shifts. During early adolescence, conformity to parents continues to decline, and both conformity to peers and peer pressure continue to rise—again, there is little change in overall behavioral autonomy. It is not until middle and late adolescence, therefore, that genuine increases in behavioral autonomy occur, for it is during this time

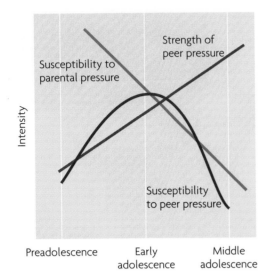

FIGURE 9.5 During adolescence, susceptibility to peer pressure increases and then falls, while susceptibility to parental pressure decreases. Perceptions of the strength of peer pressure increase throughout the period.

(between the ninth and twelfth grades) that conformity both to parents and to peers declines even though peer pressure continues to increase (see Figure 9.5).

■ **Individual Differences in Susceptibility to Peer Influence**   Within a group of teenagers of the same age, of course, some are highly autonomous, others are easily influenced by their peers, others are oriented toward their parents, and still others are swayed by both peers and parents, depending on the situation. For instance, adolescents from single-parent families, as well as those with less supportive or involved parents, appear relatively more susceptible to antisocial peer pressure (Farrell & White, 1998; Wong, Crosnoe, Laird, & Dornbusch, 2003). In general, autonomous youngsters and adult-oriented youngsters are likely to have come from homes in which their parents were warm and moderately controlling—the typical authoritative household. Peer-oriented children, especially when in antisocial situations, are likely to have parents who were less nurturant and either extremely controlling or extremely permissive.

Like emotional autonomy, then, behavioral autonomy appears to be associated with authoritative rather than permissive, authoritarian, or neglectful parenting (Devereux, 1970). Consistent with this, the sexual behavior of adolescents who have discussed sex with their parents is less influenced by peer pressure than is the behavior of adolescents who have not done so (Whitaker & Miller, 2000), and adolescents whose parents strongly disapprove of smoking are less likely to be influenced by their friends' smoking than are

adolescents whose parents do not voice their disapproval (Sargent & Dalton, 2001).

The situation may be somewhat more complicated than this, however. It turns out that the impact of having authoritative parents on adolescents' susceptibility to peer pressure depends on the nature of the peer pressure in question. Adolescents from authoritative homes are less susceptible to antisocial peer pressure, but they may be more susceptible to the influence of positive peers. Adolescents from authoritative homes, for example, are less likely than other teenagers to be influenced by having drug-using friends, but they are *more* likely than their peers to be influenced by having friends who perform well in school (Mounts & Steinberg, 1995). It is also important to distinguish between adolescents who are excessively dependent on their peers (and who forgo their parents' rules and pay less attention to their schoolwork for the sake of being popular with peers) versus those who turn to peers for counsel but do not ignore their parents' guidance (Fuligni, Eccles, Barber, & Clements, 2001). Substituting peers for parents leads to problem behavior; adding peers to the list of persons whom the adolescent turns to for advice, so long as that list includes parents, does not. In other words, it is detachment from parents, rather than attachment to peers, that is potentially harmful.

Although it is tempting to conclude from these studies that authoritative parenting fosters the development of responsible autonomy, we must be careful about drawing this conclusion, since the direction of effects could work just as plausibly the other way around. Perhaps responsible, independent children elicit warm and democratic behavior from their parents, whereas less autonomous youngsters invoke harsher discipline or parental nonchalance. In all likelihood, both processes are at work—children are affected by their parents, and parents are affected by their children. In essence, authoritative parenting probably leads to adolescent autonomy, which, in turn, leads to more authoritative parenting.

The ways in which parents and adolescents negotiate changes in behavioral autonomy have implications for adolescents' adjustment, according to several studies (e.g., Fuligni & Eccles, 1993; Goldstein, Davis-Kean, & Eccles, 2005; Sim, 2000). Not surprisingly, adolescents who have less positive relationships with their parents are more likely to be especially peer oriented, to affiliate with negative peers, and to spend time with friends in unsupervised settings, all of which heighten adolescents' risk for problem behavior. But studies also show that parents need to maintain a healthy balance between asserting control and granting autonomy. Generally, granting too much autonomy before adolescents are ready for it *or* granting too little autonomy once adolescents are mature enough to handle it creates adolescents who are the most strongly peer oriented. Adolescents whose parents become more authoritarian (that is, stricter and less likely to permit the adolescent to make decisions) over time are the most peer oriented of all. Although many parents clamp down on their teenagers' independence out of fear that not doing so will allow the youngsters to fall under the "evil" influence of the peer group, this strategy often backfires. Evidently, having parents limit their autonomy at just the time when more independence is desired and expected makes adolescents turn away from the family and toward their friends.

ETHNIC AND CULTURAL DIFFERENCES IN EXPECTATIONS FOR AUTONOMY

The development of behavioral autonomy varies across cultures because of differences in the age expectations that adolescents and parents have for independent behavior. Psychologist Shirley Feldman and colleagues have examined this issue by asking parents and adolescents from both Asian and white cultural groups to fill out a "teen timetable"—a questionnaire that asks at what age adolescents should be permitted to engage in various behaviors that signal autonomy (for example, "spend money however you want," "go out on dates," "go to rock concerts with friends") (Feldman & Wood, 1994). In general, white adolescents and their parents living in America, Australia, or Hong Kong have earlier expectations for adolescent autonomy than do Asian adolescents and parents from these same countries (Feldman & Quatman, 1988; Rosenthal & Feldman, 1990). Because of this, adolescents from Asian families may be less likely to seek autonomy from their parents than their white counterparts. And perhaps because of this, whereas individuation tends to be associated with higher self-esteem among American youth, it is associated with lower self-esteem among Asian adolescents (Chun & MacDermid, 1997). In general, though, adolescents' mental health is best when their desire for autonomy matches their expectations for what their parents are willing to grant (Juang, Lerner, McKinney, & von Eye, 1999).

Surprisingly, in these studies of expectations for behavioral autonomy, there were neither sex nor birth order differences in age expectations—contrary to the popular beliefs that boys expect more autonomy than girls and that later-born adolescents are granted earlier freedom because their older siblings have paved the way. There are sex and birth order differences in the extent to which parents grant autonomy, but the pattern varies depending on the particular constellation of sons and daughters in the household and on the parents' attitudes toward sex roles. Although it is generally thought that parents are more controlling of daughters than sons, this is more likely to be the case in households where parents have traditional views of gender roles (Bumpus, Crouter, & McHale, 2001). Sex differences in the extent to which adolescents are granted independence appear to be especially pronounced within African American households, where, compared to other ethnic groups, boys are given relatively more freedom but girls are given less (Bulcroft, Carmody, & Bulcroft, 1996; Daddis & Smetana, 2005). And, contrary to expectations, parents grant more autonomy to first-borns than to second-borns, especially when the first-born is a girl and the second-born is a boy (Bumpus et al., 2001). In addition, adolescents who feel older seek more independence than their same-aged peers who feel younger (Galambos, Kolaric, & Maggs, 1994).

Interestingly, the autonomy-granting timetable of families that have emigrated from a culture relatively slower to grant adolescents autonomy to a culture in which autonomy is granted sooner falls somewhere between the two extremes; this has been found in studies both of Chinese immigrants in America and Australia (Rosenthal & Feldman, 1990) and of East German immigrants in the former West Germany (Silbereisen & Schmitt-Rodermund, 1995). One problem facing many families that have immigrated to a new culture is that parents and adolescents may have very different expectations for what an appropriate timetable is with respect to granting autonomy—although this will depend, of course, on the degree of discrepancy in timetables in the initial and new contexts. But, as a rule, because adolescents generally acculturate more quickly to a new culture than do parents, a family that has moved from a culture in which it is normal to grant autonomy relatively later in adolescence (as in most Asian countries) to one in which it is normal to grant autonomy relatively earlier (as in the United States) may experience conflict as a result of differences in the expectations of adolescents and parents (Kwak, 2003).

FOOD FOR THOUGHT

Suppose you were writing a book for parents of teenagers. What advice would you give them about coping with adolescent peer pressure? What special advice would you give to parents who have recently moved to the United States?

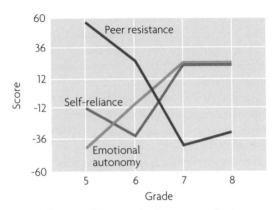

FIGURE 9.6 Age differences in three types of autonomy. (Steinberg & Silverberg, 1986)

- youngsters are particularly susceptible to peer pressure, especially on issues concerning day-to-day activities.
- Susceptibility to peer pressure increases between childhood and early adolescence, and then decreases over the high school years.
- Adolescents whose parents are extremely authoritarian or extremely permissive are the most easily influenced by their friends, especially in antisocial contexts.
- Adolescents do not experience this increased susceptibility to peer pressure as a decline in self-reliance.

CHANGES IN FEELINGS OF SELF-RELIANCE

A third approach to the study of behavioral autonomy focuses on adolescents' own judgments of how autonomous they are. When adolescents of different ages are asked to complete standardized tests of self-reliance, for example, the results show that subjective feelings of autonomy increase steadily over the adolescent years and, contrary to stereotypes, that adolescent girls report feeling more self-reliant than do adolescent boys (Greenberger, 1982; Steinberg & Silverberg, 1986). This is especially interesting in light of the findings concerning susceptibility to peer pressure, discussed earlier, since it indicates that adolescents may describe themselves as gaining in self-reliance during a period when their susceptibility to peer pressure may be increasing (see Figure 9.6). Although adults may view adolescents' giving in to peer pressure as a sign of diminished autonomy, adolescents may not see their own behavior in this light. Not surprisingly, adolescents who have a stronger sense of self-reliance report higher self-esteem and fewer behavior problems (Owens, Mortimer, & Finch, 1996; Wolfe & Truxillo, 1996).

RECAP

- As individuals mature, they become better able to seek out and weigh the advice of individuals with different degrees of expertise and to use this information in making independent decisions.
- One controversy involves whether adolescents' decision-making abilities are mature enough to warrant their treatment as adults under the law.
- Although adolescence is a time of advances in decision-making abilities, during early adolescence,

The Development of Value Autonomy

The development of value autonomy entails changes in the adolescent's conceptions of moral, political, ideological, and religious issues. Three trends in the development of value autonomy during adolescence are especially noteworthy. First, adolescents become increasingly abstract in the way they think about moral, political, ideological, and religious issues. Consider an 18-year-old who is deciding whether to participate in a disruptive demonstration in his state capital against policies he believes indirectly support the interests of environmental polluters. Instead of looking at the situation only in terms of the specifics of the situation, he might think about the implications of knowingly violating the law in general. Second, during adolescence, beliefs become increasingly rooted in general principles that have some ideological basis. An 18-year-old might say that demonstrating against pollution is acceptable because protecting the environment is more important than living in accord with the law, and so breaking a law is legitimate when the status quo leads to environmental degradation. Finally, beliefs become increasingly founded in the young person's own values, and not merely in a system of values passed on by parents or other authority figures. Thus, an 18-year-old may look at the issue of environmental protection in terms of what he himself believes, rather than in terms of what his parents have told him to think.

Much of the growth in value autonomy can be traced to the cognitive changes characteristic of the period. With adolescents' enhanced reasoning capabilities and the further development of hypothetical thinking come a heightened interest in ideological and philosophical matters, and a more sophisticated way of looking at them. The ability to consider alternate possibilities and to engage in thinking about thinking allows for the exploration of differing value systems, political ideologies, personal ethics, and religious beliefs.

But the growth of value autonomy is encouraged by the development of emotional and behavioral independence as well. As we shall see, some evidence suggests that the development of value autonomy occurs later (between ages 18 and 20) than does the development of emotional or behavioral autonomy, which take place during early and middle adolescence. As young people gain increasing distance from the emotional dependencies of childhood, they rely less on their parents' beliefs and values. The establishment of emotional autonomy provides adolescents with the ability to look at their parents' views more objectively. When young people no longer see their parents as omnipotent and infallible authorities, they may seriously reevaluate the ideas and values that they accepted without question as children. Not surprisingly, individuals with a stronger sense of value autonomy show more maturity in other psychological domains as well, such as in the realms of identity development and self-awareness (Hart & Chmeil, 1992; Hart & Fegley, 1995).

As adolescents begin to test the waters of independence behaviorally, they may experience a variety of cognitive conflicts caused by having to compare the advice of parents and friends and having to deal with competing pressures to behave in given ways. These conflicts may prompt young people to consider in more serious and thoughtful terms what they really believe. This struggle to clarify values, provoked in part by the exercise of behavioral autonomy, is a key component of the process of developing a sense of value autonomy. The development of value autonomy has been studied with regard to adolescents' beliefs about morality, politics, and religion.

MORAL DEVELOPMENT DURING ADOLESCENCE

Moral development has been the most widely studied aspect of value autonomy during adolescence. The study of moral development involves both reasoning (how individuals think about moral dilemmas) and behavior (how they behave in situations that call for moral judgments). Related to this is the study of prosocial behavior, the behaviors individuals engage in to help others.

▌ **Assessing Moral Reasoning**   The dominant theoretical viewpoint in the study of moral reasoning has

been a perspective grounded in Piaget's theory of cognitive development. As you will recall from the discussion in Chapter 2 of changes in thinking processes during adolescence, the emphasis within the Piagetian view, or cognitive-developmental perspective, is on changes in the structure and organization of thought, rather than on changes in its content. Theories of morality that stem from the cognitive-developmental viewpoint similarly emphasize shifts in the type of reasoning that individuals use in making moral decisions, rather than changes in the content of the decisions they reach or the actions they take as a result. Although the initial formulation of the cognitive-developmental perspective on morality was presented by Piaget himself, the theory was subsequently expanded by Lawrence Kohlberg, and it is Kohlberg's work that is more relevant to the study of moral development during adolescence (Eisenberg & Morris, 2004; Turiel, 1998).

Researchers assess individuals' levels of moral reasoning by examining their responses to hypothetical moral dilemmas about difficult, real-world situations. These dilemmas are presented either in an interview, in which case the adolescents' responses are recorded, transcribed, and coded (Colby & Kohlberg, 1987), or in a questionnaire, in which adolescents respond to the dilemmas in a multiple-choice format (Rest, Davison, & Robbins, 1978). Here are examples of the sorts of dilemmas researchers have used:

Judy was a twelve-year-old girl. Her mother promised her that she could go to a special rock concert coming to their town if she saved up from baby-sitting and lunch money to buy a ticket to the concert. She managed to save up the fifteen dollars the ticket cost plus another five dollars. But then her mother changed her mind and told Judy that she had to spend the money on new clothes for school. Judy was disappointed and decided to go to the concert anyway. She bought a ticket and told her mother that she had only been able to save five dollars. That Saturday she went to the performance and told her mother that she was spending the day with a friend. A week passed without her mother finding out. Judy then told her older sister, Louise, that she had gone to the performance and had lied to her mother about it. Louise wonders whether to tell their mother what Judy did.

Should Louise, the older sister, tell their mother that Judy lied about the money or should she keep quiet?

Two young men, brothers, had got into serious trouble. They were secretly leaving town in a hurry and needed money. Karl, the older one, broke into a store and stole a thousand dollars. Bob, the younger one, went to a retired old man who was known to help people in town. He told the man that he was very sick and that he needed a thousand dollars to pay for an operation. Bob asked the old man to lend him the money and promised that he would pay him back when he recovered. Really Bob wasn't sick at all, and he had no intention of paying the man back. Although the old man didn't know Bob very well, he lent him the money. So Bob and Karl skipped town, each with a thousand dollars.

Which is worse, stealing like Karl or cheating like Bob?

Perhaps Kohlberg's best-known dilemma involved a man who had to choose between stealing a drug to save his wife or letting his wife remain mortally ill:

> In Europe, a woman was near death from a very bad disease, a special kind of cancer. There was one drug that the doctors thought might save her. It was a form of radium that a druggist in the same town had recently discovered. The drug was expensive to make, but the druggist was charging ten times what the drug cost him to make. He paid $200 for the radium and charged $2,000 for a small dose of the drug. The sick woman's husband, Heinz, went to everyone he knew to borrow the money, but he could only get together about $1,000, which was half of what it cost. He told the druggist that his wife was dying, and asked him to sell it cheaper or let him pay later. But the druggist said, "No, I discovered the drug and I'm going to make money from it." Heinz got desperate and broke into the man's store to steal the drug for his wife. Should the husband have done that? Was it right or wrong?

Stages of Moral Reasoning According to Kohlberg, whether or not you think that Heinz should have stolen the drug, or that Louise should tell her mother, or that cheating someone is worse than stealing from a store is less important than the reasoning behind your answers. Kohlberg theorized that individuals' reasoning about moral issues becomes more sophisticated with development. Specifically, Kohlberg suggested that there are three levels of moral reasoning: **preconventional moral reasoning,** which is dominant during most of childhood; **conventional moral reasoning,** which is usually dominant during late childhood and early adolescence; and **postconventional moral reasoning** (sometimes called principled

The ways in which individuals think about moral dilemmas change during adolescence.

moral reasoning), which emerges sometime during the adolescent or young adult years.

Preconventional thinking is characterized by reference to external and physical events. Preconventional moral decisions are not based on society's standards, rules, or conventions (hence the label *precon*ventional). Children at this stage approach moral dilemmas in ways that focus on the rewards and punishments associated with different courses of action. One preconventional child might say that Heinz should not have stolen the drug because he could have been caught and sent to jail. Another might say that Heinz was right to steal the drug because people would have been angry with him if he had let his wife die. In either case, the chief concern to the preconventional thinker is what would happen to Heinz as a result of his choice.

Conventional thinking about moral issues focuses not so much on tangible rewards and punishments as on how an individual will be judged by others for behaving in a certain way. In conventional moral reasoning, special importance is given to the roles people are expected to play and to society's rules, institutions,

preconventional moral reasoning According to Kohlberg, the first level of moral reasoning, which is typical of children and is characterized by reasoning that is based on rewards and punishments associated with different courses of action.

conventional moral reasoning According to Kohlberg, the second level of moral development, which occurs during late childhood and early adolescence and is characterized by reasoning that is based on the rules and conventions of society.

postconventional moral reasoning In Kohlberg's theory, the stage of moral development during which society's rules and conventions are seen as relative and subjective rather than as authoritative; also called principled moral reasoning.

and conventions. Individuals behave properly because, in so doing, they receive the approval of others and help to maintain the social order. The correctness of society's rules is not questioned, however—individuals do their duty by upholding and respecting the social order. A conventional thinker might say that Heinz should not have stolen the drug because stealing is against the law. But another might counter that Heinz was right to steal the drug because it is what a good husband is expected to do. According to most studies of moral reasoning, the majority of adolescents and adults think primarily in conventional terms—they evaluate moral decisions in terms of a set of rules that people are supposed to abide by.

Postconventional reasoning is relatively rare. At this level of reasoning, society's rules and conventions are seen as relative and subjective rather than as absolute and definitive. Individuals may have a moral duty to abide by society's standards for behavior—but only insofar as those standards support and serve moral ends. Thus, occasions arise in which conventions ought to be questioned and when more important principles—such as justice, fairness, or the sanctity of human life—take precedence over established social norms. For instance, a postconventional response might be that Heinz should not have stolen the drug because in doing so he violated an implicit agreement among members of society—an agreement that gives each person the freedom to pursue his or her livelihood. However, another principled thinker might respond that Heinz was right to steal the drug because someone's life was at stake and because preserving human life is more important than respecting individual freedoms. Whereas conventional thinking is oriented toward society's rules, postconventional thinking is founded on more broadly based abstract principles. For this reason, the development of postconventional reasoning is especially relevant to the discussion of value autonomy.

Studies have confirmed Kohlberg's suggestion that moral reasoning becomes more principled over the course of childhood and adolescence (Eisenberg & Morris, 2004). Moreover, development appears to proceed through the sequence described in Kohlberg's theory (Colby, Kohlberg, Gibbs, & Lieberman, 1983). Preconventional reasoning dominates the responses of children; conventional responses begin to appear during preadolescence and continue into middle adolescence; and postconventional reasoning does not appear until late adolescence, if at all. According to Kohlberg's theory, movement into higher stages of moral reasoning occurs when the adolescent is developmentally "ready"—when his or her reasoning is predominantly at one stage but partially at the next higher one—and when he or she is exposed to the more advanced type of reasoning by other people, such as parents or peers (Eisenberg & Morris, 2004). The development of moral reasoning tends to follow a pattern in which individuals move from periods of consolidation (in which their reasoning is consistently at a particular stage of development), into periods of transition (in which there is more variability in their stages of reasoning), into new periods of consolidation (in which their reasoning is consistent, but at a higher stage than during the previous period of consolidation) (Walker, Gustafson, & Hennig, 2001).

As is the case with formal operational thought, the most advanced stage of reasoning described by Piaget (see Chapter 2), not all individuals develop the capacity to engage in postconventional moral reasoning. Advanced levels of moral reasoning are more common among children raised in authoritative families in which parents encourage their child to participate in family discussions, in which the level of conflict in family discussions is neither extremely low nor extremely high, and in which parents expose the adolescent to moral arguments that are fashioned at a higher stage than her or his own (Eisenberg & Morris, 2004). There is also some evidence that the development of advanced moral reasoning among African American youth is facilitated by commitment to traditional African values of spirituality and community (Woods & Jagers, 2003).

Although not all individuals enter a stage of postconventional thinking during adolescence, many begin to place greater emphasis on abstract values and moral principles (Rest et al., 1978). Moreover, if individuals of different ages are presented with other peoples' moral arguments, older individuals are more often persuaded by arguments that in Kohlberg's framework are more advanced. Thus, the appeal of postconventional moral reasoning increases over the course of adolescence, while the appeals of preconventional and of conventional reasoning both decline. Interestingly, the appeal of postconventional thinking appears to increase both with age and with schooling; most adults reach a plateau in moral reasoning after completing their formal education.

Moral Reasoning and Moral Behavior It is one thing to reason about hypothetical moral problems in an advanced way; it is quite another to behave in strict accordance with one's reasoning. After all, it is common for people to say one thing (for example, cheating on a test is immoral) but do another (for example, sneak a peek at a classmate's test when running out of time during an exam). Some critics have argued that although Kohlberg's theory may provide a window on how people think about abstract and hypothetical dilemmas, or about life-and-death situations, as in the

Heinz story, it does not tell us very much about the ways people reason about day-to-day problems or behave when they find themselves in situations that might evoke moral considerations.

As it turns out, research on Kohlberg's theory has answered these criticisms fairly well. As for the first of these concerns, for example, research indicates that people reason about life-and-death dilemmas in ways that parallel their reasoning about the moral dilemmas they actually encounter in everyday life (Eisenberg & Morris, 2004; Walker, de Vries, & Trevethan, 1987). And as for the second of these concerns, many studies indicate that individuals' behavior is related to the ways in which they reason about hypothetical moral dilemmas. Although individuals do not always behave in ways that are absolutely consistent with their moral reasoning, on average, individuals who reason at higher stages behave in more moral ways. For example, individuals who are capable of reasoning at higher stages of moral thought are less likely to commit antisocial acts, less likely to cheat, and less likely to bow to the pressures of others, as well as more tolerant, more likely to engage in political protests, more likely to engage in volunteer activities, and more likely to assist others in need of help. Conversely, those who reason at lower stages of moral thought are more aggressive, are more accepting of violence, and are more tolerant of others' misbehavior (Eisenberg & Morris, 2004).

FOOD FOR THOUGHT

Should schools attempt to facilitate adolescents' moral development as a part of their curriculum? If so, what sorts of activities would be most useful?

Of course, moral behavior and moral reasoning do not always go hand in hand. Most of us have found ourselves in situations in which we behaved less morally than we would have liked to. According to one writer, however, we should not expect moral behavior to follow exactly from moral reasoning, because other factors complicate moral decision making (Rest, 1983). In tests measuring moral reasoning, assessments are made in a social vacuum, but such vacuums rarely exist in the real world. For example, you probably realize in the abstract that complying with highway speed limits is important because such limits prevent accidents, and you may obey these limits most of the time. But you may have found yourself in a

situation in which you weighed your need to get somewhere in a hurry (perhaps you were late for an important job interview) against your moral belief in the importance of obeying speeding laws, and you decided that in this instance you would behave in a way inconsistent with your belief. Situational factors influence moral choices, and they also influence moral reasoning. When individuals perceive that they will be severely hurt by behaving in a morally advanced way (for example, if standing up for someone will lead to severe punishment), they are less likely to reason at a higher moral level (Sobesky, 1983). Moral reasoning is an important influence on moral behavior, but it cannot be considered out of context.

The correlation between adolescents' moral reasoning and their moral behavior is especially likely to break down when they define issues as personal choices rather than ethical dilemmas (for instance, when using drugs is seen as a personal matter rather than a moral issue) (Kuther & Higgins-D'Alessandro, 2000). This observation turns out to be especially important for understanding why adolescents' moral reasoning and risk taking are for the most part unrelated (Eisenberg & Morris, 2004). If individuals consider various risky behaviors (for example, experimenting with drugs, having unprotected sex) to be personal decisions rather than moral choices, their moral reasoning will be relatively unimportant in predicting how they will act. In other words, individuals are more likely to engage in risky behavior (even if it is unethical) when they see the behavior as a matter of personal taste than a question of right and wrong. It is not clear, however, whether viewing risk taking as a personal choice is likely to lead to more risk taking, or whether individuals, once they've engaged in a risky activity, are likely to redefine the issue as a personal rather than moral one, as a way of justifying their behavior after the fact. In either case, this suggests that interventions designed to stimulate moral reasoning will have little impact on adolescents' risk taking if they fail to convince adolescents that the behavior in question involves a moral and not just a personal choice.

Sex Differences in Moral Reasoning An important alternative to Kohlberg's model was proposed in the late 1970s by psychologist Carol Gilligan (1982), who argued that Kohlberg's view of morality places too much emphasis on a type of moral orientation characteristically employed by men. She and other feminist scholars have argued that Kohlberg's model underemphasizes an equally valid approach to morality that women happen to use more often.

Specifically, Gilligan argued that Kohlberg's theory places too much emphasis on what she calls a **justice orientation** to moral problems. The justice orientation

justice orientation In Gilligan's theory of moral development, a moral orientation that emphasizes fairness and objectivity.

holds out as its ideal a morality of reciprocity and equal respect. From this perspective, the most important consideration in resolving a moral dilemma is whether the individuals involved are treated fairly according to the ultimate decision.

A valid alternative to the justice orientation, claimed Gilligan, is a **care orientation.** From this perspective, the ideal is a morality of attention to others and responsiveness to human need. As opposed to the justice orientation, which is rooted in the premise that moral decisions are best made from a detached position of objectivity ("Rules are rules," "Fair is fair"), the care orientation is rooted in the belief that moral decisions should be shaped by individuals' attachments and responsiveness to others.

An example may help to clarify the distinction. In responding to the Heinz dilemma, discussed previously, individuals with a justice orientation cast the problem as a conflict between Heinz's desire to save his wife and the druggist's desire to engage in his business— a conflict between the values associated with life and property ownership. Individuals with a care orientation, in contrast, see the dilemma in entirely different terms: as a dilemma of responsiveness. The question is not whether the druggist has a right to personal property that outweighs other rights, but rather why the druggist is not responsive to the needs of another person. Rather than seeing society as functioning with a system of rules or abstract principles, individuals with a care orientation view society as functioning through the interconnection of human relationships. Theories of morality and of human development in general, argued Gilligan, have emphasized the sort of intellectual, individualistic, and detached reasoning characteristic of the justice orientation as the index of mental health, and have given short shrift to the emotional and interpersonal concerns characteristic of the caring orientation. Using this standard, Gilligan said, makes women appear to be less moral than men.

Despite the popularity and intuitive appeal of Gilligan's view that men and women think about ethical issues in different ways, little empirical evidence points to substantial sex differences in the ways individuals reason about moral problems (Turiel, 1998). Many studies have found that men and women approach moral problems from the perspectives of both justice and caring, depending on the problem, and explicit searches for sex differences in how individuals respond to moral dilemmas generally do not find them (Pratt, Skoe, & Arnold, 2004; Turiel, 1998; Walker et al., 1987).

How can we account for the discrepancy between Gilligan's assertions about sex differences in moral reasoning and the findings of more recent empirical studies? One explanation is that Gilligan did not study males in the research that led to her classic book *In a Different Voice* (1982). As a consequence, it is not clear whether the observations she drew from this work reflected anything unique about the moral development of women. That is, we do not know how men would have responded had they been included in Gilligan's research.

A recent study by Susan Harter and colleagues (Harter, Waters, Whitesell, & Kastelic, 1998) helps to clarify matters a bit. One of Gilligan's contentions was that at adolescence many girls feel a "loss of voice"— a suppression of their thoughts and opinions. "Gilligan argued," Harter explained, "that teenage girls quickly perceive that the desirable stereotype is being nice, polite, pleasing to others, unassertive, and quiet" (Harter et al., 1998, p. 892). This assertion formed the basis for the best-selling book *Reviving Ophelia* (Pipher, 1994), which argued that the loss of voice at early adolescence led many teenage girls to be confused and troubled.

In Harter's studies of "level of voice" among male and female adolescents, however, she did not find the sex differences hypothesized by Gilligan, nor did she find that females' voice diminished over the course of adolescence. Harter did find, however, that adolescents' gender-role orientation and the social support they received from others were predictive of loss of voice. Girls with a highly feminine gender-role orientation, as well as both boys and girls who felt that significant others in their life did not take their opinions seriously, suffered the loss of voice Gilligan had described. But androgynous girls and adolescents who felt that others supported their having strong opinions suffered no such loss. If Harter had included just girls in her study and had not examined variables other than sex, she might have drawn the same erroneous conclusions as Gilligan.

Although Gilligan's work has been popular with the general public, the scientific community has been less enamored with it (e.g., Sommers, 2000). Indeed, critics of Gilligan's work have challenged many of her other assertions, including the widely believed (but empirically unsupported) contentions that girls are more confused and more troubled than boys, that girls have more difficulty finding their "voice," and that girls are more likely to be short-changed by schools and other institutions. Indeed, some writers have argued that in many respects (for example, school problems, academic failure, trouble with the law, drug and alcohol abuse) adolescent boys are doing far worse than adolescent girls.

---

care orientation   In Gilligan's theory of moral development, a moral orientation that emphasizes responding to others' needs.

PROSOCIAL REASONING, PROSOCIAL BEHAVIOR, AND VOLUNTEERISM

▌ **Changes in Prosocial Reasoning**   Although most research on the development of morality has focused on what adolescents do under circumstances in which a law might be broken or a rule violated, researchers have increasingly turned their attention to the study of reasoning and behavior in prosocial situations. In general, the ways in which individuals think about prosocial phenomena, such as honesty or kindness, become more sophisticated during late adolescence (Eisenberg & Morris, 2004; Killen & Turiel, 1998). Over the course of adolescence, for example, individuals come to devalue prosocial acts that are done for self-serving reasons (for example, receiving a reward, returning a favor, or improving their image) and value those that are done out of genuine empathy for others (Eisenberg & Morris, 2004). During late adolescence, prosocial reasoning and perspective taking become increasingly advanced, although there are few systematic changes beyond the early 20s (Eisenberg, Cumberland, Guthrie, Murphy, & Shepard, 2005).

▌ **Prosocial Reasoning and Prosocial Behavior**   In addition, studies find important differences among adolescents in their prosocial moral reasoning, and these differences are correlated both with actual prosocial behavior and with attitudes toward helping others (Eisenberg & Morris, 2004). For example, studies of exemplary youth—adolescents who have volunteered considerable amounts of time in service activities—show that these adolescents score higher on measures of moral reasoning than do their peers, are more committed to the betterment of society, and, as children, were made aware of the suffering of those who are less fortunate (Hart & Fegley, 1995; Matsuba & Walker, 2005; Yates & Youniss, 1996). Individuals who score high on measures of prosocial moral reasoning also have been shown to be more sympathetic and empathic (Eisenberg, Carlo, Murphy, & Van Court, 1995), to engage in more prosocial behavior (Eisenberg, Zhou, & Koller, 2001), and to be less likely to behave violently after having witnessed violence themselves (Brookmeter, Henrich, & Schwab-Stone, 2005). In general, female adolescents score higher on measures of prosocial moral reasoning than do male adolescents, as do both males and females who are relatively more feminine (Carlo, Koller, Eisenberg, Da Silva, & Frohlick, 1996; Eisenberg et al., 1995, 2001).

Research on the development of prosocial *behavior* during adolescence is not as consistent, however. Some studies find that individuals become more empathic, sympathetic, and helpful as they move into and through adolescence, but many do not (Eisenberg & Morris, 2004). More consistent are research findings indicating that individuals who are relatively more prosocial tend to behave this way across different contexts (that is, adolescents who are helpful to classmates in school are more likely than their less prosocial peers to also be helpful to strangers in the mall). Also, girls are more caring and prosocial than boys, perhaps because parents emphasize prosocial development more in raising daughters than sons (Eisenberg & Morris, 2004). And individuals with prosocial friends tend to behave more prosocially themselves (Barry & Wentzel, 2006).

▌ **Volunteerism**   One of the most obvious ways in which adolescents can demonstrate prosocial behavior is through volunteerism (Flanagan, 2004). Volunteering in community service activities is more common in the United States than in most other countries and, in fact, is now required by many school districts. Researchers have been interested in both the antecedents of volunteering (that is, what leads adolescents to become involved in volunteer activities) and its consequences (that is, how adolescents are affected by volunteering). Several conclusions have emerged from this work. First, apart from attending a school in which some sort of community service is required, the best predictors of volunteerism in adolescence are being actively involved in religion (most probably because many volunteer activities are organized through religious institutions) and having parents who are active as volunteers in the community. Volunteers also tend to be female, more socially mature, more extraverted, and, not surprisingly, more altruistic (Eisenberg & Morris, 2004).

It has been more difficult to document the effects of volunteering on adolescent development because individuals who choose to volunteer are different to begin with from their peers who do not (Atkins, Hart, & Donnelly, 2005). Nevertheless, studies of volunteering that follow adolescents over time indicate that engaging in community service leads to short-term gains in social responsibility, increases in the importance individuals place on helping others, and increased commitment to tolerance, equal opportunity, and cultural diversity (Flanagan, 2004; Lawford, Pratt, Hunsburger, & Pancer, 2005). The extent to which these effects persist over time depends, in part, on how long the volunteer activity lasts; the shorter the activity, the more short-lived the results of participation. At the same time, however, studies suggest that it is important to distinguish between the effects of engaging in voluntary community service (which are generally positive) and the impact of mandatory service-learning programs in schools (which seem to have less of a lasting impact) (Flanagan, 2004).

FOOD FOR THOUGHT

Although many schools now require that students perform community service, research on the benefits of school-mandated volunteer work does not consistently find that this activity has positive effects. At the same time, no studies have found that volunteer work has negative effects on adolescent development. In light of these findings, do you support mandatory community service for all high school students?

Whereas younger adolescents believe in autocratic rule and tend to support existing laws, older adolescents are more likely to challenge authority and argue that laws should be reexamined. These Phoenix-area students are protesting proposed changes to the nation's immigration laws.

POLITICAL THINKING DURING ADOLESCENCE

Less is known about the development of political thinking during adolescence than about moral development, but research on this topic is generally consistent with the view that beliefs become more principled, more abstract, and more independent during the adolescent years. This pattern is linked in part to the general cognitive developments of adolescence and in part to the growth of specific expertise, as the adolescent is exposed to more political information and ideas (Flanagan, 2004; Torney-Purta, 1990).

■ **Changes in Political Thinking** Political thinking changes during adolescence in several important ways (Flanagan, 2004; Torney-Purta, 1990). First, it becomes more abstract. In response to the question "What is the purpose of laws?" for example, 12- and 13-year-olds are likely to reply with concrete answers—"So people don't kill or steal," "So people don't get hurt," and so on. Older adolescents, in contrast, are likely to respond with more abstract and more general statements—"To ensure safety and enforce the government" or "They are basically guidelines for people. I mean, like this is wrong and this is right and to help them understand" (Adelson, 1972, p. 108). Individuals' understanding of various rights—for example, their beliefs about whether children and adolescents have the right to have some control over their lives—becomes more abstract with age, as well (Ruck, Abramovitch, & Keating, 1998). Additionally, with age, individuals are more likely to judge the appropriateness of having certain rights (for example, freedom of speech) in light of characteristics of the individual (for example, whether the individual is mature enough to act responsibly) and the context within which the right is expressed (for example, whether the authority who is regulating speech is a parent or a government official) (Helwig, 1997).

Second, political thinking during adolescence becomes less authoritarian and less rigid (Flanagan & Gallay, 1995). Young adolescents are inclined toward obedience, authority, and an uncritical, trusting, and acquiescent stance toward government. For example, when asked what might be done in response to a law that is not working out as planned, the young adolescent will "propose that it be enforced more rigorously." An older teenager may suggest, instead, that the law needs to be reexamined and perhaps amended. In contrast to older adolescents, younger adolescents are "more likely to favor one-man rule as [opposed to] representative democracy; . . . [show] little sensitivity to individual or minority rights; [and are] indifferent to the claims of personal freedom" (Adelson, 1972, p. 108).

Of special significance is the development during late adolescence of a roughly coherent and consistent set of attitudes—a sort of ideology—that does not appear before this point. This ideology is "more or less organized in reference to a more encompassing . . . set of political principles" (Adelson, 1972, p. 121). These principles may concern a wide range of issues, including civil liberties, freedom of speech, and social equality

(Flanagan & Galay, 1995; Helwig, 1995). As is the case among adults, adolescents' views about political matters—the causes of unemployment, poverty, or homelessness, for example—are strongly linked to their social upbringing. Adolescents from higher social classes tend to attribute unemployment, poverty, and homelessness to societal factors ("People are unemployed because companies are moving a lot of jobs to Mexico"), whereas adolescents from lower-class backgrounds are more likely to attribute these problems to individual factors ("People are poor because they have problems managing money") (Flanagan & Tucker, 1999).

Shifts in all three of these directions—increasing abstraction, decreasing authoritarianism, and increasing use of principles—are similar to the shifts observed in studies of moral development, and they support the idea that value autonomy begins to emerge during late adolescence. The movement away from authoritarianism, obedience, and unquestioning acceptance of the rulings of authority is especially interesting because it suggests further that an important psychological concern for adolescents involves questioning the values and beliefs emanating from parents and other authority figures and trying to establish their own priorities.

▍ **Political Thinking and Political Behavior** As is the case with moral development, there may be gaps between adolescents' political thinking in hypothetical situations and their actual political attitudes and behavior. In general, the most important influences on the political behavior of young people tends to be the social context in which they come of age (Flanagan, 2004; Torney-Purta, 1990). This context includes both the immediate community and the larger social and historical environment. Thus, minority adolescents, especially those living in environments in which there are limited economic opportunities, tend to be more cynical about politics than their white counterparts. Similarly, a study of German youth indicates that adolescents are more likely to develop right-wing (excessively authoritarian) attitudes when they are raised by authoritarian parents within a broader context that promotes antiforeigner and antidemocratic attitudes (Noack, Kracke, & Hofer, 1994).

▍ **Attitudes of Today's College Students** Finally, studies of adolescents' political attitudes show quite clearly that young people's political attitudes and level of political participation (voting, demonstrating, letter writing, and so on)—like those of adults—fluctuate in relation to current events (Flanagan, 2004; Torney-Purta, 1990). Although we stereotypically think of late adolescence as a time of intense political activism, perhaps because of the high level of student activism in the 1960s, this image hardly characterizes

contemporary youth. Recent surveys indicate a significantly lower interest among American youth in political matters than was the case in previous eras, although interest has risen in recent years, partly as a result of the events of September 11, 2001. For example, the percentage of college freshmen who believe that it is important to keep up with political affairs is 36 percent, up from 28 percent in 2000, when it hit an all-time low. Nearly two-thirds believe that "dissent is a critical component of the political process," and nearly half participated in an organized demonstration during high school. And 12 percent worked on a political campaign during high school, the highest rate since 1971. By all of these measures, the political apathy of American college students that worried many observers finally seems to be on the decline. In general, American college students also have become somewhat more liberal in recent years—after a steady rise in political conservatism—no doubt in reaction to America's controversial involvement in the war in Iraq. Only a third believe federal military spending should be increased," down from 45 percent after September 11, 2001 (UCLA Higher Education Research Institute, 2006).

College students' interests in civic affairs also has risen in recent years, most likely in response to weather-related tragedies like the Indian Ocean tsunami and Hurricane Katrina. Two-thirds of college freshmen in 2005 believed that it is essential or very important to "help others who are in difficulty." Two-fifths of freshmen said that it is very important or essential for them to "influence social values," one-third aspired to be a community leader, and one-quarter said that it is essential or very important for them to participate in a community action program. (UCLA Higher Education Research Institute, 2006).

RELIGIOUS BELIEFS DURING ADOLESCENCE

Religious beliefs, like moral and political beliefs, also become more abstract, more principled, and more independent during the adolescent years. Specifically, adolescents' beliefs become more oriented toward spiritual and ideological matters and less oriented toward rituals, practices, and the strict observance of religious customs. For example, although close to 90 percent of all adolescents pray, and 95 percent believe in God, 40 percent of all young people feel that organized religion does not play a very important role in their lives (Gallup & Bezilla, 1992; Holder et al., 2000; Wallace, Forman, Caldwell, & Willis, 2003). Compared with children, adolescents place more emphasis on the internal aspects of religious commitment (such as what an individual believes) and less on the external manifestations (such as whether an individual goes to church) (Elkind, 1978).

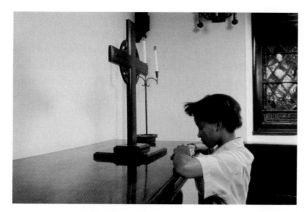

The importance of religion generally declines over the course of adolescence. Although the vast majority of adolescents have a religious affiliation, many fewer report attending services regularly.

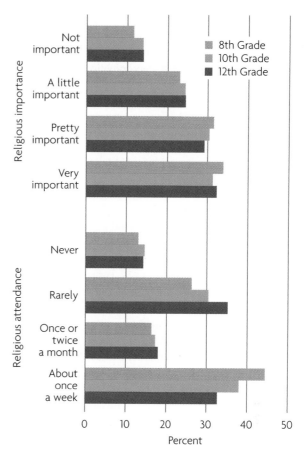

FIGURE 9.7 Age differences in religious activity. (Wallace et al., 2003)

■ **Patterns of Religious Involvement** Generally, the stated importance of religion—and especially of participation in an organized religion—declines somewhat during the adolescent years. Compared with older adolescents, younger ones are more likely to attend church regularly and to state that religion is important to them (Wallace et al., 2003) (see Figure 9.7). In addition, church attendance and religious observation are more common among rural youth, especially those from farm families (King, Elder, & Whitbeck, 1997). Several studies indicate that the decline in the importance of religion during late adolescence is more noteworthy among college than noncollege youth (Yankelovich, 1974), suggesting that college attendance may play some part in shaping (or as the case may be, in unshaping) young people's religious beliefs, although this depends on the type of institution attended. The early years of college appear to be a time when some individuals reexamine and reevaluate many of the beliefs and values they grew up with. For many, this involves a decline in regular participation in organized religious activities (perhaps because the college environment doesn't encourage this) but an increase in spirituality and religious faith (Lefkowitz, 2005). The religious context of the college environment plays an important role; religious commitment may become stronger among students who attend a college with a religious orientation (Barry & Nelson, 2005).

Although some parents may interpret this transformation as indicating a sort of rebellion against the family's values, the development of religious thinking during late adolescence might be better understood as part of the overall development of value autonomy. As the adolescent develops a stronger sense of independence, he or she may leave behind the unquestioning conventionality of earlier religious behavior as a first step toward finding a truly personal faith. According to one writer, the adolescent who continues to comply

with her or his parents' religious beliefs without ever questioning them may actually be showing signs of immature conformity or identity foreclosure, and not spiritual maturity (Hill, 1986).

■ **Individual Differences in Religiosity** Although individuals generally become less involved in formal religion during adolescence, there are differences among adolescents in their degree of religiosity. Approximately 38 percent of adolescents report weekly attendance at religious services, 17 percent attend once or twice per month, and about 45 percent rarely or never attend services; regular attendance at religious services drops over the course of high school. Adolescent religious attendance declined gradually during the 1980s and 1990s but has changed very little since then. The vast majority of adolescents (more than 85 percent) report having a religious affiliation, with about one-third identifying themselves as conservative Christians, and about one-fifth as Catholic. In general, African American and Latino adolescents are more religious than youth from other ethnic backgrounds, as are adolescents who live in the South or Midwest (Smith, Denton, Faris, & Regnerus, 2002; Wallace et al., 2003).

The Impact of Religious Involvement on Development A growing body of research suggests that religious adolescents, especially those who affiliate with more fundamentalist denominations, are less depressed than other adolescents; less likely to engage in premarital sexual intercourse, use drugs, or engage in delinquent behavior; and more altruistic, more prosocial, and more likely to be involved in the community (Chen, Dormitzer, Bejarano, & Anthony, 2004; Holder et al., 2000; King & Furrow, 2004; Litchfield, Thomas, & Li, 1997; Meier, 2003; Miller, Davies, & Greenwald, 2000; Smetana & Metzger, 2005). Although some of the apparent positive effects of religious involvement are due to the fact that adolescents who are involved in religion often have other positive influences in their life that on their own promote positive development and prevent problem behavior (for example, supportive parents, prosocial peers, adults who care about them) (King & Furrow, 2004), religiosity in and of itself appears to deter problem behavior and delay the onset of sexual activity (Hardy & Raffaelli, 2003; Jones, Darroch, & Singh, 2005; McCree, Wingood, DiClemente, Davies, & Harrington, 2003; Steinman & Zimmerman, 2004). Religious involvement may play an especially important role in buffering inner-city African American adolescents against the harmful effects of neighborhood disorganization and exposure to violence (Ball, Armistead, & Austin, 2003; Johnson, Jang, Li, & Larson, 2000; Pearce, Jones, Schwab-Stone, & Ruchkin, 2003).

FOOD FOR THOUGHT

A great deal of research indicates that adolescents who report high levels of religious involvement also report better mental health and lower levels of problem behavior. Given this, some writers advocate more religious participation in adolescence. Do you agree? Why or why not?

All in all, studies of the development of religious beliefs during adolescence indicate many parallels with the development of moral and political reasoning. According to a widely cited stage theory of religious development, during late adolescence, individuals enter into a stage in which they begin to form a system of personal religious beliefs, rather than relying solely on the teachings of their parents (Fowler, 1981). This is reminiscent, of course, of adolescents' transition to principled moral reasoning or to the development in middle to late adolescence of a coherent political ideology. In all likelihood, developments in all three

domains—moral, political, and religious—probably reflect the underlying growth of cognitive abilities and the shift from concrete to abstract reasoning that characterizes the adolescent transition. As you now know, this fundamental shift in cognitive ability affects adolescents' thinking across a wide variety of topics.

RECAP

- According to Kohlberg's theory, which is the dominant perspective on the development of moral reasoning, late adolescence is a time of potential shifting from a morality that defines right and wrong in terms of society's rules to one that defines right and wrong on the basis of one's own basic moral principles.
- Adolescents' moral behavior does not always match their moral reasoning, in part because contextual factors influence how they act when they face moral dilemmas in the real world.
- Although the assertion that there are dramatic differences in the ways males and females approach moral problems has earned a good deal of popular attention, scientific studies have not supported this proposition. Nor do studies indicate that adolescent girls have more trouble finding their "voice" than do adolescent boys.
- The ways in which individuals think about prosocial phenomena, such as honesty or kindness, become more sophisticated during adolescence, although changes in actual prosocial behavior, such as helping or empathizing with others, are not consistently found.
- Studies of volunteerism find that involvement in community service leads to gains in social responsibility, tolerance, and the importance individuals place on helping others.
- Changes in the domains of political and religious thinking during adolescence also reflect the individual's growing sense of value autonomy. As with moral reasoning, political and religious thinking become more abstract, more principled, and more independent, especially during late adolescence.
- Religious involvement during adolescence may facilitate positive development and lower the risk for problem behavior, although some of the apparent effects of religious involvement are due to the fact that it is usually accompanied by close attachments to parents and other adults and by affiliation with prosocial peers.

CHAPTER 10

Intimacy

INTIMACY AS AN ADOLESCENT ISSUE

THEORETICAL PERSPECTIVES ON ADOLESCENT INTIMACY

Sullivan's Theory of Interpersonal Development

Erikson's View of Intimacy in Adolescence

Attachment in Adolescence

THE DEVELOPMENT OF INTIMACY IN ADOLESCENCE

Changes in the Nature of Friendship

Changes in the Display of Intimacy

Sex Differences in Intimacy

Changes in the Targets of Intimacy

Friendships with the Other Sex

DATING AND ROMANTIC RELATIONSHIPS

Dating and the Development of Intimacy

The Development of Dating Relationships

The Impact of Dating on Adolescent Development

INTIMACY AND PSYCHOSOCIAL DEVELOPMENT

My boyfriend and I fell asleep together one night at my house [when I was 15]. We were curled up facing each other. I fell asleep looking at his face. I had a dream that night where I was falling.... I looked into his eyes and I knew that we were having the same dream. We immediately hugged each other and we both knew what had happened simply by looking in each other's eyes. (A 21-year-old's response when asked to recall "a vivid, highly memorable, personally important memory that 'conveys powerfully how you have come to be the person you currently are.'") (McLean & Thorne, 2003, p. 641).

ONE OF THE MOST REMARKABLE things about adolescence is the ways in which close relationships change during these years. Think about the friendships you had as a child, and compare them with those you had as a teenager. Think about the boyfriends or girlfriends that children have and the boyfriends or girlfriends adolescents have. And think about relationships between parents and their children, and about how these relationships change during adolescence. In all three cases, adolescents' relationships are closer, more personal, more involved, and more emotionally charged than children's. During adolescence, in short, relationships become more intimate. In this chapter, we examine how and why this occurs.

At the outset, we need to draw a distinction between intimacy and sexuality. The concept of **intimacy**—at least as it is used in the study of adolescence—does not have a sexual or physical connotation. Rather, an intimate relationship is an emotional attachment between two people that is characterized by concern for each other's well-being; a willingness to disclose private, and occasionally sensitive, topics; and a sharing of common interests and activities. (An easy way to remember this is "caring," "daring," and "sharing.") Two individuals can therefore have an intimate relationship without having a sexual one. And, by the same token, two people can have a sexual relationship without being especially intimate.

Although the development of intimacy during adolescence is almost always studied in relation to friendships and romantic relationships with peers, adolescents' intimate relationships are by no means limited to other teenagers. Parents often have intimate relationships with their adolescent children, especially when the children have reached a sufficient level of maturity. Siblings, even with many years between them, are often close confidants. Sometimes, young people even form intimate relationships with adults who are not in their immediate family.

Obviously, one of the central issues in the study of intimacy during adolescence is the onset of dating. Although the young person's initiation into romantic relationships is undoubtedly important, it is not the only noteworthy change that occurs in close relationships during adolescence. Adolescence is also an important time for changes in what individuals look for in friends, in their capacity to be intimate with people of both sexes, and in the way they express their closeness with friends.

Intimacy as an Adolescent Issue

Intimacy is an important concern throughout most of the life span. Friends and confidants provide support in times of emotional vulnerability, assistance when needed, and companionship in a variety of activities and contexts (Weiss, 1974). During childhood, not having friends is associated with a wide range of psychological and social problems (Hartup, 1992). And during adulthood, having at least one intimate friendship is beneficial to an individual's health: People who have others to turn to for emotional support are less likely to suffer from psychological and physical disorders (Myers, Lindentthal, & Pepper, 1975). Without question, close relationships are extremely important to people of all ages. Why, then, is the development of intimacy especially important during adolescence?

One reason is that it is not until adolescence that truly intimate relationships—relationships characterized by openness, honesty, self-disclosure, and trust—emerge. Although children certainly have important friendships, their relationships are different from those formed during adolescence. Children's friendships are activity oriented; they are built around games and shared pastimes. To a child, a friend is someone who likes to do the same things he or she does. But teenagers' close friendships are more likely to have a strong emotional foundation; they are built on the sorts of bonds that form between people who care

intimacy   The psychosocial domain concerning the formation, maintenance, and termination of close relationships.

Children's friendships center around shared activities. Not until adolescence are friendships based on the sorts of bonds that are formed between individuals who care about, know, and understand each other in a special way.

about and know and understand each other in a special way (Newcomb & Bagwell, 1995).

FOOD FOR THOUGHT

In your experience, what are the defining features of an intimate relationship? What things have been special about the relationships in your life that you consider to be intimate? Do you agree with the assertion that genuine intimacy in relationships does not appear before adolescence?

Another reason for the importance of intimacy during adolescence concerns the changing nature of the adolescent's social world—during early adolescence, the increasing importance of peers in general, and during middle and late adolescence, the increasing importance of opposite-sex peers in particular (Furman, Brown, & Feiring, 1999). In Chapter 9, we looked at the young person's growing orientation toward peers as part of the development of emotional autonomy. In this chapter, we look at changes in adolescent peer relations again, but in a different light—as part of the development of intimacy.

Puberty and the Development of Intimacy

Why do such important changes take place in close relationships during adolescence? Several theorists point to significant links between the development of intimacy during adolescence and the biological, cognitive, and social changes of the period (Berndt, 1982; Savin-Williams & Berndt, 1990). Naturally, changes in sexual impulses at puberty provoke interest in sexual

relationships, and although sexual relationships are not necessarily emotionally intimate, they frequently are. In addition, with puberty and sexuality come new issues and concerns requiring serious, intimate discussions. Some young people feel hesitant to discuss sex and dating with their parents, and turn instead to relationships outside the family. And some of the most intimate conversations adolescents have with their friends concern their feelings about and relationships with romantic partners.

Cognitive Change and the Development of Intimacy

Advances in thinking—especially in the realm of social cognition—are also related to the development of intimacy during adolescence (Hill & Palmquist, 1978). As we saw in Chapter 2, the growth of social cognition during adolescence is reflected in the young person's more sophisticated conceptions of social relationships and in improvements in interpersonal understanding and communication. These changes permit adolescents to establish and maintain far more mature relationships that are characterized by higher levels of empathy, self-disclosure, and responsiveness to each other's thoughts and feelings. The limitations in preadolescents' ability to look at things from another person's point of view may make intimate interpersonal relationships a cognitive impossibility, because it is hard to be an intimate friend to someone when you are unable to empathize with her or him (Beardslee, Schultz, & Selman, 1987; Selman, 1980). Improvements in social competence and gains in intimacy during adolescence, therefore, are partly attributable to improvements in social cognition (Ford, 1982).

Changes in Social Roles and the Development of Intimacy

We can also point to changes in the adolescent's social roles as potentially affecting the development of intimacy. Perhaps most simply, the behavioral independence that often accompanies the transition from childhood into adolescence provides greater opportunities for adolescents to be alone with their friends, engaged in intimate discussion. Adolescents spend more time in conversation with their friends than in any other activity (Csikszentimihalyi & Larson, 1984). Moreover, the recognition of adolescents as "near adults" may prompt their parents and other adults to confide in them and turn to them for support. Shared experiences such as working, as well as the development of emotional autonomy, may help give young people and their parents more of a basis for friendship and communication (Youniss & Smollar, 1985). Finally, changes in the structure of schools during early adolescence—often giving younger teenagers more contact with older ones—may promote new types of peer relationships (Blyth, Hill, & Smyth, 1981).

During the course of preadolescence and adolescence, relationships are gradually transformed from the friendly but activity-oriented friendships of childhood to the more self-conscious, more analytical, and more intimate relationships of adulthood. In the next section, we examine why and how this transformation occurs.

RECAP

- In adolescence, the development of intimacy refers to the development of relationships that are characterized by self-disclosure, trust, and concern.
- The changes of puberty, which draw young people together around common concerns and which stimulate interest in romantic relationships, contribute to the development of intimacy.
- The development of intimacy is also stimulated by the cognitive changes of the period, which allow for a more sophisticated understanding of relationships.
- Intimate relationships are facilitated by the social changes of the period, which provide for more opportunities for adolescents to be alone with each other and for them to acquire experiences that bring them closer to adults.

Theoretical Perspectives on Adolescent Intimacy

The most important theoretical perspectives on the development of intimacy during adolescence are those of Harry Stack Sullivan (1953a), Erik Erikson (1968), and various writers who have studied attachment relationships in adolescence (e.g., Allen & Land, 1999; Greenberg, Siegel, & Leitch, 1983; Kobak & Sceery, 1988; Rice, 1990). Let's look at each of these views in turn.

need for intimacy   According to Sullivan, the chief interpersonal need of preadolescence.

need for sexual contact   According to Sullivan, one of two chief interpersonal needs of early adolescence.

need for intimacy with a peer of the opposite sex   According to Sullivan, one of the two chief interpersonal needs of early adolescence.

need for integration into adult society   According to Sullivan, the chief need of late adolescence.

SULLIVAN'S THEORY OF INTERPERSONAL DEVELOPMENT

Like Erikson, whose theory of adolescent identity development was discussed at length in Chapter 8, Sullivan took a far less biological view of development than other psychoanalytic thinkers, such as Anna Freud. Instead, Sullivan emphasized the social aspects of growth, suggesting that psychological development can be best understood when looked at in interpersonal terms. Specifically, Sullivan's theory focuses on transformations in the adolescent's relationships with others. In particular, the challenges of adolescence (and indeed, according to Sullivan, of the entire life cycle) revolve around trying to satisfy changing interpersonal needs (Buhrmester, 1996). Although Sullivan's theoretical work is not especially popular today, it has had a profound influence on many contemporary researchers, and much of what Sullivan hypothesized about the development of intimacy has been confirmed in empirical studies.

Stages of Interpersonal Needs   Sullivan's perspective starts from the premise that, as children develop, different interpersonal needs surface that lead to either feelings of security (when the needs are satisfied) or feelings of anxiety (when the needs are frustrated). Sullivan charted a developmental progression of needs, beginning in infancy and continuing through adolescence (see Table 10.1): the needs for contact and for tenderness (infancy), the need for adult participation (early childhood), the need for peers and for peer acceptance (middle childhood), the **need for intimacy** (preadolescence), the **need for sexual contact** and the **need for intimacy with a peer of the opposite sex** (early adolescence), and the **need for integration into adult society** (late adolescence) (Sullivan, 1953b). These changing interpersonal needs define the course of interpersonal development through different phases of the life span. During middle childhood, for example, youngsters need to be accepted into peer groups, or else they feel rejected and ostracized.

In Sullivan's view, the security that is derived from having satisfying relationships with others is the glue that holds one's sense of self together. Identity and self-esteem are gradually built up through interpersonal relationships. Like Erikson, Sullivan viewed psychosocial development as cumulative: The frustrations and satisfactions individuals experience during earlier periods affect their later relationships and developing sense of identity. For instance, the child who as an infant has her need for contact or tenderness frustrated will approach interpersonal relationships in subsequent eras with greater anxiety, a more intense need for security, and a shakier sense of self.

TABLE 10.1   Interpersonal needs associated with different developmental eras: Sullivan's theory

Developmental Epochs	Interpersonal Needs
Infancy (0 to 2–3 yrs.)	Need for contact with people, need for tenderness from mothering one
Early childhood (2–3 to 6–7 yrs.)	Need for adult participation in child's play
Middle childhood (6–7 to 8–10 yrs.)	Need for peer playmates, need for acceptance into peer society groups
Preadolescence (8–10 to 12–14 yrs.)	Need for intimacy and consensual validation in same-sex chumships
Early adolescence (12–14 to 17–18 yrs.)	Need for sexual contact, need for intimacy with opposite-sex peer
Late adolescence (17–18 yrs. to adult)	Need for integration into adult society

Source: Sullivan, 1953a.

In contrast, the infant who has his interpersonal needs met will approach later relationships with confidence and optimism.

When important interpersonal transitions arise (for example, during childhood, when the social world is broadened to include significant relationships with peers), having a solid foundation of security in past relationships aids in the successful negotiation of the transition. An individual who is very anxious about forming relationships with others is likely to have trouble forming new types of relationships, because they threaten an already shaky sense of security. A child who does not have a strong sense of security may have many friends in elementary school but be too afraid to form intimate friendships upon reaching preadolescence. She or he may try to maintain friendships like those of childhood—friendships that focus on playing games, for example, rather than talking—long after friends have outgrown getting together to "play." As a result, that youngster may be rejected by peers and may feel lonely and isolated.

▌ **Interpersonal Development During Adolescence**   Looking back at the progression of interpersonal needs that Sullivan mapped out, we can see that he distinguished between intimacy and sexuality; perhaps more importantly, he suggested that the need for intimacy—which surfaces during preadolescence—precedes the development of romantic or sexual relationships, which do not emerge until adolescence. In other words, Sullivan believed that the capacity for intimacy first develops prior to adolescence and in the context of same-sex, not opposite-sex, relationships. This turns out to be one of most important observations in Sullivan's work, because as you will read, the quality of individuals' same-sex friendships is predictive of the quality of their later romantic relationships. One of the main challenges of adolescence, according to Sullivan, is making the transition from the nonsexual, intimate, same-sex friendships of preadolescence to the sexual, intimate, opposite-sex friendships of late adolescence.

Generally, intimacy develops first within same-sex friendships. Only later in adolescence are emotionally intimate relationships formed between males and females.

Sullivan divided the years between childhood and adulthood into three periods: preadolescence, early adolescence, and late adolescence. During preadolescence, children begin to focus their attention on relationships with a few close friends, generally of the same sex. It is through these friendships that the need for intimacy is first satisfied. With these close friends, the young person learns to disclose and receive intimate, private information and to build caring, mutual friendships based on honesty, loyalty, and trust. Sullivan believed that these relationships could even have a corrective influence, helping to repair interpersonal problems that might have developed during childhood. A good preadolescent friend, for example, can help someone overcome feelings of insecurity that have developed as a result of poor family relationships.

Not all youngsters feel secure enough as preadolescents, however, to forge these more mature, intimate friendships. The feelings of insecurity are so strong for some individuals that anxiety holds them back. As a result, some youngsters never fully develop the capacity to be intimate with others, a limitation that takes its toll on relationships throughout adolescence and adulthood. In other words, Sullivan felt that forming intimate friendships during preadolescence is a necessary precondition to forming close relationships as an adolescent or young adult.

FOOD FOR THOUGHT

According to Sullivan, intimacy first develops in same-sex friendships. Given the differences in the ways that males and females are socialized, how might we expect male and female versions of intimacy to differ?

According to Sullivan, the preadolescent era comes to an end with the onset of puberty. Early adolescence is marked by the emergence of sexuality, in the form of a powerful, biologically based sex drive. As a consequence of this development, a change in the preferred "target" of the adolescent's need for intimacy takes place. He or she must begin to make the shift from intimate relationships with members of the same sex to intimate relationships with members of the opposite sex. It is important to note that during the historical epoch when Sullivan was writing, homosexuality was considered abnormal, and like other writers of his era, Sullivan equated normal sexual development with the development of heterosexual relationships. Social scientists no longer hold this view, however, and most would say that the crucial interpersonal challenge for the young adolescent is not the movement from same-sex to opposite-sex friendships, but the transition from nonromantic to romantic relationships.

Like all interpersonal transitions, the movement from nonromantic to romantic relationships can be fraught with anxiety. For adolescents who do not have a healthy sense of security, it can be scary to leave the safety of nonsexual friendships and venture into the world of dating and sexuality.

The overarching challenge of adolescence, according to Sullivan, is to integrate the individual's established need for intimacy with the emerging need for sexual contact in a way that does not lead to excessive anxiety. Just as Erikson viewed adolescence as a time of experimentation with different identities, Sullivan saw adolescence as a time of experimentation with different types of interpersonal relationships. Some adolescents choose to date many different people to try to find out what they are looking for in a relationship. Others get involved very deeply with a boyfriend or girlfriend in a relationship that lasts throughout their entire adolescence. Others may have a series of serious relationships. And still others keep intimacy and sexuality separate. They may develop close **platonic relationships** (nonsexual relationships) with opposite-sex peers, for example, or they may have sexual relationships without getting very intimate with their sex partners. And just as Erikson viewed role experimentation as a healthy part of the adolescent's search for identity, Sullivan viewed the adolescent's experimentation with different types of relationships as a normal way of handling new feelings, new fears, and new interpersonal needs. For many young people, experimentation with sex and intimacy continues well into late adolescence.

If the interpersonal tasks of adolescence have been negotiated successfully, the young person enters late adolescence able to be intimate, able to enjoy sex, and, most critically, able to experience intimacy and sexuality in the same relationship. This accomplished, the adolescent turns to the interpersonal needs of late adolescence: carving a niche in adult society. This latter task, in some senses, is reminiscent of the adolescent identity crisis described by Erikson.

ERIKSON'S VIEW OF INTIMACY IN ADOLESCENCE

Intimacy Versus Isolation   Erikson (1968) argued that development during the adolescent and young-adult years revolves around two psychosocial crises: the crisis of identity versus identity diffusion, prominent during adolescence (see Chapter 8), and the crisis of **intimacy versus isolation,** prominent during early adulthood. Erikson's ideas about the subject of intimacy were far less developed than his ideas about

platonic relationships   Nonsexual relationships with individuals who might otherwise be romantic partners.

intimacy versus isolation   According to Erikson, the normative crisis characteristic of the sixth stage of psychosocial development, predominant during young adulthood.

the issue of identity. Nonetheless, his view of the relation between intimacy and identity provides a useful contrast to Sullivan's perspective.

Erikson believed that in a truly intimate relationship, two individuals' identities become fused in such a way that neither person's identity is lost. Together, two people who are in love form a couple that has its own life, its own future, and its own identity. Yet the partners do not lose their own sense of individuality. When two people marry, for example, being part of a couple becomes an important component of each person's identity, but it doesn't erase the sense of self that each person had before the marriage.

It follows, Erikson reasoned, that adolescents must establish a sense of identity before they are capable of real intimacy. Without a secure sense of identity, people are unwilling to make serious commitments to others: They fear that they will lose their identity in the relationship. A young woman who is struggling to establish an occupational identity, for example, may feel that getting seriously involved with someone may impede her progress toward discovering who she really is as an individual.

Relationships between individuals who have not yet established a sense of identity may look intimate, but generally, they are not. Adolescents who throw themselves into "going steady" often display a sort of **"pseudointimacy."** Their relationship may seem to be close, but a careful examination usually reveals a shallow, superficial intimacy. The couple may proclaim their faith in each other, for instance, but deep down, they are mistrustful or afraid to voice concerns or discuss problems. They may say that they are open with each other, but they don't disclose what they are really feeling for fear of losing the relationship. They may say that they will stay together forever, but they have trouble making any concrete plans for the future that include each other. In sum, they are "playing" at being a couple, the way younger children might play house. According to Erikson, this type of pseudointimacy is to be expected during adolescence. After all, it is difficult to commit yourself to someone else before you yourself know who you are.

Erikson and Sullivan: Conflicting Views?

There may seem to be a disagreement between Erikson and Sullivan about the relation between intimacy and identity. Sullivan viewed the development of intimacy as occurring primarily during preadolescence. He suggested that the development of the capacity for intimacy precedes the development of a coherent sense of identity, which does not occur until late adolescence. Erikson, in contrast, argued that the establishment of a coherent sense of identity necessarily occurs prior to the development of intimacy, since the individual must have a clear sense of who she or he is in order to avoid becoming lost in a relationship with someone else. What are we to make of this difference? Which comes first, the development of identity or the development of intimacy?

A number of studies have attempted to answer this question by assessing individuals on separate measures of identity and intimacy, and examining the relation between the two scores (e.g., Dyk & Adams, 1990; Levitz-Jones & Orlofsky, 1985; Orlofsky, Marcia, & Lesser, 1973). Unfortunately, none of the studies of the relation between identity and intimacy provides clear support for one theory over the other. Although scores on measures of identity and intimacy are generally correlated (that is, individuals who have a coherent sense of identity are more likely to have intimate interpersonal relationships, and vice versa), it has been difficult to determine whether development in one domain actually leads to development in another. Rather, individuals seem to follow different developmental routes, with some establishing a sense of identity first and then advancing in the realm of intimacy, and others following the reverse pattern.

Sex Differences in Identity and Intimacy

One hypothesis along these lines concerns sex differences in patterns of psychological development. Many theorists have argued that intimacy is a far more fundamental concern for adolescent girls than for adolescent boys and that the psychosocial crises of identity and intimacy may even be merged for female adolescents (Josselson, Greenberger, & McConochie, 1977b). For adolescent boys—actually, for males at all ages—intimacy is perhaps less important in the process of self-definition than is the case among females (Maccoby, 1990). In essence, then, Sullivan's view (that the development of intimacy precedes the development of a coherent sense of identity) may be more applicable to girls, whereas Erikson's (that the development of a sense of identity precedes the development of truly intimate relationships) may be more applicable to boys (Bakken & Romig, 1992; Dyk & Adams, 1990). Even within gender groups, however, there is considerable variation in how individuals approach and integrate the developmental tasks of identity and intimacy.

pseudointimacy   Superficial intimacy characteristic of relationships between individuals who are not emotionally mature.

FOOD FOR THOUGHT

Some writers have proposed that Sullivan's theory seems more appropriate to understanding female development, whereas Erikson's may be more applicable to males. What do you think? Looking back on your own development, did you follow one pattern (identity before intimacy) or the other (intimacy before identity)?

Rather than debating which comes first—identity (in some senses, the development of *independence*) or intimacy (in some senses, the development of *interdependence*)—it seems more sensible to suggest that the development of intimacy and of identity go hand in hand throughout adolescence, with changes in one psychosocial realm affecting changes in the other. Close relationships are a safe context in which adolescents can confront difficult questions of identity; yet, at the same time, the development of an increasingly coherent and secure sense of self provides the foundation upon which adolescents build and strengthen intimate relationships with others.

ATTACHMENT IN ADOLESCENCE

In recent decades, a third theoretical perspective has dominated the study of intimate relationships in adolescence, one that draws on theories of the development of the attachment relationship during infancy (e.g., Ainsworth, Blehar, Waters, & Wall, 1978; Bowlby, 1969; Sroufe, 1979). In order to understand how attachment theory is applied to the study of adolescence, we need to look first at how this construct has been used to understand development in infancy.

attachment   The strong affectional bond that develops between an infant and a caregiver.

secure attachment   A healthy attachment between infant and caregiver, characterized by trust.

anxious-avoidant attachment   An insecure attachment between infant and caregiver, characterized by indifference on the part of the infant toward the caregiver.

anxious-resistant attachment   An insecure attachment between infant and caregiver, characterized by distress at separation and anger at reunion.

internal working model   The implicit model of interpersonal relationships that an individual employs throughout life, believed to be shaped by early attachment experiences.

Attachment in Infancy   In writings on infant development, an **attachment** is defined as a strong and enduring emotional bond. Virtually all infants form attachment relationships with their mothers (and most do so with their fathers and other caregivers as well), but not all infants have attachment relationships of the same quality. Psychologists differentiate among three types of infant attachment: secure, anxious-avoidant, and anxious-resistant. A **secure attachment** between infant and caregiver is characterized by trust; an **anxious-avoidant attachment** is characterized by indifference on the part of the infant toward the caregiver; and an **anxious-resistant attachment** is characterized by ambivalence. The security of the early attachment relationship is important, because studies show that infants who have had a secure attachment are more likely to grow into psychologically and socially skilled children (Matas, Arend, & Sroufe, 1978).

Attachment theory has given rise to two different, but related, questions about adolescent development. First, is there a link between the quality of attachment formed in infancy and mental health or behavior in adolescence? And, second, can the same three-category framework used to characterize interpersonal relationships in infancy (secure, anxious-avoidant, anxious-resistant) be used to characterize interpersonal relationships in adolescence?

Does Infant Attachment Predict Adolescent Intimacy?   With respect to the first question, many theorists who study adolescent development believe that the nature of individuals' attachment to caregivers during infancy continues to have an influence on their capacity to form satisfying intimate relationships during adolescence and adulthood, for two reasons (Collins & Steinberg, 2006). First, some theorists have argued that the initial attachment relationship forms the basis for a more general model of interpersonal relationships employed throughout life. This so-called **internal working model** determines to a large measure whether individuals feel trusting or apprehensive in relationships with others and whether they see themselves as worthy of others' affection. We might think of an internal working model as a set of beliefs and expectations people draw on in forming close relationships with others—whether they go into relationships expecting acceptance or anticipating rejection. According to the theory, individuals who enjoyed a secure attachment relationship during infancy will have a more positive and healthy internal working model of relationships during adolescence, whereas individuals who were anxiously attached as infants will have a less positive model (e.g., Kobak & Sceery, 1988).

In support of this view, several studies have found that adolescents' working models for their relationships with parents are similar to their working models of relationships with friends, and adolescents' working models of relationships with friends are similar to their working models of relationships with romantic partners (e.g., Furman, Simon, Shaffer, & Bouchey, 2002). In addition, a number of writers have suggested that individuals who emerge from infancy with an insecure attachment relationship are more sensitive to being rejected by others in later romantic encounters, a trait that psychologists have called **rejection sensitivity** (Collins & Feeney, 2004; Downey, Bonica, & Rincón, 1999). Although studies that compare adolescents' working models of their relationships with parents, peers, and romantic partners do not directly tell us whether emotional attachments in adolescence are influenced by attachments formed during infancy (since these working models could all have been formed during adolescence), they do support the contention that our beliefs and expectations about relationships are similar across different interpersonal domains.

FOOD FOR THOUGHT

Think about your own internal working model of relationships. Are there consistencies in the ways in which you approach close relationships with different people? Would you say that you are high or low in "rejection sensitivity"?

A second reason for the continued importance of early attachment relationships during adolescence is that interpersonal development is cumulative: What happens during infancy affects what happens in early childhood, which affects what happens in middle childhood, and so on (Kerns, 1996). In other words, individuals who leave infancy with a secure attachment may be on a different interpersonal trajectory than those who leave infancy insecure. The only way to examine this proposition is to follow individuals over time and trace their interpersonal development.

A number of studies that have done just this show that anxiously attached infants are more likely to develop psychological and social problems during childhood and adolescence, including poor peer relationships (e.g., Erickson, Sroufe, & Egeland, 1985; Lewis, Feiring, McGuffog, & Jaskir, 1984; Renken, Egeland, Marvinney, Mangelsdorf, & Sroufe, 1989; Weinfeld, Ogawa, & Sroufe, 1997). It has been hypothesized that these problems in peer relations during childhood affect the development of social competence during adolescence—in essence, forming a link between

early experience and later social relations. Additionally, several studies indicate that the benefits of positive relations with peers extend beyond adolescence: Individuals who establish healthy intimate relationships with age-mates during adolescence are psychologically healthier and more satisfied with their lives as middle-aged adults (Hightower, 1990; Willits, 1988).

Of course, it is possible for interpersonal development to be cumulative without the root cause of this continuity being the individual's internal working model. In fact, both Sullivan and Erikson had theories of psychosocial development that viewed interpersonal development as cumulative, yet neither of these theorists mentioned an internal working model. Learning theory would predict a similar course of events. For example, individuals who have positive peer relationships in childhood may simply learn how to get along better with others, and this may lead to more positive peer relationships in adolescence, which, in turn, may lead to better relationships in adulthood. Similarly, individuals with more negative views of themselves may disengage from peers, which may lead to poorer-quality peer relationships and peer rejection, thereby intensifying their negative self-image (Caldwell, Rudolph, Troop-Gordon, & Kim, 2004).

How strong is the *specific* link between infant attachment and the quality of interpersonal relationships in adolescence and young adulthood? Do individuals who were securely attached as infants have more positive working models of relationships as adolescents or young adults? Only a few studies of attachment have followed individuals from infancy all the way through adolescence, and unfortunately, they have yielded conflicting results. Some have shown considerable continuity from infancy through adolescence (e.g., Hamilton, 2000; Waters, Merrick, Treboux, Crowell, & Albersheim, 2000), but others have shown no continuity whatsoever (Lewis, Feiring, & Rosenthal, 2000; Weinfeld, Sroufe, & Egelund, 2000). Some researchers have suggested that individuals' security of attachment remains stable only in the absence of major life events that could upset the course of interpersonal development (such as the loss of a parent or parental divorce), and that the lack of continuity observed in some studies is due to the importance of intervening events (Beckwith, Cohen, & Hamilton, 1999; Waters et al., 2000; Weinfeld et al., 2000). Others, however, argue that the significance of early attachment for later relationships is far outweighed by the importance of the experiences the individual has in childhood and the context in which he or she lives as an adolescent (Lewis et al., 2000). Early relationships

rejection sensitivity Heightened vulnerability to being rejected by others.

clearly matter for later interpersonal development; whether the *reason* that they matter can best be explained by attachment theory continues to be the subject of considerable debate.

■ **Attachment in Adolescence** In addition to employing the three-way attachment classification scheme to study the links among infancy, childhood, and adolescence, attachment theorists have applied similar classifications to the study of adolescents' attachments to others (e.g., Allen et al., 2003; Armsden & Greenberg, 1987; Greenberg et al., 1983; Kenny, 1987), as well as to adolescents' internal working models (Kobak, Cole, Ferenz-Gillies, Fleming, & Gamble, 1993; Kobak & Sceery, 1988). In some of these studies, adolescents' current relationships with parents and peers are assessed; in others, adolescents are asked to recount their childhood experiences through the use of a procedure called the **Adult Attachment Interview.** The Adult Attachment Interview, developed by psychologist Mary Main and her colleagues (Main, Kaplan, & Cassidy, 1985), is designed to yield insight into an individual's internal working model. The interview focuses on individuals' recollections of their early attachment experiences and obtains information on the ways in which the individual has come to terms with his or her childhood history. A variety of schemes for coding responses to the interview have been devised, but most categorize individuals as "secure", "dismissing", or "preoccupied."

Many researchers have found that adolescents in different attachment categories differ in predictable ways. Compared with dismissing or preoccupied adolescents, for example, secure adolescents interact with their mothers with less unhealthy anger and more appropriate assertiveness, suggesting that they may experience fewer difficulties in establishing emotional autonomy (Kobak et al., 1993). Individuals with dismissive or preoccupied attachment profiles are more likely to show a range of emotional and behavior problems in adolescence, including depression, maladaptive coping, anxiety, eating disorders, conduct problems, and delinquency (e.g., Allen et al., 2002; Kobak & Cole, 1994; Kobak, Sudler, & Gamble, 1992; Lieberman, Doyle, & Markiewicz, 1999; Seiffge-Krenke & Beyers, 2005; Zimmermann & Becker-Stoll, 2002). Adolescents with a secure attachment to their mother perceive her as supportive while maintaining an objective, de-idealized appraisal of her; when they disagree, they are able to discuss their differences in a way that allows for both individuation and connectedness (Allen et al., 2003). Not surprisingly, individuals who are judged to be secure have more stable romantic relationships than their insecure counterparts (Davis & Kirkpatrick, 1994).

Numerous studies also have looked at the quality of adolescents' current attachments to parents and peers as well as their early attachments. In general, individuals who have secure attachments during adolescence are more socially competent, more successful in school, and better adjusted than their insecure peers (Allen et al., 2002; Black & McCartney, 1997; Collins & Steinberg, 2006; Cooper, Shaver, & Collins, 1998; Finnegan & Perry, 1993; Jacobsen & Hofmann, 1997; Larose, Bernier, & Tarabulsy, 2005). A recent study of young Israeli adults even found that securely attached adolescents coped better with basic training in the military (Scharf, Mayseless, & Kivenson-Baron, 2004)! Of course, it is hard to say whether social competence leads to healthier attachments or vice versa (most probably, both are true).

Because interpersonal development is cumulative—influenced both by early and by later experiences—the quality of an adolescent's attachments to peers is affected not only by early experience but by her or his close relationships in childhood and early adolescence. For example, secure adolescents are more likely to come from homes with authoritative parents, whereas avoidant adolescents are more likely to come from homes where parents are neglectful (Karavasilis, Doyle, & Markiewicz, 2003). Not surprisingly, while attachment security is generally highly stable over the adolescent years, it can change if adolescents are living in dysfunctional family situations or under high amounts of stress (Allen, McElhaney, Kuperminc, & Jodl, 2004). In other words, early attachment security is not an "inoculation" that protects individuals from psychological problems forever, but rather a psychological advantage that increases the probability of developing in healthy ways.

By the same token, the degree of security in an adolescent's attachment style interacts with other experiences to shape mental health and behavior: Positive experiences (like having an authoritative parent) have even more positive effects among adolescents with a secure style, and negative experiences are not as harmful (Allen et al., 2002). Similarly, among adolescents with an insecure attachment style, negative experiences (like having excessively intrusive parents) have an even worse effect than they would otherwise (Marsh, McFarland, & Allen, 2003). As Figure 10.1 indicates, for example, maternal control and supervision seem to deter conduct problems among adolescents who are securely (but not insecurely) attached.

Adult Attachment Interview A structured interview used to assess an individual's past attachment history and "internal working model" of relationships.

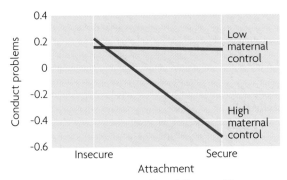

FIGURE 10.1   Maternal control has different effects on adolescent behavior depending on the security of the adolescent's working model. (Allen et al., 2002)

RECAP

- According to Sullivan, the need for intimacy emerges in preadolescence and is typically satisfied through same-sex friendships.
- In Sullivan's view, the main challenge of adolescence is to integrate an already established need for intimacy with the emerging need for sexual contact in a way that does not engender excessive anxiety.
- In Erikson's theory, the psychosocial crisis of late adolescence is one of intimacy versus isolation. According to this viewpoint, individuals must first develop a coherent sense of identity before they are able to develop genuinely intimate relationships with others.
- Most contemporary writers view the development of identity and of intimacy as complementary, not competing, tasks.
- Individuals who enjoyed a secure attachment to their caregiver during infancy develop a healthier or more secure internal working model of relationships, which is thought to permit more satisfying intimate relationships during adolescence and adulthood.
- There is also evidence that interpersonal development is cumulative: Positive experiences in early family relationships contribute to social competence, which facilitates the development of intimate relationships with peers and romantic partners.

The Development of Intimacy in Adolescence

CHANGES IN THE NATURE OF FRIENDSHIP

How do you know that someone is your best friend? When this question is posed to children and adolescents of different ages, younger and older respondents give different sorts of answers. Consider, for example, the following two responses—the first from a kindergartener, the second from a sixth-grader (from Berndt, 1981, p. 180):

> *Kindergarten child*: I sleep over at his house sometimes. When he's playing ball with his friends, he'll let me play. When I slept over, he let me get in front of him in four-squares [a playground game]. He likes me.

> *Sixth-grader*: If you can tell each other things that you don't like about each other. If you get into a fight with someone else, they'd stick up for you. If you can tell them your phone number and they don't give you crank calls. If they don't act mean to you when other kids are around.

■ **Changes in Definitions of Friendship**   These two examples illustrate the most important trend in the development of children's conceptions of friendship: It is not until early adolescence that such features as self-disclosure and loyalty are mentioned as important dimensions of friendship. Psychologist Thomas Berndt (1981), for example, compared how kindergarteners, third-graders, and sixth-graders responded to questions about their conceptions of close friendship. The children's responses were classified into one of eight categories, including play or association ("He calls me all the time"), prosocial behavior ("She helps me do things"), intimacy or trust ("I can tell her secrets"), and loyal support ("He'll stick up for me when I'm in a fight"). In general, responses mentioning prosocial behavior and association were equally frequent across all age groups—in fact, they were among the most frequent types of responses at all ages. But answers mentioning intimacy and loyalty, which were virtually absent at the kindergarten level, increased dramatically between the third and sixth grades.

A similar study revealed comparable results (Bigelow & LaGaipa, 1975). Not until seventh grade did individuals mention intimacy, or common interests or similar attitudes and values (see Figure 10.2). As in Berndt's study, the researchers found that responses mentioning prosocial behavior and common activities were high at all age levels. In other words, it may be important to differentiate between

FIGURE 10.2 Children and adolescents have different conceptions of "friendship." Some sorts of conceptions do not appear until the fifth or sixth grade.
(Derived from Bigelow & LaGaipa, 1975)

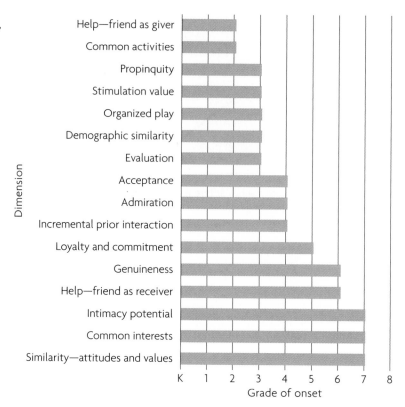

companionship, which appears much before adolescence, and intimacy, which may not emerge until considerably later (Buhrmester & Furman, 1987).

That conceptions of friendship come to place greater weight on such dimensions as intimacy, loyalty, and shared values and attitudes during early adolescence is consistent with Sullivan's theory (Savin-Williams & Berndt, 1990). As adolescents' needs for intimacy increase, so might the emphasis they place on intimacy as an important component of friendship. The findings are also consistent with what we know about other cognitive changes characteristic of early adolescence. As we saw in Chapter 2, adolescents have greater facility than children in thinking about abstract concepts such as intimacy and loyalty. And as you know, adolescents' judgments of others are more sophisticated, more psychological, and less tied to concrete attributes than are those of children.

Jealousy Several studies indicate that the importance of intimacy as a defining feature of close friendship continues to increase throughout early and middle adolescence (Berndt & Perry, 1990; McNelles & Connolly, 1999; Phillipsen, 1999). But an interesting pattern of change occurs around age 14. During middle adolescence (between ages 13 and 15), particularly among girls, concerns about loyalty and anxieties over rejection become more pronounced and may temporarily overshadow concerns about intimate self-disclosure (Berndt

& Perry, 1990; Douvan & Adelson, 1966). Consistent with this, the sorts of conflicts adolescents have with their friends change during this time; whereas older adolescents' conflicts are typically over private matters, younger adolescents' conflicts are often over perceived public disrespect (Shulman & Laursen, 2002).

Girls, in particular, show a pronounced increase in jealousy over their friends' friends during early adolescence (Parker, Low, Walker, & Gamm, 2005; Parker, Low, & Wargo, 1999). Girls who have low self-esteem and are high in rejection sensitivity are especially likely to become jealous of their friends' relationships with other girls. In some senses, then, the greater intimacy enjoyed by girls with their friends than is typical among boys is both an asset and a liability—girls get the benefits of having confidantes with whom they can easily talk about their problems, but their friendships are more fragile and more easily disrupted by feelings of betrayal. As a consequence, girls' friendships on average do not last as long as boys' do (Benenson & Christakos, 2003). As two writers noted more than 40 years ago (some things never change):

> The girls in this age group [ages 14 to 16] are unique in some respects, that is, different from both older and younger girls. What stands out in their interviews is the stress placed on security in friendships. They want the friend to be loyal, trustworthy, and a reliable source of support in any emotional crisis. She should not be the sort of person who will abandon you or who gossips

about you behind your back. . . . With so much invested in the friendship, it is no wonder that the girl is so dependent on it. . . . The girl is likely to feel like the [patient] in that famous *New Yorker* cartoon, who, getting up from the couch, takes a pistol from her purse and says [to her psychiatrist]: "You've done me a world of good, Doctor, but you know too much." (Douvan & Adelson, 1966, pp. 188–189)

How might Sullivan have explained this pattern? Why might loyalty become such a pressing concern for girls during the middle adolescent years? One possibility is that at this age, girls may start to feel more nervous about their relationships with friends because they are beginning to make the transition into opposite-sex relationships. These transitions, as Sullivan noted, can make individuals feel insecure. Perhaps it is anxiety over dating and heightened feelings of insecurity that cause adolescent girls to temporarily place a great deal of emphasis on the trust and loyalty of their close friends. Indeed, close friends who have highly intimate and exclusive relationships with each other often behave more aggressively within the friendship than they do toward peers who are not their close friends (Grotpeter & Crick, 1996).

Adolescents' close friendships also are distinguished from their casual friendships in the types of conflicts they have and in the ways in which their conflicts are resolved (Laursen, 1995, 1996; Raffaelli, 1997; Whitesell & Harter, 1996). Although conflicts between adolescents and their close friends are less frequent than they are between adolescents and other peers, arguments with close friends are more emotional (that is, lots of anger and hurt feelings). More importantly, though, conflict between close friends is more likely to provoke efforts to restore the relationship than is conflict between casual friends.

CHANGES IN THE DISPLAY OF INTIMACY

In addition to placing greater emphasis on intimacy and loyalty in defining friendship than children do, teenagers are also more likely actually to display intimacy in their relationships, with respect to what they know about their friends, how responsive they are, how empathic they are, and how they resolve disagreements.

■ **Knowing Who Their Friends Are** As individuals move into and through adolescence, they gain knowledge about more intimate aspects of their friends' lives. For example, although preadolescents and adolescents have comparable degrees of knowledge about characteristics of their best friends that are not especially personal (such as the friend's telephone number or birthdate), adolescents know significantly

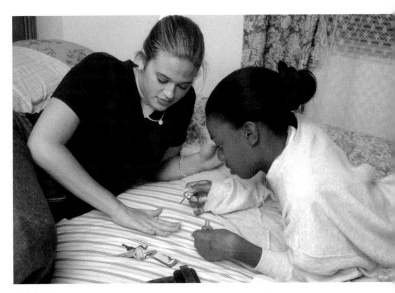

During adolescence, individuals become more knowledgeable about, more responsive to, and more sensitive to their close friends. They also become more likely to resolve disagreements through negotiation, rather than by allowing one person to overpower the other.

more things about their friends that might be classified as intimate (such as what their friends worry about or what they are proud of) (Diaz & Berndt, 1982; Jones & Dembo, 1989). Along similar lines, between the fifth and eleventh grades, increasingly more adolescents agree with such statements as "I know how [my friend] feels about things without his [or her] telling me" and "I feel free to talk to [my friend] about almost everything" (Sharabany, Gershoni, & Hofman, 1981). Over the course of adolescence, adolescents' reports of friendship quality increase steadily, a pattern observed in all ethnic groups. Although there are ethnic differences in average levels of friendship quality—Asian American adolescents report more dissatisfaction with their friendships than do other adolescents—the rate of improvement in friendship quality over time is the same (Way & Greene, 2006). Consistent with Sullivan's viewpoint, then, during preadolescence and early adolescence, youngsters' friendships become more personal.

FOOD FOR THOUGHT

Do you remember your first intimate friendship? What made the relationship different from other friendships that you had previously had?

Caring and Concern Individuals also become more responsive toward close friends, less controlling, and more tolerant of their friends' individuality during adolescence (Berndt & Perry, 1990; Estrada, 1995; Keller, Edelstein, Schmid, Fang, & Fang, 1998; Newcomb & Bagwell, 1995; Shulman, Laursen, Kalman, & Karpovsky, 1997). This can be interpreted as another indicator of their increased capacity for intimacy. Before preadolescence, for example, children are actually less likely to help and share with their friends than with other classmates (perhaps because children are more competitive with their friends than with other youngsters and do not want to feel inferior). By about fourth grade, children treat their friends and other classmates similarly when it comes to sharing and cooperation. But by the time they have reached eighth grade, one team of researchers found, friends are "more generous and more helpful toward each other than toward other classmates" (Berndt, 1982, p. 1452). Interestingly, adolescents are also physically and physiologically responsive to their friends: Studies show that the behaviors and emotional states of pairs of friends are more frequently synchronized, or "on the same wavelength," than are those of acquaintances, even when the friends and acquaintances are engaged in the same task (Field et al., 1992). Evidently, there may be something genuine about chemistry between close friends!

Interpersonal Sensitivity During the course of adolescence, individuals become more interpersonally sensitive—they show greater levels of empathy and social understanding—in situations in which they are helping or comforting others. Compared with children, adolescents are more likely to understand and acknowledge how their friends feel when those friends are having problems. For instance, one researcher asked children and adolescents how they would help a younger friend who had been scared by a horror movie on television. The children were more likely to deny their friend's feelings, whereas the adolescents were more likely to respond sensitively and supportively (Burleson, 1982). Indeed, over the course of adolescence, individuals' attempts to help their friends with personal problems of all sorts become more centered around providing support for the troubled friend, and less aimed at mere distraction (Denton & Zarbatany, 1996).

Conflict Resolution The ways in which close friends resolve conflict also change over the course of adolescence. According to a comprehensive review of research on this topic by psychologist Brett Laursen and his colleagues (Laursen, Finkelstein, & Betts, 2001), as individuals move from childhood into adolescence, and from adolescence into young adulthood, they become more likely to end their disagreements by negotiation (trying to compromise or find a solution that is acceptable to both friends) or disengagement (walking away from the situation) and less likely to end them with one person coercing or overpowering the other and getting his or her way. Negotiation is also more common between romantic partners than between friends, and more common between close friends than between acquaintances.

SEX DIFFERENCES IN INTIMACY

How Females Are More Intimate There are striking sex differences in intimacy during adolescence. When asked to name the people who are most important to them, adolescent girls—particularly in the middle adolescent years—list more friends than boys do, and girls are more likely to mention intimacy as a defining aspect of close friendship. In interviews, adolescent girls express greater interest in their close friendships, talk more frequently about their intimate conversations with friends, express greater concern about their friends' faithfulness and greater anxiety over rejection, and place greater emphasis on emotional closeness in their evaluation of romantic partners (Berndt, 1982; Feiring, 1999; Feiring & Lewis, 1991; Parker Low, Walker, Gamm, 2005). Girls are more likely than boys to make distinctions in the way they treat intimate and nonintimate friends, fight more about relationships, and prefer to keep their friendships more exclusive and are less willing to include other classmates in their cliques' activities (Berndt, 1982; Bukowski, Sippola, Gauze, Hoza, & Newcomb, 1993; Raffaelli, 1997). In conversations, girls are more collaborative, whereas boys are more controlling (Strough & Berg, 2000).

When self-disclosure is used as the measure of intimacy, boys' friendships with other boys do not approach girls' friendships with other girls until late in adolescence, if at all (Buhrmester & Furman, 1987; McNelles & Connolly, 1999; Savin-Williams & Berndt, 1990; Shulman et al., 1997). And girls appear to be more sensitive and empathic than boys, especially when comforting friends who are distressed and in knowing when their friends are depressed (Berndt, 1982; Eisenberg, Miller, Shell, McNalley, & Shea, 1991; Sharabany, Gershoni, & Hofman, 1981; Swenson & Rose, 2003). In these very numerous—and very important—respects, the expression of intimacy certainly appears to be more advanced among adolescent girls than among boys (Buhrmester, 1996). Although this carries many advantages for girls, it also carries some liabilities: Girls are more likely than boys to ruminate together about each other's problems—a phenomenon that has been called "corumination"—and this may contribute to feelings of depression (Rose, 2002).

There are also interesting sex differences in the nature of conflicts between close friends during adolescence that are consistent with other sex differences in the expression of intimacy. Boys' conflicts with their friends are briefer, typically over issues of power and control (such as whose turn it is in a game); more likely to escalate into physical aggression; and usually resolved without any explicit effort to do so, often by just "letting things slide." Girls' conflicts, in contrast, are longer, typically about some form of betrayal in the relationship (such as breaking a confidence or ignoring the other person), and only resolved when one of the friends apologizes (Raffaelli, 1997)

▌ **And How They Aren't**   On some measures of friendship, however, adolescent boys and girls show similar degrees of intimacy. Although girls are more likely to mention self-disclosure when asked to define close friendship, and although girls report more self-disclosure in their friendships, boys and girls have equivalent degrees of intimate knowledge about their best friends (Diaz & Berndt, 1982; McNelles & Connolly, 1999; Sharabany, et al., 1981; Shulman et al., 1997). When boys are with their friends, they are just as likely as girls to share each other's emotional state (McNelles & Connolly, 1999). And in group situations, boys and girls are equally likely to help their friends (Zeldin, Small, & Savin-Williams, 1982).

It seems safe to say that, at the very least, intimacy is a more conscious concern for adolescent girls than for boys. But this does not mean that intimacy is absent from boys' relationships. As Thomas Berndt, an expert on adolescent friendship has noted, "Boys may spend less time in conversations about their emotions and ideas than girls, but they may [nevertheless] acquire a deep understanding of each other by spending time together" (1982, p. 1450). In other words, boys and girls have different types of friendships, and they express intimacy in different ways. In general, boys' friendships are more oriented toward shared activities than toward the explicit satisfaction of emotional needs—as is often the case in girls' friendships; and the development of intimacy between adolescent males may be a more subtle phenomenon (McNelles & Connolly, 1999). Another possibility is that the development of close friendships among males starts at a later age than it does among females. One recent study found, for instance, that there are substantial sex differences in friendship quality at age 13, but that by age 18 these are gone (see Figure 10.3) (Way & Greene, 2006).

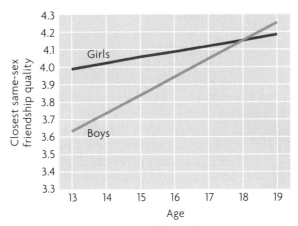

FIGURE 10.3   Changes in friendship quality over time. (Way & Greene, 2006)

▌ **Origins of Sex Differences**   Many theorists have suggested that sex differences in intimacy are the result of different patterns of socialization, with females being more strongly encouraged to develop and express intimacy—especially verbal intimacy—than males. Consistent with this, research shows that an individual's sex role (how masculine, feminine, or androgynous he or she is) is a better predictor of the person's capacity for intimate friendship than his or her sex (Jones & Costin, 1993). For instance, androgynous males (males who display both masculine and feminine traits) report levels of intimacy in their friendships that are comparable to females' levels of intimacy (Jones & Dembo, 1989).

Other factors could be at work, however, that lead to the greater expression of certain types of intimacy between females than between males. Social pressures on males and females during adolescence are quite different and may lead to differences in expressions of intimacy in certain types of relationships. For instance, theorists have noted that **homophobia**—the fear of homosexuality—is stronger among adolescent males than among adolescent females and leads to suppressed intimacy in relationships between boys (Kite, 1984). This is especially so within ethnic groups that stress the importance of machismo (a strong and sometimes exaggerated sense of masculinity), as is often the case among Mexican Americans (Stanton-Salazar & Spina, 2005). One reason that adolescent males may not be as intimate in their friendships as adolescent females may be that boys are nervous that expressions of intimacy—even without sexual contact—will be taken as a sign of their sexual orientation.

homophobia   The unwarranted fear of homosexuals or homosexuality.

FOOD FOR THOUGHT

Some sex differences in friendship quality predate adolescence—girls are more verbal than boys at an early age, for example—but others, such as differences in conflict resolution or in feelings of jealousy do not seem to emerge until this developmental period. What aspects of the transition into adolescence differ for girls and boys that might account for sex differences in intimacy?

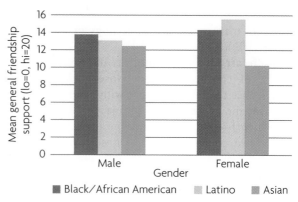

FIGURE 10.4   Patterns of sex differences in intimacy between friends vary across ethnic groups. (Way & Chen, 2000)

Although much research to date has concluded that girls experience more intimacy in their relationships than boys do (Buhrmester, 1996; Maccoby, 1990), it is important to bear in mind that these studies have been based mainly on samples of white youngsters. Several recent studies of nonwhite youth suggest that there may *not* be similar patterns of sex differences in intimacy in some ethnic groups (DuBois & Hirsch, 1990; Jones, Costin, & Ricard, 1994). Indeed, one study of African American, Asian American, and Latino adolescents found no sex differences in support between friends among African American teenagers; slight sex differences among Latino teenagers, with girls reporting more friendship support than boys; and large sex differences among Asian American teenagers, with boys reporting more support than girls (Way & Chen, 2000) (see Figure 10.4). Sanctions against intimate disclosure may be especially strong among white males, but they may be far less so among their minority counterparts.

CHANGES IN THE TARGETS OF INTIMACY

According to Sullivan, adolescence is a time of noteworthy changes in the "targets" of intimate behavior. During preadolescence and early adolescence, intimacy with peers is hypothesized to replace intimacy with parents, and during late adolescence, intimacy with peers of the opposite sex is thought to take the place of intimacy with same-sex friends. Actually, this view appears to be only somewhat accurate. As we'll see, new targets of intimacy do not *replace* old ones. Rather, new targets are *added to* old ones.

▌ **Parents and Peers as Targets of Intimacy**   Two conclusions emerge repeatedly in studies of adolescents' intimacy with parents and peers, at least in the contemporary United States. First, from early adolescence on,

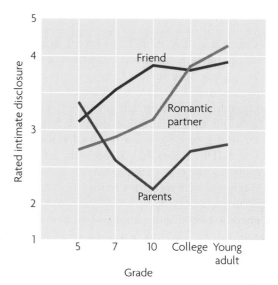

FIGURE 10.5   Age differences in self-disclosure to parents, friends, and romantic partners. (Buhrmester, 1996)

teenagers describe their relationships with their best friends and romantic partners as more intimate than those with their mother or father (Beaumont, 1996; Hunter & Youniss, 1982; Rice & Mulkeen, 1995). Second, although there may be a slight drop in intimacy between adolescents and parents sometime during adolescence, the decline reverses as young people move toward young adulthood.

Consider, for example, the results of one study of age differences in intimate self-disclosure with parents, friends, and romantic partners over the course of childhood and young adulthood (Buhrmester, 1996). As Figure 10.5 indicates, intimacy between individuals and their parents declines between the fifth and tenth grades, but increases between tenth grade and young adulthood. Intimacy with friends increases steadily throughout adolescence, although most dramatically

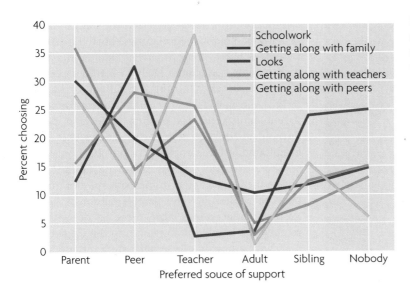

FIGURE 10.6 Preferred sources of social support among Hispanic students vary as a function of their area of concern. (Morrison et al., 1997)

during the early adolescent years. Intimacy with romantic partners also increases steadily throughout adolescence, but in this case, the most dramatic increase takes place during the late high school years.

In other words, while peers become relatively more important during adolescence as confidants and sources of emotional support, by no means do parents become unimportant. When adolescents are asked to list the important people in their lives—people they care about, go to for advice, or do things with—the number of peers listed increases over the course of adolescence. At the same time, however, there are no changes over adolescence in the percentage of individuals listing their mother or father. In one study, at each grade, among both boys and girls, about 93 percent of the adolescents sampled listed their parents (Blyth, Hill, & Thiel, 1982). More importantly, studies indicate that adolescents who spend a good deal of time with their parents also spend a good deal of time with their friends. Thus, rather than drawing distinctions between parent-oriented and peer-oriented adolescents, it makes more sense to distinguish between adolescents who have a lot of social contact and enjoy a great deal of support from others (both family and friends), and those who are socially isolated or lonely (Fallon & Bowles, 1997; Scholte, van Lieshout, & van Aken, 2001).

Indeed, one of the most consistent findings to emerge from studies of adolescents' peer and family relationships is that the qualities of these relationships are closely linked. In other words, we can see features of adolescents' relationships with their parents and their parents' relationships with each other—how close they are, how much they tolerate independence, how they deal with conflict, how much control they assert over their children's friends, and so forth—in

their relationships with their friends and romantic partners (Taradash, Connolly, Pepler, Craig, & Costa, 2001; Updegraff et al., 2004). This link between the quality of peer relationships and of family relationships has been found across ethnic groups (Way & Chen, 2000). On a theoretical level, this provides support for both social learning and attachment-based views of adolescent intimacy, in that it suggests that the lessons young people learn in close relationships at home provide a template for the close relationships they form with others. On a practical level, these findings suggest that one approach to improving the peer relationships of adolescents who are having difficulties might be to focus on improving the quality of their relationships at home (Updegraff, Madden-Derdich, Estrada, Sales, & Leonard, 2002).

Studies of adolescents' preferences for social support similarly show that the likelihood of turning to a peer during a time of trouble increases during adolescence, but that the likelihood of turning to a parent remains constant (Kneisel, 1987). In a study of African American, Hispanic American, and white youth, the researchers found that between ages 7 and 14, the amount of support received from the immediate family remained fairly constant, while the amount of support received from friends increased—a pattern seen in all three ethnic groups (Levitt, Guacci-Franci, & Levitt, 1993). In other words, even though adolescents begin to see their friends as increasingly important sources of emotional support, they do not cease needing or using their parents for the same purpose. What seems to occur, instead, is that adolescents develop preferences for social support that vary as a function of the specific issue (see Figure 10.6).

In general, adolescents interact much more often with their mother than with their father, and this is true for males as well as females. Mothers are viewed as more understanding, accepting, and willing to negotiate, and as less judgmental, guarded, and defensive.

Interestingly, adolescents may feel freer to express anger during arguments with family members than during arguments with friends, presumably because anger may lead to the end of a friendship but not to the end of a family relationship (Laursen, 1993). Perhaps because of this, adolescents report more angry feelings after conflicts with their parents than after conflicts with their friends (Adams & Laursen, 2001). And when asked to recall key events in their past that contributed to their sense of identity, college students' reminiscences of their relationships with their parents more often emphasize conflict and separation with them, whereas their recollections of their relationships with their friends more often emphasize closeness (McLean & Thorne, 2003).

■ **Cultural Differences in Patterns of Intimacy**
Patterns of adolescents' relationships with parents and peers vary across cultures, however, and it may be misleading to generalize results of studies of U.S. or Canadian teenagers to other countries. A recent comparison of American and Indonesian youth found, for instance, that Indonesian adolescents ranked parents higher in social support and ranked friends lower than was the case for the American adolescents (French, Rianasari, Pidada, Nelwan, & Buhrmester, 2001). Similarly, a comparison of adolescents from Canada, Belgium, and Italy found that Italian adolescents were closer to their family whereas Canadian adolescents were closer to their friends (Claes, 1998). It may be wrong to automatically assume that American youngsters are more peer-oriented than their counterparts in

all other cultures, however. In fact, one study found that Japanese adolescents (and Japanese boys, in particular) were less likely than American adolescents to list their parents—and more likely to list their peers—as significant others (Darling, Hamilton, & Matsuda, 1990). Another study, of Dutch youth, found that parent–adolescent relationships were least positive during late adolescence, not early adolescence, as has been found in U.S. samples (van Wel, 1994).

There are also differences among ethnic groups within the United States in the expression of intimacy between adolescents and parents, although some of these differences may have more to do with how recently the family immigrated into the United States than with ethnicity per se. One study of late adolescents found, for example, that Vietnamese American and Chinese American individuals felt less comfortable talking to their parents about such intimate matters as sex or dating than did Filipino Americans or Mexican Americans, who, in turn, felt less comfortable than European Americans. The researchers speculated that these differences reflect ethnic differences in norms of formality in family relationships, especially in relationships between adolescents and their fathers (Cooper, Baker, Polichar, & Welsh, 1994). Other studies indicate that ethnic minority American adolescents are more likely to believe that it is important to respect, assist, and support their family than are white adolescents (Fuligni, Tseng, & Lam, 1999), although ethnic differences in adolescents' beliefs and expectations appear to be more substantial than ethnic differences in how adolescents and their parents actually interact. Indeed, with the exception of families who are recent immigrants to the United States, relations between American adolescents and their parents look surprisingly similar across ethnic groups (Fuligni, 1998).

There are important differences between adolescents' relationships with mothers versus fathers, however. In general, adolescents interact much more often with, are closer to, and argue more with their mother than with their father, a pattern seen among males as well as females and across a variety of cultures (Claes, 1998; Cooper, 1994; Fuligni, 1998). Of their two parents, adolescents see their mother as being more understanding, more accepting, and more willing to negotiate, and as less judgmental, less guarded, and less defensive (see Figure 10.7). The difference between perceptions of mothers and fathers is especially large among girls: As a rule, the mother–daughter relationship tends to be the closest, and the father–daughter relationship the least intimate, with mother–son and father–son relationships falling in between (Monck, 1991; Noller & Callan, 1990; Rice & Mulkeen, 1995; Youniss & Smollar, 1985).

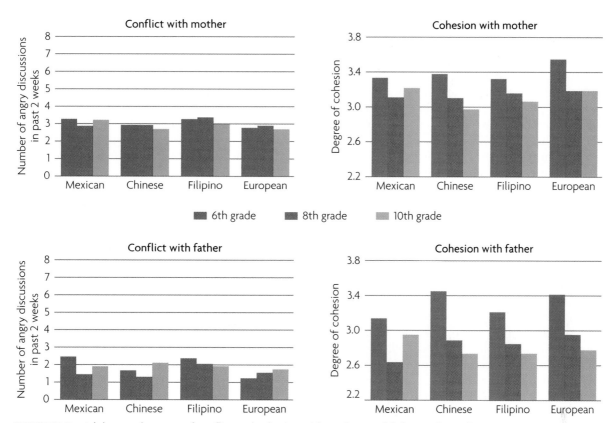

FIGURE 10.7   Adolescents' reports of conflict and cohesion with mothers and fathers in four ethnic groups. (Fuligni, 1998)

All in all, then, an important transition in intimate relationships appears to take place sometime between the fifth and eighth grades. During this period, peers become the most important source of companionship and intimate self-disclosure—surpassing parents and, interestingly, other family members such as siblings (Buhrmester & Furman, 1987; Larson & Richards, 1991). Peers may become increasingly important as targets of intimacy not simply because they are similar in age but also because they do not share the same family with the adolescent. As adolescents begin the process of individuation, they may need to seek intimacy outside the family as a means of establishing an identity beyond their family role. Although this shift in intimacy is normative, a shift in primary attachment figures at this age is not: Adolescents who report that their strongest attachment is to a friend or romantic partner are more likely to have insecure attachments with their parents (Freeman & Brown, 2001).

■ **The Different Roles of Parents and Peers**
Adolescents also have very different sorts of intimate relationships with parents and peers, and these differences point to different ways in which mothers, fathers, and friends may contribute to their social development. Even in close families, parent–adolescent

relations are characterized by an imbalance of power, with parents as nurturers, advice givers, and explainers whom adolescents turn to for their experience and expertise. Adolescents' interactions with their friends, in contrast, are more mutual, more balanced, and more likely to provide them with opportunities to express alternative views and engage in an equal exchange of feelings and beliefs (Hunter, 1984). Consistent with this, conflicts between adolescents and their parents are relatively more likely to end with a "winner" and a "loser," whereas conflicts between adolescents and their friends are relatively more likely to end in compromise or, at least, equal outcomes (Adams & Laursen, 2001).

Rather than viewing one type of relationship as more or less intimate than the other, it seems wiser to say that both types of intimacy are important, for each influences a different aspect of the adolescent's developing character in important ways. Intimacy with parents provides opportunities to learn from those older and wiser; intimacy with friends provides opportunities to share experiences with individuals who have a similar perspective and degree of expertise. Consistent with this view, studies find that adolescents who have strong attachments to both parents and peers are better adjusted than those who have strong attachments in one type of relationship but not in the other (Laible, Carlo,

& Raffaelli, 2000). In addition, the positive impact of having supportive friends in adolescence is greater when an adolescent also has supportive parents (Helsen, Vollebergh, & Meeus, 2000).

The different functions of intimacy with parents and peers are nicely illustrated in a study of social support during a transition into a new school (Dunn, Putallaz, Sheppard, & Lindstrom, 1987). As you will recall from Chapter 6, changing schools during adolescence can sometimes be stressful, and **social support**—emotional or instrumental assistance from others—can help buffer adolescents against the potential negative effects of stress (Hauser & Bowlds, 1990). The study found that support from family members was more predictive of adaptation to the demands of the new school, as indexed by grades and attendance, but that support from peers was more predictive of psychological well-being, as indexed by low levels of depression and anxiety. The absence of peer support was especially critical for boys, perhaps because girls are more likely than boys to seek out other sources of support when their peers do not provide it. Although more research on the nature and effects of social support among minority adolescents is needed, at least one study indicates that parental support is more strongly related to self-esteem among white than black adolescents (Levitt et al., 1993).

Studies show that a lack of support from parents or from friends in school is associated with low self-worth and poorer social adjustment in early adolescence. Social support from one source (such as the family) can be especially important when other sources of support (such as friends) are lacking (Ohannessian, Lerner, Lerner, & von Eye, 1994). One recent study found, for example, that having support from their family is more important for the healthy adjustment of adolescents who do not have a close friend, whereas support from friends is more crucial among adolescents whose family relationships are strained (Gauze, Bukowski, Aquan-Assee, & Sippola, 1996). Having support from parents, siblings, or non-school friends does not fully compensate for a lack of support from classmates, though, and having support from siblings, classmates, or others does not fully compensate for a lack of support from parents (East & Rook, 1992; Gore & Aseltine, 1995). In other words, optimal social development during adolescence may require healthy relationships *both* with parents and with peers (Barber & Olsen, 1997; Eccles, Early, Frasier, Belansky, & McCarthy, 1997; Young, Berenson, Cohen, & Garcia, 2005).

A study of the differential uses of parents and peers as sources of support indicates that whom adolescents turn to is likely to be highly dependent upon the specific issue at hand, which explains, in part, why adolescents may need support from both parents and peers (Boldero & Fallon, 1995; Morrison et al., 1997). This particular study asked adolescents whom they would turn to if they had a substance abuse problem; the respondents could name as many different people as desired (Windle, Miller-Tutzauer, & Barnes, 1991). Among the early adolescents surveyed, only 43 percent listed their parents among people they would turn to for help, whereas 60 percent listed friends; among the middle adolescents, the proportions were 39 percent and 70 percent, respectively. More interestingly, 10 percent of all early adolescents and almost that proportion of middle adolescents said that they would turn to no one at all—a far more common response among boys than girls. There also were interesting ethnic differences in adolescents' responses, with African American and Hispanic American youngsters twice as likely as white adolescents to report being socially isolated (that is, having *no one* to turn to). An absence of social support may be especially problematic for poor youth, who often rely on peers to provide emotional support in the face of stress and other difficulties inherent in living in high-risk environments (Stanton-Salazar & Spina, 2005).

In general, then, the results of research on changes in intimacy with parents and peers as an individual ages are similar to the findings discussed in Chapter 9 regarding autonomy: Although the importance of peer relationships undoubtedly increases during adolescence, the significance of family relationships does not decline so much as it narrows in focus. Parents do not cease to be important sources of influence or, as we see here, targets of intimacy. Throughout adolescence, parents and adolescents remain close, parents (especially mothers) remain important confidants, and both mothers and fathers continue to be significant influences on the young person's behavior and decisions. Indeed, even in adolescence, being close to one's parents has a more positive impact on psychological health than being close to one's friends (Greenberg, Siegel, & Leitch, 1983), and studies show that the quality of the relationship that adolescents have with their parents may have an influence on the quality of the relationship they have with close friends (Cooper, Carlson, Keller, Koch, & Spradling, 1993; Gold & Yanof, 1985). Family relationships and peer relationships influence, rather than compete with, each other (Fallon & Bowles, 1997; Gavin & Furman, 1996). That said, peers take on an increasingly important role in the individual's social life over the course of adolescence. Although peers do not replace parents, they

social support The extent to which an individual receives emotional or instrumental assistance from his or her social network.

clearly contribute to the adolescent's social development in a unique and influential way.

▌ Other Individuals as Targets of Intimacy

Comparatively little is known about intimacy in adolescents' relationships with siblings, with members of their extended family, or with nonfamilial adults like teachers or coaches. When asked to list people who are important in their life, only about 10 percent of adolescents who have a brother or a sister fail to list a sibling. Furthermore, more than two-thirds of the adolescents with multiple siblings list all of them as significant (Blyth, Hill, & Thiel, 1982). Adolescents typically rate their relationship with their "favorite" brother or sister as having about the same level of intimacy as their relationship with their best friend (Greenberger, Steinberg, Vaux, & McAuliffe, 1980). When researchers do not specify that the sibling be a "favorite" brother or sister, however, the relationship is usually described as less intimate than that with parents or friends (Buhrmester & Furman, 1987). Adolescents fight more with brothers and sisters than they do with close friends, and their arguments with siblings tend to be resolved less by giving in or by letting things slide than through the intervention of others, presumably parents (Raffaelli, 1997).

When teenagers are asked to list the significant people in their lives, approximately 80 percent name at least one member of their extended family (grandparents, aunts, uncles, and cousins), with extended family members constituting about one-fifth of all people listed as important (Blyth, Hill, & Thiel, 1982). Actual contact with extended family is infrequent for many adolescents, however, because those family members often live outside the adolescent's immediate area (Feiring & Lewis, 1991). There appears to be a slight increase in intimacy with extended family members during childhood but an especially steep drop-off in intimacy with grandparents and other extended family members between childhood and adolescence (Buhrmester & Furman, 1987; Creasey & Kaliher, 1994; Levitt et al., 1993).

Although a decline in intimacy with grandparents is often observed during adolescence, this may not be as common among adolescents who are living with a single, divorced mother (Clingempeel, Colyar, Brand, & Hetherington, 1992; Hirsch, Mickus, & Boerger, 2002). Divorce may be associated with increased contact between adolescents and their grandparents, especially between the adolescent and his or her maternal grandfather. Ties to grandmothers are especially strong among African American adolescents, particularly among girls from divorced households (Hirsch et al., 2002). Interestingly, puberty seems to increase the intimacy between adolescent boys from divorced homes and their grandfathers (perhaps to compensate for diminished contact with their father), whereas it seems to distance adolescent girls from their grandfathers (perhaps because of discomfort with the girl's sexuality).

Researchers also have asked whether relationships between adolescents and nonfamilial adults in schools, workplaces, or neighborhoods can play a significant role in teenagers' lives (Greenberger, Chen, & Beam, 1998; Munsch, Liang, & DeSecottier, 1996). Indeed, recent studies suggest that the development of relationships with nonfamilial adults is a normative part of adolescence, not a sign of difficulties at home (Beam, Chen, & Greenberger, 2002). Close friendships may develop naturally between adolescents and their teachers or work supervisors, or can be cultivated through community organizations, such as Big Brothers/ Big Sisters, or similar programs designed to pair young people—especially those under stress—with supportive and caring adults. One study of Latino adolescent mothers found, for example, that those who had mentors reported significantly better mental health than their peers who did not (Rhodes, Contreras, & Mangelsdorf, 1994). The benefits of having a Big Brother or Big Sister may be especially significant among adolescents with more difficulties at home, such as those living in foster care (Rhodes, Haight, & Briggs, 1999). Not all close relationships with nonparental adults are beneficial to adolescents' development, however: Adolescent boys who have close friendships with young adult men are more likely to engage in antisocial behavior when they perceive their older friends as likely to condone or commit antisocial acts themselves (Greenberger et al., 1998).

FRIENDSHIPS WITH THE OTHER SEX

It is not until late adolescence that intimate friendships with opposite-sex peers begin to be important. Consistent with Sullivan's theory, studies of preadolescents and young teenagers point to very strong sex segregation in adolescents' friendships, with boys rarely reporting friendships with girls, and girls rarely reporting friendships with boys (Hallinan, 1981). Indeed, sex is the single most important determinant of friendship during preadolescence, playing a considerably more powerful role than, say, race or socioeconomic background (Schofield, 1981). (Age is also an important determinant of preadolescents' friendships, but the organization of most elementary schools—at least in America—makes it hard for children to develop friendships with older or younger peers.)

▌ Origins of the "Sex Cleavage"

The schism between boys and girls during early adolescence results

As cross-sex relationships begin to develop, adolescents may mask their anxieties by teasing and joking around with members of the opposite sex.

from various factors. First, despite whatever changes may have taken place in American society with regard to sex-role socialization during the past 40 years, it is still the case that preadolescent and early adolescent boys and girls have different interests, engage in different sorts of peer activities, and perceive themselves to be different from each other (Schofield, 1981). In one study, for example, an interviewer asked a young adolescent boy why boys and girls sit separately in the school lunchroom. "So they can talk," the boy replied. "The boys talk about football and sports and the girls talk about whatever they talk about" (Schofield, 1981, p. 68). The sex cleavage in adolescent friendships results more from adolescents' preferring members of the same sex—and the activities they engage in—than from their actually disliking members of the opposite sex, although boys express more positive feelings about their female classmates than vice versa (Bukowski, Gauze, Hoza, & Newcomb, 1993; Bukowski, Sippola, & Hoza, 1999).

Perhaps a more interesting reason for the low frequency of cross-sex friendships during early adolescence is the concern of some adolescents that contact with members of the opposite sex could be interpreted as a sign of romantic involvement (Schofield, 1981). As one girl put it, "If you talk with boys they [other girls] say that you're almost going with him." Another girl from the same class remarked that boys and girls rarely work together on class projects "because people like to work with their friends. . . . When you're working on a project . . . your friend has to call and come over to your house. If it's a boy, it can be complicated" (Schofield, 1981, p. 69).

The discomfort that younger adolescents feel about cross-sex relationships is vividly illustrated in the following observation of three preadolescent boys in an amusement park. Although this account is more than 25 years old, it still rings true today:

> The boys seem very interested in the girls they see, and there is considerable whispering and teasing about them. Tom had received a small coin bank as a prize which he decides that he no longer wishes to keep. At this time we are standing in line for a roller coaster directly behind three girls—apparently a year or two older than these twelve-year-olds—one of whom is wearing a hooded jacket. Frank tells Tom to take the bank and "stuff it in her hood," which Tom does to the annoyance of his victim. When she turns around, Tom and Hardy tell her that Frank did it, and of course Frank denies this, blaming Tom. The girls tell the boys to shut up and leave them alone. As things work out, Hardy has to sit with one of these girls on the ride and he clearly appears embarrassed, while Tom and Frank are vastly amused. After the ride Tom and Frank claim that they saw Hardy holding her. Frank said that he saw them holding hands, and Tom said: "He was trying to go up her shirt." Hardy vehemently denies these claims. A short while later we meet these girls again, and Frank turns to Hardy, saying "Here's your honey." The girl retorts as she walks away, "Oh, stifle it." (Fine, 1981, p. 43)

Friendly interactions between early adolescent boys and girls, when they do occur, typically involve "over-acting attraction or romantic interest in such a pronounced or playful way that the indication of interest can be written off as teasing or fooling around" (Schofield, 1981, p. 71). Whereas rough play—play fighting—between boys is typically done to show who is dominant, the same behavior between boys and girls is often semisexual in nature—what some have labeled "poke and push courtship" (Pellegrini, 2003).

The transitional period—between same-sex non-sexual relationships and opposite-sex sexual ones—can be a trying time for adolescents. This period usually coincides with the peer group's shift from same-sex cliques to mixed-sex crowds, which we examined in Chapter 5. The interpersonal strains and anxieties inherent in the transition show up in the high levels of teasing, joking around, and overt discomfort that young adolescents so often display in situations that are a little too close to being romantic or sexual. As one researcher put it, intimacy between boys and girls before middle adolescence appears to be "impeded at least partly because . . . children are aware that they are approaching the age when they may begin to become deeply involved with each other in a romantic or sexual way" (Schofield, 1981, pp. 69–71). One reason for the mutual physical playfulness that boys and girls engage in is that it is ambiguous enough to be denied as motivated by genuine sexual interest (Pellegrini, 2003).

These observations support Sullivan's claim that intimacy between adolescent boys and girls is relatively slow to develop and generally is tinged with an air of sexuality. Contrary to his notion that cross-sex intimacy comes to replace intimacy with peers of the same sex, however, researchers have found that intimate relationships between adolescents of the same sex continue to develop throughout adolescence. They clearly are not displaced by the eventual emergence of intimacy between adolescent males and females (Connolly & Johnson, 1993; Sharabany et al., 1981). Although researchers find that the likelihood of opposite-sex peers appearing on adolescents' lists of people who are important to them increases during early and middle adolescence, and although the amount of time adolescents spend with opposite-sex peers increases as well, the number of same-sex peers listed also increases or remains constant, and time spent with same-sex peers does not decline (Blyth et al., 1982; Feiring & Lewis, 1991; Richards, Crowe, Larson, & Swarr, 1998; Zimmer-Gembeck, 1999). However, there are substantial individual differences in patterns of time allocation to same- and other-sex relationships; some adolescents shift their energy from same-sex friends to other-sex relationships early and abruptly, others do so gradually over the course of high school, and still others do not shift their focus at all (Zimmer-Gembeck, 1999).

Although intimacy between the sexes increases during early adolescence (Buhrmester & Furman, 1987), many adolescents do not list a single opposite-sex peer as a significant person in their lives. In middle school, only 8 percent of adolescents' friendships are with members of the opposite sex; by high school, this figure has risen only to 13 percent (Değirmencioğlu & Urberg, 1994). One exception to this general trend is seen among gay male adolescents, who tend to have more female than male friends (Diamond & Dube, 2002).

When females do include opposite-sex peers on their list of important people, the boys they mention are often older and often from another school; when boys list girls as important friends, they generally are of the same age or younger (Blyth et al., 1982). Consistent with this, the increase in time spent with opposite-sex peers that occurs in adolescence takes place much earlier among girls than boys—by the time they are in eleventh grade, girls are spending 10 hours each week alone with a boy, compared to only 5 hours per week spent by boys alone with a girl. Young

adolescents of both sexes spend a lot of time thinking about the opposite sex, but relatively little time with them. Interestingly, as adolescents get older, the time they spend thinking about the opposite sex tends to be increasingly associated with negative mood states, perhaps because the fantasies about the opposite sex experienced in early adolescence come to be replaced by more realistic longings for romantic companionship (Richards et al., 1998).

Some Functions of Opposite-Sex Friendships

Although the emergence of close opposite-sex friendships in early adolescence is not explicitly in the context of romance, it likely sets the stage for later romantic experiences. The pattern of age differences in opposite-sex friendships, for example, is consistent with what we know about age differences between dating partners in early and middle adolescence, with boys generally older than their girlfriends, rather than the reverse (Montgomery & Sorell, 1998). In addition, adolescents who have more opposite-sex friends than their peers early in adolescence tend to enter into romantic relationships at an earlier age and tend to have longer romantic relationships as well (Feiring, 1999). This could be due to many factors, including the adolescent's use of the pool of opposite-sex friends to "rehearse" for later romantic relationships or to develop a social network that is used to meet potential dates later on (Connolly, Furman, & Konarski, 2000; Connolly & Goldberg, 1999; Darling, Dowdy, Van Horn, & Caldwell, 1999). In any case, clearly, even preadolescents as young as 9 differentiate between cross-sex relationships that are friendships and those that are romantic (Connolly, Craig, Goldberg, & Pepler, 1999).

Not all relationships between males and females in adolescence are romantic, of course, and having close, opposite-sex friendships is a common experience among contemporary youth (Kuttler, La Greca, & Prinstein, 1999; Stanton-Salazar & Spina, 2005). Two very different types of adolescents appear to have close opposite-sex friends—adolescents who are socially competent and highly popular with same-sex peers, and adolescents who are socially incompetent and highly unpopular with same-sex peers (Bukowski, Sippola, & Hoza, 1999; Değirmencioğlu & Urberg, 1994; Feiring & Lewis, 1991). Among boys, having an opposite-sex friend serves as a "backup system" for those who do not have same-sex friends, leading to more positive mental health than is seen among boys without any friends at all. Among girls, however, the results are mixed. Although some studies have found that "there is no advantage, or perhaps there is even a disadvantage, to having a friendship with a boy" (Bukowski et al., 1999, p. 457), others have found that, among less sexually advanced girls, having platonic friendships with boys is associated with a more positive body image—perhaps because these friendships permit girls to feel that boys like them for themselves, without the added cost of feeling pressured to have sex (Compian, Gowen, & Hayward, 2004).

FOOD FOR THOUGHT

Anecdotal evidence suggests that nonsexual friendships between males and females have become more common in recent decades. Why do you think this might be?

In general, though, the overall picture suggests that boys have more to gain from friendships with girls than vice versa. Having an intimate relationship with an opposite-sex peer is more strongly related to boys' general level of interpersonal intimacy than it is to girls' (Buhrmester & Furman, 1987), and whereas boys report that their friendships with girls are more rewarding than their friendships with other boys, girls do not describe their friendships with boys as more rewarding than their friendships with other girls (Thomas & Daubman, 2001). These findings are not surprising, given that adolescents' friendships with girls (regardless of whether they themselves are male or female) tend to be more intimate and supportive than their friendships with boys (Kuttler et al., 1999).

A recent study of peer networks among low-income Mexican American adolescents in San Diego illustrates how important platonic friendships with girls can be for adolescent boys in the development of more mature relationships. Many boys likened their nonsexual friendships with girls to relationships with sisters, emphasizing the ease with which they could explicitly ask for emotional support, something that many adolescent males find difficult to request from their same-sex friends:

> Le tengo un cariño así con ella como si fuera también mi hermana [I have such love for her, as if she were my sister] . . . We always support each other, it doesn't matter what it is; if she asks me, I help her, and if I ask her, she helps me, with anything. (Stanton-Salazar & Spina, 2005, pp. 397–398)

Some boys also discussed the important role their female friends played in helping them manage their tempers:

> You know, I'm the kind of guy that can go around and like, you know, get mad and you know . . . siento como que quiero cingar a alguien [I feel like I wanna fuck somebody up (i.e., to hit and seriously injure

someone)]. She's the person that when she looks at me, you know [giggles], all those mad feelings go to, like, Oh God!, you know. Like she can control me, like she's holding me back, just by looking at me [laughs]. (pp. 399–400)

As in studies of non-Latino youth, this study of Mexican American adolescents indicates that the benefits of cross-sex friendships are less evident for females than for males. Many such friendships draw females into traditional caregiving roles, reinforcing traditional sex-role stereotypes.

RECAP

- With development, adolescents place more emphasis on trust and loyalty as defining features of friendship, become more self-disclosing in their relationships, and become more responsive and sensitive to their friends' needs.
- Sex differences in the expression of intimacy in adolescents' friendships are striking, with girls' relationships being more intimate than boys' across many different indicators. Boys' friendships do not lack intimacy, but intimacy is a much more conscious concern for girls than it is for boys, in part because of sex differences in the way they are socialized.
- New types of relationships are added to the adolescent's social world without replacing previous ones. Beginning in preadolescence, the network of intimate relationships widens to include peers as well as family members and, sometimes, nonfamilial adults.
- Many adolescents have nonromantic friendships with other-sex peers. Opposite-sex friendships help to set the stage for the emergence of romantic relationships later on.
- Boys may profit psychologically from opposite-sex friendships more than girls.

Dating and Romantic Relationships

Dating plays a very different role in adolescents' lives today than it did in previous times (Gordon & Miller, 1984). In earlier eras, dating during adolescence was not so much a recreational activity (as it is today) as

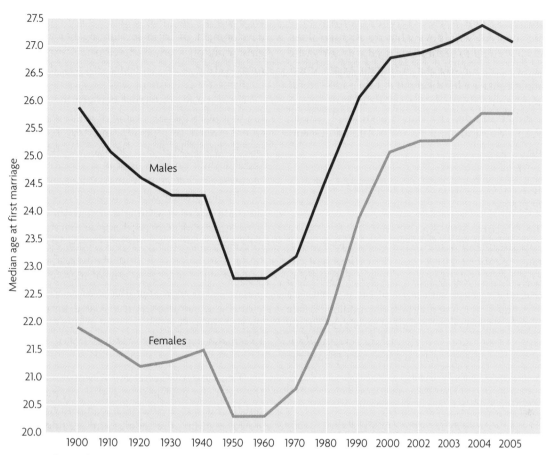

FIGURE 10.8   The median age at marriage in the United States declined from 1900 through the mid-1950s but rose markedly during the second half of the twentieth century. (U.S. Bureau of the Census, 2006)

a part of the process of courtship and mate selection. Individuals would date in order to ready themselves for marriage, and unmarried individuals would play the field—under the watchful eyes of chaperones—for a relatively long period before settling down (Montgomery, 1996). You may be surprised to learn that, at the turn of the twentieth century, most individuals did not marry until their mid-20s (Modell & Goodman, 1990). The first half of this century saw a gradual decline in the average age of marriage, however, and as a result, individuals began dating more seriously at an earlier age. By the mid-1950s, the average age at first marriage in the United States had fallen to 20 among women and 22 among men—which means that substantial numbers of individuals were courting during high school and marrying during their late adolescent years.

The function of adolescent dating changed, however, as individuals began to marry later and later—a trend that began in the mid-1950s and continues today (see Figure 10.8). Now, the average age at which people marry is considerably later than it was 40 years ago—about age 26 for women and 27 for men (U.S.

Bureau of the Census, 2006). This, of course, gives high school dating a whole new meaning, because today it is clearly divorced from its function in mate selection. Adults continue to regulate and monitor adolescent dating in order to prevent rash or impulsive commitments to early marriage (Laursen & Jensen-Campbell, 1999), but in the minds of most young people, high school dating has little to do with courtship or marriage.

Only recently have social scientists begun writing systematically about adolescents' romantic relationships, and much of what has been written is theoretical rather than data-based (Collins, 2003; Furman et al., 1999). However, recent studies of adolescent romance indicate that romantic relationships are very common: One-fourth of American 12-year-olds, one-half of 15-year-olds, and more than two-thirds of 18-year-olds report having had a romantic relationship in the past 18 months. Moreover, and contrary to the stereotypes of adolescents' romances as short-lived, one-fifth of adolescents 14 or younger, one-third of 15- and 16-year-olds, and more than half of 17- and 18-year-olds who are in dating relationships have been dating the same person for at least 11 months. Girls tend to become involved with boys who are slightly older, whereas boys tend to become involved with girls who are the same age or younger. Although Asian American adolescents are less likely than other adolescents to date, the prevalence of dating at different ages is very similar among African American, Hispanic American, American Indian, and white adolescents (Collins, 2003).

DATING AND THE DEVELOPMENT OF INTIMACY

▌ The Nature and Significance of Romance Most discussions of adolescent romance begin with Sullivan's theory of interpersonal development. As you may recall, Sullivan believed that establishing intimate relationships with peers of the opposite sex was the chief developmental task of middle and late adolescence. The capacity for intimacy, which initially develops out of same-sex friendships, eventually is brought into romantic relationships, which for the vast majority of adolescents are with members of the opposite sex. In some senses, then, Sullivan viewed relationships between romantic partners as a context in which intimacy is *expressed* rather than learned. Consistent with this, the quality of adolescents' friendships is predictive of the quality of their subsequent romantic relationships, whereas the reverse is not true (Connolly et al., 2000).

This view—that romantic relationships are *not* the context in which intimacy is first learned—may be more accurate for females than for males, however (Feiring, 1999). In American society, boys are not encouraged to develop the capacity to be emotionally expressive, particularly in their relationships with other males. During middle adolescence, as we have seen, girls are better than boys at certain types of intimacy—self-disclosure and interpersonal understanding, for example. Girls, therefore, are more likely than boys to be capable of being intimate and eager for emotional closeness upon entering a relationship. Some studies of early sexual relationships confirm this: For adolescent girls more than boys, early sexual relationships are far more likely to involve love, emotional involvement, and intimacy (Montgomery, 2005; Shulman & Scharf, 2000). For this reason, some writers have suggested that girls play an important role in teaching boys how to be more open, more sensitive, and more caring (Simon & Gagnon, 1969). In other words, whereas for girls cross-sex relationships may provide a context for further *expression* of intimacy, for boys they may provide a context for the further *development* of intimacy. This notion is consistent with the finding, discussed earlier, that opposite-sex

relationships may play a more important role in the development of intimacy among boys than among girls, who, on average, develop and experience intimacy earlier with same-sex friends than boys do (Buhrmester & Furman, 1987).

There is a big difference between the sort of learning that takes place in a long-term, intimate relationship between two people and that resulting from casual dating, however. Dating is a well-established social institution in American adolescent life. Today, the average adolescent begins dating around age 13 or 14, although nearly half of all adolescents have at least one date before they turn 12. By age 16, more than 90 percent of adolescents of both sexes have had at least one date, and during the later years of high school, more than half of all students average one or more dates weekly. Only 15 percent of high school students date less than once a month (Feiring, 1993). By age 18, virtually all adolescents have dated once, and three-fourths have had at least one steady relationship (Neemann, Hubbard, & Masten, 1995).

▌ The Role of Context Although early maturers begin dating somewhat earlier than late maturers (Lam, Shi, Ho, Stewart, & Fan, 2002; Neemann et al., 1995), age norms within the adolescent's school are more important in determining the age at which dating begins than is the adolescent's level of physical development. In other words, a physically immature 14-year-old who goes to school where it is expected that 14-year-olds will date is more likely to date than is a physically mature 14-year-old who lives in a community where dating is typically delayed until age 16 (Dornbusch et al., 1981). Sexual activity, however, as we'll see in Chapter 11, is more strongly influenced by biological development (Udry, Billy, Morris, Gruff, & Raj, 1985). Dating also begins earlier among adolescents who have older siblings, among adolescents whose parents do not monitor them well, and among those with single mothers, especially if the mother is sexually active herself (Longmore, Manning, & Giordano, 2001; Neeman et al., 1995).

The influence of context on expectations for dating is vividly illustrated in the sorts of letters that adolescents write to the advice columns in teen magazines (van Roosmalen, 2000, p. 207):

> All my friends have boyfriends and I don't (I'm 12). It makes me so depressed because I feel like I'll never have one. I'm afraid of what everyone will think.
>
> *Bummed out*

> Every kid in my class has either a boyfriend or a girlfriend. I don't have a boyfriend, so I use the excuse that boys don't look good yet. But how long can I hold out with the same excuse?
>
> *Boyfriendless*

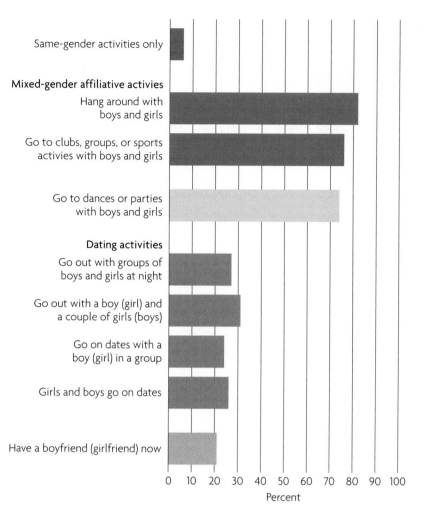

FIGURE 10.9 Participation in various romantic activities in early adolescence. (Connolly et al., 2004)

I'm just entering junior high school and all around me there are couples kissing, holding hands, and hugging. . . . It really hurts to see everyone with a boyfriend and then me just all alone.

Heartbroken

▮ **Patterns of Dating** "Dating" can mean a variety of different things, of course, from group activities that bring males and females together (without much actual contact between the sexes), to group dates in which a group of boys and girls go out jointly (and spend part of the time in couples and part of the time in the larger group), to casual dating in couples, to serious involvement with a steady boyfriend or girlfriend. Generally, casual socializing with opposite-sex peers and experiences in a mixed-sex social network generally occur before the development of romantic relationships (Connolly & Goldberg, 1999). As a consequence, more adolescents have experience in mixed-sex group activities like parties or dances than in dating, and more have experience in dating than in having a serious

boyfriend or girlfriend (see Figure 10.9) (Connolly, Craig, Goldberg, & Pepler, 2004; Tobin-Richards, 1985). Involvement in one-on-one romantic relationships does not replace same-sex or mixed-sex group activities—like other aspects of intimacy in adolescence, new forms of relationships are added to the adolescent's repertoire while old ones are retained. The sequence of transitioning into romantic relationships follows similar patterns across ethnic groups, although Asian American youth appear to make this transition at a somewhat later stage than their peers from other backgrounds, consistent with other findings on ethnic differences in beliefs about the appropriate age at which adolescents should begin dating and engaging in other adultlike activities (Connolly et al., 2004) (see Chapter 9).

Even for adolescents with a history of intimate friendships with same- and other-sex peers, the transition into romantic relationships can be difficult. In one recent study, in which adolescents were asked to discuss social situations they thought were difficult, themes having to do with communicating with the

The capacity for intimacy, which initially develops within same-sex friendships, eventually is brought into romantic relationships. Romantic relationships are more likely to be contexts in which intimacy is expressed rather than learned.

other sex were mentioned frequently. Many adolescents discussed difficulty in initiating or maintaining conversations, in person ("He will think I am an idiot," "Sometimes you don't know, if you're like sitting with a guy and you're watching a basketball game or something, you don't know if you should start talking or if you should just sit there") and on the phone ("I think it is hard to call. After it's done with, you don't know how to get off the phone"). Others mentioned problems in asking people out ("Asking a girl out on a first date—complete panic!") or in turning people down ("How about if you go on a date and you're really not interested, but he keeps calling?"). Still others noted problems in making or ending romantic commitments ("You don't know if you are going out with someone or if you are just seeing them," "It is hard to say, 'so, are we gonna make a commitment?'" "I avoided [breaking up] for two weeks because I was trying to think of what to say") (Grover & Nangle, 2003, pp. 133–134).

THE DEVELOPMENT OF DATING RELATIONSHIPS

Dating serves many purposes in adolescence, only one of which is the development of intimacy. Indeed, it is not until late adolescence that dating relationships begin to be characterized by a level of emotional depth and maturity that can be described as intimate, and it is not until late adolescence that individuals develop genuinely deep attachments to individuals other than their parents (Furman & Simon, 1999; Hazan, 1994; Montgomery, 2005). Over the course of adolescence, the importance of a romantic partner—relative to other relationships—increases, and by college, individuals typically name their romantic partner first on a list of significant others (up from fourth in grade 7 and third in grade 10) (Buhrmester, 1996; Furman & Wehner, 1994).

■ **Reasons for Dating**   Prior to middle or late adolescence, dating may be less important for the development of intimacy than it is for other purposes, including establishing emotional and behavioral autonomy from parents (Dowdy & Kliewer, 1999; Gray & Steinberg, 1999), furthering the development of gender identity (Feiring, 1999), learning about oneself as a romantic partner (Furman & Simon, 1999), and establishing and maintaining status and popularity in the peer group (Brown, 1999). For these reasons, younger adolescents' choice of dating partners may have more to do with how they will be seen by others (for example, as "grown up," "macho," or "popular") than with the actual quality of the relationship itself. Consistent with this, between elementary school and middle school, there is an increase in girls' attraction to aggressive boys who stand out in the peer group (Bukowski, Sippola, & Newcomb, 2000).

Again, letters from young adolescents to a teen magazine make the point quite clearly (van Roosmalen, 2000, p. 209):

I am really starting to like this guy at school. . . . The problem is, all my friends think he's a big annoying jerk. I'm afraid that if he asked me out and I said yes that I might lose all my friends. Yet if I say no, I might lose him. Please help!

Trapped

I'm not really popular, but I'm popular enough for a ton of guys to like me. But the problem is, they are mostly nerds. They all make such a big deal about liking me it's almost ruining my reputation. What should I do?

(Not signed)

■ **Phases of Romance**   The development of intimacy and more sophisticated social cognitive abilities is paralleled by changes in the ways adolescents think about and behave within romantic relationships. The evolution of romance in the adolescent's life proceeds through four phases (Brown, 1999; Connolly & Goldberg, 1999; Seiffge-Krenke, 2003). During the *infatuation* phase, adolescents first discover an interest in socializing with potential romantic and sexual partners. The focus of activity during this phase is primarily on learning about themselves, as adolescents broaden their self-conceptions to include seeing themselves as a potential romantic partner to someone else. Actual romantic relationships tend to be short-lived and are frequently based on superficial infatuations.

During the *status* phase, the main purpose of romantic activity involves "establishing, improving, or maintaining peer group status. Dating the 'wrong' person or conducting romantic relationships in the 'wrong' way can seriously damage one's standing in the group. . . . This makes it difficult to sustain relationships that are too heavily focused inward, on the quality of the interaction or needs of the couple" (Brown, 1999, p. 297).

During the *intimate* phase, adolescents begin to establish true and meaningful attachments to romantic partners. Although adolescents are still learning about themselves as romantic and sexual partners, and are still aware of the way their peers view their romantic relationships, they are now sufficiently involved in the emotional side of romance for this to overshadow the personal and status concerns that dominated the earlier phases of romantic involvement. Relationships become a source of passion and preoccupation—recalling the themes expressed in popular love songs that appeal to teenagers.

Finally, during the *bonding* phase, concerns about commitment begin to move to the forefront, as adolescents begin to think about the long-term survival and growth of their romantic attachments. It is not so much that adolescents in this phase are contemplating marriage—in contemporary society, this typically does not occur until individuals are at least in their mid-20s. But as conceptions of romance develop, adolescents come to value commitment and caring as features of relationships that are as important as passion and pleasure, if not more so (Brown, 1999; Seiffge-Krenke, 2003).

Although the progression through the infatuation, status, intimate, and bonding phases of dating and romance may characterize the development of most adolescents, a number of writers interested in the experiences of gay, lesbian, and bisexual adolescents have pointed out that this picture may be less applicable to **sexual-minority youth**—adolescents who are not exclusively heterosexual (Diamond, 2000; Diamond, Savin-Williams, & Dubé, 1999). Although

great strides have been made in increasing the public's tolerance and understanding of homosexuality, stigmas and stereotypes still make the development of intimate relationships—whether nonsexual friendships, dating relationships, or sexual relationships—far more complicated among sexual-minority youth than among their straight peers. For example, because few sexual-minority youth have the freedom to publicly express their romantic and sexual interests in members of the same sex, they often find it difficult, if not impossible, to engage in many of the social and interpersonal activities that their heterosexual friends are permitted to enjoy. Thus, many sexual-minority youth end up pursuing sexual activity *outside* the context of a dating relationship, because the prejudices and harassment of others may preclude any public display of romantic intimacy with a same-sex partner. At the same time, for sexual-minority youth who are even somewhat open about their sexual identity, the development of close, nonsexual friendships with same-sex peers may be hampered by the suspicions and homophobia of others. As one group of writers explains the special predicament faced by sexual-minority adolescents: "A sexual-minority adolescent may already be privately plagued by the sense that he or she is profoundly different from other youths. To have this differentness acknowledged and perhaps ridiculed by peers may prove intolerable" (Diamond et al., 1999).

■ **Sex Differences in Partner Preferences** There are both age and sex differences in what adolescents look for in romantic partners, and these differences parallel what is known about age and sex differences in romantic relationships. During middle adolescence, boys are more likely to mention physical attractiveness and girls are more likely to mention interpersonal qualities, such as support or intimacy. By late adolescence, however, both sexes emphasize interpersonal qualities, and the ingredients of a satisfying relationship are very similar for males and females (and quite similar to those mentioned by adults): passion, communication, commitment, emotional support, and togetherness (Collins, 2003; Connolly, Craig, Goldberg, & Pepler, 1999; Feiring, 1996; Levesque, 1993). Interestingly, however, adolescents' satisfaction with their romantic relationships are not as negatively affected by such qualities as conflict or possessiveness as are adults (Levesque, 1993).

Some evidence suggests that, especially for girls, it may be important to differentiate between group versus couple activities in examining the impact of dating on adolescents' psychological development.

sexual-minority youth Gay, lesbian, and bisexual youth.

Participating in mixed-sex activity in group situations—going to parties or dances, for example—may have a positive impact on the psychological well-being of young adolescent girls, while serious dating in couples may have a more negative effect (Compian et al., 2004; Tobin-Richards, 1985). The reasons for this are not entirely clear, but researchers believe that pressures on girls to engage in sexual activity when they are out alone on dates or involved with a steady boyfriend likely have a negative impact on their mental health (Simmons & Blyth, 1987)—girls who frequently go out on dates alone with boys lose their virginity at an earlier age than those who date more often in groups (Meschke, Zweig, Barber, & Eccles, 2000)—and studies show that sexual coercion and date rape are common during the high school years (Brown, 2004; McMaster, Connolly, & Craig, 1997; Patton & Mannison, 1995). Although boys may feel peer pressure to become sexually active, this may be a very different sort of pressure—with very different consequences—from what girls feel. Because boys generally begin dating at a later age than girls—and date people who are younger rather than older—beginning to date in couples may be less anxiety-provoking for boys, who have the advantage of a few additional years of "maturity."

FOOD FOR THOUGHT

Traditional, one-on-one dating is far less common today than in past generations, and relatively more interaction between males and females, even those who are romantically interested in each other, occurs in groups than in couples. What implications does it have for the development of intimacy? For preparation for marriage?

As is the case with friendships during the move from high school to college, young people are likely to report dissatisfaction with their high school romances during this transition as well. In one study, which followed a sample of students from the summer before their first year in college through the first three semesters of college, about one-half of all high school romances ended, and those that did not end became much less satisfying when one of the partners began college. Males were far more likely than females to report feeling lonely and dissatisfied with their older relationships (Shaver, Furman, & Buhrmester, 1985).

THE IMPACT OF DATING ON ADOLESCENT DEVELOPMENT

■ **Pros and Cons of Dating**   Given the generally high level of superficiality in most adolescents' dating relationships, it comes as no surprise that early and intensive dating—for example, becoming seriously involved before age 15—has a somewhat stunting effect on psychosocial development (Neemann et al., 1995) and is associated with increased alcohol use, delinquency, and, not surprisingly, sexual activity (Davies & Windle, 2000). This is probably true for both sexes, but researchers have focused primarily on girls because boys are less likely to begin serious dating quite so early. Compared with their peers, girls who begin serious dating early are worse off psychologically than their peers—less mature socially, less imaginative, less oriented toward achievement, less happy with who they are and how they look, more depressed, and more superficial—findings that have been reported consistently for at least 40 years (Douvan & Adelson, 1966; Doyle, Brendgen, Markiewicz, & Kamkar, 2003; McDonald & McKinney, 1994; Neemann et al., 1995), although this seems to be more the case among white than nonwhite girls (Compian et al., 2004) and among girls whose family relationships are more strained (Doyle et al., 2003). (In one study, the most frequently mentioned negative aspect of romantic relationships was "too much commitment" [Feiring, 1996].) Adolescents who are unpopular with same-sex peers are especially harmed by early serious dating, perhaps because having few same-sex friends makes the dating relationships excessively important (Brendgen, Vitaro, Doyle, Markiewicz, & Bukowski, 2002). Interestingly, research also shows that adolescents who begin dating early and who have multiple dating partners experience a drop in the quality of their relationships over time (Collins, 2003).

The impact of dating on adolescent development depends on the age of the adolescent and the intensity of the relationship. Early, serious dating may have a negative impact on psychological development.

FOOD FOR THOUGHT

What would Erikson say is the role of dating in adolescent development? What would Sullivan say? Given the two theorists' arguments about the development of intimacy and the research on dating, which theorist do you agree with?

This is not to say that dating is not a valuable interpersonal experience for the adolescent, only that dating may have different effects in early adolescence than in middle and late adolescence (Neemann et al., 1995). Although early involvement in serious romance has its costs for girls, adolescents who do not date at all show signs of retarded social development, excessive dependency on their parents, and feelings of insecurity (Douvan & Adelson, 1966), while adolescents who date and go to parties regularly are more popular, have a stronger self-image, and report greater acceptance by their friends (Connolly & Johnson, 1993; Long, 1989; Tobin-Richards, 1985). Conversely, stopping or cutting back on dating after having dated heavily is associated with a drop in self-image and an increase in symptoms of depression (Davies & Windle, 2000).

It is not clear, of course, whether a moderate degree of dating leads to higher levels of social development or whether more socially advanced adolescents are simply more likely to date and go to parties; both are probably true. And research shows that psychological problems both lead to and result from overinvolvement in dating (Zimmer-Gembeck, Siebenbrunner, & Collins, 2001). Nonetheless, it does seem that for girls in particular, early and intensive involvement with a boyfriend may do more harm than good. All in all, a moderate degree of dating—and a delay in serious involvement until age 15 or so—appears to be the most potentially valuable pattern. Perhaps adolescents need more time to develop the capacity to be intimate through same-sex friendships and less pressured group activities before they enter intensively into the more highly ritualized but less intimate relationships that are encouraged through dating.

Regardless of the impact that dating does or doesn't have on adolescents' psychosocial development, studies show that romance has a powerful impact on their emotional state. According to several studies, adolescents' real and fantasized relationships trigger more of their strong emotional feelings during the course of a day (one-third of girls' strong feelings and one-quarter of boys') than do family, school, or friends. Not surprisingly, the proportion of strong emotions attributed to romantic relationships increases dramatically between preadolescence and early adolescence, and between early and middle adolescence as well. And although the majority of adolescents' feelings about their romantic relationships are positive, a substantial minority of their feelings—more than 40 percent, in fact—are negative, involving anxiety, anger, jealousy, and depression (Larson, Clore, & Wood, 1999). Consistent with this, adolescents who have entered into a romantic relationship in the past year report more symptoms of depression than do those who have not (Joyner & Udry, 2000). One reason for this may be that many adolescents who are involved romantically also experience breakups during the same time period (Collins, 2003), and the breakup of a romantic relationship is the single most common trigger of the first episode of major depression (Monroe, Rohde, Seeley, & Lewinsohn, 1999).

■ **Violence in Dating Relationships** Unfortunately many romantic relationships in adolescence are characterized by hostility, aggression, and abuse (Brown, 2004), and dating violence becomes more common with age (Halpern, Oslak, Young, Martin, & Kupper, 2001). Estimates vary from study to study, but between one-fifth and two-thirds of American adolescents may have been the victim of violence within the context of a romantic relationship at one time or another (Feiring, Deblinger, Hoch-Espada, & Haworth, 2002; Gorman-Smith, Tolan, Sheidow, & Henry, 2001; Linder & Collins, 2005; Silverman, Raj, Mucci, & Hathaway, 2001). (One reason for the wide range of estimates is that studies vary considerably in how violence is defined—for example, some may include threats of violence while others may be limited to violence that actually causes physical harm.) Male and female adolescents are equally likely to be the victims of violence in dating relationships (Halpern et al., 2001; Miller & White, 2003), and violence is often associated with drinking (Buzy et al., 2004). Dating violence is more common in rural areas than in suburban or urban communities (Spencer & Bryant, 2000), and is common among both sexual-minority adolescents and heterosexual youth (Freedner, Freed, Yang, & Austin, 2002; Halpern, Young, Waler, Martin, & Kupper, 2004). Adolescents who have been the victims of violence within the context of a romantic relationship are more likely to be depressed, contemplate suicide, use illegal drugs, become pregnant during adolescence, and drop out of school (Hagan & Foster, 2001; Hyoun & Capaldi, 2004; Silverman et al., 2001). They are also more likely to be victimized again in the future (Smith, White, & Holland, 2003).

We also know that adolescents behave in a variety of ways within dating relationships that are shaped by "scripts" for how males and females are expected to behave—scripts that are learned at home and from the mass media (Feiring, 1999; Gray & Steinberg, 1999; Larson, Clore, & Wood, 1999). In general, adolescents' ways of dealing with conflict in their romantic relationships are linked to the models they had been exposed to at home. For example, adolescents who have witnessed a great deal of conflict between their parents report higher levels of verbal aggression, physical aggression, and relationship difficulties with their romantic partners (Kinsfogel & Grych, 2004; Martin, 1990). Other studies have found that adolescents who are either perpetrators or victims of violence in dating relationships are more likely to have had parents who were harsh or behaved inappropriately toward them (Lavoie et al., 2002; Linder & Collins, 2005). These studies, along with those discussed earlier about adolescent attachments, suggest that variations in adolescents' romantic relationships may have their origins—at least in part—in adolescents' family experiences.

The main point to keep in mind is that the qualities of adolescents' relationships with others—whether with parents, siblings, friends, or romantic partners—are correlated across different types of relationships (Brown, 2004). Adolescents who have supportive and satisfying relationships at home are more likely to have high-quality friendships, and adolescents who have high-quality friendships are more likely to have high-quality romantic relationships. Thus, individuals' early experiences in the family, in interaction with their cumulative experiences with peers during childhood and preadolescence, affect the nature and quality of their romantic relationships in adolescence (Brown, 2004; Collins, 2003; Collins & Sroufe, 1999), and the quality of adolescents' family relationships affect the quality of the romantic relationships they have in young adulthood (Conger, Cui, Bryant, & Elder, 2000; Donnellan, Larsen-Rife, & Conger, 2005).

RECAP

- In general, social activities with the opposite sex begin in early adolescence as group activities that bring males and females together, proceed to casual dating in couples, and later in adolescence progress to serious involvement with a steady romantic partner.
- Paralleling these changes in the context of dating are changes in the nature and function of dating. As adolescents develop, dating shifts from being based on infatuation to being oriented toward status, intimacy, and, finally, bonding.
- Although early intense dating appears to have adverse effects on adolescents' mental health and behavior, a moderate degree of dating without any serious involvement after age 15 or so is associated with better mental health and well-being than no dating at all.
- Adolescents who have supportive and satisfying relationships at home are more likely to have high-quality friendships, and adolescents who have high-quality friendships are more likely to have high-quality romantic relationships.

Intimacy and Psychosocial Development

Intimate relationships during adolescence, whether with peers or adults, inside or outside the family, or sexual or nonsexual, play an important role in young people's overall psychological development (Hartup, 1993; Hartup & Stevens, 1997). Close friends serve as a sounding board for adolescents' fantasies and questions about the future. Adolescents often talk to their friends about the careers they hope to have, the people they hope to get involved with, and the life they expect to lead after they leave home. Friends provide advice on a range of identity-related matters—from how to act in different situations to what sorts of occupational and educational paths to pursue. At least one study finds that having an intimate friendship is more central to adolescents' mental health than it is to children's (Buhrmester, 1990). It also has been found that intimacy with same-sex friends and intimacy with romantic partners make distinct contributions to adolescents' self-esteem (Connolly & Konarski, 1994). Not surprisingly, adolescents who report having at least one close friendship also report higher levels of self-esteem than their peers who do not, although we do not know whether intimacy enhances mental health, mental health facilitates intimacy, or, most likely, both (Brown, 2004).

FOOD FOR THOUGHT

Do you think changes in family life—divorce, remarriage, parental employment, and so on—have affected the nature of the development of intimacy in adolescence?

These positive aspects of close relationships notwithstanding, it is important to note that intimate relationships can have negative as well as beneficial effects on a young person's development. According to one theorist, frequent conversations with friends about personal problems and difficulties may lead to too much introspection and self-consciousness in the young person (Mechanic, 1983). Adolescent friendships may be beneficial precisely because they are not like those envisioned by Sullivan and because they involve young people in exciting activities that distract them from being preoccupied with themselves (Savin-Williams & Berndt, 1990). As noted earlier, "corumination" between friends often makes them feel depressed (Rose, 2002).

Also keep in mind that the effects of having an intimate friendship with someone depend on who that someone is and what takes place in the relationship. Being popular is less important than genuinely having friends, and having friends is less important than having *good* friendships (Asher et al., 1996; Berndt, 1996; Hartup & Stevens, 1997; Hussong, 2000; Keefe & Berndt, 1996). Not all friendships are consistently good friendships, however; friendships often provide for positive things like self-disclosure, intimacy, and companionship, but they also may give rise to insecurity, conflict, jealousy, and mistrust (Parker, Low, Walker, & Gamm, 2005; Rubin, 1980). And, as we saw in Chapter 5, adolescents who are close to peers or romantic partners who have antisocial values or habits

are themselves more likely to develop similar patterns of behavior (Haynie, Giordano, Manning, & Longmore, 2005; Hussong & Hicks, 2003). It is easy to forget, but it goes without saying, that not all close relationships foster positive developmental outcomes.

Nevertheless, studies consistently show that individuals with satisfying close friendships fare better than those without them, not only in adolescence but in adulthood as well. Adolescence is an especially important time in the development of close relationships because many of the capacities and capabilities that permit intimacy in adult relationships make their debut in adolescence.

RECAP

- Adolescents who have intimate friendships typically have better mental health than their peers who do not, although we do not know which comes first, intimacy or psychological health.
- Experts agree that close peer relationships are an essential part of healthy social development during adolescence.
- Being popular is less important than genuinely having friends, and having friends is less important than having good friendships.

CHAPTER 11

Sexuality

SEXUALITY AS AN ADOLESCENT ISSUE

HOW SEXUALLY PERMISSIVE IS CONTEMPORARY SOCIETY?
　　Sexual Socialization in Restrictive Societies
　　Sexual Socialization in Semirestrictive Societies
　　Sexual Socialization in Permissive Societies

SEXUAL ACTIVITY DURING ADOLESCENCE
　　Stages of Sexual Activity
　　Sexual Intercourse During Adolescence
　　Changes in Sexual Activity over Time

THE SEXUALLY ACTIVE ADOLESCENT
　　Psychological and Social Characteristics of Sexually Active Adolescents
　　Hormonal and Contextual Influences on Sexual Activity
　　Parental and Peer Influences on Sexual Activity
　　Sex Differences in the Meaning of Sex
　　Homosexuality During Adolescence
　　Sexual Harassment, Rape, and Sexual Abuse During Adolescence
　　Contraceptive Use
　　AIDS and Other Sexually Transmitted Diseases

TEENAGE PREGNANCY AND CHILDBEARING
　　The Nature and Extent of the Problem
　　Causes and Correlates of Teen Pregnancy
　　The Role of the Father
　　Consequences for Mother and Child
　　Teenage Pregnancy Prevention and Intervention Programs

HAVE TEENAGERS' ATTITUDES toward sex changed in recent decades? Should society be worried about sexual activity among young adolescents, or is teenage sex no more troublesome than many of the other adultlike activities that young people engage in? Does sex education prevent unwanted pregnancies, or does it encourage young people to begin sexual activity earlier? Should adolescents have access to contraceptives, and if so, should their parents be told? Have adolescents changed their sexual behavior in response to the threat of AIDS?

In this chapter, we examine adolescent sexuality in contemporary society with an eye toward dedramatizing and demystifying an aspect of adolescent behavior that has received a great deal more media attention than systematic research investigation. In order to present a more accurate picture of adolescent sexuality, we need to step back and look at sexual behavior and development during adolescence in context—in the context of society and how it has changed, and in the context of adolescence as a period in the life cycle and how it has changed.

Sexuality as an Adolescent Issue

Like other aspects of psychosocial development, sexuality is not an entirely new issue that surfaces for the first time during adolescence. Young children are curious about their sex organs, and at a very early age derive pleasure (if not what adults would label orgasm) from genital stimulation—as both Sigmund Freud and the famous sex researcher Alfred Kinsey pointed out long ago (Kinsey, Pomeroy, & Martin, 1948). And, of course, sexual activity and sexual development continue long after adolescence. Although sexual development may be more dramatic and more obvious prior to adulthood, it by no means ceases at the end of adolescence. Nonetheless, most of us would agree that adolescence is a fundamentally important time—if not the most important time in the life cycle—for the development of sexuality. There are several reasons for this.

■ **Puberty and Adolescent Sexuality**   Perhaps most obvious is the link between adolescent sexuality and puberty (Savin-Williams & Diamond, 2004; Susman & Rogol, 2004). There is a substantial increase in the sex drive in early adolescence that is clearly the result of hormonal changes. Moreover, it is not until puberty that individuals become capable of sexual reproduction. Before puberty, children are certainly capable of kissing, petting, masturbating, and even having sexual intercourse, and erotic feelings are reported by individuals prior to adolescence (Herdt & McClintock, 2000; McClintock & Herdt, 1996). But it is not until puberty that males can ejaculate semen or that females begin to ovulate, and the fact that pregnancy is a possible outcome of sexual activity changes the nature and meaning of sexual behavior markedly—for the adolescent and for others. What had previously been

innocuous sex play becomes serious business when pregnancy is a genuine possibility. Finally, as we saw in Chapter 1, not until puberty do individuals develop the secondary sex characteristics that serve as a basis for sexual attraction and as dramatic indicators that the young person is no longer physically a child.

■ **Cognitive Change and Adolescent Sexuality** The increased importance of sexuality at adolescence is not solely a result of puberty. The cognitive changes of adolescence play a part in the changed nature of sexuality as well. One obvious difference between the sex play of children and the sexual activity of adolescents is that children are not especially introspective or reflective about sexual behavior. In contrast, sex during adolescence is the subject of sometimes painful conjecture ("Will she or won't she?"), decision making ("Should I or shouldn't I?"), hypothetical thinking ("What if he wants to do it tonight?"), and self-conscious concern ("Am I good-looking enough?"). As we saw in Chapter 10, one of the chief tasks of adolescence is to figure out how to deal with sexual desires and how to incorporate sex successfully and appropriately into social relationships. Much of this task is cognitive in nature, and much of it is made possible by the expansion of intellectual abilities that takes place during the period.

■ **Social Roles and Adolescent Sexuality**   In addition to how the physical changes of puberty and the growth of sophisticated thinking capabilities influence sexuality during adolescence, the new social meaning given to sexual and dating behavior at this time in the life cycle makes sexuality an especially important psychosocial concern. For example, you may have played "doctor" with your friends when you were a little child, but—as you well know—the game meant something quite different then from what it would if you were to play it now. Although younger children may engage in sex play, and although even infants may experience sexual arousal, it is not until adolescence that sexual activity begins to take on the social meaning it will continue to have throughout adulthood. Adolescence is a turning point in the development of sexuality because it marks the onset of deliberate sexually motivated behavior that is recognized, both by oneself and by others, as primarily and explicitly sexual in nature. As noted in Chapter 1, research indicates that most individuals report having their first feelings of genuine sexual attraction around age 10—the beginning of the adolescent decade.

Healthy Sexual Development   In recent years, researchers interested in adolescent sexuality have moved away from viewing sex as a problematic aspect of adolescence and become increasingly interested in understanding the factors that lead to healthy sexual development. According to two experts, there are four distinct developmental challenges concerning sexuality in adolescence (Brooks-Gunn & Paikoff, 1993). First, the adolescent needs to come to feel comfortable with his or her maturing body—its shape, size, and attractiveness. Second, the adolescent should accept having feelings of sexual arousal as normal and appropriate. Third, the adolescent needs to feel comfortable about choosing to engage in—or not to engage in—various sexual activities; that is, healthy sexual development involves understanding that sex is a *voluntary* activity for oneself and for one's partner. Finally, the adolescent (at least, the one who is sexually active) must understand and practice safe sex—sex that avoids pregnancy and sexually transmitted infections.

FOOD FOR THOUGHT

What role, if any, should school-based sex education play in the promotion of healthy sexuality? Should the focus of sex education be on preventing sexual activity during adolescence or on promoting positive sexual development?

RECAP

- Adolescence is a fundamentally important time in the life cycle for the development of sexuality.
- The physical and hormonal changes of puberty increase sex drive, change the adolescent's appearance, and permit reproduction, all of which affect the development of sexuality.
- The cognitive changes of adolescence result in the increased capacity of the individual to understand and think about sexual feelings.

- The transition of the individual into new social roles gives new meaning to sexual behavior in the eyes of individuals, society, and social institutions.
- Four developmental challenges of adolescence are accepting one's changing body, accepting one's feelings of sexual arousal, understanding that sexual activity is voluntary, and practicing safe sex.

How Sexually Permissive Is Contemporary Society?

It is impossible to understand sexuality as a psychosocial phenomenon without taking into account the social milieu in which adolescents learn about and first experience sexuality. Although we tend to think of sex as something that adolescents are inevitably anxious or concerned about, it is no more true to suggest that sexuality is always riddled with problems during adolescence than it is to say that all adolescents have problems in establishing a sense of identity or in developing a sense of autonomy. Like any other aspect of psychosocial growth, the development of sexuality is determined largely by its context. Of particular importance is the way in which adolescents and children are exposed to and educated about sexuality—a process called **sexual socialization.**

When did you first learn about sex? How much were you exposed to as a child? Was it something that was treated casually around your house, or was there an air of mystery to it? Was your transition into adult sexual activity gradual or abrupt?

As you know from previous chapters, the passage of adolescents into adulthood is believed to be easier and less stressful when the transition between the two life stages is gradual, or continuous (Benedict, 1934). One aspect of the adolescent passage that anthropologists have examined extensively from this perspective is the transition of young people into adult sexual roles. In *Patterns of Culture* (1934), Ruth Benedict observed that anxiety about sex—which was thought to be common among teenagers—was absent in many traditional cultures. Margaret Mead's observations of young people in Samoa and New Guinea (1928/1978) provided evidence that sexual development during adolescence is smooth and nonstressful in societies in which sexual experimentation is treated openly and casually during

sexual socialization   The process through which adolescents are exposed to and educated about sexuality.

In restrictive societies, sexual activity before marriage is explicitly discouraged.

childhood, and in which special attention is not drawn to adolescents' changed sexual status.

Think about some of the things you learned gradually and casually as a child—learning your way around the kitchen, for example—and imagine how different things might have been had this process been handled the way most families handle sexual socialization. Suppose that, early in your childhood, your parents treated cooking food as though the activity had special, mysterious significance. Suppose that you were never permitted to see anyone actually cooking food, that you were prohibited from seeing TV shows and movies in which people cooked food, and that you were excluded from any discussions of cooking. Nevertheless, imagine that you knew that *something* went on in the kitchen—some special activity adults engaged in, one that you would be permitted, even expected, to perform when you grew up. Perhaps you even overheard other kids at school talking about cooking, but you still weren't sure just what the activity was or what one was supposed to do (or not do). Imagine how confused, ambivalent, and anxious you would feel.

In some respects, this is how many families in contemporary society handle sexual socialization. By

restrictive societies   Societies in which adolescents are pressured to refrain from sexual activity until they have married or undergone a formal rite of passage into adulthood.

semirestrictive societies   Societies in which pressures against adolescent sexual activity exist but are not vigilantly enforced.

being so secretive about sex when children are young and so worried about it when they are adolescents, Mead and Benedict argued, contemporary societies may have turned sexuality into a problem for young people.

Mead's and Benedict's observations of sexual socialization in traditional societies also indicated that cultures vary considerably in the ways in which they handle the sexual development of children and adolescents. Their observations were further borne out in Clellon Ford and Frank Beach's *Patterns of Sexual Behavior* (1951), perhaps the most extensive study ever done of sex in different cultures. In this enormous undertaking, the authors catalogued the sexual socialization and activity of children and adolescents in over 200 societies. Drawing on hundreds of studies undertaken by cultural anthropologists over the years, Ford and Beach categorized societies into three groups: restrictive, semirestrictive, and permissive.

SEXUAL SOCIALIZATION IN RESTRICTIVE SOCIETIES

In **restrictive societies,** the adolescent's transition into adult sexual activity is highly discontinuous. Pressure is exerted on youngsters to refrain from sexual activity until they either have undergone a formal rite of passage into adulthood or have married. In many restrictive societies, adolescents pursue sex in secrecy. Within the broad category of restrictive societies, of course, there are wide variations in the degree of restrictiveness and in the methods used to discourage sexual activity before marriage. For example, in some societies, the sexual activity of young people is controlled by separating the sexes throughout childhood and adolescence. Boys and girls are not permitted to play together, and they never associate with each other before marriage in the absence of chaperons. In other societies, sexual activity before the attainment of adult status is restricted through the physical punishment and public shaming of sexually active youngsters (Ford & Beach, 1951).

SEXUAL SOCIALIZATION IN SEMIRESTRICTIVE SOCIETIES

In **semirestrictive societies,** adults frown upon sexual activity among adolescents but do not consistently enforce prohibitions against it. For example, sexual activity among youngsters may be formally prohibited, but children playing together may imitate the sexual behavior of their elders, and unless this play is brought explicitly to the attention of adults, little is done about it. In other semirestrictive societies, "Premarital promiscuity is common, and the parents do not object as long as the love affairs are kept secret" (Ford & Beach, 1951, p. 187). It is premarital pregnancy, rather than premarital sex, that is objectionable, and unmarried adolescents whose sexual activity has resulted in pregnancy are often forced to marry.

We are frequently told that contemporary America is excessively permissive when it comes to sex, but by world standards, the sexual socialization of children and adolescents in contemporary America is semirestrictive. For the most part, for American children, masturbation, sexual exploration, and explicit sex play are frowned upon. Adults rarely mention sexual matters in the presence of children, and there are even regulations prohibiting children from being exposed to sexual activity on television or in the movies. Adults openly try to discourage young people—especially young women—from becoming sexually active by lecturing to them about the virtues of virginity, by not openly discussing matters of sex and pregnancy, and by making it difficult for young people to obtain contraception. At the same time, however, adolescent boys and girls are not typically segregated, and they usually date without chaperons present. In fact, adolescents are *encouraged* to date, even though adults know that dating provides a context for sexual activity. Adults are well aware that young people are sexually active, but for the most part, they prefer to look the other way rather than restrict adolescents' activities.

SEXUAL SOCIALIZATION IN PERMISSIVE SOCIETIES

In **permissive societies,** the transition of young people into adult sexual activity is highly continuous and usually begins in childhood. Although religious conservatives bemoan the lack of morals among the young in contemporary society, by no stretch of the imagination is America a sexually permissive culture—at least in comparison with many of the cultures described by Ford and Beach. Consider, for example, these descriptions of sexual socialization in some of the societies they categorized as permissive:

> Among the Pukapukans of Polynesia, where parents simply ignore the sexual activities of young children, boys and girls masturbate freely and openly in public.

> Lesu children playing on the beach give imitations of adult sexual intercourse, and adults in this society regard this to be a natural and normal game.

> Young Trobriand children engage in a variety of sexual activities. In the absence of adult control, typical forms of amusement for Trobriand girls and boys include manual and oral stimulation of the genitals and simulated coitus. Sexual life begins in earnest among the Trobrianders at six to eight years for girls, ten to twelve for boys. Both sexes receive explicit instruction from older companions whom they imitate in sex activities. . . . At any time a couple may retire to the bush, the bachelor's hut, an isolated yam house, or any other convenient place and there engage in prolonged sexual play with full approval of their parents. (Ford & Beach, 1951, pp. 188–191)

FOOD FOR THOUGHT

Just as we can categorize societies as restrictive, semirestrictive, or permissive when it comes to sexual socialization, we can also sort families and communities into these same categories. In light of what you've read, how would you characterize the context in which you grew up?

RECAP

- Although many people think of contemporary industrialized society as being sexually permissive, there are plenty of societies around the world that are far more lenient about sex.
- By most indications, Americans' attitudes toward adolescent sex are neither restrictive nor permissive—but semirestrictive.

Sexual Activity During Adolescence

American adolescents' attitudes toward sex—and premarital sex in particular—became more liberal during the late 1960s and 1970s, and have become only slightly more conservative since then (Chilman, 1986; UCLA Higher Education Research Institute, 1999, 2000). Although most contemporary adolescents are accepting of premarital intercourse (and most engage in it), few are proponents of "free love" or casual sex (Alan Guttmacher Institute, 1994). Surveys indicate

---

permissive societies　Societies in which sexual activity during childhood and adolescence is not greatly restrained.

Far more adolescents are sexually active at an early age today than was the case several decades ago. Sexual intercourse during high school is now part of the normative adolescent experience in contemporary America.

that the majority of American (and European) adolescents believe that openness, honesty, and fidelity are important elements of a sexual relationship (Alan Guttmacher Institute, 1994; Arnett, 2002). Although an adolescent may have a series of sexual partners over a period of time, he or she is likely to be monogamous within each relationship, a pattern known as **serial monogamy.** It is important to keep in mind, however, that adolescents as a group are as varied in their attitudes toward sex as adults are (Katchadourian, 1990).

Because of the controversies surrounding premarital intercourse, most of the research conducted into the sexual behavior of adolescents has focused on this single activity (Savin-Williams & Diamond, 2004). Although this is undoubtedly an important topic, it is also wise to remember that a good deal of the sexual activity of adolescents—even sexually experienced adolescents—involves activities other than sexual intercourse, such as kissing and touching parts of each other's body. Moreover, because most individuals do not begin their sexual experiences with intercourse

serial monogamy   Having a series of sexual relationships over time in which one is monogamous within each relationship.

autoerotic behavior   Sexual behavior that is experienced alone, such as masturbation or sexual fantasizing.

nocturnal orgasms   In males, ejaculations that occur while they are asleep, sometimes referred to as "wet dreams."

but progress toward it through stages of gradually increasing intimacy, it is important to view intercourse as one activity in a long progression, rather than as an isolated behavior (Brooks-Gunn & Paikoff, 1993).

STAGES OF SEXUAL ACTIVITY

Most adolescents' first experience with sex falls into the category of **autoerotic behavior**—sexual behavior that is experienced alone (Katchadourian, 1990). The most common autoerotic activities reported by adolescents are having erotic fantasies (about three-quarters of all teenagers report having sexual fantasies, mainly about TV or movie stars) and masturbation (different surveys yield different estimates, depending on the age of the respondents and the wording of the questions, but about half of all adolescent boys and about one-fourth of all adolescent girls masturbate prior to age 18) (Savin-Williams & Diamond, 2004). In addition, many boys have wet dreams, or **nocturnal orgasms,** during adolescence, although they generally are infrequent (Katchadourian, 1990).

By the time most adolescents reach high school, they have made the transition from autoerotic behavior to sexual activity that involves another person. Interestingly, the developmental progression of sexual behaviors, from less intimate to more intimate, has not changed very much over the past 50 years, and the sequence in which males and females engage in various sexual activities is remarkably similar. According to a recent, large-scale, nationwide study of American adolescents, holding hands comes first, followed (in this order) by kissing, necking (kissing for a long time), feeling breasts through clothes, feeling breasts under clothes, feeling a penis through clothes, feeling a penis under clothes or while naked, feeling a vagina through clothes, feeling a vagina under clothes or while naked, and intercourse or oral sex. Some studies find that adolescents' first experience with oral sex generally precedes their first experience with intercourse, whereas others find the reverse (Savin-Williams & Diamond, 2004).

Some evidence suggests that the sequence of sexual activity described above is more common among white adolescents than among African Americans (Smith & Udry, 1985). White adolescents are likely to follow this predictable pattern, and so to take longer to move toward intercourse. African Americans, in contrast, are more likely to move toward intercourse at an earlier age and without as many intervening steps (Brewster, 1994). This difference has an important implication for our understanding of adolescent pregnancy. Virtually all adolescents who are virgins find themselves unprepared for contraception when they first begin touching their partner's genitals, but the more gradual progression of sexual activity among whites is less likely to be accompanied by this lack of preparation than is the case among African Americans. In other words, faster progression of sexual activity may place young African American adolescents at greater risk for pregnancy. It is also the case that the expected timetable for progressive sexual activities is faster among adolescents who expect a relatively faster timetable for achieving autonomy from parents and experimenting with drugs and alcohol, suggesting that earlier involvement in sex may be part of a larger pattern of earlier involvement in "adult" activities (Rosenthal & Smith, 1997).

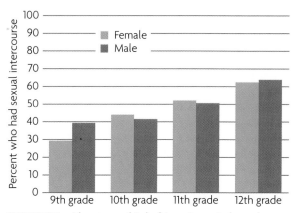

FIGURE 11.1   About one-third of American ninth-graders have had sexual intercourse. By senior year, about two-thirds have. (Centers for Disease Control and Prevention, 2006)

SEXUAL INTERCOURSE DURING ADOLESCENCE

▌ **Prevalence of Sexual Intercourse** Estimates of the prevalence of sexual intercourse among contemporary adolescents vary from study to study, depending on the nature of the sample surveyed, the year and region in which the study was undertaken, and the reliability of the data gathered (Santelli, Lindberg, Abma, McNeely, & Resnick, 2000). Some studies suggest that adolescents do not always report their sexual activity honestly or accurately, with males tending to overstate their level of activity and females tending to understate it (Alexander, Somerfield, Ensminger, Johnson, & Kim, 1993; Newcomer & Udry, 1988). The following paragraphs summarize what social scientists have concluded from recent surveys with these caveats in mind.

Although regional and ethnic variations make it difficult—if not misleading—to generalize about the average age at which American adolescents initiate sexual intercourse, national surveys indicate that more adolescents are sexually active at an earlier age today than several decades ago, although there has been a slight decrease in the proportion of sexually experienced teenagers since the mid-1990s—in other words, slightly fewer adolescents are having sexual intercourse, but those who are do so at a somewhat earlier age (Santelli et al., 2000; Singh & Darroch, 1999; Sonenstein, Ku, Lindberg, Turner, & Pleck, 1998). The best estimates we have are that, by the end of their sophomore year in high school, more than 40 percent of American adolescents have had heterosexual vaginal intercourse (that is, these estimates, which are based on large national surveys, do not include same-sex intercourse or other types of sex, like oral or anal sex). By age 18, this number has risen to about two-thirds (see Figure 11.1) (Centers for Disease Control and Prevention, 2006). Whatever we

might think about these figures, one conclusion is inescapable: Sexual intercourse during high school is now a part of the normative experience of adolescence in America.

▌ **Ethnic Differences in Age of Sexual Initiation** There are substantial ethnic differences in age of sexual initiation, especially among males (Warren et al., 1998). Among African American males, the average age of first intercourse is 15; among white and Hispanic American males, it is 16.5; and among Asian American males, it is 18 (Upchurch, Levy-Storms, Sucoff, & Aneshensel, 1998). Ethnic differences in the age of sexual initiation are far smaller among females, although Hispanic American and Asian American females generally have their first sexual intercourse at a later age than is the case among their African American and white counterparts (Grunbaum, Lowry, Kann, & Pateman, 2000). One reason for the relatively high rate of early sexual activity among African American males is the higher proportion of African American youth who grow up in single-parent homes and in poor neighborhoods, both of which, as you will read later in this chapter, are risk factors for early sexual activity (Brewster, 1994; Lauritsen, 1994). In general, Mexican American youngsters who were born in Mexico are less likely to be sexually active at an early age than Mexican Americans who are American-born, reflecting differences in norms between the two countries (Aneshensel, Becerra, Fielder, & Schuler, 1990). Consistent with this, Americanized Latino adolescents are more likely than their less acculturated peers to have sex at a younger age, to have multiple sex partners, and to become pregnant (Kaplan, Erickson, & Juarez-Reyes, 2002; Upchurch, Aneshensel, Mudgal, & McNeely, 2001).

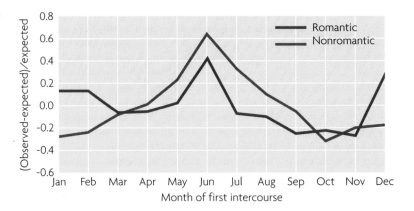

FIGURE 11.2   Adolescents are most likely to have intercourse for the first time during early summer or in December. (Levin et al., 2002)

FOOD FOR THOUGHT

Today's teenagers are growing up within a context in which sexual intercourse before high school graduation is considered normative in many segments of society. Has this changed the nature of adolescence in any profound ways? How do you think adolescence might have been different in an era in which only a minority of high school students were sexually active?

Studies also indicate that, among all ethnic groups, rates of sexual activity are higher among economically disadvantaged youth, although the gap in rates of sexual activity between rich and poor is substantially narrower now than it was a decade ago, again pointing to the increasingly normative nature of sexual intercourse among American teenagers (Singh & Darroch, 1999). Interestingly, early sexual activity is more common among African American youth attending all–African American schools than among their peers in integrated schools (Furstenberg, Morgan, & Allison, 1987), indicating the importance of the social context in which teenagers live as an influence on their sexual behavior.

It is important to note that for many girls—by some estimates, nearly 30 percent—their first sexual experience is not voluntary (Houts, 2005). Involuntary sex is especially frequent among girls who have sex for the first time when they are 13 or younger; one-fourth of younger adolescents report that their first intercourse was against their will, in contrast to 10 percent of women whose first intercourse was after age 18. Moreover, many other young women who report that they had sex voluntarily the first time nevertheless report that they did not really *want* to have sex. Young

girls whose first partner was seven or more years older were twice as likely as others to report having had voluntary but unwanted intercourse (Abma, Driscoll, & Moore, 1998). Young adolescents with a significantly older romantic partner are far more likely to have sexual intercourse than those whose boyfriend is the same age (Kaestle, Morisky, & Wiley, 2002; Leitenberg & Saltzman, 2000).

▌ **Timing of Sexual Initiation**   Adolescents are more likely to lose their virginity during certain times of the year than during others. There are two seasonal peaks in the timing of first intercourse: June and December (Levin, Xu, & Bartkowski, 2002) (see Figure 11.2). June (and to a lesser extent, May and July) are common months for first intercourse regardless of whether the adolescents were romantically involved; December, however, is a peak time only among adolescents who are with a serious boyfriend or girlfriend, and particularly so among girls. Several explanations for these seasonal trends have been offered, including the general tendency for people to be more sexually active when the weather is very hot or very cold, and the fact that adolescents have more unsupervised time when they are on summer or winter vacation. As for what has been called "the holiday effect" (the rise in sexual debuts among romantic partners in December)—well, perhaps you can figure that out for yourself.

CHANGES IN SEXUAL ACTIVITY OVER TIME

We noted earlier that attitudes toward premarital intercourse during adolescence became more liberal beginning in the mid-1960s and, especially, during the early 1970s. Not surprisingly, accompanying this shift in attitudes was an equally noteworthy shift in sexual behavior (Alan Guttmacher Institute, 1994).

Recent Historical Trends Three trends are of special interest. First, the overall percentage of American adolescents who had engaged in premarital sex accelerated markedly during the early 1970s and again during the late 1980s, and then declined between 1995 and 2001, especially among African American youth (see Figure 11.3) (Centers for Disease Control and Prevention, 2006; Hayes, 1987; Miller, Forehand, & Kotchick, 1999; Santelli et al., 2000, 2004; Savin-Williams & Diamond, 2004). Interestingly, the recent decline in the proportion of adolescents who have had sexual intercourse is not paralleled by a decline in the proportion of adolescents who are having other types of sex—in fact, today's teenagers are far more "active" sexually than were previous generations (Savin-Williams & Diamond, 2004). It is likely that the threat of AIDS and other sexually transmitted diseases (STDs) has led many adolescents to substitute a safer type of sex (such as oral sex) for intercourse.

Second, the proportion of individuals who have sexual intercourse *early* in adolescence is substantial. Although the median age at which adolescents first engage in intercourse has remained somewhere between 16 and 17, today, one-third of all contemporary American adolescents have had intercourse by the time they are ninth-graders, and more than 6 percent have had intercourse by age 13 (Blum & Rinehart, 2000; Centers for Disease Control and Prevention, 2006; Santelli et al., 2000). Among adolescents who have not had sex, fears of pregnancy and disease (including HIV/AIDS) are the most common reasons for abstaining (Blinn-Pike, 1999; Loewensen, Ireland, & Resnick, 2004). As we'll see later, these figures on sexual activity among younger adolescents are noteworthy, because the younger individuals are when they have sex, the more likely they are to have unprotected sex, exposing themselves to the risks of pregnancy and STDs (Dittus, Jaccard, & Gordon, 1997; Kaestle, Halpern, Miller, & Ford, 2005; O'Donnell, O'Donnell, & Stueve, 2001). The fact that a large number of adolescents are sexually active before high school is also an important factor in discussions of sex education, because programs that do not begin until students' later years of high school are probably too late for a substantial number of young people.

Finally, the greatest increase in the prevalence of intercourse among adolescents, and the greatest decline in the age at first intercourse, has been among females (Savin-Williams & Diamond, 2004). Before 1965, there were substantial gaps between the proportions of sexually active boys and girls. Since about 1965, the proportion of sexually experienced high school males has nearly tripled, but the proportion of sexually experienced high school females is about *five* times higher today. Sex differences in rates of sexual intercourse today are negligible (Centers for Disease Control and Prevention, 2006).

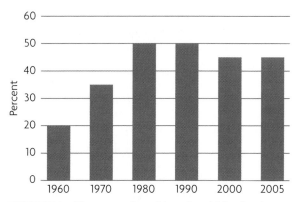

FIGURE 11.3   The proportion of American high school students who had sexual intercourse rose substantially between 1960 and 1980, but declined between 1990 and 2000. It has remained stable since then.

The bottom line: Whether adults approve or not, sexual activity has become a normative part of the American teenager's life. And while many parents, educators, and other adults are alarmed by sexual activity among the young, for most adolescents, sexual involvement is accompanied by affection, emotional involvement, and commitment to a relationship. Although many high school students are sexually active on a regular basis, promiscuity is not the norm (Singh & Darroch, 1999). According to recent data, 80 percent of sexually active high school girls, and 67 percent of sexually active high school boys, had intercourse with only one partner during the past three months, and the proportion of adolescents who have had multiple sex partners has decreased substantially over the past decade, although it is still substantial today—14 percent of high school students have had intercourse with four or more persons (Centers for Disease Control and Prevention, 2006; Santelli et al., 2000). In addition, about one-third of sexually active adolescents have had intercourse with someone they describe as a nonromantic partner—so-called friends with benefits (Manning, Longmore, & Giordano, 2005).

Sex and Alcohol One particular cause for concern is that the percentage of adolescents who use alcohol or other drugs prior to having sex has increased in recent years—in one national survey, about one-fourth of American adolescents said they drank or used drugs before the last time they had sex (Centers for Disease Control and Prevention, 2006). Not surprisingly, sexual risk taking is more likely when alcohol is involved, mainly because of impaired judgment and loss of control. One study of British adolescents found that one-fourth of those interviewed reported having been so drunk during sex that they did not even remember it (a phenomenon that by no means is limited to teenagers in England), as these two 16-year-olds (the first male, the second female) describe:

> I've actually woken up next to a girl and I didn't have a clue who she was. And when I woke up I was like, "What's your name? Like, Who were you?" She explained herself, I couldn't remember it, man. I was thinking, "How the hell couldn't I remember that?" . . . I don't remember.

> I've had previous problems with alcohol where I've been so drunk that I can't actually remember things that have happened and the next morning, or the next couple of weeks, I get told about things and then it [having sex with someone] suddenly comes back and I think, oh my God, what have I done? (Coleman & Cater, 2005, p. 656)

Although it is interesting to speculate on the causes of these changes in adolescents' sexual behavior—the increased availability of contraception, the overall liberalization of social attitudes, and the earlier age of puberty have all been suggested—the more pressing issue is how society ought to react to the changed nature of sex during adolescence. Sexual intercourse during adolescence is not limited to males, to minority youngsters, or to individuals with emotional problems. It is a part of life for the *average* teenager. Many experts contend that the longer we ignore this—by failing to provide adequate sex education, by limiting the accessibility of effective contraception methods, and by not dealing with the issue squarely—the more difficulties society in general, and young people in particular, will face.

RECAP

- Important changes in attitudes toward adolescent premarital sex occurred during the 1970s and have persisted since that time. Most teenagers today believe that it is acceptable to have intercourse before marriage as long as it takes place within the context of a loving, intimate relationship.
- Sexual intercourse, once delayed until early adulthood, is clearly now a part of the typical adolescent's experience, regardless of her or his ethnic or socioeconomic background.
- One-third of all American 14-year-olds and two-thirds of all American 18-year-olds have had sexual intercourse.
- The proportion of individuals who have had sexual intercourse before entering high school has risen significantly in recent decades.
- The most substantial change in recent decades has been in the sexual activity of females.

The Sexually Active Adolescent

PSYCHOLOGICAL AND SOCIAL CHARACTERISTICS OF SEXUALLY ACTIVE ADOLESCENTS

For many years, researchers studied the psychological and social characteristics of sexually active adolescents on the assumption that these teenagers were more troubled than their peers. This view has been replaced as sexual activity has become more prevalent.

▌ Sexual Activity and Psychological Development Indeed, numerous studies show that sexual activity during adolescence is decidedly *not* associated with psychological disturbance (Savin-Williams & Diamond, 2004). Several studies, for example, report that adolescents who become sexually active earlier than their peers have levels of self-esteem and life satisfaction similar to the levels of other adolescents (Billy, Landale, Grady, & Zimmerle, 1988; Bingham & Crockett, 1996). Another study indicates that unmarried girls who become pregnant are *more* likely to have high self-esteem and strong feelings of efficacy, rather than the reverse (Robbins, Kaplan, & Martin, 1985). Losing one's virginity does not have negative psychological repercussions, either in the short or long term (Bingham & Crockett, 1996; Langer, Zimmerman, & Katz, 1995). Nor does having premarital sex with one's future spouse threaten the stability of one's marriage (although individuals with *many* premarital sexual partners are more likely to divorce) (Teachman, 2003). Thus, both the prejudice that only "troubled" adolescents have sex and the belief that sexual activity during adolescence leads to later psychological disturbance are false.

However, *early* sexual activity (that is, having intercourse before age 16) is associated with a more general attitudinal and behavioral profile that includes experimentation with drugs and alcohol, low levels of religious involvement, tolerance of deviant behavior, lower interest in academic achievement, and a stronger orientation toward independence (Cleveland, 2003; Halpern, Joyner, Udry, & Suchindran, 2000; Lanctot & Smith, 2001; Martin et al., 2005; Paul, Fitzjohn, Herbison, & Dickson, 2000; Whitaker, Miller, & Clark, 2000). In contrast, studies of adolescents who become sexually active *at age 16 or later* do not find major differences between these youth and their virginal counterparts.

FOOD FOR THOUGHT

Why do you think the psychological correlates of early sexual intercourse are different from the correlates of sexual intercourse when it is delayed until the last years of high school? Would you be in favor of sex education courses whose focus was on persuading adolescents to wait until they were 16 before having intercourse?

■ **Causation or Correlation?** Although many studies have found a link between early sexual activity and small-scale deviance, the nature of the causal chain is not entirely clear (Zimmer-Gembeck, Siebenbrunner, & Collins, 2004). Some studies show that involvement in deviance (especially alcohol and drug use, but aggression as well) precedes early involvement with sex (Capaldi, Crosby, & Stoolmiller, 1996; Miller-Johnson et al., 1996; Underwood, Kupersmidt, & Coie, 1996). Others show that deviance follows earlier sexual activity (Elliott & Morse, 1989). And still others suggest that experimentation with deviant activity and early sex occur simultaneously and may reflect some common underlying factor, such as the propensity to take risks (e.g., Bingham & Crockett, 1996; Dorius, Heaton, & Steffen, 1993; Orr, Beiter, & Ingersoll, 1991). As you'll read in Chapter 13, many experts believe that a general inclination toward problem behavior and lack of impulse control is behind an overarching pattern that includes minor delinquency, precocious or promiscuous sex, disengagement from school, and drug and alcohol use (Costa, Jessor, Donovan, & Fortenberry, 1995; Raffaelli & Crockett, 2003; Rosenthal, Smith, & de Visser, 1999; Valois, Oeltmann, Waller, & Hussey, 1999).

Another factor that affects adolescents' sexual activity is the extent to which they are supervised by their parents or other adults. In contrast to stereotypes of adolescent couples having sex in the backseat of their car on a Friday or Saturday night, most sexual activity between teenagers takes place in one of the two individuals' homes—most often, the boy's. (The third most popular setting is at the home of a friend.) And the most common time for adolescents to have sex is not on the weekend, but on weekdays, after school. Not surprisingly, then, adolescents who are unsupervised after school and who do not participate in after-school programs are more likely to be sexually active, more likely to have multiple sexual partners, and more likely to contract an STD (Cohen, Farley, Taylor, Martin, & Schuster, 2002).

HORMONAL AND CONTEXTUAL INFLUENCES ON SEXUAL ACTIVITY

One factor that is consistently related to the age at which adolescents initiate sex is physical maturation; adolescents who mature earlier are also likely to have sex earlier (Lam et al., 2002; Miller, Norton, Fan, & Christopherson, 1998). Increased interest in sex at adolescence is likely to have social as well as biological causes, however. Specifically, adolescents are thought to become interested in sex in part because of increases in sex hormones at puberty and in part because sexual activity becomes accepted—even encouraged—in their peer group. J. Richard Udry and his colleagues, who have studied this issue extensively (Smith, Udry, & Morris, 1985; Udry, 1987; Udry, Talbert, & Morris, 1986), suggest that a fuller understanding of adolescent sexual behavior necessitates looking at biological and social influences in interaction with each other, rather than at either set of influences alone. However, the way in which hormones and friends interact to influence sexual behavior appears to be different for males than for females.

■ **Hormonal Influences** Boys' and girls' initial interest in sex is influenced primarily by the surge in certain hormones—**testosterone,** to be specific—at puberty. Adolescents with higher levels of androgens (testosterone is an androgen) are more likely than their peers to report masturbating, thinking about sex, and planning to have sexual intercourse within the next year. This hormonal change appears to increase adolescents' interest in sex as well as their arousal when exposed to sexual stimuli. This is true for both males and females, although females' interest in sex is also influenced by levels of estrogen.

Motivation to have sex is one thing; becoming sexually active is another. How important is the rise in testosterone levels at puberty in determining the onset of sexual intercourse? The answer appears to differ between boys and girls. Among boys, the increased level of androgens is directly related to the likelihood of their being sexually active (Campbell, Prossinger, & Mbzivo, 2005). Younger boys who are more mature biologically are more likely to be sexually active than older boys whose hormone levels are lower.

Boys' sexual behavior is not entirely dependent on their hormone levels, however. Boys who are more popular with girls in their school are more likely to initiate sex early than are boys who are less popular with girls. Although some evidence also suggests that boys whose friends are sexually active are themselves

testosterone One of the sex hormones secreted by the gonads, found in both sexes but in higher levels among males than females.

more likely to be involved in sex, this seems to have more to do with the influence of hormones than with the influence of friends: Boys tend to have friends who are at a similar level of pubertal development and who therefore are likely to have similar testosterone levels and rates of sexual activity. All in all, the evidence indicates a very strong biological influence on the sexual behavior of adolescent boys.

As you know from the discussion in Chapter 1 concerning biological development during adolescence, androgens, including testosterone, contribute to increases in boys' sex drive as well as to the development of secondary sex characteristics like facial hair. Because of this, it is difficult to determine whether increases in androgens lead to boys' increased sexual activity because of the increased sex drive (which may make boys with higher testosterone levels want to have sex more) or because of changes in their physical appearance (which may make them more attractive to girls).

These factors are easier to separate in girls. Although androgens are responsible for increases in girls' sex drive, a different set of hormones—estrogens—is primarily responsible for changes in their appearance, including breast development, and for changes in their receptivity to males' sexual advances. Because of this, it is possible to study whether the increased interest in sex among girls after puberty is more influenced by increases in their sex drive or by changes in their receptivity and physical appearance (both of which, presumably, influence their sexual attractiveness to boys). Research on this points mostly to the impact of estrogen on girls' receptivity to boys' sexual overtures (Udry, Halpern, & Campbell, 1991). In other words, although girls' sex drive is more influenced by androgens than estrogens, their actual sexual activity is more influenced by estrogens than by androgens.

■ **The Role of Context** Despite these effects of hormones on girls' sexual behavior, numerous studies show that social factors are far more important in influencing girls' involvement in sexual intercourse than boys', especially among white girls (Crockett, Bingham, Chopak, & Vicary, 1996; Udry & Billy, 1987). Although increases in androgens lead to increased interest in sex among girls, and although increases in estrogens lead to increased receptivity to boys' sexual advances, whether this interest and receptivity is translated into behavior depends on the social environment (Savin-Williams & Diamond, 2004). Among girls with high levels of androgens, for example, those who have sexually permissive attitudes and whose friends are sexually active are more likely to engage in intercourse. But girls whose social environment is less encouraging of sex—even those with high levels of androgens—are unlikely to be sexually active. In other words, whereas hormones seem to have a direct and powerful effect on the sexual behavior of boys, the impact of hormones on the sexual behavior of girls seems to depend on the social context.

Why might this be? One explanation is that boys develop in an environment that is more uniformly tolerant and encouraging of sexual behavior than girls do. All that boys need to become sexually active is the biological jolt from the increase in androgens at puberty—there is nothing in the environment to hold them back. For girls, however, the environment is more varied. Some girls develop within a context that permits and even encourages sexual activity; others do not. Although the increase in androgens also provides a jolt to the sex drive of the adolescent girl, and although the increase in estrogens makes her more receptive to boys' sexual overtures, if she develops within a context that places strong social controls on sexual activity, this hormonal awakening will not be translated into sexual activity.

PARENTAL AND PEER INFLUENCES ON SEXUAL ACTIVITY

Many researchers have asked whether adolescents who become sexually active earlier than their peers have different sorts of relationships with their parents or their peers. The answer is clear: Not surprisingly, given the correlation between early sexual activity and other forms of problem behavior, most studies have found that adolescents from authoritative homes—that is, homes where parents are warm, are involved in their adolescent's life, and monitor their adolescent's behavior—are less likely to become sexually active at an early age and less likely to engage in risky sexual activity, such as having sex without protection against pregnancy or STDs (Capaldi, Stoolmiller, Clark, & Owen, 2002; DiClemente et al., 2001; Frisco, 2005; Huebner & Howell, 2003; Li, Stanton, & Feigelman, 2000; Longmore et al., 2001). Parent–adolescent conflict is also associated with early sexual activity, especially among adolescents who are relatively more mature physically (McBride, Paikoff, & Holmbeck, 2003). These strong and consistent links between effective parenting and safer sexual behavior have been found across ethnic groups (Meschke, Bartholomae, & Zentall, 2000; Miller, Benson, & Galbraith, 2001).

■ **Parent–Adolescent Communication** Researchers have also devoted a great deal of attention to the study of parent–adolescent communication about sex, although it is quite clear from this research that any conclusions you might draw about the nature and impact of these conversations depends entirely on whom you ask. Many more parents report communicating with their adolescent about sex than vice versa. In addition, parents often say that they have communicated about a particular topic (such as AIDS) when their teenager says they have not (Miller, Kotchick, Dorsey, Forehand, & Ham, 1998). Other discrepancies abound as well. For instance, parents underestimate their adolescents' sexual activity and unrealistically assume that if they disapprove of sexual activity, the adolescents are not likely to be sexually active; on the other hand, sexually active adolescents underestimate their parents' disapproval of sexual activity (Jaccard, Dittus, & Gordon, 1998). Generally, teenagers are more likely to talk about sex with mothers than fathers, and they rate their mothers as better sex educators (DiIorio, Kelley, & Hockenberry-Eaton, 1999; Feldman & Rosenthal, 2000; Raffaelli & Green, 2003).

Most discussions about sex between parents and teenagers focus on issues of safety (AIDS, condom use) rather than issues of sexual behavior or relationships (DiIorio et al., 1999; Miller et al., 1998). And, despite the progressive image of countries like the Netherlands, studies indicate that parent–adolescent communication about sex is no more open in Europe than in the United States (Arnett, 2002). Across cultures, however, adolescents are more likely to be well educated about sex when their conversations with their parents are genuinely interactive, rather than dominated by the parents (Lefkowitz, Romo, Corona, Au, & Sigman, 2000). This is important because conversations between mothers and daughters about sex tend to be more interactive than conversations between mothers and sons (Lefkowitz, Boone, Sigman, & Au, 2002). Perhaps because of this, parent–adolescent communication about sex is more predictive of daughters' behavior than of sons' (McNeely et al., 2002).

The effect of parent–child communication about sex on adolescents' sexual behavior depends on who is doing the communicating and what is being communicated. Overall, most studies find that the impact of parent–adolescent communication on the likelihood of an adolescent being sexually active is very small (Casper, 1990; Miller et al., 2001; Paikoff et al., 1997), although parent–child communication about contraception in particular does appear to lower the rate of *risky* sex (Hutchinson, Jemmott, Jemmott, Braverman, & Fong, 2003; Miller & Whitaker, 2001; Rodgers, 1999), especially if the discussions take place before the adolescent becomes sexually active (Miller, Levin, Whitaker, & Xu, 1998). Communication with older siblings about safe sex is also effective (Kowal & Blinn-Pike, 2004).

A growing body of research suggests that what is most important are the attitudes and values communicated by parents during discussions of sex and, of

Most studies find that parent–adolescent communication about sex has little impact on the likelihood of an adolescent becoming sexually active, but may affect the likelihood of adolescents practicing safe sex.

course, the ways in which these attitudes and values are interpreted by the adolescent (Bersamin, Walker, Waiters, Fisher, & Grube, 2006; Jaccard, Dodge, & Dittus, 2003b; Miller et al., 2001). Among girls with liberal parents, for instance, talking about sex is associated with *more* sexual activity; this is not true among girls with parents who disapprove of premarital sex, however (Dittus & Jaccard, 2000; Fingerson, 2005; Fisher, 1989; Hovell et al., 1994). In Hispanic American families, in which parental attitudes about sex tend to be relatively more conservative, communication with adolescents about values and beliefs concerning sex is associated with less sexual activity, but the degree to which parents directly caution their teenagers against sex does not seem to make a difference (Romo, Lefkowitz, Sigman, & Au, 2002). Adolescents whose parents communicate their values and beliefs about sex to them are also less likely to be influenced by the values and beliefs of their peers (Whitaker & Miller, 2000). In addition, adolescents who speak regularly with their parents about sex are more likely to turn down unwanted sex when they are pressured by others (Sionéan et al., 2002). Moreover, studies find that it is important for parents to maintain a close relationship with their teenager after the adolescent has become sexually active and to resist the temptation to pull away in anger over the teenager's behavior (Ream & Savin-Williams, 2005)

It is important to note that parent–adolescent communication about sex is more effective in deterring *risky* sexual activity than sexual activity in general, and even here, the effect that parents have is small. Thus, despite some parents' beliefs that they can prevent their adolescent's sexual activity by talking about it, and despite other parents' fears that talking about sex will have the unintended effect of encouraging their teenager's sexual behavior, studies show that parent–adolescent communication about sex has surprisingly little impact on whether adolescents are sexually active, one way or the other. While it is possible to teach parents how to talk more effectively to their teenagers about sex, it is not clear that doing so leads to dramatic changes in teenagers' knowledge, attitudes, or behavior (Lefkowitz, Sigman, & Au, 2000). Adolescents' opportunity to have sex (for example, whether they are in a steady relationship or date frequently), their having sexually active friends, and their use of alcohol and drugs are far better predictors of early sexual initiation than is parent–adolescent communication (Black, Ricardo, & Stanton, 1997; Miller, Norton et al., 1997; Whitbeck, Yoder, Hoyt, & Conger, 1999).

▍ Sexual Activity and Household Composition

One family factor that does predict adolescent sexual involvement, however—especially among girls—is household composition. Researchers consistently find that adolescents whose parents are in the process of divorcing as well as girls who live in single-parent households—regardless of when (or if) a divorce took place—are more likely to be sexually active earlier than their peers (Crockett et al., 1996; Ellis et al., 2003; Hogan, Sun, & Cornwell, 2000; Lammers, Ireland, Resnick, & Blum, 2000; Lauritsen, 1994; Miller, Norton et al., 1997; Murry, 1996; Wu & Thomson, 2001). One hypothesis, consistent with what we know about divorce and parent–adolescent relationships, is that parental divorce temporarily disrupts the parent–child relationship, leading the adolescent into early involvement with drugs, alcohol, and minor delinquency, which, according to some studies, increases the likelihood of sex. At least one study has found that what takes place within the family context helps explain why girls from single-parent homes are more sexually active at an earlier age (Davis & Friel, 2001).

But why should growing up in a single-parent home affect *girls'* sexual behavior more than boys'? At least four possibilities exist. One is that social influences on girls' sexual behavior are stronger and more varied than are the influences on boys' behavior (Whitbeck, Simons, & Kao, 1994). Boys' parents simply may not attempt to exert much control over their sexual activity, regardless of whether the household has one parent or two, and as a result, boys from single- and two-parent homes may be equally likely to be sexually active. Girls' sexual behavior, in contrast, may be more subject to parental controls. Single-parent homes are typically more permissive than two-parent homes (Dornbusch et al., 1985), and this difference in control may be enough to make a difference in girls' sexual activity.

A second possibility is that many single-parent mothers are likely to be dating and, in so doing, may inadvertently be role models of sexual activity to their adolescents (Miller & Moore, 1990; Whitbeck et al., 1994). Other research shows, for example, that adolescents whose mothers had been sexually active at an early age are themselves more likely to begin having sex early (Mott et al., 1996). To the extent that this modeling effect is stronger between parents and children of the same sex, we would expect to find a more powerful effect of growing up in a single-parent home on the sexual behavior of daughters than sons.

Yet a third possibility is that girls are more likely than boys to respond to problems at home by going outside the family for alternative sources of warmth and support; if their family environment is not satisfying, girls (whether in divorced homes or not) may be more likely than boys to seek the attention of a romantic partner (Whitbeck, Hoyt, Miller, & Kao, 1992). During or immediately following their parents' divorce, girls may seek the support of individuals with whom they become sexually involved.

Finally, some researchers suggest that the link between growing up in a single-parent household and earlier involvement in sex is genetic. They have shown that the same gene that makes men more likely to leave their family may, when passed on to daughters, make adolescent girls more likely to go through puberty early and become sexually active at an earlier age (Comings, Muhleman, Johnson, & MacMurray, 2002).

▍ Influences Other Than Parents

Other studies have examined the influence of forces other than parents on adolescents' sexual behavior. Generally, adolescents are more likely to be sexually active when their peers are (DiBlasio & Benda, 1992; East, Felice, & Morgan, 1993; Udry, 1987); when they *believe* that their friends are sexually active, whether or not their friends actually are (Babalola, 2004; Brooks-Gunn & Furstenberg, 1989; DiIorio et al., 2001; Prinstein, Meade, & Cohen, 2003); and when they have older siblings who model more sexually advanced behavior (East et al., 1993; Rodgers & Rowe, 1988; Widmer, 1997). Consistent with this, although religious involvement deters adolescents' sexual activity, regular church attendance is associated with delayed sexual activity only among adolescents whose friends attend the same church (Mott, Fondell, Hu, Kowaleski-Jones, & Menaghan, 1996). There are age and ethnic differences in the relative importance of parental and peer influence, however. As you would expect, peers become increasingly more influential with age (Treboux & Busch-Rossnagel, 1990). In addition, African American adolescents report relatively less familial influence over their sexual behavior than do white adolescents, whereas Hispanic adolescents report relatively more (Scott & Owen, 1990).

Peer influences on adolescents' sexual activity appear to operate in two different, but compatible, ways. First, when an adolescent's peers are sexually active, they establish a normative standard that having sex is acceptable (Furstenberg et al., 1987; Gillmore et al., 2002; Miller & Moore, 1990; Stack, 1994). One of the reasons that minor drug use is associated with earlier involvement in sexual activity is that drug use may lead an adolescent to form friendships with a different group of friends, a group that is sexually more permissive (French & Dishion, 2003; Whitbeck, Conger, Simons, & Kao, 1993). Consistent with this, adolescents' initiation of sexual activity varies from neighborhood to neighborhood, with earlier sexual activity more likely in relatively more disorganized neighborhoods, where adults have little control over teenagers and where peer groups are relatively more powerful (Upchurch et al., 1999). Generally, the more individual **risk factors** there are in an adolescent's life for involvement in early sexual activity (for example, drug and alcohol use, poor parental monitoring, sexually active friends, antisocial peers, disengagement from school, a disadvantaged neighborhood), the more likely the adolescent is to be sexually active (see Figure 11.4) (Small & Luster, 1994). The factors that place adolescents at risk for early sexual activity are the same across ethnic groups (Perkins, Luster, Villaruel, & Small, 1998).

Peers also influence each other's sexual behavior directly, either through communication among friends ("You haven't done it yet! What's the matter with you?" "You're thinking of doing what?") or, more commonly, between potential sex partners. Several studies show that sexual activity spreads within a community of adolescents much like an epidemic, with sexually experienced adolescents initiating their less experienced partners into increasingly more advanced sex (Rodgers & Rowe, 1993). Once they become sexually experienced, previously inexperienced adolescents then "infect" other adolescents. Over time, the percentage of sexually experienced adolescents within a community grows and grows.

▌ **Virginity Pledges** A recent analysis of "virginity pledges" also sheds light on the way in which the social context can influence adolescent sexual activity (Bearman & Brückner, 2001). Over the past decade, several million American adolescents have taken a virginity pledge, promising to abstain from sex until they are married. Not surprisingly, adolescents who take such a pledge are less likely to have intercourse than those who do not, although pledging only works for younger adolescents—it has no effect among older high school students. But the impact of pledging varies as a function of how many other adolescents in the

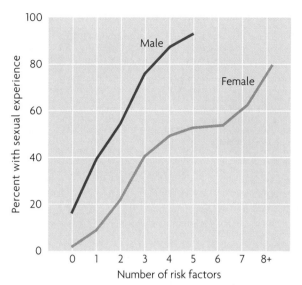

FIGURE 11.4 Sexual experience status as a function of number of risk factors. (Small & Luster, 1994)

same school have taken the pledge. Pledging has little effect in schools in which few students take virginity pledges (presumably, because there is little social support for abstinence) or in schools in which nearly everyone pledges (because one of the ways in which pledging works is by allowing those who pledge to make a statement about their values). By the way, it turns out that making a promise to *oneself* to delay becoming sexually active is more effective than making a formal, public pledge (Bersamin, Walker, Waiters, Fisher, & Grube, 2005).

Finally, several studies have examined the role of the broader environment in influencing adolescent sexual behavior. Adolescents growing up in poor neighborhoods, for example, are more likely to engage in early sexual activity than adolescents from more affluent communities (Billy, Brewster, & Grady, 1994; Brewster, Billy, and Grady, 1993; Brooks-Gunn, Duncan, Klebanov, & Sealand, 1993; Crane, 1991). When adolescents grow up in poverty, they may see little hope for the future, and they therefore may be more likely to risk their occupational and economic future by becoming sexually active (Benda & Corwyn, 1998; Lauritsen, 1994; Murry, 1994). To a young person who believes that the chances of getting a good job are slim, an early pregnancy does not seem as costly as it might to someone who hopes to complete high school, attend college, and secure a good job. Adolescents' sexual behavior is more strongly influenced by the values and attitudes of their schoolmates than the characteristics of their neighborhood, however (Teitler & Weiss, 2000).

risk factors Factors that increase the likelihood of some behavior or condition.

There are substantial sex differences in the way in which early sexual activity is experienced psychologically. For adolescent boys, early sexual relationships are often brief, impersonal, and associated with a sense of achievement.

SEX DIFFERENCES IN THE MEANING OF SEX

Any discussion of the psychosocial significance of sexual experience during adolescence must be sensitive to the very substantial sex differences in the ways in which early sexual activity is experienced. Despite the convergence of males' and females' rates of sexual activity in recent decades, the early sexual experiences of adolescent boys and girls are still very different and, as a consequence, are imbued with very different *meanings* (Savin-Williams & Diamond, 2004). In other words, the sexual behavior of males and females may be similar, but the sexual socialization of males and females is quite different.

❚ **The Way Boys Feel**   As noted earlier, the typical adolescent boy's first sexual experience is in early adolescence through masturbation (Savin-Williams & Diamond, 2004). At the outset, then, the sexual socialization of males typically places sex outside of an interpersonal context. Before adolescent boys begin dating, they have generally already experienced orgasm and know how to arouse themselves sexually. For males, the development of sexuality during adolescence revolves around efforts to integrate the capacity to form close relationships into an already-existing sense of sexual capability.

Perhaps because of this, at the time of first intercourse, boys are likely to keep matters of sex and intimacy separate. Boys often have as their first partner someone they just met or describe as a casual date, and

it is generally the male partner of a couple who is likely to initiate sex (Savin-Williams & Diamond, 2004). These findings suggest that the early sexual experiences of males are often interpreted not in terms of intimacy and emotional involvement, but in terms of recreation (Hendrick & Hendrick, 1994). Consistent with this, boys are more likely than girls to mention sexual arousal (rather than emotional factors) as a reason for having sex (Eyre & Millstein, 1999). And males typically report that the people to whom they describe their first sexual liaison—generally, male peers—are overwhelmingly approving (Miller & Simon, 1980). Not surprisingly, the most common immediate reactions among adolescent males to having intercourse for the first time are excitement, satisfaction, exhilaration, and happiness (Gordon & Gilgun, 1987; Oswald, Bahne, & Feder, 1994; Savin-Williams & Diamond, 2004).

❚ **The Way Girls Feel**   The typical girl's first experience is likely to be very different and leave her feeling very differently. Masturbation is a far less prevalent activity among girls than boys, and it is far less regularly practiced (Larsson & Svedin, 2002; Savin-Williams & Diamond, 2004). As a consequence, the typical adolescent girl, in contrast to the typical boy, is more likely to experience sex for the first time with another person. For girls, unlike boys, the development of sexuality involves the integration of sexual activity into an already existing capacity for intimacy and emotional involvement. As a consequence, the girl's sexual script is one that, from the outset, tinges sex with romance, love, friendship, and intimacy (Aitken & Chaplin, 1990; Hendrick & Hendrick, 1994; Savin-Williams & Diamond, 2004).

Boys and girls also encounter very different social attitudes about sex. Because of the possibility of pregnancy, the potential adverse consequences of sexual activity are far more serious for girls than for boys. For this reason, society monitors the sexual activity of girls more carefully, and girls are more likely to be encouraged to approach sex cautiously (Rosenthal, 1994). Girls' feelings of sexual desire are "tempered by their knowledge that girls are not supposed to be sexual or that if they are, they will be marked as bad and unlovable" (Tolman, 1993, p. 4). Perhaps because of this, girls have an easier time saying no to unwanted sex than boys do (Zimmerman, Sprecher, Langer, & Holloway, 1995).

Not surprisingly, then, at the time of first intercourse, the adolescent girl's sexual partner is likely to be someone she says she was in love with at the time (Savin-Williams & Diamond, 2004). After having intercourse for the first time, she is more likely to encounter disapproval or mixed feelings on the part of others in whom she confides (generally, peers) than is the typical boy (Savin-Williams & Diamond, 2004). And although the majority of girls report more positive than negative feelings about their first sexual experience, girls are more likely than boys to report feeling afraid, guilty, and worried as well as happy or excited about the experience (Gordon & Gilgun, 1987; Oswald et al., 1994; Savin-Williams & Diamond, 2004). The ambivalence expressed in this adolescent girl's letter to an advice column in *Teen* magazine is not unusual (van Roosmalen, 2000, p. 219):

> Every time I watch a freaky movie, I get really uptight and scared. My boyfriend is always there to comfort me, but we end up having sex when I don't know if I want to, but I am so freaked out I don't care. It doesn't comfort me at all. Now I am afraid we will have sex on every date.
>
> *Freaky*

It is important to keep in mind that differences between males and females in the meaning of sex are neither inevitable nor consistent across cultures or historical time. Nor is it the case that all adolescent boys follow the male "script" and all adolescent girls follow the female "script." As Ritch Savin-Williams and Lisa Diamond, two experts on adolescent sexuality, recently noted, "Girls are more sexually oriented and boys more romantically oriented than previous research might suggest" (Savin-Williams & Diamond, 2004).

FOOD FOR THOUGHT

Can you think of any evolutionary explanations for the different ways in which males and females react to their first sexual experiences?

HOMOSEXUALITY DURING ADOLESCENCE

▌ Prevalence of Homosexuality It is not uncommon for young adolescents to engage in sex play with members of the same sex, to have sexual fantasies about people of the same sex, or to have questions about the nature of their feelings for same-sex peers (Savin-Williams & Diamond, 2004). According to the national (and confidential) Add Health survey, about 8 percent of boys and 6 percent of girls reported having had strong

same-sex attractions or engaged in same-sex activity during adolescence. (Males are more likely to experiment with same-sex activity during adolescence, whereas females are more likely to experiment with it in young adulthood, often during college.) A smaller number of adolescents—between 3 and 4 percent—identify themselves as gay, lesbian, or bisexual, and this number increases to about 8 percent among adults (Michael, Laumann, & Kolata, 1994; Savin-Williams & Diamond, 2004). Researchers have not found consistent predictors that distinguish individuals who experiment with same-sex relations in adolescence and who later identify themselves as gay, lesbian, or bisexual from those whose experimentation during adolescence is passing and who later identify themselves as exclusively heterosexual. By the same token, the majority of gay, lesbian, and bisexual adults engaged in heterosexual activity during adolescence (Savin-Williams & Diamond, 2004).

It is important to distinguish between homosexuality as an exclusive preference and homosexuality as an interest that may exist simultaneously with strong heterosexual interests (Diamond et al., 1999). Many people mistakenly view sexual orientation as an "either-or" attribute, with individuals being either exclusively heterosexual or exclusively homosexual. In fact, however, of the individuals who do not develop an exclusive preference for heterosexual relationships, only one-third are exclusively homosexual in their orientation. Nearly twice as many describe themselves as bisexual—having both heterosexual and homosexual interests. Recent surveys indicate that only about 3 percent of adult males and 1 percent of adult females are exclusively homosexual (Michael et al., 1994). Interestingly, males are more likely to have had same-sex relations before identifying themselves as gay or bisexual, whereas the reverse sequence is more characteristic among females (Savin-Williams & Diamond, 2004).

A great deal of confusion about homosexuality results because people tend to confuse **sexual orientation** (the extent to which someone is oriented toward heterosexual activity, homosexual activity, or both), **sex-role behavior** (the extent to which an individual behaves in traditionally masculine or feminine ways), and **gender identity** (the gender an individual believes he or she is psychologically). There is no connection between an adolescent's sexual orientation and his or

sexual orientation An individual's orientation toward same- or opposite-sex sex partners.

sex-role behavior Behavior that is consistent with prevailing expectations for how individuals of a given sex are to behave.

gender identity The gender an individual identifies with.

Sexual orientation is influenced by a complex interplay of biological and contextual factors.

her sex-role behavior. Individuals with strong, or even exclusive, preferences for homosexual relationships exhibit the same range of masculine and feminine behaviors seen among individuals with strong or exclusive heterosexual interests. In other words, exclusively gay men (like exclusively heterosexual men) may act in very masculine, very feminine, or both masculine and feminine ways, and the same holds true for exclusively lesbian and exclusively heterosexual women, as it does for bisexual individuals. Along similar lines, individuals with homosexual interests are generally not confused about their gender identity—or, at least, they are no more confused than are individuals with heterosexual interests.

Origins of Homosexuality Studies of the antecedents of homosexuality generally have focused on two sets of factors: biological influences, such as hormones, and social influences, such as the parent–child relationship. More is known about the development of homosexuality among men than among women, but the weight of the evidence thus far suggests that an adolescent's sexual orientation is likely to be shaped by a complex interaction of social and biological influences (Bem, 1996; Green, 1980, 1987; Paul, 1993; Savin-Williams, 1988).

Support for the contention that homosexuality is determined at least partly by biological factors comes from two sources. You may recall that in Chapter 1 we distinguished between the organizational and the activational roles of hormones on behavior. The hormonal changes of puberty activate sexual behavior, but the particular pattern of sexual behavior that is activated may depend on the way in which hormonal pathways in the brain were organized early in life. There is suggestive evidence that gay and lesbian adults may have been exposed prenatally to certain hormones that, in theory, could affect sexual orientation through their effects on early brain organization (Meyer-Bahlburg et al., 1995; Savin-Williams, 1988). Second, some evidence indicates that homosexuality has a strong genetic component, since sexual orientation is more likely to be similar among close relatives than distant relatives and between identical twins than fraternal twins (Savin-Williams, 1988). Although environmental explanations for this similarity cannot be ruled out, chances are that at least some of the predisposition to develop a homosexual orientation is inherited.

Several studies suggest as well that a higher proportion of homosexuals than heterosexuals report having had problems in their early family relationships—

specifically, in their relationship with their father. The stereotype of the homosexual's father as cold and distant once was rejected as an artifact of popular stereotype and poor research designs. But more carefully designed studies have offered at least partial confirmation of this notion. Both gay and lesbian adults are more likely than heterosexuals to describe their fathers as distant and rejecting. Whereas gay men are more likely than heterosexuals to report having had close and generally positive relationships with their mothers, lesbians are more likely than heterosexuals to describe their mothers as cold and unpleasant (Bell, Weinberg, & Hammersmith, 1981). However, gay and lesbian adolescents are no more likely than heterosexual youth to have had gay or lesbian parents—in fact, studies of adolescents with same-sex parents find few differences between them and their peers with opposite-sex parents (Wainwright, Russell, & Patterson, 2004)

Although these studies point to certain factors that appear more often than not in the early histories of homosexuals, they hardly indicate that all individuals who show patterns of gender nonconformity or who have distant relations with their fathers inevitably become homosexual (Golombock & Tasker, 1996). Nor does research show that all homosexuals have identical developmental histories. For example, although, on average, homosexuals are more likely than heterosexuals to describe their parents in negative terms, not all gay and lesbian individuals feel this way. Indeed, only about half do, suggesting that a large number of gay and lesbian individuals had quite positive family relationships growing up. And, of course, many heterosexuals describe their parents in exceedingly negative terms. Similarly, although the majority of boys with persistently feminine behavior preferences may grow up to be gay, a substantial number of feminine boys do not.

Development of Sexual Identity Several writers have described the process through which gay, lesbian, and bisexual individuals discover, come to terms with, and disclose their sexual-minority identity (Diamond, 1998; Dubé & Savin-Williams, 1999; Savin-Williams, 1998). Although the traditional model of this progression—feeling different as a child, engaging in gender-atypical behavior, being attracted to members of the same sex and disinterested in those of the opposite sex, realizing one's sexual attraction to others of the same sex, and consciously questioning one's sexual identity—describes the experience of many sexual-minority adolescents, it by no means is universal. Indeed, some writers have suggested that this may be more applicable to the development of white gay men than to lesbians, bisexual adolescents, or ethnic minority gay men (Diamond, 1998; Dubé & Savin-Williams, 1999). There is also evidence that females' sexual orientation may be more fluid than males', which some have taken

as evidence that homosexuality has a stronger biological component among men and a stronger volitional component among women (Bem, 1998; Diamond, 1998). This may also help explain why same-sex sexual activity typically precedes the identification of oneself as homosexual among males but follows it among females.

FOOD FOR THOUGHT

Should social scientists be interested the antecedents of homosexuality? Is it important to know whether homosexuality is biologically or contextually determined? Why or why not?

Regardless of its origins, it is important to bear in mind that homosexuality is not considered by mental health experts to be a form of psychopathology, an indicator of an underlying psychological disturbance, or a condition warranting psychological treatment. Perhaps as we begin to understand more about the interplay among biological and social factors that contribute to the development of a homosexual orientation, our attitudes toward homosexuality will change for the better. Indeed, as one expert noted, "Society tends to treat . . . homosexuals as if they had a choice about their sexual orientation, when in fact they have no more choice about how they develop than heterosexuals do" (Marmor, quoted in Brody, 1987, p. 17).

Society's prejudice and ignorance about homosexuality likely cause significant psychological distress for gay and lesbian adolescents, especially if they encounter hostility from those around them. As you know by now, the developmental tasks in the domains of identity, intimacy, and sexuality present formidable challenges for many teenagers. These challenges may be exacerbated for sexual-minority adolescents, who are forced to resolve these issues without the same degree of social support as their heterosexual peers (Diamond & Lucas, 2004). Indeed, many studies have found that a substantial number of gay, lesbian, and bisexual adolescents had been harassed, physically abused, or verbally abused by peers or adults while growing up (Hershberger & D'Augelli, 1995; Pilkington & D'Augelli, 1995; Russell, Franz, & Driscoll, 2001; Russell & Joyner, 2001; Savin-Williams, 1994). Abuse of this sort may account for the relatively higher rates of depression, suicide, substance abuse, running away from home, and school difficulties reported by gay, lesbian, and bisexual adolescents (Bontempo & D'Augelli, 2002; Cochran, Stewart, Ginzler, & Cauce, 2002; Galliher, Rostosky, & Hughes, 2004; Rosario, Rotheram-Borus, &

Reid, 1996; Savin-Williams, 1994). Recent research indicates that patterns of mental health differ between gay and bisexual youth, however, and that it may be misleading to group all sexual-minority adolescents into one category. For example, involvement in risky behavior is higher among bisexual adolescents than among heterosexual or exclusively homosexual youth; and while emotional distress is higher among gay males than other males, it is not any more prevalent among lesbians than among other females (Udry & Chantala, 2002).

SEXUAL HARASSMENT, RAPE, AND SEXUAL ABUSE DURING ADOLESCENCE

▌ **Sexual Harassment and Date Rape**   Although most research on adolescent sexual activity has focused on voluntary sexual behavior between consenting individuals, there is growing public awareness that a large proportion of teenagers are sexually harassed, and that a significant minority are forced to have sex against their will (Lee, Croninger, Linn, & Chen, 1996; Lewin, 1997; Stein, 1995; Vicary, Klingaman, & Harkness, 1995). This latter group includes adolescents who have been the victims of forcible rape by a stranger, sexual abuse within the family, or **date rape**—when a young person, typically a woman, is forced by a date to have sex when she does not want to. Sexual coercion and sex under the influence of alcohol or drugs are more likely to occur when there is a large age difference (three years or more) between a girl and her partner (Gowen, Feldman, Diaz, & Yisrael, 2004).

Recent studies indicate that sexual harassment—both cross-gender and between members of the same sex—is widespread within American public schools (Lee et al., 1996; Loredo, Reid, & Deaux, 1995; McMaster, Connolly, Pepler, & Craig, 2002; Stein, 1995). According to one study of a nationally representative sample of middle and secondary school students, more than 80 percent of girls and 60 percent of boys reported having received unwanted sexual attention while in school (Lee at al., 1996) (see Figure 11.5). Because the majority of those who had been sexually harassed had themselves harassed others, and because many incidents occurred within full view of teachers and other school personnel—indeed, a significant percentage of students report having been sexually harassed by their *teachers*—numerous experts have suggested the need for wholesale changes in the moral and ethical climate of secondary schools (Lee et al., 1996; Stein, 1995; Timmerman, 2002). This is easier said than done, however; one evaluation of a school-based program called Safe

Dates found significant reductions in psychological abuse and sexual violence one month after the program was implemented, but these effects had disappeared within one year (Foshee et al., 2000). Other research, on the histories of individuals who commit dating violence, indicates that perpetrators themselves were likely to have been exposed to physical punishment and abuse at home (Capaldi & Clark, 1998; Simons, Lin, & Gordon, 1998; Wolfe, Wekerle, Reitzel-Jaffe, & Lefebvre, 1998).

FOOD FOR THOUGHT

If you were asked to devise a sexual harassment policy for a high school, what would be the main elements of your policy? Should policies governing adolescents' conduct in school be the same as those governing adults in the workplace?

▌ **Sexual Abuse**   Because both perpetrators and victims of sexual assaults are often reluctant to admit their experiences, it is difficult to obtain accurate estimates of the numbers of adolescents who have been sexually victimized. We do know that adolescent victims of sexual abuse are disproportionately female and poor (Cappelleri, Eckenrode, & Powers, 1993). According to several studies, more than 10 percent of American females and 5 percent of males report having had nonvoluntary sexual intercourse before age 18 (Howard & Wang, 2005; Luster & Small, 1997; Moore, Nord, & Peterson, 1989). (These figures on sexual abuse do not include adolescents who have been physically forced to engage in sexual activity other than intercourse and, as such, clearly underestimate the proportion of teenagers who have been sexually abused.) Women who were most likely to have been raped during adolescence were those who lived apart from their parents before age 16; who were physically, emotionally, or mentally impaired; who were raised at or below the poverty level; or whose parents abused alcohol or used other drugs. Indeed, two-thirds of all women who had three or more of these risk factors were raped as adolescents. In contrast to popular perception, adolescents are abused (sexually, physically, and emotionally) and neglected at a higher rate than are younger children (Cappelleri et al., 1993).

Several studies have examined the psychological consequences of having been the victim of sexual abuse during adolescence. Adolescents who have been sexually abused have relatively lower self-esteem, more academic difficulties, and higher rates of anxiety, fear,

date rape   Being forced by a date to have sex against one's will.

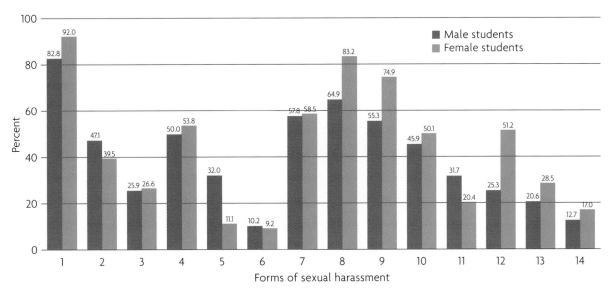

1. Made sexual comments, jokes, gestures, or looks
2. Showed you sexual pictures, photographs, messages, etc.
3. Wrote sexual messages about you on bathroom walls, etc.
4. Spread sexual rumors about you
5. Said you were gay or lesbian
6. Spied on you as you dressed or showered at school
7. Flashed or mooned you
8. Touched, grabbed, or pinched you in a sexual way
9. Intentionally brushed up against you in a sexual way
10. Pulled at your clothing in a sexual way
11. Pullead your clothing off or down
12. Blocked your way or cornered you in a sexual way
13. Forced you to kiss him/her
14. Forced you to do something sexual, other than kissing

FIGURE 11.5 The percentage of male and female students having ever experienced different forms of sexual harassment. (Lee et al., 1996)

eating disorders, and depression (Calverley, Fischer, & Ayoub, 1994; Nagy, DiClimente, & Adcock, 1995; Perkins, Luster, & Jank, 2002; Trickett, McBride-Chang, & Putnam, 1994; Williamson, Borduin, & Howe, 1991); are more likely to engage in risky behavior (Nagy, Adcock, & Nagy, 1994; Tubman, Montgomery, Gil, & Wagner, 2004; Whitbeck, Hoyt, & Ackley, 1997; Widom & Kuhns, 1996); and are more likely to have multiple sexual partners, to be sexually victimized, and to become pregnant as teenagers (Butler & Burton, 1990; Stock, Bell, Boyer, & Connell, 1997; Tyler, Hoyt, Whitbeck, & Cauce, 2001). Girls who have been chronically sexually abused by their biological father are at greatest risk for problems (Trickett, Noll, Reiffman, & Putnam, 2001). There is also some evidence that sexual abuse prior to adolescence may lead to precocious (that is, very early) puberty (Herman-Giddens, Sandler, & Friedman, 1988).

At the same time, it is worth noting that there are substantial differences among individuals in the extent to which they show problems as a result of having been sexually abused and in the form those problems take (Bauserman & Rind, 1997). Generally, individuals who have been both sexually and physically abused fare worse than those who experience sexual

abuse alone. But adolescents who have been sexually abused fare better psychologically when they have parents (presumably not the perpetrators of the abuse) who are authoritative (firm and supportive) and when they are successful in school (Luster & Small, 1997).

CONTRACEPTIVE USE

One reason for the great concern among adults over the sexual activity of adolescents is the failure of many sexually active young people to use contraception regularly. Among late adolescent males, nearly one-third report using either no contraception or an ineffective method (such as withdrawing before ejaculating) the first time they had sex (Manning, Longmore, & Giordano, 2000). Nor is failure to use contraception limited to adolescents' first experiences with intercourse; studies indicate that between 20 and 30 percent of young people did not use contraception the last time they had sex (Coleman, 1999; Hogan et al., 2000; Santelli et al., 2000). It is estimated that in the United States alone, more than 1.5 million pregnancies among adolescents are averted each year as a result of contraception (Kahn, Brindis, & Glei, 1999).

FIGURE 11.6   Condom use by sexually active adolescents increased substantially during the 1990s.
(Santelli et al., 2004)

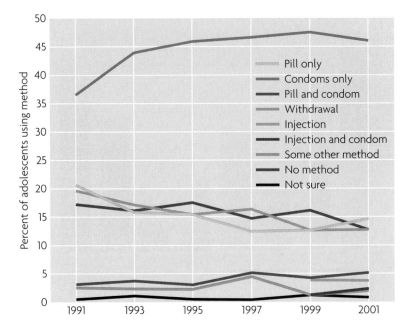

Trends in Contraceptive Use   Although findings of adolescents' poor contraceptive behavior are worrisome, there has been a clear improvement in this behavior in recent decades, both in the United States and abroad (Häggström-Nordin, Hanson, & Tydén, 2002; Hogan et al., 2000). In 1976, for example, nearly two-thirds of sexually active young women reported that they had not used contraception during their first intercourse (as opposed to about one-fourth today), and more than 35 percent reported never using birth control (as opposed to about 15 percent today) (Kahn et al., 1999). During the late 1980s, partly in response to the threat of AIDS, condom use among older teenagers more than doubled (Miller & Moore, 1990), and it continued to increase during the 1990s (see Figure 11.6) (Santelli et al., 2004). Still, surveys indicate that close to 40 percent of all American high school students did not use a condom the last time they had sex (Centers for Disease Control and Prevention, 2006).

Among adolescents who do use contraception, the most popular method by far is using a condom, which are used by close to 60 percent of sexually active teenage couples, followed by the birth control pill, which is used by about one-fifth of couples; this is a significant change from previous generations of adolescents, who were far more likely to depend on the birth control pill than on condoms (Everett et al., 2000). (About 20 percent of girls who are on the pill report that their partner uses a condom as well [Santelli et al., 1997].) Withdrawal, a highly ineffective method of preventing pregnancy, unfortunately is still used by a large number of teenagers, as is the rhythm method—a method of birth control that requires more regular menstrual cycling than many teenagers have and more careful

One of the reasons for adults' concern about adolescent sexual activity is the failure of many sexually active teenagers to use contraception regularly.

monitoring of menstrual cycling than most teenagers are capable of. Studies also show that a large proportion of condom users do not use condoms correctly (for example, not putting the condom on before first entry and not holding onto the condom while withdrawing) (Oakley & Bogue, 1995).

Adolescents' Reasons for Not Using Contraception   Why do so few adolescents use contraception regularly and effectively? Social scientists point to several factors. First, for a sizable minority of adolescents, contraceptives are not readily available. This is an especially important barrier among younger adolescents, who may feel uncomfortable discussing their sexual activity with parents or other adults whose help or consent may be necessary in order to obtain birth control. Having ready access to a free, confidential family

planning service that does not require parents' consent is a strong predictor of whether adolescents will use contraceptives at all or will use them consistently (Averett, Rees, & Argys, 2002; Blake et al., 2003; Mauldon & Luker, 1996). One study found that teen pregnancies and childbearing rose after the imposition of a requirement that adolescents get their parents' consent in order to obtain contraception (Zavodny, 2004), and surveys of sexually active teenagers who use contraceptives indicate that one-fifth of them would stop using them if they had to notify their parents in order to get them (Jones, Purcell, Singh, & Finer, 2005). Also, adolescents who are health conscious in general are more likely to use contraception, suggesting that it may be beneficial to incorporate education about contraception into broader health promotion efforts (Fortenberry, Costa, Jessor, & Donovan, 1997).

FOOD FOR THOUGHT

Think back to your own sexual experience as an adolescent. If you were sexually active, what factors influenced your use (or lack of use) of contraception? Based on the research reviewed here, as well as your own experience, what sorts of interventions hold the most promise for increasing contraceptive use among teenagers?

Second, many young people are insufficiently educated about sex, contraception, and pregnancy (Trussell, 1989), although knowledge alone does not seem to be sufficient to promote contraceptive use; individuals must be *motivated* to use contraception as well as know why they need to (Sheeran, Abraham, & Orbell, 1999). Nevertheless, many young people do not fully understand that the likelihood of pregnancy varies over the course of a woman's menstrual cycle, and more than half mistakenly believe that it is during menstruation that the risk of pregnancy is greatest (Zelnick & Kantner, 1973). At the time of first intercourse, about one-third of all teenagers who do not use contraception fail to do so because they don't know about contraception or don't think about using contraceptives (Hayes, 1987). Among sexually active teenagers, many "just trust to luck" that pregnancy will not result from intercourse (Sorensen, 1973). Consistent with this, adolescents who have pregnancy tests but who learn that they are not pregnant—that is, those who believe that they *are* lucky—are less likely to use contraceptives regularly during subsequent months (Zabin, Sedivy, & Emerson, 1994). Unfortunately, few

sexually active adolescents who fail to use contraception remain lucky for very long.

Psychological factors also play a role in adolescents' failure to use contraception. Many young people do not recognize the seriousness of pregnancy and take the possibility lightly (Hayes, 1987). More than 25 percent of nonusers of contraception report that they or their partners simply did not want to use birth control. From a cognitive perspective, the limited ability of young adolescents to engage in long-term hypothetical thinking, and their occasionally egocentric tendency to believe that they are immune from the forces that affect others, may impede their consideration of pregnancy or an STD as a likely outcome of sexual activity (Burns & Dillon, 2005).

Perhaps most importantly, many adolescents fail to use birth control because doing so would be tantamount to admitting that they are choosing to be sexually active (Miller & Moore, 1990). Many teenagers do not anticipate having intercourse (Trussell, 1989). Going on the pill or purchasing a condom requires an adolescent to acknowledge that he or she is having or is going to have sexual relations. For many young people, this is an extremely difficult admission to make—especially for young women who feel ambivalent and guilty about having sex with someone for the first time. Consistent with this, studies show that one of the best predictors of condom use is the individual's intent to use a condom and willingness to communicate about it with his or her partner (Sheeran et al., 1999; Tschann & Adler, 1997). Interventions designed to strengthen adolescents' intentions and their ability to communicate with their partner about contraception, and not just increase their knowledge, have been shown to be effective in promoting condom use, even within high-risk populations (DiClemente et al., 2004; Jemmott, Jemmott, Fong, & McCaffree, 1999)

Given all these reasons, not surprisingly, one of the best predictors of contraceptive use is the adolescent's age: Older teenagers are better informed, less guilty about having sex, more likely to be able to discuss contraception with their partner, and better able to grasp the potential negative consequences of an unwanted pregnancy (Miller & Moore, 1990; Sheeran et al., 1999). Relatively younger women are even less likely to use contraception if their partner is older (Glei, 1999; Miller, Clark, & Moore, 1997). It is also important for adolescents to understand the need to use contraception every time they have sex. A very large proportion of teenagers who have had sex with contraception have also had sex *without* contraception (Arnett & Balle-Jensen, 1993; Gillmore, Morrison, Lowery, & Baker, 1994).

One study illustrates well the role that emotional factors play in influencing contraceptive use. Individuals

FIGURE 11.7 Pregnancies among women ages 19 and younger in selected industrialized countries. (Alan Guttmacher Institute, 1994)

who feel very guilty about having sex are less likely to be sexually active, but when they are, they are also less inclined to use effective contraception—perhaps because their guilt inhibits their ability to plan for sex (Gerrard, 1987). When sexual standards become more permissive, many individuals who would otherwise feel guilty about having sex are drawn into sexual relationships. Unfortunately, their feelings of guilt are not changed by the aura of permissiveness, and, as a consequence, they have sex without using effective contraception. Along these lines, studies indicate that conservatively religious adolescents are less likely to be sexually active but also are less likely to use birth control if they do have sex (Miller & Gur, 2002; Studer & Thornton, 1987), and that adolescents who promise to remain virgins but who break their pledge are less likely to use contraception the first time they have sex than are those who do not make so-called virginity pledges (Brückner & Bearman, 2005).

■ **Cross-National Comparisons** More interesting, perhaps, is research indicating that the rate of adolescent pregnancy is substantially higher in the United States than in other industrialized countries—despite the fact that the rate of teenage sexual activity in the United States is comparable to that in other countries (Jones et al., 1987) (see Figure 11.7). For numerous reasons, American teenagers are less likely than their counterparts in other industrialized countries to use contraception regularly and effectively (Darroch, Singh, & Frost, 2001). According to one widely cited study, this is because nonmarital sex is portrayed in the United States as "romantic, exciting, and titillating . . . [while] at the same time, young people get the message that good girls should say no" (Jones et al., 1987, p. 239). As yet another expert wrote, "Sex saturates American life—in television programs, movies, and advertisements—yet the media generally fail to communicate responsible

attitudes toward sex, with birth control remaining a taboo subject" (Westoff, 1988, p. 254). One result of this set of mixed messages is that the rates of STDs, teenage childbearing, and teenage abortion are substantially higher in the United States than in many industrialized nations (Darroch et al., 2001).

A fascinating comparison of the way in which having intercourse for the first time is portrayed in teen magazines aimed at adolescent girls in the United States (*Seventeen*) and Germany (*Bravo!*) further illustrates the different sorts of messages adolescents receive in America and Europe. Keep in mind that rates of sexual activity are similar in the two countries, but that American teenagers are far less likely than German adolescents to use contraception regularly. In both magazines, the nature of individuals' first sexual experience was a common topic of discussion, both in advice columns and in stories that readers told about themselves (the German magazine actually had a regular column called "My First Time"), but the similarities ended there. In the American publication, the event was usually discussed in negative terms, emphasizing the loss of virginity and the potential harmful consequences of the act (such as feeling guilty afterwards). In the German publication, the event was almost always described in positive terms, emphasizing sexual pleasure and romance. More strikingly, in the German magazine, contraceptive use was presented as a regular part of sexual activity, whereas in the American magazine, it was rarely mentioned by adolescent readers and generally presented by the editors as "a necessary but disagreeable responsibility" (Carpenter, 2001, p. 47).

■ **Improving Contraceptive Behavior** Taken together, research suggests that there is a great deal that adults can do to improve the contraceptive behavior of adolescents. First, adults can see that contraceptives are made accessible to the young people who feel they need them. Second, adults can provide sex education at an early enough age to instruct young people in the fundamentals of contraceptive use before, rather than after, adolescents have become sexually active; such education should be aimed at strengthening adolescents' intentions to use contraception, and not just their contraceptive knowledge. Third, parents and teachers can make adolescents feel more free to talk about their sexual interests and concerns, so that young people will be more apt to look at their own behavior seriously and thoughtfully. Finally, the mass media should portray sex in a more responsible fashion, showing contraception use along with sexual activity. When, for instance, was the last time you saw a couple in a film or on television interrupt sex in order to discuss birth control?

AIDS AND OTHER SEXUALLY TRANSMITTED DISEASES

Helping youngsters understand sex, pregnancy, and contraception is an important goal of sex education programs for adolescents. Helping them avoid the risks of **sexually transmitted diseases (STDs)** is another. STDs are caused by viruses, bacteria, or parasites that are transmitted through sexual contact (Mahoney, 1983). Several million adolescents contract an STD each year, and one in four teenagers contracts an STD before graduating from high school (Gans, 1990; Luster & Small, 1994). Some of the most common STDs among adolescents are **gonorrhea** and **chlamydia** (both caused by a bacterium), and **herpes** and **human papilloma virus** (both caused by a virus) (Slap & Jablow, 1994). These infections pose a significant health risk to young people, because they are associated with increased rates of cancer and infertility. They also place a tremendous financial burden on taxpayers—in 2000, the treatment of new cases of STDs among young Americans cost taxpayers $6.5 billion (Chesson, Blandford, Gift, Tao, & Irwin, 2004). Countries vary considerably in rates of STD infection, with the United States having one of the highest rates in the world (Panchaud, Singh, Feivelson, & Darroch, 2000).

▌ **HIV/AIDS** During the 1980s, a new and far more serious STD commanded the world's attention: **AIDS, or acquired immune deficiency syndrome**. AIDS is transmitted through bodily fluids, especially semen, during sex, or blood when drug users share needles. Before information was available about the transmission of AIDS, some individuals were infected through blood transfusions in hospitals. Now hospitals routinely screen blood for the AIDS virus—**HIV, or human immunodeficiency virus**—and this means of transmission is extremely rare today.

AIDS itself has no symptoms, but HIV attacks the body's immune system, interfering with the body's ability to defend itself against life-threatening diseases like pneumonia or cancer. About 25 percent of all individuals who are infected with the virus develop complications within five years; about half of all people in the United States known to have AIDS have died as a result.

Although the incidence of AIDS in the United States was initially concentrated within two groups, gay men and drug users who use needles, surveys indicate that the transmission of AIDS through heterosexual activity is a clear danger within the adolescent community, particularly among inner-city minority youngsters (D'Angelo, Getson, Luban, & Gayle, 1991), among homeless youth (Rotheram-Borus, Koopman, & Ehrhardt, 1991), and among high school dropouts (St. Louis et al., 1991). Among infected females, the major source of infection is heterosexual intercourse (Futterman, Hein, Reuben, Dell, & Shaffer, 1993). Because there is a long period of time between HIV infection and the actual manifestation of illness, however—sometimes as long as 10 years—many more adolescents are likely to be asymptomatic carriers of the HIV virus who may develop AIDS in young adulthood (Hein, 1988b). You should be aware that HIV infection is not limited to poor, inner-city adolescents, however: In 1990, it was estimated that 1 in 500 college students (and 1 in 200 male college students) would test HIV-positive (Gayle et al., 1990). Studies of adolescents' behavior and beliefs indicate that heterosexual, bisexual, and homosexual youth are all at high risk for HIV (Rotheram-Borus, Marelich, & Srinivasan, 1999).

The chances of contracting HIV are greatest among individuals who use drugs, have unprotected sex, have many sexual partners, and already have another STD (such as gonorrhea) (Hein, Dell, Futterman,

sexually transmitted disease (STD)   Any of a group of infections—including gonorrhea, herpes, chlamydia, and AIDS—passed on through sexual contact.

gonorrhea   A sexually transmitted infection caused by a bacterium.

chlamydia   A sexually transmitted infection caused by a bacterium.

herpes   A sexually transmitted infection caused by a virus.

human papilloma virus   One of several viruses that causes a sexually transmitted disease.

AIDS (acquired immune deficiency syndrome)   A disease, transmitted by means of bodily fluids, that devastates the immune system.

HIV (human immunodeficiency virus)   The virus associated with AIDS.

Rotheram-Borus, & Shaffer, 1995; Lowry et al., 1994). Because these risk factors are more common among young people than adults, the risk of HIV infection among adolescents is substantial. Accordingly, in recent years, efforts have been made to develop AIDS education programs specifically aimed at teenagers (e.g., DiClemente et al., 2004; Fang, Stanton, Feigelman, & Baldwin, 1998; Jemmott et al., 1999). Unfortunately, despite the existence of many programs designed to reduce the prevalence of HIV infection among adolescents, many young people, especially minority youth, remain confused and misinformed about AIDS (Stevenson, Davis, Weber, Weiman, & Abdul-Kabir, 1995). Some evidence suggests, however, that educational efforts can be successful in preventing continued sexual risk taking among adolescents who are already HIV-infected (Rotheram-Borus et al., 2001).

■ **Protecting Against STDs** Most experts believe that, short of abstinence, the best way for teenagers to protect themselves against contracting HIV and many other STDs is by using condoms during sex; adolescents who consistently use condoms are half as likely as those who do not to contract an STD (Crosby, DiClemente, Wingood, Lang, & Harrington, 2003). Educating young people about the risk factors associated with AIDS is also important, because studies show that adolescents who believe that they are at risk for HIV infection and who are motivated to avoid the risk are more likely to take precautions during intercourse (DiClemente et al., 1992; Hausser & Michaud, 1994; Jemmott et al., 1999; Orr & Langefeld, 1993; Rotheram-Borus & Koopman, 1991). Increasing adolescents' perceptions of vulnerability to HIV infection is not sufficient to motivate them to use condoms, however (Gerrard, Gibbons, & Bushman, 1996).

Adults often forget that adolescents' sexual behavior is as much, if not more, influenced by their perceptions of benefits (for example, the fun of having different partners) as it is by their perceptions of costs (for example, the risks of having different partners) (Levinson, Jaccard, & Beamer, 1995). Even adolescents who know they are vulnerable to infection are less likely to protect themselves when they feel negatively about using condoms, when they are positively inclined toward risk taking, and when their friends are actively engaged in risky sex (Romer et al., 1994; Serovich & Greene, 1997; Shoop & Davidson, 1994; St. Lawrence, Brasfield, Jefferson, Allyene, & Shirley, 1994). Interestingly, adolescents who are part of the "jock" crowd are more likely to engage in sexual risk taking, although this is due to peer norms and not to participation in sports, which actually is associated with *healthier* sex behaviors among both boys and

girls, most likely because adolescents who care about their physical health avoid many of the behaviors that lead to sexual risk taking, such as drinking or using drugs (Lehman & Koerner, 2004; Miller, Farrell, Barnes, Melnick, & Sabo, 2005; Waller & Dubois, 2004).

In short, while most adolescents are aware of the risk of STDs, it has been difficult to convince them to translate this knowledge into safer behavior (Gerrard et al., 1996; Langer, Tubman, & Duncan, 1998). More promising strategies emphasize adolescents' motives and social relationships, rather than their knowledge (Fang et al., 1998; Jemmott et al., 1999). For example, one study found that adolescents are often not aware when their sex partner is having sex with others as well, which increases their chances of contracting an STD (Lenoir, Adler, Borzekowski, Tschann, & Ellen, 2006). It also may be important to use different strategies with sexually active versus inexperienced adolescents (Silver & Bauman, 2006).

RECAP

- In general, sexual activity during adolescence does not carry the psychological risks that many adults associate with it. Adolescents who are sexually active have psychological profiles that are similar to, rather than different from, their nonactive peers.
- Some evidence suggests that early sexual activity (having intercourse before age 16) is more common among teenagers growing up in single-parent households and is associated with higher rates of problem behaviors, such as drug and alcohol use.
- Any discussion of the psychological aspects of adolescent sexuality must differentiate between the experiences of males and females. Early sexuality for males is tinged with elements of recreation, whereas for females it is more linked to feelings of intimacy and love.
- Approximately 4 percent of adolescents and 8 percent of young adults are gay, lesbian, or bisexual. Experts agree that homosexuality is not a form of psychopathology, an indicator of an underlying psychological disturbance, or a condition warranting psychological treatment. Many difficulties experienced by gay and lesbian youth result from their being harassed by peers and adults.
- A majority of teenagers report having been sexually harassed in school, and a significant minority of young people, mainly females, are forced to have sex against their will.

- Adolescents who have been sexually abused show higher-than-average rates of academic difficulties, anxiety, fear, and depression; are more likely to engage in risky behavior; and are more likely to become pregnant as teenagers.
- Most experts agree that the reasons so few adolescents use birth control regularly are that contraceptives are not as accessible as they might be, that adolescents are insufficiently educated about pregnancy and contraception, that they seldom anticipate having intercourse until they become sexually active on a regular basis, and that using birth control requires the sort of long-term planning that many young people are reluctant or unable to engage in.
- Several million adolescents contract a sexually transmitted disease each year. While most adolescents are now aware of the risk of HIV infection, it has been difficult to convince them to translate this knowledge into safer behavior. Programs that simply advocate abstinence have not been successful, and providing information alone appears to do little to change adolescents' sexual behavior.

Nearly one-fourth of American young women become pregnant before their 18th birthday. A little more than half of these pregnancies result in the birth of a baby.

Teenage Pregnancy and Childbearing

THE NATURE AND EXTENT OF THE PROBLEM

Given the high rate of sexual activity and poor record of contraceptive use among contemporary adolescents, it comes as little surprise to learn that many young women become pregnant before the end of adolescence. Each year, between 800,000 and 900,000 American adolescents become pregnant—giving the United States the highest rate of teen pregnancy in the industrialized world (Alan Guttmacher Institute, 2004).

▌ Prevalence of Teen Pregnancy Recent statistics indicate that nearly one-third of American young women become pregnant at least once by age 20, although rates of teen pregnancy vary considerably by ethnicity: The rate is twice as high among African American youth as among white youth, and the rate among Hispanic teenagers falls somewhere between (Alan Guttmacher Institute, 2004). These rates are lower than they were in the past several decades (Coley & Chase-Lansdale, 1998), in part because of increased

contraceptive use and in part because fewer younger teenagers are sexually active (Santelli et al., 2004).

Keep in mind that not all adolescent pregnancies result in childbirth. In the United States, about 30 percent of all teenage pregnancies are aborted, and slightly more than 15 percent end in miscarriage (Centers for Disease Control and Prevention, 2004). The proportion of teen pregnancies that are aborted differs from country to country, from a low of about 20 percent in Ireland to a high of close to 70 percent in Sweden (Singh & Darroch, 2000). Among American adolescents who carry their pregnancy full term, the vast majority—over 90 percent—keep and raise the infant; only 1 in 10 put the child up for adoption. Thus, approximately 45 percent of teenage pregnancies end in abortion or miscarriage, about 50 percent result in the birth of an infant who will be raised by his or her mother (with or without the help of a partner or other family members), and about 5 percent result in an adoption (Coley & Chase-Lansdale, 1998).

It is important to distinguish between pregnancies and actual births—a distinction that often is lost in debates over the consequences of teenage pregnancy. Because of the many pregnant adolescents choosing abortion, the birthrate among teenage women is far lower than it would otherwise be, and it may surprise you to learn that the birthrate among adolescent women today is considerably lower than it was in previous eras. Contrary to the popular idea that teenage childbearing has reached epidemic proportions in this country is the truth of the matter: Relatively more women gave birth to an infant before reaching adulthood in previous decades than do so today—by a large margin.

Nevertheless, the rate of teenage births in the United States continues to be twice as high as in Great Britain and Canada; 3 times greater than in Israel; 7 times greater than in Spain, Sweden, and Italy; and 14 times greater than in Japan. And while the teen birthrate has fallen considerably in most industrialized countries over the past 25 years (one dramatic exception is in many of the former republics of the Soviet Union, where the birthrate has risen), the decline has been far more modest in the United States (Singh & Darroch, 2000) (see Figure 11.8)

If teenage childbearing is less prevalent today than in earlier eras, why does the issue receive so much attention in the media? First, although the rate of childbearing may be lower today than previously, the proportion of teenage childbearing that occurs out of wedlock is much higher. In earlier eras, adolescents who became pregnant were much more likely to marry before their child was born. Their pregnancy and childbearing did not cause as much concern, because they were "legitimized" by marriage. One source estimates that about half of all adolescent women who married during the late 1950s were pregnant at the time of marriage (Furstenberg, Brooks-Gunn, & Morgan, 1987). As recently as 1955, out-of-wedlock births accounted for only about 14 percent of all births to young women. But by 1995, this figure had skyrocketed to 75 percent (Coley & Chase-Lansdale, 1998).

■ **Causes for Concern**   Society is now more tolerant of single parenthood and of nonmarital pregnancy than it was 50 years ago, and many more women choose this option today than did so in the past. Nonetheless, one reason for the special concern about teenage childbearing in the media is that such a high proportion of it occurs outside of marriage. Whether this should be a concern, however—setting issues of morality aside—is still hotly debated, as we'll see in a moment. Indeed, some evidence suggests that the fates of a large group of adolescent mothers are worsened, not bettered, by marrying the father of their child.

A second reason for widespread concern is that rates of teenage childbearing vary markedly across ethnic and socioeconomic groups. Middle-class women are far more likely to abort their pregnancies than are poor women, and as a consequence, the problem of

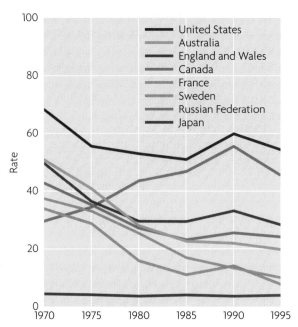

FIGURE 11.8   Adolescent birthrates in selected countries. (Singh & Darroch, 2000)

teenage childbearing is densely concentrated among economically disadvantaged youth (Miller & Moore, 1990; Russell, 1994). Part of the controversy surrounding teenage childbearing is linked to the public's concern about the large number of teenage mothers who spend extended periods of time on welfare— more than half of all welfare funding in the United States is spent on families resulting from teenage births (Coley & Chase-Lansdale, 1998).

Because minority adolescents are more likely to grow up poor, teenage childbearing is especially prevalent in nonwhite communities. Among white adolescents, nearly two-thirds of all births occur outside of marriage, but a large proportion of these births occur within the context of cohabitation; among African American adolescents, virtually all childbirths are out of wedlock, and relatively few of these even occur among cohabiting couples (Manning & Landale, 1996; Schellenbach, Whitman, & Borkowski, 1992). The rate for Hispanic teenagers falls somewhere in between; interestingly, young Mexican American women are more likely to bear their first child within marriage, whereas young Puerto Rican women are more likely to bear children out of wedlock but within the context of cohabitation. This suggests that cultural attitudes toward marriage and cohabitation influence the context of childbearing in important ways (Darabi & Ortiz, 1987; East & Blaustein, 1995; Manning & Landale, 1996). Because minority youth are more likely to experience problems such as school failure or unemployment, early childbearing is likely to take place in the context of limited social and economic resources.

Indeed, the main reason for the high rate of nonmarital childbearing among African Americans is the higher proportion of adolescents growing up in single-parent homes (Bumpass & McLanahan, 1987), which experience more stress. In addition, many poor, young, African American women believe that it is perfectly normal to become a mother while still a teenager and to become a grandmother before turning 40 (Perez-Febles, Allison, & Burton, 1999), norms that may be handed down from one generation to the next (Hardy, Astone, Brooks-Gunn, Shapiro, & Miller, 1998).

CAUSES AND CORRELATES OF TEEN PREGNANCY

Many myths permeate discussions of the causes of adolescent pregnancy and complicate what is actually a fairly simple matter. The most important differences between young women who do and do not become pregnant during adolescence are in their sexual activity and contraceptive use. As you have read, sexual activity among American young people is high while contraceptive use is sporadic and inadequate. Although some evidence indicates that African American and Hispanic teenagers are more likely than white teenagers to say they intend to have a baby at an early age, the large racial difference in teenage childbearing is due mainly to racial differences in *unintended* pregnancies (Mosher & Bachrach, 1996; Trent & Crowder, 1997).

Deep down inside, though, do adolescents who become pregnant actually want to have a baby? This has been an extremely difficult question for social scientists to answer. According to national surveys, 85 percent of births to women ages 15–19 are unintended, a figure suggesting that the vast majority of adolescent mothers did not become pregnant intentionally. Yet, studies that plumb the issue a bit deeper find that many young women who say they do not want to become pregnant are actually ambivalent, and not unequivocally negative, about the prospect of having a child (Jaccard, Dodge, & Dittus, 2003a). More importantly, those who are ambivalent about childbearing or who believe that having a child will be a positive experience are less likely to use contraception effectively (Unger, Molina, & Teran, 2000; Zabin, Astone, & Emerson, 1993). Thus, while the vast majority of sexually active teenagers do not actively wish to become pregnant, a significant minority feel less troubled by the prospect of early parenthood than do their peers, and these youngsters are more likely to risk pregnancy by having unprotected sex. As you know, risky sex may be part of a larger constellation of risky behaviors, including delinquency and experimentation

with drugs and alcohol (Guo et al., 2002; Scaramella, Conger, Simons, & Whitbeck, 1998; Woodward, Fergusson, & Horwood, 2001; Zweig, Lindberg, & McGinley, 2001). As one team of authors wrote, "Adolescent childbearing is more an unintended result of risky behaviors than a result of rational choice" (Trent & Crowder, 1997, p. 532). Research also indicates that the younger sisters of adolescent mothers may be more likely to become adolescent parents themselves, in part because the older sisters may communicate some acceptance of early motherhood (East, 1996a, 1996b; East & Felice, 1992).

There are important differences between pregnant teenagers who do and do not seek abortion. Although studies show that teenagers can make well-reasoned decisions about abortion (Adler, Ozer, & Tschann, 2003), this option is not chosen equally often within all segments of the adolescent population. Unplanned pregnancies are much more likely to be terminated by abortion among young women who are academically successful and ambitious, who come from middle- or upper-class families, whose parents are well educated, who live in wealthier neighborhoods, and whose significant others support the decision to terminate the pregnancy (Hayes, 1987; Miller & Moore, 1990; South & Baumer, 2001). An important factor accounting for the racial and socioeconomic differences in adolescent childbearing, therefore, is that white and middle-class adolescent women perceive themselves as having more to lose—economically and in terms of their careers— by having a child so early in life than do their minority and poor counterparts. It has also been suggested that, because teenage childbearing is so prevalent in the African American community, it is more accepted by adults and therefore more acceptable to teenagers (Coley & Chase-Lansdale, 1998). Consistent with this, research shows strong neighborhood influences on teenage childbearing: Among urban African American adolescents, childbearing is more common in segregated neighborhoods than in integrated ones (Sucoff & Upchurch, 1998).

▌ Psychological Consequences of Abortion

Several studies have examined whether teenagers who choose to abort an unwanted pregnancy are harmed psychologically by the experience. The consensus among experts is that they are not (Adler, Ozer, & Tschann, 2003). Indeed, several studies indicate that pregnant teenage women who abort their pregnancy are significantly better off, psychologically as well as socially and economically, than comparable women who choose to give birth to their child, both in the United States (Zabin, Hirsch, & Emerson, 1989) and abroad (Bailey et al., 2001). Among the most important differences between pregnant adolescents who do versus do not have an abortion is that young women who terminate their pregnancy by abortion are less likely over the next two years to experience a subsequent pregnancy and more likely to practice contraception. Given the apparent psychological and economic benefits of terminating an unwanted adolescent pregnancy, it is easy to understand why many social scientists have questioned the wisdom of court decisions designed to restrict adolescents' access to abortion services (Blum, Resnick, & Stark, 1990). While some studies show that laws requiring parental notification or limiting access to legal abortion do, in fact, result in fewer terminated pregnancies among adolescents (Joyce & Mocan, 1990; Rogers, Boruch, Storms, & DeMoya, 1991), not all studies reach the same conclusion (e.g., Henshaw, 1995). One possible reason for these inconsistent findings is that states requiring parental notification also tend to have high levels of religious involvement, both of which are associated with a lower teen abortion rate (Tomal, 2001).

■ **Adoption**   Less research has examined pregnant adolescents who choose adoption. In general, formal adoption, like abortion, is selected by adolescents from more affluent backgrounds and with higher educational aspirations (Donnelly & Voydanoff, 1996). However, informal adoption—in particular, having one's child raised by one's own mother—is widely practiced within the poor, African American community (Resnick, Blum, Bose, Smith, & Toogood, 1990; Sandven & Resnick, 1990). Like adolescents who choose to abort their pregnancy, those who choose to have their infant adopted (formally or informally) show no negative psychological effects of the decision. In fact, in terms of occupational and educational attainment, adolescents who select adoption are better off than those who choose to rear their child (Donnelly & Voydanoff, 1996; Kalmuss, Namerow, & Bauer, 1992; Sandven & Resnick, 1990). Unfortunately, many adolescents are ill informed about adoption procedures, and this lack of information likely makes adoption a relatively less frequent choice among pregnant teenagers (Daly, 1994).

THE ROLE OF THE FATHER

A number of studies have focused on the male partners of pregnant adolescents. In general, research indicates that these males share a number of distinguishing characteristics that differentiate them from their peers who have not gotten a teenager pregnant. Most important is the fact that they are relatively more likely to have problems with self-esteem, school, work, aggression, drugs and alcohol, and the law, and to have fathered a child previously (Dearden, Hale, & Woolley, 1995; Fagot, Pears, Capaldi, Crosby, & Leve, 1998;

Males & Chew, 1996; Miller-Johnson, Winn, Coie, Malone, & Lochman, 2004; Thornberry, Smith, & Howard, 1997). Much has been made in the popular media about the age gap between teenage mothers and the men who have fathered their children, but the proportion of teenage births fathered by adult men (that is, age 20 or older) actually has declined over the past 40 years, and the age difference between teenage mothers (most of whom are 18 or 19) and their sexual partners is generally about two or three years—a gap not substantially different than the age gap between husbands and wives in the general population (Elo, King, & Furstenberg, 1999). Moreover, girls who choose to get involved with older partners have more psychological problems than girls who do not, before the relationship begins (Young & d'Arcy, 2005). Regardless of the age difference between mother and father, however, the higher rates of problem behavior among the male partners of pregnant adolescents help to explain why marriage may not be the best response to pregnancy for teenage women, as we'll see shortly.

Although many of their problems precede the pregnancy, young men's educational development and mental health are adversely affected by fathering a child early in life, even if they do not marry the child's mother (Buchanan & Robbins, 1990; Furstenberg, Brooks-Gunn, & Chase-Lansdale, 1989; Nock, 1998; Sigle-Rushton, 2005; Vera Institute of Justice, 1990). Men who impregnate adolescent women are more likely to drop out of school and to report feeling anxious and depressed as young adults than their peers. The adverse effects of teenage fatherhood appear to be greater among white and Hispanic American men than among African American men, however, perhaps because teenage fatherhood is more disruptive and is seen as less acceptable within the white and Hispanic American communities (Buchanan & Robbins, 1990). In general, however, teenage fathers receive little in the way of supportive services or assistance in becoming responsible parents (Kiselica & Sturmer, 1993).

CONSEQUENCES FOR MOTHER AND CHILD

Because teenage childbearing tends to go hand in hand with a variety of other problems—the most critical of which is poverty—it is extremely difficult to know whether any problems of teenage mothers or their children result from the mother's young age or from other, correlated factors. Separating the effects of early childbearing from poverty is a matter of more than theoretical importance: If early childbearing is, in fact, a problem in and of itself, it becomes important to direct preventive programs at deterring adolescent pregnancy (either by discouraging sexual activity or by encouraging effective contraceptive use) and child-bearing (by encouraging adoption and abortion). But if poverty, not the mother's age, is the key, an entirely different set of strategies is called for, aimed not at youngsters' sexual behavior but at all individuals' economic circumstances. It is extremely important, therefore, to ask whether and in what ways a mother's age at the time she gives birth affects her and her child's well-being.

Children of Teen Mothers

We now know that many of the problems that plague children born to adolescent mothers result primarily from the environment of poverty and single parenthood in which these children are raised, and from other qualities that often characterize young women who become teen parents (such as poor school achievement), rather than from the mother's youth (e.g., Kalil & Kunz, 2002; Levine, Pollack, & Comfort, 2001; Schellenbach et al., 1992). In other words, infants born to middle-class adolescents differ little from their counterparts born to older middle-class mothers, and infants born to poor adolescents are similar to children born to equally poor adults.

One important exception to this general similarity between the children of adolescent and adult mothers is that adolescent mothers—even of similar socioeconomic status—may perceive their babies as being especially difficult and may interact with their infants less often in ways that are known to be beneficial to the child's cognitive and social development (Coley & Chase-Lansdale, 1998; Furstenberg et al., 1989; Miller & Moore, 1990; Schellenbach et al., 1992; Sommer et al., 1993). To what extent this directly jeopardizes the child's development is not known, although studies suggest that children born to adolescent mothers are more likely to have school problems, more likely to be involved in misbehavior and delinquent activity, and more likely themselves to be sexually active at an early age (Coley & Chase-Lansdale, 1998; Conseur, Rivara, Barnoski, & Emanuel, 1997; Hofferth & Reid, 2002; Wakschlag et al., 2000). In general, and for reasons that are not known, the cognitive and psychosocial problems of children born to adolescent mothers grow increasingly more apparent with age (that is, the differences between children born to teen versus adult mothers are more evident in adolescence than infancy). Again, though, studies show that the adverse outcomes of being born to an adolescent mother—even outcomes not visible until the children have reached young adulthood—are attributable both to characteristics of young women who are likely to become teen parents (for example, the adverse effects of being raised by someone who is poorly educated) and to the circumstances that characterize the family environments of young mothers (for example, the

adverse effects of growing up in poverty) (Jaffee, Caspi, Moffitt, Belsky, & Silva, 2001; Pogarsky, Lizotte, & Thornberry, 2003). Not surprisingly, then, adolescent mothers who were relatively more intelligent and better adjusted *before* the birth of their infant have greater parenting skills later (Mylod, Whitman, & Borkowski, 1997; O'Callaghan, Borkowski, Whitman, Maxwell, & Keogh, 1999), and children whose adolescent mothers are better educated, married, and better off financially do better in school than those whose mothers are less accomplished and single (Luster, Bates, Fitzgerald, Vandenbelt, & Key, 2000).

Because adolescent mothers are more likely than adult mothers to be both unmarried and poor, their children are at greater risk of developing a variety of psychological and social problems. Indeed, many of the problem behaviors seen among children of adolescent mothers are prevalent among poor children growing up in single-parent homes generally. In other words, the greater incidence of problems among offspring of adolescent mothers may reflect the overall environment in which their children grow up, rather than the ways in which they are raised. Although in theory we can separate the effects of poverty on children from the effects of adolescent childbearing, in reality, the two usually go together, and the end result is that children born to adolescent mothers are more likely than other children to suffer the effects both of malnutrition—in the womb as well as in the world—and of environmental deprivation.

Consequences for Teen Mothers

Studies of the long-term consequences of adolescent parenthood indicate that the problems associated with it may actually be greater for the mothers than for their children (Furstenberg et al., 1989). In general, women who bear children early suffer disruptions in their educational and occupational careers (Fergusson & Woodward, 2000; Hofferth, Reid, & Mott, 2001; Klepinger, Lundberg, & Plotnick, 1995; Otterblad Olausson, Haglund, Ringback, Weitoft, & Cnattingius, 2001). Not only are adolescent mothers more likely to come from a poor background and to have a history of academic difficulties, but they are also more likely to remain poor than their equally disadvantaged peers who delay childbearing until after their schooling is completed (Hoffman, Foster, & Furstenberg, Jr., 1993; Moore et al., 1993; Richardson, 1996). It is important to bear in mind, however, that many adolescent mothers were poor students *before* becoming pregnant, and the limited educational attainment of teenage mothers is at least partly due to factors that were in play long before the pregnancy, perhaps even during early childhood (Fergusson & Woodward, 2000; Miller-Johnson et al., 1999; Roenkae & Pulkkinen, 1998; Russell, 2002; Shearer et

In order to be effective, sex education courses that focus on increasing youngsters' knowledge about sex, contraception, and pregnancy need to begin early and include lessons in decision making and interpersonal assertiveness.

al., 2002). In short, poverty and low achievement are both causes *and* consequences of early childbearing.

Having a child early in life does not inevitably cast in concrete a life of poverty and misery for the mother and her youngster, however. Studies show that there is considerable diversity among teenage mothers in the routes that their adult lives take (Ahn, 1994; Coley & Chase-Lansdale, 1998). One recent study identified three distinct groups: a problem-prone group (15 percent of the sample), who had chronic problems in many areas of life, including antisocial behavior; a psychologically vulnerable group (42 percent), who had relatively high rates of mental health problems but who were able to transition into adult roles with some degree of success; and a normative group (43 percent), who defied common stereotypes of adolescent mothers as doomed to failure and poverty, and who were able to make a successful transition to adulthood (Oxford et al., 2005). Some research suggests that the long-term consequences of early childbearing may not be as negative among African Americans as among whites or Hispanic Americans, especially among African Americans living in communities in which early childbearing is accepted as normative (Moore et al., 1993; Smith & Zabin, 1993).

In general, young mothers who remain in, or return to, high school and delay subsequent childbearing fare a great deal better over the long run—as do their children—than their counterparts who drop out of school or have more children relatively early on (Furstenberg et al., 1987; Leadbeater, 1996; Upchurch & McCarthy, 1990). Indeed, remaining in school and living at home with one's parents significantly diminishes the chances

of a second unwanted pregnancy (Manlove, Mariner, & Papillo, 2000). Marriage, in contrast, tends to be a high-risk strategy (Furstenberg et al., 1987). In some cases, when a stable relationship is formed and economic resources are available, marriage improves the mother's and the child's chances for life success; this seems to be especially true for women who marry somewhat later. In other cases, however, a hasty decision to marry in the absence of a stable relationship and economic security actually exacerbates many other problems (Teti & Lamb, 1989).

TEENAGE PREGNANCY PREVENTION AND INTERVENTION PROGRAMS

Although there are stories of young women whose lives are not devastated by early childbearing, in general, studies suggest that the successes are young women who have avoided poverty, rather than achieving great economic success. Although the picture of adolescent parenthood appears less uniformly or dire than typically painted in the media, there is still consensus among experts that it is important to try to prevent teenage pregnancy and childbearing. Unfortunately, this task is more easily said than done. To date, few strategies have proven effective on a large scale.

■ **Sex Education in Schools** The first line of teenage pregnancy prevention has been classroom-based sex education. Today, many adolescents receive some sort of classroom instruction about sex—whether through high school health classes, biology classes, classes designated exclusively for the purpose of sex education, or educational programs administered through youth or religious organizations. Most evaluations of formal sex education programs administered through schools have shown them to have no effect on adolescents' sexual activity but small effects on their contraceptive behavior (Franklin, Grant, Corcoran, Miller, & Bultman, 1997). The consensus among experts has been that most traditional sex education programs fail because they emphasize the biological over the emotional aspects of sex (and thus do not prepare adolescents for making decisions about sexual involvement); because they come too late in high school (and thus do not reach adolescents before they become sexually active); and because they focus primarily on changing students' knowledge rather than their behavior (and thus do not directly affect patterns of sexual activity or contraceptive use) (Landry, Singh, & Darroch, 2000).

During the mid-1980s, the emphasis in sex education shifted from encouraging "responsible" sex to encouraging sexual abstinence, an emphasis that still

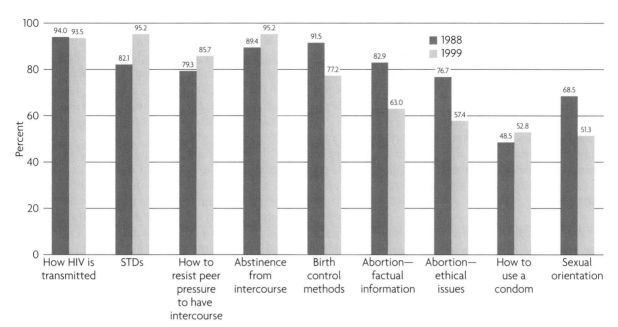

FIGURE 11.9   During the 1990s, there was a steep increase in the proportion of American sex education classes that emphasized abstinence, and a substantial decline in the proportion that discussed birth control and abortion. This graph shows the
percentages of classes covering various topics in 1988 and 1999. (Adapted from Darroch, Landry, & Singh, 2000)

prevails in many school districts (Landry, Kaeser, &
Richards, 1999). As you can see in Figure 11.9, during
the 1990s, there were significant increases in the number of schools in which sex education included information on abstinence and resisting peer pressure to
have sex, and significant declines in discussion of birth
control and abortion; indeed, in 1999, nearly one-
fourth of sex education teachers taught abstinence as
the *only* means of protection against pregnancy or
STDs, compared with just 2 percent 10 years earlier
(Darroch, Landry, & Singh, 2000). In addition to ses-
sions about sexual decision making and values and
exercises designed to enhance students' self-esteem,
such programs teach adolescents to "just say no" to
sexual intercourse. It was hoped that by encouraging
sexual abstinence these programs would also have the
effect of reducing teenage pregnancy. Unfortunately,
careful evaluations of these programs have shown that
they are not usually successful, either in changing adolescents' sexual behavior or in reducing rates of nonmarital pregnancy (Christopher, 1995; Christopher &
Roosa, 1990; Kirby, Korpi, Barth, & Cagampang, 1997;
Leiberman, Gray, Wier, Fiorentino, & Maloney, 2000;
Roosa & Christopher, 1990).

▋ **What Works?**   Does anything work? One approach that experts are cautiously optimistic about involves a combination of school-based sex education
and community-based health clinics through which
adolescents can receive information about sex and

pregnancy as well as contraception. Some evaluations
indicate that this combination of sex education and
clinical care may diminish the rate of teen pregnancy,
even within inner-city communities characterized by
high rates of adolescent pregnancy and childbearing
(Christopher, 1995; Frost & Forrest, 1995; Koo, Dunteman, George, Green, & Vincent, 1994; Tiezzi, Lipshutz,
Wrobleski, Vaughan, & McCarthy, 1997). Unfortunately, as you might suspect, many parents have ob-
jected to having such programs in their community,
fearing that they will stimulate teenage sexual activity.
However, most studies indicate that these fears—however intuitively reasonable—are unwarranted; in general, condom distribution programs increase adolescents' condom use but have little impact on the rate of
sexual activity (Christopher, 1995; Furstenberg, Geitz,
Teitler, & Weiss, 1997; Guttmacher et al., 1997; Kaplan
et al., 2001; Richardson, 1997; Schuster, Bell, Berry, &
Kanouse, 1998).

At the same time, programs that provide family
planning services to adolescents are unlikely, on their
own, to solve the problems of teenage pregnancy and
sexually transmitted diseases. Even the best programs
only affect the sexual behavior of teenagers who actually use the services (Brindis, Starbuck-Morales,
Wolfe, & McCarter, 1994; Christopher, 1995; Erikson, 1994; Hughes, Furstenberg, Jr., & Teitler, 1995).
As a consequence, many communities that implement these sorts of prevention programs do not
experience overall declines in rates of teen pregnancy

(Christopher, 1995). Clearly, effective prevention programs must find ways to motivate sexually active adolescents to make use of whatever health care services are provided. One program, for example, had success by combining service learning with classroom discussions about life options (Allen & Philliber, 2001; Allen, Philliber, Herrling, & Kuperminc, 1997). Other promising approaches focus more generally on facilitating positive youth development than on preventing pregnancy or sexual activity (East, Kierman, & Chavez, 2003; Philliber, Kaye, Herrling, & West, 2002).

After the Baby Is Born   Research on the consequences of adolescent childbearing also suggests that many of the negative effects of having children early can be prevented or at least minimized by lessening the disruptive economic impact of teenage parenthood on young women's lives (Sandfort & Hill, 1996). What do we know about the factors that work toward this end? First, it is clear that marrying the father of the child may place the adolescent mother at greater risk if the father is not capable of supporting himself economically, much less his family. Studies show, in contrast, that if the father is able to find a good job and remain employed, he can be an important source of psychological and economic support, and a healthy influence on the mother and child. Given the characteristic problems of male partners of adolescent mothers that we discussed earlier, however, it is all too likely that marriage may diminish, rather than enhance, an adolescent mother's economic circumstances. In addition, marriage places the adolescent mother at greater risk of having another child relatively soon, which further jeopardizes her already precarious economic situation. One of the factors most likely to worsen the problems of teenage mothers is having yet another child (Apfel & Seitz, 1997; Furstenberg et al., 1987; Kalmuss & Namerow, 1994). Moreover, teenage marriage is very likely to end in divorce, which itself is an additional stressor on the mother and child.

Adolescent mothers therefore cannot always look to the father of the child to help break the cycle of poverty that afflicts many young parents. However, they can, in many cases, look to their own parents for support, and this may be an effective strategy for some (Stevens, 1988). Teenage mothers who move in with their own family *for a short time*—a practice far more common among African Americans than among Hispanic Americans or white adolescents—are more likely to enjoy educational and occupational success than their counterparts who live on their own, because the family's help allows the young mother to return to school or find employment (Miller & Moore, 1990;

Roye & Balk, 1996; Trent & Harlan, 1994). Without this help, many young mothers must drop out of school and find and pay for child care, which often is more costly than the income their low-paying jobs generate. Without a high school diploma, these women have little chance of improving their economic situation and, consequently, of improving the opportunities for their child.

Although having the support of her own family is important for the adolescent mother's development and well-being, living with the family of origin for an extended period after having a baby is not uniformly beneficial, as several studies of three-generational African American families show. On the negative side, when the adolescent mother lives with her own mother, the living arrangement may undermine the development of her own parenting skills and increase the risk of getting pregnant again (Chase-Lansdale, Brooks-Gunn, & Zamsky, 1994; Gillmore, Lewis, Lohr, Spencer, & White, 1997; Spieker & Bensley, 1994), and problems in the relationship between the adolescent and her mother can adversely affect the teen parent's mental health (Davis & Rhodes, 1994; East & Felice, 1996; Musick, 1994). On the positive side, living with one's mother is associated with continued schooling, which confers long-term economic advantages (Spieker & Bensley, 1994). Interestingly, several studies have found that support from the adolescent's father, in addition to that of her mother, may be especially beneficial (Davis, Rhodes, & Hamilton-Leaks, 1997; Oyserman, Radin, & Benn, 1993).

FOOD FOR THOUGHT

Based on what you've read in this section, what advice would you give a 17-year-old young woman who was pregnant and unsure about what she should do?

One fact is certain, though: Adolescent mothers who receive social support fare better, are better parents, and have healthier children than do adolescent mothers who lack support (Barratt, Roach, Morgan, & Colbert, 1996; Leadbeater & Bishop, 1994; Riggs, Holmbeck, Paikoff, & Bryant, 2004; Turner, Sorenson, & Turner, 2000). Studies suggest that a lack of support is an especially dire problem among poor Hispanic adolescent mothers (Wasserman et al., 1990). Taken together, these and other studies suggest that the best arrangement for a teenage mother may be to live independently from her own parents but rely on them for emotional support and child care (Coley & Chase-Lansdale, 1998).

Because it is so important for young mothers to have an adequate income and the chance for adequate employment, many policymakers have called for changes in the ways that schools and other social institutions treat pregnant students, and changes in the provision of day care (Sandfort & Hill, 1996; Seitz & Apfel, 1993, 1994). Among the most important are adaptations in school schedules and the development of school-based child care centers, so that pregnant students can remain in school after the birth of their child; the expansion of subsidized child care for young mothers who are out of school, so that the economic benefits of having a job are not outweighed by the costs of child care; and the expansion of family planning services to adolescent mothers so that they can prevent yet another pregnancy. Unfortunately, evaluations of programs aimed at enhancing teen mothers' employability, decreasing their reliance on welfare, or preventing their subsequent pregnancies have been largely disappointing (Coley & Chase-Lansdale, 1998), although occasional successes have been reported in the literature (e.g., Solomon & Liefeld, 1998).

RECAP

- Preventing teenage pregnancy has been extremely difficult, and most sex education programs developed during the past two decades have failed in this respect.
- About half of all teenage pregnancies result in the birth of a child who is raised by the teen parent; the majority of other pregnancies are aborted.
- Teenagers are not harmed psychologically by aborting their pregnancy or by placing their infant up for adoption, but studies of the consequences of teenage childbearing indicate that both short- and long-term problems for the teenage mother may be considerable.
- While there are occasional success stories, teenage parents are more likely than their peers to experience disruptions in their educational and occupational development.
- Adolescent mothers who have social support from family or friends and who are able to complete high school fare far better than those who do not.

CHAPTER 12

Achievement

ACHIEVEMENT AS AN ADOLESCENT ISSUE

ACHIEVEMENT MOTIVES AND BELIEFS

The Motive to Achieve

The Importance of Beliefs

ENVIRONMENTAL INFLUENCES ON ACHIEVEMENT

The Influence of the Home Environment

The Influence of Friends

EDUCATIONAL ACHIEVEMENT

The Importance of Socioeconomic Status

Ethnic Differences in Educational Achievement

Changes in Educational Achievement over Time

Dropping Out of High School

OCCUPATIONAL ACHIEVEMENT

The Development of Occupational Plans

Influences on Occupational Choices

BECAUSE ADOLESCENCE IS typically a time of preparation for the roles of adulthood, considerable attention has been paid to the development and expression of achievement during these years. Broadly defined, **achievement** concerns the development of motives, capabilities, interests, and behavior that have to do with performance in evaluative situations. More specifically, the study of achievement during adolescence has focused on young people's performance in educational settings and on their hopes and plans for future scholastic and occupational careers. Since most young people form their first realistic educational and vocational plans during adolescence, researchers have long been interested in the factors that play the greatest role in influencing individuals' futures.

Achievement is a particularly important consideration in the study of adolescence in contemporary society. Industrialized societies place an extraordinary emphasis on achievement, competition, and success. During childhood and adolescence, youngsters are continually tested to determine how they stand scholastically in relation to their peers. In most industrialized societies, the amount of education a person has completed and the job he or she holds—two of the most important indicators of achievement—provide a basis for the individual's self-conceptions and his or her image in the eyes of others (Featherman, 1980).

A second reason for the importance of the concept of achievement in the study of adolescence in contemporary society concerns the range and rapidly changing nature of the choices faced by today's young people. Unlike youth in most traditional cultures, adolescents in modern societies are confronted with an array of difficult occupational and educational decisions before they turn 25. Beyond such fundamental questions as what type of career to follow and whether to continue with schooling after high school, issues to ponder include what specific sorts of jobs should be pursued within a particular career path, what kind of educational preparation would be most appropriate, and how entry into the labor force is best negotiated. For the college student contemplating a career in business, for instance, is it better to major in business administration or to follow a liberal arts course of study? How early is it necessary to decide which aspects of business to specialize in? Is it necessary to go to graduate school, or do employers prefer applicants with work experience in place of an advanced degree? These are all difficult questions to answer. And they are made more difficult because the nature of education and work changes so rapidly in contemporary society.

Finally, achievement is a particularly important issue in the study of adolescence in contemporary society because of the wide variation in levels of educational and occupational success. By the end of high school, many adolescents demonstrate a high enough level of academic achievement to enter selective colleges and universities; yet a sizable number of their peers enter adulthood unable even to read a newspaper or understand a bus schedule. Although three-quarters of adolescents in the United States today complete high school and go on to college, some leave high school before graduating. Similar disparities exist in the occupational achievements of young people: Most youth make the transition from school to work without a great deal of difficulty, but a significant number experience long bouts of unemployment. Even within the population of young people who enter the labor force, there is considerable variation in earnings and in occupational status. Many important questions in the study of adolescent achievement, therefore, concern factors that distinguish between young people who are successful—however success is defined—and those who are not.

Achievement as an Adolescent Issue

As noted above, in contemporary society, achievement is a lifelong concern. Educational institutions—even for young children—stress performance, competition, and success on tests of knowledge and ability. Concerns over achievement continue throughout adulthood as well. Like their younger counterparts, adults for the most part place a premium on success. Work and occupational attainment play an important role in shaping the adult's values, self-concept, and self-esteem (Featherman, 1980). Development in the realm of achievement neither begins nor ends during adolescence.

achievement The psychosocial domain concerning behaviors and feelings in evaluative situations.

Achievement during the adolescent years, though, merits special attention for several reasons (Masten et al., 1995). First, the fact that adolescence is a time of preparation for adult work roles raises questions about the nature of the preparation young people receive and the processes through which they sort themselves (or are sorted) into the occupational roles that may influence the remainder of their lives. Many of the factors that narrow an individual's educational options and vocational alternatives are prominent during the high school and college years, and it is important to ask how such options are defined and at what age educational and occupational decisions are made.

FOOD FOR THOUGHT

Adults disagree about the extent to which achievement is, and should be, made an especially salient issue among adolescents. Some contend that we place too much pressure on teenagers to succeed in school. Others argue that we do not place enough. What's your view?

Second, although differences in school performance and achievement are apparent as early as the first grade, not until adolescence do individuals begin to appreciate fully the implications of these differences for immediate and future success. During childhood, for example, children's occupational plans are to a large extent made on the basis of fantasy and passing interests, without any realistic assessment of their practicality or feasibility. Not until adolescence do individuals begin to evaluate their occupational choices in light of their talents, abilities, opportunities, and the performance of those around them. For example, high-achieving students who attend schools in which average achievement levels are high do not feel as good about themselves as their high-achieving counterparts in schools with lower average achievement levels (Marsh, Kong, & Hau, 2000).

Third, the educational and occupational decisions made during adolescence are more numerous, and the consequences of such decisions more serious, than the decisions characteristic of childhood. For example, in most elementary schools, although children may be grouped by ability—groupings that have implications for subsequent achievement—they generally are all exposed to fairly similar curricula and have few opportunities to veer from the educational program established by their school system. In high school, however, students can select how much science and math they want to take (in the view of some experts [e.g., Schmidt, 2003], this is one of the reasons American students do so poorly in international achievement comparisons), whether they wish to study a foreign language, whether they want to pursue an academic or vocational track—even whether they want to remain in school once they have reached the legal age for leaving school. Moreover, it is during adolescence that most individuals decide whether they want to pursue postsecondary education or enter a full-time job directly from high school. All these decisions have important implications for the sort of choices and plans the adolescent will make in the future, which, in turn, will influence his or her earnings, lifestyle, identity, and subsequent psychosocial development.

Social Roles and Achievement in Adolescence

It is neither surprising nor coincidental that many achievement-related issues surface for the first time during adolescence. One major reason for this relates to the social transition of adolescence. In virtually all societies, adolescence is the period when important educational and occupational decisions are made, and society has structured its educational and work institutions accordingly. In America, for example, it is not until adolescence that individuals attain the status necessary to decide whether they will continue or end their formal education. And it is not until adolescence that individuals are allowed to enter the labor force in an official capacity, since child labor regulations typically prohibit the formal employment of youngsters under the age of 14 or so. The transition from school to work—one of the central issues in the study of achievement during adolescence—is a socially defined transition, a passage that society has determined will be negotiated during adolescence.

Cognitive Change and Achievement in Adolescence

The special significance of achievement in adolescence does not derive solely from the transitional nature of the period, however. The intellectual changes of the period are important as well. Not until adolescence are individuals cognitively capable of seeing the long-term consequences of educational and occupational choices or of realistically considering the range of scholastic and work possibilities open to them. Thus, a second reason for the prominence of achievement-related issues during adolescence relates to the advent of more sophisticated forms of thinking. The ability to think in hypothetical terms, for example, raises new achievement concerns for the individual ("Should I go to college after I graduate, or should I work for a while?"); it also permits the young person to think through such questions in a logical and systematic fashion ("If I decide to go to college, then . . .").

▌Puberty and Achievement in Adolescence

Although the biological changes of puberty are probably less important influences on achievement than are the cognitive and social-role transitions of the period, they may nevertheless affect adolescents' school performance in important ways. Individuals who look more mature may elicit different reactions from teachers and other students. Some writers, for instance, have suggested that going through puberty early may disadvantage girls in school, because they may feel conflicts between their desire to be physically attractive to boys and their desire to do well in school (which they may feel undermines their attractiveness). Although girls who mature at a later age may also experience these conflicting demands, older girls are more likely to have the confidence and maturity to realize that they can be both successful in the classroom and popular with their peers. And to the extent that early physical maturation also draws adolescents into older peer groups, in which experimentation with alcohol and drugs is more likely, going through puberty early may disadvantage boys as well, since using drugs and alcohol can undermine students' motivation (Zimmerman & Schmeelk-Cone, 2003).

In this chapter, we look at the nature of achievement during the adolescent years. As you will see, the extent to which an adolescent is successful in school and in preparing for work is influenced by a complex array of personal and environmental factors. In addition, development in the realm of achievement is cumulative, in that youngsters who are successful early on are likely to reap the benefits of the educational system, to continue to succeed in school, and to complete more years of education than their peers. This success, in turn, gives them an advantage in the labor market, since the prestige and status of individuals' entry-level jobs are largely dependent on their educational background.

If there is a theme to this chapter, it is, at least with respect to achievement over the course of adolescence, that the rich get richer and the poor get poorer. More often than not, personal and environmental influences on achievement complement rather than correct each other, in the sense that individuals who bring personal advantages to the world of achievement—talent, motivation to succeed, high aspirations for the future—are also likely to grow up in an environment that supports and maintains success in school and work.

We begin with a look at one set of factors that may differentiate the "rich" from the "poor" early in their schooling—long before adolescence, in fact: their motive to succeed and their beliefs about the causes of their successes and failures.

RECAP

- Achievement is an important issue during adolescence because society typically designates adolescence as a time for preparation for adult work roles, because individuals now can understand the long-term implications of their educational and career decisions, and because during adolescence schools begin making distinctions among individuals that potentially have profound effects on their long-term occupational development.
- The fundamental changes of adolescence affect the development of achievement in several ways. Society has structured the worlds of school and work so that major transitions in the domain of achievement necessarily take place in adolescence.
- The cognitive changes of adolescence allow individuals to engage in longer-term, hypothetical thinking and planning about their educational and occupational futures.
- Puberty may affect the development of achievement by transforming the physical appearance of the adolescent, which may affect the way he or she is perceived by adults and peers.
- Because educational and occupational achievement are so cumulative, during adolescence the rich tend to get richer, while the poor get poorer.

Achievement Motives and Beliefs

THE MOTIVE TO ACHIEVE

One of the oldest notions in the study of achievement is that individuals differ in the extent to which they strive for success, and that this differential striving—which can be measured independently of sheer ability—helps to account for different degrees of actual achievement. Two students may both score 100 on an intelligence test, but if one student simply tries much harder than the other to do well in school, their actual grades may differ. The extent to which an individual strives for success is referred to as his or her **need for achievement** (McClelland, Atkinson, Clark, & Lowell, 1953). Need for achievement is an intrinsically motivated desire to perform well that operates even in the absence of external rewards for success. A student who works very hard on an assignment that is not going to be graded probably has a very strong need

need for achievement A need that influences the extent to which an individual strives for success in evaluative situations.

for achievement. All other factors being equal, a student who tries hard to succeed in school is, in fact, more likely to succeed than one who tries less (Wentzel, 1989).

One of the oldest findings in the study of adolescent development is that adolescents who have a strong need for achievement come from families in which parents have set high performance standards, have rewarded achievement success during childhood, and have encouraged autonomy and independence (Rosen & D'Andrade, 1959; Winterbottom, 1958). Equally important, however, is the fact that this training for achievement and independence generally takes place in the context of a warm parent–child relationship in which the child forms close identifications with his or her parents (Shaw & White, 1965). Put most succinctly, authoritative parenting, coupled with parents' encouragement of success, is likely to lead to the development of a strong need for achievement.

▌ Fear of Failure One psychological factor that interacts with an adolescent's need for achievement is a related, and in some senses complementary, motive—**fear of failure.** Fear of failure, which is often manifested in feelings of anxiety during tests or in other evaluative situations, can interfere with successful performance. Generally, when the achievement situation involves an easy task, and when a little anxiety helps to focus attention (if, for example, the task is boring), a moderate amount of fear of failure may improve performance by increasing one's concentration. Usually, however, the anxiety generated by a strong fear of failure interferes with successful performance. This is often the case in situations in which the task involves learning something new or solving a complex problem—like many tasks faced by adolescents in school settings. Individuals with a high fear of failure often come from family environments in which parents have set unrealistically high standards for their children's achievement and react very negatively to failure (rather than simply reacting positively to success) (Spielberger, 1966).

An adolescent's need for achievement and her or his fear of failure work together to pull the individual toward (or repel the individual from) achievement situations. Individuals with a relatively strong need for achievement and a relatively weak fear of failure are more likely to actively approach challenging achievement situations—by taking more difficult classes, for example—and to look forward to them. In contrast, those whose fear of failure is relatively intense and whose need for achievement is relatively weak will dread challenging situations and do what they can to avoid them. Many students who have trouble persisting at tasks and who fear failure become **underachievers**— their grades are far lower than one would expect based on their intellectual ability.

▌ Self-Handicapping It is important to distinguish between students whose underachievement is due mainly to anxiety and those who underperform for other reasons (Midgley, Arunkumar, & Urdan, 1996; Midgley & Urdan, 1995). Some students, for example, want to appear uninterested in school because in some contexts this presentation may garner more respect and admiration from peers than academic success. Others want to make sure that they have an excuse for poor performance other than a lack of ability (Nurmi, Onatsu, & Haavisto, 1995). Still others may downplay the importance of academics as a response to their poor performance (Gibbons, Benbow, & Gerrard, 1994). These students may use various **self-handicapping** strategies—such as fooling around in class, waiting until the last minute to study for a test, turning in incomplete homework, or partying excessively the night before a big exam—as a way of self-protection ("I failed the test because I didn't try hard, not because I'm stupid") or as a means of enhancing their self-presentation ("I'm too cool to care about doing well in school"). Although self-handicapping is common among both males and females, there are sex differences in the ways in which adolescent girls and boys undermine their own success in school: Boys who self-handicap tend to attribute their poor performance to a lack of effort, whereas girls are more likely to mention emotional problems (Warner & Moore, 2004). A number of writers have drawn special attention to the use of self-handicapping strategies among ethnic minority youth, who may disengage from school because they perceive their long-term prospects as being limited by discrimination and prejudice (Mickelson, 1990; Taylor, Casten, Flickinger, Roberts, & Fulmore, 1994).

THE IMPORTANCE OF BELIEFS

In recent years, researchers have questioned the usefulness of asserting the existence of global achievement-related motives that are expressed equally in a variety of situations. The relation between an individual's internal needs and his or her actual effort and performance varies in different situations. Someone who has a strong need for achievement might express this need to different degrees in academic and in social situations—or even in different sorts of academic and

---

fear of failure   Fear of the consequences of failing in achievement situations.

underachievers   Individuals whose actual school performance is lower than what would be expected on the basis of objective measures of their aptitude or intelligence.

self-handicapping   Deliberately behaving in ways that will likely interfere with doing well, in order to have an excuse for failing.

social situations—depending on past experiences and his or her perception of the specific situation. Because of this, individuals' actual performance in achievement situations may not be strongly related to their general achievement motives. Some students who want very much to succeed, for example, are susceptible to feelings of anxiety and helplessness in performance settings.

We now know that adolescents make judgments about their likelihood of succeeding or failing and that they exert different degrees of effort accordingly. For example, adolescents' choices of what classes to take in school are influenced by their beliefs about their abilities. Students who believe that they are good at math, for instance, will take more, and more difficult, math courses than their peers. But because course selection influences subsequent achievement (students who take more challenging math classes perform better on math tests), and achievement, in turn, influences students' beliefs about their abilities (students who do well on math tests come to see themselves as better math students), a cycle is set in motion in which students' beliefs, abilities, and actual achievement have a reciprocal influence on each other (Marsh & Yeung, 1997).

▌ **Two Types of Motivation**   A number of studies indicate that students' beliefs about their abilities exert a particularly strong influence on their motivation and effort, which, in turn, influences their scholastic performance (Harter, Whitesell, & Kowalski, 1991; Little, Oettingen, Stensenko, & Baltes, 1995; MacIver, Stipek, & Daniels, 1991; Pintrich, Roeser, & De Groot, 1994). In order to understand this process, it is necessary to draw a distinction between **intrinsic motivation** (sometimes referred to as "mastery motivation") and **extrinsic motivation** (sometimes referred to as "performance motivation"). Individuals who are intrinsically motivated strive to achieve because of the pleasure they get out of learning and mastering the material. Individuals who are extrinsically motivated strive to achieve because of the rewards they get for performing well and the punishments they receive for performing poorly. Early theories of achievement motivation did not draw this distinction and, as a consequence, may have grouped together students who—while highly motivated to do well in achievement situations—may have been motivated for very different reasons.

We all know individuals who are genuinely interested in what they learn in school, and we know others

Individuals who are intrinsically motivated strive to achieve because of the pleasure they get out of mastering the material.

whose main concern is really just their grade point average. These two approaches to achievement have very different psychological consequences for the individual adolescent. Adolescents who believe that they are competent are more likely to be intrinsically motivated and to maintain their efforts to do well in school (Pintrich et al., 1994). In contrast, adolescents who have doubts about their abilities are more likely to be extrinsically motivated and to be more susceptible to feelings of anxiety and hesitation in the face of challenge. That is, although extrinsically motivated adolescents want to do well in school, the source of their motivation puts them on shaky ground. Being intrinsically motivated in school is a stable trait, by the way—children who are relatively more intrinsically motivated in elementary school tend to be relatively more intrinsically motivated through high school (Gottfried, Fleming, & Gottfried, 2001).

You read earlier that adults—parents and teachers, for instance—can affect adolescents' degree of achievement motivation. Adults can also affect the extent to which an adolescent's achievement motives are intrinsic

intrinsic motivation   Motivation based on the pleasure one will experience from mastering a task.

extrinsic motivation   Motivation based on the rewards one will receive for successful performance.

or extrinsic. When adults attempt to control an adolescent's achievement behavior by rewarding good grades (such as by giving prizes or money), punishing bad grades (such as by restricting privileges), or excessively supervising their performance (such as by constantly checking up on their homework), adolescents are more likely to develop an extrinsic orientation and, as a result, are less likely to do well in school. In contrast, adolescents whose parents encourage their autonomy, provide a cognitively stimulating home environment, and are supportive of school success (without rewarding it concretely) tend to perform better in the classroom (Deci & Ryan, 1985; Ginsburg & Bronstein, 1993; Gottfried, Fleming, & Gottfried, 1998). Research also suggests that low-achieving students are more affected—for better or for worse—by their teachers' expectations than are high-achieving students (Madon, Jussim, & Eccles, 1997).

▌ **Stereotype Threat**   Student's beliefs about their abilities, and as a consequence, their performance, can also be affected by situational factors operating when they take an exam. Psychologist Claude Steele (1997) has demonstrated that when students are told that members of their ethnic group usually perform poorly on a particular test (for example, before the test is administered, students are told that previous studies have shown that members of their ethnic group do not score as well as other students), their performance actually suffers, whereas the reverse is true when students are told that members of their ethnic group usually perform better than others. This so-called **stereotype threat** effect has also been demonstrated to depress females' performance when they are told before taking a test that males usually outperform females (Keller, 2002). To the extent that adolescents believe widely held stereotypes about ethnic or sex differences in ability (for example, that boys are just better at math than girls), their achievement may be enhanced or depressed, depending on how they think they are expected to perform.

Although for many years experts who studied adolescents expressed special concern about the motives and beliefs of adolescent girls, particular with regard to performance in math and science, in recent years studies have shown that many previously observed sex differences have gotten much smaller or have disappeared (Vermeer, Boekaerts, & Seegers, 2000). One possible reason for this is that stereotypes about sex differences in cognitive ability have weakened considerably. Indeed, in contrast to several decades ago, when raters in experiments judged successful females as less likable, less attractive, and less likely to be happy, similar experiments conducted more recently show the opposite effect, perhaps because we have become that much more accustomed to seeing suc-

cessful girls and women in a variety of settings and endeavors (Quatman, Sokolik, & Smith, 2000). With improvements in girls' achievement—across all subject areas—the achievement gap is closing, even in subjects that traditionally have been dominated by males. When sex differences in math and science achievement are reported today, they are very slight, especially in the United States (Evans, Schweingruber, & Stevenson, 2002; Leahy, 2001). Indeed, observations that boys are not doing as well in school in girls, that boys are disciplined more in school than girls, and that boys are more likely to perceive their schools and teachers as unfair (Nichols & Good, 1998; Pomerantz, Altermatt, & Saxon, 2002) have prompted numerous writers to express concern about the achievement problems of boys (Marsh & Yeung, 1998; Sommers, 2000). Sex differences in educational attainment have grown in recent years, with females far outnumbering males on American college campuses (Lewin, 2006). Sex differences in educational attainment, favoring females, are especially great among African American adolescents (King, 2006; Saunders, Davis, Williams, & Williams, 2004).

▌ **Beliefs About Intelligence**   Other studies suggest that the way in which adolescents think about intelligence in general (in addition to how they view their own capability) also enters into the achievement equation; what's especially crucial is whether intelligence is thought of as something that is fixed or as something that is changeable (Stipek & Gralinski, 1996). Thus, three factors interact to predict students' behavior in school: whether the student believes that intelligence is fixed or malleable, whether the student is oriented more toward extrinsic rewards (performance) or intrinsic rewards (mastery), and whether the student is confident about his or her abilities, or, as some theorists have put it, has a strong sense of **self-efficacy** (Bandura, Barbaranelli, Caprara, & Pastorelli, 1996). Although it is possible to make general statements about where students' beliefs fall with regard to these three dimensions, it is also true that their beliefs, reward orientation, and sense of self-efficacy will vary somewhat from subject to subject (that is, it is possible to feel very confident about one's math ability but less so about one's skills in social studies); this is especially true once students reach high school (Bong, 2001).

What do these different achievement profiles look like? Students who believe that intelligence is fixed

stereotype threat   The harmful effect that exposure to stereotypes about ethnic or sex differences in ability has on student performance.

self-efficacy   The sense that an individual has some control over his or her life.

tend to be oriented toward their performance and to be greatly affected by their degree of confidence (Stipek & Gralinski, 1996). If they are confident about their abilities, they tend to work hard and to seek out challenges. If they are insecure, however, they tend to give up easily and to feel helpless. In other words, if you believe that intelligence is fixed, it's important to have confidence in your own abilities.

Students who believe that intelligence is malleable, in contrast, approach achievement situations from a different perspective. These students are more likely to have learning goals than performance goals; for them, satisfaction comes from mastering the material, not simply from gaining a good evaluation. They are also far less affected by their level of confidence, because they are less concerned about their performance. Whether assured or insecure, these students exert extra effort and seek out challenges, because they are motivated by learning rather than by performing (Purdie, Hattie, & Douglas, 1996).

▍ **The Importance of Context** Although students' orientation toward mastery versus performance is determined in part by psychological factors, the educational context matters as well. When classroom conditions change so that performance becomes more important than learning, students' motives and beliefs change as a result. You have probably experienced this when you enrolled in a course in which the instructor stressed grades rather than mastery of the material. This sort of emphasis brings out the worst in students—literally. Under some circumstances, performance goals make students more extrinsically motivated, more insecure about their abilities, more hesitant to challenge themselves, and less likely to ask for help to improve their performance (Newman & Schwager, 1995). This is especially likely when students are motivated mainly by trying to avoid looking stupid (which diminishes their performance) rather than by trying to compete with and outperform their classmates (which enhances their performance) (Pintrich, 2000). In classrooms in which teachers are very performance-oriented (rather than master-oriented), students, on average, engage in self-handicapping behavior (Urdan, 2004).

One of the most interesting applications of this perspective on achievement has been in studies of changes in adolescents' academic motivation during the transition from elementary school to junior high school (Eccles et al., 1993). As you read in Chapter 6, it has been widely reported that students' motivation and school performance decline when they move into

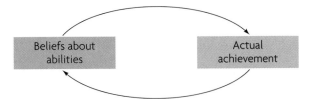

FIGURE 12.1 Adolescents' beliefs about their abilities influence their actual achievement, which, in turn, shapes their beliefs about their abilities. (Simpkins et al., 2006)

secondary school (Eccles, 2004; Elmen, 1991; Yoon, Eccles, Wigfield, & Barber, 1996). Why might this be? Among the other important changes that take place during this school transition is a shift on the part of teachers toward a more performance-oriented style of instruction and evaluation. Elementary school teachers tend to stress the importance of mastering the material. During secondary school, however, students discover that more of an emphasis is placed on grades. This shift in emphasis undermines many students' intrinsic motivation and their self-confidence, which, in turn, diminishes their performance. Indeed, during the early years of high school, there is a general decline in adolescents' feelings of self-efficacy and in their mastery motivation, and an increase in their use of self-handicapping strategies (Gottfried et al., 2001; Pintrich, 2000). In addition, studies find that individuals' beliefs about intelligence change as they move into and through adolescence, with older students more likely to view intelligence as stable (Ablard & Mills, 1996).

These newer models of the psychological aspects of achievement during adolescence suggest that across all ethnic groups, students' beliefs (about the nature of ability in general and the nature of their own ability in particular) influence their motivation, which, in turn, influences their performance (Bandura et al., 1996; Gordon, 1995). Psychologist Jacquelynne Eccles and her colleagues have shown in several studies that students' beliefs about their abilities influence the academic activities they participate in (both in and out of school), which influences their achievement, which further shapes their beliefs (see Figure 12.1) (Simpkins, Davis-Kean, & Eccles, 2006).

▍ **Attributions for Success and Failure** How students interpret their successes and failures is also important. Researchers who are interested in what are called **achievement attributions** (Dweck & Wortman, 1980) have studied how the explanations that individuals give for their success or failure influence their performance. According to these theorists, individuals attribute their performance to a combination of four factors: ability, effort, task difficulty, and luck. When

achievement attributions The beliefs an individual holds about the causes of her or his successes and failures.

individuals succeed and attribute their success to internal causes such as their ability or effort, they are more likely to approach future tasks confidently and with self-assurance. If, however, they attribute their success to external factors outside their control, such as luck or an easy task, they are more likely to remain unsure of their abilities. Not surprisingly, scholastically successful individuals, who tend to be high in achievement motivation, are likely to attribute their successes to internal causes (Carr, Borkowski, & Maxwell, 1991; Randel, Stevenson, & Witruk, 2000; Vispoel, 1995).

FOOD FOR THOUGHT

When you succeed in school, to what do you attribute your success? When you fail, how do you explain your failure? Have you had teachers who influenced your beliefs about your own abilities?

How adolescents interpret their failures is also important in influencing their subsequent behavior. Some youngsters try harder in the face of failure, whereas others withdraw and exert less effort. According to psychologist Carol Dweck (Dweck & Light, 1980), when individuals attribute their failures to a lack of effort, they are more likely to try harder on future tasks. But individuals who attribute their failure to factors that they feel cannot be changed (such as bad luck, or lack of intelligence, or task difficulty) are more likely to feel helpless and to exert less effort in subsequent situations.

Suppose, for instance, a student takes the SAT and receives a combined score of 1000. He then is told by his guidance counselor that the SAT is a measure of intelligence, that intelligence is fixed, and that his score reflects how smart he is. The counselor tells the student that he can retake the test if he wants to but that he should not expect to score much higher than 1000. Now imagine a different student, who also scores 1000 on the test. She is told by her guidance counselor that effort has a great deal to do with scores on the SAT and that she can raise her score by trying harder. In all likelihood, the next time these students take the test, the first student will not try as hard as the second student, because he is more likely to feel helpless.

Students who are led to believe that their efforts do not make a difference—by being told, for example, that they are stupid or that the work is too difficult for them—develop what psychologists call **learned helplessness:** the belief that failure is inevitable (Dweck & Light, 1980). As a result of learned helplessness, some students try less hard than their peers, and they do not do as well as they might.

Students who suffer from learned helplessness and who use a lot of self-handicapping strategies tend not only to perform worse in school but also to have more overall adjustment problems than their peers (Määta, Stattin, & Nurmi, 2002). Research on adolescents' attributions for success and failure suggests that, instead of dismissing low-achieving students as having "low needs for achievement" or "low intelligence," teachers and other school personnel can help students achieve more by helping them learn to attribute their performance to factors that are under their own control (Hudley, 1997; Wilson & Linville, 1985).

RECAP

- Adolescents' need for achievement and their fear of failure work together to pull them toward or repel them from achievement situations.
- Although some students underachieve because they have an intense fear of failure, which makes them anxious, others engage in "self-handicapping" strategies in order to appear nonchalant about school. Often, self-handicapping is done so that students have an excuse for poor performance other than a lack of ability.
- Contemporary theories tend to stress the interaction of motives, beliefs, attributions, and goals as influencing adolescents' achievement orientation. Adolescents who believe that ability is malleable, who are motivated by intrinsic rather than extrinsic rewards, who are confident about their abilities, and who attribute their successes and failures to effort rather than to things they can't control achieve more in school than their peers.
- Some students perform poorly because they have been led to believe that members of their ethnic group or gender are inherently less able than others, a phenomenon that is called "stereotype threat."
- Observations that boys are not doing as well in school in girls, that boys are disciplined for school misbehavior more than girls, that boys are more likely to perceive their schools and teachers as unfair, and that females now outnumber males on college campuses by a substantial margin are now prompting numerous writers to express concern about the achievement problems of boys.

learned helplessness The acquired belief that an individual is not able to influence events through his or her own efforts or actions.

Adolescents who attend schools in which there are ample resources—such as computers—have a distinct advantage over their peers who attend schools in impoverished communities.

Environmental Influences on Achievement

Ability, beliefs, and motivation may play a large role in influencing individual performance, but opportunity and situational factors also have a great deal to do with achievement (Eccles, 2004). Many of the differences in academic or occupational achievement that are observed among adolescents result not from differences in their abilities, motives, or beliefs but from differences in the schools and classrooms where their abilities and motives are expressed.

School environments differ markedly—in physical facilities, in opportunities for pursuing academically enriched programs, and in classroom atmospheres. For example, students are more engaged and achieve more in schools that are more personal, less departmentalized, and less rigidly tracked, and in which team teaching is used more frequently (Gamoran, 1992; Lee & Smith, 1993). Unfortunately, many school districts, plagued with shrinking tax bases, are characterized by decaying school buildings, outdated equipment, and textbook and teacher shortages. In some schools, problems of crime and discipline have become so overwhelming that attention to these matters has taken precedence over learning and instruction. In short, many young people who genuinely want to succeed are impeded not by a lack of talent or motivation but by a school environment that makes their academic success virtually impossible. Students who attend schools with a high concentration of poor, minority students are especially disadvantaged, as are

students who attend schools with a high proportion of students from single-parent families (Bankston & Caldas, 1996, 1998; Pong, 1997, 1998).

THE INFLUENCE OF THE HOME ENVIRONMENT

The school, of course, is not the only environment that makes a difference in adolescents' achievement, and few would argue that schools should accept full responsibility for adolescents who do not succeed at a level consonant with their abilities. If anything, the evidence suggests that important aspects of the home environment are better predictors of adolescents' academic achievement than are features of the school environment (Coleman et al., 1966; Steinberg, 1996). Researchers have studied three ways in which the adolescent's home may influence his or her level of achievement.

▍ Parental Values and Expectations   First, studies have shown that adolescents' achievement is directly related to their parents' values and expectations (Jodl, Michael, Malanchiuk, Eccles, & Sameroff, 2001). Adolescents whose parents expect them to go to college are more likely to do so than are adolescents of equal ability whose parents expect less of them (Featherman, 1980). Parental encouragement of academic success may be manifested in a number of ways, all of which have been shown to be beneficial to adolescents' school performance.

First, parents who encourage school success set higher standards for their child's school performance and homework, and they have higher aspirations for their child, which, in turn, contributes to school success (Entwisle & Hayduk, 1988; Patrikakou, 1996; Wilson & Wilson, 1992). Second, parents who encourage school success also have values that are consistent with doing well in school, and they structure the home environment to support academic pursuits so that the messages children receive from their teachers are echoed at home (Jodl et al., 2001; Kurdek & Sinclair, 1988; Sui-Chu & Willms, 1996). Studies show that even high school students profit from having parents who help them learn more effective time management strategies and healthier work habits (Xu, 2004). Finally, parents who encourage success are likely to be more involved in their child's education—more likely to attend school programs, to help in course selection, to maintain interest in school activities and assignments, and the like—all of which contribute to students' success (Bogenschneider, 1997; Hill et al., 2004; Hoover-Dempsey & Sandler, 1995; Muller, 1998; Shumow & Miller, 2001). Parental involvement in schooling may make academics seem both more important and more conquerable to the adolescent, which may enhance the young person's academic self-conceptions (Grolnick & Slowiaczek, 1994; Ibañez, Kuperminc, Jurkovic, & Perilla, 2004). In contrast, parental disengagement from school may make students themselves more likely to disengage and do poorly (Roeser, Lord, & Eccles, 1994). Interestingly, parental involvement in schooling has a more substantial effect when the adolescent attends a school in which a large proportion of other students' parents are involved as well (Darling & Steinberg, 1997; Pong, 1998). Parental involvement seems to be an especially strong influence on the achievement of Mexican American youth, perhaps because of the importance of the family in Mexican culture (Trusty, Plata, & Salazar, 2003).

■ **Authoritative Parenting** A second way in which parents influence student achievement is more indirect—through their general approach to parenting. Numerous studies have shown that authoritative parenting—parenting that is warm, firm, and fair—is linked to school success during adolescence, as indexed by better performance, better attendance, higher expectations, more positive academic self-conceptions, and stronger engagement in the classroom (Bronstein et al., 1996; Corville-Smith, Ryan, Adams, & Dalicandro, 1998; Sirin & Rogers-Sirin, 2004; Steinberg, Lamborn, Darling, Mounts, & Dornbusch, 1994; Wentzel, 1998). In contrast, parenting that is especially punitive, harsh, strict, or inept is associated with lower school engagement and diminished achievement (Clark, Dogan, & Akbar, 2003; DeBaryshe, Patterson, & Capaldi, 1993; Eamon, 2005; Melby & Conger, 1996).

In one study, for example, sociologist Sanford Dornbusch and his colleagues (Dornbusch, Ritter, Liederman, Roberts, & Fraleigh, 1987) demonstrated that adolescents whose parents were authoritative consistently performed better in school than did peers whose parents were indulgent or authoritarian. Interestingly, the poorest school performance was observed among adolescents whose parents were inconsistent in their child rearing. That is, even though adolescents whose parents were autocratic received lower grades than did students whose parents were authoritative, adolescents whose parents used a mixture of authoritarian and indulgent techniques performed even worse. Interestingly, extreme parental permissiveness, not authoritarianism, is associated with higher rates of dropping out of school (Rumberger, Ghatak, Poulos, Ritter, & Dornbusch, 1990). Authoritative parenting has also been shown to help adolescents adjust to middle school (Bronstein et al., 1998) and help poorly performing early adolescents turn their academic performance around in high school (Catterall, 1998).

Why do adolescents achieve more in school when they come from authoritative homes? One reason is that authoritative parenting promotes the development of a healthy achievement orientation—including an emphasis on intrinsic motivation and a healthier attributional style—which, in turn, enhances adolescent school performance (Aunola, Stattin, & Nurmi, 2000; Bronstein, Ginsburg, & Herrera-Leavitt, 2000; DeBaryshe et al., 1993; Glasgow, Dornbusch, Ritter, Troyer, & Steinberg, 1997). This is in part because authoritative parents are more likely themselves to hold healthier beliefs about their child's achievement and less likely to be overly controlling—two factors that strengthen adolescents' work ethic and intrinsic motivation (Arbeton, Eccles, & Harold, 1994; Grolnick & Slowiaczek, 1994). Having a strong work orientation enhances achievement both directly, as we saw earlier, and indirectly through the positive impression it makes on teachers (Farkas, Grobe, & Shuan, 1990).

In general, these findings are in line with a good deal of research suggesting that consistent, authoritative parenting is associated with a wide array of benefits to the adolescent, including higher achievement motivation, greater self-esteem, and enhanced competence (Maccoby & Martin, 1983; Wentzel, 1994). Authoritative parents also tend to be more involved in school activities, which is associated with scholastic success, although parents' involvement both affects and is affected by adolescents' achievement (Crosnoe, 2001; Juang & Silbereisen, 2002; Paulson, 1994; Steinberg, Dornbusch, & Brown, 1992). Students also perform better when the values and expectations they encounter at home are consistent with those they encounter in school (Arunkumar, Midgley, & Urdan, 1999).

■ **The Quality of the Home Environment** A third mechanism of familial influence is through the quality of the home environment provided. Studies have shown that the quality of an adolescent's home environment—as measured simply in terms of the presence of such items as a television, dictionary, encyclopedia, newspaper, vacuum cleaner, and other indicators of family income—is more strongly correlated with youngsters' level of academic achievement than is the quality of the physical facility of the school they attend, the background and training of their teachers, or the level of teachers' salaries paid by the school district (Armor, 1972). A number of researchers have also shown that the extent to which the adolescent's parents provide the youngster with what is called **cultural capital**—by exposing the adolescent to art, music, literature, and so forth—exerts a positive impact

cultural capital The resources provided within a family through the exposure of the adolescent to art, music, literature, and other elements of "high culture."

Having friends who value school can positively affect academic achievement; by the same token, however, having friends who disparage school success can depress school performance.

on achievement above and beyond the effects of the parents' own level of education (Buechel & Duncan, 1998; DiMaggio, 1982; Roscigno & Ainsworth-Darnell, 1999).

Several researchers have asked whether adolescents' school achievement is affected by genetic factors. Interestingly, evidence on the heritability of school achievement suggests that while intelligence and cognitive achievement have strong genetic components, school performance is highly influenced by environmental factors, both inside and outside the family (Teachman, 1997). With this in mind, it is important to point out that a disheartening number of young people in this country live in overcrowded, inadequate housing and come from families that are under severe economic and social stress—so much so that parental encouragement and involvement are often undermined by neighborhood conditions (Gonzales, Cauce, Friedman, & Mason, 1996). It is extremely difficult for a parent to provide a supportive home environment when he or she is under severe economic stress. And environmental obstacles to success disproportionately afflict youngsters from minority backgrounds.

Put succinctly, many American youngsters do not grow up in an atmosphere that is conducive to academic achievement. Many communities lack what social scientists sometimes call **social capital**—the support, encouragement, and involvement of adults necessary to facilitate youngsters' success in school

(Coleman & Hoffer, 1987). Social capital, which is strengthened when families have strong ties to other families in the community, has been shown to be an important contributor to success in school, above and beyond the contribution of adolescents' family income, their parents' education, or their household composition (Pong, 1997, 1998). Not surprisingly, students whose families lack social capital are more likely to have difficulty in school (Teachman, Paasch, & Carver, 1997).

FOOD FOR THOUGHT

What sorts of programs for parents existed in the district in which you attended high school? In view of what we know about the home environments of high-achieving students, how likely are these sorts of activities to succeed?

THE INFLUENCE OF FRIENDS

There is also evidence that friends influence adolescents' achievement, in addition to the influence of their parents. Indeed, some studies suggest that friends, not parents, are the most salient influences on adolescents' day-to-day school behaviors, such as doing homework and exerting effort in class (Kurdek, Fine, & Sinclair, 1995; Midgely & Urdan, 1995; Steinberg et al., 1996). Parents are stronger influences on long-range educational plans, but what adolescents do in school on a daily basis is more affected by their friends. Indeed, one of the main reasons that adolescents growing up in poor neighborhoods achieve less is that they are often surrounded by peers who are disengaged from school (South, Baumer, & Lutz, 2003).

When most of us think about the influence of adolescents' peers on achievement, we tend immediately to think of the ways in which peers undermine academic success. But contrary to the notion that the influence of the peer group is always negative, studies suggest that the impact of friends on adolescents' school performance depends on the academic orientation of the peer group. Having friends who earn high grades and aspire to further education can enhance adolescents' achievement, whereas having friends who earn low grades or disparage school success may interfere with it (Natriello & McDill, 1986; Steinberg et al., 1996).

According to one extensive study of friends in school (Epstein, 1983a), students' grades change

social capital The interpersonal resources available to an adolescent or family.

over time in relation to the grades of their friends. Students with best friends who achieve high grades in school are more likely to show improvements in their own grades than are students who begin at similar levels of achievement but whose friends are not high achievers. Peers also exert a small but significant influence on each other's college plans. Among low-achieving adolescents, for example, those with high-achieving friends are more likely to plan to continue their education than are those with low-achieving friends.

In the contemporary United States, the influence of the peer culture on academic achievement is far more negative than positive (Bishop, Bishop, Gelbwasser, Green, & Zuckerman, 2003; Steinberg et al., 1996). Perhaps because of this, adolescents with an extremely high orientation toward peers tend to perform worse in school (Fuligni & Eccles, 1993). Conversely, adolescents who are neglected by their peers often have a stronger academic orientation than relatively more popular students (Luthar & McMahon, 1996; Wentzel & Asher, 1995). As they move into middle school, adolescents become increasingly worried about their friends' reactions to success in school; one study found, for example, that by eighth grade students did not want their classmates to know that they worked hard in school, even though they knew that it would be helpful to convey this impression to their teachers (Juvonen & Murdock, 1995).

Recently, a number of researchers have begun to study how the influences of parents and peers operate together to affect adolescents' achievement (Brown, Mounts, Lamborn, & Steinberg, 1993; Fletcher, Darling, Steinberg, & Dornbusch, 1995; Gonzales et al., 1996; Kurdek et al., 1995; Steinberg et al., 1996). These studies show that the family environment has an effect on adolescents' choice of friends, and this, in turn, can influence school achievement (Brown et al., 1993). In addition, having friends who value school can positively affect academic achievement, even among teenagers who do not come from nonauthoritative homes. By the same token, having friends who disparage school success may offset the benefits of authoritative parenting (Steinberg et al., 1996). Rather than asking whether family or friends influence adolescents' school performance, then, it may make more sense to ask how these two forces—along with the influence of the school itself—work together.

A recent study examining the influence of peers and parents on school achievement in 12 different countries shows that the broader context in which schooling takes place can affect the degree to which peers and parents influence adolescents' achievement. Peers and parents more strongly influence student achievement in countries where schools serve more heterogeneous groups of students, as in the United States. In countries where students with different long-term educational aspirations attend different schools (that is, where there are separate schools for adolescents who are planning to go to college versus those who are not), as is the case in Germany, for example, peers and parents are less influential (Buchmann & Dalton, 2002).

In sum, although psychological factors play a key role in determining occupational and scholastic success, it is important to take into account the broader environment in which individuals pursue their educational and occupational careers (Gonzales et al., 1996; Steinberg et al., 1996). Moreover, distinguishing between motivational and environmental factors is hard, because they typically go hand in hand. Living in an environment that offers few opportunities for success induces feelings of learned helplessness, which, in turn, leads individuals to feel that exerting any effort to succeed is futile. Attending school in an environment in which achievement is not encouraged engenders attitudes and beliefs inconsistent with striving to do well. Rather than viewing achievement during adolescence as being determined by one single factor, such as ability, it is more accurate to say that patterns of achievement are the result of a cumulative process that includes a long history of experience and socialization in school, in the family, in the peer group, and in the community.

RECAP

- In addition to the influence of beliefs, motives, attributions, and goals, individuals' levels of achievement are affected by the social context in which they develop.
- Adolescents perform better and are more engaged in school when they come from authoritative homes in which their parents are highly involved in their education.
- In addition, adolescents whose friends support academic achievement perform better in school than do peers whose friends disparage doing well in school.
- Researchers now understand that patterns of achievement are the result of a cumulative process that includes a long history of experience and socialization in school, in the family, in the peer group, and in the community.

Educational Achievement

Educational achievement is usually defined in one of three ways: **school performance** (the grades students earn in school), **academic achievement** (their performance on standardized tests), or **educational attainment** (the number of years of schooling they complete). These different measures of educational achievement are, not surprisingly, interrelated, but they are less tied to each other than you might expect.

No single factor adequately accounts for differences in adolescents' levels of educational achievement. Generally, intellectual ability—as assessed by IQ tests—is highly correlated with performance on achievement tests (hardly a surprise, since IQ tests and achievement tests are designed to tap similar abilities). Intellectual ability is only moderately correlated with school grades, however, and even less strongly correlated with educational attainment (Featherman, 1980).

The truth of the matter is that grades in school—and to an even greater extent, educational attainment—are influenced by a wider range of factors than simply the adolescent's intellectual abilities. Grades, for example, are influenced by teachers' judgments of students' mastery of the material, and these judgments may be influenced by teachers' evaluations of students' efforts and behaviors in the classroom (Farkas, Grobe, & Shuan, 1990). How many years of school an adolescent completes is likely to be influenced by his or her family background and living circumstances, as well as by school performance. Two adolescents may have similar grade point averages, but if one comes from a poor family and cannot afford to go to college, the two will have different levels of educational attainment (Featherman, 1980). Even as early as elementary school, for example, many inner-city youth have very limited occupational expectations, and these low expectations affect their educational achievement and attainment (Cook et al., 1996).

Regardless of what influences it, educational attainment has important implications for subsequent earnings (Ceci & Williams, 1999). The gap in earnings between high school graduates and college graduates is considerable, and this is true across all ethnic groups. When they enter the labor force, individuals with a college degree earn nearly twice as much per hour as do individuals with only a high school diploma (Economic Policy Institute, 1994).

school performance   A measure of achievement based on an individual's grades in school.

academic achievement   Achievement that is measured by standardized tests of scholastic ability or knowledge.

educational attainment   The number of years of schooling completed by an individual.

THE IMPORTANCE OF SOCIOECONOMIC STATUS

■ **A Head Start for the More Affluent**   One of the most powerful influences on educational achievement is the socioeconomic status of the adolescent's family. Five decades of studies have shown over and over that middle-class adolescents score higher on basic tests of academic skills, earn higher grades, and complete more years of schooling than their working-class and lower-class peers (Featherman, 1980; Muller, Stage, & Kinzie, 2001; Schoon, Parsons, & Sacker, 2004; Sewell & Hauser, 1972). Adolescents who come from lower socioeconomic levels are more likely to score lower than their more advantaged peers on standardized tests of achievement. Similarly, youngsters whose parents have gone to college are more likely to attend college themselves than are those whose parents did not attend college. And youngsters whose parents completed high school are also more likely to attend college than are youngsters whose parents did not complete high school (Johnson, 1975). Although some of the socioeconomic gaps in school achievement have narrowed, and although families influence student achievement through additional pathways—by providing cultural and social capital, for example—disparities in achievement between the social classes remain strong, and the importance of socioeconomic status in determining educational achievement remains substantial across all ethnic groups (Goyette & Xie, 1999; Hanson, 1994; Kao & Tienda, 1998; Lucas, 1996; Teachman & Paasch, 1998). Socioeconomic status also influences adolescent achievement through neighborhood processes. For example, one recent study found that poor African American students who live in neighborhoods with a relatively higher proportion of middle-class neighbors place more value on education and try harder in school than comparably poor students who live in less advantaged communities (Ceballo, McLoyd, & Toyokawa, 2004).

Socioeconomic status, therefore, influences both educational achievement and attainment and, as a consequence, influences occupational achievement as well. However, keep in mind that variations within socioeconomic categories are often as substantial as differences between categories. Not all youngsters from affluent backgrounds have higher levels of educational achievement than adolescents from poorer families, and many youngsters from economically disadvantaged households go on to earn college and post-college degrees.

One big reason that family background is related to educational achievement is that children from lower socioeconomic levels are more likely to enter elementary school scoring low on tests of basic academic competence. These initial differences reflect both genetic and environmental factors. Middle-class adults generally have higher IQs than lower-class adults, and this advantage is passed on to their children—both through inheritance and through the benefit that middle-class youngsters receive from growing up under more favorable environmental conditions (Chen, Lee, & Stevenson, 1996; Featherman, 1980; Teachman, 1996). Affluent youngsters receive better health care and better nutrition, for example, both of which contribute to their higher performance on IQ tests. The disadvantages of poorer youngsters in achievement test scores persist—and may even increase—throughout elementary and secondary school (Coleman et al., 1966; Entwisle & Hayduk, 1988). Because progress in high school depends so heavily on having a solid foundation of basic academic competence, adolescents who enter secondary school without having mastered basic academic skills quickly fall behind, and some leave high school before graduating.

▌ **Early Intervention**   One bit of encouraging news on this front comes from long-term evaluations of interventions designed to improve the academic achievement of very poor youngsters who, by virtue of their poverty, are at high risk for academic failure (Campbell & Ramey, 1995; Reynolds & Temple, 1998). In these evaluations, researchers compared groups of adolescents who had participated in an intensive educational program during their preschool and elementary school years with matched samples of adolescents who had had the preschool intervention only, the elementary school intervention only, or no educational intervention at all. The interventions were targeted at improving the children's school skills and at strengthening the links between parents and their child's school.

Long-term evaluations show that individuals who participated in preschool interventions (with or without participation in elementary school interventions) perform significantly better in school during adolescence than those who did not (Campbell & Ramey, 1995). In one study, participating in both the preschool and the elementary school programs provided additional advantages over the preschool program alone (Reynolds, Temple, Robertson, & Mann, 2001). Interestingly, however, adolescents who had been in the elementary school program but not the preschool program had no advantages over those who had been in no intervention at all (Campbell & Ramey, 1995). These findings suggest that intervening prior to entering first grade may be extremely important in preventing long-term academic problems among impoverished youngsters, and that extended participation in educational programs may be better than short-term participation. Consistent

with this, longitudinal research shows that school difficulties as early as kindergarten are predictive of poor school performance in adolescence (Hamre & Pianta, 2001).

One reason for the relatively poorer school performance of disadvantaged youth, therefore, is that these youngsters begin school at a distinct academic disadvantage. A second reason for the disparity is stress, however—both before and during adolescence. Adolescents who come from lower-class backgrounds experience more stressful life events, report more daily hassles, and attend schools with more negative climates (DuBois, Felner, Meares, & Krier, 1994; Felner et al., 1995; Gillock & Reyes, 1999; Pungello, Kupersmidt, Burchinal, & Patterson, 1996). Stress has been shown to adversely affect adolescents' mental health, well-being, and school performance (DuBois, Felner, Brand, Adan, & Evans, 1992; Felner et al., 1995).

▌ **Parental Involvement**   Some studies also suggest that parents from higher social classes are more likely to be involved in their adolescent's education, especially through formal parent–teacher organizations, like the PTA or PTO (Shumow & Miller, 2001; Stevenson & Baker, 1987). Middle- and upper-middle-class parents are also more likely to have information about their child's school, to be responsive to their child's school problems, and to help select more rigorous courses for their child to take (Baker & Stevenson, 1986). Because adolescents whose parents are involved in their schooling perform better than those whose parents are not involved, youngsters from higher social classes may achieve more in school than their less advantaged peers in part because of their parents' more active involvement (Lee & Croninger, 1994; Stevenson & Baker, 1987). In addition, parents with greater economic resources are able to provide their children with more cultural capital, which, as we have seen, is an important contributor to school success (Roscigno & Ainsworth-Darnell, 1999).

FOOD FOR THOUGHT

In light of the profound impact that socioeconomic status has on student achievement, what would you suggest as policies or practices to raise the achievement of poor youth? Think about people you know who overcame economic disadvantage and were highly successful in school (perhaps *you* are in this category). To what would you attribute this success?

Adolescents whose parents are involved in their schooling perform better than adolescents whose parents are not. One reason that students from higher social classes do better in school is that their parents tend to be more involved.

Socioeconomic differences in school achievement obviously reflect the cumulative and combined effects of a variety of influences, and it is simplistic to explain social class differences in achievement without considering these factors simultaneously. What is perhaps more interesting—and more worthy of scientific study—is the question of what it is about the many youngsters from economically disadvantaged backgrounds who are successful that accounts for their overcoming the tremendous odds against them. Put concretely, the successful college student who comes from an environment of severe economic disadvantage has to overcome incredible barriers.

Although more research on successful students from poor backgrounds is sorely needed, several findings suggest that what might be most important is social support for academic achievement: the presence of warm and encouraging parents who raise their children authoritatively, take an interest in their children's academic progress, and hold high aspirations for their children's educational attainment, as well as the availability of peers who support and encourage academic success (Brody, Stoneman, & Flor, 1995; Gregory, 1995; Simpson, 1962; Steinberg et al., 1996; Sui-Chu & Willms, 1996). In other words, positive relations at home and the encouragement of significant others can in some circumstances overcome the negative influence of socioeconomic disadvantage.

ETHNIC DIFFERENCES IN EDUCATIONAL ACHIEVEMENT

Among the most controversial—and intriguing—findings in research on adolescents' achievement are those concerning ethnic differences in school success. On average, the educational achievement of African American and Hispanic American students—virtually however indexed—lags behind that of white students, and all three groups achieve less in school than do Asian American students. Although some of these differences can be attributed to socioeconomic differences among these ethnic groups, the group disparities persist even after socioeconomic factors are taken into account (Call & McNall, 1992; Chen & Stevenson, 1995; Goyette & Xie, 1999; Hedges & Nowell, 1999; Mickelson, 1990; Muller et al., 2001; Steinberg, Dornbusch, & Brown, 1992; Sue & Okazaki, 1990). The academic superiority of Asian American students tends to emerge during the transition into junior high school—when most other students' grades typically decline, and it persists through high school and into college (Fuligni, 1994; Fuligni & Witkow, 2004). What has been most intriguing to social scientists is the observation that African American and Hispanic American students have educational aspirations and attitudes that are similar to those of Asian American and white students but significantly poorer academic skills, habits, and behavior (Ainsworth-Darnell & Downey, 1998). If African American and Hispanic American students ostensibly have the same long-term goals as other students, why do they not behave in similar ways?

█ False Optimism Rather Than Realistic Pessimism Several theories have been advanced to explain this finding. One set of theories involves the perceptions that adolescents have about the likely payoff of hard work in school. Some writers, for instance, have argued that even though they have high aspirations in the abstract, many minority youth do not believe that educational success will have substantial occupational payoff for them, because of a prejudicially imposed job ceiling on the career development of African American, Hispanic American, and American Indian individuals (Mickelson, 1990; Ogbu, 1974). Although intuitively appealing, this theory has not received convincing empirical support. It is true that adolescents who believe they have been victims of discrimination, or who believe that their opportunities for occupational success are unfairly constrained by society, achieve less in school and report more emotional distress than do peers who do not hold these beliefs (Fisher, Wallace, & Fenton, 2000; Taylor, Casten, Flickinger, Roberts, & Fulmore, 1994; Wood & Clay, 1996). It is also true that students who are more confident about and oriented to the future do better in school (Brown & Jones, 2004). It is not true, however, that African American or Hispanic American youngsters are more likely than other adolescents to believe that their opportunities for success are blocked (Ainsworth-Darnell & Downey, 1998; Downey & Ainsworth-Darnell, 2002; Kao & Tienda, 1998; Steinberg et al., 1992). Indeed, several studies indicate that African American and Hispanic American youth may actually have more optimistic beliefs and positive feelings about school than other students (e.g., Ainsworth-Darnell & Downey, 1998; Voelkl, 1997). Actually, some research suggests that beliefs about the likelihood of future discrimination may motivate adolescents to perform better in school (perhaps because they feel that they will need to be even better prepared than others to overcome prejudicial treatment), but that feeling discriminated against in the present, by classmates or teachers, hinders academic achievement (perhaps by causing psychological distress or hopelessness) (Eccles, 2004).

If anything, it may be adolescents' fear of failure, rather than their desire (or lack of desire) to succeed, that matters most (Steinberg et al., 1992). Asian American youngsters not only believe in the value of school success but also are very anxious about the possible negative repercussions of not doing well in school, in terms of both occupational success and their parents' disappointment (Chung & Walkey, 1989; Eaton & Dembo, 1997; Steinberg et al., 1996). Moreover, many Asian American youth believe that the only way they can succeed in mainstream American society is through educational achievement (Sue & Okazaki, 1990). Interestingly, Asian American students' sense of obligation to their parents—a factor frequently suggested as a reason for their high rates of school success—does not seem to play a very important role in predicting school achievement. In addition, being expected to assist the family by performing household chores and other family work—something that is especially salient in Asian American and Hispanic American households—has a negative impact on school performance (Fuligni, Tseng, & Lam, 1999). As one team of researchers explains:

> One Mexican youth . . . , when asked to describe the thoughts of a girl in a picture who is holding school books while watching her parents labor in the fields, said: " . . . she is watching her parents working so hard . . . she feels like they have a big problem. She tries to help her parents, but she has to study. In the end, she tries to help them." . . . Education remains important to these youths, but the families may face more pressing needs that demand the students' attention. These periodic compromises, in turn, may cumulatively erode the students' progress at school over time. (Fuligni et al., 1999, p. 104)

■ **The Burden of "Acting White"** One popular explanation for ethnic differences in achievement that

has not received much support is that some ethnic minority students underperform in school because they are stigmatized for "acting white" if they try to do well. This view, originally proposed by two researchers who observed African American male peer groups in an inner-city school (Fordham & Ogbu, 1986), has not held up under more thorough investigation, perhaps because the extent of this negative peer pressure varies from school to school and from peer group to peer group (e.g., Akom, 2003; Downey & Ainsworth-Darnell, 2002; Farkas, Lleras, & Maczuga, 2002; Horvat & Lewis, 2003; Tyson, Darity, & Castellino, 2005). In other words, the original observations of African American students being ostracized as "brainiacs" may have been specific to the particular school studied, and not true in general (Fordham & Ogbu, 1986). African American peer groups are not all the same, and while some may disparage academic achievement, many admire it. Here's how one academically successful African American student replied when asked if students from different peer groups treated her differently:

> I think, yes. The black people who, say, aren't as smart as me or Renée or whoever else they say, "Oh, you act white" because we're in high classes or whatever, and that really upsets me. They say we talk white. I don't even have like proper English or whatever, but they say we talk white because we use all these big words and everything. To me, that's total ignorance.

When asked to describe her own friends, however, she said:

> They're always, "I'm so proud of you. You have a job, you're still in school, and you're not pregnant." All this other good stuff. But it makes me feel good. (Horvat & Lewis, 2003, pp. 270–272)

Another successful student from the same school noted that even her friends who had dropped out of school in the eighth or ninth grade were supportive of her achievement:

> They just treat me as one of them. School's not a subject that really comes up as far as my neighborhood is concerned. They'll say, "How was your day at school?" "Fine." They accept me for what I am and what I do. If I am smart, I am smart. It seems they really congratulated me, if anything, especially now. So many of my friends have told me, "I'm so proud of you." Basically pushing me on. (Horvat & Lewis, 2003, p. 272)

■ **Ethnic Differences in Beliefs** An alternative account of ethnic differences in achievement stresses differences in ethnic groups' beliefs about ability. We noted earlier that adolescents who believe that intelligence is malleable are more likely to be intrinsically motivated, mastery oriented, and, as a consequence, academically successful. It is therefore interesting to note that Asian cultures tend to place more emphasis on effort than on ability in explaining school success and are more likely to believe that all students have the capacity to succeed (Hess, Chih-Mei, & McDevitt, 1987; Holloway, 1988; Stevenson & Stigler, 1992). By and large, students from Asian backgrounds tend to be more invested in mastering the material than in simply performing well—an orientation that, as we saw earlier, contributes to school success (Li, 2006). It is also important to note that Asian students—both in the United States and in Asia—spend significantly more time each week on homework and other school-related activities, and significantly less time socializing and watching television, than do other youth (Asakawa & Csikzentmihalyi, 2000; Caplan, Choy, & Whitmore, 1992; Fuligni & Stevenson, 1995; Steinberg et al., 1996).

You may be interested to know that, contrary to popular belief, Asian students do not pay a price for their superior achievement in terms of increased anxiety, depression, stress, or social competence; the suicide rate among American teenagers is substantially higher than it is among Japanese youth, for example (Chen, Rubin, & Li, 1997; Crystal et al., 1994; King, Akiyama, & Elling, 1996). However, there is some evidence that the long hours of studying that Korean high school seniors must endure while in "examination hell"—the period of preparation for that country's college entrance exam—may take its toll on adolescents' mental health (Lee & Larson, 2000). During regular periods of school in the United States, however, Asian American students' moods while studying are significantly more positive than those of other students (Asakawa & Csikszentmihalyi, 1998), and the links between academic motivation and various indices of happiness and adjustment are stronger among Asian American adolescents than other youth (Asakawa & Csikzentmihalyi, 2000). Among Asian American students more than their peers from other ethnic groups, then, engagement in academics is linked to positive emotion and well-being.

▌ **The Success of Immigrants**   Of course, as is the case with research on socioeconomic differences in educational achievement, research on ethnic differences indicates that there are large and important variations within as well as between ethnic groups. First, there are differences in educational achievement among youngsters from different countries of origin who may be classified together by researchers into the same larger ethnic group for purposes of statistical comparison. For example, although both groups are classified as Asian, Chinese American adolescents have much higher academic achievement than Filipino Americans; similarly, there are large differences in academic achievement

among Puerto Rican, Cuban American, and Mexican American adolescents, all of whom are classified as Hispanic (Blair & Qian, 1998; Kao, 1995; Lee, 2001; Portes & MacLeod, 1996; Schmid, 2001; Velez, 1989; Wojtkiewicz & Donato, 1995).

Second, studies of ethnic minority youngsters show that foreign-born adolescents, as well as those who are children of immigrants, tend to achieve more in school than do minority youngsters who are second- or third-generation Americans, a finding that has now emerged in many studies of Asian, Latino, and Caribbean youth (Fuligni, 1997; Kao, 1999; Kao & Tienda, 1995; Rong & Brown, 2001; Steinberg et al., 1996). One explanation for this has been that part of becoming acculturated to American society—at least among teenagers—may be learning to devalue academic success. There is also some evidence that the higher school achievement of immigrant youth—at least among adolescents who have immigrated from Mexico—may be due to the higher quality of the schooling they receive before coming to the United States (Padilla & Gonzalez, 2001). As psychologist Andrew Fuligni has pointed out, the exceptional achievement of immigrant youth is all the more remarkable in light of the fact that these adolescents typically have much greater family obligations—providing financial support to their parents, for instance—than their American-born peers (Fuligni & Witkow, 2004).

FOOD FOR THOUGHT

Many immigrant adolescents in the United States achieve more in school than their counterparts from the same ethnic group who were born in America—despite the fact that adolescents who are immigrants often arrive without proficiency in English or familiarity with American culture. How do you account for this?

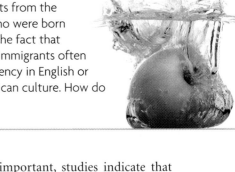

Third, and most important, studies indicate that within all ethnic groups, students achieve more when they feel a sense of belonging to their school, when they see the connection between academic accomplishment and future success, when their friends and parents value and support educational achievement, and when their parents are effective monitors of their children's behavior and schooling (Alva, 1993; Chen & Stevenson, 1995; Chen et al., 1996; Conchas, 2001; Connell, Spencer, & Aber, 1994; Ford and Harris, 1996; Goodenow, 1992; Luthar, 1994; Murdock, 1994;

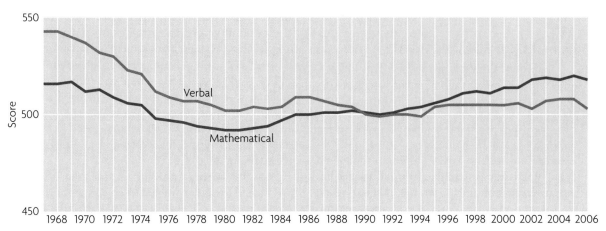

FIGURE 12.2 Changes in SAT scores over time. (College Entrance Examination Board, 2006)

Reyes & Jason, 1993; Steinberg et al., 1996). There is also some evidence that having a positive role model who is the same sex and from the same ethnic group can help facilitate adolescents' academic success (Zirkel, 2002).

CHANGES IN EDUCATIONAL ACHIEVEMENT OVER TIME

As we noted in Chapter 6, more students are going on to postsecondary education today than ever before. Today, three-fourths of high school graduates enroll in college, two-thirds of them immediately after graduation (National Center for Education Statistics, 1999; Pennington, 2003). Although ethnic differences in educational attainment have narrowed over the past 40 years, there remain substantial gaps in attainment between white and nonwhite individuals, and especially between white and Hispanic American individuals. Thus, whereas about 28 percent of all white adults ages 25 and over, and 49 percent of all Asian American adults of this age, are college graduates, only 17 percent of African American adults and only 12 percent of Hispanic American adults are (U.S. Census Bureau, 2006). (There is considerable variation within the Hispanic American population in rates of college graduation, however—only 8 percent of Mexican American adults ages 25 and older are college graduates, compared with 14 percent of Puerto Rican adults and 24 percent of Cuban American adults.) Discrepancies in rates of high school graduation between Hispanic and non–Hispanic Americans are also substantial—86 percent of white adults have completed high school, compared with 81 percent of African Americans and 87 percent of Asian Americans, but only 58 percent of Hispanic American adults have (U.S. Census Bureau, 2006). In light of the rapidly increasing size of the Latino population in the United States, the gap in educational attainment between Latinos and non-Latinos is one of the most important chellenges facing American educational institutions.

▌ **More Schooling, But Less Learning** Trends in academic achievement (what students know) have not paralleled trends in educational attainment (how many years of schooling they have completed), however. In other words, although more students are staying in school longer, they are not necessarily learning more. For example, as Figure 12.2 indicates, between 1970 and 1980, average scores on the Scholastic Assessment Test (SAT) declined by about 35 points on the verbal portion and 20 points on the math. Scores remained more or less flat between 1980 and 1990, when math (but not verbal) scores began to rise; in fact, verbal scores dropped between 2004 and 2006 (see Figure 12.2). Moreover, the gap in SAT scores between African American and Hispanic American students on the one hand, and Asian American and white students on the other, remains substantial (College Entrance Examination Board, 2006).

The relatively poor showing of American adolescents on standardized tests of achievement was carefully documented in a series of reports based on the **National Assessment of Educational Progress (NAEP)** (National Assessment of Educational Progress, 1999). This national assessment of student achievement is conducted by the federal government in order to track trends in educational achievement over time. Because the NAEP tests have been administered regularly for nearly 40 years, it is possible to compare the achievement levels of today's adolescents with their counterparts four decades ago.

National Assessment of Educational Progress (NAEP) A periodic testing of American fourth-, eighth-, and twelfth-graders by the federal government, used to track achievement.

FOOD FOR THOUGHT

Why do you think it has been so difficult to improve the educational achievement of American youth?

According to recent NAEP reports, adolescent achievement in reading, writing, math, and science has not improved significantly over the past 40 years, despite massive national efforts at education reform. Contemporary 17-year-olds, for example, score no better than their counterparts did in the early 1970s in reading or math, and *worse* than their counterparts did in science. Among 13-year-olds, reading scores in 2004 were slightly better than they had been in the 1970s, but only by about 2 percent, and science scores showed no improvement between 1970 and 2000. In fact, science scores actually declined in the late 1990s and have remained flat since then. The only bit of good news has been in math scores among 13-year-olds, with scores improving steadily since the 1970s (National Assessment of Educational Progress, 2006).

Perhaps more importantly, most analyses of the NAEP data indicate that the modest gains in achievement that have occurred during the past two decades or so have been in relatively simple skills. In reading and writing, for example, although more than half of all American 13-year-olds today can read well enough to be able to search for specific information and can make generalizations from reading material, only 10 percent can understand and summarize relatively complicated information. Only one-third are able to read or write at their grade level, and fewer than one-third are able to write a persuasive essay. The news is even more dismal with regard to twelfth-graders: 25 percent cannot even write the simplest of essays, and only 25 percent can write at their grade level (the other 50 percent fall somewhere between these two points). Only about one-third of high school seniors can read at grade level or better.

Levels of achievement in math and science show a similarly worrisome pattern. The picture is rosier among 13-year-olds than 17-year-olds, but, as the old saying goes, everything is relative. Much has been made of the improved math performance of 13-year-olds, and while this is technically true, the fact remains that fewer than one-third of eighth-graders are performing at grade level (Perie, Grigg, & Dion, 2005). The data are even more depressing with respect to older students. Thus, while virtually all 17-year-olds can add, subtract, multiply, and divide using whole numbers, only half can perform computations with decimals, fractions, and percents and solve

simple equations, and only 6 percent can do basic algebra. And according to the latest NAEP data, the low level of science achievement among American students is equally alarming: Fewer than one-third of eighth-graders, and fewer than one-fifth of twelfth-graders, scored in the "proficient" range (that is, at grade level). More than 40 percent of eighth-graders and nearly 50 percent of all seniors scored in the lowest possible category on the science test (Grigg, Lauko, & Brockway, 2006).

As is the case in rates of high school graduation and SAT scores, the gap in achievement among ethnic groups narrowed during the 1970s, but a wide disparity still exists. The achievement gap did not shrink at all during the 1980s and, if anything, widened a bit during the 1990s (Education Trust, 1996; National Assessment of Educational Progress, 1999). About three times as many white and Asian American students score in the proficient range in writing, for example, as do African American students, and nearly twice as many white and Asian American students score in the proficient range as do Hispanic American students. The gaps are even larger in math, especially—about eight times as many white and Asian American students are competent in algebra as are African American or Hispanic American students (National Center for Education Statistics, 2006). This gap has tremendously important implications for the labor market success of adolescents from different ethnic groups.

▌ **International Competitions**   There is no reason to be sanguine about the performance of white students, however. Since the 1970s, their achievement test scores have remained more or less stagnant, and U.S. scores on standardized tests of math and science are mediocre in comparison with scores of other industrialized countries. More importantly, the gap between American students' performance and that of students from other countries widens as they move from elementary to middle to high school. That is, when elementary school students from around the world are compared, American students fare just about as well as students from other countries. But once the comparison focuses on secondary school students, the gap between the United States and other countries becomes apparent, and it grows even larger when the comparison involves high school seniors (Schmidt, 2003).

The relatively poor performance of American students in international competitions persists despite the fact that spending on education in the United States is among the world's highest (Walberg, 1998). Especially distressing have been studies of students in advanced classes from various countries; here, the best U.S. students fare worse than their counterparts all over the world, especially in science and math, a situation

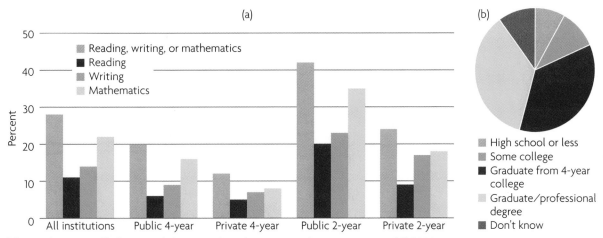

(a) Freshmen enrolled in remedial courses, by subject area and institution type, fall 2000.
(b) High school sophomores' educational expectations, 2002.

FIGURE 12.3 There is a large disconnect between adolescents' academic skills and their expectations. Although the proportion of college students who require remedial education is alarmingly high, the vast majority of high school sophomores expect to graduate from college, and more than one-third expect to obtain a graduate or professional degree. (National Center for Education Statistics, 2002b, 2004)

that threatens the long-term economic well-being of the United States, which increasingly must compete in a global economy dominated by high-tech industries (National Research Council, 2006). Employers and postsecondary educational institutions alike today devote vast amounts of money to remedial education. Indeed, nearly one-third of entering college freshmen in the United States now require some sort of remedial education in order to do college-level work (see Figure 12.3a) (National Center for Education Statistics, 2004), and one-third of American corporations report that they have trouble finding skilled employees (Steinberg, 1998). Ironically, more than 70 percent of American high school sophomores expect to earn a college degree, and half of these expect to earn a graduate or professional degree (National Center for Education Statistics, 2002b) (see Figure 12.3b).

If more American students are remaining in high school, and so many are going on to college, why are their achievement test scores so low according to absolute, historical, and international standards? Experts suggest several reasons: that teachers are not spending enough time on basic instruction in the classroom; that there has been a pervasive decline in the difficulty of textbooks; that parents are not encouraging academic pursuits at home; that students are not spending sufficient time on their studies outside of school; that students are permitted to choose what courses they take; and that students know that, thanks to "grade inflation," they can earn good grades without working very hard (Hayes, Wolfer, & Wolfe, 1996; Owen, 1995; Public Agenda, 1997; Schmidt, 2003; Steinberg, 2003).

DROPPING OUT OF HIGH SCHOOL

There was a time when leaving high school before graduating did not have the dire consequences that it does today. With changes in the labor force, however, have come changes in the educational requirements for entry into the world of work. Today, educational attainment is a powerful predictor of adult occupational success and earnings. Not surprisingly, high school dropouts are far more likely than graduates to live at or near the poverty level, to experience unemployment, to depend on government-subsidized income maintenance programs, to become pregnant while still a teenager, and to be involved in delinquent and criminal activity (Manlove, 1998; Rumberger, 1995).

Because there are different ways of counting dropouts, different studies often report very different figures. For example, many students drop out of school temporarily but return in their early 20s and obtain a diploma or GED—so while these students would be classified as dropouts at the age of 17, they would be classified as graduates if they were surveyed just a few years later. No matter how it is computed, however, the proportion of individuals who have not completed high school has declined steadily over the past half-century, to about 12 percent. There are huge variations in dropout rates from region to region, however; indeed, in some urban areas, well over 50 percent of students leave school prematurely (Alexander, Entwisle, & Kabbani, 2001). African American youngsters drop out of high school at a rate only slightly greater than that of white youngsters (both are near the national average), but Hispanic American youngsters drop out at more than twice the rate of

FIGURE 12.4 Ethnic differences in rates of dropping out of high school. (U.S. Census Bureau, 2005)

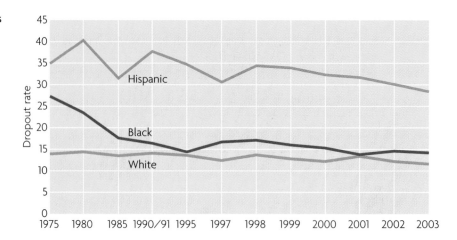

other youth (see Figure 12.4) (U.S. Bureau of the Census, 2006). One reason for this is the large proportion of Hispanic American youth who are not English-speaking; among these youth, a lack of proficiency in English is a major determinant of dropping out (Singh & Hernandez-Gantes, 1996; Stanton-Salazar & Dornbusch, 1995).

▌ **Correlates of Dropping Out**   Given the findings on educational achievement discussed earlier, the other correlates of dropping out come as no surprise. In addition to the higher prevalence of dropping out among Hispanic American youngsters and among those who are not fluent in English, adolescents who leave high school before graduating are more likely to come from lower socioeconomic levels, poor communities, large families, single-parent families, permissive or disengaged families, and households where little reading material is available. In short, adolescents who drop out of school are more likely to come from backgrounds with limited financial, social, and cultural capital (Alexander et al., 2001; Davis, Ajzen, Saunders, & Williams, 2002; Entwisle, 1990; Pong & Ju, 2000; Rumberger, 1995).

Coupled with this disadvantage in background, adolescents who drop out of high school also are more likely to have a history of poor school performance, low school involvement, multiple changes of schools, poor performance on standardized tests of achievement and intelligence, negative school experiences, and a variety of behavioral problems, such as excessive aggression (Battin-Pearson et al., 2000; Jordan, Lara, & McPartland, 1996; Kasen, Cohen, & Brook, 1998; Rumberger & Larson, 1998). Many high school dropouts had to repeat one or more grades in elementary school; indeed, having been held back is one of the strongest predictors of dropping out (Janosz, LeBlanc, Boulerice, & Tremblay, 1997; Roderick, 1994; Rumberger, 1995).

The picture that emerges, then, is that dropping out of high school is not so much a discrete decision made

Dropping out of high school is not so much a discrete event as it is the culmination of a long process that began many years earlier. Dropouts are far more likely than graduates to experience poverty and unemployment, to depend on government-subsidized income maintenance programs, to become pregnant while still a teenager, and to be involved in delinquent and criminal activity.

during the adolescent years as, like other aspects of adolescent achievement, the culmination of a long process (Alexander et al., 2001; Garnier, Stein, & Jacobs, 1997). Specific factors may instigate a student's final decision to leave school—a suspension for misbehavior, a failed course, an unintended pregnancy, the lure of a job—but by and large, dropping out is a process characterized by a history of repeated academic failure and increasing alienation from school (Jordan et al., 1996). While programs designed to enhance adolescents' academic skills have been largely unsuccessful in preventing dropping out, one approach that has met with success has focused on involving at-risk adolescents in service learning and in guided discussions of their life options, which may help them see how important it is to graduate from high school (Allen et al., 1997).

Although adolescents who drop out of school often share certain characteristics in common (for example, a history of poor school performance), there is nevertheless diversity within this population. According to one extensive study of Canadian students (Janosz, Le Blanc, Boulerice, & Tremblay, 2000), there are at least four distinct groups of dropouts: (1) quiet dropouts (whose histories and personal characteristics actually look very similar to students who do not drop out of school, but who appear somewhat withdrawn—they almost seem to "fade out" rather than drop out, perhaps as a result of depression), (2) disengaged dropouts (whose dropping out appears mainly to be the result of low commitment to school and poor academic motivation), (3) low achiever dropouts (whose dropping out is primarily the result of very poor school performance), and (4) maladjusted dropouts (whose dropping out is part of a larger constellation of behavioral and psychological problems). The idea that different developmental histories lead to dropping out is important to the design of preventive interventions, because it suggests that different sorts of programs may work for different sorts of students. Other studies indicate that it is important to distinguish between students who temporarily drop out of school but return at some later point and obtain their GED—as do between one-third and one-half of all dropouts—and those who leave and never return (Entwisle, Alexander, & Olson, 2004).

FOOD FOR THOUGHT

Based on what we know about the causes and consequences of dropping out, what steps should be taken to reduce the dropout rate?

▌ **School Factors**   Although most research on the causes of dropping out has focused on characteristics of adolescents who leave school prematurely, some studies have focused on the schools that dropouts leave (Rumberger & Palardy, 2005). In general, dropping out is less likely from schools where the environment is orderly, where academic pursuits are emphasized, and where the faculty is supportive and committed (Lee & Burkham, 2003). Students who are at particularly high

risk of dropping out (low-achieving, economically disadvantaged youth) are helped especially by having teachers who are sources of social support and guidance (Croninger & Lee, 2001). Dropout rates are also higher in larger schools that group students according to ability and that fail a relatively high proportion of students in the early years of high school (Bryk & Thum, 1989; Roderick & Camburn, 1999). Consistent with this, some research suggests that dropout rates may be reduced in some cases by permitting students who are having educational difficulties to change schools, rather than leaving school altogether (Lee & Burkam, 1992). Although some educators have expressed concern about the recent trend toward toughening graduation requirements and ending **social promotion**—the practice of promoting students from one grade to the next on the basis of age rather than actual achievement—evaluations of policies such as the use of high school exit examinations to determine whether students can graduate show that they do not increase the rate of dropping out (Bishop, 2001; Hoffer, 1997; Warren & Jenkins, 2005).

RECAP

- Socioeconomic status is an extremely powerful influence on educational achievement. Generally, adolescents from higher social classes perform better in school and complete more years of schooling than do their less advantaged counterparts.
- Studies also indicate that there are ethnic differences in educational achievement above and beyond those attributable to socioeconomic status. In general, Asian American adolescents outperform white students, who, in turn, do better than African American, Hispanic American, or American Indian students. One reason for the superior performance of Asian American students is that they are more likely to hold the sorts of beliefs about achievement that are predictive of success in school in all ethnic groups.
- The low level of educational achievement among American youth in general has been a concern for several decades. Although some gains in scores on standardized tests of achievement were reported during the mid-1980s, test scores by and large have not improved since then, and American students continue to fare poorly in international comparisons.

social promotion   The practice of promoting students from one grade to the next automatically, regardless of their school performance.

- Dropouts are more likely than their peers to be Latino, to come from economically disadvantaged backgrounds, to come from single-parent homes, and to have had a poor record of educational achievement throughout their school years. Dropping out is not so much a decision that is made during adolescence as it is the culmination of a long process that begins early on.

Occupational Achievement

School, rather than work, is the setting in which achievement is most often studied by contemporary scholars interested in teenagers. Although many individuals in previous generations began their occupational careers during adolescence, this is very rare today in most industrialized societies, where the majority of individuals pursue some form of postsecondary education before entering into full-time work. With the exception of apprenticeships, which, as we noted in earlier chapters, are popular in only a handful of European countries, the work individuals perform during adolescence is rarely relevant to their future careers—it is a means of earning spending money. Work experiences in adolescence, in general, have little or no impact on adolescents' plans or aspirations for adult work, especially among students from non-poor families (Entwisle et al., 2005; Johnson, 2002). During late adolescence, however, at least for some individuals, the focus of their achievement shifts to the world of work and careers.

Although we often think of school and work as separate domains, achievement is one aspect of psychosocial development during adolescence that links them together. The number of years of schooling an individual completes is the single best indicator of his or her eventual occupational success (Arum & Hout, 1998). It is not simply that adolescents benefit in the labor force by having a high school diploma or a college degree. Although these credentials matter, research shows that each year of education—even without graduating—adds significantly to occupational success. In other words, individuals who have completed three years of college earn more money, on average, than individuals who have completed only one year, even though neither group has a college

degree in hand. You may be surprised to learn, however, that *grades* in high school and college are virtually unrelated to occupational success. A few years after graduation, A students and C students hold similarly prestigious jobs and earn comparable amounts of money (Garbarino & Asp, 1981).

Researchers who are interested in occupational achievement during adolescence have examined several issues, including the ways in which young people make decisions about their careers and the influences on their occupational aspirations and expectations. We begin with a look at the development of adolescents' occupational plans.

THE DEVELOPMENT OF OCCUPATIONAL PLANS

The development of occupational plans during adolescence can be viewed in many respects as paralleling, or even as part of, the identity development process. As with developing a coherent sense of identity, the development of occupational plans follows a sequence that involves an examination of one's traits, abilities, and interests; a period of experimentation with different work roles; and an integration of influences from one's past (primarily, identification with familial role models) with one's hopes for the future. And as is also the case with identity development, occupational role development is profoundly influenced by the social environment in which it takes place.

According to many theories of occupational development, occupational plans form in stages, with late adolescence being an important time for the crystallization of plans that are more realistic, less based on fantasy, and more grounded in the adolescent's assessment of his or her talents. According to one theory (Super, 1967), between ages 14 and 18, individuals first begin to crystallize a vocational preference. During this period of **crystallization,** they begin to formulate ideas about appropriate work and begin to develop occupational self-conceptions that will guide subsequent educational decisions. Although adolescents may not settle on a particular career at this point, they do begin to narrow their choices according to their interests, values, and abilities. One adolescent may decide that she wants a career in which she works with people. Another may decide that he wants a career in which he can earn a great deal of money. A third may think about a career in science. During this period, the adolescent begins to seek out information on her or his tentative choice and make plans for the future (Osipow, 1973). The process is reminiscent of the sort of role experimentation described by Erik Erikson (1968) in his theory of adolescent identity development (see Chapter 8). In both cases, during middle

crystallization   According to Super, the stage during which individuals, typically ages 14–18, first begin to formulate their ideas about appropriate occupations.

adolescence, alternative identities are considered and evaluated on the basis of exploration, experimentation, and self-examination (Crites, 1989).

Following the period of crystallization is a period of **specification,** occurring roughly between the ages of 18 and 21, or during the college years. During this period, the young person recognizes the need to specify his or her vocational interests and begins to seek appropriate information to accomplish this. In many regards, a similar process is followed during the stage of specification as during the stage of crystallization: Alternatives are considered, information is sought, decisions are made, and preferences are consolidated. The chief difference, however, is that during the period of specification, more narrowly defined career pursuits within a general career category are considered (rather than general career categories themselves). For example, during the period of crystallization, an adolescent may decide to pursue a career in the field of mental health, without being able to specify a vocational preference within this general category. During the specification stage, he or she might begin to consider and compare a variety of careers within the mental health profession—social work, educational counseling, clinical psychology, psychiatry, and so on—and make choices among them.

Although many theories of occupational plans originally focused on adolescence, changes in the labor force, requiring individuals to complete more and more education before beginning their careers, have made young adulthood a far more important phase than adolescence for the development of occupational plans. Changes in the broader environment in which adolescents develop—in this case, changes in the need for and accessibility of higher education—have exerted a powerful influence on the developmental course of occupational planning. For many individuals, the crystallization of occupational plans may not take place until the final years of college, and the specification process may not even begin until after graduation.

INFLUENCES ON OCCUPATIONAL CHOICES

What makes one individual choose to become an attorney and another decide to be a teacher? Why do some students pursue careers in psychology while others major in computer science? Researchers have long been interested in the reasons that individuals end up in certain careers.

▌ The Role of Personality and Work Values

Many theorists who are interested in why people enter different occupational fields have examined the role of personality factors—traits, interests, and values—in the

An individual's choice of occupation is influenced by many factors, including the work values he or she has. Contextual factors, such as job opportunities, are important as well.

process of career selection. They believe that individuals select careers that match, in one way or another, certain elements of their personality. Perhaps the most widely cited perspective of this sort is that of John Holland (1985).

After years of extensive analysis of jobs and the people who select them, Holland determined that career choices can be viewed as a reflection of basic personality styles. Certain occupational environments are well suited to individuals with certain personalities, and others are not. Successful career choice, in Holland's model, entails the matching of a particular personality type—a given set of interests and characteristics—with a vocation that allows the expression of these traits. By answering questions on a standardized personality inventory, an individual can determine which basic personality dimensions are characteristic of him or herself and can then examine directories in which occupations have been classified according to the same typology.

After completing Holland's personality inventory—called the **Self-Directed Search**—an individual can better understand his or her vocational profile (which of the personality dimensions are dominant and which are less important). Because different occupations typically offer different degrees of opportunity to express different traits, a good career choice in Holland's view is one that provides the best fit between a person's personality and a vocation's characteristics. Someone who is artistic, social, and enterprising, for example, would be better suited to a career in acting than in accounting.

specification   According to Super, the stage during which individuals, typically ages 18–21, first begin to consider narrowly defined occupational pursuits.

Self-Directed Search   A personality designed by Holland and used to help individuals better understand their vocational interests.

TABLE 12.1 People look for different things in a job. Which types of rewards are most important to you?

Type of Reward	Example
Extrinsic	Earning a good income
Security	Enjoying job stability
Intrinsic	Having opportunities for creativity
Influence	Wielding power over others
Altruistic	Helping others
Social	Enjoying one's co-workers
Leisure	Having opportunities for vacation or time off

A different approach to understanding vocational choice focuses on **work values,** which reflect the different sorts of rewards individuals seek from their work (e.g., Johnson, 2002). When you think about your future work, what will you look for in a job? For example, are you most interested in making a lot of money, in having a secure job, or in having a job that permits you to have a lot of vacation time? According to most theories of work values, seven basic types of work rewards define individuals' work values: extrinsic rewards (earning a high income), security (enjoying job stability), intrinsic rewards (being able to be creative or to learn things from work), influence (having authority over others or power over decision making), altruistic rewards (helping others), social rewards (working with people you like), and leisure (having an opportunity for free time or vacation). Individuals choose jobs based on the relative importance of these various work rewards to them (see Table 12.1).

Several writers have noted that many contemporary adolescents have unrealistic and overly ambitious ideas about the rewards they will derive from their future work. One set of authors noted that a very large proportion of adolescents aspire to levels of work rewards that they are highly unlikely to attain (Schneider & Stevenson, 1999). One specific problem is that adolescents tend to rate almost all work rewards very highly, optimistically believing that they can find jobs that satisfy multiple rewards simultaneously. When they actually enter their first full-time adult jobs, though, they soon discover that it is difficult, if not impossible, to have a career in which, say, one makes a lot of money, is creative, helps other people, enjoys job security, and has a lot of free time. Over the course of young adulthood, then, one of the most important changes that occurs in the domain of occupational development is that individuals become both somewhat disillusioned and more focused on what they want from a job, abandoning the unrealistic notion that one can "have it all" (Roberts, O'Donnell, &

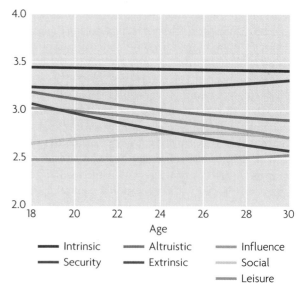

FIGURE 12.5 As adolescents move into young adulthood, the value they place on the extrinsic, altruistic, and social rewards of a job declines, whereas the value they place on intrinsic job rewards and job security remains strong. (Johnson, 2002)

Robins, 2004). As adolescents move into young adulthood, the degrees to which they value the extrinsic, altruistic, and social rewards of jobs, which are all strongly valued when individuals are seniors in high school, decline most dramatically, whereas the values they place on intrinsic rewards and job security, which are also strong at the end of high school, remain strong (Johnson, 2002) (see Figure 12.5).

There are important limitations to theories of career choice that are based solely on personality traits or reward preferences assessed in adolescence, however. First, interests and abilities are not fixed during adolescence and young adulthood (Mortimer & Lorence, 1979), but continue to develop and change during the adult years (Johnson, 2002). Indeed, one of the most important influences on personality development during adulthood is work itself. Thus, through working in a job that emphasizes certain personality characteristics, requires certain abilities, or provides

work values The particular sorts of rewards an individual looks for in a job (extrinsic, intrinsic, social, altruistic, security, influence, leisure).

certain types of rewards, individuals begin to change their personality, skills, and values. Consequently, a job that seems like a bad match during early adulthood may, over time, become a good match, as the individual grows and changes in response to the work environment. For example, someone may not be especially interested in social interactions but may, because of a tight job market, end up in a teaching position after graduating from college. Over time, the more he interacts with students, the more appealing the interpersonal aspects of the job may become. Eventually, he may come to feel that having opportunities for social interaction on the job is very important.

A second problem with theories of career choice that emphasize adolescents' personality dimensions or work values is that they may underestimate the importance of other factors that influence and shape vocational decisions. Many career decisions are influenced more by individuals' beliefs about what sorts of jobs are accessible or "appropriate" for them than by their interests and preferences (Johnson, 2002). It is all well and good, for example, for an adolescent to discover that he is well suited for a career in medicine, but the realization is of little value if his family cannot afford the cost of college or medical school. Or an adolescent girl may discover through taking a vocational preference inventory that she is well suited for work in the area of construction or building, but she may find that her parents, peers, teachers, and potential employers all discourage her from following this avenue of employment. One recent study found that early adolescent Mexican American girls, in particular, were more likely than African American or white girls to have stereotypically female career goals (Hill, Ramirez, & Dumka, 2003).

Put most simply, career choices are not made solely on the basis of individual preference; they are the result of an interaction among individual preferences, social influences, and important forces in the broader social environment. It is to these influences and forces that we now turn.

■ **The Influence of Parents and Peers** No influence on occupational choice is stronger than socioeconomic status, and as a result, adolescents' occupational ambitions and achievements are highly correlated with the ambitions and achievements of those around them (Duncan, Featherman, & Duncan, 1972). Youngsters from middle-class families are more likely than their less advantaged peers to aspire to and enter middle-class occupations. In addition, apart from their own socioeconomic status, youngsters who have many friends from middle-class backgrounds are more likely than those who have many friends from lower socioeconomic levels to aspire to high-status occupations (Simpson, 1962). Socioeconomic status also influences

work values, with individuals from higher classes more likely to value intrinsic rewards and influence, and less likely to value extrinsic rewards and security. The importance of social class as a determinant of what people look for in their jobs is strong and constant throughout adolescence and young adulthood (Johnson, 2002).

A variety of explanations have been offered for the fit between adolescents' ambitions and the socioeconomic status of those around them. First, and perhaps most important, **occupational attainment**—the prestige or status an individual achieves in the world of work—depends strongly on educational attainment (Alexander & Eckland, 1975). As we saw earlier, educational attainment is greatly influenced by socioeconomic status. Thus, because middle-class adolescents are likely to complete more years of schooling than their lower-class peers, economically advantaged adolescents are more likely to seek and enter higher-status occupations.

Second, middle-class parents, as noted earlier, are more likely to raise their children in ways that foster the development of strong needs for achievement (Rosen, 1956) and interest in career exploration (Grotevant & Cooper, 1988). The development of achievement motivation, which has an impact on school performance, also has an impact on youngsters' occupational ambitions—both directly (in that individuals with strong needs for achievement will express these needs by aspiring to occupations that provide opportunities to achieve status or wealth) and indirectly, through the effects of achievement motivation on academic achievement (in that youngsters who are successful in school are likely to be encouraged to seek higher-status occupations and engage in identity exploration). Indeed, parents influence their adolescents' career aspirations mainly by influencing their educational achievement (Jodl, Michael, Malanchuk, Eccles, & Sameroff, 2001).

Third, the same opportunities that favor economically advantaged youngsters in the world of education—better facilities, more opportunities for enrichment, greater accessibility of higher education—also favor middle-class youngsters in the world of work. Because their parents, for example, are more likely to work in positions of power and leadership, middle-class youngsters often have important family connections and sources of information about the world of work that are less available to youngsters from poorer families. In addition, coming from a family that is economically well off may provide an adolescent with more time to explore career options and to wait for an especially desirable position, rather than having to take the first job that becomes available out of economic necessity.

occupational attainment A measure of achievement based on the status or prestige of the job an individual holds.

Fourth, parents, siblings, and other important sources of influence serve as models for adolescents' occupational choices (Barber & Eccles, 1992; Grotevant & Cooper, 1988). Although some young people establish career choices through the explicit rejection of their parents' careers, the weight of the evidence suggests that adolescents' and parents' vocations are more similar than different, particularly when the adolescent's family relationships have been warm and close, and when strong identifications have formed between the adolescent and his or her parents. As we saw in our discussion of mothers' employment in Chapter 4, adolescents are especially influenced by the work roles of the parent of the same sex. This finding has become increasingly important as growing numbers of women enter the labor force and hold high-status occupations. Daughters of women who are happily employed outside the home are far more likely themselves to seek careers in addition to marriage and family responsibilities than are adolescent girls whose mothers are not employed (Leslie, 1986). Young women whose mothers are in high-status occupations are more likely to do so themselves when they enter the labor force (Hoffman, 1974). And both sons and daughters are less likely to have sex-stereotyped attitudes about work and more likely to prefer a dual-career arrangement if they come from dual-career families themselves (Barber & Eccles, 1992).

Finally, parents—and, to a lesser extent, peers—influence adolescents' occupational plans by establishing a value context in which certain occupational choices are encouraged and others are discouraged. According to sociologist Melvin Kohn (1977), middle-class families and middle-class schools encourage children to value autonomy, self-direction, and independence—three features that are more likely to be found in middle-class than in working-class jobs. The children are told, implicitly and explicitly, how important it is to have freedom, power, and status. Adolescents who have been raised to value attributes that are characteristic of middle-class jobs, not surprisingly, will seek those attributes when they plan their careers. They will look for jobs that offer independence and power. In working-class families, in contrast, children are more likely to be raised to value obedience and conformity—two characteristics that are highly valued in most working-class jobs. For youngsters from this socioeconomic background, jobs that appeal to these values will be relatively more attractive. They will have been raised to value such things as job security and not having to worry too much about making high-pressured decisions. Indeed, to many working-class youngsters, the high-stress world of the business executive is not at all an attractive career possibility.

The Broader Context of Occupational Choice

Adolescents' occupational choices are made, of course, within a broader social context that profoundly influences the nature of their plans. At different times, different employment opportunities arise, and young people—particularly by the time they reach the end of their formal schooling—are often very aware of the prospects for employment in different fields. Indeed, one study of inner-city youngsters found that many had developed ideas about their future job prospects by the time they were in second grade (Cook et al., 1996). Understandably, young people often tailor their plans in response to what they perceive as the future needs and demands of the labor market, and the acceptability of given occupational choices within their community. One study found, for example, that many rural adolescents experience great conflicts between wanting to pursue a career that would take them away from their rural community and wanting to remain close to their roots (Hektner, 1994).

FOOD FOR THOUGHT

Think about your own occupational development. What factors have most influenced your choices? How did your occupational plans change during adolescence?

Unfortunately, adolescents also tailor their plans based on their beliefs regarding which jobs society says are "acceptable" for individuals of particular social class, ethnicity, or sex (Johnson, 2002). Despite the substantial liberalization in sex-role stereotypes that has occurred during the past 40 years, for example, adolescent girls' vocational choices still tend to be concentrated among jobs that have historically been occupied by women, such as secretarial work, teaching, and nursing, and they are more oriented toward occupations that involve working with people and that allow the expression of compassion and altruism (Beutel & Marini, 1995; Marini, Fan, Finley, & Beutel, 1996). In contrast, relatively fewer adolescent girls plan to enter jobs in which the main tasks involve working with things, rather than people, as is the case in science or engineering (Jozefowicz, Barber, Eccles, & Mollasis, 1994). Girls are more likely than boys to value the intrinsic, altruistic, and social rewards of work, whereas boys are more likely to value influence and leisure; sex differences in the value placed on extrinsic rewards are small (Johnson, 2002).

Moreover, many more adolescent girls than boys express concern about having to balance family and work demands in adulthood, and this further affects their occupational decision making, since they may be reluctant to pursue careers that they believe will interfere with family life (Astin, 1984). This task may vary between daughters who grow up in divorced versus nondivorced households, since they probably have been exposed to very different models of how to balance work and family obligations (Barber & Eccles, 1992).

One problem faced by all young people in making career plans is obtaining accurate information about the labor market needs of the future and the appropriate means of pursuing positions in various fields. The majority of young people do not have educational plans that are consistent with the educational requirements of the jobs they hope to enter, and many adolescents are overly optimistic about their chances for success (Schneider & Stevenson, 1999). One goal of career educators is to help adolescents make more informed and more realistic choices about their careers and to free them from stereotypes that constrain their choices.

RECAP

- Adolescence is a time for the development of realistic occupational plans.
- Adolescents' career choices are influenced by a number of factors, including their personality, their work values, their social background, and their perceptions of the labor market and their potential place within it.
- As is the case with educational achievement, occupational attainment is strongly influenced by socioeconomic status.
- Occupational plans are also influenced by the broader context, including adolescents' perceptions of what occupations are "appropriate" for them given their sex, ethnicity, and social background.

CHAPTER 13

Psychosocial Problems in Adolescence

SOME GENERAL PRINCIPLES ABOUT PROBLEMS IN ADOLESCENCE

PSYCHOSOCIAL PROBLEMS: THEIR NATURE AND COVARIATION

    Comorbidity of Externalizing Problems

    Comorbidity of Internalizing Problems

SUBSTANCE USE AND ABUSE

    Prevalence of Substance Use and Abuse

    Causes and Consequences of Substance Use and Abuse

    Prevention and Treatment of Substance Use and Abuse

EXTERNALIZING PROBLEMS

    Categories of Externalizing Problems

    Developmental Progression of Antisocial Behavior

    Changes in Juvenile Offending over Time

    Causes of Antisocial Behavior

    Prevention and Treatment of Externalizing Problems

INTERNALIZING PROBLEMS

    The Nature and Prevalence of Depression

    Sex Differences in Depression

    Suicide

    Causes of Depression and Internalizing Disorders

    Treatment and Prevention of Internalizing Problems

STRESS AND COPING

ALTHOUGH THE VAST MAJORITY of young people move through the adolescent years without experiencing major difficulty, some encounter serious psychological and behavioral problems that disrupt not only their lives but also the lives of those around them. Problems such as substance abuse, delinquency, and depression—while certainly not the norm during adolescence—do affect a worrisome number of teenagers. Moreover, these problems indirectly touch the lives of all of us, either directly, through the personal contact we may have with a troubled young person, or indirectly, through increased taxes for community services or heightened anxiety about the safety of our neighborhoods.

In the previous chapters, which examined normative aspects of adolescent development, the more problematic aspects of behavior and development were deliberately deemphasized, in order to dispel the erroneous stereotype of adolescence as an inherently troubled time. As you now know, most individuals emerge from adolescence with positive feelings about themselves and their parents; with the ability to form, maintain, and enjoy close relationships with same- and opposite-sex peers; and with the basic capabilities needed to take advantage of a range of educational, occupational, and recreational opportunities. Most settle into adulthood relatively smoothly and begin establishing their work and family careers with little serious difficulty. Although the transition into adulthood may appear forbidding to the young adolescent approaching many weighty decisions about the future, statistics tell us that, for a remarkably high proportion of youth, the transition is relatively peaceful. Yes, it is true that one in three adolescent girls gets pregnant before she is 21, but it is also true that two of three do not. Although 20 percent of teenagers do not complete high school by the societally expected age, 80 percent do, and more than half of the students who drop out later receive a high school diploma or GED. And despite popular media portrayals to the contrary, the majority of inner-city ethnic minority youth are not poorly adjusted (Barbarin, 1993; McDermott & Spencer, 1997). By the same token, however, we should not assume that white suburban youth are trouble-free; one recent study of suburban teenagers found very high rates of depression and substance use, especially among students who were under tremendous pressure to achieve (Luthar & Ansary, 2005; Luthar & Becker, 2002).

We should not gloss over the fact that many healthy adolescents at one time or another experience self-doubt, family squabbles, academic setbacks, or broken hearts. But it is important to keep in mind as we look at psychosocial problems during adolescence that there is an important distinction between the normative, and usually transitory, difficulties encountered by many young people—and by many adults, for that matter—and the serious psychosocial problems experienced by a relatively small minority of youth.

Some General Principles About Problems in Adolescence

The mass media like nothing more than to paint extreme pictures of the world in which we live. This exaggerated worldview is obvious in the presentation of teenage problem behavior. Rarely are popular portrayals of behavioral disorders, psychological distress, drug use, or delinquency accurate: One experiment with marijuana inevitably leads to drug addiction and school failure. A breakup with a boyfriend is followed by a suicide attempt. An after-school prank develops into a life of crime. A couple's passionate make-out session on the beach fades into a commercial, and when the program returns, the adolescent girl is on her way to a life of single parenthood and welfare dependency. Those of you for whom adolescence was not that long ago know that these "facts" about adolescent problem behavior are rarely true. But we are so often bombarded with images of young people in trouble that it is easy to be fooled into believing that "adolescence" equals "problems."

One of the purposes of this chapter is to put these problems in perspective. It is therefore helpful, before we look at several specific sorts of problems in detail, to lay out some general principles about adolescent psychosocial problems that apply to a range of issues.

Most Problems Reflect Transitory Experimentation First, we need to distinguish between

FOOD FOR THOUGHT

Why do you think stereotypes of problem behavior in adolescence differ from reality? What are some dangers of holding on to the stereotypic view?

It is important to differentiate between occasional experimentation with risky or unhealthful activities and enduring patterns of troublesome behavior.

occasional experimentation and enduring patterns of dangerous or troublesome behavior. Research shows that rates of occasional, usually harmless, experimentation far exceed rates of enduring problems. For example, the majority of adolescents experiment with alcohol sometime before high school graduation, and the majority will have been drunk at least once; but, as we'll see, relatively few teenagers develop drinking problems or permit alcohol to adversely affect their school or personal relationships. Similarly, although the vast majority of teenagers do something during adolescence that is against the law, very few of these young people go on to have criminal careers. In a period of development during which it is normal, even expected, that individuals will seek independence and explore themselves and their relationships with others, it is hardly surprising that some of the experimentation in which individuals engage is risky (Siegel & Scovill, 2000). In fact, adolescents who experiment occasionally with risky behavior report a quality of life that is more similar to that reported by adolescents who abstain from risk taking entirely than it is to the quality of life reported by frequent risk takers (Topolski et al., 2001).

Not All Problems Begin in Adolescence

Second, we need to distinguish between problems that have their origins and onset during adolescence, and those that have their roots during earlier periods of development. It is true, for example, that some teenagers fall into patterns of criminal or delinquent behavior during adolescence, and for this reason, we tend to associate delinquency with the adolescent years. But most teenagers who have recurrent problems with the law had problems at home and at school from an early age; in some samples of delinquents, the problems were evident as early as preschool (Farrington, 2004). Many individuals who develop depression during adolescence suffered from other types of psychological distress, such as excessive anxiety, as children. In other words, simply because a problem may be displayed during adolescence does not mean that it is a problem of adolescence.

Most Problems Do Not Persist into Adulthood

Third, it is important to remember that many, although not all, of the problems experienced by adolescents are relatively transitory in nature and are resolved by the beginning of adulthood, with few long-term repercussions in most cases. Substance abuse, delinquency, and unemployment are three good examples of problems that tend to follow this pattern: Rates of drug and alcohol use, unemployment, and delinquency are all higher within the adolescent population than in the adult population, but most individuals who have abused drugs and alcohol, been unemployed, or committed delinquent acts as teenagers grow up to be sober, employed, law-abiding adults. Individuals for whom problem behavior persists into adulthood are likely to have had a problematic childhood as well as a problematic adolescence. The fact that some of the problems of adolescence seem to fade away with time does not make their prevalence during adolescence any less significant, but it should be kept in mind when rhetoric about the inevitable decline of civilization at the hands of contemporary youth is bandied about.

Problems During Adolescence Are Not Caused by Adolescence

Finally, problem behavior during adolescence is virtually never a direct consequence of the normative changes of adolescence itself.

Popular theories about "raging hormones" causing oppositional or deviant behavior have no scientific support whatsoever, for example, nor do the widely held beliefs that problem behaviors are manifestations of an inherent need to rebel against authority or that bizarre behavior results from an identity crisis. As you learned in previous chapters, the hormonal changes of puberty have only a modest direct effect on adolescent behavior; rebellion during adolescence is atypical, not normal; and few adolescents experience a tumultuous identity crisis. When a young person exhibits a serious psychosocial problem, such as depression, the worst possible interpretation is that it is a normal part of growing up. It is more likely a sign that something is wrong.

RECAP

- The vast majority of individuals do not develop serious psychological or social problems during the adolescent years, but a significant minority do.
- It is important to distinguish between experimentation and enduring patterns of behavior, between problems that have their origins during adolescence and those that do not, and between problems that are transitory and those that persist into adulthood.
- Serious problem behavior during adolescence is almost never a direct consequence of the normative changes of adolescence itself.

Psychosocial Problems: Their Nature and Covariation

Clinical practitioners (psychologists, psychiatrists, social workers, and counselors) and other experts on the development and treatment of psychosocial problems during adolescence typically distinguish among three broad categories of problems: substance abuse, internalizing disorders, and externalizing disorders (Achenbach & Edelbrock, 1987). **Substance abuse** refers to the maladaptive use of drugs, including legal drugs like alcohol or nicotine; illegal drugs like marijuana, cocaine, and ecstasy; and prescription drugs such as stimulants or sedatives. **Internalizing disorders** are those in which the young person's problems are turned inward and are manifested in emotional and cognitive distress, such as depression, anxiety, or phobia. **Externalizing disorders** are those in which the young person's problems are turned outward and are manifested in behavioral problems (some writers use the expression "acting out" to refer to this set of problems). Common externalizing problems during adolescence are delinquency, antisocial aggression, and truancy. Some adolescents also have problems that do not fit neatly into one of these three categories, such as academic problems (for example, low motivation, poor attention) or peer problems (for example, low popularity, poor social skills) (Wångby, Bergman, & Magnusson, 1999).

Although we often think of adolescent substance abuse as an externalizing disorder, more recent research indicates that it is just as likely to accompany depression and other internalizing disorders as it is to be a part of "acting out" behavior. We are simply more likely to be aware of substance abuse problems when they are seen among adolescents who are antisocial (such as a rowdy group of drunk delinquent youth) than when they occur in the context of internalizing problems (such as a depressed teenager who drinks herself to sleep each night). Because substance abuse problems co-occur, or are **comorbid,** with both externalizing and internalizing problems, and because many adolescents who experiment with drugs have neither internalizing nor externalizing problems, we look at substance abuse as a separate category of problem behavior.

While the distinction between internalizing disorders and externalizing disorders is useful for organizing information about psychosocial problems during adolescence, it is important to bear in mind that some adolescents experience problems in both domains simultaneously. That is, some adolescents who engage in delinquency or show other behavior problems also suffer from depression (Beyers & Loeber, 2003; Capaldi, 1991, 1992; Garnefski & Diekstra, 1997; Hinden, Compas, Howell, & Achenbach, 1997; Kiesner, 2002). And, as noted earlier, many depressed or anxious adolescents as well as many antisocial adolescents also abuse drugs and alcohol (Armstrong & Costello, 2002; Garnefski & Diekstra, 1997; Flisher et al., 2000; Henry et al., 1993). Many researchers believe that it is

substance abuse   The misuse of alcohol or other drugs to a degree that causes problems in the individual's life.

internalizing disorders   Psychosocial problems that are manifested in a turning of the symptoms inward, as in depression or anxiety.

externalizing disorders   Psychosocial problems that are manifested in a turning of the symptoms outward, as in aggression or delinquency.

comorbid   Co-occurring, as when an individual has more than one problem at the same time.

Problem behaviors tend to cluster together—that is, adolescents who smoke and drink are also more likely to engage in risk taking and antisocial behavior.

FOOD FOR THOUGHT

How might the recognition that there is considerable comorbidity of problems in adolescence change our approaches to prevention and intervention?

important to distinguish among adolescents who exhibit one specific problem without any others (for example, depressed adolescents who do not have other internalizing or externalizing problems), adolescents who exhibit more than one problem within the same general category (for example, violent delinquent youth or anxious-depressed youth), and adolescents who exhibit both internalizing and externalizing problems (for example, depressed delinquents). These adolescents may have followed very different pathways to deviance and may require very different types of treatment (Capaldi, 1991, 1992; Ensminger, 1990; McCord, 1990). In general, studies show that multiproblem teenagers have had far worse family experiences than those with one problem (Aseltine, Gore, & Colten, 1998; Capaldi, 1992; Ge, Best, Conger, & Simons, 1996).

COMORBIDITY OF EXTERNALIZING PROBLEMS

One of the reasons it is helpful to differentiate between internalizing and externalizing disorders is that the specific problems within each broad category are often highly intercorrelated. Delinquency, for example, is often associated with problems such as truancy, defiance, sexual promiscuity, academic difficulties, and violence (Farrington, 2004; Resnick & Blum, 1994). All these problems are different sorts of manifestations of a lack of impulse control, and adolescents who engage in these behaviors are often described as "undercontrolled" (Robins, John, Caspi, Moffitt, & Stouthamer-Loeber, 1996).

Problem Behavior Syndrome Researchers have devoted a great deal of attention to studying the covariation among externalizing problems during adolescence in general—and the comorbidity of externalizing and substance abuse problems in particular—and a number of theories about the origins of what some experts call **problem behavior syndrome** have been proposed. The most widely cited perspective, now more than 30 years old, comes from the work of social psychologist Richard Jessor and his colleagues (Jessor & Jessor, 1977). According to Jessor, the underlying cause of externalizing problems during adolescence is unconventionality in both the adolescent's personality and the social environment (Donovan & Jessor, 1985; Menard & Huizinga, 1994). Unconventional individuals are tolerant of deviance in general, are not highly connected to educational or religious institutions, and are very liberal in their views. Unconventional environments are those in which a large number of individuals share these same attitudes. Unconventional individuals in unconventional environments are more likely to engage in a wide variety of risk-taking behavior, including experimentation with illegal drugs, sex without contraception, delinquent activity, and even risky driving (Brack, Brack, & Orr, 1996; Cooper, Wood, Orcutt, & Albino, 2003; Fergusson & Lynskey, 1996; Jakobsen, Rise, Aas, & Anderssen, 1997; Spingarn & DuRant, 1996). A recent comparison of adolescents in the United States and China found that the same factors heighten or diminish adolescents' risk for problem behavior in both countries (Jessor et al., 2003).

Although Jessor's theory does not specifically hypothesize about the origins of unconventionality, a number of possibilities have been proposed. One set of theories emphasizes the biological underpinnings of risk taking or unconventionality and argues that a predisposition toward deviance may actually be inherited (e.g., Mednick, Gabrielli, & Hitchings, 1987; Rowe, Rodgers, Meseck-Bushey, & St. John, 1989). A second view stresses biologically based differences (either inherited or acquired through experience) among individuals in arousal, sensation seeking, and

problem behavior syndrome The covariation among various types of externalizing disorders believed to result from an underlying trait of unconventionality.

FIGURE 13.1 One explanation for cormorbidity is that problems in one domain can create problems in another. (Masten et al., 2005)

fearlessness (e.g., Ortiz & Raine, 2004; Zuckerman, 1983). Yet a third view emphasizes the early family context in which deviance-prone children are reared and frames problem behavior as a sort of adaptive response to a hostile environment (Belsky, Steinberg, & Draper, 1991).

■ **Problem Clusters** An alternative to the view that there is an underlying trait that drives all problem behavior has been proposed by sociologist Denise Kandel. She and her associates argue that different types of deviance have distinctly different origins, but that involvement in a given problem behavior may itself lead to involvement in a second one. For example, the use of illicit drugs other than marijuana (cocaine, heroin) increases the chances that an adolescent will become premaritally pregnant (Elliott & Morse, 1989; Yamaguchi & Kandel, 1987) or suicidal (Kandel, Raveis, & Davies, 1991). Thus, problem behaviors may cluster together not mainly because of a common underlying trait like unconventionality, but because involvement in some problematic activities (such as drug and alcohol use) leads to involvement in others (such as delinquency) (Bingham & Shope, 2004; Hussong, Curran, & Moffitt, 2004; Malone, Taylor, & Marmorstein, 2004; Mason & Windle, 2002; Ridenour et al., 2002; Rohde, Lewinsohn, Kahler, Seeley, & Brown, 2001). Some writers have talked about "cascading" effects, where one sort of problem leads to another, which leads to a third. For example, one recent analysis of individuals followed from preadolescence into adulthood found that externalizing problems in childhood led to academic difficulties in adolescence, which, in turn, led to internalizing problems in adulthood (see Figure 13.1) (Masten et al., 2005). Similarly, a longitudinal study of African American youth found that problems in school led to drug and alcohol use, which led to dropping out (Zimmerman & Schmeelk-Cone, 2003).

■ **Social Control Theory** According to a third view, **social control theory** (Gottfredson & Hirschi, 1990), individuals who do not have strong bonds to society's institutions—such as the family, school, or workplace—will be likely to deviate and behave unconventionally in a variety of ways. This view suggests that the apparent clustering of different problem behaviors

may stem not from a problem "in" the person (such as inherent unconventionality or a biological predisposition toward risky behavior), but from an underlying weakness in the attachment of certain youngsters to society. This underlying problem leads to the development of an unconventional attitude, to membership in an unconventional peer group, or to involvement in one or several problem behaviors that may set a chain of problem activities in motion. Social control theory helps to explain why behavior problems are not just clustered together but are far more prevalent among poor, inner-city, minority youngsters.

■ **Overstating the Case?** Finally, a number of researchers stress that we should be careful about overstating the case for a single problem behavior "syndrome" (Farrell, Sullivan, Esposito, Meyer, & Valois, 2005; McCord, 1990; Resnicow, Ross-Gaddy, & Vaughan, 1995; Willoughby, Chalmers, & Busseri, 2004). They note that although engaging in one type of problem behavior increases the likelihood of engaging in another, the overlap among behavior problems is far from perfect. Indeed, in one study, it was found that the vast majority of delinquents are *not* serious drug users (Elliott, Huizinga, & Menard, 1989). Other studies suggest that it is important to differentiate between problem behavior that adults disapprove of but that many adolescents consider normative (such as smoking, drinking, having sex) versus problem behavior that both adults and adolescents view as serious (such as, violent crime) (Basen-Engquist, Edmundson, & Parcel, 1996; Willoughby et al., 2004; Zweig, Lindberg, & McGinley, 2001). Such evidence makes it difficult to embrace a theory that identifies a single cause of problem behavior. Like other types of behavior, problem behavior has multiple and complex causes that vary from one individual to the next. It may be just as erroneous to generalize about the troubled adolescent as it is to generalize about young people overall. Indeed, risky activities cluster together in different ways among different adolescents, creating very different risk profiles (Zweig et al., 2001) (see Figure 13.2).

It is also true that the clustering of different problem behaviors is seen more often in some populations than others, and more often in studies of adolescents than in studies of either children or young adults (Gillmore et al., 1991; McGee & Newcomb, 1992). For instance, some studies find that two factors that often are correlated with externalizing problems such as

social control theory A theory of delinquency that links deviance with the absence of bonds to society's main institutions.

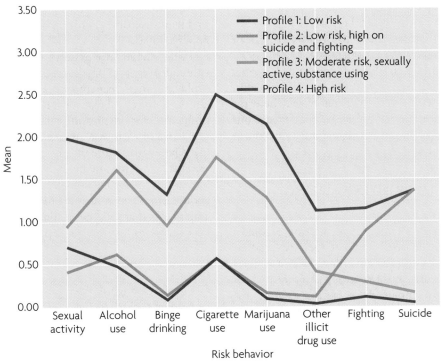

Profiles of risk—Females, grades 9–12

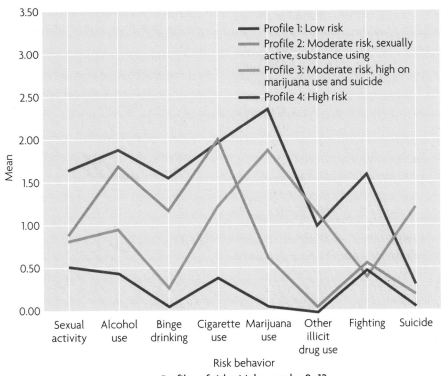

Profiles of risk—Males, grades 9–12

FIGURE 13.2   Different risky activities cluster together in different ways for different individuals. In one study, four different risk profiles were identified for male and female adolescents. (Zweig et al., 2001)

delinquency—disengagement from school and early sexual intercourse—may not be part of a problematic syndrome among inner-city African American youth or American Indians (Mitchell & O'Nell, 1998; Neumark-Sztainer et al., 1996; Resnicow et al., 1995; Rotheram-Borus, Rosario, Van Rossem, Reid, & Gillis, 1995; Stanton et al., 1993). It therefore may be erroneous to view certain behaviors, such as precocious sexual activity, as indicative of underlying problems in certain communities.

COMORBIDITY OF INTERNALIZING PROBLEMS

Although covariation among internalizing problems has been less extensively studied than covariation among externalizing problems, there is also a good deal of comorbidity in internalizing disorders, which tend to have in common the subjective state of distress. For example, depressed adolescents are more likely than their peers to experience anxiety, panic, phobia, obsessional thinking, suicidal ideation, eating disorders, and various psychosomatic disturbances (that is, physical problems that have psychological causes) (Attie & Brooks-Gunn, 1989; Gerhardt, Compas, Connor, & Achenbach, 1999; Graber, 2004; Johnson, Cohen, Kotler, Kasen, & Brook, 2002; Masi et al., 2004; Petersen et al., 1993; Zaider, Johnson, & Cockell, 2003). Some experts question whether it even makes sense to consider some of these problems as separate entities when speaking about children or adolescents (for example, to draw a distinction between anxiety and depression), because rates of comorbidity are so high (Graber, 2004).

Just as different externalizing problems are hypothesized to reflect an underlying antisocial syndrome, various indicators of internalizing problems may be thought of as different manifestations of a common underlying factor. This factor is often referred to as **negative affectivity** (Lonigan, Carey, & Finch, Jr., 1994; Watson & Kendall, 1989). Individuals who are high in negative affectivity—who become distressed easily—are at greater risk for depression, anxiety disorders, and a range of internalizing problems. As is the case with the underpinnings of externalizing problems, the underpinnings of internalizing problems are believed to have both biological and environmental origins, including high levels of biological reactivity to stress (Katainen, Raeikkoenen, & Keltikangas-Jaervinen, 1998; Susman, Dorn, Inoff-Germain, Nottelmann, & Chrousos, 1997). These common underpinnings contribute to a certain degree

of stability in predispositions toward internalizing problems over time (Bardone, Moffitt, Caspi, Dickson, & Silva, 1996).

In this chapter, we examine the nature, prevalence, consequences, and amelioration of the three sets of problems often seen during adolescence: substance abuse, antisocial behavior and other externalizing problems, and depression and other internalizing problems. In each case, we ask four central questions: (1) What is the nature of this sort of problem in adolescence? (2) How many, and which, young people have problems in this domain? (3) What do we know about factors that contribute to problems in this area? and, (4) what approaches to prevention and intervention appear to have the most promise?

RECAP

- Experts distinguish among three categories of problems in adolescence: substance abuse, internalizing problems, and externalizing problems.
- There is a great deal of covariation, or "comorbidity," among different psychosocial problems during adolescence within and across these broad categories.
- Adolescents who engage in delinquency are more likely than their peers to be truant, to engage in precocious sexual behavior, and to commit acts of aggression—a pattern that has been termed problem behavior syndrome.
- Adolescents who are high in negative affectivity are more likely to suffer from depression, feel anxious, and report other symptoms of distress.

Substance Use and Abuse

Our society sends young people mixed messages about drugs and alcohol. Television programs aimed at preadolescents urge viewers to "Just Say No!" but the football games and sitcoms that many of these same viewers watch tell them, no less subtly, that having a good time with friends is virtually impossible without something alcoholic to drink. Many celebrities who are idolized by teenagers speak out against cocaine and marijuana, but many equally famous stars admit to using these same drugs. Tobacco companies spend enormous amounts of money marketing cigarettes to teenagers, and research shows that adolescents are especially drawn to cigarette advertisements that are presumed to be aimed at teenagers

negative affectivity The presumed underlying cause of internalizing disorders, characterized by high levels of subjective distress.

(Arnett, 2001; Biener & Siegel, 2000). On music videos, tobacco and alcohol use is common and often linked to sex, and more often than not, the lead performer is the individual doing the drinking, smoking, and lovemaking (DuRant et al., 1997). Although there is no solid evidence that exposure to alcohol or cigarette advertising *causes* adolescents to start drinking or smoking—advertising is mainly effective in increasing brand recognition (National Research Council, 2004)—the messages these ads communicate is that these are pleasurable activities (hardly a surprise, since the ads are designed to get people to buy the products).

The mixed signals sent to young people about drugs reflect, no doubt, the inconsistent way that we view these substances as a society: Some drugs (like alcohol or Prozac) are fine, as long as they are not abused, but others (like cocaine or ecstasy) are not; some drinking (enough to relax at a party) is socially appropriate, but too much (enough to impair an automobile driver) is not; some people (those over 21) are old enough to handle drugs, but others (those under 21) are not. It is easy to see why teenagers do not follow the dictates of their elders when it comes to alcohol and other drugs. How, then, should we view substance use and abuse among teenagers, when our backdrop is a society that much of the time tolerates, if not actively encourages, adults to use these same substances?

As with most of the problem behaviors that are common during adolescence, discussions of teenage substance use are often filled more with rhetoric than reality. The popular stereotype of contemporary young people is that they use and abuse a wide range of drugs more than their counterparts did previously, that the main reason adolescents use drugs is peer pressure, and that the "epidemic" level of substance use among American teenagers is behind many of the other problems associated with this age group—including academic underachievement, early pregnancy, suicide, and crime. The simplicity of these assertions is certainly tempting—after all, what could be more reassuring than to identify the "real" culprit (drugs) and the "real" causes (peers) of all the maladies of young people? And what could be even more comforting than the belief that, if we simply teach young people to "say no" to their peers, these problems will disappear?

Unfortunately, what we might like to believe about adolescent drug use is not necessarily correct. As we shall see, although there are grains of truth to many of the popular claims about the causes, nature, and consequences of teenage substance use and abuse, there are many widely held misconceptions about the subject, too.

PREVALENCE OF SUBSTANCE USE AND ABUSE

Each year since 1975, a group of researchers from the University of Michigan has surveyed a nationally representative sample of about 15,000 American high school seniors on several aspects of their lifestyle and values, including their use and abuse of a variety of drugs. Beginning in 1991, comparable samples of eighth- and tenth-graders were added to the annual survey. Because of the size and representativeness of the sample of respondents, this survey, called **Monitoring the Future,** is an excellent source of information about patterns of adolescent drug and alcohol use, at least among young people who have not dropped out of school. (The latest survey results can be accessed via the Internet, at www.monitoringthefuture.org.)

▌ **Drugs of Choice** The surveys consistently indicate that the two major legal drugs—alcohol and nicotine—are by far the most commonly used and abused substances, in terms of both prevalence (the percentage of teenagers who have ever used the drug) and recency of use (the percentage of teenagers who have used the drug within the last month). By the time they are seniors in high school, three-fourths of teenagers have tried alcohol and half have smoked cigarettes. Experimentation with marijuana is also common: 45 percent of all seniors have tried marijuana, 33 percent

Alcohol and cigarettes and, to a lesser extent, marijuana, remain the drugs of choice for contemporary adolescents.

Monitoring the Future An annual survey of a nationwide sample of American eighth-, tenth-, and twelfth-graders, mainly known for its data on adolescent substance use.

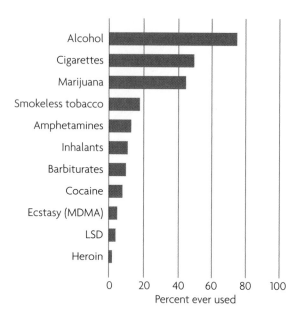

FIGURE 13.3   Percentages of American high school seniors who have ever used various drugs. (Johnston et al., 2006)

have smoked marijuana at least once within the last year, and 25 percent have done so within the past 30 days. After marijuana, however, the percentage of young people who have tried various other drugs drops precipitously, and only about 10 percent of teenagers have used an illicit drug other than marijuana within the last month (Monitoring the Future, 2006). And, notwithstanding all the media attention given in recent years to ecstasy and steroids, fewer high school seniors have ever taken ecstasy (5 percent) or steroids (3 percent) than have tried smokeless tobacco (18 percent), amphetamines (13 percent), or inhalants (11 percent) (see Figure 13.3). In recent years, public health experts have expressed particular concern about the rapidly increasing recreational use of prescription opioids, like OxyContin or Vicodin (Sung, Richter, Vaughan, Johnson, & Thom, 2005). In general, although alcohol and tobacco use among adolescents in most other industrialized countries is comparable to that in the United States, illicit drug use by adolescents is less prevalent abroad than in America (Arnett, 2002).

Prevalence statistics, especially those that tap whether an individual has ever tried the substance in question, tell us little about the nature and extent of drug use from the standpoint of adolescents' health and well-being. It is one thing to have tried alcohol or marijuana; it is something else to use either of these substances so often that one's life and behavior are markedly affected.

One of the best ways to examine this issue is to look at the percentage of young people who report using various substances daily or nearly daily. It turns out that cigarettes are the only substances used by a substantial number of high school seniors daily (about one-sixth smoke daily), and of the remaining drugs, only alcohol and marijuana are used daily by even a modest percentage of teenagers (alcohol is used daily by about 3 percent of seniors, and marijuana by about 5 percent). Although daily use of alcohol is relatively infrequent among adolescents, nearly 30 percent of all seniors, 20 percent of all tenth-graders, and 10 percent of all eighth-graders report having abused alcohol (had more than five drinks in a row, sometimes called **binge drinking**) at least once during the past two weeks (Monitoring the Future, 2005).

Taken together, the findings from these surveys cast doubt on some of the most fervently held stereotypes about adolescent drug use. It is true that too many adolescents smoke cigarettes, which is certainly cause for concern, and that many adolescents who drink do so to excess. But only a very small proportion of young people have serious drug dependency problems (which would lead to daily use) or use hard drugs at all. Moreover, it is very unlikely that drug and alcohol use lurks behind the wide assortment of adolescent problems for which it is so frequently blamed. Rather, the pattern suggests that most adolescents have experimented with alcohol and marijuana, that many have used one or both of these drugs regularly, that alcohol is clearly the drug of choice among teenagers (a substantial minority of whom drink to excess), and that most teenagers have not experimented with other drugs. From a health and safety standpoint, therefore, education about alcohol and cigarette use and abuse is more urgently needed and may potentially affect a larger percentage of young people than education about any other drug type.

Changes in Substance Use over Time   The Monitoring the Future study has also been used to chart changes over time in adolescent substance use, and recent administrations of the survey have given experts cause for concern (see Figure 13.4). Marijuana use, which had been on a steady decline since the late 1970s, rose quite sharply during the mid-1990s and has not declined to its former levels (Monitoring the Future, 2005). Alcohol use, which had been declining steadily since the early 1980s (when more than 70 percent of seniors reported having consumed alcohol within the past month), also has leveled off, with about 50 percent of seniors reporting alcohol use in the last month. One bit of good news is that cigarette use by teenagers, which increased during the 1990s, has declined significantly since 1997—probably because there

binge drinking   Consuming five or more drinks in a row on one occasion, an indicator of alcohol abuse.

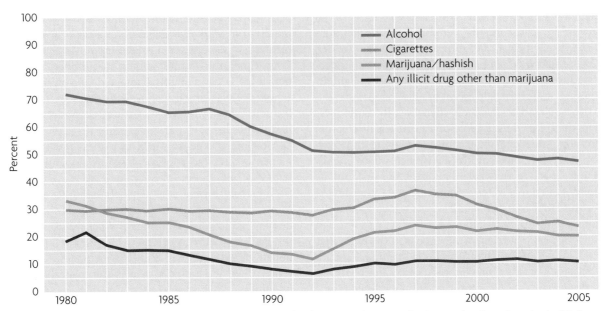

FIGURE 13.4 Over-time trends in the proportion of high school seniors who report having used various drugs in the 30 days preceding the survey. (Monitoring the Future, 2005)

was a 70 percent increase in the price of cigarettes between 1997 and 2001 (Monitoring the Future, 2005). Despite the massive amounts of money spent on anti-smoking education, the high price of cigarettes is a far more powerful deterrent to teen smoking (Centers for Disease Control and Prevention, 2002; Gruber & Zinman, 2001; Johnston, Bachman, & O'Malley, 2002).

Although pundits and political commentators frequently claim to have discovered the "real" reason for changes in rates of adolescent substance use, no one really knows why rates of adolescent substance use fluctuate over time, except, perhaps, because of fluctuations in the price and availability of various substances. We know that adolescents' drug use fluctuates with changes in their perceptions of how harmful and disapproved of drug use is, but scientists have not been able to determine what influences these perceptions, although it is likely that the messages teenagers receive about drugs—from parents, teachers, and mass media—are important (Bachman, Johnston, & O'Malley, 1998). What is clear, however, is that cohorts of U.S. adolescents born after World War II use more legal and illegal drugs at an earlier age than did their counterparts who were born in the first half of the century (Johnson & Gerstein, 1998). Interestingly, the once-existent gender gap in drug use, with males more likely to use and abuse drugs, has all but disappeared for alcohol, marijuana, and cigarettes, and has narrowed substantially for other drugs as well (Johnson & Gerstein, 1998).

Perhaps the most worrisome finding to emerge in recent surveys is that experimentation with drugs

begins at an earlier age now than previously, so that the most pressing problem may not be the prevalence of drug use among high school seniors but early experimentation with drugs among younger teenagers. Nearly 1 in 5 of all eighth-graders drink alcohol regularly, and nearly 1 in 10 smokes cigarettes at least once a month (Monitoring the Future, 2005). One-sixth of eighth-graders have tried inhalants, one-sixth have tried marijuana, and 20 percent have been drunk at least once (Monitoring the Future, 2005).

Rates of substance use among eight-graders are important to watch, because evidence strongly suggests that the chances of becoming addicted to alcohol or nicotine are dramatically increased when substance use begins before age 14. Because the typical adolescent who smokes cigarettes begins around the seventh or eighth grade, looking at changes in the number of eighth-graders who smoke is a good way of forecasting rates of smoking among adults in the future. Unfortunately, the rate of smoking among eighth-graders, which had been declining rapidly, has leveled off in recent years.

▌ **Drugs and the Adolescent Brain**   Researchers have long speculated that, because the brain is still very malleable early in adolescence, experimentation with drugs is more harmful then than later in development. In recent years, experimental research, in which researchers compared the brains of animals exposed to drugs either close to the time of puberty or after reaching full maturity, has illuminated some of the specific neurobiological pathways that explain why the potential for addiction to both nicotine and alcohol is much greater in adolescence than adulthood (Schochet, Kelley, & Landry, 2004, 2005; Sturmhöfel & Swartzwelder, 2004; Volkow & Ting-Kai, 2005). In order to understand what these studies say, we need to take a slight digression and revisit adolescent brain development.

As you read in Chapter 2, changes in the limbic system take place during adolescence that affect receptors for **dopamine,** one of the neurotransmitters that influence our experience of pleasure. When we experience things that are enjoyable, like great sex or fabulous food, the reason we experience these as rewarding is because they result in higher levels of dopamine in the brain, which permits more electrical activity through the synapses that connect the circuits in the brain that regulate feelings of pleasure. Keep in mind, though, that levels of dopamine are monitored and regulated so that feelings of pleasure stay within a normal range; when they get too high, dopamine levels are diminished, and when they get too low, they are increased.

The main reason that certain drugs feel good is that they affect the same receptors that are sensitive to the dopamine that is in the brain naturally. In fact, the molecules of addictive drugs are so similar to dopamine molecules that the dopamine receptors act in the same way in their presence as they do in the presence of actual dopamine. As a result, when drugs enter the brain (which is where they go whether they enter the body through the mouth, nose, or blood vessels), they are "read" by dopamine receptors as the real thing. On the positive side, this makes the user feel good (the same way that natural dopamine does)—which, of course, is why people take drugs. The problem, though, is that frequent drug use signals the brain to reduce levels of natural dopamine, in order to maintain the proper level, because the dopamine receptors can't tell the difference between the drug molecules and dopamine molecules. As a result, the more you use drugs, the less natural dopamine circulates in your brain.

This would not be a problem if it were easily reversed—if, say, as soon as you stopped using a drug, your brain upped its production of dopamine to compensate. But the animal studies referred to earlier have shown that experiences in early adolescence, when the limbic system is changing naturally, can *permanently* affect the way the dopamine system functions. (As you know, various brain systems and regions change during different periods of development, and it is during periods of change that these brain systems are most easily and irreversibly affected by outside influences.) Repeated exposure to drugs during this period of

heightened malleability in the limbic system can affect the brain in ways that make it *necessary* to use drugs in order to experience normal amounts of pleasure. Over time, the brain's ability to produce natural dopamine is permanently hampered, and in order to experience pleasurable feelings, it is necessary to "supplement" the low levels of natural dopamine in the brain with drugs.

How many exposures to a drug does it take to permanently alter the adolescent brain's dopamine system? No one knows for sure, and the answer varies from person to person, largely because of genetic factors (this is why some people are more likely to develop addictions than others). What we now know, though, is that this permanent alteration in the dopamine system is more likely to happen in adolescence, when the limbic system is still malleable, than in adulthood, when it is less changeable.

If this is true, we should expect to find that exposure to drugs during adolescence is more likely to lead to addiction than is exposure during adulthood. And, in fact, studies show that, compared with individuals who delay drinking until they are 21, people who begin drinking in early adolescence (before age 14) are *seven times* more likely to binge drink as teenagers and *five times* more likely to develop a substance abuse or dependence disorder at some point in their life (Hingson, Heeren, & Winter, 2006). Similar evidence suggests that individuals who begin smoking regularly before age 14 are at greater risk for nicotine dependence as adults than are those who start in late adolescence (Orlando, Tucker, Ellickson, & Klein, 2004), and, as well, that early use of inhalants is associated with higher rates of abuse and dependence (Wu, Pilowsky, & Schlenger, 2004) (see Figure 13.5).

There is also solid evidence that the effects of nicotine and alcohol on brain functioning are worse in adolescence than in adulthood—again, because the brain is more vulnerable to influences during periods of change. One area of the adolescent brain that appears especially vulnerable to the harmful effects of alcohol is the hippocampus, which is important for memory and, along with the prefrontal cortex, for "putting the brakes" on impulsive behavior (Sturmhöfel & Swartzwelder, 2004; Walker et al., 2004). Evidence also indicates that alcohol has harmful effects on the development of regions of the brain involved in higher-order cognitive abilities, such as planning, and in the regulation of impulses (Butler, 2006). Although there is some evidence that the harmful neurobiological consequences of drinking in early adolescence can be reversed, the fact that early exposure is more likely to lead to addiction and long-term use indicates that interventions designed to prevent substance abuse should begin prior to adolescence.

dopamine A neurotransmitter especially important in the brain circuits that regulate the experience of pleasure.

FIGURE 13.5 Animal studies show that first exposure to nicotine during adolescence is more likely to lead to addiction than first exposure in adulthood. (Zickler, 2004)

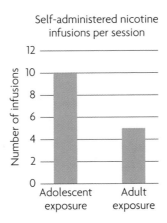

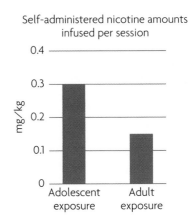

Ethnic Differences in Substance Use

Several national surveys have examined ethnic differences in rates of adolescent substance use and abuse. In general, white adolescents are more likely to use drugs and alcohol than minority youngsters, especially African American and Asian American youth. Rates of drug use among Hispanic American adolescents are comparable to those of white youngsters, and use among American Indian adolescents is the highest (Chassin et al., 2004). In general, foreign-born and less Americanized minority youngsters—whether Asian or Hispanic in background—use alcohol, drugs, and tobacco at a lower rate than do American-born and more acculturated minority youth, suggesting, unfortunately, that part of becoming an "American" teenager means experimenting with drugs (Delva et al., 2005; Georgiades, Boyle, Duku, & Racine, 2006; Gfroerer & Tan, 2003; Hahm, Lahif, & Guterman, 2004). Indeed, the rate of drug use among immigrant adolescents is *half* the rate of use among adolescents from the same ethnic group who were born in the United States (Harris, 1999).

Does Substance Use Follow a Particular Progression?

Researchers have also been interested in the sequence through which adolescents experiment with different drugs. In general, young people experiment with beer and wine before trying cigarettes or hard liquor, which precedes marijuana use, which, in turn, precedes the use of other illicit drugs (cocaine, stimulants, LSD) (Kandel, 1980). However, although experimentation may follow this sequence, this does not mean that alcohol use invariably leads to marijuana use, or that marijuana use necessarily leads to experimentation with harder drugs. In fact, there is little evidence to support the idea that marijuana is an inevitable stepping-stone to hard-drug use (much appears to depend on how frequently marijuana is used) (Treaster, 1994).

The fact that there is a fairly standard sequence of drug use, however, suggests that virtually all users of hard drugs have also tried alcohol, cigarettes, and

marijuana and, moreover, that one way to prevent adolescents from experimenting with more serious drugs is to stop them from experimenting with alcohol and marijuana. In fact, studies show that adolescents who have not experimented with alcohol or marijuana by the time they are in their 20s are unlikely ever to use these or any other drugs (Chen & Kandel, 1996; Kandel & Logan, 1984). For this reason, alcohol and marijuana are considered **gateway drugs,** in the sense that they represent a gate through which individuals pass on the way to using harder drugs. Whether an individual passes through the gate, however, is influenced by many factors beyond his or her previous patterns of drug use, including the period in which he or she grows up. For example, progression from tobacco and alcohol to marijuana and other illegal drugs was far more common among people who were born around 1960 than among people born before 1950 or after 1970 (Golub & Johnson, 2001).

Several studies that followed adolescents over time have identified several distinct **developmental trajectories** of alcohol, tobacco, and drug use (Chassin et al., 2004; Flory, Lynam, & Milich, 2004; Sher, Gotham, & Watson, 2004; Windle & Wiesner, 2004). In one study, six distinct groups were identified. Nonusers (who made up one-third of the sample) rarely experimented with substances at any point in adolescence. Alcohol experimenters (25 percent of the sample) first tried alcohol early in adolescence and continued to drink occasionally, but did not try other drugs and did not increase their drinking over time. Low escalators (5 percent of the sample) began using substances early in adolescence and increased their use slowly but steadily over time. Early starters (6 percent of the sample) showed very high substance use in early adolescence and escalated gradually over time, so that by the end of high

gateway drugs　Drugs that, when used over time, lead to the use of other, more dangerous substances.

developmental trajectories　Patterns of change over time.

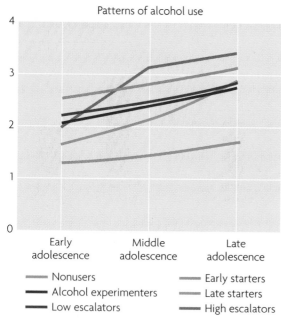

Patterns of alcohol use

— Nonusers
— Alcohol experimenters
— Low escalators
— Early starters
— Late starters
— High escalators

FIGURE 13.6 Adolescents follow different over-time trajectories in their use of tobacco, alcohol, and other drugs. (Adapted from Zapert et al., 2002)

TABLE 13.1 DSM-IV diagnostic criteria for substance abuse

A maladaptive pattern of substance use leading to clinically significant impairment or distress as manifested by one (or more) of the following, occurring within a 12-month period:

1. Recurrent substance use resulting in a failure to fulfill major role obligations at work, school, or home (such as repeated absences or poor work performance related to substance use; substance-related absences, suspensions, or expulsions from school; or neglect of children or household)

2. Recurrent substance use in situations in which it is physically hazardous (such as driving an automobile or operating a machine when impaired by substance use)

3. Recurrent substance-related legal problems (such as arrests for substance related disorderly conduct)

4. Continued substance use despite having persistent or recurrent social or interpersonal problems caused or exacerbated by the effects of the substance (for example, arguments with spouse about consequences of intoxication and physical fights)

school they were smoking and drinking frequently and experimenting with drugs. Late starters (20 percent of the sample) used substances infrequently during early adolescence but increased their use rapidly during high school—so much so that by the end of high school their substance use was similar to that of the early starters. Finally, High escalators (8 percent of the sample) showed moderate use in early adolescence, escalated rapidly between early and middle adolescence, and continued to increase their use throughout high school (Zapert, Snow, & Tebes, 2002) (see Figure 13.6).

CAUSES AND CONSEQUENCES OF SUBSTANCE USE AND ABUSE

In looking at the causes and consequences of substance use and abuse in adolescence, it is especially important to keep in mind the distinction between occasional experimentation and problematic use. Psychologists distinguish between two levels of severity of pathological substance use: **substance abuse,** whereby the use causes problems (see Table 13.1), and **substance dependence,** whereby the individual is physically addicted. All individuals who are substance dependent by definition are substance abusers, but the reverse is not true.

substance abuse The misuse of alcohol or other drugs to a degree that causes problems in the individual's life.

substance dependence The misuse of alcohol or other drugs to a degree that causes physical addiction.

■ **Users, Abusers, and Abstainers** Because the majority of adolescents have experimented with alcohol and marijuana, we can speculate that occasional alcohol and marijuana use has become normative among American high school students, and consequently, that there are plenty of normal, healthy young people who have used these drugs at least once. In fact, several studies indicate that adolescents who experiment with alcohol and marijuana are as well adjusted as—if not somewhat better adjusted and more socially skilled than—their peers who abstain completely from alcohol and marijuana (e.g., Baumrind, 1991; Scheier & Botvin, 1998; Shedler & Block, 1990). This substantial body of research shows quite clearly that it is important to differentiate among four groups of adolescents: frequent drug users (for example, at least once a week) or hard-drug users (that is, drugs other than alcohol, tobacco, or marijuana); those who experiment with marijuana and alcohol but who do not use them frequently (that is, no more than once a month); those who abstain out of irrational fear; and those who abstain out of rational choice (Baumrind, 1991; Hughes, Power, & Francis, 1992; Mitchell et al., 1996; Wills, McNamara, Vacaro, & Hirky, 1996). Experimenters and rational abstainers score higher on measures of psychological adjustment than either frequent users or irrational abstainers. Longer-term follow-up studies also show that moderate alcohol use during adolescence does not have negative long-term effects (Newcomb & Bentler, 1988; Paschall, Freisthler,

& Lipton, 2005). Indeed, cigarette use during adolescence has more harmful long-term health consequences than does experimentation with alcohol or marijuana, partly because nicotine is a more addictive drug, and its use is more likely to persist into middle adulthood (Chen & Kandel, 1996; Elders, Perry, Eriksen, & Giovino, 1994; Pierce & Gilpin, 1996).

These results do not mean that occasional experimentation with drugs during adolescence *leads* to better adjustment, of course. In fact, research shows that the psychological advantages observed among adolescents who experiment with alcohol and marijuana were evident when these individuals were younger children (Shedler & Block, 1990). Taken together, though, the studies suggest that moderate alcohol and marijuana use has become normative among adolescents in contemporary society (however troublesome some adults may find this), that these substances are typically used in social situations, and that better-adjusted and more interpersonally competent young people are likely to participate in social activities in which alcohol and other drugs are present (Scheier & Botvin, 1998; Shedler & Block, 1990). Relative to experimenters, abstainers—and "irrational" abstainers, in particular—tend to be overcontrolled, narrow in their interests, anxious, and inhibited (Shedler & Block, 1990).

Predictors and Consequences of Substance Abuse

Substance abuse (using drugs in a way that causes significant problems at home, school, work, or with the law) is a different matter. Adolescents who are frequent users of alcohol, tobacco, and other drugs score lower on measures of psychological adjustment as teenagers and were more likely to be maladjusted as children (Shedler & Block, 1990). Indeed, a team of researchers who followed a sample of individuals from preschool into young adulthood report that, at age 7, individuals who would later become frequent drug users as adolescents were described as "not getting along well with other children, not showing concern for moral issues . . . not planful or likely to think ahead, not trustworthy or dependable . . . [and] not self-reliant or confident" (Shedler & Block, 1990, p. 618). As 11-year-olds, these individuals were described as deviant, emotionally labile (unstable), stubborn, and inattentive. In other words, drug and alcohol abuse during adolescence is often a symptom of prior psychological disturbance.

Substance abuse during adolescence, whatever its antecedents, is associated with a host of other problems. Young people who abuse alcohol, tobacco, and other drugs are more likely to experience problems at school, suffer from psychological distress and depression, have physical health problems, engage in unprotected sexual activity, abuse alcohol as young adults, and become involved in dangerous or deviant activities, including crime, delinquency, and truancy (Chassin et al., 2004; Holmen, Barrett-Connor, Holmen, & Bjermer, 2000; Kandel, Johnson, Bird, & Canino, 1997; Wu & Anthony, 1999). These problems are especially severe among adolescents who are involved in drug dealing (Centers & Weist, 1998). Alcohol and other drugs are typically implicated in adolescent automobile crashes, the leading cause of death and disability among American teenagers (Lang, Waller, & Shope, 1996; O'Malley & Johnston, 1999), and in other fatal and nonfatal accidents, such as drownings, falls, and burns (Irwin, 1986; Wintemute, Kraus, Teret, & Wright, 1987). Adolescent substance abusers also expose themselves to the long-term health risks of excessive drug use that stem from addiction or dependency; in the case of cigarettes, alcohol, and marijuana, these risks are substantial and well documented—among them, cancer, heart disease, and kidney and liver damage. It is also now well established that heavy cigarette smoking during adolescence can exacerbate feelings of emotional distress and lead to depression and anxiety disorders (Goodman & Capitman, 2000; Johnson et al., 2000; Orlando, Ellickson, & Jinnett, 2001; Windle & Windle, 2001).

Risk Factors for Substance Abuse

Which adolescents are most likely to become substance abusers? Generally, four sets of risk factors—psychological, familial, social, and contextual—for substance abuse have been identified, and the more risk factors that are present for an individual, the more likely she or he is to use and abuse drugs (Hawkins, Catalano, & Miller, 1992; Newcomb & Felix-Ortiz, 1992; Petraitis, Flay, & Miller, 1995; Ritchey, Reid, & Hasse, 2001; Shoal & Giancola, 2003). These same risk factors have been found across a variety of studies and in samples of adolescents from a wide range of ethnic and socioeconomic backgrounds, with little variation in the potency of risk factors across different socioeconomic, ethnic, or gender groups. In other words, the factors that place an adolescent at risk for substance abuse are more or less the same regardless of the adolescent's sex, social class, or ethnicity (Choi, Harachi, Gillmore, & Catalano, 2005). As one team of researchers point out, this is good news, because it suggests that preventive interventions do not need to be specifically tailored to different subgroups of adolescents (Hu, Davies, & Kandel, 2006).

The first set of risk factors is psychological. Individuals with certain personality characteristics—which typically are present prior to adolescence—are more likely to develop drug and alcohol problems than their peers. These characteristics include anger, impulsivity, and inattentiveness (Chassin et al., 2004; Scheer & Unger, 1998; Tapert, Baratta, Abrantes, & Brown, 2002; Wills, Sandy, Yaeger, & Shinar, 2001). In addition, individuals who have more tolerant attitudes about drug use (and about deviance in general) are at greater risk for drug abuse (Schulenberg, Wadsworth, O'Malley, Bachman, & Johnston, 1996; Petraitis et al., 1995), as are those who expect alcohol or other drugs to improve their social relationships (Griffin, Epstein, Botvin, & Spoth, 2001; Smith & Goldman, 1994; Smith, Goldman, Greenbaum, & Christiansen, 1995). Even as children, for example, individuals who eventually become heavy drinkers as adolescents expect alcohol to have positive effects on them (Dunn & Goldman, 1998).

Second, individuals with distant, hostile, or conflicted family relationships are more likely to develop substance abuse problems than are their peers who grow up in close, nurturing families (Dishion, Capaldi, & Yoerger, 1999; Kilpatrick et al., 2000; Sale et al., 2005). Drug-abusing youngsters are also more likely than their peers to have parents who are excessively permissive, uninvolved, neglectful, or rejecting (Barnes, Reifman, Farrel, & Dintcheff, 2000; Chassin et al., 2004). In addition, they are more likely to come from homes in which one or more other family members (parents or siblings) smokes, drinks, or uses drugs; there are both genetic and family environmental influences on adolescent alcohol and drug use (Chassin et al., 2004; Hill, Hawkins, Catalano, Abbott, & Guo, 2005).

Third, individuals with substance abuse problems are more likely to have friends who use and tolerate the use of drugs, both because they are influenced by these friends and because they are drawn to them (Beal, Ausiello, & Perrin, 2001; Bray, Adams, Getz, & McQueen, 2003; Ennett et al., 2006; Killen et al., 1997; Kim, Zane, & Hong, 2002; Rose, Chassin, Presson, & Sherman, 1999). As you read in Chapter 5, whether and how often adolescents use drugs is an important defining characteristic of peer groups—abstainers tend to have other abstainers as friends, and users tend to be friends with other users. Drug-using adolescents seek drug-using peers, and drug-using peers encourage even more drug use among their friends (Chassin, Presson, Todd, Rose, & Sherman, 1998; Schulenberg et al., 1999; Steinberg, Fletcher, & Darling, 1994). Indeed, the most common setting in which adolescents use alcohol and drugs is in a friend's home (Hussong, 2000). Substance-using adolescents who have many substance-using friends may also overestimate how common substance use is because they are so much more likely to see other people engaged in it (Unger & Rohrbach, 2002).

Finally, adolescents who become substance abusers are more likely to live in a social context that makes drug use easier (Chassin et al., 2004). Important contextual factors are the availability of drugs, the community's norms regarding drug use, the degree to which drug laws are enforced, and the ways in which drug use is presented via the mass media (Allison et al., 1999; Li, Stanton, & Feigelman, 1996; Petraitis et al., 1995; Robinson, Klesges, Zbikowski, & Glaser, 1997). All other factors being equal, adolescents who have easy access to drugs, who believe that there are ample opportunities to use drugs, and who are exposed to messages that tolerate or even encourage drug use are more likely to use and abuse drugs. And adolescents who attend schools with a high proportion of substance-using students are more likely to have friends who use substances, which elevates their own use (Cleveland & Wiebe, 2003).

Researchers have also identified important **protective factors** that decrease the likelihood of adolescents' engaging in substance abuse (Jessor, Van Den Bos, Vanderryn, Costa, & Turbin, 1995). Among the most important protective factors are positive mental health (including high self-esteem and the absence of depressive symptoms), high academic achievement, engagement in school, close family relationships, and involvement in religious activities (Albers & Biener, 2003; Bahr, Maughan, Marcos, & Li, 1998; Bryant, Schulenberg, O'Malley, Bachman, & Johnston, 2003; Flannery, Vazsonyi, & Rowe, 1996; Jessor, Turbin, & Costa, 1998; Jordan & Lewis, 2005). These protective factors appear to operate over and above the effects of the risk factors discussed previously. As with the factors that place adolescents at risk for substance abuse, the protective factors identified operate similarly among adolescents from different ethnic groups and explain why some groups of adolescents use drugs more than others do (Barnes & Farrell, 1992; Flannery, Vazsonyi, & Rowe, 1996; Peterson, Hawkins, Abbott, & Catalano, 1994). One of the reasons for the lower rate of drinking among African American youth, for example, is that their parents are less likely to drink or to tolerate adolescent drinking (Peterson et al., 1994).

PREVENTION AND TREATMENT OF SUBSTANCE USE AND ABUSE

Efforts to prevent substance use and abuse among teenagers focus on one of three factors: the supply of drugs, the environment in which teenagers may be exposed to drugs, and characteristics of the potential drug user (Newcomb & Bentler, 1989). Although a good deal of government spending and media attention have

protective factors Factors that limit individual vulnerability to harm.

One of the strongest deterrents against teen smoking is not providing antismoking education, but raising the financial cost of smoking. Researchers believe that the drop in teen smoking in recent years is mainly attributable to increases in the price of cigarettes.

been devoted to the first of these approaches—attempts to control or limit the availability of drugs—the consensus among experts is that it is more realistic to try to change adolescents' motivation to use drugs and the environment in which they live, since it has proven virtually impossible to remove drugs totally from society. Indeed, the two most commonly used and abused drugs—cigarettes and alcohol—are both legal and widely available, and laws prohibiting the sale of these substances to minors are not well enforced (Centers for Disease Control and Prevention, 2006). Research does show, however, that raising the price of alcohol and cigarettes does reduce adolescents' use of them (Biener, Aseltine, Cohen, & Anderka, 1998; Grossman, Chaloupka, Saffer, & Laixuthai, 1994; Gruber & Zinman, 2001). Attempts to enforce laws governing the purchase of cigarettes are less effective, in part because many adolescents obtain cigarettes through means other than purchasing them from stores (for example, bumming them from older friends, stealing them from parents) (Fichtenberg & Glantz, 2002).

Many different types of drug abuse prevention interventions have been tried, either alone or in combination. In programs designed to change some characteristic of the adolescent, drug use is targeted indirectly either by attempting to enhance adolescents' psychological development in general or by helping adolescents develop other interests and participate in other activities that will make drug use less likely. The idea behind these sorts of efforts is that adolescents who have high self-esteem, for example, or who are gainfully employed will be less likely to use drugs. In other programs, the intervention is directly focused on preventing drug use. These programs include information-based efforts (in which adolescents are educated about the dangers of drugs), social skills

training (in which adolescents are taught how to turn down drugs), and some combination of informational and general psychological intervention (in which adolescents are educated about drug abuse and exposed to a program designed to enhance their self-esteem, for instance) (Newcomb & Bentler, 1989).

FOOD FOR THOUGHT

Why do you think that interventions designed to change individuals' knowledge about drug use and its consequences have been such failures? How do you explain the fact that many individuals continue to engage in behaviors that they know are dangerous or unhealthy, such as smoking?

Generally, the results of research designed to evaluate these sorts of individual-focused approaches have not been especially encouraging (Dielman, 1994; Leventhal & Keeshan, 1993). Careful evaluations of Project DARE, for example—the most widely implemented drug education program in the United States—show that the program is largely ineffective (Ennett, Tobler, Ringwall, & Flewelling, 1994). Experts are now fairly confident that drug education alone, whether based on rational information or scare tactics, does not prevent drug use. This is reminiscent of research on sex education, which, as we saw in Chapter 11, has shown that informational programs are simply not effective on their own. As a rule, educational programs may change individuals' knowledge, but they rarely affect their behavior. In addition, a recent large-scale study of drug testing in schools found that the practice has no effect on adolescents' drug use (Yamaguchi, Johnston, & O'Malley, 2003).

The most encouraging results have been found in programs that focus not just on the individual adolescent but rather combine some sort of social competence training with a communitywide intervention aimed not only at adolescents but also at their peers, parents, and teachers (Chou et al., 1998; Dielman, 1994; Kellam & Anthony, 1998; Leventhal & Keeshan, 1993; Siegel & Biener, 2000). These multifaceted efforts have been shown to be effective in reducing adolescents' use of alcohol, cigarettes, and other drugs, especially if the programs begin when youngsters are preadolescents and continue well into high school (Bruvold, 1993; Dielman, 1994; Ellickson, Bell, & McGuigan, 1993; Flynn et al., 1994; Perry et al., 1996). Overall, most experts agree that efforts designed simply to change the potential adolescent drug user without transforming the environment in which the adolescent lives are not likely to succeed. Despite their intuitive appeal, efforts to help adolescents "Just Say No" have been remarkably unsuccessful.

One of the problems with all prevention programs is that they often do not distinguish between drug *use* (which is not always problematic) and drug *abuse* (which is). Trying to stop teenagers from *ever* using alcohol, for instance, is both unlikely to succeed and probably not a very wise allocation of resources, whereas preventing binge drinking or drunk driving is a far more important—and attainable—goal.

Distinguishing between use and abuse is also important in treatment. Some experts worry that adolescents who are mistakenly enrolled in treatment programs (because their parents have overreacted to the adolescent's normative and probably harmless experimentation with drugs) may end up more alienated and more distressed—and more likely to become drug abusers—as a result of the "treatment." Evaluations of treatment programs for adolescents who are genuine drug abusers suggest that efforts that involve the adolescent's family, and not just the teenager, are more likely to be successful (Dielman, 1994; Dishion & Andrews, 1995; St. Pierre, Mark, Kaltreider, & Aikin, 1997; Zavela et al., 1997).

RECAP

- Among contemporary adolescents, alcohol and cigarettes are still the drugs of choice, although a substantial number of young people have experimented with marijuana as well.
- Experts have expressed particular concern about the use of substances early in adolescence, especially in light of new brain research indicating that the potential for addiction and for other harmful physical consequences is significantly greater when the first use of substances occurs before age 14.
- Research indicates a clear need to distinguish between experimentation with alcohol and marijuana (which has not been shown to be harmful) and regular or heavy use (which has).

conduct disorder   A repetitive and persistent pattern of antisocial behavior that results in problems at school or work, or in relationships with others.

oppositional-defiant disorder   A disorder of childhood and adolescence characterized by excessive anger, spite, and stubbornness.

antisocial personality disorder   A disorder of adulthood characterized by antisocial behavior and persistent disregard for the rules of society and the rights of others.

- Adolescents who abuse alcohol and other drugs are more likely to come from hostile family environments, to have friends who use drugs, and to have other problems in school as well as in interpersonal relationships.
- The most promising interventions for substance abuse problems in adolescence are those that target the adolescent's social environment as well as the individual.

Externalizing Problems

Generally, experts distinguish among three main categories of externalizing problems in adolescence: conduct disorder, aggression, and delinquency. Although these three classes of problems are highly interrelated, their definitions differ.

CATEGORIES OF EXTERNALIZING PROBLEMS

■ **Conduct Disorder**   The first category of externalizing problems is **conduct disorder,** which is a clinical diagnosis that refers to a repetitive and persistent pattern of antisocial behavior in which the rights of others or age-appropriate societal norms are violated, and where, as a result of this behavior, the individual has problems in social relationships, school, or the workplace (see Table 13.2) (Farrington, 2004). (A related, but less serious, diagnosis is **oppositional-defiant disorder,** which refers to behavior that is spiteful, angry, and argumentative, but not necessarily aggressive.) An estimated 6–16 percent of adolescent males and 2–9 percent of adolescent females have conduct disorder (Farrington, 2004), although these estimates vary considerably from sample to sample. Estimates of the prevalence of conduct disorder have been increasing in recent years, although it is hard to know whether this is due to increases in the numbers of children who genuinely have the disorder or to increases in the number of badly behaving children who are diagnosed. Conduct disorder is very stable between childhood and adolescence—about half of all individuals who are diagnosed with it as children are also diagnosed with it as teenagers, and many had oppositional-defiant disorder when they were younger.

Individuals who have been diagnosed with conduct disorder and who persist in their antisocial behavior after age 18 may subsequently be diagnosed with **antisocial personality disorder,** which is characterized by

TABLE 13.2 DSM-IV diagnostic criteria for conduct disorder

A repetitive and persistent pattern of behavior in which the basic rights of others or major age-appropriate societal norms or rules are violated, as manifested by the presence of three (or more) of the following criteria in the past 12 months, with at least one criterion present in the past 6 months, and where the behavior causes impairment in school, work, or relationships:

1. Often bullies, threatens, or intimidates others
2. Often initiates physical fights
3. Has used a weapon that can cause serious physical harm to others (e.g., a bat, brick, broken bottle, knife, gun)
4. Has been physically cruel to people
5. Has been physically cruel to animals
6. Has stolen while confronting a victim (e.g., mugging, purse snatching, extortion, armed robbery)
7. Has forced someone into sexual activity
8. Has deliberately engaged in fire setting with the intention of causing serious damage
9. Has deliberately destroyed others' property (other than by fire setting)
10. Has broken into someone else's house, building, or car
11. Often lies to obtain goods or favors or to avoid obligations (i.e., "cons" others)
12. Has stolen items of nontrivial value without confronting a victim (e.g., shoplifting, but without breaking and entering; forgery)
13. Often stays out at night despite parental prohibitions, beginning before age 13 years
14. Has run away from home overnight at least twice while living in parental or parental surrogate home (or once without returning for a lengthy period)
15. Is often truant from school, beginning before age 13 years

a lack of regard for the moral or legal standards of the community and a marked inability to get along with others or abide by societal rules. Some individuals with antisocial personality disorder are called **psychopaths,** which refers to individuals who are not only antisocial in their behavior but manipulative, superficially charming, impulsive, and indifferent to the feelings of others (Hare, 1991). Because the terms "antisocial personality disorder" and "psychopath" imply a deep-seated personality problem that is unlikely to change, experts advise against applying them to people younger than 18, because, as you will read, most individuals who engage in antisocial behavior as teenagers do not continue to do so after their mid-20s. Social scientists disagree about whether it is possible to identify "juvenile psychopaths" or "fledgling psychopaths"—individuals who, despite their youth, exhibit many of the same characteristics of adult psychopaths. Some contend that it is possible to do so (e.g., Campbell, Porter, & Santor, 2004; Frick, Kotov, Loney, & Vasey, 2005; Lynam, 1996), while others note that some of the distinguishing features of adult psychopaths that are considered pathological (impulsivity, irresponsibility, instability in romantic relationships) may be transient characteristics that are normative during adolescence and that reflect immaturity, not pathology (Edens, Skeem, Cruise, & Cauffman, 2000; Skeem & Cauffman, 2003; Vincent, Vitacco, Grisso, & Corrado, 2003).

■ **Aggression** A second category of externalizing problems is **aggression,** which is behavior that is done to intentionally hurt someone. "Aggression" is a very broad term that includes physical fighting, relational aggression, and intimidation, and it can be either instrumental (planned) or reactive (unplanned). It is very difficult to estimate the prevalence of aggression during adolescence, because the category is so far-reaching. Virtually everyone has done *something* aggressive at one time or another. Most psychologists are concerned with adolescents whose aggression is persistent and causes serious injury to others. Aggressive behavior actually declines over the course of childhood and adolescence—in sheer quantity, the most aggressive period of development is the preschool years, when children frequently hit, kick, or bite each other—although aggression committed by adolescents is generally more serious than that committed by children (see Figure 13.7) (Bongers, Koot, van der Ende, & Verhulst, 2004). Like conduct disorder, aggression is also very stable over time, although much more so in boys than girls (Broidy et al., 2003). One likely reason for this sex difference is that aggressive little girls are more often forced to curtail their bad behavior than aggressive little boys are, which will make girls' aggression less stable over time.

psychopaths Individuals who are not only antisocial but also manipulative, superficially charming, impulsive, and indifferent to the feelings of others.

aggression Acts done to be intentionally harmful.

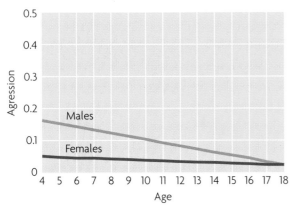

FIGURE 13.7   Aggression actually is higher during preschool than during adolescence. (Bongers et al., 2004)

■ **Juvenile Offending**   The third main category of externalizing problems is **juvenile offending,** which includes **delinquency** (crimes committed by minors that are dealt with in the juvenile justice system) and **criminal behavior** (crimes that are dealt with in the criminal justice system, regardless of the age of the offender). A special category of delinquent acts are called **status offenses,** which are behaviors that are not against the law for adults but that nevertheless violate established codes of conduct for juveniles, like truancy or running away from home (Scott & Woolard, 2004). Unlike conduct disorder or aggression, which are defined by in terms of behavior, juvenile offending is defined legally. A large proportion of juvenile offenders have conduct disorder, and most are aggressive, but not all adolescents who have conduct disorder or who are aggressive are juvenile offenders, because that depends entirely on whether they have broken the law.

Both violent crimes (such as assault, rape, robbery, and murder) and property crimes (such as burglary, theft, and arson) increase in frequency between the preadolescent and adolescent years, peak during the late high school years (slightly earlier for property than for violent crimes), and decline during young adulthood. The so-called **age–crime curve** has been remarkably stable over time and is consistently seen around the world (Piquero, Farrington, & Blumstein, 2003). In the United States, almost one-third of arrests for serious crimes involves a suspect under 18, and individuals under 18 account for well over one-sixth of all violent crimes (Federal Bureau of Investigation, 1999) (see Figure 13.8). About 10 percent of serious delinquency is committed by children who are younger than 13 (Loeber & Farrington, 2000). The onset of serious delinquency generally begins between the ages of 13 and 16 (Farrington, 2004) (see Figure 13.9).

DEVELOPMENTAL PROGRESSION OF ANTISOCIAL BEHAVIOR

Antisocial behavior can take different forms: **authority conflicts** (such as truancy or running away from home), **covert antisocial behavior** (such as stealing), and **overt antisocial behavior** (such as attacking someone with a weapon). Within these broad categories, there are some fairly predictable progressions (Loeber & Farrington, 2000). Authority conflicts usually first appear as stubborn behavior, which escalates into defiance and disobedience, and then progresses to more serious signs of problems with authority, such as truancy and running away from home. Covert antisocial behavior typically begins with acts like lying and shoplifting; progresses to property damage, such as vandalism; and then to more serious property crimes, such as burglary. Overt antisocial behavior generally first presents itself as fighting or bullying, which escalates to things like gang fighting and, ultimately, to violent criminal activity.

This is not to say that all bullies grow up to be violent criminals, or that all stubborn preschoolers end up running away from home as teenagers. But the reverse is almost always true: Virtually all violent juveniles have a history of escalating aggressive behavior; most adolescents who commit serious property crimes started with less serious forms of overt behavior; and most chronically rebellious teenagers were oppositional children. Of course, some juveniles commit all three types of acts; generally, the more serious an adolescent's behavior is in one category, the more likely he or she is to have displayed the others. That is, most

juvenile offending   An externalizing problem that includes delinquency and criminal behavior.

delinquency   Juvenile offending that is processed within the juvenile justice system.

criminal behavior   Crimes that are dealt with in the criminal justice system, regardless of the age of the offender.

status offenses   Violations of the law that pertain to minors but not adults.

age–crime curve   The relationship between chronological age and offending, showing that the prevalence of offending peaks in late adolescence.

authority conflicts   A type of antisocial behavior characterized by stubbornness and rebelliousness.

covert antisocial behavior   A type of antisocial behavior characterized by misdeeds that are not always detected by others, such as lying or stealing.

overt antisocial behavior   A type of antisocial behavior characterized by aggression toward others.

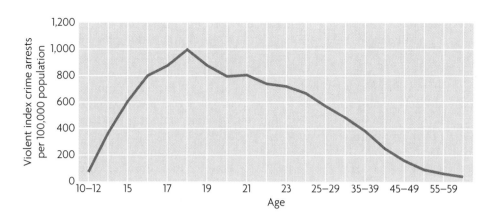

FIGURE 13.8 Age differences in violent criminal activity. (Federal Bureau of Investigation, 1999)

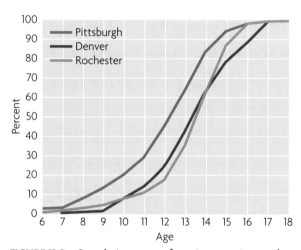

FIGURE 13.9 Cumulative onset of persistent serious and violent delinquency in three inner-city samples. Most serious delinquency begins between the ages of 13 and 16. (Loeber & Farrington, 2000)

adolescents who commit violent crimes have also engaged in covert and authority-related antisocial behavior, but not all adolescents who have conflicts with authority or who engage in covert antisocial behavior are necessarily aggressive. The authority conflict pathway almost always starts in childhood (contrary to the stereotype, few people suddenly develop serious authority problems for the first time as teenagers). The covert and overt pathways, in contrast, can begin either in childhood or in adolescence—and as you will read, individuals whose antisocial behavior begins in childhood are very different from those whose antisocial behavior doesn't start until adolescence (Moffitt, 2006).

CHANGES IN JUVENILE OFFENDING OVER TIME

When social scientists track changes in antisocial behavior over time, they generally look at juvenile

offending, because statistics are kept on the numbers of juveniles arrested each year and the crimes with which they have been charged. Between 1965 and 1988, and especially after 1984, arrests for the most serious violent crimes—murder, rape, armed robbery, and aggravated assault—increased substantially among young people. Since 1993, though, violent crime among young people has declined dramatically, contradicting the hysterical claims of some that the United States was going to be ravaged by a wave of "superpredators" (Zimring, 1998). In addition, the average age at which individuals are arrested has fallen during the past several decades, as criminal behavior has become increasingly prevalent among younger boys and girls (Snyder & Sickmund, 1996)—not unlike, and probably related to, the drop in age of initiation into drug and alcohol use discussed earlier in this chapter.

▌ **Bad Girls** Much recent attention has been devoted to what appears to be a substantial decline in the gender gap in serious offending over the past several decades (Office of Juvenile Justice and Delinquency Prevention, 2002). Although antisocial behavior is still far more common among males than females, the male-to-female ratio in juvenile arrests today is half (about four to one) what it was in 1980. However, it is not clear whether this change is mainly due to changes in actual offending or to changes in arrest practices. We need to be careful not to make the same mistake about the growing numbers of violent girls that was made about the coming wave of "superpredators" a decade ago. Changes in arrest rates can occur without there being any changes in actual offending (if, for example, the police crack down on crime, more people will be arrested, even if more people are not offending), and studies that rely on official statistics often reach conclusions different from those that rely on police or court records (Farrington et al., 2003). In fact, a recent analysis of data on actual offending found that there has *not* been an increase in violent acts committed by adolescent girls;

rather, girls are simply being arrested more frequently for the same things they did in the past but were not arrested for (Steffensmeier, Schwartz, Zhong, & Ackerman, 2005). It is also possible that the ratio of males to females who have been arrested has changed not because of an increase in female offending, but because the drop in juvenile offending since 1993 was steeper for males than females. If female offending increased just a little since then, but male offending dropped by more than 50 percent, the ratio of male-to-female offending would be cut in half. Regardless of the size or causes of the gender gap in arrests, there is good evidence that violent females have significantly more mental health problems than do violent males (Cauffman, 2004), consistent with the notion that gender-inappropriate displays of aggression may be indicative of greater maladjustment (Cauffman, Feldman, Waterman, & Steiner, 1998; Crick, 1997; Ellickson, Saner, & McGuigan, 1997; McCabe, Lansing, Garland, & Hough, 2002).

■ **Adolescents as Crime Victims** Violent crime among young people is a significant source of worry to adults, of course. But crime is also a significant source of worry to adolescents themselves, who are the age group most likely to be *victims* of crimes such as theft, robbery, rape, and assault. Indeed, although adolescents under age 18 account for only 10 percent of the population, they constitute nearly one-fourth of all victims of crime (Perkins, 1997). Victims of violent crimes are more likely to report a wide range of problems than are other adolescents, including posttraumatic stress disorder, depressed mood, sleep deprivation, and academic difficulties, and they are more likely themselves to engage in aggression and antisocial behavior (Boney-McCoy & Finkelhor, 1995; Cooley-Quille & Lorion, 1999; DuRant, Pendergrast, & Cadenhead, 1994; Moses, 1999). African American and Hispanic American adolescents living in the inner city are disproportionately likely to be the victims of violent crime (Hutson, Anglin, & Pratts, 1994). Among 12- to 24-year-olds, for example, homicide accounts for 42 percent of all deaths among African Americans and 35 percent of all deaths among Hispanic Americans, but "only" 6 percent of white deaths (Blum, Ireland, & Blum, 2003). Indeed, for many young adolescents growing up in the inner city, gang violence and victimization are chronic problems.

Most researchers agree that violence and aggression among youth are strongly linked to poverty for a number of reasons. First, when families live in impoverished neighborhoods, parents are less effective in nurturing and monitoring their children, and this diminished effectiveness leads to increased aggression and crime (Sampson & Laub, 1994). One study of an American Indian community before and after it had benefited

from the added income generated by the opening of a casino on the reservation found a substantial drop in adolescents' behavioral problems as a result of the increase in parental monitoring (Costello, Compton, Keeler, & Angold, 2003). Second, concentrated poverty upsets the social fabric of a neighborhood, making it more difficult for adults and social institutions to provide the guidance and supervision that adolescents need (Sampson, 1992; Sampson & Groves, 1989). (Interestingly, however, there is no evidence that communitywide curfews for adolescents affect juvenile crime [Fried, 2001].) Third, in many inner-city communities devastated by unemployment, aggression is used by males to demonstrate their standing and power—characteristics that are typically demonstrated in middle-class communities through occupational success (Wilson & Daley, 1985). Finally, the widespread prevalence of guns in inner-city neighborhoods changes the sorts of interactions that take place when adolescents fight, transforming what might have been aggressive disputes into lethal exchanges (Cook & Ludwig, 2004; Wilkinson & Fagan, 1996). The significance of neighborhood influences on violence was confirmed in a recent experiment, in which poor families with adolescents were randomly selected to be relocated into better neighborhoods: After their relocation, rates of violent behavior among the juveniles dropped significantly (Kling, Ludwig, & Katz, 2005).

■ **Official Statistics Versus Adolescents' Reports** Official figures about adolescent crime both underreport and selectively report rates of juvenile offending (Farrington, Loeber, & Stouthamer-Loeber, 2003). Underreporting results from the fact that many adolescents commit offenses that are undetected by authorities or that are handled outside official reporting procedures—for example, when an adolescent who is caught shoplifting is reprimanded by the storekeeper instead of being referred to the police. Selective reporting results from the fact that poor and minority youngsters are more likely to be arrested and, if convicted, to be treated more harshly than other youngsters who commit similar offenses, so that official statistics may artificially inflate the proportion of crimes committed by poor, minority youth (Bridges & Steen, 1998; Farrington et al., 2003; Feld, 1997; Poe-Yamagata & Jones, 2000). One recent experiment found that people hold such strong negative stereotypes about African American males that when provided with information about a crime and asked to evaluate the perpetrator, individuals who were unconsciously led to believe that the offender was black were significantly more likely than those who were not to rate him as likely to reoffend in the future and as deserving of harsh punishment, an effect that

A very large proportion of adolescents—between 60 and 80 percent, depending on the survey—have engaged in delinquent behavior at one time or another. Although most of these behaviors are not serious crimes, they are often chargeable offenses.

was consistent regardless of the race of the rater (Graham & Lowery, 2004). Racial bias is especially strong in the processing of relatively more *minor* crimes; when a very serious crime, like armed robbery, is committed, juveniles of different ethnic backgrounds are likely to receive similar treatment (Cauffman, Piquero, Kimonis, Steinberg, & Chassin, 2007).

An alternative to relying on official records is to go to adolescents directly and ask them about their involvement in various criminal or status offenses. Several researchers have done this, promising the respondents anonymity and confidentiality. The results of these surveys do not necessarily provide a more accurate picture of juvenile crime, but they certainly suggest a different one. Two conclusions are especially interesting.

First, a very large proportion of adolescents—between 60 and 80 percent, depending on the survey sample—report having engaged in delinquent behavior at one time or another; nearly one-third of American 17-year-old boys have committed a violent crime in

the past year, and nearly half of all males report being responsible for an assault sometime during adolescence (Farrington, 2004; Huizinga & Elliot, 1985; Zimring, 1998). Second, ethnic differences in the prevalence of actual offending are smaller than what you might think based on official records (Farrington et al., 2003). More minority than white youth admit to having committed a serious crime, but ethnic differences in self-reported offending are far smaller than ethnic differences in rates of arrest. There also are social class and neighborhood differences in rates of serious criminal activity, and because minority youth are overrepresented among the poor, they are also overrepresented among those who commit crimes (McNulty & Bellair, 2003). Delinquency is by no means limited to poor adolescents, however. One-third of adolescents in affluent neighborhoods report involvement in violent and serious delinquency (Beyers, Loeber, Wikström, & Stouthamer-Loeber, 2001).

FOOD FOR THOUGHT

Why do you think antisocial behavior follows the developmental course reflected in the age–crime curve? How do you explain the fact that this pattern is seen around the world?

Although studies indicate that most adolescents—regardless of their social backgrounds—do something that violates the law at one time or another, the vast majority of teenagers who violate the law do so only once, and not violently. In fact, a relatively small number of adolescents account for a relatively high proportion of serious criminal activity; one estimate indicates that fewer than 10 percent of adolescents account for about two-thirds of all recorded offenses (Yoshikawa, 1994), and another notes that half of all violent acts are committed by just 6 percent of the population (Dodge & Pettit, 2003). It is important, therefore, in thinking about the causes of delinquent behavior, to distinguish between delinquent behavior that is serious and chronic and delinquent behavior that is less worrisome. As you will see momentarily, these two sets of delinquent behavior have very different antecedents (Moffitt, 1993).

CAUSES OF ANTISOCIAL BEHAVIOR

In general, the earlier an adolescent's "criminal career" begins—in particular, if it begins before adolescence—the more likely he or she is to become a chronic offender, to commit serious and violent crimes, and to continue committing crimes as an adult (Farrington, 2004). Conversely, the older an adolescent is when the delinquent activity first appears, the less worrisome his or her behavior is likely to become. For purposes of discussion, therefore, it is helpful to distinguish between youngsters who begin misbehaving before adolescence and those whose delinquent activity first appears during adolescence.

■ **Two Types of Offenders** One of the most influential ways of characterizing these two groups of delinquents has been suggested by psychologist Terrie Moffitt (2006), who distinguishes between **life-course-persistent offenders** and **adolescence-limited offenders**. The first group demonstrates antisocial behavior before adolescence, is involved in delinquency during adolescence, and is at great risk for continuing criminal activity in adulthood. The second group engages in antisocial behavior *only* during adolescence; some adolescence-limited offenders become involved in crime relatively early in adolescence, whereas others begin during midadolescence (Fergusson & Horwood, 2002). Some researchers have suggested that there are other groups of offenders as well (for example, individuals who do not start offending until adolescence but who continue on into adulthood, and those who display antisocial behavior as children but desist before adulthood) (e.g., Côté, Zoccolillo, Tremblay, Nagin, & Vitaro, 2001; Raskin-White, Bates, & Buyske, 2001; Weisner & Windle, 2004), and others have pointed out that virtually everybody desists from crime by midlife, so that there really is no such thing as "life-course-persistent" offending (Sampson & Laub, 2003). Nevertheless, experts agree that the causes and consequences of delinquent behavior that begins during childhood or preadolescence are quite different from those of delinquency that begins—and typically ends—during adolescence or young adulthood (e.g., McCabe, Hough, Wood, & Yeh, 2001). Although many more males than females are life-course-persistent offenders, the risk factors for early-onset antisocial behavior are similar for the sexes (Fergusson & Horwood, 2002; Storvoll & Wichtström, 2002).

One important ramification of Moffitt's theory is that it is extremely difficult to predict which antisocial adolescents will persist in their bad behavior solely on the basis of their behavior during adolescence. Indeed, social scientists who have attempted to assess juvenile offenders' risk for future reoffending based solely on their adolescent characteristics have a remarkably poor track record (Mulvey et al., 2004). According to Moffitt's model, it is necessary to have information on the juvenile's behavior and history *before* adolescence in order to predict whether her or his offending is likely to be adolescence-limited or life-course-persistent, because the best predictor of continued offending in adulthood is the presence of serious antisocial behavior in childhood.

■ **Life-Course-Persistent Offenders** Many studies indicate that youngsters whose problems with the law begin before adolescence are often psychologically troubled. Most of these delinquents are male, many are poor, and a disproportionate number come from homes in which divorce has occurred (Farrington, 2004). More importantly, a large and consistent body of research shows that chronic delinquents typically come from disorganized families with hostile, inept, or neglectful parents who have mistreated their children and failed to instill in them proper standards of behavior or the psychological foundations of self-control (Compton, Snyder, & Schrepferman, 2003; Dishion, Patterson, Stoolmiller, & Skinner, 1991; Laub & Sampson, 1995; Patterson, DeGarmo, & Knutson, 2000; Stouthamer-Loeber, Loeber, Homish, & Wei, 2001). There is some evidence that exposure to harsh parenting may adversely affect the developing child's brain chemistry—in particular, the activity of serotonin receptors—which may increase the risk of antisocial behavior (Pine et al., 1996). Exposure to harsh or abusive parenting early in life (before age 5) is especially harmful (Keily, Howe, Dodge, Bates, & Petit, 2001). Because antisocial behavior in the child typically provokes further parental ineffectiveness, association with other antisocial children, and school problems, aggressive children often get caught up in a vicious cycle (O'Connor et al., 1998; Patterson & Yoerger, 1993; Vuchinich, Bank, & Patterson, 1992). As a consequence, early involvement in antisocial activity tends to escalate and to become self-perpetuating over time (Dodge & Pettit, 2003; Kim, Conger, Elder, & Lorenz, 2003).

The idea that family factors may underlie chronic delinquency—because of genetic factors, environmental influences, or both—is supported by observations that preadolescent delinquency tends to run in families (Farrington et al., 2001; Thornberry, Freeman-Gallant, Lizotte, Krohn, & Smith, 2003). Many adolescents who have been in trouble with the law from an early age have siblings and parents who have had similar problems (Farrington, 2004; Loeber & Stouthamer-Loeber, 1986; Rowe, Rodgers, & Meseck-Bushey, 1992).

life-course-persistent offenders Individuals who begin demonstrating antisocial or aggressive behavior during childhood and continue their antisocial behavior throughout adolescence and into adulthood.

adolescence-limited offenders Antisocial adolescents whose delinquent or violent behavior begins and ends during adolescence.

Although studies have identified genetic influences on all types of antisocial behavior, aggression is especially heritable (Deater-Deckard & Plomin, 1999; Eley, Lichtenstein, & Stevenson, 1999; Rutter, 1997).

There is also considerable evidence that, apart from family factors, certain characteristics distinguish persistently delinquent youngsters from their peers at a relatively early age. First and most importantly, children who become delinquent—especially those who engage in violence—have histories of aggressive and antisocial behavior that were identifiable as early as age 8 (Broidy et al., 2003; Farrington, 2004; Loeber & Farrington, 2000; Patterson, Forgatch, Yoerger, & Stoolmiller, 1998). Although this fact has been confirmed in hundreds of studies, it is important to keep in mind that the majority of children who have histories of aggressive behavior problems do *not* grow up to be delinquent. (If this seems confusing, think about it this way: The majority of delinquents probably have eaten in fast-food restaurants at some point in their childhood, but the majority of children who eat in fast-food restaurants do not grow up to be delinquent.)

Second, studies show that many children who become persistent offenders have problems in self-regulation—they are more impulsive, less able to control their anger, and more likely than their peers to suffer from hyperactivity, or as it is technically known, **attention deficit/hyperactivity disorder (ADHD)** (Colder & Stice, 1998; Farrington, 2004; Henry, Caspi, Moffitt, Harrington, & Silva, 1999; Patterson, DeGarmo, & Knutson, 2000; Steiner, Cauffman, & Duxbury, 1999). ADHD is believed to be primarily biological in origin and is characterized by impulsivity, inattentiveness, restlessness, and inappropriately high levels of activity, especially in learning situations. Although ADHD does not directly cause antisocial behavior, it does elevate the risk for other family and academic problems, which, in turn, increase the likelihood of an adolescent developing externalizing problems (Nagin & Tremblay, 1999; Patterson et al., 2000). The current thinking is that chronically conduct-disordered adolescents are born with strong biological predispositions toward antisocial behavior, including low levels of serotonin (which diminishes their ability to delay gratification), an emotional system that is easily aroused and difficult to regulate, and a temperament than makes them hard to control (Dodge & Pettit, 2003). There is also evidence that antisocial adolescents have a significantly lower resting heart rate than other youth, which may indicate a biologically inherited tendency toward fearlessness (Ortiz & Raine, 2004).

Third, and probably as a result of these biological inclinations, children who become chronically delinquent are more likely than their peers to score low in

standardized tests of intelligence and neuropsychological functioning and to perform poorly in school (Cauffman, Steinberg, & Piquero, 2005; Fergusson and Horwood, 1995; Henry et al., 1999; Raine et al., 2005). Some of this is due to genetic factors, but some is also due to conditions surrounding their birth and prenatal care. A disproportionate number of persistently violent adolescents were born to poor mothers who abused drugs during pregnancy and had medical complications during delivery that likely affected their baby's neuropsychological and intellectual development (Arseneault, Tremblay, Boulerice, & Saucier, 2002; Brennan, Hall, Bor, Najman, & Williams, 2003; Piquero & Chung, 2001).

Finally, as you read in Chapter 5, aggressive adolescents often have a prior history of poor relations with peers (Agnew & Brezina, 1997; Lewin, Davis, & Hops, 1999; Loeber & Farrington, 2000; Lyon, Henggeler, & Hall, 1992; Stattin & Magnusson, 1994). The combination of early aggression and peer rejection is especially devastating. As you may recall from Chapter 5, not all aggressive children are unpopular; one recent study of girls found, for example, that aggressive elementary school girls who were nevertheless liked by their classmates were not at elevated risk for later problem behavior (Prinstein & La Greca, 2004).

Research by psychologist Kenneth Dodge and his colleagues into the cognitive aspects of antisocial behavior indicates that especially aggressive youngsters are likely to suffer from a tendency toward what has been called a **hostile attributional bias** (Crick & Dodge, 1994; Dodge & Petit, 2003; Lochman & Dodge, 1994, 1998). Individuals with a hostile attributional bias are more likely than their peers to interpret ambiguous interactions with other children as deliberately hostile and to react aggressively. What might be viewed by the average adolescent as an innocent and accidental bump on the basketball court may be interpreted as an intentional shove by someone with a biased viewpoint, and it may lead to a fight. Such problematic information processing has been linked to aggression among white, African American, and Hispanic American youngsters alike (Graham, Hudley, & Williams, 1992). Adolescents who have this sort of attributional bias are also likely to interpret teachers' behavior as hostile when it is not (Wyatt & Haskett, 2001). There is also evidence that some adolescents have more positive views about using aggression as a means to solve problems and that this inclination, in

attention deficit/hyperactivity disorder (ADHD) A biologically based psychological disorder characterized by impulsivity, inattentiveness, and restlessness, often in school situations.

hostile attributional bias The tendency to interpret ambiguous interactions with others as deliberately hostile.

Some aggressive adolescents are prone to having a "hostile attributional bias"—they are more likely to interpret ambiguous interactions with others as intentionally hostile.

combination with a hostile attributional bias, leads to aggressive behavior that is almost automatic (Griffith Fontaine, Salzer Burks, & Dodge, 2002).

Because aggressiveness, hyperactivity, and intelligence are relatively stable traits over childhood, there is a great deal of continuity in problem behaviors over time. Studies that have followed individuals from childhood through adolescence and into adulthood find very high correlations between behavior problems at one point in time and antisocial behavior later in life (Farrington, 1991; Fergusson, Lynskey, & Horwood, 1996; Henry, Caspi, Moffitt, & Silva, 1996; Lahey et al., 1995; Robins, 1986; Rönkä & Pulkkinen, 1995). As noted earlier, this does not mean that all individuals who show antisocial behavior early invariably show it later—in fact, the majority do not. Nevertheless, many chronically antisocial adolescents grow up to be adults who persist in their antisocial behavior and who are at increased risk for other problems as well, such as substance abuse and depression (Wiesner, Kim, & Capaldi, 2005; Wiesner & Windle, 2006).

▌ Adolescence-Limited Offenders In contrast to youngsters who begin their delinquent behaviors prior to adolescence (and who often continue their antisocial behavior into adulthood), those who begin during adolescence do not ordinarily show signs of psychological abnormality or severe family pathology (Moffitt, 1993; Moffitt & Caspi, 2001). Typically, the offenses committed by these youngsters do not develop into serious criminality, and these individuals do not commit serious violations of the law after adolescence, although they may be more likely to have subsequent problems with drugs and alcohol (Nagin, Farrington, & Moffitt, 1995). In general, individuals who are involved in adolescence-limited antisocial activities have learned the norms and standards of society, and are far better socialized than life-course-persistent antisocial individuals. Nor do adolescence-limited offenders show the sorts of temperamental difficulties and neuropsychological problems seen among life-course-persistent offenders (Moffitt, Caspi, Harrington, & Milne, 2002). Interestingly, in contrast to the greatly disproportionate number of males who make up the life-course-persistent population (10 times more of these offenders are males than females), the ratio of males to females whose delinquency begins in adolescence is much smaller (about 1.5 to 1) (Moffitt & Caspi, 2001).

Although adolescence-limited offenders do not show the same degree of pathology as life-course-persistent offenders, they do have more problems both during adolescence and in early adulthood than youth who are not at all delinquent (Aguilar, Sroufe, Egeland, & Carlson, 2000; Moffitt et al., 2002). Indeed, a long-term follow-up of individuals who had earlier been classified as life-course-persistent offenders, adolescence-limited offenders, or neither found that as young adults the adolescence-limited offenders had more mental health, substance abuse, and financial problems than individuals who had not been delinquent at all as teenagers (Moffitt et al., 2002). It would be incorrect, therefore, to assume that just because an adolescent's antisocial behavior is limited to adolescence that he or she is not troubled. These individuals' serious offending may be limited to adolescence, but their other problems may persist into early adulthood.

The main risk factors for adolescence-limited offending are well established: poor parenting (especially poor monitoring) and affiliation with antisocial peers (Ary et al., 1999; Forgatch & Stoolmiller, 1994; Jones, Forehand, Brody, & Armistead, 2002; Lacourse, Nagin, & Tremblay, 2003; McCabe et al., 2001). The first of these (poor parenting) usually leads to the second (hanging around with antisocial peers) (Dishion et al., 1991; Lansford, Criss, Pettit, Dodge, & Bates, 2003; Patterson, 1986; Patterson,

DeBaryshe, & Ramsey, 1989). Influences on adolescence-limited offending are virtually identical for males and females and among adolescents from different ethnic groups (Choi, Harachi, Gillmore, & Catalano, 2005; Dekovi, Buist, & Reitz, 2004; Fergusson & Horwood, 2002; Sameroff, Peck, & Eccles, 2004).

The role of the peer group in adolescence-limited offending is extremely important, especially in industrialized countries, where peer influence tends to be relatively strong (Cheung, 1997; Dishion, Andrews, & Crosby, 1995; Greenberger, Chen, Beam, Whang, & Dong, 2000; Heimer & Matsueda, 1994; Keenan, Loeber, Zhang, Stouthamer-Loeber, & Van Kammen, 1995; Tremblay, Mâsse, Vitaro, & Dobkin, 1995). As you read in Chapter 7, one of the strongest predictors of delinquency and other forms of problem behavior is the extent to which the adolescent spends unsupervised time in unstructured activities with peers—activities like hanging out, cruising around, and going to parties (Osgood, Wilson, O'Malley, Bachman, & Johnston, 1996). Arrest statistics show that most delinquent activity occurs in group situations in which adolescents are pressured by their friends to go along with the group (Zimring, 1998). It is not coincidental that the peak years of susceptibility to peer pressure overlap with the peak years for this sort of delinquency. Indeed, one of the central tenets of Moffit's theory is that adolescence-limited offending is largely done in an effort to impress other adolescents with one's bravado and independence from adult authority; nondelinquent youth may mimic antisocial peers to increase their status and popularity (Moffitt, 2006). Consistent with this, adolescents who do not have friends—that is, loners—are much less delinquent than those who do (Demuth, 2004).

▌ **Runaways** Despite a good deal of attention in the popular media, little systematic research has focused on adolescent runaways. The little research that has been done paints a different picture than is portrayed in most made-for-television melodramas. First, the alleged epidemic of teenage runaways is grossly overstated, despite all those faces you see on milk cartons (most of whom, by the way, have been "kidnapped" by the child's noncustodial divorced parent). Nationally representative samples of adolescents suggest that only between 4 and 10 percent of adolescents have ever run away from home (running away is more common among poor adolescents), and that fewer than half of all runaways have done so more than once. Second, in contrast to images of teenage runaways traveling across the country, surveys indicate that half of all runaways stay within their community with relatives or friends. Finally, despite frequent portrayals of "long-lost" runaways, half of all runaways return home within

a few days, and more than 75 percent return home within a week. Public concern about runaways is high not because the numbers are large but because of the dangers faced on the streets by the 20 percent who do not return home promptly. These young people are exposed to numerous psychological and physical risks, including prostitution and other criminal behaviors, AIDS and other sexually transmitted diseases, victimization, and drug and alcohol abuse (Darling, Palmer, & Kipke, 2005; Terrell, 1997; Whitbeck, Hoyt, & Yoder, 1999; Windle, 1989).

Running away from home is typically another manifestation of externalizing problems in general, along with delinquency, aggression, truancy, and precocious sexuality. Consistent with this view, runaways—and repeat runaways, in particular—are more likely than other adolescents to be delinquent, drop out of school, and be aggressive. The antecedents of running away are similar to those for deviance in general: poverty, low scores on intelligence tests, and family conflict (Garbarino, Wilson, & Garbarino, 1986; Windle, 1989).

PREVENTION AND TREATMENT OF EXTERNALIZING PROBLEMS

Given the important differences between the causes of life-course-persistent and adolescence-limited antisocial behavior it makes sense that these two groups of adolescents would be best served by different sorts of preventive and after-the-fact interventions. In order to lower the rate of chronic antisocial behavior, experts argue that we need mainly to prevent disruption in early family relationships and to head off early academic problems through a combination of family support and preschool intervention (Butts & Mears, 2001; Loeber & Farrington, 2000; Tolan & Gorman-Smith, 2002; Tremblay, Pagani-Kurtz, Mâsse, Vitaro, & Pihl, 1995; Yoshikawa, 1994). There is also some evidence that interventions designed to improve the transition into school and work roles in young adulthood may prove helpful (Roisman, Aguilar, & Egeland, 2004; Stouthamer-Loeber, Wei, & Loeber, 2004).

These sorts of preventive strategies are easier proposed than done, however. Our society is hesitant to intervene to prevent family problems, and we typically wait until we see a sign of trouble in a family before acting. Unfortunately, waiting until after family relationships have become disrupted to intervene may have little benefit, for research shows that the outlook for delinquents who have begun criminal careers early is not very good. Various attempts at therapy and other sorts of treatment have not, by and large, proven successful. While it is not true that nothing works, it is true that even the very best programs for treating serious juvenile offenders have very small effects

(Lipsey, 1997). This is the case for treatment approaches that employ individual psychotherapy, group therapy, and diversion programs designed to remove delinquents from the juvenile justice system (to avoid the harmful effects of being labeled "delinquent") and to provide them with alternative opportunities for productive behavior (McCord, 1990). Nor have "boot camps" proven to be effective (Butts & Mears, 2001). One potential problem with interventions that group antisocial youth together is that these programs may have the unintended effect of increasing delinquency, by fostering friendships among delinquent peers (Poulin, Dishion, & Haas, 1997). And, of course, there is the possibility that in group situations, relatively more antisocial adolescents may teach less antisocial ones some of the "tricks of the trade" (Mager, Milich, Harris, & Howard, 2005).

Programs that attempt to change delinquents' beliefs about the value of aggression as a means of solving problems and to teach socially acceptable alternatives to aggression have shown some promise (e.g., Farrell & Meyer, 1997; Guerra & Slaby, 1990; Lochman, 1992), but even these programs have been only modestly successful in changing offenders' actual behavior (McCord, 1990). Some evidence suggests that family-based interventions (such as parent training, family therapy, or therapeutic foster care) may be more successful than interventions that focus on the individual adolescent (Butts & Mears, 2001; Chamberlain & Reid, 1998; Eddy & Chamberlain, 2000; Henggeler, Clingempeel, Brondino, & Pickrel, 2002; Lacourse et al., 2002), but these programs tend to be extremely expensive and time consuming (Bank, Marlowe, Reid, Patterson, & Weinrott, 1991; Henggeler, Melton, & Smith, 1992). Of course, no intervention is as expensive as incarceration—which in many states costs more than $100,000 per adolescent per year.

The prognosis for delinquents whose antisocial behavior is adolescence-limited is considerably better. Because they have internalized a basic foundation of norms and moral standards, it is easier to help these youngsters control their own behavior and stop misbehaving. Four types of strategies have been proposed. First, we can help youngsters by teaching them how to learn to resist peer pressure and to settle conflicts without resorting to aggression (DuRant et al., 1996). Second, by training parents to monitor their children more effectively, we can minimize the number of opportunities adolescents have to engage in peer-oriented misbehavior (Loeber & Stouthamer-Loeber, 1986). Third, by intervening within classrooms, schools, and neighborhoods, we may be able to alter the broader climate in ways that discourage antisocial behavior and encourage prosocial behavior (Felson, Liska, South, & McNulty, 1994; Hausman, Pierce, &

Briggs, 1996; Kellam, Ling, Merisca, Brown, & Ialongo, 1998). Finally, by treating delinquency seriously when it occurs—by making sure that an adolescent knows that misbehavior has definite consequences—we can deter her or him from doing the same thing again in the future.

RECAP

- Experts distinguish among three broad categories of externalizing problems in adolescence: conduct disorder, aggression, and juvenile offending. Although there is considerable overlap among them, they have different definitions.
- Antisocial behavior takes three forms: authority-related conflicts, covert antisocial behavior, and overt antisocial behavior. Within each of these types, there are predictable patterns of progression from less serious to more serious forms.
- Although the juvenile crime rate has declined in recent years, adolescents still account for a disproportionately high number of crimes, including violent crimes.
- It is important to distinguish between life-course-persistent offenders, whose antisocial behavior begins before adolescence and continues into adulthood, and adolescence-limited offenders, whose antisocial behavior typically begins and ends during the teenage years.
- Life-course-persistent offenders typically have histories of early family problems, childhood aggression, and neuropsychological deficits, and strong biological predispositions toward antisocial behavior.
- Adolescence-limited offenders, in contrast, are normal adolescents whose problems usually stem from poor parental monitoring and affiliation with antisocial peers.
- Because few approaches to the treatment of life-course-persistent offenders have proven successful, many efforts today in the area of crime and delinquency are being directed at prevention through early intervention and parent education.

Internalizing Problems

Most individuals emerge from adolescence confident, with a healthy sense of who they are and where they are headed. But in some instances, the changes and demands of adolescence may leave a teenager feeling

TABLE 13.3 DSM-IV diagnostic criteria for mild depressive disorder (dysthymic disorder)

1. Depressed or irritable mood for most of the day, for more days, than not, for at least one year.
2. The presence, while depressed, of at least two of the following:
   a. Poor appetite or overeating
   b. Insomnia or hypersomnia (sleeping too much)
   c. Low energy or fatigue
   d. Low self-esteem
   e. Poor concentration or difficulty making decisions
   f. Feelings of hopelessness
3. The symptoms cause clinically significant distress or impairment in social, school, or other important areas of functioning.

helpless, confused, and pessimistic about the future. Although minor fluctuations in self-esteem during early adolescence are commonplace—as you read in Chapter 8—it is not normal for adolescents (or adults, for that matter) to feel a prolonged or intense sense of hopelessness or frustration. Such young people are likely to be psychologically depressed and in need of professional help. Depression is by far the most significant internalizing problem in adolescence.

THE NATURE AND PREVALENCE OF DEPRESSION

In its mild form, **depression** is the most common psychological disturbance among adolescents (Graber, 2004; Steinberg et al., 2006; Zahn-Waxler, Klimes-Dougan, & Slattery, 2000). Although we typically associate depression with feelings of sadness, there are other symptoms that are important signs of the disturbance, and sadness alone without any other symptoms may not indicate depression in the clinical sense of the term. Depression has emotional symptoms, including dejection, decreased enjoyment of pleasurable activities, and low self-esteem. It has cognitive symptoms, such as pessimism and hopelessness. It has motivational symptoms, including apathy and boredom. Finally, it usually has physical symptoms, such as a loss of appetite, difficulty sleeping, and loss of energy. The symptoms of major depression are the same in adolescence as in adulthood and among males and females, although, as you'll read, there are sex differences in the prevalence of the illness (Lewinsohn, Pettit, Joiner, & Seeley, 2003).

▌ **Mood, Syndromes, and Disorder** Many people use the term "depression" imprecisely, to refer to a wide range of affective problems. Psychologists believe that it is important to distinguish among depressed mood (feeling sad), depressive syndromes (having multiple symptoms of depression), and depressive disorder (having enough symptoms to be diagnosed with the illness) (Compas, Ey, & Grant, 1993; Graber, 2004; Petersen et al., 1993). All individuals experience periods of sadness or depressed mood at one time or another. According to one large-scale survey, nearly one-third of all adolescents feel so sad and hopeless so often that they stop engaging in their usual activities (Centers for Disease Control and Prevention, 2006). According to other surveys, about 25 percent of adolescents regularly feel depressed (Avenevoli & Steinberg, 2001).

Fewer individuals report a pattern of depressive symptoms that includes a wider range of symptoms than sadness alone. At any one point in time, somewhat fewer than 10 percent of American teenagers report moderate or severe symptoms of depression—about 5 percent have the symptoms of a depressive syndrome, and approximately 3 percent meet the DSM-IV diagnostic criteria for depressive disorder (see Table 13.3) (Compas et al., 1993; Lewinsohn, Hops, Roberts, Seeley, & Andrews, 1993; Rushton, Forcier, & Schectman, 2002). Some studies estimate that as many as 25 percent of individuals will experience at least one bout of depression by the end of adolescence (Forbes & Dahl, 2005).

Depressed mood, depressive syndrome, and depressive disorder all become more common over adolescence, in part because of the increasing prevalence of stressful events during the adolescent years (Graber, 2004) and in part because the cognitive changes of adolescence permit the sort of introspection and rumination that often accompanies depression (Avenevoli & Steinberg, 2001; Chen, Mechanic, & Hansell, 1998). Although most adolescents are able to cope with the challenges of the period, some are not.

There is a dramatic increase in the prevalence of depressive feelings around the time of puberty; depression is half as common during childhood as it

depression A psychological disturbance characterized by low self-esteem, decreased motivation, sadness, and difficulty in finding pleasure in formerly pleasurable activities.

is during adolescence (Avenevoli & Steinberg, 2001). Symptoms of depression increase steadily throughout adolescence, and then start to decline—making late adolescence the period of the life span with the highest risk for the disorder (Wight, Sepúlveda, & Anashensel, 2004). Some studies also indicate that there have been historical increases in the prevalence of depression and other signs of internalized distress, especially among adolescents, with the rates increasing in each generation (Lewinsohn, Rohde, Seeley, & Fischer, 1993). Indeed, one recent analysis found that the *average* American child in the 1980s reported feeling more anxious than child psychiatric patients did in the 1950s; increases in stressors such as divorce and crime seem to have played a major role (Twenge, 2000). Several recent studies have also indicated that there may be ethnic differences in the prevalence of depression during adolescence, with significantly more Mexican American teenagers reporting depressive symptoms than their white, African American, or Asian American peers, especially within samples of girls (Roberts, Roberts, & Chen, 1997; Siegel, Aneshensel, Taub, Cantwell, & Driscoll, 1998). At this point, it is not known why this is the case or whether similar patterns are found when the comparison group is drawn from other Hispanic American subpopulations (such as Puerto Rican adolescents).

▌ Problems in Diagnosing Depression in Adolescence Diagnosing and studying depression among adolescents has been a tricky business for three very different reasons. First, depression during adolescence is often accompanied by other psychosocial or behavioral problems, including anxiety, phobias, psychosomatic complaints, and substance abuse (Brady & Kendall, 1992). Low-income urban adolescents who are depressed are especially likely to report psychosomatic symptoms such as headaches and stomachaches, rather than the symptoms we more automatically associate with depression, like apathy or sadness (Reynolds, O'Koon, Papademetriou, Szczygiel, & Grant, 2001).

Second, many professionals have been tempted to attribute nearly all observable difficulties in adolescence to unseen depression. In the past, for example, behaviors such as school phobia, running away from home, and anorexia nervosa were thought to hide the "real" problem—depression. Now, however, it is widely recognized that not all adolescents with behavior problems are "really" depressed; rather, as we saw earlier, depression and other problems are often comorbid (Avenevoli & Steinberg, 2001; Compas et al., 1993; Graber, 2004). In cases in which the main problem seems not to be depression, a careful clinician would certainly want to probe to see whether depressive symptoms were present but would not necessarily

jump to the conclusion that depression and behavior problems always go hand in hand.

Third, the popular stereotype of adolescents as normally disturbed leads many parents and teachers to fail to recognize genuine psychological problems when they appear. You can probably imagine a parent's description of an adolescent daughter who is critical of herself (which can be an emotional manifestation of depression), unduly negative (a possible cognitive manifestation), bored with everything (a possible motivational manifestation), and uninterested in eating (a possible physical manifestation). It would be easy for this parent to overlook a potentially very real problem and dismiss the daughter's mood and behavior as normal. Obviously, not all instances of self-criticism or apathy reflect psychological disturbance. But a good rule of thumb is that an individual who displays three or more of the signs of depression (see Table 13.3) for two weeks should probably consult a professional.

SEX DIFFERENCES IN DEPRESSION

One of the most consistent findings in the study of adolescent depression involves the emergence of a very large sex difference in rates of depression in early adolescence. As Figure 13.10 indicates, before adolescence, boys are somewhat more likely to exhibit depressive symptoms than girls, but after puberty, the sex difference in prevalence of depression reverses. From early adolescence until very late in adulthood, twice as many females as males suffer from depressive disorder, and females are somewhat more likely than males to report depressed mood (Compas et al., 1997; Holsen, Kraft, & Vitterso, 2000; Twenge & Nolen-Hoeksema, 2002; Wade, Cairney, & Pevalin, 2002). The increased risk for depression among girls emerges during puberty, rather than at a particular age or grade in school (Angold, Costello, & Worthman, 1998). Although sex differences in major depression persist beyond adolescence, reports of depressive symptoms tend to diminish somewhat in early adulthood; both sexes report less depression in their mid-20s than late teens, but the decline is steeper among females (Galambos, Barker, & Krahn, 2006; Stoolmiller, Kim, & Capaldi, 2005).

Psychologists do not have a certain explanation for the emergence of sex differences in depressive disorder at adolescence. Although the fact that the emergence of a strong sex differential coincides with puberty suggests a biological explanation, there actually is little evidence that the sex difference in depression is directly attributable to sex differences in hormones (Rutter & Garmezy, 1983). Some evidence indicates that females are more susceptible than males to genetic influences on depression, such that even when males

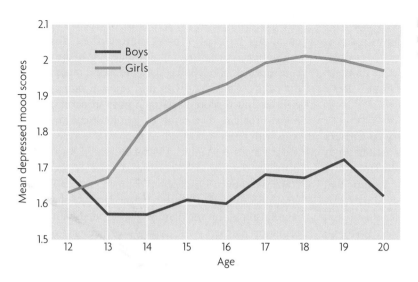

FIGURE 13.10 Depressed mood among males and females as a function of age. (Wichstrøm, 1999)

Rates of depression are twice as high among adolescent girls as they are among adolescent boys, although there is no clear consensus for why this is the case. Many scientists think the sex difference has something to do with the fact that adolescence is more stressful for females than for males and that, when faced with stress, girls are more likely than boys to ruminate.

and females inherit the same genetic predisposition toward depression from their parents, the predisposition is more likely to be manifested among girls

(Jacobson & Rowe, 1999), but it is not known why this is the case. More likely, changes in social relationships around the time of puberty may leave girls more vulnerable than boys to some forms of psychological distress (with some individuals inheriting a stronger predisposition than others), and depression may be a stereotypically feminine way of manifesting it.

■ **Gender Roles**　More specifically, social scientists speculate that the emergence of sex differences in depression has something to do with the social role that the adolescent girl may find herself in as she enters the world of boy–girl relationships (Petersen et al., 1993; Wichstrøm, 1999). As you read in previous chapters, this role may bring heightened self-consciousness over her physical appearance and increased concern over popularity with peers. Since many of these feelings may provoke helplessness, hopelessness, and anxiety, adolescent girls may be more susceptible to depressive feelings. To make matters worse, pressures on young women to behave in sex-stereotyped ways, which intensify during adolescence (Hill & Lynch, 1983), may lead girls to adopt some behaviors and dispositions—passivity, dependency, and fragility, for example—that they have been socialized to believe are part of the feminine role, and that may contribute to their depressed mood. Consistent with this, studies show that depression in girls is significantly correlated with having a poor body image and with having low scores on measures of masculinity (Allgood-Merten, Lewinsohn, & Hops, 1990; Obeidallah, McHale, & Silbereisen, 1996; Seiffge-Krenke & Stemmler, 2002; Stice & Bearman, 2001; Stice, Hayward, Cameron, Killen, & Taylor, 2000; Wichstrøm, 1999).

The gender-role intensification hypothesis is only one explanation for sex differences in the prevalence of depression during adolescence. Three other accounts focus on sex differences in the degree to which adolescence is stressful, in the ways of coping with stress, and in vulnerability to different types of stress (Cryanowski & Frank, 2000; Leadbeater, Blatt, & Quinlan, 1995; Nolen-Hoeksema & Girgus, 1994; Rudolph & Hammen, 1999).

▌ Stress, Rumination, and Sensitivity to Others
With respect to the first of these explanations, it is important to note that the link between stress and depression during adolescence is well documented among both males and females; individuals who experience more stress are more vulnerable to depression and other internalizing problems (Petersen et al., 1993). Of interest, then, is evidence that early adolescence is generally a more stressful time for girls than boys (Allgood-Merten et al., 1990; Petersen, Sarigiani, & Kennedy, 1991; Rudolph & Hammen, 1999). This is because the bodily changes of puberty, especially when they occur early in adolescence, are more likely to be stressful for girls than boys; because girls are more likely than boys to experience multiple stressors at the same time (for example, going through puberty while making the transition into junior high school); and because girls are likely to experience more stressful life events than boys (Graber, 2004). In addition, girls are much more likely than boys to have been sexually abused during childhood, which is a very strong risk factor for depression during adolescence (Cutler & Nolen-Hoeksema, 1991).

Second, there is evidence that girls are more likely than boys to react to stress by turning their feelings inward—for instance, by ruminating about the problem and feeling helpless—whereas boys are more likely to respond either by distracting themselves or by turning their feelings outward, in aggressive behavior or in drug and alcohol abuse (Calvete & Cardeñoso, 2005; Grant et al., 2004; Hart & Thompson, 1996; Nolen-Hoeksema & Girgus, 1994; Sethi & Nolen-Hoeksema, 1997). As a result, even when exposed to the same degree of stress, girls are more likely to respond to the stressors by becoming depressed (Angold et al., 1996; Ge, Lorenz, Conger, Elder, & Simons, 1994; Rudolph & Hammen, 1999). This difference in the ways that boys and girls react to stress helps explain why the prevalence of externalizing disorders is higher in boys, while the prevalence of internalizing disorders is higher in girls.

The third explanation emphasizes girls' generally greater orientation toward and sensitivity to interpersonal relations (Cyranowski & Frank, 2000). Sex differences in levels of the hormone **oxytocin** may both encourage females to invest more in their close relationships and make them more vulnerable to the adverse consequences of relational disruptions and interpersonal difficulties. Consistent with this, research indicates that girls are much more likely than boys to develop emotional problems as a result of family discord or problems with peers (Crawford, Cohen, Midlarsky, & Brook, 2001; Davies & Windle, 1997; Leadbeater, Kuperminc, Blatt, & Hertzog, 1999; Seiffge-Krenke & Stemmler, 2002; Washburn-Ormachea, Hillman, & Sawilowsky, 2004). Because adolescence is a time of many changes in relationships—in the family, with friends, and with romantic partners—the capacity of females to invest heavily in their relationships with others may be both a strength and a source of vulnerability.

FOOD FOR THOUGHT
In light of what we know about the likely causes of sex differences in depression, what preventive interventions should be targeted at young adolescent girls?

SUICIDE
▌ Prevalence of Suicide   According to recent national surveys, in any given year, more than 10 percent of American female high school students and more than 6 percent of males attempt suicide; about one-third of these attempts are serious enough to require treatment by a physician or nurse. A much larger proportion (close 20 percent) think about killing themselves—referred to as **suicidal ideation**—and the vast majority of these have gone so far as to make a plan (Centers for Disease Control and Prevention, 2006). Suicidal ideation increases during early adolescence, peaks around age 15, and then declines (see Figure 13.11) (Rueter & Kwon, 2005). Adolescents who attempt to kill themselves usually have made appeals for help and have tried but failed to get emotional support from family or friends. They report feeling trapped, lonely, worthless, and hopeless (Kidd, 2004).

The adolescent suicide rate among 15- to 19-year-olds increased alarmingly between 1950 and 1990, fueled by the increased use of drugs and alcohol and the increased availability of firearms (Judge & Billick, 2004). The rate peaked and declined somewhat during the 1990s, as new forms of antidepressant medication were more widely prescribed to adolescents (Zametkin, Alter, & Yemini, 2001; Zito et al., 2002). You may have read that suicide is a leading cause of death among

oxytocin   A hormone known to influence emotional bonding to others.

suicidal ideation   Thinking about ending one's life.

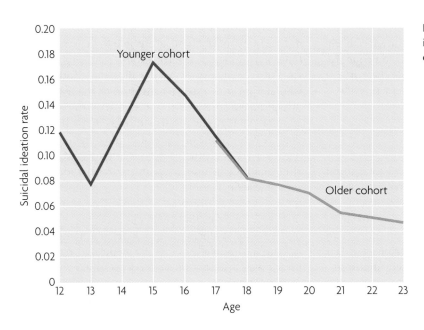

FIGURE 13.11 Suicidal ideation peaks in middle adolescence and then declines. (Rueter & Kwon, 2005)

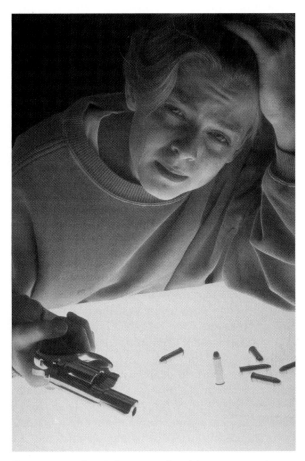

Contrary to myth, suicide attempts by adolescents are rarely impulsive reactions to specific events. Rather, adolescents who attempt to kill themselves typically have had a history of depression and have not been able to find emotional support from family or friends.

young people, but this is primarily because very few young people die from other causes, such as disease. Although the rate of suicide rises rapidly during the middle adolescent years, it continues to rise throughout adulthood, and suicide is a much more common cause of death among adults than it is among young people, largely because very few suicide attempts by adolescents are successful. The most common method of suicide among adolescents is with a firearm, followed by hanging. Drug overdoses and carbon monoxide poisoning are also common (Judge & Billick, 2004). The suicide rate is highest among American Indian and Alaskan Native adolescents and lowest among African Americans; rates among white, Hispanic American, and Asian American adolescents fall in between these extremes (Judge & Billick, 2004).

■ **Risk Factors for Suicide** Systematic studies have identified four established sets of risk factors for attempting suicide during adolescence, and they are similar for males and females and among African American, Hispanic American, and white adolescents: having a psychiatric problem, especially depression or substance abuse; having a history of suicide in the family; being under stress, especially in the areas of achievement and sexuality; and experiencing parental rejection, family disruption, or extensive family conflict (Judge & Billick, 2004). Adolescents who have one of these risk factors are significantly more likely to attempt suicide than their peers, and adolescents who have more than one risk factor are dramatically more likely to try to kill themselves. Adolescents who have attempted suicide once are at risk for attempting it again (Lewinsohn, Rohde, & Seely, 1994). Adolescents are also more likely to attempt suicide if one of their friends or someone else in their community has committed suicide (Bearman & Moody, 2004; Gould, Wallenstein, & Kleinman, 1990).

CAUSES OF DEPRESSION AND INTERNALIZING DISORDERS

A variety of theories have been proposed to account for the onset of depression and other types of internalizing problems during adolescence, and the current consensus is that internalizing problems are likely to result from interacting environmental conditions and individual predispositions rather than either set of factors alone. Today, most experts endorse a **diathesis–stress model** of depression, which suggests that depression may occur when individuals who are predisposed toward internalizing problems (the term "diathesis" refers to this predisposition) are exposed to chronic or acute stressors that precipitate a depressive reaction (Hilsman & Garber, 1995; Lewinsohn, Joiner, & Rohde, 2001). Individuals without the diathesis—who are not predisposed toward depression—are able to withstand a great deal of stress, for instance, without developing any psychological problems. Individuals who have strong predispositions toward the disorder may become depressed in the face of stressful circumstances that most of us would consider to be quite normal, however. Research has focused both on the diathesis and the stress—on identifying individual predispositions toward depression and on identifying the environmental circumstances likely to precipitate the disorder.

▌ **The Diathesis** Two categories of diatheses, or predispositions, have received the most attention. First, because depression has been found to have a strong genetic component, it is believed that at least some of the diathesis is biological and may be related to problematic patterns of neuroendocrine functioning (**neuroendocrine** refers to hormonal activity in the brain and nervous system). In particular, researchers have focused on the predisposition toward intense problems in regulation of activity in one or more of the hypothalamic-pituitary axes, including those involving the adrenal, thyroid, gonadal, and somatotropic axes (Graber, 2004). This biological predisposition may make it diffi-

cult for individuals to regulate their emotions, which, in turn, may make them susceptible to depression and other psychological problems (Silk, Steinberg, & Morris, 2003; Steinberg & Avenevoli, 2000). Individuals who are prone to intense activation of the hypothalamic-pituitary-adrenocortical (HPA) axis, in particular, are more biologically reactive to stress than others, and they are more prone to depression and other internalizing disorders. Scientists have recently discovered that abnormalities in one gene, in particular, may make some individuals more likely to develop depression in the face of stress (Caspi et al., 2003). Not surprisingly, then, given the role that genes play in the development of depression, vulnerability to depression tends to run in families—adolescents with a depressed parent are three times as likely to develop depression as are other youth (Graber, 2004).

Other researchers have focused more on the cognitive style of depressed individuals, suggesting that people with tendencies toward hopelessness, pessimism, and self-blame are more likely to interpret events in their lives in ways that lead to the development of depression (Kaslow, Adamson, & Collins, 2000; Prinstein & Atkins, 2004; Robinson, Garber, & Hilsman, 1995). These sorts of cognitive sets, which may be linked to the ways in which children think they are viewed first by parents and later by peers, develop during childhood and are thought to play a role in the onset of depression during adolescence (Cole & Jordan, 1995; Cole, Martin, & Powers, 1997; Garber, Weiss, & Shanley, 1993; Nolen-Hoeksema, Girgus, & Seligman, 1992). Because there is evidence that negative cognitions result from as well as contribute to depression, it is difficult to say with precision what the cause-and-effect relationship is, however (Cole, Martin, Peeke, Seroczynski, & Hoffman, 1998).

▌ **The Stress** Researchers who have been more concerned with the stress component of the diathesis–stress model—that is, with environmental influences on depression—have focused on three broad sets of stressors (Aseltine, Gore, & Colten, 1994; Lewinsohn et al., 1994; Lewinsohn, Gotlib, & Seeley, 1997; Petersen et al., 1993). By and large, these factors have been found to be linked to depression among adolescents from very different cultures (Greenberger, Chen, Tally, & Dong, 2000; Kim & Ge, 2000; Xia & Qian, 2001). First, depression is more common among adolescents from families characterized by high conflict and low cohesion, and it is higher among adolescents from divorced homes. Second, depression is more prevalent among adolescents who are unpopular or who have poor peer relations. Third, depressed adolescents report more chronic and acute stress than nondepressed

diathesis–stress model A perspective on disorder that posits that problems are the result of an interaction between a preexisting condition (the diathesis) and exposure to a stressful event or condition.

neuroendocrine Hormonal activity in the brain and nervous system.

adolescents do. These psychosocial factors may both contribute to and exacerbate the development of negative cognitive sets (Garber, Robinson, & Valentiner, 1997). There is also evidence that academic difficulties are correlated with depression, especially among adolescents from Asian cultures, in which relatively more stress may be placed on achievement (Chan, 1997; Greenberger et al., 2000). Similar findings on the connection between academic pressure and depression have emerged from studies of affluent suburban youth (Luthar & Becker, 2002). Although all sorts of stressors have been linked to the onset of psychological problems (Steinberg & Avenevoli, 2000), the single most common trigger of the first episode of major depression in adolescence is the breakup of a romantic relationship (Monroe, Rohde, Seeley, & Lewinsohn, 1999).

You read earlier that the prevalence of depression rises during adolescence. Can diathesis–stress models of depression account for this increase? For the most part, they can. Biological theorists can point to the hormonal changes of puberty, which are likely to have implications for neuroendocrine activity; as you read in Chapter 1, one of the effects of pubertal hormones is to make individuals more sensitive to stress (Walker, Sabuwalla, & Huot, 2004). Depression and negative affect among both boys and girls are correlated with various hormones known to change at puberty (Angold, Costello, Erkanli, & Worthman, 1999; Graber, 2004). Many studies show that the increase in depression in adolescence is more closely linked to puberty than age (Hayward, Gotlib, Schraedley, & Litt, 1999), although it is difficult to pinpoint puberty as the cause of the problem, since many other changes typically occur around the same time (such as the transition out of elementary school). Cognitive theorists can point to the onset of hypothetical thinking at adolescence, which may result in new (and perhaps potentially more depressing) ways of viewing the world (Keating, 2004). And theorists who emphasize environmental factors draw attention to the new environmental demands of adolescence, such as changing schools, beginning to date, or coping with transformations in family relationships—all of which may lead to heightened stress (Graber, 2004). Thus, there are many good reasons to expect that the prevalence of depression would increase as individuals pass from childhood into adolescence. It is also important to note that individuals who develop internalizing disorders such as depression and anxiety in adolescence are at elevated risk to suffer from these problems as adults (Lewinsohn, Rohde, Seeley, Klein, & Gotlib, 2003; Pine, Cohen, Gurley, Brook, & Ma, 1998).

TREATMENT AND PREVENTION OF INTERNALIZING PROBLEMS

The treatment of depression during adolescence is very similar to its treatment at other points in the life span. Clinicians use a wide range of approaches, including biological therapies employing antidepressant medication (these address the neuroendocrine problem, if one exists); psychotherapies designed to help depressed adolescents understand the roots of their depression, to increase the degree to which they experience reinforcement in their daily activities, or to change the nature of their cognitive set; and family therapy, which focuses on changing patterns of family relationships that may be contributing to the adolescent's symptoms (Weisz & Hawley, 2002). Generally, behavioral and cognitive-behavioral approaches to psychotherapy with depressed and anxious adolescents are more effective than insight-oriented or family therapy, and psychotherapy appears to be more effective with female adolescents than with males (Marcotte, 1997; Silverman et al., 1999; Weisz, Weiss, Han, Granger, & Morton, 1995). With regard to antidepressants, research has confirmed the effectiveness of a class of drugs called **selective serotonin reuptake inhibitors (SSRIs),** such as Prozac, in the treatment of depression in adolescence (Graber, 2004). These medications are also effective in treating other types of internalizing problems, such as anxiety disorders and social phobias (Pine et al., 2001).

Efforts are also being made to prevent adolescent depression on a larger scale, since this strategy may be more effective than delivering treatment to individuals once they have become depressed. **Primary prevention** approaches emphasize teaching all adolescents social competencies and life skills that will help them cope with stress (Weissberg, Caplan, & Harwood, 1991). **Secondary prevention** approaches aim at adolescents who are believed to be at high risk for developing depression, such as teenagers with a depressed parent (who are at risk because of the genetic and environmental risks associated with this) (e.g., Hammen, Shih, & Brennan, 2004) or adolescents who are under stress (e.g., Grych & Fincham, 1992). Screening high school students to identify those at greatest risk

selective serotonin reuptake inhibitors (SSRIs) A class of antidepressant medications that have proven to be effective with adolescents suffering from internalizing problems, such as depression.

primary prevention An approach to health promotion that emphasizes teaching all adolescents certain behaviors, values, and information.

secondary prevention An approach to health promotion that is specifically aimed at adolescents believed to be at high risk for a particular disease or disturbance.

for suicide has been found to be safe and does not, as some fear, cause adolescents to think more about killing themselves (Gould et al., 2005).

RECAP

- Depression is the most common internalizing disorder of adolescence, afflicting as many as 25 percent of individuals by the time they enter adulthood.
- Significant sex differences in depression emerge in early adolescence that are maintained throughout adulthood. Females are more likely to be depressed than males, although experts disagree about why this is the case.
- Nearly 10 percent of adolescents have attempted suicide, and twice this number have seriously thought about killing themselves.
- Depression is the result of an interacting set of environmental conditions (especially stress) and individual predispositions, or diatheses (including biological and cognitive predispositions).
- Depression during adolescence can be successfully treated through a combination of biological, psychological, and family therapies.

Stress and Coping

Nearly half of all adolescents report difficulty in coping with stressful situations at home or at school (Gans, 1990). These stressors include major life changes (such as going through parental divorce, changing schools, on having someone in the family suddenly become seriously ill), chronically stressful conditions (such as poverty, a disabling illness, or constant family conflict), and day-to-day hassles (such as school exams, fights with friends, and arguments with siblings and parents) (Compas, 2004).

Research indicates that stress can affect individuals in different ways (Steinberg & Avenevoli, 2000). For some teenagers, stress can lead to internalized disorders, such as anxiety, depression, headaches, and indigestion—even compromised immune system functioning (Birmaher et al., 1994). For others, the consequences of stress are externalized, in behavior and conduct problems. For still others, the impact of stress is manifested in drug and alcohol abuse. These links between stress and psychosocial problems have been documented in studies of youngsters from all ethnic groups and family backgrounds (Dornbusch, Mont-Reynaud, Ritter, Chen, & Steinberg, 1991) and among youth exposed to both relatively common stressors (such as breaking up with a romantic partner) and relatively severe ones (such as exposure to war trauma) (Macksoud & Aber, 1996; Sack & Clarke, 1996).

Yet, for some adolescents, the very same sources and levels of stress do not seem to be associated with psychological or physical upset at all. Thus, although we tend to think of stress as having negative effects on our well-being, the connection between stress and dysfunction is not clear-cut. Some adolescents show enormous **resilience** in the face of enormous adversity (Compas, 2004; Luthar, Cicchetti, & Becker, 2000; Masten, 2001). What makes some adolescents more vulnerable to the effects of stress than others? Psychologists point to three sets of factors.

First, the effect of any one stressor is exacerbated if it is accompanied by other stressors. Studies show that stress tends to have a multiplicative effect: An adolescent who faces two stressors at the same time (parental divorce and school change, for example) is more than twice as likely to experience psychological problems as someone who has experienced only one of the two stressors (Compas, 2004; Forehand, Biggar, & Kotchick, 1998; Rutter, 1978).

Second, adolescents who have other resources—either internal resources such as high self-esteem, healthy identity development, high intelligence, or strong feelings of competence; or external resources such as social support from others—are less likely to be adversely affected by stress than their peers (Compas, 2004; Hauser, 1999; Luthar, 1991; Masten et al., 1999; Steinberg et al., 2006; Wills & Cleary, 1996). Adolescents with close friends and good social skills seem to be better able to handle stressors such as parental divorce or starting junior high school than are teenagers who lack close friendships or have fewer interpersonal resources. Most importantly, teenagers who have warm and close family relationships are less likely to be distressed by a stressful experience than are teenagers without such familial support (Weist, Freedman, Paskewitz, Proescher, & Flaherty, 1995). Indeed, studies consistently show that the presence of a close parent–adolescent relationship is probably the single most important factor in protecting adolescents from psychological harm (Resnick et al., 1997). The importance of social support as a buffer against the adverse effects of stress has been documented in studies of adolescents around the world.

Finally, some adolescents use more effective coping strategies than do others. Specialists who study coping

---

resilience The ability of an individual to continue to function competently in the face of adversity or stress.

strategies distinguish between strategies that involve taking steps to change the source of the stress, called **primary control strategies,** and those that involve efforts to adapt to the problem, called **secondary control strategies** (Compas, 2004; Compas, Connor-Smith, Saltzman, Thomsen, & Wadsworth, 2001; Weisz, McCabe, & Dennig, 1994). For instance, if you are very worried about an upcoming exam in this course, a primary control strategy might be to form a study group with other students in order to review the material, whereas a secondary control strategy might be to go out to a movie or to a party in order to distract yourself.

FOOD FOR THOUGHT

How do you cope with stress? Are you more likely to use primary or secondary control strategies?

In some situations, secondary control strategies are quite effective. These tend to be stressful situations that are clearly uncontrollable, such as getting an injection at the doctor's office or learning that a loved one has a terminal illness. In these instances, trying to distract and calm oneself may help alleviate some of the stress. But, in general, research shows that adolescents who employ primary control strategies are less vulnerable to the detrimental health consequences of stress, especially if the source of the stress is control-

lable. Studies of a wide range of male and female adolescents from different ethnic groups show that individuals who use primary control strategies are better adjusted, less depressed, and less likely to have behavioral problems than those who react to stress through disengagement or avoidance (Compas, 2004; Dumont & Provost, 1999; Ebata & Moos, 1994; Herman-Stahl, Stemmler, & Petersen, 1995; Lee & Larson, 1996; Sandler, Tein, & West, 1994; Scott & House, 2005; Seiffge-Krenke & Klessinger, 2000; Tolan, Gorman-Smith, Henry, Chung, & Hunt, 2002; Windle & Windle, 1996.

RECAP
- For some adolescents, exposure to chronic or severe stress can result in psychological or physical difficulties, but for others, the very same sources and levels of stress do not seem to be associated with upset at all.
- In general, the effect of stress is exacerbated if it is accompanied by other stressors, if the adolescent lacks sufficient internal or external resources, or if the adolescent has poorly developed coping skills.
- Coping with stress by trying to change to source of stress (if it is controllable) or to adapt to the problem (if it is not) is generally more effective than coping through distraction or avoidance.

primary control strategies Coping strategies in which an individual attempts to change the stressor.

secondary control strategies Coping strategies that involve attempts by the individual to adapt to the stressor.

Glossary

A

academic achievement Achievement that is measured by standardized tests of scholastic ability or knowledge.

achievement The psychosocial domain concerning behaviors and feelings in evaluative situations.

achievement attributions The beliefs an individual holds about the causes of her or his successes and failures.

activational role of hormones The process through which changes in hormone levels, especially at puberty, stimulate changes in the adolescent's behavior, appearance, or growth.

adolescence The second decade of life.

adolescence-limited offenders Antisocial adolescents whose delinquent or violent behavior begins and ends during adolescence.

adolescent growth spurt The dramatic increase in height and weight that occurs during puberty.

adolescent health care A field of study and health care devoted to understanding the health care needs of individuals during the second decade of life.

adrenarche The maturation of the adrenal glands that takes place in preadolescence.

Adult Attachment Interview A structured interview used to assess an individual's past attachment history and "internal working model" of relationships.

age of majority The designated age at which an individual is recognized as an adult member of the community.

age–crime curve The relationship between chronological age and offending, showing that the prevalence of offending peaks in late adolescence.

age grading The process of grouping individuals within social institutions on the basis of chronological age.

agency The sense that one has an impact on one's world.

aggression Acts done to be intentionally harmful.

AIDS (acquired immune deficiency syndrome) A disease, transmitted by means of bodily fluids, that devastates the immune system.

androgens A class of sex hormones secreted by the gonads, found in both sexes, but in higher levels among males than females following puberty.

androgyny The combination of both highly masculine and highly feminine traits.

anorexia nervosa An eating disorder found chiefly among young women, characterized by dramatic and severe self-induced weight loss.

antisocial personality disorder A disorder of adulthood characterized by antisocial behavior and persistent disregard for the rules of society and the rights of others.

anxious-avoidant attachment An insecure attachment between infant and caregiver, characterized by indifference on the part of the infant toward the caregiver.

anxious-resistant attachment An insecure attachment between infant and caregiver, characterized by distress at separation and anger at reunion.

attachment The strong affectional bond that develops between an infant and caregiver.

attention deficit/hyperactivity disorder (ADHD) A biologically based psychological disorder characterized by impulsivity, inattentiveness, and restlessness, often in school situations.

authoritarian parents Parents who use punitive, absolute, and forceful discipline, and who place a premium on obedience and conformity.

authoritative parents Parents who use warmth, firm control and rational, issue-oriented discipline, in which emphasis is placed on the development of self-direction.

authority conflicts A type of antisocial behavior characterized by stubbornness and rebelliousness.

autoerotic behavior Sexual behavior that is experienced alone, such as masturbation or sexual fantasizing.

autonomy The psychosocial domain concerning the development and expression of independence.

B

baby boom The period following World War II, during which the number of infants born was extremely large.

Bar (Bas) Mitzvah In Judaism, the religious ceremony marking the young person's transition to adulthood.

barometric self-esteem The aspect of self-esteem that fluctuates across situations.

basal metabolism rate The minimal amount of energy used by the body during a resting state.

baseline self-esteem The aspect of self-esteem that is relatively stable across situations and over time.

behavioral autonomy The capacity to make independent decisions and to follow through with them.

behavioral decision theory An approach to understanding adolescent risk taking, in which behaviors are seen as the outcome of systematic decision-making processes.

behavioral genetics The scientific study of genetic influences on behavior.

biculturalism The successful maintenance of an identification with more than one cultural background.

big fish–little pond effect The phenomenon whereby individuals who attend school with high-achieving peers feel worse about themselves than comparably successful individuals with lower-achieving peers.

binge drinking Consuming five or more drinks in a row on one occasion, an indicator of alcohol abuse.

biracial Having two parents of different ethnic or racial backgrounds.

body mass index (BMI) A measure of an individual's body fat, the ratio of weight to height; used to gauge overweight and obesity.

brother–sister avoidance The avoidance of any contact or interaction between brothers and sisters from the onset of puberty until one or both persons are married, part of the process of social re-definition at adolescence in many societies.

bulimia   An eating disorder found chiefly among young women, characterized primarily by a pattern of binge eating and self-induced vomiting.

C

care orientation   In Gilligan's theory of moral development, a moral orientation that emphasizes responding to others' needs.

causation   When one thing actually causes another.

charter schools   Public schools that have been given the autonomy to establish their own curricula and teaching practices.

child protectionists   Individuals who argued, early in the twentieth century, that adolescents needed to be kept out of the labor force in order to protect them from the hazards of the workplace.

chlamydia   A sexually transmitted infection caused by a bacterium.

circumcision   A procedure in which some part of the genitals is cut and permanently altered.

cliques   Small, tightly knit groups of between 2 and 12 friends, generally of the same sex and age.

cluster suicides   Outbreaks of suicides, in which an unusually high number of suicides occur within a limited time period or small geographic area.

cognitive-developmental view   A perspective on development, based on the work of Piaget, that takes a qualitative, stage-theory approach.

cohort   A group of individuals born during the same general historical era.

collective efficacy   A community's social capital, derived from its members' common values and goals.

community service   The involvement of young people in activities that serve some social or economic need of society.

comorbid   Co-occurring, as when an individual has more than one problem at the same time.

competence–performance distinction   The distinction between what individuals are capable of and what they actually do, important in the study of cognitive development.

comprehensive high school   An educational institution that evolved during the first half of the twentieth century, offering a varied curriculum and designed to meet the needs of a diverse population of adolescents.

concrete operations   The third stage of cognitive development, according to Piaget, spanning the period roughly between age 6 and early adolescence.

conduct disorder   A repetitive and persistent pattern of antisocial behavior that results in problems and school or work, or in relationships with others.

continuous transitions   Passages into adulthood in which adult roles and statuses are entered into gradually.

conventional moral reasoning   According to Kohlberg, the second level of moral development, which occurs during late childhood and early adolescence and is characterized by reasoning that is based on the rules and conventions of society.

correlation   When two things go hand in hand.

cortisol   A hormone produced when we are exposed to stress.

covert antisocial behavior   A type of antisocial behavior characterized by misdeeds that are not always detected by others, such as lying or stealing.

criminal behavior   Crimes that are dealt with in the criminal justice system, regardless of the age of the offender.

criminal justice system   The system of courts and related institutions developed to handle adult crime.

critical thinking   Thinking that involves analyzing, evaluating, and interpreting information, rather than simply memorizing it.

cross-sectional study   A study that compares two or more groups of individuals at one point in time.

crowds   Large, loosely organized groups of young people, composed of several cliques and typically organized around a common shared activity.

crystallization   According to Super, the stage during which individuals, typically aged 14–18, first begin to formulate their ideas about appropriate occupations.

cultivation theory   A perspective on media use that emphasizes the impact media exposure has on individuals.

cultural capital   The resources provided within a family through the exposure of the adolescent to art, music, literature, and other elements of "high culture."

culture-fair tests   Standardized tests that do not, by virtue of their construction, favor one cultural or ethnic group over another.

curvilinear pattern   In statistical analyses, a pattern of relations between two variables that resembles a U-shaped or an inverted U-shaped curve.

D

date rape   Being forced by a date to have sex against one's will.

deductive reasoning   A type of logical reasoning in which one draws logically necessary conclusions from a general set of premises, or givens.

delayed phase preference   A pattern of sleep characterized by later sleep and wake times, which usually emerges during puberty.

delinquency   Juvenile offending that is processed within the juvenile justice system.

demographers   Social scientists who study large-scale changes in the makeup of the population.

depression   A psychological disturbance characterized by low self-esteem, decreased motivation, sadness, and difficulty finding pleasure in formerly enjoyable activities.

detachment   In psychoanalytic theory, the process through which adolescents sever emotional attachments to their parents or other authority figures.

developmental trajectories   Patterns of change over time.

diathesis–stress model   A perspective on disorder that posits that problems are the result of an interaction between a preexisting condition (the diathesis) and exposure to a stressful event or condition.

diffusion tensor imaging (DTI)   A technique used to produce images of the brain that show connections among different regions.

discontinuous transitions   Passages into adulthood in which adult roles and statuses are entered into abruptly.

disordered eating   Mild, moderate, or severe disturbance in eating habits and attitudes.

divided attention   The process of paying attention to two or more stimuli at the same time.

dopamine   A neurotransmitter especially important in the brain circuits that regulate the experience of pleasure.

dorsolateral prefontal cortex   The outer and upper areas of the front of the brain, important for skills such as planning ahead and controlling impulses.

E

early adolescence   The period spanning roughly ages 11–14, corresponding approximately to the junior or middle high school years.

ecological perspective on human development   A perspective on development that emphasizes the broad context in which development occurs.

educational attainment   The number of years of schooling completed by an individual.

emerging adulthood   The period spanning roughly ages 18–25, during which individuals make the transition from adolescence into adulthood.

emotional autonomy   The establishment of more adultlike and less childish close relationships with family members and peers.

endocrine system   The system of the body that produces, circulates, and regulates hormones.

ephebephobia   The irrational fear of adolescents.

epiphysis   The closing of the ends of bones, which terminates growth after the adolescent growth spurt has been completed.

estrogens   A class of sex hormones secreted by the gonads, found in both sexes but in higher levels among females than males following puberty.

ethnic identity   The aspect of one's sense of identity concerning ancestry or racial group membership.

ethnography   A type of research in which individuals are observed in their natural settings.

exo-system   In the ecological perspective on human development, the layer of the environment that does not directly contain the developing person but that affects the settings in which the person lives.

experience sampling method (ESM)   A method for collecting data about adolescents' emotional states, in which individuals are paged and asked to report on their mood and activity.

externalizing disorders   Psychosocial problems that are manifested in a turning of the symptoms outward, as in aggression or delinquency.

extrinsic motivation   Motivation based on the rewards one will receive for successful performance.

extrusion   The practice of separating children from their parents and requiring them to sleep in other households, part of the process of social redefinition at adolescence in many societies.

F

false-self behavior   Behavior that intentionally presents a false impression to others.

family systems theory   A perspective on family functioning that emphasizes interconnections among different family relationships (such as marital, parent–child, or sibling).

fear of failure   Fear of the consequences of failing in achievement situations.

feedback loop   A cycle through which two or more bodily functions respond to and regulate each other, such as that formed by the hypothalamus, the pituitary gland, and the gonads.

five-factor model   The theory that there are five basic dimensions to personality: extraversion, agreeableness, conscientiousness, neuroticism, and openness to experience.

formal operations   The fourth stage of cognitive development, according to Piaget, spanning the period from early adolescence through adulthood.

functional magnetic resonance imaging (fMRI)   A technique used to produce images of the brain, often while the subject is performing some sort of mental task.

future orientation   The extent to which an individual is able and inclined to think about the potential consequences of decisions and choices.

G

gangs   Organized peer groups of antisocial individuals.

gateway drugs   Drugs that, when used over time, lead to the use of other, more dangerous substances.

gender identity   The aspects of an individual's sense of self that concern masculinity and femininity.

gender intensification hypothesis   The idea that pressures to behave in sex-appropriate ways intensify during adolescence.

generation gap   The popular phrase for the alleged conflict between young people and adults over values and attitudes.

gifted students   Students who are unusually talented in some aspect of intellectual performance.

glands   Organs that stimulate particular parts of the body to respond in specific ways to particular hormones.

gonadotropin-releasing hormone (GnRH) neurons   Specialized neurons that are activated by certain pubertal hormones.

gonads   The glands that secrete sex hormones: in males, the testes; in females, the ovaries.

gonorrhea   A sexually transmitted infection caused by a bacterium.

H

health-compromising behaviors   Behaviors that place individuals at risk for health problems.

health-enhancing behaviors   Behaviors that lessen individuals' risk for health problems or that increase well-being.

herpes   A sexually transmitted infection caused by a virus.

HIV (human immunodeficiency virus)   The virus associated with AIDS.

homophobia   The unwarranted fear of homosexuals or homosexuality.

hormones   Highly specialized substances secreted by one or more endocrine glands.

hostile attributional bias   The tendency to interpret ambiguous interactions with others as deliberately hostile.

HPG (hypothalamic-pituitary-gonadal) axis   The neurophysiological pathway that involves the hypothalamus, pituitary gland, and gonads.

human papilloma virus   One of several viruses that causes a sexually transmitted disease.

hypothalamus   A part of the lower brain stem that controls the functioning of the pituitary gland.

I

iatrogenic effects   Unintended adverse consequences of a treatment or intervention.

identity   The domain of psychosocial development involving self-conceptions, self-esteem, and the sense of who one is.

identity diffusion (identity confusion)   The incoherent, disjointed, incomplete sense of self characteristic of not having resolved the crisis of identity.

identity foreclosure   The premature establishment of a sense of identity, before sufficient role experimentation has occurred.

identity versus identity diffusion   According to Erikson, the normative crisis characteristic of the fifth stage of psychosocial development, predominant during adolescence.

imaginary audience   The belief, often brought on by the heightened self-consciousness of early adolescence, that everyone is watching and evaluating one's behavior.

implicit personality theory   An intuitive understanding of human behavior and motivation that emerges during early adolescence.

indifferent parents   Parents who are characterized by low levels of both responsiveness and demandingness.

individuation   The progressive sharpening of one's sense of being an autonomous, independent person.

inductive reasoning   Reasoning that involves drawing an inference from the evidence that one has.

indulgent parents   Parents who are characterized by high responsiveness but low demandingness, and who are mainly concerned with the child's happiness.

information-processing perspective   A perspective on cognition that derives from the study of artificial intelligence and attempts to explain cognitive development in terms of the growth of specific components of the thinking process (for example, memory).

initiation ceremony   The formal induction of a young person into adulthood.

instrumental aggression   Aggressive behavior that is deliberate and planned.

internal working model   The implicit model of interpersonal relationships that an individual employs through life, believed to be shaped by early attachment experiences.

internalizing disorders   Psychosocial problems that are manifested in a turning of the symptoms inward, as in depression or anxiety.

intimacy   The psychosocial domain concerning the formation, maintenance, and termination of close relationships.

intimacy versus isolation   According to Erikson, the normative crisis characteristic of the sixth psychosocial stage of development, predominant during young adulthood.

intrinsic motivation   Motivation based on the pleasure one will experience from mastering a task.

inventionists   Theorists who argue that the period of adolescence is mainly a social invention.

J

junior high school   An educational institution designed during the early era of public secondary education, in which young adolescents are schooled separately from older adolescents.

justice orientation   In Gilligan's theory of moral development, a moral orientation that emphasizes fairness and objectivity.

juvenile offending   An externalizing problem that includes delinquency and criminal behavior.

juvenile justice system   A separate system of courts and related institutions developed to handle juvenile crime and delinquency.

L

late adolescence   The period spanning roughly ages 18–21, corresponding approximately to the college years.

learned helplessness   The acquired belief that an individual is not able to influence events through his or her own efforts or actions.

learning disability   A difficulty with academic tasks that cannot be traced to an emotional problem or sensory dysfunction.

leptin   A protein produced by fat cells that may play a role in the onset of puberty.

life-course-persistent offenders   Individuals who begin demonstrating antisocial or aggressive behavior during childhood and continue their antisocial behavior through adolescence and into adulthood.

limbic system   An area of the brain that plays an important role in emotional experience.

longitudinal study   A study following the same group of individuals over time.

long-term memory   The ability to recall something from a long time ago.

M

macro-system   In the ecological perspective on human development, the outermost layer of the environment, containing forces such as history and culture.

mainstreaming   The integration of adolescents who have educational handicaps into regular classrooms.

marginal man   Lewin's term that refers to the transitional nature of adolescence—poised on the margin of adulthood.

media practice model   A perspective on media use that emphasizes the fact that adolescents not only choose what media they are exposed to but also interpret the media in ways that shape their impact.

melatonin   A hormone secreted by the brain that contributes to sleepiness.

menarche   The time of first menstruation, one of the important changes to occur among females during puberty.

meso-system   In the ecological perspective on human development, the layer of the environment formed by the intersection of two or more immediate settings, as in the home–school linkage.

metacognition   The process of thinking about thinking itself.

micro-systems   In the ecological perspective on human development, the immediate settings in which adolescents develop, such as the family or the peer group.

middle adolescence   The period spanning roughly ages 15–18, corresponding approximately to the high school years.

middle school   An educational institution housing seventh- and eighth-grade students along with adolescents who are one or two years younger.

midlife crisis   A psychological crisis over identity believed to occur between the ages of 35 and 45, the age range of most adolescents' parents.

Monitoring the Future   An annual survey of a national sample of American eighth-, tenth-, and twelfth-graders, mainly known for its data on adolescent substance use.

multidimensional model of racial identity (MMRI)   Sellers's perspective on ethnic identity, which emphasizes three different phenomena: racial centrality (how important race is in defining individuals' identity), private regard (how individuals feel about being a member of their race), and public regard (how individuals think others feel about their race).

mutual role taking   In Selman's theory, the stage of social perspective taking during which the young adolescent can be an objective third party and can see how the thoughts or actions of one person can influence those of another.

myelination   The process through which brain circuits are insulated with myelin, which improves the efficiency of information processing.

N

National Assessment of Educational Progress (NAEP)   A periodic testing of American fourth-, eighth-, and twelfth-graders by the federal government, used to track achievement.

need for achievement   A need that influences the extent to which an individual strives for success in evaluative situations.

need for integration into adult society   According to Sullivan, the chief need of late adolescence.

need for intimacy   According to Sullivan, the chief interpersonal need of preadolescence.

needs for sexual contact and for intimacy with a peer of the other sex   According to Sullivan, the chief interpersonal needs of early adolescence.

negative affectivity   The presumed underlying cause of internalizing disorders, characterized by high levels of subjective distress.

negative identity   The selection of an identity that is obviously undesirable in the eyes of significant others and the broader community.

neuroendocrine   Hormonal activity in the brain and nervous system.

neurons   Nerve cells.

neurotransmitters   Chemical substances in the brain that carry electrical impulses across synapses.

nocturnal orgasms   In males, ejaculations that occur while they are asleep, sometimes referred to as "wet dreams."

O

occupational attainment   A measure of achievement based on the status or prestige of the job an individual holds.

oppositional-defiant disorder   A disorder of childhood and adolescence characterized by excessive anger, spite, and stubbornness.

orbitofrontal cortex   The region of the brain located directly behind the eyes, important for the evaluation of risk and reward.

organizational role of hormones   The process through which early exposure to hormones, especially prenatally, organizes the brain or other organs in anticipation of later changes in behavior or patterns of growth.

ovaries   The female gonads.

overt antisocial behavior   A type of antisocial behavior characterized by aggression toward others.

oxytocin   A hormone known to influence emotional bonding to others.

P

parental demandingness   According to Baumrind, one of the two important dimensions of parenting; demandingness refers to the degree to which the parent expects and insists on mature, responsible behavior from the child.

parental responsiveness   According to Baumrind, one of the two important dimensions of parenting; responsiveness refers to the degree to which the parent responds to the child's needs in an accepting, supportive manner.

participant observation   A research technique in which the researcher "infiltrates" a group of individuals in order to study their behavior and relationships.

particularistic norms   Guidelines for behavior that vary from one individual to another; more commonly found in less industrialized societies.

peak height velocity   The point at which the adolescent is growing most rapidly.

peer groups   Groups of individuals of approximately the same age.

permissive societies   Societies in which sexual activity during childhood and adolescence is not greatly restrained.

personal fable   An adolescent's belief that he or she is unique and therefore not subject to the rules that govern other people's behavior.

pheromones   A class of chemicals secreted by animals that stimulate certain behaviors in other members of the species.

Piagetian perspective   See *cognitive-developmental view*.

pituitary gland   One of the chief glands responsible for regulating levels of hormones in the body.

platonic relationships   Nonsexual relationships with individuals who might otherwise be romantic partners.

positive youth development   The goal of programs designed to facilitate healthy psychosocial development and not simply to deter problematic development.

positron emission tomography (PET)   A technique used to produce images of the brain, often while the subject is performing some sort of mental task; it is more invasive than fMRI.

possible selves   The various identities an adolescent might imagine for him- or herself.

postconventional moral reasoning   In Kohlberg's theory, the stage of moral development during which society's rules and conventions are seen as relative and subjective rather than as authoritative; also called principled moral reasoning.

preconventional moral reasoning   According to Kohlberg, the first level of moral development, which is typical of children and is characterized by reasoning that is based on the rewards and punishments associated with different courses of action.

prefrontal cortex   The part of the brain responsible for many higher-order cognitive skills, such as decision making and planning.

premature affluence   Having more income than one can manage maturely, especially during adolescence.

preoperational period   The second stage of cognitive development, according to Piaget, spanning roughly ages 2–5.

primary control strategies   Coping strategies in which an individual attempts to change the stressor.

primary prevention   An approach to health promotion that emphasizes teaching all adolescents certain behaviors, values, and information.

problem behavior syndrome   The covariation among various types of externalizing disorders believed to result from an underlying trait of unconventionality.

propositional logic   An abstract system of logic that forms the basis for formal operational thinking.

protective factors   Factors that lessen individual vulnerability to harm.

pseudointimacy   Superficial intimacy characteristic of relationships between individuals who are not emotionally mature.

psychological control   Parenting that attempts to control the adolescent's emotions and opinions.

psychopaths   Individuals who are not only antisocial but manipulative, superficially charming, impulsive, and indifferent to the feelings of others.

psychosocial   Referring to aspects of development that are both psychological and social in nature, such as developing a sense of identity or sexuality.

psychosocial moratorium   A period during which individuals are free from excessive obligations and responsibilities, and can therefore experiment with different roles and personalities.

puberty   The biological changes of adolescence leading to reproductive maturity.

Q

quinceañera   An elaborate sort of "coming-out" celebration for adolescent girls that is practiced in many Latino communities.

R

racial socialization   The process through which individuals develop an understanding of their racial or ethnic background.

reactive aggression   Aggressive behavior that is unplanned and impulsive.

reference group   A group against which an individual compares him- or herself.

rejection sensitivity   Heightened vulnerability to being rejected by others.

relational aggression   Acts intended to harm another through the manipulation of his or her relationships with others, as in malicious gossip.

resilience   The ability of an individual to continue to function competently in the face of adversity or stress.

restrictive societies   Societies in which adolescents are pressured to refrain from sexual activity until they have married or undergone a formal rite of passage into adulthood.

reverse causation   When the correlation between two things is due not to the first thing causing the second, but to the second causing the first.

risk factors   Factors that increase individual vulnerability to harm.

rite of passage   A ceremony or ritual marking an individual's transition from one social status to another, especially marking the young person's transition into adulthood.

routine activity theory   A perspective on adolescence that views unstructured, unsupervised time with peers as a main cause of misbehavior.

S

scaffolding   Structuring a learning situation so that it is just within the reach of the student.

scarification   The intentional creation of scars on some part or parts of the body, often done as part of an initiation ceremony.

school performance   A measure of achievement based on an individual's grades in school.

school-based health centers   A relatively new approach to the delivery of health care services to adolescents, that places health care providers in offices located in or adjacent to schools.

schools within schools   Subdivisions of the student body within large schools created to foster feelings of belongingness.

school vouchers   Government-subsidized vouchers that can be used for private school tuition.

secondary control strategies   Coping strategies that involve attempts by the individual to adapt to the stressor.

secondary education   The system of middle schools, junior high schools, and high schools.

secondary prevention   An approach to health promotion that is specifically aimed at adolescents believed to be at high risk for a particular disease or disturbance.

secondary sex characteristics   The manifestations of sexual maturation at puberty, including the development of breasts, the growth of facial and body hair, and changes in the voice.

secular trend   The tendency, over the past two centuries, for individuals to be larger in stature and to reach puberty earlier, primarily because of improvements in health and nutrition.

secure attachment   A healthy attachment between infant and caregiver, characterized by trust.

selective attention   The process through which we focus on one stimulus while tuning out another.

selective serotonin reuptake inhibitors (SSRIs)   A class of antidepressant medications that have proven to be effective with adolescents suffering from internalizing problems, such as depression.

self-conceptions   The collection of traits and attributes that individuals use to describe or characterize themselves.

self-consciousness   The degree to which an individual is preoccupied with his or her self-image.

self-directed search   A personality inventory developed by Holland and used to help individuals better understand their vocational interests.

self-efficacy   The sense that an individual has some control over his or her life.

self-esteem   The degree to which individuals feel positively or negatively about themselves.

self-fulfilling prophecy   The idea that individuals' behavior is influenced by others' expectations for them.

self-handicapping   Deliberately behaving in ways that will likely interfere with doing well, in order to have an excuse for failing.

self-image stability   The degree to which an individual's self-image changes from day to day.

semirestrictive societies   Societies in which pressures against adolescent sexual activity exist but are not vigilantly enforced.

sensation seeking   The enjoyment of novel and intense experiences.

sense of identity   The extent to which individuals feel secure about who they are and who they are becoming.

sensorimotor period   The first stage of cognitive development, according to Piaget, spanning the period roughly between birth and age 2.

serial monogamy   Having a series of sexual relationships over time in which one is monogamous within each relationship.

service learning   Structured educational experiences that involve volunteering in the community.

set point   A physiological level or setting (of a specific hormone, for example) that the body attempts to maintain through a self-regulating system.

sex cleavage   The separation of girls and boys into different cliques, common during late childhood and early adolescence.

sex-role behavior   Behavior that is consistent with prevailing expectations for how individuals of a given sex are to behave.

sexual orientation   An individual's orientation toward same- or opposite-sex sex partners.

sexual socialization   The process through which adolescents are exposed to and educated about sexuality.

sexuality   The psychosocial domain concerning the development and expression of sexual feelings.

sexually transmitted disease (STD)   Any of a group of infections—including gonorrhea, herpes, chlamydia, and AIDS—passed on through sexual contact.

sexual minority youth   Gay, lesbian, and bisexual youth.

sibling deidentification   The process through which siblings deliberately try to be different from each other.

sibling rivalry   Competition between siblings, often for parental attention.

social capital   The interpersonal resources available to an adolescent or family.

social cognition   The aspect of cognition that concerns thinking about other people, about interpersonal relationships, and about social institutions.

social control theory   A theory of delinquency that links deviance with the absence of bonds to society's main institutions.

social conventions   The norms that govern everyday behavior in social situations.

social perspective taking   The ability to view events from the perspective of others.

social promotion   The practice of promoting students from one grade to the next automatically, regardless of their school performance.

social redefinition   The process through which an individual's position or status is redefined by society.

social support   The extent to which an individual receives emotional or instrumental assistance from his or her social network.

specification   According to Super, the stage during which individuals, typically ages 18–21, first begin to consider narrowly defined occupational pursuits.

spurious correlation   When the correlation between two things is due to the fact that each of them is correlated with some third factor.

standards-based reform   Policies designed to improve achievement by holding schools and students to a predetermined set of standards measured by achievement tests.

status offense   A violation of the law that pertains to minors but not to adults.

stereotype threat   The harmful effect that exposure to stereotypes about ethnic or sex differences in ability has on student performance.

substance abuse   The misuse of alcohol or other drugs to a degree that causes problems in the individual's life.

substance dependence   The misuse of alcohol or other drugs to a degree that causes physical addiction.

suicidal ideation   Thinking about ending one's life.

synaptic pruning   The process through which unnecessary connections between neurons are eliminated, improving the efficiency of information processing.

T

Tanner stages   A widely used system to describe the five stages of pubertal development.

teenager   A term popularized about 50 years ago to refer to young people; it connoted a more frivolous and lighthearted image than did "adolescent."

testes   The male gonads.

testosterone   One of the sex hormones secreted by the gonads, found in both sexes but in higher levels among males than females.

tracking   The grouping of students, according to ability, into different levels of classes within the same school grade.

U

underachievers   Individuals whose actual school performance is lower than what would be expected on the basis of objective measures of their aptitude or intelligence.

universalistic norms   Guidelines for behavior that apply to all members of a community; more common in industrialized societies.

V

value autonomy   The establishment of an independent set of values and beliefs.

uses and gratifications approach   A perspective on media use that emphasizes the active role users play in selecting the media to which they are exposed.

ventromedial prefontal cortex   The lower and central area at the front of the brain, important for gut-level decision making.

viral marketing   A way of promoting products or services by encouraging individuals to pass information on to others.

W

work values   The particular sorts of rewards one looks for in a job (extrinsic, intrinsic, social, altruistic, security, influence, leisure).

working memory   That aspect of memory in which information is held for a short time while a problem is being solved.

Y

youth   Today, a term used to refer to individuals ages 18–22; it once referred to individuals ages of 12–24.

youth apprenticeship   A structured, work-based learning experience that places an adolescent under the supervision of a skilled adult.

Z

zero tolerance   A get-tough approach to adolescent misbehavior that responds seriously or excessively to the first infraction.

zone of proximal development   In Vygotsky's theory, the level of challenge that is still within the individual's reach but that forces an individual to develop more advanced skills.

References

Abecassis, M., Hartup, W. W., Haselager, G. T., Scholte, R. J., & Van Lieshout, C. M. (2002). Mutual antipathies and their significance in middle childhood and adolescence. *Child Development, 73*(5), 1543–1556.

Ablard, K., & Mills, C. (1996). Implicit theories of intelligence and self-perceptions of academically talented adolescents and children. *Journal of Youth and Adolescence, 25,* 137–148.

Abma, J., Driscoll, A., & Moore, K. (1998). Young women's degree of control over first intercourse: an exploratory analysis. *Family Planning Perspectives, 30,* 12–18.

Abrahamson, A., Baker, L. A., & Caspi, A. (2002). Rebellious teens? Genetic and environmental influences on the social attitudes of adolescents. *Journal of Personality and Social Psychology, 83*(6), 1392–1408.

Abrams, L., & Stormer, C. (2002). Sociocultural variations in the body image perceptions of urban adolescent females. *Journal of Youth and Adolescence, 31*(6), 443–450.

Achenbach, T., & Edelbrock, C. (1987). *The manual for the Youth Self-Report and Profile.* Burlington: University of Vermont.

Adalbjarnardottir, S., & Hafsteinsson, L. G. (2001). Adolescents' perceived parenting styles and their substance use: Concurrent and longitudinal analyses. *Journal of Research on Adolescence, 11*(4), 401–423.

Adam, E., & Chase-Lansdale, P. (2002). Home sweet home(s): Parental separations, residential moves, and adjustment problems in low-income adolescent girls. *Developmental Psychology, 38*(5), 792–805.

Adamczyk-Robinette, S. L., Fletcher, A. C., & Wright, K. (2002). Understanding the authoritative parenting–early adolescent tobacco use link: The mediating role of peer tobacco use. *Journal of Youth and Adolescence, 31*(4), 311–318.

Adams, G., & Fitch, S. (1982). Ego stage and identity status development: A cross-sequential analysis. *Journal of Personality and Social Psychology, 43,* 574–583.

Adams, G., & Jones, R. (1983). Female adolescents' identity development: Age comparisons and perceived child-rearing experience. *Developmental Psychology, 19,* 249–256.

Adams, G., Gullotta, T., & Montemayor, R. (Eds.). (1992). *Adolescent identity formation.* Newbury Park, CA: Sage.

Adams, R., & Laursen, B. (2001). The organization and dynamics of adolescent conflict with parents and friends. *Journal of Marriage and the Family, 63*(1), 97–110.

Adams, R. E., Bukowski, W. M., & Bagwell, C. (2005). Stability of aggression during early adolescence as moderated by reciprocated

friendship status and friend's aggression. *International Journal of Behavioral Development, 29,* 139.

Adan, A., & Felner, R. (1995). Ecological congruence and adaptation of minority youth during the transition to college. *Journal of Community Psychology, 23,* 256–269.

Adegoke, A. (1993). The experience of spermarche (the age of onset of sperm emission) among selected adolescent boys in Nigeria. *Journal of Youth and Adolescence, 22,* 201–209.

Adelson, J. (1972). The political imagination of the young adolescent. In J. Kagan & R. Coles (Eds.), *Twelve to sixteen: Early adolescence.* New York: Norton.

Adler, N., Boyce, T., Chesney, M., Cohen, S., Folkman, S., Kahn, R., & Syme, S. L. (1994). Socioeconomic status and health: The challenge of the gradient. *American Psychologist, 49,* 15–24.

Adler, N. E., Ozer, E. J., & Tschann, J. (2003). Abortion among adolescents. *American Psychologist, 58,* 211–217.

Agnew, R., & Brezina, T. (1997). Relational problems with peers, gender, and delinquency. *Youth & Society, 29,* 84–111.

Agras, W. S., Schneider, J., Arnow, B., Raeburn, S., and Telch, C. (1989). Cognitive-behavioral and response-prevention treatments for bulimia nervosa. *Journal of Consulting and Clinical Psychology, 57,* 215–221.

Aguilar, B., Sroufe, L. A., Egeland, B., & Carlson, E. (2000). Distinguishing the early onset/persistent and adolescence-onset antisocial behavior types: From birth to 16 years. *Development and Psychopathology, 12,* 109–132.

Ahn, N. (1994). Teenage childbearing and high school completion: Accounting for individual heterogeneity. *Family Planning Perspectives, 26,* 17–21.

Ainsworth, J. W. (2002). Why does it take a village? The mediation of neighborhood effects on educational achievement. *Social Forces, 81*(1), 117–152.

Ainsworth, M., Blehar, M., Waters, E., & Wall, S. (1978). *Patterns of attachment.* Hillsdale, NJ: Erlbaum.

Ainsworth-Darnell, J., & Downey, D. (1998). Assessing the oppositional culture explanation for racial/ethnic differences in school performance. *American Sociological Review, 63,* 536–553.

Aitken, D., & Chaplin, J. (1990). Sex miseducation. *Family Therapy Networker, 14,* 24–25.

Akom, A. A. (2003). Reexamining resistance as oppositional behavior: The nation of Islam and the creation of a black achievement ideology. *Sociology of Education, 76*(4), 305–325.

Alan Guttmacher Institute. (1994). *Sex and America's teenagers.* New York: Author.

Alan Guttmacher Institute (2004). *U.S. teenage pregnancy statistics: Overall trends, trends by race and ethnicity and state-by-state information.* New York: Author.

Alasker, F., & Flammer, A. (1999). Time use by adolescents in an international perspective. II: The case of necessary activities. In F. Alasker & A. Flammer (Eds.), *The adolescent experience: European and American adolescents in the 1990s,* pp. 61–83. Hillsdale, NJ: Erlbaum.

Alasker, F., & Olweus, D. (1992). Stability of global self-evaluations in early adolescence: A cohort longitudinal study. *Journal of Research on Adolescence, 1,* 123–145.

Albers, A. B., & Biener, L. (2003). Adolescent participation in tobacco promotions: The role of psychosocial factors. *Pediatrics, 111*(2), 402–406.

Albrecht, C., & Teachman, J. D. (2003). Childhood living arrangements and the risk of premarital intercourse. *Journal of Family Influence, 24,* 867–894.

Alexander, C., Somerfield, M., Ensminger, M., Johnson, K., & Kim, Y. (1993). Consistency of adolescents' self-report of sexual behavior in a longitudinal study. *Journal of Youth and Adolescence, 22,* 455–471.

Alexander, K., & Cook, M. (1982). Curricula and coursework: A surprise ending to a familiar story. *American Sociological Review, 47,* 626–640.

Alexander, K., & Eckland, B. (1975). School experience and status attainment. In S. Dragastin & G. Elder, Jr. (Eds.), *Adolescence in the life cycle.* Washington, DC: Hemisphere.

Alexander, K., Natriello, G., & Pallas, A. (1985). For whom the cognitive bell tolls: The impact of dropping out on cognitive performance. *American Sociological Review, 50,* 409–420.

Alexander, K. L., Entwisle, D. R., & Kabbani, N. S. (2001). The dropout process in life course perspective: Early risk factors at home and school. *Teachers College Record, 103*(5), 760–822.

Alfieri, T., Ruble, D., & Higgins, E. (1996). Gender stereotypes during adolescence: Developmental changes and the transition to junior high school. *Developmental Psychology, 32,* 1129–1137.

Allen, J., Hauser, S., Bell, K., & O'Connor, T. (1994). Longitudinal assessment of autonomy and relatedness in adolescent–family interactions as predictors of adolescent ego development and self-esteem. *Child Development, 65,* 179–194.

Allen, J., Hauser, S., Eickholt, C., Bell, K., & O'Connor, T. (1994). Autonomy and relatedness in family interactions as predictors of expressions of negative adolescent affect. *Journal of Research on Adolescence, 4,* 535–552.

Allen, J., Hauser, S., O'Connor, T., & Bell, K. (2002). Prediction of peer-rated adult hostility from autonomy struggles in adolescent-family interactions. *Development and Psychopathology, 14,* 123–137.

Allen, J., Hauser, S., O'Connor, T., Bell, K., & Eickholt, C. (1996). The connection of observed hostile family conflict to adolescents' developing autonomy and relatedness with parents. *Development and Psychopathology, 8,* 425–442.

Allen, J., & Land, D. (1999). Attachment in adolescence. In J. Cassidy & P. Shaver (Eds.), *Handbook of attachment theory and research.* New York: Guilford Press.

Allen, J., & McElhaney, K. (March, 2000). Autonomy in discussions vs. autonomy in decision-making as predictors of developing close friendship competence. Paper presented at the Biennial Meetings of the Society for Research on Adolescence, Chicago.

Allen, J., McElhaney, K., Kuperminc, G., & Jodl, K. (2004). Stability and change in attachment security across adolescence. *Child Development, 75,* 1792–1805.

Allen, J., McElhaney, K., Land, D., Kuperminc, G., Moore, C., O'Beime-Kelly, H., & Kilmer, S. (2003). A secure base in adolescence: Markers of attachment security in the mother–adolescent relationship. *Child Development, 74,* 292–307.

Allen, J., & Philliber, S. (2001). Who benefits most from a broadly targeted prevention program? Differential efficacy across populations in the Teen Outreach program. *Journal of Community Psychology, 29*(6), 637–655.

Allen, J., Philliber, S., Herrling, S., & Kuperminc, G. (1997). Preventing teen pregnancy and academic failure: Experimental evaluation of a developmentally based approach. *Child Development, 64,* 729–742.

Allen, J., Porter, M., McFarland, F., Marsh, P., & McElhaney, K. (2005). The two faces of adolescents' success with peers: Adolescent popularity, social adaptation, and deviant behavior. *Child Development, 76,* 747–760.

Allen, R., & Mirabell, J. (1990, May). Shorter subjective sleep of high school students from early compared to late starting schools. Paper presented at the second meeting of the Society for Research on Biological Rhythms, Jacksonville, FL.

Alleyne, S. I., & LaPoint, V. (2004). Obesity among black adolescent girls: Genetic, psychosocial, and cultural influences. *Journal of Black Psychology, 30,* 344–365.

Allgood-Merten, B., Lewinsohn, P., & Hops, H. (1990). Sex differences and adolescent depression. *Journal of Abnormal Psychology, 99,* 55–63.

Allgood-Merten, B., & Stockard, J. (1991). Sex role identity and self-esteem: A comparison of children and adolescents. *Sex Roles, 25,* 129–140.

Allison, K., Crawford, I., Leone, P., Trickett, E., Perez-Febles, A., Burton, L., & Le Blanc, R. (1999). Adolescent substance use: Preliminary examinations of school and neighborhood context. *American Journal of Community Psychology, 27,* 111–141.

Allison, P., & Furstenberg, F., Jr. (1989). How marital dissolution affects children: Variations by age and sex. *Developmental Psychology, 25,* 540–549.

Althaus, F. (1997). Female circumcision: Rite of passage or violation of rights? *International Family Planning Perspectives, 23,* 130–133.

Alva, S. (1993). Differential patterns of achievement among Asian-American adolescents. *Journal of Youth and Adolescence, 22,* 407–423.

Amato, P., & Booth, A. (1996). A prospective study of divorce and parent–child relationships. *Journal of Marriage and the Family, 58,* 356–365.

Amato, P., & Keith, B. (1991a). Parental divorce and the well-being of children: A meta-analysis. *Psychological Bulletin, 110,* 26–46.

Amato, P., & Keith, B. (1991b). Separation from a parent during childhood and adult socioeconomic attainment. *Social Forces, 70,* 187–206.

Amato, P., & Rezac, S. (1994). Contact with nonresidential parents, interparental conflict, and children's behavior. *Journal of Family Issues, 15,* 191–207.

Amato, P. R., & Fowler, F. (2002). Parenting practices, child adjustment, and family diversity. *Journal of Marriage and the Family, 64*(3), 703–716.

Amato, P. R., & Sobolewski, J. M. (2001). The effects of divorce and marital discord on adult children's psychological well being. *American Sociological Review, 66*(6), 900–921.

American Psychiatric Association. (1994). *Diagnostic and statistical manual of the American Psychiatric Association (DSM-IV).* Washington, DC: Author.

Anastasi, A. (1988). *Psychological testing,* 6th ed. New York: Macmillan.

Anderman, E. (2002). School effects on psychological outcomes during adolescence. *Journal of Educational Psychology, 94*(4), 795–809.

Anderman, E., & Midgley, C. (1996, March). Changes in achievement goal orientations after the transition to middle school. Paper presented at the biennial meetings of the Society for Research on Adolescence, Boston.

Anderson, C. A., Carnagey, N. L., & Eubanks, J. (2003). Exposure to violent media: The effects of songs with violent lyrics on aggressive thoughts and feelings. *Journal of Personality and Social Psychology, 84,* 960–971.

Anderson, E. (1992, March). Consistency of parenting in stepfather families. Paper presented at the biennial meetings of the Society for Research on Adolescence, Washington, DC.

Anderson, E., Hetherington, E. M., & Clingempeel, W. (1989). Transformations in family relations at puberty: Effects of family context. *Journal of Early Adolescence, 9,* 310–334.

Anderson, E., Hetherington, E. M., Reiss, D., & Howe, G. (1994). Parents' nonshared treatment of siblings and the development of social competence during adolescence. *Journal of Family Psychology, 8,* 303–320.

Anderson, M., Kaufman, J., Simon, T. R., Barrios, L., Paulozzi, L., Ryan, G., et al. (2001). School-associated violent deaths in the United States, 1994–1999. *Journal of the American Medical Association, 286,* 2695–2702.

Anderson, S. E., Dallal, G. E., & Must, A. (2003). Relative weight and race influence average age at menarche: Results from two nationally representative surveys of U.S. girls studied 25 years apart. *Pediatrics, 111,* 844–891.

Andersson, T., & Magnusson, D. (1990). Biological maturation in adolescence and the development of drinking habits and alcohol abuse among young males: A prospective longitudinal study. *Journal of Youth and Adolescence, 19,* 33–42.

Ando, M., Asakura, T., & Simons-Morton, B. (2005). Psychosocial influences on physical, verbal, and indirect bullying among Japanese early adolescents. *Journal of Early Adolescence 25,* 268–297.

Andrews, J., Alpert, A., Hops, H., & Davis, B. (1996, March). The relation of competence in middle adolescence to depression and antisocial behavior: A multi-method assessment. Paper presented at the biennial meetings of the Society for Research on Adolescence, Boston.

Andrews, J., Hops, H., Davis, B., & Duncan, S. (1995, March). The structure of competence among middle adolescents: A multi-method assessment. Paper presented at the biennial meetings of the Society for Research in Child Development, Indianapolis.

Aneshensel, C., Becerra, R., Fielder, E., & Schuler, R. (1990). Onset of fertility-related events during adolescence: A prospective comparison of Mexican American and Non-Hispanic White females. *American Journal of Public Health, 80,* 959–963.

Angold, A., Costello, E. J., & Worthman, C. (1998). Puberty and depression: The roles of age, pubertal status, and pubertal timing. *Psychological Medicine, 28,* 51–61.

Apfel, N., & Seitz, V. (1997). The firstborn sons of African American teen mothers: Perspectives on risk and resilience. In S. Luthar, J. Burack, D. Cicchetti, & J. Weisz (Eds.), *Developmental psychopathology: Perspectives on risk and disorder,* pp. 484–506. New York: Cambridge University Press.

Apter, T. (1990). *Altered loves: Mothers and daughters during adolescence.* New York: St. Martin's Press.

Aquilino, W. (1991). Family structure and home-leaving: A further specification of the relationship. *Journal of Marriage and the Family, 53,* 999–1010.

Aquilino, W. S. (2005). Impact of family structure on parental attitudes toward the economic support of adult children over the transition to adulthood. *Journal of Family Influence, 26,* 143–167.

Aquilino, W. S., & Supple, A. J. (2001). Long-term effects of parenting practices during adolescence on well-being: Outcomes in young adulthood. *Journal of Family Issues, 22*(3), 289–308.

Arbeton, A., Eccles, J., & Harold, R. (1994, February). Parents' perceptions of their children's competence: The role of parent attributions. Paper presented at the biennial meetings of the Society for Research on Adolescence, San Diego.

Archer, S. (1982). The lower age boundaries of identity development. *Child Development, 53,* 1551–1556.

Archibald, A., Linver, M., Graber, J., & Brooks-Gunn, J. (2002). Parent–adolescent relationships and girls' unhealthy eating: Testing reciprocal effects. *Journal of Research on Adolescence, 12*(4), 451–461.

Archibald, A., Graber, J., & Brooks-Gunn, J. (1999). Associations among parent–adolescent relationships, pubertal growth, dieting, and body image in young adolescent girls: A short-term longitudinal study. *Journal of Research on Adolescence, 9*(4), 395–415.

Ardelt, M., & Day, L. (2002). Parents, siblings, and peers: Close social relationships and adolescent deviance. *Journal of Early Adolescence, 22*(3), 310–349.

Armor, D. (1972). School and family effects on black and white achievement: A reexamination of the USOE data. In F. Mosteller & D. Moynihan (Eds.), *On equality of educational opportunity.* New York: Random House.

Armsden, G., & Greenberg, M. (1987). The inventory of parent and peer attachment: Individual differences and their relationship to psychological well-being in adolescence. *Journal of Youth and Adolescence, 16,* 427–453.

Armstrong, T. D., & Costello, E. (2002). Community studies on adolescent substance use, abuse, or dependence and psychiatric comorbidity. *Journal of Consulting and Clinical Psychology, 70*(6), 1224–1239.

Arnett, J. (1994). Are college students adults? Their conceptions of the transition to adulthood. *Journal of Adult Development, 1,* 213–224.

Arnett, J. (1996). *Metalheads.* Boulder, CO: Westview Press.

Arnett, J. (1998). Learning to stand alone: The contemporary American transition to adulthood in cultural and historical context. *Human Development, 41,* 295–315.

Arnett, J. (2000). Emerging adulthood: A theory of development from the late teens through the twenties. *American Psychologist, 55,* 469–480.

Arnett, J. (2001). Adolescents' responses to cigarette advertisements for five "youth brands" and one "adult brand." *Journal of Research on Adolescence, 11*(4), 425–443.

Arnett, J. (2002). Adolescents in Western countries on the threshold of the 21st century. In B. Brown, R. Larson, & T. Saraswathi (Eds.), *The world's youth: Adolescence in eight regions of the globe.* New York: Cambridge University Press.

Arnett, J. (2004). *Emerging adulthood: The winding road from the late teens through the twenties.* New York: Oxford University Press.

Arnett, J., & Balle-Jensen, L. (1993). Cultural bases of risk behavior: Danish adolescents. *Child Development, 64,* 1842–1855.

Aro, H., & Taipale, V. (1987). The impact of timing of puberty on psychosomatic symptoms among fourteen- to sixteen-year-old Finnish girls. *Child Development, 58,* 261–268.

Arseneault, L., Tremblay, R. E., Boulerice, B., & Saucier, J. (2002). Obstetrical complications and violent delinquency: Testing two developmental pathways. *Child Development, 73*(2), 496–508.

Arum, R., & Hout, M. (1998). The early returns: The transition from school to work in the United States. In Y. Shavit & W. Mueller (Eds.), *From school to work: A comparative study of educational qualifications and occupational destinations,* pp. 471–510. Oxford: Clarendon Press.

Arunkumar, R., Midgley, C., & Urdan, T. (1999). Perceiving high or low home–school dissonance: Longitudinal effects on adolescent emotional and academic well-being. *Journal of Research on Adolescence, 9,* 441–466.

Ary, D., Duncan, T., Biglan, A., Metzler, C., Noell, J., & Smolkowski, K. (1999). Development of adolescent problem behavior. *Journal of Abnormal Child Psychology, 27,* 141–150.

Asakawa, K., & Csikszentmihalyi, M. (1998). The quality of experience of Asian American adolescents in academic activities: An exploration of educational achievement. *Journal of Research on Adolescence, 8,* 241–262.

Asakawa, K., & Csikszentmihalyi, M. (2000). Feelings of connectedness and internalization of values in Asian American adolescents. *Journal of Youth and Adolescence, 29*(2), 121–145.

Aseltine, R., Jr., & Gore, S. (1994, February). The occurrence and co-occurrence of affective disorder and substance abuse during the transition to adulthood. Paper presented at the biennial meetings of the Society for Research on Adolescence, San Diego.

Aseltine, R., Jr., Gore, S., & Colten, M. (1998). The co-occurrence of depression and substance abuse in late adolescence. *Development & Psychopathology, 10,* 549–570.

Asher, S., Parker, J., & Walker, D. (1996). Distinguishing friendship from acceptance: Implications for intervention and assessment. In W. Bukowski, A. Newcomb, & W. Hartup (Eds.), *The company they keep: Friendship in childhood and adolescence,* pp. 366–405. New York: Cambridge University Press.

Asmussen, L., & Larson, R. (1991). The quality of family time among young adolescents in single-parent and married-parent families. *Journal of Marriage and the Family, 53,* 1021–1030.

Astin, H. (1984). The meaning of work in women's lives: A sociopsychological model of career choice and work behavior. *Counseling Psychologist, 12,* 117–126.

Astone, N., & McLanahan, S. (1991). Family structure, parental practices, and high school completion. *American Sociological Review, 56,* 309–320.

Astor, R. (1994). Children's moral reasoning about family and peer violence: The role of provocation and retribution. *Child Development, 65,* 1054–1067.

Atkins, R., Hart, D., & Donnelly, T. M. (2005). The association of childhood personality type with volunteering during adolescence. *Merrill-Palmer Quarterly, 2,* 145–162.

Attie, I., & Brooks-Gunn, J. (1989). The development of eating problems in adolescent girls: A longitudinal study. *Developmental Psychology, 25,* 70–79.

Aunola, K., Stattin, H., & Nurmi, J.-E. (2000). Parenting styles and adolescents' achievement strategies. *Journal of Adolescence, 23*(2), 205–222.

Austin, S. B., & Gortmaker, S. L. (2001). Dieting and smoking initiation in early adolescent girls and boys: A prospective study. *American Journal of Public Health, 91*(3), 446–450.

Avenevoli, S., & Steinberg, L. (2001). The continuity of depression across the adolescent transition. In H. Reese & R. Kail (Eds.), *Advances in child development and behavior,* Vol. 28, pp. 139–173. New York: Academic Press.

Averett, S. L., Rees, D. I., & Argys, L. M. (2002). The impact of government policies and neighborhood characteristics on teenage sexual activity and contraceptive use. *American Journal of Public Health, 92*(11), 1773–1778.

Ayalon, H. (1994). Monopolizing knowledge? The ethnic composition and curriculum of high schools. Paper presented at the biennial meetings of the Society for Research on Adolescence, Boston. *Sociology of Education, 67,* 264–278.

Babalola, S. (2004). Perceived peer behavior and the timing of sexual debut in Rwanda: A survival analysis of youth data. *Journal of Youth and Adolescence, 33,* 353–363.

Bachman, J. (1983, Summer). Premature affluence: Do high school students earn too much? *Economic Outlook USA,* 64–67.

Bachman, J., Johnston, L., & O'Malley, P. (1998). Explaining recent increases in students' marijuana use: Impacts of perceived risks and disapproval, 1976 through 1996. *American Journal of Public Health, 88,* 887–892.

Bachman, J., & O'Malley, P. (1986). Self-concepts, self-esteem, and educational experiences: The frog pond revisited (again). *Journal of Personality and Social Psychology, 50,* 35–46.

Bachman, J., & Schulenberg, J. (1993). How part-time work intensity relates to drug use, problem behavior, time use, and satisfaction among high school seniors: Are these consequences or merely correlates? *Developmental Psychology, 29,* 220–235.

Baer, J. (2002). Is family cohesion a risk or protective factor during adolescent development? *Journal of Marriage and the Family, 64*(3), 668–675.

Bagwell, C., Newcomb, A., & Bukowski, W. (1998). Preadolescent friendship and peer rejection as predictors of adult adjustment. *Child Development, 69,* 140–153.

Bahr, S., Maughan, S., Marcos, A., & Li, B. (1998). Family, religiosity, and the risk of adolescent drug use. *Journal of Marriage and the Family, 60,* 979–992.

Bailey, P. E., Bruno, Z. V., Bezerra, M. F., Queiroz, I., Oliveira, C. M., & Chen-Mok, M. (2001). Adolescent pregnancy 1 year later: The effects of abortion vs. motherhood in Northeast Brazil. *Journal of Adolescent Health, 29*(3), 223–232.

Bakan, D. (1972). Adolescence in America: From idea to social fact. In J. Kagan & R. Coles (Eds.), *Twelve to sixteen: Early adolescence.* New York: Norton.

Baker, D., & Stevenson, D. (1986). Mothers' strategies for school achievement: Managing the transition to high school. *Sociology of Education, 59,* 156–167.

Baker, L., & Brown, A. (1984). Metacognitive skills and reading. In P. Pearson (Ed.), *Handbook of reading research,* Part 2. New York: Longman.

Baker, M., Milich, R., & Manolis, M. (1996). Peer interactions of dysphoric adolescents. *Journal of Abnormal Child Psychology, 24,* 241–255.

Bakken, L., & Romig, C. (1992, March). The relationship of intimacy and identity development in middle adolescents. Paper presented at the biennial meetings of the Society for Research on Adolescence, Washington, DC.

Ball, J., Armistead, L., & Austin, B. (2003). The relationship between religiosity and adjustment among African American, female, urban adolescents. *Journal of Adolescence, 26,* 431–446.

Bandura, A., & Walters, R. (1959). *Adolescent aggression.* New York: Ronald Press.

Bandura, A., Barbaranelli, C., Caprara, G., & Pastorelli, C. (1996). Multifaceted impact of self-efficacy beliefs on adcademic functioning. *Child Development, 67,* 1206–1222.

Bank, L., Burraston, B., & Snyder, J. (2004). Sibling conflict and ineffective parenting as predictors of adolescent boys' antisocial behavior and peer difficulties: Additive and interactional effects. *Journal of Research on Adolescence, 14,* 99–125.

Bank, L., Marlowe, J., Reid, J., Patterson, G., & Weinrott, M. (1991). A comparative evaluation of parent-training interventions for families of chronic delinquents. *Journal of Abnormal Child Psychology, 19,* 15–33.

Bank, L., Reid, J., & Greenley, K. (1994, February). Middle childhood predictors of adolescent and early adult aggression. Paper presented at the biennial meetings of the Society for Research on Adolescence, San Diego.

Bankston, C., III., & Caldas, S. (1996). Majority African American schools and social injustice: The influence of de facto segregation on academic achievement. *Social Forces, 75,* 535–555.

Barbarin, O. (1993). Coping and resilience: Exploring the inner lives of African-American children. *Journal of Black Psychology, 19,* 478–492.

Barbarin, O., & Soler, R. (1993). Behavioral, emotional, and academic adjustment in a national probability sample of African-American children. *Journal of Black Psychology, 19,* 423–446.

Barber, B. (1994). Cultural, family, and personal contexts of parent-adolescent conflict. *Journal of Marriage and the Family, 56,* 375–386.

Barber, B. (1996). Parental psychological control: Revisiting a neglected construct. *Child Development, 67,* 3296–3319.

Barber, B., & Eccles, J. (1992). Long-term influence of divorce and single parenting on adolescent family- and work-related values, behaviors, and aspirations. *Psychological Bulletin, 111,* 108–126.

Barber, B., Eccles, J., & Stone, M. (2001). Whatever happened to the jock, the brain, and the princess? Young adult pathways linked to adolescent activity involvement and social identity. *Journal of Adolescent Research, 16*(5), 429–455.

Barber, B., & Olsen, J. (1997). Socialization in context: Connection, regulation, and autonomy in the family, school, neighborhood, and with peers. *Journal of Adolescent Research, 12,* 287–315.

Barber, B., & Olsen, J. (2004). Assessing the transitions to middle and high school. *Journal of Adolescent Research, 19,* 3–30.

Barber, B., Stone, M., Hunt, J., & Eccles, J. (2005). Benefits of activity participation: The roles of identity affirmation and peer norm sharing. In J. Mahoney, R. Larson, & J. Eccles (Eds.), *Organized activities as contexts of development,* pp. 185–210. Hillsdale, NJ: Erlbaum.

Bardone, A., Moffitt, T., Caspi, A., Dickson, N., & Silva, P. (1996). Adult mental health and social outcomes of adolescent girtls with depression and conduct disorder. *Development and Psychopathology, 8,* 811–829.

Barenboim, C. (1981). The development of person perception in childhood and adolescence: From behavioral comparisons to psychological constructs to psychological comparisons. *Child Development, 52,* 129–144.

Barker, R., & Gump, P. (1964). *Big school, small school: High school size and student behavior.* Stanford, CA: Stanford University Press.

Barnes, E. (1980). The black community as the source of positive self-concept for black children: A theoretical perspective. In R. Jones (Ed.), *Black psychology,* pp. 106–130. New York: Harper & Row.

Barnes, G., & Farrell, M. (1992). Parental support and control as predictors of adolescent drinking, delinquency, and related problem behaviors. *Journal of Marriage and the Family, 54,* 763–776.

Barnes, G., Reifman, A., Farrell, M., & Dintcheff, B. (2000). The effects of parenting on the development of adolescent alcohol misuse: A six-wave latent growth model. *Journal of Marriage and the Family, 62,* 175–186.

Barratt, M., Roach, M., Morgan, K., & Colbert, K. (1996). Adjustment to motherhood by single adolescents. *Family Relations, 45,* 209–215.

Barrera, M., Jr., Li, S., & Chassin, L. (1995). Effects of parental alcoholism and life stress on Hispanic and non-Hispanic Caucasian adolescents: A prospective study. *American Journal of Community Psychology, 23,* 479–507.

Barrera, M., Jr., Prelow, H. M., Dumka, L. E., Gonzales, N. A., Knight, G. P., Michaels, M., et al. (2002). Pathways from family economic conditions to adolescents' distress: Supportive parenting, stressors outside the family, and deviant peers. *Journal of Community Psychology, 30,* 135–152.

Barrett-Singer, A. T., & Weinstein, R. S. (2000). Differential parent treatment predicts achievement and self-perceptions in two cultural contexts. *Journal of Family Psychology, 14*(3), 491–509.

Barry, C. M., & Nelson, L. J. (2005). The role of religion in the transition to adulthood for young emerging adults. *Journal of Youth and Adolescence 34,* 245–255.

Barry, C. M., & Wentzel, K. R. (2006). Friend influence on prosocial behavior: The role of motivational factors and friendship characteristics. *Developmental Psychology, 42,* 153–163.

Bartko, W. T., & Eccles, J. S. (2003). Adolescent participation in structured and unstructured activities: A person-oriented analysis. *Journal of Youth and Adolescence, 32,* 233–241.

Basen-Engquist, K., Edmundson, E., & Parcel, G. (1996). Structure of health risk behavior among high school students. *Journal of Consulting and Clinical Psychology, 64,* 764–775.

Battin-Pearson, S., Newcomb, M. D., Abbott, R. D., Hill, K. G., Catalano, R. F., & Hawkins, J. (2000). Predictors of early high school dropout: A test of five theories. *Journal of Educational Psychology, 92*(3), 568–582.

Bauer, L., & Hesselbrock, V. (2002). Brain maturation and subtypes of conduct disorder: Interactive effects on P300 amplitude and topography in male adolescents. *Journal of the American Academy of Child and Adolescent Psychiatry, 42,* 106–115.

Baumeister, R., & Tice, D. (1986). How adolescence became the struggle for self: A historical transformation of psychological development. In J. Suls & A. Greenwald (Eds.), *Psychological perspectives on the self,* Vol. 3, pp. 183–201. Hillsdale, NJ: Erlbaum.

Baumer, E. P., & South, S. J. (2001). Community effects on youth sexual activity. *Journal of Marriage and the Family, 63*(2), 540–554.

Baumrind, D. (1978). Parental disciplinary patterns and social competence in children. *Youth and Society, 9,* 239–276.

Baumrind, D. (1991). The influence of parenting style on adolescent competence and substance use. *Journal of Early Adolescence, 11,* 56–95.

Bauserman, R., & Rind, B. (1997). Psychological correlates of male child and adolescent sexual experiences with adults: A review of the nonclinical literature. *Archives of Sexual Behavior, 26,* 105–141.

Beal, A. C., Ausiello, J., & Perrin, J. M. (2001). Social influences on health-risk behaviors among minority middle school students. *Journal of Adolescent Health, 28*(6), 474–480.

Beam, M. R., Chen, C., & Greenberger, E. (2002). The nature of adolescents' relationship with their "very important" nonparental adults. *American Journal of Community Psychology, 30*(2), 305–325.

Bean, R. A., Bush, K. R., McKenry, P. C., & Wilson, S. M. (2003). The impact of parental support, behavioral control, and psychological control on the academic achievement and self-esteem of African American and European American adolescents. *Journal of Adolescent Research, 18,* 523–541.

Beardslee, W., Schultz, L., & Selman, R. (1987). Level of social-cognitive development, adaptive functioning, and DSM-III diagnoses in adolescent offspring of parents with affective disorders: Implications for the development of the capacity for mutuality. *Developmental Psychology, 23,* 807–815.

Bearman, P. S., & Brückner, H. (2001). Promising the future: Virginity pledges and first intercourse. *American Journal of Sociology, 106*(4), 859–912.

Beaumont, S. (1996). Adolescent girls' perceptions of conversations with mothers and friends. *Journal of Adolescent Research, 11,* 325–346.

Bechara, A. (2005). Decision making, impulse control and loss of willpower to resist drugs: A neurocognitive perspective. *Nature Neuroscience, 8,* 1458–63.

Becker, A., Burwell, R., Herzog, D., Hamburg, P., & Gilman, S. (2002). Eating behaviors and attitudes following prolonged exposure to television among ethnic Fijian adolescent girls. *British Journal of Psychiatry, 180,* 509–514.

Beckwith, L., Cohen, S., & Hamilton, C. (1999). Maternal sensitivity during infancy and subsequent life events relate to attachment representation at early adulthood. *Developmental Psychology, 35,* 693–700.

Bell, A., Weinberg, M., & Hammersmith, S. (1981). *Sexual preference: Its development in men and women.* Bloomington: Indiana University Press.

Bell, J., & Bromnick, R. (2000, March). A grounded approach to understanding modern dilemmas of individuality. Paper presented at the eighth biennial meeting of the Society for Research on Adolescence, Chicago.

Bell, L. G., & Bell., D. C. (2005). Family dynamics in adolescence affect midlife well-being. *Journal of Family Psychology, 19,* 198–207.

Belsky, J., Steinberg, L., & Draper, P. (1991). Childhood experience, interpersonal development, and reproductive strategy: An evolutionary theory of socialization. *Child Development, 62,* 647–670.

Bem, D. (1996). Exotic becomes erotic: A developmental theory of sexual orientation. *Psychological Review, 103,* 320–335.

Bem, S. (1975). Sex-role adaptability: One consequence of psychological androgyny. *Journal of Personality and Social Psychology, 31,* 634–643.

Bence, P. (1992, March). Patterns of the experience of mood. Paper presented at the biennial meetings of the Society for Research on Adolescence, Washington, DC.

Benda, B., & Corwyn, R. (1998). Race and gender differences in theories of sexual behavior among rural adolescents residing in AFDC families. *Youth and Society, 30,* 59–88.

Benenson, J. F., & Christakos, A. (2003). The greater fragility of females' versus males' closest same-sex friendships. *Child Development, 74,* 1123–1129.

Bengtsson, S. L., Nagy, Z., Skare, S., Forsman, L., Forssberg, H., & Ullen, F. (2005). Extensive piano practicing has regionally specific effects on white matter development. *Nature Neuroscience 8,* 1148–1150.

Benjet, C., & Hernandez-Guzman, L. (2002). A short-term longitudinal study of pubertal change, gender, and psychological well-being of Mexican early adolescents. *Journal of Youth and Adolescence, 31*(6), 429–442.

Ben-Zur, H., & Reshef-Kfir, Y. (2003). Risk taking and coping strategies among Israeli adolescents. *Journal of Adolescence, 26,* 255–265.

Berk, L. (1992). The extracurriculum. In P. Jackson (Ed.), *Handbook of research on curriculum.* New York: Macmillan.

Berkowitz, R. I., Wadden, T. A., Tershakovec, A. M., & Cronquist, J. L. (2003). Behavior therapy and sibutramine for the treatment of adolescent obesity. *Journal of the American Medical Association, 289,* 1805–1812.

Berliner, D., & Biddle, B. (1995). *The manufactured crisis: Myths, fraud, and attack on America's public schools.* Reading, MA: Addison-Wesley.

Berndt, T. (1979). Developmental changes in conformity to peers and parents. *Developmental Psychology, 15,* 608–616.

Berndt, T. (1981). Relations between social cognition, nonsocial cognition, and social behavior: The case of friendship. In J. Flavell and L. Ross (Eds.), *Social cognitive development: Frontiers and possible futures.* Cambridge: Cambridge University Press.

Berndt, T. (1982). The features and effects of friendship in early adolescence. *Child Development, 53,* 1447–1460.

Berndt, T. (1996). Exploring the effects of friendship quality on social development. In W. Bukowski, A. Newcomb, & W. Hartup, W. (Eds.), *The company they keep: Friendship in childhood and adolescence,* pp. 346–365. New York: Cambridge University Press.

Berndt, T., & Keefe, K. (1995). Friends' influence on adolescents' adjustment to school. *Child Development, 66,* 1312–1329.

Berndt, T., & Mekos, D. (1995). Adolescents' perceptions of the stressful and desirable aspects of the transition to junior high. *Journal of Research on Adolescence, 5,* 123–142.

Berndt, T., & Perry, T. (1990). Distinctive features and effects of early adolescent friendships. In R. Montemayor, G. Adams, & T. Gullota (Eds.), *Advances in adolescence research,* Vol. 2., pp. 269–287. Beverly Hills, CA: Sage.

Bersamin, M. M., Walker, S., Waiters, E. D., Fisher, D. A., & Grube, J. W. (2005). Promising to wait: Virginity pledges and adolescent sexual behavior. *Journal of Adolescent Health, 36,* 428–436.

Berzonsky, M. (2004). Identity style, parental authority, and identity commitment. *Journal of Youth and Adolescence, 33,* 213–220.

Berzonsky, M., & Adams, G. (1999). Commentary: Reevaluating the identity status paradigm: Still useful after 35 years. *Developmental Review, 19,* 557–590.

Beutel, A., & Marini, M. (1995). Gender and values. *American Sociological Review, 60,* 436–448.

Beyers, J. M., Bates, J. E., Pettit, G. S., & Dodge, K. A. (2003). Neighborhood structure, parenting processes, and the development of youths' externalizing behaviors: A multilevel analysis. *American Journal of Community Psychology, 31,* 35–53.

Beyers, J. M., & Loeber, R. (2003). Untangling developmental relations between depressed mood and delinquency in male adolescents. *Journal of Abnormal Child Psychology, 31,* 247–266.

Beyers, J. M., Loeber, R., Wikstrom, P. H., & Stouthamer-Loeber, M. (2001). What predicts adolescent violence in better-off neighborhoods? *Journal of Abnormal Psychology, 29*(5), 369–381.

Beyers, W., Goossens, L., Vasant, I., & Moors, E. (2003). A structural model of autonomy in middle and late adolescence; Connectedness, separation, detachment, and agency. *Journal of Youth and Adolescence, 32,* 351–365.

Beyth-Marom, R., Austin, L., Fischoff, B., Palmgren, C., & Jacobs-Quadrel, M. (1993). Perceived consequences of risky behaviors: Adults and adolescents. *Developmental Psychology, 29,* 549–563.

Biehl, M., & Halpern-Felsher, B. L. (2001). Adolescents' and adults' understanding of probability expressions. *Journal of Adolescent Health, 28*(1), 30–35.

Biener, L., Aseltine, R., Cohen, B., & Anderka, M. (1998). Reactions of adult and teenaged smokers to the Massachusetts Tobacco Tax. *American Journal of Public Health, 88,* 1389–1391.

Biener, L., & Siegel, M. (2000). Tobacco marketing and adolescent smoking: More support for a causal inference. *American Journal of Public Health, 90*(3), 407–411.

Bierman, K., & Furman, W. (1984). The effects of social skills training and peer involvement on the social adjustment of preadolescents. *Child Development, 55,* 151–162.

Bierman, K., & Wargo, J. (1995). Predicting the longitudinal course associated with aggressive-rejected, aggressive-nonrejected, and rejected non-aggressive status. *Development and Psychopathology, 7,* 669–682.

Bigelow, B., & LaGaipa, J. (1975). Children's written descriptions of friendship. *Developmental Psychology, 11,* 857–858.

Bills, D., Helms, L., & Ozcan, M. (1995). The impact of student employment on teachers' attitudes and behaviors toward working students. *Youth and Society, 27,* 169–193.

Billy, J., Brewster, K., & Grady, W. (1994). Contextual effects on the sexual behavior of adolescent women. *Journal of Marriage and the Family, 56,* 387–404.

Billy, J., Landale, N., Grady, W., & Zimmerle, D. (1988). Effects of sexual activity on adolescent social and psychological development. *Social Psychology Quarterly, 51,* 190–212.

Bingenheimer, J. B. (2005). Firearm violence exposure and serious violent behavior. *Science, 308,* 1323–1326.

Bingham, C., & Crockett, L. (1996). Longitudinal adjustment patterns of boys and girls experiencing early, middle, and late sexual intercourse. *Developmental Psychology, 32,* 647–658.

Bingham, C. R., & Shope, J. T. (2004). Adolescent problem behavior and problem driving in young adulthood. *Journal of Adolescent Research, 19,* 205–223.

Birmaher, B., Rabin, B., Garcia, M., Jain, U., Whiteside, T., Williamson, D., Al-Shabbout, M., Nelson, B., Dahl, R., & Ryan, N. (1994). Cellular immunity in depressed, conduct disorder, and normal adolescents: Role of adverse life events. *Journal of the American Academy of Child and Adolescent Psychiatry, 33,* 671–678.

Birman, D., Trickett, E. J., & Vinokurov, A. (2002). Acculturation and adaptation of Soviet Jewish refugee adolescents: Predictors of adjustment across life domains. *American Journal of Community Psychology, 30*(5), 585–607.

Biro F., Huang, B., Crawford, P., Lucky, A., Striegel-Moore, R., Barton, B., & Daniels, S. (2006). Pubertal correlates in black and white girls. *Journal of Pediatrics, 148,* 234–240.

Bishop, J. (1999) Nerd harrassment, incentives, school priorities and learning. In S. Mayer & P. Peterson (Eds.), *Earning and learning.* Washington, DC: Brookings Institution.

Bishop, J. (2001). The role of end-of-course exams and minimum competency exams in standards-based reforms. In D. Ravitch (Ed.), *Brookings papers on educational policy.* Washington, DC: Brookings Institution.

Bishop, J., Bishop, M., Gelbwasser, L., Green, S., & Zuckerman, A. (2003). Why do we harass nerds and freaks?: Towards a theory of student culture and norms. In D. Ravitch (Ed.), *Brookings papers on education policy.* Washington, DC: Brookings Institution.

Bjorklund, D. (1997). In search of a metatheory for cognitive development (or, Piaget is dead and I don't feel so good myself). *Child Development, 68,* 144–148.

Black, K., & McCartney, K. (1997). Adolescent females' security with parents predicts the quality of peer interactions. *Social Development, 6,* 91–110.

Black, M., Ricardo, I., & Stanton, B. (1997). Social and psychological factors associated with AIDS risk behaviors among low-income, urban, African American adolescents. *Journal of Research on Adolescence, 7,* 173–195.

Blair, S., & Qian, Z. (1998). Family and Asian students' educational performance: A consideration of diversity. *Journal of Family Issues, 19,* 355–374.

Blake, S. M., Ledsky, R., Goodenow, C., Sawyer, R., Lohrmann, D., & Windsor, R. (2003). Condom availability programs in Massachusetts high schools: Relationships with condom use and sexual behavior. *American Journal of Public Health, 93,* 955–962.

Blash, R., & Unger, D. (1992, March). Cultural factors and the self-esteem and aspirations of African-American adolescent males. Paper presented at the biennial meetings of the Society for Research on Adolescence, Washington, DC.

Blinn-Pike, L. (1999). Why abstinent adolescents report they have not had sex: Understanding sexually resilient youth. *Family Relations, 48,* 295–301.

Block, J., & Robins, R. (1993). A longitudinal study of consistency and change in self-esteem from early adolescence to early adulthood. *Child Development, 64,* 909–923.

Bloom, A. (1987). *The closing of the American mind.* New York: Simon & Schuster.

Blos, P. (1967). The second individuation process of adolescence. In R. S. Eissler et al. (Eds.), *Psychoanalytic study of the child,* Vol. 15. New York: International Universities Press.

Blos, P. (1979). *The adolescent passage.* New York: International Universities Press.

Blum, J., Ireland, M., & Blum, R. W. (2003). Gender differences in juvenile violence: A report from Ad. Health. *Journal of Adolescent Health, 32,* 234–240.

Blum, R., Beuhring, T., Wunderlich, M., & Resnick, M. (1996). Don't ask, they won't tell: The quality of adolescent health screening in five practice settings. *American Journal of Public Health, 86,* 1767–1772.

Blum, R., Resnick, M., & Stark, T. (1990). Factors associated with the use of court bypass by minors to obtain abortions. *Family Planning Perspectives, 22,* 158–160.

Blum, R., & Rinehart, P. (2000). *Reducing the risk: Connections that make a difference in the lives of youth.* Minneapolis: Division of General Pediatrics and Adolescent Health, University of Minnesota.

Blum, R. W., & Nelson-Mmari, K. (2004). The health of young people in a global context. *Journal of Adolescent Health, 35,* 402–418.

Blyth, D., Hill, J., & Smyth, C. (1981). The influence of older adolescents on younger adolescents: Do grade-level arrangements make a difference in behaviors, attitudes, and experiences? *Journal of Early Adolescence, 1,* 85–110.

Blyth, D., Hill, J., & Thiel, K. (1982). Early adolescents' significant others: Grade and gender differences in perceived relationships with familial and non-familial adults and young people. *Journal of Youth and Adolescence, 11,* 425–450.

Blyth, D., Simmons, R., & Zakin, D. (1985). Satisfaction with body image for early adolescent females: The impact of pubertal timing within different school environments. *Journal of Youth and Adolescence, 14,* 227–236.

Bogenschneider, K. (1997). Parental involvement in adolescent schooling: A proximal process with transcontextual validity. *Journal of Marriage and the Family, 59,* 1–16.

Bogenschneider, K., Small, S., & Tsay, J. (1997). Child, parent, and contextual influences on perceived parenting competence among parents of adolescents. *Journal of Marriage and the Family, 59*, 345–362.

Boldero, J., & Fallon, B. (1995). Adolescent help-seeking: What do they get help for and from whom? *Journal of Adolescence, 18*, 193–209.

Bolland, J. M., Lian, B. E., & Formichella, C. M. (2005). The origins of hopelessness among inner-city African American adolescents. *American Journal of Community Psychology, 36*, 293–305.

Bomar, J., & Sabatelli, R. (1996). Family system dynamics, gender, and psychosocial maturity in late adolescence. *Journal of Adolescent Research, 11*, 421–439.

Boney-McCoy, S., & Finkelhor, D. (1995). The psychosocial impact of violent victimization in a national youth sample. *Journal of Consulting and Clinical Psychology, 63*, 726–736.

Bong, M. (2001). Between- and within-domain relations of academic motivation among middle and high school students: Self-efficacy, task value, and achievement goals. *Journal of Educational Psychology, 93*(1), 23–34.

Bongers, I. L., Koot, H. M., van der Ende, J., & Verhulst, F. C. (2004). Developmental trajectories of externalizing behaviors in childhood and adolescence. *Child Development, 75*, 1523–1537.

Bontempo, D. E., & D'Augelli, A. R. (2002). Effects of at-school victimization and sexual orientation on lesbian, gay, or bisexual youths' health risk behavior. *Journal of Adolescent Health, 30*(5), 364–374.

Booth, A., Johnson, D. R., Granger, D. A., Crouter, A. C., & McHale, S. (2003). Testosterone and child and adolescent adjustment: The moderating role of parent–child relationships. *Developmental Psychology, 39*(1), 85–98.

Botstein, L. (1997). *Jefferson's children: Education and the promise of American culture.* New York: Doubleday.

Botvin, M., & Vitaro, F. (1995). The impact of peer relationships on aggression in childhood: Inhibition through coercion or promotion through peer support. In J. McCord (Ed.), *Coercion and punishment in long-term perspectives*, pp. 183–197. New York: Cambridge University Press.

Bowen, N. K., & Bowen, G. L. (2002). Neighborhood social disorganization, families, and the educational behavior of adolescents. *Journal of Adolescent Research, 17*(5), 468–490.

Bowker, A. (2004). Predicting friendship stability during early adolescence. *Journal of Early Adolescence, 24*, 85–112.

Bowker, A., Bukowski, W., Hymel, S., & Sippola, L. (2000). Coping with daily hassles in the peer group: Variations as a function of peer experience. *Journal of Research on Adolescence, 10*, 211–243.

Bowlby, J. (1969). *Attachment and loss,* Vol. 1: *Attachment.* New York: Basic Books.

Boyer, E. (1986, December). Transition from school to college. *Phi Delta Kappan*, 293–287.

Boykin McElhaney, K., & Allen, J. P. (2001). Autonomy and adolescent social functioning: The moderating effect of risk. *Child Development, 72*(1), 220–235.

Boykin, A., & Toms, F. (1985). Black child socialization: A conceptual framework. In H. McAdoo and J. McAdoo (Eds.), *Black children: Social, educational, and parental environments.* Newbury Park, CA: Sage.

Brack, C., Brack, G., & Orr, D. (1996). Adolescent health promotion: Testing a model using multidimensional scaling. *Journal of Research on Adolescence, 6*, 139–149.

Braddock, J. (1985). School desegregation and black assimilation. *Journal of Social Issues, 41*, 9–22.

Bradley, L., & Bradley, G. (1977). The academic achievement of black students in desegregated schools: A critical review. *Review of Educational Research, 47*, 399–449.

Bradley, R. H., Corwyn, R. F., Pipes McAdoo, H., & Garcia-Coll, C. (2001). The home environments of children in the United States, part 1: Variations by age, ethnicity, and poverty status. *Child Development, 72*(6), 1844–1867.

Brady, E., & Kendall, P. (1992). Comorbidity of anxiety and depression in children and adolescents. *Psychological Bulletin, 111*, 244–255.

Branch, C. (1995, August). Gang bangers: Ethnic variations. Paper presented at APA, New York.

Braun, H., Jenkins, F., & Grigg, W. (2006). Comparing private schools and public schools using hierarchical linear modeling (NCES 2006-461). U.S. Department of Education, National Center for Education Statistics, Institute of Education Sciences. Washington, DC: U.S. Government Printing Office.

Bray, J., Berger, S., Tiuch, G., & Boethel, C. (1993, March). Nonresidential parent–child relationships following divorce and remarriage: A longitudinal perspective. Paper presented at the biennial meetings of the Society for Research in Child Development, New Orleans.

Bray, J. H., Adams, J., Getz, J., & Baer, P. E. (2001). Developmental, family, and ethnic in influences on adolescent alcohol usage: A growth curve approach. *Journal of Family Psychology, 15*(2), 301–314.

Bray, J. H., Adams, G., Getz, J., & McQueen, A. (2003). Individuation, peers, and adolescent alcohol use: A latent growth analysis. *Journal of Consulting and Clinical Psychology, 71*, 553–564.

Brendgen, M., Markiewicz, D., & Kamkar, K. (2003). Family relationships as moderators of the association between romantic relationships and adjustment in early adolescence. *Journal of Early Adolescence, 23*, 316–340.

Brendgen, M., Vitaro, F., & Bukowski, W. (2000). Deviant friends and early adolescents' emotional and behavioral adjustment. *Journal of Research on Adolescence, 10*, 173–189.

Brendgen, M., Vitaro, F., Doyle, A., Markiewicz, D., & Bukowski, W. M. (2002). Same-sex peer relations and romantic relationships during early adolescence: Interactive links to emotional, behavioral, and academic adjustment. *Merrill-Palmer Quarterly, 48*(1), 77–103.

Brennan, P. A., Hall, J., Bor, W., Najman, J. M., & Williams, G. (2003). Integrating biological and social processes in relation to early-onset persistent aggression in boys and girls. *Developmental Psychology, 39*(2), 309–323.

Brewster, K. (1994). Race differences in sexual activity among adolescent women: The role of neighborhood characteristics. *American Sociological Review, 59*, 408–424.

Brewster, K., Billy, J., & Grady, W. (1993). Social context and adolescent behavior: The impact of community on the transition to sexual activity. *Social Forces, 71*, 713–740.

Bridges, G., & Steen, S. (1998). Racial disparities in official assessments of juvenile offenders: Attributional stereotypes as mediating mechanisms. *American Sociological Review, 63*, 554–570.

Brindis, C., Starbuck-Morales, S., Wolfe, A., & McCarter, V. (1994). Characteristics associated with contraceptive use among adolescent females in school-based family planning programs. *Family Planning Perspectives, 26*, 160–164.

Brittain, C. (1963). Adolescent choices and parent/peer cross-pressures. *American Sociological Review, 28*, 385–391.

Brody, G., Ge, X., Yeong, K., McBride, M., Simons, R., Gibbons, F., Gerrard, M., & Conger, R. (2003). Neighborhood disadvantage moderates associations of parenting and older sibling problem attitudes and behavior with conduct disorders in African American children. *Journal of Consulting and Clinical Psychology, 71*, 211–222.

Brody, G., Moore, K., & Glei, D. (1994). Family processes during adolescence as predictors of parent–young adult attitude similarity: A six-year longitudinal analysis. *Family Relations, 43*, 369–373.

Brody, G., Murry, V. M., McNair, L., Chen, Y., Gibbons, F. X., Gerrard, M., & Willis, T. A. (2005). Linking changes in parenting to parent–child relationship quality and youth self-control: The strong African American families program. *Journal of Research on Adolescence, 15*, 47–69.

Brody, G., Stoneman, Z., & Burke, M. (1987). Child temperaments, maternal differential treatment, and sibling relationships. *Developmental Psychology, 23*, 354–362

Brody, G., Stoneman, Z., & Flor, D. (1995). Linking family processes and academic competence among rural African American youths. *Journal of Marriage and the Family, 57*, 567–579.

Brody, G., Stoneman, Z., Flor, D., & McCrary, C. (1994). Religion's role in organizing family relationships: Family process in rural, two-parent African American families. *Journal of Marriage and the Family, 56*, 878–888.

Brody, G., Stoneman, Z., & Flor, D. (1996). Parental religiosity, family processes, and youth competence in rural, two-parent African-American families. *Developmental Psychology, 32,* 696–706.

Brody, G., Stoneman, Z., & McCoy, J. (1994). Forecasting sibling relationships in early adolescence from child temperaments and family processes in middle childhood. *Child Development, 65,* 771–784.

Brody, J. (1987, June 3). Personal health column. *New York Times.*

Broh, B. A. (2002). Linking extracurricular programming to academic achievement: Who benefits and why? *Sociology of Education, 75*(1), 69–95.

Broidy, L. M., Nagin, D. S., Tremblay, R. E., Bates, J. E., Brame, B., Dodge, K. A., et al. (2003). Developmental trajectories of childhood disruptive behaviors and adolescent delinquency: A six-site, cross-national study. *Developmental Psychology, 39*(2), 222–245.

Bronfenbrenner, U. (1974). The origins of alienation. *Scientific American, 231,* 53–61.

Bronfenbrenner, U. (1979). *The ecology of human development.* Cambridge, MA: Harvard University Press.

Bronstein, P., Duncan, P., Clauson, J., Abrams, C. L., Yannett, N., Ginsburg, G., & Milne, M. (1998). Preventing middle school adjustment problems for children from lower-income families: A program for aware parenting. *Journal of Applied Developmental Psychology, 19*(1), 129–152.

Bronstein, P., Duncan, P., D'Ari, A., Pieniadz, J., Fitzgerald, M., Abrams, C., Frankowski, B., Franco, O., Hunt, C., & Oh Cha, S. (1996). Family and parenting behaviors predicting middle school adjustment: A longitudinal study. *Family Relations, 45,* 415–426.

Bronstein, P., Ginsburg, G., & Herrera-Leavitt, I. (2000). Parental predictors of motivational orientation and academic performance in early adolescence: A longitudinal study. Manuscript submitted for publication. Burlington: Department of Psychology, University of Vermont.

Brookmeyer, K. A., Henrich, & Schwab-Stone, M. (2005). Adolescents who witness community violence: Can parent support and prosocial cognitions protect them from committing violence? *Child Development, 76,* 917–929.

Brooks-Gunn, J., Duncan, G., Klebanov, P., & Sealand, N. (1993). Do neighborhoods influence child and adolescent development? *American Journal of Sociology, 99,* 353–395.

Brooks-Gunn, J., & Furstenberg, F., Jr. (1989). Adolescent sexual behavior. *American Psychologist, 44,* 249–257.

Brooks-Gunn, J., Graber, J., & Paikoff, R. (1994). Studying links between hormones and negative affect: Models and measures. *Journal of Research on Adolescence, 4,* 469–486.

Brooks-Gunn, J., Newman, D., Holderness, C., & Warren, M. (1994). The experience of breast development and girls' stories about the purchase of a bra. *Journal of Youth and Adolescence, 23,* 539–565.

Brooks-Gunn, J., & Paikoff, R. (1993). "Sex is a gamble, kissing is a game": Adolescent sexuality and health promotion. In S. Millstein, A. Petersen, & E. Nightingale (Eds.), *Promoting the health of adolescents: New directions for the twenty-first century,* pp. 180–208. New York: Oxford University Press.

Brooks-Gunn, J., & Reiter, E. (1990). The role of pubertal processes. In S. Feldman & G. Elliott (Eds.), *At the threshold: The developing adolescent,* pp. 16–23. Cambridge, MA: Harvard University Press.

Brooks-Gunn, J., & Ruble, D. (1979). The social and psychological meaning of menarche. Paper presented at the biennial meetings of the Society for Research in Child Development, San Francisco.

Brooks-Gunn, J., & Ruble, D. (1982). The development of menstrual-related beliefs and behaviors during early adolescence. *Child Development, 53,* 1567–1577.

Brooks-Gunn, J., & Warren, M. (1985). The effects of delayed menarche in different contexts: Dance and nondance students. *Journal of Youth and Adolescence, 14,* 285–300.

Broverman, I., Vogel, S., Broverman, D., Clarkson, F., & Rosenkrantz, P. (1972). Sex-role stereotypes: A current appraisal. *Journal of Social Issues, 28,* 59–78.

Brown, A. (1975). The development of memory: Knowing, knowing about knowing, and knowing how to know. In H. Reese (Ed.), *Advances in child development and behavior,* Vol. 10. New York: Academic Press.

Brown, B. (1990). Peer groups. In S. Feldman & G. Elliott (Eds.), *At the threshold: The developing adolescent,* pp. 171–196. Cambridge, MA: Harvard University Press.

Brown, B. (1996). Visibility, vulnerability, development, and context: Ingredients for a fuller understanding of peer rejection in adolescence. *Journal of Early Adolescence, 16,* 27–36.

Brown, B. (1999). "You're going out with who?": Peer group influences on adolescent romantic relationships. In W. Furman, B. Brown, & C. Feiring (Eds.), *Contemporary perspectives on adolescent romantic relationships,* pp. 291–329. New York: Cambridge University Press.

Brown, B. (2004). Adolescents' relationships with peers. In R. Lerner & L. Steinberg (Eds.), *Handbook of adolescent psychology.* New York: Wiley.

Brown, B., Clasen, D., & Eicher, S. (1986). Perceptions of peer pressure, peer conformity dispositions, and self-reported behavior among adolescents. *Developmental Psychology, 22,* 521–530.

Brown, B., Dolcini, M., & Leventhal, A. (1995, March). The emergence of peer crowds: Friend or foe to adolescent health? Paper presented at the biennial meetings of the Society for Research in Child Development, Indianapolis.

Brown, B., Freeman, H., Huang, B., & Mounts, N. (1992, March). "Crowd hopping": Incidence, correlates and consequences of change in crowd affiliation during adolescence. Paper presented at the biennial meetings of the Society for Research on Adolescence, Washington, DC.

Brown, B., Lamborn, S., & Newmann, F. (1992). "You live and you learn": The place of school engagement in the lives of teenagers. In F. Newmann (Ed.), *Student engagement and achievement in American high schools.* New York: Teachers College Press.

Brown, B., Larson, R., & Saraswathi, T. (Eds.). (2002). *The world's youth: Adolescence in eight regions of the globe.* New York: Cambridge University Press.

Brown, B., & Lohr, M. J. (1987). Peer group affiliation and adolescent self-esteem: An integration of ego-identity and symbolic interaction theories. *Journal of Personality and Social Psychology, 52,* 47–55.

Brown, B., Mory, M., & Kinney, D. (1994). Casting crowds in a relational perspective: Caricature, channel, and context. In R. Montemayor, G. Adams, & T. Gullotta (Eds.), *Advances in adolescent development,* Vol. 5: *Personal relationships during adolescence.* Newbury Park, CA: Sage.

Brown, B., & Mounts, N. (1989, April). Peer group structures in single versus multiethnic high schools. Paper presented at the biennial meetings of the Society for Research in Child Development, Kansas City.

Brown, B., Mounts, N., Lamborn, S., & Steinberg, L. (1993). Parenting practices and peer group affiliation in adolescence. *Child Development, 64,* 467–482.

Brown, J. (1994, February). Adolescents' uses of mass media and bedroom culture. Paper presented at the biennial meetings of the Society for Research on Adolescence, San Diego.

Brown, J., & Cantor, J. (2000). An agenda for research on youth and the media. *Journal of Adolescent Health, 27,* 2–7.

Brown, K., McMahon, R., Biro, F., Crawford, P., Schreiber, G., Similo, S. L., Waclawiw, M., & Striegel-Moore, R. (1998). Changes in self-esteem in Black and White girls between the ages of 9 and 14 years: The NHLBI Growth and Health Study. *Journal of Adolescent Health, 23,* 7–19.

Brown, W. T., & Jones, J. M. (2003). The substance of things hoped for: A study of the future orientation, minority status perceptions, academic engagement, and academic performance of black high school students. *Journal of Black Psychology, 30,* 248–273.

Browning, C. R., Leventhal, T., & Brooks-Gunn, J. (2005). Sexual initiation in early adolescence:

The nexus of parental and community control. *American Sociological Review, 70,* 758–778.

Brubacher, J., & Rudy, W. (1976). *Higher education in transition,* 3rd ed. New York: Harper & Row.

Brückner, H., & Bearman, P. (2005). After the promise: The STD consequences of adolescent virginity pledges. *Journal of Adolescent Health, 36,* 271–278.

Brumberg, J. (1997). *The body project: An intimate history of American girls.* New York: Random House.

Bruvold, W. (1993). A meta-analysis of adolescent smoking prevention programs. *American Journal of Public Health, 83,* 872–880.

Bryant, A. L., Schulenberg, J. E., O'Malley, P. M., Bachman, J. G., & Johnston, L. D. (2003). How academic achievement, attitudes, and behaviors relate to the course of substance use during adolescence: A 60-year, multiwave national longitudinal study. *Journal of Research on Adolescence, 13,* 361–397.

Bryant, A. L., & Zimmerman, M. A. (2002). Examining the effects of academic beliefs and behaviors on changes in substance use among urban adolescents. *Journal of Educational Psychology, 94*(3), 621–637.

Bryant, A. L., & Zimmerman, M. A. (2003). Role models and psychosocial outcomes among African American adolescents. *Journal of Adolescent Research, 18*(1), 36–67.

Bryk, A., & Thum, Y. (1989). The effects of high school organization on dropping out: An exploratory investigation. *American Educational Research Journal, 26,* 353–383.

Buchanan, C. (2003). Mother's generalized beliefs about adolescents: Links to expectations for a specific child. *Journal of Early Adolescence, 23,* 29–50.

Buchanan, C., Eccles, J., & Becker, J. (1992). Are adolescents the victims of raging hormones? Evidence for activational effects of hormones on moods and behavior at adolescence. *Psychological Bulletin, 111,* 62–107.

Buchanan, C., & Holmbeck, G. (1998). Measuring beliefs about adolescent personality and behavior. *Journal of Youth and Adolescence, 27,* 607–627.

Buchanan, C., & Maccoby, E. (1993, March). Relationships between adolescents and their nonresidential parents: A comparison of nonresidential mothers and fathers. Paper presented at the biennial meetings of the Society for Research in Child Development, New Orleans.

Buchanan, C., Maccoby, E., & Dornbusch, S. (1996). *Adolescents after divorce.* Cambridge, MA: Harvard University Press.

Buchanan, M., & Robbins, C. (1990). Early adult psychological consequences for males of adolescent pregnancy and its resolution. *Journal of Youth and Adolescence, 19,* 413–424.

Buchmann, C., & Dalton, B. (2002). Interpersonal influences and educational aspirations in 12 countries: The importance of institutional context. *Sociology of Education, 75*(2), 99–122.

Buechel, F., & Duncan, G. (1998). Do parents' social activities promote children's school attainments? Evidence from the German Socioeconomic Panel. *Journal of Marriage and the Family, 60,* 95–108.

Buehler, C., Benson, M., & Gerard, J. (2006). Interpersonal hostility and early adolescent problem behavior: The mediating role of specific aspects of parenting. *Journal of Research on Adolescence, 16,* 265–292.

Buehler, C., Krishnakumar, A., Stone, G., Anthony, C., Pemberton, S., Gerard, J., & Barber, B. (1998). Interparental conflict styles and youth problem behaviors: A two-sample replication study. *Journal of Marriage and the Family, 60,* 119–132.

Buhrmester, D. (1990). Intimacy of friendship, interpersonal competence, and adjustment during preadolescence and adolescence. *Child Development, 61,* 1101–1111.

Buhrmester, D. (1996). Need fulfillment, interpersonal competence, and the developmental contexts of early adolescent friendship. In W. Bukowski, A. Newcomb, & W. Hartup, W. (Eds.), *The company they keep: Friendship in childhood and adolescence,* pp. 158–185. New York: Cambridge University Press.

Buhrmester, D., & Furman, W. (1987). The development of companionship and intimacy. *Child Development, 58,* 1101–1113.

Buhrmester, D., & Furman, W. (1990). Perceptions of sibling relationships during middle childhood and adolescence. *Child Development, 61,* 1387–1396.

Buhrmester, D., & Yin, J. (1997, April). A longitudinal study of friends' influence on adolescents' adjustment. Paper presented at the biennial meetings of the Society for Research in Child Development, Washington, DC.

Bukowski, W., Gauze, C., Hoza, B., & Newcomb, A. (1993). Differences and consistency between same-sex and other-sex peer relationships during early adolescence. *Developmental Psychology, 29,* 255–263.

Bukowski, W., Peters, P., Sippola, L., & Newcomb, A. (1993, March). Patterns in the selection of same- and other-sex friends among aggressive and nonaggressive early adolescent boys and girls. Paper presented at the biennial meetings of the Society for Research in Child Development, New Orleans.

Bukowski, W., Sippola, L., Gauze, C., Hoza, B., & Newcomb, A. (1993, March). On which aspects of friendship are there differences between boys and girls? Paper presented at the biennial meetings of the Society for Research in Child Development, New Orleans.

Bukowski, W., Sippola, L., & Hoza, B. (1999). Same and other: Interdependency between participation in same- and other-sex friendships. *Journal of Youth and Adolescence, 28*(4), 439–459.

Bukowski, W., Sippola, L., & Newcomb, A. F. (2000). Variations in patterns of attraction of same- and other-sex peers during early adolescence. *Developmental Psychology, 36*(2), 147–154.

Bulcroft, R., Carmody, D., & Bulcroft, K. (1996). Patterns of parental independence giving to adolescents: Variations by race, age, and gender of child. *Journal of Marriage and the Family, 58,* 866–883.

Bullock, B., & Dishion, T. J. (2002). Sibling collusion and problem behavior in early adolescence: Toward a process model for family mutuality. *Journal of Abnormal Child Psychology, 30,* 143–153.

Bumpass, L., & McLanahan, S. (1987, April). Unmarried motherhood: A note on recent trends, composition and black-white differences. Paper presented at the annual meeting of the Population Association of America, Chicago.

Bumpus, M. F., Crouter, A. C., & McHale, S. M. (2001). Parental autonomy granting during adolescence: Exploring gender differences in context. *Developmental Psychology, 37*(2), 163–173.

Burleson, B. (1982). The development of comforting communication skills in childhood and adolescence. *Child Development, 53,* 1578–1588.

Burns, M. J., & Dillon, F. R. (2005). AIDS health locus of control, self-efficacy for safer sexual practices, and future time orientation as predictors of condom use in African American college students. *Journal of Black Psychology, 31,* 172–188.

Butler, J., & Burton, L. (1990). Rethinking teenage childbearing: Is sexual abuse a missing link? *Family Relations, 39,* 73–80.

Butler, K. (2006). The grim neurology of teenage drinking. *The New York Times,* July 4.

Butts, J. A., & Mears, D. P. (2001). Reviving juvenile justice in a get-tough era. *Youth and Society, 33*(2), 169–198.

Buzy, W. M., McDonald, R. Jouriles, E. N., Swank, P. R., Rosenfield, D., Shimek, J. S., & Corbitt-Shindler, D. (2004). Adolescent girls' alcohol use as a risk factor for relationship violence. *Journal of Research on Adolescence, 14,* 449–470.

Byrne, B., & Shavelson, R. (1996). On the structure of social self-concept for pre-, early, and late adolescents: A test of the Shavelson, Hubner, and Stanton (1976) model. *Journal of Personality and Social Psychology, 70,* 599–613.

Byrnes, J. (1997). *The nature and development of decision-making: A self-regulation model.* Hillsdale, NJ: Erlbaum.

Byrnes, J., Miller, D., & Schafer, W. (1999). Gender differences in risk taking: A meta-analysis. *Psychological Bulletin, 125,* 367–383.

Cairns, R., Cairns, B., & Neckerman, H. (1989). Early school dropout: Configurations and determinants. *Child Development, 60,* 1437–1452.

Cairns, R., Cairns, B., Neckerman, H., Gest, S., & Gariepy, J. L. (1988). Social networks and aggressive behavior: Peer support or peer rejection? *Developmental Psychology, 24,* 815–823.

Cairns, R., Leung, M., Buchanan, L., & Cairns, B. (1995). Friendships and social networks in childhood and adolescence: Fluidity, reliability, and interrelations. *Child Development, 66,* 1330–1345.

Caldwell, C. H., Kohn-Wood, L. P., Schmeelk-Cone, K. H., Chavous, T. M., & Zimmerman, M. A. (2004). Racial discrimination and racial identity as risk or protective factors for violent behaviors in African American young adults. *American Journal of Community Psychology, 33,* 91–105.

Caldwell, C. H., Sellers, R. M., Bernat, D. H., & Zimmerman, M. A. (2004). Racial identity, parental support, and alcohol use in a sample of academically at-risk African American high school students. *American Journal of Community Psychology, 34,* 71–82.

Caldwell, L., & Darling, N. (1999). Leisure context, parental control, and resistance to peer pressure as predictors of adolescent partying and substance use: An ecological perspective. *Journal of Leisure Research, 31,* 57–77.

Caldwell, M. S., Rudolph, K. D., Troop-Gordon, W., & Kim, D. Y. (2004). Reciprocal influence among relational self-views, social disengagement, and peer stress during early adolescence. *Child Development, 75,* 1140–1154.

Call, K. T., Riedel, A. A., Hein, K., McLoyd, V., Petersen, A., & Kipke, M. (2002). Adolescent health and well-being in the twenty-first century: A global perspective. *Journal of Research on Adolescence, 12*(1), 69–98.

Call, K., & McNall, M. (1992). Poverty, ethnicity, and youth adjustment: A comparison of poor Hmong and non-Hmong adolescents. In W. Meeus, M. de Goede, W. Knox, & K. Hurrelmann (Eds.), *Adolescence, careers, and cultures,* pp. 373–392. New York: de Gruyter.

Callahan, R. (2005). Tracking and English learners: Limiting opportunity to learn. *American Educational Research Journal, 42,* 305–328.

Calverley, R., Fischer, K., & Ayoub, C. (1994). Complex splitting of self-representations in sexually abused adolescent girls. *Development and Psychopathology, 6,* 195–213.

Calvete, E., & Cardeñoso, O. (2005). Gender differences in cognitive vulnerability to depression and behavior problems in adolescents. *Journal of Abnormal Child Psychology, 33,* 179–192.

Campbell, B. (1977). The impact of school desegregation: An investigation of three mediating factors. *Youth and Society, 9,* 79–111.

Campbell, B. C., Prossinger, H., & Mbzivo, M. (2005). Timing of pubertal maturation and the onset of sexual behavior among Zimbabwe school boys. *Archives of Sexual Behavior, 34,* 505–516.

Campbell, C., & Schwartz, D. (1996). Prevalence and impact of exposure to interpersonal violence among suburban and urban middle school students. *Pediatrics, 98,* 396–402.

Campbell, E., Adams, G., & Dobson, W. (1984). Familial correlates of identity formation in late adolescence: A study of the predictive utility of connectedness and individuality in family relations. *Journal of Youth and Adolescence, 13,* 509–526.

Campbell, F., Pungello, E., Miller-Johnson, S., Burchinal, M., & Ramey, C. (2001). The development of cognitive and academic abilities: Growth curves from an early childhood educational experiment. *Developmental Psychology, 37*(2), 231–242.

Campbell, F., & Ramey, C. (1995). Cognitive and school outcomes for high-risk African-American students at middle adolescence: Positive effects of early intervention. *American Educational Research Journal, 32,* 743–772.

Campbell, M. A., Porter, S., & Santor, D. (2004). Psychopathic traits in adolescent offenders: An evaluation of criminal history, clinical, and psychosocial correlates. *Behavioral Sciences and the Law, 22,* 23–47.

Campione-Barr, N., & Smetana, J. G. (2004). In the eye of the beholder: Subjective and observer ratings of middle-class African American mother–adolescent interactions. *Developmental Psychology, 40,* 927–934.

Cantor, J. (2000). Media violence. *Journal of Adolescent Health, 27,* 30–34.

Capaldi, D. (1991). Co-occurrence of conduct problems and depressive symptoms in early adolescent boys, I: Familial factors and general adjustment at grade 6. *Development and Psychopathology, 3,* 277–300.

Capaldi, D. (1992). Co-occurrence of conduct problems and depressed mood in early adolescent boys, II: A two-year follow-up at grade 8. *Development and Psychopathology, 4,* 125–144.

Capaldi, D., & Clark, S. (1998). Prospective family predictors of aggression toward female partners for at-risk young men. *Developmental Psychology, 34,* 1175–1188.

Capaldi, D., Crosby, L., & Stoolmiller, M. (1996). Predicting the timing of first sexual intercourse for at-risk adolescent males. *Child Development, 67,* 344–359.

Capaldi, D., Dishion, T., Stoolmiller, M., & Yoerger, K. (2001). Aggression toward female partners by at-risk young men: The contribution of male adolescent friendships. *Developmental Psychology, 37*(1), 61–73.

Capaldi, D., Stoolmiller, M., Clark, S., & Owen, L. (2002). Heterosexual risk behaviors in at-risk young men from early adolescence to young adulthood: Prevalence, prediction, and association with STD contraction. *Developmental Psychology, 38*(3), 394–406.

Caplan, N., Choy, M., & Whitmore, J. (1992, February). Indochinese refugee families and academic achievement. *Scientific American,* pp. 36–42.

Cappelleri, J., Eckenrode, J., & Powers, J. (1993). The epidemiology of child abuse: Findings from the Second National Incidence and Prevalence Study of Child Abuse and Neglect. *American Journal of Public Health, 83,* 1622–1624.

Carbonaro, W. (2005). Tracking, students' effort, and academic achievement. *Sociology of Education, 78,* 27–49.

Carlo, G., Koller, S., Eisenberg, N., Da Silva, M., & Frohlich, C. (1996). A cross-national study of the relations among prosocial moral reasoning, gender role orientations, and prosocial behaviors. *Developmental Psychology, 32,* 231–240.

Carlson Jones, D. (2004). Body image among adolescent girls and boys: A longitudinal study. *Developmental Psychology, 40,* 823–835.

Carlson, E., Sroufe, L. A., Collins, W. A., Jimerson, S., Weinfield, N., Henninghausen, K., Egeland, B., Hyson, D., Anderson, F., & Meyer, S. (1999). Early environmental support and elementary school adjustment as predictors of school adjustment in middle adolescence. *Journal of Adolescent Research, 14,* 72–94.

Carnegie Council on Adolescent Development. (1989). Turning points: Preparing youth for the 21st century. New York: Carnegie Corporation of New York.

Carnegie Council on Adolescent Development. (1992). A matter of time: Risk and opportunity in the after-school hours. Washington, DC: Carnegie Council on Adolescent Development.

Carpenter, L. M. (2001). The first time/das erstes mal: Approaches to virginity loss in U.S. and German teen magazines. *Youth and Society, 33*(1), 31–61.

Carr, M., Borkowski, J., & Maxwell, S. (1991). Motivational components of underachievement. *Developmental Psychology, 27,* 108–118.

Carr, R., Wright, J., & Brody, C. (1996). Effects of high school work experience a decade later: Evidence from the National Longitudinal Survey. *Sociology of Education, 69,* 66–81.

Carskadon, M., & Acebo, C. (2002). Regulation of sleepiness in adolescence: Update, insights, and speculation. *Sleep, 25,* 606–616.

Carskadon, M., Acebo, C., Richardson, G., Tate, B., & Seifer, R. (1997). Long nights protocol: Access to circadian parameters in adolescents. *Journal of Biological Rhythms, 12,* 278–289.

Carson, D., Chowdhury, A., Perry, C., & Pati, C. (1999). Family characteristics and adolescent competence in India: Investigation of youth in southern Orissa. *Journal of Youth and Adolescence, 28,* 211–233.

Casella, R. (2003). Zero tolerance policy in schools: Rationale, consequences, and alternatives. *Teachers College Review, 105,* 872–892.

Casey, B.J., Tottenham, N., Liston, C., & Durston, S. (2005). Imaging the developing brain: What have we learned about cognitive development? *Trends in Cognitive Science, 9,* 104–110.

Cash, T. F., Morrow, J., Hrabosky, J. I., & Perry, A. A. (2004). How has body image changed? A cross-sectional investigation of college women and men from 1983 to 2001. *Journal of Consulting and Clinical Psychology, 72,* 1081–1089.

Casper, L. (1990). Does family interaction prevent adolescent pregnancy? *Family Planning Perspectives, 22,* 109–114.

Caspi, A. (2000). The child is father of the man: Personality continuities from childhood to adulthood. *Journal of Personality and Social Psychology, 78*(1), 158–172.

Caspi, A., Henry, B., McGee, R. O., Moffitt, T. E., & Silva, P. A. (1995). Temperamental origins of child and adolescent behavior problems: From age 3 to age 15. *Child Development, 66,* 55–68.

Caspi, A., Lynam, D., Moffitt, T., & Silva, P. (1993). Unraveling girls' delinquency: Biological, dispositional, and contextual contributions to adolescent misbehavior. *Developmental Psychology, 29,* 19–30.

Caspi, A., & Moffitt, T. (1991). Individual differences and personal transitions: The sample case of girls at puberty. *Journal of Personality and Social Psychology, 61,* 157–168.

Caspi, A., & Silva, P. (1995). Temperamental qualities at age three predict personality traits in young adulthood: Longitudinal evidence from a birth cohort. *Child Development, 66,* 486–498.

Cassidy, J., Ziv, Y., Mehta, T. G., & Feeney, B. C. (2003). Feedback seeking in children and adolescents: Associations with self-perceptions, attachment representations, and depression. *Child Development, 74,* 612–628.

Casteel, M. (1993). Effects of inference necessity and reading goal on children's inferential generation. *Developmental Psychology, 29,* 346–357.

Catsambis, S. (1992, March). The many faces of tracking in middle school grades: Between- and within-school differentiation of students and resources. Paper presented at the biennial meetings of the Society for Research on Adolescence, Washington, DC.

Catterall, J. (1998). Risk and resilience in student transitions to high school. *American Journal of Education, 106,* 302–333.

Cauffman, E., Feldman, S., Waterman, J., & Steiner, H. (1998). Posttraumatic stress disorder among incarcerated females. *Journal of the American Academy of Child and Adolescent Psychiatry, 37,* 1209–1216.

Cauffman, E., Piquero, A., Kimonis, E., Steinberg, L., & Chassin, L. (2007). Legal, individual, and contextual predictors of court disposition. *Law and Human Behavior.*

Cauffman, E., & Steinberg, L. (1996). Effects of menarche, dating, and heterosocial involvement on dieting behavior in early adolescence. *Developmental Psychology, 32,* 631–635.

Cauffman, E., Steinberg, L., & Piquero, A. R. (2005). Psychological, neuropsychological and physiological correlates of serious antisocial behavior in adolescence: The role of self-control. *Criminology, 43,* 133–175.

Ceballo, R., McLoyd, V. C., & Toyokawa, T. (2004). The influence of neighborhood quality on adolescents' educational values and school effort. *Journal of Adolescent Research, 19,* 716–739.

Ceci, S., & Williams, W. (1999). Schooling, intelligence, and income. *American Psychologist, 52,* 1051–1058.

Centers for Disease Control and Prevention. (2002). Trends in cigarette smoking among high school students: United States, 1991–2001. *Journal of the American Medical Association, 288,* 308–309.

Centers for Disease Control and Prevention. (2004). NCHS data on teenage pregnancy. Washington, DC: Author.

Centers for Disease Control and Prevention. (2006). Youth behavior surveillance—United States, 2005. *Morbidity and Mortality Weekly Report, 55* (SS-5), 1–108.

Centers, N., & Weist, M. (1998). Inner city youth and drug dealing: A review of the problem. *Journal of Youth and Adolescence, 27,* 395–411.

Cepeda, A., & Valdez, A. (2003). Risk behaviors among young Mexican American gang-associated females: Sexual relations, partying, substance abuse, and crime. *Journal of Adolescent Research, 18*(1), 90–106.

Chalmers, D., & Lawrence, J. (1993). Investigating the effects of planning aids on adults' and adolescents' organisation of a complex task. *International Journal of Behavioural Development, 16,* 191–214.

Chamberlain, P., & Reid, J. (1998). Comparison of two community alternatives to incarceration for chronic juvenile offenders. *Journal of Consulting and Clinical Psychology, 66,* 624–633.

Chan, D. (1997). Depressive symptoms and perceived competence among Chinese secondary school students in Hong Kong. *Journal of Youth and Adolescence, 26,* 303–319.

Chandler, M. (1987). The Othello effect: Essay on the emergence and eclipse of skeptical doubt. *Human Development, 30,* 137–159.

Chanoine, J., Hampl, S., Jensen, C., Boldrin, M., & Hauptman, J. (2005). Effect of orlistat on weight and body composition in obese adolescents: A randomized controlled trial. *Journal of the American Medical Association, 293,* 1873–1883.

Chao, R. (1994). Beyond parental control and authoritarian parenting style: Understanding Chinese parenting through the cultural notion of training. *Child Development, 65,* 1111–1119.

Chao, R. K. (2001). Extending research on the consequences of parenting style for Chinese Americans and European Americans. *Child Development, 72*(6), 1832–1843.

Charner, I., & Fraser, B. (1987). *Youth and work.* Washington, DC: William T. Grant Foundation Commission on Work, Family, and Citizenship.

Chase-Landsdale, P., Brooks-Gunn, J., & Zamsky, E. (1994). Young African-American multigenerational families in poverty: Quality of mothering and grandmothering. *Child Development, 65,* 373–393.

Chase-Landsdale, P. L., Moffit, R. A., Lohman, B. J., Cherlin, A. J., Coley, R. L., Pittman, L. D., Roff, J., & Votruba-Drzal, E. (2003). Mothers' transitions from welfare to work and the well-being of preschooler and adolescents. *Science, 299,* 1528.

Chassin, L., Hussong, A., Barrera, M., Jr., Molina, B., Trim, R., & Ritter, J.(2004). Adolescent substance use. In R. Lerner & L. Steinberg (Eds.), *Handbook of adolescent psychology.* New York: Wiley.

Chassin, L., Presson, C., Todd, M., Rose, J., & Sherman, S. (1998). Maternal socialization of adolescent smoking: The intergenerational transmission of parenting and smoking. *Developmental Psychology, 34,* 1189–1201.

Chavous, T. M., Bernat, D. H., Schmeelk-Cone, K., Caldwell, C., Kohn-Wood, L., & Zimmerman, M. A. (2003). Racial identity and academic attainment among African American adolescents. *Child Development, 74,* 1076–1090.

Chen, C., Greenberger, E., Lester, J., Dong, Q., & Guo, M. (1998). A cross-cultural study of family and peer correlates of adolescent misconduct. *Developmental Psychology, 34,* 770–781.

Chen, C., & Stevenson, H. (1995). Motivation and mathematics achievement: A comparative study of Asian-American, Caucasian-American, and East Asian high school students. *Child Development, 66,* 1215–1234.

Chen, C. S., Lee, S. Y., & Stevenson, H. W. (1996). Academic achievement and motivation of Chinese students: A cross-national perspective. In S. Lau (Ed.), *Growing up the Chinese way: Chinese child and adolescent development.* Hong Kong: Chinese University Press.

Chen, C. Y., Dormitzer, C. M., Bejarno, J., & Anthony, J. C. (2004). Religiosity and the earliest stages of adolescent drug involvement in seven countries of Latin America. *American Journal of Epidemiology, 159,* 1180–1188.

Chen, E., Langer, D. A., Raphaelson, Y. E., & Matthews, K. (2004). Socioeconomic status and health in adolescents: The role of stress interpretations. *Child Development, 75,* 1039–1052.

Chen, H., Mechanic, D., & Hansell, S. (1998). A longitudinal study of self-awareness and depressed mood in adolescence. *Journal of Youth and Adolescence, 27,* 719–734.

Chen, K., & Kandel, D. (1996). The natural history of drug use from adolescence to the mid-thirties in a general population sample. *American Journal of Public Health, 85,* 41–47.

Chen, X., Rubin, K., & Li, D. (1997). Relation between academic achievement and social adjustment: Evidence from Chinese children. *Developmental Psychology, 33,* 518–525.

Cherlin, A., Chase-Lansdale, P., & McRae, C. (1998). Effects of parental divorce on mental health throughout the life course. *American Sociological Review, 63,* 239–249.

Cherlin, A., Furstenberg, F., Jr., Chase-Lansdale, L., Kiernan, K., Robins, P., Morrison, D., & Teitler, J. (1991). Longitudinal studies of effects of divorce on children in Great Britain and the United States. *Science, 252,* 1386–1389.

Chesson, H. W., Blandford, J. M., Gift, T. L., Tao, G., & Irwin, K. L. (2004). The estimated direct medical cost of sexually transmitted diseases among American youth. *Perspectives on Sexual and Reproductive Health, 36,* 11–19.

Cheung, Y. (1997). Family, school, peer, and media predictors of adolescent deviant behavior in Hong Kong. *Journal of Youth and Adolescence, 26,* 569–596.

Children's Defense Fund. (1989). *Service opportunities for youths.* Washington, DC: Children's Defense Fund.

Chilman, C. (1986). Some psychosocial aspects of adolescent sexual and contraceptive behaviors in a changing American society. In J. Lancaster and B. Hamburg (Eds.), *School-age pregnancy and parenthood: Biosocial dimensions.* New York: Aldine de Gruyter.

Chisholm, L., & Hurrelmann, K. (1995). Adolescence in modern Europe: Pluralized transition patterns and their implications for personal and social risks. *Journal of Adolescence, 18,* 129–158.

Choi, Y., Harachi, T. W., Gillmore, M. R., & Catalano, R. F. (2005). Applicability of the social development model to urban ethnic minority youth: Examining the relationship between external constraints, family socialization, and problem behaviors. *Journal of Research on Adolescence, 15,* 505–534.

Chou, C., Montgomery, S., Pentz, M., Rohrbach, L., Johnson, C., Flay, B., & MacKinnon, D. (1998). Effects of a community-based prevention program in decreasing drug use in high-risk adolescents. *American Journal of Public Health, 88,* 944–948.

Christopher, F. (1995). Adolescent pregnancy prevention. *Family Relations, 44,* 384–391.

Christopher, F. S., & Roosa, M. (1990). An evaluation of an adolescent pregnancy prevention program: Is "Just say no" enough? *Family Relations, 39,* 68–72.

Chumlea, W., Schubert, C., Roche, A., Kulin, H., Lee, P., Himes, J., et al. (2003). Age at menarche and racial comparisons in U.S. girls. *Pediatrics, 111*(1), 110–113.

Chun, Y.-J., & MacDermid, S. M. (1997). Perceptions of family differentiation, individuation, and self-esteem among Korean adolescents. *Journal of Marriage and the Family, 59*(2), 451–462.

Chung, H. L., & Steinberg, L. (2006). Relations between neighborhood factors, parenting behaviors, peer deviance, and delinquency among serious juvenile offenders. *Developmental Psychology, 42,* 319–331.

Chung, R., & Walkey, F. (1989). Educational and achievement aspirations of New Zealand Chinese and European secondary school students. *Youth and Society, 21,* 139–152.

Church, R. (1976). *Education in the United States.* New York: Free Press.

Claes, M. (1998). Adolescents' closeness with parents, siblings, and friends in three countries: Canada, Belgium, and Italy. *Journal of Youth and Adolescence, 27*(2), 165–184.

Clancy, S., & Dollinger, S. (1993). Identity, self, and personality, I: Identity status and the five-factor model of personality. *Journal of Research on Adolescence, 3,* 227–246.

Clark, J., & Barber, B. (1994). Adolescents in postdivorce and always-married families: Self-esteem and perceptions of fathers' interest. *Journal of Marriage and the Family, 56,* 608–614.

Clark, R., & Delia, J. (1976). The development of functional persuasive skills in childhood and early adolescence. *Child Development, 47,* 1008–1014.

Clark, R., Dogan, R. R., & Akbar, N. J. (2003). Youth and parental correlates of externalizing symptoms, adaptive functioning, and academic performance: An exploratory study in preadolescent blacks. *Journal of Black Psychology, 29,* 210–229.

Clark, R., Novak, J. D., & Dupree, D. (2002). Relationship of perceived parenting practices to anger regulation and coping strategies in African American adolescents. *Journal of Adolescence, 25*(4), 373–384.

Clasen, D., & Brown, B. (1985). The multidimensionality of peer pressure in adolescence. *Journal of Youth and Adolescence, 14,* 451–468.

Cleveland, H. (2003). The influence of female and male risk on the occurrence of sexual intercourse within adolescent relationships. *Journal of Research on Adolescence, 13*(1), 81–112.

Cleveland, H. H., & Wiebe, R. P. (2003). The moderation of adolescent-to-peer similarity in tobacco and alcohol use by school levels of substance use. *Child Development, 74,* 279–291.

Cleveland, M. J., Gibbons, F. X., Gerrard, M., Pomery, E. A., & Brody, G. H. (2005). The impact of parenting on risk cognitions and risk behavior: A study of mediation and moderation in a panel of African American adolescents. *Child Development, 76,* 900–916.

Clingempeel, W., Colyar, J., Brand, E., & Hetherington, E. (1992). Children's relationships with maternal grandparents: A longitudinal study of family structure and pubertal status effects. *Child Development, 63,* 1404–1422.

Coatsworth, J. D., Sharp, E. H., Palen, L., Darling, N., Cumsille, P., & Marta, E. (2005). Exploring adolescent self-defining leisure activities and identity experiences across three countries. *International Journal of Behavioral Development, 29,* 361–370.

Cochran, B. N., Stewart, A. J., Ginzler, J. A., & Cauce, A. (2002). Challenges faced by homeless sexual minorities: Comparison of gay, lesbian, bisexual, and transgender homeless adolescents with their heterosexual counterparts. *American Journal of Public Health, 92*(5), 773–777.

Coe, C., Hayashi, K., & Levine, S. (1988). Hormones and behavior at puberty: Activation or concatenation. In M. Gunnar & W. A. Collins (Eds.), *The Minnesota Symposia on Child Psychology,* Vol. 21, pp. 17–41. Hillsdale, NJ: Erlbaum.

Cohen, D., Farley, T., Taylor, S., Martin, D., & Schuster, M. (2002). When and where do youths have sex? The potential role of adult supervision. *Pediatrics, 110*(6), E66.

Cohen, P. K., Chen, H., Hartmark, C., & Gordon, K. (2003). Variations in patterns of developmental transmissions in the emerging adulthood period. *Developmental Psychology, 39,* 657–669.

Cohen, Y. (1964). *The transition from childhood to adolescence.* Chicago: Aldine.

Coie, J., Terry, R., Lenox, K., Lochman, J., & Hyman, C. (1995). Childhood peer rejection and aggression as predictors of stable patterns of adolescent disorder. *Development and Psychopathology, 7,* 697–713.

Coiro, M., & Emery, R. (1996, March). Adolescents' adjustment as a function of their involvement in post-divorce conflict. Paper presented at the biennial meetings of the Society for Research on Adolescence, Boston.

Colby, A., & Kohlberg, L. (1987). *The measurement of moral judgment.* New York: Cambridge University Press.

Colby, A., Kohlberg, L., Gibbs, J., & Lieberman, M. (1983). A longitudinal study of moral judgment. *Monographs of the Society for Research in Child Development, 48,* Serial No. 200.

Colder, C., & Stice, E. (1998). A longitudinal study of the interactive effects of impulsivity and anger on adolescent problem behavior. *Journal of Youth and Adolescence, 27*, 255–274.

Cole, A., & Kerns, K. A. (2001). Perceptions of sibling qualities and activities of early adolescents. *Journal of Early Adolescence, 21*(2), 204–226.

Cole, D., & Jordan, A. (1995). Competence and memory: Integrating psychosocial and cognitive correlates of child depression. *Child Development, 66*, 459–473.

Cole, D., Martin, J., Peeke, L., Seroczynski, A., & Hoffman, K. (1998). Are cognitive errors of underestimation predictive or reflective of depressive symptoms in children: A longitudinal study. *Journal of Abnormal Psychology, 107*, 481–496.

Cole, D., Martin, J., & Powers, B. (1997). A competency-based model of child depression: A longitudinal study of peer, parent, teacher, and self-evaluations. *Journal of Child Psychology and Psychiatry and Allied Disciplines, 38*, 505–514.

Cole, D., Maxwell, S., Martin, J., Peeke, L., Seroczynski, A., Tram, J., et al. (2001). The development of multiple domains of child and adolescent self-concept: A cohort sequential longitudinal design. *Child Development, 72*(6), 1723–1746.

Cole, D., Peeke, L., Dolezal, S., Murray, N., & Canzoniero, A. (1999). A longitudinal study of negative affect and self-perceived competence in young adolescents. *Journal of Personality and Social Psychology, 77*, 851–862.

Coleman, J. (1961). *The adolescent society.* Glencoe, IL: Free Press.

Coleman, J., Campbell, E., Hobson, C., McPartland, J., Mood, A., Weinfeld, F., & York, R. (1966). *Equality of educational opportunity.* Washington, DC: U.S. Government Printing Office.

Coleman, J., & Hoffer, T. (1987). *Public and private high schools: The impact of communities.* New York: Basic Books.

Coleman, J., Hoffer, T., & Kilgore, S. (1982). *High school achievement: Public, Catholic and other private schools compared.* New York: Basic Books.

Coleman, L. (1999). Comparing contraceptive use surveys of young people in the United Kingdom. *Archives of Sexual Behavior, 28*, 255–264.

Coleman, L. M., & Cater, S. M. (2005). A qualitative study of the relationship between alcohol consumption and risky sex in adolescents. *Archives of Sexual Behavior, 34*, 649–661.

Coley, R. L. (2003). Daughter–father relationships and adolescent psychosocial functioning in low-income African American families. *Journal of Marriage and the Family, 65*, 867–875.

Coley, R. L., & Chase-Lansdale, P. L. (1998). Adolescent pregnancy and parenthood: Recent evidence and future directions. *American Psychologist, 53*, 152–166.

Coley, R. L., Morris, J. E., & Hernandez, D. (2004). Out-of-school care and problem behavior trajectories among low-income adolescents: Individual, family, and neighborhood characteristics as added risks. *Child Development, 75*, 948–965.

Coll, C., Hoffman, J., & Oh, W. (1987). The social ecology and early parenting of Caucasian adolescent mothers. *Child Development, 58*, 955–963.

Collaer, M., & Hines, M. (1995). Human behavioral sex differences: A role for gonadal hormones during early development? *Psychological Bulletin, 118*, 55–107.

College Entrance Examination Board (2006). *2005 college-bound seniors.* New York: Author.

Collins, N. L., & Feeney, B. C. (2004). Working models of attachment shape perceptions of social support: Evidence from experimental and observational studies. *Journal of Personality and Social Psychology, 87*, 363–383.

Collins, W. A. (2003). More than a myth: The developmental significance of romantic relationships during adolescence. *Journal of Research on Adolescents, 13*(1), 1–24.

Collins, W. A. (1988). Research on the transition to adolescence: Continuity in the study of developmental processes. In M. Gunnar & W. A. Collins (Eds.), Minnesota Symposium on Child Psychology, Vol. 21, pp. 1–15. Hillsdale, NJ: Erlbaum.

Collins, W. A. (1990). Parent–child relationships in the transition to adolescence: Continuity and change in interaction, affect, and cognition. In R. Montemayor, G. Adams, & T. Gullotta (Eds.), *Advances in adolescent development,* Vol. 2: *The transition from childhood to adolescence,* pp. 85–106. Beverly Hills, CA: Sage.

Collins, W. A., & Laursen, B. (2004). Changing relationships, changing youth interpersonal contexts of adolescent development. *Journal of Early Adolescence, 24*, 55–62.

Collins, W. A., & Laursen, B. (2004). Parent–adolescent relationships and influences. In R. Lerner & L. Steinberg (Eds.), *Handbook of adolescent psychology.* New York: Wiley.

Collins, W. A., Maccoby, E., Steinberg, L., Hetherington, E. M., & Bornstein, M. (2000). Contemporary research on parenting: The case for nature and nurture. *American Psychologist, 55*, 218–232.

Collins, W. A., & Russell, G. (1991). Mother–child and father–child relationships in middle adolescence: A developmental analysis. *Developmental Review, 11*, 99–136.

Collins, W. A., & Sroufe, L. A. (1999). Capacity for intimate relationships: A developmental construction. In W. Furman, B. Brown, & C. Feiring (Eds.). *Contemporary perspectives on adolescent romantic relationships,* pp. 125–147. New York: Cambridge University Press.

Collins, W. A., & Steinberg, L. (2006). Adolescent development in interpersonal context. In N.

Eisenberg (Vol. Ed.), *Social, emotional, and personality development. Handbook of child psychology* (W. Damon and R. Lerner, Eds.), pp. 1003–1067. New York: Wiley.

Comer, J., Haynes, N., Joyner, E., & Ben Avie, M. (1996). *Rallying the whole village: The Comer process for reforming education.* New York: Teachers College Press.

Comings, D. E., Muhleman, D., Johnson, J. P., & MacMurray, J. P. (2002). Parent–daughter transmission of the androgen receptor gene as an explanation of the effect of father absence on age of menarche. *Child Development, 73*(4), 1046–1051.

Compas, B. (2004). Processes of risk and resilience during adolescence: Linking contexts and individuals. In R. Lerner & L. Steinberg (Eds.), *Handbook of adolescent psychology* (2nd ed.). New York: Wiley.

Compas, B., Connor-Smith, J., Saltzman, H., Thomsen, A., & Wadsworth, M. (2001). Coping with stress during childhood and adolescence: Problems, progress, and potential in theory and research. *Psychological Bulletin, 127*, 87–127.

Compas, B., Ey, S., & Grant, K. (1993). Taxonomy, assessment, and diagnosis of depression during adolescence. *Psychological Bulletin, 114*, 323–344.

Compas, B., Oppedisano, G., Connor, J., Gerhardt, C., Hinden, B., Achenbach, T., & Hammen, C. (1997). Gender differences in depressive symptoms in adolescence: Comparison of national samples of clinically referred and nonreferred youths. *Journal of Consulting and Clinical Psychology, 65*, 617–626.

Compian, L., Gowen, L., & Hayward, C. (2004). Peripubertal girls' romantic and platonic involvement with boys: Associations with body image and depression symptoms. *Journal of Research on Adolescents, 14*, 23–47.

Compton, K., Snyder, J., & Schrepferman, L. (2003). The contribution of parents and siblings to antisocial and depressive behavior in adolescents: A double jeopardy coercion model. *Development and Psychopathology, 15*, 163–182.

Conant, J. (1959). *The American high school today.* New York: McGraw-Hill.

Condit, V. (1990). Anorexia nervosa: Levels of causation. *Human Nature, 1*, 391–413.

Conduct Problems Prevention Research Group (1999). Initial impact of the Fast Track Prevention Trial for Conduct Problems, II: Classroom effects. *Journal of Consulting and Clinical Psychology, 67*, 648–657.

Conger, K., & Conger, R. (1994). Differential parenting and change in sibling differences in delinquency. *Journal of Family Psychology, 8*, 287–302.

Conger, K., Conger, R., & Elder, G., Jr. (1994). Sibling relationships during hard times. In R.

Conger & G. Elder, Jr. (Eds.), *Families in troubled times: Adapting to change in rural America*, pp. 235–252. New York: Aldine.

Conger, R., Conger, K., Elder, G., Jr., Lorenz, F., Simons, R., & Whitbeck, L. (1992). A family process model of economic hardship and adjustment of early adolescent boys. *Child Development, 63*, 526–541.

Conger, R., Conger, K., Elder, G., Jr., Lorenz, F., Simons, R., & Whitbeck, L. (1993). Family economic stress and adjustment of early adolescent girls. *Developmental Psychology, 29*, 206–219.

Conger, R., Conger, K., Matthews, L., & Elder, G. H., Jr. (1999). Pathways of economic influence on adolescent adjustment. *American Journal of Community Psychology, 27*, 519–541.

Conger, R., Cui, M., Bryant, C. M., & Elder, G. H., Jr. (2000). Competence in early adult romantic relationships: A developmental perspective on family influences. *Journal of Personality and Social Psychology, 79*(2), 224–237.

Conger, R., Ge, X., Elder, G., Jr., Lorenz, F., & Simons, R. (1994). Economic stress, coercive family process, and developmental problems of adolescents. *Child Development, 65*, 541–561.

Conger, R., Patterson, G., & Ge, X. (1995). It takes two to replicate: A mediational model for the impact of parents' stress on adolescent adjustment. *Child Development, 66*, 80–97.

Connell, J., Spencer, M., & Aber, J. (1994). Educational risk and resilience in African-American youth: Context, self, action, and outcomes in school. *Child Development, 65*, 493–506.

Connolly, J., Craig, W., Goldberg, A., & Pepler, D. (1999). Conceptions of cross-sex friendships and romantic relationships in early adolescence. *Journal of Youth and Adolescence, 28*(4), 481–494.

Connolly, J., Craig, W., Goldberg, A., & Pepler, D. (2004). Mixed-gender groups, dating, and romantic relationships in early adolescence. *Journal of Research on Adolescence, 14*, 185–207.

Connolly, J., Furman, W., & Konarski, R. (2000). The role of peers in the emergence of heterosexual romantic relationships in adolescence. *Child Development, 71*(5), 1395–1408.

Connolly, J., & Goldberg, A. (1999). Romantic relationships in adolescence: The role of friends and peers in their emergence and development. In W. Furman, B. Brown, & C. Feiring (Eds.), *Contemporary perspectives on adolescent romantic relationships*, pp. 266–290. New York: Cambridge University Press.

Connolly, J., & Johnson, A. (1993, March). The psychosocial context of romantic relationships in adolescence. Paper presented at the biennial meetings of the Society for Research in Child Development, New Orleans.

Connolly, J., & Konarski, R. (1994). Peer self-concept in adolescence: Analysis of factor structure and of associations with peer experience. *Journal of Research on Adolescence, 4*, 385–403.

Conseur, A., Rivara, F., Barnoski, R., & Emanuel, I. (1997). Maternal and perinatal risk factors for later delinquency. *Pediatrics, 99*, 785–790.

Consortium on Productivity in the Schools. (1995). *Using what we have to get the schools we need: A productivity focus for American education.* New York: Author, Institute on Education and the Economy, Teachers College, Columbia University.

Consortium on Renewing Education. (1998). *20/20 vision: A strategy for doubling America's academic achievement by the year 2020.* Nashville, TN: Peabody Center for Education Policy, Vanderbilt University.

Cook, P. J., & Ludwig, J. (2004). Does gun prevalence affect teen gun carrying after all? *Criminology, 42*, 27–54.

Cook, T., Church, M., Ajanaku, S., Shadish, W., Jr., Kim, J., & Cohen, R. (1996). The development of occupational aspirations and expectations among inner-city boys. *Child Development, 67*, 3368–3385.

Cook, T., Habib, F., Phillips, M., Settersen, R., Shagle, S., & Degirmencioglu, S. (1999). Comer's school development program in Prince George's County, Maryland: A theory-based evaluation. *American Educational Research Journal, 36*, 543–597.

Cook, T., Herman, M., Phillips, M., & Settersten, R., Jr. (2002). Some ways in which neighborhoods, nuclear families, friendship groups, and schools jointly affect changes in early adolescent development. *Child Development, 73*(4), 1283–1309.

Cook, T., Murphy, R., & Hunt, H. (2000). Comer's school development program in Chicago: A theory-based evaluation. *American Educational Research Journal, 37*(2), 535–597.

Cook, W. L. (2001). Interpersonal influence in family systems: A social relations model analysis. *Child Development, 72*(4), 1179–1197.

Cooksey, E. C., Mott, F. L., & Neubauer, S. A. (2002). Friendships and early relationships: Links to sexual initiation among American adolescents born to young mothers. *Perspectives on Sexual and Reproductive Health, 34*(3), 118–126.

Cooley-Quille, M., & Lorion, R. (1999). Adolescents' exposure to community violence: Sleep and psychophysiological functioning. *Journal of Community Psychology, 27*, 367–375.

Cooper, C. (1988). Commentary: The role of conflict in adolescent–parent relationships. In M. Gunnar & W. A. Collins (Eds.), *Minnesota Symposium on Child Psychology*, Vol 21, pp. 181–187. Hillsdale, NJ: Erlbaum.

Cooper, C. (1994). Cultural perspectives on continuity and change in adolescents' relationships. In R. Montemayor, G. Adams, & T. Gullotta (Eds.), *Personal relationships during adolescence.* Thousand Oaks, CA: Sage.

Cooper, C., Baker, H., Polichar, D., & Welsh, M. (1994). Values and communication of Chinese, European, Filipino, Mexican, and Vietnamese American adolescents with their families and friends. In S. Shulman & W. A. Collins (Eds.), *The role of fathers in adolescent development: New directions for child development*, pp. 73–89. San Francisco: Jossey-Bass.

Cooper, C., Carlson, C., Keller, J., Koch, P., & Spradling, V. (1993, March). Conflict negotiation in early adolescence: Links between family and peer relational patterns. Paper presented at the biennial meetings of the Society for Research in Child Development, New Orleans.

Cooper, C., Grotevant, H., & Condon, S. (1983). Individuality and connectedness in the family as a context for adolescent identity formation and role taking skill. In H. Grotevant & C. Cooper (Eds.), *Adolescent development in the family.* San Francisco: Jossey-Bass.

Cooper, H., Charlton, K., Valentine, J., & Muhlenbruck, L. (2000). Making the most of summer school: A meta-analytic and narrative review. *Monographs of the Society for Research in Child Development, 65*, Serial No. 260.

Cooper, M. L., Shaver, P. R., & Collins, N. L. (1998b). Attachment styles, emotion regulation, and adjustment in adolescence. *Journal of Personality and Social Psychology, 74*(5), 1380–1397.

Cooper, M., L., Wood, P. K., Orcutt, H. K., & Albino, A. (2003). Personality and the predisposition to engage in risky or problem behaviors during adolescence. *Journal of Personality and Social Psychology, 84*, 390–410.

Cornwell, G., Eggebeen, D., & Meschke, L. (1996). The changing family context of early adolescence. *Journal of Early Adolescence, 16*, 141–156.

Corville-Smith, J., Ryan, B., Adams, G., & Dalicandro, T. (1998). Distinguishing absentee students from regular attenders: The combined influence of personal, family, and school factors. *Journal of Youth and Adolescence, 27*, 629–640.

Costa, F., Jessor, R., Donovan, J., & Fortenberry, J. (1995). Early initiation of sexual intercourse: The influence of psychosocial unconventionality. *Journal of Research on Adolescence, 5*, 93–121.

Costello, E. J., Compton, S. N., Keeler, G., & Angold, A. (2003). Relationships between poverty and psychopathology. *Journal of the American Medical Association, 290*, 2023–2029.

Cota-Robles, S., Neiss, M., & Rowe, D. C. (2002). The role of puberty in violent and nonviolent delinquency among Anglo American, Mexican American, and African American boys. *Journal of Adolescent Research, 17*(4), 364–376.

Côté, J. (2000). *Arrested adulthood: The changing nature of maturity and identity.* New York: New York University Press.

Cote, S., Zoccolillio, M., Tremblay, R. E., Nagin, D., & Vitaro, F. (2001). Predicting girls' conduct disorder in adolescence from childhood trajectories of disruptive behaviors. *Journal of the American Academy of Child and Adolescent Psychiatry, 40,* 678–684.

Coulten, C., & Pandey, S. (1992). Geographic concentration of poverty and risk to children in urban environments. *American Behavioral Scientist, 35,* 238–257.

Courtney, M., & Cohen, R. (1996). Behavior segmentation by boys as a function of aggressiveness and prior information. *Child Development, 67,* 1034–1047.

Crandall, C. (1988). Social contagion of binge eating. *Journal of Personality and Social Psychology, 55,* 588–598.

Crane, D. R., So Wa, N., Larson, J. H., & Hafen, M., Jr. (2005). The influence of family functioning and parent-adolescent acculturation on North American Chinese adolescent outcomes. *Family Relations, 54,* 400–410.

Crane, J. (1991). The epidemic theory of ghettos and neighborhood effects on dropping out and teenage childbearing. *American Journal of Sociology, 96,* 1226–1259.

Crawford, T. N., Cohen, P., Midlarsky, E., & Brook, J. S. (2001). Internalizing symptoms in adolescents: Gender differences in vulnerability to parental distress and discord. *Journal of Research on Adolescence, 11*(1), 95–118.

Creasey, G., & Kaliher, G. (1994). Age differences in grandchildren's perceptions of relations with grandparents. *Journal of Adolescence, 17,* 411–426.

Crick, N. (1996). The role of overt aggression, relational aggression, and prosocial behavior in the prediction of children's future social adjustment. *Child Development, 67,* 2317–2327.

Crick, N. (1997). Engagement in gender normative versus nonnormative forms of aggression: Links to social-psychological adjustment. *Developmental Psychology, 33,* 610–617.

Crick, N., Bigbee, M., & Howes, C. (1996). Gender differences in children's normative beliefs about aggression: How do I hurt thee? Let me count the ways. *Child Development, 67,* 1003–1014.

Crick, N., & Dodge, K. (1994). A review and reformulation of social information-processing mechanisms in children's social adjustment. *Psychological Bulletin, 115,* 74–101.

Crick, N., & Dodge, K. (1996). Social information-processing mechanisms in reactive and proactive aggression. *Child Development, 67,* 993–1002.

Crick, N., & Grotpeter, K. (1995). Relational aggression, gender, and social-psychological adjustment. *Child Development, 66,* 710–722.

Criss, M. M., & Shaw, D. (2005). Sibling relationships as contexts for delinquency training in low-income families. *Journal of Family Psychology, 19,* 592–600.

Crites, H. (1989). Career differentiation in adolescence. In D. Stern & D. Eichorn (Eds.), *Adolescence and work.* Hillsdale, NJ: Erlbaum.

Crittenden, P., Claussen, A., & Sugarman, D. (1994). Physical and psychological maltreatment in middle childhood and adolescence. *Development and Psychopathology, 6,* 145–164.

Crockett, L., & Bingham, R. (2000). Anticipating adulthood: Expected timing of work and family transitions among rural youth. *Journal of Research on Adolescence, 10,* 151–172.

Crockett, L., Bingham, C., Chopak, J., & Vicary, J. (1996). Timing of first sexual intercourse: The role of social control, social learning and problem behavior. *Journal of Youth and Adolescence, 25,* 89–111.

Croll, J., Neumark-Sztainer, D., Story, M., & Ireland, M. (2002). Prevalence and risk and protective factors related to disordered eating behaviors among adolescents: Relationship to gender and ethnicity. *Journal of Adolescent Health, 31*(2), 166–175.

Croninger, R. G., & Lee, V. E. (2001). Social capital and dropping out of school: Benefits to at-risk students of teachers' support and guidance. *Teachers College Record, 103*(4), 548–581.

Crosbie-Burnett, M., & Giles-Sims, J. (1994). Adolescent adjustment and stepparenting styles. *Family Relations, 43,* 394–399.

Crosby, R. A., DiClemente, R. J., Wingood, G. M., Lang, D., & Harrington, K. F. (2003). Value of consistent condom use: A study of sexually transmitted disease prevention among African American adolescent females. *American Journal of Public Health, 93,* 901–902.

Crosnoe, R. (2001). Academic orientation and parental involvement in education during high school. *Sociology of Education, 74*(3), 210–230.

Crosnoe, R. (2002). High school curriculum track and adolescent association with delinquent friends. *Journal of Adolescent Research, 17*(2), 143–167.

Crosnoe, R., Erickson, K., & Dornbusch, S. M. (2002). Protective functions of family relationships and school factors on the deviant behavior of adolescent boys and girls: Reducing the impact of risky friendships. *Youth and Society, 33*(4), 515–544.

Crosnoe, R., Mistry, R. S., & Elder, G. H., Jr. (2002). Economic disadvantage, family dynamics, and adolescent enrollment in higher education. *Journal of Marriage and the Family, 64*(3), 690–702.

Crosnoe, R., & Needham, B. (2004). Holism, contextual variability, and the study of friendships in adolescent development. *Child Development, 75,* 264–279.

Cross, W. (1978). The Thomas and Cook models of psychological nigrescence: A literature review. *Journal of Black Psychology, 4,* 13–31.

Crouter, A., Manke, B., & McHale, S. (1995). The family context of gender intensification in early adolescence. *Child Development, 66,* 317–329.

Crouter, A. C., Bumpus, M. F., Davis, K. D., & McHale, S. M. (2005). How do parents learn about adolescents' experiences? Implications for parental knowledge and adolescent risky behavior. *Child Development, 76,* 869–882.

Crystal, D., Chen, C., Fuligni, A., Stevenson, H., Hsu, C., Ko, H., Kitamura, S., & Kimura, S. (1994). Psychological maladjustment and academic achievement: A cross-cultural study of Japanese, Chinese, and American high school students. *Child Development, 65,* 738–753.

Crystal, D., Watanabe, H., Weinfurt, K., & Wu, C. (1998). Concepts of human differences: A comparison of American, Japanese, and Chinese children and adolescents. *Developmental Psychology, 34,* 714–722.

Csikszentmihalyi, M., & Larson, R. (1984). *Being adolescent.* New York: Basic Books.

Cubbin, C., Santelli, J., Brindis, C. D., & Braveman, P. (2005). Neighborhood context and sexual behaviors among adolescents: Findings from the National Longitudinal Study of Adolescent Health. *Perspectives on Sexual and Reproductive Health, 37,* 125–134.

Cui, M., Conger, R. D., Bryant, C. M., & Elder, G. H. (2002). Parental behavior and the quality of adolescent friendships: A social contextual perspective. *Journal of Marriage and the Family, 64*(3), 676–689.

Cui, M., Conger, R. D., & Lorenz, F. O. (2005). Predicting change in adolescent adjustment from change in marital problems. *Developmental Psychology, 41,* 812–823.

Cummings, E., Ballard, M., El-Sheikh, M., & Lake, M. (1991). Resolution and children's responses to interadult anger. *Developmental Psychology, 27,* 462–470.

Cunningham, M. (1999). African-American adolescent males' perceptions of their community resources and constraints: A longitudinal analysis. *Journal of Community Psychology, 27,* 569–588.

Cunningham, M., Bhattacharyya, S., & Benes, F. (2002). Amygdalo-cortical sprouting continues into early adulthood: Implications for the development of normal and abnormal function during adolescence. *Journal of Comparative Neurology, 453,* 116–130.

Curran, P., Stice, E., & Chassin, L. (1997). The relation between adolescent alcohol use and peer alcohol use: A longitudinal random coefficients model. *Journal of Consulting and Clinical Psychology, 65,* 130–140.

Curtner-Smith, M., & MacKinnon-Lewis, C. (1994). Family process effects on adolescent males' susceptibility to antisocial peer pressure. *Family Relations, 43,* 462–468.

Cusick, P. A. (1973). *Inside high school.* New York: Holt, Rinehart & Winston.

Cutler, S., & Nolen-Hoeksema, S. (1991). Accounting for sex differences in depression through female victimization: Childhood sexual abuse. *Sex Roles, 24,* 425–438.

Cvijanovich, N. Z., Cook, L. J., Mann, N. C., & Dean, J. M. (2001). A population-based study of crashes involving 16- and 17-year-old drivers: The potential benefit of graduated driver licensing restrictions. *Pediatrics, 107*(4), 632–637.

Cyranowski, J., & Frank, E. (2000). Adolescent onset of the gender difference in lifetime rates of major depression. *Archives of General Psychiatry, 57,* 21–27.

D'Angelo, L., Getson, P., Luban, N., & Gayle, H. (1991). Human immunodeficiency virus infection in urban adolescents: Can we predict who is at risk? *Pediatrics, 88,* 982–986.

Daddis, C., & Smetana, J. (2005). Middle-class African American families' expectations for adolescents' behavioral autonomy. *International Journal of Behavioral Development, 29,* 371–381.

Dahl, R. E., & Hariri, A. R. (2005). Lessons from G. Stanley Hall: Connecting new research in biological science to the study of adolescent development. *Journal of Research on Adolescence 15,* 367–382.

Dalton, S. (1992). Overuse injuries in adolescent athletes. *Sports Medicine, 13,* 58–70.

Daly, K. (1994). Adolescent perceptions of adoption. *Youth and Society, 25,* 330–350.

Damico, R. (1984). Does working in high school impair academic progress? *Sociology of Education, 57,* 157–164.

Daniel, D. B., & Klaczynski, P. A. (2006). Developmental and individual differences in conditional reasoning: Effects of logic instructions and alternative antecedents. *Child Development, 77,* 339–354.

Daniels, D., Dunn, J., Furstenberg, F., Jr., & Plomin, R. (1985). Environmental differences within the family and adjustment differences within pairs of adolescent siblings. *Child Development, 56,* 764–774.

Danner, F., & Day, M. (1977). Eliciting formal operations. *Child Development, 48,* 1600–1606.

Darabi, K., & Ortiz, V. (1987). Childbearing among young Latino women in the United States. *American Journal of Public Health, 77,* 25–28.

Darling, N., & Steinberg, L. (1997). Community influences on adolescent achievement and deviance. In J. Brooks-Gunn, G. Duncan, & L. Aber (Eds.), *Neighborhood poverty: Context and consequences for children,* Vol. 2: *Conceptual, methodological, and policy approaches to studying neighborhoods,* pp 120–131. New York: Russell Sage Foundation.

Darling, N., Dowdy, B. B., Van Horn, M. L., & Caldwell, L. L. (1999). Mixed-sex settings and the perception of competence. *Journal of Youth and Adolescence, 28*(4), 461–480.

Darling, N., Hamilton, S., & Matsuda, S. (1990, March). Functional roles and social roles: Adolescents' significant others in the United States and Japan. Paper presented at the biennial meetings of the Society for Research on Adolescence, Atlanta.

Darling, N., Palmer, R. F., & Kirpke, M. D. (2005). Do street youths' perceptions of their caregivers predict HIV-risk behavior? *Journal of Family Psychology, 19,* 456–464.

Darroch, J. E., Landry, D. J., & Singh, S. (2000). Changing emphases in sexuality education in U.S. public secondary schools. *Family Planning Perspectives, 32*(5), 204–211, 265.

Darroch, J. E., Singh, S., Frost, J. J., & Study Team. (2001). Differences in teenage pregnancy rates among five developed countries: The roles of sexual activity and contraceptive use. *Family Planning Perspectives, 33*(5), 244–250, 281.

Dauber, S., Alexander, K., & Entwisle, D. (1996). Tracking and transitions through the middle grades: Chanelling educational trajectories. *Sociology of Education, 69,* 290–307.

Davenport, E., Davison, M., Kuang, H., Ding, S., Kim, S., & Kwak, N. (1998). High school mathematics course-taking by gender and ethnicity. *American Educational Research Journal, 35,* 497–514.

Davies, P., & Cummings, M. (1994). Marital conflict and child adjustment: An emotional security hypothesis. *Psychological Bulletin, 116,* 387–411.

Davies, P., & Lindsay, L. (2004). Interparental conflict and adolescent adjustment: Why does gender moderate early adolescent vulnerability? *Journal of Family Psychology, 18,* 160–170.

Davies, P., & Windle, M. (1997). Gender-specific pathways between maternal depressive symptoms, family discord, and adolescent adjustment. *Developmental Psychology, 33,* 657–668.

Davies, P., & Windle, M. (2001). Interparental discord and adolescent adjustment trajectories: The potentiating and protective role of intrapersonal attributes. *Child Development, 72*(4), 1163–1178.

Davis, A., & Rhodes, J. (1994). African-American teenage mothers and their mothers: An analysis of supportive and problematic interactions. *Journal of Community Psychology, 22,* 12–19.

Davis, A., Rhodes, J., & Hamilton-Leaks, J. (1997). When both parents may be a source of support and problems: An analysis of pregnant and parenting female African American adolescents' relationships with their mothers and fathers. *Journal of Research on Adolescence, 7,* 331–348.

Davis, E., & Friel, L. V. (2001). Adolescent sexuality: Disentangling the effects of family structure and family context. *Journal of Marriage and the Family, 63*(3), 669–681.

Davis, K., & Kirkpatrick, L. (1994). Attachment style, gender, and relationship stability: A longitudinal analysis. *Journal of Personality and Social Psychology, 66,* 502–512.

Davis, L. E., Ajzen, I., Saunders, J., & Williams, T. (2002). The decision of African American students to complete high school: An application of the theory of planned behavior. *Journal of Educational Psychology, 94*(4), 810–819.

Dearden, K., Hale, C., & Woolley, T. (1995). The antecedents of teen fatherhood: A retrospective case-control study of Great Britain youth. *American Journal of Public Health, 85,* 551–554.

Deardorff, J., Gonzales, N. A., Christopher, F. S., Roosa, M. W., & Millsap, R. E. (2005). Early puberty and adolescent pregnancy: The influence of alcohol use. *Pediatrics 116,* 1451–1456.

Deater-Deckard, K., & Plomin, R. (1999). An adoption study of etiology of teacher and parent reports of externalizing behavior problems in middle childhood. *Child Development, 70,* 144–154

DeBaryshe, K., Patterson, G., & Capaldi, D. (1993). A performance model for academic achievement in early adolescent boys. *Developmental Psychology, 29,* 795–804.

DeBerry, K., Scarr, S., & Weinberg, R. (1996). Family racial socialization and ecological competence: Longitudinal assessments of African-American transracial adoptees. *Child Development, 67,* 2375–2399.

Deci, E., & Ryan, R. (1985). Intrinsic motivation and self-determination in human behavior. New York: Plenum.

Dee, T., & Evans, W. (2001). Teens and traffic safety. In J. Gruber (Ed.). *Risky behavior among youths: An economic analysis,* pp. 121–165. Chicago: University of Chicago Press.

Değirmencioğlu, S., & Urberg, K. (1994, February). Cross-gender friendships in adolescence: Who chooses the "other"? Paper presented at the biennial meetings of the Society for Research on Adolescence, San Diego.

Değirmencioğlu, S., Tolson, J., & Urberg, K. (1993, March). Stability of adolescent social networks over the school year. Paper presented at the biennial meetings of the Society for Research in Child Development, New Orleans.

Değirmencioğlu, S., Urberg, K., Tolson, J., & Richard, P. (1998). Adolescent friendship networks: Continuity and change over the school year. *Merrill-Palmer Quarterly, 44,* 313–337.

Dekovi, M., Buist, K. L., & Reitz, E. (2004). Stability and changes in problem behavior during adolescence: Latent growth analysis. *Journal of Youth and Adolescence, 33,* 1–12.

Delva, J., Wallace, J. M., Jr., O'Malley, P. M., Bachman, J. G., Johnston, L. D., & Schulenberg, J. E. (2005). The epidemiology of alcohol, marijuana, and cocaine use among Mexican American, Puerto Rican, Cuban American, and other Latin American eighth-grade students in the United States: 1991–2002. *American Journal of Public Health, 95,* 696–702.

Demetriou, A., Christou, C., Spanoudis, G., & Platsidou, M. (2002). The development of mental processing: Efficiency, working memory, and thinking. *Monographs of the Society for Research in Child Development, 67*(1), Serial No. 268.

Demo, D., & Acock, A. (1996). Family structure, family process, and adolescent well-being. *Journal of Research on Adolescence, 6,* 457–488.

Demorest, A., Meyer, C., Phelps, E., Gardner, H., & Winner, E. (1984). Words speak louder than actions: Understanding deliberately false remarks. *Child Development, 55,* 1527–1534.

Demuth, S. (2004). Understanding the delinquency and social relationships of loners. *Youth and Society, 35,* 366–392.

Denton, K., & Zarbatany, L. (1996). Age differences in support processes in conversations between friends. *Child Development, 67,* 1360–1373.

DeRosier, M., Kupersmidt, J., & Patterson, C. (1994). Children's academic and behavioral adjustment as a function of the chronicity and proximity of peer rejection. *Child Development, 65,* 1799–1813.

Devereux, E. (1970). The role of peer group experience in moral development. In J. Hill (Ed.), *Minnesota Symposium on Child Psychology,* Vol. 4. Minneapolis: University of Minnesota Press.

Deyhle, D. (1995). Navajo youth and Anglo racism: Cultural integrity and resistance. *Harvard Educational Review, 65,* 403–444.

Diamond, L. (1998). Development of sexual orientation among adolescent and young adult women. *Developmental Psychology, 34,* 1085–1095.

Diamond, L. M. (2000). Passionate friendships among adolescent sexual-minority women. *Journal of Research on Adolescence, 10*(2), 191–209.

Diamond, L. M., & Dubé, E. M. (2002). Friendship and attachment among heterosexual and sexual-minority youths: Does the gender of your friend matter? *Journal of Youth and Adolescence, 31*(2), 155–166.

Diamond, L., & Lucas, S. (2004). Sexual-minority and heterosexual youths' peer relationships: Experiences, expectations, and implications for well-being. *Journal of Research of Adolescence, 14,* 313–340.

Diamond, L., Savin-Williams, R., & Dubé, E. (1999). Sex, dating, passionate friendships, and romance: Intimate peer relations among lesbian, gay, and bisexual adolescents. In W.

Furman, B. Brown, & C. Feiring (Eds.), *Contemporary perspectives on adolescent romantic relationships,* pp. 175–210. New York: Cambridge University Press.

Diaz, R., & Berndt, T. (1982). Children's knowledge of a best friend: Fact or fancy? *Developmental Psychology, 18,* 787–794.

DiBlasio, F., & Benda, B. (1992). Gender differences in theories of adolescent sexual activity. *Sex Roles, 27,* 221–240.

Dick, D. M., Rose, R. J., Viken, R. J., & Kaprio, J. (2000). Pubertal timing and substance use: Associations between and within families across late adolescence. *Developmental Psychology, 36*(2), 180–189.

Dick, D., Rose, R., Pulkkinen, L., & Kaprio, J. (2001). Measuring puberty and understanding its impact: A longitudinal study of adolescent twins. *Journal of Youth and Adolescence, 30*(4), 385–400.

Dickenson, G. (1975). Dating behavior of black and white adolescents before and after desegregation. *Journal of Marriage and the Family, 37,* 602–608.

DiClemente, R. (1990). The emergence of adolescents as a risk group for Human Immunodeficiency Virus infection. *Journal of Adolescent Research, 5,* 7–17.

DiClemente, R., Boyer, C., & Morales, E. (1988). Minorities and AIDS: Knowledge, attitudes, and misconceptions among Black and Latino adolescents. *American Journal of Public Health, 78,* 55–57.

DiClemente, R., Durbin, M., Siegel, D., Krasnovsky, F., Lazarus, N., & Comacho, T. (1992). Determinants of condom use among junior high school students in a minority, inner-city school district. *Pediatrics, 89,* 197–202.

DiClemente, R., Lodico, M., Grinstead, O., Harper, G., Rickman, R., Evans, P., & Coates, T. (1996). African-American adolescents residing in high-risk urban environments do use condoms: Correlates and predictors of condom use among adolescents in public housing developments. *Pediatrics, 98,* 269–278.

DiClemente, R., Wingood, G., Crosby, R., Sionean, C., Cobb, B., Harrington, K., et al. (2001). Parental monitoring: Association with adolescents' risk behaviors. *Pediatrics, 107*(6), 1363–1368.

DiClemente, R., Wingood, G. M., Harrington, K. F., Lang, D. L., Davies, S. L., Hook, E. W., Oh, M. K., Corsby, R. A., Hertzberg, V. S., Gordon, A. B., Hardin, J. W., Parker, S., & Robillard, A. (2004). Efficacy of an HIV prevention intervention for African American adolescent girls: A randomized controlled trial. *Journal of the American Medical Association, 292,* 171–179.

Diehl, L., Vicary, J., & Deike, R. (1997). Longitudinal trajectories of self-esteem from early to middle adolescence and related psychosocial variables among rural adolescents. *Journal of Research on Adolescence, 7,* 393–411.

Dielman, T. (1994). School-based research on the prevention of adolescent alcohol use and misuse: Methodological issues and advances. *Journal of Research on Adolescence, 4,* 271–293.

DiFranza, J., Savageau, J., & Aisquith, B. (1996). Youth access to tobacco: The effects of age, gender, vending machine locks, and "It's the Law" programs. *American Journal of Public Health, 86,* 221–224.

DiIorio, C., Dudley, W. N., Kelly, M., Soet, J. E., Mbwara, J., & Sharpe Potter, J. (2001). Social cognitive correlates of sexual experience and condom use among 13- through 15-year-old adolescents. *Journal of Adolescent Health, 29*(3), 208–216.

DiIorio, C., Kelley, M., & Hockenberry-Eaton, M. (1999). Communication about sexual issues: Mothers, fathers, and friends. *Journal of Adolescent Health, 24,* 181–189.

DiMaggio, P. (1982). Cultural capital and school success: The impact of status culture participation on the grades of U.S. high school students. *American Sociological Review, 47,* 189–201.

Dishion, T., & Andrews, D. (1995). Preventing escalation in problem behaviors with high-risk young adolescents: Immediate and 1-year outcomes. *Journal of Consulting and Clinical Psychology, 63,* 538–548.

Dishion, T., Andrews, D., & Crosby, L. (1995). Antisocial boys and their friends in early adolescence: Relationship characteristics, quality, and interactional process. *Child Development, 66,* 139–151.

Dishion, T., Capaldi, D., & Yoerger, K. (1999). Middle childhood antecedents to progressions in male adolescent substance use: An ecological analysis of risk and protection. *Journal of Adolescent Research, 14*(2), 175–205.

Dishion, T., McCord, J., & Poulin, F. (1999). When interventions harm: Peer groups and problem behavior. *American Psychologist, 54,* 755–764.

Dishion, T., Nelson, S., & Bullock, B. (2004). Premature adolescent autonomy: Parent disengagement and deviant peer process in the amplification of problem behavior. *Journal of Adolescence, 27,* 515–530.

Dishion, T., Nelson, S., Winter, C., & Bullock, B. (2004). Adolescent friendship as a dynamic system: Entropy and deviance in the etiology and course of male antisocial behavior. *Journal of Abnormal Child Psychology, 32,* 651–663.

Dishion, T., & Owen, L. (2002). A longitudinal analysis of friendships and substance use: Bidirectional influence from adolescence to adulthood. *Developmental Psychology, 38*(4), 480–491.

Dishion, T., Patterson, G., Stoolmiller, M., & Skinner, M. (1991). Family, school, and behavioral antecedents to early adolescent involvement with antisocial peers. *Developmental Psychology, 27,* 172–180.

Dittus, P. J., & Jaccard, J. (2000). Adolescents' perceptions of maternal disapproval of sex:

Relationship to sexual outcomes. *Journal of Adolescent Health, 26*(4), 268–278.

Dittus, P., Jaccard, J., & Gordon, V. (1997). The impact of African American fathers on adolescent sexual behavior. *Journal of Youth and Adolescence, 26*, 445–465.

Dmitrieva, J., Chen, C., Greenberger, E., & Gil-Rivas, V. (2004). Family relationships and adolescent psychosocial outcomes: Converging findings from eastern and western cultures. *Journal of Research on Adolescence, 14*, 425–447.

Dobkin, P., Tremblay, R., Mâsse, L., & Vitaro, F. (1995). Individual and peer characteristics in predicting boys' early onset of substance abuse: A seven-year longitudinal study. *Child Development, 66*, 1198–1214.

Dobkin, P., Tremblay, R., & Sacchitelle, C. (1997). Predicting boys' early-onset substance abuse from father's alcoholism, son's disruptiveness, and mother's parenting behavior. *Journal of Consulting and Clinical Psychology, 65*, 86–92.

Dodge, K. (1986). A social information-processing model of social competence in children. In M. Perlmutter (Ed.), *Minnesota Symposium on Child Psychology,* Vol. 18, pp. 77–125. Hillsdale, NJ: Erlbaum.

Dodge, K., & Coie, J. (1987). Social information-processing factors in reactive and proactive aggression in children's peer groups. *Journal of Personality and Social Psychology, 53*, 1146–1158.

Dodge, K., & Pettit, G. (2003). A biopsychosocial model of the development of chronic conduct problems in adolescence. *Developmental Psychology, 39*, 349–371.

Donnellan, M. B., Larsen-Rife, D., & Conger, R. D. (2005). Personality, family history, and competence in early adult romantic relationship. *Journal of Personality and Social Psychology, 88*, 562–576.

Donnelly, B., & Voydanoff, P. (1996). Parenting versus placing for adoption: Consequences for adolescent mothers. *Family Relations, 42*, 427–434.

Donnelly, D., & Finkelhor, D. (1992). Does equality in custody arrangement improve the parent–child relationship? *Journal of Marriage and the Family, 54*, 837–845.

Donovan, J., & Jessor, R. (1985). Structure of problem behavior in adolescence and young adulthood. *Journal of Consulting and Clinical Psychology, 53*, 890–904.

Dorfman, L., Woodruff, K., Chavez, V., & Wallack, L. (1997). Youth and violence on local television news in California. *American Journal of Public Health, 87*(8), 1311–1316.

Dorius, G., Heaton, T., & Steffen, P. (1993). Adolescent life events and their association with the onset of sexual intercourse. *Youth and Society, 25*, 3–23.

Dorn, L., Dahl, R., Woodward, H., & Biro, F. (2006). Defining the boundaries of early adolescence: A user's guide to assessing pubertal status and pubertal timing in research with adolescents. *Applied Developmental Science, 1*, 30–56.

Dorn, L. D., Nottelmann, E. D., Susman, E. J., Inoff-Germain, G., Cutler, G. B., Jr., & Chrousos, G. P. (1999). Variability in hormone concentrations and self-reported menstrual histories in young adolescents: Menarche as an integral part of a developmental process. *Journal of Youth and Adolescence, 28*(3), 283–304.

Dornbusch, S. (1994, February). Off the track. Presidential address to the Society for Research on Adolescence, San Diego.

Dornbusch, S., Carlsmith, J., Bushwall, S., Ritter, P., Leiderman, P., Hastorf, A., & Gross, R. (1985). Single parents, extended households, and the control of adolescents. *Child Development, 56*, 326–341.

Dornbusch, S., Carlsmith, J., Gross, R., Martin, J., Jennings, D., Rosenberg, A., & Duke, P. (1981). Sexual development, age, and dating: A comparison of biological and social influences upon one set of behaviors. *Child Development, 52*, 179–185.

Dornbusch, S., Erickson, K., Laird, J., & Wong, C. (2001). The relation of family and school attachment to adolescent deviance in diverse groups and communities. *Journal of Adolescent Research, 16*(4), 396–422.

Dornbusch, S., Mont-Reynaud, R., Ritter, P., Chen, Z., & Steinberg, L. (1991). Stressful events and their correlates among adolescents of diverse backgrounds. In M. Colten & S. Gore (Eds.), *Adolescent stress: Causes and consequences,* pp. 111–130. Hawthorne, NY: Aldine de Gruyter.

Dornbusch, S., Ritter, P., Liederman, P., Roberts, D., & Fraleigh, M. (1987). The relation of parenting style to adolescent school performance. *Child Development, 58*, 1244–1257.

Douvan, E., & Adelson, J. (1966). *The adolescent experience.* New York: Wiley.

Dowdy, B. B., & Kliewer, W. (1998). Dating, parent–adolescent conflict, and behavioral autonomy. *Journal of Youth and Adolescence, 27*(4), 473–492.

Downey, D. (1995). Understanding academic achievement among children in stephouseholds: The role of parental resources, sex of stepparent, and sex of child. *Social Forces, 73*, 875–894.

Downey, D. B., & Pribesh, S. (2004). When race matters: Teachers' evaluations of students' classroom behavior. *Sociology of Education, 77*, 267–282.

Downey, D. B., & Ainsworth-Darnell, J. W. (2002). The search for oppositional culture among black students. *American Sociological Review, 67*(1), 156–164.

Downey, D., Ainsworth-Darnell, J., & Dufur, M. (1998). Sex of parent and children's well-being in single-parent households. *Journal of Marriage and the Family, 60*, 878–893.

Downey, G., Bonica, C., & Rincón, C. (1999). Rejection sensitivity and adolescent romantic relationships. In W. Furman, B. Brown, & C. Feiring (Eds.), *Contemporary perspectives on adolescent romantic relationships,* pp. 148–174. New York: Cambridge University Press.

Downey, G., Lebolt, A., Rincón, C., & Freitas, A. (1998). Rejection sensitivity and children's interpersonal difficulties. *Child Development, 69*, 1074–1091.

Doyle, A. B., & Markiewicz, D. (2005). Parenting, marital conflict, and adjustment from early to mid-adolescence: Mediated by adolescent attachment style? *Journal of Youth and Adolescence 34*, 97–110.

Drumm, P., & Jackson, D. (1996). Developmental changes in questioning strategies during adolescence. *Journal of Adolescent Research, 11*, 285–305.

Dryfoos, J. (1990). *Adolescents at risk: Prevalence and prevention.* New York: Oxford University Press.

Dryfoos, J. (1993). Schools as places for health, mental health, and social services. *Teachers College Record, 94*, 540–567.

Dubas, J., Graber, J., & Petersen, A. (1991). A longitudinal investigation of adolescents' changing perceptions of pubertal timing. *Developmental Psychology, 27*, 580–586.

Dubé, E., & Savin-Williams, R. (1999). Sexual identity development among ethnic sexual-minority male youths. *Developmental Psychology, 35*, 1389–1398.

Dube, S. R., Felitti, V. J., Dong, M., Chapman, D. P., Giles, W. H., & Anda, R. F. (2003). Childhood abuse, neglect, and household dysfunction and the risk of illicit drug use: The adverse childhood experiences study. *Pediatrics, 111*(3), 564–572.

DuBois, D., Burk-Braxton, C., Swenson, L. P., Tevendale, H. D., & Hardesty, J. L. (2002). Race and gender influences on adjustment in early adolescence: Investigation of an integrative model. *Child Development, 73*(5), 1573–1592.

DuBois, D., Bull, C., Sherman, M., & Roberts, M. (1998). Self-esteem and adjustment in early adolescence: A social-contextual perspective. *Journal of Youth and Adolescence, 27*, 557–583.

DuBois, D., Felner, R., Brand, S., Adan, A., & Evans, E. (1992). A prospective study of life stress, social support, and adaptation in early adolescence. *Child Development, 63*, 542–557.

DuBois, D., Felner, R., Brand, S., & George, G. (1999). Profiles of self-esteem in early adolescence: Identification and investigation of adaptive correlates. *American Journal of Community Psychology, 27*, 899–932.

DuBois, D., Felner, R., Brand, S., Phillips, R., & Lease, A. (1996). Early adolescent self-esteem: A developmental-ecological framework and assessment strategy. *Journal of Research on Adolescence, 6*, 543–579.

DuBois, D., Felner, R., Meares, H., & Frier, M. (1994). Prospective investigation of the effects of socioeconomic disadvantage, life stress, and social support on early adolescent adjustment. *Journal of Abnormal Psychology, 103,* 511–522.

DuBois, D., & Hirsch, B. (1990). School and neighborhood friendship patterns of blacks and whites in early adolescence. *Child Development, 61,* 524–536.

DuBois, D., Holloway, B., Valentine, J., & Cooper, H. (2002). Effectiveness of mentoring programs for youth: A meta-analytic review. *American Journal of Community Psychology, 30,* 157–197.

DuBois, D., & Silverthorn, N. (2005). Natural mentoring relationships and adolescent health: Evidence from a national study. *American Journal of Public Health, 95,* 518–524.

DuBois, D., & Tevendale, H. (1999). Self-esteem in childhood and adolescence: Vaccine or epiphenomenon. *Applied and Preventive Psychology, 8,* 103–117.

Duchesne, S., Larose, S., Guay, F., Vitaro, F., & Tremblay, R. (2005). The transition from elementary to high school: The pivotal role of mother and child characteristics in explaining trajectories of academic functioning. *International Journal of Behavioral Development, 29,* 409–417.

Dukes, R., Martinez, R., & Stein, J. (1997). Precursors and consequences of membership in youth gangs. *Youth and Society, 29,* 139–165.

Dumont, M., & Provost, M. (1999). Resilience in adolescents: Protective role of social support, coping strategies, self-esteem, and social activities on experience of stress and depression. *Journal of Youth and Adolescence, 28,* 343–363.

Duncan, G. (1994). Families and neighbors as sources of disadvantage in the schooling decisions of white and black adolescents. *American Journal of Education, 103,* 20–53.

Duncan, O., Featherman, D., & Duncan, B. (1972). *Socioeconomic background and achievement.* New York: Semmar Press.

Duncan, P., Ritter, P., Dornbusch, S., Gross, R., & Carlsmith, J. (1985). The effects of pubertal timing on body image, school behavior, and deviance. *Journal of Youth and Adolescence, 14,* 227–236.

Dunn, J., Slomkowski, C., & Beardsall, L. (1994). Sibling relationships from the preschool period through middle childhood and early adolescence. *Developmental Psychology, 30,* 315–324.

Dunn, S., Putallaz, M., Sheppard, B., & Lindstrom, R. (1987). Social support and adjustment in gifted adolescents. *Journal of Educational Psychology, 79,* 467–473.

Dunphy, D. (1969). *Cliques, crowds, and gangs.* Melbourne: Chesire.

DuRant, R., Cadenhead, C., Pendergrast, R., Slavens, G., & Linder, C. (1994). Factors associated with the use of violence among urban Black adolescents. *American Journal of Public Health, 84,* 612–617.

DuRant, R., Getts, A., Cadenhead, C., & Woods, E. (1995). The association between weapon-carrying and the use of violence among adolescents living in or around public housing. *Journal of Adolescence, 18,* 579–592.

DuRant, R., Pendergrast, R., & Cadenhead, C. (1994). Exposure to violence and victimization and fighting behavior by urban Black adolescents. *Journal of Adolescent Health, 15,* 311–318.

DuRant, R., Rome, E., Rich, M., Allred, E., Emans, S., & Woods, E. (1997). Tobacco and alcohol use behaviors portrayed in music videos: A content analysis. *American Journal of Public Health, 87,* 1131–1135.

DuRant, R., Treiber, F., Getts, A., McCloud, K., Linder, C., & Woods, E. (1996). Comparison of two violence prevention curricula for middle school adolescents. *Journal of Adolescent Health, 19,* 111–117.

Dusek, J., & Flaherty, J. (1981). The development of the self-concept during the adolescent years. *Monographs of the Society for Research in Child Development, 46,* Serial No. 191.

Dweck, C., & Light, B. (1980). Learned helplessness and intellectual achievement. In J. Garber and M. Seligman (Eds.), *Human helplessness.* New York: Academic Press.

Dweck, C., & Wortman, C. (1980). Achievement, test anxiety, and learned helplessness: Adaptive and maladaptive cognitions. In H. Krohne and L. Laux (Eds.), *Achievement, stress, and anxiety.* Washington, DC: Hemisphere.

Dyer, G., & Tiggemann, M. (1996). The effects of school environment on body concerns in adolescent women. *Sex Roles, 34,* 127–138.

Dyk, P., & Adams, G. (1990). Identity and intimacy: An initial investigation of three theoretical models using cross-lag panel correlations. *Journal of Youth and Adolescence, 19,* 91–110.

Eamon, M. K. (2005). Social-demographic, school, neighborhood, and parenting influences on the academic achievement of Latino young adolescents. *Journal of Youth and Adolescence, 34,* 163–174.

Earls, F., Cairns, R., & Mercy, J. (1993). The control of violence and the promotion of nonviolence in adolescents. In S. Millstein, A. Petersen, & E. Nightingale (Eds.), *Promoting the health of adolescents: New directions for the twenty-first century,* pp. 285–304. New York: Oxford University Press.

Early, D., & Eccles, J. (1994, February). Predicting parenting behavior: The role of SES, neighborhood risk, and parental values. Paper presented at the biennial meetings of the Society for Research on Adolescence, San Diego.

East, P. (1996a). Do adolescent pregnancy and childbearing affect younger siblings? *Family Planning Perspectives, 28,* 148–153.

East, P. (1996b). The younger sisters of childbearing adolescents: Their attitudes, expectations, and behaviors. *Child Development, 67,* 267–282.

East, P., & Blaustein, E. (1995, March). Perceived timing of life-course transitions: Race differences in early adolescent girls' sexual, marriage, and childbearing expectations. Paper presented at the biennial meetings of the Society for Research in Child Development, Indianapolis.

East, P., & Felice, M. (1992). Pregnancy risk among the younger sisters of pregnant and childbearing adolescents. *Developmental and Behavioral Pediatrics, 13,* 128–136.

East, P., & Felice, M. (1996). *Adolescent pregnancy and parenting: Findings from a racially diverse sample.* Mahwah, NJ: Erlbaum.

East, P., Felice, M., & Morgan, M. (1993). Sisters' and girlfriends' sexual and childbearing behavior: Effects on early adolescent girls' sexual outcomes. *Journal of Marriage and the Family, 55,* 953–963.

East, P., & Jacobson, L. (2001). The younger siblings of teenage mothers: A follow-up of their pregnancy risk. *Developmental Psychology, 37*(2), 254–264.

East, P., & Jacobson, L. (2003). Mothers' differential treatment of their adolescent childbearing and nonchildbearing children: Contrasts between and within families. *Journal of Family Psychology, 19,* 384–396.

East, P., & Khoo, S. (2005). Longitudinal pathways linking family factors and sibling relationship qualities to adolescent substance use and sexual risk behaviors. *Journal of Family Psychology, 19,* 571–580.

East, P., & Kierman, E. (2001). Risks among youths who have multiple sisters who were adolescent parents. *Family Planning Perspectives, 33*(2), 75–80.

East, P., Kierran, E., & Chavez, G. (2003). An evaluation of California's adolescent sibling pregnancy prevention program. *Perspectives on Sexual and Reproductive Health, 35,* 62–70.

East, P., & Rook, K. (1992). Compensatory patterns of support among children's peer relationships: A test using school friends, nonschool friends, and siblings. *Developmental Psychology, 28,* 163–172.

Eaton, M. J., & Dembo, M. H. (1997). Differences in the motivational beliefs of Asian American and non-Asian students. *Journal of Educational Psychology, 89*(3), 433–440.

Ebata, A., & Moos, R. (1994). Personal, situational, and contextual correlates of coping in adolescence. *Journal of Research on Adolescence, 4,* 99–126.

Ebin, V. J., Sneed, C. D., Morisky, D. E., Rotherman-Borus, M., Magnusson, A. M., & Malotte,

C. (2001). Acculturation and interrelation-ships between problem and health-promoting behaviors among Latino adolescents. *Journal of Adolescent Health, 28*(1), 62–72.

Ebstyne King, P., & Furrow, J. L. (2004). Religion as a resource for positive youth development: Religion, social capital, and moral outcomes. *Developmental Psychology, 40,* 703–713.

Eccles, J. (2004). Schools, academic motivation, and stage-environment fit. In R. Lerner & L. Steinberg (Eds.), *Handbook of adolescent psychology.* New York: Wiley.

Eccles, J., & Barber, B. (1999). Student council, volunteering, basketball, or marching band: What kind of extracurricular involvement matters? *Journal of Adolescent Research, 14,* 10–43.

Eccles, J., Early, D., Frasier, K., Belansky, E., & McCarthy, K. (1997). The relation of connection, regulation, and support for autonomy to adolescents' functioning. *Journal of Adolescent Research, 12,* 263–286.

Eccles, J., Lord, S., & Midgley, C. (1991). What are we doing to early adolescents? The impact of educational contexts on early adolescents. *American Journal of Education, 99,* 521–542.

Eccles, J., Midgley, C., Wigfield, A., Buchanan, C., Reuman, D., Flanagan, C., & MacIver, D. (1993). Development during adolescence: The impact of stage-environment fit on young adolescents' experiences in schools and families. *American Psychologist, 48,* 90–101.

Economic Policy Institute. (1994). *The state of working in America, 1992–93.* Washington, DC: Economic Policy Institute.

Eddy, M., & Chamberlain, P. (2000). Family management and deviant peer association as mediators of the impact of treatment condition on youth antisocial behavior. *Journal of Consulting and Clinical Psychology, 68,* 857–863.

Edens, J., Skeem, J., Cruise, K., & Cauffman, E. (2000). The assessment of juvenile psychopathy and its association with violence: A critical review. *Behavioral Sciences and the Law,* 18.

Eder, D. (1985). The cycle of popularity: Interpersonal relations among female adolescence. *Sociology of Education, 58,* 154–165.

Eder, D., & Kinney, D. (1995). The effect of middle school extracurricular activities on adolescents' popularity and peer status. *Youth and Society, 26,* 298–324.

Eder, D., & Parker, S. (1987). The cultural production and reproduction of gender: The effect of extracurricular activities on peer-group culture. *Sociology of Education, 60,* 200–213.

Education Trust. (1996). *Education watch: The 1996 Education Trust state and national data book.* Washington: Author.

Egan, S., & Perry, D. (1998). Does low self-regard invite victimization? *Developmental Psychology, 34,* 299–309.

Eisenberg, N., Carlo, G., Murphy, B., & Van Court, P. (1995). Prosocial development in late adolescence: A longitudinal study. *Child Development, 66,* 1179–1197.

Eisenberg, N., Cumberland, A., Guthrie, I. K., Murphy, B. C., & Shepard, S. A (2005). Age changes in prosocial responding and moral reasoning in adolescence and early adulthood. *Journal of Research on Adolescence, 15,* 235–260.

Eisenberg, N., Miller, P., Shell, R., McNalley, S., & Shea, C. (1991). Prosocial development in adolescence: A longitudinal study. *Developmental Psychology, 27,* 849–857.

Eisenberg, N., & Morris, A. (2004). Moral cognitions and prosocial responding in adolescence. In R. Lerner & L. Steinberg (Eds.), *Handbook of adolescent psychology.* New York: Wiley.

Eisenberg, N., Zhou, Q., & Koller, S. (2001). Brazilian adolescents' prosocial moral judgment and behavior: Relations to sympathy, perspective taking, gender-role orientation, and demographic characteristics. *Child Development, 72*(2), 518–534.

Eisenstadt, S. (1956). *From generation to generation.* Glencoe, IL: Free Press.

Elder, G. H., Jr. (1974). *Children of the Great Depression.* Chicago: University of Chicago Press.

Elder, G. H., Jr. (1980). Adolescence in historical perspective. In J. Adelson (Ed.), *Handbook of adolescent psychology.* New York: Wiley.

Elder, G. H., Jr., & Ardelt, M. (1992, March). Families adapting to economic pressure: Some consequences for parents and adolescents. Paper presented at the biennial meetings of the Society for Research on Adolescence, Washington, DC.

Elder, G. H., Jr., Caspi, A., & van Nguyen, T. (1986). Resourceful and vulnerable children: Family influences in stressful times. In R. Silbereisen, K. Eyferth, & G. Rudinger (Eds.), *Development as action in context.* Heidelberg: Springer.

Elder, G. H., Jr., & Conger, R. (2000). *Children of the land.* Chicago: University of Chicago Press.

Elder, G. H., Jr., Conger, R., Foster, E., & Ardelt, M. (1992). Families under economic pressure. *Journal of Family Issues, 13,* 5–37.

Elder, G. H., Jr., van Nguyen, T., & Caspi, A. (1985). Linking family hardship to children's lives. *Child Development, 56,* 361–375.

Elders, M., Perry, C., Eriksen, M., & Giovino, G. (1994). The report of the Surgeon General: Preventing tobacco use among young people. *American Journal of Public Health, 84,* 543–547.

Eley, T., Lichenstein, P., & Stevenson, J. (1999). Sex differences in the etiology of aggressive and nonaggressive antisocial behavior: Results from two twin studies. *Child Development, 70,* 155–168.

Elkind, D. (1967). Egocentrism in adolescence. *Child Development, 38,* 1025–1034.

Elkind, D. (1978). Understanding the young adolescent. *Adolescence, 13,* 127–134.

Elkind, D. (1985). Egocentrism redux. *Developmental Review, 5,* 218–226.

Ellickson, P., Bell, R., & McGuigan, K. (1993). Preventing adolescent drug use: Long-term results of a junior high program. *American Journal of Public Health, 83,* 856–861.

Ellickson, P., Saner, H., & McGuigan, K. (1997). Profiles of violent youth: Substance use and other concurrent problems. *American Journal of Public Health, 87,* 985–991.

Elliott, B., & Richards, M. (1991, July). Children and divorce: Educational performance and behaviour before and after parental separation. Paper presented at the meetings of the International Society for the Study of Behavioural Development, Minneapolis.

Elliott, D., Huizinga, D., & Menard, S. (1989). *Multiple problem youth: Delinquency, substance abuse, and mental health problems.* New York: Springer-Verlag.

Elliott, D., & Morse, B. (1989). Delinquency and drug use as risk factors in teenage sexual activity. *Youth and Society, 21,* 32–57.

Ellis, B. (2004). Timing of pubertal maturation in girls: An integrated life history approach. *Psychological Bulletin, 130,* 920–958.

Ellis, B. J., Bates, J. E., Dodge, K. A., Fergusson, D. M., Horwood, L. J., Pettit, G. S., & Woodward, L. (2003). Does father absence place daughters at special risk for early sexual activity and teenage pregnancy? *Child Development, 74,* 801–821.

Elmen, J. (1991). Achievement orientation in early adolescence: Developmental patterns and social correlates. *Journal of Early Adolescence, 11,* 125–151.

Elo, I., King, R., & Furstenberg, F., Jr. (1999). Adolescent females: Their sexual partners and the fathers of their children. *Journal of Marriage and the Family, 61,* 74–84.

Ennett, S., & Bauman, K. (1996). Adolescent social networks: School, demographic, and longitudinal considerations. *Journal of Adolescent Research, 11,* 194–215.

Ennett, S., Bauman, K., Hussong, A., Faris, R., Foshee, V., Cai, L., & DuRant, R (2006). The peer context of adolescent substance use: Findings from social network analysis. *Journal of Research on Adolescence, 16,* 159–186.

Ennett, S., Tobler, N., Ringwalt, C., & Flewelling, R. (1994). How effective is drug abuse resistance education? A meta-analysis of Project DARE outcome evaluations. *American Journal of Public Health, 84,* 1394–1401.

Enright, R., Levy, V., Harris, D., & Lapsley, D. (1987). Do economic conditions influence how theorists view adolescents? *Journal of Youth and Adolescence, 16,* 541–560.

Ensminger, M. (1990). Sexual activity and problem behaviors among Black, urban adolescents. *Child Development, 61,* 2032–2046.

Ensminger, M., Lamkin, R., & Jacobson, N. (1996). School leaving: A longitudinal perspective including neighborhood effects. *Child Development, 67,* 2400–2416.

Entwisle, D. (1990). Schools and the adolescent. In S. Feldman & G. Elliott (Eds.), *At the threshold: The developing adolescent,* pp. 197–224. Cambridge, MA: Harvard University Press.

Entwisle, D., Alexander, K., & Olson, L. (2004). Temporary as compared to permanent high school dropout. *Social Forces, 82,* 1181–1205.

Entwisle, D., Alexander, K., & Olson, L. (2005). Urban teenagers work and dropout. *Youth and Society, 37,* 3–32.

Entwisle, D., & Hayduk, L. (1988). Lasting effects of elementary school. *Sociology of Education, 61,* 147–159.

Ephron, N. (1980). *Teenage romance, or how to die of embarrassment.* New York: Viking Press.

Epstein, J. (1983a). Selecting friends in contrasting secondary school environments. In J. Epstein & N. Karweit (Eds.), *Friends in school.* New York: Academic Press.

Epstein, J. (1983b). The influence of friends on achievement and affective outcomes. In J. Epstein & N. Karweit (Eds.), *Friends in school,* pp. 177–200. New York: Academic Press.

Erel, O., & Burman, B. (1995). Interrelatedness of marital relations and parent–child relations: A meta-analytic review. *Psychological Bulletin, 118,* 108–132.

Erickson, K., Crosnoe, R., & Dornbusch, S. M. (2000). A social process model of adolescent deviance: Combining social control and differential association perspectives. *Journal of Youth and Adolescence, 29*(4), 395–425.

Erickson, M. F., Sroufe, L. A., & Egeland, B. (1985). The relationship between quality of attachment and behavior problems in preschool in a high-risk sample: Growing points of attachment theory and research. *Monographs of the Society for Research in Child Development, 50,* 147–193.

Erickson, P. (1994). Lessons from a repeat pregnancy prevention program for Hispanic teenage mothers in East Los Angeles. *Family Planning Perspectives, 26,* 174–178.

Erikson, E. (1959). Identity and the life cycle. *Psychological Issues, 1,* 1–171.

Erikson, E. (1963). *Childhood and society.* New York: Norton.

Erikson, E. (1968). *Identity: Youth and crisis.* New York: Norton.

Erkut, S., Szalacha, L. A., Garcia Coll, C., & Alarcon, O. (2000). Puerto Rican early adolescents' self-esteem patterns. *Journal of Research on Adolescence, 10*(3), 339–364.

Ernst, M., Nelson, E., Jazbec, S., McClure, E., Monk, C., Leibenluft, E., Blair, J., & Pine, D. (2005). Amygdala and nucleus accumbens in response to receipt and omission of gains in adults and adolescents. *Neuroimage, 25,* 1279–1291.

Esbensen, F., Deschenes, E., & Winfree, L., Jr. (1999). Differences between gang girls and gang boys: Results from a multisite survey. *Youth and Society, 31,* 27–53.

Espelage, D. L., Holt, M. K., & Henkel, R. R. (2003). Examination of peer-group contextual effects on aggression during early adolescence. *Child Development, 74,* 205–220.

Espenshade, T. J., Hale, L. E., & Chung, C. Y. (2005). The frog pond revisited: High school academic context, class rank, and elite college admission. *Sociology of Education, 78,* 269–293.

Estrada, P. (1995). Adolescents' self-reports of prosocial responses to friends and acquaintances: The role of sympathy-related cognitive, affective, and motivational processes. *Journal of Research on Adolescence, 5,* 173–200.

Evans, D. (1993, March). A model of structural self-complexity: Its relation to age, symptomatology and self-perception. Paper presented at the biennial meetings of the Society for Research in Child Development, New Orleans.

Evans, E., Rutberg, J., Sather, C., & Turner, C. (1991). Content analysis of contemporary teen magazines for adolescent females. *Youth and Society, 23,* 99–120.

Evans, E., Schweingruber, H., & Stevenson, H. W. (2002). Gender differences in interest and knowledge acquisition: The United States, Taiwan, and Japan. *Sex Roles, 47*(3–4), 153–167.

Eveleth, P., & Tanner, J. (1990). *Worldwide variation in human growth* (2nd ed.). New York: Cambridge University Press.

Everett, S. A., Warren, C. W., Santelli, J. S., Kann, L., Collins, J. L., & Kolbe, L. J. (2000). Use of birth control pills, condoms, and withdrawal among U.S. high school students. *Journal of Adolescent Health, 27*(2), 112–118.

Eyre, S., & Millstein, S. (1999). What leads to sex? Adolescent preferred partners and reasons for sex. *Journal of Research on Adolescence, 9,* 277–307.

Fagan, J, & Zimring, F. (Eds.). (2000). *The changing borders of juvenile justice: Transfer of adolescents to the criminal court.* Chicago: University of Chicago Press.

Fagot, B., Pears, K., Capaldi, D., Crosby, L., & Leve, C. (1998). Becoming an adolescent father: Precursors and parenting. *Developmental Psychology, 34,* 1209–1219.

Falk, R., & Wilkening, F. (1998). Children's construction of fair chances: Adjusting probabilities. *Developmental Psychology, 34,* 1340–1357.

Fall, R., Webb, N. M., & Chudowsky, N. (2000). Group discussion and large-scale language arts assessment: Effects on students' comprehension. *American Educational Research Journal, 37*(4), 911–941.

Fallon, B. J., & Bowles, T. V. (1997). The effect of family structure and family functioning on adolescents' perceptions of intimate time spent with parents, siblings, and peers. *Journal of Youth and Adolescence, 26*(1), 25–43.

Fang, X., Stanton, B., Li, X., Feigelman, S., & Baldwin, R. (1998). Similarities in sexual activity and condom use among friends within groups before and after a risk-reduction intervention. *Youth and Society, 29,* 431–450.

Farkas, G., Grobe, R., & Shuan, Y. (1990). Cultural resources and school success: Gender, ethnicity, and poverty groups within an urban school district. *American Sociological Review, 55,* 127–142.

Farkas, G., Lleras, C., & Maczuga, S. (2002). Does oppositional culture exist in minority and poverty peer groups? *American Sociological Review, 67,* 148–155.

Farmer, T. W., Estell, D. B., Bishop, J. L., O'Neal, K. K., & Cairns, B. D. (2003). Rejected bullies or popular leaders? The social relations of aggressive subtypes of rural African American early adolescents. *Developmental Psychology, 39,* 992–1004.

Farrell, A. D., & Sullivan, T. (2004). Impact of witnessing violence on growth curves for problem behaviors among early adolescents in urban and rural settings. *Journal of Community Psychology, 32,* 505–525.

Farrell, A. D., Sullivan, T. N., Esposito, L. E., Meyer, A. L., & Valois, R. F. (2005). A latent growth curve analysis of the structure of aggression, drug use, and delinquent behaviors and their interrelations over time in urban and rural adolescents. *Journal of Research on Adolescence, 15,* 179–203.

Farrell, A. D., & White, K. S. (1998). Peer influences and drug use among urban adolescents: Family structure and parent–adolescent relationship as protective factors. *Journal of Consulting and Clinical Psychology, 66*(2), 248–258.

Farrell, A., & Meyer, A. (1997). The effectiveness of a school-based curriculum for reducing violence among urban sixth-grade students. *American Journal of Public Health, 87,* 979–984.

Farrell, M., & Rosenberg, S. (1981). *Men at midlife.* Boston: Auburn House.

Farrelly, M. C., Davis, K. C., Haviland, M. L., Healton, C. G., & Messeri, P. (2005). Evidence of a dose-response relationship between "truth" antismoking ads and youth smoking prevalence. *American Journal of Public Health, 95,* 425–431.

Farrington, D. (1991). Childhood aggression and adult violence: Early precursors and later-life outcomes. In D. Pepler & K. Rubin (Eds.), *The development and treatment of childhood aggression,* pp. 5–29. Hillsdale, NJ: Erlbaum.

Farrington, D. (2004). Conduct disorder, aggression, and delinquency. In R. Lerner & L. Steinberg (Eds.), *Handbook of adolescent psychology.* New York: Wiley.

Farrington, D., Jolliffe, D., Hawkins, J., Catalano, R., Hill, K., & Kosterman, R. (2003). Comparing delinquency careers in court records and self-reports. *Criminology, 41,* 933–958.

Farrington, D., Jolliffe, D., Loeber, R., Stouthamer-Loeber, M., & Kalb, L. M. (2001). The concentration of offenders in families, and family criminality in the prediction of boys' delinquency. *Journal of Adolescence, 24*(5), 579–596.

Farrington, D., Loeber, R., & Stouthamer-Loeber, M. (2003). How can the relationship between race and violence be explained? In D. Hawkins (Ed.), *Violent crimes: Assessing race and ethnic differences,* pp. 213–237. New York: Cambridge University Press.

Fasick, F. (1994). On the "invention" of adolescence. *Journal of Early Adolescence, 14,* 6–23.

Featherman, D. (1980). Schooling and occupational careers: Constancy and change in worldly success. In O. Brim, Jr., & J. Kagan (Eds.), *Constancy and change in human development.* Cambridge, MA: Harvard University Press.

Federal Bureau of Investigation. (1999). *Uniform crime reports for the United States.* Washington, DC: U.S. Government Printing Office.

Federal Interagency Forum on Child and Family Statistics. (1997). *America's children: Key national indicators of well-being.* Washington, DC: Author.

Federal Interagency Forum on Child and Family Statistics. (2005). *America's children: Key national indicators of well-being 2005.* Washington, DC: Author.

Feinberg, M. E., & Hetherington, E. (2000). Sibling differentiation in adolescence: Implications for behavioral genetic theory. *Child Development, 71*(6), 1512–1524.

Feinberg, M. E., Howe, G. W., Reiss, D., & Hetherington, E. (2000). Relationship between perceptual differences of parenting and adolescent antisocial behavior and depressive symptoms. *Journal of Family Psychology, 14*(4), 531–555.

Feinberg, M. E., McHale, S. M., Crouter, A. C., & Cumsille, P. (2003). Sibling differentiation: Sibling and parent relationship trajectories in adolescence. *Child Development, 74,* 1261–1274.

Feinberg, M. E., Neiderhiser, J. M., Simmens, S., Reiss, D., & Hetherington, E. (2000). Sibling comparison of differential parental treatment in adolescence: Gender, self-esteem, and emotionality as mediators of the parenting-adjustment association. *Child Development, 71*(6), 1611–1628.

Feiring, C. (1993, March). Developing concepts of romance from 15 to 18 years. Paper presented at the biennial meetings of the Society for Research in Child Development, New Orleans.

Feiring, C. (1996). Concepts of romance in 15-year-old adolescents. *Journal of Research on Adolescence, 6,* 181–200.

Feiring, C. (1999). Gender identity and the development of romantic relationships in adolescence. In W. Furman, B. Brown, & C. Feiring (Eds.), *Contemporary perspectives on adolescent romantic relationships,* pp. 211–232. New York: Cambridge University Press.

Feiring, C. (1999). Other-sex friendship networks and the development of romantic relationships in adolescence. *Journal of Youth and Adolescence, 28*(4), 495–512.

Feiring, C., Deblinger, E., Hoch-Espada, A., & Haworth, T. (2002). Romantic relationship aggression and attitudes in high school students: The role of gender, grade, and attachment and emotional styles. *Journal of Youth and Adolescence, 31*(5), 373–385.

Feiring, C., & Lewis, M. (1991). The transition from middle childhood to early adolescence: Sex differences in the social network and perceived self-competence. *Sex Roles, 24,* 489–510.

Feiring, C., & Lewis, M. (1993). Do mothers know their teenagers' friends? Implications for individuation in early adolescence. *Journal of Youth and Adolescence, 22,* 337–354.

Feld, B. (1997). Juvenile and criminal justice systems' responses to youth violence. In M. T. Moore (Ed.), *Crime and justice,* Vol. 24. Chicago: University of Chicago Press.

Feldman, C., Stone, A., & Renderer, B. (1990). Stage, transfer, and academic achievement in dialect-speaking Hawaiian adolescents. *Child Development, 61,* 472–484.

Feldman, S., & Fisher, L. (1997). The effect of parents' marital satisfaction on young adults' adaptation: A longitudinal study. *Journal of Research on Adolescence, 7,* 55–80.

Feldman, S., & Gehring, T. (1988). Changing perceptions of family cohesion and power across adolescence. *Child Development, 59,* 1034–1045.

Feldman, S., & Quatman, T. (1988). Factors influencing age expectations for adolescent autonomy: A study of early adolescents and parents. *Journal of Early Adolescence, 8,* 325–343.

Feldman, S., & Rosenthal, D. (2000). The effect of communication characteristics on family members' perceptions of parents as sex educators. *Journal of Research on Adolescence, 10,* 119–150.

Feldman, S., Rosenthal, D., Brown, N., & Canning, R. (1995). Predicting sexual experience in adolescent boys from peer rejection and acceptance during childhood. *Journal of Research on Adolescence, 5,* 387–411.

Feldman, S., & Wentzel, K. (1995). Relations of marital satisfaction to peer outcomes in adolescent boys: A longitudinal study. *Journal of Early Adolescence, 15,* 220–237.

Feldman, S., & Wood, D. (1994). Parents' expectations for preadolescent sons' behavioral autonomy: A longitudinal study of correlates and outcomes. *Journal of Research on Adolescence, 4,* 45–70.

Felner, R., Brand, S., DuBois, D., Adan, A., Mulhall, P., & Evans, E. (1995). Socioeconomic disadvantage, proximal environmental experiences, and socioemotional and academic adjustment in early adolescence: Investigation of a mediated effects model. *Child Development, 66,* 774–792.

Felson, R., Liska, A., South, S., & McNulty, T. (1994). The subculture of violence and delinquency: Individual vs. school context effects. *Social Forces, 73,* 155–173.

Felson, R., & Zielinski, M. (1989). Children's self-esteem and parental support. *Journal of Marriage and the Family, 51,* 727–735.

Fenzel, L. (2001). Prospective study of changes in global self-worth and strain during the transition to middle school. *Journal of Early Adolescence, 20*(1), 93–116.

Fergusson, D., & Horwood, L. (1995). Early disruptive behavior, IQ, and later school achievement and delinquent behavior. *Journal of Abnormal Child Psychology, 23,* 183–199.

Fergusson, D., & Horwood, L. (2002). Male and female offending trajectories. *Development and Psychopathology, 14,* 159–177.

Fergusson, D., & Lynskey, M. (1996). Alcohol misuse and adolescent sexual behaviors and risk taking. *Pediatrics, 98,* 91–96.

Fergusson, D., Lynskey, M., & Horwood, L. (1996). Factors associated with continuity and changes in disruptive behavior patterns between childhood and adolescence. *Journal of Abnormal Child Psychology, 24,* 533–553.

Fergusson, D., & Woodward, L. (2000). Teenage pregnancy and female educational underachievement: A prospective study of a New Zealand birth cohort. *Journal of Marriage and the Family, 62,* 147–161.

Fichtenberg, C. M., & Glantz, S. A. (2002). Youth access interventions do not affect youth smoking. *Pediatrics, 109*(6), 1088–1092.

Field, T., Greenwald, P., Morrow, C., Healy, B., Foster, T., Guthertz, M., & Frost, P. (1992). Behavior state matching during interactions of preadolescent friends versus acquaintances. *Developmental Psychology, 28,* 242–250.

Fields, J. (2003). *Children's living arrangements and characteristics: March 2002.* Current Population Reports P20-547. Washington, DC: U.S. Census Bureau.

Filardo, E. (1996). Gender patterns in African American and white adolescents' social interactions in same-race, mixed-gender groups. *Journal of Personality and Social Psychology, 71,* 71–82.

Fincham, F. (1994). Understanding the association between marital conflict and child adjustment: Overview. *Journal of Family Psychology, 8,* 123–127.

Fine, G. (1981). Friends, impression management, and preadolescent behavior. In S. Asher & J. Gottman (Eds.), *The development of children's friendships.* Cambridge: Cambridge University Press.

Fine, G., Mortimer, J., & Roberts, D. (1990). Leisure, work, and the mass media. In S. Feldman & G. Elliott (Eds.), *At the threshold: The developing adolescent,* pp. 225–252. Cambridge, MA: Harvard University Press.

Fine, M., & Kurdek, L. (1995). Relation between marital quality and (step)parent–child relationship quality for parents and stepparents in stepfamilies. *Journal of Family Psychology, 9,* 216–223.

Fingerson, L. (2005). Do mother's opinions matter in teens' sexual activity? *Journal of Family Influence, 26,* 947–974.

Finkelhor, D., Mitchell, K., & Wolak, J. (2005). Online victimization: What youth tell us. In S. Cooper, R. Estes, A. Giardino, N. Kellogg, & V. Vieth (Eds.), *Medical, legal, and social science aspects of child sexual exploitation: A comprehensive review of pornography, prostitution, and Internet crimes,* Vol. 1, pp. 437–467. St. Louis: GW Medical.

Finken, L., & Jacobs, J. (1996). Consultant choice across decision contexts: Are abortion decisions different? *Journal of Adolescent Research, 11,* 235–260.

Finkenauer, C., Engles, R., & Meeus, W. (2002). Keeping secrets from parents: Advantages and disadvantages of secrecy in adolescence. *Journal of Youth and Adolescence, 31*(2), 123–136.

Finn, C., Jr. (1991). *We must take charge: Our schools and our future.* New York: Free Press.

Finn, J., Gerber, S. B., & Boyd-Zaharias, J. (2005). Small classes in the early grades, academic achievement, and graduating from high school. *Journal of Educational Psychology, 97,* 214–223.

Finnegan, R., & Perry, D. (1993, March). Preadolescents' self-reported attachments to their mothers and their social behavior with peers. Paper presented at the biennial meetings of the Society for Research in Child Development, New Orleans.

Fischoff, B., & Quadrel, M. (1995). Adolescent alcohol decisions. In G. Boyd, J. Howard, & R. Zucker (Eds.), *Alcohol problems among adolescents: Current directions in prevention research,* pp. 59–84. Hillsdale, NJ: Erlbaum.

Fisher, C., Wallace, S. A., & Fenton, R. E. (2000). Discrimination distress during adolescence. *Journal of Youth and Adolescence, 29*(6), 679–695.

Fisher, M., Golden, N., Katzman, D., Kriepe, R., Rees, J., Schebendach, J., Sigman, G., Ammerman, S., & Hoberman, H. (1995). Eating disorders in adolescents: A background paper. *Journal of Adolescent Health, 16,* 420–437.

Fisher, T. (1989). An extension of the findings of Moore, Peterson, & Furstenberg [1986] regarding family sexual communication and adolescent sexual behavior. *Journal of Marriage and the Family, 51,* 637–639.

Flammer, A., Alasker, F., & Noack, P. (1999). Time use by adolescents in an international perspective, I: The case of leisure activities. In F. Alasker & A. Flammer (Eds.), *The adolescent experience: European and American adolescents in the 1990s,* pp. 33–60. Hillsdale, NJ: Erlbaum.

Flammer, A., & Schaffner, B. (2003). Adolescent leisure across European nations. *New Directions for Child and Adolescent Development, 99,* 65–78.

Flanagan, C. (1990). Change in family work status: Effects on parent–adolescent decision making. *Child Development, 61,* 163–177.

Flanagan, C. (2004). Volunteerism, leadership, political socialization, and civic engagement. In R. Lerner & L. Steinberg (Eds.), *Handbook of adolescent psychology.* New York: Wiley.

Flanagan, C., & Galay, L. (1995). Reframing the meaning of "political" in research with adolescents. *Perspectives on Political Science, 24,* 34–41.

Flanagan, C., & Tucker, C. (1999). Adolescents' explanations for political issues: Concordance with their views of self and society. *Developmental Psychology, 35,* 1198–1209.

Flannery, D., Torquati, J., & Lindemeier, L. (1994). The method and meaning of emotional expression and experience during adolescence. *Journal of Adolescent Research, 9,* 8–27.

Flannery, D., Vazsonyi, A., Torquati, J., & Rowe, D. (1993, March). Parenting, personality, and school influences on substance use in Caucasian and Hispanic early adolescents. Paper presented at the biennial meetings of the Society for Research in Child Development, New Orleans.

Flannery, D., Weseter, K., & Singer, M. (2004). Impact of exposure to violence in school on child and adolescent mental health and behavior. *Journal of Community Psychology, 32,* 559–573.

Flavell, J., Green, F., & Flavell, E. (1998). The mind has a mind of its own: Developing knowledge about mental uncontrollability. *Cognitive Development, 13,* 127–138.

Fletcher, A., Darling, N., Steinberg, L., & Dornbusch, S. (1995). The company they keep: Relation of adolescents' adjustment and behavior to their friends' perceptions of authoritative parenting in the social network. *Developmental Psychology, 31,* 300–310.

Fletcher, A., Elder, G., Jr., & Mekos, D. (2000). Parental influences on adolescent involvement in community activities. *Journal of Research on Adolescence, 10,* 29–48.

Fletcher, A., Steinberg, L., & Williams-Wheeler, M. (2004). Parental influences on adolescent problem-behavior: Revisiting Stattin and Kerr. *Child Development, 75,* 781–796.

Flieller, A. (1999). Comparison of the development of formal thought in adolescent cohorts aged 10 to 15 years (1967–1996 and 1972–1993). *Developmental Psychology, 35,* 1048–1058.

Flisher, A. J., Kramer, R. A., Hoven, C. W., King, R. A., Bird, H. R., Davies, M., et al. (2000). Risk behavior in a community sample of children and adolescents. *Journal of the American Academy of Child and Adolescent Psychiatry, 39,* 881–887.

Flory, K., Lynam, D., & Milich, R. (2004). Early adolescent through young adult alcohol and marijuana use trajectories: Early predictors, young adult outcomes, and predictive utility. *Development and Psychopathology, 16,* 193–213.

Flynn, B., Worden, J., Secker-Walker, R., Pirie, P., Badger, G., Carpenter, J., & Geller, B. (1994). Mass media and school interventions for cogarette smoking prevention: Effects 2 years after completion. *American Journal of Public Health, 84,* 1148–1150.

Forbes, E. E., & Dahl, R. E. (2005). Neural systems of positive affect: Relevance to understanding child and adolescent depression? *Development and Psychopathology, 17,* 827–850.

Ford, C., & Beach, F. (1951). Patterns of sexual behavior. New York: Harper & Row.

Ford, D., & Harris, J. I. (1996). Perceptions and attitudes of Black students toward school, achievement, and other educational variables. *Child Development, 67,* 1141–1152.

Ford, M. (1982). Social cognition and social competence in adolescence. *Developmental Psychology, 18,* 323–340.

Fordham, C., & Ogbu, J. (1986). Black students' school success: Coping with the burden of "acting white." *Urban Review, 18,* 176–206.

Forehand, R., Armistead, L., & David, C. (1997). Is adolescent adjustment following parental divorce a function of predivorce adjustment? *Journal of Abnormal Child Psychology, 25,* 157–164.

Forehand, R., Biggar, H., & Kotchick, B. (1998). Cumulative risk across family stressors: Short- and long-term effects for adolescents. *Journal of Abnormal Child Psychology, 26,* 119–128.

Forehand, R., Neighbors, B., Devine, D., & Armistead, L. (1994). Interparental conflict and parental divorce: The individual, relative, and interactive effects on adolescents across four years. *Family Relations, 43,* 387–393.

Forehand, R., Thomas, A. M., Wierson, M., Brody, G., & Fauber, R. (1990). Role of maternal functioning and parenting skills in adolescent functioning following parental divorce. *Journal of Abnormal Psychology, 99,* 278–283.

Forehand, R., Wierson, M., Thomas, A., Fauber, R., Armistead, L., Kemptom, T., & Long, N. (1991). A short-term longitudinal examination of young adolescent functioning following divorce: The role of family factors. *Journal of Abnormal Child Psychology, 19,* 97–111.

Forgatch, M., & Stoolmiller, M. (1994). Emotions as contexts for adolescent delinquency. *Journal of Research on Adolescence, 4,* 601–614.

Forgatch, M., DeGarmo, D., & Knutson, N. (1994, February). Transitions within transitions: The impact of adolescence and family structure on boys' antisocial behavior. Paper presented at the biennial meetings of the Society for Research on Adolescence, San Diego.

Formoso, D., Ruiz, S., & Gonzales, N. (1997, March). Parent–adolescent conflict: Resolution strategies reported with African-American, Mexican-American, and Anglo-American families. Paper presented at the SRCD, Washington, DC.

Fortenberry, J., Costa, F., Jessor, R., & Donovan, J. (1997). Contraceptive behavior and adolescent lifestyles: A structural modeling approach. *Journal of Research on Adolescence, 7,* 307–329.

Fortner, M. R., Crouter, A. C., & McHale, S. M. (2004). Is parents' work involvement responsive to the quality of relationships with adolescent offspring? *Journal of Family Psychology, 19,* 530–538.

Foshee, V., Bauman, K., Greene, W., Koch, G., Linder, G., & MacDougall, J. (2000). The safe dates program: 1-year follow-up results. *American Journal of Public Health, 90*(10), 1619–1622.

Foss, R. D., Feaganes, J. R., & Rodgman, E. A. (2001). Initial effects of graduated driver licensing on 16-year-old driver crashes in North Carolina. *Journal of the American Medical Association, 286,* 1588–1592.

Foster, E. (1995). Why teens do not benefit from work experience programs: Evidence from brother comparisons. *Journal of Policy Analysis and Management, 14,* 393–414.

Foster, L., & Ritter, J. (1995, March). Independence from parents as a predictor of happiness and life satisfaction. Paper presented at the SRCD, Indianapolis.

Foster, S. E., Vaughan, R. D., Foster, W. H., & Califano, J. A. (2003). Alcohol consumption and expenditures for underage drinking and adult excessive drinking. *Journal of the American Medical Association, 289,* 989–995.

Fowler, J. (1981). *Stages of faith.* New York: Harper & Row.

Fox, C., & Harding, D. J. (2005). School shootings as organizational deviance. *Sociology of Education, 78,* 69–97.

Frabutt, J. M., Walker, A. M., & MacKinnon-Lewis, C. (2002). Racial socialization messages and the quality of mother/child interactions in African American families. *Journal of Early Adolescence, 22*(2), 200–217.

Frank, S., & Jackson, S. (1996). Family experiences as moderators of the relationship between eating symptoms and personality disturbance. *Journal of Youth and Adolescence, 25,* 55–72.

Frank, S., Pirsch, L., & Wright, V. (1990). Late adolescents' perceptions of their relationships with their parents: Relationships among deidealization, autonomy, relatedness, and insecurity and implications for adolescent adjustment and ego identity status. *Journal of Youth and Adolescence, 19,* 571–588.

Frankenberger, K. D. (2000). Adolescent egocentrism: A comparison among adolescents and adults. *Journal of Adolescence, 23*(3), 343–354.

Franklin, C., Grant, D., Corcoran, J., Miller, P., & Bultman, L. (1997). Effectiveness of prevention programs for adolescent pregnancy: A meta-analysis. *Journal of Marriage and the Family, 59,* 551–567.

Franzoi, S., Davis, M., & Vasquez-Suson, K. (1994). Two social worlds: Social correlates and stability of adolescent status groups. *Journal of Personality and Social Psychology, 67,* 462–473.

Fredricks, J. A., & Eccles, J. S. (2002). Children's competence and value beliefs from childhood through adolescence: Growth trajectories in two male-sex-typed domains. *Developmental Psychology, 38*(4), 519–533.

Fredriksen, K., Rhodes, J., Reddy, R., & Way, N. (2004). Sleepless in Chicago: Tracking the effects of adolescent sleep loss during the middle school years. *Child Development, 75,* 84–95

Freedle, R. O. (2003). Correcting the SAT's ethnic and social-class bias: A method for reestimating SAT scores. *Harvard Educational Review, 73,* 1–43.

Freedner, N., Freed, L. H., Yang, Y., & Austin, S. (2002). Dating violence among gay, lesbian, and bisexual adolescents: Results from a community survey. *Journal of Adolescent Health, 31*(6), 469–474.

Freeman, H., & Brown, B. (2001). Primary attachment to parents and peers during adolescence: Differences by attachment style. *Journal of Youth and Adolescence, 30*(6), 653–674.

Freeman, R., & Wise, D. (Eds.). (1982). *The youth labor market problem: Its nature, causes, and consequences.* Chicago: University of Chicago Press.

French, D., & Conrad, J. (2001). School dropout as predicted by peer rejection and antisocial behavior. *Journal of Research on Adolescence, 11*(3), 225–244.

French, D., Conrad, J., & Turner, T. (1995). Adjustment of antisocial and nonantisocial rejected adolescents. *Development and Psychopathology, 7,* 857–874.

French, D., & Dishion, T. (2003). Predictors of early initiation of sexual intercourse among high-risk adolescents. *Journal of Early Adolescence, 23,* 295–315.

French, D., Jansen, E., & Pidada, S. (2002). United States and Indonesian children's and adolescents' reports of relational aggression by disliked peers. *Child Development, 73*(4), 1143–1150.

French, D., Rianasari, M., Pidada, S., Nelwan, P., & Buhrmester, D. (2001). Social support of Indonesian and U.S. children and adolescents by family members and friends. *Merrill-Palmer Quarterly, 47*(3), 377–394.

French, S., Story, M., Downes, B., Resnick, M., & Blum, R. (1995). Frequent dieting among adolescents: Psychosocial and health behavior correlates. *American Journal of Public Health, 85,* 695–701.

French, S. E., Seidman, E., Allen, L., & Aber, J. L. (2006). The development of ethnic identity during adolescence. *Developmental Psychology, 42,* 1–10.

Freud, A. (1958). Adolescence. *Psychoanalytic Study of the Child, 13,* 255–278.

Freud, S. (1938). *An outline of psychoanalysis.* London: Hogarth Press.

Frick, P., Kotov, R., Loney, B., & Vasey, M. (2005). The latent structure of psychopathy in youth: A taxometric investigation. *Journal of Abnormal Child Psychology, 33.*

Frick, P. J., Stickle, T. R., Dandreaux, D. M., Farrell, J. M., & Kimonis, E. R. (2005). Callous-unemotional traits in predicting the severity and stability of conduct problems and delinquency. *Journal of Abnormal Child Psychology, 33,* 471–487.

Fried, C. S. (2001). Juvenile curfews: Are they an effective and constitutional means of combating juvenile violence? *Behavioral Sciences and the Law, 19*(1), 127–141.

Fried, C. S., & Reppucci, N. (2001). Criminal decision-making: The development of adolescent judgment, criminal responsibility, and culpability. *Law and Human Behavior, 25*(1), 45–61.

Fried, M., & Fried, M. (1980). *Transitions: Four rituals in eight cultures.* New York: Norton.

Friedenberg, E. (1959). *The vanishing adolescent.* Boston: Beacon Press.

Friedenberg, E. (1967). *Coming of age in America.* New York: Vintage Books.

Frijns, T., Finkenauer, C., Vermulst, A. A., & Engels, R. C. M. E. (2005). Keeping secrets from parents: Longitudinal associations of secrecy in adolescence. *Journal of Youth and Adolescence, 34,* 137–148.

Frisch, R. (1983). Fatness, puberty, and fertility: The effects of nutrition and physical training on menarche and ovulation. In J. Brooks-Gunn & A. Petersen (Eds.), *Girls at puberty.* New York: Plenum.

Frisco, M. L. (2005). Parental involvement and young women's contraceptive use. *Journal of Marriage and the Family 67,* 110

Frome, P., & Eccles, J. (1996, March). Gender-role identity and self-esteem. Paper presented at the biennial meetings of the Society for Research on Adolescence, Boston.

Frost, J., & Forrest, J. (1995). Understanding the impact of effective teenage pregnancy prevention programs. *Family Planning Perspectives, 27,* 188–195.

Fuhrman, T., & Holmbeck, G. (1995). A contextual-moderator analysis of emotional autonomy and adjustment in adolescence. *Child Development, 66,* 793–811.

Fuligni, A. (1994, February). Academic achievement and motivation among Asian-American and European-American early adolescents. Paper presented at the biennial meetings of the Society for Research on Adolescence, San Diego.

Fuligni, A. (1997). The academic achievement of adolescents from immigrant families: The roles of family background, attitudes, and behavior. *Child Development, 68,* 351–363.

Fuligni, A. (1998). Authority, autonomy, and parent–adolescent conflict and cohesion: A study of adolescents from Mexican, Chinese, Filipino, and European backgrounds. *Developmental Psychology, 34,* 782–792.

Fuligni, A., & Eccles, J. (1993). Perceived parent–child relationships and early adolescents' orientation toward peers. *Developmental Psychology, 29,* 622–632.

Fuligni, A., Eccles, J., Barber, B., & Clements, P. (2001). Early adolescent peer orientation and adjustment during high school. *Developmental Psychology, 37,* 28–36.

Fuligni, A., & Stevenson, H. (1995). Time-use and mathematics achievement among American, Chinese, and Japanese high school students. *Child Development, 66,* 830–842.

Fuligni, A., Tseng, V., & Lam, M. (1999). Attitudes toward family obligations among American adolescents from Asian, Latin American, and European backgrounds. *Child Development, 70,* 1030–1044.

Fuligni, A., & Witkow, M. (2004). The postsecondary educational progress of youth from immigrant families. *Journal of Research on Adolescence, 14,* 159–183.

Fuligni, A., Witkow, M., & Garcia, C. (2005). Ethnic identity and the academic adjustment of adolescents from Mexican, Chinese and European backgrounds. *Developmental Psychology, 41,* 799–811.

Fuligni, A., Yip, T., & Tseng, V. (2002). The impact of family obligation on the daily activities and psychological well-being of Chinese American adolescents. *Child Development, 73*(1), 302–314.

Fuligni, A., & Zhang, W. (2004). Attitudes toward family obligation among adolescents in contemporary urban and rural China. *Child Development, 75,* 180–192.

Fulkerson, J. A., & French, S. A. (2003). Cigarette smoking for weight loss or control among adolescents: Gender and racial/ethnic differences. *Journal of Adolescent Health, 32,* 306–313.

Fulton, A. (1997). Identity status, religious orientation, and prejudice. *Journal of Youth and Adolescence, 26,* 1–11.

Funk, J., Flores, G., Buchman, D., & Germann, J. (1999). Rating electronic games: Violence is in the eye of the beholder. *Youth and Society, 30,* 283–312.

Furbey, M., & Beyth-Marom, R. (1992). Risk-taking in adolescence: A decision-making perspective. *Developmental Review, 12,* 1–44.

Furman, W., Brown, B., & Feiring, C. (Eds.). (1999). *Contemporary perspectives on adolescent romantic relationships.* New York: Cambridge University Press.

Furman, W., & Buhrmester, D. (1985). Children's perceptions of the personal relationships in their social networks. *Developmental Psychology, 21,* 1016–1024.

Furman, W., & Simon, V. (1999). Cognitive representations of adolescent romantic relationships. In W. Furman, B. Brown, & C. Feiring (Eds.), *Contemporary perspectives on adolescent romantic relationships,* pp. 75–98. New York: Cambridge University Press.

Furman, W., Simon, V. A., Shaffer, L., & Bouchey, H. A. (2002). Adolescents' working models and styles for relationships with parents, friends, and romantic partners. *Child Development, 73*(1), 241–255.

Furman, W., & Wehner, E. (1994). Romantic views: Toward a theory of adolescent romantic relationships. In R. Montemayor (Ed.), *Advances in adolescent development,* Vol. 3: *Relationships in adolescence,* pp. 168–195. Newbury Park, CA: Sage.

Furstenberg, F., Jr. (1990). Coming of age in a changing family system. In S. Feldman & G. Elliott (Eds.), *At the threshold: The developing adolescent,* pp. 147–170. Cambridge, MA: Harvard University Press.

Furstenberg, F., Jr. (1996). Family management of adolescent success in inner-city Philadelphia. Paper presented at the biennial meetings of the Society for Research on Adolescence, Boston.

Furstenberg, F., Jr. (2000). The sociology of adolescence and youth in the 1990s: A critical commentary. *Journal of Marriage and Family, 62*(4), 896–910.

Furstenberg, F., Jr. (2006, March). Diverging development: The not-so-invisible hand of social class in the United States. Invited address, Society for Research on Adolescence, San Francisco.

Furstenberg, F., Jr., et al. (1987). Race differences in the timing of adolescent intercourse. *American Sociological Review, 52,* 511–518.

Furstenberg, F., Jr., Brooks-Gunn, J., & Morgan, S. (1987). Adolescent mothers in later life. New York: Cambridge University Press.

Furstenberg, F., Jr., Brooks-Gunn, J., & Chase-Landsdale, L. (1989). Teenaged pregnancy and childbearing. *American Psychologist, 44,* 313–320.

Furstenberg, F., Jr., Cook, T., Eccles, J., Elder, G., Jr., & Sameroff, A. (1999). *Managing to make it: Urban families and adolescent success.* Chicago: University of Chicago Press.

Furstenberg, F., Jr., Geitz, L., Teitler, J., & Weiss, C. (1997). Does condom availability make a difference? An evaluation of Philadelphia's health resource centers. *Family Planning Perspectives, 29,* 123–127.

Furstenberg, F., Jr., Morgan, S. P., & Allison, P. (1987). Paternal participation and children's well-being after marital dissolution. *American Sociological Review, 52,* 695–701.

Fussell, M., & Greene, M. (2002). Demographic trends affecting youth around the world. In B. Brown, R. Larson, & T. Saraswathi (Eds.), *The world's youth: Adolescence in eight regions of the globe.* New York: Cambridge University Press.

Futterman, D., Hein, K., Reuben, N., Dell, R., & Shaffer, N. (1993). Human immunodeficiency virus–infected adolescents: The first 50 patients in a New York City program. *Pediatrics, 91,* 730–735.

Gaddis, A., & Brooks-Gunn, J. (1985). The male experience of pubertal change. *Journal of Youth and Adolescence, 14,* 61–70.

Gage, J. C., Overpeck, M. D., Nansel, T. R., & Kogan, M. D. (2005). Peer activity in the evenings and participation in aggressive and problem behaviors. *Journal of Adolescent Health, 37,* 517.e7–517.e14.

Galambos, N. (2004). Gender and gender role development in adolescence. In R. Lerner & L. Steinberg (Eds.), *Handbook of adolescent psychology.* New York: Wiley.

Galambos, N., Almeida, D., & Petersen, A. (1990). Masculinity, femininity, and sex role attitudes in early adolescence: Exploring gender intensification. *Child Development, 61,* 1905–1914.

Galambos, N., Barker, E., & Almeida, D. (2003). Parents do matter: Trajectories of change in externalizing and internalizing problems in adolescence. *Child Development, 74,* 578–594.

Galambos, N., Barker, E., & Krahn, H. (2006). Depression, self-esteem, and anger in emerging adulthood: Seven-year trajectories. *Developmental Psychology, 42,* 350–365.

Galambos, N., Barker, E., & Tilton-Weaver, L. (2003). Who gets caught at maturity gap? A study of pseudomature, immature, and mature adolescents. *International Journal of Behavioral Development, 27,* 253–263.

Galambos, N., & Garbarino, J. (1985). Adjustment of unsupervised children in a rural setting. *Journal of Genetic Psychology, 146,* 227–231.

Galambos, N., Kolaric, G., & Maggs, J. (1994, February). Adolescents' subjective age: An Indicator of phenomenological maturity. Paper presented at the biennial meetings of the Society for Research on Adolescence, San Diego.

Galambos, N., Kolaric, G., Sears, H., & Maggs, J. (1999). Adolescents' subjective age: An indicator of perceived maturity. *Journal of Research on Adolescence, 9,* 309–337.

Galambos, N., & Maggs, J. (1991). Out-of-school care of young adolescents and self-reported behavior. *Developmental Psychology, 27,* 644–655.

Galambos, N., & Silbereisen, R. (1987). Income change, parental life outlook, and adolescent expectations for job success. *Journal of Marriage and the Family, 49,* 141–149.

Galambos, N., Turner, P., & Tilton-Weaver, L. (2005). Chronological and subjective age in emerging adulthood: The crossover effect. *Journal of Adolescent Research, 20,* 538–556.

Galen, B., & Underwood, M. (1997). A developmental investigation of social aggression among children. *Developmental Psychology, 33,* 589–600.

Gallatin, J. (1975). *Adolescence and individuality.* New York: Harper & Row.

Galliher, R. V., Rostosky, S. S., & Hughes, H. K. (2004). School belonging, self-esteem, and depressive symptoms in adolescents: An examination of sex, sexual attraction status, and urbanicity. *Journal of Youth and Adolescence, 33,* 235–245.

Gallup, G., & Bezilla, R. (1992). *The religion life of young Americans.* Princeton, NJ: Gallup Institute.

Galotti, K., Komatsu, L., & Voelz, S. (1997). Children's differential performance on deductive and inductive syllogisms. *Developmental Psychology, 33,* 70–78.

Gamoran, A. (1987). The stratification of high school learning opportunities. *Sociology of Education, 60,* 135–155.

Gamoran, A. (1992). The variable effects of high school tracking. *American Sociological Review, 57,* 812–828.

Gamoran, A. (1993). Alternative uses of ability grouping in secondary schools: Can we bring high-quality instruction to low-ability classes? *American Journal of Education, 102,* 1–22.

Gamoran, A. (1996). Curriculum standardization and equality of opportunity in Scottish secondary education: 1984–90. *Sociology of Education, 69,* 1–21.

Gamoran, A., & Mare, R. (1989). Secondary school tracking and educational inequality: Compensation, reinforcement, or neutrality? *American Journal of Sociology, 94,* 1146–1183.

Gans, J. (1990). *America's adolescents: How healthy are they?* Chicago: American Medical Association.

Garbarino, J., & Asp, C. (1981). *Successful schools and competent students.* Lexington, MA: Lexington Books.

Garbarino, J., Burston, N., Raber, S., Russell, R., & Crouter, A. (1978). The social maps of children approaching adolescence: Studying the ecology of youth development. *Journal of Youth and Adolescence, 7,* 417–428.

Garbarino, J., Wilson, J., & Garbarino, J. (1986). The adolescent runaway. In J. Garbarino & J. Sebes (Eds.), *Troubled youth, troubled families,* pp. 315–351. New York: Aldine.

Garber, J., Robinson, N., & Valentiner, D. (1997). The relation between parenting and adolescent depression: Self-worth as a mediator. *Journal of Adolescent Research, 12,* 12–33.

Garber, J., Weiss, B., & Shanley, N. (1993). Cognitions, depressive symptoms, and development in adolescents. *Journal of Abnormal Psychology, 102,* 47–57.

Garcia Coll, C., Lamberty, G., Jenkins, R., McAdoo, H., Crnic, K., Wasik, B., & Vazquez Garcia, H. (1996). An integrative model for the study of developmental competencies in minority children. *Child Development, 67,* 1891–1914.

Gardner, H. (1983). *Frames of mind.* New York: Basic Books.

Gardner, M., & Steinberg, L. (2005). Peer influence on risk taking, risk preference, and risky decision making in adolescence and adulthood: An experimental study. *Developmental Psychology, 41,* 625–635.

Gardner, W., Scherer, D., & Tester, M. (1989). Asserting scientific authority: Cognitive development and adolescent legal rights. *American Psychologist, 44,* 895–902.

Gargiulo, J., Attie, I., Brooks-Gunn, J., & Warren, M. (1987). Girls' dating behavior as a function of social context and maturation. *Developmental Psychology, 23,* 730–737.

Garnefski, N. (2000). Age differences in depressive symptoms, antisocial behavior, and negative perceptions of family, school, and peers among adolescents. *Journal of the American Academy of Child and Adolescent Psychiatry, 39,* 1175–1181.

Garnefski, N., & Diekstra, R. (1997). "Comorbidity" of behavioral, emotional, and cognitive problems in adolescence. *Journal of Youth and Adolescence, 26,* 321–338.

Garnier, H., & Stein, J. (2002). An 18-year model of family and peer effects on adolescent drug use and delinquency. *Journal of Youth and Adolescence, 31*(1), 45–56.

Garnier, H., Stein, J., & Jacobs, J. (1997). The process of dropping out of high school: A 19-year perspective. *American Educational Research Journal, 34,* 395–419.

Gathercole, S. E., Pickering, S. J., Ambridge, B., & Wearing, H. (2004). The structure of working memory from 4 to 15 years of age. *Developmental Psychology, 40,* 177–190.

Gau, S. S., Soong, W., & Merikangas, K. R. (2004). Correlates of sleep-wake patterns among children and young adolescents in Taiwan. *Sleep, 27,* 512–519.

Gauze, C., Bukowski, W., Aquan-Assee, J., & Sippola, L. (1996). Interactions between family environment and friendship and associations with self-perceived well-being during early adolescence. *Child Development, 67,* 2201–2216.

Gavin, L., & Furman, W. (1989). Age differences in adolescents' perceptions of their peer groups. *Developmental Psychology, 25,* 827–834.

Gavin, L., & Furman, W. (1996). Adolescent girls' relationships with mothers and best friends. *Child Development, 67,* 375–386.

Gayle, H., Keeling, R., Garcia-Tunon, M., Kilbourne, B., Narkunas, J., Ingram, F., Rogers, M., & Curran, J. (1990). Prevalence of the human immunodeficiency virus among university students. *New England Journal of Medicine, 323,* 1538–1541.

Ge, X., Best, K., Conger, R., & Simons, R. (1996). Parenting behaviors and the occurrence and co-occurrence of adolescent depressive symptoms and conduct problems. *Developmental Psychology, 32,* 717–731.

Ge, X., Brody, G. H., Conger, R. D., Simons, R. L., & Murry, V. (2002). Contextual amplification of pubertal transition effects on deviant peer affiliation and externalizing behavior among African American children. *Developmental Psychology, 38*(1), 42–54.

Ge, X., & Conger, R. (1995, March). Parents' depressive symptoms, hostile behaviors, and adolescent degressive symptoms. Paper presented at the SRCD, Indianapolis.

Ge, X., Conger, R., Cadoret, R., Neiderhiser, J., Yates, W., Throughton, E., & Stewart, M. (1996). The developmental interface between nature and nurture: A mutual influence model of child antisocial behavior and parent behaviors. *Developmental Psychology, 32,* 574–589.

Ge, X., Conger, R. D., & Elder, G. H., Jr. (2001). The relation between puberty and psychological distress in adolescent boys. *Journal of Research on Adolescence, 11*(1), 49–70.

Ge, X., Conger, R., Lorenz, F., Shanahan, M., & Elder, G., Jr. (1995). Mutual influences in parent and adolescent psychological distress. *Developmental Psychology, 31,* 406–419.

Ge, X., Kim, I. J., Brody, G. H., Conger, R. D., Simons, R. L., Gibbons, F. X., & Cutrona, C. E. (2003). It's about timing and change: Pubertal transition effects on symptoms of major depression among African American youths. *Developmental Psychology, 39,* 430–439.

Ge, X., Lorenz, F., Conger, R., Elder, G., Jr., & Simons, R. (1994). Trajectories of stressful life events and depressive symptoms during adolescence. *Developmental Psychology, 30,* 467–483.

Gecas, V., & Seff, M. (1990). Families and adolescents: A review of the 1980s. *Journal of Marriage and the Family, 52,* 941–958.

Gennetian, L. A., Duncan, G., Knox, V., Vargas, W., Clark-Kauffman, E., & London, A. S. (2004). How welfare policies affect adolescents' school outcomes: A synthesis of evidence from experimental studies. *Journal of Research on Adolescence, 14,* 399–423.

Gentile, D. A., Lynch, P. J., Linder, J. R., & Walsh, D. A. (2004). The effects of violent video game habits on adolescent hostility, aggressive behaviors, and school performance. *Journal of Adolescence, 27,* 5–22.

Gentry, M., Gable, R. K., & Rizza, M. G. (2002). Students' perceptions of classroom activities: Are there grade-level and gender differences? *Journal of Educational Psychology, 94*(3), 539–544.

Georgiades, K., Boyle, M. H., Duku, E., & Racine, Y. (2006). Tobacco use among immigrant and nonimmigrant adolescents: Individual and family level influences. *Journal of Adolescent Health, 38,* 443.e1–443.e7.

Gerard, J. M., & Buehler, C. (2004). Cumulative environmental risk and youth maladjustment: The role of youth attributes. *Child Development, 75,* 1832–1849.

Gerbner, G., Gross, L., Morgan, M., & Signorelli, N. (1994). Growing up with television: The cultivation perspective. In J. Bryant & D. Zillman (Eds.), *Media effects: Advances in theory and research,* pp. 17–41. Hillsdale, NJ: Erlbaum.

Gerhardt, C., Compas, B., Connor, J., & Achenbach, T. (1999). Association of a mixed anxiety-depression syndrome and symptoms of major depressive disorder during adolescence. *Journal of Youth and Adolescence, 28,* 305–323.

Gerrard, M. (1987). Sex, sex guilt, and contraceptive use revisited: The 1980s. *Journal of Personality and Social Psychology, 52,* 975–980.

Gerrard, M., Gibbons, F., & Bushman, B. (1996). Relation between perceived vulnerability to HIV and precautionary sexual behavior. *Psychological Bulletin, 119,* 390–409.

Gest, S. (1997). Behavioral inhibition: Stability and associations with adaptation from childhood to early adulthood. *Journal of Personality and Social Psychology, 72,* 467–475.

Gfroerer, J. C., & Tan, L. L. (2003). Substance use among foreign-born youths in the United States: Does the length of residence matter? *American Journal of Public Health, 93,* 1892–1895.

Gibbons, F., Benbow, C., & Gerrard, M. (1994). From top dog to bottom half: Social comparison strategies in response to poor performance. *Journal of Personality and Social Psychology, 67,* 638–652.

Giedd, J. N., Blumenthal, J., Jeffries, N. O., Castellanos, F. X., Liu, H., Zijdenbos, A., Paus, T., Evans, A. C., & Rapoport, J. L. (1999). Brain development during childhood and adolescence: A longitudinal MRI study. *Nature Neuroscience, 2,* 861–863.

Gil, A., Vega, W., & Dimas, J. (1994). Acculturative stress and personal adjustment among Hispanic adolescent boys. *Journal of Community Psychology, 22,* 43–54.

Gilliam, F., & Bales, S. (2001). Strategic frame analysis: Reframing America's youth. *SRCD Social Policy Report, 15*(3).

Gilligan, C. (1982). *In a different voice.* Cambridge, MA: Harvard University Press.

Gilligan, C. (1993). Joining the resistance: Psychology, politics, and girls. In L. Weis & M. Fine (Eds.), *Beyond silenced voices,* pp. 143–168. Albany: SUNY Press.

Gilligan, C., Lyons, N., & Hanmer, T. (Eds.). (1990). *Making connections: The relational worlds of adolescent girls at Emma Willard School.* Cambridge, MA: Harvard University Press.

Gillmore, M., Archibald, M. E., Morrison, D. M., Wilsdon, A., Wells, E. A., Hoppe, M. J., et al. (2002). Teen sexual behavior: Applicability of the theory of reasoned action. *Journal of Marriage and the Family, 64*(4), 885–897.

Gillmore, M., Hawkins, J., Catalano, R., Jr., Day, L., Moore, M., & Abbott, R. (1991). Structure of problem behaviors in preadolescence. *Journal of Consulting and Clinical Psychology, 59,* 499–506.

Gillmore, M., Lewis, S., Lohr, M., Spencer, M., & White, R. (1997). Repeat pregnancies among adolescent mothers. *Journal of Marriage and the Family, 59,* 536–550.

Gillmore, M., Morrison, D., Lowery, C., & Baker, S. (1994). Beliefs about condoms and their association with intentions to use condoms among youths in detention. *Journal of Adolescent Health, 15,* 228–237.

Gillock, K., & Reyes, O. (1996). High school transition-related changes in urban minority students' academic performance and perceptions of self and school environment. *Journal of Community Psychology, 24,* 245–261.

Gillock, K., & Reyes, O. (1999). Stress, support, and academic performance of urban, low-income, Mexican-American adolescents. *Journal of Youth and Adolescence, 28,* 259–282.

Gilsanz, V., Roe, T., Mora, S., Costin, G., & Goodman, W. (1991). Changes in vertebral bone density in Black girls and White girls during childhood and puberty. *New England Journal of Medicine, 325,* 1597–1600.

Ginsburg, G., & Bronstein, P. (1993). Family factors related to children's intrinsic/extrinsic motivational orientation and academic performance. *Child Development, 64,* 1461–1474.

Ginzberg, E. (1977). The job problem. *Scientific American, 237,* 43–51.

Gittler, J., Quigley-Rick, M., & Saks, M. (1990). *Adolescent health care decision making: The law and public policy.* Washington, DC: Carnegie Council on Adolescent Development.

Gjerde, P. (1995, March). A typological analysis of girls' personality: A longitudinal study of developmental pathways. Paper presented at the SRCD, Indianapolis.

Glasgow, K., Dornbusch, S., Ritter, P., Troyer, L., & Steinberg, L. (1997). Parenting styles, dysfunctional attributions, and adolescent outcomes in diverse groups. *Child Development, 67,* 507–529.

Glasgow, K., Dornbusch, S., Troyer, L., Steinberg, L., & Ritter, P. (1997). Parenting styles, adolescents' attributions, and educational outcomes in nine heterogeneous high schools. *Child Development, 68,* 507–529.

Glei, D. (1999). Measuring contraceptive use patterns among teenage and adult women. *Family Planning Perspectives, 31,* 73–80.

Gold, M., & Yanof, D. (1985). Mothers, daughters, and girlfriends. *Journal of Personality and Social Psychology, 49,* 654–659.

Goldsmith, P. A. (2004). Schools' racial mix, students' optimism, and the black-white and Latino-white achievement gaps. *Sociology of Education, 77,* 121–147.

Goldstein, B. (1976). *Introduction to human sexuality.* Belmont, CA: Star.

Goldstein, S. E., Davis-Kean, P. E., & Eccles, J. S. (2005). Parents, peers, and problem behavior: A longitudinal investigation of the impact of relationship perceptions and characteristics on the development of adolescent problem behavior. *Developmental Psychology, 41,* 401–413.

Goleman, D. (1995). *Emotional intelligence.* New York: Bantam Books.

Golombok, S., & Tasker, F. (1996). Do parents influence the sexual orientation of their children? Findings from a longitudinal study of lesbian families. *Developmental Psychology, 32,* 3–11.

Gonzales, N., Cauce, A., Friedman, R., & Mason, C. (1996). Family, peer, and neighborhood influences on academic achievement among African-American adolescents: One-year prospective effects. *American Journal of Community Psychology, 24,* 365–387.

Gonzales, N., Cause, A., & Mason, C. (1996). Interobserver agreement in the assessment of parental behavior and parent–adolescent conflict: African American mothers, daughters, and independent observers. *Child Development, 67,* 1483–1498.

Good, T., & Brophy, J. (1948). *Looking in classrooms.* New York: Harper & Row.

Goodenow, C. (1992, April). School motivation, engagement, and sense of belonging among urban adolescent students. Paper presented at the annual meeting of the American Educational Research Association, San Francisco.

Goodlad, J. (1984). *A place called school.* New York: McGraw-Hill.

Goodman, E., & Capitman, J. (2000). Depressive symptoms and cigarette smoking among teens. *Pediatrics, 106*(4), 748–755.

Goossens, L., Seiffge-Krenke, I., & Marcoen, A. (1992, March). The many faces of adolescent egocentrism: Two European replications. Paper presented at the biennial meetings of the Society for Research on Adolescence, Washington, DC.

Goran, M., et al. (1998). Developmental changes in energy expenditure and physical activity in children: Evidence for a decline in physical activity in girls before puberty. *Pediatrics, 101*(5), 887–891.

Gordis, E., Margolin, G., & St. John, R. (1997). Marital aggression, observed parental hostility, and child behavior during triadic family interaction. *Journal of Family Psychology, 11,* 76–89.

Gordon, K. (1995). Self-concept and motivational patterns of resilient African American high school students. *Journal of Black Psychology, 21,* 239–255.

Gordon, M., & Miller, R. (1984). Going steady in the 1980s: Exclusive relationships in six Connecticut high schools. *Sociology and Social Research, 68,* 463–479.

Gordon, R. A., Lahey, B. B., Kawai, E., Loeber, R., Stouthamer-Loeber, M., & Farrington, D. P. (2004). Antisocial behavior and youth gang membership. *Criminology, 42,* 55–87.

Gordon, S., & Gilgun, J. (1987). Adolescent sexuality. In V. Van Hasselt & M. Hersen (Eds.), *Handbook of adolescent psychology.* New York: Pergamon Press.

Gore, S., & Aseltine, R., Jr. (1995). Protective processes in adolescence: Matching stressors with social resources. *American Journal of Community Psychology, 23,* 301–327.

Gore, S., Farrell, F., & Gordon, J. (2001). Sports involvement as protection against depressed mood. *Journal of Research on Adolescence, 11*(1), 119–130.

Gorman-Smith, D., & Tolan, P. (1998). The role of exposure to community violence and developmental problems among inner-city youth. *Development and Psychopathology, 10*(1), 101–116.

Gorman-Smith, D., Tolan, P., Sheidow, A., & Henry, D. (2001). Partner violence and street violence among urban adolescents: Do the same family factors relate? *Journal of Research on Adolescence, 11*(3), 273–295.

Gottfredson, D. (1985). Youth employment, crime, and schooling: A longitudinal study of a national sample. *Developmental Psychology, 21,* 419–432.

Gottfredson, M., & Hirschi, T. (1990). A general theory of crime. Stanford, CA: Stanford University Press.

Gottfried, A., Fleming, J., & Gottfried, A. (1998). Role of cognitively stimulating home environment in children's academic intrinsic motivation: A longitudinal study. *Child Development, 69,* 1448–1460.

Gottfried, A., Fleming, J. S., & Gottfried, A. W. (2001). Continuity of academic intrinsic motivation from childhood through late adolescence: A longitudinal study. *Journal of Educational Psychology, 93*(1), 3–13.

Gould, M., Marrocco, F. A., Kleinman, M., Thomas, J. G., Mostkoff, K., Cote, J., & Davies, M. (2005). Evaluating iatrogenic risk of youth suicide screening programs: A randomized controlled trial. *Journal of the American Medical Association, 293,* 1635–1643.

Gould, M., Munfakh, J., Lubell, K., Kleinman, M., & Parker, S. (2002). Seeking help from the Internet during adolescence. *Journal of the American Academy of Child and Adolescent Psychiatry, 41,* 1182–1189.

Gould, M., Wallenstein, S., & Kleinman, M. (1990). Time-space clustering of teenage suicide. *American Journal of Epidemiology, 131,* 71–78.

Gould, R. (1972). The phases of adult life. *American Journal of Psychiatry, 129,* 521–531.

Gowen, L. K., Feldman, S. S., Diaz, R., & Yisrael, D. S. (2004). A comparison of the sexual behaviors and attitudes of adolescent girls with older vs. similar-aged boyfriends. *Journal of Youth and Adolescence, 33,* 167–175.

Gowen, L., Hayward, C., Killen, J., Robinson, T., & Taylor, C. (1999). Acculturation and eating disorder symptoms in adolescent girls. *Journal of Research on Adolescence, 9,* 67–83.

Goyette, K., & Xie, Y. (1999). Educational expectations of Asian American youths: Determinants and ethnic differences. *Sociology of Education, 72,* 22–36.

Graber, J. (2004). Internalizing problems during adolescence. In R. Lerner & L. Steinberg (Eds.), *Handbook of adolescent psychology.* New York: Wiley.

Graber, J., Brooks-Gunn, J., Paikoff, R., & Warren, M. (1994). Prediction of eating problems: An 8-year study of adolescent girls. *Developmental Psychology, 30,* 823–834.

Graber, J., Brooks-Gunn, J., & Warren, M. P. (2006). Pubertal effects on adjustment in girls: Moving from demonstrating effects to identifying pathways. *Journal of Youth and Adolescence, 35,* 391–401.

Graber, J., Lewinsohn, P., Seeley, J., & Brooks-Gunn, J. (1997). Is psychopathology associated with the timing of pubertal development? *Journal of the American Academy of Child and Adolescent Psychiatry, 36,* 1768–1776.

Graber, J., Seeley, J., Brooks-Gunn, J., & Lewinsohn, P. (2004). Is pubertal timing associated with psychopathology in young adulthood? *Journal of the American Academy of Child and Adolescent Psychiatry, 43,* 718–726.

Graham, C. (1991). Menstrual synchrony: An update and review. *Human Nature, 2,* 293–311.

Graham, E. (1988, January 19). As kids gain power of purse, marketing takes aim at them. *The Wall Street Journal,* pp. 1ff.

Graham, S. (1993, March). Peer-directed aggression in African-American youth from an attributional perspective. Paper presented at the biennial meetings of the Society for Research in Child Development, New Orleans.

Graham, S., Bellmore, A., Nishina, A., & Juvonen, J. (in press). "It must be me": Ethnic context and attributions for peer victimization. *Child Development.*

Graham, S., & Hudley, C. (1994). Attributions of aggressive and nonaggressive African-American male early adolescents: A study of construct accessibility. *Developmental Psychology, 30,* 365–373.

Graham, S., Hudley, C., & Williams, E. (1992). Attributional and emotional determinants of aggression among African-American and Latino young adolescents. *Developmental Psychology, 28,* 731–740.

Graham, S., & Juvonen, J. (1998). Self-blame and peer victimization in middle school: An attributional analysis. *Developmental Psychology, 34,* 587–599.

Graham, S., & Juvonen, J. (2002). Ethnicity, peer harassment, and adjustment in middle school: An exploratory study. *Journal of Early Adolescence, 22*(2), 173–199.

Graham, S., & Lowery, B. S. (2004). Priming unconscious racial stereotypes about adolescent offenders. *Law and Human Behavior, 28,* 483–504.

Granic, I., Hollenstein, T., Dishion, T. K., & Patterson, G. R. (2003). Longitudinal analysis of flexibility and reorganization in early adolescence: A dynamic systems study of family interactions. *Developmental Psychology, 39,* 606–617.

Grant, K. E., Lyons, A. L., Finkelstein, J. A., Conway, K. M., Reynolds, L K., O'Koon, J. H., Waitkoff, G. R., & Hicks, K. J. (2004). Gender differences in rates of depressive symptoms among low-income, urban, African American youth: A test of two mediational hypotheses. *Journal of Youth and Adolescence, 33,* 523–533.

Gray, M., & Steinberg, L. (1999). Adolescent romance and the parent–child relationship: A contextual perspective. In W. Furman, B. Brown, & C. Feiring (Eds.), *Contemporary perspectives on adolescent romantic relationships,* pp. 235–265. New York: Cambridge University Press.

Gray, P., & Feldman, J. (1997). Patterns of age mixing and gender mixing among children and adolescents at an ungraded democratic school. *Merrill-Palmer Quarterly, 43,* 67–86.

Gray, W., & Hudson, L. (1984). Formal operations and the imaginary audience. *Developmental Psychology, 20,* 619–627.

Gray-Little, B., & Carels, R. (1997). The effect of racial dissonance on academic achievement in elementary, junior high, and high school students. *Journal of Research on Adolescence, 7,* 109–131.

Gray-Little, B., & Hafdahl, A. (2000). Factors influencing racial comparisons of self-esteem: A quantitative review. *Psychological Bulletin, 126,* 26–54.

Graziano, W., Jensen-Campbell, L., & Finch, J. (1997). The self as a mediator between personality and adjustment. *Journal of Personality and Social Psychology, 73*(2), 392–404.

Green, R. (1980). Homosexuality. In H. Kaplan, A. Freedman, & B. Sadock (Eds.), *Comprehensive textbook of psychiatry,* Vol. 2 (3rd ed.). Baltimore: Williams & Wilkins.

Green, R. (1987). *The "Sissy Boy" syndrome and the development of homosexuality.* New Haven, CT: Yale University Press.

Greenberg, M., & Kusche, C. (1998). *Promoting alternative thinking strategies.* Boulder: Institute of Behavioral Sciences, University of Colorado.

Greenberg, M., Siegel, J., & Leitch, C. (1983). The nature and importance of attachment relationships to parents and peers during adolescence. *Journal of Youth and Adolescence, 12,* 373–386.

Greenberger, E. (1982). Education and the acquisition of psychosocial maturity. In D. McClelland (Ed.), *The development of social maturity.* New York: Irvington.

Greenberger, E., & Chen, C. (1996). Perceived family relationships and depressed mood in early and late adolescence: A comparison of European and Asian Americans. *Developmental Psychology, 32,* 707–716.

Greenberger, E., Chen, C., & Beam, M. R. (1998). The role of "very important" nonparental adults in adolescent development. *Journal of Youth and Adolescence, 27*(3), 321–343.

Greenberger, E., Chen, C., Beam, M., Whang, S., & Dong, Q. (2000). The perceived social contexts of adolescents' misconduct: A comparative study of youths in three cultures. *Journal of Research on Adolescence, 10*(3), 365–388.

Greenberger, E., Chen, C., Tally, S., & Dong, Q. (2000). Family, peer, and individual correlates of depressive symptomatology among U.S. and Chinese adolescents. *Journal of Consulting and Clinical Psychology, 68,* 209–219.

Greenberger, E., & Sorenson, A. (1974). Toward a concept of psychosocial maturity. *Journal of Youth and Adolescence, 3,* 329–358.

Greenberger, E., & Steinberg, L. (1981). The workplace as a context for the socialization of youth. *Journal of Youth and Adolescence, 10,* 185–210.

Greenberger, E., & Steinberg, L. (1983). Sex differences in early work experience: Harbinger of things to come? *Social Forces, 62,* 467–486.

Greenberger, E., & Steinberg, L. (1986). *When teenagers work: The psychological and social costs of adolescent employment.* New York: Basic Books.

Greenberger, E., Steinberg, L., & Ruggiero, M. (1982). A job is a job is a job . . . Or is it? Behavioral observations in the adolescent workplace. *Work and Occupations, 9,* 79–96.

Greenberger, E., Steinberg, L., & Vaux, A. (1981). Adolescents who work: Health and behavioral consequences of job stress. *Developmental Psychology, 17,* 691–703.

Greenberger, E., Steinberg, L., Vaux, A., & McAuliffe, S. (1980). Adolescents who work: Effects of part-time employment on family and peer relations. *Journal of Youth and Adolescence, 9,* 189–202.

Greene, M. L., & Way, N. (2005). Self-esteem trajectories among ethnic minority adolescents: A growth curve analysis of the patterns and predictors of change. *Journal of Research on Adolescence, 15,* 151–177.

Greene, M. L., Way, N., & Pahl, K. (2006). Trajectories of perceived adult and peer discrimination among Black, Latino, and Asian American adolescents: Patterns and psychological correlates. *Developmental Psychology, 42,* 218–236.

Gregory, A., & Weinstein, R. S. (2004). Connection and regulation at home and in school: Predicting growth in achievement for adolescents. *Journal of Adolescent Research, 19,* 405–427.

Gregory, L. (1995). The "turnaround" process: Factors influencing the school success of urban youth. *Journal of Adolescent Research, 10,* 136–154.

Greif, E., & Ulman, K. (1982). The psychological impact of menarche on early adolescent females: A review of the literature. *Child Development, 53,* 1413–1430.

Griffin, K. W., Epstein, J. A., Botvin, G. J., & Spoth, R. L. (2001). Social competence and substance use among rural youth: Mediating role of social benefit expectancies of use. *Journal of Youth and Adolescence, 30*(4), 485–498.

Griffith Fontaine, R., Salzer Burks, V., & Dodge, K. A. (2002). Response decision processes and externalizing behavior problems in adolescents. *Development and Psychopathology, 14,* 107–122.

Grigg, W. S., Lauko, M. A., & Brockway, D. M. (2006). *The nation's report card: Science 2005.* U.S. Department of Education, National Center for Education Statistics (NCES 2006-466). Washington, DC: U.S. Government Printing Office.

Grisso, T., & Schwartz, R. (2000). *Youth on trial.* Chicago: University of Chicago Press.

Grisso, T., Steinberg, L., Woolard, J., Cauffman, E., Scott, E., Graham, S., Lexcen, F., Reppucci, N., & Schwartz, R. (2003). Juveniles' competence to stand trial: A comparison of adolescents' and adults' capacities as trial defendants. *Law and Human Behavior, 27,* 333–363.

Grolnick, W., Kurowki, C. O., Dunlap, K. G., & Hevey, C. (2000). Parental resources and the transition to junior high. *Journal of Research on Adolescence, 10*(4), 465–488.

Grolnick, W., & Slowiaczek, M. (1994). Parents' involvement in children's schooling: A multidimensional conceptualization and motivational model. *Child Development, 65,* 237–252.

Grossman, M., Chaloupka, F., Saffer, H., & Laixuthai, A. (1994). Effects of alcohol price policy on youth: A summary of economic research. *Journal of Research on Adolescence, 4,* 347–364.

Grotevant, H. (1997). Adolescent development in family contexts. In N. Eisenberg (Ed.), *Handbook of child psychology* (5th ed.), Vol. 3: *Social, emotional, and personality development,* pp. 1097–1149. New York: Wiley.

Grotevant, H., & Cooper, C. (1986). Individuation in family relationships: A perspective on individual differences in the development of identity and role-taking skill in adolescence. *Human Development, 29,* 82–100.

Grotevant, H., & Cooper, C. (1988). The role of family experience in career exploration during adolescence. In P. Baltes, D. Featherman, & R. Lerner (Eds.), *Life-span development and behavior,* Vol. 8., pp. 231–258. Hillsdale, NJ: Erlbaum.

Grotpeter, J., & Crick, N. (1996). Relational aggression, overt aggression, and friendship. *Child Development, 67,* 2328–2338.

Grover, R. L., & Nangle, D. W. (2003). Adolescent perceptions of problematic heterosocial situations: A focus group study. *Journal of Youth and Adolescence, 32*(2), 129–139.

Gruber, J. (Ed.). (2001). *Risky behavior among youths: An economic analysis.* Chicago: University of Chicago Press.

Gruber, J., & Zinman, J. (2001). Youth smoking in the United States. In J. Gruber (Ed.), *Risky behavior among youths: An economic analysis,* pp. 69–120. Chicago: University of Chicago Press.

Grunbaum, J., Lowry, R., Kann, L., & Pateman, B. (2000). Prevalence of health risk behaviors among Asian American/Pacific Islander high school students. *Journal of Adolescent Health, 27*(5), 322–330.

Grych, J., & Fincham, F. (1992). Interventions for children of divorce: Toward greater integration of research and action. *Psychological Bulletin, 111,* 434–454.

Grych, J. H., Raynor, S. R., & Fosco, G. M. (2004). Family processes that shape the impact of interparental conflict on adolescents. *Development and Psychopathology, 16,* 649–665.

Guberman, S. (1996). The development of everyday mathematics in Brazilian children with limited formal education. *Child Development, 67,* 1609–1623.

Guerra, N., & Slaby, R. (1990). Cognitive mediators of aggression in adolescent offenders, 2: Intervention. *Developmental Psychology, 26,* 269–277.

Guest, A., & Schneider, B. (2003). Adolescents' extracurricular participation in context: The mediating effects of schools, communities, and identity. *Sociology of Education, 76,* 89–109.

Guillen, E., & Barr, S. (1994). Nutrition, dieting, and fitness messages in a magazine for adolescent women, 1970–1990. *Journal of Adolescent Health, 15,* 464–472.

Guisinger, S., & Blatt, S. (1994). Individuality and relatedness: Evolution of a fundamental dialectic. *American Psychologist, 49,* 104–111.

Guldi, M., Page, M., & Stevens, A. (2007). Family background and children's transition to adulthood over time. In S. Danziger & C. Rouse (Eds.), *The price of independence: The economics of early adulthood.* New York: Russell Sage Foundation.

Gunnoe, M. (1994, February). Noncustodial mothers' and fathers' contributions to the adjustment of adolescents in stepfamilies. Paper presented at the biennial meetings of the Society for Research on Adolescence, San Diego.

Gunnoe, M., Hetherington, E. M., & Reiss, D. (1999). Parental religiosity, parenting style, and adolescent social responsibility. *Journal of Early Adolescence, 19,* 199–225.

Gunnoe, M., Hetherington, E. M., & Reiss, D. (2006). The differential impact of fathers' authoritarian parenting on early adolescent adjustment in conservative Protestant vs. other families. *Journal of Family Psychology, 20,* 589–596.

Guo, G. (1998). The timing of the influences of cumulative poverty on children's cognitive ability and achievement. *Social Forces, 77,* 257–287.

Guo, J., Chung, I.-J., Hill, K. G., Hawkins, J., Catalano, R. F., & Abbott, R. D. (2002). Developmental relationships between adolescent substance use and risky sexual behavior in young adulthood. *Journal of Adolescent Health, 31*(4), 354–362.

Gutierrez, R. (2000). Advancing African American, urban youth in mathematics: Unpacking the success of one math department. *American Journal of Education, 109*(1), 63–111.

Gutman, L., McLoyd, V. C., & Tokoyawa, T. (2005). Financial strain, neighborhood stress, parenting behaviors, and adolescent adjustment in urban African American families. *Journal of Research on Adolescence, 15,* 425–449.

Gutman, L., & Midgley, C. (2000). The role of protective factors in supporting the academic achievement of poor African American students during the middle school transition. *Journal of Youth and Adolescence, 29*(2), 223–248.

Guttmacher, S., Lieberman, L., Ward, D., Freudenberg, N., Radosh, A., & Des Jarlais, D. (1997). Condom availability in New York City public high schools: Relationships to condom use and sexual behavior. *American Journal of Public Health, 87,* 1427–1433.

Hacker, D. (1994). An existential view of adolescence. *Journal of Early Adolescence, 14,* 300–327.

Hafetz, E. (1976). Parameters of sexual maturity in man. In E. Hafetz (Ed.), *Perspectives in human reproduction,* Vol. 3: *Sexual maturity: Physiological and clinical parameters.* Ann Arbor, MI: Ann Arbor Science Publishers.

Hagan, J., & Foster, H. (2001). Youth violence and the end of adolescence. *American Sociological Review, 66*(6), 874–899.

Hagan, J., MacMillan, R., & Wheaton, B. (1996). New kid in town: Social capital and the life course effects of family migration on children. *American Sociological Review, 61,* 368–385.

Haggstrom-Nordin, E., Hanson, U., & Tyden, T. (2002). Sex behavior among high school students in Sweden: Improvement in contraceptive use over time. *Journal of Adolescent Health, 30*(4), 288–295.

Hahm, H., Lahif, M., & Buterman, N. (2004). Asian American adolescents' acculturation, binge drinking, and alcohol- and tobacco-using peers. *Journal of Community Psychology, 32,* 295–308.

Haj-Yahia, M. M., Musleh, K., & Haj-Yahia, Y. (2002). The incidence of adolescent maltreatment in Arab society and some of its psychological effects. *Journal of Family Issues, 23*(8), 1032–1064.

Hale, S., Bronik, M., & Fry, A. (1997). Verbal and spatial working memory in school-age children: Developmental differences in susceptibility to interference. *Developmental Psychology, 33,* 364–371.

Hale, S. (1990). A global developmental trend in cognitive processing speed. *Child Development, 61,* 653–663.

Hall, G. S. (1904). *Adolescence.* New York: Appleton.

Hallinan, M. (1981). Recent advances in sociometry. In S. Asher & J. Gottman (Eds.), *The development of children's friendship.* New York: Cambridge University Press.

Hallinan, M. (1992). The organization of students for instruction in the middle school. *Sociology of Education, 65,* 114–127.

Hallinan, M. (1996). Track mobility in secondary school. *Social Forces, 74,* 983–1002.

Hallinan, M., & Williams, R. (1989). Interracial friendship choices in secondary schools. *American Sociological Review, 54,* 67–78.

Hallinan, M., & Sorensen, A. (1987). Ability grouping and sex differences in mathematics achievement. *Sociology of Education, 60,* 63–72.

Halperin, S. (Ed.). (2001). *The forgotten half revisited: American youth and young families, 1988–2008.* Washington: American Youth Policy Forum.

Halpern, C., Joyner, K., Udry, J., & Suchindran, C. (2000). Smart teens don't have sex (or kiss much either). *Journal of Adolescent Health, 26*(3), 213–225.

Halpern, C., King, R., Oslak, S., & Udry, J. (2005). Body mass index, dieting, romance, and sexual activity in adolescent girls: Relationships over time. *Journal of Research on Adolescence, 15,* 535–559.

Halpern, C., Oslak, S., Young, M., Martin, S., & Kupper, L. (2001). Partner violence among adolescents in opposite-sex romantic relationships: Findings from the National Longitudinal Study of Adolescent Health. *American Journal of Public Health, 91,* 1679–1685.

Halpern, C., & Udry, J. (1994, February). Pubertal increases in body fat and implications for dieting, dating, and sexual behavior among Black and White females. Paper presented at the biennial meetings of the Society for Research on Adolescence, San Diego.

Halpern, C., Udry, J., Campbell, B., & Suchindran, C. (1999). Effects of body fat on weight concerns, dating, and sexual activity: A longitudinal analysis of black and white adolescent girls. *Developmental Psychology, 35,* 721–736.

Halpern, C., Udry, J., & Suchindran, C. (1996, March). Monthly measures of salivary testosterone predict sexual activity in adolescent males. Paper presented at the biennial meetings of the Society for Research on Adolescence, Boston.

Halpern, C., Young, M., Waller, M., Martin, S., & Kupper, L. (2004). Prevalence of partner violence in same-sex romantic and sexual relationships in a national sample of adolescents. *Journal of Adolescent Health, 35,* 124–131.

Halpern-Felsher, B., & Cauffman, E. (2001). Costs and benefits of a decision: Decision-making competence in adolescents and adults. *Journal of Applied Developmental Psychology, 22,* 257–273.

Hamburg, D. (1986). *Preparing for life: The critical transition of adolescence.* New York: Carnegie Corporation of New York.

Hamill, S. (1994). Parent–adolescent communication in sandwich generation families. *Journal of Adolescent Research, 9,* 458–482.

Hamilton, C. (2000). Continuity and discontinuity of attachment from infancy through adolescence. *Child Development, 71,* 690–694.

Hamilton, H. A. (2005). Extended families and adolescent well-being. *Journal of Adolescent Health, 36,* 260–266.

Hamilton, S., & Hamilton, M. (2004). Contexts for mentoring: Adolescent–adult relationships in workplaces and communities. In R. Lerner & L. Steinberg (Eds.), *Handbook of adolescent psychology.* New York: Wiley.

Hamilton, S., & Hurrelmann, K. (1994). The school-to-career transition in Germany and the United States. *Teachers College Record, 96,* 329–344.

Hamm, J. V. (2000). Do birds of a feather flock together? The variable bases for African American, Asian American, and European American adolescents' selection of similar friends. *Developmental Psychology, 36*(2), 209–219.

Hamm, J. V., & Coleman, H. K. (2001). African American and White adolescents' strategies for managing cultural diversity in predominantly White high schools. *Journal of Youth and Adolescence, 30*(3), 281–303.

Hammen, C., Shih, H., & Brennan, P. (2004). Intergenerational transmission of depression: Test of an interpersonal stress model in a community sample. *Journal of Consulting and Clinical Psychology, 72,* 511–522.

Hamre, B. K., & Pianta, R. C. (2001). Early teacher–child relationships and the trajectory of children's school outcomes through eighth grade. *Child Development, 72*(2), 625–638.

Hansen, D. M., Larson, R. W., & Dworkin, J. B. (2003). What adolescents learn in organized youth activities: A survey of self-reported developmental experiences. *Journal of Research on Adolescence, 13*(1), 25–55.

Hansen, M., Janssen, I., Schiff, A., Zee, P. C., & Dubocovich, M. L. (2005). The impact of school daily schedule on adolescent sleep. *Pediatrics, 115,* 1555–1561.

Hanson, S. (1994). Lost talent: Unrealized educational aspirations and expectations among U.S. youths. *Sociology of Education, 67,* 159–183.

Hanson, S., & Kraus, R. (1998). Women, sports, and science: Do female athletes have an advantage? *Sociology of Education, 71,* 93–110.

Hanson, T., McLanahan, S., & Thomson, E. (1996). Double jeopardy: Parental conflict and stepfamily outcomes for children. *Journal of Marriage and the Family, 58,* 141–154.

Harding, D. J. (2003). Counterfactual models of neighborhood effects: The effect of neighborhood poverty on dropping out and teenage pregnancy. *American Journal of Sociology, 109,* 676–719.

Hardy, D., Astone, N., Brooks-Gunn, J., Shapiro, X., & Miller, X. (1998). Like mother, like child: Intergenerational patterns of age at first birth and associations with childhood and adolescent characteristics and adult outcomes in the second generation. *Developmental Psychology, 34,* 1220–1232.

Hardy, S. A., & Raffaelli, M. (2003). Adolescent religiosity and sexuality: An investigation of reciprocal influences. *Journal of Adolescence, 26,* 731–739.

Hargreaves, D., & Tiggemann, M. (2003). The effect of thin ideal television commercials on body dissatisfaction and schema activation during early adolescence. *Journal of Youth and Adolescence, 32,* 367–373.

Harker, K. (2001). Immigrant generation, assimilation and adolescent psychological well-being. *Social Forces, 79,* 969–1004.

Harold, G., & Conger, R. (1997). Marital conflict and adolescent distress: The role of adolescent awareness. *Child Development, 68,* 333–350.

Harper, G., & Robinson, W. L. (1999). Pathways to risk among inner-city African-American adolescent females: The influence of gang membership. *American Journal of Community Psychology, 27,* 383–404.

Harre, N. (2000). Risk evaluation, driving, and adolescents: A typology. *Developmental Review, 20*(2), 206–226.

Harris, J. (1995). Where is the child's environment? A group socialization theory of development. *Psychological Bulletin, 102,* 458–489.

Harris, J. R. (1998). *The nurture assumption: Why children turn out the way they do.* New York: Free Press.

Harris, K. (1999). The health status and risk behavior of adolescents in immigrant families. In D. Hernandez (Ed.), *Children of immigrants: Health, adjustment, and public assistance,* pp. 286–347. Washington, DC: National Academy Press.

Harris, M. (1994). Cholas, Mexican-American girls, and gangs. *Sex Roles, 30,* 289–301.

Hart, B., & Thompson, J. (1996). Gender role characteristics and depressive symptomatology among adolescents. *Journal of Early Adolescence, 16,* 407–426.

Hart, D., & Chmiel, S. (1992). Influence of defense mechanisms on moral judgment development: A longitudinal study. *Developmental Psychology, 28,* 722–730.

Hart, D., & Fegley, S. (1995). Prosocial behavior and caring in adolescence: Relations to self-understanding and social judgment. *Child Development, 66,* 1346–1359.

Hart, D., Fegley, S., & Brengelman, D. (1993). Perceptions of past, present, and future selves among children and adolescents. *British Journal of Developmental Psychology, 11,* 265–282.

Hart, D., Hofmann, V., Edelstein, W., & Keller, M. (1997). The relation of childhood personality types to adolescent behavior and development: A longitudinal study of Icelandic children. *Developmental Psychology, 33,* 195–205.

Harter, S. (1990). Identity and self development. In S. Feldman & G. Elliott (Eds.), *At the threshold: The developing adolescent,* pp. 352–387. Cambridge, MA: Harvard University Press.

Harter, S. (1998). The development of self-representations. In W. Damon (Series Ed.) & N. Eisenberg (Vol. Ed.), *Handbook of child psychology* (5th ed.), pp. 53–617. New York: Wiley.

Harter, S. (1999). *The construction of the self.* New York: Guilford Press.

Harter, S., & Monsour, A. (1992). Developmental analysis of conflict caused by opposing attributes in the adolescent self-portrait. *Developmental Psychology, 28,* 251–260.

Harter, S., Marold, D., Whitesell, N., & Cobbs, G. (1996). A model of the effects of parent and peer support on adolescent false self behavior. *Child Development, 67,* 360–374.

Harter, S., Stocker, C., & Robinson, N. (1996). The perceived directionality of the link between approval and self-worth: The liabilities of a looking glass self orientation among young adolescents. *Journal of Research on Adolescence, 6,* 285–308.

Harter, S., Waters, P., & Whitesell, N. (1998). Relational self-worth: Differences in perceived worth as a person across interpersonal contexts among adolescents. *Child Development, 69,* 756–766.

Harter, S., Waters, P., Whitesell, N., & Kastelic, D. (1998). Level of voice among female and male high school students: Relational context, support, and gender orientation. *Developmental Psychology, 34,* 892–901.

Harter, S., Whitesell, N., & Kowalski, P. (1991). The effects of educational transitions on children's perceptions of competence and motivational orientation. Manuscript submitted for publication. Department of Psychology, University of Denver.

Hartney, C. (2006). *Youth under 18 in the criminal justice system.* Oakland: National Council on Crime and Delinquency.

Hartup, W. (1977). Adolescent peer relations: A look to the future. In J. Hill & F. Monks (Eds.), *Adolescence and youth in prospect.* Guildford, England: IPC Press.

Hartup, W. (1983). Peer relations. In E. M. Hetherington (Ed.), *Handbook of child psychology: Socialization, personality, and social development,* Vol. 4. New York: Wiley.

Hartup, W. (1993). Adolescents and their friends. In. In B. Laursen (Ed.), *Close friendships during adolescence: New directions for child development,* pp. 3–22. San Francisco: Jossey-Bass.

Hartup, W. (1996). The company they keep: Friendships and their developmental significance. *Child Development, 67*, 1–13.

Hartup, W., & Stevens, N. (1997). Friendships and adaptation in the life course. *Psychological Bulletin, 121*, 335–370.

Hasebe, Y., Nucci, L., & Nucci, M. S. (2004). Parental control of the personal domain and adolescent symptoms of psychopathology: A cross-national study in the United States and Japan. *Child Development, 75*, 815–828.

Hatzichristou, C., & Hopf, D. (1996). A multiperspective comparison of peer sociometric status groups in childhood and adolescence. *Child Development, 67*, 1085–1102.

Hauser, S. (1999). Understanding resilient outcomes: Adolescent lives across time and generations. *Journal of Research on Adolescence, 9*, 1–24.

Hauser, S., & Bowlds, M. (1990). Stress, coping, and adaptation. In S. Feldman & G. Elliott (Eds.), *At the threshold: The developing adolescent*, pp. 388–413. Cambridge, MA: Harvard University Press.

Hauser, S., & Kasendorf, E. (1983). *Black and white identity formation*. Malabar, FL: Kreiger.

Hauser, S., Powers, S., & Noam, G. (1991). *Adolescents and their families*. New York: Free Press.

Hausman, A., Pierce, G., & Briggs, L. (1996). Evaluation of comprehensive violence prevention education: Effects on student behavior. *Journal of Adolescent Health, 19*, 104–110.

Hausser, D., & Michaud, P. (1994). Does a condom-promoting strategy (the Swiss STOP-AIDS campaign) modify sexual behavior among adolescents? *Pediatrics, 93*, 580–585.

Havighurst, R. (1952). *Developmental tasks and education*. New York: McKay.

Hawkins, J., Catalano, R., & Miller, J. (1992). Risk and protective factors for alcohol and other drug problems in adolescence and early adulthood: Implications for substance abuse prevention. *Psychological Bulletin, 112*, 64–105.

Hayes, C. (Ed.). (1987). *Risking the future: Adolescent sexuality, pregnancy, and childbearing*, Vol. 1. Washington, DC: National Academy Press.

Hayes, D., Wolfer, L., & Wolfe, M. (1996). Schoolbook simplification and its relation to the decline in SAT-Verbal scores. *American Educational Research Journal, 33*, 489–508.

Haynie, D. L. (2003). Contexts of risk? Explaining the link between girls' pubertal development and their delinquency involvement. *Social Forces, 82*, 355–397.

Haynie, D. L., Giordano, P. C., Manning, W. D., & Longmore, M. A. (2005). Adolescent romantic relationships and delinquency involvement. *Criminology, 43*, 177–210.

Haynie, D. L. & McHugh, S. (2003). Sibling deviance in the shadows of mutual and unique friendship effects? *Criminology, 41*, 355–391.

Haynie, D. L., Nansel, T., Eitel, P., Crump, A., Saylor, K., Yu, K., et al. (2001). Bullies, victims, and bully/victims: Distinct groups of at-risk youth. *Journal of Early Adolescence, 21*(1), 29–49.

Haynie, D. L., & Osgood, D. W. (2005). Reconsidering peers and delinquency: How do peers matter? *Social Forces, 84*, 1109–1130.

Hayward, C., Gotlib, I., Schraedley, P., & Litt, I. (1999). Ethnic differences in the association between pubertal status and symptoms of depression in adolescent girls. *Journal of Adolescent Health, 25*, 143–149.

Hayward, C., Killen, J., Wilson, D., Hammer, L., Litt, I., Kraemer, H., Haydel, F., Varady, A., & Taylor, B. (1997). Psychiatric risk associated with early puberty in adolescent girls. *Journal of the American Academy of Child and Adolescent Psychiatry, 36*, 255–261.

Hazan, C. (1994, February). The role of sexuality in peer attachment formation. Paper presented at the biennial meetings of the Society for Research on Adolescence, San Diego.

Hechinger, F. (1993). Schools for teenagers: A historic dilemma. *Teachers College Record, 94*, 522–539.

Heck, R. H., Price, C. L., & Thomas, S. L. (2004). Tracks as emergent structures: A network analysis of student differentiation in a high school. *American Journal of Education, 110*, 321–353.

Hedges, L., & Nowell, A. (1999). Changes in the Black-White gap in achievement test scores. *Sociology of Education, 72*, 111–135.

Heimer, K., & Matsueda, R. (1994). Role-taking, role commitment, and delinquency: A theory of differential social control. *American Sociological Review, 59*, 365–390.

Hein, K. (1988a). *Issues in adolescent health: An overview*. Washington, DC: Carnegie Council on Adolescent Development.

Hein, K. (1988b). *AIDS in adolescence: A rationale for concern*. Washington, DC: Carnegie Council on Adolescent Development.

Hein, K., Dell, R., Futterman, D., Rotheram-Borus, M., & Shaffer, N. (1995). Comparison of HIV+ and HIV− adolescents: Risk factors and psychosocial determinants. *Pediatrics, 95*, 96–104.

Hektner, J. (1994, April). When moving up implies moving out: How rural adolescents and their parents think about higher education and careers. Paper presented at the annual meeting of the American Educational Research Association, New Orleans.

Helsen, M., Vollebergh, W., & Meeus, W. (2000). Social support from parents and friends and emotional problems in adolescence. *Journal of Youth and Adolescence, 29*(3), 319–335.

Helwig, C. (1997). The role of agent and social context in judgments of freedom of speech and religion. *Child Development, 68*, 484–495.

Helwig, C. C., Arnold, M. L., Tan, D., & Boyd, D. (2003). Chinese adolescents' reasoning about democratic and authority-based decision-making in peer, family, and school contexts. *Child Development, 74*, 783–800.

Hendrick, S., & Hendrick, C. (1994, February). Gender, sexuality, and close relationships. Paper presented at the biennial meetings of the Society for Research on Adolescence, San Diego.

Henggeler, S. W., Clingempeel, W., Brondino, M. J., & Pickrel, S. G. (2002). Four-year follow-up of multisystemic therapy with substance-abusing and substance-dependent juvenile offenders. *Journal of the American Academy of Child and Adolescent Psychiatry, 41*, 868–874.

Henggeler, S., Melton, G., & Smith, L. (1992). Family prevention using multisystemic therapy: An effective alternative to incarcerating serious juvenile offenders. *Journal of Consulting and Clinical Psychology, 60*, 953–961.

Henry, B., Caspi, A., Moffitt, T., & Silva, P. (1996). Temperamental and familial predictors of violent and nonviolent criminal convictions: age 3 to age 18. *Developmental Psychology, 32*, 614–623.

Henry, B., Caspi, A., Moffitt, T., Harrington, H., & Silva, P. (1999). Staying in school protects boys with poor self-regulation in childhood from later crime: A longitudinal study. *International Journal of Behavioral Development, 23*, 1049–1073.

Henry, B., Feehan, M., McGee, R., Stanton, W., Moffitt, T., & Silva, P. (1993). The importance of conduct problems and depressive symptoms in predicting adolescent substance use. *Journal of Abnormal Child Psychology, 21*, 469–480.

Henry, C., & Lovelace, S. (1995). Family resources and adolescent life satisfaction in remarried households. *Journal of Family Issues, 16*, 765–786.

Henshaw, S. (1995). The impact of requirements for parental consent on minors' abortions in Mississippi. *Family Planning Perspectives, 27*, 120–122.

Herdt, G., & McClintock, M. (2000). The magical age of 10. *Archives of Sexual Behavior, 29*(6), 587–606.

Herman, M. (2004). Forced to choose: Some determinants of racial identification in multiracial adolescents. *Child Development, 75*, 730–748.

Herman-Giddens, M., Sandler, A., & Friedman, N. (1988). Sexual precocity in girls: An association with sexual abuse? *American Journal of the Diseases of Childhood, 142*, 431–433.

Herman-Giddens, M., Slora, E., Wasserman, R., Bourdony, C., Bhapkar, M., Koch, G., & Hasemeier, C. (1997). Secondary sexual characteristics and menses in young girls seen in office practice: A study from the Pediatric Research in Office Settings Network. *Pediatrics, 88,* 505–512.

Herman-Stahl, M., Stemmler, M., & Petersen, A. (1995). Approach and avoidant coping: Implications for adolescent mental health. *Journal of Youth and Adolescence, 24,* 649–665.

Hernandez, D. (1997). Child development and the social demography of childhood. *Child Development, 68,* 149–169.

Herrenkohl, T. I., Maguin, E., Hill, K. G., Hawkins, J., Abbott, R. D., & Catalano, R. F. (2000). Developmental risk factors for youth violence. *Journal of Adolescent Health, 26*(3), 176–186.

Hershberger, S., & D'Augelli, A. (1995). The impact of victimization on the mental health and suicidality of lesbian, gay, and bisexual youths. *Developmental Psychology, 31,* 65–74.

Hess, R., Chin-Mei, C., & McDevitt, T. (1987). Cultural variations in family beliefs about children's performance in mathematics: Comparisons among People's Republic of China, Chinese-American, and Caucasian-American families. *Journal of Educational Psychology, 79,* 179–188.

Hetherington, E. M. (1991). The role of individual differences and family relationships in children's coping with divorce and remarriage. In P. Cowan & E. M. Hetherington, (Eds.), *Advances in family research,* Vol. 2: *Family transitions.* Hillsdale, NJ: Erlbaum.

Hetherington, E. M. (1993). An overview of the Virginia longitudinal study of divorce and remarriage with a focus on early adolescence. *Journal of Family Psychology, 7,* 39–56.

Hetherington, E. M., Bridges, M., & Insabella, G. (1998). What matters? What does not? Five perspectives on the association between marital transitions and children's adjustment. *American Psychologist, 53,* 167–184.

Hetherington, E. M., Clingempeel, W., Anderson, E., Deal, J., Hagan, M., Hollier, E., & Lindner, M. (1992). Coping with marital transitions: A family systems perspective. *Monographs of the Society for Research in Child Development,* Serial No. 227.

Hetherington, E. M., Henderson, S., & Reiss, D. (1999). Adolescent siblings in stepfamilies: Family functioning and adolescent adjustment. *Monographs of the Society for Research in Child Development, 64,* Serial No. 259.

Hetherington, E. M., Reiss, D., & Plomin, R. (Eds.). (1994). *Separate social worlds of siblings: The impact of nonshared environment on development.* Hillsdale, NJ: Erlbaum.

Hetherington, E. M., & Stanley-Hagan, M. (1995). Parenting in divorced and remarried families. In M. Bornstein (Ed.), *Handbook of parenting,*

Vol. 3: *Status and social conditions of parenting,* pp. 233–254. Mahwah, NJ: Erlbaum.

Higgins, A., & Turnure, J. (1984). Distractibility and concentration of attention in children's development. *Child Development, 44,* 1799–1810.

Hightower, E. (1990). Adolescent interpersonal and familial predictors of positive mental health at midlife. *Journal of Youth and Adolescence, 19,* 257–276.

Hill, C. (1986). A developmental perspective on adolescent "rebellion" in the church. *Journal of Psychology and Theology, 14,* 306–318.

Hill, C., & Holzer, H. (2007). Labor market experiences and the transition to adulthood. In S. Danziger & C. Rouse (Eds.), *The price of independence: The economics of early adulthood.* New York: Russell Sage Foundation.

Hill, J. (1983). Early adolescence: A framework. *Journal of Early Adolescence, 3,* 1–21.

Hill, J., & Holmbeck, G. (1986). Attachment and autonomy during adolescence. In G. Whitehurst (Ed.), *Annals of child development.* Greenwich, CT: JAI Press.

Hill, J., & Lynch, M. (1983). The intensification of gender-related role expectations during early adolescence. In J. Brooks-Gunn & A. Petersen (Eds.), *Girls at puberty,* pp. 201–228. New York: Plenum.

Hill, J., & Palmquist, W. (1978). Social cognition and social relations in early adolescence. *International Journal of Behavioral Development, 1,* 1–36.

Hill, K. G., Hawkins, J. D., Catalano, R. F., Abbott, R. D., & Guo, J. (2005). Family influences on the risk of daily smoking initiation. *Journal of Adolescent Health, 37,* 202–210.

Hill, N. E., Ramirez, C., & Dumka, L. E. (2003). Early adolescents' career aspirations: A qualitative study of perceived barriers and family support among low-income, ethnically diverse adolescents. *Journal of Family Issues, 24,* 934–959.

Hill, N. E., Castellino, D. R., Lansford, J. E., Nowlin, P., Dodge, K. A., Bates, J. E., & Pettit, G. S. (2004). Parent academic involvement as related to school behavior, achievement, and aspirations: Demographic variations across adolescence. *Child Development, 75,* 1491–1509.

Hilsman, R., & Garber, J. (1995). A test of the cognitive diathesis-stress model of depression in children: Academic stressors, attributional style, perceived competence, and control. *Journal of Personality and Social Psychology, 69,* 370–380.

Hinden, B., Compas, B., Howell, D., & Achenbach, T. (1997). Covariation of the anxious-depressed syndrome during adolescence: Separating fact from artifact. *Journal of Consulting and Clinical Psychology, 65,* 6–14.

Hine, T. (1999). *The rise and fall of the American teenager.* New York: Bard Books.

Hines, A. (1997). Divorce-related transitions, adolescent development, and the role of the parent–child relationship: A review of the literature. *Journal of Marriage and the Family, 59,* 375–388.

Hingson, R., Heeren, T., & Winter, M. (2006). Age at drinking onset and alcohol dependence: Age at onset, duration, and severity. *Archives of Pediatric and Adolescent Medicine, 160,* 739–746.

Hirsch, B., & DuBois, D. (1991). Self-esteem in early adolescence: The Identification and prediction of contrasting longitudinal trajectories. *Journal of Youth and Adolescence, 20,* 53–72.

Hirsch, B., Mickus, M., & Boerger, R. (2002). Ties to influential adults among Black and White adolescents: Culture, social class, and family networks. *American Journal of Community Psychology, 30*(2), 289–303.

Hirsch, E. D. (1996). *The schools we need.* New York: Doubleday.

Hock, E., Eberly, M., Bartle-Haring, S., Ellwanger, P., & Widaman, K. F. (2001). Separation anxiety in parents of adolescents: Theoretical significance and scale development. *Child Development, 72*(1), 284–298.

Hodges, E., Boivin, M., Vitaro, F., & Bukowski, W. (1998). The power of friendship: Protection against an escalating cycle of peer victimization. *Developmental Psychology, 35,* 94–101.

Hodges, E., Finnegan, R., & Perry, D. (1999). Skewed autonomy-relatedness in preadolescents' conceptions of their relationships with mother, father, and best friend. *Developmental Psychology, 35,* 737–748.

Hodges, E., & Perry, D. (1999). Personal and interpersonal antecedents and consequences of victimization by peers. *Journal of Personality and Social Psychology, 76,* 677–685.

Hoffer, T. (1997). High school graduation requirements: Effects on dropping out and student achievement. *Teachers College Record, 98,* 584–607.

Hofferth, S. L., & Reid, L. (2002). Early childbearing and children's achievement and behavior over time. *Perspectives on Sexual and Reproductive Health, 34*(1), 41–49.

Hofferth, S. L., Reid, L., & Mott, F. L. (2001). The effects of early childbearing on schooling over time. *Family Planning Perspective, 33*(5), 259–267.

Hoffman, J. P. (2002). The community context of family structure and adolescent drug use. *Journal of Marriage and the Family, 64*(2), 314–330.

Hoffman, J. P. (2003). A contextual analysis of differential association, social control, and strain theories of delinquency. *Social Forces, 81*(3), 753–785.

Hoffman, K. L., Kiecolt, J., & Edwards, J. N. (2005). Physical violence between siblings: A theoretical and empirical analysis. *Journal of Family Issues, 26,* 1103–1130.

Hoffman, L. (1974). Effects of maternal employment on the child: A review of the research. *Developmental Psychology, 10,* 204–228.

Hoffman, S., Foster, E., & Furstenberg, F., Jr., (1993). Reevaluating the costs of teenage childbearing. *Demography, 30,* 1–13.

Hogan, D., Sun, R., & Cornwell, G. (2000). Sexual and fertility behaviors of American females aged 15–19 years: 1985, 1990, and 1995. *American Journal of Public Health, 90*(9), 1421–1425.

Hogue, A., & Steinberg, L. (1995). Homophily of internalized distress in adolescent peer groups. *Developmental Psychology, 31,* 897–906.

Holder, D. W., DuRant, R. H., Harris, T. L., Henderson Daniel, J., Obeidallah, D., & Goodman, E. (2000). The association between adolescent spirituality and voluntary sexual activity. *Journal of Adolescent Health, 26*(4), 295–302.

Holland, A., & Andre, T. (1994). Athletic participation and the social status of adolescent males and females. *Youth and Society, 25,* 388–407.

Holland, J. (1985). *Making vocational choice: A theory of careers* (2nd ed.). Englewood Cliffs, NJ: Prentice-Hall.

Hollingshead, A. ([1949]1975). *Elmtown's youth and Elmtown revisited.* New York: Wiley.

Holloway, S. (1988). Concepts of ability and effort in Japan and the United States. *Review of Educational Research, 58,* 327–345.

Holmbeck, G. (1996). A model of family relational transformations during the transition to adolescence: Parent–adolescent conflict and adaptation. In J. Graber, J. Brooks-Gunn, & A. Petersen (Eds.), *Transitions through adolescence: Interpersonal domains and context,* pp. 167–199. Mahwah, NJ: Erlbaum.

Holmbeck, G., & Hill, J. (1991). Conflictive engagement, positive affect, and menarche in families with seventh-grade girls. *Child Development, 62,* 1030–1048.

Holmbeck, G., & O'Donnell, K. (1991). Longitudinal study of discrepancies between maternal and adolescent perceptions of decision-making and desired behavioral autonomy. In R. Paikoff & W. A. Collins (Eds.), *New directions for child development: Shared views of the family during adolescence,* pp. 51–69. San Francisco: Jossey-Bass.

Holmbeck, G., Durbin, D., & Kung, E. (1995, March). Attachment, autonomy, and adjustment before and after leaving home: Sullivan and Sullivan revisited. Paper presented at the SRCD, Indianapolis.

Holmbeck, G., Paikoff, R., & Brooks-Gunn, J. (1995). Parenting adolescents. In M. Bornstein (Ed.), *Handbook of parenting,* Vol. 1: *Children and parenting,* pp. 91–118. Mahwah, NJ: Erlbaum.

Holmbeck, G., Shapera, W., Westhoven, V., Johnson, S., Millstein, R., & Hommeyer, J. (2000, March). A longitudinal study of observed and perceived parenting behaviors and autonomy development in families of young adolescents with spina bifida. Paper presented at the biennial meetings of the Society for Research on Adolescence, Chicago.

Holmen, T., Barrett-Connor, E., Holmen, J., & Bjerner, L. (2000). Health problems in teenage daily smokers versus nonsmokers, Norway, 1995–1997. *American Journal of Epidemiology, 151,* 148–155.

Holsen, I., Kraft, P., & Vitterso, J. (2000). Stability in depressed mood in adolescence: Results from a 6-year longitudinal panel study. *Journal of Youth and Adolescence, 29*(1), 61–78.

Hooper, C. J., Luciana, M., Conklin, H. M., & Yarger, R. S. (2004). Adolescents' performance on the Iowa gambling task: Implications for the development of decision making and ventromedial prefrontal cortex. *Developmental Psychology, 40,* 1148–1158.

Hoover-Dempsey, K., & Sandler, H. (1995). Parental involvement in children's education: Why does it make a difference? *Teachers College Record, 97,* 310–331.

Horan, P., & Hargis, P. (1991). Children's work and schooling in the late nineteenth-century family economy. *American Sociological Review, 56,* 583–596.

Horn, S. S. (2003). Adolescents' reasoning about exclusion from social groups. *Developmental Psychology, 39*(1), 71–84.

Horvat, E. M., & Lewis, K. S. (2003). Reassessing the "burden of 'acting white'": The importance of peer group in managing academic success. *Sociology of Education, 76,* 265–280.

Houts, L. A. (2005). But was it wanted? Young women's first voluntary sexual intercourse. *Journal of Family Influence, 26,* 1082–1102.

Hovell, M., Sipan, C., Blumberg, E., Atkins, C., Hofsterrer, C., & Kreitner, S. (1994). Family influences on Latino and Anglo adolescents' sexual behavior. *Journal of Marriage and the Family, 56,* 973–986.

Howard, D. E., & Wang, M. Q. (2005). Psychosocial correlates of U.S. adolescents who report a history of forced sexual intercourse. *Journal of Adolescent Health, 36,* 372–379.

Howell, W., & Peterson, P. (2002). *The education gap: Vouchers and urban schools.* Washington, DC: Brookings Institution.

Hoza, B., Molina, B., Bukowski, W., & Sippola, L. (1995). Peer variables as predictors of later childhood adjustment. *Development and Psychopathology, 7,* 787–802.

Hu, M., Davies, M., & Kandel, D. B. (2006). Epidemiology and correlates of daily smoking and nicotine dependence among young adults in the United States. *American Journal of Public Health, 96,* 299–308.

Hudley, C. (1995). Assessing the impact of separate schooling for African American male adolescents. *Journal of Early Adolescence, 15,* 38–57.

Hudley, C. (1997). Supporting achievement beliefs among ethnic minority adolescents: Two case examples. *Journal of Research on Adolescence, 7,* 133–152.

Huebner, A. J., & Howell, L. W. (2003). Examining the relationship between adolescent sexual risk-taking and perceptions of monitoring, communication, and parenting styles. *Journal of Adolescent Health, 33,* 71–78.

Huebner, A. J., & Mancini, J. A. (2003). Shaping structured out-of-school time use among youth: The effects of self, family, and friend systems. *Journal of Youth and Adolescence, 32,* 453–463.

Huesmann, L., Moise-Titus, J., Podolski, C., & Eron, L. (2003). Longitudinal relations between children's exposure to TV violence and their aggressive and violent behavior in young adulthood: 1977–1992. *Developmental Psychology, 39,* 201–221.

Hughes, M., Furstenberg, F., Jr., & Teitler, J. (1995). The impact of an increase in family planning on the teenage population of Philadelphia. *Family Planning Perspectives, 27,* 60–65, 78.

Hughes, S., Power, T., & Francis, D. (1992). Defining patterns of drinking in adolescence: A cluster analytic approach. *Journal of Studies on Alcohol, 53,* 40–47.

Huizinga, D., & Elliot, D. (1985). *Juvenile offenders prevalence, offender incidence, and arrest rates by race.* Boulder, CO: Institute of Behavioral Science.

Hunter, F. (1984). Socializing procedures in parent–child and friendship relations during adolescence. *Developmental Psychology, 18,* 806–811.

Hunter, F., & Youniss, J. (1982). Changes in functions of three relations during adolescence. *Developmental Psychology, 18,* 806–811.

Hunter, J., & Csikszentmihalyi, M. (2003). The positive psychology of interested adolescents. *Journal of Youth and Adolescnce, 32,* 27–35.

Hurley, D. (2005, April 19). Divorce rate: It's not as high as you think. *The New York Times.*

Hussong, A. M. (2000). Perceived peer context and adolescent adjustment. *Journal of Research on Adolescence, 10*(4), 391–415.

Hussong, A. M., Curran, P. J., & Moffitt, T. E. (2004). Substance abuse hinders desistance in young adults' antisocial behavior. *Development and Psychopathology, 16,* 1029–1046.

Hussong, A. M., & Hicks, R. E. (2003). Affect and peer context interactively impact adolescent substance use. *Journal of Abnormal Child Psychology, 31,* 413–426.

Huston, A., & Alvarez, M. (1990). The socialization context of gender role development in early adolescence. In R. Montemayor, G. Adams, & T. Gullotta (Eds.), *Advances in adolescent development,* Vol. 2: *The transition from childhood to adolescence,* pp. 156–179. Beverly Hills, CA: Sage.

Hutchinson, M. K., Jemmott, J. B., III, Jemmott, L. S., Braverman, P., & Fong, G. T. (2003). The role of mother–daughter sexual risk communication in reducing sexual risk behaviors among urban adolescent females: A prospective study. *Journal of Adolescent Health, 33,* 98–107.

Hutson, H., Anglin, D., & Pratts, M., Jr. (1994). Adolescents and children injured or killed in drive-by shootings in Los Angeles. *New England Journal of Medicine, 330,* 324–327.

Hymel, S., Bowker, A., & Woody, E. (1993). Aggressive versus withdrawn unpopular children: Variations in peer and self-perceptions in multiple domains. *Child Development, 64,* 879–896.

Hymel, S., Rubin, K., Rowden, L., & LeMare, L. (1990). Children's peer relationships: Longitudinal prediction of internalizing and externalizing problems from middle to late childhood. *Child Development, 61,* 2004–2021.

Ibañez, G. E., Kuperminc, G. P., Jurkovic, G., & Perilla, J. (2004). Cultural attributes and adaptations linked to achievement motivation among Latino adolescents. *Journal of Youth and Adolescence 33,* 559–568.

Iglowstein, I., Jenni, O., Molinari, L., & Largo, R. (2003). Sleep duration from infancy to adolescence: Reference values and generational trends. *Pediatrics, 111*(2), 302–307.

Inhelder, B., & Piaget, J. (1958). *The growth of logical thinking from childhood to adolescence.* New York: Basic Books.

Institute of Medicine (2006). *Food marketing to children and youth: Threat or opportunity?* Washington, DC: National Academies Press.

Irwin, C., Jr. (1986). Biopsychosocial correlates of risk-taking behavior during adolescence: Can the physician intervene? *Journal of Adolescent Health Care, 7,* 82–96.

Irwin, K. (2004). The violence of adolescent life experiencing and managing everyday threats. *Youth and Society, 35,* 452–479.

Isakson, K., & Jarvis, P. (1999). The adjustment of adolescents during the transition into high school: A short term longitudinal study. *Journal of Youth and Adolescence, 28,* 1–26.

Jaccard, J., Blanton, H. & Dodge, T. (2005). Peer influences on risk behavior: An analysis of the effects of a close friend. *Developmental Psychology, 41,* 135–147.

Jaccard, J., Dittus, P., & Gordon, V. (1998). Parent–adolescent congruency in reports of adolescent sexual behavior and in communications about sexual behavior. *Child Development, 69,* 247–261.

Jaccard, J., Dodge, T., & Dittus, P. (2003a). Do adolescents want to avoid pregnancy? Attitudes toward pregnancy as predictors of pregnancy. *Journal of Adolescent Health, 33,* 79–83.

Jaccard, J., Dodge, T., & Dittus, P. (2003b). Maternal discussion about pregnancy and adolescents' attitudes towards pregnancy. *Journal of Adolescent Health, 33,* 84–87.

Jacklin, C. (1989). Female and male: Issues of gender. *American Psychologist, 44,* 127–133.

Jackson, C. (2002). Perceived legitimacy of parental authority and tobacco and alcohol use during early adolescence. *Journal of Adolescent Health, 31*(5), 425–432.

Jackson, L., Hodge, C., & Ingram, J. (1994). Gender and self-concept: A reexamination of stereotypic differences and the role of gender attitudes. *Sex Roles, 30,* 615–630.

Jacobi, C., Hayward, C., de Zwaan, M., Kraemer, H. C., & Agras, W. S. (2004). Coming to terms with risk factors for eating disorders: Application of risk terminology and suggestions for a general taxonomy. *Psychological Bulletin, 130,* 19–65.

Jacobs, J. E., Chin, C. S., & Shaver, K. (2005). Longitudinal links between perceptions of adolescence and the social beliefs of adolescents: Are parents' stereotypes related to beliefs held about and by their children? *Journal of Youth and Adolescence, 34,* 61–72.

Jacobs, J. E., Lanza, S., Osgood, D., Eccles, J. S., & Wigfield, A. (2002). Changes in children's self-competence and values: Gender and domain differences across grades one through twelve. *Child Development, 73*(2), 509–527.

Jacobs, J. E., & Portenza, M. (1991). The use of judgment heuristics to make social and object decisions: A developmental perspective. *Child Development, 62,* 166–178.

Jacobs, J. E., Vernon, M. K., & Eccles, J. S. (2004). Relations between social self-perceptions, time use, and prosocial or problem behaviors during adolescence. *Journal of Adolescent Research, 19,* 45–62.

Jacobsen, T., & Hofmann, W. (1997). Children's attachment representations: Longitudinal relations to school behavior and academic competency in middle childhood and adolescence. *Developmental Psychology, 35,* 703–710.

Jacobsen, T., Edelstein, W., & Hofmann, V. (1994). A longitudinal study of the relation between representations of attachment in childhood and cognitive functioning in childhood and adolescence. *Developmental Psychology, 30,* 112–124.

Jacobson K., & Rowe, D. (1999). Genetic and environmental influences on the relationships between family connectedness, school connectedness, and adolescent depressed mood: Sex differences. *Developmental Psychology, 35,* 926–939.

Jaffee, S., Caspi, A., Moffitt, T. E., Belsky, J., & Silva, P. (2001). Why are children born to teen mothers at risk for adverse outcomes in young adulthood? Results from a 20-year longitudinal study. *Development and Psychopathology, 13,* 377–397.

Jakobsen, R., Rise, J., Aas, H., & Anderssen, N. (1997). Noncoital sexual interactions and problem behaviour among young adolescents: The Norwegian Longitudinal Health Behaviour Study. *Journal of Adolescence, 20,* 71–83.

Jang, S., & Thornberry, T. (1998). Self-esteem, delinquent peers, and delinquency: A test of the self-enhancement thesis. *American Sociological Review, 63,* 586–598.

Janosz, M., LeBlanc, M., Boulerice, B., & Tremblay, R. E. (1997). Disentangling the weight of school dropout predictors: A test on two longitudinal samples. *Journal of Youth & Adolescence, 26,* 733–762.

Janosz, M., Le Blanc, M., Boulerice, B., & Tremblay, R. E. (2000). Predicting different types of school dropouts: A typological approach with two longitudinal samples. *Journal of Educational Psychology, 92*(1), 171–190.

Jarrett, R. (1995). Growing up poor: The family experiences of socially mobile youth in low-income African American neighborhoods. *Journal of Adolescent Research, 10,* 111–135.

Jarvinen, D., & Nicholls, J. (1996). Adolescents' social goals, beliefs about the causes of social success, and satisfaction in peer relations. *Developmental Psychology, 32,* 435–441.

Jemmott, J., III, Jemmott, L., Fong, G., & McCaffree, K. (1999). Reducing HIV risk-associated sexual behavior among African American adolescents: Testing the generality of intervention effects. *American Journal of Community Psychology, 27,* 161–187.

Jensen, L. A., Arnett, J. J., Feldman, S. S., & Cauffman, E., (2004). The right to do wrong: Lying to parents among adolescents and emerging adults. *Journal of Youth and Adolescence, 33,* 101–112.

Jessor, R., & Jessor, S. (1977). Problem behavior and psychosocial development: A longitudinal study of youth. New York: Academic Press.

Jessor, R., Turbin, M., & Costa, F. (1998). Protective factors in adolescent health behavior. *Journal of Personality and Social Psychology, 75,* 788–800.

Jessor, R., Turbin, M. S., Costa, F. M., Dong, Q., Zhang, H., & Wang, C. (2003). Adolescent problem behavior in China and the United States: A cross-national study of psychosocial protective factors. *Journal of Research on Adolescence, 13,* 329–360.

Jessor, R., Van Den Bos, J., Vanderryn, J., Costa, F., & Turbin, M. (1995). Protective factors in adolescent problem behavior: Moderator effects and developmental change. *Developmental Psychology, 31,* 923–933.

Jeynes, W. (1999). Effects of remarriage following divorce on the academic achievement of children. *Journal of Youth and Adolescence, 28,* 385–393.

Jeynes, W. (2000). The effects of recent parental divorce on their children's consumption of alcohol. *Journal of Youth and Adolescence, 30,* 305–319.

Jodl, K. M., Michael, A., Malanchuk, O., Eccles, J. S., & Sameroff, A. (2001). Parents' roles in shaping early adolescents' occupational aspirations. *Child Development, 72*(4), 1247–1265.

Johnson, B. R., Jang, S., Li, S., & Larson, D. (2000). The "invisible institution" and Black youth crime: The church as an agency of local social control. *Journal of Youth and Adolescence, 29*(4), 479–498.

Johnson, E., & Meade, A. (1987). Developmental patterns of spatial ability: An early sex difference. *Child Development, 58,* 725–740.

Johnson, E., Roth, T., Schultz, L., & Breslau, N. (2006). Epidemiology of DSM-IV insomnia in adolescence: Lifetime prevalence, chronicity, and emergent gender difference. *Pediatrics, 117,* 247–256.

Johnson, J. G., Cohen, P., Kotler, L., Kasen, S., & Brook, J. S. (2002). Psychiatric disorders associated with risk for the development of eating disorders during adolescence and early adulthood. *Journal of Consulting and Clinical Psychology, 70*(5), 1119–1128.

Johnson, J. G., Cohen, P., Smailes, E. M., Kasen, S., & Brook, J. S. (2002). Television viewing and aggressive behavior during adolescence and adulthood. *Science, 295,* 2468–2471.

Johnson, M. (2002). Social origins, adolescent experiences, and work value trajectories during the transition to adulthood. *Social Forces, 80,* 1307–1341.

Johnson, R., & Gerstein, D. (1998). Initiation of use of alcohol, cigarettes, marijuana, cocaine, and other substances in U.S. birth cohorts since 1919. *American Journal of Public Health, 88,* 27–33.

Johnson, R., Johnson, D., Wang, M., Smiciklas-Wright, H., & Guthrie, H. (1994). Characterizing nutrient intakes of adolescents by sociodemographic factors. *Journal of Adolescent Health, 15,* 149–154.

Johnson, S. (1975). *Update on education: A digest of the National Assessment of Education Progress.* Denver: Education Commission of the States.

Johnston, L., Bachman, G., & O'Malley, P. (2002). *Monitoring the future.* Ann Arbor, MI: Institute for Social Research.

Johnston, M., Crosnoe, R., & Elder, G. H., Jr. (2001). Students' attachment and academic engagement: The role of race and ethnicity. *Sociology of Education, 74*(4), 318–340.

Jones, D., & Costin, S. (1993, March). Helping orientations, sex role characteristics, and friendship satisfaction during preadolescence and adolescence. Paper presented at the biennial meetings of the Society for Research in Child Development, New Orleans.

Jones, D., Costin, S., & Ricard, R. (1994, February). Ethnic and sex differences in best friendship characteristics among African-American, Mexican-American, and European-American adolescents. Paper presented at the biennial meetings of the Society for Research on Adolescence, San Diego.

Jones, D. C., Vigfusdottir, T. H., & Lee, Y. (2004). Body image and the appearance culture among adolescent girls and boys: An examination of friend conversations, peer criticism, appearance magazines, and the internalization of appearance ideals. *Journal of Adolescent Research, 19,* 323–339.

Jones, D. J., Forehand, R., Brody, G., & Armistead, L. (2002). Psychosocial adjustment of African American children in single-mother families: A test of three risk models. *Journal of Marriage and the Family, 64*(1), 105–115.

Jones, E., et al. (1987). *Teenage pregnancy in industrialized countries.* New Haven, CT: Yale University Press.

Jones, G., & Dembo, M. (1989). Age and sex role differences in intimate friendships during childhood and adolescence. *Merrill-Palmer Quarterly, 35,* 445–462.

Jones, J., Vanfossen, B., & Ensminger, M. (1995). Individual and organizational predictors of track placement. *Sociology of Education, 68,* 287–300.

Jones, M. C., & Bayley, N. (1950). Physical maturing among boys as related to behavior. *Journal of Educational Psychology, 41,* 129–148.

Jones, N., Pieper, C., & Robertson, L. (1992). The effect of legal drinking age on fatal injuries of adolescents and young adults. *American Journal of Public Health, 82,* 112–115.

Jones, R. K., Darroch, J. E., & Singh, S. (2005). Religious differentials in the sexual and reproductive behaviors of young women in the United States. *Journal of Adolescent Health, 36,* 279–288.

Jones, R. K., Purcell, A., Singh, S., & Finer, L. B. (2005). Adolescents' reports of parental knowledge of adolescents' use of sexual health services and their reactions to mandated parental notification for prescription contraception. *Journal of the American Medical Association, 293,* 340–348.

Jordan, A., & Cole, D. (1996). Relation of depressive symptoms to the structure of self-knowledge in childhood. *Journal of Abnormal Psychology, 105,* 530–540.

Jordan, L. C., & Lewis, M. L. (2005). Paternal relationship quality as a protective factor: Preventing alcohol use among African American adolescents. *Journal of Black Psychology, 31,* 152–171.

Jordan, W., Lara, J., & McPartland, J. (1996). Exploring the causes of early dropout among race-ethnic and gender groups. *Youth and Society, 28,* 62–94.

Josselson, R. (1980). Ego development in adolescence. In J. Adelson (Ed.), *Handbook of adolescent psychology,* pp. 188–210. New York: Wiley.

Josselson, R., Greenberger, E., & McConochie, D. (1977a). Phenomenological aspects of psychosocial maturity in adolescence, Part I: Boys. *Journal of Youth and Adolescence, 6,* 25–56.

Josselson, R., Greenberger, E., & McConochie, D. (1977b). Phenomenological aspects of psychosocial maturity in adolescence, Part II: Girls. *Journal of Youth and Adolescence, 6,* 145–167.

Joyce, T., & Mocan, N. (1990). The impact of legalized abortion on adolescent childbearing in New York City. *American Journal of Public Health, 80,* 273–278.

Jozefowicz, D., Barber, B., Eccles, J., & Mollasis, C. (1994, February). Relations between maternal and adolescent values and beliefs: Gender differences and implications for occupational choice. Paper presented at the biennial meetings of the Society for Research on Adolescence, San Diego.

Juang, L., & Silbereisen, R. K. (2002). The relationship between adolescent academic capability beliefs, parenting and school grades. *Journal of Adolescence, 25*(1), 3–18.

Juang, L., Lerner, J., McKinney, J., & von Eye, A. (1999). The goodness of fit in autonomy timetable expectations between Asian-Americans late adolescents and their parents. *International Journal of Behavioral Development, 23,* 1023–1048.

Judge, B., & Billick, S. B. (2004). Suicidality in adolescence: Review and legal considerations. *Behavioral Sciences and the Law, 22,* 681–695.

Juvonen, J., Graham, S., & Schuster, M., A. (2003). Bullying among young adolescents: The strong, the weak, and the troubled. *Pediatrics, 112,* 1231–1237.

Juvonen, J., & Murdock, T. (1995). Grade-level differences in the social value of effort: Implications for self-presentation tactics of early adolescents. *Child Development, 66,* 1694–1705.

Juvonen, J., Nishina, A., & Graham, S. (2000). Peer harassment, psychological adjustment, and school functioning in early adolescence. *Journal of Educational Psychology, 92*(2), 349–359.

Juvonen, J., Nishina, A., & Graham, S. (2006). Ethnic diversity and perceptions of safety in urban middle schools. *Psychological Science, 17,* 393–400.

Kaestle, C. E., Halpern, C. T., Miller, W. C. & Ford, C. A. (2005). Young age at first sexual intercourse and sexually transmitted infections in adolescents and young adults. *American Journal of Epidemiology, 161,* 774–780.

Kaestle, C. E., Morisky, D. E., & Wiley, D. J. (2002). Sexual intercourse and the age difference between adolescent females and their romantic partners. *Perspectives on Sexual and Reproductive Health, 34*(6), 304–305.

Kahn, J., Brindis, C., & Glei, D. (1999). Pregnancies averted among U.S. teenagers by the use of contraceptives. *Family Planning Perspectives, 31,* 29–34.

Kahneman, D., Slovic, P., & Tversky, A. (Eds.). (1982). *Judgment under uncertainty: Heuristics and biases.* New York: Cambridge University Press.

Kail, R. (1991a). Processing time declines exponentially during childhood and adolescence. *Developmental Psychology, 27,* 259–266.

Kail, R. (1991b). Developmental change in speed of processing during childhood and adolescence. *Psychological Bulletin, 109,* 490–501.

Kail, R., & Hall, L. (1994). Processing speed, naming speed, and reading. *Developmental Psychology, 30,* 949–954.

Kalakoski, V., & Nurmi, J.-E. (1998). Identity and educational transitions: Age differences in adolescent exploration and commitment related to education, occupation, and family. *Journal of Research on Adolescence, 8,* 29–47.

Kalil, A., & Eccles, J. (1998). Does welfare affect family processes and adolescent adjustment? *Child Development, 69,* 1597–1613.

Kalil, A., & Kunz, J. (2002). Teenage childbearing, marital status, and depressive symptoms in later life. *Child Development, 73*(6), 1748–1760.

Kalmuss, D., & Namerow, P. (1994). Subsequent childbearing among teenage mothers: The determinants of a closely spaced second birth. *Family Planning Perspectives, 26,* 149–153, 159.

Kalmuss, D., Namerow, P., & Bauer, U. (1992). Short-term consequences of parenting versus adoption among young unmarried women. *Journal of Marriage and the Family, 54,* 80–90.

Kamenetz, A. (2006, May 30). Take this internship and shove it. *The New York Times,* p. A19.

Kandel, D. (1978). Homophily, selection, and socialization in adolescent friendships. *American Journal of Sociology, 84,* 427–436.

Kandel, D. (1980). Drug and drinking behavior among youth. *Annual Review of Sociology, 6,* 235–285.

Kandel, D., & Lesser, G. (1972). *Youth in two worlds.* San Francisco: Jossey-Bass.

Kandel, D., & Logan, J. (1984). Patterns of drug use from adolescence to young adulthood, I: Periods of risk for initiation, continued use, and discontinuation. *American Journal of Public Health, 74,* 660–666.

Kandel, D., Johnson, J., Bird, H., & Canino, G. (1997). Psychiatric disorders associated with substance use among children and adolescents: Findings from the Methods for the Epidemiology of Child and Adolescent Mental Disorders (MECA) Study. *Journal of Abnormal Child Psychology, 25,* 121–132.

Kandel, D., Raveis, V., & Davies, M. (1991). Suicidal ideation in adolescence: Depression, substance abuse, and other risk factors. *Journal of Youth and Adolescence, 20,* 289–310.

Kantor, H. (1994). Managing the transition from school to work: The false promise of youth apprenticeship. *Teachers College Record, 95,* 442–461.

Kantor, H., & Brenzel, B. (1992). Urban education and the "truly disadvantaged": The historical roots of the contemporary crisis, 1945–1990. *Teachers College Record, 94,* 278–314.

Kao, G. (1995). Asian Americans as model minorities? A look at their academic performance. *American Journal of Education, 103,* 121–159.

Kao, G. (1999). Psychological well-being and educational achievement among immigrant youth. In D. Hernandez (Ed.), *Children of immigrants: Health, adjustment, and public assistance,* pp. 410–477. Washington, DC: National Academy Press.

Kao, G., & Tienda, M. (1995). Optimism and achievement: The educational performance of immigrant youth. *Social Science Quarterly, 76,* 1–19.

Kao, G., & Tienda, M. (1998). Educational aspirations of minority youth. *American Journal of Education, 106,* 349–384.

Kaplan, C., Erickson, P., & Juarez-Reyes, M. (2002). Acculturation, gender role orientation, and reproductive risk-taking behavior among Latina adolescent family planning. *Journal of Adolescent Research, 17*(2), 103–121.

Kaplan, D., Feinstein, R., Fisher, M., Klein, J., Lomedo, L., Rome, F., et al. (2001). Condom use by adolescents. *Pediatrics, 107*(6), 1463–1469.

Kaplowitz, P. B., Slora, E. J., Wasserman, R. C., Pedlow, S. E., & Herman-Giddens, M. E. (2001). Earlier onset of puberty in girls: Relation to increased body mass index and race. *Pediatrics, 108*(2), 347–353.

Karavasilis, L., Doyle, A. B., & Markiewicz, D. (2003). Associations between parenting style and attachment to mother in middle childhood and adolescence. *International Journal of Behavioral Development, 27,* 153–164.

Karpati, A. M., Rubin, C. H., Kieszak, S. M., Marcus, M., & Troiano, R. P. (2002). Stature and pubertal stage assessment in American boys: The 1988–1994 Third National Health and Nutrition Examination Survey. *Journal of Adolescent Health, 30*(3), 205–212.

Kasen, S., Cohen, P., & Brook, J. (1998). Adolescent school experiences and dropout, adolescent pregnancy, and young adult deviant behavior. *Journal of Adolescent Research, 13,* 49–72.

Kaslow, N. J., Adamson, L. B., & Collins, M. H. (2000). A developmental psychopathology perspective on the cognitive components of child and adolescent depression. In A. J. Sameroff, M. Lewis & S. M. Miller (Eds.), *Handbook of developmental psychopathology* (2nd ed.), pp. 491–510. New York: Plenum.

Katainen, S., Raeikkoenen, K., & Keltikangas-Jaervinen, L. (1998). Development of temperament: Childhood temperament and the mother's childrearing attitudes as predictors of adolescent temperament in a 9-year follow-up study. *Journal of Research on Adolescence, 8,* 485–509.

Katchadourian, H. (1990). Sexuality. In S. Feldman & G. Elliott (Eds.), *At the threshold: The developing adolescent,* pp. 330–351. Cambridge, MA: Harvard University Press.

Katz, M. (1975). *The people of Hamilton, Canada West: Family and class in a mid-nineteenth-century city.* Cambridge, MA: Harvard University Press.

Katz, P., & Ksansnak, K. (1994). Developmental aspects of gender role flexibility and traditionality in middle childhood and adolescence. *Developmental Psychology, 30,* 272–282.

Kaufman, K., Gregory, W., & Stephan, W. (1990). Maladjustment in statistical minorities within ethnically unbalanced classrooms. *American Journal of Community Psychology, 18,* 757–762.

Kazis, R. (1993). *Improving the transition from school to work in the United States.* Washington, DC: American Youth Policy Forum, Competitiveness Policy Council, and Jobs for the Future.

Keating, D. (1990). Adolescent thinking. In S. Feldman & G. Elliott (Eds.), *At the threshold: The developing adolescent,* pp. 54–89. Cambridge, MA: Harvard University Press.

Keating, D. (1995). Habits of mind: Developmental diversity in competence and coping. In D. Detterman (Ed.), *Current topics in human intelligence: The role of the environment,* pp. 31–44. Norwood, NJ: Ablex.

Keating, D. (2004). Cognitive and brain development. In R. Lerner & L. Steinberg (Eds.), *Handbook of adolescent psychology* (2nd ed.). New York: Wiley.

Keating, D., & Hertzman, C. (Eds.). (2000). *Developmental health and the wealth of nations: Social, biological, and educational dynamics.* New York: Guilford Press.

Keefe, K., & Berndt, T. (1996). Relations of friendship quality to self-esteem in early adolescence. *Journal of Early Adolescence, 16,* 110–129.

Keel, P. K., & Klump, K. L. (2003). Are eating disorders culture-bound syndromes? Implications for conceptualizing their etiology. *Psychological Bulletin, 129,* 747–769.

Keenan, K., Loeber, R., Zhang, Q., Stouthamer-Loeber, M., & Van Kammen, W. (1995). The influence of deviant peers on the development of boys' disruptive and delinquent behavior: A temporal analysis. *Development and Psychopathology, 7,* 715–726.

Keener, D., & Boykin, K. (1996, March). Parental control, autonomy, and adolescent ego development.Paper presented at the biennial meetings of the Society for Research on Adolescence, Boston.

Keiley, M. K., Howe, T. R., Dodge, K. A., Bates, J. E., & Pettit, G. S. (2001). The timing of child physical maltreatment: A cross-domain growth analysis of impact on adolescent externalizing and internalizing problems. *Development and Psychopathology, 13,* 891–912.

Kellam, S., Ling, X., Merisca, R., Brown, C., & Ialongo, N. (1998). The effect of the level of aggression in the first grade classroom on the course and malleability of aggressive behavior into middle school. *Development and Psychopathology, 10,* 165–185.

Keller, J. (2002). Blatant stereotype threat and women's math performances: Self-handicapping as a strategic means to cope with obtrusive negative performance expectations. *Sex Roles, 47*(3–4), 193–198.

Keller, M., Edelstein, W., Schmid, C., Fang, F., & Fang, G. (1998). Reasoning about responsibilities and obligations in close relationships: A comparison across two cultures. *Developmental Psychology, 34,* 731–741.

Kelley, J., & de Armaa, A. (1989). Social relationships in adolescence: Skill development and training. In J. Worell & F. Danner (Eds.), *The adolescent as decision-maker.* San Diego: Academic Press.

Kelly, A., Wall, M., Eisenberg, M., Story, M., & Neumark-Sztainer, D. (2005). Adolescent girls with high body satisfaction: Who are they and what can they teach us? *Journal of Adolescent Health, 37,* 391–396.

Keniston, K. (1970). Youth: A "new" stage of life. *American Scholar, 39,* 631–641.

Kenny, M. (1987). The extent and function of parental attachment among first-year college students. *Journal of Youth and Adolescence, 16,* 17–27.

Kerr, M., & Stattin, H. (2000). What parents know, how they know it, and several forms of adolescent adjustment: Further support for a reinterpretation of monitoring. *Developmental Psychology, 36,* 366–380.

Kett, J. (1977). *Rites of passage: Adolescence in America, 1790 to the present.* New York: Basic Books.

Khoury-Kassibri, M., Benbensihty, R., Astor, R. A., & Zeira, A. (2004). The contributions of community, family, and school variables to student victimization. *American Journal of Community Psychology, 34,* 187–204.

Kiesner, J. (2002). Depressive symptoms in early adolescence: Their relations with classroom problem behavior and peer status. *Journal of Research on Adolescence, 12*(4), 463–478.

Kiesner, J., Cadinu, M., Poulin, F., & Bucci, M. (2002). Group identification in early adolescence: Its relation with peer adjustment and its moderator effect on peer influence. *Child Development, 73*(1), 196–208.

Kiesner, J., & Pastore, M. (2005). Differences in the relations between antisocial behavior and peer acceptance across contexts and across adolescence. *Child Development, 76,* 1278–1293.

Kiesner, J., Poulin, F., & Nicotra, E. (2003). Peer relations across contexts: Individual–network homophily and network inclusion in and after school. *Child Development, 74,* 1328–1343.

Kilborn, P. (1996, November 27). Shifts in families reach a plateau, study says. *The New York Times,* p. A16.

Killen, J., Robinson, T., Haydel, K., Hayward, C., Wilson, D., Hammer, L., Litt, I., & Taylor, C. (1997). Prospective study of risk factors for the initiation of cigarette smoking. *Journal of Consulting and Clinical Psychology, 65,* 1011–1016.

Killen, M., & Nucci, L. (1995). Morality, autonomy, and social conflict. In M. Killen & D. Hart (Eds.), *Morality in everyday life: A developmental perspective,* pp. 52–86. Cambridge: Cambridge University Press.

Killen, M., & Turiel, E. (1998). Adolescents' and young adults' evaluations of helping and sacrificing for others. *Journal of Research on Adolescence, 8*(3), 355–375.

Killian, K. (1994). Fearing fat: A literature review of family systems understandings and treatments of anorexia and bulimia. *Family Relations, 43,* 311–318.

Kilpatrick, D., Acierno, R., Saunders, B., Resnick, H., Best, C., & Schnurr, P. (2000). Risk factors for adolescent substance abuse and dependence: Data from a national sample. *Journal of Consulting and Clinical Psychology, 68,* 19–30.

Kilpatrick, D., Ruggiero, K., Acierno, R., Saunders, B., Resnick, H., & Best, C. (2003). Violence and risk of PTSD, major depression, substance abuse/dependence and comorbidity: Results from the national survey of adolescents. *Journal of Consulting and Clinical Psychology, 71,* 692–700.

Kim, H. K., & Capaldi, D. M. (2004). The association of antisocial behavior and depressive symptoms between partners and risk for aggression in romantic relationships. *Journal of Family Psychology, 18,* 82–96.

Kim, H. K., Capaldi, D. M., & Stoolmiller, M. (2003). Depressive symptoms across adolescence and young adulthood in men: Predictions from parental and contextual risk factors. *Development and Psychopathology, 15,* 469–495.

Kim, I. J., Zane, N., & Hong, S. (2002). Protective factors against substance use among Asian American youth: A test of the peer cluster theory. *Journal of Community Psychology, 30*(5), 565–584.

Kim, J., Hetherington, E. M., & Reiss, D. (1999). Associations among family relationships, antisocial peers, and adolescents' externalizing behaviors: Gender and family type differences. *Child Development, 70,* 1209–1230.

Kim, K., Conger, R. D., Lorenz, F. O., & Elder, G. H., Jr. (2001). Parent–adolescent reciprocity in negative affect and its relation to early adult social development. *Developmental Psychology, 37*(6), 775–790.

Kim, K. J., Conger, R. D., Elder, G. H., Jr., & Lorenz, F. O. (2003). Reciprocal influences between stressful life events and adolescent internalizing and externalizing problems. *Child Development, 74,* 127–143.

Kim, S., & Brody, G. H. (2005). Longitudinal pathways to psychological adjustment among black youth living in single-parent households. *Journal of Family Psychology, 19,* 305–313.

Kim, S., & Ge, X. (2000). Parenting practices and adolescent depressive symptoms in Chinese American families. *Journal of Family Psychology, 14*(3), 420–435.

Kimm, S. Y., Barton, B. A., Obarzanek, E., McMahon, R. P., Kronsberg, S. S., Waclawiw, M. A., et al. (2002). Obesity development during adolescence in a biracial cohort: The NHLBI Growth and Health study. *Pediatrics, 110*(5), Article e54.

King, C., Akiyama, M., & Elling, K. (1996). Self-perceived competencies and depression among middle school students in Japan and the United States. *Journal of Early Adolescence, 16,* 192–210.

King, J. (2006). *Gender equity in higher education, 2006.* Washington: American Council on Education.

King, V., Elder, G. H., Jr., & Whitbeck, L. B. (1997). Religious involvement among rural youth: An ecological and life-course perspective. *Journal of Research on Adolescence, 7*(4), 431–456.

Kinney, D. (1993). From nerds to normals: The recovery of identity among adolescents from middle school to high school. *Sociology of Education, 66,* 21–40.

Kinsey, A., Pomeroy, W., & Martin, C. (1948). *Sexual behavior in the human male.* Philadelphia: Saunders.

Kinsfogel, K. M., & Grynch, J. H. (2004). Interparental conflict and adolescent dating relationships: Integrating cognitive, emotional, and peer influences. *Journal of Family Psychology, 18,* 505–515.

Kirby, D., Coyle, K., & Gould, J. B. (2001). Manifestations of poverty and birthrates among young teenagers in California zip code areas. *Family Planning Perspectives, 33*(2), 63–69.

Kirby, D., Korpi, M., Barth, R., & Cagampang, H. (1997). The impact of the Postponing Sexual Involvement curriculum among youths in California. *Family Planning Perspectives, 29,* 100–108.

Kiselica, M., & Sturmer, P. (1993). Is society giving teenage fathers a mixed message? *Youth and Society, 24,* 487–501.

Kisker, E., & Brown, R. (1996). Do school-based health centers improve adolescents' access to health care, health status, and risk-taking behavior? *Journal of Adolescent Health, 18,* 335–343.

Kite, M. (1984). Sex differences in attitudes towards homosexuals: A meta-analytic review. *Journal of Homosexuality, 10,* 69–81.

Klaczynski, P. (2000). Motivated scientific reasoning biases, epistemological beliefs, and theory polarization: A two-process approach to adolescent cognition. *Child Development, 71*(5), 1347–1366.

Klaczynski, P. (2001). Analytic and heuristic processing influences on adolescent reasoning and decision making. *Child Development, 72,* 844–861.

Klaczynski, P., & Narasimham, G. (1998). Development of scientific reasoning biases: Cognitive versus ego-protective explanations. *Developmental Psychology, 34,* 175–187.

Klepinger, D., Lundberg, S., & Plotnick, R. (1995). Adolescent fertility and the educational attainment of young women. *Family Planning Perspectives, 27,* 23–28.

Klerman, L. (1993). The influence of economic factors on health-related behaviors in adolescents. In S. Millstein, A. Petersen, & E. Nightingale (Eds.), *Promoting the health of adolescents: New directions for the twenty-first century,* pp. 38–57. New York: Oxford University Press.

Kling, J. R., Ludwig, J., & Katz, L. F. (2005). Neighborhood effects on crime for female and male youth: Evidence from a randomized housing voucher experiment. *Quarterly Journal of Economics, 120,* 87–130.

Kling, K., Hyde, J., Showers, C., & Buswell, B. (1999). Gender differences in self-esteem: A meta-analysis. *Psychological Bulletin, 125,* 470–500.

Kloep, M. (1995). Concurrent and predictive correlates of girls' depression and antisocial behaviour under conditions of economic crisis and value change: The case of Albania. *Journal of Adolescence, 18,* 445–458.

Knafo, A., & Schwartz, S. H. (2003). Parenting and adolescents' accuracy in perceiving parental values. *Child Development, 74,* 595–611.

Kneisel, P. (1987). Social support preferences of female adolescents in the context of interpersonal stress. Paper presented at the biennial meetings of the Society for Research in Child Development, Baltimore.

Knight, G., Virdin, L., & Roosa, M. (1994). Socialization and family correlates of mental health outcomes among Hispanic and Anglo American children: Consideration of cross-ethnic scalar equivalence. *Child Development, 65,* 212–224.

Knoester, C. (2003). Transitions in young adulthood and the relationship between parent and offspring well-being. *Social Forces, 81,* 1431–1457.

Knoester, C., & Haynie, D. L. (2005). Community context, social integration into family, and youth violence. *Journal of Marriage and the Family, 67,* 767.

Kobak, R., & Cole, H. (1994). Attachment and meta-monitoring: Implications for adolescent autonomy and psychopathology. In D. Cicchetti & S. Toth (Eds.), *Rochester symposium on developmental psychopathology,* Vol. 5: *Disorders and dysfunctions of the self,* pp. 267–297. Rochester, NY: University of Rochester Press.

Kobak, R., Cole, H., Ferenz-Gillies, R., Fleming, W., & Gamble, W. (1993). Attachment and emotion regulation during mother–teen problem-solving: A control theory analysis. *Child Development, 64,* 231–245.

Kobak, R., & Sceery, A. (1988). Attachment in late adolescence: Working models, affect regulation, and representations of self and others. *Child Development, 59,* 135–146.

Kobak, R., Sudler, N., & Gamble, W. (1992). Attachment and depressive symptoms during adolescence: A developmental pathways analysis. *Development and Psychopathology, 3,* 461–474.

Koenig, L. (1995, March). Change in self-esteem from 8th to 10th grade: Effects of gender and disruptive life events. Paper presented at the biennial meetings of the Society for Research in Child Development, Indianapolis.

Koerner, S., Jacobs, S., & Raymond, M. (2000). When mothers turn to their adolescent daughters: Predicting daughters' vulnerability to negative adjustment outcomes. *Family Relations, 49,* 301–309.

Koerner, S., Wallace, S. J., Lee, S, & Escalante, K. A. (2004). Sensitive mother-to-adolescent disclosures after divorce: Is the experience of sons different from that of daughters? *Journal of Family Psychology, 18,* 46–57.

Koff, E., & Rierdan, J. (1996). Premenarcheal expectations and postmenarcheal experiences of positive and negative menstrual related changes. *Journal of Adolescent Health, 18,* 286–291.

Kohler, J. K., Grotevant, H. D., & McRoy, R. G. (2002). Adopted adolescents' preoccupation with adoption: The impact on adoptive family relationships. *Journal of Marriage and Family, 64*(1), 93–104.

Kohn, M. (1977). *Class and conformity* (2nd ed.). Chicago: University of Chicago Press.

Kolburn Kowal, A., & Blinn-Pike, L. (2004). Sibling influences on adolescents' attitudes toward safe sex practices. *Family Relations, 53,* 377–384.

Koo, H., Dunteman, G., George, C., Green, Y., & Vincent, M. (1994). Reducing adolescent pregnancy through a school- and community-based intervention: Denmark, South Carolina revisited. *Family Planning Perspectives, 26,* 206–211, 217.

Kowal, A., & Kramer, L. (1997). Children's understanding of parental differential treatment. *Child Development, 68,* 113–126.

Kowaleski-Jones, L. (2000). Staying out of trouble: Community resources and problem behavior among high-risk adolescents. *Journal of Marriage and the Family, 62*(2), 449–464.

Kramer, L., & Kowal, A. K. (2005). Sibling relationship quality from birth to adolescence: The enduring contributions of friends. *Journal of Family Psychology, 19,* 503–511.

Kreager, D. A. (2004). Strangers in the halls: Isolation and delinquency in social networks. *Social Forces, 83*(1), 351–390.

Krei, M., & Rosenbaum, J. E. (2001). Career and college advice to the forgotten half: What do counselors and vocational teachers advise? *Teachers College Record, 103*(5), 823–842.

Krevans, J., & Gibbs, J. (1996). Parents' use of inductive discipline: Relations to children's empathy and prosocial behavior. *Child Development, 67,* 3263–3277.

Krishnakumar, A., & Buehler, C. (1996, March). Interparental conflict styles and youth problem behaviors: The mediational role of parental behavioral control. Paper presented at the biennial meetings of the Society for Research on Adolescence, Boston.

Kroger, J. (1993). The role of historical context in the identity formation process of late adolescence. *Youth and Society, 24,* 363–376.

Kroger, J. (1995). The differentiation of "firm" and "developmental" foreclosure identity statuses: A longitudinal study. *Journal of Adolescent Research, 10,* 317–337.

Kroger, J. (1996). Identity, regression, and development. *Journal of Adolescence, 19,* 203–222.

Kroger, J., & Green, K. (1996). Events associated with identity status change. *Journal of Adolescence, 19,* 477–490.

Krosnick, J., & Judd, C. (1982). Transitions in social influence at adolescence: Who induces cigarette smoking? *Developmental Psychology, 18,* 359–368.

Kuhn, D., Garcia-Mila, M., Zohar, A., & Andersen, C. (1995). Strategies of knowledge acquisition. *Monographs of the Society for Research in Child Development, 60*(4) (Serial No. 245).

Kuhn, D., Langer, J., Kohlberg, L., & Haan, N. (1977). The development of formal operations in logical and moral judgment. *Genetic Psychology Monographs, 95,* 97–188.

Kulis, S., Marsiglia, F., & Hurdle, D. (2003). Gender identity, ethnicity, acculturation, and drug use: Exploring differences among adolescents in the southwest. *Journal of Community Psychology, 31,* 167–188.

Kumpfer, K. L., & Alvarado, R. (2003). Family-strengthening approaches for the prevention of youth problem behaviors. *American Psychologist, 58,* 457–465.

Kunkel, D., Eyal, E., Finnerty, K., Biely, E., & Donnerstein, E. (2005). *Sex on TV.* Menlo Park, CA: Kaiser Family Foundation.

Kuperminc, G. P., Blatt, S. J., Shahar, B., Henrich, C., & Leadbeater, B. J. (2004). Cultural equivalence and cultural variance in longitudinal associations of young adolescents' self-definition and interpersonal relatedness to psychological and school adjustment. *Journal of Youth and Adolescence, 33,* 13–30.

Kupersmidt, J., Burchinal, M., & Patterson, C. (1995). Developmental patterns of childhood peer relations as predictors of externalizing behavior problems. *Development and Psychopathology, 7,* 825–843.

Kupersmidt, J., & Coie, J. (1990). Preadolescent peer status, aggression, and school adjustment as predictors of externalizing problems in adolescents. *Child Development, 61,* 1350–1362.

Kurdek, L., & Fine, M. (1993). The relation between family structure and young adolescents' appraisals of family climate and parenting behavior. *Journal of Family Issues, 14,* 279–290.

Kurdek, L., & Fine, M. (1994). Family acceptance and family control as predictors of adjustment in young adolescents: Linear, curvilinear, or interactive effects. *Child Development, 65,* 1137–1146.

Kurdek, L., Fine, M., & Sinclair, R. (1995). School adjustment in sixth graders: Parenting transitions, family climate, and peer norm effects. *Child Development, 66,* 430–445.

Kurdek, L., & Sinclair, R. (1988). Relation of eighth graders' family structure, gender, and family environment with academic performance and school behavior. *Journal of Educational Psychology, 80,* 90–94.

Kurlychek, M. C., & Johnson, B. D. (2004). The juvenile penalty: A comparison of juvenile and young adult sentencing outcomes in criminal court. *Criminology, 42,* 485–517.

Kuther, T. L., & Higgins-D'Alessandro, A. (2000). Bridging the gap between moral reasoning and adolescent engagement in risky behavior. *Journal of Adolescence, 23*(4), 409–422.

Kuttler, A. F., & La Greca, A. M. (2004). Linkages among adolescent girls' romantic relationships, best friendships, and peer networks. *Journal of Adolescence, 27,* 395–414.

Kuttler, A. F., La Greca, A. M., & Prinstein, M. J. (1999). Friendship qualities and social-emotional functioning of adolescents with close, cross-sex friendships. *Journal of Research on Adolescence, 9*(3), 339–366.

Kwak, K. (2003). Adolescents and their parents: A review of intergenerational family relations for immigrant and non-immigrant families. *Human Development (Karger AG), 46,* 115–136.

Lacourse, E., Cote, S., Nagin, D. S., Vitaro, F., Brendgen, M., & Tremblay, R. E. (2002). A longitudinal-experimental approach to testing theories of antisocial behavior development. *Development and Psychopathology, 14,* 909–924.

Lacourse, R., Nagin, D., & Tremblay, R. E. (2003). Developmental trajectories of boys' delinquent group membership and facilitation of violent behaviors during adolescence. *Development and Psychopathology, 15,* 183–197.

Lahey, B., Loeber, R., Hart, E., Frick, P., Applegate, B., Zhang, Q., Green, S., & Russo, M. (1995). Four-year longitudinal study of conduct disorder in boys: Patterns and predictors of persistence. *Journal of Abnormal Psychology, 104,* 83–93.

Laible, D., Carlo, G., & Raffaelli, M. (2000). The differential relations of parent and peer attachment to adolescent adjustment. *Journal of Youth and Adolescence, 29*(1), 45–59.

Laird, R., Pettit, G., Bates, J., & Dodge, K. (2003). Parents' monitoring-relevant knowledge and adolescents' delinquent behavior: Evidence of correlated developmental changes and reciprocal influences. *Child Development, 74,* 752–768.

Laird, R., Pettit, G., Dodge, K., & Bates, J. (1999). Best friendships, group relationships, and antisocial behavior in early adolescence. *Journal of Early Adolescence, 19,* 413–437.

Lam, T., Shi, H., Ho, L., Stewart, S. M., & Fan, S. (2002). Timing of pubertal maturation and heterosexual behavior among Hong Kong Chinese adolescents. *Archives of Sexual Behavior, 31*(4), 359–366.

Lamborn, S., Dornbusch, S., & Steinberg, L. (1996). Ethnicity and community context as moderators of the relation between family decision-making and adolescent adjustment. *Child Development, 66,* 283–301.

Lamborn, S., & Nguyen, D. T. (2004). African American adolescents' perceptions of family interactions: Kinship support, parent–child relationships, and teen adjustment. *Journal of Youth and Adolescence, 33,* 547–558.

Lamborn, S., & Steinberg, L. (1993). Emotional autonomy redux: Revisiting Ryan and Lynch. *Child Development, 64,* 483–499.

Lammers, C., Ireland, M., Resnick, M., & Blu, R. (2000). Influences on adolescents' decision to postpone onset of sexual intercourse: A survival analysis of virginity among youths aged 13 to 18 years. *Journal of Adolescent Health, 26*(1), 42–48.

Lanctot, N., & Smith, C. A. (2001). Sexual activity, pregnancy, and deviance in a representative urban sample of African American girls. *Journal of Youth and Adolescence, 30*(3), 349–372.

Landry, D., Kaeser, L., & Richards, C. (1999). Abstinence promotion and the provision of information about contraception in public school district sexuality education policies. *Family Planning Perspectives, 31,* 280–286.

Landry, D., Singh, S., & Darroch, J. E. (2000). Sexuality education in fifth and sixth grades in U.S. public schools, 1999. *Family Planning Perspectives, 32*(5), 212–219.

Lang, S., Waller, P., & Shope, J. (1996). Adolescent driving: Characteristics associated with single-vehicle and injury crashes. *Journal of Safety Research, 27,* 241–257.

Langer, J. A. (2001). Beating the odds: Teaching middle and high school students to read and write well. *American Educational Research Journal, 38*(4), 837–880.

Langer, L., Tubman, J. G., & Duncan, S. (1998). Anticipated mortality, HIV vulnerability, and psychological distress among adolescents and young adults at higher and lower risk for HIV infection. *Journal of Youth and Adolescence, 27,* 513–538.

Langer, L., Zimmerman, R., & Katz, J. (1995). Virgins' expectations and nonvirgins' reports: How adolescents feel about themselves. *Journal of Adolescent Research, 10,* 291–306.

Langhout, R. D., Rhodes, J. E., & Osborne, L. N. (2004). An exploratory study of youth mentoring in an urban context: Adolescents' perceptions of relational styles. *Journal of Youth and Adolescence, 33,* 293–306.

Lansford, J. E., Criss, M. M., Pettit, G. S., Dodge, K. A., & Bastes, J. E. (2003). Friendship quality, peer group affiliation, and peer antisocial behavior as moderators of the link between negative parenting and adolescent externalizing behavior. *Journal of Research on Adolescence, 13,* 161–184.

Lanz, M., Scabini, E., Vermulst, A. A., & Gerris, J. M. (2001). Congruence on child rearing in families with early adolescent and middle adolescent children. *International Journal of Behavioral Development, 25*(2), 133–139.

Lapsley, D. (1989). Continuity and discontinuity in adolescent social cognitive development. In R. Montemayor, G. Adams, & T. Gullota (Eds.), *Advances in adolescence research,* Vol. 2. Beverly Hills, CA: Sage.

Lapsley, D., Enright, R., & Serlin, R. (1985). Toward a theoretical perspective on the legislation of adolescence. *Journal of Early Adolescence, 5,* 441–466.

Lapsley, D., Flannery, D., Gottschlich, H., & Raney, M. (1996, March). Sources of risk and resilience in adolescent mental health. Paper presented at the biennial meetings of the Society for Research on Adolescence, Boston.

Larkin, R. W. (1979). *Suburban youth in cultural crisis.* New York: Oxford.

Larose, S., Bernier, A., & Tarabulsy, G. M. (2005). Attachment state of mind, learning dispositions, and academic performance during the college transition. *Developmental Psychology, 41,* 281–289.

Larson, M. (1996). Sex roles and soap operas: What adolescents learn about single motherhood. *Sex Roles, 35,* 97–110.

Larson, R. (1983). Adolescents' daily experience with family and friends: Contrasting opportunity systems. *Journal of Marriage and the Family, 11,* 739–750.

Larson, R. (1990). The solitary side of life: An examination of the time people spend alone from childhood to old age. *Developmental Review, 10,* 155–183.

Larson, R. (1994, February). Secrets in the bedroom: Adolescents' private music listening. Paper presented at the biennial meetings of the Society for Research on Adolescence, San Diego.

Larson, R. (1995). Secrets in the bedroom: Adolescents' private use of media. *Journal of Youth and Adolescence, 24,* 535–550.

Larson, R. (1997). The emergence of solitude as a constructive domain of experience in early adolescence. *Child Development, 68,* 80–93.

Larson, R. (2000). Toward a psychology of positive youth development. *American Psychologist, 55,* 170–183.

Larson, R., Clore, G., & Wood, G. (1999). The emotions of romantic relationships: Do they wreak havoc on adolescents? In W. Furman, B. Brown, & C. Feiring (Eds.), *Contemporary perspectives on adolescent romantic relationships,* pp. 19–49. New York: Cambridge University Press.

Larson, R., & Gillman, S. (1996, March). Daily processes in single parent families. Paper presented at the biennial meetings of the Society for Research on Adolescence, Boston.

Larson, R., & Lampman-Petraitis, C. (1989). Daily emotional states as reported by children and adolescents. *Child Development, 60,* 1250–1260.

Larson, R., Moneta, G., Richards, M. H., & Wilson, S. (2002). Continuity, stability, and change in daily emotional experience across adolescence. *Child Development, 73*(4), 1151–1165.

Larson, R., & Richards, M. (Eds.). (1989). The changing life space of early adolescence. *Journal of Youth and Adolescence, 18*(6). Special issue devoted to a series of studies of how adolescents spend their time.

Larson, R., & Richards, M. (1991). Daily companionship in late childhood and early adolescence: Changing developmental contexts. *Child Development, 62,* 284–300.

Larson, R., & Richards, M. (1994). Family emotions: Do young adolescents and their parents experience the same states? *Journal of Research on Adolescence, 4,* 567–583.

Larson, R., & Richards, M. (1998). Waiting for the weekend: Friday and Saturday night as the emotional climax of the week. *New Directions for Child and Adolescent Development,* Winter, 37–51.

Larson, R., Richards, M., Moneta, G., Holmbeck, G., & Duckett, E. (1996). Changes in adolescents' daily interactions with their families from ages 10 to 18: Disengagement and transformation. *Developmental Psychology, 32,* 744–754.

Larson, R., Richards, M., Sims, B., & Dworkin, J. (2001). How urban African American young adolescents spend their time: Time budgets for locations, activities, and companionship. *American Journal of Community Psychology, 29,* 565–597.

Larson, R., & Seepersad, S. (2003). Adolescents' leisure time in the United States: Partying, sports, and the American experiment. *New Directions for Child and Adolescent Development, 99,* 53–64.

Larson, R., & Verma, S. (1999). How children and adolescents spend time across the world: Work, play, and developmental opportunities. *Psychological Bulletin, 125,* 701–736.

Larson, R., & Wilson, S. (2004). Adolescence across place and time: Globalization and the changing pathways to adulthood. In R. Lerner & L. Steinberg (Eds.), *Handbook of adolescent psychology.* New York: Wiley.

Larsson, I., & Svedin, C.-G. (2002). Sexual experience in childhood: Young adults' recollections. *Archives of Sexual Behavior, 31*(3), 263–273.

Lau, S. (1989). Sex role orientation and domains of self-esteem. *Sex Roles, 21,* 415–422.

Laub, J., & Sampson, R. (1995). The long-term effect of punitive discipline. In J. McCord (Ed.), *Coercion and punishment in long-term perspectives,* pp. 247–258. New York: Cambridge University Press.

Lauritsen, J. (1994). Explaining race and gender differences in adolescent sexual behavior. *Social Forces, 72,* 859–884.

Laursen, B. (1993). The perceived impact of conflict on adolescent relationships. *Merrill-Palmer Quarterly, 39,* 535–550.

Laursen, B. (1995). Conflict and social interaction in adolescent relationships. *Journal of Research on Adolescence, 5,* 55–70.

Laursen, B. (1996). Closeness and conflict in adolescent peer relationships: Interdependence with friends and romantic partners. In W. Bukowski, A. Newcomb, & W. Hartup (Eds.), *The company they keep: Friendship in childhood and adolescence,* pp. 186–210. New York: Cambridge University Press.

Laursen, B., Coy, K., & Collins, W. A. (1998). Reconsidering changes in parent–child conflict across adolescence: A meta-analysis. *Child Development, 69,* 817–832.

Laursen, B., Finkelstein, B. D., & Townsend Betts, N. (2001). A developmental meta-analysis of peer conflict resolution. *Developmental Review, 21*(4), 423–449.

Laursen, B., & Jensen-Campbell, L. (1999). The nature and functions of social exchange in adolescent romantic relationships. In W. Furman, B. Brown, & C. Feiring (Eds.), *Contemporary perspectives on adolescent romantic relationships,* pp. 50–74. New York: Cambridge University Press.

Lavoie, F., Hebert, M., Tremblay, R., Vitaro, F., Vezina, L., & McDuff, P. (2002). History of family dysfunction and perpetration of dating violence by adolescent boys: A longitudinal study. *Journal of Adolescent Health, 30*(5), 375–383.

LaVoie, J. (1994). Identity in adolescence: Issues of theory, structure, and transition. *Journal of Adolescence, 17,* 17–28.

Lawford, H., Pratt, M. W., Hunsberger, B., & Pancer, S. M. (2005). Adolescent generativity: A longitudinal study of two possible contexts for learning concern for future generations. *Journal of Research on Adolescence, 15,* 261–273.

Leadbeater, B. (1996). School outcomes for minority-group adolescent mothers at 28 to 36 months postpartum: A longitudinal follow-up. *Journal of Research on Adolescence, 6,* 629–648.

Leadbeater, B., & Bishop, S. (1994). Predictors of behavior problems in preschool children of inner-city Afro-American and Puerto Rican adolescent mothers. *Child Development, 65,* 638–648.

Leadbeater, B., Blatt, S., & Quinlan, D. (1995). Gender-linked vulnerabilities to depressive symptoms, stress, and problem behaviors in adolescents. *Journal of Research on Adolescence, 5,* 1–29.

Leadbeater, B., Kuperminc, G., Blatt, S., & Hertzog, C. (1999). A multivariate model of gender differences in adolescents' internalizing and externalizing problems. *Developmental Psychology, 35,* 1268–1282.

Leahy, E. (2001). Gender differences in mathematical trajectories. *Social Forces, 80*(2), 713–732.

LeBlanc, A. (2003). *Random family: Love, drugs, trouble, and coming of age in the Bronx.* New York: Scribner.

Lee, M., & Larson, R. (1996). Effectiveness of coping in adolescence: The case of Korean examination stress. *International Journal of Behavioral Development, 19,* 851–869.

Lee, M., & Larson, R. (2000). The Korean "examination hell": Long hours of studying, distress, and depression. *Journal of Youth and Adolescence, 29*(2), 249–271.

Lee, S. (2001). More than "model minorities" or "delinquents": A look at Hmong American high school students. *Harvard Educational Review, 71,* 505–528.

Lee, V., & Bryk, A. (1989). A multilevel model of the social distribution of high school achievement. *Sociology of Education, 62,* 172–192.

Lee, V., & Burkham, D. (1992). Transferring high schools: An alternative to dropping out? *American Journal of Education, 100,* 420–453.

Lee, V., & Burkam, D. (2003). Dropping out of high school: The role of school organization and structure. *American Educational Research Journal, 40,* 353–393.

Lee, V., Burkham, D., Zimiles, H., & Ladewski, B. (1994). Family structure and its effect on behavioral and emotional problems in young adolescents. *Journal of Research on Adolescence, 4,* 405–437.

Lee, V., & Croninger, R. (1994). The relative importance of home and school in the development of literacy skills for middle-grade students. *American Journal of Education, 102,* 286–329.

Lee, V., Croninger, R., Linn, E., & Chen, X. (1996). The culture of sexual harassment in secondary schools. *American Educational Research Journal, 33,* 383–417.

Lee, V., Marks, H., & Byrd, T. (1994). Sexism in single-sex and coeducational independent secondary school classrooms. *Sociology of Education, 67,* 92–120.

Lee, V., & Smith, J. (1993). Effects of school restructuring on the achievement and engagement of middle-grade students. *Sociology of Education, 66,* 164–187.

Lee, V., & Smith, J. (1995). Effects of high school restructuring and size in early gains in achievement and engagement. *Sociology of Education, 68,* 241–270.

Lee, V., & Smith, J. (1996). Collective responsibility for learning and its effects on gains in achievement for early secondary school students. *American Journal of Education, 104,* 103–147.

Lee, V., Smith, J., & Croninger, R. (1997). How high school organization influences the equitable distribution of learning in mathematics and science. *Sociology of Education, 70,* 128–150.

Lefkowitz, E. (2005). "Things have gotten better": Developmental changes among emerging adults after the transition to university. *Journal of Adolescent Research, 20,* 40–63.

Lefkowitz, E., Boone, T. L., Sigman, M., & Au, T. (2002). He said, she said: Gender differences in mother–adolescent conversations about sexuality. *Journal of Research on Adolescence, 12*(2), 217–242.

Lefkowitz, E., Romo, L., Corona, R., Au, T., & Sigman, M. (2000). How Latino American and European American adolescents discuss conflicts, sexuality, and AIDS with their mothers. *Developmental Psychology, 36,* 315–325.

Lefkowitz, E., Sigman, M., & Au, T. (2000). Helping mothers discuss sexuality and AIDS with adolescents. *Child Development, 71*(5), 1383–1394.

Lehman, S. J., & Koerner, S. S. (2004). Adolescent women's sports involvement and sexual behavior/health: A process-level investigation. *Journal of Youth and Adolescence, 33,* 443-455.

Leiberman, L. D., Gray, H., Wier, M., Fiorentino, R., & Maloney, P. (2000). Long-term outcomes of an abstinence-based, small-group pregnancy prevention program in New York city schools. *Family Planning Perspectives, 32*(5), 237–245.

Leitenberg, H., & Saltzman, H. (2000). A statewide survey of age at first intercourse for adolescent females and age of their male partners: Relation to other risk behaviors and statutory rape implications. *Archives of Sexual Behavior, 29*(3), 203–215.

Lempers, J., & Clark-Lempers, D. (1992). Young, middle, and late adolescents' comparisons of the functional importance of five significant relationships. *Journal of Youth and Adolescence, 21,* 53–96

Lempers, J., Clark-Lempers, D., & Simmons, R. (1989). Economic hardship, parenting, and distress in adolescence. *Child Development, 60,* 25–49.

L'Engle, K. L., Brown, J. D., & Kenneavy, K. (2006). The mass media are an important context for adolescents' sexual behavior. *Journal of Adolescent Health, 38,* 186–192.

Lenhart, L., & Rabiner, D. (1995). An integrative approach to the study of social competence in adolescence. *Development and Psychopathology, 7,* 543–561.

Lenoir, C. D., Adler, N. E., Borzekowski, D. L. G., Tschann, J. M., & Ellen, J. M. (2006). What you don't know can hurt you: Perceptions of sex-partner concurrency and partner-reported behavior. *Journal of Adolescent Health, 38,* 179–185.

Leon, G., Fulkerson, J. A., Perry, C. L., Keel, P. K., & Klump, K. L. (1999). Three to four year prospective evaluation of personality and behavioral risk factors for later disordered eating in adolescent girls and boys. *Journal of Youth and Adolescence, 28,* 181–196.

Lerner, J., Castellino, D., & Perkins, D. (1994, February). The influence of adolescent behavioral and psychosocial characteristics on maternal behaviors and satisfaction. Paper presented at the biennial meetings of the Society for Research on Adolescence, San Diego.

Lerner, R., Lerner, J. V., Almerigi, J. B., Theokas, C., Phelps, E., Gestsdottir, S., Naudeau, S., Jelicic, H., Alberts, A., Ma, L., Smith, L. M., Bobek, D. L., Richman-Raphael, D., Simpson, I., Christiansen, E. D., & von Eye, A. (2005). Positive youth development, participation in community youth development programs, and community contributions of fifth-grade adolescents findings from the first wave of the 4-H study of positive youth development. *Journal of Early Adolescence, 25,* 17–71.

Lerner, R., & Steinberg, L. (2004). The scientific study of adolescence: Past, present, and future. In R. Lerner & L. Steinberg (Eds.), *Handbook of adolescent psychology.* New York: Wiley.

Lesko, N. (1996). Denaturalizing adolescence: The politics of contemporary representations. *Youth and Society, 28,* 139–161.

Leslie, L. (1986). The impact of adolescent females' assessments of parenthood and employment on plans for the future. *Journal of Youth and Adolescence, 15,* 29–49.

Lesthaeghe, R., & Neidert, L. (2006). *The second demographic transition in the U.S: Spatial patterns and correlates.* Population Studies Center, Institute for Social Research, University of Michigan (Report 06-592).

Leventhal, H., & Keeshan, P. (1993). Promoting healthy alternatives to substance abuse. In S. Millstein, A. Petersen, & E. Nightingale (Eds.), *Promoting the health of adolescents: New directions for the twenty-first century,* pp. 260–284. New York: Oxford University Press.

Leventhal, T., & Brooks-Gunn, J. (2004). Diversity in developmental trajectories across adolescence: Neighborhood influences. In R. Lerner & L. Steinberg (Eds.), *Handbook of adolescent psychology.* New York: Wiley.

Leventhal, T., Fauth, R. C., & Brooks-Gunn, J. (2005). Neighborhood poverty and public policy: A 5-year follow-up of children's educational outcomes in the New York City Moving to Opportunity demonstration. *Developmental Psychology, 41,* 933–952.

Leventhal, T., Graber, J. A., & Brooks-Gunn, J. (2001). Adolescent transitions to young adulthood: Antecedents, correlates, and consequences of adolescent employment. *Journal of Research on Adolescence, 11*(3), 297–323.

Levesque, R. (1993). The romantic experience of adolescents in satisfying love relationships. *Journal of Youth and Adolescence, 22,* 219–251.

Levin, M., Xu, X., & Bartkowski, J. (2002). Seasonality of sexual debut. *Journal of Marriage and the Family, 64,* 871–884.

Levine, J. A., Pollack, H., & Comfort, M. E. (2001). Academic and behavioral outcomes among the children of young mothers. *Journal of Marriage and the Family, 63*(2), 355–369.

Levine, M., Smolak, L., & Hayden, H. (1994). The relation of sociocultural factors to eating attitudes and behaviors among middle school girls. *Journal of Early Adolescence, 14,* 471-490.

Levine, P. (2001). The sexual activity and birth control use of American teenagers. In J. Gruber (Ed.), *Risky behavior among youths: An economic analysis,* pp. 167–218. Chicago: University of Chicago Press.

Levinson, D. (1978). *The seasons of a man's life.* New York: Knopf.

Levinson, R., Jaccard, J., & Beamer, L. (1995). Older adolescents' engagement in casual sex: Impact of risk perception and psychosocial motivations. *Journal of Youth and Adolescence, 24,* 349–364.

Levitt, M., Guacci-Franci, N., & Levitt, J. (1993). Convoys of social support in childhood and early adolescence: Structure and function. *Developmental Psychology, 29,* 811–818.

Levitt, S., & Dubner, S. (2005). *Freakonomics.* New York: William Morrow.

Levitz-Jones, E., & Orlofsky, J. (1985). Separation-individuation and intimacy capacity in college women. *Journal of Personality and Social Psychology, 49,* 156–169.

Lewin, K. (1948). *Resolving social conflict.* New York: Harper & Row.

Lewin, K. (1951). *Field theory and social science.* New York: Harper & Row.

Lewin, L., Davis, B., & Hops, H. (1999). Childhood social predictors of adolescent antisocial behavior: Gender differences in predictive accuracy and efficacy. *Journal of Abnormal Child Psychology, 27,* 277–292.

Lewin, T. (1997, October 1). Sexual abuse tied to 1 in 4 girls in teens. *The New York Times,* p. A24.

Lewin, T. (July 9, 2006). At colleges, women are leaving men in the dust. *The New York Times,* pp. 1ff.

Lewin-Epstein, N. (1981). *Youth employment during high school.* Washington, DC: National Center for Education Statistics.

Lewinsohn, P. M., Joiner, T. E., Jr., & Rohde, P. (2001). Evaluation of cognitive diathesis-stress models in predicting major depressive disorder in adolescents. *Journal of Abnormal Psychology, 110*(2), 203–215.

Lewinsohn, P. M., Rohde, P., Seeley, J. R., & Baldwin, C. L. (2001). Gender differences in suicide attempts from adolescence to young adulthood. *Journal of the American Academy of Child and Adolescent Psychiatry, 40,* 427–434.

Lewinsohn, P., Gotlib, I., & Seeley, J. (1997). Depression-related psychosocial variables: Are they specific to depression in adolescents? *Journal of Abnormal Psychology, 106,* 365–375.

Lewinsohn, P., Hops, H., Roberts, R., Seeley, J., & Andrews, J. (1993). Adolescent psychopathology, I: Prevalence and incidence of depression and other DSM-III-R disorders in high school students. *Journal of Abnormal Psychology, 102,* 133–144.

Lewinsohn, P., Pettit, J., Joiner, T., Jr., & Seeley, J. (2003). The symptomatic expression of major depressive disorder in adolescents and young adults. *Journal of Abnormal Psychology, 112,* 244–252.

Lewinsohn, P., Roberts, R., Seeley, J., Rohde, P., Gotlib, I., & Hops, H. (1994). Adolescent psychopathology, II: Psychosocial risk factors for depression. *Journal of Abnormal Psychology, 103,* 302–325.

Lewinsohn, P., Rohde, P., & Seeley, J. (1994). Psychosocial risk factors for future adolescent suicide attempts. *Journal of Consulting and Clinical Psychology, 62,* 297–305.

Lewinsohn, P., Rohde, P., Seeley, J., Klein, D., & Gotlib, I. (2003). Psychosocial functioning of young adults who have experienced and recovered from major depressive disorder during adolescence. *Journal of Abnormal Psychology, 112,* 353–363.

Lewis, C. (1981a). The effects of parental firm control. *Psychological Bulletin, 90,* 547–563.

Lewis, C. (1981b). How adolescents approach decisions: Changes over grades seven to twelve and policy implications. *Child Development, 52,* 538–544.

Lewis, C. (1987). Minors' competence to consent to abortion. *American Psychologist, 41,* 84–88.

Lewis, M., Feiring, C., McGuffog, C., & Jaskir, J. (1984). Predicting psychopathology in six-year-olds from early social relations. *Child Development, 55,* 123–136.

Lewis, M., Feiring, C., & Rosenthal, S. (2000). Attachment over time. *Child Development, 71,* 707–720.

Li, J. (2006). Self in learning: Chinese adolescents' goals and sense of agency. *Child Development, 77,* 482–501.

Li, X., Stanton, B., & Feigelman, S. (2000). Impact of perceived parental monitoring on adolescent risk behavior over 4 years. *Journal of Adolescent Health, 27*(1), 49–56.

Li, X., Stanton, B., Pack, R., Harris, C., Cottrell, L., & Burns, J. (2002). Risk and protective factors associated with gang involvement among urban African American adolescents. *Youth and Society, 34*(2), 172–194.

Lieberman, M., Doyle, A., & Markiewicz, D. (1999). Developmental patterns in security of attachment to mother and father in late childhood and early adolescence: Associations with peer relations. *Child Development, 70,* 202–213.

Liebkind, K., Jasinkaja-Lahti, I., & Solheim, E. (2004). Cultural identity, perceived discrimination, and parental support as determinants of immigrants' school adjustments: Vietnamese youth in Finland. *Journal of Adolescent Research, 19,* 635–656.

Linder, J. R., & Collins, W. A. (2005). Parent and peer predictors of physical aggression and conflict management in romantic relationships in early adulthood. *Journal of Family Psychology, 19,* 252–262.

Linn, M., & Songer, N. (1991). Cognitive and conceptual change in adolescence. *American Journal of Education,* August, 379–417.

Linn, M., & Songer, N. (1993). How do students make sense of science? *Merrill-Palmer Quarterly, 39,* 47–73.

Linney, J., & Seidman, E. (1989). The future of schooling. *American Psychologist, 44,* 336–340.

Lipsey, M. (1997, May). Can intervention rehabilitate serious delinquents? Research on a central premise of the juvenile justice system. Paper presented at the Symposium on the Future of the Juvenile Court, University of Pennsylvania, Philadelphia.

Litchfield, A., Thomas, D., & Li, B. (1997). Dimensions of religiosity as mediators of the relations between parenting and adolescent deviant behavior. *Journal of Adolescent Research, 12,* 199–226.

Little, S. A. & Garber, J. (2004). Interpersonal and achievement orientations and specific stressors predict depressive and aggressive symptoms. *Journal of Adolescent Research, 19,* 63–84.

Little, T., Oettingen, G., Stetsenko, A., & Baltes, P. (1995). Children's action-control beliefs about school performance: How do American children compare with German and Russian children? *Journal of Personality and Social Psychology, 69,* 686–700.

Little, T. D., Brauner, J., Jones, S. M., Nock, M. K., & Hawley, P. H. (2003). Rethinking aggression: A typological examination of the functions of aggression. *Merrill-Palmer Quarterly, 49,* 343–369.

Liu, X., Kaplan, H., & Risser, W. (1992). Decomposing the reciprocal relationships between academic achievement and general self-esteem. *Youth and Society, 24,* 123–148.

Livson, N., & Peskin, H. (1980). Perspectives on adolescence from longitudinal research. In J. Adelson (Ed.), *Handbook of adolescent psychology,* pp. 47–98. New York: Wiley.

Lobel, T. E., Nov-Crispin, N., Schiller, D., Lobel, O., & Feldman, A. (2004). Gender discriminatory behavior during adolescence and young adulthood: A developmental analysis. *Journal of Youth and Adolescence, 33,* 535–546.

Lochman, J. (1992). Cognitive-behavioral intervention with aggressive boys: Three-year follow-up and preventive effects. *Journal of Consulting and Clinical Psychology, 60,* 426–432.

Lochman, J., & Dodge, K. (1994). Social-cognitive processes of severely violent, moderately aggressive, and nonaggressive boys. *Journal of Consulting and Clinical Psychology, 62,* 366–374.

Lochman, J., & Dodge, K. (1998). Distorted perceptions in dyadic interactions of aggressive and nonaggressive boys: Effects of prior expectations, context, and boys' age. *Development and Psychopathology, 10,* 495–512.

Loeber, R., & Farrington, D. P. (2000). Young children who commit crime: Epidemiology, developmental origins, risk factors, early interventions, and policy implications. *Development and Psychopathology, 12,* 737–762.

Loeber, R., & Stouthamer-Loeber, M. (1986). Family factors as correlates and predictors of juvenile conduct problems and delinquency. In M. Tonry & N. Morris (Eds.), *Crime and justice,* Vol. 7, pp. 219–339. Chicago: University of Chicago Press.

Loehlin, J. C., Neiderheiser, J. M., & Reiss, D. (2005). Genetic and environmental components of adolescent adjustment and parental behavior: A multivariate analysis. *Child Development, 76,* 1104–1115.

Loewenson, P. R., Ireland, M., & Resnick, M. D. (2004). Primary and secondary sexual abstinence in high school students. *Journal of Adolescent Health, 34,* 209–215.

Long, B. (1989). Heterosexual involvement of unmarried undergraduate females in relation to self-evaluations. *Journal of Youth and Adolescence, 18,* 489–500.

Longmore, M. A., Manning, W. D., & Giordano, P. C. (2001). Preadolescent parenting strategies and teens' dating and sexual initiation: A longitudinal analysis. *Journal of Marriage and the Family, 63*(2), 322–335.

Lonigan, C., Carey, M., & Finch, A., Jr. (1994). Anxiety and depression in children and adolescents: Negative affectivity and the utility of self-reports. *Journal of Consulting and Clinical Psychology, 62,* 1000–1008.

Lord, S., Eccles, J., & McCarthy, K. (1994). Surviving the junior high transition: Family processes and self-perceptions as protective and risk factors. *Journal of Early Adolescence, 14,* 162–199.

Loredo, C., Reid, A., & Deaux, K. (1995). Judgments and definitions of sexual harassment by high school students. *Sex Roles, 32,* 29–45.

Louis, K., & Smith, B. (1992). Breaking the iron law of social class: The renewal of teachers' professional status and engagement. In F. Newmann (Ed.), *Student engagement and achievement in American high schools.* New York: Teachers College Press.

Loveless, T. (2002). *How well are American students learning? The 2002 Brown Center Report on American Education.* Washington, DC: Brookings Institution.

Lovitt, T. (1989). *Introduction to learning disabilities.* Boston: Allyn & Bacon.

Lucas, S. (1996). Selective attrition in a newly hostile regime: The case of 1980 sophomores. *Social Forces, 75,* 511–533.

Lucas, S. R., & Berends, M. (2002). Sociodemographic diversity, correlated achievement, and De Facto tracking. *Sociology of Education, 75*(4), 328–348.

Luciana, M., Conklin, H. M., Hooper, C. J., & Yarger, R. S. (2005). The development of nonverbal working memory and executive control processes in adolescents. *Child Development, 76,* 697

Ludwig, J., Duncan, G., & Hirschfield, P. (2001). Urban poverty and juvenile crime: Evidence from a randomized housing-mobility experiment. *Quarterly Journal of Economics, 116,* 665–679.

Luna, B., Thulborn, K. R., Munoz, D. P., Merriam, E. P., Garver, K. E., Minshew, N. J., et al. (2001). Maturation of widely distributed brain function subserves cognitive development. *Neuroimage, 13,* 786–793.

Luo, Q., Urberg, K., & Rao, P. (1995, March). Selection of best friends among Chinese adolescents. Paper presented at the biennial meetings of the Society for Research in Child Development, Indianapolis.

Luster, T., Bates, L., Fitzgerald, H., Vandenbelt, M., & Key, J. (2000). Factors related to successful outcomes among preschool children born to low-income adolescent mothers. *Journal of Marriage and the Family, 62*(1), 133–146.

Luster, T., & McAdoo, H. (1995). Factors related to self-esteem among African American youths: A secondary analysis of the High/Scope Perry Preschool data. *Journal of Research on Adolescence, 5,* 451–467.

Luster, T., & Small, S. (1994). Factors associated with sexual risk-taking behaviors among adolescents. *Journal of Marriage and the Family, 56,* 622–632.

Luster, T., & Small, S. (1997). Sexual abuse history and problems in adolescence: Exploring the effects of moderating variables. *Journal of Marriage and the Family, 59,* 131–142.

Luthar, S. (1991). Vulnerability and resilience: A study of high-risk adolescents. *Child Development, 62,* 600–616.

Luthar, S. (1994, February). Social competence of inner-city adolescents: A six-month prospective study. Paper presented at the biennial meetings of the Society for Research on Adolescence, San Diego.

Luthar, S., & Ansary, N. (2005). Dimensions of adolescent rebellion: Risks for academic failure among high- and low-income youth. *Development and Psychopathology, 17,* 231–250.

Luthar, S., & Becker, B. (2002). Privileged but pressured? A study of affluent youth. *Child Development, 73*(5), 1593–1610.

Luthar, S., Cicchetti, D., & Becker, B. (2000). The construct of resilience: A crtical evaluation and guidelines for future work. *Child Development, 71,* 543–562.

Luthar, S., & Cushing, G. (1997). Substance use and personal adjustment among disadvantaged teenagers: A six-month prospective study. *Journal of Youth and Adolescence, 26,* 353–372.

Luthar, S., & Latendresse, S. (2005). Comparable "risks" at the socioeconomic status extremes: Preadolescents' perceptions of parenting. *Development and Psychopathology, 17,* 207–230.

Luthar, S., & McMahon, T. (1996). Peer reputation among inner-city adolescents: Structure and correlates. *Journal of Research on Adolescence, 6,* 581–603.

Luyckx, K., Goossens, L., & Soenens, B. (2006). A developmental contextual perspective on identity construction in emerging adulthood: Change dynamics in commitment formation and commitment evaluation. *Developmental Psychology, 42,* 366–380.

Lynam, D. R., Caspi, A., Moffitt, T. E., Wikstroem, P.-O., Loeber, R., & Novak, S. (2000). The interaction between impulsivity and neighborhood context on offending: The effects of impulsivity are stronger in poorer neighborhoods. *Journal of Abnormal Psychology, 109*(4), 563–574.

Lynn, D. (1966, November). The process of learning parental and sex-role identification. *Journal of Marriage and the Family, 28,* 446–470.

Lyon, J., Henggeler, S., & Hall, J. (1992). The family relations, peer relations, and criminal activities of Caucasian and Hispanic-American gang members. *Journal of Abnormal Child Psychology, 20,* 439–449.

Määta, S., Stattin, H., & Nurmi, J.-E. (2002). Achievement strategies at school: Types and correlates. *Journal of Adolescence, 25*(1), 31–46.

Maccoby, E. (1990). Gender and relationships: A developmental account. *American Psychologist, 45,* 513–520.

Maccoby, E., & Martin, J. (1983). Socialization in the context of the family: Parent–child interaction. In E. M. Hetherington (Ed.), *Handbook of child psychology: Socialization, personality, and social development,* Vol. 4., pp. 1–101. New York: Wiley.

MacDonald, W., & DeMaris, A. (1995). Remarriage, stepchildren, and marital conflict: Challenges to the incomplete institutionalization hypothesis. *Journal of Marriage and the Family, 57,* 387–398.

MacIver, D., Stipek, D., & Daniels, D. (1991). Explaining within-semester changes in student effort in junior high school and senior high school courses. *Journal of Educational Psychology, 83,* 201–211.

Mackey, K., Arnold, M. L., & Pratt, M. W. (2001). Adolescents' stories of decision making in more and less authoritative families: Representing the voices of parents in narrative. *Journal of Adolescent Research, 16*(3), 243–268.

Macksoud, M., & Aber, J. (1996). The war experiences and psychosocial development of children in Lebanon. *Child Development, 67,* 70–88.

Macmillan, R., & Hagan, J. (2004). Violence in the transition to adulthood: Adolescent victimization, education, and socioeconomic attainment in later life. *Journal of Research on Adolescence, 14,* 127–158.

Madon, S., Jussim, L., & Eccles, J. (1997). In search of the powerful self-fulfilling prophecy. *Journal of Personality and Social Psychology, 72,* 791–809.

Mager, W., Milich, R., Harris, M. J., & Howard, A. (2005). Intervention groups for adolescents with conduct problems: Is aggregation harmful or helpful? *Journal of Abnormal Child Psychology, 33,* 349–362.

Maggs, J., Almeida, D., & Galambos, N. (1995). Risky business: The paradoxical meaning of problem behavior for young adolescents. *Journal of Early Adolescence, 15,* 344–362.

Magnusson, D., Stattin, H., & Allen, V. (1986). Differential maturation among girls and its relation to social adjustment in a longitudinal perspective. In P. Baltes, D. Featherman, & R. Lerner (Eds.), *Life span development and behavior,* Vol. 7. Hillsdale, NJ: Erlbaum.

Maharaj, S., & Connolly, J. (1994). Peer network composition of acculturated and ethnoculturally-affiliated adolescents in a multicultural setting. *Journal of Adolescent Research, 9,* 218–240.

Mahoney, A., Donelly, W. O., Boxer, P., & Lewis, T. (2003). Marital and severe parent-to-adolescent physical aggression in clinic-referred families: Mother and adolescent reports on co-occurrence and links to child behavior problems. *Journal of Family Psychology, 17,* 3–19.

Mahoney, E. (1983). *Human sexuality.* New York: McGraw-Hill.

Mahoney, J., & Cairns, R. (1997). Do extracurricular activities protect against early school dropout? *Developmental Psychology, 33,* 241–253.

Mahoney, J., Larson, R., Eccles, J., & Lord, H. (2005). Organized activities as developmental contexts for children and adolescents. In J. Mahoney, R. Larson, & J. Eccles (Eds.), *Organized activities as contexts of development,* pp. 3–22. Hillsdale, NJ: Erlbaum.

Mahoney, J., Schweder, A. E., & Stattin, H. (2002). Structured after-school activities as a moderator of depressed mood for adolescents with detached relations to their parents. *Journal of Community Psychology, 30*(1), 69–86.

Mahoney, J., & Stattin, H. (2000). Leisure activities and adolescent antisocial behavior: The role of structure and social context. *Journal of Adolescence, 23*(2), 113–127.

Mahoney, J., Stattin, H., & Lord, H. (2004). Unstructured youth recreation centre participation and antisocial behaviour development: Selective influences and the moderating role of antisocial peers. *International Journal of Behavioral Development, 28,* 553–560.

Main, M., Kaplan, N., & Cassidy, J. (1985). Security in infancy, childhood and adulthood: A move to the level of representation. In I. Bretherton and E. Waters (Eds.), *Growing points of attachment theory and research,* pp. 66–106. *Monographs of the Society for Research on Child Development, 50*(1–2), Serial No. 209.

Malanchuk, O., & Eccles, J. (April, 1999). Determinants of self-esteem in African-American and White adolescent girls. Paper presented at the biennial meetings of the Society for Research on Child Development, Albuquerque.

Males, M. (1998). *Framing Youth: 10 Myths about the next generation.* Monroe, ME: Common Courage Press.

Males, M., & Chew, K. (1996). The ages of fathers in California adolescent births. *American Journal of Public Health, 86,* 565–568.

Malone, S. M., Taylor, J., & Marmorstein, N. R. (2004). Genetic and environmental influences on antisocial behavior and alcohol dependence from adolescence to early adulthood. *Development and Psychopathology, 16,* 943–966.

Mandara, J., & Murray, C. B. (2000). Effects of parental marital status, income, and family functioning on African American adolescent self-esteem. *Journal of Family Psychology, 14*(3), 475–490.

Manlove, J., Mariner, C., & Papillo, A. (2000). Subsequent fertility among teen mothers: Longitudinal analyses of recent national data. *Journal of Marriage and the Family, 62*(2), 430–448.

Mannheim, K. (1952). The problem of generations. In K. Mannheim (Ed.), *Essays on the sociology of knowledge.* London: Routledge & Kegan Paul.

Manning, W., & Lamb, K. (2003). Adolescent well-being in cohabiting, married, and single-parent families. *Journal of Marriage and Family, 65* 876.

Manning, W., & Landale, N. (1996). Racial and ethnic differences in the role of cohabitation in premarital childbearing. *Journal of Marriage and the Family, 58,* 63–77.

Manning, W., Longmore, M., & Giordano, P. (2000). The relationship context of contraceptive use at first intercourse. *Family Planning Perspectives, 32*(3), 104–110.

Manning, W., Longmore, M, & Giordano, P. (2005). Adolescents' involvement in non-romantic sexual activity. *Social Science Research, 34,* 384–407.

Marcia, J. (1966). Development and validation of ego identity status. *Journal of Personality and Social Psychology, 3,* 551–558.

Marcia, J. (1976). Identity six years after: A follow-up study. *Journal of Youth and Adolescence, 5,* 145–150.

Marcia, J. (1980). Identity in adolescence. In J. Adelson (Ed.), *Handbook of adolescent psychology,* pp. 159–187. New York: Wiley.

Marcotte, D. (1997). Treating depression in adolescence: A review of the effectiveness of cognitive-behavioral treatments. *Journal of Youth* and *Adolescence, 26,* 273–283.

Marini, M., Fan, P., Finley, E., & Beutel, A. (1996). Gender and job values. *Sociology of Education, 69,* 49–65.

Markovits, H., & Valchon, R. (1989). Reasoning with contrary-to-fact propositions. *Journal of Experimental Child Psychology, 47,* 398–412.

Markovits, H., & Valchon, R. (1990). Conditional reasoning, representation, and level of abstraction. *Developmental Psychology, 26,* 942–951.

Markovits, H., Venet, M., Janveau-Brennan, G., Malfait, N., Pion, N., & Vadeboncoeur, I. (1996). Reasoning in young children: Fantasy and information retrieval. *Child Development, 67,* 2857–2872.

Marks, H. M. (2000). Student engagement in instructional activity: Patterns in the elementary, middle, and high school years. *American Educational Research Journal, 37*(1), 153–184.

Markstom, C. A., & Iborra, A. (2003). Adolescent identity formation and rites of passage: The Navajo kinaalda ceremony for girls. *Journal of Research on Adolescence, 13,* 399–426.

Markstrom, C. A., Li, X., Blackshire, S. L., & Wilfong, J. J. (2005). Ego strength development of adolescents involved in adult-sponsored structured activities. *Journal of Youth and Adolescent, 34,* 85–95.

Markstrom-Adams, C. (1989). Androgyny and its relation to adolescent psychological well-being: A review of the literature. *Sex Roles, 21,* 469–473.

Markstrom-Adams, C., & Adams, G. (1995). Gender, ethnic group, and grade differences in psychosocial functioning during middle adolescence? *Journal of Youth and Adolescence, 24,* 397–417.

Markstrom-Adams, C., Hofstra, G., & Dougher, K. (1994). The ego virtue of fidelity: A case for the study of religion and identity formation in adolescence. *Journal of Youth and Adolescence, 23,* 453–469.

Markus, H., & Nurius, P. (1986). Possible selves. *American Psychologist, 41,* 954–969.

Marsh, H. (1989a). Age and sex effects in multiple dimensions of self-concept: Preadolescence to early adulthood. *Journal of Educational Psychology, 81,* 417–430.

Marsh, H. (1989b). Sex differences in the development of verbal and mathematical constructs: The High School and Beyond Study. *American Educational Research Journal, 26,* 191–225.

Marsh, H., et. al. (2005). Consequences of employment during high school: Character building, subversion of academic goals, or a threshold? *American Educational Research Journal, 42,* 331–369.

Marsh, H., Chessor, D., Craven, R., & Roche, L. (1995). The effects of gifted and talented programs on academic self-concept: The big fish strikes again. *American Educational Research Journal, 32,* 285–319.

Marsh, H., & Hau, K. (2003). Big-fish—little-pond effect on academic self-concept: A cross-cultural (26-country) test of the negative effects of academically selective schools. *American Psychologist, 58*, 364–376.

Marsh, H. & Hau, K. (2004). Explaining paradoxical relationship between academic self-concepts and achievements: Cross-cultural generalizability of the internal/external frame of reference predictions across 26 countries. *Journal of Educational Psychology, 96*, 56–67.

Marsh, H., & Kleitman, S. (2002). Extracurricular school activities: The good, the bad, and the nonlinear. *Harvard Educational Review, 72*(4), 464–514.

Marsh, H., Kong, C., & Hau, K. (2000). Longitudinal multilevel models of the big-fish-little-pond effect on academic self-concept: Counterbalancing contrast and reflected-glory effects in Hong Kong schools. *Journal of Personality and Social Psychology, 78*, 337–349.

Marsh, P., McFarland, F. C., & Allen, J. P. (2003). Attachment, autonomy, and multifinality in adolescent internalizing and risky behavioral symptoms. *Development and Psychopathology, 15*, 451–467.

Marsh, H., & Yeung, A. (1997). Coursework selection: Relations to academic self-concept and achievement. *American Educational Research Journal, 34*, 691–720.

Marshall, S. (1994, February). Ethnic socialization of African American children: Implications for parenting, identity development and academic achievement. Paper presented at the biennial meetings of the Society for Research on Adolescence, San Diego.

Marshall, S. (1995). Ethnic socialization of African American children: Implications for parenting, identity development, and academic achievement. *Journal of Youth and Adolescence, 24*, 377–396.

Marshall, W. (1978). Puberty. In F. Falkner & J. Tanner (Eds.), *Human growth*, Vol. 2. New York: Plenum.

Marsiglia, F., Kulis, S., & Hecht, M. L. (2001). Ethnic labels and ethnic identity as predictors of drug use among middle school students in the southwest. *Journal of Research on Adolescence, 11*(1), 21–48.

Martin, A., Ruchkin, V., Caminis, A., Vermeiren, R., Henrich, C. C., & Schwab-Stone, M. (2005). Early to bed: A study of adaptation among sexually active urban adolescent girls younger than age sixteen. *Journal of the American Academy of Child and Adolescent Psychiatry, 44*, 358–367.

Martin, B. (1990). The transmission of relationship difficulties from one generation to the next. *Journal of Youth and Adolescence, 19*, 181–200.

Martinez, R., & Dukes, R. (1997). The effects of ethnic identity, ethnicity, and gender on adolescent well-being. *Journal of Youth and Adolescence, 26*, 503–516.

Masi, G., Millepiedi, S., Mucci, M., Poll, P., Bertini, N., & Milantoni, L. (2004). Generalized anxiety disorder in referred children and adolescents. *Journal of the American Academy of Child and Adolescent Psychiatry, 43*, 752–760.

Mason, C., Cauce, A., Gonzales, N., & Hiraga, Y. (1994). Adolescent problem behavior: The effect of peers and the moderating role of father absence and the mother–child relationship. *American Journal of Community Psychology, 22*, 723–743.

Mason, C., Cauce, A., Gonzales, N., & Hiraga, N. (1996). Neither too sweet nor too sour: Problem peers, maternal control, and problem behavior in African American adolescents. *Child Development, 67*, 2115–2130.

Mason, C., Cauce, A., Gonzales, N., Hiraga, Y., & Grove, K. (1994). An ecological model of externalizing behaviors in African-American adolescents: No family is an island. *Journal of Research on Adolescence, 4*, 639–655.

Mason, W. (2001). Self-esteem and delinquency revisited (again): A test of Kaplan's self-derogation theory of delinquency using latent growth curve modeling. *Journal of Youth and Adolescence, 30*(1), 83–102.

Mason, W. A., & Windle, M. (2002). Reciprocal relations between adolescent substance use and delinquency: A longitudinal latent variable analysis. *Journal of Abnormal Psychology, 111*(1), 63–76.

Massad, C. (1981). Sex role identity and adjustment during adolescence. *Child Development, 52*, 1290–1298.

Masten, A. (2001). Ordinary magic: Resilience processes in development. *American Psychologist, 56*, 227–238.

Masten, A., Burt, K. B., & Roisman, G. I. (2004). Resources and resilience in the transition to adulthood: Continuity and change. *Development and Psychopathology, 16*, 1071–1094.

Masten, A., Coatsworth, J., Neemann, J., Gest, S., Tellegen, A., & Garmezy, N. (1995). The structure and coherence of competence from childhood through adolescence. *Child Development, 66*, 1635–1659.

Masten, A., Hubbard, J., Gest, S., Tellegen, A., Garmezy, N., & Ramirez, M. (1999). Competence in the context of adversity: Pathways to resilience and maladaptation from childhood to late adolescence. *Development and Psychopathology, 11*, 143–169.

Masten, A., Miliotis, D., Graham-Bermann, S., Ramirez, M., & Neemann, J. (1993). Children in homeless families: Risks to mental health and development. *Journal of Consulting and Clinical Psychology, 61*, 335–343.

Masten, A., Roisman, G. I., Long, J. D., Burt, K. B., Obradovic, J., Riley, J. R., Boelcke-Stennes, K., & Tellegen, A. (2005). Developmental cascades: Linking academic achievement and externalizing and internalizing symptoms over 20 years. *Developmental Psychology, 41*, 733–746.

Matas, L., Arend, R., & Sroufe, L. (1978). Continuity in adaptation in the second year: The relationship between quality of attachment and later competence. *Child Development, 49*, 547–556.

Matsuba, M. K., & Walker, L. J. (2005). Young adult moral exemplars: The making of self through stories. *Journal of Research on Adolescence, 15*, 275–297.

Matsueda, R. L., Kreager, D. A., & Huizinga, D. (2006). Deterring delinquents: A rational choice model of theft and violence. *American Sociological Review, 71*, 95–122.

Matthews, L. S., & Conger, R. D. (2004) "He did it on purpose!" Family correlates of negative attributions about an adolescent sibling. *Journal of Research on Adolescence, 14* 257–284.

Matza, L. S., Kupersmidt, J. B., & Glenn, D. (2001). Adolescents' perceptions and standards of their parents as a function of sociometric status. *Journal of Research on Adolescence, 11*(3), 245–272.

Mauldon, J., & Luker, K. (1996). The effects of contraceptive education on method use at first intercourse. *Family Planning Perspectives, 28*, 19–24, 41.

May, J. C., Delgado, M. R., Dahl, R., Fiez, J. A., Stenger, V. A., Ryan, N., & Carter, C. S. (2004). Event-related fMRI of reward related brain activity in children and adolescents. *Biological Psychiatry, 55*(4), 359–366.

Mayer, C. (2006, May 3). Sugary drinks to be pulled from schools. *The Washington Post*, pp. D1ff.

Mayseless, O., Scharf, M., & Sholt, M. (2003). From authoritative parenting practices to an authoritarian context: Exploring the person–environment fit. *Journal of Research on Adolescence, 13*, 427–457.

Mazor, A., & Enright, R. (1988). The development of the individuation process from a social-cognitive perspective. *Journal of Adolescence, 11*, 29–47.

Mazor, A., Shamir, R., & Ben-Moshe, J. (1990). The individuation process from a social-cognitive perspective in kibbutz adolescents. *Journal of Youth and Adolescence, 19*, 73–90.

McBride, C. K., Paikoff, R. L., & Holmbeck, G. N. (2003). Individual and familial influences on the onset of sexual intercourse among urban African American adolescents. *Journal of Consulting and Clinical Psychology, 71*(1), 159–167.

McCabe, K. (1997, April). Early adolescents at risk: Familial factors that mediate and moderate the effect of risk on child adjustment. Paper presented at the biennial meetings of the Society for Research in Child Development.

McCabe, K., Hough, R., Wood, P. A., & Yeh, M. (2001). Childhood and adolescent onset conduct disorder: A test of the developmental taxonomy. *Journal of Abnormal Child Psychology, 29*(4), 305–316.

McCabe, K., Lansing, A. E., Garland, A., & Hough, R. (2002). Gender differences in psychopathology, functional impairment, and familial risk factors among adjudicated delinquents. *Journal of the American Academy of Child and Adolescent Psychiatry, 41,* 860–867.

McCarthy, K., Lord, S., Eccles, J., Kalil, A., & Furstenberg, F., Jr. (1992, March). The impact of family management strategies on adolescents in high risk environments. Paper presented at the biennial meetings of the Society for Research on Adolescence, Washington.

McClelland, D., Atkinson, J., Clark, R., & Lowell, E. (1953). *The achievement motive.* New York: Appleton-Century-Crofts.

McClintock, M. (1980). Major gaps in menstrual cycle research: Behavioral and physiological controls in a biological context. In P. Komenich, M. McSweeney, J. Noack, & N. Elder (Eds.), *The menstrual cycle,* Vol. 2, pp. 7–23. New York: Springer.

McClintock, M., & Herdt, G. (1996). Rethinking puberty: The development of sexual attraction. *Psychological Sciences, 5,* 178–183.

McCord, J. (1990). Problem behaviors. In S. Feldman & G. Elliott (Eds.), *At the threshold: The developing adolescent,* pp. 414–430. Cambridge, MA: Harvard University Press.

McCoy, J. (1996, March). Parents' involvement in youths' peer relationships as a predictor of youths' later psychological well-being. Paper presented at the biennial meetings of the Society for Research on Adolescence, Boston.

McCoy, J., Brody, G., & Stoneman, Z. (1994). A longitudinal analysis of sibling relationships as mediators of the link between family processes and youths' best friendships. *Family Relations, 43,* 400–408.

McCrae, R., Costa, P. T., Jr., Terracciano, A., Parker, W. D., Mills, C. J., De Fruyt, F., et al. (2002). Personality trait development from age 12 to age 18: Longitudinal, cross-sectional and cross-cultural analyses. *Journal of Personality and Social Psychology, 83*(6), 1456–1468.

McCrae, R., & John, O. (1992). An introduction to the Five-Factor Model and its applications. *Journal of Personality, 60,* 175–215.

McCree, D. J., Wingood, G. M., DiClemente, R., Davies, S., & Harrington, K. F. (2003). Religiosity and risky sexual behavior in African-American adolescent females. *Journal of Adolescent Health, 33,* 2–8.

McCullers, C. (1946). *The member of the wedding.* New York: Bantam Books.

McDermott, P., & Spencer, M. (1997). Racial and social class prevalence of psychopathology among school-age youth in the United States. *Youth and Society, 28,* 387–414.

McDonald, D., & McKinney, J. (1994). Steady dating and self-esteem in high school students. *Journal of Adolescence, 17,* 557–564.

McGee, L., & Newcomb, M. (1992). General deviance syndrome: Expanded hierarchical evaluations at four ages from early adolescence to adulthood. *Journal of Consulting and Clinical Psychology, 60,* 766–776.

McGee, R., Wolfe, D., & Wilson, S. (1997). Multiple maltreatment experiences and adolescent behavior problems: Adolescents' perspectives. *Development and Psychopathology, 9,* 131–149.

McGue, M., Elkins, I., Walden, B., & Iacono, W. G. (2005). Perceptions of the parent–adolescent relationship: A longitudinal investigation. *Developmental Psychology, 41,* 971–984.

McGue, M., Sharma, A., & Benson, P. (1996). The effects of common rearing on adolescent adjustment: Evidence from a U.S. adoption cohort. *Developmental Psychology, 32,* 604–613.

McGuire, J. K., & Gamble, W. C. (2006). Community service for youth: The value of psychological engagement over number of hours spent. *Journal of Adolescence, 29,* 289–298.

McGuire, S., Manke, B., Saudino, K., Reiss, D., Hetherington, E. M., & Plomin R. (1999). Perceived competence and self-worth during adolescence: A longitudinal behavioral genetic study. *Child Development, 70,* 1283–1296

McGuire, S., Neiderhiser, J., Reiss, D., Hetherington, E. M., & Plomin, R. (1994). Genetic and environmental influences on perceptions of self-worth and competence in adolescence: A study of twins, full siblings, and step-siblings. *Child Development, 65,* 785–799.

McHale, S. M., Corneal, D. A., Crouter, A. C., & Birch, L. L. (2001). Gender and weight concerns in early and middle adolescence: Links with well-being and family characteristics. *Journal of Clinical Child Psychology, 30,* 338–348.

McHale, S. M., Kim, J., Whiteman, S., & Crouter, A. C. (2004). Links between sex-typed time use in middle childhood and gender development in early adolescence. *Developmental Psychology, 40,* 868–881.

McHale, S. M., Shanahan, L., Updegraff, K. A., Crouter, A. C., & Booth, A. (2004). Developmental and individual differences in girls' sex-typed activities in middle childhood and adolescence. *Child Development, 75,* 1575–1593.

McKeough, A., & Genereaux, R. (2003). Transformations in narrative thought during adolescence: The structures and content of story compositions. *Journal of Educational Psychology, 95,* 537–552.

McKeown, R., Garrison, C., Jackson, K., Cuffe, S., Addy, C., & Waller, J. (1997). Family structure and cohesion, and depressive symptoms in adolescents. *Journal of Research on Adolescence, 7,* 267–281.

McLanahan, S., & Bumpass, L. (1988). Intergenerational consequences of family disruption. *American Journal of Sociology, 94,* 130–152.

McLean, K. C., (2005). Late adolescent identity development: Narrative meaning making and memory telling. *Developmental Psychology, 41,* 683–691.

McLean, K. C. & Thorne, A. (2003). Late adolescents' self-defining memories about relationships. *Developmental Psychology, 39,* 635–645.

McLellan, J. A., & Youniss, J. (2003). Two systems of youth service: Determinants of voluntary and required youth community service. *Journal of Youth and Adolescence, 32*(1), 47–58.

McLoyd, V. (1990). The impact of economic hardship on black families and children: Psychological distress, parenting, and socioemotional development. *Child Development, 61,* 311–346.

McLoyd, V., Jayaratne, T., Ceballo, R., & Borquez, J. (1994). Unemployment and work interruption among African American single mothers: Effects on parenting and adolescent socioemotional functioning. *Child Development, 65,* 562–589.

McMahon, S. D., & Watts, R. J. (2002). Ethnic identity in urban African American youth: Exploring links with self-worth, aggression, and other psychosocial variables. *Journal of Community Psychology, 30*(4), 411–431.

McMaster, L., Connolly, J., & Craig, W. (1997, March). Sexual harassment and dating violence among early adolescents. Paper presented at the biennial meetings of the Society for Research in Child Development, Washington, DC.

McMaster, L., Connolly, J., Pepler, D., & Craig, W. (2002). Peer to peer sexual harassment in early adolescence: A developmental perspective. *Development and Psychopathology, 14,* 91–105.

McNeal, R., Jr. (1997). Are students being pulled out of high school? The effect of adolescent employment on dropping out. *Sociology of Education, 70,* 206–220.

McNeely, C., Shew, M. L., Beurhing, T., Sieving, R., Miller, B. C., & Blum, R. (2002). Mothers' influence on the timing of first sex among 14- and 15-year olds. *Journal of Adolescent Health, 31*(3), 256–265.

McNeil, L. (1984). *Lowering expectations: The impact of student employment on classroom knowledge.* Madison: Wisconsin Center for Education Research.

McNelles, L. R., & Connolly, J. A. (1999). Intimacy between adolescent friends: Age and gender differences in intimate affect and intimate behaviors. *Journal of Research on Adolescence, 9*(2), 143-159.

McNulty, T. L., & Bellair, P. E. (2003). Explaining racial and ethnic differences in serious adolescent violent behavior. *Criminology, 41,* 709–748.

McQueen, A., Getz, J. G., & Bray, J. H. (2003). Acculturation, substance use, and deviant behavior: Examining separation and family conflict as mediators. *Child Development, 74*, 1737–1750.

Mead, M. ([1928]1978). *Coming of age in Samoa.* New York: Morrow.

Mechanic, D. (1983). Adolescent health and illness behavior: Review of the literature and a new hypothesis for the study of stress. *Journal of Human Stress, 9*, 4–13.

Mednick, S., Gabrielli, W., & Hitchings, B. (1987). Genetic factors in the etiology of criminal behavior. In S. Mednick, T. Moffitt, & S. Stack (Eds.), *The causes of crime: New biological approaches,* pp. 74–91. Cambridge: Cambridge University Press.

Medrich, E., Roizen, J., Rubin, V., & Buckley, S. (1982). *The serious business of growing up.* Berkeley: University of California Press.

Meeus, W. (1996). Studies on identity development in adolescence: An overview of research and some new data. *Journal of Youth and Adolescence, 25*, 569–598.

Meeus, W., Iedema, J., & Vollebergh, W., (1999). Rejoinder: Identity formation re-revisited: A rejoinder to Waterman in developmental and cross-cultural issues. *Developmental Review, 19*, 480–496.

Meeus, W., Iedema, J., Helsen, M., & Vollebergh, W. (1999). Patterns of adolescent identity development: Review of literature and longitudinal analysis. *Developmental Review, 19*, 419–461.

Meier, A. M. (2003). Adolescents' transition to first intercourse, religiosity, and attitudes about sex. *Social Forces, 81*(3), 1031–1052.

Mekos, D., Hetherington, E. M., & Reiss, D. (1996). Sibling differences in problem behavior and parental treatment in nondivorced and remarried families. *Child Development, 67*, 2148–2165.

Melby, J. (1995, March). Early family and peer predictors of later adolescent tobacco use. Paper presented at the biennial meetings of the Society for Research in Child Development, Indianapolis.

Melby, J., & Conger, R. (1996). Parental behaviors and adolescent academic performance: A longitudinal analysis. *Journal of Research on Adolescence, 6*, 113–137.

Melton, G. (1990). Knowing what we do know: APA and adolescent abortion. *American Psychologist, 45*, 1171–1173.

Menard, S., & Huizinga, D. (1994). Changes in conventional attitudes and delinquent behavior in adolescence. *Youth and Society, 26*, 23–53.

Menning, C. L. (2002). Absent parents are more than money: The joint effect of activities and financial support on youths' educational attainment. *Journal of Family Issues, 23*(5), 648–671.

Merten, D. (1997). The meaning of meanness: Popularity, competition and conflict among junior high school girls. *Sociology of Education, 70*, 175–191.

Merten, D. E. (1996). Visibility and vulnerability: Responses to rejection by nonaggressive junior high school boys. *Journal of Early Adolescence, 16*, 5–26.

Meschke, L. L., Bartholomae, S., & Zentall, S. R. (2000). Adolescent sexuality and parent-adolescent processes: Promoting healthy teen choices. *Family Relations: Interdisciplinary Journal of Applied Family Studies, 49*(2), 143–154.

Meschke, L. L., Zweig, J. M., Barber, B. L., & Eccles, J. S. (2000). Demographic, biological, psychological, and social predictors of the timing of first intercourse. *Journal of Research on Adolescence, 10*(3), 315–338.

Meyer, L. (1994). *Teenspeak.* Princeton, NJ: Peterson.

Meyer-Bahlburg, H., Ehrhardt, A., Rosen, L., Gruen, R., Veridiano, N., Vann, F., & Neuwalder, H. (1995). Prenatal estrogens and the development of homosexual orientation. *Developmental Psychology, 31*, 12–21.

Michael, R., Laumann, E., & Kolata, G. (1994). *Sex in America.* Boston: Little, Brown.

Mickelson, R. (1990). The attitude–achievement paradox among black adolescents. *Sociology of Education, 63*, 44–61.

Mickelson, R. (2001). Subverting swann: First- and second-generation segregation in the Charlotte-Mecklenburg schools. *American Educational Research Journal, 38*(2), 215–252.

Midgley, C., Arunkumar, R., & Urban T. (1996). If I don't do well tomorrow, there's a reason: Predictors of adolescents' use of academic self-handicapping strategies. *Journal of Educational Psychology, 88*, 423–434.

Midgley, C., Berman, E., & Hicks, L. (1995). Differences between elementary and middle school teachers and students: A goal theory approach. *Journal of Early Adolescence, 15*, 90–113.

Midgley, C., Feldlaufer, H., & Eccles, J. (1988). The transition to junior high school: Beliefs of pre- and posttransition teachers. *Journal of Youth and Adolescence, 17*, 543–562.

Midgley, C., & Urdan, T. (1995). Predictors of middle school students' use of self-handicapping strategies. *Journal of Early Adolescence, 15*, 389–411.

Mihalic, S., & Elliot, D. (1997). Short- and long-term consequences of adolescent work. *Youth and Society, 28*, 464–498.

Miller, B., Benson, B., & Galbraith, K. A. (2001). Family relationships and adolescent pregnancy risk: A research synthesis. *Developmental Review, 21*(1), 1–38.

Miller, B., Fan, X., Christensen, M., Grotevant, H. D., & van Dulmen, M. (2000). Comparisons of adopted and nonadopted adolescents in a large, nationally represented sample. *Child Development, 71*(5), 1458–1473.

Miller, B., & Moore, K. (1990). Adolescent sexual behavior, pregnancy, and parenting: Research through the 1980s. *Journal of Marriage and the Family, 52*, 1025–1044.

Miller, B., Norton, M., Curtis, T., Hill, E., Schvaneveldt, P., & Young, M. (1997). The timing of sexual intercourse among adolescents: Family, peer, and other antecedents. *Youth and Society, 29*, 54–83.

Miller, B., Norton, M., Fan, X., & Christopherson, C. (1998). Pubertal development, parental communication, and sexual values in relation to adolescent sexual behaviors. *Journal of Early Adolescence, 18*, 27–52.

Miller, D., & Byrnes, J. (1997). The role of contextual and personal factors in children's risk taking. *Developmental Psychology, 33*, 814–823.

Miller, J., & White, N. (2003). Gender and adolescent relationship violence: A contextual examination. *Criminology, 41*, 1207–1248.

Miller, J., & Yung, S. (1990). The role of allowances in adolescent socialization. *Youth and Society, 17*, 57–63.

Miller, K., Clark, L., & Moore, J. (1997). Sexual initiation with older male partners and subsequent HIV risk behavior among female adolescents. *Family Planning Perspectives, 29*, 212–214.

Miller, K. E., Farrell, M. P., Barnes, G. M., Melnick, M. J., & Sabo, D. (2005). Gender/racial differences in jock identity, dating, and adolescent sexual risk. *Journal of Youth and Adolescence, 34*, 123–136.

Miller, K., Forehand, R., & Kotchick, B. (1999). Adolescent sexual behavior in two ethnic minority samples: The role of family variables. *Journal of Marriage and the Family, 61*, 85–98.

Miller, K., Kotchick, B., Dorsey, S., Forehand, R., & Ham, A. (1998). Family communication about sex: What are parents saying and are their adolescents listening? *Family Planning Perspectives, 30*, 218–222, 235.

Miller, K., Levin, M., Whitaker, D., & Xu, X. (1998). Patterns of condom use among adolescents: The impact of mother–adolescent communication. *American Journal of Public Health, 88*, 1542–1544.

Miller, K., & Whitaker, D. (2001). Predictors of mother–adolescent discussions about condoms: Implications for providers who serve youth. *Pediatrics, 108*(2), E28.

Miller, L., & Gur, M. (2002). Religiousness and sexual responsibility in adolescent girls. *Journal of Adolescent Health, 31*(5), 401–406.

Miller, L., Davies, M., & Greenwald, S. (2000). Religiosity and substance use and abuse among adolescents in the National Comorbidity Survey. *Journal of the American Academy of Child and Adolescent Psychiatry, 39*, 1190–1197.

Miller, N. (1928). *The child in primitive society.* New York: Bretano.

Miller, P., & Simon, W. (1980). The development of sexuality in adolescence. In J. Adelson (Ed.), *Handbook of adolescent psychology*, pp. 383–407. New York: Wiley.

Miller-Johnson, S., Winn, D., Coie, J., Hyman, C., Terry, R., Lochman, J., & Maumary-Gremaud, A. (1996, March). Parenthood during the teen years: A developmental perspective on risk factors for childbearing. Paper presented at the biennial meetings of the Society for Research on Adolescence, Boston.

Miller-Johnson, S., Winn, D., Coie, J., Malone, P., & Lochman, J. (2004). Risk factors for adolescent pregnancy reports among African American males. *Journal of Research on Adolescence, 14*, 471–495.

Miller-Johnson, S., Winn, D., Coie, J., Maumary-Gremaud, A., Hyman, C., Retty, R., & Lochman, J. (1999). Motherhood during the teen years: A developmental perspective on risk factors for childbearing. *Development and Psychopathology, 11*, 85–100.

Miller-Jones, D. (1989). Culture and testing. *American Psychologist, 44*, 360–366.

Millstein, S. G., & Halpern-Felsher, B. L. (2002). Judgments about risk and perceived invulnerability in adolescents and young adults. *Journal of Research on Adolescence, 12*(4), 399–422.

Millstein, S., Petersen, A., & Nightingale, E. (Eds.). (1993). *Promoting the health of adolescents: New directions for the twenty-first century.* New York: Oxford University Press.

Milnitsky-Sapiro, C., Turiel, E., & Nucci, L. (2006). Brazilian adolescents' conceptions of autonomy and parental authority. *Cognitive Development, 21*, 317–331.

Minuchin, S., Rosman, B., & Baker, L. (1978). *Psychosomatic families: Anorexia nervosa in context.* Cambridge, MA: Harvard University Press.

Mitchell, B., Wister, A., & Burch, T. (1989). The family environment and leaving the parental home. *Journal of Marriage and the Family, 51*, 605–613.

Mitchell, C., & O'Nell, T. (1998). Problem and conventional behavior among American Indian adolescents: Structure and validity. *Journal of Research on Adolescence, 8*, 97–122.

Mitchell, C., O'Nell, T., Beals, J., Dick, R., Keane, E., & Manson, S. (1996). Dimensionality of alcohol use among American Indian adolescents: Latent structure, construct validity, and implications for developmental research. *Journal of Research on Adolescence, 6*, 151–180.

Mitchell, E. (Ed.). (1985). *Anorexia nervosa and bulimia: Diagnosis and treatment.* Minneapolis: University of Minnesota Press.

Mitru, G., Millrood, D. L., & Mateika, J. H. (2002). The impact of sleep on learning and behavior in adolescents. *Teachers College Record, 104*(4), 704–726.

Modell, J., Furstenberg, F., Jr., & Hershberg, T. (1976). Social change and transitions to adulthood in historical perspective. *Journal of Family History, 1*, 7–32.

Modell, J., & Goodman, M. (1990). Historical perspectives. In S. Feldman & G. Elliott (Eds.), *At the threshold: The developing adolescent*, pp. 93–122. Cambridge, MA: Harvard University Press.

Moffitt, T. (1993). Adolescence-limited and life-course persistent antisocial behavior: A developmental taxonomy. *Psychological Review, 100*, 674–701.

Moffitt, T. (2006). Life-course persistent versus adolescence-limited antisocial behavior. In D. Cicchetti & D. Cohen (Eds.), *Developmental Psychopathology* (2nd ed.). New York: Wiley.

Moffitt, T., & Caspi, A. (2001). Childhood predictors differentiate life-course persistent and adolescence-limited antisocial pathways among males and females. *Development and Psychopathology, 13*, 355–375.

Moffitt, T., Caspi, A., Harkness, A., & Silva, P. (1993). The natural history of change in intellectual performance: Who changes? How much? Is it meaningful? *Journal of Child Psychology and Psychiatry, 34*, 455–506.

Moffitt, T., Caspi, A., Harrington, H., & Milne, B. J. (2002). Males on the life-course-persistent and adolescence-limited antisocial pathways: Follow-up at age 26 years. *Development and Psychopathology, 14*, 179–207.

Molina, B., & Chassin, L. (1996). The parent–adolescent relationship at puberty: Hispanic ethnicity and parent alcoholism as moderators. *Developmental Psychology, 32*, 675–686.

Moll, R. (1986). *Playing the private college admissions game.* New York: Penguin Books.

Monck, E. (1991). Patterns of confiding relationships among adolescent girls. *Journal of Child Psychology and Psychiatry, 32*, 333–345.

Monitoring the Future. (2005). The Monitoring the Future Study, University of Michigan (available at www.monitoringthefuture.org).

Monroe, S. M., Rohde, P., Seeley, J. R., & Lewinsohn, P. M. (1999). Life events and depression in adolescence: Relationship loss as a prospective risk factor for first onset of major depressive disorder. *Journal of Abnormal Psychology, 108*, 606–614.

Montemayor, R. (1982). The relationship between parent-adolescent conflict and the amount of time adolescents spend alone and with parents and peers. *Child Development, 53*, 1512–1519.

Montemayor, R. (1983). Parents and adolescents in conflict: All families some of the time and some families most of the time. *Journal of Early Adolescence, 3*, 83–103.

Montemayor, R. (1986). Family variation in parent–adolescent storm and stress. *Journal of Adolescent Research, 1*, 15–31.

Montemayor, R., Brown, B., & Adams, G. (1985). Changes in identity status and psychological adjustment after leaving home and entering college. Paper presented at the biennial meetings of the Society for Research in Child Development, Toronto.

Montemayor, R., & Eisen, M. (1977). The development of self-conceptions from childhood to adolescence. *Developmental Psychology, 13*, 314–319.

Montgomery, M. (1996). "The fruit that hangs highest": Courtship and chaperonage in New York High Society, 1880–1920. *Journal of Family History, 21*, 172–191.

Montgomery, M. J. (2005). Psychosocial intimacy and identity: From early adolescence to emerging adulthood. *Journal of Adolescent Research, 20*, 346–374.

Montgomery, M.J., & Sorell, G. T. (1998). Love and dating experience in early and middle adolescence: Grade and gender comparisons. *Journal of Adolescence, 21*(6), 677–689.

Moody, J. (2001). Race, school integration, and friendship segregation in America. *American Journal of Sociology, 107*(3), 679–716.

Moore, K., Myers, D., Morrison, D., Nord, C., Brown, B., & Edmonston, B. (1993). Age at first childbirth and later poverty. *Journal of Research on Adolescence, 3*, 393–422.

Moore, K., Nord, C., & Peterson, J. (1989). Nonvoluntary sexual activity among adolescents. *Family Planning Perspectives, 21*, 110–114.

Moore, M. (1992). The family as portrayed on prime-time television, 1947–1990: Structure and characteristics. *Sex Roles, 26*, 41–62.

Moore, M., Petrie, C., Braga, A., & McLaughlin, B. (2003). *Deadly lessons: Understanding lethal school violence.* Washington, DC: National Academies Press.

Moore, M. J., & Werch, C. E. (2005). Sport and physical activity participation and substance use among adolescents. *Journal of Adolescent Health, 36*, 486–493.

Moore, M. R., & Chase-Lansdale, P. (2001). Sexual intercourse and pregnancy among African American girls in high-poverty neighborhoods: The role of family and perceived community environment. *Journal of Marriage and the Family, 63*(4), 1146–1157.

Moore, S. (1995). Girls' understanding and social construction of menarche. *Journal of Adolescence, 18*, 87–104.

Moore, S., & Gullone, E. (1996). Predicting adolescent risk behavior using a personalized cost-benefit analysis. *Journal of Youth and Adolescence, 25*, 343–359.

Moos, R. (1978). A typology of junior high and high school classrooms. *American Educational Research Journal, 15*, 53–66.

Morabia, A. Costanza, M., & World Health Organization Collaborative Study of Neoplasia and Steroid Contraceptives. (1998). International variability in ages at menarche, first livebirth, and menopause. *American Journal of Epidemiology, 148,* 1195–1205.

Morison, P., & Masten, A. (1991). Peer reputation in middle childhood as a predictor of adaptation in adolescence: A seven-year follow-up. *Child Development, 62,* 991–1007.

Morris, A., & Sloutsky, V. (1998). Understanding of logical necessity: Developmental antecedents and cognitive consequences. *Child Development, 69,* 721–741.

Morris, B., & Sloutsky, V. (2001). Children's solutions of logical versus empirical problems: What's missing and what develops? *Cognitive Development, 16,* 907–928.

Morrison, G. M., Laughlin, J., Miguel, S. S., Smith, D. C., & Widaman, K. (1997). Sources of support for school-related issues: Choices of Hispanic adolescents varying in migrant status. *Journal of Youth and Adolescence, 26*(2), 233–252.

Morrison Gutman, L., Sameroff, A. J., & Eccles, J. S. (2002). The academic achievement of African American students during early adolescence: An examination of multiple risk, promotive, and protective factors. *American Journal of Community Psychology, 30*(3), 367–399.

Mortimer, J. (2003). *Working and growing up in America.* Cambridge, MA: Harvard University Press.

Mortimer, J., & Finch, M. (1986). The effects of part-time work on adolescent self-concept and achievement. In P. Borman & J. Reisman (Eds.), *Becoming a worker.* Norwood, NJ: Ablex.

Mortimer, J., & Johnson, M. (1998). New perspectives on adolescent work and the transition to adulthood. In R. Jessor & M. Chase (Eds.), *New perspectives on adolescent risk behavior.* New York: Cambridge University Press.

Mortimer, J., & Larson, R. (2002). Adolescence in the 21st century: A worldwide perspective. Introduction: Macro societal trends and the changing experiences of adolescence. In J. Mortimer & R. Larson (Eds.), *The future of adolescent experience: Societal trends and the transition to adulthood.* New York: Cambridge University Press.

Mortimer, J., & Lorence, J. (1979). Work experience and occupational value socialization: A longitudinal study. *American Journal of Sociology, 84,* 1361–1385.

Mortimer, J., Pimentel, E., Ryu, S., Nash, K., & Lee, C. (1996). Part-time work and occupational value formation in adolescence. *Social Forces, 74,* 1405–1418.

Mortimer, J. T., & Staff, J. (2004). Early work as a source of developmental discontinuity during the transition to adulthood. *Development and Psychopathology, 16,* 1047–1070.

Mory, M. (1992, March). "Love the ones you're with": Conflict and consensus in adolescent peer group stereotypes. Paper presented at

the biennial meetings of the Society for Research on Adolescence, Washington, DC.

Mory, M. (1994, February). When people form or perceive sets, they tend to be fuzzy: The case of adolescent crowds. Paper presented at the biennial meetings of the Society for Research on Adolescence, San Diego.

Moses, A. (1999). Exposure to violence, depression, and hostility in a sample of inner city high school youth. *Journal of Adolescence, 22,* 21–32.

Mosher, W., & Bachrach, C. (1996). Understanding U.S. fertility: Continuity and change in the National Survey of Family Growth, 1988–1995. *Family Planning Perspectives, 28,* 4–12.

Moshman, D. (1993). Adolescent reasoning and adolescent rights. *Human Development, 36,* 27–40.

Mosteller, F., Light, R., & Sachs, J. (1996). Sustained inquiry in education: Lessons from skill grouping and class size. *Harvard Educational Review, 66,* 797–842.

Motl, R. W., McAuley, E., Birnbaum, A. S., & Lytle, L. A. (2006). Naturally occurring changes in time spent watching television are inversely related to frequency of physical activity during early adolescence. *Journal of Adolescence, 29,* 19–32.

Mott, F., Fondell, M., Hu, P., Kowaleski-Jones, P., & Menaghan, E. (1996). The determinants of first sex by age 14 in a high-risk adolescent population. *Family Planning Perspectives, 28,* 13–18.

Mounts, N., & Steinberg, L. (1995). An ecological analysis of peer influence on adolescent grade point average and drug use. *Developmental Psychology, 31,* 915–922.

Mounts, N. S. (2002). Parental management of adolescent peer relationships in context: The role of parenting style. *Journal of Family Psychology, 16*(1), 58–69.

Mounts, N. S. (2004). Adolescents' perceptions of parental management of peer relationships in an ethnically diverse sample. *Journal of Adolescent Research, 19,* 446–467.

Muise, A. M., Stein, D. G., & Arbess, G. (2003). Eating disorders in adolescent boys: A review of the adolescent and young adult literature. *Journal of Adolescent Health, 33,* 427–435.

Mukai, T. (1996). Mothers, peers, and perceived pressure to diet among Japanese adolescent girls. *Journal of Research on Adolescence, 6,* 309–324.

Muller, C. (1998). Gender differences in parental involvement and adolescents' mathematics achievement. *Sociology of Education, 71,* 336–356.

Muller, P. A., Stage, F. K., & Kinzie, J. (2001). Science achievement growth trajectories: Understanding factors related to gender and racial-ethnic differences in precollege science achievement. *American Educational Research, 3*(4), 981–1012.

Mulvey, E., & Cauffman, E. (2001). The inherent limits of predicting school violence. *American Psychologist, 56*(10), 797–802.

Mulvey, E., Steinberg, L., Fagan, J., Cauffman, E., Piquero, A., Chassin, L., Knight, G., Brame, R., Schubert, C., Hecker, T., & Losoya, S. (2004). Theory and research on desistance from antisocial activity among serious adolescent offenders. *Youth Violence and Juvenile Justice, 2,* 213–236.

Munsch, J., Liang, S., & DeSecottier, L. (1996, March). Natural mentors: Who they are and the roles they fill. A gender and ethnic comparison. Paper presented at the biennial meetings of the Society for Research on Adolescence, Boston.

Munsch, J., & Wampler, R. (1993). Ethnic differences in early adolescents' coping with school stress. *American Journal of Orthopsychiatry, 63,* 633–646.

Murdock, T. (1994, February). Who are you and how do you treat me? Student withdrawal as motivated alienation. Paper presented at the biennial meetings of the Society for Research on Adolescence, San Diego.

Murdock, T. B., Anderman, L. H., & Hodge, S. A. (2000). Middle-grade predictors of students' motivation and behavior in high school. *Journal of Adolescent Research, 15*(3), 327–351.

Murry, V. (1994). Black adolescent females: A comparison of early versus late coital initiators. *Family Relations, 43,* 342–348.

Murry, V. (1996). An ecological analysis of coital timing among middle-class African American adolescent females. *Journal of Adolescent Research, 43,* 400–408.

Musick, J. (1994). Grandmothers and grandmothers-to-be: Effects on adolescent mothers and adolescent mothering. *Infancy and Young Children, 6,* 1–9.

Mustanski, B. S., Viken, R. J., Kaprio, J., Pulkkinen, L., & Rose, R. J. (2004). Genetic and environmental influences on pubertal development: Longitudinal data from Finnish twins at ages 11 and 14. *Developmental Psychology, 40,* 1188–1198.

Myers, J., Lindentthal, J., & Pepper, M. (1975). Life events, social integration, and psychiatric symptomatology. *Journal of Health and Social Behavior, 16,* 421–429.

Mylod, D., Whitman, T., & Borkowski, J. (1997). Predicting adolescent mothers' transition to adulthood. *Journal of Research on Adolescence, 7,* 457–478.

Nadeem, E., & Graham, S. (2005). Early puberty, peer victimization, and internalizing symptoms in ethnic minority adolescents. *Journal of Early Adolescence, 25,* 197–222.

Nagin, D., Farrington, D., & Moffitt, T. (1995). Life-course trajectories of different types of offenders. *Criminology, 33,* 111–139.

Nagin, D., & Tremblay, R. (1999). Trajectories of boys' physical aggression, opposition, and hyperactivity on the path to physically violent and nonviolent juvenile delinquency. *Child Development, 70,* 1181–1196.

Nagy, S., Adcock, A., & Nagy, C. (1994). A comparison of risky health behaviors of sexually active, sexually abused, and abstaining adolescents. *Pediatrics, 93,* 570–575.

Nagy, S., DiClimente, R., & Adcock, A. (1995). Adverse factors associated with forced sex among Southern adolescent girls. *Pediatrics, 96,* 944–946.

Nansel, T. R., Overpeck, M., Pilla, R. S., Ruan, W., Simons-Morton, B., & Scheidt, P. (2001). Bullying behaviors among U.S. youth. *Journal of the American Medical Association, 285,* 2094–2100.

Nation, M., Crusto, C., Wandersman, A., Kumpfer, K. L., Seybolt, D., Morrissey-Kane, E., & Davino, K. (2003). What works in prevention: Principles of effective prevention programs. *American Psychologist, 58,* 449–456.

National Assessment of Educational Progress (NAEP). (1999). *NAEP 1999 trends in academic progress.* Washington, DC: U.S. Department of Education.

National Assessment of Educational Progress (NAEP). (2006). Up to date reports available on line at nces.ed.gov/nationsreportcard/.

National Center for Education Statistics. (1999). *The condition of education.* Washington, DC: U.S. Department of Education.

National Center for Education Statistics (2002a). *Educational Longitudinal Study of 2002.* Washington, DC: U.S. Department of Education.

National Center for Education Statistics (2002b). *Digest of education statistics, 2001.* Washington, DC: U.S. Department of Education.

National Center for Educational Statistics. (2003). *Digest of educational statistics, 2002.* Washington, DC: U.S. Department of Education.

National Center for Education Statistics. (2004). *Digest of education statistics, 2003.* Washington, DC: U.S. Department of Education.

National Center for Education Statistics (2006a). *Comparing private schools and public schools using Hierarchical Linear Modeling.* Washington, DC: U.S. Department of Education.

National Center for Education Statistics (2006b). *Annual expenditures on public and private institutions per student and as a percentage of gross domestic product (GDP) in OECD countries, by level of education: 2002.* Washington, DC: U.S. Department of Education.

National Commission on Excellence in Education. (1983). *A nation at risk: The imperative for educational reform.* Washington, DC: U.S. Department of Education.

National Education Commission on Time and Learning. (1994). *Prisoners of time.* Washington, DC: U.S. Government Printing Office.

National Heart, Lung, and Blood Institute Growth and Health Study Research Group. (1992). Obesity and cardiovascular disease risk factors in Black and White girls: The NHLBI Growth and Health Study. *American Journal of Public Health, 82,* 1613–1620.

National Institute on Out-of-School Time. (2006). *Making the case: A fact sheet on children and youth in out-of-school time.* Wellesley, MA: Center for Research on Women, Wellesley College.

National Research Council. (1993). *Losing generations.* Washington, DC: National Academy Press.

National Research Council. (1998). *Protecting youth at work.* Washington, DC: National Academy Press.

National Research Council. (2004). *Reducing underage drinking: A collective responsibility.* Washington, DC: National Academies Press.

National Research Council. (2005). *Growing up global.* Washington, DC: National Academies Press.

National Research Council (2006). *Rising above the gathering storm.* Washington, DC: National Academies Press.

Natriello, G., & McDill, E. (1986). Performance standards, student effort on homework, and academic achievement. *Sociology of Education, 59,* 18–31.

Neckerman, H., Cairns, B., & Cairns, R. (1993, March). Peers and families: Developmental changes, constraints, and continuities. Paper presented at the biennial meetings of the Society for Research on Child Development, New Orleans.

Needle, R., Su, S., & Doherty, W. (1990). Divorce, remarriage, and adolescent substance use: A prospective longitudinal study. *Journal of Marriage and the Family, 52,* 157–169.

Neemann, J., Hubbard, J., & Masten, A. (1995). The changing importance of romantic relationship involvement to competence from late childhood to late adolescence. *Development and Psychopathology, 7,* 727–750.

Neiderhiser, J., Pike, A., Hetherington, E. M., & Reiss, D. (1999). Adolescent perceptions as mediators of parenting: Genetic and environmental contributions. *Developmental Psychology, 34,* 1459–1469.

Neiderhiser, J., Reiss, D., Hetherington, E. M., Plomin, R. (1999). Relationships between parenting and adolescent adjustment over time: Genetic and environmental contributions. *Developmental Psychology, 35,* 680–92.

Neiderhiser, J. M., Reiss, D., Pedersen, N. L., Lictenstein, P., Spotts, E. L., Hansson, K., Cederblad, M., & Ellhammer, O. (2004). Genetic and environmental influences on mothering of adolescents: A comparison of two samples. *Developmental Psychology, 40,* 335–351.

Nelson, E., Leibenluft, E., McClure, E., & Pine, D. (2005). The social re-orientation of adolescence: A neuroscience perspective on the process and its relation to psychopathology. *Psychological Medicine, 35,* 163–174.

Nelson, E., McClure, E., Parrish, J., Leibenluft, E., Ernst, M., Fox, N., & Pine, D. (2007). Brain systems underlying peer social acceptance in adolescents. Unpublished paper, Development and Anxiety Neuroscience Section, Mood and Activity Disorders Program, National Institute of Mental Health, Washington, DC.

Nelson, L. J., Badger, S., & Bo, W. (2004). The influence of culture in emerging adulthood: Perspectives of Chinese college students. *International Journal of Behavioral Development, 28,* 26–36.

Nelson, L. J., & Barry, C. M. (2005). Distinguishing features of emerging adulthood. *Journal of Adolescent Research, 20,* 242–262.

Neugarten, B., & Datan, N. (1974). The middle years. In S. Arieti (Ed.), *American handbook of psychiatry,* (2nd ed.), Vol. 1, Part 3. New York: Basic Books.

Neumark-Sztainer, D., Story, M., Dixon, L., & Murray, D. (1998). Adolescents engaging in unhealthy weight control behaviors: Are they at risk for other health-compromising behaviors? *American Journal of Public Health, 88*(6), 952–955.

Neumark-Sztainer, D., Story, M., French, S., Cassuto, N., Jacobs, J. D., & Resnick, M. (1996). Patterns of health-compromising behaviors among Minnesota adolescents: Sociodemographic variations. *American Journal of Public Health, 86,* 1599–1606.

Newacheck, P. W., Park, M. J., Brindis, C. D., Biehl, M., & Irwin, C. E. (2004). Trends in private and public health insurance for adolescents. *Journal of the American Medical Association, 291,* 1231–1237.

Newcomb, A., & Bagwell, C. (1995). Children's friendship relations: A meta-analytic review. *Psychological Review, 117,* 306–347.

Newcomb, M., & Bentler, P. (1988). Impact of adolescent drug use and social support on problems of young adults: A longitudinal study. *Journal of Abnormal Psychology, 97,* 64–75.

Newcomb, M., & Bentler, P. (1989). Substance use and abuse among children and teenagers. *American Psychologist, 44,* 242–248.

Newcomb, M., & Felix-Ortiz, M. (1992). Multiple protective and risk factors for drug use and abuse: Cross-sectional and prospective findings. *Journal of Personality and Social Psychology, 63,* 280–296.

Newcomer, S., & Udry, J. (1988). Adolescents' honesty in a survey of sexual behavior. *Journal of Adolescence Research, 3,* 419–423.

Newman, B., & Newman, P. (2001). Group identity and alienation: Giving the we its due. *Journal of Youth and Adolescence, 30*(5), 515–538.

Newman, D. L. (2005). Ego development and ethnic identity formation in rural American Indian adolescents. *Child Development, 76,* 734–746.

Newmann, F. (1992). Higher order thinking and prospects for classroom thoughtfulness. In F. Newmann (Ed.), *Student engagement and achievement in American high schools.* New York: Teachers College Press.

Newmann, F., Marks, H., & Gamoran, A. (1996). Authentic pedagogy and student performance. *American Journal of Education, 104,* 280–312.

Newman, K. (1999). *No shame in my game.* New York: Knopf.

Newman, R., & Schwager, M. (1995). Students' help seeking during problem solving: Effects of grade, goal, and prior achievement. *American Educational Research Journal, 32,* 352–376.

Nichols, S., & Good, T. (1998). Students' perceptions of fairness in school settings: A gender analysis. *Teachers College Record, 100,* 369–401.

Nieto, M., Lambert, S., Briggs, E., McCoy, J., Brunson, L., & Aber, M. (1996, March). Untangling the relationship between ethnic composition of neighborhood and school adjustment. Paper presented at the biennial meetings of the Society for Research on Adolescence, Boston.

Nightingale, E., & Wolverton, L. (1993). Adolescent rolelessness in modern society. *Teachers College Record, 94,* 472–486.

Nishina, A., & Juvonen, J. (2005). Daily reports of witnessing and experience peer harassment in middle school. *Child Development, 76,* 435–450.

Noack, P., Kracke, B., & Hofer, M. (1994, February). The family context of rightist attitudes among adolescents in East and West Germany. Paper presented at the biennial meetings of the Society for Research on Adolescence, San Diego.

Nock, S. (1998). The consequences of premarital fatherhood. *American Sociological Review, 63,* 250–263.

Noguera, P. (1995). Preventing and producing violence: A critical analysis of responses to school violence. *Harvard Educational Review, 65,* 189–212.

Nolen-Hoeksema, S., & Girgus, J. (1994). The emergence of gender differences in depression during adolescence. *Psychological Bulletin, 115,* 424–443.

Nolen-Hoeksema, S., Girgus, J., & Seligman, M. (1992). Predictors and consequences of childhood depressive symptoms: A 5-year longitudinal study. *Journal of Abnormal Psychology, 101,* 405–422.

Noller, P., & Callan, V. (1990). Adolescents' perceptions of the nature of their communication with parents. *Journal of Youth and Adolescence, 19,* 349–362.

Noom, M. J., Dekovic, M., & Meeus, W. (2001). Conceptual analysis and measurement of adolescent autonomy. *Journal of Youth and Adolescence, 30*(5), 577–595.

Nottelmann, E. (1987). Competence and self-esteem during transition from childhood to adolescence. *Developmental Psychology, 23,* 441–450.

Nurmi, J. (1993). Adolescent development in an age-graded context: The role of personal beliefs, goals, and strategies in the tackling of developmental tasks and standards. *International Journal of Behavioural Development, 16,* 169–189.

Nurmi, J. (2004). Socialization and self-development: Channeling, selection, adjustment, and reflection. In R. Lerner & L. Steinberg (Eds.), *Handbook of adolescent psychology.* New York: Wiley.

Nurmi, J., Onatsu, T., & Haavisto, T. (1995). Underachievers' cognitive and behavioral strategies: Self-handicapping at school. *Contemporary Educational Psychology, 20,* 188–200.

Oakes, J. (1995). Two cities' tracking and within-school segregation. *Teachers College Record, 96,* 681–690.

Oakley, D., & Bogue, E. (1995). Quality of condom use as reported by female clients of a family planning clinic. *American Journal of Public Health, 85,* 1526–1530.

Obeidallah, D., Brennan, R. T., Brooks-Gunn, J., & Earls, F. (2004). Links between pubertal timing and neighborhood contexts: Implications for girls' violent behavior. *Journal of the American Academy of Child and Adolescent Psychiatry, 43,* 1460–1468.

Obeidallah, D., McHale, S., & Silbereisen, R. (1996). Gender role socialization and adolescents' reports of depression: Why some girls and not others? *Journal of Youth and Adolescence, 25,* 775–786.

O'Brien, S., & Bierman, K. (1988). Conceptions and perceived influence of peer groups: Interviews with preadolescents and adolescents. *Child Development, 59,* 1360–1365.

O'Callaghan, M., Borkowski, J., Whitman, T., Maxwell, S., & Keogh, D. (1999). A model of adolescent parenting: The role of cognitive readiness to parent. *Journal of Research on Adolescence, 9,* 203–225.

O'Connor, T., Caspi, A., DeFries, J., & Plomin, R. (2000). Are associations between parental divorce and children's adjustment genetically mediated? An adoption study. *Developmental Psychology, 36,* 429–437.

O'Connor, T., Deater-Deckard, K., Fulker, D., Rutter, M., & Plomin, R. (1998). Genotype-environment correlations in late childhood and early adolescence: Antisocial behavioral problems and coercive parenting. *Developmental Psychology, 34,* 970–981.

O'Connor, T., Hetherington, E. M., Reiss, D., & Plomin, R. (1995). A twin-sibling study of

observed parent–adolescent interactions. *Child Development, 66,* 812–829.

O'Donnell, L., O'Donnell, C. R., & Stueve. (2001). Early sexual initiation and subsequent sex-related risks among urban minority youth: The reach for health study. *Family Planning Perspectives, 33*(5), 268–275.

Oettinger, G. (1999). Does high school employment affect high school academic performance? *Industrial and Labor Relations Review, 53,* 136–151.

Office of Juvenile Justice and Delinquency Prevention. (2002). Trends in juvenile violent offending: An analysis of victim survey data. *OJJDP Bulletin,* October, pp. 1ff.

Ogbu, J. (1974). *The next generation: An ethnography of education in an urban neighborhood.* New York: Academic Press.

Ogle, J. P., & Damhorst, M. L., (2003). Mothers' and daughters' interpersonal approaches to body and dieting. *Journal of Family Influence, 24,* 448–487.

Ogletree, M. D., Jones, R. M., & Coyl, D. D. (2002). Fathers and their adolescent sons: Pubertal development and paternal involvement. *Journal of Adolescent Research, 17*(4), 418–424.

Ohannessian, C., Lerner, R., Lerner, J., & von Eye, A. (1994). A longitudinal study of perceived family adjustment and emotional adjustment in early adolescence. *Journal of Early Adolescence, 14,* 371–390.

Ohida, T., Osaki, Y., Doi, Y., Tanihata, T., Minowa, M., Suzuki, K., Wada, K., Suzuki, K., & Kaneita, Y., (2004). An epidemiologic stud of self-reported sleep problems among Japanese adolescents. *Sleep, 27,* 978–985.

Olatunji, A. N. (2005). Dropping out of high school among Mexican-origin youths: Is early work experience a factor? *Harvard Educational Review, 75,* 286–305.

Olweus, D. (1993). Victimization by peers: Antecedents and long-term outcomes. In K. Rubin & J. Asendorf (Eds.), *Social withdrawal, inhibition, and shyness in childhood.* Hillsdale, NJ: Erlbaum.

O'Malley, P., & Bachman, J. (1983). Self-esteem: Change and stability between ages 13 and 23. *Developmental Psychology, 19,* 257–268.

O'Malley, P., & Johnston, L. (1999). Drinking and driving among U.S. high school seniors, 1984–1997. *American Journal of Public Health, 89,* 678–684.

Oppedal, B., Røysamb, E., & Sam, D.L. (2004). The effect of acculturation and social support on change in mental health among young immigrants. *International Journal of Behavioral Development, 28,* 481–494.

Orlando, M., Ellickson, P. L., & Jinnett, K. (2001). The temporal relationship between emotional distress and cigarette smoking during adolescence and young adulthood. *Journal of Consulting and Clinical Psychology, 69*(6), 959–970.

Orlando, M., Tucker, J. S., Ellickson, P., & Klein, D. (2004). Developmental trajectories of cigarette smoking and their correlates from early adolescence to young adulthood. *Journal of Consulting and Clinical Psychology, 72,* 400–410.

Orlofsky, J., Marcia, J., & Lesser, I. (1973). Ego identity status and the intimacy versus isolation crisis of young adulthood. *Journal of Personality and Social Psychology, 27,* 211–219.

Orr, D., Beiter, M., & Ingersoll, G. (1991). Premature sexual activity as an indicator of psychosocial risk. *Pediatrics, 87,* 141–147.

Orr, D., & Langefeld, C. (1993). Factors associated with condom use by sexually active male adolescents at risk for sexually transmitted disease. *Pediatrics, 91,* 873–879.

Orr, E., & Ben-Eliahu, E., (1993). Gender differences in idiosyncratic sex-typed self-images and self-esteem. *Sex Roles, 29,* 271–296.

Ortiz, J., & Raine, A. (2004). Heart rate level and antisocial behavior in children and adolescents. *Journal of the American Academy of Child and Adolescent Psychiatry, 43,* 154–162.

Osgood, D. W., & Anderson, A. (2004). Unstructured socializing and rates of delinquency. *Criminology, 42,* 519–549.

Osgood, D. W., Anderson, A., & Shafer, J. (2005). Unstructured leisure in the after-school hours. In J. Mahoney, R. Larson, & J. Eccles (Eds.), *Organized activities as contexts of development,* pp. 45–64. Hillsdale, NJ: Erlbaum.

Osgood, D. W., Wilson, J., O'Malley, P., Bachman, J., & Johnston, L. (1996). Routine activities and individual deviant behavior. *American Sociological Review, 61,* 635–655.

Osgood, W., Ruth, G., Eccles, J., Jacobs, J., & Barber, B. (2005). Six paths to adulthood. In R. Settersten, R., Furstenberg, F., Jr., & R. Rumbaut (Eds.), *On the frontier of adulthood,* pp. 340–355. Chicago: University of Chicago Press.

Osofsky, J. (1995). The effects of exposure to violence on young children. *American Psychologist, 50,* 782–788.

Oswald, H., Bahne, J., & Feder, M. (1994, February). Love and sexuality in adolescence: Gender-specific differences in East and West Berlin. Paper presented at the biennial meetings of the Society for Research on Adolescence, San Diego.

Otterblad Olausson, P., Haglund, B., Ringback Weitoft, G., & Cnattingius, S. (2001). Teenage childbearing and long-term socioeconomic consequences: A case study in Sweden. *Family Planning Perspectives, 33*(2), 70–74.

Overbaugh, K., & Allen, J. (1994). The adolescent athlete, II: Injury patterns and prevention. *Journal of Pediatric Health Care, 8,* 203–211.

Overton, W. (1990). Competence and procedures: Constraints on the development of logical reasoning. In W. Overton (Ed.), *Rea-soning, necessity, and logic: Developmental perspectives,* pp. 1–32. Hillsdale, NJ: Erlbaum.

Owen, J. (1995). *Why our kids don't study.* Baltimore: Johns Hopkins University Press.

Owens, T., Mortimer, J., & Finch, M. (1996). Self-determination as a source of self-esteem in adolescence. *Social Forces, 74,* 1377–1404.

Oxford, M. L., Gilchrist, L. D., Lohr, M. J., Gillmore, M. R., Morrison, D. M., & Spieker, S. J. (2005). Life course heterogeneity in the transition from adolescence to adulthood among adolescent mothers. *Journal of Research on Adolescence, 15,* 479–504.

Oyserman, D., & Markus, H. (1990). Possible selves and delinquency. *Journal of Personality and Social Psychology, 59,* 112–125.

Oyserman, D., Radin, N., & Benn, R. (1993). Dynamics in a three-generational family: Teens, grandparents, and babies. *Developmental Psychology, 29,* 564–572.

Ozer, E., Macdonald, T., & Irwin, C., Jr. (2002). Adolescent health: Implications and projections for the new millennium. In J. Mortimer & R. Larson (Eds.), *The changing adolescent experience: Societal trends and the transition to adulthood.* New York: Cambridge University Press

Ozer, E. J. (2005). The impact of violence on urban adolescents: Longitudinal effects of perceived school connection and family support. *Journal of Adolescent Research, 20,* 167–192.

Pabon, E., Rodriguez, O., & Gurin, G. (1992). Clarifying peer relations and delinquency. *Youth and Society, 24,* 149–165.

Padilla, A. M., & Gonzalez, R. (2001). Academic performance of immigrant and U.S.-born Mexican heritage students: Effects of schooling in Mexico and bilingual/English language instruction. *American Educational Research Journal, 38*(3), 727–742.

Paikoff, R., & Brooks-Gunn, J. (1991). Do parent–child relationships change during puberty? *Psychological Bulletin, 110,* 47–66.

Paikoff, R., Parfenoff, S., Williams, S., McCormick, A., Greenwood, G., & Holmbeck, G. (1997). Parenting, parent–child relationships, and sexual possibility situations among urban African American preadolescents: Preliminary findings and implications for HIV prevention. *Journal of Family Psychology, 11,* 11–22.

Paley, B., Conger, R. D., & Harold, G. T. (2000). Parents' affect, adolescent cognitive representations, and adolescent social development. *Journal of Marriage and the Family, 62*(3), 761–776.

Panchaud, C., Singh, S., Feivelson, D., & Darroch, J. E. (2000). Sexually transmitted diseases among adolescents in developed countries. *Family Planning Perspectives, 32*(1), 24–32, 45.

Paquette, J., & Underwood, M. (1999). Gender differences in young adolescents' experiences of peer victimization: Social and physical aggression. *Merrill-Palmer Quarterly, 45,* 242–266.

Pardini, D. A., Loeber, R., & Stouthamer-Loeber, M. (2005). Developmental shifts in parent and peer influences on boys' beliefs about delinquent behavior. *Journal of Research on Adolescence 15,* 299–323.

Parke, R. (1988). Families in life-span perspective: A multilevel developmental approach. In E. M. Hetherington & M. Perlmutter (Eds.), *Child development in life-span perspective,* pp. 159–190. Hillsdale, NJ: Erlbaum.

Parke, R. D., & Buriel, R. (1998). Socialization in the family: Ethnic and ecological perspectives. In W. Damon (Series Ed.) & N. Eisenberg (Vol. Ed.), *Handbook of child psychology* (5th ed.), pp. 463–552. New York: Wiley.

Parker, J., & Asher, S. (1987). Peer acceptance and later personal adjustment. Are low accepted children at risk? *Psychological Bulletin, 102,* 357–389.

Parker, J., Low, C., & Wargo, J. (1999, April). Children's jealousy over their friends' friends: Personal and relational correlates in preadolescent and adolescent boys and girls. Paper presented at the biennial meetings of the Society for Research in Child Development, Albuquerque.

Parker, J., Low, C., Walker, A. R., & Gamm, B. K. (2005). Friendship jealousy in young adolescents: Individual differences and links to sex, self-esteem, aggression, and social adjustment. *Developmental Psychology, 41,* 235–250.

Parker, J., & Seal, J. (1996). Forming, losing, renewing, and replacing friendships: Applying temporal parameters to the assessment of children's friendship experiences. *Child Development, 67,* 2248–2268.

Parkhurst, J., & Asher, S. (1992). Peer rejection in middle school: Subgroup differences in behavior, loneliness, and interpersonal concerns. *Developmental Psychology, 28,* 231–241.

Paschall, M., & Hubbard, M. (1998). Effects of neighborhood and family stressors on African American male adolescents' self-worth and propensity for violent behavior. *Journal of Consulting and Clinical Psychology, 66*(5), 825–831.

Paschall, M. J., Flewelling, R. L., & Russell, T. (2004). Why is work intensity associated with heavy alcohol use among adolescents? *Journal of Adolescent Health, 34,* 79–87.

Paschall, M. J., Freisthler, B., & Lipton, R. I. (2005). Moderate alcohol use and depression in young adults: Findings from a national longitudinal study. *American Journal of Public Health, 95,* 453–457.

Pasley, K., & Gecas, V. (1984). Stresses and satisfactions of the parental role. *Personnel and Guidance Journal, 2,* 400–404.

Pastore, D., Fisher, M., & Friedman, S. (1996). Abnormalities in weight status, eating attitudes, and eating behaviors among urban high school students: Correlations with self-esteem and anxiety. *Journal of Adolescent Health, 18*, 312–319.

Pasupathi, M., Staudinger, U. M., & Baltes, P. B. (2001). Seeds of wisdom: Adolescents' knowledge and judgment about difficult life problems. *Developmental Psychology, 37*(3), 351–361.

Paternoster, R., Bushway, S., Brame, R., & Apel, R. (2003). The effect of teenage employment on delinquency and problem behaviors. *Social Forces, 82*, 297–335.

Patrikakou, E. (1996). Investigating the academic achievement of adolescents with learning disabilities: A structural modeling approach. *Journal of Education Psychology, 88*, 435–450.

Patten, C. A., Choi, W. S., Gillin, C. J., & Pierce, J. P. (2000). Depressive symptoms and cigarette smoking predict development and persistence of sleep problems in U. S. adolescents. *Pediatrics, 106*(2), Article e23.

Patterson, G. (1986). Performance models for antisocial boys. *American Psychologist, 41*, 432–444.

Patterson, G., DeBaryshe, B., & Ramsey, E. (1989). A developmental perspective on antisocial behavior. *American Psychologist, 44*, 329–335.

Patterson, G., DeGarmo, D., & Knutson, M. (2000). Hyperactive and antisocial behaviors: Comorbid or two points in the same process? *Development and Psychopathology, 12*, 91–106.

Patterson, G., Forgatch, M., Yoerger, K., & Stoolmiller, M. (1998). Variables that initiate and maintain an early-onset trajectory for juvenile offending. *Development and Psychopathology, 10*, 531–547.

Patterson, G., & Stoolmiller, M. (1991). Replications of a dual failure model for boys' depressed mood. *Journal of Consulting and Clinical Psychology, 59*, 491–498.

Patton, W., & Mannison, M. (1995). Sexual coercion in high school dating. *Sex Roles, 33*, 447–457.

Paul, C., Fitzjohn, J., Herbison, P., & Dickson, N. (2000). The determinants of sexual intercourse before age 16. *Journal of Adolescent Health, 27*(2), 136–147.

Paul, J. (1993). Childhood cross-gender behavior and adult homosexuality: The resurgence of biological models of sexuality. *Journal of Homosexuality, 24*, 41–54.

Paulson, S. (1994). Relations of parenting style and parental involvement with ninth-grade students' achievement. *Journal of Early Adolescence, 14*, 250–267.

Paus, T., Zijdenbos, A., Worsley, K., Collins, D. L., Blumenthal, J., Giedd, J. N., Rapoport, J. L., &

Evans, A. C. (1999). Structural maturation of neural pathways in children and adolescents: In vivo study. *Science, 283*, 1908–1911.

Pavlidis, K., & McCauley, E. (1995, March). Autonomy and relatedness in family interactions with depressed adolescents. Paper presented at the biennial meetings of the Society for Research in Child Development, Indianapolis.

Paxton, S., Wertheim, E., Gibbons, K., Szmukler, G., Hillier, L., & Petrovich, J. (1991). Body image satisfaction, dieting beliefs, and weight loss behaviors in adolescent girls and boys. *Journal of Youth and Adolescence, 20*, 361–380.

Pearce, M. J., Jones, S. M., Schwab-Stone, M. E., & Ruchkin, V. (2003). The protective effects of religiousness and parent involvement on the development of conduct problems among youth exposed to violence. *Child Development, 74*, 1682–1696.

Pechmann, C., Levine, L., Loughlin, S., & Leslie, F. (2005). Impulsive and self-conscious: Adolescents' vulnerability to advertising and promotion. *Journal of Public Policy and Marketing, 24*, 202–221.

Pedersen, S., Seidman, E., Yoshikawa, H., Rivera, A. C., Allen, L., & Aber, J. L. (2005). Contextual competence: Multiple manifestations among urban adolescents. *American Journal of Community Psychology, 35*, 65–82.

Pellegrini, A. D. (2003). Perceptions and functions of play and real fighting in early adolescence. *Child Development, 74*, 1522–1533.

Pellerin, L. A. (2005). Student disengagement and the socialization styles of high schools. *Social Forces, 84*, 1159–1179.

Penner, D., & Klahr, D. (1996). The interaction of domain-specific knowledge and domain-general discovery strategies: A study with sinking objects. *Child Development, 67*, 2709–2727.

Pennington, H. (2003). Accelerating advancement in school and work. In D. Ravitch (Ed.), *Brookings papers on education policy.* Washington, DC: Brookings Institution.

Perez-Febles, A., Allison, K., & Burton, L. (April, 1999). Sociocultural context and the construction of research questions: The case of adolescent childbearing. Paper presented at the biennial meetings of the Society for Research on Child Development, Albuquerque.

Perie, M., Grigg, W. S., & Dion, G. S. (2005). *The nation's report card: Mathematics 2005* (NCES 2006-453). U.S. Department of Education, Institute of Education Sciences, National Center for Education Statistics. Washington, DC: U.S. Government Printing Office.

Perkins, C. (1997). *Age patterns of victims of serious violent crime.* Washington, DC: U.S. Department of Justice.

Perkins, D., Jacobs, J. E., Barber, B. L., & Eccles, J. (2003). Childhood and adolescent sports

participation as predictors of participation in sports and physical fitness activities during young adulthood. *Youth and Society, 35*, 295–520.

Perkins, D., Luster, T., & Jank, W. (2002). Protective factors, physical abuse, and purging from community-wide surveys of female adolescents. *Journal of Adolescent Research, 17*(4), 377–400.

Perosa, L., Perosa, S., & Tam, H. (1996). The contribution of family structure and differentiation to identity development in females. *Journal of Youth and Adolescence, 25*, 817–837.

Perry, C., Williams, C., Veblen-Mortenson, S., Toomey, T., Komro, K., Anstine, P., McGivern, P., Finnegan, J., Forster, J., Wagenar, A., & Wolfson, M. (1996). Project Northland: Outcomes of a communitywide alcohol use prevention program during early adolescence. *American Journal of Public Health, 86*, 956–965.

Peskin, H. (1967). Pubertal onset and ego functioning: A psychoanalytic approach. *Journal of Abnormal Psychology, 72*, 1–15.

Peskin, H. (1973). Influence of the developmental schedule of puberty on learning and ego functioning. *Journal of Youth and Adolescence, 2*, 273–290.

Petersen, A. (1985). Pubertal development as a cause of disturbance: Myths, realities, and unanswered questions. *Genetic, Social, and General Psychology Monographs, 111*, 205–232.

Petersen, A. (1988). Adolescent development. *Annual Review of Psychology, 39*, 583–607.

Petersen, A., Compas, B., Brooks-Gunn, J., Stemmler, M., Ey, S., & Grant, K. (1993). Depression in adolescence. *American Psychologist, 48*, 155–168.

Petersen, A., Sarigiani, P., & Kennedy, R. (1991). Adolescent depression: Why more girls? *Journal of Youth and Adolescence, 20*, 247–272.

Petersen, A., & Taylor, B. (1980). The biological approach to adolescence: Biological change and psychological adaptation. In J. Adelson (Ed.), *Handbook of adolescent psychology*, pp. 117–155. New York: Wiley.

Peterson, P., Hawkins, J., Abbott, R., & Catalano, R. (1994). *Journal of Research on Adolescence, 4*, 203–227.

Petraitis, J., Flay, B., & Miller, T. (1995). Reviewing theories of adolescent substance use: Organizing pieces in the puzzle. *Psychological Bulletin, 117*, 67–86.

Pettit, G., Bates, J., Dodge, K., & Meece, D. (1999). The impact of after-school peer contact on early adolescent externalizing problems is moderated by parental monitoring, perceived neighborhood safety, and prior adjustment. *Child Development, 70*, 768–778.

Phares, V., Steinberg, A. R., & Thompson, J. K. (2004). Gender differences in peer and parental influences: Body image disturbance, self-worth, and psychological functioning in preadolescent children. *Journal of Youth and Adolescence, 33,* 421–429.

Phelan, P., Yu, H., & Davidson, A. (1994). Navigating the psychosocial pressures of adolescence: The voices and experiences of high school youth. *American Educational Research Journal, 31,* 415–447.

Philliber, S., Kaye, J., Herrling, S., & West, E. (2002). Preventing pregnancy and improving health care access among teenagers: An evaluation of the Children's Aid Society–Carrera program. *Perspectives on Sexual and Reproductive Health, 34*(5), 244.

Phillipsen, L. C. (1999). Associations between age, gender, and group acceptance and three components of friendship quality. *Journal of Early Adolescence, 19*(4), 438–464.

Phinney, J., & Alipuria, L. (1987). Ethnic identity in older adolescents from four ethnic groups. Paper presented at the biennial meetings of the Society for Research in Child Development, Baltimore.

Phinney, J., Cantu, C., & Kurtz, D. (1997). Ethnic and American identity as predictors of self-esteem among African American, Latino, and White adolescents. *Journal of Youth and Adolescence, 26,* 165–185.

Phinney, J., & Chavira, V. (1995). Parental ethnic socialization and adolescent coping with problems related to ethnicity. *Journal of Research on Adolescence, 5,* 31–53.

Phinney, J., & Devich-Navarro, M. (1997). Variations in bicultural identification among African American and Mexican American adolescents. *Journal of Research on Adolescence, 7,* 3–32.

Phinney, J., Devich-Navarro, M., DuPont, S., Estrada, A., & Onwughala, M. (1994, February). Bicultural identity orientations of African American and Mexican American adolescents. Paper presented at the biennial meetings of the Society for Research on Adolescence, San Diego.

Phinney, J., DuPont, S., Espinosa, C., Revill, J., & Sanders, K. (1994). Ethnic identity and American identification among ethnic minority adolescents. In F. van de Vijver (Ed.), *Proceedings of 1992 conference of the international association for cross-cultural psychology.* Tilburg, Netherlands: Tilburg University Press.

Phinney, J., Ferguson, D., & Tate, J. (1997). Intergroup attitudes among ethnic minority adolescents: A causal model. *Child Development, 68,* 955–969.

Phinney, J., & Ong, A. D. (2002). Adolescent–parent disagreements and life satisfaction in families from Vietnamese- and European-American backgrounds. *Journal of Behavioral Development, 26*(6), 556–561.

Phinney, J., Romero, I., Nava, M., & Huang, D. (2001). The role of language, parents, and peers in ethnic identity among adolescents in immigrant families. *Journal of Youth and Adolescence, 30*(2), 135–153.

Pierce, J., & Gilpin, E. (1996). How long will today's new adolescent smoker be addicted to cigarettes? *American Journal of Public Health, 86,* 253–256.

Pierce, K. (1993). Socialization of teenage girls through teen-magazine fiction: The making of a new woman or an old lady? *Sex Roles, 29,* 59–68.

Pietilainen, K. H., Kaprio, J., Rasanen, M., Winter, T., Rissanen, A., & Rose, R. (2001). Tracking of body size from birth to late adolescence: Contributions of birth length, birth weight, duration of gestation, parents' body size, and twinship. *American Journal of Epidemiology, 154*(1), 21–29.

Pike, A., McGuire, S., Hetherington, E. M., Reiss, D., et al. (1996). Family environment and adolescent depressive symptoms and antisocial behavior: A multivariate genetic analysis. *Developmental Psychology, 32,* 590–604.

Pilgrim, C., Luo, Q., Urberg, K. A., & Fang, X. (1999). Influence of peers, parents, and individual characteristics on adolescent drug use in two cultures. *Merrill-Palmer Quarterly, 45,* 85–107.

Pilkington, N., & D'Augelli, A. (1995). Victimization of lesbian, gay, and bisexual youth in community settings. *Journal of Community Psychology, 23,* 34–56.

Pillay, Y. (2005). Racial identity as a predictor of the psychological health of African American students at a predominantly white university. *Journal of Black Psychology, 31,* 46–66.

Pine, D., Cohen, P., Gurley, D., Brook, J., & Ma,Y. (1998). The risk for early-adulthood anxiety and depressive disorders in adolescents with anxiety and depressive disorders. *Archives of General Psychiatry, 55,* 56–64.

Pine, D., Grun, J., Fyer, A., Zarahn, E., Koda, V., Szeszko, P., Ardekani, B., Li W., & Bilder, R. (2000). Cortical brain regions engaged by masked emotional faces in adolescents and adults: An fMRI study. Manuscript submitted for publication.

Pine, D., Walkup, J. T., Labellarte, M. J., Riddle, M. A., Greenhill, L., Klein, R., et al. (2001). Fluvoxamine for the treatment of anxiety disorders in children and adolescents. *New England Journal of Medicine, 344*(17), 1279–1285.

Pine, D., Wasserman, G., Coplan, J., Fried, J., Huang, Y., Kassir, S., Greenhill, L., Shaffer, D., & Parsons, B. (1996). Platelet serotonin 2A ($5HT_{2A}$) receptor characteristics and parenting factors for boys at risk for delinquency: A preliminary report. *American Journal of Psychiatry, 153,* 538–544.

Pinquart, M., & Silbereisen, R. K. (2002). Changes in adolescents' and mothers' auton-

omy and connectedness in conflict discussions: An observation study. *Journal of Adolescence, 25*(5), 509–522.

Pintrich, P. (2000). Multiple goals, multiple pathways: The role of goal orientation in learning and achievement. *Journal of Educational Psychology, 92*(3), 544–555.

Pintrich, P., Roeser, R., & De Groot, E. (1994). Classroom and individual differences in early adolescents' motivation and self-regulated learning. *Journal of Early Adolescence, 14,* 139–161.

Piquero, A., & Chung, H. L. (2001). On the relationship between gender, early onset, and the seriousness of offending. *Journal of Criminal Justice, 29,* 189–206.

Piquero, A., Farrington, D., & Blumstein, A. (2003). The criminal career paradigm. In M. Tonry (Ed.), Crime and justice: A review of research, Vol. 30, pp. 359–506. Chicago: University of Chicago Press.

Pitner, R. O., Astor, R. A., Benbenishty, R., Haj-Yahia, M. M., & Zeira, A. (2003). The effects of group stereotypes on adolescents' reasoning about peer retribution. *Child Development, 74,* 413–425.

Pittman, L. D., & Chase-Lansdale, P. (2001). African American adolescent girls in impoverished communities: Parenting style and adolescent outcomes. *Journal of Research on Adolescence, 11*(2), 199–224.

Pleck, J., Sonenstein, F., & Ku, L. (1994). Problem behaviors and masculinity ideology in adolescent males. In R. Ketterlinus & M. Lamb. (Eds.), *Adolescent problem behaviors: Issues and research,* pp. 165–186. Hillsdale, NJ: Erlbaum.

Plomin, R., & Daniels, D. (1987). Why are children in the same family so different from one another? *Behavioral and Brain Sciences, 10,* 1–60.

Plumert, J. (1994). Flexibility in children's use of spatial and categorical organizational strategies in recall. *Developmental Psychology, 30,* 738–747.

Poe-Yamagata, E., & Jones, M. (2000). *And justice for some: Differential treatment of minority youth in the justice system.* Washington, DC: Youth Law Center.

Pogarsky, G., Lizotte, A. J., & Thornberry, T. P. (2003). The delinquency of children born to young mothers: Results from the Rochester Youth Development Study. *Criminology, 41,* 1249–1286.

Polce-Lynch, M., Myers, B., Kilmartin, C., Forssmann-Falck, R., & Kliewer, W. (1998). Gender and age patterns in emotional expression, body image, and self-esteem: A qualitative analysis. *Sex Roles, 38,* 1025–1048.

Polce-Lynch, M., Myers, B. J., Kliewer, W., & Kilmartin, C. (2001). Adolescent self-esteem and gender: Exploring relations to sexual harassment, body image, media influence, and emotional expression. *Journal of Youth and Adolescence, 30,* 225–244.

Pollack, C., & Bright, D. (2003). Caffeine consumption and weekly sleep patterns in U.S. seventh-, eighth-, and ninth-graders. *Pediatrics, 111*(1), 42–46.

Pomerantz, E. (2001). Parent–child socialization: Implications for the development of depressive symptoms. *Journal of Family Psychology, 15*(3), 510–525.

Pomerantz, E., Altermatt, E., & Saxon, J. L. (2002). Making the grade but feeling distressed: Gender differences in academic performance and internal distress. *Journal of Educational Psychology, 94*(2), 396–404.

Pong, S. (1997). Family structure, school context and eighth-grade math and reading achievement. *Journal of Marriage and the Family, 59,* 734–746.

Pong, S. (1998). The school compositional effect of single parenthood on 10th-grade achievement. *Sociology of Education, 71,* 23–42.

Pong, S., & Ju, D. (2000). The effects of change in family structure and income on dropping out in middle and high school. *Journal of Family Issues, 21,* 147–169.

Pope, A., & Bierman, K. (1999). Predicting adolescent peer problems and antisocial activities: The relative roles of aggression and dysregulation. *Developmental Psychology, 35,* 335–346.

Portes, A., & MacLeod, D. (1996). Educational progress of children of immigrants: The roles of class, ethnicity, and school context. *Sociology of Education, 69,* 255–275.

Poulin, F., Dishion, T., & Haas, E. (1999). The peer influence paradox: Friendship quality and deviancy training within male adolescent friendships. *Merrill-Palmer Quarterly, 45,* 42–61.

Powell, A., Farrar, E., & Cohen, D. (1985). *The shopping mall high school.* Boston: Houghton Mifflin.

Pratt, M. W., Skoe, E. E., & Arnold, M. L. (2004). Care reasoning development and family socialisation patterns in later adolescence: A longitudinal analysis. *International Journal of Behavioural Development, 28,* 139–147.

Prelow, H., Danoff-Burg, S., Swenson, R., & Pulgiano, D. (2004). The impact of ecological risk and perceived discrimination on the psychological adjustment of African American and European American youth. *Journal of Community Psychology, 32,* 375–389.

Prelow, H., & Loukas, A. (2003). The role of resource, protective, and risk factors in academic achievement–related outcomes of economically disadvantaged Latino youth. *Journal of Community Psychology, 31,* 513–529.

President's Science Advisory Committee. (1974). *Youth: Transition to adulthood.* Chicago: University of Chicago Press.

Prinstein, M, Meade, C., & Cohen, G. (2003). Adolescent oral sex, peer popularity, and perceptions of best friends' sexual behavior. *Journal of Pediatric Psychology, 28,* 243–249.

Prinstein, M. J., & Aikins, J. W. (2004). Cognitive moderators of the longitudinal association between peer rejection and adolescent depressive symptoms. *Journal of Abnormal Child Psychology, 32,* 147–158.

Prinstein, M. J., & Cillessen, A. H. (2003). Forms and functions of adolescent peer aggression associated with high levels of peer status. *Merrill-Palmer Quarterly, 49,* 310–342.

Prinstein, M. J., & Greca, A. M. L. (2004). Childhood peer rejection and aggression as predictors of adolescent girls' externalizing and health risk behaviors: A 6-year longitudinal study. *Journal of Consulting and Clinical Psychology, 71,* 103–112.

Prinstein, M. J., & La Greca, A. M. (2002). Peer crowd affiliation and internalizing distress in childhood and adolescence: A longitudinal follow-back study. *Journal of Research on Adolescence, 12*(3), 325–351.

Prosser, E., & Carlson, C. (April, 1999). Ethnic differences in fluctuations in female self-esteem during early adolescence. Paper presented at the biennial meetings of the Society for Research on Child Development, Albuquerque.

Public Agenda. (1997). *Getting by: What American teenagers really think about their schools.* New York: Public Agenda.

Public Agenda. (1999). *Kids these days '99: What Americans really think about the next generation.* New York: Public Agenda.

Punamaki, R., Qouta, S., et al. (1997). Models of traumatic experiences and children's psychological adjustment: The roles of perceived parenting and the children's own resources and activity. *Child Development, 68,* 718–728.

Punch, S. (2004). The impact of primary education on school-to-work transitions for young people in rural Bolivia. *Youth and Society, 36,* 163–182.

Pungello, E., Kupersmidt, J., Burchinal, M., & Patterson, C. (1996). Environmental risk factors and children's achievement from middle childhood to early adolescence. *Developmental Psychology, 32,* 755–767.

Purdie, N., Hattie, J., & Douglas, G. (1996). Student conceptions of learning and their use of self-regulated learning strategies: A cross-cultural comparison. *Journal of Educational Psychology, 88,* 87–100.

Quadrel, M., Fischhoff, B., & Davis, W. (1993). Adolescent (in)vulnerability. *American Psychologist, 48,* 102–116.

Quatman, T., Sokolik, E., & Smith, K. (2000). Adolescent perception of peer success: A gendered perspective over time. *Sex Roles, 43*(1–2), 61–84.

Quillian, L., & Campbell, M. E. (2003). Beyond black and white: The present and future of multiracial friendship segregation. *American Sociological Review, 68,* 540–566.

Quintana, S., Castaneda-English, P., & Ybarra, V. C. (1999). Role of perspective-taking abilities and ethnic socialization in development of adolescent ethnic identity. *Journal of Research on Adolescence, 9,* 161–184.

Raeff, C. (1997). Individuals in relationships: Cultural values, children's social interactions, and the development of an American individualistic self. *Developmental Review, 17,* 205–238.

Raffaelli, M. (1997). Young adolescents' conflicts with siblings and friends. *Journal of Youth and Adolescence, 26*(5), 539–558.

Raffaelli, M., & Crockett, L. J. (2003). Sexual risk taking in adolescence: The role of self-regulation and attraction to risk. *Developmental Psychology, 39,* 1036–1046.

Raffaelli, M., & Green, S. (2003). Parent–adolescent communication about sex: Retrospective reports by Latino college students. *Journal of Marriage and the Family, 65,* 474.

Raffaelli, M., & Larson, R. (1987). Sibling interactions in late childhood and early adolescence. Paper presented at the biennial meetings of the Society for Research in Child Development, Baltimore.

Raine, A., Loeber, R., Stouthamer-Loeber, M., Moffitt, T. E., Caspi, A., & Lynam, D. (2005). Neurocognitive impairments in boys on the life-course persistent antisocial path. *Journal of Abnormal Psychology, 114,* 38–49.

Ramirez-Valles, J., Zimmerman, M. A., & Juarez, L. (2002). Gender differences of neighborhood and social control processes: A study of the timing of first intercourse among low-achieving, urban, African American youth. *Youth and Society, 33*(3), 418–441.

Randel, B., Stevenson, H. W., & Witruk, E. (2000). Attitudes, beliefs, and mathematics achievement of German and Japanese high school students. *International Journal of Behavioral Development, 24*(2), 190–198.

Rankin, J. L., Lane, D. J., Gibbons, F. X., & Gerrard, M. (2004). Adolescent self-consciousness: Longitudinal age changes and gender differences in two cohorts. *Journal of Research on Adolescence, 14,* 1–21.

Raskin-White, H., Bates, M. E., & Buyske, S. (2001). Adolescence-limited versus persistent delinquency: Extending Moffitt's hypothesis into adulthood. *Journal of Abnormal Psychology, 110*(4), 600–609.

Ravitch, D. (1995). *National standards in American education: A citizen's guide.* Washington, DC: Brookings Institution.

Ravitch, D. (2000). *Left back: A century of failed school reforms.* New York: Simon & Schuster.

Ravitch, D. (Ed.). (2001). *Brookings papers on education policy.* Washington, DC: Brookings Institution.

Ready, D. D., Lee, V. E., & Welner, K. G. (2004). Educational equity and school structure: School size, overcrowding, and schools-within-schools. *Teachers College Review, 106,* 1989–2014.

Ream, G. L., & Savin Williams, R. C. (2005). Reciprocal associations between adolescent sexual activity and quality of youth–parent interactions. *Journal of Family Psychology, 19,* 171–179.

Reddy, R., Rhodes, J. E., & Mulhall, P. (2003). The influence of teacher support on student adjustment in the middle school years: A latent growth curve study. *Development and Psychopathology, 15,* 119–138.

Redlich, A. D., & Goodman, G. S. (2003). Taking responsibility for an act not committed: The influence of age and suggestibility. *Law and Human Behavior, 27*(2), 141–156.

Redlich, A. D., Silverman, A. D., & Steiner, H. (2003). Pre-adjudicative competence in juveniles and young adults. *Behavioral Sciences and the Law, 21,* 393–410.

Reese-Weber, M. (2000). Middle and late adolescents' conflict resolution skills and siblings: Associations with interparental and parent–adolescent conflict resolution. *Journal of Youth and Adolescence, 29*(6), 697–711.

Reich, K., Oser, F., & Valentin, P. (1994). Knowing why I now know better: Children's and youth's explanations of their worldview changes. *Journal of Research on Adolescence, 4,* 151–173.

Reimer, M. (1996). "Sinking into the ground": The development and consequences of shame in adolescence. *Developmental Review, 16,* 321–363.

Reimer, M., Overton, W., Steidl, J., Rosenstein, D., & Horowitz, H. (1996). Familial responsiveness and behavioral control: Influences on adolescent psychopathology, attachment, and cognition. *Journal of Research on Adolescence, 6,* 87–112.

Reis, O., & Youniss, J. (2004). Patterns in identity change and development in relationships with mothers and friends. *Journal of Adolescent Research, 19,* 31–44.

Reiss D., Hetherington, E. M., Plomin, R., Howe, G., Simmens, S., Henderson S., et al. (1995). Genetic questions for environmental studies. *Archives of General Psychiatry, 52,* 925–936

Renken, B., Egeland, B., Marvinney, D., Mangelsdorf, S., & Sroufe, L. A. (1989). Early childhood antecedents of aggression and passive withdrawal in early elementary school. *Journal of Personality, 57,* 257–282.

Repetti, R. (1996). The effects of perceived daily social and academic failure experiences on school-age children's subsequent interactions with parents. *Child Development, 67,* 1467–1482.

Repinski, D., & Leffert, N. (1994, February). Adolescents' relations with friends: The effects of a psychoeducational intervention. Paper presented at the biennial meetings of the Society for Research on Adolescence, San Diego.

Resnick, M., & Blum, R. (1994). The association of consensual sexual intercourse during childhood with adolescent health risk and behaviors. *Pediatrics, 94,* 907–913.

Resnick, M., Bearman, P., Blum, R., Bauman, K., Harris, K., Jones, J., Tabor, J., Beuhring, T., Sieving, R., Shew, M., Ireland, M., Bearinger, L., & Udry, J. (1997). Protecting adolescents from harm: Findings from the National Longitudinal Study of Adolescent Health. *Journal of the American Medical Association, 278,* 823–832.

Resnick, M., Blum, R., Bose, J., Smith, M., & Toogood, R. (1990). Characteristics of unmarried adolescent mothers: Determinants of child rearing versus adoption. *American Journal of Orthopsychiatry, 60,* 577–583.

Resnicow, K., Ross-Gaddy, D., & Vaughan, R. (1995). Structure of problem and positive behaviors in African American youths. *Journal of Consulting and Clinical Psychology, 63,* 594–603.

Rest, J. (1983). Morality. In J. Flavell & E. Markman (Eds.), *Handbook of child psychology,* Vol. III: *Cognitive development,* pp. 556–629. New York: Wiley.

Rest, J., Davison, M., & Robbins, S. (1978). Age trends in judging moral issues: A review of cross-sectional, longitudinal, and sequential studies of the Defining Issues Test. *Child Development, 49,* 263–279.

Reuman, D. (1989). How social comparison mediates the relation between ability-grouping practices and students' achievement expectancies in mathematics. *Journal of Educational Psychology, 81,* 178–189.

Reviere, S., & Bakeman, R. (1992, March). Measuring multicultural competence: American Whites, American Blacks, and immigrants. Paper presented at the biennial meetings of the Society for Research on Adolescence, Washington, DC.

Reyes, O., & Jason, L. (1993). Pilot study examining factors associated with academic success for Hispanic high school students. *Journal of Youth and Adolescence, 22,* 57–71.

Reyna, V., & Farley, F. (2006). Risk and rationality in adolescent decision making: Implications for theory, practice, and public policy. *Psychological Science in the Public Interest, 7,* 1–44.

Reynolds, A., & Temple, J. (1998). Extended early childhood intervention and school achievement: Age thirteen findings from the Chicago Longitudinal Study. *Child Development, 69,* 231–246.

Reynolds, A., Temple, J., Robertson, D. L., & Mann, E. A. (2001). Long-term effects of an early childhood intervention on educational achievement and juvenile arrest: A 15-year follow-up of low-income children in public schools. *Journal of the American Medical Association, 285,* 2339–2346.

Reynolds, L. K., O'Koon, J. H., Papademetriou, E., Szczygiel, S., & Grant, K. E. (2001). Stress and somatic complaints in low-income urban adolescents. *Journal of Youth and Adolescence, 30*(4), 499–514.

Rhodes, J. (2004). *Stand by me.* Canbridge, MA: Harvard University Press.

Rhodes, J. E., Contreras, J., & Mangelsdorf, S. (1994). Natural mentor relationships among Latina adolescent mothers: Psychological adjustment, moderating processes, and the role of early parental acceptance. *American Journal of Community Psychology, 22,* 211–227.

Rhodes, J. E., Grossman, J. B., & Resche, N. L. (2000). Agents of change: Pathways through which mentoring relationships influence adolescents' academic adjustment. *Child Development, 71*(6), 1662–1671.

Rhodes, J. E., Haight, W. L., & Briggs, E. C. (1999). The influence of mentoring on the peer relationships of foster youth in relative and nonrelative care. *Journal of Research on Adolescence, 9*(2), 185–201.

Ricciardelli, L. A., & McCabe, M. P. (2001). Self-esteem and negative affect as moderators of sociocultural influences on body dissatisfaction, strategies to decrease weight, and strategies to increase muscles among adolescent boys and girls. *Sex Roles, 44*(3–4), 189–207.

Ricciardelli, L. A., & McCabe, M. P. (2004). A biopsychosocial model of disorder eating and the pursuit of muscularity in adolescent boys. *Psychological Bulletin, 130,* 179–205.

Rice, K. (1990). Attachment in adolescence: A narrative and meta-analytic review. *Journal of Youth and Adolescence, 19,* 511–538.

Rice, K., & Mulkeen, P. (1995). Relationships with parents and peers: A longitudinal study of adolescent intimacy. *Journal of Adolescent Research, 10,* 338–357.

Rich, L. M., & Kim, S.-B. (2002). Employment and the sexual and reproductive behavior of female adolescents. *Perspectives on Sexual and Reproductive Health, 34*(3), 127–134.

Richards, M., Boxer, A., Petersen, A., & Albrecht, R. (1990). Relation of weight to body image in pubertal girls and boys from two communities. *Developmental Psychology, 26,* 313–321.

Richards, M., Crowe, P., Larson, R., & Swarr, A. (1998). Developmental patterns and gender differences in the experience of peer companionship during adolescence. *Child Development, 69,* 154–163.

Richards, M., & Larson, R. (1993). Pubertal development and the daily subjective states of young adolescents. *Journal of Research on Adolescence, 3,* 145–169.

Richardson, J., Dwyer, K., McGuigan, K., Hansen, W., Dent, C., Johnson, C., Sussman, S., Brannon, B., & Flay, B. (1989). Substance use among eighth-grade students who take care of themselves after school. *Pediatrics, 84,* 556–566.

Richardson, J., Radziszewska, B., Dent, C., & Flay, B. (1993). Relationship between after-school care of adolescents and substance use, risk taking, depressed mood, and academic achievement. *Pediatrics, 92,* 32–38.

Richardson, L. (1997, September 30). Condoms in school said not to affect teen-age sex rate. *The New York Times,* pp. A1ff.

Richardson, R. (1996, March). Competence in the transition to adulthood: Exploring the influence of adolescent motherhood for low-income, urban, African-American women. Paper presented at the biennial meetings of the Society for Research on Adolescence, Boston.

Ridenour, T. A., Cottier, L. B., Robins, L. N., Campton, W. M., Spitznagel, E. L., & Cunningham-Williams, R. M. (2002). Test of the plausibility of adolescent substance use playing a causal role in developing adulthood antisocial behavior. *Journal of Abnormal Psychology, 111*(1), 144–155.

Riggs, L., Holmbeck, G., Paikoff, R., & Bryant, F. B. (2004). Teen mothers parenting their own teen offspring: The moderating role of parenting support. *Journal of Early Adolescence, 24,* 200–230.

Rigsby, L., & McDill, E. L. (1975). Value orientations of high school students. In H. R. Stub (Ed.), *The sociology of education: A sourcebook* (3rd ed.), pp. 53–74. Homewood, IL: Dorsey.

Riley, T., Adams, G., & Neilsen, E. (1984). Adolescent egocentrism: The association among imaginary audience behavior, cognitive development, and parental support and rejection. *Journal of Youth and Adolescence, 13,* 401–438.

Ringwalt, C., Greene, J., Robertson, M., & McPheeters, M. (1998). The prevalence of homelessness among adolescents in the United States. *American Journal of Public Health, 88,* 1325–1329.

Risch, S. C., Jodl, K. M., & Eccles, J. S. (2004). Role of the father–adolescent relationship in shaping adolescents' attitudes toward divorce. *Journal of Marriage and the Family, 66,* 46.

Ritchey, P. N., Reid, G. S., & Hasse, L. A. (2001). The relative influence of smoking on drinking and drinking on smoking among high school students in a rural tobacco-growing country. *Journal of Adolescent Health, 29*(6), 386–394.

Rivkin, S. (1994). Residential segregation and school integration. *Sociology of Education, 67,* 279–292.

Robbins, C., Kaplan, H., & Martin, S. (1985, August). Antecedents of pregnancy among unmarried adolescents. *Journal of Marriage and the Family,* 567–583.

Robbins, R. N., & Bryan, A. (2004). Relationships between future orientation, impulsive sensation seeking, and risk behavior among adjudicated adolescents. *Journal of Adolescent Research, 19,* 428–445.

Roberts, A., Seidman, E., Pederson, S., Chesir-Teran, D., Allen, L., Aber, J., et al. (2000). Perceived family and peer transactions and self-esteem among urban early adolescents. *Journal of Early Adolescence, 20*(1), 68–92.

Roberts, B., & DelVecchio, W. F. (2000). The rank-order consistency of personality traits from childhood to old age: A quantitative review of longitudinal studies. *Psychological Bulletin, 126*(1), 3–25.

Roberts, B., Caspi, A., & Moffitt, T. E. (2001). The kids are alright: Growth and stability in personality development from adolescence to adulthood. *Journal of Personality and Social Psychology, 81*(4), 670–683.

Roberts, B., O'Donnell, M., & Robins, R.. (2004). Goal and personality trait development in emerging adulthood. *Journal of Personality and Social Psychology, 87,* 541–550.

Roberts, B., Walton, K., & Viechtbauer, W. (2006). Patterns of mean-level change in personality traits across the life course: A meta-analysis of longitudinal studies. *Psychological Bulletin, 132,* 1–25.

Roberts, D. (1993). Adolescents and the mass media: From "Leave It to Beaver" to "Beverly Hills 90210." *Teachers College Record, 94,* 629–644.

Roberts, D., & Foehr, U. (2003). *Kids and media in America: Patterns of use at the millennium.* New York: Cambridge University Press.

Roberts, D., Foeher, U., & Rideout, V. (2005). *Generation M: Media in the lives of 8–18-Year-olds.* Menlo Park, CA: Kaiser Family Foundation.

Roberts, D., Henriksen, L., & Foehr, U. (2004). Adolescents and media. In R. Lerner & L. Steinberg (Eds.), *Handbook of adolescent psychology.* New York: Wiley.

Roberts, R., Roberts, C., & Chen, Y. (1997). Ethnocultural differences in prevalence of adolescent depression. *American Journal of Community Psychology, 25,* 95–110.

Robins, L. (1986). Changes in conduct disorder over time. In D. Farran & J. McKinney (Eds.), *Risk in intellectual and psychosocial development,* pp. 227–259. New York: Academic Press.

Robins, R., John, O., Caspi, A., Moffitt, T., & Stouthamer-Loeber, M. (1996). Resilient, overcontrolled, and undercontrolled boys: Three replicable personality types. *Journal of Personality and Social Psychology, 70,* 157–171.

Robinson, L., Klesges, R., Zbikowski, S., & Glaser, R. (1997). Predictors of risk for different stages of adolescent smoking in a biracial sample. *Journal of Consulting and Clinical Psychology, 65,* 653–662.

Robinson, N. (1995). Evaluating the nature of perceived support and its relation to perceived self-worth in adolescents. *Journal of Research on Adolescence, 5,* 253–280.

Robinson, N., Garber, J., & Hilsman, R. (1995). Cognitions and stress: Direct and moderating effects on depressive versus externalizing symptoms during the junior high school transition. *Journal of Abnormal Psychology, 104,* 453–463.

Roche, K. M., Ensminger, M. E., Chilcoat, H., & Storr, C. (2003). Establishing independence in low-income urban areas: The relationship to adolescent aggressive behavior. *Journal of Marriage and the Family, 65,* 668.

Roderick, M. (1994). Grade retention and school dropout: Investigating the association. *American Educational Research Journal, 31,* 729–759.

Roderick, M., & Camburn, E. (1999). Risk and recovery from course failure in the early years of high school. *American Educational Research Journal, 36*(2), 303–343.

Rodgers, J., & Rowe, D. (1988). Influence of siblings on adolescent sexual behavior. *Developmental Psychology, 24,* 722–728.

Rodgers, J., & Rowe, D. (1993). Social contagion and adolescent sexual behavior: A developmental EMOSA model. *Psychological Review, 100,* 479–510.

Rodgers, K. (1999). Parenting processes related to sexual risk-taking behaviors of adolescent males and females. *Journal of Marriage and the Family, 61,* 99–109.

Rodgers, K., & Rose, H. A. (2002). Risk and resiliency factors among adolescents who experience marital transitions. *Journal of Marriage and the Family, 64*(4), 1024–1037.

Rodkin, P., Farmer, T., Pearl, R., & Van Acker, R. (2000). Heterogeneity of popular boys: Antisocial and prosocial configurations. *Developmental Psychology, 36,* 14–24.

Rodman, H., Pratto, D., & Nelson, R. (1988). Toward a definition of self-care children: A commentary on Steinberg (1986). *Developmental Psychology, 24,* 292–294.

Roe, K. (1995). Adolescents' use of socially disvalued media: Towards a theory of media delinquency. *Journal of Youth and Adolescence, 24,* 617–631.

Roenkae, A., & Pulkkinen, L. (1998). Work involvement and timing of motherhood in the accumulation of problems in social functioning in young women. *Journal of Research on Adolescence, 8,* 221–239.

Roenneberg, T., Kuehnle, T., Pramstaller, P., Ricken, J., Havel, M., Guth, A., & Merrow, M. (2004). A marker for the end of adolescence. *Current Biology, 14,* 1038–1039.

Roeser, R., Eccles, J., & Freedman-Doan, C. (1999). Academic functioning and mental health in adolescence: Patterns, progressions, and routes from childhood. *Journal of Adolescent Research, 14,* 135–174.

Roeser, R., Eccles, J., & Sameroff, A. (1998). Academic and emotional functioning in early adolescence: Longitudinal relations, patterns, and prediction by experience in middle school. *Development and Psychopathology, 10,* 321–352.

Roeser, R., Lord, S., & Eccles, J. (1994, February). A portrait of academic alienation in adolescence: Motivation, mental health, and family experience. Paper presented at the biennial meetings of the Society for Research on Adolescence, San Diego.

Roeser, R., Midgley, C., & Urdan, T. (1996). Perceptions of the school psychological environment and early adolescents' psychological and behavioral functioning in school: The mediating role of goals and belonging. *Journal of Educational Psychology, 88,* 408–422.

Rogers, A. (1993). Voice, play, and a practice of ordinary courage in girls' and women's lives. *Harvard Educational Review, 63,* 265–295.

Rogers, J., Boruch, R., Stoms, G., & DeMoya, D. (1991). Impact of the Minnesota parental notification law on abortion and birth. *American Journal of Public Health, 81,* 294–298.

Rogers, M., & Holmbeck, G. (1997). Effects of brief interparental aggression on children's adjustment: The moderating role of cognitive appraisal and coping. *Journal of Family Psychology, 11,* 125–130.

Rohde, P., Lewinsohn, P. M., Kahler, C. W., Seeley, J. R., & Brown, R. A. (2001). Natural course of alcohol use disorders from adolescence to young adulthood. *Journal of the American Academy of Child and Adolescent Psychiatry, 40,* 83–90.

Rohner, R., Bourque, S., & Elordi, C. (1996). Children's perceptions of corporal punishment, caretaker acceptance, and psychological adjustment in a poor, biracial Southern community. *Journal of Marriage and the Family, 58,* 842–852.

Roisman, G. I. (2002). Beyond main effect models of adolescent work intensity, family closeness and school disengagement: Mediational and conditional hypotheses. *Journal of Adolescent Research, 17*(4), 331–345.

Roisman, G. I., Aguilar, B., & Egeland, B. (2004). Antisocial behavior in the transition to adulthood: The independent and interactive roles of developmental history and emerging developmental tasks. *Development and Psychopathology, 16,* 857–871.

Roisman, G. I., Masten, A. S., Coatsworth, J. D., & Tellegen, A. (2004). Salient and emerging developmental tasks in the transition to adulthood. *Child Development, 75,* 123–133.

Romer, D., Black, M., Ricardo, I., Feigelman, S., Kaljee, L., Galbraith, J., Nesbit, R., Hornik, R., & Stanton, B. (1994). Social influences on the sexual behavior of youth at risk for HIV exposure. *American Journal of Public Health, 84,* 977–985.

Romo, L. F., Lefkowitz, E. S., Sigman, M., & Au, T. K. (2002). A longitudinal study of maternal messages about dating and sexuality and their influence on Latino adolescents. *Journal of Adolescent Health, 31*(1), 59–69.

Rong, X., & Brown, F. (2001). The effects of immigrant generation and ethnicity on educational attainment among young African and Caribbean Blacks in the United States. *Harvard Educational Review, 71*(3), 536–565.

Rönká, A., & Pulkkinen, L. (1995). Accumulation of problems in social functioning in young adulthood: A developmental approach. *Journal of Personality and Social Psychology, 69,* 381–391.

Roosa, M., & Christopher, F. S. (1990). Evaluation of an abstinence-only adolescent pregnancy prevention program: A replication. *Family Relations, 39,* 363–367.

Rosario, M., Rotheram-Borus, M., & Reid, H. (1996). Gay-related stress and its correlates among gay and bisexual adolescents of predominantly black and Hispanic background. *Journal of Community Psychology, 24,* 136–159.

Roscigno, V., & Ainsworth-Darnell, J. (1999). Race, cultural capital and educational resources: Persistent inequalities and achievement returns. *Sociology of Education, 72,* 158–178.

Rose, A. J. (2002). Co-rumination in the friendships of girls and boys. *Child Development, 73*(6), 1830–1843.

Rose, A. J., Swenson, L. P., & Walker, E. M. (2004). Overt and relational aggression and perceived popularity: Developmental differences in concurrent and prospective relations. *Developmental Psychology, 40,* 378–387.

Rose, J., Chassin, L., Presson, C., & Sherman, S. (1999). Peer influences on adolescent cigarette smoking: A prospective sibling analysis. *Merrill-Palmer Quarterly, 45,* 62–84.

Rose, R. (1988). Genetic and environmental variance in content dimensions of the MMPI. *Journal of Personality and Social Psychology, 55,* 302–311.

Rose, S., & Feldman, J. (1995). Prediction of IQ and specific cognitive abilities at 11 years from infancy measures. *Developmental Psychology, 31,* 685–696.

Rosen, B., & D'Andrade, R. (1959). The psychosocial origins of achievement motivation. *Sociometry, 22,* 185–218.

Rosenbaum, J. (1976). *Making inequality: The hidden curriculum of high school tracking.* New York: Wiley.

Rosenbaum, J. (1996). Policy uses of research on the high school-to-work transition. *Sociology of Education,* Extra Issue, 102–122.

Rosenbaum, J., Stern, D., Hamilton, M., Hamilton, S., Berryman, S., & Kazis, R. (1992). *Youth apprenticeship in America: Guidelines for building an effective system.* Washington, DC: William T. Grant Foundation Commission on Youth and America's Future.

Rosenberg, M. (1975). The dissonant context and the adolescent self-concept. In S. Dra-

gastin & G. Elder, Jr. (Eds.), *Adolescence in the life cycle.* Washington, DC: Hemisphere.

Rosenberg, M. (1986). Self concept from middle childhood through adolescence. In J. Suls & A. Greenwald (Eds.), *Psychological perspectives on the self,* Vol. 3. Hillsdale, NJ: Erlbaum.

Rosenberg, M., Schooler, C., & Schoenbach, C. (1989). Self-esteem and adolescent problems: Modeling reciprocal effects. *American Sociological Review, 54,* 1004–1018.

Rosenbloom, S. R., & Way, N. (2004). Experiences of discrimination among African American, Asian American, and Latino adolescents in an urban high school. *Youth and Society, 35,* 420–451.

Rosenblum, G., & Lewis, M. (1999). The relations among body image, physical attractiveness, and body mass in adolescence. *Child Development, 70,* 50–64.

Rosenthal, D. (1994, February). Gendered constructions of adolescent sexuality. Paper presented at the biennial meetings of the Society for Research on Adolescence, San Diego.

Rosenthal, D., & Feldman, S. (1990). The acculturation of Chinese immigrants: The effects on family functioning of length of residence in two cultural contexts. *Journal of Genetic Psychology, 151,* 493–514.

Rosenthal, D., & Smith, A. (1997). Adolescent sexual timetable. *Journal of Youth and Adolescence, 26,* 619–636.

Rosenthal, D., Smith, A., & de Visser, R. (1999). Personal and social factors influencing age at first sexual intercourse. *Archives of Sexual Behavior, 28,* 319–333.

Rosenthal, R., & Jacobson, E. (1968). *Pygmalion in the classroom.* New York: Holt, Rinehart & Winston.

Roth, J., Brooks-Gunn, J., Murray, L., & Foster, W. (1998). Promoting healthy adolescents: Synthesis of youth development program evaluations. *Journal of Research on Adolescence, 8*(4), 423–459.

Rotheram-Borus, M., & Koopman, C. (1991). Sexual risk behaviors, AIDS knowledge, and beliefs about AIDS among runaways. *American Journal of Public Health, 81,* 206–208.

Rotheram-Borus, M., Koopman, C., & Ehrhardt, A. (1991). Homeless youths and HIV infection. *American Psychologist, 46,* 1188–1197.

Rotheram-Borus, M., Lee, M., Murphy, D., Futterman, D., Duan, N., Birnbaum, J., et al. (2001). Efficacy of a preventive intervention for youths living with HIV. *American Journal of Public Health, 91*(3), 400–405.

Rotheram-Borus, M., Marelich, W., & Srinivasan, S. (1999). HIV risk among homosexual, bisexual, and heterosexual male and female youths. *Archives of Sexual Behavior, 28,* 159–177.

Rotheram-Borus, M., & Phinney, J. (1990). Patterns of social expectations among black and Mexican-American children. *Child Development, 61,* 542–556.

Rotheram-Borus, M., Rosario, M., Van Rossem, R., Reid, H., & Gillis, R. (1995). Prevalence, course, and predictors of multiple problem behaviors among gay and bisexual male adolescents. *Developmental Psychology, 31,* 75–85.

Rousseau, J. ([1762]1911). *Emile* (B. Foxley, trans.). London: Dent.

Rowan, B., Chiang, F., & Miller, R. (1997). Using research on employees' performance to study the effects of teachers on students' achievement. *Sociology of Education, 70,* 256–284.

Rowe, D., Jacobson, K., & Van den Oord, E. (1999). Genetic and environmental influences on vocabulary IQ: Parental education level as moderator. *Child Development, 70,* 1151–1162

Rowe, D., Rodgers, J., & Meseck-Bushey, S. (1992). Sibling delinquency and the family environment: Shared and unshared influences. *Child Development, 63,* 59–67.

Rowe, D., Rodgers, J., Meseck-Bushey S., & St. John, C. (1989). Sexual behavior and nonsexual deviance: A sibling study of their relationship. *Developmental Psychology, 25,* 61–69

Rowe, D., Vazsonyi, A., & Flannery, D. (1994). No more than skin deep: Ethnic and racial similarity in developmental processes. *Psychological Review, 101,* 396–413.

Rozin, P., Bauer, R. & Catanese, D. (2003). Food and life, pleasure and worry, among American college students; Gender differences and regional similarities. *Journal of Personality and Social Psychology, 85,* 132–141.

Rubin, K., Chen, X., McDougall, P., Bowker, A., & McKinnon, J. (1995). The Waterloo Longitudinal Project: Predicting internalizing and externalizing problems in adolescence. *Development and Psychopathology, 7,* 751–764.

Rubin, K., LeMare, L., & Lollis, S. (1990). Social withdrawal in childhood: Developmental pathways to peer rejection. In S. Asher & J. Coie (Eds.), *Peer rejection in childhood,* pp. 217–249. New York: Cambridge University Press.

Rubin, Z. (1980). *Children's friendships.* Cambridge, MA: Harvard University Press.

Ruble, D., & Brooks-Gunn, J. (1982). The experience of menarche. *Child Development, 53,* 1557–1566.

Ruck, M., Abramovitch, R., & Keating, D. (1998). Children and adolescents' understanding of rights: Balancing nurturance and self-determination. *Child Development, 64,* 404–417.

Ruck, M., Peterson-Badali, M., & Day, D. M. (2002). Adolescents' and mothers' understanding of children's rights in the home. *Journal of Research on Adolescence, 12*(3), 373–398.

Rudolph, K., & Hammen, C. (1999). Age and gender as determinants of stress exposure, generation, and reactions in youngsters: A transactional perspective. *Child Development, 70,* 660–677.

Rueter, M., & Conger, R. (1995a). Interaction style, problem-solving behavior, and family problem-solving effectiveness. *Child Development, 66,* 98–115.

Rueter, M., & Conger, R. (1995b). Antecedents of parent–adolescent disagreements. *Journal of Marriage and the Family, 57,* 435–448.

Rueter, M., & Conger, R. (1998). Reciprocal influences between parenting and adolescent problem-solving behavior. *Developmental Psychology, 34,* 1470–1482.

Rueter, M., & Kwon, H. (2005). Developmental trends in adolescent suicidal ideation. *Journal of Research on Adolescence, 15,* 205–222.

Ruggiero, M., Greenberger, E., & Steinberg, L. (1982). Occupational deviance among first-time workers. *Youth and Society, 13,* 423–448.

Ruggles, S. (1994). The origins of African-American family structure. *American Sociological Review, 59,* 136–151.

Ruiz, S. Y., Roosa, M. W., & Gonzales, N. A. (2002). Predictors of self-esteem for Mexican-American and European American youths: A reexamination of the influence of parenting. *Journal of Family Psychology, 16*(1), 70–80.

Rumbaut, R. (1997). Assimilation and its discontents: Between rhetoric and reality. *International Migration Review, 31,* 923–960.

Rumbaut, R., & Cornelius, W. (Eds.). (1995). *California's immigrant children: Theory, research, and implications for educational policy.* San Diego: University of California, Center for U.S.-Mexican Studies.

Rumberger, R. (1995). Dropping out of middle school: A multilevel analysis of students and schools. *American Educational Research Journal, 32,* 583–625.

Rumberger, R., Ghatak, R., Poulos, G., Ritter, P., & Dornbusch, S. (1990). Family influences on dropout behavior in one California high school. *Sociology of Education, 63,* 283–299.

Rumberger, R., & Palardy, G. (2005). Test scores, dropout rates, and transfer rates as alternative indicators of high school performance. *American Education Research Journal, 42,* 3–42.

Rusby, J. C., Forrester, K. K., Biglan A., & Metzler, C. W. (2005). Relationships between peer harassment and adolescent problem behaviors. *Journal of Early Adolescence, 25,* 453–477.

Rushton, J., Forcier, M., & Schectman, R. M. (2002). Epidemiology of depressive symptoms in the National Longitudinal Study of Adolescent Health. *Journal of the American Academy of Child and Adolescent Psychiatry, 41,* 199–205.

Russell, S. (1994). Life course antecedents of premarital conception in Great Britain. *Journal of Marriage and the Family, 56,* 480–492.

Russell, S. (2002). Childhood development risk for teen childbearing in Britain. *Journal of Research on Adolescence, 12*(3), 305–324.

Russell, S., & Joyner, K. (2001). Adolescent sexual orientation and suicide risk: Evidence from a national study. *American Journal of Public Health, 91*(8), 1276–1281.

Russell, S., Elder, G. H., Jr., & Conger, R. (1997, April). School transitions and academic achievement. Paper presented at the biennial meetings of the Society for Research in Child Development, Washington, DC.

Russell, S., Franz, B., & Driscoll, A. (2001). Same-sex romantic attraction and experiences of violence in adolescence. *American Journal of Public Health, 91*(6), 903–906.

Rutter, M. (1978). Protective factors in children's responses to stress and disadvantage. In M. Kent & J. Rolf (Eds.), *Primary prevention of psychopathology,* Vol. 3: *Promoting social competence and coping in children.* Hanover, NH: University Press of New England.

Rutter, M. (1983). School effects on pupil progress: Research findings and policy implications. *Child Development, 54,* 1–29.

Rutter, M. (1997). Nature-nurture integration: The example of antisocial behavior. *American Psychologist, 52,* 390–398.

Rutter, M., & Garmezy, N. (1983). Developmental psychopathology. In E. M. Hetherington (Ed.), *Handbook of child psychology,* Vol. IV: *Socialization, personality, and social development,* pp. 775–911. New York: Wiley.

Rutter, M., Graham, P., Chadwick, F., & Yule, W. (1976). Adolescent turmoil: Fact or fiction? *Journal of Child Psychiatry and Psychology, 17,* 35–56.

Ryan, A. M. (2001). The peer group as a context for the development of young adolescent motivation and achievement. *Child Development, 72*(4), 1135–1150.

Ryan, A. M., & Patrick, H. (2001). The classroom social environment and changes in adolescents' motivation and engagement during middle school. *American Educational Research Journal, 38*(2), 437–460.

Ryan, R., & Lynch, J. (1989). Emotional autonomy versus detachment: Revisiting the vicissitudes of adolescence and young adulthood. *Child Development, 60,* 340–356.

Rys, G., & Bear, G. (1997). Relational aggression and peer relations: Gender and developmental issues. *Merrill-Palmer Quarterly, 43,* 87–106.

Sack, W., & Clarke, G. (1996). Multiple forms of stress in Cambodian adolescent refugees. *Child Development, 67,* 107–116.

Safron, J., Sy, S., & Schulenberg, J. (2003). Wishing to work: New perspectives on how adolescents' part-time work intensity is linked to educational disengagement, substance use, and other problem behaviours. *International Journal of Behavioral Development, 27,* 301–315.

Sagar, H., Schofield, J., & Snyder, H. (1983). Race and gender barriers: Preadolescent peer behavior in academic classrooms. *Child Development, 54,* 1032–1040.

Sagrestano, L., McCormick, S., Paikoff, R., & Holmbeck, G. (1999). Pubertal development and parent–child conflict in low-income, urban, African American adolescents. *Journal of Research on Adolescence, 9,* 85–107.

Sale, E., Sambrano, S., Springer, J. F., Pena, C., Pan, W., & Kasim, R. (2005). Family protection and prevention of alcohol use among Hispanic youth at high risk. *American Journal of Community Psychology, 36,* 195–205.

Salem, D., Zimmerman, M., & Notaro, P. (1998). Effects of family structure, family process, and father involvement on psychosocial outcomes among African American adolescents. *Family Relations, 47,* 331–341.

Salinger, J. D. ([1951]1964). *The catcher in the rye.* New York: Bantam Books.

Salmivalli, C. (1998). Intelligent, attractive, well-behaving, unhappy: The structure of adolescents' self-concept and its relations to their social behavior. *Journal of Research on Adolescence, 8,* 333–354.

Samaniego, R., & Gonzales, N. (1999). Multiple mediators of the effects of acculturation status on delinquency for Mexican American adolescents. *American Journal of Community Psychology, 27,* 189–210.

Sameroff, A. J., Peck, S. C., & Eccles, J. S. (2004). Changing ecological determinants of conduct problems from early adolescence to early adulthood. *Development and Psychopathology, 16,* 873–896.

Sampson, R. (1992). Family management and child development: Insights from social disorganization theory. In J. McCord (Ed.), *Advances in criminological theory,* Vol. 3., pp. 63–93. New Brunswick, NJ: Transaction.

Sampson, R. (1997). Collective regulation of adolescent misbehavior: Validation results from eighty Chicago neighborhoods. *Journal of Adolescent Research, 12,* 227–244.

Sampson, R., & Groves, W. (1989). Community structure and crime: Testing social-disorganization theory. *American Journal of Sociology, 94,* 774–802.

Sampson, R., & Laub, J. (1994). Urban poverty and the family context of delinquency: A new look at structure and process in a classic study. *Child Development, 65,* 523–540.

Sampson, R., & Laub, J. (2003). Life-course desistors? Trajectories of crime among delinquent boys followed to age 70. *Criminology, 41,* 555–592.

Sampson, R., Raudenbush, S., & Earls, F. (1997, August 15). Neighborhoods and violent crime: A multilevel study of collective efficacy for children. *Science, 277,* 918–924.

Sandefur, G., McLanahan, S., & Wojtkiewicz, R. (1992). The effects of parental marital status during adolescence on high school graduation. *Social Forces, 71,* 103–121.

Sandfort, J., & Hill, M. (1996). Assisting young, unmarried mothers to become self-sufficient: The effects of different types of early economic support. *Journal of Marriage and the Family, 58,* 311–326.

Sandler, I., Tein, J., & West, S. (1994). Coping, stress, and the psychological symptoms of children of divorce: A cross-sectional and longitudinal study. *Child Dedvelopment, 65,* 1744–1763.

Sandven, K., & Resnick, M. (1990). Informal adoption among Black adolescent mothers. *American Journal of Orthopsychiatry, 60,* 210–224.

Santelli, J., Abma, J., Ventura, S., Lindberg, L., Morrow, B., Anderson, J. E., Lyss, S., & Hamilton, B. E. (2004). Can changes in sexual behaviors among high school students explain the decline in teen pregnancy rates in the 1990s? *Journal of Adolescent Health, 35,* 80–90.

Santelli, J., Lindberg, L., Abma, J., McNeely, C., & Resnick, M. (2000). Adolescent sexual behavior: Estimates and trends from four nationally representative surveys. *Family Planning Perspectives, 32*(4), 156–165.

Santelli, J., Warren, C., Lowry, R., Sogolow, E., Collins, J., Kann, L., Kaufmann, R., & Celentano, D. (1997). The use of condoms with other contraceptive methods among young men and women. *Family Planning Perspectives, 29,* 261–267.

Sargent, J., & Dalton, M. (2001). Does parental disapproval of smoking prevent adolescents from becoming established smokers? *Pediatrics, 108*(6), 1256–1262.

Saunders, J., Davis, L., Williams, T., & Williams, J. H. (2004). Gender differences in self-perceptions and academic outcomes: A study of African American high school students. *Journal of Youth and Adolescence, 33,* 81–90.

Savage, M., & Holcomb, D. (1999). Adolescent female athletes' sexual risk-taking behaviors. *Journal of Youth and Adolescence, 28,* 595–602.

Savage, M., & Scott, L. (1998). Physical activity and rural middle school adolescents. *Journal of Youth and Adolescence, 27*(2), 245–253.

Savin-Williams, R. (1988). Theoretical perspectives accounting for adolescent homosexuality. *Journal of Adolescent Health Care, 9,* 95–104.

Savin-Williams, R., & Berndt, T. (1990). Friendship and peer relations. In S. Feldman & G. Elliott (Eds.), *At the threshold: The developing adolescent,* pp. 277–307. Cambridge, MA: Harvard University Press.

Savin-Williams, R., & Demo, D. (1983). Situational and transituational determinants of adolescent self-feelings. *Journal of Personality and Social Psychology, 44,* 824–833.

Savin-Williams, R., & Demo, D. (1984). Developmental change and stability in adolescent self-concept. *Developmental Psychology, 20,* 1100–1110.

Savin-Williams, R., & Diamond, L. (2004). Sex. In R. Lerner & L. Steinberg (Eds.), *Handbook of adolescent psychology.* New York: Wiley.

Scales, P. (1991). *A portrait of young adolescents in the 1990s: Implications for promoting healthy growth and development.* Chapel Hill, NC: Center for Early Adolescence.

Scales, P., Blyth, D. A., Berkas, T. H., & Kielsmeier, J. C. (2000). The effects of service-learning on middle school students' social responsibility and academic success. *Journal of Early Adolescence, 20*(3), 332–358.

Scanlan, T., Bakes, M., & Scanlan, L. (2005), Participation in sport: A developmental glimpse at emotion. In J. Mahoney, R. Larson, & J. Eccles (Eds.), *Organized activities as contexts of development,* pp. 275–309. Hillsdale, NJ: Erlbaum.

Scaramella, L., Conger, R., Simons, R., & Whitbeck, L. (1998). Predicting risk for pregnancy by late adolescence: A social contextual perspective. *Developmental Psychology, 34,* 1233–1245.

Scaramella, L., Conger, R. D., Spoth, R., & Simons, R. L. (2002). Evaluation of a social contextual model of delinquency: A cross-study replication. *Child Development, 73*(1), 175–195.

Scharf, M., Shulman, S., & Avigad-Spitz, L. (2005). Sibling relationships in emerging adulthood and in adolescence. *Journal of Adolescent Research, 20,* 64–90.

Scheer, S., & Unger, D. (1998). Russian adolescents in the era of emergent democracy: The role of family environment in substance use and depression. *Family Relations: Interdisciplinary Journal of Applied Family Studies, 47*(3), 297–303.

Scheier, L., & Botvin, G. (1998). Relations of social skills, personal competence, and adolescent alcohol use: A developmental exploratory study. *Journal of Early Adolescence, 18,* 77–114.

Scheier, L., Botvin, G. J., Griffin, K. W., & Diaz, T. (2000). Dynamic growth models of self-esteem and adolescent alcohol use. *Journal of Early Adolescence, 20*(2), 178–209.

Schellenbach, C., Whitman, T., & Borkowski, J. (1992). Toward an integrative model of adolescent parenting. *Human Development, 35,* 81–99.

Scherer, D., & Gardner, W. (1990). Reasserting the authority of science. *American Psychologist, 45,* 1173–1174

Schiff, A., & Knopf, I. (1985). The effects of task demands on attention allocation in children of different ages. *Child Development, 56,* 621–630.

Schlegel, A., & Barry, H. (1991). *Adolescence: An anthropological inquiry.* New York: Free Press.

Schmid, C. L. (2001). Educational achievement, language-minority students, and the new second generation. *Sociology of Education, 74,* 71–87.

Schmidt, J., & Padilla, B. (2003). Self-esteem and family challenge: An investigation of their effects on achievement. *Journal of Youth and Adolescence, 32*(1), 37–46.

Schmidt, J. A. (2003). Correlates of reduced misconduct among adolescents facing adversity. *Journal of Youth and Adolescence, 32,* 439–452.

Schmidt, M. G., Reppucci, N. D., & Woolard, J. L. (2003). Effectiveness of participation as a defendant: The attorney-juvenile client relationships. *Behavioral Sciences and the Law, 21,* 175–198.

Schmidt, W. (2003). Too little too late: American high schools in an international context. In D. Ravitch (Ed.), *Brookings papers on education policy.* Washington, DC: Brookings Institution.

Schmitt-Rodermund, E., & Silbereisen, R. (1993, March). Adolescents' age expectations during acculturation of German families from Eastern Europe. Paper presented at the biennial meetings of the Society for Research in Child Development, New Orleans.

Schneider, B., & Shouse, R. (1991, April). The work lives of eighth graders: Preliminary findings from the National Educational Longitudinal Study of 1988. Paper presented at the biennial meetings of the Society for Research in Child Development, Seattle.

Schneider, B., & Stevenson, D. (1999). *The ambitious generations: America's teenagers, motivated but directionless.* New Haven, CT: Yale University Press.

Schneider, B., Clegg, M., Byrne, B., Ledingham, J., & Crombie, G. (1989). Social relations of gifted children as a function of age and school program. *Journal of Educational Psychology, 81,* 48–56.

Schochet, T., Kelley, A., & Landry, C. (2004). Differential behavioral effects of nicotine exposure in adolescent and adult rats. *Psychopharmacology, 175,* 265–273.

Schochet, T., Kelley, A., & Landry, C. (2005). Differential expression of arc mRNA and other plasticity-related genes induced by nicotine in adolescent rat forebrain. *Neuroscience, 135,* 285–297.

Schoen, E., Wiswell, T., & Moses, S. (2000). New policy on circumcision—causes for concern. *Pediatrics, 105,* 620–623.

Schoenhals, M., Tienda, M., & Schneider, B. (1998). The educational and personal consequences of adolescent employment. *Social Forces, 77,* 723–762.

Schofield, J. (1981). Complementary and conflicting identities: Images and interaction in an interracial school. In S. Asher & J. Gottman (Eds.), *The development of children's friendships.* Cambridge: Cambridge University Press.

Scholte, R., & van Lieshout, C. (2001). Perceived relational support in adolescence: Dimensions, configurations, and adolescent adjustment. *Journal of Research on Adolescence, 11*(1), 71–94.

Schommer, M., Calvert, C., Gariglietti, G., & Bajaj, A. (1997). The development of epistemological beliefs among secondary school students: A longitudinal study. *Journal of Educational Psychology, 89,* 37–40.

Schoon, I., Bynner, J., Joshi, H., Parsons, S., Wiggins, R. D., & Sacker, A. (2002). The influence of context, timing, and duration of risk experiences for the passage from childhood to midadulthood. *Child Development, 73*(5), 1486–1504.

Schoon, I., Parsons, S., & Sacker, A. (2004). Socioeconomic adversity, educational resilience, and subsequent levels of adult adaptation. *Journal of Adolescent Research, 19,* 383–404.

Schulenberg, J., & Bachman, J. (1993, March). Long hours on the job? Not so bad for some adolescents in some types of jobs: The quality of work and substance use, affect, and stress. Paper presented at the biennial meetings of the Society for Research in Child Development, New Orleans.

Schulenberg, J., Bryant, A. L., & O'Malley, P. (2004). Taking hold of some kind of life: How developmental tasks relate to trajectories of well-being during the transition to adulthood. *Development and Psychopathology, 16,* 1119–1140.

Schulenberg, J., Maggs, J., Dielman, T., Leech, S., Kloska, D., Shope, J., & Laetz, V. (1999). On peer influences to get drunk: A panel study of young adolescents. *Merrill-Palmer Quarterly, 45,* 108–142.

Schulenberg, J., Wadsworth, K., O'Malley, P., Bachman, J., & Johnston, L. (1996). Adolescent risk factors for binge drinking during the transition to young adulthood: Variable- and pattern-centered approaches to change. *Developmental Psychology, 32,* 659–674.

Schuster, M., Bell, R., Berry, S., & Kanouse, D. (1998). Impact of a high school condom availability program on sexual attitudes and behaviors. *Family Planning Perspectives, 30,* 67–72, 88.

Schwab, J., Kulin, H. E., Susman, E. J., Finkelstein, J. W., Chinchilli, V. M., Kunselman, S. J., et al. (2001). The role of sex hormone replacement therapy on self-perceived competence in adolescents with delayed puberty. *Child Development, 72*(5), 1439–1450.

Schwartz, S. J., Côté, J. E., & Arnett, J. J. (2005). Identity and agency in emerging adulthood: Two developmental routes in the individualization process. *Youth and Society, 37,* 201–229.

Schwartz, S. J., Pantin, H., Prado, G., Sullivan, S., & Szapocznik, J. (2005). Family functioning, identity and problem behavior in Hispanic immigrant early adolescents. *Journal of Early Adolescence 25,* 392–420.

Schweder, R. (Ed.). (1998). *Welcome to middle age! And other cultural fictions.* Chicago: University of Chicago Press.

Schweingruber, H. A., & Kalil, A. (2000). Decision making and depressive symptoms in Black and White multigenerational teen-parent families. *Journal of Family Psychology, 14*(4), 556–569.

Scott, C., & Owen, R. (1990, March). Similarities and differences in sexuality socialization of males in three cultural/ethnic groups. Paper presented at the biennial meetings of the Society for Research on Adolescence, Atlanta.

Scott, E., Reppucci, N., & Woolard, J. (1995). Evaluating adolescent decision making in legal contexts. *Law and Human Behavior, 19,* 221–244.

Scott, E., & Woolard, J. (2004). The legal regulation of adolescence. In R. Lerner & L. Steinberg (Eds.), *Handbook of adolescent psychology.* New York: Wiley.

Scott, L. D., & House, L. E. (2005). Relationship of distress and perceived control to coping with perceived racial discrimination among black youth. *Journal of Black Psychology, 31,* 254–272.

Sebald, H. (1986). Adolescents' shifting orientation toward parents and peers: A curvilinear trend over recent decades. *Journal of Marriage and the Family, 48,* 5–13.

Segalowitz, S. J., & Davies, P. L. (2004). Charting the maturation of the frontal lobe: An electrophysiological strategy. *Brain and Cognition, 55,* 116–133.

Seginer, R. (1998). Adolescents' perceptions of relationships with older siblings in the context of other close relationships. *Journal of Research on Adolescence, 8,* 287–308.

Seidman, E., Aber, J., Allen, L., & French, S. (1996). The impact of the transition to high school on the self-system and perceived social context of poor urban youth. *American Journal of Community Psychology, 24,* 489–515.

Seidman, E., Allen, L., Aber, J., Mitchell, C., & Feinman, J. (1994). The impact of school transitions in early adolescence on the self-system and perceived social context of poor urban youth. *Child Development, 65,* 507–522.

Seidman, E. & French, S. E. (2004). Developmental trajectories and ecological transitions: A two-step procedure to aid in the choice of prevention and promotion interventions. *Development and Psychopathology, 16,* 1141–1159.

Seidman, E., Lambert, L. E., Allen, L., & Aber, J. L. (2003). Urban adolescents' transition to junior high school and protective family transactions. *Journal of Early Adolescence, 23,* 166–193.

Seiffge-Krenke, I. (2003). Testing theories of romantic development from adolescence to young adulthood: Evidence of a developmental sequence. *International Journal of Behavioral Development, 27,* 519–531.

Seiffge-Krenke, I., & Beyers, W. (2005). Coping trajectories from adolescence to young adulthood: Links to attachment state of mind. *Journal of Research on Adolescence, 15,* 561–582.

Seiffge-Krenke, I., & Klessinger, N. (2000). Long-term effects of avoidant coping on adolescents' depressive symptoms. *Journal of Youth and Adolescence, 29*(6), 617–630.

Seiffge-Krenke, I., & Stemmler, M. (2002). Factors contributing to gender differences in depressive symptoms: A test of three developmental models. *Journal of Youth and Adolescence, 31*(6), 405–417.

Seitz, V., & Apfel, N. (1993). Adolescent mothers and repeated childbearing: Effects of a school-based intervention program. *American Journal of Orthopsychiatry, 63,* 572–581.

Seitz, V., & Apfel, N. (1994). Effects of a school for pregnant students on the incidence of low-birthweight deliveries. *Child Development, 65,* 666–676.

Sellers, R. M., Copeland-Linder, N., Martin, P. P., & Lewis, R. L. (2006). Racial identity matters: The relationship between racial discrimination and psychological functioning in African American adolescents. *Journal of Research on Adolescence, 16,* 187–216.

Sellers, R. M., & Shelton, N. (2003) The role of racial identity in perceived racial discrimination. *Journal of Personality and Social Psychology, 84,* 1079–1092.

Sells, C., & Blum, R. (1996). Morbidity and mortality among U.S. adolescents: An overview of data and trends. *American Journal of Public Health, 86,* 513–519.

Selman, R. (1980). *The growth of interpersonal understanding: Developmental and clinical analyses.* New York: Academic Press.

Serovich, J., & Greene, K. (1997). Predictors of adolescent sexual risk taking behaviors which put them at risk for contracting HIV. *Journal of Youth and Adolescence, 26,* 429–444.

Sessa, F., & Steinberg, L. (1991). Family structure and the development of autonomy in adolescence. *Journal of Early Adolescence, 11,* 38–55.

Sethi, S., & Nolen-Hoeksema, S. (1997). Gender differences in internal and external focusing among adolescents. *Sex Roles, 37,* 687–700.

Settersten, R., Furstenberg, F., & Rumbaut, R. (Eds.). (2005). *On the frontier of adulthood.* Chicago: University of Chicago Press.

Sewell, W., & Hauser, R. (1972). Causes and consequences of higher education: Models of the status attainment process. *American Journal of Agricultural Economics, 54,* 851–861.

Shahinfar, A., Kupersmidt, J. B., & Matza, L. S. (2001). The relation between exposure to violence and social information processing among incarcerated adolescents. *Journal of Abnormal Psychology, 110*(1), 136–141.

Shanahan, M. J., & Flaherty, B. P. (2001). Dynamic patterns of time use in adolescence. *Child Development, 72*(2), 385–401.

Shanahan, M. J., Mortimer, J. T., & Krueger, H. (2002). Adolescence and adult work in the twenty-first century. *Journal of Research on Adolescence, 12*(1), 99–120.

Shanahan, M. J., Porfeli, E., Mortimer, J. T., & Erickson, L. (2005). Subjective age identity and the transition to adulthood: When do adolescents become adults? In R. Settersten, F. Furstenberg, Jr.., & R. Rumbaut (Eds.), *On the frontier of adulthood,* pp. 225–255. Chicago: University of Chicago Press.

Shanahan, M. J., & Bauer, D. J. (2004). Developmental properties of transactional models: The case of life events and mastery from adolescence to young adulthood. *Development and Psychopathology, 16,* 1095–1117.

Sharabany, R., & Wiseman, H. (1993). Close relationships in adolescence: The case of the kibbutz. *Journal of Youth and Adolescence, 22,* 671–695.

Sharabany, R., Gershoni, R., & Hofman, J. (1981). Girlfriend, boyfriend: Age and sex differences in intimate friendship. *Developmental Psychology, 17,* 800–808.

Shaver, P., Furman, W., & Buhrmester, D. (1985). Transition to college: Network changes, social skills, and loneliness. In S. Duck & D. Perlman (Eds.), *Understanding personal relationships: An interdisciplinary approach,* pp. 193–219. London: Sage.

Shaw, M., & White, D. (1965). The relationship between child–parent identification and academic underachievement. *Journal of Clinical Psychology, 21,* 10–13.

Shaw, P., Greenstein, D., Lerch, J., Klasen, L., Lenroot, R., Gotgay, N., Evans, A., Rapoport, J., & Giedd, J. (2006). Intellectual ability and cortical development in children and adolescents. *Nature, 440,* 676–679.

Shearer, D. L., Mulvihill, B. A., Klerman, L. V., Wallander, J. L., Hovinga, M. E., & Redden, D. T. (2002). Association of early childbearing and low cognitive ability. *Perspectives on Sexual and Reproductive Health, 34*(5), 236.

Shedler, J., & Block, J. (1990). Adolescent drug use and psychological health: A longitudinal inquiry. *American Psychologist, 45,* 612–630.

Sheeber, L., Hops, H., Alpert, A., Davis, B., & Andrews, J. (1997). Family support and conflict: Prospective relations to adolescent depression. *Journal of Abnormal Child Psychology, 25,* 333–344.

Sheeran, P., Abraham, C., & Orbell, S. (1999). Psychosocial correlates of heterosexual condom use: A meta-analysis. *Psychological Bulletin, 125,* 90–132.

Sheidow, A. J., Gorman-Smith, D., Tolan, P. H., & Henry, D. B. (2001). Family and community characteristics: Risk factors for violence exposure in inner-city youth. *Journal of Community Psychology, 29*(3), 345–360.

Sher, K. J., Gotham, H. J., & Watson, A. L. (2004). Trajectories of dynamic predictors of disorder: Their meanings and implications. *Development and Psychopathology, 16,* 825–856.

Shih, T. (1998). Finding the niche: Friendship formation of immigrant adolescents. *Youth and Society, 30,* 209–240.

Shiner, R. L., Masten, A. S., & Tellegen, A. (2002). A developmental perspective on personality in emerging adulthood: Childhood antecedents and concurrent adaptation. *Journal of Personality and Social Psychology, 83*(5), 1165–1177.

Shoal, G. D., & Giancola, P. R. (2003). Negative affectivity and drug use in adolescent boys: Moderating and mediating mechanisms. *Journal of Personality and Social Psychology, 84*(1), 221–233.

Shoop, D., & Davidson, P. (1994). AIDS and adolescents: The relation of parent and partner communication to adolescent condom use. *Journal of Adolescence, 17,* 137–148.

Shope, J. T., Molnar, L. J., Elliott, M. R., & Waller, P. F. (2001). Early impact on motor vehicle crashes among 16-year-old drivers. *Journal of the American Medical Association, 286,* 1593–1598.

Shrum, W., Cheek, N., Jr., & Hunter, S. (1988). Friendship in school: Gender and racial homophily. *Sociology of Education, 61,* 227–239.

Shucksmith, J., Glendinning, A., & Hendry, L. (1997). Adolescent drinking behaviour and the role of family life: A Scottish perspective. *Journal of Adolescence, 20,* 85–101.

Shulman, S., Feldman, B., Blatt, S. J., Cohen, O., & Mahler, A. (2005). Emerging adulthood: Age-related tasks and underlying self processes. *Journal of Adolescent Research, 20,* 577–603.

Shulman, S., & Laursen, B. (2002). Adolescent perceptions of conflict in interdependent and disengaged friendships. *Journal of Research on Adolescence, 12*(3), 353–372.

Shulman, S., Laursen, B., Kalman, Z., & Karpovsky, S. (1997). Adolescent intimacy revisited. *Journal of Youth and Adolescence, 26*(5), 597–617.

Shulman, S., & Scharf, M. (2000). Adolescent romantic behaviors and perceptions: Age- and gender-related differences, and links with family and peer relationships. *Journal of Research on Adolescence, 10,* 99–118.

Shumow, L., & Miller, J. D. (2001). Parents' at-home and at-school academic involvement with youth adolescents. *Journal of Early Adolescence, 21*(1), 68–91.

Siegel, A., & Scovill, L. C. (2000). Problem behavior: The double symptom of adolescence. *Development and Psychopathology, 12,* 763–793.

Siegel, J., Aneshensel, C., Taub, B., Cantwell, D., & Driscoll, A. (1998). Adolescent depressed mood in a multiethnic sample. *Journal of Youth and Adolescence, 27,* 413–427.

Siegel, J., Yancey, A., Aneshensel, C., & Schuler, R. (1999). Body image, perceived pubertal timing, and adolescent mental health. *Journal of Adolescent Health, 25,* 155–165.

Siegel, L. (1994). Working memory and reading: A life-span perspective. *International Journal of Behavioural Development, 17,* 109–124.

Siegel, M., & Biener, L. (2000). The impact of an antismoking media campaign on progression to established smoking: Results of a longitudinal study. *American Journal of Public Health, 90,* 380–386.

Siegler, R. (1988). Individual differences in strategy choices: Good students, not-so-good students, and perfectionists. *Child Development, 59,* 833–851.

Siegler, R., Liebert, D., & Liebert, R. (1973). Inhelder and Piaget's pendulum problem: Teaching adolescents to act as scientists. *Developmental Psychology, 9,* 97–101.

Sigler-Rushton, W. (2005). Young fatherhood and subsequent disadvantage in the United Kingdom. *Journal of Marriage and the Family, 67,* 735.

Signorielli, N. (1993). Television and adolescents' perceptions about work. *Youth and Society, 24,* 314–341.

Silbereisen, R., Petersen, A., Albrecht, H., & Kracke, B. (1989). Maturational timing and the development of problem behavior: Longitudinal studies in adolescence. *Journal of Early Adolescence, 9,* 247–268.

Silbereisen, R., & Schmitt-Rodermund, E. (1995). German immigrants in Germany: Adaptation of adolescents' timetables for autonomy. In M. Hofer, P. Noack, & J. Youniss (Eds.), *Psychological responses to social change: Human development in changing environments,* pp. 105–125. Berlin: de Gruyter.

Silbereisen, R., Schwarz, B., Nowak, M., Kracke, B., & von Eye, A. (1993, March). Psychosocial adversities and timing of adolescent transitions: A comparison of the former East and West Germanies. Paper presented at the biennial meetings of the Society for Research in Child Development, New Orleans.

Silk, J., Morris, A., Kanaya, T., & Steinberg, L. (2003). Psychological control and autonomy granting: Opposite ends of a continuum or distinct constructs? *Journal of Research on adolescence, 13*(1), 113–128.

Silk, J., Steinberg, L., & Morris, A. (2003). Adolescents' emotion regulation in daily life: Links to depressive symptoms and problem behavior. *Child Development, 74,* 1869–1880.

Silver, E., & Bauman, L. (2006). The association of sexual experience with attitudes, beliefs, and risk behaviors of inner-city adolescents. *Journal of Research on Adolescence, 16,* 29–45.

Silverberg, S. (1986). Psychological well-being of parents with early adolescent children. Unpublished doctoral dissertation, Department of Child and Family Studies, University of Wisconsin–Madison.

Silverberg, S., Marczak, M., & Gondoli, D. (1996). Maternal depressive symptoms and achievement-related outcomes among adolescent daughters: Variations by family structure. *Journal of Early Adolescence, 16,* 90–109.

Silverberg, S., & Steinberg, L. (1987). Adolescent autonomy, parent–adolescent conflict, and parental well-being. *Journal of Youth and Adolescence, 16,* 293–312.

Silverberg, S., & Steinberg, L. (1990). Psychological well-being of parents at midlife: The impact of early adolescent children. *Developmental Psychology, 26,* 658–666.

Silverberg, S., Tennenbaum, D., & Jacob, T. (1992). Adolescence and family interaction. In V. Van Hasselt & M. Hersen (Eds.), *Handbook of social development: A lifespan perspective,* pp. 347–370. New York: Plenum.

Silverman, J., Raj, A., Mucci, L. A., & Hathaway, J. E. (2001). Dating violence against adolescent girls and associated substance abuse, unhealthy weight control, sexual risk behavior, pregnancy, and suicidality. *Journal of the American Medical Association, 286,* 572–579.

Silverman, W., Kurtines, W., Ginsburg, G., Weems, C., Lumpkin, P., & Carmichael, D. (1999). Treating anxiety disorders in children with group cognitive-behavioral therapy: A randomized clinical trial. *Journal of Consulting and Clinical Psychology, 67,* 995–1003.

Sim, H., & Vuchinich, S. (1996). The declining effects of family stressors on antisocial behavior from childhood to adolescence and early adulthood. *Journal of Family Issues, 17,* 408–427.

Sim, T. (2000). Adolescent psychosocial competence: The importance and role of regard for parents. *Journal of Research on Adolescence, 10,* 49–64.

Sim, T., & Koh, S. (2003). A domain conceptualization of adolescent susceptibility to peer pressure. *Journal of Research on Adolescence, 13*(1), 57–80.

Simmons, R. (2003). *Odd girl out.* New York: Harvest Books.

Simmons, R., & Blyth, D. (1987). *Moving into adolescence.* New York: Aldine de Gruyter.

Simmons, R., Blyth, D., & McKinney, K. (1983). The social and psychological effects of puberty on white females. In J. Brooks-Gunn & A. Petersen (Eds.), *Girls at puberty,* pp. 229–272. New York: Plenum.

Simmons, R., & Rosenberg, F. (1975). Sex, sex roles, and self-image. *Journal of Youth and Adolescence, 4,* 229–258.

Simmons, R., Rosenberg, F., & Rosenberg, M. (1973). Disturbance in the self-image at adolescence. *American Sociological Review, 38,* 553–568.

Simon, W., & Gagnon, J. (1969). On psychosexual development. In D. Goslin (Ed.), *Handbook of socialization theory and research.* Chicago: Rand McNally.

Simons, R., Chao, W., Conger, R. D., & Elder, G. H. (2001). Quality of parenting as mediator of the effect of childhood defiance on adolescent friendship choice and delinquency: A growth curve analysis. *Journal of Marriage and the Family, 63*(1), 63–79.

Simons, R., Johnson, C., Beaman, J., Conger, R., & Whitbeck, L. (1996). Parents and peer group as mediators of the effect of community structure on adolescent problem behavior. *American Journal of Community Psychology, 24,* 145–171.

Simons, R., Johnson, C., & Conger, R. (1994). Harsh corporal punishment versus quality of parental involvement as an explanation of adolescent maladjustment. *Journal of Marriage and the Family, 56,* 591–607.

Simons, R., Lin, K., & Gordon, L. (1998). Socialization in the family of origin and male dating violence: A prospective study. *Journal of Marriage and the Family, 60,* 467–478.

Simons, R., Simons, L. G., Burt, C. H., Brody, G. H., & Cutrona, C. (2005). Collective efficacy, authoritative parenting and delinquency: A longitudinal test of a model integrating community- and family-level processes. *Criminology, 43,* 989–1029.

Simons, R., Whitbeck, L., Beaman, J., & Conger, R. (1994). The impact of mothers' parenting, involvement by nonresidential fathers, and parental conflict on the adjustment of adolescent children. *Journal of Marriage and the Family, 56,* 356–374.

Simons, R., Whitbeck, L., Conger, R., & Chyi-In, W. (1991). Intergenerational transmission of harsh parenting. *Developmental Psychology, 27,* 159–171.

Simons-Morton, B., Hartos, J., Leaf, W., & Preusser, D. (2005). Persistence of effects of the Checkpoints Program on parental restrictions on teen driving privileges. *American Journal of Public Health, 95,* 447–452.

Simpkins, S. D., Davis-Kean, P. E., & Eccles, J. S. (2006). Math and science motivation: A longitudinal examination of the links between choices and beliefs. *Developmental Psychology, 42,* 70–83.

Simpson, R. (1962). Parental influence, anticipatory socialization, and social mobility. *American Sociological Review, 27,* 517–522.

Singh, G., & Yu., S. (1996). U.S. childhood mortality, 1950 through 1993: Trends and socioeconomic differentials. *American Journal of Public Health, 86,* 505–512.

Singh, K., & Hernandez-Gantes, V. (1996). The relation of English language proficiency to educational aspirations of Mexican-American eighth graders. *Journal of Early Adolescence, 16,* 253–273.

Singh, S., & Darroch, J. (1999). Trends in sexual activity among adolescent American women: 1982–1995. *Family Planning Perspectives, 31,* 212–219.

Singh, S., & Darroch, J. E. (2000). Adolescent pregnancy and childbearing: Levels and trends in developed countries. *Family Planning Perspectives, 32*(1), 14–23.

Sionean, C., DiClemente, R. J., Wingood, G. M., Crosby, R., Cobb, B. K., Harrington, K., et al. (2002). Psychosocial and behavioral correlates of refusing unwanted sex among African-American adolescent females. *Journal of Adolescent Health, 30*(1), 55–63.

Sirin, S. R., & Rogers-Sirin, L. (2004). Exploring school engagement of middle-class African American adolescents. *Youth and Society, 35,* 323–340.

Sisk, C. L., & Foster, D. L. (2004). The neural basis of puberty and adolescence. *Nature Neuroscience, 7,* 1040–1047.

Skeem, J., & Cauffman. E. (2003). Views of the downward extension: Comparing the youth version of the Psychopathy Checklist with the Youth Psychopathic Traits Inventory. *Behavioral Sciences and the Law, 21,* 737–770.

Skinner, B. F. (1953). *Science and human behavior.* New York: Free Press.

Slap, G., Goodman, E., & Huang, B. (2001). Adoption as a risk factor for attempted suicide during adolescence. *Pediatrics, 108*(2), Article E30.

Slap, G., & Jablow, M. (1994). *Teenage health care.* New York: Pocket Books.

Slyper, A. (2006). The pubertal timing controversy in the USA, and a review of possible causative factors for the advance in timing of onset of puberty. *Clinical Endocrinology, 65,* 1–8.

Small, S., Eastman, G., & Cornelius, S. (1988). Adolescent autonomy and parental stress. *Journal of Youth and Adolescence, 17,* 377–391.

Small, S., & Luster, T. (1994). Adolescent sexual activity: An ecological, risk-factor approach. *Journal of Marriage and the Family, 56,* 181–192.

Small, S., & Memmo, M. (2004). Contemporary models of youth development and problem prevention: Toward an integration of terms, concepts and models. *Family Relations, 53,* 3–11.

Smetana, J. (1988). Concepts of self and social convention: Adolescents' and parents' reasoning about hypothetical and actual family conflicts. In M. Gunnar & W. A. Collins (Eds.), *Minnesota Symposium on Child Psychology, Vol 21,* pp. 79–122. Hillsdale, NJ: Erlbaum.

Smetana, J. (1989). Adolescents' and parents' reasoning about actual family conflict. *Child Development, 59,* 1052–1067.

Smetana, J. (1995). Parenting styles and conceptions of parental authority during adolescence. *Child Development, 66,* 299–316.

Smetana, J. (2000). Middle-class African American adolescents' and parents' conceptions of parental authority and parenting practices: A longitudinal investigation. *Child Development, 71*(6), 1672–1686.

Smetana, J. (2005). Adolescent–parent conflict: Resistance and subversion as developmental process. In L. Nucci (Ed.), *Conflict, contradiction, and contrarian elements in moral development and education,* pp. 69–91. Mahwah, NJ: Erlbaum.

Smetana, J. (in press). Social-cognitive domain theory: Consistencies and variations in children's moral and social judgments. In M. Killen & J. G. Smetana (Eds.), *Handbook of moral development.* Mahwah, NJ: Erlbaum.

Smetana, J., & Asquith, P. (1994). Adolescents' and parents' conceptions of parental authority and personal autonomy. *Child Development, 65,* 1147–1162.

Smetana, J., & Bitz, B. (1996). Adolescents' conceptions of teachers' authority and their relations to rule violations in school. *Child Development, 67,* 1153–1172.

Smetana, J., Campione-Barr, N., & Daddis, C. (2004). Longitudinal development of family decision making: Defining healthy behavioral autonomy for middle-class African American adolescents. *Child Development, 75,* 1418–1434.

Smetana, J., Crean, H. F., & Daddis, C. (2002). Family processes and problem behaviors in middle-class African American adolescents. *Journal of Research on Adolescence, 12*(2), 275–304.

Smetana, J., & Chuang, S. (2001). Middle-class African American parents' conceptions of parenting in the transition to adolescence. *Journal of Research on Adolescence,* 11, 177–198.

Smetana, J., & Daddis, C. (2002). Domain-specific antecedents of parental psychological control and monitoring: The role of parenting beliefs and practices. *Child Development, 73*(2), 563–580.

Smetana, J., Daddis, C., & Chuang, S. (2003). "Clean your room!" *Journal of Adolescent Research, 18,* 631–650.

Smetana, J., & Gaines, C. 2000. Adolescent–parent conflict in middle-class African-American families. *Child Development, 70,* 1447–1463.

Smetana, J., & Metzger, A. (2005). Family and religious antecedents of civic involvement in middle class African American late adolescents. *Journal of Research on Adolescence, 15,* 325–352.

Smetana, J., Metzger, A., & Campione-Barr, N. (2004). African American late adolescents' relationships with parents: Developmental transitions and longitudinal patterns. *Child Development, 75,* 932–947.

Smetana, J., Metzger, A., Gettman, D., & Campione-Barr, N. (2006). Disclosure and secrecy in adolescent–parent relationships. *Child Development, 77,* 201–217.

Smetana, J., Yau, J., Restrepo, A., & Braeges, J. (1991). Adolescent–parent conflict in married and divorced families. *Developmental Psychology, 27,* 1000–1010.

Smith, A., & Lalonde, R. N. (2003). "Racelessness" in a Canadian context? Exploring the link between black students' identity, achievement, and mental health. *Journal of Black Psychology, 29,* 142–164.

Smith, C., Denton, M., Faris, R., & Regnerus, M. (2002). Mapping American adolescent religious participation. *Journal for the Scientific Study of Religion, 41,* 597–612.

Smith, E. (1996, March). Ethnic identity in African-American youth: Definition, components, and measurement. Paper presented at the biennial meetings of the Society for Research on Adolescence, Boston.

Smith, E., & Udry, J. (1985). Coital and noncoital sexual behaviors of white and black adolescents. *American Journal of Public Health, 75,* 1200–1203.

Smith, E., Udry, J., & Morris, N. (1985). Pubertal development and friends: A biosocial explanation of adolescent sexual behavior. *Journal of Health and Social Behavior, 26,* 183–192.

Smith, E., & Zabin, L. (1993). Marital and birth expectations of urban adolescents. *Youth and Society, 25,* 62–74.

Smith, G., & Goldman, M. (1994). Alcohol expectancy theory and the identification of high-risk adolescents. *Journal of Research on Adolescence, 4,* 229–247.

Smith, G., Goldman, M., Greenbaum, P., & Christiansen, B. (1995). Expectancy for social facilitation from drinking: The divergent paths of high-expectancy and low-expectancy adolescents. *Journal of Abnormal Psychology, 104,* 32–40.

Smith, P. H., White, J. W., & Holland, L. J. (2003). A longitudinal perspective on dating violence among adolescent and college-age women. *American Journal of Public Health, 93,* 1104–1109.

Smith, T. (1993, March). Federal employment training programs for youth: Failings and opportunities. Paper presented at the biennial meetings of the Society for Research in Child Development, New Orleans.

Smith, T. E., & Leaper, C. (2005). Self-perceived gender typicality and the peer context during adolescence. *Journal of Research on Adolescence, 16,* 91–103.

Smolak, L., Levine, M., & Gralen, S. (1993). The impact of puberty and dating on eating problems among middle school girls. *Journal of Youth and Adolescence, 22,* 355–368.

Smoll, F., & Schutz, R. (1990). Quantifying gender differences in physical performance: A developmental perspective. *Developmental Psychology, 26,* 360–369.

Smollar, J., & Youniss, J. (1985). Transformation in adolescents' perceptions of parents. Paper presented at the biennial meetings of the Society for Research in Child Development, Baltimore.

Snyder, H., & Sickmund, M. (1995). *Juvenile offenders and victims: A national report.* Washington, DC: Office of Juvenile Justice and Delinquency Prevention.

Snyder, J., Bank, L., & Burraston, B. (2005). The consequences of antisocial behavior in older male siblings for younger brothers and sisters. *Journal of Family Psychology, 19,* 643–653.

Sobesky, W. (1983). The effects of situational factors on moral judgments. *Child Development, 54,* 575–584.

Soenens, B., Vansteenkiste, M., Luyckx, K., & Goossens, L. (2006). Parenting and adolescent problem behavior: An integrated model with adolescent self-disclosure and perceived parental knowledge as intervening variables. *Developmental Psychology, 42,* 305–318.

Solomon, R., & Liefeld, C. (1998). Effectiveness of a family support center approach to adolescent mothers: Repeat pregnancy and school drop-out rates. *Family Relations, 47,* 139–144.

Sommers, C. (2000). *The war against boys.* New York: Simon & Schuster.

Sonenstein, F., Ku, L., Lindberg, L., Turner, C., & Pleck, J. (1998). Changes in sexual behavior and condom use among teenaged males: 1988 to 1995. *American Journal of Public Health, 88,* 956–959.

Sorensen, R. (1973). *Adolescent sexuality in contemporary society.* New York: World Book.

Sorensen, S., Richardson, B., & Peterson, J. (1993). Race/ethnicity patterns in the homicide of children in Los Angeles, 1980 through 1989. *American Journal of Public Health, 83,* 725–727.

South, S. J., & Baumer, E. P. (2000). Deciphering community and race effects on adolescent premarital childbearing. *Social Forces, 78*(4), 1379–1407.

South, S. J., & Baumer, E. P. (2001). Community effects on the resolution of adolescent premarital pregnancy. *Journal of Family Issues, 22*(8), 1025–1043.

South, S. J., Baumer, E. P., & Lutz, A. (2003). Interpreting community effects on youth educational attainment. *Youth and Society, 35,* 3–36.

South, S. J., & Haynie, D. L. (2004). Friendship networks of mobile adolescents. *Social Forces, 83,* 315–350.

Sowell, E. R., Trauner, D. A, Gamst, A., & Jernigan, T. L. (2002). Development of cortical and subcortical brain structures in childhood and adolescence: A structural MRI study. *Developmental Medicine and Child Neurology, 44,* 4–16.

Spear, P. (2000). The adolescent brain and age-related behavioral manifestations. *Neuroscience and Biobehavioral Reviews, 24,* 417–463.

Spence, J., & Helmreich, R. (1978). *Masculinity and femininity: Their psychological dimensions, correlates, and antecedents.* Austin: University of Texas Press.

Spencer, G. A., & Bryant, S. A. (2000). Dating violence: A comparison of rural, suburban, and urban teens. *Journal of Adolescent Health, 27*(5), 302–305.

Spencer, M., & Dornbusch, S. (1990). Challenges in studying minority youth. In S. Feldman & G. Elliott (Eds.), *At the threshold: The developing adolescent,* pp. 123–146. Cambridge, MA: Harvard University Press.

Spencer, M., & Markstrom-Adams, C. (1990). Identity processes among racial and ethnic minority children in America. *Child Development, 61,* 290–310.

Spencer, M. B. (2005). Crafting identities and accessing opportunities post-Brown. *American Psychologist, 60,* 821–830.

Spieker, S., & Bensley, L. (1994). Roles of living arrangements and grandmother social support in adolescent mothering and infant attachment. *Developmental Psychology, 30,* 102–111.

Spielberger, C. (1966). The effects of anxiety on complex learning and academic achievement. In C. Spielberger (Ed.), *Anxiety and behavior.* New York: Academic Press.

Spingarn, R., & DuRant, R. (1996). Male adolescents involved in pregnancy: Associated health risk and problem behaviors. *Pediatrics, 98,* 262–268.

Spotts, E. L., Neiderheiser, J. M., Hetherington, E., & Reiss, D. (2001). The relation between observational measures of social problem solving and familial antisocial behavior: Genetic and environmental influences. *Journal of Research on Adolescence, 11*(4), 351–374.

Spreitzer, E. (1994). Does participation in interscholastic athletics affect adult development? *Youth and Society, 25,* 368–387.

Sroufe, L. A. (1979). The coherence of individual development. *American Psychologist, 34,* 834–841.

St. George, I., Williams, S., & Silva, P. (1994). Body size and menarche: The Dunedin study. *Journal of Adolescent Health, 15,* 573–576.

St. John, N. (1975). *School desegregation outcomes for children.* New York: Wiley.

St. Lawrence, J., Brasfield, T., Jefferson, K., Allyene, E., & Shirley, A. (1994). Social support as a factor in African-American adolescents' sexual risk behavior. *Journal of Adolescent Research, 9,* 292–310.

St. Louis, M., Conway, M., Hayman, C., Miller, C., Petersen, L., & Dondero, T. (1991). Human immunodeficiency virus infection in disadvantaged adolescents. *Journal of the American Medical Association, 266,* 2387–2391.

St. Pierre, T., Mark, M., Kaltreider, D., & Aikin, K. (1997). Involving parents of high-risk youth in drug prevention. *Journal of Early Adolescence, 17,* 21–50.

Stack, S. (1994). The effect of geographic mobility on premarital sex. *Journal of Marriage and the Family, 56,* 204–208.

Staff, J., Mortimer, J., & Uggen, C. (2004). Work and leisure in adolescence. In R. Lerner & L. Steinberg (Eds.), *Handbook of adolescent psychology.* New York: Wiley.

Stanton, B., Romer, D., Ricardo, I., Black, M., Feigelman, S., & Galbraith, J. (1993). Early initiation of sex and its lack of association with risk behaviors among African-Americans. *Pediatrics, 92,* 13–19.

Stanton-Salazar, R., & Dornbusch, S. (1995). Social capital and the reproduction of inequality: Information networks among Mexican-origin high school students. *Sociology of Education, 68,* 116–135.

Stanton-Salazar, R., & Spina, S. (2005). Adolescent peer networks as a context for social and emotional support. *Youth and Society, 36,* 379–417.

Stattin, H., & Kerr, M. (2000). Parental monitoring: A reinterpretation. *Child Development, 71*(4), 1072–1085.

Stattin, H., & Magnusson, D. (1994, February). Onset of official delinquency: Its co-occurrence in time with educational, behavioral, and interpersonal problems. Paper presented at the biennial meetings of the Society for Research on Adolescence, San Diego.

Stearns, E. (2004). Interracial friendliness and the social organization of schools. *Youth and Society 35,* 395–419.

Steele, C. M. (1997). A threat in the air: How stereotypes shape intellectual identity and performance. *American Psychologist, 52,* 613–619.

Steele, J., & Brown, J. (1995). Adolescent room culture: Studying media in the context of everyday life. *Journal of Youth and Adolescence, 24,* 551–576.

Steffensmeier, D., Schwartz, J., Zhong, H., & Ackerman, J. (2005). An assessment of recent trends in girls' violence using diverse longitudinal sources: Is the gender gap closing? *Criminology, 43,* 355–406.

Stein, J., Newcomb, M., & Bentler, P. (1987). An 8-year study of multiple influences on drug use and drug use consequences. *Journal of Personality and Social Psychology, 53*, 1094–1105.

Stein, J., & Reiser, L. (1994). A study of white middle-class adolescent boys' responses to "semenarche" (the first ejaculation). *Journal of Youth and Adolescence, 23*, 373–384.

Stein, J., Newcomb, M., & Bentler, P. (1992). The effect of agency and communion on self-esteem: Gender differences in longitudinal data. *Sex Roles, 26*, 465–484.

Stein, N. (1995). Sexual harassment in school: The public performance of gendered violence. *Harvard Educational Review, 65*, 145–162.

Steinberg, L. (1986). Latchkey children and susceptibility to peer pressure: An ecological analysis. *Developmental Psychology, 22*, 433–439.

Steinberg, L. (1987b). The impact of puberty on family relations: Effects of pubertal status and pubertal timing. *Developmental Psychology, 23*, 451–460.

Steinberg, L. (1987c). Single parents, stepparents, and the susceptibility of adolescents to antisocial peer pressure. *Child Development, 58*, 269–275.

Steinberg, L. (1989). Pubertal maturation and parent–adolescent distance: An evolutionary perspective. In G. Adams, R. Montemayor, & T. Gullotta (Eds.), *Advances in adolescent development*, Vol. 1, pp. 71–97. Beverly Hills, CA: Sage.

Steinberg, L. (1990). Autonomy, conflict, and harmony in the family relationship. In S. Feldman & G. Elliott (Eds.), *At the threshold: The developing adolescent*, pp. 255–276. Cambridge, MA: Harvard University Press.

Steinberg, L. (1996). *Beyond the classroom: Why school reform has failed and what parents need to do.* New York: Simon & Schuster.

Steinberg, L. (1998). Standards outside the classroom. In D. Ravitch (Ed.), *The state of student performance in American schools: Brookings papers on education policy*, Vol. 1, pp. 319–357. Washington, DC: Brookings Institution.

Steinberg, L. (2000). Youth violence: Do parents and families make a difference? *National Institute of Justice Journal*, April, 30–38.

Steinberg, L. (2001). We know some things: Adolescent–parent relationships in retrospect and prospect. *Journal of Research on Adolescence, 11*, 1–19.

Steinberg, L. (2003). The state of adolescence. In D. Ravitch (Ed.), *Brookings papers on education policy.* Washington, DC: Brookings Institution.

Steinberg, L. (2004). Risk-taking in adolescence: What changes, and why? *Annals of the New York Academy of Sciences, 1021*, 51–58.

Steinberg, L. (2005a). Cognitive and affective development in adolescence. *Trends in Cognitive Sciences, 9*, 69–74.

Steinberg, L. (2005b). *The 10 basic principles of good parenting.* New York: Simon & Schuster.

Steinberg, L. (2007). Risk-taking in adolescence: New perspectives from brain and behavioral science. *Current Directions in Psychological Science, 16*, 55–59.

Steinberg, L., & Avenevoli, S. (2000). The role of context in the development of psychopathology: A conceptual framework and some speculative propositions. *Child Development, 71*, 66–74.

Steinberg, L., Blatt-Eisengart, I., & Cauffman, E. (2006). Patterns of competence and adjustment among adolescents from authoritative, authoritarian, indulgent, and neglectful homes: Replication in a sample of serious juvenile offenders. *Journal of Research on Adolescence, 16*, 47–58.

Steinberg, L., & Cauffman, E. (1995). The impact of employment on adolescent development. In R. Vasta (Ed.), *Annals of Child Development*, Vol. 11, pp. 131–166. London: Jessica Kingsley.

Steinberg, L., & Cauffman, E. (1996). Maturity of judgment in adolescence: Psychosocial factors in adolescent decisionmaking. *Law and Human Behavior, 20*, 249–272.

Steinberg, L., & Cauffman, E. (2000). Developmental perspectives on jurisdictional boundary. In J. Fagan & F. Zimring (Eds.), *The changing borders of juvenile justice: Transfer of adolescents to the criminal court.* Chicago: University of Chicago Press.

Steinberg, L., Dahl, R., Keating, D., Kupfer, D., Masten, A., & Pine, D. (2006). Psychopathology in adolescence: Integrating affective neuroscience with the study of context. In D. Cicchetti & D. Cohen (Eds.), *Developmental psychopathology, Vol. 2: Developmental neuroscience*, pp. 710–741. New York: Wiley.

Steinberg, L., & Dornbusch, S. (1991). Negative correlates of part-time work in adolescence: Replication and elaboration. *Developmental Psychology, 17*, 304–313.

Steinberg, L., Dornbusch, S., & Brown, B. (1992). Ethnic differences in adolescent achievement: An ecological perspective. *American Psychologist, 47*, 723–729.

Steinberg, L., Elmen, J., & Mounts, N. (1989). Authoritative parenting, psychosocial maturity, and academic success among adolescence. *Child Development, 60*, 1424–1436.

Steinberg, L., Fegley, S., & Dornbusch, S. (1993). Negative impact of part-time work on adolescent adjustment: Evidence from a longitudinal study. *Developmental Psychology, 29*, 171–180.

Steinberg, L., Fletcher, A., & Darling, N. (1994). Parental monitoring and peer influences on adolescent substance use. *Pediatrics, 93*, 1060–1064.

Steinberg, L., Greenberger, E., Garduque, L., Ruggiero, M., & Vaux, A. (1982). Effects of working on adolescent development. *Developmental Psychology, 18*, 385–395.

Steinberg, L., Lamborn, S., Darling, N., Mounts, N., & Dornbusch, S. (1994). Over-time changes in adjustment and competence among adolescents from authoritative, authoritarian, indulgent, and neglectful families. *Child Development, 65*, 754–770.

Steinberg, L., Lamborn, S., Dornbusch, S., & Darling, N. (1992). Impact of parenting practices on adolescent achievement: Authoritative parenting, school involvement, and encouragement to succeed. *Child Development, 63*, 1266–1281.

Steinberg, L., & Levine, A. (1991). *You and your adolescent: A parent's guide for ages 10 to 20.* New York: Harper Perennial.

Steinberg, L., & Morris, A. (2001). Adolescent development. *Annual Review of Psychology, 52*, 83–110.

Steinberg, L., & Scott, E. (2003). Less guilty by reason of adolescence. *American Psychologist.*

Steinberg, L., & Silk, J. (2002). Parenting adolescents. In M. Bornstein (Ed.), *Handbook of parenting, Vol. 1: Children and parenting* (2nd ed.), pp. 103–133. Mahwah, NJ: Erlbaum.

Steinberg, L., & Silverberg, S. (1986). The vicissitudes of autonomy in early adolescence. *Child Development, 57*, 841–851.

Steinberg, L., & Silverberg, S. (1987). Influences on marital satisfaction during the middle stages of the family life cycle. *Journal of Marriage and the Family, 49*, 751–760.

Steinberg, L., & Steinberg, W. (1994). *Crossing paths: How your child's adolescence triggers your own crisis.* New York: Simon & Schuster.

Steiner, H., Cauffman, E., & Duxbury, E. (1999). Personality traits in juvenile delinquents: Relation to criminal behavior and recidivism. *Journal of the Academy of Child and Adolescent Psychiatry, 38*, 256–262.

Steinman, K. J., & Zimmerman, M. A. (2004). Religious activity and risk behavior among African American adolescents: Concurrent and developmental effects. *American Journal of Community Psychology, 33*, 151–161.

Stephens, L. (1996). Will Johnny see Daddy this week? An empirical test of three theoretical perspectives of postdivorce contact. *Journal of Family Issues, 17*, 466–494.

Stern, D., Finkelstein, N., Stone, J., Latting, J., & Dornsife, C. (1994). Research on school-to-work transition programs in the United States. Berkeley, CA: National Center for Research in Vocational Education.

Sternberg, R. (1988). *The triarchic mind.* New York: Viking Penguin.

Sternberg, R. (1994). Commentary: Reforming school reform: Comments on multiple intelligences. *Teachers College Record, 95*, 561–569.

Sternberg, R., & Nigro, G. (1980). Developmental patterns in the solution of verbal analogies. *Child Development, 51*, 27–38.

Stevens, E. A., & Prinstein, M. J. (2005). Peer contagion of depressogenic attributional styles among adolescents: A longitudinal study. *Journal of Abnormal Child Psychology, 33*, 25–38.

Stevens, J. (1988). Social support, locus of control, and parenting in three low-income groups of mothers: Black teenagers, Black adults, and White adults. *Child Development, 59*, 635–642.

Stevenson, D., & Baker, D. (1987). The family-school relation and the child's school performance. *Child Development, 58,* 1348–1357.

Stevenson, D., Schiller, K., & Schneider, B. (1994). Sequences of opportunities for learning. *Sociology of Education, 67,* 184–198.

Stevenson, H. (1994). Extracurricular programs in East Asian schools. *Teachers College Record, 95*, 389–407.

Stevenson, H., & Stigler, J. (1992). *The learning gap: Why our schools are failing and what we can learn from Japanese and Chinese education.* New York: Simon & Schuster.

Stevenson, H., Jr. (1995). Relationship of adolescent perceptions of racial socialization to racial identity. *Journal of Black Psychology, 21,* 49–70.

Stevenson, H., Jr. (1998). Raising safe villages: Cultural-ecological factors that influence the emotional adjustment of adolescents. *Journal of Black Psychology, 24*(1), 44–59.

Stevenson, H., Jr., Davis, G., Weber, E., Weiman, D., & Abdul-Kabir, S. (1995). HIV prevention beliefs among urban African-American youth. *Journal of Adolescent Health, 16,* 316–323.

Stevenson, H., Jr., Reed, J., Bodison, P., & Bishop, A. (1997). Racism stress management: Racial social beliefs and the experience of depression and anger in African American youth. *Youth and Society, 29,* 197–222.

Stewart, S. D. (2003). Nonresident parenting and adolescent adjustment: The quality of nonresident father–child interaction. *Journal of Family Issues, 24,* 217–244.

Stice, E., & Barrera, M., Jr. (1995). A longitudinal examination of the reciprocal relations between perceived parenting and adolescents' substance use and externalizing behaviors. *Developmental Psychology, 31,* 322–334.

Stice, E., & Bearman, S. (2001). Body-image and eating disturbances prospectively predict increases in depressive symptoms in adolescent girls: A growth curve analysis. *Developmental Psychology, 37*(5), 597–607.

Stice, E., Cameron, R., Killen, J., Hayward, C., & Taylor, C. (1999). Naturalistic weight-reduction efforts prospectively predict growth in relative weight and onset of obesity among female adolescents. *Journal of Consulting and Clinical Psychology, 67*(6), 967–974.

Stice, E., & Gonzales, N. (1998). Adolescent temperament moderates the relation of parenting to antisocial behavior and substance use. *Journal of Adolescent Research, 13*(1), 5–31.

Stice, E., Hayward, C., Cameron, R. P., Killen, J., & Taylor, C. (2000). Body-image and eating disturbances predict onset of depression among female adolescents: A longitudinal study. *Journal of Abnormal Psychology, 109*(3), 438–444.

Stice, E., Presnell, K., & Bearman, S. (2001). Relation of early menarche to depression, eating disorders, substance abuse, and comorbid psychopathology among adolescent girls. *Developmental Psychology, 37*(5), 608–619.

Stice, E., Presnell, K., Shaw, H., & Rohde, P. (2005). Psychological and behavioral risk factors for obesity onset in adolescent girls: A prospective study. *Journal of Consulting and Clinical Psychology, 73*, 195–202.

Stice, E., & Shaw, H. (2003). Prospective relations of body image, eating, and affective disturbances to smoking onset in adolescent girls: How Virginia slims. *Journal of Consulting and Clinical Psychology, 71*(1), 129–135.

Stice, E., & Whitenton, K. (2002). Risk factors for body dissatisfaction in adolescent girls: A longitudinal investigation. *Developmental Psychology, 38*(5), 669–678.

Sticke, E., Burton, E., & Shaw, H. (2004). Prospective relations between bulimic pathology, depression, and substance abuse: Unpacking comorbidity in adolescent girls. *Journal of Consulting and Clinical Psychology, 72,* 62–71.

Stipek, D., & Gralinski, J. (1996). Children's beliefs about intelligence and school performance. *Journal of Educational Psychology, 88,* 397–407.

Stock, J., Bell, M., Boyer, D., & Connell, F. (1997). Adolescent pregnancy and sexual risk-taking among sexually abused girls. *Family Planning Perspectives, 29,* 200–203, 227.

Stocker, C. M., Burwell, R. A., & Briggs, M. L. (2002). Sibling conflict in middle childhood predicts children's adjustment in early adolescence. *Journal of Family Psychology, 16*(1), 50–57.

Stoller, C., Offer, D., Howard, K., & Koenig, L. (1996). Psychiatrists' concept of adolescent self-image. *Journal of Youth and Adolescence, 25,* 273–284.

Stoolmiller, M., Kim, H. K., & Capaldi, D. M. (2005). The course of depressive symptoms in men from early adolescence to young adulthood: Identifying latent trajectories and early predictors. *Journal of Abnormal Psychology, 114,* 331–345.

Storvoll, E. E., & Wichström, L. (2002). Do the risk factors associated with conduct problems vary according to gender? *Journal of Adolescence, 25*(2), 183–202.

Stouthamer-Loeber, M., Loeber, R., Homish, D., & Wei, E. (2001). Maltreatment of boys and the development of disruptive and delinquent behavior. *Development and Psychopathology, 13,* 941–955.

Stouthamer-Loeber, M., Wei, E., & Loeber, R. (2004). Desistance from persistent serious delinquency in the transition to adulthood. *Development and Psychopathology, 16,* 897–918.

Strasburger, V., & Donnerstein, E. (1999). Children, adolescents, and the media: Issues and solutions. *Pediatrics, 103,* 129–139.

Straub, D. M., Hills, N. K., Thompson, P. J., & Moscicki, A. (2003). Effects of pro- and antitobacco advertising on nonsmoking adolescents' intentions to smoke. *Journal of Adolescent Health, 32,* 36–43.

Strauss, M., & Yodanis, C. (1996). Corporal punishment in adolescence and physical assaults on spouses in layer life: What accounts for the link? *Journal of Marriage and the Family, 58,* 825–841.

Strough, J., & Berg, C. (2000). Goals as a mediator of gender differences in high-affiliation dyadic conversations. *Developmental Psychology, 36,* 117–125.

Strouse, J., Goodwin, M., & Roscoe, B. (1994). Correlates of attitudes toward sexual harassment among early adolescents. *Sex Roles, 31,* 559–577.

Studer, M., & Thornton, A. (1987). Adolescent religiosity and contraceptive usage. *Journal of Marriage and the Family, 49,* 117–128.

Stukas, A., Jr., Clary, E., & Snyder, M. (1999). Service learning: Who benefits and why. *Social Policy Report of the Society for Research in Child Development, 13.*

Sturmhöfel, S., & Swartzwelder, H. (2004). Alcohol's effects on the adolescent brain: What can be learned from animal models? *Alcohol Research and Health, 28,* 213–221.

Sucoff, C., & Upchurch, D. (1998). Neighborhood context and the risk of childbearing among metropolitan-area Black adolescents. *American Sociological Review, 63,* 571–585.

Sue, S., & Okazaki, S. (1990). Asian-American educational achievements: A phenomenon in search of an explanation. *American Psychologist, 45,* 913–920.

Sui-Chu, E., & Williams, J. (1996). Effects of parental involvement on eighth-grade achievement. *Sociology of Education, 69,* 126–141.

Sullivan, H. S. (1953a). *The interpersonal theory of psychiatry.* New York: Norton.

Sullivan, H. S. (1953b). *Conceptions of modern psychiatry.* New York: Norton.

Sullivan, K., & Sullivan, A. (1980). Adolescent–parent separation. *Developmental Psychology, 16,* 93–99.

Sullivan, M. (1989). *Getting paid: Youth crime and work in the inner city.* New York: Cornell University Press.

Summers, P., Forehand, R., Armistead, L., & Tannenbaum, L. (1998). Parental divorce during early adolescence in Caucasian families: The role of family process variables in predicting the long-term consequences for early adult psychosocial adjustment. *Journal of Consulting and Clinical Psychology, 66,* 327–336.

Sun, S. S., Schubert, C. M., Liang, R., Roche, A. F., Kulin, H. E., Lee, P. A., Himes, J. H., & Chumlea, W. C. (2005). Is sexual maturity occurring earlier among U.S. children? *Journal of Adolescent Health, 37,* 345–355.

Sun, Y. (2003). The well-being of adolescents in households with no biological parents. *Journal of Marriage and Family 65,* 894

Sun, Y., & Li, Y. (2002). Children's well-being during the parents' marital disruption process: A pooled time-series analysis. *Journal of Marriage and the Family, 64*(2), 472–488.

Sung, H., Richter, L., Vaughan, R., Johnson, P. B., & Thom, B. (2005). Nonmedical use of prescription opioids among teenagers in the United States: Trends and correlates. *Journal of Adolescent Health, 37,* 44–51.

Super, D. (1967). *The psychology of careers.* New York: Harper & Row.

Supple, A. J., Peterson, G. W., & Bush, K. R. (2004). Assessing the validity of parenting measures in a sample of Chinese adolescents. *Journal of Family Psychology, 18,* 539–544.

Susman, E. (1997). Modeling developmental complexity in adolescence: Hormones and behavior in context. *Journal of Research on Adolescence, 7,* 283–306.

Susman, E., & Rogol, A. (2004). Puberty and psychological development. In R. Lerner & L. Steinberg (Eds.), *Handbook of adolescent psychology.* New York: Wiley.

Susman, E., Dorn, L., Inoff-Germain, G., Nottelmann, E., & Chrousos, G. (1997). Cortisol reactivity, distress behavior, and behavioral and psychological problems in young adolescents: A longitudinal perspective. *Journal of Resreach on Adolescence, 7,* 81–105.

Susman, E., Koch, P., Maney, D., & Finkelstein, J. (1993). Health promotion in adolescence: Developmental and theoretical considerations. In R. Lerner (Ed.), *Early adolescence: Perspectives on research, policy, and intervention,* pp. 247–260. Hillsdale, NJ: Erlbaum.

Sussman, S., Dent, C., McAdams, L., Stacy, A., Burton, D., & Flay, B. (1994). Group self-identification and adolescent cigarette smoking: A 1-year prospective study. *Journal of Abnormal Psychology, 103,* 576–580.

Swarr, A., & Richards, M. (1996). Longitudinal effects of adolescent girls' pubertal development, perceptions of pubertal timing, and parental relations on eating problems. *Developmental Psychology, 32,* 636–646.

Swenson, L. P., & Rose, A. J. (2003). Friends as reporters of children's and adolescents' depressive symptoms. *Journal of Abnormal Child Psychology, 31,* 619–631.

Tang, C. S., Yeung, D. Y. L., & Lee, A. M. (2004). A comparison of premenarcheal expectations and postmenarcheal experiences in Chinese early adolescents. *Journal of Early Adolescence, 24,* 180–195.

Tang, C. S., Yeung, D. Y., & Lee, A. M. (2003). Psychosocial correlates of emotional responses to menarche among Chinese adolescent girls. *Journal of Adolescent Health, 33,* 193–201.

Tanner, D. (1972). *Secondary education.* New York: Macmillan.

Tanner, J. (1972). Sequence, tempo, and individual variation in growth and development of boys and girls aged twelve to sixteen. In J. Kagan & R. Coles (Eds.), *Twelve to sixteen: Early adolescence.* New York: Norton.

Tapert, S. F., Baratta, M. V., Abrantas, A. M., & Brown, S. A. (2002). Attention dysfunction predicts involvement in community youths. *Journal of the American Academy of Child and Adolescent Psychiatry, 41,* 680–686.

Taradash, A., Connolly, J., Pepler, D., Craig, W., & Costa, M. (2001). The interpersonal context of romantic autonomy in adolescence. *Journal of Adolescence, 24*(3), 365–377.

Tasker, F., & Richards, M. (1994). Adolescents' attitudes toward marriage and marital prospects after parental divorce: A review. *Journal of Adolescent Research, 9,* 340–362.

Taveras, E. M., Rifas-Shiman, S. L., Field, A. E., Frazier, A. L., Colditz, G. A., & Gillman, M. W. (2004). The influence of wanting to look like media figures on adolescent physical activity. *Journal of Adolescent Health, 35,* 41–50.

Taylor, D., Jenni, O., Acebo, C., & Carskadon, M. (2005). Sleep tendency during extended wakefulness: Insights into adolescent sleep regulation and behavior. *Journal of Sleep Research, 14,* 239–244.

Taylor, R. (1996). Adolescents' perceptions of kinship support and family management practices: Association with adolescent adjustment in African American families. *Developmental Psychology, 32,* 697–695.

Taylor, R., Casten, R., Flickinger, S., Roberts, D., & Fulmore, C. (1994). Explaining the school performance of African-American adolescents. *Journal of Research on Adolescence, 4,* 21–44.

Taylor, R., & Roberts, D. (1995). Kinship support and maternal and adolescent well-being in economically disadvantaged African-American families. *Child Development, 66,* 1585–1597.

Taylor, R., Rodriguez, A. U., Seaton, E. K., & Dominguez, A. (2004). Association of financial resources with parenting and adolescent adjustment in African American families. *Journal of Adolescent Research, 19,* 267–283.

Teachman, J. (1996). Intellectual skill and academic performance: Do families bias the relationship? *Sociology of Education, 69,* 35–48.

Teachman, J. (1997). Gender of siblings, cognitive achievement, and academic performance: Familial and nonfamilial influences on children. *Journal of Marriage and the Family, 59,* 363–374.

Teachman, J. (2003). Premarital sex, premarital cohabitation, and the risk of subsequent marital dissolution among women. *Journal of Marriage and Family, 65,* 444.

Teachman, J., & Paasch, K. (1998). The family and educational aspirations. *Journal of Marriage and the Family, 60,* 704–714.

Teachman, J., Paasch, K., & Carver, K. (1996). Social capital and dropping out of school early. *Journal of Marriage and the Family, 58,* 773–783.

Teachman, J., Paasch, K., & Carver, K. (1997). Social capital and the generation of human capital. *Social Forces, 75,* 1343–1359.

Teen Research Unlimited. (2006). *The TRU Study (Wave 47).* Northbrook, IL: TRU.

Teitler, J. O., & Weiss, C. C. (2000). Effects of neighborhood and school environments on transitions to first sexual intercourse. *Sociology of Education, 73*(2), 112–132.

Terrell, N. (1997). Street life: Aggravated and sexual assaults among homeless and runaway adolescents. *Youth and Society, 28,* 267–290.

Teti, D., & Lamb, M. (1989). Socioeconomic and marital outcomes of adolescent marriage, adolescent childbirth, and their co-occurrence. *Journal of Marriage and the Family, 51,* 203–212.

Tevendale, H., DuBois, D., Lopez, C., & Prindiville, S. (1997). Self-esteem stability and early adolescent adjustment: An exploratory study. *Journal of Early Adolescence, 17,* 216–237.

Thomas, G., Farrell, M., & Barnes, G. (1996). The effects of single-mother families and nonresident fathers on delinquency and substance abuse in black and white adolescents. *Journal of Marriage and the Family, 58,* 884–894.

Thomas, J., & Daubman, K. A. (2001). The relationship between friendship quality and self-esteem in adolescent girls and boys. *Sex Roles, 45*(1–2), 53–65.

Thompson, P., Giedd, J. N., Woods, R. P., MacDonald, D., Evans, A. C., & Toga, A. W. (2000). Growth patterns in the developing brain detected by using continuum mechanical tensor maps. *Nature, 404,* 190–193.

Thompson, R., & Larson, R. (1995). Social context and the subjective experience of different types of rock music. *Journal of Youth and Adolescence, 24,* 731–744.

Thompson, R., & Zuroff, D. C. (1999a). Dependency, self-criticism, and mothers' responses to adolescent sons' autonomy and competence. *Journal of Youth and Adolescence, 28*(3), 365–384.

Thomson, E., Hanson, T., & McLanahan, S. (1994). Family structure and child well-being: Economic resources vs. parental behaviors. *Social Forces, 73,* 221–242.

Thornberry, T., Smith, C., & Howard, G. (1997). Risk factors for teenage fatherhood. *Journal of Marriage and the Family, 59,* 505–522.

Thornberry, T., Freeman-Gallant, A., Lizotte, A. J., Krohn, M. D., & Smith, C. (2003). Linked lives: The intergenerational transmission of antisocial behavior. *Journal of Abnormal Child Psychology, 31,* 171–184.

Thornton, A., Orbuch, T. L., & Axinn, W. G. (1995). Parent–child relationships during the transition to adulthood. *Journal of Family Issues, 16,* 538–564.

Thornton, M., Chatters, L., Taylor, R., & Allen, W. (1990). Sociodemographic and environmental correlates of racial socialization by Black parents. *Child Development, 61,* 401–409.

Thurber, C. (1995). The experience and expression of homesickness in preadolescent and adolescent boys. *Child Development, 66,* 1162–1178.

Tiezzi, L., Lipshutz, J., Wrobleski, N., Vaughan, R., & McCarthy, J. (1997). Pregnancy prevention among urban adolescents younger than 15: Results of the "In Your Face" Program. *Family Planning Perspectives, 29,* 173–176, 197.

Tilton-Weaver, L. C., & Galambos, N. L. (2003). Adolescents' characteristics and parents' beliefs as predictors of parents' peer management behaviors. *Journal of Research on Adolescence, 13,* 269–300.

Timmerman, G. (2002). A comparison between unwanted sexual behavior by teachers and by peers in secondary schools. *Journal of Youth and Adolescence, 31*(5), 397–404.

Tisak, M., Tisak, J., & Rogers, M. (1994). Adolescents' reasoning about authority and friendship relations in the context of drug usage. *Journal of Adolescence, 17,* 265–282.

Tobin-Richards, M. (1985). Sex differences and similarities in heterosexual activity in early adolescence. Paper presented at the biennial meetings of the Society for Research in Child Development, Toronto.

Toch, T. (1993). Violence in schools. *U.S. News & World Report, 115,* 31–37.

Tolan, P., & Gorman-Smith, D. (2002). What violence prevention research can tell us about developmental psychopathology. *Development and Psychopathology, 14,* 713–729.

Tolan, P., Gorman-Smith, D., & Henry, D. (2003). The developmental ecology of urban males' youth violence. *Developmental Psychology, 39*(2), 274–291.

Tolan, P., Gorman-Smith, D., Henry, D., Chung, K., & Hunt, M. (2002). The relation of patterns of coping inner-city youth to psychopathology symptoms. *Journal of Research on Adolescence, 12*(4), 423–449.

Tolman, D. (1993, March). "When my body says yes": Adolescent girls' experiences of sexual desire. Paper presented at the biennial meetings of the Society for Research in Child Development, New Orleans.

Tolson, J., Halliday-Scher, K., & Mack, V. (1994, February). Similarity and friendship quality in African-American adolescents. Paper presented at the biennial meetings of the Society for Research on Adolescence, San Diego.

Tomal, A. (2001). The effect of religious membership on teen abortion rates. *Journal of Youth and Adolescence, 30*(1), 103–116.

Topolski, T. D., Patrick, D. L., Edwards, T. C., Huebner, C. E., Connell, F. A., & Mount, K. K. (2001). Quality of life and health-risk behaviors among adolescents. *Journal of Adolescent Health, 29*(6), 426–435.

Torney-Purta, J. (1990). Youth in relation to social institutions. In S. Feldman & G. Elliott (Eds.), At the threshold: The developing adolescent, pp. 457–478. Cambridge, MA: Harvard University Press.

Tram, J. M., & Cole, D. A. (2000). Self-perceived competence and the relation between life events and depressive symptoms in adolescence: Mediator or moderator? *Journal of Abnormal Psychology, 109*(4), 753–760.

Treaster, J. (1994, February 1). Survey finds marijuana use is up in high schools. *The New York Times,* pp. A1ff.

Treboux, D., & Busch-Rossnagel, N. (1995). Age differences in parent and peer influences on female sexual behavior. *Journal of Research on Adolescence, 5,* 469–487.

Tremblay, R., Mâsse, L., Vitaro, F., & Dobkin, P. (1995). The impact of friends' deviant behaior on early onset of delinquency: Longitudinal data from 6 to 13 years of age. *Development and Psychopathology, 7,* 649–667.

Tremblay, R., Pagani-Kurtz, L., Mâsse, L., Vitaro, F., & Pihl, R. (1995). A bimodal preventive intervention for disruptive kindergarten boys: Its impact through mid-adolescence. *Journal of Consulting and Clinical Psychology, 63,* 560–568.

Trent, K., & Crowder, K. (1997). Adolescent birth intentions, social disadvantage and behavioral outcomes. *Journal of Marriage and the Family, 59,* 523–535.

Trent, K., & Harlan, S. (1994). Teenage mothers in nuclear and extended households: Differences by marital status and race/ethnicity. *Journal of Family Issues, 15,* 309–337.

Trickett, P., McBride-Chang, C., & Putnam, F. (1994). The classroom performance and behavior of sexually abused females. *Development and Psychopathology, 6,* 183–194.

Trickett, P., Noll, J. G., Reiffman, A., & Putnam, F. W. (2001). Variants of intrafamilial sexual abuse experience: Implications for short- and long-term development. *Development and Psychopathology, 13,* 1001–1019.

Trussell, J. (1989). Teenage pregnancy in the United States. *Family Planning Perspectives, 21,* 262–269.

Trusty, J., Plata, M., & Salazar, C. F. (2003). Modeling Mexican Americans' educational expectations: Longitudinal effects of variables across adolescence. *Journal of Adolescent Research, 18,* 131–153.

Trzesniewski, K. H., Donnellan, M. B., Moffitt, T. E., Robins, R. W., Poulton, R., & Caspi, A. (2006). Low self-esteem during adolescence predicts poor health, criminal behavior, and limited economic prospects during adulthood. *Developmental Psychology, 42,* 381–390.

Trzesniewski, K. H., Donnellan, M., & Robins, R. W. (2003). Stability of self-esteem across the life span. *Journal of Personality and Social Psychology, 84*(1), 205–220.

Tschann, J., & Adler, N. (1997). Sexual self-acceptance, communication with partner, and contraceptive use among adolescent females: A longitudinal study. *Journal of Research on Adolescence, 7,* 413–430.

Tschann, J., Flores, E., VanOss Marin, B., Pasch, L. A., Baisch, E., & Wibbelsman, C. J. (2002). Interparental conflict and risk behaviors among Mexican American adolescents: A cognitive-emotional model. *Journal of Abnormal Psychology, 30*(4), 373–385.

Tseng, V. (2004). Family interdependence and academic adjustment in college: Youth from immigrant and U.S.-born families. *Child Development, 75,* 966–983.

Tseng, V., & Fuligni, A. J. (2000). Parent–adolescent language use and relationship among immigrant families with East Asian, Filipino and Latin American backgrounds. *Journal of Marriage and the Family, 62*(2), 465–476.

Tubman, J. G., Montgomery, M. J., Gil, A. G., & Wagner, E. F. (2004). Abuse experiences in a community sample of young adults: Relations with psychiatric disorders, sexual risk behaviors, and sexually transmitted diseases. *American Journal of Community Psychology, 34,* 147–162.

Tucker, C., Barber, B., & Eccles, J. (1997). Advice about life plans and personal problems in late adolescent sibling relationships. *Journal of Youth and Adolescence, 26,* 63–76.

Tucker, C., McHale, S. M., & Crouter, A. C. (2001). Conditions of sibling support in adolescence. *Journal of Family Psychology, 15*(2), 254–271.

Tucker, C., McHale, S. M., & Crouter, A. C. (2003a). Dimensions of mothers' and fathers' differential treatment of siblings: Links with adolescents' sex-typed personal qualities. *Family Relations: Interdisciplinary Journal of Applied Family Studies, 52*(1), 82–89.

Tucker, C., McHale, S., & Crouter, A. (2003b). Conflict resolution links with adolescents' family relationships and individual well-being. *Journal of Family Influence, 24,* 715–736.

Turiel, E. (1998). The development of morality. In W. Damon (Series Ed.) and N. Eisenberg (Vol. Ed.), *Handbook of child psychology,* Vol. 3: *Social, emotional, and personality development* (5th ed.), pp. 863–932. New York: Wiley.

Turkheimer, E., & Waldron, M. (2000). Nonshared environment: A theoretical, methodological, and quantitative review. *Psychological Bulletin, 126,* 78–108.

Turner, R., Sorenson, A. M., & Turner, J. (2000). Social contingencies in mental health: A seven-year follow-up study of teenage mothers. *Journal of Marriage and the Family, 62*(3), 777–791.

Twenge, J. (2000). The age of anxiety? The birth cohort change in anxiety and neuroticism, 1952–1993. *Journal of Personality and Social Psychology, 79*(6), 1007–1021.

Twenge, J., & Crocker, J. (2002). Race and self-esteem: Meta-analyses comparing Whites, Blacks, Hispanics, Asians, and American Indians and comment on Gray-Little and Hafdahl. *Psychological Bulletin, 128*(3), 371–408.

Twenge, J., & Nolen-Hoeksema, S. (2002). Age, gender, race, socioeconomic status, and birth cohort difference on the children's depression inventory: A meta-analysis. *Journal of Abnormal Psychology, 111*(4), 578–588.

Tyler, K. A., Hoyt, D. R., Whitbeck, L. B., & Cauce, A. (2001). The impact of childhood sexual abuse on later sexual victimization among runaway youth. *Journal of Research on Adolescence, 11*(2), 151–176.

Tyrka, A. R., Graber, J. A., & Brooks-Gunn, J. (2000). The development of disordered eating: Correlate and predictors of eating problems in the context of adolescence. In A. J. Sameroff, M. Lewis, & S. M. Miller (Eds.), *Handbook of developmental psychopathology* (2nd ed.), pp. 607–624. New York: Kluwer Academic/Plenum.

Tyson, K., Darity, W., & Castellino, D. R. (2005). It's not "a black thing." Understanding the burden of acting white and other dilemmas of high achievement. *American Sociological Review, 70,* 582–605.

U.S. Bureau of the Census. (1994). *Who's minding the kids?* Washington, DC: U.S. Bureau of the Census.

U.S. Bureau of the Census. (2000). *Projections of the total resident population by 5-year age groups and sex with special age categories: Middle series, 1999 to 2100.* Washington, DC: U.S. Department of Commerce.

U.S. Bureau of the Census. (2006). *Current population survey.* Washington, DC: Author.

U.S. Census Bureau. (2002). *Statistical abstract of the United States.* Washington, DC: Author.

U.S. Census Bureau. (2003). *Current population survey, March 2002.* Washington: U.S. Department of Commerce.

U.S. Census Bureau. (2005). *Statistical abstract of the United States.* Washington, DC: Author.

U.S. Department of Education. (2006). *No Child Left Behind.* Available at www.ed.gov/nclb/landing.html.

U.S. Department of Commerce, Bureau of the Census. (1940). *Characteristics of the population.* Washington, D.C.: U.S. Government Printing Office.

UCLA Higher Education Research Institute (1999). *The American freshman: National norms for Fall, 1998.* Los Angeles: Author.

UCLA Higher Education Research Institute (2000). *The American Freshman: National norms for Fall, 1999.* Los Angeles: Author.

Udry, J. (1987). Hormonal and social determinants of adolescent sexual initiation. In J. Bancroft (Ed.), *Adolescence and puberty.* New York: Oxford University Press.

Udry, J. R., & Billy, J. (1987). Initiation of coitus in early adolescence. *American Sociological Review, 52,* 841–855.

Udry, J., & Chantala, K. (2002). Risk assessment of adolescents with same-sex relationships. *Journal of Adolescent Health, 31*(1), 84–92.

Udry, J., Billy, J., Morris, N., Gruff, T., & Raj, M. (1985). Serum androgenic hormones motivate sexual behavior in boys. *Fertility and Sterility, 43,* 90–94.

Udry, J., Halpern, C., & Campbell, B. (1991, April). Hormones, pubertal development, and sexual behavior in adolescent females. Paper presented at the biennial meetings of the Society for Research in Child Development, Seattle.

Udry, J., Talbert, L., & Morris, N. (1986). Biosocial foundations for adolescent female sexuality. *Demography, 23,* 217–230.

Uhlenberg, P., & Eggebeen, D. (1986). The declining well-being of American adolescents. *Public Interest, 82,* 25–38.

Umana-Taylor, A. J., & Bámaca-Gómez, M. Y. (2003). Generational differences in resistance to peer pressure among Mexican-origin adolescents. *Youth and Society, 35,* 183–203.

Umaña-Taylor, A. J. (2004). Ethnic identity and self-esteem: Examining the role of social context. *Journal of Adolescence, 27,* 139–146.

Underwood, M., Kupersmidt, J., & Coie, J. (1996). Childhood peer sociometric status and aggression as predictors of adolescent childbearing. *Journal of Research on Adolescence, 6,* 201–223.

Unger, J., Kipke, M., Simon, T., Montgomery, S., & Johnson, C. (1997). Homeless youths and young adults in Los Angeles: Prevalence of mental health problems and the relationship between mental health and substance abuse disorders. *American Journal of Community Psychology, 25,* 371–394.

Unger J., Molina G., & Teran, L. (2002). Perceived consequences of teenage childbearing among adolescent girls in an urban sample. *Journal of Adolescent Health, 26,* 205–212.

Unger, J., & Rohrbach, L. (2002). Why do adolescents overestimate their peers' smoking prevalence? Correlates of prevalence estimates among California 8th-grade students. *Journal of Youth and Adolescence, 31*(2), 147–153.

Upchurch, D., Aneshensel, C., Sucoff, C., & Levy-Storms, L. (1999). Neighborhood and family contexts of adolescent sexual activity. *Journal of Marriage and the Family, 61,* 920–933.

Upchurch, D., Levy-Storms, L., Sucoff, C., & Aneshensel, C. (1998). Gender and ethnic differences in the timing of first sexual intercourse. *Family Planning Perspectives, 30,* 121–127.

Upchurch, D., & McCarthy, J. (1990). The timing of a first birth and high school completion. *American Sociological Review, 55,* 224–234.

Updegraff, K. A., Helms, H. M., McHale, S. M., Crouter, A. C., Thayer, S. M., & Sales, L. H. (2004). Who's the boss? Patterns of perceived control in adolescents' friendships. *Journal of Youth and Adolescence, 33,* 403–420.

Updegraff, K. A., Madden-Derdich, D. A., Estrada, A., Sales, L. J., & Leonard, S. A. (2002). Young adolescents' experiences with parents and friends: Exploring the connections. *Family Relations, 51*(1), 72–80.

Updegraff, K., McHale, S. M., & Crouter, A. C. (2000). Adolescents' sex-typed friendship experiences: Does having a sister versus and brother matter? *Child Development, 71*(6), 1597–1610.

Updegraff, K., McHale, S. M., Crouter, A. C., & Kupanoff, K. (2001). Parents' involvement in adolescents' peer relationships: A comparison of mothers' and fathers' roles. *Journal of Marriage and the Family, 63*(3), 655–668.

Urberg, K., Değirmencioğlu, S., & Pilgrim, C. (1997). Close friend and group influence on adolescent cigarette smoking and alcohol use. *Developmental Psychology, 33,* 834–844.

Urberg, K., Değirmencioğlu, S., Tolson, J., & Halliday-Scher, K. (1995). The structure of adolescent peer networks. *Developmental Psychology, 31,* 540–547.

Usmiani, S., & Daniluk, J. (1997). Mothers and their adolescent daughters: Relationship between self-esteem, gender role identity, and body image. *Journal of Youth and Adolescence, 26,* 45–62.

Valois, R., Oeltmann, J., Waller, J., & Hussey, J. (1999). Relationship between number of sexual intercourse partners and selected health risk behaviors among public high school adolescents. *Journal of Adolescent Health, 25,* 328–335.

Vandell, D., & Corasaniti, M. (1988). The relation between third graders' after-school care and social, academic, and emotional functioning. *Child Development, 59,* 868–875.

Vandell, D., & Ramanan, J. (1991). Children of the National Longitudinal Survey of Youth: Choices in after-school care and child development. *Developmental Psychology, 27,* 637–643.

Van den Bulck, J. (2004). Television viewing, computer game playing, and Internet use and self-reported time to bed and time out of bed in secondary-school children. *Sleep, 27,* 101–104.

Vandewater, E., & Lansford, J. (1998). Influences of family structure and parental conflict on children's well-being. *Family Relations, 47,* 323–330.

Vanfossen, B., Jones, J., & Spade, J. (1987). Curriculum tracking and status maintenance. *Sociology of Education, 60,* 104–122.

van Hoof, A. (1999). The identity status field re-reviewed: An update of unresolved and neglected issues with a view on some alternative approaches. *Developmental Review, 19,* 497–556.

Van Leeuwen, K. G., Mervielda, I., Braet, C., & Bosmans, G. (2004). Child personality and parental behavior as moderators of problem behavior: Variable- and person-centered approaches. *Developmental Psychology, 40,* 1028–1046.

van Roosmalen, E. (2000). Forces of patriarchy: Adolescent experiences of sexuality and conceptions of relationships. *Youth and Society, 32*(2), 202–227.

van Wel, F. (1994). "I count my parents among my best friends:" Youths' bonds with parents and friends in the Netherlands. *Journal of Marriage and the Family, 56,* 835–843.

Varenne, H. (1982). Jocks and freaks: The symbolic structure of the expression of social interaction among American senior high school students. In G. Spindler (Ed.), *Doing the ethnography of schooling,* pp. 213–235. New York: Holt, Rinehart & Winston.

Vaughan, R., McCarthy, J., Armstrong, B., Walter, H., Waterman, P., & Tiezzi, L. (1996). Carrying and using weapons: A survey of minority junior high school students in New York City. *American Journal of Public Health, 86,* 568–572.

Vazsonyi, A. T., Hibbert, J. R., & Black, S. J. (2003). Exotic enterprise no more? Adolescent reports of family and parenting processes from youth in four countries. *Journal of Research on Adolescence, 13,* 129–160.

Vega, W., Khoury, E., Zimmerman, R., Gil, A., & Warheit, G. (1995). Cultural conflicts and problem behaviors of Latino adolescents in home and school environments. *Journal of Community Psychology, 23,* 167–179.

Velez, W. (1989). High school attrition among Hispanic and non-Hispanic White youths. *Sociology of Education, 62,* 119–133.

Vera Institute of Justice. (1990). *The male role in teenage pregnancy and parenting.* New York: Vera Institute of Justice.

Verkuyten, M. (1995). Self-esteem, self-concept stability, and aspects of ethnic identity among minority and majority youth in the Netherlands. *Journal of Youth and Adolescence, 24,* 155–185.

Verma, S., & Larson, R. (Eds.). (2003). Examining adolescent leisure time across cultures. *New Directions for Child and Adolescent Development, 99.*

Vermeer, H. J., Boekaerts, M., & Seegers, G. (2000). Motivational and gender differences: Sixth-grade students' mathematical problem-solving behavior. *Journal of Educational Psychology, 92*(2), 308–315.

Vermeiren, R., Ruchkin, V., Leckman, P. E., Deboutte, D., & Schwab-Stone, M. (2002). Exposure to violence and suicide risk in adolescents: A community study. *Journal of Abnormal Child Psychology, 30*(5), 529–537.

Vicary, J., Klingaman, L., & Harkness, W. (1995). Risk factors associated with date rape and sexual assault of adolescent girls. *Journal of Adolescence, 18,* 289–306.

Videon, T. M. (2002). The effects of parent–adolescent relationships and parental separation on adolescent well-being. *Journal of Marriage and the Family, 64*(2), 489–503.

Vieno, A., Perkins, D. D., Smith, T. M., & Santinello, M. (2005). Democratic school climate and sense of community in the school: A multilevel analysis. *American Journal of Community Psychology, 36,* 327–341.

Vigersky, R. (Ed.). (1977). *Anorexia nervosa.* New York: Raven Press.

Viljoen, J. L., Klaver, J., & Roesch, R. (2005). Legal decisions of preadolescent and adolescent defendants: Predictors of confessions, pleas, communication with attorneys, and appeals. *Law and Human Behavior, 29,* 253–277.

Vincent, G. M., Vitacco, M. J., Grisso, T., & Corraso, R. R. (2003). Subtypes of adolescent offenders: Affective traits and antisocial behavior patterns. *Behavioral Sciences and the Law, 21,* 695–712.

Vispoel, W. A. J. (1995). Success and failure in junior high school: A critical incident approach to understanding students' attributional beliefs. *American Educational Research Journal, 32,* 377–412.

Vitaro, F., Brendgen, M., & Tremblay, R. E. (2000). Influence of deviant friends on delinquency: Searching for moderator variables. *Journal of Abnormal Child Psychology, 28*(4), 313–325.

Vitaro, F., Tremblay, R., Kerr, M., Pagani, L., & Bukowski, W. (1997). Disruptiveness,

friends' characteristics, and delinquency in early adolescence: A test of two competing models. *Child Development, 68,* 676–689.

Voelkl, K. (1997). Identification with school. *American Journal of Education, 105,* 294–318.

Volkow, N., & Ting-Kai, L. (2005). The neuroscience of addiction. *Nature Neuroscience, 8,* 1429–1430.

Voyer, D., Voyer, S., & Bryden, M. (1995). Magnitude of sex differences in spatial abilities: A meta-analysis and consideration of critical variables. *Psychological Bulletin, 117,* 250–270.

Vuchinich, S., Angeletti, J., & Gatherum, A. (1996). Context and development in family problem solving with preadolescent children. *Child Development, 67,* 1276–1288.

Vuchinich, S., Hetherington, E. M., Vuchinich, R., & Clingempeel, W. (1991). Parent–child interaction and gender differences in early adolescents' adaptation to stepfamilies. *Developmental Psychology, 27,* 618–626.

Vygotsky, L. ([1930]1978). *Mind in society.* Cambridge, MA: Harvard University Press.

Wade, T. J., Cairney, J., & Pevalin, D. J. (2002). Emergence of gender differences in depression during adolescence: National panel results from three countries. *Journal of the American Academy of Child and Adolescent Psychiatry, 41,* 190–198.

Wadsworth, M. E., & Compas, B. E. (2002). Coping with family conflict and economic strain: The adolescent perspective. *Journal of Research on Adolescence, 12*(2), 243–274.

Wagner, B., Cohen, P., & Brook, J. (1996). Parent/adolescent relationships: Moderators of the effects of stressful life events. *Journal of Adolescent Research, 11,* 347–374.

Wainer, H., & Steinberg, L. (1992). Sex differences in performance on the mathematics section of the Scholastic Aptitude Test: A bidirectional validity study. *Harvard Educational Review, 62,* 323–336.

Wainright, J. L., Russell, S. T., & Patterson, C. J. (2004). Psychosocial adjustment, school outcomes, and romantic relationships of adolescents with same-sex parents. *Child Development, 75,* 1886–1898.

Wainryb, C., Shaw, L. A., Laupa, M., & Smith, K. R. (2001). Children's, adolescents', and young adults' thinking about different types of disagreements. *Developmental Psychology, 37*(3), 373–386.

Waite, L., Goldscheider, F., & Witsberger, C. (1986). Nonfamily living and the erosion of traditional family orientations among young adults. *American Sociological Review, 51,* 541–554.

Waizenhofer, R., Buchanan, C. M., & Jackson-Newsom, J. (2004). Mothers' and fathers' knowledge of adolescents' daily activities: Its sources and its links with adolescent adjustment. *Journal of Family Psychology, 18,* 348–360.

Wakschliag, L. S., Gordon, R. A., Lahey, B. B., Loeber, R., Green, S. M., & Leventhal, B. L. (2000). Maternal age at first birth and boys' risk for conduct disorder. *Journal of Research on Adolescence, 10*(4), 417–441.

Walberg, H. (1998). *Spending more while learning less.* New York: Thomas B. Fordham Foundation.

Wald, M. (2005). Foreword. In D. Osgood, M. Foster, C. Flanagan, & G. Ruth (Eds.), *On your own without a net: The transition to adulthood for vulnerable populations,* pp. vii–xi. Chicago: University of Chicago Press.

Waldman, I. (1996). Aggressive boys' hostile perceptual and response biases: The role of attention and impulsivity. *Child Development, 67,* 1015–1033.

Walker, E. F., Sabuwalla, Z., & Huot, R. (2004). Pubertal neuromaturation, stress sensitivity, and psychopathology. *Development and Psychopathology, 16,* 807–824.

Walker, L., de Vries, B., & Trevethan, S. (1987). Moral stages and moral orientations in real-life and hypothetical dilemmas. *Child Development, 58,* 842–858.

Walker, L., Gustafson, P., & Hennig, K. H. (2001). The consolidation/transition model in moral reasoning development. *Developmental Psychology, 37*(2), 187–197.

Walker-Barnes, C. J., & Mason, C. A. (2004). Delinquency and substance use among gang-involved youth: The moderating role of parenting practices. *American Journal of Community Psychology, 34,* 235–250.

Wall, J., Power, T., & Arbona, C. (1993). Susceptibility to antisocial peer pressure and its relation to acculturation in Mexican-American adolescents. *Journal of Adolescent Research, 8,* 403–418.

Wallace, J. M., Forman, T. A., Caldwell, C. H., & Willis, D. S. (2003). Religion and U.S. secondary school students current patterns, recent trends, and sociodemographic correlates. *Youth and Society, 35,* 98–125.

Wallace-Broscious, A., Serafica, F., & Osipow, S. (1994). Adolescent career development: Relationships to self-concept and identity status. *Journal of Research on Adolescence, 4,* 127–149.

Waller, E., M., & DuBois, D. L. (2004). Investigation of stressful experiences, self-evaluations, and self-standards as predictors of sexual activity during early adolescence. *Journal of Early Adolescence, 24,* 431–459.

Wallerstein, J., & Blakeslee, S. (1989). *Second chances.* New York: Ticknor & Fields.

Wallerstein, J., & Kelley, J. (1974). The effects of parental divorce: The adolescent experience. In E. Anthony & A. Koupernik (Eds.), *The child in his family: Children as a psychiatric risk,* Vol. 3. New York: Wiley.

Wallis, C. (2004, May 10). What makes teens tick? *Time.*

Walsh, B., Kaplan, A., Attia, E., Olmsted, M., Parides, M., Carter, J., Pike, K., Devlin, M., Woodside, B., Roberto, C., & Rockert, W. (2006). Fluoxetine after weight restoration in anorexia nervosa: A randomized controlled trial. *Journal of the American Medical Association, 295,* 2605–2612.

Walsh, S., Shulman, S., Bar-On, Z., & Tsur, A. (2006). The role of parentification and family climate in adaptation among immigrant descendants in Israel. *Journal of Research on Adolescence, 16,* 321–350.

Wang, R., Bianchi, S. M., & Raley, S. B. (2005). Teenagers' Internet use and family rules: A research note. *Journal of Marriage and Family, 67,* 1249.

Wang, Y. (2002). Is obesity associated with early sexual maturation? A comparison of the association in American boys versus girls. *Pediatrics, 110*(5), 903–910.

Wångby, M., Bergman, L., & Magnusson, D. (1999). Development of adjustment problems in girls: What syndromes emerge? *Child Development, 70,* 678–699.

Ward, L. M., & Friedman, K. (2006). Using TV as a guide: Associations between television viewing and adolescents' sexual attitudes and behavior. *Journal of Research on Adolescence, 16,* 133–156.

Ward, L. M., Hansbrough, E., & Walker, E. (2005). Contributions of music video exposure to black adolescents' gender and sexual schemas. *Journal of Adolescent Research, 20,* 143–166.

Ward, M. (1995). Talking about sex: Common themes about sexuality in the prime-time television programs children and adolescents view most. *Journal of Youth and Adolescence, 24,* 595–615.

Ward, M. (2003). Understanding the role of entertainment media in the sexual socialization of American youth: A review of empirical research. *Developmental Review, 23,* 347–388.

Warneke, C., & Cooper, S. (1994). Child and adolescent drownings in Harris County, Texas, 1983 through 1990. *American Journal of Public Health, 84,* 593–598.

Warner, S., & Moore, S. (2004). Excuses, excuses: Self-handicapping in an Australian adolescent sample. *Journal of Youth and Adolescence, 33,* 271–281.

Warren, C., Santelli, J., Everett, S., Kann, L., Collins, J., Cassell, C., Morris, L., & Kolbe, L. (1998). *Sexual behavior among U.S. high school students, 1990–1995. Family Planning Perspectives, 30,* 170–172, 200.

Warren, J. (2002). Reconsidering the relationship between student employment and academic outcomes: A new theory and better data. *Youth and Society, 33*(3), 366–393.

Warren, J. R., & Jenkins, K. N. (2005). High school exit examinations and high school

dropout in Texas and Florida, 1971–2000. *Sociology of Education, 78,* 122–143.

Washburn-Ormachea, J. M., Hillman, S. B., & Sawilowsky, S. S. (2004). Gender and gender-role orientation differences on adolescents' coping with peer stressors. *Journal of Youth and Adolescent, 33,* 31–40.

Wasserman, G., Rauh, V., Brunelli, S., Garcia-Castro, M., & Necos, B. (1990). Psychosocial attributes and life experiences of disadvantaged minority mothers: Age and ethnic variations. *Child Development, 61,* 566–580.

Waterman, A. (1982). Identity development from adolescence to adulthood: An extension of theory and a review of research. *Developmental Psychology, 18,* 341–358.

Waterman, A. (1999a). Commentary: Identity, the identity statuses, and identity status development: A contemporary statement. *Developmental Review, 19,* 591–621.

Waterman, A. (1999b). Issues of identity formation revisited: United States and the Netherlands. *Developmental Review, 19,* 462–279.

Waterman, A., Geary, P., & Waterman, A. (1974). A longitudinal study of changes in ego identity status from the freshman to the senior year at college. *Developmental Psychology, 10,* 387–392.

Waterman, A., & Goldman, J. (1976). A longitudinal study of ego identity development at a liberal arts college. *Journal of Youth and Adolescence, 5,* 361–369.

Waters, E., Merrick, S., Treboux, D., Crowell, J., & Albersheim, L. (2000). Attachment security in infancy and early adulthood: A twenty-year longitudinal study. *Child Development, 71,* 684–689.

Watson, D., & Kendall, P. (1989). Understanding anxiety and depression: Their relation to negative and positive affective states. In P. Kendall (Ed.), *Anxiety and depression,* pp. 3–26. New York: Academic Press.

Watt, H. M. (2004). Development of adolescents' self-perceptions, values, and task perceptions according to gender and domain in 7th- through 11th-grade Australian students. *Child Development, 75,* 1556–1574.

Watt, T. T. (2003). Are small schools and private schools better for adolescents' emotional adjustment? *Sociology of Education, 76,* 344–367.

Way, N., & Chen, L. (2000). Close and general friendships among African American, Latino, and Asian American adolescents from low-income families. *Journal of Adolescent Research, 15*(2), 274–301.

Way, N., & Greene, M. L. (2006). Trajectories of perceived friendship quality during adolescence: The patterns and contextual predictors. *Journal of Research on Adolescence, 16,* 293–320.

Way, N., & Pahl, K. (2001). Individual and contextual predictors of perceived friendship quality among ethnic minority, low-income adolescents. *Journal of Research on Adolescence, 11*(4), 325–349.

Way, N., & Robinson, M. G. (2003). A longitudinal study of the effects of family, friends, and school experiences on the psychological adjustment of ethnic minority, low-SES adolescents. *Journal of Adolescent Research, 18,* 324–346.

Weinfield, N., Ogawa, J. R., & Sroufe, L. A. (1997). Early attachment as a pathway to adolescent peer competence. *Journal of Research on Adolescence, 7*(3), 241–265.

Weinfeld, N., Sroufe, A., & Egeland, B. (2000). Attachment from infancy to early adulthood in a high-risk sample: Continuity, discontinuity, and their correlates. *Child Development, 71,* 695–702.

Weisner, T., & Garnier, H. (1995, March). Family values and nonconventional family lifestyles: An 18-year longitudinal study at adolescence. Paper presented at the biennial meetings of the Society for Research in Child Development, Indianapolis.

Weiss, R. (1974). The provisions of social relationships. In Z. Rubin (Ed.), *Doing unto others.* Englewood Cliffs, NJ: Prentice-Hall.

Weiss, R. (1979). Growing up a little faster: The experience of growing up in a single parent household. *Journal of Social Issues, 35,* 97–111.

Weissberg, R., Caplan, M., & Harwood, R. (1991). Promoting competent young people in competence-enhancing environments: A systems-based perspective on primary prevention. *Journal of Consulting and Clinical Psychology, 59,* 830–841.

Weist, M., Freedman, A., Paskewitz, D., Proescher, E., & Flaherty, L. (1995). Urban youth under stress: Empirical identification of protective factors. *Journal of Youth and Adolescence, 24,* 705–729.

Weisz, J., & Hawley, K. M. (2002). Developmental factors in the treatment of adolescents. *Journal of Consulting and Clinical Psychology, 70*(1), 21–43.

Weisz, J., McCabe, M., & Dennig, M. (1994). Primary and secondary control among children undergoing medical procedures: Adjustment as a function of coping style. *Journal of Consulting and Clinical Psychology, 62,* 324–332.

Weisz, J., Weiss, B., Han, S., Granger, D., & Morton, T. (1995). Effects of psychotherapy with children and adolescents revisited: A meta-analysis of treatment outcome studies. *Psychological Bulletin, 117,* 450–468.

Wells, A. (1995). Reexamining social science research on desegregation: Long- versus short-term effects. *Teachers College Record, 96,* 691–706.

Wells, A., & Serna, I. (1996). The politics of culture: Understanding local political resistance

to detracking in racially mixed schools. *Harvard Educational Review, 66,* 93–118.

Wentzel, K. (1989). Adolescent classroom goals, standards for performance, and academic achievement: An interactionist perspective. *Journal of Educational Psychology, 81,* 131–142.

Wentzel, K. (1994). Relations of social goal pursuit to social acceptance, classroom behavior, and perceived social support. *Journal of Educational Psychology, 86,* 173–182.

Wentzel, K. (1998). Social relationships and motivation in middle school: The role of parents, teachers, and peers. *Journal of Educational Psychology, 90,* 202–209.

Wentzel, K. (2002). Are effective teachers like good parents? Teaching styles and student adjustment in early adolescence. *Child Development, 73*(1), 287–301.

Wentzel, K. (2003). Sociometric status and adjustment in middle school: A longitudinal study. *Journal of Early Adolescence, 23*(1), 5–28.

Wentzel, K., & Asher, S. (1995). The academic lives of neglected, rejected, popular, and controversial children. *Child Development, 66,* 754–763.

Wentzel, K., & Caldwell, K. (1997). Friendships, peer acceptance, and group membership: Relations to academic achievement in middle school. *Child Development, 68,* 1198–1209.

Wentzel, K., & Erdley, C. (1993). Strategies for making friends: Relations to social behavior and peer acceptance in early adolescence. *Developmental Psychology, 29,* 819–826.

Werner, N. E., & Nixon, C. L. (2005). Normative beliefs about relational aggression: An investigation of the cognitive bases of adolescent aggressive behavior. *Journal of Youth and Adolescence, 34,* 229–243.

Werner, N. E., & Silbereisen, R. K. (2003). Family relationship quality and contact with deviant peers as predictors of adolescent problem behaviors: The moderating role of gender. *Journal of Adolescent Research, 18,* 454–480.

Westoff, C. (1988). Unintended pregnancy in America and abroad. *Family Planning Perspectives, 20,* 254–261.

Whitaker, D., & Miller, K. (2000). Parent–adolescent discussions about sex and condoms: Impact on peer influences of sexual risk behavior. *Journal of Adolescent Research, 15*(2), 251–273.

Whitaker, D., Miller, K., & Clark, L. F. (2000). Reconceptualizing adolescent sexual behavior: Beyond did they or didn't they? *Family Planning Perspectives, 32*(3), 111–117.

Whitbeck, L., Conger, R., Simons, R., & Kao, M. (1993). Minor deviant behaviors and adolescent sexuality. *Youth and Society, 25,* 24–37.

Whitbeck, L., Hoyt, D., & Ackley, K. (1997). Abusive family backgrounds and later victimization among runaway and homeless

adolescents. *Journal of Research on Adolescence, 7,* 375–392.

Whitbeck, L., Hoyt, D., & Bao, W. (2000). Depressive symptoms and co-occurring depressive symptoms, substance abuse, and conduct problems among runaway and homeless adolescents. *Child Development, 71*(3), 721–732.

Whitbeck, L., Hoyt, D., Miller, M., & Kao, M. (1992). Parental support, depressed affect, and sexual experience among adolescents. *Youth and Society, 24,* 166–177.

Whitbeck, L., Simons, R., & Kao, M. (1994). The effects of divorced mothers' dating behaviors and sexual attitudes on the sexual attitudes and behaviors of their adolescent children. *Journal of Marriage and the Family, 56,* 615–621.

Whitbeck, L., Hoyt, D., & Yoder, K. (1999). A risk-amplification model of victimization and depressive symptoms among runaway and homeless adolescents. *American Journal of Community Psychology, 27,* 273–296.

Whitbeck, L., Yoder, K., Hoyt, D., & Conger, R. (1999). Early adolescent sexual activity: A developmental study. *Journal of Marriage and the Family, 61,* 934–946.

White, K., Speisman, J., & Costos, D. (1983). Young adults and their parents. In H. Grotevant & C. Cooper (Eds.), *Adolescent development in the family,* pp. 61–76. San Francisco: Jossey-Bass.

White, L., & Brinkerhoff, D. (1981). The sexual division of labor: Evidence from childhood. *Social Forces, 60,* 170–181.

Whiteman, S., & Buchanan, C. (2002). Mothers and children's expectations for adolescence: The impact of perceptions of an older sibling's experience. *Journal of Family Psychology, 16*(2), 157–171.

Whitesell, N., & Harter, S. (1996). The interpersonal context of emotion: Anger with close friends and classmates. *Child Development, 67,* 1345–1359.

Whiting, B., & Whiting, J. (1975). Children of six cultures. Cambridge, MA: Harvard University Press.

Wichstrøm, L. (1999). The emergence of gender difference in depressed mood during adolescence: The role of intensified gender socialization. *Developmental Psychology, 35,* 232–245.

Wichstrøm, L. (2001). The impact of pubertal timing on adolescents' alcohol use. *Journal of Research on Adolescence, 11*(2), 131–150.

Wickrama, K. A., Merton, M., & Elder, G. (2005). Community influence on precocious transitions to adulthood: Racial differences and mental health consequences. *Journal of Community Psychology, 33,* 639–653.

Widmer, E. (1997). Influence of older siblings on initiation of sexual intercourse. *Journal of Marriage and the Family, 59,* 928–938.

Widom, C., & Kuhns, J. (1996). Childhood victimization and subsequent risk for promiscuity, prostitution, and teenage pregnancy: A prospective study. *American Journal of Public Health, 86*, 1607–1612.

Wiesner, M., Kim, H. K., & Capaldi, D. M. (2005). Developmental trajectories of offending: Validation and prediction to young adult alcohol use, drug use, and depressive symptoms. *Development and Psychopathology, 17*, 251–270.

Wiesner, M., & Windle, M. (2004). Assessing covariates of adolescent delinquency trajectories: A latent growth mixture modeling approach. *Journal of Youth and Adolescence, 33*, 431–442.

Wigfield, A., Eccles, J., MacIver, D., Reuman, D., & Midgley, C. (1991). Transitions during early adolescence: Changes in children's domain-specific self-perceptions and general self-esteem across the transition to junior high school. *Developmental Psychology, 27*, 552–565.

Wight, R. G., Sepúlveda, J. E., & Aneshensel, C. S. (2004). Depressive symptoms: How do adolescents compare with adults? *Journal of Adolescent Health, 34*, 314–323.

Wilcox, W. (1998). Conservative Protestant childrearing: Authoritarian or authoritative? *American Sociological Review, 63*, 796–809.

Wilkinson, D., & Fagan, J. (1996). The role of firearms in violence "scripts:" The dynamics of gun events among adolescent males. *Law and Contemporary Problems, 59*, 55–89.

Wilkinson, R. B. (2004). The role of parental and peer attachment in the psychological health and self-esteem of adolescents. *Journal of Youth and Adolescence, 33*, 479–493.

William T. Grant Foundation Commission on Work, Family, and Citizenship. (1988). *The forgotten half: Non-college youth in America.* Washington, DC: Author.

Williams, A. (2003). Teenage drivers: Patterns of risk. *Journal of Safety Research, 34*, 5–15.

Williams, P., Holmbeck, G. N., & Greenley, R. N. (2002). Adolescent health psychology. *Journal of Consulting and Clinical Psychology, 70*(3), 828–842.

Williams, S. K., & Kelly, F. D. (2005). Relationships among involvement, attachment, and behavioral problems in adolescence: Examining fathers' influence. *Journal of Early Adolescence, 25*, 168–196.

Williams, W., Blythe, T., White, N., Li, J., Gardner, H., & Sternberg, R. J. (2002). Practical intelligence for school: Developing metacognitive sources of achievement in adolescence. *Developmental Review, 22*(2), 162–210.

Williamson, J., Borduin, C., & Howe, B. (1991). The ecology of adolescent maltreatment: A multilevel examination of adolescent physical abuse, sexual abuse, and neglect. *Journal of Consulting and Clinical Psychology, 59*, 449–457.

Willits, F. (1988). Adolescent behavior and adult success and well-being. *Youth and Society, 20*, 68–69.

Willoughby, T., Chalmers, H., & Busseri, M. A. (2004). Where is the syndrome? Examining co-occurrence among multiple problem behaviors in adolescence. *Journal of Consulting and Clinical Psychology, 72*, 1022–1037.

Wills, T., & Cleary, S. (1996). How are social support effects mediated? A test with parental support and adolescent substance use. *Journal of Personality and Social Psychology, 71*, 937–952.

Wills, T., McNamara, G., Vaccaro, D., & Hirky, A. (1996). Escalated substance use: A longitudinal grouping analysis from early to middle adolescence. *Journal of Abnormal Psychology, 105*, 166–180.

Wills, T., Sandy, J. M., Yaeger, A., & Shinar, O. (2001). Family risk factors and adolescent substance use: Moderation effects for temperament dimensions. *Developmental Psychology, 37*(3), 283–297.

Wilson, M., & Daly, M. (1985). Competitiveness, risk taking, and violence: The young male syndrome. *Ethology and Sociobiology, 6*, 59–73.

Wilson, P., & Wilson, J. (1992). Environmental influences on adolescent educational aspirations: A logistic transform model. *Youth and Society, 24*, 52–70.

Wilson, R. (February 1, 2005). The six simple principles of viral marketing. *Web Marketing Today.* Available at www.wilsonweb.com/wmt5/viral-principles.htm.

Wilson, T., & Linville, P. (1985). Improving the performance of college freshmen with attributional techniques. *Journal of Personality and Social Psychology, 49*, 287–293.

Wilson, W. (1987). *The truly disadvantaged: The inner city, the underclass, and public policy.* Chicago: University of Chicago Press.

Windle, M. (1989). Substance use and abuse among adolescent runaways: A four-year follow-up study. *Journal of Youth and Adolescence, 18*, 331–344.

Windle, M. (1994). A study of friendship characteristics and problem behaviors among middle adolescents. *Child Development, 65*, 1764–1777.

Windle, M. & Weisner, M. (2004). Trajectories of marijuana use from adolescence to young adulthood: Predictors and outcomes. *Development and Psychopathology, 16*, 1007–1027.

Windle, M., & Windle, R. (1996). Coping strategies, drinking motives, and stressful life events among middle adolescents: Associations with emotional and behavioral problems and with academic functioning. *Journal of Abnormal Psychology, 105*, 551–560.

Windle, M., & Windle, R. (2001). Depressive symptoms and cigarette smoking among middle adolescents: Prospective associations

and intrapersonal and interpersonal influences. *Journal of Consulting and Clinical Psychology, 69*(2), 215–226.

Windle, M., Miller-Tutzauer, C., & Barnes, G. (1991). Adolescent perceptions of help-seeking resources for substance abuse. *Child Development, 62*, 179–189.

Winfree, J., L., Bäckström, T., & Mays, G. (1994). Social learning theory, self-reported delinquency, and youth gangs: A new twist on a general theory of crime and delinquency. *Youth and Society, 26*, 147–177.

Wingood, G., DiClemente, R. J., Bernhardt, J. M., Harrington, K., Davies, S. L., Robillard, A., et al. (2003). A prospective study of exposure to rap music videos and African American female adolescents' health. *American Journal of Public Health, 93*, 437–439.

Winstok, Z., Eisikovits, Z., & Fishman, G. (2004). Towards the development of a conflict escalation model: The case of Israeli youth. *Journal of Youth and Adolescence 33*, 283–292.

Wintemute, G., Kraus, J., Teret, S., & Wright, M. (1987). Drowning in childhood and adolescence: A population-based study. *American Journal of Public Health, 77*, 830–832.

Winterbottom, M. (1958). The relation of need for achievement to learning experiences in independence and mastery. In J. Atkinson (Ed.), *Motives in fantasy, action, and society.* Princeton, NJ: Van Nostrand.

Wintre, M., Hicks, R., McVey, G., & Fox, J. (1988). Age and sex differences in choice of consultant for various types of problems. *Child Development, 59*, 1046–1055.

Wiseman, R. (2003). *Queen bees and wannabes.* New York: Three Rivers Press.

Wojtkiewicz, R., & Donato, K. (1995). Hispanic educational attainment: The effects of family background and nativity. *Social Forces, 74*, 559–574.

Wolak, J., Mitchell, K. J., & Finkelhor, D. (2003). Escaping or connecting? Characteristics of youth who form close online relationships. *Journal of Adolescence, 26*(1), 105–119.

Wolak, J., Mitchell, K., & Finkelhor, D. (2006). Online victimization of youth: Five years later. Durham: National Center for Missing and Exploited Children, University of New Hampshire.

Wolf, A., Gortmaker, S., Cheung, L., Gray, H., Herzog, D., & Colditz, G. (1993). Activity, inactivity, and obesity: Racial, ethnic, and age differences among schoolgirls. *American Journal of Public Health, 83*, 1625–1627.

Wolfe, D., Wekerle, C., Reitzel-Jaffe, D., & Lefebvre, L. (1998). Factors associated with abusive relationships among maltreated and nonmaltreated youth. *Development and Psychopathology, 10*, 61–85.

Wolfe, S., & Truxillo, C. (1996, March). The relationship between decisional control, responsibility and positive and negative outcomes during early adolescence. Paper presented at the biennial meetings of the Society for Research on Adolescence, Boston.

Wolfson, A., & Carskadon, M. (1998). Sleep schedules and daytime functioning in adolescents. *Child Development, 69,* 875–887.

Wong, C., Crosnoe, R., Laird, J., & Dornbusch, S. (2003). Relations with parents and teachers, susceptibility to friends' negative influences, and adolescent deviance. Manuscript under review, Department of Sociology, University of Texas at Austin.

Wong, M., & Csikszentmihalyi, M. (1991). Affiliation motivation and daily experience: Some issues on gender differences. *Journal of Personality and Social Psychology, 60,* 154–164.

Wood, P., & Clay, W. (1996). Perceived structural barriers and academic performance among American Indian high school students. *Youth and Society, 28,* 40–61.

Woods, L. N., & Jagers, R. J. (2003). Are cultural values predictors of moral reasoning in African American adolescents? *Journal of Black Psychology, 29,* 102–118.

Woodward, L., Fergusson, D., & Belsky, J. (2000). Timing of parental separation and attachment to parents in adolescence: Results of a prospective study from birth to age 16. *Journal of Marriage and the Family, 62*(1), 162–174.

Woodward, L., Fergusson, D., & Horwood, L. (2001). Risk factors and life processes associated with teenage pregnancy: Results of a prospective study from birth to 20 years. *Journal of Marriage and the Family, 63*(4), 1170–1184.

Wright, J., Cullen, F., & Williams, N. (1997). Working while in school and delinquent involvement: Implications for social policy. *Crime and Delinquency, 43,* 203–221.

Wu, L., & Anthony, J. (1999). Tobacco smoking and depressed mood in late childhood and early adolescence. *American Journal of Public Health, 89,* 1837–1840.

Wu, L., Pilowsky, D. J., & Schlenger, W. E. (2004). Inhalant abuse and dependence among adolescents in the United States. *Journal of the American Academy of Child and Adolescent Psychiatry, 43,* 1206–1214.

Wu, L., Schlenger, W. E., & Galvin, D. M. (2003). The relationship between employment and substance use among students aged 12 to 17. *Journal of Adolescent Health, 32,* 5–15.

Wu, L., & Thomson, E. (2001). Race differences in family experience and early sexual initiation: Dynamic models of family structure and family change. *Journal of Marriage and the Family, 63*(3), 682–696.

Wu, T., Mendola, P., & Buck, G. (2002). Ethnic differences in the presence of secondary sex characteristics and menarche among U.S. girls: The Third National Health and Nutrition Examination Survey, 1988–1994. *Pediatrics, 110*(4).

Wyatt, L. W., & Haskett, M. E. (2001). Aggressive and nonaggressive young adolescents' attributions of intent in teacher/student interactions. *Journal of Early Adolescence, 21*(4), 425–446.

Xia, G., & Qian, M. (2001). The relationship of parenting style to self-reported mental health among two subcultures of Chinese. *Journal of Adolescence, 24*(2), 251–260.

Xu, J. (2004). Family help and homework management in urban and rural secondary schools. *Teachers College Review, 106,* 1786–1803.

Yamaguchi, K., & Kandel, D. (1987). Drug use and other determinants of premarital pregnancy and its outcome: A dynamic analysis of competing life events. *Journal of Marriage and the Family, 49,* 257–270.

Yamaguchi R., Johnston L., & O'Malley, P. (2003). Relationship between student illicit drug use and school drug-testing policies. *Journal of School Health, 73,* 159–164.

Yankelovich, D. (1974). *The new morality: A profile of American youth in the 1970s.* New York: McGraw-Hill.

Yasui, M., Dorham, C. L., & Dishion, T. J. (2004). Ethnic identity and psychological adjustment: A validity analysis for European American and African American adolescents. *Journal of Adolescent Research, 19,* 807–825.

Yates, A., Edman, J., & Aruguete, M. (2004). Ethnic differences in BMI and body/self-dissatisfaction among Whites, Asian subgroups, Pacific Islanders, and African Americans. *Journal of Adolescent Health, 34,* 300–307.

Yates, M., & Youniss, J. (1996). Community service and political-moral identity in adolescents. *Journal of Research on Adolescence, 6,* 271–284.

Yau, J., & Smetana, J. (1996). Adolescent–parent conflict among Chinese adolescents in Hong Kong. *Child Development, 67,* 1262–1275.

Yau, J., & Smetana, J. (2003). Adolescent–parent conflict in Hong Kong and Shenzhen: A comparison of youth in two cultural contexts. *International Journal of Behavioral Development, 27,* 201–211.

Ybarra, M. L., Alexander, C., & Mitchell, K. J. (2005). Depressive symptomatology, youth Internet use, and online interactions: A national survey. *Journal of Adolescent Health, 36,* 9–18.

Yeh, H., & Lempers, J. D. (2004). Perceived sibling relationships and adolescent development. *Journal of Youth and Adolescence, 33,* 133–147.

YMCA. (2000). Telephone survey conducted for the White House Conference on Teenagers. Chicago: Author.

YMCA. (2006). Information on the history of the organization is available at www.ymca.net/about_the_ymca/history_of_the_ymca.html.

Yoon, J. S., Barton, E., & Taiarol, J. (2004). Relational aggression in middle school educational implications of developmental research. *Journal of Early Adolescence, 24,* 303–318.

Yoon, K., Eccles, J., Wigfield, A., & Barber, B. (1996, March). Developmental trajectories of early to middle adolescents' academic achievement and motivation. Paper presented at the biennial meetings of the Society for Research on Adolescence, Boston.

Yoshikawa, H. (1994). Prevention as cumulative protection: Effects of early family support and education on chronic delinquency and its risks. *Psychological Bulletin, 115,* 28–54.

Young, A. M. & d'Arcy, H. (2005). Older boyfriends of adolescent girls: The cause or a sign of the problem? *Journal of Adolescent Health, 36,* 410–419.

Young, J. F., Berenson, K., Cohen, P., & Garcia, J. (2005). The role of parent and peer support in predicting adolescent depression: A longitudinal community study. *Journal of Research on Adolescence 15,* 407–423.

Young, H., & Ferguson, L. (1979). Developmental changes through adolescence in the spontaneous nomination of reference groups as a function of decision context. *Journal of Youth and Adolescence, 8,* 239–252.

Young, S. K., Yun-Joo, K., & Leventhal, B. (2005). School bullying and suicidal risk in Korean middle school students. *Pediatrics, 115,* 357–363.

Youngstrom, E., Weist, M. D., & Albus, K. E. (2003). Exploring violence exposure, stress, protective factors and behavioral problems among inner-city youth. *American Journal of Community Psychology, 32,* 115–129.

Youniss, J., & Smollar, J. (1985). *Adolescent relations with mothers, fathers, and friends.* Chicago: University of Chicago Press.

Zabin, L., Astone, N., & Emerson, M. (1993). Do adolescents want babies? The relationship between attitudes and behavior. *Journal of Research on Adolescence, 3,* 67–86.

Zabin, L., Hirsch, M., & Emerson, M. (1989). When urban adolescents choose abortion: Effects on education, psychological status and subsequent pregnancy. *Family Planning Perspectives, 21,* 248–255.

Zabin, L., Sedivy, V., & Emerson, M. (1994). Subsequent risk of childbearing among adolescents with a negative pregnancy test. *Family Planning Perspectives, 26,* 212–217.

Zaff, J. F., Moore, K. A., Papillo, A. R., & Williams, S. (2003). Implications of extracurricular activity participation during adolescence on positive outcomes. *Journal of Adolescent Research, 18,* 599–630.

Zahn-Waxler, C., Klimes-Dougan, B., & Slattery, M. (2000). Internalizing problems of childhood and adolescence: Prospects, pitfalls, and progress in understanding the development of anxiety and depression. *Development and Psychopathology, 12,* 443–466.

Zaider, T., Johnson, J. G., & Cockell, S. J. (2002). Psychiatric disorders associated with the onset and persistence of bulimia nervosa and binge eating disorder during adolescence. *Journal of Youth and Adolescence, 31*(5), 319–329.

Zametkin, A. J., Alter, M. R., & Yemini, T. (2001). Suicide in teenagers. *Journal of the American Medical Association, 286,* 3120–3125.

Zametkin, A. J., Zoon, C. K., Klein, H. W., & Munson, S. (2004). Psychiatric aspects of child and adolescent obesity: A review of the past 10 years. *Journal of the American Academy of Child and Adolescent Psychiatry, 43,* 134–150.

Zapert, K., Snow, D. L., & Tebes, J. K. (2002). Patterns of substance use in early through late adolescence. *American Journal of Community Psychology, 30*(6), 835–852.

Zavela, K., Battistich, V., Dean, B., Flores, R., Barton, R., & Delaney, R. (1997). Say yes first: A longitudinal, school-based alcohol and drug prevention project for rural youth and families. *Journal of Early Adolescence, 17,* 67–96.

Zavodny, M. (2004). Fertility and parental consent for minors to receive contraceptives. *American Journal of Public Health, 94,* 1347–1351.

Zeldin, R., Small, S., & Savin-Williams, R. (1982). Prosocial interactions in two mixed-sex adolescent groups. *Child Development, 53,* 1492–1498.

Zeldin, S., & Topitzes, D. (2002). Neighborhood experiences, community connection, and positive beliefs about adolescents among urban adults and youth. *Journal of Community Psychology, 30*(6), 647–669.

Zelnick, M., & Kantner, L. (1973). Sex and contraception among unmarried teenagers. In C. Westoff et al. (Eds.), *Toward the end of growth: Population in America.* Englewood Cliffs, NJ: Prentice-Hall.

Zeman, J., & Shipman, K. (1997). Social-contextual influences on expectancies for managing anger and sadness: The transition from middle childhood to adolescence. *Developmental Psychology, 33,* 917–924.

Zickler, P. (2004). Early nicotine initiation increases severity of addiction, vulnerability to some effects of cocaine. *NIDA Notes, 19,* 2.

Zillman, D. (2000). Influence of unrestrained access to erotica on adolescents' and young adults' dispositions toward sexuality. *Journal of Adolescent Health, 27,* 41–44.

Zima, B., Wells, K., & Freeman, H. (1994). Emotional and behavioral problems and severe academic delays among sheltered homeless children in Los Angeles County. *American Journal of Public Health, 84,* 260–264.

Zimiles, H., & Lee, V. (1991). Adolescent family structure and educational progress. *Developmental Psychology, 27,* 314–320.

Zimmer-Gembeck, M. J. (1999). Stability, change and individual differences in involvement with friends and romantic partners among adolescent females. *Journal of Youth and Adolescence, 28*(4), 419–438.

Zimmer-Gembeck, M. J., Siebenbruner, J., & Collins, W. (2001). Diverse aspects of dating: Associations with psychosocial functioning from early to middle adolescence. *Journal of Adolescence, 24*(3), 313–336.

Zimmer-Gembeck, M. J., Siebenbruner, J., & Collins, W. A. (2004). A prospective study of intraindividual and peer influences on adolescents' heterosexual romantic and sexual behavior. *Archives of Sexual Behavior, 33,* 381–394.

Zimmerman, M., Bingenheimer, J. B., & Notaro, P. C. (2002). Natural mentors and adolescent resiliency: A study with urban youth. *American Journal of Community Psychology, 30*(2), 221–243.

Zimmerman, M., Copeland, L., Shope, J., & Dielman, T. (1997). A longitudinal study of self-esteem: Implications for adolescent development. *Journal of Youth and Adolescence, 26,* 117–141.

Zimmerman, M., & Schmeelk-Cone, K. (2003). A longitudinal analysis of adolescent substance use and school motivation among African American youth. *Journal of Research on Adolescence, 13,* 185–210.

Zimmermann, P., & Becker-Stoll, F. (2002). Stability of attachment representations during adolescence: The influence of ego-identity status. *Journal of Adolescence, 25*(1), 107–124.

Zimmerman, R., Sprecher, S., Langer, L., & Holloway, C. (1995). Adolescents' perceived ability to say "No" to unwanted sex. *Journal of Adolescent Research, 10,* 383–399.

Zimring, F. (1982). *The changing legal world of adolescence.* New York: Free Press.

Zimring, F. (1998). *American youth violence.* New York: Oxford University Press.

Zirkel, S. (2002). Is there a place for me? Role models and academic identity among white students and students of color. *Teachers College Record, 104*(2), 357–376.

Zito, J. M., Safer, D. J., DosReis, S., Gardner, J. F., Soeken, K., Boles, M., et al. (2002). Rising prevalence of antidepressants among U.S. youths. *Pediatrics, 109*(5), 721–727.

Zollo, P. (2004). *Getting wiser to teens: More insights into marketing to teenagers.* Ithaca, NY: New Strategist Publications.

Zuckerman, M. (Ed.). (1983). *Biological basis of sensation seeking, impulsivity, and anxiety.* Hillsdale, NJ: Erlbaum.

Zweig, J. M., Lindbergh, L., & McGinley, K. (2001). Adolescent health risk profiles: The co-occurrence of health risks among females and males. *Journal of Youth and Adolescence, 30*(6), 707–728.

Credits

TEXT AND ILLUSTRATIONS

Chapter 1 Figure 1.1 From M. Grumbach, J. Roth, S. Kaplan, & R. Kelch, 1974, "Hypothalamic-Pituitary Regulation of Puberty in Man: Evidence and Concepts Derived from Clinical Research," in *Control of the Onset of Puberty*, M. Grumbach, G. Grave, & F. Mayer (eds.). Copyright © 1974 Lippincott Williams & Wilkins. Reprinted by permission. **Figure 1.2** From W. Marshall, 1978, "Puberty," in *Human Growth*, vol. 2, F. Faulkner & J. Tanner (eds.). Copyright © 1978 Plenum Publishers. Reprinted with kind permission from Springer Science and Business Media. **Figure 1.3** From L. Dorn, R. Dahl, H. Woodward, & F. Biro, 2006, "Defining the Boundaries of Early Adolescence: A User's Guide to Assessing Pubertal Status and Pubertal Timing in Research with Adolescents," *Applied Developmental Science*, 1, pp. 30–56. Reprinted with permission from Lawrence Erlbaum Associates. **Table 1.1** From B. Goldstein, *Introduction to Human Sexuality*, Copyright © 1976. Reprinted by permission of Star Publishing Company, Belmont, CA. **Figure 1.4** From N. Morris & J. Udry, 1980, "Validation of a Self-Administered Instrument to Assess Stage of Adolescent Development," *Journal of Youth and Adolescence*, 9, pp. 271–280. Reprinted with kind permission from Springer Science and Business Media. **Figure 1.5** From W. Marshall & J. Tanner, 1969, "Variations in the Pattern of Pubertal Change in Girls," *Archive of Disease of Childhood*, 44, 130. BMJ Publishing Group. Reprinted with the permission of BMJ Publishing Group. **Figure 1.7** From P. Eveleth & J. Tanner, 1976, *Worldwide Variation in Human Growth*. Cambridge University Press. Reprinted with the permission of Cambridge University Press. **Figure 1.10** From A. Booth, D. R. Johnson, D. A. Granger, A. C. Crouter, & S. McHale, 2003, "Testosterone and Child and Adolescent Adjustment: The Moderating Role of Parent-Child Relationships," *Developmental Psychology*, 39 (1), 85–98. Copyright © 2003 by the American Psychological Association. Reprinted by permission. **Table 1.2** From Patricia Bence, "Patterns of the Experience of Mood," paper presented at the biennial meetings of the Society for Research on Adolescence, Washington, March 1992. **Figure 1.11** From D. Dick, R. Rose, R. Viken, & J. Kaprio, 2000, "Pubertal Timing and Substance Use: Associations Between and Within Families Across Late Adolescence," *Developmental Psychology*, 36(2), 180–189. Copyright © 2000 by the American Psychological Association. Reprinted by permission. **Figure 1.12** "Prevalence of Obesity Among U.S. Children and Adolescents by Age Group and Selected Period, 1963–2002," from: http://www.cdc.gov/nchs/products/pubs/pubd/hestats/overwght99.htm.

Chapter 2 Figure 2.2, Figure 2.5 From N. Bayley, 1949, "Consistency and Variability in the Growth of Intelligence from Birth to Eighteen Years," *Journal of Genetic Psychology*, 75, 165–196. Reprinted with the permission of the Helen Dwight Reid Educational Foundation. Published by Heldref Publications, 1319 Eighteenth Street, NW, Washington, DC 20036-1802. Copyright © 1949. **Figure 2.6** From B. Fischoff, J. Howard, & R. Zucker, 1995, *Alcohol Problems Among Adolescents: Current Directions in Prevention Research*, pp. 59–84. Lawrence Erlbaum Associates. Reprinted with permission from Lawrence Erlbaum Associates. **Figure 2.7** Reprinted from A. Williams, 2003, "Teenage Drivers: Patterns of Risk," *Journal of Safety Research*, Vol. 34, 5–15, Fig. 13, with permission from Elsevier.

Chapter 3 Figure 3.1 From W. Osgood, G. Ruth, J. Eccles, J. Jacobs, & B. Barber, 2005, "Six Paths to Adulthood," in R. Settersten, F. Furstenberg, Jr., & R. Rumbaut (Eds.), *On the Frontier of Adulthood*, pp. 320–355. Chicago: University of Chicago Press. Reprinted with permission. **Figure 3.2** From N. L. Galambos, E. T. Barker, & H. J. Krahn, 2006, "Depression, Self-Esteem, and Anger in Emerging Adulthood: Seven-Year Trajectories," *Developmental Psychology*, 42, 350–365. Copyright © 2006 by the American Psychological Association. Reprinted by permission. **Table 3.1** From J. E. Schulenberg, A. L. Bryant, & P. M. O'Malley, 2004, "Taking Hold of Some Kind of Life: How Developmental Tasks Relate to Trajectories of Well-Being

During the Transition to Adulthood," *Development and Psychopathology*, 16(4), p. 1124. Reprinted with the permission of Cambridge University Press. **Figure 3.5** Copyright © European Foundation for the Improvement of Living and Working Conditions, 2007, Wyattville Road, Loughlinstown, Dublin 18, Ireland. **Figure 3.7** Reprinted from V. J. Ebin, C. D. Sneed, D. E. Morisky, M. Rotherman-Borus, A. M. Magnusson, & C. Malotte, 2001, "Acculturation and Interrelationships Between Problem and Health-Promoting Behaviors Among Latino Adolescents," *Journal of Adolescent Health*, 28, Fig. 1., 62–72, with permission from the Society for Adolescent Medicine and Elsevier. **Figure 3.9** From H. L. Chung & L. Steinberg, 2006, "Relations Between Neighborhood Factors, Parenting Behaviors, Peer Deviance, and Delinquency Among Serious Juvenile Offenders," *Developmental Psychology*, 42, 319–331. Copyright © 2006 by the American Psychological Association. Reprinted by permission. **Figure 3.10** From J. M. Beyers, J. E. Bates, G. S. Pettit, & K. A. Dodge, 2003, "Neighborhood Structure, Parenting Processes, and the Development of Youths' Externalizing Behaviors: A Multilevel Analysis," *American Journal of Community Psychology*, 31, 35–53. Reprinted with kind permission from Springer Science and Business Media. **Figure 3.11** From T. Cook, M. Herman, M. Phillips, & R. Settersten, Jr., 2002, "Some Ways in Which Neighborhoods, Nuclear Families, Friendship Groups, and Schools Jointly Affect Changes in Early Adolescent Development," *Child Development*, 73(4), 1283–1309. Reprinted with permission of the Society for Research in Child Development and Blackwell Publishing.

Chapter 4 Figure 4.1 From R. Larson, M. Richards, G. Moneta, G. Holmbeck, & E. Duckett, 1996, "Changes in Their Families From Ages 10 to 18: Disengagement and Transformation," *Developmental Psychology*, 32, 744–754. Copyright © 1996 by the American Psychological Association. Reprinted by permission. **Figure 4.2** From E. Stice & N. Gonzales, 1998, "Adolescent Temperament Moderates the Relation of Parenting to Antisocial Behavior and Substance Use," *Journal of Adolescent Research*, 13(1), 5–31. Reprinted by permission of Sage Publications, Inc. **Figure 4.3** From E. Maccoby & J. Martin, 1983, "Socialization in the Context of the Family: Parent-Child Interaction," in *Handbook of Child Psychology: Socialization, Personality and Social Development*, vol. 4, E. M. Hetherington (ed.). This material is used by permission of John Wiley & Sons, Inc. **Table 4.1** Reprinted with the permission of Simon and Schuster Adult Publishing Group from *The Ten Basic Principles of Good Parenting*, by Laurence Steinberg, Ph.D. Copyright © 2004 by Laurence Steinberg, Ph.D. **Figure 4.8** From A. Cherlin, P. Lindsay Chase-Lansdale, & C. McRae, 1998, "Effects of Parental Divorce on Mental Health Throughout the Life Course," *American Sociological Review*, 63, 239–249. Copyright © 1998. Reprinted by permission of the American Sociological Association. **Figure 4.9** From R. Conger, K. Conger, G. Elder, Jr., F. Lornez, R. Simons, & L. Whitbeck, 1993, "Family Economic Stress and Adjustment of Early Adolescent Girls," *Developmental Psychology*, 29, 206–219. Copyright © 1993 by the American Psychological Association. Reprinted by permission.

Chapter 5 Figure 5.1 From R. Larson & M. Richards, 1998, "Waiting for the Weekend," *New Directions for Child and Adolescent Development*, Winter, no. 82, 37–51. Reprinted by permission of John Wiley & Sons. Inc. **Figure 5.3** From R. Larson & M. Richards, 1991, "Daily Companionship in Late Childhood and Early Adolescence: Changing Developmental Contexts," *Child Development*, 62, pp. 284–300. Reprinted with permission of the Society for Research in Child Development and Blackwell Publishing. **Figure 5.4** From S. Ennett & K. Bauman, 1996, "Adolescent Social Networks: School, Demographic & Longitudinal Considerations," *Journal of Adolescent Research*, 11, 194–215. Reprinted by permission of Sage Publications, Inc. **page 175** From D. Kinney, 1993, "From Nerds to Normals: The Recovery of Identity Among Adolescents from Middle School to High School," *Sociology of Education*, 66, pp. 21–40. **Figure 5.6** From B. Brown, 1990, "Peer Groups," in *At the Threshold: The Developing Adolescent*, S. Feldman & G. Elliot (eds.), Harvard University Press. Reprinted by permission. **Figure 5.7** From M. L. Greene, N. Way, & K. Pahl, 2006, "Trajectories of

Perceived Adult and Peer Discrimination Among Black, Latino, and Asian American Adolescents: Patterns and Psychological Correlates," *Developmental Psychology*, 42, 227, Fig 2. Copyright © 2006 by the American Psychological Association. Reprinted by permission. **Figure 5.10** From R. Crosnoe & B. Needham, 2004, "Holism, Contextual Variability, and the Study of Friendships in Adolescent Development," *Child Development*, 75, p. 271, Fig. 1. Reprinted by permission of Blackwell Publishing. **Figure 5.11** From R. Macmillan & J. Hagan, 2004, "Violence in the Transition to Adulthood: Adolescent Victimization, Education, and Socioeconomic Attainment Later in Life," *Journal of Research on Adolescence*, 14, pp. 127–158. Reprinted by permission of Blackwell Publishing. **Figure 5.12** From A. Nishima & J. Juvonen, 2005, "Daily Reports of Witnessing and Experiencing Peer Harassment in Middle School," *Child Development*, 76, p. 442, Figure 2; p. 446, Figure 3. Reprinted by permission of Blackwell Publishing.

Chapter 6 Figure 6.1 From D. Tanner, 1972, *Secondary Education*. New York: Macmillan; William T. Grant Foundation Commission on Work, Family, and Citizenship. (1988). *The Forgotten Half: Non-College Youth in America*. Washington, D.C.: William T. Grant Foundation Commission on Work, Family, and Citizenship. **Figure 6.2** From R. Roeser, J. Eccles, & C. Freedman-Doan, 1999, "Academic Functioning and Mental Health," *Journal of Adolescent Research*, 14, 135–174. Reprinted by permission of Sage Publications, Inc. **Figure 6.3** From L. Gutman & C. Midgley, 2000, "The Role of Protective Factors in Supporting the Academic Achievement of Poor African American Students During the Middle School Transition," *Journal of Youth and Adolescence*, 29(2), 223–248. Reprinted with kind permission from Springer Science and Business Media. **p. 214** From P. Phelan, H. Yu, & A. Davidson, 1994, "Navigating the Psychosocial Pressures of Adolescence: The Voices and Experiences of High School Youth," *American Educational Research Journal*, 31, pp. 415–447. **Figure 6.5** From R. Roeser, C. Midgley, & T. Urdan, 1996, "Perceptions of the School Psychological Environment and Early Adolescents' Psychological and Behavioral Functioning in School: The Mediating Role of Goals and Belonging," *Journal of Educational Psychology*, 88, 408–422. Copyright © 1996 by the American Psychological Association. Reprinted by permission. **Figure 6.7** From R. Larson & M. Richards, 1998, "Waiting for the Weekend," *New Directions for Child and Adolescent Development*, Winter, no. 82, 37–51. Reprinted by permission of John Wiley & Sons, Inc.

Chapter 7 Figure 7.1 From R. Larson, M. Richards, B. Sims, & J. Dworkin, 1999, "How Urban African-American Young Adolescents Spend Their Time: Time Budgets for Locations, Activities and Companionship," *American Journal of Community Psychology*, 29(4), 565–597. Reprinted with kind permission from Springer Science and Business Media. **Figure 7.4** From R. Larson & M. Richards, 1991, "Daily Companionship in Late Childhood and Early Adolescence: Changing Developmental Contexts," *Child Development*, 62. Reprinted with permission of the Society for Research in Child Development and Blackwell Publishing. **Figure 7.5** From R. Larson, 2000, "Toward a Psychology of Positive Youth Development," *American Psychologist*, 55, 170–183. Copyright © 2000 by the American Psychological Association. Reprinted by permission. **Figure 7.7** From H. Snyder & M. Sickmund, 1995, *Juvenile Offenders and Victims: A National Report*, Washington, D.C.: Office of Juvenile Justice and Delinquency Prevention. **Figure 7.9** This information was reprinted with permission from the Henry J. Kaiser Family Foundation. The Kaiser Family Foundation, based in Menlo Park, California, is a nonprofit, independent national health care philanthropy and is not associated with Kaiser Permanente or Kaiser Industries. **Figure 7.11** Reprinted by permission from J. Johnson, P. Cohen, E. Smailes, S. Kasen, & J. Brook, 2002, "Television Viewing and Aggressive Behavior During Adolescence and Childhood," *Science*, 295(5564), 2468–2471. Copyright © 2002 American Association for the Advancement of Science.

Chapter 8 Page 268 From S. Harter, 1999, *The Construction of the Self*. New York: Guilford. Reprinted by permission of Guilford Publications, Inc. **p. 271** Quote from S. Harter, 1990, "Identity and Self-Development," in *At the Threshold: The Developing Adolescent*, S. Feldman & G. Elliott (eds.), pp. 352–387. Harvard University Press. Reprinted by permission. **p. 272** From S. Shulman, B. Feldman, S. J. Blatt, O. Cohen, & A. Mahler, 2005, "Emerging Adulthood: Age-Related Tasks and Underlying Self Processes," *Journal of Adolescent Research*, 20(5), p. 591. **Figure 8.1** From S. Harter, 1999, *The Construction of the Self*, New York: Guilford Press. Reprinted by permission of Guilford Publications, Inc. **Figure 8.2** From R. Larson, G. Moneta, M. Richards & S. Wilson, 2002, "Continuity, Stability, and Change in Daily Emotional Experience Across Adolescence," *Child Development*, 73(4), pp. 1151–1165. Reprinted with permission of the Society for Research in Child Development. **Figure 8.3** From B. Hirsch & D. DuBois, 1991, "Self-Esteem in Early Adolescence: The Identification and Prediction of Contrasting Longitudinal Trajectories," *Journal of Youth and Adolescence*, 20, 53–72. Reprinted with kind permission from Springer Science and Business Media. **Figure 8.4** From S. Harter, 1999, *The Construction of the Self*, Guilford Press. Reprinted by permission of Guilford Publications, Inc. **Figure 8.5** Reprinted from K. Brown, R. McMahon, F. Biro, P. Cranford, G. Schrieber, S. L. Similo, M. Waclawiw, & R. Striegel-Moore, 1998, "Changes in Self Esteem in Black and White Girls Between the Ages of 9 and 14 years: The NHLBI Growth and Health Study," *Journal of Adolescent Health*, 23, 7–19, with permission from the Society for Adolescent Medicine and Elsevier. **Figure 8.6** From M. L. Greene & N. Way, 2005, "Self-Esteem Trajectories Among Ethic Minority Adolescents: A Growth Curve Analysis of the Patterns and Predictors of Change," *Journal of Research on Adolescence*, 15, p. 165. Reprinted by permission of Blackwell Publishing. **p. 284** From K. C. McLean, 2005, "Late Adolescent Development: Narrative Meaning Making and Memory Telling," *Developmental Psychology*, 41, 683–691. Copyright © 2005 by the American Psychological Association. Reprinted by permission. **Figure 8.8** From Jean S. Phinney, 1990, "Ethnic Identity in Adolescence and Adults: A Review of Research," *Psychological Bulletin*, 108, 499–514. Copyright © 1990 by the American Psychological Association. Reprinted by permission. **Table 8.1** From M. Herman, 2004, "Forced to Choose: Some Determinants of Racial Identification in Multiracial Adolescents," *Child Development*, 75, pp. 730–748, Table 2. Reprinted by permission of Blackwell Publishing.

Chapter 9 Page 302 "How to Talk to Your Mother," from *Teenage Romance: or How to Die of Embarrassment*, by Delia Ephron, illustrated by Edward Koren. Copyright © 1981 by Delia Ephron. Used by permission of Viking Penguin, a division of Penguin Group (USA) Inc. **Figure 9.1** From L. Steinberg & S. Silverberg, 1986, "The Vicissitudes of Autonomy in Early Adolescence," *Child Development*, 57. Reprinted with permission of the Society for Research in Child Development and Blackwell Publishing. **Figure 9.3** From T. Grisso, L. Steinberg, J. Woolard, E. Cauffman, E. Scott, S. Graham, F. Lexcen, N. Reppucci, & R. Schwartz, 2003, "Juveniles' Competence to Stand Trial: A Comparison of Adolescents' and Adults' Capabilities as Trial Defendants," *Law and Human Behavior*, 27, 333–363. Reprinted with kind permission from Springer Science and Business Media. **Figure 9.4** From A. Redlich & G. Goodman, 2003, "Taking Responsibility for an Act Not Committed: The Influence of Age and Suggestibility," *Law and Human Behavior*, 27(2), 141–156. Reprinted with kind permission from Springer Science and Business Media. **Figure 9.6** From L. Steinberg & S. Silverberg, 1986, "The Vicissitudes of Autonomy in Early Adolescence," *Child Development*, 57, pp. 841–851. Reprinted with permission of the Society for Research in Child Development.

Chapter 10 Page 334 From K. C. McLean & A. Thorne, 2003, "Late Adolescents' Self-Defining Memories About Relationships," *Developmental Psychology*, 39, 635–645. Copyright © 2003 by the American

Psychological Association. Reprinted by permission. **Table 10.1** From *Conceptions of Modern Psychiatry*, by Henry Stack Sullivan. Copyright © 1940, 1945, 1947, 1953 by the William Alanson White Psychiatric Foundation. Used by permission of W. W. Norton & Company, Inc. **p. 343** From T. Berndt, 1981, "Relationships Between Social Cognition, Nonsocial Cognition, and Social Behavior: The Case of Friendship," in J. Flavell and L. Ross (eds.), *Social Cognitive Development: Frontiers and Possible Futures*, p. 180. Cambridge, England: Cambridge University Press. Reprinted with the permission of Cambridge University Press. **Figure 10.1** From J. Allen, C. Moore, G. Kupermine, & K. Bell, 1998, "Attachment and Adolescent Psychosocial Functioning," *Child Development*, 69, 1406–1419. Reprinted with permission of the Society for Research in Child Development. **Figure 10.2** From B. J. Bigelow & J. J. LaGaipa, 1975, "Children's Written Descriptions of Friendship: A Multidimensional Analysis," *Developmental Psychology*, 11, 857–858. Copyright © 1975 by the American Psychological Association. Reprinted by permission. **Figure 10.3** From N. Way, & M. L. Greene, 2006, "Trajectories of Perceived Friendship Quality During Adolescence: The Patterns and Contextual Predictors," *Journal of Research on Adolescence*, 16(2), p. 308. Reprinted by permission of Blackwell Publishing. **Figure 10.4** From N. Way & L. Chen, 2000, "Close and General Friendships Among African American, Latino, and Asian American Adolescents from Low-Income Families," *Journal of Adolescent Research*, 15(2), 274–301. Reprinted by permission of Sage Publications, Inc. **Figure 10.5** From D. Buhrmester, 1996, "Need Fulfillment, Interpersonal Competence and the Developmental Contexts of Early Adolescent Friendship," in *The Company They Keep: Friendship in Childhood and Adolescence*, W. Bukowski, A. Newcomb & W. Hartup (eds.), pp. 158–185. Cambridge University Press. Reprinted with the permission of Cambridge University Press. **Figure 10.6** From G. M. Morrison, J. Laughlin, S. S. Miguel, D. C. Smith, & K. Widaman, 1997, "Sources of Support for School-Related Issues: Choices of Hispanic Adolescents Varying in Migrant Status," *Journal of Youth and Adolescence*, 26(2), pp. 233–252. Reprinted with kind permission from Springer Science and Business Media. **Figure 10.7** From A. Fuligni, 1998, "Authority, Autonomy, and Parent-Adolescent Conflict and Cohesion: A Study of Adolescents from Mexican, Chinese, Filipino and European Backgrounds," *Developmental Psychology*, 34, 782–792. Copyright © 1998 by the American Psychological Association. Reprinted by permission. **p. 354** From G. Fine, 1981, "Friends, Impression Management, and Preadolescent Behavior," in S. Asher and J. Gottman (eds.), *The Development of Children's Friendships*, p. 43. Cambridge, England: Cambridge University Press. Reprinted with the permission of Cambridge University Press. **p. 356** From R. D. Stanton-Salazar & S. U. Spina, 2005, "Adolescent Peer Networks as a Context for Social and Emotional Support," *Youth and Society*, 36(4), pp. 397–398; pp. 399–400. **p. 358** From E. van Roosmalen, 2000, "Forces of Patriarchy: Adolescent Experiences of Sexuality and Concepts of Relationships," *Youth and Society*, 32(2), p. 207. **p. 360** From E. van Roosmalen, 2000, "Forces of Patriarchy: Adolescent Experiences of Sexuality and Concepts of Relationships," *Youth and Society*, 32(2), p. 209.

Chapter 11 Figure 11.2 From M. Levin, X. Xu, & J. Bartkowski, 2002, "Seasonality of Sexual Debut," *Journal of Marriage and the Family*, 64, 871–884. Copyright © 2002 by the National Council on Family Relations, 3989 Central Avenue, NE, Suite 550, Minneapolis, MN 55421. Reprinted by permission of the National Council on Family Relations and Blackwell Publishing. **p. 376** From L. M. Coleman & S. M. Cater, 2005, "A Qualitative Study of the Relationship Between Alcohol Consumption and Risky Sex in Adolescents," *Archives of Sexual Behavior*, 34, 649–661. Reprinted with kind permission from Springer Science and Business Media. **Figure 11.4** From S. Small & T. Luster, 1994, "Adolescent Sexual Activity: An Ecological, Risk-Factor Approach," *Journal of Marriage and the Family*, 56, 181–192. Copyright © 1994 by the National Council on Family Relations, 3989 Central Avenue, NE, Suite 550, Minneapolis, MN 55421. Reprinted by permission of the National Council on Family Relations and Blackwell Publishing. **p. 383** From E. van Roosmalen, 2000, "Forces of Patriarchy: Adolescent Experiences of Sexuality and Concepts of Relationships," *Youth and Society*, 32(2), p. 219. **Figure 11.5** From V. Lee, R. Croninger, E. Linn, & X. Chen, 1996,

"The Culture of Sexual Harassment in Secondary Schools," *American Educational Research Journal*, 33, pp. 383–417. Copyright © Sage Publications. Reprinted with permission. **Figure 11.6** Reprinted from J. S. Santelli, J. Abma, S. Ventura, L. Lindberg, B. Morrow, J. E. Anderson, S. Lyss, & B. E. Hamilton, 2004, "Can Changes in Sexual Behaviors Among High School Students Explain the Decline in Teen Pregnancy Rates in the 1990s?" *Journal of Adolescent Health*, 35, pp. 80–90, Table 3, with permission from the Society for Adolescent Medicine and Elsevier. **Figure 11.8** From S. Singh & J. Darroch, 2000, "Adolescent Pregnancy and Childbearing: Levels and Trends in Developed Countries," *Family Planning Perspectives*, 32(1), 14–23. Reprinted by permission of The Alan Guttmacher Institute and Blackwell Publishing.

Chapter 12 Page 419 From E. M. Horvat & K. S. Lewis, 2003, "Reassessing the Burden of 'Acting White': The Importance of Peer Group in Managing Academic Success," *Sociology of Education*, 76(4), pp. 270–272. **Figure 12.5** From M. Johnson, 2002, "Social Origins, Adolescent Experiences, and Work Value Trajectories During the Transition to Adulthood," *Social Forces*, 80, pp. 1307–1341. Copyright © 2002 by The University of North Carolina Press. Used by permission of the publisher. www.uncpress.unc.edu.

Chapter 13 Figure 13.2 From J. Zweig, L. Lindbergh, & K. McGinley, 2001, "Adolescent Health Risk Profiles: The Co-Occurrence of Health Risks Among Females and Males," *Journal of Youth and Adolescence*, 30(6), 707–728. Reprinted with kind permission from Springer Science and Business Media. **Figure 13.4** Figure from L. Johnston, G. Bachman, & P. O'Malley, 2002, *Monitoring the Future*. Ann Arbor, MI: Institute for Social Research. **Figure 13.5** From P. Zickler, 2004, "Early Nicotine Initiation Increases Severity of Addiction, Vulnerability to Some Effects of Cocaine," *NIDA Notes*, vol. 19, p. 2. **Table 13.1** Table: DSM-IV Diagnostic Criteria for Substance Abuse, from DSM-IV-R. Reprinted with permission from *The Diagnostic and Statistical Manual of Mental Disorders*, Text Revision, Copyright © 2000. American Psychiatric Association. **Figure 13.6** From K. Zapert, D. L. Snow, & J. K. Tebes, 2002, "Patterns of Substance Use in Early Through Late Adolescence," *American Journal of Community Psychology*, 30(6), 835–852. Reprinted with kind permission from Springer Science and Business Media. **Table 13.2** Table: DSM-IV Diagnostic Criteria for Conduct Disorder, from DSM-IV-R. Reprinted with permission from *The Diagnostic and Statistical Manual of Mental Disorders*, Text Revision, Copyright © 2000. American Psychiatric Association. **Figure 13.7** From I. L. Bongers, H. M. Koot, J. van der Ende, & F. C. Verhulst, 2004, "Developmental Trajectories of Externalizing Behaviors in Childhood and Adolescence," *Child Development*, vol. 75, p. 1530. Reprinted by permission of the Society for Research in Child Development and Blackwell Publishing. **Figure 13.9** From R. Loeber & D. P. Farrington, 2000, "Young Children Who Commit Crime: Epidemiology, Developmental Origins, Risk Factors, Early Interventions, and Policy Implications," *Development and Psychopathology*, 12, 737–762. Reprinted with the permission of Cambridge University Press. **Table 13.3** Table of Diagnostic Criteria for Mild Depressive Disorder (Dysthymic Disorder), from DSM-IV-R. Reprinted with permission from *The Diagnostic and Statistical Manual of Mental Disorders*, Text Revision, Copyright © 2000. American Psychiatric Association. **Figure 13.10** From L. Wichstrøm, 1999, "The Emergence of Gender Difference in Depressed Mood During Adolescence: The Role of Intensified Gender Socialization," *Developmental Psychology*, 35, 232–245. Copyright ©1999 by the American Psychological Association. Reprinted by permission. **Figure 13.11** From M. A. Rueter & H. Kwon, 2005, "Developmental Trends in Adolescent Suicidal Ideation," *Journal of Research on Adolescence*, 15, p. 211. Reprinted by permission of Blackwell Publishing.

PHOTOS

Introduction Page 2 © Tom Grill/Corbis; **5** © Michael Newman/PhotoEdit; **8** © BananaStock/PunchStock; **9** (all) © David Young-Wolff/PhotoEdit; **12** © BananaStock/PunchStock; **18** © AP Photo/The Daily Sentinel, Andrew D. Brosig/Wide World Photos

Name Index

A

Aas, H., 437
Abbott, R., 438, 448
Abbott, R. D., 123, 395, 424, 448
Abdul-Kabir, S., 392
Abecassis, M., 192
Aber, J., 207, 209, 281, 234, 291, 420, 468
Aber, M., 214
Ablard, K., 410
Abma, J., 373, 374, 375, 387, 388, 393
Abraham, C., 389
Abrahamson, A., 145
Abramovitch, R., 327
Abrams, C., 209, 413
Abrantas, A. M., 448
Acebo, C., 41, 42, 140
Achenbach, T., 436, 440, 462
Acierno, R., 448
Ackerman, J., 454
Ackley, K., 387
Acock, A., 150
Adalbjarnardottir, S., 140
Adam, E., 156
Adams, G., 66, 273, 287, 288, 289, 290, 339, 413
Adams, J., 308, 448
Adams, R., 136, 350, 351
Adams, R. E., 186
Adamson, L. B., 466
Adan, A., 158, 214, 417
Adcock, A., 387
Addy, C., 150
Adegoke, A., 45
Adelson, J., 304, 327, 344, 345, 362, 363
Adler, N., 389, 392, 395
Agnew, R., 457
Agras, W. S., 52, 53, 54, 55
Aguilar, B., 458, 459
Ahn, N., 398
Aikin, K., 450
Aikins, J. W., 466
Ainsworth, J. W., 123
Ainsworth, M., 340
Ainsworth-Darnell, J., 154, 414, 417, 418, 419
Aitken, D., 382
Ajanaku, S., 416, 430
Ajzen, I., 424
Akbar, N. J., 413
Akiyama, M., 420
Akom, A. A., 419
Alan Guttmacher Institute., 371, 372, 374, 390, 393
Alarcon, O., 279
Alasker, F., 234, 274
Albers, A. B., 448
Albersheim, L., 341
Alberts, A., 252
Albino, A., 437
Albrecht, C., 156
Albrecht, H., 46, 47, 48
Albrecht, R., 47
Albus, K. E., 124
Alexander, C., 256, 373

Alexander, K., 210, 211, 212, 228, 242, 423, 424, 425, 426, 429
Alfieri, T., 297
Alipuria, L., 291, 292
Allen, J., 143, 188, 249, 307, 309, 310, 336, 342, 343, 400, 425
Allen, L., 207, 209, 234, 281, 291
Allen, V., 48, 49
Allen, W., 291
Alleyne, S. I., 50
Allgood-Merten, B., 298, 463, 464
Allison, K., 395, 448
Allison, P., 150, 151, 153, 374
Allison, S., 154
Allred, E., 441
Allyene, E., 392
Almeida, D., 89, 140, 298
Almerigi, J. B., 252
Alpert, A., 140, 282
Al-Shabbout, M., 468
Alter, M. R., 464
Altermatt, E., 409
Althaus, F., 112
Alva, S., 420
Alvarado, R., 159
Alvarez, M., 297
Amaral, D., 77
Amato, P., 142, 150, 151, 152, 153, 154
Ambridge, B., 73
American Psychiatric Association., 52
Ammerman, S., 51, 52
Anastasi, A., 82
Anda, R. F., 140
Anderka, M., 449
Anderman, E., 205, 207, 214
Anderman, L. H., 207, 208
Andersen, C., 71
Anderson, A., 100, 118, 250, 251
Anderson, C. A., 258
Anderson, E., 43, 146, 151, 156
Anderson, J. E., 388, 393
Anderson, M., 222, 223
Anderson, S. E., 34, 38
Anderssen, N., 437
Andersson, T., 46
Ando, M., 192
Andre, T., 249
Andrews, D., 282, 450, 459
Andrews, J., 140, 277, 282, 461
Aneshensel, C., 40, 373, 381, 462
Angeletti, J., 310
Anglin, D., 454
Angold, A., 454, 462, 464, 467
Ansary, N., 434
Anstine, P., 449
Anthony, C., 152
Anthony, J., 447
Anthony, J. C., 330
Apel, R., 242
Apfel, N., 400, 401
Applegate, B., 458
Apter, T., 137

Aquan-Assee, J., 352
Aquilino, W., 115
Aqulino, W. S., 156
Arbess, G., 52
Arbeton, A., 413
Arbona, C., 316
Archer, S., 289
Archibald, A., 51
Archibald, M. E., 381
Ardelt, M., 145, 157, 158
Arend, R., 340
Argys, L. M., 389
Armistead, L., 125, 151, 152, 153, 330, 458
Armor, D., 413
Armsden, G., 342
Armstrong, B., 222
Armstrong, T. D., 436
Arnett, J., 7, 99, 110, 111, 172, 256, 288, 308, 372, 379, 389, 441, 442
Arnold, M. L., 141, 315, 325
Arnow, B., 55
Aro, H., 47
Arseneault, L., 457
Aruguete, M., 30
Arunkumar, R., 407, 413
Ary, D., 458
Asakawa, K., 420
Asakura, T., 192
Aseltine, R., 226, 352, 437, 449, 466
Asher, S., 189, 190, 191, 194, 365, 415
Asmussen, L., 150
Asp, C., 426
Asquith, P., 131, 141, 310
Astin, H., 431
Astone, N., 153, 395
Astor, R., 191
Astor, R. A., 182, 222
Atkins, C., 379
Atkins, R., 326
Atkinson, J., 406
Attia, E., 54
Attie, I., 44, 52
Au, T., 379, 380
Aunola, K., 413
Ausiello, J., 448
Austin, B., 330
Austin, L., 87, 88
Austin, S., 363
Austin, S. B., 52, 440
Avenevoli, S., 461, 462, 466, 467, 468
Averett, S. L., 389
Avigad-Spitz, L., 144
Axinn, W. G., 136
Ayalon, H., 210
Ayoub, C., 387

B

Babalola, S., 380
Bachman, J., 239, 241, 242, 250, 251, 275, 276, 281, 443, 445, 448, 459

Bachrach, C., 395
Backstrom, T., 183
Badger, G., 449
Badger, S., 99
Baer, J., 136
Baer, P. E., 308, 448
Bagwell, C., 186, 194, 335, 346
Bahne, J., 382, 383
Bahr, S., 448
Bailey, P. E., 395
Baisch, E., 152
Bajaj, A., 65
Bakan, D., 17, 164, 200
Bakeman, R., 292
Baker, D., 221, 417
Baker, H., 350
Baker, L., 54, 73
Baker, L. A., 145
Baker, M., 186
Baker, S., 389
Baker, T., 224
Bakes, M., 249
Bakken, L., 339
Baldwin, R., 392
Bales, S., 19
Ball, J., 330
Ballard, M., 157
Balle-Jensen, L., 389
Baltes, P., 86, 408
Bámaca-Gómez, M. Y., 316
Bandura, A., 15f, 16, 18, 409, 410
Bank, L., 144, 145, 460
Bankston, C., III, 412
Bao, W., 158
Baratta, M. V., 448
Barbaranelli, C., 409, 410
Barbarin, O., 152, 434
Barber, B., 7, 99, 119, 131, 143, 145, 150, 152,
    178, 207, 212, 262, 309, 318, 352, 362, 410,
    430, 431
Bardone, A., 440
Barenboim, C., 84
Barker, E., 462
Barker, E. T., 45, 100, 101, 140, 180
Barker, R., 205
Barnes, E., 280
Barnes, G., 151, 352, 392, 448
Barnoski, R., 397
Barr, S., 51
Barratt, M., 400
Barrera, M., Jr., 14, 140, 141, 445, 447, 448
Barrett Singer, A. T., 146
Barrett-Connor, E., 447
Barrios, L., 222, 223
Barry, C., 209
Barry, C. M., 76, 258, 326, 329
Barry, H., 108
Barth, R., 399
Bartholomae, S., 378
Bartkowski, J., 374
Bartle-Haring, S., 308
Barton, B., 38
Barton, E., 190
Barton, R., 450
Basen-Engquist, K., 438
Bastes, J. E., 458

Bates, J., 124, 141, 183, 251, 380, 412, 451, 456,
    457
Bates, L., 397
Bates, M. E., 456
Battin-Pearson, S., 424
Battistich, V., 450
Bauer, D. J., 101
Bauer, L., 75
Bauer, R., 51
Bauer, U., 396
Bauman, K., 171, 172, 179, 180, 181, 185, 186,
    386, 448, 468
Bauman, L., 392
Baumer, E. P., 123, 395, 414
Baumrind, D., 138, 139, 141, 310, 446
Bauserman, R., 387
Bayley, N., 45, 80
Beach, F., 9, 108, 111, 369, 370
Beal, A. C., 448
Beals, J., 446
Beam, M., 459, 467
Beam, M. R., 353
Beaman, J., 123, 154
Beamer, L., 392
Bean, R. A., 309
Bear, G., 190
Beardsall, L., 144
Beardslee, W., 335
Bearinger, L., 468
Bearman, P., 381, 390, 468
Bearman, S., 47, 48, 52
Beaumont, S., 348
Becerra, R., 373
Bechara, A., 76
Becker, A., 260
Becker, B., 434, 467, 468
Becker, J., 40
Becker-Stoll, F., 287, 342
Beckwith, L., 341
Beiter, M., 377
Bejarno, J., 330
Belansky, E., 352
Bell, A., 385
Bell, D. C., 310
Bell, J., 66
Bell, K., 143, 307, 309, 310, 342, 343
Bell, L. G., 310
Bell, M., 387
Bell, R., 399, 449
Bellair, P. E., 455
Bellmore, A., 192
Belsky, J., 153, 397, 438
Bem, D., 384
Bem, S., 297, 298
Ben Avie, M., 221
Benbenishty, R., 182, 222
Benbow, C., 407
Bence, P., 41
Benda, B., 380, 381
Benedict, R., 15, 15f, 18, 103, 104, 112
Ben-Eliahu, E., 298
Benenson, J. F., 344
Benes, F., 75
Bengtsson, S. L., 75
Benjet, C., 45
Ben-Moshe, J., 304

Benn, R., 400
Bensley, L., 142, 400
Benson, B., 378, 379
Benson, P., 146
Bentler, P., 185, 298, 446, 448, 449
Ben-Zur, H., 88
Berends, M., 211
Berenson, K., 352
Berg, C., 346
Bergman, L., 436
Berk, L., 247, 248
Berkas, T. H., 244
Berkowitz, R. I., 51
Berliner, D., 204
Berman, E., 207
Bernat, D. H., 281, 296
Berndt, T., 183, 194, 209, 316, 335, 343, 344, 345,
    346, 347, 365
Bernhardt, J. M., 259
Bernier, A., 342
Berry, S., 399
Berryman, S., 113
Bersamin, M. M., 379, 381
Bertini, N., 440
Berzonsky, M., 287, 288
Best, C., 448
Best, K., 47, 437
Bettis, P., 117
Beuhring, T., 57, 379, 468
Beutel, A., 430
Beyers, J. M., 124, 436, 455
Beyers, W., 308, 342
Beyth-Marom, R., 86, 87, 88
Bezerra, M. F., 395
Bezilla, R., 328
Bhapkar, M., 34
Bhattacharyya, S., 75
Bianchi, S. M., 253
Biddle, B., 204
Biehl, M., 57, 88
Biely, E., 257, 258
Biener, L., 441, 448, 449
Bierman, K., 175, 176, 188, 189, 193
Bigbee, M., 189
Bigelow, B., 343, 344
Biggar, H., 468
Biglan, A., 193, 458
Billick, S. B., 464, 465
Bills, D., 242
Billy, J., 358, 376, 378, 381
Bingenheimer, J. B., 121, 124
Bingham, C., 376, 377, 378, 380, 438
Bingham, R., 117
Birch, L. L., 251, 299
Bird, H., 447
Bird, H. R., 436
Birmaher, B., 468
Birman, D., 295
Birnbaum, A. S., 254
Birnbaum, J., 392
Biro, F., 31, 38, 279
Bishop, A., 291, 292
Bishop, J., 167, 188, 221, 415, 425
Bishop, M., 415
Bishop, S., 400
Bitz, B., 316

Bjerner, L., 447
Bjorklund, D., 70
Black, K., 342
Black, M., 380, 392, 440
Blackshire, S. L., 247
Blair, S., 420
Blake, S. M., 389
Blakeslee, S., 153
Blandford, J. M., 391
Blanton, H., 186
Blash, R., 292
Blatt, S., 306, 464
Blatt, S. J., 207, 272
Blatt-Eisengart, I., 142
Blaustein, E., 394
Blehar, M., 340
Blinn-Pike, L., 144, 375, 379
Block, J., 275, 276, 446, 447
Bloom, A., 202
Bloom, F., 77
Blos, P., 15, 306
Blum, J., 454
Blum, R., 51, 57, 159, 217, 314, 375, 379, 380, 396, 437, 454, 468
Blumberg, E., 379
Blumenthal, J., 75
Blumler, J., 256
Blumstein, A., 452
Blyth, D., 39, 47, 164, 180, 209, 244, 335, 349, 353, 355, 362
Blyth, T., 91
Bo, W., 99
Bobek, D. L., 252
Bodison, P., 291, 292
Boekaerts, M., 409
Boelcke-Stennes, K., 438
Boerger, R., 353
Bogenschneider, K., 141, 412
Bogue, E., 388
Boldero, J., 352
Boldrin, M., 51
Boles, M., 464
Bolland, J. M., 124
Bomar, J., 309
Boney-McCoy, S., 454
Bong, M., 409
Bongers, I. L., 451, 452
Bonica, C., 341
Bontempo, D. E., 385
Boone, T. L., 379
Booth, A., 40, 152, 297
Bor, W., 457
Borduin, C., 387
Borkowski, J., 394, 397, 411
Bornstein, M., 138, 145
Borquez, J., 158
Boruch, R., 396
Borzekowski, D. L. G., 392
Bose, J., 396
Bosmans, G., 138
Botstein, L., 113, 202
Botvin, G., 282, 446, 447, 448
Botvin, M., 186
Bouchey, H. A., 341
Boulerice, B., 424, 425, 457
Bourdony, C., 34

Bourque, S., 140
Bouvin, M., 192
Bowen, G. L., 123
Bowen, N. K., 123
Bowker, A., 187, 188, 189, 191
Bowlby, J., 340
Bowlds, M., 352
Bowles, T. V., 349, 352
Boxer, A., 47
Boxer, P., 153
Boyd, D., 315
Boyd-Zaharias, J., 206
Boyer, D., 387
Boyer, E., 225
Boykin, A., 291
Boykin, K., 309
Boykin McElhaney, K., 143
Boyle, M. H., 445
Brack, C., 437
Brack, G., 437
Braddock, J., 214
Bradley, G., 213
Bradley, L., 213
Bradley, R. H., 123
Brady, E., 462
Braeges, J., 132, 151
Braet, C., 138
Braga, A., 222, 223
Brame, B., 451, 457
Brame, R., 242, 456
Branch, C., 183
Brand, E., 353
Brand, S., 158, 277, 281, 417
Brannon, B., 250, 251
Brasfield, T., 392
Braun, H., 215
Brauner, J., 188
Braveman, P., 123
Braverman, P., 379
Bray, J. H., 120, 308, 448
Brendgen, M., 183, 185, 194, 362, 458, 460
Brengelman, D., 272
Brennan, P., 457, 467
Brennan, R. T., 49
Brenzel, A., 76
Brenzel, B., 204
Brewster, K., 372, 373, 381
Breyer (Justice), 4
Brezina, T., 457
Bridges, G., 454
Bridges, M., 149, 151
Briggs, E., 214
Briggs, E. C., 353
Briggs, L., 460
Briggs, M. L., 144
Bright, D., 43
Brindis, C., 57, 123, 387, 388, 399
Brinkerhoff, D., 108
Brittain, C., 315
Brockway, D. M., 422
Brody, C., 237, 241
Brody, G., 46, 47, 48, 124, 125, 140, 141, 144, 146, 158, 418, 458
Brody, J., 385
Brogli, B. R., 76
Broh, B. A., 248

Broidy, L. M., 451, 457
Bromnick, R., 66
Brondino, M. J., 460
Bronfenbrenner, U., 10, 11, 12, 167
Bronstein, P., 209, 409, 413
Brook, J., 140, 424, 467
Brook, J. S., 259, 440, 464
Brookmeyer, K. A., 124, 326
Brooks-Gunn, J., 39, 40, 44, 45, 47, 48, 49, 51, 52, 54, 121, 122, 123, 124, 125, 137, 242, 369, 380, 381, 394, 395, 396, 397, 398, 400, 440, 461, 463, 464, 466
Brophy, J., 218
Broverman, D., 297
Broverman, I., 297
Brown, A., 73
Brown, B., 11, 13, 142, 162, 163, 167, 168, 170, 171, 172, 173, 175, 176, 177, 178, 181, 182, 184, 186, 187, 194, 220, 221, 228, 289, 293, 316, 317, 335, 351, 357, 360, 361, 362, 363, 364, 397, 398, 413, 415, 418
Brown, C., 460
Brown, F., 420
Brown, J., 232, 255, 257
Brown, J. D., 259
Brown, K., 279
Brown, N., 191
Brown, R., 57
Brown, R. A., 438
Brown, S. A., 448
Brown, W. T., 418
Browning, C. R., 123, 124
Brubacher, J., 224, 225
Bruch, H., 54
Brückner, H., 381, 390
Brumberg, J., 39, 51, 260
Brunelli, S., 400
Bruno, Z. V., 395
Brunson, L., 214
Bruvold, W., 449
Bryan, A., 89
Bryant, A. L., 100, 102, 121, 186, 448
Bryant, C. M., 364
Bryant, F. B., 400
Bryant, S. A., 363
Bryden, M., 81
Bryk, A., 212, 425
Bucci, M., 183
Buchanan, C., 19, 20, 40, 137, 141, 150, 151, 154, 156, 207, 410
Buchanan, L., 186
Buchanan, M., 396
Buchman, D., 260
Buchmann, C., 194, 415
Buck, G., 35
Buckley, S., 108, 163
Buechel, F., 414
Buehler, C., 152, 282
Buhrmester, D., 54, 143, 144, 194, 336, 344, 346, 347, 348, 350, 351, 353, 355, 356, 358, 360, 362, 364
Buist, K. L., 459
Bukowski, W., 183, 184, 186, 188, 191, 192, 194, 346, 352, 354, 355, 360, 362
Bulcroft, K., 319
Bulcroft, R., 319
Bull, C., 281

Bullock, B., 145
Bullock, B. M., 142, 185
Bultman, L., 398
Bumpass, L., 153, 395
Bumpus, M. F., 137, 319
Burch, T., 115
Burchinal, M., 80, 131, 190, 417
Buriel, R., 148
Burk-Braxton, C., 278, 280, 281, 292
Burke, M., 146
Burkham, D., 155, 425
Burleson, B., 346
Burman, B., 152
Burns, J., 183
Burns, M. J., 389
Burraston, B., 144, 145
Burston, N., 44
Burt, C. H., 124
Burt, K. B., 101, 438
Burton, D., 178
Burton, E., 54
Burton, L., 387, 395, 448
Burwell, R., 260
Burwell, R. A., 144
Busch-Rossnagel, N., 380
Bush, George W., 99
Bush, K. R., 142, 309
Bushman, B., 392
Bushwall, S., 153, 155, 380
Bushway, S., 242
Busseri, M. A., 438
Buswell, B., 279
Buterman, N., 445
Butler, J., 387
Butler, K., 444
Butts, J. A., 459, 460
Buyske, S., 456
Buzy, W. M., 363
Bynner, J., 120
Byrd, T., 211
Byrne, B., 213, 270
Byrnes, J., 86, 89

C

Cadenhead, C., 124, 454
Cadinu, M., 183
Cagampang, H., 399
Cai, L., 448
Cairney, J., 462
Cairns, B., 122, 183, 186, 188, 273
Cairns, R., 57, 183, 186, 248, 273
Caldas, S., 412
Caldwell, C., 281, 296, 328, 329
Caldwell, K., 209
Caldwell, L., 251
Caldwell, L. L., 355
Caldwell, M. S., 341
Califano, J. A., 261
Call, K., 58, 418
Callan, V., 350
Calverley, R., 387
Calvert, C., 65
Calvete, E., 464
Cambell, C., 124

Camburn, E., 425
Cameron, J., 77
Cameron, R., 52, 463
Caminis, A., 376
Campbell, B., 38, 214, 377, 378
Campbell, C., 124
Campbell, E., 288, 412, 417
Campbell, F., 417
Campbell, F. A., 80
Campbell, M. A., 451
Campbell, M. E., 181, 182, 214
Campione-Barr, N., 116, 136, 137
Campton, W. M., 438
Canino, G., 447
Canning, R., 191
Cantor, J., 232, 258, 259
Cantu, C., 292
Cantwell, D., 462
Canzoniero, A., 282
Capaldi, D., 100, 185, 377, 378, 386, 396, 413,
    436, 437, 448, 458, 462
Capitman, J., 447
Caplan, M., 193, 467
Caplan, N., 420
Cappelleri, J., 212, 386
Caprara, G., 409, 410
Carbonaro, W., 212
Cardeñoso, O., 464
Carels, R., 214
Carey, M., 440
Carlo, G., 326, 351
Carlsmith, J., 30, 44, 46, 153, 155, 358, 380
Carlson, C., 280, 352
Carlson, E., 458
Carmichael, D., 467
Carmody, D., 319
Carnagey, N. L., 258
Carnegie Council on Adolescent Development.,
    207, 250, 251
Carpenter, J., 449
Carpenter, L. M., 390
Carr, M., 411
Carr, R., 237, 241
Carskadon, M., 41, 42, 43, 140
Carson, D., 140
Carter, C. S., 76
Carter, J., 54
Carver, K., 207, 216, 414
Casella, R., 222
Casey, BJ., 75, 76, 81
Cash, T. F., 53
Casper, L., 379
Caspi, A., 48, 80, 124, 145, 151, 157, 273, 282,
    397, 437, 440, 457, 458
Cassell, C., 373
Cassidy, J., 282, 342
Cassuto, N., 440
Castaneda-English, P., 291
Casteel, M., 71
Castellanos, F. X., 75
Castellino, D., 138, 142
Castellino, D. R., 179, 412, 419
Casten, R., 407, 418
Catalano, R., 123, 395, 424, 438, 447, 448, 453,
    455, 459
Catanese, D., 51

Cater, S. M., 376
Catsambis, S., 212
Catterall, J., 413
Cauce, A., 140, 142, 143, 151, 158, 184, 385,
    387, 414, 415
Cauffman, E., 54, 88, 89, 104, 105, 142, 223,
    236, 242, 246, 308, 312, 314, 451, 454,
    455, 456, 457
Caulfield, Holden, 286
Ceballo, R., 158, 416
Ceci, S., 80, 416
Cederblad, M., 145, 146
Celentano, D., 388
Centers for Disease Control and Prevention., 86,
    204, 373, 375, 388, 393, 445, 449, 461, 464
Centers, N., 447
Cepeda, A., 183
Chalmers, D., 65
Chalmers, H., 438
Chaloupka, F., 449
Chamberlain, P., 460
Chan, D., 467
Chandler, M., 68
Chanoine, J., 51
Chantala, K., 386
Chao, R., 142
Chao, W., 184
Chaplin, J., 382
Chapman, D. P., 140
Charlton, K., 228
Charner, I., 238
Chase-Lansdale, L., 140, 152, 153, 154, 156, 393,
    394, 395, 396, 397, 398, 400, 401
Chassin, L., 14, 43, 140, 185, 186, 445, 447, 448,
    455, 456
Chatters, L., 291
Chavez, G., 400
Chavez, V., 19
Chavira, V., 291
Chavous, T. M., 296
Cheek, N., Jr., 180, 181
Chen, C., 140, 186, 193, 353, 417, 418, 420, 459,
    466, 467
Chen, C. Y., 330
Chen, E., 124
Chen, H., 112, 461
Chen, K., 445, 447
Chen, L., 181, 214, 348, 349
Chen, X., 188, 191, 386, 387, 420
Chen, Y., 140, 462
Chen, Z., 468
Chen-Mok, M., 395
Cherlin, A., 152, 153, 154, 158
Chesir-Teran, D., 281
Chesson, H. W., 391
Chessor, D., 212, 213
Cheung, L., 57
Cheung, Y., 459
Chew, K., 396
Chiang, F., 217
Chilcoat, H., 242
Chilman, C., 371
Chin, C. S., 130
Chinchilli, V. M., 46, 47
Chin-Mei, C., 420
Chisholm, L., 96, 115, 116

Chmiel, S., 321
Choi, W. S., 43
Choi, Y., 447, 459
Chopak, J., 378, 380
Chou, C., 449
Chowdhury, A., 140
Choy, M., 420
Christakos, A., 344
Christensen, M., 147
Christiansen, B., 448
Christiansen, E. D., 252
Christopher, F., 48, 400
Christopherson, C., 377
Christou, C., 71
Chrousos, G., 440
Chrousos, G. P., 34
Chuang, S., 142
Chuang, S. S., 131
Chudowsky, N., 203
Chumlea, W., 34, 38
Chumlea, W. C., 38
Chun, Y.-J., 319
Chung, C. Y., 213
Chung, H. L., 123, 124, 125, 457
Chung, I.-J., 395
Chung, K., 469
Chung, R., 419
Church, M., 416, 430
Church, R., 200, 224
Chyi-In, W., 157
Cicchetti, D., 468
Cillessen, A. H., 188
Claes, M., 350
Clancy, S., 288
Clark, J., 150
Clark, L., 389
Clark, L. F., 376
Clark, R., 63, 84, 140, 406, 413
Clark, S., 378, 386
Clarke, G., 468
Clark-Kauffman, E., 158
Clark-Lempers, D., 144, 157
Clarkson, F., 297
Clary, E., 244
Clasen, D., 168, 178, 194, 221, 316, 317
Clauson, J., 209
Claussen, A., 140
Clay, W., 418
Cleary, S., 468
Clegg, M., 213
Clements, P., 318
Cleveland, H., 124, 376
Cleveland, H. H., 186, 448
Cleveland, M. J., 124, 140
Clingempeel, W., 43, 151, 155, 156, 353, 460
Clore, G., 363, 364
Cnattingius, S., 397
Coatsworth, J., 111, 263, 277, 405
Cobb, B., 378, 379
Cobbs, G., 272
Cochran, B. N., 385
Cockell, S. J., 440
Coe, C., 27
Cohen, B., 449
Cohen, D., 202, 251, 377
Cohen, G., 380

Cohen, O., 272
Cohen, P., 140, 259, 352, 424, 440, 464, 467
Cohen, P. K., 112
Cohen, R., 191, 416, 430
Cohen, S., 341
Cohen, Y., 104, 106, 107, 108
Coie, J., 189, 190, 191, 194, 377, 396, 397
Coiro, M., 154
Colbert, K., 400
Colby, A., 321, 323
Colder, C., 457
Colditz, G., 57, 254
Cole, A., 144
Cole, D., 272, 275, 278, 282, 466
Cole, H., 342
Coleman, H. K., 294
Coleman, J., 17, 167, 215, 216, 218, 227, 279, 412, 414, 417
Coleman, L., 387
Coleman, L. M., 376
Coley, R. L., 151, 158, 251, 393, 394, 395, 397, 398, 401
Collaer, M., 27
College Entrance Examination Board, 421
Collins, D. L., 75
Collins, J., 373, 388
Collins, J. L., 388
Collins, M. H., 466
Collins, N. L., 341, 342
Collins, W., 3, 11, 13, 43, 130, 131, 133, 136, 137, 138, 140, 143, 145, 303, 306, 308, 340, 342, 357, 358, 361, 362, 363, 364, 377
Colten, M., 437, 466
Colyar, J., 353
Comacho, T., 392
Comer, J., 221
Comfort, M. E., 397
Comings, D. E., 380
Compas, B., 158, 436, 440, 461, 462, 463, 464, 466, 468, 469
Compian, L., 44, 356, 362
Compton, K., 456
Compton, S. N., 454
Conant, J., 201
Condit, V., 53, 55
Condon, S., 310
Conduct Problems Prevention Research Group, 193
Conger, K., 145, 146, 157
Conger, R., 46, 47, 48, 123, 124, 138, 140, 141, 143, 144, 145, 146, 152, 154, 156, 157, 158, 184, 205, 208, 364, 380, 381, 395, 413, 437, 456, 464
Conklin, H. M., 73, 75
Connell, F., 387
Connell, F. A., 435
Connell, J., 420
Connolly, J., 174, 182, 278, 306, 344, 346, 347, 349, 355, 358, 359, 361, 362, 363, 364, 386
Connor, J., 440, 462
Connor-Smith, J., 469
Conrad, J., 189, 190, 191
Conseur, A., 397
Consortium on Productivity in the Schools., 198, 202
Consortium on Renewing Education., 202
Contreras, J., 353

Conway, K. M., 464
Conway, M., 391
Cook, L. J., 56
Cook, M., 210, 211
Cook, P. J., 454
Cook, T., 158, 221, 416, 430
Cook, T. D., 125, 221
Cook, W. L., 141
Cooksey, E. C., 174
Cooley-Quille, M., 454
Cooper, C., 143, 288, 308, 309, 310, 350, 352, 429, 430
Cooper, H., 121, 228
Cooper, M. L., 342, 437
Cooper, S., 57
Copeland, L., 277
Copeland-Linder, N., 281, 294, 295, 296
Corasaniti, M., 250
Corbitt-Shindler, D., 363
Corcoran, J., 398
Corneal, D. A., 251, 299
Cornelius, S., 134
Cornelius, W., 295
Cornwell, G., 148, 380, 387, 388
Corona, R., 379
Corraso, R. R., 451
Corsby, R. A., 389, 392
Corville-Smith, J., 413
Corwyn, R., 381
Corwyn, R. F., 123
Costa, F., 437, 377, 389, 448
Costa, M., 306, 349
Costa, P. T., Jr., 273
Costanza, M., 36
Costello, E., 436, 454, 462, 464, 467
Costin, G., 29
Costin, S., 348
Costos, D., 307
Cota-Robles, S., 46
Côté, J., 7, 288
Cote, S., 456, 458, 460
Cottier, L. B., 438
Cottrell, L., 183
Coulten, C., 122
Courtney, M., 191
Coy, K., 43, 136
Coyl, D. D., 43
Coyle, K., 123
Craft, L. L., 54
Craig, W., 306, 349, 355, 359, 361, 362, 386
Crandall, C., 54
Crane, D. R., 135
Crane, J., 123, 381
Craven, R., 212, 213
Crawford, A., 448
Crawford, P., 38, 279
Crawford, T. N., 464
Crean, H. F., 141
Creasey, G., 353
Crick, N., 189, 190, 191, 345, 454, 457
Criss, M. M., 144, 458
Crites, H., 427
Crittenden, P., 140
Crnic, K., 119, 292
Crocker, J., 280
Crockett, L., 117, 376, 377, 378, 380

Croll, J., 52
Crombie, G., 213
Croninger, R., 205, 227, 386, 387, 417, 425
Cronquist, J. L., 51
Crosbie-Burnett, M., 156
Crosby, L., 282, 377, 396, 459
Crosby, R., 378, 379
Crosby, R. A., 392
Crosnoe, R., 158, 183, 185, 186, 187, 212, 214,
    316, 318, 347, 413
Cross, W., 291
Crouter, A., 40, 44, 135, 136, 137, 144, 145, 146,
    147, 251, 297, 298, 299, 319, 349
Crowder, K., 395
Crowe, P., 355
Crowell, J., 341
Cruise, K., 451
Crump, A., 192
Crusto, C., 57
Crystal, D., 83, 420
Csikszentmihalyi, M., 40, 194, 232, 245, 246,
    255, 263, 335, 420
Cubbin, C., 123
Cuffe, S., 150
Cui, M., 152, 157, 364
Cullen, F., 239, 242
Cumberland, A., 326
Cummings, E., 157
Cummings, M., 152, 153
Cumsille, P., 147, 263
Cunningham, M., 75, 299
Cunningham-Williams, R. M., 438
Curran, J., 391
Curran, P., 185, 186, 438
Curtis, T., 380
Curtner-Smith, M., 184
Cusick, P. A., 173, 177
Cutler, G. B., Jr., 34
Cutler, S., 464
Cutrona, C., 124
Cvijanovich, N. Z., 56
Cyranowski, J., 464

D

Da Silva, M., 326
Daddis, C., 131, 132, 141, 319
Dahl, R., 6, 15, 31, 38, 76, 77, 461, 468
Dalicandro, T., 413
Dallal, G. E., 34, 38
Dalton, B., 194, 415
Dalton, M., 318
Dalton, S., 249
Daly, K., 396
Daly, M., 454
Damhorst, M. L., 51, 54
Damico, S., 241
D'Andrade, R., 407
D'Angelo, L., 391
Daniel, D. B., 63
Daniels, D., 145, 146, 408
Daniels, S., 38
Daniluk, J., 278
Danner, F., 90
Danoff-Burg, S., 125

Darabi, K., 394
d'Arcy, H., 396
D'Ari, A., 413
Darity, W., 179, 419
Darling, N., 141, 142, 221, 251, 263, 350, 355,
    413, 415, 419, 448, 459
Darroch, J., 330, 373, 374, 375, 390, 391, 393,
    394, 398, 399
Darwin, C., 14
Datan, N., 134
Dauber, S., 210, 211
Daubman, K. A., 356
D'Augelli, A., 385
Davenport, E., 211
Davidson, A., 214
Davidson, P., 392
Davies, M., 330, 436, 438, 447
Davies, P., 151, 152, 153, 362, 363, 464
Davies, P. L., 75
Davies, P. T., 152
Davies, S., 330
Davies, S. L., 259, 389, 392
Davino, K., 57
Davis, A., 400
Davis, B., 140, 277, 282, 457
Davis, E., 380
Davis, G., 392
Davis, K., 342
Davis, K. C., 259
Davis, K. D., 137
Davis, L., 409
Davis, L. E., 424
Davis, M., 189
Davis, W., 66, 88
Davis-Kean, P. E., 318, 410
Davison, M., 211, 321, 323
Day, D. M., 308
Day, L., 145, 438
Day, M., 90
de Armaa, A., 193
De Fruyt, F., 273
De Groot, E., 408
de Visser, R., 377
de Vries, B., 324, 325
De Winter, A. F., 42
de Zwaan, M., 52, 53, 54
Deal, J., 151
Dean, B., 450
Dean, J. M., 56
Dearden, K., 396
Deardorff, J., 48
Deater-Deckard, K., 145, 146, 456, 457
Deaux, K., 386
DeBaryshe, B., 458
DeBaryshe, K., 413
DeBerry, K., 291, 292
Deblinger, E., 363
Deboutte, D., 124
Deci, E., 409
Dee, T., 56
DeFries, J., 151
DeGarmo, D., 156, 456, 457
Degirmencioglu, S., 172, 173, 186, 187, 221, 355
Deike, R., 276, 277
Dekovi, M., 459
Dekovic, M., 304

Delaney, R., 450
Delgado, M. R., 76
Delia, J., 63, 84
Dell, R., 391
Delva, J., 445
DelVecchio, W. F., 273
DeMaris, A., 155
Dembo, M., 345, 347
Dembo, M. H., 419
Demetriou, A., 71
Demo, D., 150, 275, 276, 280
Demorest, A., 67
DeMoya, D., 396
Demuth, S., 459
Dennig, M., 469
Dent, C., 178, 250, 251
Denton, K., 346
Denton, M., 329
DeRosier, M., 190
Deschenes, E., 184
DeSecottier, L., 353
Devereux, E., 311, 318
Devich-Navarro, M., 291, 294
Devinne, D., 152
Devlin, M., 54
Deyhle, D., 292
Diamond, L., 13, 180, 355, 361, 364, 368, 375,
    376, 378, 382, 383, 385
Diaz, R., 345, 347, 386
Diaz, T., 282
DiBlasio, F., 380
Dick, D., 35, 46
Dick, D. M., 48
Dick, R., 446
Dickson, N., 376, 440
DiClemente, R., 259, 330, 378, 379, 387,
    389, 392
Diehl, L., 276, 277
Diekstra, R., 436
Dielman, T., 277, 448, 449, 450
DiIorio, C., 379, 380
Dillon, F. R., 389
DiMaggio, P., 414
Dimas, J., 294, 295
Ding, S., 211
Dintcheff, B., 448
Dion, G. S., 422
Dishion, T., 142, 145, 183, 184, 185, 186, 282,
    295, 381, 448, 450, 456, 458, 459, 460
Dishion, T. K., 133
Dittus, P., 375, 379, 395
Dmitrieva, J., 140
Dobkin, P., 138, 185, 186, 459
Dobson, W., 288
Dodge, K., 124, 141, 183, 191, 251, 380, 412,
    451, 455, 456, 457, 458
Dodge, T., 186, 379, 395
Dogan, R. R., 413
Doherty, W., 155
Dolcini, M., 172
Dolezal, S., 282
Dollinger, S., 288
Dominguez, A., 158
Donato, K., 420
Dondero, T., 391
Donelly, W. O., 153

Dong, M., 140
Dong, Q., 186, 437, 459, 466, 467
Donnellan, M., 274, 282, 364
Donnelly, B., 396
Donnelly, D., 154
Donnelly, T. M., 326
Donnerstein, E., 257, 258, 259
Donovan, J., 377, 389, 437
Dorfman, L., 19
Dorham, C. L., 295
Dorius, G., 377
Dormitzer, C. M., 330
Dorn, L., 31, 34, 38, 440
Dornbusch, S., 30, 44, 46, 140, 142, 150, 151,
     153, 154, 155, 156, 159, 182, 185, 194, 211,
     221, 238, 239, 240, 242, 292, 293, 316, 318,
     358, 380, 413, 415, 418, 419, 424, 468
Dornsife, C., 113
Dorsey, S., 379
DosReis, S., 464
Dougher, K., 289
Douglas, G., 410
Douvan, E., 304, 344, 345, 362, 363
Dowdy, B. B., 355, 360
Downes, B., 51
Downey, D., 154, 218, 418, 419
Downey, G., 191, 341
Doyle, A., 342, 362
Doyle, A. B., 153, 342
Draper, P., 153, 438
Driscoll, A., 374, 385, 462
Drumm, P., 73
Dryfoos, J., 120, 201
Duan, N., 392
Dubas, J., 45
Dubé, E., 180, 355, 361, 383, 385
Dube, S. R., 140
Dubner, S., 201
Dubocovich, M. L., 42
DuBois, D., 121, 158, 276, 277, 278, 280, 281,
     282, 292, 348, 392, 417
Duchesne, S., 209
Duckett, E., 133, 136
Dufur, M., 154
Duke, P., 30, 44, 358
Dukes, R., 184, 291, 292
Duku, E., 445
Dumka, L. E., 429
Dumont, M., 469
Duncan, B., 429
Duncan, G., 122, 123, 158, 381, 414
Duncan, O., 429
Duncan, P., 46, 209, 413
Duncan, S., 277, 392
Duncan, T., 458
Dunlap, K. G., 143
Dunn, J., 144, 147
Dunn, S., 352
Dunphy, D., 171
Dunteman, G., 399
DuPont, S., 294, 296
Dupree, D., 140
DuRant, R., 124, 328, 330, 437, 441, 448,
     454, 460
Durbin, D., 309
Durbin, M., 392

Durston, S., 75, 76, 81
Dusek, J., 274
Duxbury, E., 457
Dweck, C., 410, 411
Dworkin, J., 170, 233, 244
Dwyer, K., 250, 251
Dyer, G., 47
Dyk, P., 339

E

Eamon, M. K., 413
Earls, F., 49, 57, 123
Early, D., 158, 352
East, P., 144, 145, 146, 352, 380, 394, 395, 400
Eastman, G., 134
Eaton, M. J., 419
Ebata, A., 469
Eberly, M., 308
Ebin, V. J., 120
Eccles, J., 7, 12, 13, 40, 99, 119, 125, 142, 145,
     156, 158, 170, 178, 199, 207, 208, 209, 210,
     212, 217, 218, 221, 232, 245, 251, 262, 275,
     278, 279, 280, 298, 318, 352, 362, 409, 410,
     411, 412, 413, 415, 419, 429, 430, 431,
     454, 459
Eckenrode, J., 212, 386
Eckland, B., 429
Economic Policy Institute., 416
Eddy, M., 460
Edelbrock, C., 436
Edelstein, W., 70, 273, 346
Edens, J., 451
Eder, D., 171, 188, 248, 249
Edman, J., 30
Edmonston, B., 397, 398
Edmundson, E., 438
Education Trust, 203, 422
Edwards, J. N., 144
Edwards, T. C., 435
Egan, S., 282, 299
Egeland, B., 341, 458, 459
Eggebeen, D., 148
Ehrhardt, A., 384, 391
Eicher, S., 168, 194, 316, 317
Eickholt, C., 307
Eisen, M., 270
Eisenberg, M., 51
Eisenberg, N., 13, 85, 86, 141, 321, 323,
     324, 326, 346
Eisenstadt, S., 169
Eitel, P., 192
Elder, G., 17, 48, 109, 117, 122, 138, 146, 156,
     157, 158, 184, 205, 208, 214, 239, 247, 329,
     347, 364, 456, 464
Elders, M., 447
Eley, T., 146, 457
Elkind, D., 65, 66, 328
Elkins, I., 136, 145, 146
Ellen, J. M., 392
Ellhammer, O., 145, 146
Ellickson, P., 444, 447, 449, 454
Elling, K., 420
Elliot, D., 241, 242, 455
Elliott, B., 152

Elliott, D., 377, 438
Elliott, M. R., 56
Ellis, B., 36
Ellis, B. J., 380
Ellwanger, P., 308
Elmen, J., 142, 410
Elo, I., 396
Elordi, C., 140
El-Sheikh, M., 157
Emans, S., 441
Emanuel, I., 397
Emerson, M., 389, 395
Emery, R., 154
Engels, R. C. M. E., 308
Engles, R., 308
Ennett, S., 171, 172, 179, 180, 181, 185, 186,
     448, 449
Enright, R., 20, 96, 97, 304, 308
Ensminger, M., 122, 210, 242, 373, 437
Entwisle, D., 206, 210, 211, 214, 215, 242, 412,
     423, 424, 425, 426
Epstein, J., 183, 194, 414, 448
Erdley, C., 188
Erel, O., 152
Erickson, K., 185, 316
Erickson, K. G., 159
Erickson, L., 7, 99
Erickson, M. F., 341
Erickson, P., 373, 399
Eriksen, M., 447
Erikson, E., 15, 15f, 16, 18, 283, 285, 286, 287,
     290, 291, 303, 336, 338, 339, 341, 426
Erkut, S., 279
Ernst, M., 76
Eron, L., 259
Esbensen, F., 184
Escalante, K. A., 155
Espelage, D. L., 183, 186
Espenshade, T. J., 213
Espinosa, Revill, J., 294, 296
Esposito, L. E., 438
Estell, D. B., 188
Estrada, A., 294, 349
Estrada, P., 346
Eubanks, J., 258
European Quality of Life Survey, 116
Evans, A., 75, 76
Evans, D., 272
Evans, E., 158, 260, 409, 417
Evans, W., 56
Eveleth, P., 24, 36, 37
Everett, S., 373, 388
Ey, S., 440, 461, 462, 463, 464, 466
Eyal, E., 257, 258
Eyre, S., 382

F

Fagan, J., 105, 314, 454, 456
Fagot, B., 396
Falk, R., 67
Fall, R., 203
Fallon, B., 349, 352
Fan, P., 430
Fan, S., 358, 377

Fan, X., 147, 377
Fang, F., 346
Fang, G., 346
Fang, X., 392
Faris, R., 329, 448
Farkas, G., 413, 416, 419
Farley, T., 251, 377
Farmer, T., 188
Farmer, T. W., 122, 188
Farrar, E., 202
Farrell, A., 460
Farrell, A. D., 124, 438
Farrell, F., 247
Farrell, M., 133, 151, 448
Farrell, M. P., 392
Farrelly, M. C., 259
Farrington, D., 14, 186, 435, 437, 450, 452, 453, 454, 455, 456, 457, 458, 459
Fasick, F., 96, 97, 98
Fauber, R., 151
Fauth, R. C., 122
Feaganes, J. R., 56
Featherman, D., 404, 416, 417, 429
Feder, M., 382, 383
Federal Bureau of Investigation., 452, 453
Federal Interagency Forum on Child and Family Statistics., 119, 243
Feehan, M., 436
Feeney, B. C., 282, 341
Fegley, S., 238, 239, 240, 242, 272, 326
Feigelman, S., 378, 392, 440, 448
Feinberg, M. E., 143, 146, 147
Feinman, J., 209
Feinstein, R., 399
Feiring, C., 13, 307, 335, 341, 346, 353, 355, 357, 358, 360, 361, 362, 363, 364
Feivelson, D., 391
Feld, B., 454
Feldlaufer, H., 208
Feldman, A., 297
Feldman, B., 272
Feldman, C., 91
Feldman, J., 80, 164
Feldman, S., 137, 152, 191, 308, 319, 379, 386, 454
Felice, M., 380, 395, 400
Felitti, V. J., 140
Felix-Ortiz, M., 447
Felner, R., 158, 214, 277, 281, 417
Felson, R., 280, 460
Fenton, R. E., 418
Fenzel, L., 208
Ferenz-Gillies, R., 342
Ferguson, D., 292
Ferguson, L., 315
Fergusson, D., 153, 194, 380, 395, 397, 437, 456, 457, 458, 459
Fichtenberg, C. M., 449
Field, A. E., 254
Field, T., 346
Fielder, E., 373
Fields, J., 148
Fiez, J. A., 76
Filardo, E., 180
Finch, A., Jr., 440
Finch, J., 277

Finch, M., 241, 320
Fincham, F., 152, 467
Fine, G., 239, 261, 354
Fine, M., 153, 156, 414, 415
Finer, L. B., 389
Fingerson, L., 379
Finkelhor, D., 154, 256, 454
Finkelstein, B. D., 346
Finkelstein, J., 56
Finkelstein, J. A., 464
Finkelstein, J. W., 46, 47
Finkelstein, N., 113
Finken, L., 315
Finkenauer, C., 308
Finley, E., 430
Finn, C., Jr., 202
Finn, J., 206
Finnegan, J., 449
Finnegan, R., 310, 342
Finnerty, K., 257, 258
Fiorentino, R., 399
Fischer, K., 387
Fischoff, B., 66, 87, 88
Fisher, C., 418
Fisher, D. A., 379, 381
Fisher, L., 152
Fisher, M., 51, 52, 124, 399
Fisher, T., 379
Fitch, S., 290
Fitzgerald, H., 397
Fitzgerald, M., 413
Fitzjohn, J., 376
Flaherty, B. P., 232, 233
Flaherty, J., 274
Flaherty, L., 468
Flammer, A., 234, 237
Flanagan, C., 157, 207, 326, 327, 328, 410
Flannery, D., 40, 43, 66, 222, 273, 281
Flavell, E., 65
Flavell, J., 65
Flay, B., 178, 250, 251, 447, 448, 449
Fleming, J., 409
Fleming, J. S., 408, 409
Fleming, W., 342
Fletcher, A., 141, 247, 415, 448
Flewelling, R., 449
Flickinger, S., 407, 418
Flielier, A., 70
Flisher, A. J., 436
Flor, D., 158, 418
Flores, E., 152
Flores, G., 260
Flores, R., 450
Flory, K., 445
Flynn, B., 449
Foeher, U., 12, 232, 253, 254, 255, 256, 258, 259, 260
Folkman, S., 58
Fondell, M., 380
Fong, G., 389, 392
Fong, G. T., 379
Forbes, E. E., 461
Forcier, M., 461
Ford, C., 9, 108, 111, 369, 370
Ford, C. A., 375
Ford, D., 420

Ford, M., 335
Fordham, C., 178, 179, 419
Forehand, R., 125, 151, 152, 153, 375, 379, 458, 468
Forgatch, M., 156, 457, 458
Forman, T. A., 328, 329
Formichella, C. M., 124
Formoso, D., 142
Forrest, J., 399
Forrester, K. K., 193
Forsman, L., 75
Forssberg, H., 75
Forssmann-Falck, R., 297
Forster, J., 449
Fortenberry, J., 377, 389
Fortner, M. R., 135
Fosco, G. M., 152
Foshee, V., 386, 448
Foss, R. D., 56
Foster, D., 25, 26, 27
Foster, E., 157, 244, 397
Foster, H., 363
Foster, L., 309
Foster, S. E., 261
Foster, T., 346
Foster, W., 121
Foster, W. H., 261
Fowler, F., 142
Fowler, J., 330
Fox, C., 222
Fox, J., 315
Fox, N., 76
Frabutt, J. M., 292
Fraleigh, M., 142, 221, 413
Francis, D., 446
Franco, O., 413
Frank, E., 464
Frank, S., 54, 308
Frankenberger, K. D., 66
Franklin, C., 398
Frankowski, B., 413
Franz, B., 385
Franzoi, S., 189
Fraser, B., 238
Frasier, K., 352
Frazier, A. L., 254
Fredricks, J. A., 278
Fredriksen, K., 41, 43
Freed, L. H., 363
Freedle, R. O., 82
Freedman, A., 468
Freedman-Doan, C., 208, 209
Freedner, N., 363
Freeman, H., 158, 173, 351
Freeman, R., 243
Freeman-Gallant, A., 456
Freisthler, B., 446
Freitas, A., 191
French, D., 54, 189, 190, 191, 350, 381
French, S., 51, 209, 440
French, S. A., 52
French, S. E., 275, 291
Freud, A., 15, 303, 305
Freud, S., 15, 16, 18, 368
Frick, P., 451, 458
Fried, C. S., 314, 454

Fried, M., 104, 109
Friedenberg, E., 12, 228
Friedman, N., 387
Friedman, R., 142, 414
Friedman, S., 124
Friel, L. V., 380
Frier, M., 417
Frijns, T., 308
Frisch, R., 26, 35
Frisco, M. L., 378
Frohlich, C., 326
Frome, P., 298, 415
Frost, J., 399
Frost, J. J., 390
Frost, P., 346
Fry, A., 72
Fuhrman, T., 309, 310
Fuligni, A., 116, 135, 136, 212, 291, 318, 350, 351, 418, 419, 420
Fulker, D., 456
Fulkerson, J. A., 51, 52
Fulmore, C., 407, 418
Fulton, A., 287
Funk, J., 260
Furbey, M., 86, 88
Furman, W., 13, 143, 144, 174, 176, 193, 335, 341, 344, 346, 351, 352, 353, 355, 356, 357, 358, 360, 362
Furstenberg, F., 6, 7, 17, 98, 115, 118, 147, 150, 151, 152, 153, 158, 163, 235, 374, 380, 381, 394, 396, 397, 398, 399, 400, 454
Fussell, M., 58
Futterman, D., 391, 392

G

Gable, R. K., 207
Gabrielli, W., 437
Gaddis, A., 45
Gage, J. C., 250
Gagnon, J., 358
Gaines, C., 142
Galambos, N., 45, 89, 100, 101, 110, 111, 140, 180, 184, 250, 251, 297, 298, 319, 462
Galay, L., 327, 328
Galbraith, J., 392, 440
Galbraith, K. A., 378, 379
Galen, B., 189
Gallatin, J., 285
Galliher, R. V., 385
Gallup, G., 328
Galotti, K., 64
Galvin, D. M., 242
Gamble, W., 244, 342
Gamm, B. K., 344, 346, 365
Gamoran, A., 203, 212, 219, 227, 412
Gamst, A., 75
Gans, J., 391, 468
Garbarino, J., 44, 250, 426, 459
Garber, J., 209, 466, 467
Garcia, C., 119, 279, 291, 292
Garcia, J., 352
Garcia, M., 468
Garcia-Castro, M., 400
Garcia-Coll, C., 119, 123

Garcia-Mila, M., 71
Garcia-Tunon, M., 391
Gardner, H., 67, 78, 79, 83, 91
Gardner, J. F., 464
Gardner, M., 90
Gardner, W., 314
Garduque, L., 239
Gargiulo, J., 44
Gariepy, J. L., 183
Gariglietti, G., 65
Garland, A., 454
Garmezy, N., 277, 405, 462, 468
Garnefski, N., 159, 436
Garnier, H., 148, 184, 424
Garrison, C., 150
Garver, K. E., 63, 75
Gathercole, S. E., 73
Gatherum, A., 310
Gau, S. S., 42
Gauze, C., 346, 352, 354
Gavin, L., 176, 352
Gayle, H., 391
Ge, X., 46, 47, 48, 124, 138, 140, 146, 157, 158, 437, 464, 466
Geary, P., 290
Gecas, V., 131, 134, 168
Gehring, T., 137
Geitz, L., 399
Gelbwasser, L., 415
Geller, B., 449
Genereaux, R., 84
Gennetian, L. A., 158
Gentile, D. A., 258
Gentry, M., 207
George, C., 399
George, G., 281
Georgiades, K., 445
Gerard, J., 152
Gerard, J. M., 282
Gerber, S. B., 206
Gerbner, G., 256
Gerhardt, C., 440, 462
Germann, J., 260
Gerrard, M., 65, 124, 140, 390, 392, 407
Gerris, J. M., 137
Gershoni, R., 345, 346, 347, 355
Gerstein, D., 443
Gest, S., 183, 273, 277, 405, 468
Gestsdottir, S., 252
Getson, P., 391
Getts, A., 124, 460
Getz, J., 308, 448
Getz, J. G., 120
Gfroerer, J. C., 119, 445
Ghatak, R., 413
Giancola, P. R., 447
Gibbons, F., 124, 392, 407
Gibbons, F. X., 46, 47, 65, 124, 140
Gibbons, K., 52
Gibbs, J., 141, 323
Giedd, J. N., 75
Gift, T. L., 391
Gil, A., 291, 294, 295
Gil, A. G., 387
Gilchrist, L. D., 398
Giles, W. H., 140

Giles-Sims, J., 156
Gilgun, J., 382, 383
Gilliam, F., 19
Gilligan, C., 298, 324, 325
Gillin, C. J., 43
Gillis, R., 440
Gillman, M. W., 254
Gillman, S., 151
Gillmore, M., 381, 389, 398, 400, 438, 447, 459
Gillock, K., 207, 417
Gilman, S., 260
Gilpin, E., 447
Gil-Rivas, V., 140
Gilsanz, V., 29
Ginsburg (Justice), 4
Ginsburg, G., 209, 409, 413, 467
Ginzberg, E., 235
Ginzler, J. A., 385
Giordano, P., 358, 365, 375, 378, 387
Giovino, G., 447
Girgus, J., 464, 466
Gittler, J., 314
Gjerde, P., 273
Glantz, S. A., 449
Glaser, R., 448
Glasgow, K., 140, 413
Glei, D., 141, 387, 388, 389
Glendinning, A., 151
Glenn, D., 140
Goforth, J. B., 122
Gold, M., 352
Goldberg, A., 355, 359, 361
Golden, N., 51, 52
Goldman, J., 290
Goldman, M., 448
Goldscheider, F., 115
Goldsmith, P. A., 214
Goldstein, S. E., 318
Goleman, D., 78
Golombok, S., 385
Gondoli, D., 134
Gonzales, N., 48, 138, 140, 142, 143, 151, 158, 184, 296, 414, 415
Gonzalez, R., 420
Good, T., 218, 409
Goodenow, C., 389, 420
Goodlad, J., 227
Goodman, E., 147, 316, 328, 330, 447
Goodman, G. S., 316
Goodman, M., 97, 98, 115, 164, 232, 357
Goodman, W., 29
Goodwin, M., 259
Goossens, L., 65, 66, 141, 289, 290, 308
Goran, M., 30
Gordis, E., 152
Gordon, A. B., 389, 392
Gordon, J., 247
Gordon, K., 112, 410
Gordon, L., 386
Gordon, M., 356
Gordon, R. A., 186, 397
Gordon, S., 382, 383
Gordon, V., 375, 379
Gore, S., 226, 247, 352, 437, 466
Gorman-Smith, D., 123, 124, 158, 184, 363, 459, 469

Gortmaker, S., 52, 57, 440
Gotgay, N., 76
Gotham, H. J., 445
Gotlib, I., 466, 467
Gottfredson, D., 242
Gottfredson, M., 438
Gottfried, A., 408, 409
Gottschlich, H., 66
Gould, J. B., 123
Gould, M., 134, 256, 466
Gowen, L., 44, 51, 356, 362, 386
Goyette, K., 416, 418
Graber, J., 14, 38, 40, 45, 47, 49, 51, 52, 242, 369, 440, 461, 462, 464, 466, 467
Grady, W., 376, 381
Graham, C., 36
Graham, E., 261
Graham, S., 46, 105, 191, 192, 193, 214, 455, 457
Graham-Bermann, S., 158
Gralen, S., 30, 54
Gralinski, J., 409, 410
Granger, D., 467
Granger, D. A., 40
Granic, I., 133
Grant, D., 398
Grant, K., 440, 461, 462, 463, 464, 466
Gray, H., 57, 399
Gray, M., 360, 364
Gray, P., 164
Gray, W., 66
Gray-Little, B., 214, 280, 292
Graziano, W., 277
Greca, A. M. L., 457
Green, F., 65
Green, K., 290
Green, R., 384
Green, S., 379, 415, 458
Green, S. M., 397
Green, Y., 399
Greenbaum, P., 448
Greenberg, M., 193, 336, 342, 352
Greenberger, E., 98, 140, 162, 186, 193, 236, 237, 238, 239, 240, 242, 309, 320, 339, 353, 459, 466, 467
Greene, J., 158
Greene, K., 392
Greene, M., 58
Greene, M. L., 181, 280, 281, 296, 345, 347
Greene, W., 386
Greenhill, L., 467
Greenley, K., 144
Greenley, R. N., 55, 56, 65, 91
Greenstein, D., 76
Greenwald, P., 346
Greenwald, S., 330
Greenwood, G., 379
Gregory, A., 221
Gregory, L., 418
Gregory, W., 281
Greif, E., 44
Griffin, K. W., 282, 448
Griffith Fontaine, R., 458
Grigg, W., 215
Grigg, W. S., 422
Grisso, T., 105, 314, 451
Grobe, R., 413, 416

Grolnick, W., 143, 413
Gross, L., 256
Gross, R., 30, 44, 46, 153, 155, 358, 380
Grossman, J. B., 121
Grossman, M., 449
Grotevant, H., 136, 143, 147, 288, 306, 309, 310, 429, 430
Grotpeter, J., 345
Grotpeter, K., 189
Grove, K., 151
Grover, R. L., 360
Groves, W., 454
Grube, J. W., 379, 381
Gruber, J., 57, 87, 89, 443, 449
Gruen, R., 384
Gruff, T., 358
Grumbach, M., 25
Grunbaum, J., 373
Grych, J., 467
Grych, J. H., 152
Grynch, J. H., 364
Guacci-Franci, N., 349, 352, 353
Guay, F., 209
Guberman, S., 81
Guerra, N., 460
Guest, A., 248
Guillen, E., 51
Guisinger, S., 306
Guldi, M., 120
Gullone, E., 88
Gullotta, T., 288
Gump, P., 205
Gunnore, M., 156
Guo, G., 120
Guo, J., 395, 448
Guo, M., 186
Gur, M., 390
Gurevitch, M., 256
Gurin, G., 184
Gurley, D., 467
Gustafson, P., 323
Guterman, N. B., 120
Guth, A., 42
Guthertz, M., 346
Guthrie, H., 30
Guthrie, I. K., 326
Gutierrez, R., 217
Gutman, L., 207, 209
Gutman, L. M., 123, 158

H

Haan, N., 70
Haas, E., 185, 460
Haavisto, T., 407
Habib, F., 221
Hacker, D., 65
Hafdahl, A., 280, 292
Hafen, M., Jr., 135
Hafetz, E., 34
Hafsteinsson, L. G., 140
Hagan, J., 140, 192, 363
Hagan, M., 151
Haggstrom-Nordin, E., 388
Haglund, B., 397

Hahm, H., 445
Hahm, H. C., 120
Haight, W. L., 353
Haj-Yahia, M. M., 140, 182
Haj-Yahia, Y., 140
Hale, Bronik, 72
Hale, C., 396
Hale, L. E., 213
Hale, S., 72
Hall, G. S., 14–16, *15*, 15f, 19, 96
Hall, J., 457
Hall, L., 72
Halliday-Scher, K., 172, 173, 183
Hallinan, M., 180, 182, 211, 212, 353
Halperin, S., 226
Halpern, C., 30, 38, 52, 363, 375, 376, 378
Halpern-Felsher, B., 88, 312
Ham, A., 379
Hamburg, D., 118
Hamburg, P., 260
Hamill, S., 134
Hamilton, B. E., 388, 393
Hamilton, C., 341
Hamilton, H. A., 152
Hamilton, M., 113, 226, 237, 244
Hamilton, S., 113, 226, 237, 244, 350
Hamilton-Leaks, J., 400
Hamm, J. V., 181, 182, 183, 294
Hamm, M, 79
Hammen, C., 462, 464, 467
Hammer, L., 448
Hammersmith, S., 385
Hampl, S., 51
Hamre, B. K., 417
Han, S., 467
Handbrough, E., 259
Hanmer, T., 298
Hansell, S., 461
Hansen, D. M., 241, 244
Hansen, M., 42
Hansen, W., 250, 251
Hanson, S., 250, 416
Hanson, T., 151, 155
Hanson, U., 388
Hansson, K., 145, 146
Harachi, T. W., 447, 459
Hardesty, J. L., 278, 280, 281
Hardin, J. W., 389, 392
Harding, D. J., 122, 222
Hardy, D., 395
Hardy, S. A., 330
Hargis, P., 235
Hargreaves, D., 51
Hariri, A. R., 6, 15
Harker, K., 296
Harkness, A., 80
Harkness, W., 386
Harlan, S., 400
Harold, G., 152
Harold, R., 413
Harper, G., 184
Harre, N., 56
Harrington, H., 457, 458
Harrington, K., 259, 378, 379
Harrington, K. F., 330, 389, 392
Harris, C., 183

Harris, D., 20, 97
Harris, J., 162, 167, 168, 169
Harris, J. I., 420
Harris, J. R., 159
Harris, K., 119, 445, 468
Harris, M., 183, 184
Harris, M. J., 460
Harris, T. L., 328, 330
Hart, B., 464
Hart, D., 272, 273, 321, 326
Hart, E., 458
Harter, S., 268, 270, 271, 272, 277, 278, 281, 282, 298, 325, 345, 408
Hartman, C. A., 42
Hartmark, C., 112
Hartney, C., 110
Hartos, J., 56
Hartup, W., 163, 188, 192, 194, 325, 364, 365
Harwood, R., 193, 467
Hasebe, Y., 132
Haselager, G. T., 192
Hasemeier, C., 34
Haskett, M. E., 457
Hasse, L. A., 447
Hastorf, A., 153, 155, 380
Hathaway, J. E., 363
Hattie, J., 410
Hatzichristou, C., 189
Hau, K., 213, 278, 405
Hauptman, J., 51
Hauser, R., 416
Hauser, S., 143, 292, 307, 309, 310, 342, 343, 352, 468
Hausman, A., 460
Hausser, D., 392
Havel, M., 42
Havighurst, R., 17
Haviland, M. L., 259
Hawkins, J., 123, 395, 424, 438, 447, 448, 453, 455
Hawley, K. M., 467
Hawley, P. H., 188
Haworth, T., 363
Hayashi, K., 27
Haydel, K., 448
Hayden, H., 54
Hayduk, L., 412
Hayes, C., 375, 389, 395
Hayes, D., 423
Hayman, C., 391
Haynes, N., 221
Haynie, D. L., 48, 124, 172, 186, 192, 365
Hayward, C., 44, 51, 52, 53, 54, 356, 362, 448, 463, 467
Hazan, C., 360
Healton, C. G., 259
Healy, B., 346
Heaton, T., 377
Hebert, M., 364
Hechinger, F., 207
Hecht, M. L., 292
Heck, D. J., 181, 182
Heck, R. H., 211
Hecker, T., 456
Hedges, L., 418
Heeren, T., 444

Heimer, K., 459
Hein, K., 56, 391
Hektner, J., 430
Helmreich, R., 298
Helms, H. M., 349
Helms, L., 242
Helsen, M., 287, 352
Helwig, C., 327
Helwig, C. C., 315
Henderson Daniel, J., 328, 330
Henderson, S., 144, 146, 148, 149, 150, 156, 255
Hendrick, C., 382
Hendrick, S., 382
Hendry, L., 151
Henggeler, S., 457, 460
Henkel, R. R., 183, 186
Hennig, K. H., 323
Henrich, C., 207
Henrich, C. C., 376
Henrich, Schwab-Stone, M., 124, 326
Henriksen, L., 12, 232, 256, 258, 259, 260
Henry, B., 273, 436, 457, 458
Henry, C., 156
Henry, D., 363, 469
Henry, D. B., 123, 124, 158, 184
Henshaw, S., 396
Herbison, P., 376
Herdt, G., 26, 27, 368
Herman, M., 280, 292, 293
Herman, M. R., 125
Herman-Giddens, M., 26, 34, 387
Herman-Stahl, M., 469
Hernandez, D., 11, 148, 149, 251
Hernandez-Gantes, V., 424
Hernandez-Guzman, L., 75
Herrenkohl, T. I., 123
Herrera-Leavitt, I., 413
Herrling, S., 400, 425
Hershberg, T., 115, 163, 235
Hershberger, S., 385
Hertzberg, V. S., 389, 392
Hertzman, C., 58
Hertzog, C., 464
Herzog, D., 57, 260
Hess, R., 420
Hesselbrock, V., 75
Hetherington, E., 10, 43, 138, 140, 141, 143, 144, 145, 146, 147, 148, 149, 150, 151, 153, 154, 156, 184, 255, 353
Hevey, C., 143
Hicks, K. J., 464
Hicks, L., 207
Hicks, R., 315
Hicks, R. E., 186, 365
Higgins, A., 71
Higgins, E., 297
Higgins-D'Alessandro, A., 324
Hightower, E., 341
Hill, C., 329
Hill, E., 380
Hill, J., 8, 43, 83, 108, 164, 180, 194, 297, 306, 308, 310, 311, 335, 349, 353, 355, 463
Hill, K., 453, 455
Hill, K. G., 123, 395, 424, 448
Hill, M., 400, 401
Hill, N. E., 412, 429

Hillier, L., 52
Hillman, S. B., 464
Hills, N. K., 259
Hilsman, R., 466
Himes, J., 34, 38
Himes, J. H., 38
Hinden, B., 436, 462
Hine, T., 17, 98, 232
Hines, A., 150
Hines, M., 27
Hingson, R., 444
Hiraga, N., 142
Hiraga, Y., 140, 151, 158, 184
Hirky, A., 446
Hirsch, B., 276, 348, 353
Hirsch, E. D., 202, 203
Hirsch, M., 395
Hirschfield, P., 122
Hirschi, T., 438
Hitchings, B., 437
Ho, L., 358, 377
Hoberman, H., 51, 52
Hobson, C., 412, 417
Hock, E., 308
Hockenberry-Eaton, M., 379, 380
Hodge, C., 276
Hodge, S. A., 207, 208
Hodges, E., 192, 310
Hofer, M., 328
Hoffer, T., 215, 216, 218, 227, 414, 425
Hofferth, S. L., 397
Hoffman, J. P., 124, 150
Hoffman, K., 466
Hoffman, K. L., 144
Hoffman, L., 430
Hoffman, S., 397
Hofman, J., 345, 346, 347, 355
Hofmann, V., 70, 273
Hofmann, W., 342
Hofsterrer, C., 379
Hofstra, G., 289
Hogan, D., 380, 387, 388
Hogue, A., 186
Holcomb, D., 248
Holder, D. W., 328, 330
Holderness, C., 44
Holland, A., 249
Holland, J., 427
Holland, L. J., 363
Hollenstein, T., 133
Hollier, E., 151
Hollingshead, A., 17, 171, 180
Holloway, B., 121
Holloway, C., 382
Holloway, S., 420
Holmbeck, G., 20, 43, 55, 56, 65, 91, 133, 136, 137, 152, 154, 194, 303, 306, 308, 309, 310, 311, 378, 379, 400
Holmen, J., 447
Holmen, T., 447
Holsen, I., 462
Holt, M. K., 183, 186
Homish, D., 456
Hommeyer, J., 309
Hong, S., 50, 448
Hook, E. W., 389, 392

Hooper, C. J., 73, 75
Hoover-Dempsey, K., 412
Hopf, D., 189
Hoppe, M. J., 381
Hops, H., 140, 277, 282, 457, 461, 463, 464
Horan, P., 235
Horn, S. S., 175, 176, 190
Hornik, R., 392
Horowitz, H., 275
Horvat, E. M., 179, 419
Horwood, L., 395, 456, 457, 458, 459
Horwood, L. J., 380
Hough, R., 454, 456
House, L. E., 469
Houts, L. A., 374
Hovell, M., 379
Hoven, C. W., 436
Hovinga, M. E., 397
Howard, A., 460
Howard, D. E., 386
Howard, G., 396
Howard, K., 19
Howe, B., 387
Howe, G., 146
Howe, G. W., 143
Howe, T. R., 456
Howell, D., 436
Howell, L. W., 378
Howell, W., 216
Howes, C., 189
Hoyt, D., 380, 387, 459
Hoyt, D. R., 158, 387
Hoza, B., 191, 346, 354, 355
Hrabosky, J. I., 53
Hsu, C., 420
Hu, M., 447
Hu, P., 380
Huang, B., 38, 147, 173
Huang, D., 295
Hubbard, J., 358, 362, 363, 468
Hubbard, M., 123
Hudley, C., 191, 214, 411, 457
Hudson, L., 66
Huebner, A. J., 247, 378
Huebner, C. E., 435
Huesmann, L., 259
Hughes, H. K., 385
Hughes, J., 154
Hughes, M., 399
Hughes, S., 446
Huizinga, D., 88, 437, 438, 455
Hunsberger, B., 326
Hunt, C., 413
Hunt, H., 221
Hunt, J., 262
Hunt, M., 469
Hunter, F., 306, 348, 351
Hunter, S. MacD., 180, 181
Huot, R., 26, 444, 467
Hurdle, D., 295, 299
Hurley, D., 148
Hurrelmann, K., 96, 115, 116, 237
Hussey, J., 377
Hussong, A., 14, 186, 365, 438, 445, 447, 448
Huston, A., 297
Hutchinson, M. K., 379

Hutson, H., 454
Hyde, J., 279
Hyman, C., 189, 194, 377, 397
Hymel, S., 188, 189, 191, 194
Hyoun, C., 363

I

Iacono, W. G., 136, 145, 146
Ialongo, N., 460
Ibanez, G. E., 413
Iborra, A., 106, 107
Iedema, J., 287
Iglowstein, I., 42
Ingersoll, G., 377
Ingram, F., 391
Ingram, J., 276
Inhelder, B., 15
Inoff-Germain, G., 34, 440
Insabella, G., 149, 151
Institute of Medicine, 50, 51
Ireland, M., 52, 375, 380, 454, 468
Irwin, C., 55, 56, 57, 58, 86, 447
Irwin, K., 223
Irwin, K. L., 391
Isakson, K., 209

J

Jablow, M., 391
Jaccard, J., 186, 375, 379, 392, 395
Jacklin, C., 81
Jackson, C., 132
Jackson, D., 73
Jackson, K., 150
Jackson, L., 276
Jackson, S., 54
Jackson-Newsom, J., 137, 141
Jacob, T., 142
Jacobin, C., 52, 53, 54
Jacobs, J., 7, 99, 119, 315, 424
Jacobs, J. D., 440
Jacobs, J. E., 130, 170, 248, 275, 279
Jacobs, S., 155
Jacobsen, T., 70, 342
Jacobson, E., 218
Jacobson, K., 146, 463
Jacobson, L. J., 145, 146
Jacobson, N., 122
Jacobs-Quadrel, M., 87, 88
Jaffee, S., 397
Jagers, R. J., 323
Jain, U., 468
Jakobsen, R., 437
Jang, S., 282, 330, 447
Jank, W., 387
Janosz, M., 424, 425
Jansen, E. A., 189
Janssen, I., 42
Janveau-Brennan, G., 69
Jarrett, R., 158
Jarvinen, D., 188
Jarvis, P., 209
Jarvis, P. A., 241

Jasinkaja-Lahti, I., 295
Jaskir, J., 341
Jason, L., 421
Jayaratne, T., 158
Jefferson, K., 392
Jeffries, N. O., 75
Jelicic, H., 252
Jemmott, J. B., III, 379, 389, 392
Jemmott, L., 389, 392
Jemmott, L. S., 379
Jenkins, F., 215
Jenkins, K. N., 425
Jenkins, R., 119, 292
Jenni, O., 42
Jennings, D., 30, 44, 358
Jensen, C., 51
Jensen, L. A., 308
Jensen-Campbell, L., 277, 357
Jernigan, T. L., 75
Jessor, R., 377, 389, 437, 448
Jessor, S., 437
Jeynes, W., 150, 151
Jinnett, K., 447
Jodl, K., 342
Jodl, K. M., 156, 412, 429
John, O., 273, 437
Johnson, A., 355, 363
Johnson, B. D., 104
Johnson, B. R., 330, 447
Johnson, C., 123, 140, 158, 250, 251, 449
Johnson, D., 30
Johnson, D. R., 40
Johnson, E., 81
Johnson, J., 447
Johnson, J. G., 259, 440
Johnson, J. P., 380
Johnson, K., 373
Johnson, M., 235, 239, 242, 426, 428, 429, 430
Johnson, P. B., 442
Johnson, R., 30, 443
Johnson, S., 309, 416
Johnston, L., 250, 251, 443, 445, 447, 448, 449, 459
Johnston, M., 214, 347
Joiner, T., 461
Joiner, T. E., Jr., 466
Jolliffe, D., 453, 455, 456
Jones, D., 348
Jones, D. C., 54
Jones, D. J., 125, 458
Jones, E., 390
Jones, G., 345, 347
Jones, J., 210, 468
Jones, J. M., 418
Jones, M., 454
Jones, M. C., 45
Jones, N., 57
Jones, R., 289
Jones, R. K., 330, 389
Jones, R. M., 43
Jones, S. M., 124, 140, 188, 330
Jordan, A., 272, 466
Jordan, Michael, 79
Jordan, W., 424
Joshi, H., 120
Josselson, R., 306, 309, 339

Jouriles, E. N., 363
Joyce, T., 396
Joyner, E., 221
Joyner, K., 376, 385
Jozefowicz, D., Jr., 430, 438, 461
Ju, D., 151, 424
Juang, L., 319, 413
Juarez, L., 123
Juarez-Reyes, M., 373
Judd, C., 316
Judge, B., 464, 465
Jurkovic, G., 413
Jussim, L., 218, 409
Juvonen, J., 120, 191, 192, 193, 214, 415

K

Kabbani, N. S., 423, 424
Kaeser, L., 399
Kaestle, C. E., 374, 375
Kahler, C. W., 438
Kahn, J., 387, 388
Kahn, R., 58
Kahneman, D., 87
Kail, R., 72
Kalakoski, V., 290
Kalb, L. M., 456
Kaliher, G., 353
Kalil, A., 142, 158, 397, 454
Kaljee, L., 392
Kalman, Z., 346, 347
Kalmuss, D., 396, 400
Kaltreider, D., 450
Kamenetz, A., 115
Kanaya, T., 132
Kandel, D., 185, 186, 309, 438, 445, 447
Kann, L., 373, 388
Kanouse, D., 399
Kantner, L., 389
Kantor, H., 204, 244
Kao, G., 119, 416, 419, 420
Kao, M., 380, 381
Kaplan, A., 54
Kaplan, C., 373
Kaplan, D., 399
Kaplan, H., 282, 376
Kaplan, N., 342
Kaplan, S., 25
Kaplowitz, P. B., 26
Kaprio, J., 34, 35, 46, 48
Karavasilis, L., 342
Karpati, A. M., 37
Karpovsky, S., 346, 347
Kasen, S., 259, 424, 440
Kasendorf, E., 292
Kasim, R., 448
Kaslow, N. J., 466
Kastelic, D., 298, 325
Katainen, S., 440
Katchadourian, H., 372
Katz, E., 256
Katz, J., 376
Katz, L. F., 122, 454
Katz, M., 107, 112, 115
Katz, P., 297

Katzman, D., 51, 52
Kaufman, J., 222, 223
Kaufman, K., 281
Kaufmann, R., 388
Kawai, E., 186
Kaye, J., 400
Kazis, R., 113, 120
Keane, E., 446
Keating, D., 8, 58, 62, 68, 70, 71, 73, 74, 76, 79, 82, 327, 467
Keefe, K., 183, 365
Keel, P. K., 51, 53, 54
Keeler, G., 454
Keeling, R., 391
Keenan, K., 459
Keener, D., 309
Keeshan, P., 57, 449
Keiley, M. K., 456
Keith, B., 150, 151, 153
Kelch, R., 25
Kellam, S., 460
Keller, J., 352, 409
Keller, M., 273, 346
Kelley, A., 444
Kelley, J., 193, 308
Kelley, M., 379, 380
Kelly, A., 51
Kelly, F. D., 137
Kelly, T. H., 76
Keltikangas-Jaervinen, L., 440
Kemptom, T., 151
Kendall, P., 440, 462
Keniston, K., 98
Kenneavy, K., 259
Kennedy (Justice), 4
Kennedy, R., 464
Kenny, M., 342
Keogh, D., 397
Kerns, K. A., 144
Kerr, M., 184
Kerry, John, 99
Kett, J., 17, 107, 112, 115, 235
Key, J., 397
Khoo, S. T., 144
Khoury, E., 291, 294, 295
Khoury-Kassibri, M., 222
Kiecolt, J., 144
Kielsmeier, J. C., 244
Kierman, E. A., 145
Kiernan, K., 152
Kierran, E., 400
Kiesner, J., 183, 189, 436
Kieszak, S. M., 37
Kilborn, P., 148
Kilbourne, B., 391
Kilgore, S., 215, 216, 218
Killen, J., 51, 52, 448, 463
Killen, M., 326
Killian, K., 55
Kilmartin, C., 297
Kilmer, S., 342
Kilpatrick, D., 448
Kim, D. Y., 341
Kim, H. K., 100, 458, 462
Kim, I. J., 46, 47, 50, 448
Kim, J., 140, 141, 184, 297, 416, 430

Kim, K., 138
Kim, K. J., 156, 456
Kim, S., 140, 158, 211, 346
Kim, S.-B., 242
Kim, Y., 373
Kimonis, E., 455
Kimura, S., 420
King, C., 420
King, J., 409
King, R., 396
King, R. A., 436
King, R. G., 52
King, V., 329
Kinney, D., 171, 172, 173, 175, 176, 248, 249
Kinsey, A., 368
Kinsfogel, K. M., 364
Kinzie, J., 416, 418
Kipke, M., 158
Kirby, D., 123, 399
Kirkpatrick, L., 342
Kirpke, M. D., 459
Kiselica, M., 396
Kisker, E., 57
Kitamura, S., 420
Kite, M., 347
Klaczynski, P., 63, 64, 70
Klahr, D., 90
Klasen, L., 76
Klaver, J., 106
Klebanov, P., 381
Klein, D., 444, 467
Klein, D. F., 259
Klein, H. W., 50
Klein, J., 399
Klein, R., 467
Kleinman, M., 133, 134, 256, 466
Klepinger, D., 397
Klerman, L., 58
Klerman, L. V., 397
Klesges, R., 448
Klessinger, N., 469
Kliewer, W., 297, 360
Klimes-Dougan, B., 461
Kling, J. R., 122, 454
Kling, K., 279
Klingaman, L., 386
Kloep, M., 157
Kloska, D., 448
Klump, K. L., 51, 53, 54
Knafo, A., 131
Kneisel, P., 349
Knight, G., 142, 456
Knoester, C., 124, 133
Knopf, I., 71
Knox, V., 158
Knutson, M., 456, 457
Knutson, N., 156
Ko, H., 420
Kobak, R., 336, 340, 342
Koch, G., 34, 386
Koch, P., 56, 352
Koenig, L., 19, 277
Koerner, S., 155
Koerner, S. S., 155, 392
Koff, E., 45
Kogan, M. D., 250

Koh, S., 316
Kohlberg, L., 70, 321, 322, 323, 324, 330
Kohler, J. K., 147
Kohn, M., 430
Kohn-Wood, L., 296
Kolaric, G., 45, 111, 319
Kolata, G., 383
Kolbe, L., 373
Kolbe, L. J., 388
Kolburn Kowal, A., 144, 379
Koller, S., 326
Komatsu, L., 64
Komro, K., 449
Konarski, R., 174, 278, 355, 358, 364
Kong, C., 405
Koo, H., 399
Koopman, C., 391, 392
Koot, H. M., 451, 452
Korpi, M., 399
Kosterman, R., 453, 455
Kotchick, B., 375, 379, 468
Kotler, L., 440
Kotov, R., 451
Kowal, A., 147
Kowal, A. K., 144
Kowaleski-Jones, L., 125
Kowaleski-Jones, P., 380
Kowalski, P., 408
Kracke, B., 46, 47, 48, 117, 328
Kraemer, H. C., 52, 53, 54
Kraft, P., 462
Krahn, H., 462
Krahn, H. J., 100, 101
Kramer, L., 144, 147
Kramer, R. A., 436
Krasnovsky, F., 392
Kraus, J., 447
Kraus, R., 250
Kreager, D. A., 88, 183
Krei, M., 113, 226
Kreitner, S., 379
Krevans, J., 141
Kriepe, R., 51, 52
Krishnakumar, A., 152
Kroger, J., 284, 287, 290
Krohn, M. D., 456
Krosnick, J., 316
Krueger, H., 113
Ksansnak, K., 297
Ku, L., 299, 373
Kuang, H., 211
Kuhn, D., 70, 71
Kuhns, J., 387
Kulin, H., 34, 38
Kulin, H. E., 38, 46, 47
Kulis, S., 292, 295, 299
Kumpfer, K. L., 57, 159
Kung, E., 309
Kunkel, D., 257, 258
Kunselman, S. J., 46, 47
Kunz, J., 397
Kupanoff, K., 137
Kuperminc, G., 207, 342, 400, 413, 425, 464
Kupersmidt, J., 124, 131, 140, 190, 191, 194, 377, 417
Kupfer, D., 76

Kupper, L., 363
Kurdek, L., 153, 156, 412, 414, 415
Kurlychek, M. C., 104
Kurowki, C. O., 143
Kurtines, W., 467
Kurtz, D., 292
Kusche, C., 193
Kuther, T. L., 324
Kuttler, A. F., 174, 355, 356
Kwak, K., 319
Kwak, N., 211
Kwon, H., 464, 465

L

La Greca, A. M., 174, 178, 355, 356
Labellarte, M. J., 467
Lacourse, E., 458, 460
Ladewski, B., 155
Laetz, V., 448
LaGaipa, J., 343, 344
Lahey, B., 458
Lahey, B. B., 186, 397
Lahif, M., 445
Lahiff, M., 120
Laible, D., 351
Laird, J., 159, 318
Laird, R., 183
Laird, R. D., 141, 191
Laixuthai, A., 449
Lake, M., 157
Lalonde, R. N., 295
Lam, M., 350, 419
Lam, T., 358, 377
Lamb, K. A., 155
Lamb, M., 398
Lambert, L. E., 207
Lambert, S., 214
Lamberty, G., 119, 292
Lamborn, S., 142, 151, 184, 220, 221, 228, 308, 310, 413, 415, 419
Lamkin, R., 122
Lammers, C., 380
Lampman-Petraitis, C., 40, 245
Lanctot, N., 376
Land, D., 336, 342
Landale, N., 376, 394
Landry, C., 444
Landry, D., 398, 399
Landry, D. J., 399
Lane, D. J., 65
Lang, D., 392
Lang, D. L., 389, 392
Lang, S., 447
Langefeld, C., 392
Langer, D. A., 124
Langer, J., 70
Langer, J. A., 217
Langer, L., 376, 382, 392
Langhout, R. D., 121
Lansford, J. E., 412, 458
Lansing, A. E., 454
Lanz, M., 137
Lanza, S., 275, 279
LaPoint, V., 50

Lapsley, D., 20, 66, 83, 96, 97
Lara, J., 424
Largo, R., 42
Larkin, R. W., 176
Larose, S., 209, 342
Larsen-Rife, D., 364
Larson, D., 330, 447
Larson, J. H., 135
Larson, M., 260
Larson, R., 6, 11, 19, 20, 40, 45, 98, 108, 114, 118, 119, 133, 135, 136, 137, 143, 150, 151, 162, 163, 170, 194, 198, 219, 232, 233, 234, 236, 237, 244, 245, 246, 247, 251, 254, 255, 263, 274, 275, 335, 351, 355, 363, 364, 420, 428, 469
Larsson, I., 382
Latting, J., 113
Lau, S., 298
Laub, J., 123, 454, 456
Laughlin, J., 315, 349, 352
Lauko, M. A., 422
Laumann, E., 383
Laupa, M., 84
Lauritsen, J., 373, 380, 381
Laursen, B., 11, 43, 130, 131, 133, 136, 303, 306, 308, 344, 345, 346, 347, 350, 351, 357
Lavoie, F., 364
LaVoie, J., 290
Lawford, H., 326
Lawrence, J., 65
Lazar, N. A., 63
Lazarus, N., 392
Le Blanc, R., 448
Leadbeater, B., 398, 400, 464
Leadbeater, B. J., 180, 207
Leaf, W., 56
Leahy, E., 409
Leaper, C., 298
Lease, A., 277
LeBlanc, A., 123
LeBlanc, M., 424, 425
Lebolt, A., 191
Leckman, P. E., 124
Ledingham, J., 213
Ledsky, R., 389
Lee, A. M., 45
Lee, C., 238
Lee, M., 392, 420, 469
Lee, P., 34, 38
Lee, P. A., 38
Lee, S., 135, 155, 420
Lee, S. Y., 417, 420
Lee, V., 153, 155, 205, 206, 208, 211, 212, 227, 386, 387, 412, 417, 425
Lee, Y., 54
Leech, S., 448
Lefebvre, L., 386
Leff, S., 131
Leffert, N., 193
Lefkowitz, E., 306, 329, 379, 380
Lehman, S. J., 392
Leibenluft, E., 40, 66, 76, 136
Leiberman, L. D., 399
Leiderman, P., 153, 155, 380
Leitch, C., 336, 342, 352
Leitenberg, H., 374

LeMare, L., 191, 194
Lempers, J., 144, 157
Lempers, J. D., 144
L'Engle, K. L., 259
Lenhart, L., 83, 86
Lenoir, C. D., 392
Lenox, K., 189, 194
Lenroot, R., 76
Leon, G., 51
Leonard, S. A., 349
Leone, P., 448
Lerch, J., 76
Lerner, J., 138, 142, 252, 319, 352
Lerner, R., 6, 252, 352
Lerner, R. M., 252
Lesko, N., 20
Leslie, F., 261
Leslie, L., 430
Lesser, G., 309
Lesser, I., 339
Lester, J., 186
Lesthaeghe, R., 99
Leung, M., 186
Leung, M. C., 122
Leve, C., 396
Leventhal, A., 172
Leventhal, B. L., 397
Leventhal, H., 57, 449
Leventhal, T., 121, 122, 123, 124, 125, 242
Levesque, R., 361
Levin, M., 374, 379
Levine, A., 252
Levine, J. A., 397
Levine, L., 261
Levine, M., 30, 54
Levine, P., 89
Levine, S., 27
Levinson, D., 133
Levinson, R., 392
Levitt, J., 349, 352, 353
Levitt, M., 349, 352, 353
Levitt, S., 201
Levitz-Jones, E., 339
Levy, V., 20, 97
Levy-Storms, L., 373, 381
Lewin, K., 15f, 17, 110
Lewin, L., 457
Lewin, T., 386, 409
Lewin-Epstein, N., 235
Lewinsohn, P., 45, 49, 363, 438, 461, 463, 464, 466, 467
Lewis, C., 88, 141, 312, 313
Lewis, K. S., 179, 419
Lewis, M., 40, 52, 307, 341, 346, 353, 355
Lewis, R. L., 281, 294, 295, 296
Lewis, S., 400
Lewis, T., 153
Lexcen, F., 105
Li, B., 330, 448
Li, D., 420
Li, J., 91, 420
Li, S., 140, 330, 447
Li, X., 183, 247, 378, 392, 448
Li, Y., 151
Li, Z., 188
Lian, B. E., 124

Liang, R., 38
Liang, S., 353
Lichenstein, P., 146, 457
Lichtenstein, P., 145, 146
Lieberman, M., 323, 342
Liebert, D., 90
Liebert, R., 90
Liebkind, K., 295
Liederman, P., 142, 221, 413
Liefeld, C., 401
Light, B., 411
Light, R., 206
Lin, K., 386
Lindberg, L., 373, 375, 387, 388, 393
Lindbergh, L., 395, 438, 439
Lindemeier, L., 40, 43
Lindentthal, J., 334
Linder, C., 460
Linder, G., 386
Linder, J. R., 258, 363, 364
Lindner, M., 151
Lindsay, L. L., 152
Lindstrom, R., 352
Ling, X., 460
Linn, E., 386, 387
Linn, M., 90
Linney, J., 227
Linville, P., 411
Lipsey, M., 460
Lipshutz, J., 399
Lipton, R. I., 446
Liska, A., 460
Liston, C., 75, 76, 81
Litchfield, A., 330
Litt, I., 448, 467
Little, S.A., 209
Little, T., 408
Little, T. D., 188
Liu, H., 75
Liu, X., 282
Livson, N., 46
Lizotte, A. J., 397, 456
Lleras, C., 419
Lobel, O., 297
Lobel, T. E., 297
Lochman, J., 189, 194, 377, 396, 397, 457, 460
Lockerd, E. M., 292
Loeber, R., 124, 184, 186, 397, 436, 452, 453, 454, 455, 456, 457, 458, 459, 460
Loehlin, J. C., 146
Loewenson, P. R., 375
Logan, J., 445
Lohr, M., 400
Lohr, M. J., 178, 398
Lohrmann, D., 389
Lollis, S., 191
Lomedo, L., 399
London, A. S., 158
Loney, B., 451
Long, B., 363
Long, J. D., 438
Long, N., 151
Longmore, M., 358, 365, 375, 378, 387
Lonigan, C., 440
Lopez, C., 276
Lord, H., 185, 232, 245, 250, 251

Lord, S., 158, 207, 413, 454
Loredo, C., 386
Lorenz, F., 138, 152, 156, 157, 456, 464
Lorion, R., 454
Losoya, S., 456
Loughlin, S., 261
Louis, K., 208
Loukas, A., 125
Lourenco, O., 71
Lovelace, S., 156
Loveless, T., 203, 216
Lovitt, T., 212, 213
Low, C., 344, 346, 365
Lowell, E., 406
Lowery, B. S., 455
Lowery, C., 389
Lowry, R., 373, 388
Luban, N., 391
Lubell, K., 256
Lucas, S., 385, 416
Lucas, S. R., 211
Luciana, M., 73, 75
Lucky, A., 38
Ludwig, J., 122, 454
Luker, K., 389
Lumpkin, P., 467
Luna, B., 63, 75
Lundberg, S., 397
Luo, Q., 186
Luster, T., 280, 281, 381, 386, 387, 391, 397
Luthar, S., 415, 420, 434, 467, 468
Lutz, A., 414
Luyckx, K., 141, 289, 290
Lynam, D., 48, 445, 457
Lynam, D. R., 124
Lynch, J., 308, 309
Lynch, M., 108, 297, 463
Lynch, P. J., 258
Lynn, D., 298
Lynskey, M., 437, 458
Lyon, J., 457
Lyons, A. L., 464
Lyons, N., 298
Lyss, S., 388, 393
Lytle, L. A., 254

M

Ma, L., 252
Määta, S., 411
Mac Iver, D., 207, 410
Maccoby, E., 138, 139, 145, 150, 151, 154, 156, 170, 180, 339, 348, 413
MacDermid, S. M., 319
MacDonald, D., 75
Macdonald, T., 55, 56, 57, 58, 86
MacDonald, W., 155
MacDougall, J., 386
Machado, A., 71
MacIver, D., 208, 408
Mack, V., 183
Mackey, K., 141
MacKinnon, D., 449
MacKinnon-Lewis, C., 184, 292
Macksoud, M., 468

MacLeod, D., 420
MacMillan, R., 140
Macmillan, R., 192
MacMurray, J. P., 380
Maczuga, S., 419
Madden-Derdich, D. A., 349
Madon, S., 218, 409
Mager, W., 460
Maggs, J., 45, 89, 111, 251, 319, 448
Magnusson, A. M., 120
Magnusson, D., 46, 48, 49, 436, 457
Maguin, E., 123
Maharaj, S., 182
Mahler, A., 272
Mahoney, A., 153
Mahoney, J., 185, 232, 245, 248, 250, 251, 308
Main, M., 342
Malanchuk, O., 280, 412, 429
Males, M., 19, 20, 396
Malfait, N., 69
Malone, P., 396
Malone, S. M., 438
Maloney, P., 399
Malotte, C., 120
Mancini, J. A., 247
Mandara, J., 150
Maney, D., 56
Mangelsdorf, S., 341, 353
Manke, B., 146, 297, 298
Manlove, J., 398
Mann, E. A., 417
Mann, N. C., 56
Mannheim, K., 17
Mannheim, Karl, 15f
Manning, W., 155, 358, 365, 375, 378, 387, 394
Mannison, M., 362
Manolis, M., 186
Manson, S., 446
Marcia, J., 287, 289, 339
Marcoen, A., 65, 66
Marcos, A., 448
Marcotte, D., 467
Marcus, M., 37
Marczak, M., 134
Mare, R., 212
Marelich, W., 391
Margolin, G., 152
Mariner, C., 398
Marini, M., 430
Mark, M., 450
Markiewicz, D., 153, 342, 362
Markovits, H., 64, 69
Marks, H., 203, 211, 219, 227
Markstrom, C. A., 106, 107, 247
Markstrom-Adams, C., 273, 289, 291, 298
Markus, H., 269, 272, 273
Marlowe, J., 460
Marmorstein, N. R., 438
Marold, D., 272
Marsh, H., 212, 213, 270, 278, 405, 408, 409
Marsh, P., 188, 342
Marshall, S., 291
Marshall, W., 24, 29, 33, 35
Marsiglia, F., 292, 295, 299
Marta, E., 263
Martin, A., 376

Martin, B., 364
Martin, C., 368
Martin, C. A., 76
Martin, D., 251, 377
Martin, J., 30, 44, 138, 139, 275, 278, 358, 413, 466
Martin, P. P., 281, 294, 295, 296
Martin, S., 363, 376
Martinez, R., 184, 291, 292
Marvinney, D., 341
Masi, G., 440
Mason, C., 140, 142, 143, 151, 158, 184, 185, 414, 415
Mason, W., 282
Mason, W. A., 438
Massad, C., 298
Masse, L., 185, 186
Mâsse, L., 459
Masten, A., 76, 101, 111, 158, 190, 191, 273, 277, 358, 362, 363, 405, 438, 468
Matas, L., 340
Mateika, J. H., 42
Matsuba, M. K., 326
Matsuda, S., 350
Matsueda, R., 459
Matsueda, R. L., 88
Matthews, D., 79
Matthews, K., 124
Matthews, L., 157
Matthews, L. S., 144
Matza, L. S., 124, 140
Maugham, B., 130
Maughan, S., 448
Mauldon, J., 389
Maumary-Gremaud, A., 377, 397
Maxwell, S., 275, 278, 397, 411
Ma, Y., 467
May, J. C., 76
Mayer, C., 50
Mays, G., 183
Mazor, A., 304, 308
Mbzivo, M., 377
McAdams, L., 178
McAdoo, H., 119, 280, 281, 292
McAuley, E., 254
McAuliffe, S., 353
McBride, C. K., 378
McBride, M., 124
McBride-Chang, C., 387
McCabe, K., 140, 454, 456
McCabe, M., 469
McCabe, M. P., 53, 54
McCaffree, K., 389, 392
McCarter, V., 399
McCarthy, J., 222, 398, 399
McCarthy, K., 158, 207, 352, 454
McCartney, K., 342
McCauley, E., 310
McClelland, D., 406
McClintock, M., 26, 27, 36, 368
McCloud, K., 460
McClure, E., 40, 66, 76, 136
McConochie, D., 309, 339
McCord, J., 185, 437, 438, 460
McCormick, A., 379
McCormick, S., 43

McCoy, J., 144, 158, 194, 214
McCracy, C., 158
McCrae, R., 273
McCree, D. J., 330
McCullers, C., 283
McDermott, P., 434
McDevitt, T., 420
McDill, E., 414
McDill, E. L., 177
McDonald, D., 362
McDonald, R., 363
McDougall, P., 191
McDuff, P., 364
McElhaney, K., 309, 342
McElhaney, K. B., 188
McFarland, F. C., 188, 342
McGee, L., 438
McGee, R., 140, 436
McGee, R. O., 273
McGinley, K., 395, 438, 439
McGivern, P., 449
McGue, M., 136, 145, 146
McGuffog, C., 341
McGuigan, K., 250, 251, 449, 454
McGuire, J. K., 244
McGuire, S., 146
McHale, S., 40, 135, 136, 137, 144, 145, 146, 147, 251, 297, 298, 299, 319, 349, 463
McKenry, P. C., 309
McKeough, A., 84
McKeown, R., 150
McKinney, J., 319, 362
McKinney, K., 47
McKinnon, J., 191
McLanahan, S., 151, 153, 155, 395
McLaughlin, B., 222, 223
McLean, K. C., 284
McLellan, J. A., 120
McLoyd, V., 157, 158
McLoyd, V. C., 123, 158, 416
McMahon, R., 279
McMahon, S. D., 292
McMahon, T., 415
McMaster, L., 362, 386
McNair, L., 140
McNall, M., 58, 418
McNalley, S., 346
McNamara, G., 446
McNeal, J., 248
McNeal, R., Jr., 236, 238, 241
McNeely, C., 373, 375, 379, 387
McNeil, L., 242
McNelles, L. R., 344, 346, 347
McNulty, T., 460
McNulty, T. L., 455
McPartland, J., 412, 417, 424
McPheeters, M., 158
McQueen, A., 120
McRae, C., 152, 153, 154
McRoy, R. G., 147
McVey, G., 315
Mead, M., 18, 104, 114, 369
Mead, Margaret, 114
Meade, A., 81
Meade, C., 380
Meares, H., 417

Mears, D. P., 459, 460
Mechanic, D., 365, 461
Mednick, S., 437
Medrich, E., 108, 163
Meece, D., 251
Meeus, W., 287, 304, 308, 352
Mehta, T. G., 282
Meier, A. M., 330
Mekos, D., 146, 209, 247
Melby, J., 184, 413
Melnick, M. J., 392
Melton, G., 314, 460
Memmo, M., 252
Menaghan, E., 380
Menard, S., 437, 438
Mendola, P., 35
Menning, C. L., 151
Mercy, J., 57
Merikangas, K. R., 42
Merisca, R., 460
Merriam, E. P., 75
Merrick, S., 341
Merrow, M., 42
Merten, D., 188, 189
Merten, D. E., 176
Merton, M., 122
Mervielda, I., 138
Meschke, L., 148, 362, 378
Meseck-Bushey, S., 145, 456
Meseck-Bushey S., 437
Messeri, P., 259
Metzger, A., 116, 137, 330
Metzler, C., 458
Metzler, C. W., 193
Meyer, A., 460
Meyer, A. L., 438
Meyer, C., 67
Meyer, L., 167, 168, 261, 362
Meyer-Bahlburg, H., 384
Michael, A., 412, 429
Michael, R., 383
Michaud, P., 392
Mickelson, R., 214, 407, 418
Mickus, M., 353
Midgley, C., 205, 207, 208, 218, 407, 410, 413
Midlarsky, E., 464
Miguel, S. S., 315, 349, 352
Mihalic, S., 241, 242
Milantoni, L., 440
Milich, R., 186, 445, 460
Miliotis, D., 158
Millepiedi, S., 440
Miller, B., 147, 377, 378, 379, 380, 381, 388, 389, 394, 395, 397, 400
Miller, C., 391
Miller, D., 86, 89
Miller, J., 240, 363, 447
Miller, J. D., 412, 417
Miller, K., 318, 375, 376, 379, 389
Miller, K. E., 392
Miller, L., 330, 390
Miller, M., 380
Miller, N., 104, 109, 114
Miller, P., 346, 382, 398
Miller, R., 217, 356
Miller, T., 447, 448

Miller, W. C., 375
Miller, X., 395
Miller-Johnson, S., 80, 377, 396, 397
Miller-Jones, D., 82
Miller-Tutzauer, C., 352
Millrood, D. L., 42
Mills, C., 410
Mills, C. J., 273
Millsap, R. E., 48
Millstein, R., 309
Millstein, S., 56, 88, 382
Milne, B. J., 458
Milne, M., 209
Milnitsky-Sapiro, C., 132
Minshew, N. J., 75
Minuchin, S., 54
Mistry, R. S., 158
Mitchell, B., 115
Mitchell, C., 209, 440, 446
Mitchell, E., 55
Mitchell, K., 256
Mitchell, K. J., 256
Mitru, G., 42
Mocan, N., 396
Modell, J., 97, 98, 115, 163, 164, 232, 235, 357
Moffitt, T., 48, 80, 124, 273, 282, 397, 436, 437, 438, 440, 453, 455, 456, 457, 458, 459
Moise-Titus, J., 259
Molina, B., 14, 43, 191, 445, 447, 448
Molina G., 395
Molinari, L., 42
Moll, R., 81
Mollasis, C., 430
Molnar, L. J., 56
Monck, E., 350
Moneta, G., 133, 136, 274, 275
Monitoring the Future, 442, 443
Monroe, S. M., 363, 467
Monsour, A., 271
Montemayor, R., 131, 136, 194, 270, 288, 289, 303
Montgomery, M., 355, 357, 358, 360, 387
Montgomery, S., 158, 449
Mont-Reynaud, R., 468
Mood, A., 412, 417
Moody, J., 181
Moore, C., 342
Moore, J., 389
Moore, K., 141, 374, 380, 381, 386, 388, 389, 394, 395, 397, 398, 400
Moore, K. A., 246
Moore, M., 222, 223, 260, 438
Moore, M. J., 248
Moore, M. R., 153
Moore, S., 44, 88, 407
Moors, E., 308
Moos, R., 217, 469
Mora, S., 29
Morabia, A., 36
Moran, B. L., 292
Morgan, K., 400
Morgan, M., 256, 380
Morgan, S., 394, 398, 400
Morgan, S. P., 151, 374
Morisky, D. E., 120, 374
Morison, P., 190, 191

Morris, A., 13, 14, 19, 64, 70, 85, 86, 132, 141, 321, 323, 324, 326, 466
Morris, J. E., 251
Morris, L., 373
Morris, N., 32, 358, 377
Morrison, D., 152, 381, 389, 397, 398
Morrison, G. M., 315, 349, 352
Morrison Gutman, L., 125, 142
Morrissey-Kane, E., 57
Morrow, B., 388, 393
Morrow, C., 346
Morrow, J., 53
Morse, B., 377, 438
Mortimer, J., 7, 12, 99, 113, 118, 221, 232, 235, 236, 237, 238, 239, 240, 241, 242, 261, 320, 428
Mortimore, P., 130
Morton, T., 467
Mory, M., 171, 172, 173
Moscicki, A., 259
Moses, A., 454
Mosher, W., 395
Moshman, D., 106
Mosteller, F., 206
Motl, R. W., 254
Mott, F., 380
Mott, F. L., 174, 397
Mount, K. K., 435
Mounts, N., 140, 141, 142, 173, 178, 184, 185, 318, 413, 415
Mucci, L. A., 363
Mucci, M., 440
Muhleman, D., 380
Muhlenbruck, L., 228
Muise, A. M., 52
Mukai, T., 54
Mulhall, P., 158, 217, 417
Mulkeen, P., 348, 350
Muller, C., 412
Muller, P. A., 416, 418
Mulvey, E., 456
Mulvey, E. P., 223
Mulvihill, B. A., 397
Munfakh, J., 256
Munoz, D. P., 75
Munsch, J., 209, 353
Munson, S., 50
Murdock, T., 415, 420
Murdock, T. B., 207, 208
Murphy, B., 326
Murphy, B. C., 326
Murphy, D., 392
Murphy, R. F., 221
Murray, C. B., 150
Murray, L., 121
Murray, N., 282
Murry, V., 46, 48, 380, 381
Murry, V. M., 140
Musick, J., 400
Musleh, K., 140
Must, A., 34, 38
Mustanski, B. S., 35
Myers, B., 297
Myers, B. J., 297
Myers, D., 397, 398
Myers, J., 334
Mylod, D., 397

N

Nadeem, E., 46
Nagin, D., 451, 456, 457, 458, 460
Nagy, C., 387
Nagy, S., 387
Nagy, Z., 75
Najman, J. M., 457
Namerow, P., 396, 400
Nangle, D. W., 360
Nansel, T., 192
Nansel, T. R., 192, 250
Narasimham, G., 64
Narkunas, J., 391
Nash, K., 238
Nation, M., 57
National Assessment of Educational Progress, 421, 422
National Center for Children in Poverty., 149
National Center for Education Statistics, 198, 216, 219, 220, 224, 225, 226, 235, 247, 421, 422, 423
National Commission on Excellence in Education., 198, 202
National Education Commission on Time and Learning., 198, 202
National Heart, Lung, and Blood Institute Growth and Health Study Research Group., 57
National Institute on Out-of-School Time., 164
National Research Council., 19, 95, 118, 120, 122, 155, 198, 236, 237, 238, 241, 423, 441
Natriello, G., 212, 228, 414
Naudeau, S., 252
Nava, M., 295
Neckerman, H., 183, 186, 273
Necos, B., 400
Needham, B., 183, 186, 187
Needle, R., 155
Neemann, J., 158, 277, 358, 362, 363, 405
Neiderhiser, J., 145, 146, 147
Neidert, L., 99
Neighbors, B., 152
Neilsen, E., 66
Neiss, M., 46
Nelson, B., 468
Nelson, C., 77
Nelson, E., 40, 66, 76, 136
Nelson, L. J., 76, 99, 258, 329
Nelson, R., 250
Nelson, S. E., 142, 185
Nelwan, P., 54, 350
Nesbit, R., 392
Neubauer, S. A., 174
Neugarten, B., 134
Neumark-Sztainer, D., 51, 52, 440
Neuwalder, H., 384
Newacheck, P. W., 57
Newcomb, A., 188, 194, 335, 346, 354, 360
Newcomb, M., 185, 298, 424, 438, 446, 447, 448, 449
Newcomer, S., 373
Newman, B., 176, 178
Newman, D., 44
Newman, D. L., 291
Newman, K., 242

Newman, P., 176, 178
Newman, R., 410
Newmann, F., 202, 203, 219, 220, 227, 228
Nguyen, D. T., 151
Nicholls, J., 188
Nichols, S., 409
Nicotra, E., 189
Nieto, M., 214
Nightingale, E., 56, 96, 120
Nishina, A., 120, 191, 192, 214
Nixon, C. L., 190
Noack, P., 234, 328
Noam, G., 309
Nock, M. K., 188
Nock, S., 396
Noell, J., 458
Noguera, P., 222
Nolen-Hoeksema, S., 462, 464, 466
Noll, J. G., 387
Noller, P., 350
Noom, M. J., 304
Nord, C., 386, 397, 398
Norton, M., 377, 380
Notaro, P., 151
Notaro, P. C., 121
Nottelmann, E., 34, 275, 440
Novak, J. D., 140
Novak, S., 124
Nov-Crispin, N., 297
Nowak, M., 117
Nowell, A., 418
Nowlin, P., 412
Nucci, L., 132
Nucci, M. S., 132
Nurius, P., 269, 273
Nurmi, J., 13, 110, 269, 289, 290, 407, 411, 413

O

Oakes, J., 210, 211
Oakley, D., 388
Obeidallah, D., 49, 328, 330, 463
O'Beime-Kelly, H., 342
Obradovic, J., 438
O'Brien, S., 175, 176
O'Callaghan, M., 397
O'Connor (Justice), 4
O'Connor, T., 143, 151, 307, 309, 310, 342, 343, 456
O'Donnell, C. R., 375
O'Donnell, K., 303
O'Donnell, L., 375
O'Donnell, M., 232, 428
Oeltmann, J., 377
Oettingen, G., 408
Oettinger, G., 241
Offer, D., 19
Office of Juvenile Justice and Delinquency Prevention., 453
Ogawa, J. R., 341
Ogbu, J., 178, 179, 418, 419
Ogle, J. P., 51, 54
Ogletree, M. D., 43
Oh Cha, S., 413
Oh, M. K., 389, 392

Ohannessian, C., 352
Okazaki, S., 418, 419
O'Koon, J. H., 462, 464
Olatunji, A. N., 242
Oldehinkel, A. J., 42
Oliveira, C. M., 395
Olmsted, M., 54
Olsen, J., 207, 352
Olson, L., 425, 426
Olson, L. S., 242
Olweus, D., 189, 190, 191, 274
O'Malley, P., 100, 102, 250, 251, 275, 276, 281, 443, 445, 447, 448, 449, 459
Onatsu, T., 407
O'Neal, K. K., 122, 188
O'Nell, T., 440, 446
Ong, A. D., 135
Onwughala, M., 294
Oppedal, B., 296
Oppedisano, G., 462
Orbell, S., 389
Orbuch, T. L., 136
Orcutt, H. K., 437
Orlando, M., 444, 447
Orlofsky, J., 339
Orr, D., 377, 392, 437
Orr, E., 298
Ortiz, J., 438, 457
Ortiz, V., 394
Osborne, L. N., 121
Oser, F., 65
Osgood, D., 275, 279
Osgood, D. W., 100, 118, 186, 250, 251, 459
Osgood, W., 7, 99, 119
Osipow, S., 288
Oslak, S., 363
Oslak, S. G., 52
Osofsky, J., 152
Oswald, H., 382, 383
Otterblad Olausson, P., 397
Ouston, J., 130
Overbaugh, K., 249
Overpeck, M., 192
Overpeck, M. D., 250
Overton, W., 70, 275
Owen, J., 220, 423
Owen, L. D., 186, 378
Owen, R., 380
Owens, T., 320
Oxford, M. L., 398
Oyserman, D., 272, 400
Ozcan, M., 242
Ozer, E., 55, 56, 57, 58, 86, 124, 395

P

Paasch, K., 207, 216, 414, 416
Pabon, E., 184
Pack, R., 183
Padilla, A. M., 420
Padilla, B., 282
Pagani, L., 184
Pagani-Kurtz, L., 459
Page, M., 120
Pahl, K., 181, 218, 296

Paikoff, R., 38, 40, 43, 44, 51, 137, 369, 378, 379, 400
Palardy, G., 425
Palen, L., 263
Pallas, A., 212, 228
Palmer, R. F., 459
Palmgren, C., 87, 88
Palmquist, W., 83, 335
Pan, W., 448
Pancer, S. M., 326
Panchaud, C., 391
Pandey, S., 122
Pantin, H., 288
Papademetriou, E., 462
Papillo, A., 398
Papillo, A. R., 246
Paquette, J., 189
Parcel, G., 438
Pardinin, D. A., 184
Parfenoff, S., 379
Parides, M., 54
Park, M. J., 57
Parke, R., 134
Parke, R. D., 148
Parker, J., 189, 190, 194, 344, 346, 365
Parker, S., 249, 256, 389, 392
Parker, W. D., 273
Parkhurst, J., 189, 191
Parrish, J., 76
Parsons, S., 120, 416
Pasch, L. A., 152
Paschall, M., 123
Paschall, M. J., 446
Paskewitz, D., 468
Pasley, K., 134
Pastore, D., 124
Pastorelli, C., 409, 410
Pasupathi, M., 86
Pateman, B., 373
Paternoster, R., 242
Pati, C., 140
Patil, S. M., 180, 181
Patrick, D. L., 435
Patrick, H., 218
Patrikakou, E., 412
Patten, C. A., 43
Patterson, C., 131, 190, 417
Patterson, C. J., 385
Patterson, G., 133, 158, 183, 184, 190, 413, 456, 457, 458, 460
Patton, W., 362
Paul, C., 376
Paul, J., 384
Paulozzi, L., 222, 223
Paulson, S., 413
Paus, T., 75
Pavlidis, K., 310
Paxton, S., 52
Pearce, M. J., 124, 140, 330
Pearl, R., 188
Pears, K., 396
Pechmann, C., 261
Peck, S. C., 459
Pedersen, N. L., 145, 146
Pedersen, S., 116, 234
Pederson, S., 281

Pedlow, S. E., 26
Peeke, L., 275, 278, 282, 466
Pellegrini, A. D., 354, 355
Pellerin, L. A., 217
Pemberton, S., 152
Pena, C., 448
Pendergrast, R., 124, 454
Penner, D., 90
Pennington, H., 224, 226, 421
Pentz, M., 449
Pepler, D., 306, 349, 355, 359, 361, 386
Pepper, M., 334
Perez-Febles, A., 395, 448
Perie, M., 422
Perilla, J., 413
Perkins, C., 454
Perkins, D., 138, 142, 387
Perkins, D. D., 217
Perkins, D. F., 248
Perosa, L., 288
Perosa, S., 288
Perrin, J. M., 448
Perry, A. A., 53
Perry, C., 140, 447, 449
Perry, C. L., 51
Perry, D., 192, 282, 299, 310, 342
Perry, T., 344, 346
Peskin, H., 46, 47, 49
Petersen, A., 26, 30, 40, 45, 46, 47, 48, 56, 298, 440, 461, 463, 464, 466, 469
Petersen, L., 391
Peterson, G. W., 142
Peterson, J., 57, 386, 389
Peterson, P., 216, 448
Peterson-Badali, M., 308
Petraitis, J., 447, 448
Petrie, C., 222, 223
Petrovich, J., 52
Pettit, G., 124, 141, 183, 191, 251, 380, 412, 455, 456, 457, 458
Pettit, J., 461
Pevalin, D. J., 462
Pfeiffer, K. A., 54
Phares, V., 51
Phelan, P., 214
Phelps, E., 67, 252
Philliber, S., 400, 425
Phillips, M., 125, 221
Phillips, R., 277
Phillipsen, L. C., 344
Phinney, J., 135, 191, 291, 292, 294, 295, 296
Piaget, J., 15, 15f, 16, 18, 321
Pianta, R. C., 417
Pickering, S. J., 73
Pickrel, S. G., 460
Pidada, S., 54, 189, 350
Pieniadz, J., 413
Pieper, C., 57
Pierce, G., 460
Pierce, J., 447
Pierce, J. P., 43
Pierce, K., 260
Pietilainen, K. H., 34
Pihl, R., 459
Pike, A., 146

Pike, K., 54
Pilgrim, C., 186
Pilkington, N., 385
Pilla, R. S., 192
Pillay, Y., 295
Pilowsky, D. J., 444
Pimentel, E., 238
Pine, D., 40, 66, 76, 77, 136, 259, 467
Pinquart, M., 308
Pintrich, P., 408, 410
Pion, N., 69
Pipes McAdoo, H., 123
Piquero, A., 452, 455, 456, 457
Piquero, A. R., 457
Pirie, P., 449
Pirsch, L., 308
Pitner, R. O., 182
Pittman, L. D., 140, 158
Pivarnik, J. M., 54
Plata, M., 413
Platsidou, M., 71
Pleck, J., 299, 373
Plomin, R., 145, 146, 147, 151, 456, 457
Plotnick, R., 397
Plumert, J., 72
Podolski, C., 259
Poe-Yamagata, E., 454
Pogarsky, G., 397
Polce-Lynch, M., 297
Polichar, D., 350
Poll, P., 440
Pollack, H., 397
Pollak, C., 43
Pomerantz, E., 309, 409
Pomeroy, W., 368
Pomery, E. A., 124, 140
Pong, S., 151, 412, 414, 424
Pope, A., 188
Porfeli, E., 7, 99
Porter, M. R., 188
Porter, S., 451
Portes, A., 420
Poulin, F., 183, 185, 189, 460
Poulos, G., 413
Poulton, R., 282
Powell, A., 202
Power, T., 316, 446
Powers, B., 466
Powers, J., 212, 386
Powers, S., 309
Prado, G., 288
Pratt, M. W., 141, 325, 326
Pratto, D., 250
Pratts, M., 454
Prelow, H., 125
President's Science Advisory Committee., 115, 163, 201, 225
Presnell, K., 47, 48, 51
Presson, C., 448
Preusser, D., 56
Pribesh, S., 218
Price, C. L., 211
Price, L. N., 122
Prindiville, S., 276
Prinstein, M., 178, 186, 188, 355, 356, 380, 457, 466

Proescher, E., 468
Prosser, E., 280
Prossinger, H., 377
Provost, M., 469
Public Agenda., 20, 220, 423
Pulgiano, D., 125
Pulkkinen, L., 35, 46, 397, 458
Punamaki, R., 140
Punch, S., 236
Pungello, E., 417
Pungello, E. P., 80
Purcell, A., 389
Purdie, N., 410
Putallaz, M., 352
Putnam, F., 387
Putnam, F. W., 387

Q

Qian, M., 466
Qian, Z., 420
Qouta, S., 140
Quadrel, M., 66, 87, 88
Quatman, T., 308, 319, 409
Queiroz, I., 395
Quigley-Rick, M., 314
Quillian, L., 181, 182, 214
Quinlan, D., 464
Quintana, S., 291

R

Raber, S., 44
Rabin, B., 468
Rabiner, D., 83, 86
Racine, Y., 445
Radin, N., 400
Radziszewska, B., 250, 251
Raeburn, S., 55
Raeikkoenen, K., 440
Raffaelli, M., 143, 330, 345, 346, 347, 351,
     353, 377, 379
Raine, A., 438, 457
Raj, A., 363
Raj, M., 358
Raley, S. B., 253
Ramanan, J., 251
Ramey, C., 417
Ramey, C. T., 80
Ramirez, C., 429
Ramirez, M., 158, 468
Ramirez-Valles, J., 123
Ramsey, E., 458
Randel, B., 411
Raney, M., 66
Rankin, J. L., 65
Rao, P., 186
Raphaelson, Y. E., 124
Rapoport, J., 76
Rapoport, J. L., 75
Rasanen, M., 34
Raskin-White, H., 456
Rathunde, K., 143
Raudenbusch, S., 123

Rauh, V., 400
Raveis, V., 438
Ravitch, D., 90, 201, 202, 203
Rayens, M., 76
Raymond, M., 155
Raynor, S. R., 152
Ready, D. D., 205, 206
Ream, G. L., 379
Redden, D. T., 397
Reddy, R., 41, 43, 217
Redlich, A. D., 106, 316
Reed, J., 291, 292
Rees, D. I., 389
Rees, J., 51, 52
Reese, L. E., 122
Reese-Weber, M., 144
Regnerus, M., 329
Rehnquist (Chief Justice), 4
Reich, K., 65
Reichhardt, T., 258
Reid, A., 386
Reid, G. S., 447
Reid, H., 385, 440
Reid, J., 144, 460
Reid, L., 397
Reiffman, A., 387
Reifman, A., 448
Reimer, M., 275
Reirdan, J., 45
Reis, O., 289
Reiser, L., 45
Reiss, D., 140, 141, 143, 144, 145, 146, 147, 148,
     149, 150, 156, 184, 255
Reiter, E., 44, 47
Reitz, E., 459
Reitzel-Jaffe, D., 386
Renderer, B., 91
Renken, B., 341
Repetti, R., 142
Repinski, D., 193
Reppucci, N., 89, 105, 312, 314
Resche, N. L., 121
Reshef-Kfir, Y., 88
Resnick, H., 448
Resnick, M., 51, 57, 314, 373, 375, 380, 387, 396,
     437, 440, 468
Resnicow, K., 438, 440
Rest, J., 321, 323, 324
Restrepo, A., 132, 151
Retty, R., 397
Reuben, N., 391
Reuman, D., 207, 208, 212, 410
Reviere, S., 292
Reyes, O., 207, 417, 421
Reyna, V., 87, 88
Reynolds, A., 417
Reynolds, L. K., 462, 464
Rezac, S., 154
Rhodes, J., 41, 43, 121, 217, 353, 400
Rianasari, M., 54, 350
Ricard, R., 348
Ricardo, I., 380, 392, 440
Ricciardelli, L. A., 53, 54
Rice, K., 336, 348, 350
Rich, L. M., 242
Rich, M., 441

Richard, P., 187
Richards, C., 399
Richards, M., 45, 47, 54, 133, 135, 136, 137, 152,
     153, 162, 170, 219, 233, 245, 246, 255, 274,
     275, 351, 355
Richardson, B., 57, 389
Richardson, G., 140
Richardson, J., 250, 251
Richardson, L., 399
Richardson, R., 397
Richman-Raphael, D., 252
Richter, L., 442
Ricken, J., 42
Riddle, M. A., 467
Ridenour, T. A., 438
Rideout, V., 253, 254, 255, 256
Rifas-Shiman, S. L., 254
Riggs, L., 400
Rigsby, L., 177
Riley, J. R., 438
Riley, T., 66
Rincón, C., 191, 341
Rind, B., 387
Rinehart, P., 159, 217, 375
Ringback Weitoft, G., 397
Ringwalt, C., 158, 449
Risch, S. C., 156
Rise, J., 437
Rissanen, A., 34
Risser, W., 282
Ritchey, P. N., 447
Ritter, J., 14, 309, 445, 447, 448
Ritter, P., 46, 140, 142, 153, 155, 221, 380, 413, 468
Rivara, F., 397
Rivera, A. C., 234
Rivkin, S., 213
Rizza, M. G., 207
Roach, M., 400
Robbins, C., 376, 396
Robbins, R. N., 89
Robbins, S., 321, 323
Roberto, C., 54
Roberts, A., 281
Roberts, B., 232, 273, 428
Roberts, C., 462
Roberts, D., 12, 142, 151, 158, 221, 232, 239,
     253, 254, 255, 256, 258, 259, 260, 261, 407,
     413, 418
Roberts, M., 281
Roberts, R., 461, 462
Robertson, D. L., 417
Robertson, L., 57
Robertson, M., 158
Robillard, A., 259, 389, 392
Robins, L., 458
Robins, L. N., 438
Robins, P., 152
Robins, R., 232, 275, 276, 428, 437
Robins, R. W., 274, 282
Robinson, L., 448
Robinson, M. G., 217
Robinson, N., 280, 281, 466, 467
Robinson, T., 51, 448
Robinson, W. L., 184
Roche, A., 34, 38
Roche, A. F., 38

Roche, K. M., 242
Roche, L., 212, 213
Rockert, W., 54
Roderick, M., 424, 425
Rodgers, J., 145, 380, 381, 437, 456
Rodgers, K., 151, 379
Rodgman, E. A., 56
Rodkin, P., 188
Rodman, H., 250
Rodriguez, A. U., 158
Rodriguez, O., 184
Roe, K., 256
Roe, T., 29
Roenkae, A., 397
Roesch, R., 106
Roeser, R., 205, 208, 209, 217, 218, 408, 413
Roff, J., 158
Rogers, A., 298
Rogers, J., 396
Rogers, M., 152, 316, 391
Rogers-Sirin, L., 413
Rogol, A., 8, 24, 26, 28, 368
Rohde, P., 51, 363, 438, 466, 467
Rohner, R., 140
Rohrbach, L., 448, 449
Roisman, G. I., 101, 111, 438, 459
Roizen, J., 108, 163
Rome, E., 441
Rome, F., 399
Romer, D., 392, 440
Romero, I., 295
Romig, C., 339
Romo, L., 379
Romo, L. F., 379
Rong, X., 420
Rönká, A., 458
Rook, K., 144, 352
Roosa, M., 142, 399
Roosa, M. W., 48, 142
Rosario, M., 385, 440
Roscigno, V., 414, 417
Roscoe, B., 259
Rose, A. J., 190, 346, 347, 365
Rose, H. A., 151
Rose, J., 448
Rose, R., 34, 35, 46, 273
Rose, R. J., 35, 48
Rose, S., 80
Rosen, B., 407
Rosen, L., 384
Rosenbaum, J., 113, 210, 243
Rosenbaum, J. E., 113, 226
Rosenberg, A., 30, 44, 358
Rosenberg, F., 275, 276, 279
Rosenberg, M., 214, 275, 276, 281, 282
Rosenberg, S., 133
Rosenbloom, S. R., 219, 222
Rosenblum, G., 40, 52
Rosenfield, D., 363
Rosenkrantz, P., 297
Rosenstein, D., 275
Rosenthal, D., 191, 319, 373, 377, 379, 382
Rosenthal, R., 218
Rosenthal, S., 341
Rosman, B., 54
Ross-Gaddy, D., 438, 440

Rostosky, S. S., 385
Roth, J., 25, 121
Rotheram-Borus, M., 191, 385, 391, 392, 440
Rotherman-Borus, M., 120
Rousseau, J., 19
Rowan, B., 217
Rowden, L., 191, 194
Rowe, D., 145, 146, 273, 281, 380, 381, 437, 456, 463
Rowe, D. C., 46
Røysamb, E., 296
Rozin, P., 51
Ruan, W., 192
Rubin, C. H., 37
Rubin, K., 188, 191, 194, 420
Rubin, V., 108, 163
Rubin, Z., 365
Ruble, D., 44, 297
Ruchkin, V., 124, 140, 330, 376
Ruck, M., 308, 327
Rudolph, K., 464
Rudolph, K. D., 341
Rudy, W., 224, 225
Rueter, M., 140, 141, 143, 464, 465
Ruggiero, M., 238, 239
Ruggles, S., 152
Ruiz, S., 142
Ruiz, S. Y., 142
Rumbaut, R., 6, 7, 119, 295
Rumberger, R., 413, 423, 424, 425
Rusby, J. C., 193
Rushton, J., 461
Russell, G., 137
Russell, R., 44
Russell, S., 208, 385, 394, 397
Russo, M., 458
Rutberg, J., 260
Ruth, G., 7, 99, 119
Rutter, M., 130, 138, 210, 217, 456, 457, 462, 468
Ryan, A. M., 172, 194, 218
Ryan, B., 413
Ryan, G., 222, 223
Ryan, N., 76, 468
Ryan, R., 308, 309, 409
Rys, G., 190
Ryu, S., 238

S

Sabatelli, R., 309
Sabo, D., 392
Sabuwalla, Z., 26, 444, 467
Sacchitelle, C., 138
Sachs, J., 206
Sack, W., 468
Sacker, A., 120, 416
Safer, D. J., 464
Saffer, H., 449
Safron, J., 241, 242
Sagar, H., 180, 182
Sagrestano, L., 43
Saks, M., 314
Salazar, C. F., 413
Sale, E., 448
Salem, D., 151

Sales, L. H., 349
Sales, L. J., 349
Salinger, J. D., 283, 286
Salmivalli, C., 191
Saltzman, H., 374, 469
Salzer Burks, V., 458
Sam, D. L., 296
Samaniego, R., 296
Sambrano, S., 448
Sameroff, A., 125, 142, 158, 217, 412, 429, 459
Sampson, R., 122, 123, 454, 456
Sandefur, G., 153
Sanders, K., 294, 296
Sandfort, J., 400, 401
Sandler, A., 387
Sandler, H., 412
Sandler, I., 469
Sandven, K., 396
Sandy, J. M., 446
Saner, H., 454
Santelli, J., 123, 373, 375, 387, 388, 393
Santinello, M., 217
Santor, D., 451
Saraswathi, T., 11
Sargent, J., 318
Sarigiani, P., 464
Sather, C., 260
Saucier, J., 457
Saudino, K., 146
Saunders, B., 448
Saunders, J., 409, 424
Savage, M., 30, 248
Savin-Williams, R., 13, 194, 275, 276, 280, 335, 344, 346, 347, 361, 364, 365, 368, 375, 376, 378, 379, 382, 383, 384, 385, 386
Sawilowsky, S. S., 464
Sawyer, R., 389
Saxon, J. L., 409
Saylor, K., 192
Scabini, E., 137
Scales, P., 57, 244
Scalia (Justice), 4
Scanlan, L., 249
Scanlan, T., 249
Scaramella, L., 145, 184, 395
Scarr, S., 291, 292
Sceery, A., 336, 340, 342
Schafer, W., 86
Schaffner, B., 237
Scharf, M., 144, 358
Schebendach, J., 51, 52
Schectman, R. M., 461
Scheer, S., 448
Scheidt, P., 192
Scheier, L., 282, 446, 447
Schellenbach, C., 394, 397
Scherer, D., 314
Schiff, A., 42, 71
Schiller, D., 297
Schiller, K., 209, 211
Schlegel, A., 108
Schlenger, W. E., 242, 444
Schmeelk-Cone, K., 296, 406, 438
Schmid, C., 346
Schmid, C. L., 119, 420
Schmidt, J., 282

Schmidt, J. A., 221
Schmidt, M. G., 312
Schmidt, W., 405, 422, 423
Schmitt-Rodermund, E., 319
Schneider, B., 211, 213, 241, 248, 428, 431
Schneider, J., 55
Schnurr, P., 448
Schochet, T., 444
Schoenbach, C., 282
Schoenhals, M., 241
Schofield, J., 180, 182, 353, 354, 355
Scholte, R., 349
Scholte, R. J., 192
Schommer, M., 65
Schooler, C., 282
Schoon, I., 120, 416
Schraedley, P., 467
Schreiber, G., 279
Schrepferman, L., 456
Schubert, C., 34, 38, 456
Schulenberg, J., 100, 102, 239, 241, 242, 445, 448
Schuler, R., 40, 373
Schultz, L., 335
Schuster, M., 251, 377, 399
Schuster, M. A., 193
Schutz, R., 29, 30
Schvaneveldt, P., 380
Schwab, J., 46, 47
Schwab-Stone, M., 124, 140, 330, 376
Schwager, M., 410
Schwartz, D., 124
Schwartz, J., 454
Schwartz, R., 105, 314
Schwartz, S. H., 131
Schwartz, S. J., 288
Schwarz, B., 117
Schweder, A. E., 308
Schweder, R., 101
Schweingruber, H., 409
Schweingruber, H. A., 142
Scott, C., 380
Scott, E., 4, 20, 89, 94, 95, 104, 105, 314, 452
Scott, L., 30
Scott, L. D., 469
Scovill, L. C., 20, 435
Seal, J., 194
Sealand, N., 381
Sears, H., 45, 111
Seaton, E. K., 158
Sebald, H., 168
Secker-Walker, R., 449
Sedivy, V., 389
Seegers, G., 409
Seeley, J., 45, 49, 363, 438, 461, 466, 467
Seepersad, S., 234, 236, 237
Seff, M., 131, 134, 168
Segalowitz, S. J., 75
Seginer, R., 144
Seidman, E., 207, 209, 227, 234, 275, 281, 291
Seifer, R., 140
Seiffge-Krenke, I., 65, 66, 342, 361, 463, 464, 469
Seitz, V., 400, 401
Seligman, M., 464, 466
Sellers, R. M., 281, 294, 295, 296
Sells, C., 57
Selman, R., 84, 335

Sepúlveda, J. E., 462
Serafica, F., 288
Serlin, R., 96
Serna, I., 210, 211, 212
Seroczynski, A., 275, 278, 466
Serovich, J., 392
Sessa, F., 153, 308
Sethi, S., 464
Settersen, R., 221
Settersten, R., 6, 7
Settersten, R. A., Jr., 125
Sewell, W., 416
Seybolt, D., 57
Shadish, W., Jr., 416, 430
Shafer, J., 100, 118, 250, 251
Shaffer, L., 341
Shaffer, N., 391
Shagle, S., 221
Shahar, B., 207
Shahinfar, A., 124
Shamir, R., 304
Shanahan, L., 297
Shanahan, M., 7, 99, 101, 113, 138, 232, 233
Shanley, N., 466
Shapera, W., 309
Shapiro, X., 395
Sharabany, R., 345, 346, 347, 355
Sharma, A., 146
Sharp, E. H., 263
Shavelson, R., 270
Shaver, K., 130
Shaver, P., 362
Shaver, P. R., 342
Shaw, D., 144
Shaw, H., 51, 52, 54
Shaw, L. A., 84
Shaw, M., 407
Shaw, P., 76
Shea, C., 346
Shearer, D. L., 397
Shedler, J., 446, 447
Sheeber, L., 140
Sheeran, P., 389
Sheidow, A., 363
Sheidow, A. J., 158
Shell, R., 346
Shelton, N., 296
Shepard, S. A., 326
Sheppard, B., 352
Sher, K. J., 445
Sherman, M., 281
Sherman, S., 448
Shew, M., 468
Shew, M. L., 379
Shi, H., 358, 377
Shih, H., 467
Shih, T., 182
Shimek, J. S., 363
Shinar, O., 446
Shiner, R. L., 273
Shipman, K., 307
Shirley, A., 392
Shoal, G. D., 447
Shoop, D., 392
Shope, J., 277, 447, 448
Shope, J. T., 56, 180, 181, 438

Showers, C., 279
Shrum, W., 180, 181
Shuan, Y., 413, 416
Shucksmith, J., 151
Shulman, S., 144, 272, 344, 346, 347, 358
Shumow, L., 412, 417
Sickmund, M., 453
Siebenbruner, J., 363, 377
Siegel, A., 20, 435
Siegel, D., 392
Siegel, J., 40, 336, 342, 352, 462
Siegel, L., 72
Siegel, M., 441, 449
Siegler, R., 72, 90
Sieving, R., 379, 468
Sigler-Rushton, W., 396
Sigman, G., 51, 52
Sigman, M., 379, 380
Signorelli, N., 256
Signorielli, N., 260
Silbereisen, R., 46, 47, 48, 117, 186, 308, 319, 413, 463
Silk, J., 132, 137, 466
Silva, P., 34, 35, 48, 80, 273, 397, 436, 440, 457, 458
Silver, E., 392
Silverberg, S., 84, 134, 135, 142, 306, 311, 316, 317, 320
Silverman, A. D., 106
Silverman, J., 363
Silverman, W., 467
Silverthorn, N., 121
Sim, H., 152
Sim, T., 141, 316, 318
Similo, S. L., 279
Simmens, S., 146, 147
Simmons, R., 39, 47, 157, 190, 209, 275, 276, 279, 362
Simmons-Morton, B., 192
Simon, T., 158
Simon, T. R., 222, 223
Simon, V., 360
Simon, V. A., 341
Simon, W., 358, 382
Simons, L. G., 124
Simpkins, S. D., 410
Simpson, I., 252
Simpson, R., 418, 429
Sims, B., 170, 233
Sinclair, R., 156, 412, 414, 415
Singer, M., 222
Singh, G., 57
Singh, K., 424
Singh, S., 330, 373, 374, 375, 389, 390, 391, 393, 394, 398, 399
Sionean, C., 378, 379
Sipan, C., 379
Sippola, L., 188, 191, 346, 352, 354, 355, 360
Sirin, S. R., 413
Sisk, C., 25, 26, 27
Skare, S., 75
Skeem, J., 451
Skinner, B. F., 16, 18
Skinner, M., 183, 184, 456, 458

Skoe, E. E., 325
Slaby, R., 460
Slap, G., 147, 391
Slattery, M., 461
Slomkowski, C., 144
Slora, E., 34
Slora, E. J., 26
Sloutsky, V., 64, 70
Slovic, P., 87
Slowiaczek, M., 413
Slyper, A., 38
Small, S., 134, 141, 252, 347, 381, 386, 387, 391
Smetana, J., 63, 85, 116, 131, 132, 136, 137, 141,
    142, 151, 308, 310, 316, 319, 330
Smiciklas-Wright, H., 30
Smith, A., 295, 373, 377
Smith, B., 208
Smith, C., 329, 396, 456
Smith, C. A., 376
Smith, D. C., 315, 349, 352
Smith, E., 292, 372, 377, 398
Smith, G., 448
Smith, J., 205, 208, 227, 412
Smith, K., 409
Smith, K. R., 84
Smith, L., 460
Smith, L. M., 252
Smith, M., 396
Smith, P. H., 363
Smith, T., 244
Smith, T. E., 298
Smith, T. M., 217
Smith, W., 76
Smolak, L., 30, 54
Smolkowski, K., 458
Smoll, F., 29, 30
Smollar, J., 137, 307, 335, 350
Smyth, C., 335
Sneed, C. D., 120
Snow, D. L., 446
Snyder, H., 180, 182, 453
Snyder, J., 144, 145, 456
Snyder, M., 244
So Wa, N., 135
Sobesky, W., 324
Sobolewski, J. M., 151, 153
Soeken, K., 464
Soenens, B., 141, 289, 290
Sogolow, E., 388
Sokolik, E., 409
Soler, R., 152
Solheim, E., 295
Solomon, R., 401
Somerfield, M., 373
Sommers, C., 325, 409
Sonenstein, F., 299, 373
Songer, N., 90
Soong, W., 42
Sorell, G. T., 355
Sorensen, A., 211
Sorensen, S., 57, 389
Sorenson, A. M., 400
Souter (Justice), 4
South, S., 460
South, S. J., 123, 172, 395, 414
Sowell, E. R., 75

Spade, J., 210
Spanoudis, G., 71
Sparks, C., 241
Spear, P., 76
Speisman, J., 307
Spence, J., 298
Spencer, G. A., 363
Spencer, M., 218, 291, 292, 294, 400, 420, 434
Spieker, S., 142, 400
Spieker, S. J., 398
Spielberger, C., 407
Spina, S., 347, 352, 355, 356
Spingarn, R., 437
Spitznagel, E. L., 438
Spoth, R., 184
Spoth, R. L., 448
Spotts, E. L., 145, 146
Spradling, V., 352
Sprecher, S., 382
Spreitzer, E., 247
Springer, J. F., 448
Srinivasan, S., 391
Sroufe, L., 340, 341, 364, 458
St. George, I., 34, 35
St. John, C., 437
St. John, N., 215
St. John, R., 152
St. Lawrence, J., 392
St. Louis, M., 391
St. Pierre, T., 450
Stack, S., 381
Stacy, A., 178
Staff, J., 12, 221, 232, 235, 239, 241
Stage, F. K., 416, 418
Stanley-Hagan, M., 153, 154
Stanton, B., 183, 378, 380, 392, 440, 448
Stanton, W., 436
Stanton-Salazar, R., 347, 352, 355, 356, 424
Starbuck-Morales, S., 399
Stark, T., 314, 396
Stattin, H., 48, 49, 185, 250, 251, 308, 411,
    413, 457
Staudinger, U. M., 86
Stedman, L., 204
Steele, C. M., 409
Steele, J., 255, 257
Steen, S., 454
Steffen, P., 377
Steffensmeier, D., 454
Steidl, J., 275
Stein, D. G., 52
Stein, J., 45, 184, 185, 298, 424
Stein, J. A., 184
Stein, N., 386
Steinberg, A. R., 51
Steinberg, L., 3, 4, 6, 13, 14, 19, 26, 43, 54, 64, 74,
    76, 77, 81, 88, 89, 90, 98, 104, 105, 123, 124,
    125, 130, 132, 133, 134, 135, 136, 137, 138,
    139, 140, 141, 142, 143, 145, 153, 155, 159,
    162, 182, 184, 185, 186, 194, 203, 221, 223,
    236, 237, 238, 239, 240, 242, 246, 251, 252,
    303, 305, 306, 308, 309, 310, 311, 314, 316,
    317, 318, 320, 340, 342, 353, 360, 364, 412,
    413, 415, 418, 419, 423, 438, 448, 455, 456,
    457, 461, 462, 466, 467, 468
Steinberg, W., 133, 134, 135, 308
Steiner, H., 106, 454, 457

Steinman, K. J., 330
Stemmler, M., 440, 461, 463, 464, 466, 469
Stenger, V. A., 76
Stephan, W., 281
Stephens, L., 154
Stern, D., 113
Sternberg, R., 64, 78, 83, 90, 91
Stetsenko, A., 408
Stevens (Justice), 4
Stevens, A., 120
Stevens, E. A., 186
Stevens, J., 400
Stevens, N., 364, 365
Stevenson, D., 211, 221, 417, 428, 431
Stevenson, H., 246, 418, 420
Stevenson, H., Jr., 124, 291, 292, 392
Stevenson, H. W., 409, 411, 417, 420
Stevenson, J., 146, 457
Stewart, A. J., 385
Stewart, S. D., 154
Stewart, S. M., 358, 377
Stice, E., 47, 48, 51, 52, 54, 138, 141, 185, 186,
    457, 463
Sticke, E., 54
Stigler, J., 420
Stipek, D., 408, 409, 410
Stock, J., 387
Stockard, J., 298
Stocker, C., 281
Stocker, C. M., 144
Stoller, C., 19
Stoms, G., 396
Stone, A., 91
Stone, G., 152
Stone, J., 113
Stone, M., 262
Stone, M. R., 178
Stoneman, Z., 144, 146, 158, 418
Stoolmiller, M., 100, 183, 184, 185, 190, 377,
    378, 456, 457, 458, 462
Storr, C., 242
Storvoll, E. E., 456
Story, M., 51, 52, 440
Stouthamer-Loeber, M., 184, 186, 437, 454, 455,
    456, 457, 459, 460
Strasburger, V., 258, 259
Straub, D. M., 259
Strauss, M., 140, 157
Striegel-Moore, R., 38, 279
Strough, J., 346
Strouse, J., 259
Studer, M., 390
Study Team., 390
Stueve, 375
Stukas, A., Jr., 244
Sturmer, P., 396
Sturmhöfel, S., 444
Su, S., 155
Suchindran, C., 38, 376
Sucoff, C., 373, 381, 395
Sudler, N., 342
Sue, S., 418, 419
Sugarman, D., 140
Sui-Chu, E., 412, 418
Sullivan, A., 309
Sullivan, H. S., 194, 336, 337, 339, 341

Sullivan, K., 309
Sullivan, M., 242
Sullivan, S., 288
Sullivan, T., 124
Sullivan, T. N., 438
Summers, P., 153
Sun, R., 380, 387, 388
Sun, S. S., 38
Sun, Y., 147, 151, 152
Sung, H., 442
Super, D., 426
Supple, A. J., 142
Susman, E., 8, 24, 26, 28, 34, 39, 40, 46, 47, 56, 368, 440
Sussman, S., 178, 250, 251
Svedin, C.-G., 382
Swank, P. R., 363
Swarr, A., 54, 355
Swartzwelder, H., 444
Sweeney, J. A., 63
Swenson, L. P., 190, 278, 280, 281, 292, 346
Swenson, R., 125
Sy, S., 241, 242
Syme, S. L., 58
Szalacha, L. A., 279
Szapocznik, J., 288
Szczygiel, S., 462
Szmukler, G., 52

T

Tabor, J., 468
Taiariol, J., 190
Taipale, V., 47
Talbert, L., 377
Tally, S., 466
Tam, H., 288
Tan, D., 315
Tan, L. L., 119, 445
Tang, C. S., 45
Tannenbaum, L., 153
Tanner, D., 199, 200
Tanner, J., 24, 29, 32, 33, 34, 36, 37
Tao, G., 391
Tapert, S. F., 448
Tarabulsy, G. M., 342
Taradash, A., 306, 349
Tasker, F., 153, 385
Tate, B., 140
Tate, J., 292
Taub, B., 462
Taveras, E. M., 254
Taylor, B., 26, 30
Taylor, C., 52, 448, 463
Taylor, D., 42
Taylor, J., 438
Taylor, R., 151, 158, 291, 407, 418
Taylor, S., 251, 377
Teachman, J., 146, 207, 216, 376, 414, 416, 417
Teachman, J. D., 156
Tebes, J. K., 446
Teen Research Unlimited., 256
Tein, J., 469
Teitler, J., 152, 399
Teitler, J. O., 125, 381

Telch, C., 55
Tellegen, A., 111, 273, 277, 405, 438, 468
Temple, J., 417
Tennenbaum, D., 142
Teran, L., 395
Teret, S., 447
Terracciano, A., 273
Terrell, N., 459
Terry, R., 189, 194, 377
Tershakovec, A. M., 51
Tester, M., 314
Teti, D., 398
Tevendale, H., 276, 282
Tevendale, H. D., 278, 280, 281, 292
Thayer, S. M., 349
Theokas, C., 252
Thiel, K., 164, 180, 349, 353, 355
Thom, B., 442
Thomas (Justice), 4
Thomas, A., 151
Thomas, D., 330
Thomas, G., 151
Thomas, J., 356
Thomas, S. L., 211
Thompson, J., 464
Thompson, J. K., 51
Thompson, P., 75
Thompson, P. J., 259
Thompson, R., 254, 255, 309
Thomsen, A., 469
Thomson, E., 151, 155, 380
Thornberry, T., 282, 396, 397, 456
Thornton, A., 136, 390
Thornton, M., 291
Thulborn, K. R., 75
Thum, Y., 425
Thurber, C., 307
Tienda, M., 241, 416, 419, 420
Tiezzi, L., 222, 399
Tiggemann, M., 47
Tiggermann, M., 51
Tilton-Weaver, L. C., 45, 110, 111, 184
Timmerman, G., 386
Ting-Kai, L., 444
Tisak, J., 316
Tisak, M., 316
Tobin-Richards, M., 359, 362, 363
Tobler, N., 449
Toch, T., 222
Todd, M., 448
Toga, A. W., 75
Tokoyawa, T., 123, 158
Tolan, P., 124, 363, 459, 469
Tolan, P. H., 123, 124, 158, 184
Tolman, D., 382
Tolson, J., 172, 173, 183, 186, 187
Tomal, A., 396
Toms, F., 291
Toogood, R., 396
Toomey, T., 449
Topitzes, D., 125
Topolski, T. D., 435
Torney-Purta, J., 327, 328
Torquati, J., 40, 43
Tottenham, N., 75, 76, 81
Townsend Betts, N., 346

Toyokawa, T., 416
Tram, J., 275, 278
Tram, J. M., 282
Trauner, D. A., 75
Treaster, J., 445
Treboux, D., 341, 380
Treiber, F., 460
Tremblay, R., 138, 184, 185, 186, 209, 364, 424, 425, 451, 456, 457, 458, 459, 460
Trent, K., 395, 400
Trevethan, S., 324, 325
Trickett, E., 295, 448
Trickett, P., 387
Trim, R., 14, 445, 447, 448
Trivellore, E. R., 180, 181
Troiano, R. P., 37
Troop-Gordon, W., 341
Troyer, L., 140, 413
Trussell, J., 389
Trusty, J., 413
Truxillo, C., 320
Trzesniewski, K. H., 274, 282
Tsay, J., 141
Tschann, J., 152, 389, 392, 395
Tseng, V., 116, 135, 136, 350, 419
Tubman, J. G., 387, 392
Tucker, C., 136, 144, 145, 146, 328
Tucker, J. S., 444
Turbin, M., 448
Turbin, M. S., 437
Turiel, E., 132, 321, 325, 326
Turkheimer, E., 145
Turner, C., 260, 373
Turner, J., 400
Turner, P. K., 110, 111
Turner, R., 400
Turner, T., 189, 191
Turnure, J., 71
Tversky, A., 87
Twenge, J., 280, 462
Tyden, T., 388
Tyler, K. A., 387
Tyrka, A. R., 52
Tyson, K., 179, 419

U

UCLA Higher Education Research Institute, 328, 371
Udry, J., 30, 32, 38, 358, 372, 373, 376, 377, 378, 380, 386, 468
Udry, J. R., 52, 378
Uggen, C., 12, 221, 232, 235, 239, 241
Ullen, F., 75
Ulman, K., 44
Umaña-Taylor, A. J., 295, 316
Underwood, M., 189, 191, 377
Unger, D., 292, 448
Unger, J., 158, 395, 448
Upchurch, D., 373, 381, 395, 398
Updegraff, K., 137, 144, 297, 349
Urban T., 407
Urban, T. A., 63
Urberg, K., 172, 173, 186, 187, 355
Urdan, T., 205, 218, 407, 413

U.S. Bureau of the Census., 112, 149, 165, 243, 250, 357, 421, 424
U.S. Department of Commerce, Bureau of the Census., 235
Usmiani, S., 278

V

Vaccaro, D., 446
Vadeboncoeur, I., 69
Valchon, R., 64, 70
Valdez, A., 183
Valentin, P., 65
Valentine, J., 121, 228
Valentiner, D., 467
Valois, R., 377
Valois, R. F., 438
Van Acker, R., 188
Van Court, P., 326
Van Den Bos, J., 448
Van den Bulck, J., 42
Van den Oord, E., 146
van der Ende, J., 451, 452
van Dulmen, M., 147
van Hoof, A., 287
Van Horn, M. L., 355
Van Kammen, W., 459
Van Leeuwen, K. G., 138
van Lieshout, C., 192, 349
van Nguyen, T., 157
van Roosmallen, E., 358, 360, 383
Van Rossem, R., 440
van Wel, F., 350
Vandell, D., 250, 251
Vandenbelt, M., 397
Vanderryn, J., 448
Vanfossen, B., 210
Vann, F., 384
VanOss Marin, B., 152
Vansteenkiste, M., 141
Varenne, H., 176
Vargas, W., 158
Vasant, I., 308
Vasey, M., 451
Vasquez-Suson, K., 189
Vaughan, R., 222, 399, 438, 440, 442
Vaughan, R. D., 261
Vaux, A., 239, 242, 353
Vazquez Garcia, H., 119, 292
Vazsonyi, A., 273, 281
Veblen-Mortenson, S., 449
Vega, W., 291, 294, 295
Velez, W., 224, 420
Venet, M., 69
Ventura, S., 388, 393
Vera Institute of Justice., 396
Verhulst, F. C., 451, 452
Veridiano, N., 384
Verkuyten, M., 292
Verma, S., 162, 163, 198, 232, 233, 234, 236, 237
Vermeer, H. J., 409
Vermeiren, R., 124, 376
Vermulst, A. A., 137, 308
Vernon, M. K., 170
Vezina, L., 364

Vicary, J., 276, 277, 378, 380, 386
Videon, T. M., 154
Viechtbauer, W., 273
Vieno, A., 217
Vieria, C., 140
Vigersky, R., 55
Vigfusdottir, T. H., 54
Viken, R. J., 35, 48
Viljoen, J. L., 106
Vincent, G. M., 451
Vincent, M., 399
Vinokurov, A., 295
Virdin, L., 142
Vispoel, W. A. J., 411
Vitacco, M. J., 451
Vitaro, F., 183, 184, 185, 186, 192, 194, 209, 362, 364, 456, 458, 459, 460
Vitterso, J., 462
Voelkl, K., 419
Voelz, S., 64
Vogel, S., 297
Volkow, N., 444
Vollebergh, W., 287, 352
von Eye, A., 117, 252, 319, 352
Votruba-Drzal, E., 158
Voydanoff, P., 396
Voyer, D., 81
Voyer, S., 81
Vuchinich, R., 155, 156
Vuchinich, S., 152, 155, 156, 310

W

Waclawiw, M., 279
Wadden, T. A., 51
Wade, T. J., 462
Wadsworth, K., 448
Wadsworth, M., 469
Wadsworth, M. E., 158
Wagenar, A., 449
Wagner, B., 140
Wagner, E. F., 387
Wainer, H., 81
Wainright, J. L., 385
Wainryb, C., 84
Waite, L., 115
Waiters, E. D., 379, 381
Waitkoff, G. R., 464
Waizenhofer, R., 137, 141
Wakschlag, L. S., 397
Walberg, H., 422
Wald, M., 118, 227
Walden, B., 136, 145, 146
Waldman, I., 191
Walker, A. M., 292
Walker, A. R., 344, 346, 365
Walker, D., 189, 365
Walker, E., 259
Walker, E. F., 26, 444, 467
Walker, E. M., 190
Walker, L., 323, 324, 325, 326
Walker, S., 379, 381
Walker-Barnes, C. J., 140, 142, 185
Walkey, F., 419
Walkup, J. T., 467

Wall, J., 316
Wall, M., 51
Wall, S., 340
Wallace, J. M., 328, 329
Wallace, J. M., Jr., 445
Wallace, S. A., 418
Wallace, S. J., 155
Wallace-Broscious, A., 288
Wallack, L., 19
Wallander, J. L., 397
Wallenstein, S., 133, 134, 466
Waller, E. M., 392
Waller, J., 150, 377
Waller, M., 363
Waller, P., 447
Waller, P. F., 56
Wallerstein, J., 153, 308
Wallis, C., 74
Walrodn, M., 145
Walsh, B., 54
Walsh, D. A., 258
Walter, H., 222
Walters, R., 16
Walton, K., 273
Wampler, R., 209
Wandersman, A., 57
Wang, C., 437
Wang, M., 30
Wang, M. Q., 386
Wang, R., 253
Wang, Y., 26
Wångby, M., 436
Ward, L. M., 259
Ward, M., 258, 280
Ward, M. L., 258, 260
Ward, S., 70
Wargo, J., 189, 344
Warheit, G., 291, 294, 295
Warneke, C., 57
Warner, S., 407
Warren, C., 373, 388
Warren, C. W., 388
Warren, J. R., 425
Warren, M., 44, 48, 51
Warren, M. P., 47
Washburn-Ormachea, J. M., 464
Wasik, B., 119, 292
Wasserman, G., 400
Wasserman, R., 34
Wasserman, R. C., 26
Watanabe, H., 83
Waterman, A., 287, 289, 290
Waterman, J., 454
Waterman, P., 222
Waters, E., 340, 341
Waters, P., 278, 298, 325
Watson, A. L., 445
Watson, D., 440
Watt, H. M., 297
Watt, T. T., 205
Watts, R. J., 292
Way, N., 41, 43, 181, 214, 217, 218, 219, 222, 280, 281, 296, 345, 347, 348, 349
Wearing, H., 73
Webb, N. M., 203
Weber, E., 392

Weems, C., 467
Wehner, E., 360
Wei, E., 456, 459
Weiman, D., 392
Weinberg, M., 385
Weinberg, R., 291, 292
Weinfeld, F., 412, 417
Weinfeld, N., 341
Weinfield, N., 341
Weinfurt, K., 83
Weinrott, M., 460
Weinstein, R. S., 146, 221
Weisner, M., 445
Weisner, T., 148
Weiss, B., 466, 467
Weiss, C., 399
Weiss, C. C., 125, 381
Weiss, R., 308, 334
Weissberg, R., 193, 467
Weist, M., 447, 468
Weist, M. D., 124
Weisz, J., 467, 469
Wekerle, C., 386
Wells, A., 210, 211, 212, 214
Wells, E. A., 381
Wells, K., 158
Welner, K. G., 205, 206
Welsh, M., 350
Wentzel, K., 152, 188, 190, 209, 217, 326, 407, 413, 415
Werch, C. E., 248
Werner, N. E., 186, 190
Wertheim, E., 52
Weseter, K., 222
West, E., 400
West, S., 469
Westhoven, V., 309
Westoff, C., 390
Whang, S., 459, 467
Wheaton, B., 140
Whitaker, D., 318, 376, 379
Whitbeck, L., 123, 154, 157, 158, 329, 380, 381, 387, 395, 459
White, D., 407
White, J. W., 363
White, K., 307
White, L., 108
White, N., 91, 363
White, R., 400
Whiteman, S., 137, 297
Whitenton, K., 54
Whitesell, N., 272, 278, 298, 325, 345, 408
Whiteside, T., 468
Whiting, B., 236
Whiting, J., 236
Whitman, T., 394, 397
Whitmore, J., 420
Wibbelsman, C. J., 152
Wichstrom, L., 46, 48
Wichström, L., 456
Wichstrøm, L., 463
Wickraman, K. A., 122
Widaman, K., 315, 349, 352
Widaman, K. F., 308
Widmer, E., 380
Widom, C., 387

Wiebe, R. P., 186, 448
Wier, M., 399
Wierson, M., 151
Wiesner, M., 458
Wigfield, A., 207, 208, 275, 279, 410
Wiggins, R. D., 120
Wight, R. G., 462
Wikstroem, P.-O., 124
Wikstrom, P. H., 455
Wilcox, W., 143
Wiley, D. J., 374
Wilfong, J. J., 247
Wilkening, F., 67
Wilkinson, D., 454
Wilkinson, R. B., 281
William T. Grant Foundation Commission on Work, Family, and Citizenship., 118, 198, 226
Williams, A., 89, 90
Williams, C., 449
Williams, E., 457
Williams, G., 457
Williams, J., 412, 418
Williams, J. H., 409
Williams, N., 239, 242
Williams, P., 55, 56, 65, 91
Williams, R., 182
Williams, S., 34, 35, 246, 379
Williams, S. K., 137
Williams, T., 409, 424
Williams, W., 80, 91, 416
Williamson, D., 468
Williamson, J., 387
Williams-Wheeler, M., 141
Willis, D. S., 328, 329
Willis, T. A., 140
Willits, F., 341
Willoughby, T., 438
Wills, T., 446, 468
Wilsdon, A., 381
Wilson, D., 448
Wilson, J., 250, 251, 412, 459
Wilson, M., 454
Wilson, P., 412
Wilson, R., 261
Wilson, S., 6, 19, 20, 98, 108, 114, 119, 140, 274, 275
Wilson, S. M., 309
Wilson, T., 411
Wilson, W., 120
Windle, M., 151, 194, 352, 362, 363, 438, 445, 447, 458, 459, 464, 469
Windle, R., 447, 469
Windsor, R., 389
Winfree, J. L., 183
Winfree, L., Jr., 184
Wingood, G., 259, 378
Wingood, G. M., 330, 379, 389, 392
Winn, D., 377, 396, 397
Winner, E., 67
Wintemute, G., 447
Winter, C. E., 185
Winter, M., 444
Winter, T., 34
Winterbottom, M., 407
Wintre, M., 315
Wise, D., 243

Wiseman, R., 190
Wister, A., 115
Witkow, M., 291, 418, 420
Witruk, E., 411
Witsberger, C., 115
Wojtkiewicz, R., 153, 420
Wolak, J., 256
Wolf, A., 57
Wolfe, A., 399
Wolfe, D., 140, 386
Wolfe, M., 423
Wolfe, S., 320
Wolfer, L., 423
Wolfson, A., 42, 43
Wolfson, M., 449
Wolverton, L., 96, 120
Wong, C., 318
Wong, C. A., 159
Wong, M., 255
Wood, D., 319
Wood, G., 363, 364
Wood, P., 418
Wood, P. A., 456
Wood, P. K., 437
Woodruff, K., 19
Woods, E., 124, 441, 460
Woods, L. N., 323
Woods, R. P., 75
Woodside, B., 54
Woodward, H., 31, 38
Woodward, L., 153, 194, 380, 395, 397
Woody, E., 189
Woolard, J., 20, 89, 94, 95, 104, 105, 452
Woolard, J. L., 312
Woolley, T., 396
Worden, J., 449
World Health Organization Collaborative Study of Neoplasia and Steroid Contraceptives, 36
Worsley, K., 75
Worthman, C., 462, 464, 467
Wortman, C., 410
Wright, J., 237, 239, 241, 242
Wright, K., 141
Wright, M., 447
Wright, V., 308
Wrobleski, N., 399
Wu, C., 83
Wu, L., 242, 380, 444, 447
Wu, T., 35
Wunderlich, M., 57
Wyatt, L. W., 457

X

Xia, G., 466
Xie, Y., 416, 418
Xu, J., 412
Xu, X., 374, 379

Y

Yaeger, A., 446
Yamaguchi, K., 438
Yamaguchi, R., 449

Yancey, A., 40
Yang, Y., 363
Yankelovich, D., 329
Yannett, N., 209
Yanof, D., 352
Yarger, R. S., 73, 75
Yasui, M., 295
Yates, A., 30
Yates, M., 326
Yau, J., 131, 142, 151
Ybarra, M. L., 256
Ybarra, V. C., 291
Yeh, H., 144
Yeh, M., 456
Yemini, T., 464
Yeong, K., 124
Yeung, A., 408, 409
Yeung, D. Y., 45
Yeung, D. Y. L., 45
Yin, J., 194
Yip, T., 135
Yisrael, D. S., 386
YMCA., 130, 252
Yodanis, C., 140, 157
Yoder, K., 380, 459
Yoerger, K., 185, 448, 457
Yoon, J. S., 190
Yoon, K., 410
York, R., 412, 417
Yoshikawa, H., 234, 455, 459
Young, A. M., 396
Young, H., 315

Young, J. F., 352
Young, M., 363, 380
Youngstrom, E., 124
Youniss, J., 120, 137, 289, 306, 307, 326, 335, 348, 350
Yu, H., 214
Yu, K., 192
Yu, S., 57
Yung, S., 240

Z

Zabin, L., 389, 395, 398
Zaff, J. F., 246
Zahn-Waxler, C., 461
Zaider, T., 440
Zakin, D., 47
Zametkin, A. J., 50, 464
Zamsky, E., 400
Zane, N., 50, 448
Zapert, K., 446
Zarbatany, L., 346
Zavela, K., 450
Zavodny, M., 389
Zbikowski, S., 448
Zee, P. C., 42
Zeira, A., 182, 222
Zeldin, R., 347
Zeldin, S., 125
Zelnick, M., 389
Zeman, J., 307

Zentall, S. R., 378
Zhang, H., 437
Zhang, Q., 458, 459
Zhang, W., 116
Zhong, H., 454
Zhou, Q., 326
Zickler, P., 445
Zielinski, M., 280
Zijdenbos, A., 75
Zillman, D., 259
Zima, B., 158
Zimiles, H., 153, 155
Zimmer-Gembeck, M. J., 355, 363, 377
Zimmerle, D., 376
Zimmerman, M., 121, 123, 151, 186, 277, 281, 296, 330, 406, 438
Zimmerman, R., 291, 294, 295, 376, 382
Zimmermann, P., 287, 342
Zimring, F., 105, 106, 314, 453, 455, 459
Zinman, J., 57, 443, 449
Zirkel, S., 421
Zito, J. M., 464
Ziv, Y., 282
Zoccolillo, M., 456
Zohar, A., 71
Zollo, P., 232, 261
Zoon, C. K., 50
Zuckerman, A., 415
Zuckerman, M., 438
Zuroff, D. C., 309
Zweig, J. M., 362, 395, 438, 439

Subject Index

A

abortion, 395–396, 399f
abstinence, 399
abstract concepts, 64–65
academic achievement, 416, **416**
    ethnicity and, 182, 183, 209, 418–422, 419, 420, 422, 433
achievement, **13**, 403–431, **404**. *See also* academic achievement; educational achievement; occupational achievement
    attributions, 410, **410**, 410f
    belief importance for, 407–411
    cognitive transitions and, 405
    environment influencing, 412–415
    identity, 289
    motivation, 406–409
    success and failures, 410–411
    tracking and student, 212
acquired immune deficiency syndrome (AIDS), **391**, 391–392
'acting white' stigma, 419
activational role (of hormones), 27, **27**
ADHD. *See* attention deficit/hyperactivity disorder
adolescence, 8, 24–58. *See also* puberty
    adult differences in values and priorities, 88–89
    behavior implications, 77
    contexts of, 9–12
    crime victims during, 454
    criminal defendants during, 105–106
    development of, 4–20
    divorce of parents during, 150–152, 155
    ecology of, 11
    family influence, 11, 130–159
    financial strain in family during, 157–158, 157f
    free time in contemporary society, 232–235
    fundamental changes of, 8–9
    industrialization impact on invention of, 97
    interpersonal development during, 337–338
    as invention, 17–18
    legal status inconsistencies, 106
    leisure time during, 245–252
    length of, 95–96
    -limited offenders, 456, **456**, 458–459
    marital conflict impact on, 152–153
    motherhood during, 400–401
    multidisciplinary approach to, 5–6
    origins of, 97–98
    positive influences and success of, 125, 125f
    pre-adolescence thinking different from, 85–86, 86t
    problem behavior, 138, 138f
    rebelling against parents, 132
    rejection during, 189
    responsibility developing through jobs, 239–241
    risk-taking, 86–90
    school influence, 11–12

social transitions, 8, 93–125
stereotypes v. scientific study, 19–20
structured leisure activities, 246–250, 247f
adolescent development, 8–14
    achievement, 403–431
    behavioral autonomy, 311–320
    behavioral genetics and, 145–147
    dating impacting, 362–364
    emotional autonomy, 304–312
    employment and, 239–243
    family importance in, 138–145, 159
    free time and, 262–263
    hormones influencing, 27
    identity, 267–299
    identity crisis, 283–287
    intimacy, 334–365
    neighborhood conditions influencing, 121–125, 122f, 123f, 124f, 125f
    psychosocial problems in early periods of, 435
    schools and, 227–229
    sexuality, 367–401
    value autonomy, 320–330
adolescent growth spurt, **28**, 28–34
adolescent health care, **55**, 55–58
The Adolescent Society (Coleman), 167, 221
adolescent-parent relationships, 130–159
    anti-social peer groups influenced by, 184–185
    autonomy and, 306–309
    change in needs and function of family, 135
    communication about sex, 378–379
    conflicts, 131–132
    development of adolescent, 138–145
    expectations, 136–137
    family relations transformed, 135–137
    family systems theory, 133, **133**
    intimacy and, 348–350, 351f
    midlife crisis and, **133**, 133–134
    parenting styles, 138–142
    popular books, 130
    puberty influencing, 136
    reciprocity of, 141, 142f
    struggle and rebellion, 132
adoption, 147, 396
adrenal axis maturation, 30–31, 31f
adrenarche, 26, **26**
Adult Attachment Interview, 342, **342**
adulthood. *See also* emerging adulthood
    criteria for, 111
    legal age of, 95
    preparing adolescents for, 108–109
    psychosocial problems ending in, 435
    risk-taking in, 88–89
    transition to, in contemporary society, 118–121
affluence, premature, 241, **241**
African Americans
    academic achievement of, 209, 418, 419, 420, 422, 423
    'acting white' stigma, 419
    anti-social behavior of, 48

body satisfaction among, 30, 55
bone density of, 29
crowds and, 178
dating and, 53f, 358
discrimination of, 181–182, 181f
extracurricular activities of, 233, 234, 255, 259
family influence of, 136, 149, 152, 153, 170, 319, 353
health of, 132, 196
muscular development of, 30
obesity of, 50
parent relationships of, 116, 308, 349
peer groups and, 54
poverty influencing, 119, 120, 149, 416
pregnancy and childbearing of, 393–400
puberty timing among, 34, 35f, 38
religion influencing, 329–330
school desegregation and, 181–182, 214, 248
self-esteem and, 214, 278–281
sexual activity of, 348, 372, 373, 374, 375, 380
stress impacting, 123
suicide among, 465
age
    -crime curve, 452, **452**
    grading, 163, **163**
    of majority, 95, **95**
    segregation, 180
agency, 288, **288**
aggression, 188–191, 451, **451**, 452f, 457–458. *See also* antisocial behavior; criminal behavior
AIDS. *See* acquired immune deficiency syndrome
alcohol, 242, 251. *See also* binge drinking
    sex and, 375–376
American Idol, 258
America's Next Top Model, 258
androgens, **25**, 25f, 25–26
androgyny, 297, **297**
    masculinity, femininity and, 298–299
anorexia nervosa, 51, **52**
    prevalence and causes of, 53–55
anthropological perspectives, 18–19
anti-social behavior, 48, 184–186
    causes of, 455–459
    developmental progression of, 452–453
antisocial personality disorder, **450**, 450–451
anxious-avoidant attachment, 340, **340**
anxious-resistant attachment, 340, **340**
Asian Americans. *See also* ethnicity
    academic achievement of, 182, 183, 418–422
    adult transition challenges for, 119, 120
    crowd membership of, 178, 181
    dating of, 358, 359
    depression among, 462
    discrimination, 181–182, 181f
    eating disorders among, 53
    family relationships of, 136, 142, 149
    friendships of, 345
    school violence among, 222
    self-esteem, 280, 281

sexual activity among, 373
substance use among, 445
suicide among, 465
attachment, 342, 343f. *See also* Adult Attachment Interview; anxious-avoidant attachment; anxious-resistant attachment
in family, 143
intimacy, **340,** 340–343
secure, 340, **340**
attention, 71
attention deficit/hyperactivity disorder
(ADHD), 457
authoritarian parents, 139, **139,** 310
influencing achievement, 413
authoritative parents, 139, **139,** 221, 223, 251,
310, 342, 413
how it works, 140–142
power of, 139–140
authority conflicts, 452, **452**
autoerotic behavior, 372, **372**
autonomy, **13,** 302–330. *See also* behavioral autonomy; emotional autonomy; value autonomy
adolescent-parent relationships and, 306–309
cognitive changes and, 304
in family, 143
puberty and development of, 303–304
socialization and, 204
types of, 304–305

B

baby boom, 112, **112, 164,** 164–165, 165f, 166t
Bar (Bas) Mitzvah, 108, **108,** 110
barometric self-esteem, 275–276, **276**
basal metabolism rate, 49, **49**
baseline self-esteem, 275–276, **276**
Beavis and Butthead, 67
behavioral autonomy, **304,** 304–305, 311–320
ethnic and cultural differences in, 319
self-reliant feelings, 320
susceptibility to influence, 314–318
behavioral decision theory, 86–87, **87,** 87f
behavioral genetics, **145,** 145–147
behaviorism, 16
biculturalism, 294, **294**
Big Brothers/Big Sisters, 121, 353
big fish-little pond effect, 213, **213**
binge drinking, 442, **442**
biological development
health paradox, 55–56
hormones influence development of, 27
moodiness, puberty and, 40–41, 41t
physical health and health care, 55–58
promoting health of, 56–57
biological transitions, 8, 39f
dating and, 358
eating disorders, 49–55
health care, 55–58
psychological impact of puberty, 38–49
puberty, 24–28
puberty timing and tempo, 34–38
social impact of puberty, 38–49
biosocial theories, 14–15
biracial, 292–294
birth control, 399f. *See also* contraceptive use

BMI. *See* body mass index
Board of Education v. Mergens, 106
body
changes in stature and dimensions of, 28–30,
29f, 55
dissatisfaction, 52–53
image and opposite sex friendships, 355–356
body mass index (BMI), 50, **50**
Bolivia, adolescent employment in, 237
boys. *See* males
brain
of adolescent, 73–78
drugs and, 443–444
Bravo! magazine, 390
breast development, 32–33, 33d
brother-sister avoidance, 108, **108**
Brown v. Board of Education of Topeka, 213
bulimia, 51–55, **52**
prevalence and causes of, 53–55
bullies, 191–192, 193f

C

care orientation, 325, **325**
The Catcher in the Rye (Salinger), 283
Catholic schools, 215–216
causation, 257, **257,** 257f
Central Park jogger, 316
charter schools, 203, **203**
child protectionists, 97, **97**
childbearing, 393–401
prevalence of teen, 393–394, 394f
China, adolescent employment in, 237
chlamydia, **391,** 391–392
chronic poverty, 158
circumcision, **111,** 111–112
classroom climate, 90–91, 217–223
ideal, 217–218, 217f
cliques, 171, **171,** 179–187
changes in, 173–174
similarities among, 179–182
social networks and, 171–172
closeness, 309–310
cognitive transitions, 8, 62–91
abstract concepts, 64–65
achievement and, 405
adolescent relativism, 67–68
autonomy and, 304
decision making and, 314
egocentrism, 65–66
hypothetical thinking, 64
identity development and, 269
intelligence, 78–82
intimacy development and, 335
reasoning, 63–64
sarcasm, 67
sexuality and, 368
social cognition, **83,** 83–86, 86t
cognitive-development view, 68, **68,** 69t
cohort, **106,** 106–107
collective efficacy, **122,** 122–123
college, 223–227, 224f, 225f
attitudes of, students, 328
high school transition to, 225–226
Columbine High School shootings, 222

Coming of Age in Samoa (Mead), 114
community service, 243, **243**
comorbid, 436, **436**
comorbidity
of externalizing problems, 437–440,
437f, 438f
of internalizing problems, 440
competence-performance distinction, 70,
70, 70f
compulsory education, 199–200, 232
computer technology, 253, 262
concrete operations, 68, **68,** 69t
condoms, 388, 388f, 399
preventing STDs, 392
conduct disorder, **450,** 450–451, 451t
conflict
authority, 452, **452**
after divorce, 154–155
in family, 151
intergenerational, 17
marital, 152–153, 152f
in parent-adolescent relationships, 131–132
resolution, 346
consumer, adolescent, 261
context
of adolescence, 9–12
dating influenced by, 358–359
identity development in social, 284–285
importance of, for achievement, 410
of risk-taking, 89–90
sexual activity influenced by, 377–378
continuity of passage, 113–115
continuous transitions, 113, **113**
contraceptive use, 387–391
abstaining from, 388–389
improving, 390–391
lack of education about, 389
STDs and, 392
trends in, 388, 388f
conventional moral reasoning, **322,** 322–323
correlation, 257, **257,** 257f
cortisol, 26, **26**
covert antisocial behavior, 452, **452**
crash rates, 90f
criminal behavior, 452, **452**
unreported, 454–455
criminal justice system, **104,** 104–105
critical thinking, 90, **90, 202,** 202–203
cross-sectional study, 39, **39**
cross-sex friendships, 353–356
crowds, 171–173, **172**
adolescent identity and, 178
changes in, 173–175
ethnicity in, 178–179, 181
identity and, 178–179
membership and adolescent identity, 178
pressure exerted by, 176, 176f
as reference groups, 177–178
in schools, 206
social map of adolescence, 177–179
crystallization, 426, **426**
cultivation theory, 256, **256**
cultural capital, **413,** 413–414
cultural differences. *See also* biculturalism
behavioral autonomy and, 319
Bolivian adolescent employment, 237

China's adolescent employment, 237
European adolescent employment, 237, 244
Germany's adolescent employment, 237
immigrants' achievements in education, 420–421
in intimacy patterns, 350–351
Latino's acculturation, 119–120, 120f
pregnancy, 390, 390f
sex and alcohol, 375–376
sexually permissive societies, 369–371
Taiwan's adolescent employment, 237
teen pregnancy, 394, 394f
United States adolescent employment, 237
weight issues, 53–54, 53f
culture
-fair tests, 82, **82**
intelligence and, 81–82
curvilinear pattern, 246, **246**
custody issues, 154–155

D

Darwin's theory of evolution, 14
date rape, 386, **386**
dating, 53f, 356–364
context influence on, 358–359
development of, relationships, 360–362
impact of, 362–364
intimacy development from, 358–360
partner preferences, 361–362
patterns of, 359–360, 359f
reasons for, 360
violence and, 363–364
death penalty, 4–5
decision making, 88–89. *See also* behavioral decision theory
abilities changing, 311–314
cognitive and psychosocial influences in, 314
improvements in, 312, 313f
legal, 312–313, 313f
deductive reasoning, 63, **63**
de-idealization, emotional autonomy and, 307
delayed phase preference, 41, **41**
delinquency, 251, 251f, 452, **452**
democracy, as social invention, 101
demographers, 148, **148**
depression, **461**
causes of, 466–467
diagnosing, 462
gender roles and, 463–464
nature and prevalence of, 461–462, 461t
sex differences and, 462–464, 463f
desegregation, 181–182, 213–214, 248
detachment, **305**
emotional autonomy and, 305
research on, 305–306
developmental task domains, 102t
developmental trajectories, 445, **445**, 446f
diathesis-stress model, 466, **466**
diffusion tensor imaging (DTI), 74, **74**
discontinuous passages, 113, **113**
discrimination, 181, 181f, 296
disordered eating, **51**, 51–52
diversity, 148
divided attention, 71, **71**

divorce, 148, 149f, 150
adolescents and, 150–152, 155
consequences of, 151
custody issues, 154–155
living arrangements after, 154–155
long-term effects of, 153, 154f
reactions to, differing, 151–152
remarriage, 149, 150, 155–156
dopamine, 444, **444**
dorsolateral prefrontal cortex, 76, **76**
drugs, 242, 251, 441–446
adolescent brain and, 443–444
gateway, 445, **445**
mass media and, 258–259
prevention and treatment for, 448–450
used by high school students, 441–446, 442f
users, abusers, and abstainers, 446–447
DTI. *See* diffusion tensor imaging

E

early adolescence, 7, **7**, 9
early adulthood. *See* emerging adulthood
eating disorders, 49–55
anorexia nervosa, 51–55
bulimia, 51–55, **52**
obesity, 49–51
ecological perspective on human development, 10, **10**
economic status, 103t, 104. *See also* socioeconomic status
affluence and achievement, 416–418
living with parents and, 116–117
education. *See also* schools; secondary education
about contraceptives, 389
age grouping and school transitions, 206–210
beyond high school, 223–227
changing school climate, 221–222
charter schools, 203, **203**
class size, 205–206
classroom boredom, 90–91, 219–221, 219f
classroom climate, 217–223, 217f
college enrollment growth, 224–225, 224f
comprehensive high school, 200, **200**
compulsory, 199–200, 232
ethnicity and, 204, 416, 418–422
immigrants' achievements in, 420–421
in inner cities, 204
learning decreasing in, 421–422
learning theories, 16
No Child Left Behind, 201
non-college bound, 226–227
origin of peer groups in, 163–165
overcrowding in schools, 206
postsecondary, in America, 225
school reform, 201–202
school responsibilities, 202–203
school size, 205–206
school vouchers, 203, **203**
secondary school transition, 207–209
sex, 398–399, 399f
standards-based reform, 203, **203**
student attendance, 220, 220f
student engagement, 219–221, 219f
student performance, 218–219

teaching expectations, 218–219
tracking, 210–213
violence in schools, 222–223
educational achievement, 410, 416–425
changes over time, 421–422, 421f
dropping out, 423–425
influencing parenting, 417–418
pessimism v. optimism in, 418–419
educational attainment, 416, **416**
egocentrism, 65–66
ejaculation, reaction to, 45
elementary schools, 207–208, 209f
Elmstown's Youth, 180, 181
emerging adulthood, 7, **7**, 18, 99–103
lifestyle patterns, 99, 100f
mental health and, 100–101, 100f
in previous eras, 112
study of, 100–101, 102t
universality of, 99
emotional autonomy, **304**, 304–312
age differences and, 307, 307f
de-idealization and, 307
detachment and, 305
ethnicity and, 308
parenting practices and, 309–311
research on, 306–309
endocrine system, **23**, 25–26
environment
achievement influenced by, 412–415
adolescent development influencing, 145–146
obesity influenced by, 50
puberty influenced by, 35–38
shared influences of, 145
work, 238–239
ephebephobia, 20, **20**
epiphysis, 28, **28**
Eriksonian theory, 15–16, 283, 285, 287, 336
intimacy v. isolation, **338**, 338–339
Sullivan's theory compared to, 339
ESM. *See* experience sampling method
estrogens, **25**, 25f, 25–26
ethnic identity, **291**, 291–297
alternative orientations to, 294–296
development, 291–292
MMRI, 296, **296**
ethnicity. *See also* biracial; cultural differences;
multiethnic adolescents
academic achievement and, 182, 183, 209,
418–422, 433
achievement and, 410
'acting white' stigma, 419
adolescent mothers, 400
African American discrimination, 181–182,
181f
Asian Americans discrimination, 181–182,
181f
behavioral autonomy and, 319
beliefs about success, 419–420
classroom thinking and, 91
college and, 224–225
composition in schools, 213–215
crowd membership, 178–179
desegregation, 213–214
discrimination, 181, 181f, 296
education changes over time, 421–422
education in inner cities, 204

educational achievement and, 416, 418–421
emotional autonomy and, 308
health care, mortality and, 57–58
identity development, 291–297
immigrant success, 420–421
international competitions in school,
    422–423
intimacy patterns, 350–351, 351f
leisure time and, 250–251
living as minority, 214–215
mass media and, 255–256
moral reasoning and, 323
Navajo initiation ceremony, 107
opposite sex friendships and, 356
parenting practices influenced by, 142–143
patterns of activity, 234
poverty, neighborhood conditions and,
    123–124
pregnancy and role of father, 396
race-related hassles, 294, 295f
racial identity group, 296, 296f
religion and, 329
school drop-outs and, 423–425, 424f
school transitions and, 209
school violence and, 222
segregation, 181–182
self-esteem and, 278–281, 279f, 281f
sex differences and, 348, 348f
sexual activity and, 372–375, 380–381
social support of Hispanic students, 348–349,
    349f
substance abuse differences, 445
teacher's expectations and, 218
teen pregnancy, 395, 398
thinness and, 53–54, 53f
and transitional problems, 119–120
unemployment and, 243
in United States, 119, 119f
use of time and, 233
weight issues, dating and, 53f
ethnography, 175, **175**
Europe, adolescent employment in, 237, 244
executions, 4–5
exo-systems, **11**
experience sampling method (ESM), **245,**
    245–246
externalizing disorders, 436, **436**
    prevention and treatment of, 459–460
extracurricular activities, 233, 234, 241, 255,
    259, 262
    impact on development of adolescents,
        247–248, 248f
    sex roles, 249–250
extrinsic motivation, 408, **408**
extrusion, 107, **107**

F

facial hair, 8, 31, 378
false confessions, 316, 316f
false-self behavior, **272,** 272–273
family, 11, 130–159. See also divorce; sibling(s)
    adolescent development and relationship of,
        138–145, 159
    adolescent peer groups and, 144–145,
        144f, 164

age differences and time spent with, 133–134,
    133f
attachment in, 143
autonomy in, 143
balance of power changing, 135–136
brother-sister avoidance, 108, **108**
change in needs and function of, 135
in changing society, 148–159
conflicts of parents, 151
economic stress and poverty, 156–159
ethnicity and, 136, 142, 149, 151–152, 153,
    170, 319, 353
expectations of adolescents, 136–137
extended, and intimacy, 353
financial strain in, 157–158, 157f
importance of, 159
influence on adolescence, 11, 130–159, 157f
latchkey youth, 250, 251
nature of, 148–150
parenting styles, 138–142
peer groups and, 164
puberty influenced by, 36
puberty influencing, 136
relations transformation, 135–137
relationships at adolescence, 133–137
remarriage in, 149, 150, 155–156
sex differences in relationship of, 137
sexual activity influenced by, 380
systems theory, 133, **133**
The Family Guy, 67
fear of failure, 407, **407**
feedback loop, **25,** 25–26
female circumcision, 112
females. See also dating; romantic relationships;
        sex differences
    androgyny and, 298–299
    body dissatisfaction of, 30
    breast development, 32–33, 33d
    college enrollment and, 224, 224f
    cross-sex friendships of, 353–356
    depression in, 462–464, 463f
    early/late maturation among, 46–49, 48f
    extracurricular activities and, 249–250
    family relationships of, 137
    hormonal influences and, 377–378
    identity and, 284
    intimacy of, 346–348
    mass media, 255
    meaning of sex to, 383–384
    moodiness during puberty, 40, 40f
    occupational choices for, 430–431
    pubic hair growth, 32–33, 33d
    self-esteem and, 279, 279f
    as sex objects, 258
    sexual maturation in, 32–34
    stress, rumination and sensitivity to
        others, 464
    as teen mothers, 396–398
    violent crimes of, 453–454
fighting, between parents and adolescents,
    131–132
five-factor model, 273, **273**
fMRI. See functional magnetic reasoning
        imaging
formal operations, 68, **68,** 69t
formal-operational thinking, 69–70

free time, 245–252
    adolescent development and, 262–263
    in contemporary society, 232–235
Freudian theory, 15
Friends, 280
friendships, 186f. See also cliques; crowds;
        gangs; intimacy; peer groups
    achievement influenced by, 414–415
    antisocial activity involvement, 183
    caring and concern in, 346
    changes in, 347, 347f
    common interest in, 182–185
    conflict resolution in, 346
    cross-sex, 353–356
    definitions of, 343–344, 344f
    group profiles, 186, 187f
    jealousy, 344–345
    nature of, 343–345
    occupation choice influenced by, 429–431
    with opposite sex, 353–356
    opposite sex, and body image, 355–356
    role of family, 184–185
    school orientations of, 183
    significant knowledge of, 345–346
    similarities in, 185–187
    stability of adolescent, 186–187
    teen culture orientations of, 183
frontal cortex, 75–76, 76f
functional magnetic reasoning imaging (fMRI),
    74, **74,** 74
future orientation, 269, **269**

G

gangs, 183, **183,** 216f
Gardner's theory of multiple intelligences, 79
gateway drugs, 445, **445**
Gen X, 165
gender identification hypothesis, 297, **297**
gender identity, **383,** 383–384
gender role
    depression and, 463–464
    development, 297–299
    socialization and, 297–298
generation gap, 130–131, **131**
genetics, 35–38, 50
    behavioral, **145,** 145–147
Germany, adolescent employment in, 237
gifted students, **212,** 212–213
girls. See females
GnRH. See gonadotropin-releasing hormone
        neurons
gonadal axis maturation, 30–31, 31f
gonadotropin-releasing hormone (GnRH)
        neurons, **25**
gonads, **25,** 25f
gonorrhea, **391,** 391–392
Great Depression, 117, 166t
Greatest Generation, 166t

H

Hall's theory of recapitulation, 14–15
Happy Days Generation, 166t

harassment, 191–193
  sexual, 386–387, 387*f*
Hazelwood v. Kuhlmeier, 106
health care, 55–58. *See also* mental health
health-compromising behaviors, **56,** 56–57
health-enhancing behaviors, **56,** 56–57
height, 28–29
helplessness, learned, 411, **411**
herpes, **391,** 391–392
Hispanic Americans
  academic achievement of, 418
  dating and, 358
  parent relationships of, 349
  poverty influencing, 119, 120
  suicide among, 465
historical theories, 17–19
  adolescence as invention, 17–18
  of sexual activity, 375
HIV. *See* human immunodeficiency virus
Hodgson v. Minnesota, 106
Holland's personality inventory, 427
home
  environment influencing achievement,
    412–414
  living, 116, 116*f*
homophobia, 347, **347**
homosexuality, 383–386
  origins of, 384–385
  prejudice and ignorance about, 385–386
  prevalence of, 383–384
hormonal feedback loop, 24–26, 25*f*
hormones, **24**
  activational role of, 27, **27**
  adolescent development influenced by, 27
  influences on sexual activity, 377–378
  organizational role of, 27, **27**
  sex, 25*f*, 25–26
hostile attributional bias, 191, **191,** 457, **457**
HPG. *See* hypothalamic-pituitary-gonadic axis
human immunodeficiency virus (HIV), **391,**
  391–392, 399*f*
human papilloma virus, **391,** 391–392
Hurricane Katrina, 117
hypothalamic-pituitary-gonadic (HPG) axis, **25**
hypothalamus, **25,** 25*f*
hypothesized causation, 257, 257*f*
hypothetical thinking, 64

I

iatrogenic effects, 185, **185**
identity, **13**
  achievement, 289
  crisis, 17, 283–288
  crowds and adolescent, 178–179
  diffusion, **283,** 283–284, **286,** 289
  foreclosure, 286, **286,** 289
  versus identity diffusion, **283,** 283–284
  sex differences in, 339–340
  status of, 287–288, 287*f*
identity development, 267–299
  gender roles, 297–299
  research on, 287–20
  self-conception, 270–274
  shifts in status, 290

social context of, 284–285
  studying, 289
imaginary audience, 65, **65**
imagination, 62
immigrants, 420–421
implicit personality theory, **83,** 83–84
impression formation, 83–84
In a Different Voice (Gilligan), 325
indifferent parents, 139, **139**
individuation, 306, **306**
  closeness and, 309–310
  emotional autonomy and, 306
  triggers of, 308–309
inductive reasoning, **63,** 63–64
indulgent parents, 139, **139**
industrialization, 97
infatuation, 361
information-processing perspective, **71,** 71–73
initiation
  ceremonies, 104, **104,** 106–109
  sexual, 374
instrumental aggression, 188, **188**
intelligence
  beliefs about, 409–410
  cognitive transitions, 78–82
  culture and, 81–82
  tests, 80–81
  types, 78–79
intelligence quotient (IQ), 78, 146
intergenerational conflict, 17
internal working model, 340, **340**
internalizing disorders, 436, **436,** 440, 460–468
  causes of, 466–467
  treatment and prevention of, 467–468
Internet usage, 253–254
interpersonal development, 336–338
interpersonal security, 346
interpersonal status, 103, 103*t*
intimacy, **13, 334,** 334–365, 351*f*
  attachment, **340,** 340–343
  cultural differences in patterns of, 350–351
  dating and romantic relationships, 356–364
  development of, 343–356
  display of, 345–346
  friendships, 343–345
  v. isolation, **338,** 338–339
  need for, 336
  opposite sex friendships, 353–356
  pseudo-, 339, **339**
  psychosocial development and, 364–365
  sex differences in, 339–340, 346–348
  siblings, 353
  targets of, 348–353
intrinsic motivation, 408, **408**
inventionists, **96,** 96
invulnerability, 88
IQ. *See* intelligence quotient

J

jealousy, 344–345
jobs. *See* work
junior high school, 207, **207**
justice orientation, **324,** 324–325
juveniles

death penalty, 4–5
justice system, **104,** 104–105
offending, **452,** 452–455

K

Kinaaldá, 107

L

latchkey youth, 250, 251
late adolescence, 7, **7,** 9
Latino adolescents
  academic achievement of, 420–421
  acculturation, 119–120, 120*f*
  aggression of, 191
  discrimination of, 181, 181*f*
  education of, 204, 218, 222
  friendships of, 356
  as mothers, 353
  parenting of, 288
  peer pressure of, 316
  religion of, 329
  self-esteem of, 280–281
  sexual activity of, 373
learned helplessness, 411, **411**
learning disability, **212,** 212–213
Leave It To Beaver, 112
legal status, 95, 103*t,* 104–106
leisure time, 12, 170, 170*f*
  adolescents and, 245–252
  structured activities, 246–250, 247*f*
  unstructured time, 250–252
leptin, 26, **26**
lesbians. *See* homosexuality
life-course-persistent offenders, **456,** 456–457
limbic system, 76, **76**
logical reasoning, 77, 77*f*
longitudinal study, 39, **39**
long-term memory, **71,** 71–72
Lost Generation, 166*t*

M

macro-systems, 11, **11**
mainstreaming, **212,** 212–213
males. *See also* dating; romantic relationships;
    sex differences
  androgyny and, 298–299
  cross-sex friendships of, 353–356
  depression in, 462–464, 463*f*
  early/late maturation among, 45–46
  ejaculation, reaction to, 45
  extracurricular activities and, 249–250
  family relationships of, 137
  intimacy of, 347–348
  mass media, 255
  meaning of sex to, 383
  moodiness during puberty, 40, 40*f*
  occupational choices for, 430–431
  penis growth, 31–32, 32*f*
  pregnancy and role of father, 396
  pubic hair growth, 31–32, 32*f*

sexual maturation in, 30–32
stress, rumination and sensitivity to others, 464
marginal man, 110, **110**
marginality, 17
marital conflict, 152–153, 152*f. See also* divorce; parenting
marriage, 357, 357*f*
　re-, 149, 150, 155–156
mass media, 12, 254
　adolescence and, 253–262, 253*f*
　adolescence problems portrayed by, 434
　adolescent consumer, 261
　age difference in patterns of use, 254, 255*f*
　controversial, impact, 258–259
　influences of, 234
　misleading messages of, 259–260
　preferences of, 255–256
　saturation of, 253–254
　sex-role socialization and, 260
　television, 254–255
　theories of use, 256–258
　work, leisure and, 231–263
masturbation, 382
maternal employment, 149–150
maturation
　adrenal axis, 30–31, 31*f*
　early/late, among females, 46–49, 48*f*
　gonadal axis, 30–31, 31*f*
　individual differences in, 35–36
　of males, 30–32, 45–46
　puberty and early/late, 45–49
　sexual, and somatic development, 30–34
　sexual, in females, 32–34, 46–49, 48*f*
maturing, early/late, 45–49, 48*f*
media practice model, 257, **257**
melatonin, 41, **41**
The Member of the Wedding (McCullers), 283
memory, 71–72
menarche, 24, **24**
　reaction to, 44–45
　in 20th century, 37–38, 38*f*
　variations in, by location, 36–37, 37*f*
mental abilities, growth of, 80, 80*f*
mental health
　in early adulthood, 100–101, 101*f*
　of parents, 134–135
mentoring programs, 120–121
meso-systems, 11, **11**
metacognition, 65, **65**, 73
micro-systems, **11**
middle adolescence, 7, **7**, 9
middle school, 207, **207**, 208*f*, 209*f*
midlife crisis, of parents, **133**, 133–134
Millennial Generation, 165, 166*t*
mixed-sex cliques, 174, 362
MMRI. *See* multidimensional model of racial identity
Monitoring the Future survey, 441, **441**
monogamy, serial, 372, **372**
moodiness, 40–41, 40*f*, 40*t*, 245–246, 275*f*, 298, 461
　student engagement and, 219*f*
moral development, 321–325
moral reasoning, 322–323
　moral behavior and, 323–324
　postconventional, **322**, 322–323

preconventional, **322**, 322–323
　sex differences in, 324–325
　stages of, 322–323
morality, 84–86
motivation, 406–409
multidimensional model of racial identity (MMRI), 296, **296**
multiethnic adolescents, 292–294, 293*f*
mutual role taking, 84, **84**
myelination, **74**, 74–75

N

NAEP. *See* National Assessment of Educational Progress
National Assessment of Educational Progress (NAEP), **421**, 421–422
Native Americans, self-esteem, 280
Navajo initiation ceremony, 107
need for achievement, **406**, 406–407
need for integration into adult society, 336, **336**
need for intimacy, 336, **336**
need for intimacy with a peer of opposite sex, 336, **336**
need for sexual contact, 336, **336**
negative identity, 287, **287**
negativity affectivity, 440, **440**
neighborhood conditions, 121–125, 122*f*
　disadvantaged, 123–124, 123*f*
　influence processes, 122–125
　positive influences in, 125, 125*f*
　resource limitations, 124–125
　stability of, 124, 124*f*
　stress impact, 123–124
nerds, 175–176
neuroendocrine, 466, **466**
neurons, 74, **74**
neurotransmitters, 76, **76**
nicotine, 443, 443*f*
No Child Left Behind, 201
nocturnal orgasms, 372, **372**
nonfamilial adults, 353
nonshared environmental influences, 145, **145**

O

obesity, 49–51
　genetic and environmental influences on, 50
　preventing and treating, 50–51
　rate of, 50, 51*f*
occupational achievement, 426–431
　influences on choices, 427–429
　plan development, 426–427
occupational attainment, 429, **429**
Odd Girl Out (Simmons), 190
opposite-sex friendships, 353–356
oppositional-defiant disorder, 450, **450**
optimism, false, 418–419
orbitofrontal cortex, 76, **76**, 76*f*
organismic theories, 15–16
　Eriksonian theory, 15–16, 283, 285, 287, 336, 338–339
　Freudian theory, 15
　Piagetian theory, 16

organization, of thoughts, 73
organizational role (of hormones), 27, **27**
ovaries, 25, **25**
overprotectiveness, 309
overt antisocial behavior, 452, **452**
oxytocin, 464, **464**

P

Parent Team, 221
parent-adolescent relationships, 130–159
　anti-social peer groups influenced by, 184–185
　autonomy and, 306–309
　change in needs and function of family, 135
　communication about sex, 378–379
　conflicts, 131–132
　development of adolescent, 138–145
　expectations, 136–137
　family relations transformed, 135–137
　family systems theory, 133, **133**
　intimacy and, 348–350, 351*f*
　midlife crisis and, **133**, 133–134
　parenting styles, 138–142
　popular books, 130
　puberty influencing, 136
　reciprocity of, 141, 142*f*
　struggle and rebellion, 132
parental demandingness, 139, **139**
parental responsiveness, 138, **138**
parents and parenting, 349. *See also* authoritarian parents; authoritative parents; parent-adolescent relationships
　adolescence-limited offenders and, 458–459
　conflicts of, 151
　divorced, and adolescents, 155
　educational achievement influenced by, 417–418
　emotional autonomy and practices of, 309–311
　ethnic differences in style of, 142–143, 288
　four styles of, 139
　indulgent, 139, **139**
　influence of two, 150, 315–316
　influence on achievement, 412–414
　as intimacy targets, 348–350, 348*f*
　maternal control, 343*f*
　mental health of, 134–135
　midlife crisis of, **133**, 133–134
　occupation choice influenced by, 429–431
　peer intimacy differing from role of, 351–353
　poor, and deviance, 184–185, 184*f*
　problem behavior and response of, 138, 138*f*
　quality of, 150–151
　remarriage of, 149, 155–156
　separation from, 107
　sexual activity influencing, 378–381
　single, 148–149
　styles of, 138–142
　ten basic principles of, 140, 140*t*
　values and expectations of, 412–413
　young adults living with, 116, 116*f*
participant observation, 173, **173**
particularistic norms, **168**, 168–169

PATH. *See* Promoting Alternative Thinking
    Strategies
Patterns of Culture (Benedict), 103, 369
Patterns of Sexual Behavior (Ford & Beach), 370
PDAs. *See* personal digital assistants
peak height velocity, 28, **28**
peer groups, 11, 54, 144–145, 144*f*, **162**, 162–197,
    162*f*. *See also* cliques; crowds; friendships
    achievement influenced by, 414–415
    changes in, 169–171
    educational origins of, 163–164
    false confessions, 316, 316*f*
    family life and, 164
    harm of youth culture, 168
    influence of, 315–316
    as intimacy targets, 348–350, 348*f*
    leisure time, 170, 170*f*
    in modern society, 168–169
    nature of, 169–176
    occupation choice influenced by, 429–431
    origins of, 163–165
    parent intimacy differing from role of,
        351–353
    popularity and rejection in, 187–193
    pressure from, 316–319, 318*f*
    problem or necessity, 167–177
    psychosocial development and, 194
    during puberty, 44
    romance changing, 173–175
    separate world of, 167–168
    sexual activity influenced by, 378–381
    social map of, 177, 177*f*
    stability of, 186–187
    work and, 164
    youth culture, 167–168
penis growth, 31–32, 32*f*
permissive societies, 371, **371**
personal digital assistants (PDAs), 245
personal fable, 66, **66**
personality, 427
    antisocial, disorder, **450**, 450–451
    dimensions of, 273–274
    implicit, theory, **83**, 83–84
    occupational choice influenced by, 427–429
pessimism, realistic, 418–419
PET. *See* positron emission tomography
pheromones, 36, **36**
physical health, 55–58
Piagetian theory, 16, 71, 73, 321
Piaget's theory of cognitive development, 68–69
pituitary gland, 25, 25*f*
platonic relationships, 338, **338**
political behavior, 328
political status, 103–104, 103*t*
political thinking, 327–328
    behavior and, 328
popularity, 187–193
    aggression and, 188
    determinants of, 187–188
    dynamics of, 188–189
pornography, 258–259
Portrait of the Artist as a Young Man (Joyce), 283
positive youth development, 252, **252**
    promoting, 252–253
positron emission tomography (PET), 74, **74**
possible selves, 269, **269**

postconventional moral reasoning, **322**,
    322–323
postsecondary education, 225
poverty, 416
    chronic, 158
    economic stress and, 156–159
    family and, 149–150
    neighborhood conditions and, 123–124
    sexual activity and, 381
    social transitions and, 119–120
    teen pregnancy and, 394–395, 397–398
preconventional moral reasoning, **322**, 322–323
prefrontal cortex, **75**, 75–76
pregnancy, 390, 390*f*, 393–401
    abortion, 395–396, 399*f*
    adoption, 147, 396
    after birth, 400–401
    causes and correlates of teen, 395–396
    children of teen mothers, 397
    consequences for mother and child, 396–398
    cultural differences, 390, 390*f*
    father's role, 396
    intervention programs, 398–401
    prevalence of teen, 393–394
    prevention programs, 398–401
    SES and, 394–395
prejudice, 280
    homosexual, 385–386
premature affluence, 241, **241**
preoperational period, 68, **68**, 69*t*
primary control strategies, 469, **469**
primary prevention, 467, **467**
priorities, 88–89
private schools, 215–216
    gangs in, 216*f*
problem(s)
    behavior syndrome, 437, 437*f*, 438–439
    clusters, 438, 438*f*
    comorbidity of externalizing, 437–440
    externalizing, 450–460
Promoting Alternative Thinking Strategies
    (PATH), 193
propositional logic, 69, **69**
prosocial behavior, 326
prosocial reasoning, 326
protectionists, child, 97, **97**
protective factors, 448, **448**
pseudointimacy, 339, **339**
psychoanalytic theory, and detachment, 305
psychological development
    cognitive transitions of, 62–91
    emerging adulthood and well-being, 100–102
    puberty impacted by, 38–49
    sexual activity and, 376–377
psychopaths, 451, **451**
psychosocial development, **12**, 12–14, 94–95
    decision making and, influences, 314
    intimacy and, 364–365
    peer group and, development, 194
    problems in adolescence, 433–469
    sexuality, 369–371
psychosocial maturity, 77, 77*f*
psychosocial moratorium, **284**, 284–285
psychosocial problems, 433–469
    ending in adulthood, 435
    externalizing problems, 450–460

factors causing, 435–436
    internalizing problems, 460–468
    nature and covariation of, 436–440
    stress and coping, 468–469
    substance use and abuse, 440–450
    transitory experiences causing, 434–435
puberty, 8, **8**, 9–10, 24–28. *See also* initiation
    achievement and, 406
    adolescent behavior influenced by, 38–39, 39*f*
    adolescent growth spurt, **28**, 28–34
    adolescent moodiness and, 40–41, 41*t*
    adolescent-parent relationships and, 136
    adrenarche, 26, **26**
    autonomy development and, 303–304
    early/late maturation, 45–49
    endocrine system, 25–26
    environmental influences on, 35–38
    ethnic differences in timing of, 35*f*
    familial influences on, 35–36, 136
    genetic influences on, 35–38
    group differences in maturation, 36–37, 37*f*
    hormonal feedback loop, 25*f*, 25–26
    identity development and, 269
    immediate impact of, 39–44
    individual differences in maturation, 35
    intimacy development and, 335, 353
    moodiness during, 40, 40*f*
    peer relationships during, 44
    physical manifestations of, 24
    secular trend, 37–38
    self-esteem and, 39–40
    sequence of physical change during, 31*t*
    sex differences in muscle and fat, 29–30
    sexuality and, 368
    sleep changes during, 41–44
    social impact of, 38–49
    timing and tempo of, 34–38
    triggering of, 26
pubic hair growth, 31–32, 32*f*
    of boys, 31–32, 32*f*
    of girls, 32–33, 33*d*
public schools, 216*f*

Q

Queen Bees and Wannabees (Wiseman), 190
quinceañera, 107, **107**

R

racial socialization, 291, **291**
racism, 280
rape, date, 386, **386**
reactive aggression, 188, **188**
reasoning, 63–64
reference groups, 177–178, **178**
rejection, 187–193
    consequences of, 190
    sensitivity, 341, **341**
relational aggression, **189**, 189–191
relativism, 67–68
religion
    age differences and activities of, 329, 329*f*
    development impacted by, 330

individual differences in involvement, 329
    patterns of involvement, 329
    value autonomy and, 328–331
remarriage, 149, 150, 155–156
    difficulties adjusting to, 156
resilience, 468, **468**
responsibility, development of, 239–241
restrictive societies, 370, **370**
reverse causation, 257, **257**, 257*f*
Reviving Ophelia (Pipher), 325
risk factors, 381, **381**, 381*f*, 447, **447**
risk-taking, 86–90, 89*f*
    adult differences from adolescents, 88–89
    behavioral decision theory, 86–87, **87**, 87*f*
    emotional and contextual influences, 89–90
    invulnerability, 88
    priorities, 88–89
    values, 88–89
rite of passage, 9, **9**, 106–109
romantic relationships, 355–356. *See also* dat-
    ing; intimacy
    activities of, 359, 359*f*
    nature and significance of, 358
    phases of, 360–361
Roper v. Simmons, 4, 106
routine activity theory, 250, **250**
runaways, 459

S

SAT, 81, 82
scaffolding, 81, **81**
scarification, 109, **109**
School Planning and Management Team, 221
school-based health centers, 57, **57**
schools, 11–12, 198–229. *See also* charter
    schools; education; elementary schools
    adolescent development and, 227–229
    characteristics of good, 227
    classroom climate, 217–223
    climate change in, 221–221
    desegregation, 181–182, 213–214, 248
    drop-outs, 423–425, 424*f*
    as environment for achievement, 412
    ethnic composition in, 213–215
    gifted students, **212**, 212–213
    high, to college, 225–226
    large, 205–206
    less learning in, 421–422
    overcrowding in, 206
    performance in, 416, **416**
    private, 215–216, 216*f*
    public, 215–216, 216*f*
    responsibilities of, 202–203
    within schools, 205, **205**
    sex education in, 398–399, 399*f*
    single-sex, 211
    small, 205–206
    social organization of, 204–216
    teaching basics, 202
    tracking in, 210–213
    violence in, 222–223
    work and, in early 20th century, 235
    work impacting, 241–242
scientific study, stereotypes v., 19–20

secondary control strategies, 469, **469**
secondary education, **198**, 198–204, 199*f*,
    206–208
    transition to, 207–209
secondary prevention, 467, **467**
secondary sex characteristics, 30, **30**
secular trend, 37–38, **38**
secure attachment, 340, **340**
selection, 185–187
selective attention, 71, **71**
selective serotonin reuptake inhibitors (SSRIs),
    467, **467**
self-care, 251
self-conception, **270**, 270–274, 271*f. See also*
    personality
    changes in, 270–273
    differentiation in, 270
    false self behavior, 272–273
    organization and integration of, 270–272
self-consciousness, 275, **275**
Self-Directed Search, 427, **427**
self-efficacy, 409, **409**
self-esteem, 39–40, 214, **270**, 275*f*
    barometric, 275–277, **276**
    baseline, 275–277, **276**
    components of, 278
    consequences of high, 281–283
    ethnicity and, 214, 278–281, 279*f*, 281*f*
    female, 279, 279*f*
    influences on, 281
    patterns of, 276–277, 277*f*
    puberty and, 39–40
    sexual activity and, 376
    social class segregation and, 280
    stability and changes in, 274–283
self-fulfilling prophecy, 130, **130**
self-handicapping, 407, **407**
self-image stability, 275, **275**
self-reliance, 320
semirestrictive societies, **370**, 370–371
sensation seeking, 89, **89**
sense of identity, **270**
sensorimotor period, 68, **68**, 69*t*
serial monogamy, 372, **372**
service learning, 243, **243**
SES. *See* socioeconomic status
set point, 25, **25**
Seventeen magazine, 260, 390
sex
    differences and self-esteem, 278, 279*f*
    education, 398–399, 399*f*
    hormones, 25, 25*f*
    mass media and, 258
    -role behavior, **383**, 383–384
    roles and extracurricular activities, 249–250
    segregation, 180
sex cleavage, 170
    origins of, 353–355
sex differences
    in depression, 462–464, 463*f*
    ethnicity and, 348, 348*f*
    in identity/intimacy, 339–340, 346–348
    meaning of sex, 382–383
    in moral reasoning, 324–325
    in muscle and fat, 29–30
    origins of, 347–348

in partner preferences, 361–362
in relationship of family, 137
self-esteem and, 278, 279*f*
sexism, tracking and, 211
sex-role socialization, mass media and, 260
sexual abstinence, 399
sexual abuse, 386–387, 387*f*
sexual activity, 348, 371–393
    alcohol and, 375–376
    changes in, 374–376
    contextual influences, 377–378
    early, and deviance, 377
    historical trends, 375
    hormonal influences on, 377–378
    non-parental influences, 380–381
    risk factors, 381, **381**, 381*f*
    stages of, 372–373
    virginity pledges, 381
sexual development
    contraceptive use, 387–391
    harassment, rape, and abuse, 386–387, 387*f*
    homosexuality, 383–386
    pregnancy and childbearing, 393–401
    sexual identity, 385–386
    sexually active, 376–393
sexual harassment, 386–387, 387*f*
sexual identity, 385–386
sexual initiation, 374
sexual intercourse, 373, 373*f*, 374, 374*f*
    peer pressure resistance, 399*f*
sexual maturation
    in boys, 30–32, 45–46
    in girls, 32–34, 46–49, 48*f*
sexual orientation, **383**, 383–384, 399*f*
sexual socialization, 369–371
    in permissive societies, 369–370
    in restrictive societies, 370
    in semirestrictive societies, 370–371
sexuality, **13**, 367–401. *See also* homosexuality
    adolescent development, 367–401
    cognitive transitions and, 368
    healthy development of, 369
    permissiveness, 369–371
    as psychosocial phenomenon, 369–371
    puberty and, 368
    social roles and, 368–369
sexually active adolescents, 376–393
sexually transmitted diseases (STDs), **391**,
    391–392, 399*f*
    protecting against, 392
sexual-minority youth, 361, **361**
shared environmental influences, 145, **145**
sibling(s), 353
    identification, 147, **147**
    occupation choice influenced by, 429–430
    relationships of, 143–147
    rivalry, 147, **147**
The Simpsons, 67
single parenthood, 148–149, 150
single-sex schools, 211
sleep, puberty and changes in, 41–44
sleeper effects, 153
social capital, 216, **216**, 414, **414**
social class segregation, 180
    self-esteem and, 280
social cognition, **83**, 83–86, 86*t*

social control theory, 438, **438**
social conventions, 84–86, **85**
social inventions, 103–106
social learning theory, 16
social networking, 171–172, 172f
social perspective taking, 84, **84**
social promotion, 201, **201**, 425, **425**
social redefinition, 94, **94**
    common practices in, 107–109
    in contemporary society, 110
    differences between sexes, 108–109
    passing on of information, 108–109
    in previous eras, 112
    process of, 106–109
    psychosocial development and, 94–95
    separation from parents, 107
    in traditional cultures, 111
    variations in continuity, 112–117
social roles
    achievement and, 405
    identity development and, 269
    intimacy development and, 335–336
    occupation choice influenced by, 430–431
    sexuality and, 368–369
social status, 110
social support, 348–350, 349f, 352, **352**
social transitions, 8, 93–125
    easing, 120–121
    elongation of adolescence, 95–96
    minority youth challenges, 119–120
    poverty challenges, 119–120
    social invention of adolescence, 96–103
    social redefinition and psychosocial development, 94–95
    variations in, 109–117
socialization, 185–187. *See also* racial socialization; sexual socialization
    autonomy and, 204
    gender role development, 297–298
    sex-role, and mass media, 260
society
    adolescent family in changing, 148–159
    family in changing, 148–159
    free time in contemporary, 232–235
    need for integration into adult, 336, **336**
    peer groups in, 168–169
    social definition in contemporary, 110
    transition to, 118–121
socioeconomic status (SES), 228
    importance of, for achievement, 416–418
    pregnancy and, 394–395
sociological theories, 17
solitude, 246, 246f
somatic development, 28–34
    body and stature changes, 28–30, 29f
    sexual maturation, 30–34
South Park, 67
specification, 427, **427**
speed, of thinking, 72
spurious causation, 257, **257**, 257f
SSRIs. *See* selective serotonin reuptake inhibitors
stages of moral reasoning, 322–323
standards-based reform, 203, **203**
Stanford-Binet, 78
stature, 28–30, 29f

status. *See also* socioeconomic status
    adult, consequences, 103t
    economic, 103t, 104, 116–117, 416–418
    of identity, 287–288, 287f
    in identity development, 290
    interpersonal, 103, 103t
    legal, 95, 103t, 104–106
    legal inconsistencies, 106
    offense, 104, **104**
    offenses, 452, **452**
    political, 103–104, 103t
STDs. *See* sexually transmitted diseases
stereotypes
    scientific study v., 19–20
    as threat to achievement, 409
Sternberg's triarchic theory, 79
stress
    coping with psychosocial problems, 468–469
    depression and, 464
    diathesis-, model, 466, **466**
    economic, and poverty, 156–159
    neighborhood conditions and, 123–124
students
    attendance of, 220, 220f
    attitudes of college, 328
    drugs used by, 441–446, 442f
    engagement by, 219–221, 219f
    gifted, **212**, 212–213
    high school, with jobs, 235–236, 236f
    out-of-school influences on, 221
    performance by, 218–219
    social support of, 348–349, 349f
    tracking and, achievement of, 212
    as workers, 235–236
substance abuse, 436, **436**, 440–450, **446**. *See also* drugs
    changes in use over time, 442–443, 443f
    diagnostic criteria for, 446t
    predictors and consequences of, 447
    prevalence of, 441–446
    prevention and treatment for, 448–450
    progression of, 445–446
    risk factors for, 447–448
    users, abusers, and abstainers, 446–447
substance abuse use over, time, 442–443
substance dependence, 446, **446**
suicidal ideation, 464, **464**, 465f
suicide, 464–466
Sullivan's theory on interpersonal development, 336–338, 355
    Eriksonian theory compared to, 339
    stages of needs, 336–337, 337t
Surviving Your Dog's Adolescence, 19
synaptic pruning, **74**, 74–75, 75f

T

Taiwan, adolescent employment in, 237
Tanner stages, 30, **30**, 31–32, 32f, 34
technology, 262
    computer, 253
teenagers, 98, **98**
    employment of, 236–237
    invention of, 232
    time spending of, 233f

testes, 25, **25**
testosterone, 40, 40f, 377, **377**
theoretical perspectives, 14–18, 15f, 68–73
    on adolescent intimacy, 336–343
    biosocial theories, 14–15
    formal-operational thinking, 69–70
    learning theories, 16
    organismic theories, 15–16
    Piaget's theory of cognitive development, 68–69
thinking, 193. *See also* cognitive transitions; critical thinking; formal-operational thinking; hypothetical thinking; moral reasoning; political thinking
    classroom, 90–91
    influences of cognitive development, 83–91, 86t
    information-processing view of, 71–73
    in multiple dimensions, 66–67
Tikopia, 104
time. *See also* free time
    educational achievement over, 421–422, 421f
    ethnicity and leisure, 250–251
    with family members, 133–134, 133f
    free, 245–252
    leisure, 170, 170f, 245–252
    substance abuse use over, 443f
    suburban and urban teenagers spending, 233f
    use of, in contemporary America, 232–234
    use of, in other countries, 234
tracking, **210**, 210–213
    early placement, 211–212
    pros and cons of, 210–211
    sexism, single-sex schools and, 211
    student achievement and, 212
    students at extremes, 212–213
The Truly Disadvantaged (Wilson), 120, 121

U

underachievers, 407, **407**
unemployment, of youths, 243–244
United States, ethnic composition of, 119f, 237
universalistic norms, 168–169, **169**
unpopular teens, 193
unstructured leisure time, 250–252
uses and gratification approach, 256, **256**

V

value autonomy, **304**, 304–305, 320–330
    moral development, 321–325
    political thinking and, 327–328
    prosocial reasoning, prosocial behavior, and, 326
    religious beliefs, 328–331
    volunteerism, 326
values, 88–89
    parents, 412–413
    work, 427–429, **428**, 428f, 428t
ventromedial prefrontal cortex, 76, **76**
victimization, 191–193, 192f, 193f, 454
views of social status, 110
violence, 159f, 259–260

age differences in crimes of, 453, 453*f*
   dating and, 363–364
   mass media and, 258
   in school, 222–223
viral marketing, 261, **261**
virginity
   losing, 374
   pledges, 381
volunteerism, 326
Vygotsky's perspective, 81

W

Wechsler Adult Intelligence Scale (WAIS-III), 78
Wechsler Intelligence Scale for Children
   (WISC-IV), 78

WIAS-III. *See* Wechsler Adult Intelligence Scale
WISC-IV. *See* Wechsler Intelligence Scale for
   Children
wisdom, 86
work, 12. *See also* occupational achievement
   adolescents and, 164, 235–244
   common adolescent jobs, 238
   environments of adolescents, 238–239
   leisure, and mass media, 231–263
   school and, in early 20th century, 235
   school impacted by, 241–242
   students at, 235–236
   values, 427–429, **428**, 428*f*, 428*t*
working memory, **71**, 71–72

Y

youth, 98, **98**
   apprenticeship, 113, **113**
   culture, 167–168
   development, 252, 252*t*

Z

zero sum phenomenon, 234
zero tolerance, 222, **222**
zone of proximal development, 81, **81**